Financial Accounting

GLOBAL EDITION

ELEVENTH EDITION

International Financial Reporting Standards

International Financial Reporting Standards

Walter T. Harrison Jr.
Baylor University

Charles T. Horngren
Stanford University

C. William (Bill) Thomas
Baylor University

Wendy M. Tietz
Kent State University

Themin Suwardy
Singapore Management University

Harlow, England • London • New York • Boston • San Francisco • Toronto • Sydney • Dubai • Singapore • Hong Kong
Tokyo • Seoul • Taipei • New Delhi • Cape Town • Sao Paulo • Mexico City • Madrid • Amsterdam • Munich • Paris • Milan

Vice President, Business Publishing: Donna Battista
Editor-in-Chief: Adrienne D'Ambrosio
Senior Acquisitions Editor: Lacey Vitetta
Editorial Assistant: Christine Donovan
Managing Editor, Global Edition: Yajnaseni Das
Associate Acquisitions Editor, Global Edition: Ananya Srivastava
Associate Project Editor, Global Edition: Paromita Banerjee
Project Editor, Global Edition: Punita Kaur Mann
Vice President, Product Marketing: Maggie Moylan
Director of Marketing, Digital Services and Products: Jeanette Koskinas
Field Marketing Manager: Natalie Wagner
Product Marketing Assistant: Jessica Quazza
Team Lead, Program Management: Ashley Santora
Program Manager: Mary Kate Murray
Team Lead, Project Management: Jeff Holcomb
Content Producer, Global Edition: Nikhil Rakshit
Content Producer, Global Edition: Purnima Narayanan
Senior Manufacturing Controller, Global Edition: Angela Hawksbee
Project Manager: Heather Pagano
Operations Specialist: Carol Melville
Creative Director: Blair Brown
Art Director: Jonathan Boylan
Vice President, Director of Digital Strategy and Assessment: Paul Gentile
Manager of Learning Applications: Paul DeLuca
Digital Editor: Sarah Peterson
Director, Digital Studio: Sacha Laustsen
Digital Studio Manager: Diane Lombardo
Digital Studio Project Manager: Andra Skaalrud
Digital Studio Project Manager: Robin Lazrus
Digital Content Team Lead: Noel Lotz
Digital Content Project Lead: Martha LaChance
Manager, Media Production, Global Edition: Vikram Kumar
Senior Media Editor, Global Edition: Gargi Banerjee
Full-Service Project Management and Composition: Cenveo® Publisher Services
Interior Designer: Cenveo® Publisher Services
Cover Designer: Lumina Datamatics, Inc.
Cover Art: antishock/Shutterstock

Acknowledgments of third-party content appear on the appropriate page within the text, or are as follows: Decision Guidelines and Ethical Issue icons: Micromaniac/Shutterstock. Global View and Cooking the Books icons: Pearson Education.

Pearson Education Limited

KAO Two
KAO Park
Harlow
CM17 9NA
United Kingdom
and Associated Companies throughout the world

Visit us on the World Wide Web at: www.pearsonglobaleditions.com

Authorized adaptation from the United States edition, entitled Financial Accounting, 11th Edition, ISBN 978-0-13-412762-0 by Walter T. Harrison Jr., Charles T. Horngren, C. William (Bill) Thomas, and Wendy M. Tietz, published by Pearson Education © 2017.

ISBN 10: 1-292-21114-8
ISBN 13: 978-1-292-21114-5

British Library Cataloguing-in-Publication Data
A catalogue record for this book is available from the British Library

10 9 8 7 6 5 4 3 2 1

Typeset in Helvetica Neue LT W 1 G by Cenveo® Publisher Services
Printed and bound by Vivar in Malaysia

For my wife, Mary Ann.

C. William (Bill) Thomas

To my husband, Russ, who steadfastly supports me in every endeavor.

Wendy M. Tietz

ABOUT THE AUTHORS

Walter T. Harrison, Jr., is professor emeritus of accounting at the Hankamer School of Business, Baylor University. He received his BBA from Baylor University, his MS from Oklahoma State University, and his PhD from Michigan State University.

Professor Harrison, recipient of numerous teaching awards from student groups as well as from university administrators, has also taught at Cleveland State Community College, Michigan State University, the University of Texas, and Stanford University.

A member of the American Accounting Association and the American Institute of Certified Public Accountants, Professor Harrison has served as chairman of the Financial Accounting Standards Committee of the American Accounting Association, on the Teaching/Curriculum Development Award Committee, on the Program Advisory Committee for Accounting Education and Teaching, and on the Notable Contributions to Accounting Literature Committee.

Professor Harrison has lectured in several foreign countries and published articles in numerous journals, including *Journal of Accounting Research*, *Journal of Accountancy*, *Journal of Accounting and Public Policy*, *Economic Consequences of Financial Accounting Standards*, *Accounting Horizons*, *Issues in Accounting Education*, and *Journal of Law and Commerce*.

Professor Harrison has received scholarships, fellowships, and research grants or awards from PricewaterhouseCoopers, Deloitte & Touche, the Ernst & Young Foundation, and the KPMG Foundation.

Charles T. Horngren was the Edmund W. Littlefield Professor of Accounting, emeritus, at Stanford University. A graduate of Marquette University, he received his MBA from Harvard University and his PhD from the University of Chicago. He also received honorary doctorates from Marquette University and DePaul University.

A certified public accountant, Horngren served on the Accounting Principles Board, the Financial Accounting Standards Board Advisory Council, and the Council of the American Institute of Certified Public Accountants and served as a trustee of the Financial Accounting Foundation, which oversees the Financial Accounting Standards Board and the Government Accounting Standards Board.

Horngren is a member of the Accounting Hall of Fame. As a member of the American Accounting Association, Horngren was its president and its director of research. He received its first annual Outstanding Accounting Educator Award. The California Certified Public Accountants Foundation gave Horngren its Faculty Excellence Award and its Distinguished Professor Award. He was the first person to have received both awards. The American Institute of Certified Public Accountants presented its first Outstanding Educator Award to Horngren. Horngren was named Accountant of the Year, in Education, by the national professional accounting fraternity, Beta Alpha Psi. Professor Horngren was also a member of the Institute of Management Accountants, from whom he received its Distinguished Service Award. He was a member of the institute's Board of Regents, which administers the certified management accountant examinations.

Horngren is an author of these other accounting books published by Pearson: *Cost Accounting: A Managerial Emphasis*, Fifteenth Edition, 2015 (with Srikant M. Datar and Madhav V. Rajan); *Introduction to Financial Accounting*, Eleventh Edition, 2014 (with Gary L. Sundem, John A. Elliott, and Donna Philbrick); *Introduction to Management Accounting*, Sixteenth Edition, 2014 (with Gary L. Sundem, Jeff Schatzberg, and Dave Burgstahler);

Horngren's Financial & Managerial Accounting, Fifth Edition, 2016 (with Tracie L. Miller-Nobles, Brenda L. Mattison, and Ella Mae Matsumura); and *Horngren's Accounting*, Eleventh Edition, 2016 (with Tracie L. Miller-Nobles, Brenda L. Mattison, and Ella Mae Matsumura). Horngren was the consulting editor for Pearson's Charles T. Horngren Series in Accounting.

C. William (Bill) Thomas is the J. E. Bush Professor of Accounting and a Master Teacher at Baylor University. A Baylor University alumnus, he received both his BBA and MBA there and went on to earn his PhD from The University of Texas at Austin.

With primary interests in the areas of financial accounting and auditing, Bill Thomas has served as the J. E. Bush Professor of Accounting since 1995. He has been a member of the faculty of the Accounting and Business Law Department of the Hankamer School of Business since 1971, and served as chair of the department for 12 years. He was recognized as an Outstanding Faculty Member of Baylor University as well as a Distinguished Professor for the Hankamer School of Business. Dr. Thomas has received several awards for outstanding teaching, including the Outstanding Professor in the Executive MBA Programs as well as the designation as Master Teacher.

Thomas is the author of textbooks in auditing and financial accounting, as well as many articles in auditing, financial accounting and reporting, taxation, ethics, and accounting education. His scholarly work focuses on the subject of fraud prevention and detection, and ethical issues among accountants in public practice. He presently serves as the accounting and auditing editor of *Today's CPA*, the journal of the Texas Society of Certified Public Accountants, with a circulation of approximately 28,000.

Thomas is a certified public accountant in Texas. Prior to becoming a professor, Thomas was a practicing accountant with the firms of KPMG, LLP, and BDO Seidman, LLP. He is a member of the American Accounting Association, the American Institute of Certified Public Accountants, and the Texas Society of Certified Public Accountants.

Wendy M. Tietz is a professor in the Department of Accounting in the College of Business Administration at Kent State University, where she has taught since 2000. She teaches introductory financial and managerial accounting in a variety of formats, including large sections, small sections, and web-based sections. She has received numerous college and university teaching awards while at Kent State University. Most recently she was named the Beta Gamma Sigma Professor of the Year for the College of Business Administration.

Dr. Tietz is a certified public accountant, a certified management accountant, and a chartered global management accountant. She is a member of the American Accounting Association (AAA), the Institute of Management Accountants (IMA), and the American Institute of Certified Public Accountants (AICPA). She has published articles in such journals as *Issues in Accounting Education, Accounting Education: An International Journal,* and *Journal of Accounting & Public Policy*. She received the 2014 Bea Sanders/AICPA Innovation in Teaching Award for her accounting educator blog entitled "Accounting in the Headlines." She regularly presents at AAA regional and national meetings. Dr. Tietz is also the coauthor of a managerial accounting textbook, *Managerial Accounting*, with Dr. Karen Braun.

Dr. Tietz received her PhD from Kent State University. She received both her MBA and BSA from the University of Akron. She worked in industry for several years, both as a controller for a financial institution and as the operations manager and controller for a recycled plastics manufacturer.

Themin Suwardy is the Dean of Postgraduate Professional Programmes and Associate Professor of Accounting at SMU. Prior to joining academia, Themin was an auditor with KPMG Peat Marwick. He graduated with a BBA in Accountancy, a Bachelor of Computing (Information System), and received his PhD from Monash University, Australia.

He has received over 20 SMU and international teaching awards, including SMU Best MBA Core Teacher Award five times, EMBA Most Outstanding Faculty Award three times, and three SMU university-wide teaching awards. He is a recipient of the Hewlett-Package Mobile Technology for Teaching Grant Award (2004) and the inaugural CEEMAN's Champion Award for Management Teaching (2010). In 2011, he was accorded Singapore's Public Administration Medal (Bronze) for his contribution to education.

Dr. Suwardy has been active member of the accounting profession through his involvement over the years in numerous professional bodies, including CPA Australia (President of Singapore Division, 2013–2014), IIA Singapore, SAC, ISCA, and served as the vice-president of the International Association for Accounting Education and Research. In 2015, he was conferred the Lifetime Achievement Award by CPA Australia for his contributions to the accounting profession.

Dr. Suwardy's main research areas include financial reporting and analysis, corporate governance, and accounting education. He is an associate editor of *Accounting Education*. He has consulted and worked with KPMG Forensics Singapore, DFS Singapore, Singapore Airlines, HP, the Accounting and Corporate Regulatory Authority of Singapore (ACRA), among others.

BRIEF CONTENTS

CONTENTS

With

Financial Accounting

Student Text, Study Resources, and Pearson MyLab Accounting, students will have more

"I get it!"

moments!

PREFACE

Financial Accounting: *International Financial Reporting Standards* (IFRS) continues to give readers a solid foundation in the fundamentals of accounting and the basics of financial statements under IFRS, and then builds upon that foundation to offer more advanced and challenging concepts and problems. This approach helps students to better understand the meaning and relevance of financial information and develop the skills needed to analyze financial information in both their courses and careers.

Written in a manner suitable for accounting and non-accounting majors, *Financial Accounting: IFRS* is the ideal text for a first course in financial accounting with a focus on IFRS. With its long-standing reputation in the marketplace for being easy to read and understand, this text drives home fundamental concepts in a reader-friendly way without adding unnecessary complexity. While maintaining the hallmark features of accuracy, readability, and ease of understanding, this Global Edition includes updated explanations, coverage, new real-world examples, and most importantly, updates to the *Conceptual Framework*.

CHANGES FOR THE ELEVENTH EDITION

1. The first three chapters of the book cover the accounting cycle and how financial statements are constructed. In previous editions of the book, we used separate companies in each of Chapters 1, 2, and 3 to illustrate various phases of the accounting cycle. For this edition, in Chapter 1, we give an overview of the company's financial statements and explain what each contains. The Chapter Spotlight focuses on a new company, Alibaba, which provides an excellent illustration of how companies and accounting frameworks interact in a globalized setting. The updated coverage of the *Conceptual Framework* includes the latest changes made to the IFRS framework, setting the tone for relevant study in the subject. In Chapter 2, we cover business transactions—how they impact the accounting equation and how they are journalized, posted, and summarized. Chapters 3 and 4 come with updated Chapter Spotlights, featuring the latest financial statements and accounting practices of companies. New and updated box features reflect the latest discussions in the IFRS and harmonization contexts. Improved organization of material makes the sequence and flow of the topics easier to follow and retain. New adapted excerpts from real-world companies' notes to the financial statements illustrate how additional information is factored into the main statements.
2. A scaffolding approach has been implemented in the book and its resources. Chapter content and the end-of-chapter material builds from the basic short exercise featuring one basic concept to more advanced problems featuring multiple learning objectives. This allows the student to practice at the basic level and then build upon that success to advance to more challenging problems.
3. Short exercises, exercises, and problems are more clearly labeled by learning objective (LO). Most short exercises have been shortened and simplified in this edition to cover only one LO each. They can be used better to briefly cover single concepts as illustrations or class exercises. Exercises might cover two or three LOs, and problems cover multiple LOs.
4. Chapter 5 has been revised to include a new Chapter Spotlight on The LEGO Group to illustrate the use of internal controls and corporate governance; updated examples of accounting scandals and their repercussions to emphasize the significance of the need for internal controls under IFRS; and new A Closer Look boxes provide snapshots into upcoming changes in IFRS under the topics covered in this chapter and their relevance with International Accounting Standards (IAS) and harmonization. The updated sequence of the topics provides a better flow of the material.
5. Chapter 6 has been updated with a new Chapter Spotlight on Fast Retailing to provide a relevant illustration of a company accounting for merchandise operations across multiple brands. Updated excerpts adapted from various companies' financial statements offer a focused look into inventory management in modern business organizations. New Stop & Think boxes are tailored to act as important checkpoints for concepts on which later topics build. Updated illustrations provide a comparative look into real-world companies' accounts in terms of inventory management.
6. A new Chapter Spotlight focusing on Airbus Group in Chapter 7 illustrates how major companies with operations in multiple countries account for property, plant, and equipment along with intangibles. Adapted excerpts are used as snapshots into the group's classification of assets and methods of accounting.

7. Chapter 9 comes with a new Chapter Spotlight on Jardine Matheson Holdings Ltd. to represent how companies operating in multiple sectors account for liabilities. Updated explanations of the company's financial statements and adapted excerpts shed light on the specifics of the various categories of liabilities. New adapted excerpts from BP's notes to the accounts refer to the Gulf of Mexico oil spill to apply concepts to relatable, real-world incidents. Updated coverage on leases brings the chapter on a par with the latest developments in accounting for liabilities under IFRS.
8. The updated Chapter Spotlight for Chapter 10 and the new Chapter Spotlight on Singtel for Chapter 11 illustrate the management and accounting for shareholders' equity and cash flows. Revised coverage of the cash realization ratio and the direct method to account for cash flows allow a holistic understanding of the concept. New Stop & Think boxes and adapted excerpts from real-world companies' cash flow statements improve the understanding of concepts discussed in these chapters.
9. New Chapter Spotlight on Nestlé for Chapter 12 provides a significantly updated and comprehensive look into financial statement analysis for a company operating in multiple geographies and brands. A detailed look into the company's financial statements covers the various aspects involved in analysis. New Stop & Think boxes offer an opportunity for the students to try their hand at interpreting financial statements and assessing their interpretation.
10. In certain sections, the "Try It in Excel" feature has been added to illustrate the use of Excel and a business problem-solving tool. Students should be exposed to such Excel applications early and frequently in their business education. Throughout the book, most exhibits and journal entries are formatted as Excel worksheets. In addition, at certain points in the text, we include examples that show students step-by-step how to build Excel templates to facilitate the solutions of specific accounting problems.
11. Ethics is a vital part of accounting. Several sections of the text are dedicated to discussing ethical problems that can arise in dealing with that particular subject matter and how they should be properly handled.
12. In all chapters, there is an emphasis on how accounting information covered in that chapter is analyzed and used to help individuals make various kinds of business decisions. User-relevant information and key ratios that are covered in various chapters include the following:

    Chapter 3: Debt-paying ability: net working capital, current ratio, debt ratio

    Chapter 5: Liquidity: acid-test (quick) ratio, accounts receivable turnover, days' sales in receivables

    Chapter 6: Profitability: gross profit percentage, inventory turnover, inventory resident period

    Chapter 9: Time value: time value of money and how it impacts investing and lending decisions

    Chapter 9: Liquidity: accounts payable turnover, days' payable outstanding, cash collection cycle (days' sales in receivables + days inventory outstanding − days' payable outstanding)

    Chapter 10: Profitability: rate of return on ordinary equity, often simply called return on equity (ROE) (net income – preference dividends / total shareholders' equity – preference equity)

    Chapter 11: Cash flow: use of cash flow information by creditors and investors; free cash flow

    Chapter 13: Financial statement analysis: comprehensive financial statement analysis, incorporating all of the ratios covered in the previous chapters, applying them to the book's appendix focus company, Nestlé

13. Emphasis on *Conceptual Framework:* The *Conceptual Framework* is the best way to understand accounting in an IFRS setting. The Eleventh Edition includes updates in the *Conceptual Framework* and combines it with new and updated real-world applications. This approach ensures that students learn basic concepts in accounting in a way that is relevant, stimulating, and fun.
14. Integrated coverage of International Financial Reporting Standards (IFRS): This text offers detailed coverage of the accounting framework and how financial statements provide information for decision making. References to various standards from the IFRS framework offer students insights into the way accounting principles are expressed. A list of resources related to IFRS is available in Appendix D.

VISUAL WALK-THROUGH

Try It in Excel

Describes line-by-line how to retrieve and prepare accounting information (such as adjusted trial balance worksheets, ratio computations, depreciation schedules, bond discount and premium amortization schedules, and financial statement analysis) in Excel.

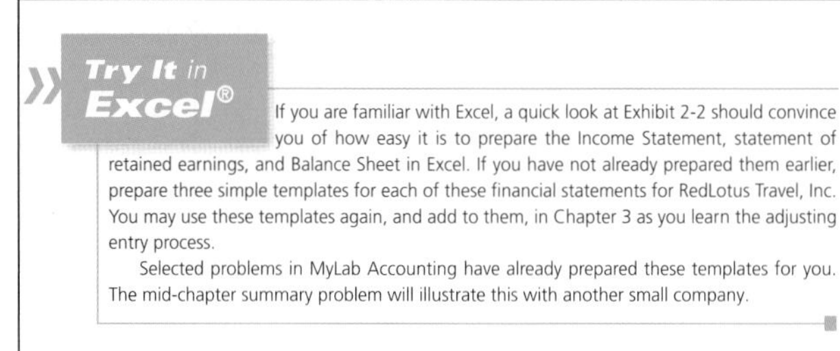

Try It in Excel®

If you are familiar with Excel, a quick look at Exhibit 2-2 should convince you of how easy it is to prepare the Income Statement, statement of retained earnings, and Balance Sheet in Excel. If you have not already prepared them earlier, prepare three simple templates for each of these financial statements for RedLotus Travel, Inc. You may use these templates again, and add to them, in Chapter 3 as you learn the adjusting entry process.

Selected problems in MyLab Accounting have already prepared these templates for you. The mid-chapter summary problem will illustrate this with another small company.

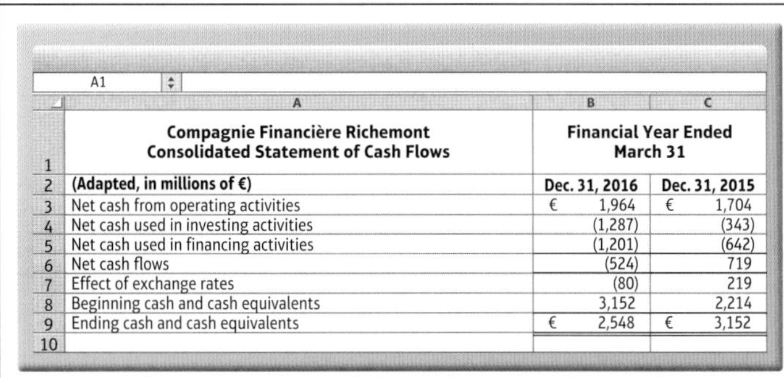

	A	B	C
1	**Compagnie Financière Richemont Consolidated Statement of Cash Flows**	**Financial Year Ended March 31**	
2	**(Adapted, in millions of €)**	**Dec. 31, 2016**	**Dec. 31, 2015**
3	Net cash from operating activities	€ 1,964	€ 1,704
4	Net cash used in investing activities	(1,287)	(343)
5	Net cash used in financing activities	(1,201)	(642)
6	Net cash flows	(524)	719
7	Effect of exchange rates	(80)	219
8	Beginning cash and cash equivalents	3,152	2,214
9	Ending cash and cash equivalents	€ 2,548	€ 3,152
10			

Excel Integrated Throughout Text!

Excel-based financial statements are used so that students will familiarize themselves with the accounting information format actually used in the business world.

Box Features Throughout Text!

Stop & Think boxes are found at various points in a chapter; this tool includes a question-and-answer snapshot asking students to apply what they just learned. A Closer Look boxes provide a snapshot into upcoming changes in IFRS (and IAS) under the topics covered in the chapters.

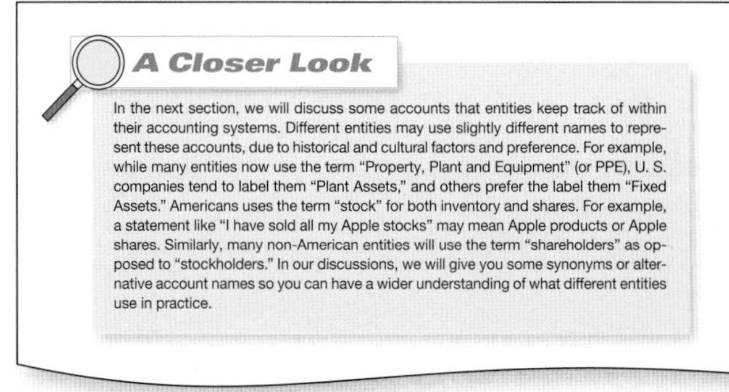

A Closer Look

In the next section, we will discuss some accounts that entities keep track of within their accounting systems. Different entities may use slightly different names to represent these accounts, due to historical and cultural factors and preference. For example, while many entities now use the term "Property, Plant and Equipment" (or PPE), U. S. companies tend to label them "Plant Assets," and others prefer the label them "Fixed Assets." Americans uses the term "stock" for both inventory and shares. For example, a statement like "I have sold all my Apple stocks" may mean Apple products or Apple shares. Similarly, many non-American entities will use the term "shareholders" as opposed to "stockholders." In our discussions, we will give you some synonyms or alternative account names so you can have a wider understanding of what different entities use in practice.

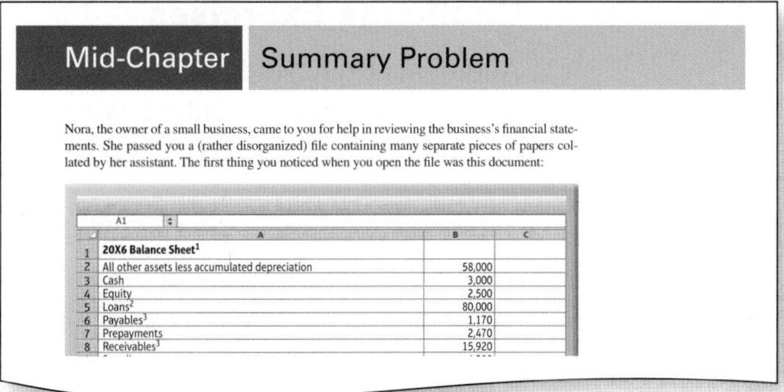

Mid-Chapter Summary Problem

Nora, the owner of a small business, came to you for help in reviewing the business's financial statements. She passed you a (rather disorganized) file containing many separate pieces of papers collated by her assistant. The first thing you noticed when you open the file was this document:

	A	B	C
1	**20X6 Balance Sheet**[1]		
2	All other assets less accumulated depreciation	58,000	
3	Cash	3,000	
4	Equity	2,500	
5	Loans[2]	80,000	
6	Payables[3]	1,170	
7	Prepayments	2,470	
8	Receivables[3]	15,920	

Chapter Summary Problems

Found in the middle and then at the end of each chapter along with solutions, this feature provides students with additional guided learning. By appearing twice in each chapter, it breaks down information and enables students to absorb and master the material in manageable pieces.

Decision Guidelines

Illustrates how financial statements are used and how accounting information aids companies in decision making.

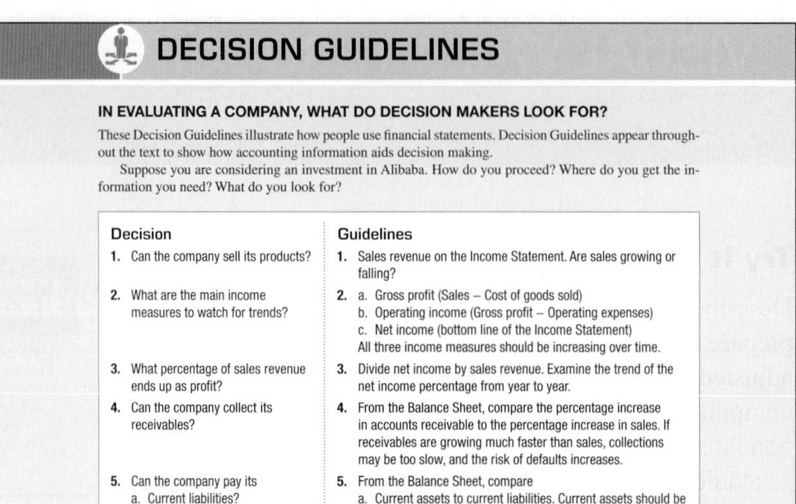

DECISION GUIDELINES

IN EVALUATING A COMPANY, WHAT DO DECISION MAKERS LOOK FOR?

These Decision Guidelines illustrate how people use financial statements. Decision Guidelines appear throughout the text to show how accounting information aids decision making.

Suppose you are considering an investment in Alibaba. How do you proceed? Where do you get the information you need? What do you look for?

Decision	Guidelines
1. Can the company sell its products?	**1.** Sales revenue on the Income Statement. Are sales growing or falling?
2. What are the main income measures to watch for trends?	**2.** a. Gross profit (Sales – Cost of goods sold) b. Operating income (Gross profit – Operating expenses) c. Net income (bottom line of the Income Statement) All three income measures should be increasing over time.
3. What percentage of sales revenue ends up as profit?	**3.** Divide net income by sales revenue. Examine the trend of the net income percentage from year to year.
4. Can the company collect its receivables?	**4.** From the Balance Sheet, compare the percentage increase in accounts receivable to the percentage increase in sales. If receivables are growing much faster than sales, collections may be too slow, and the risk of defaults increases.
5. Can the company pay its a. Current liabilities? b. Current and long-term liabilities?	**5.** From the Balance Sheet, compare a. Current assets to current liabilities. Current assets should be somewhat greater than current liabilities. b. Total assets to total liabilities. Total assets must be somewhat greater than total liabilities.

Ethical Issue

This end-of-chapter feature presents students with ethical situations and requires them to work through the decision framework for making ethical judgments. Finally, they are asked to come to a decision and support it.

Ethical Issue

For each of the following situations, answer the following questions:

1. What is the ethical issue in this situation?
2. What are the alternatives?
3. Who are the stakeholders? What are the possible consequences to each? Analyze from the following standpoints: (a) economic, (b) legal, and (c) ethical.
4. Place yourself in the role of the decision maker. What would you do? How would you justify your decision?

Issue 1. Sunrise Bank recently appointed the accounting firm of Smith, Godfroy, and Hannaford as the bank's auditor. Sunrise quickly became one of Smith, Godfroy, and Hannaford's largest clients. Subject to banking regulations, Sunrise must provide for any expected losses on notes receivable that Sunrise may not collect in full.

During the course of the audit, Smith, Godfroy, and Hannaford determined that three large notes receivable of Sunrise seem questionable. Smith, Godfroy, and Hannaford discussed these loans with Susan Carter, controller of Sunrise. Carter assured the auditors that these notes were good and that the makers of the notes will be able to pay their notes after the economy improves.

Challenge Exercises

E2-37. *(Learning Objective 5: Computing financial statement amounts)* The manager of Pierce Furniture needs to compute the following amounts: LO 5

a. Total cash paid during October.
b. Cash collections from customers during October. Analyze Accounts Receivable.
c. Cash paid on a note payable during October. Analyze Notes Payable.

Here's the additional data you need to analyze the accounts:

Account	Balance Sep 30	Balance Oct 31	Additional Information for the Month of October
1. Cash	$ 12,000	$ 6,000	Cash receipts, $ 85,000
2. Accounts Receivable	27,500	26,000	Sales on account, $ 50,000
3. Notes Payable	16,100	23,000	New borrowing, $ 15,000

Challenge Exercises

Additional exercises have been developed to provide students with the opportunity for applied critical thinking.

DIGITAL WALK-THROUGH

Pearson eText

The Pearson eText, available through MyLab Accounting, gives students access to their textbook anytime, anywhere. In addition to note taking, highlighting, and bookmarking, the Pearson eText offers interactive and sharing features. Rich media options let students watch lecture and example videos as they read or do their homework. Instructors can share their comments or highlights, and students can add their own, creating a tight community of learners in your class.

The Pearson eText companion app allows existing subscribers to access their titles on an iPad or Android tablet for either online or offline viewing. The app is available on Google's Play Store and Apple's App Store.

- Now available on smartphones and tablets
- Seamlessly integrated videos and other rich media
- Accessible (screen-reader ready)
- Configurable reading settings, including resizable type and night-reading mode
- Instructor and student note taking, highlighting, bookmarking, and search

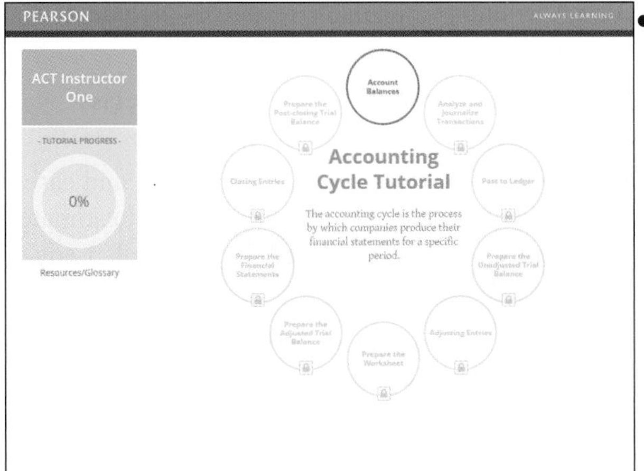

Accounting Cycle Tutorial (ACT) NEW!

MyLab Accounting's new interactive tutorial helps students master the accounting cycle for early and continued success in the Introduction to Accounting course. The tutorial, accessed by computer, Smartphone, or tablet, provides students with brief explanations of each concept of the accounting cycle through engaging videos and animations. Students are immediately assessed on their understanding, and their performance is recorded in the MyLab Accounting grade book. Whether the Accounting Cycle Tutorial is used as a remediation self-study tool or course assignment, students have yet another resource within MyLab Accounting to help them be successful with the accounting cycle.

Learning Catalytics

Learning Catalytics, available through MyLab Accounting, is a "bring your own device" assessment and classroom activity system that expands the possibilities for student engagement. Using Learning Catalytics, you can deliver a wide range of automatically graded or open-ended questions that test content knowledge and build critical thinking skills.

STUDENT AND INSTRUCTOR RESOURCES

For Students

MyLab Accounting online Homework and Assessment Manager includes:

- Pearson eText
- Student PowerPoint® Presentations
- Accounting Cycle Tutorial
- Videos
- Demo Docs
- Flash Cards
- Dynamic Study Modules
- QuickBooks Data Files
- Excel in Practice Data Files
- Working Papers

Student resource website: http://www.pearsonglobaleditions.com/harrison
This website contains the following:

- The QuickBooks Data Files and the Excel in Practice Data Files, related to select end-of-chapter problems
- Working Papers, for completing end-of-chapter questions in preformatted templates
- Student PowerPoint® Presentations

For Instructors

Instructor Resource Center: http://www.pearsonglobaleditions.com/harrison
For the instructor's convenience, the instructor resources can be downloaded from the textbook's catalog page and MyLab Accounting. Available resources include the following:

- *Instructor's Resource Manual*: Includes chapter outlines, suggested in-class activities, topics with which students struggle, as well as the following:
  - Assignment grid that outlines all end-of-chapter exercises, problems, and cases; the topic being covered in that particular exercise, problem, or cases; estimated completion time; level of difficulty; and availability in General Ledger, QuickBooks, or Excel templates.
- *Instructor's Solutions Manual*: Contains solutions to all end-of-chapter questions, including short exercises, exercises, problems, and cases.
- *Test Bank*: Includes more than 2,000 questions. Both objective-based questions and computational problems are available.
- *PowerPoint Presentations*: These presentations help facilitate classroom discussion.
  - Instructor PowerPoint Presentations with lecture notes
  - Student PowerPoint Presentations
- *Working Paper Templates and Solutions* in Excel and PDF Format
- *Image Library*
- *Data and Solution Files*: These include QuickBooks Data Files and Excel in Practice Data Files, related to select end-of-chapter problems. Corresponding solution files are also provided.

ACKNOWLEDGMENTS

We sincerely thank the many friends and colleagues who have helped in the process of writing and revising this book. Betsy Willis deserves special mention for her dedication, feedback, and hard work throughout this project. We thank Carolyn Streuly for her amazing accuracy checking. We are also deeply grateful to Lacey Vitetta and Heather Pagano for their endless patience and support. Thank you to Donna Battista, Natalie Wagner, Mary Kate Murray, Sarah Peterson, Kathy Smith, and Martha LaChance for their continued help and support. Thanks also to Sheila Ammons for preparing the Test Bank, to Betsy Willis for preparing the *Instructor's Resource Manual*, and to Michelle Franz for preparing the PowerPoint presentation. Thank you also to the many professors and students who have used the book and provided feedback for improving it.

We would like to thank the following reviewers for the Eleventh Edition for their valuable input: Patricia Derrick, Drexel University; Shuai Ma, American University; Susan Machuga, University of Hartford; Dorothy Thompson, Ave Maria University; Gary Olsen, Carroll University; Reed Easton, Seton Hall University; Randall Serrett, University of Houston–Downtown; Ada Duffey, University of Wisconsin–Waukesha; Alesha Graves, Mount St. Joseph University; Brian Routh, University of Southern Indiana; Regan Garey, Lock Haven University; Michelle Watts, Boise State University; David Parker, Saint Xavier University; Brian Porter, Hope College; Rosemary Nurre, College of San Mateo.

In revising previous editions of *Financial Accounting*, we had the help of instructors from across the country who have participated in online surveys, chapter reviews, and focus groups. Their comments and suggestions for both the text and the supplements have been a great help in planning and carrying out revisions, and we thank them for their contributions.

GLOBAL EDITION ACKNOWLEDGMENTS

We would like to thank the following people for reviewing the Global Edition. Their inputs, comments, and suggestions helped us to improve the content for the Eleventh Edition: Diane Bonneau, The American University of Paris; Loo Choo Hong, Wawasan Open University; Gagan Kukreja, Ahlia University; Jeff Ng, Chinese University of Hong Kong; Jan Renaud, Utrecht University; Gretha Steenkamp, Stellenbosch University; and Gunawan Wibisono, Universitas Gadjah Mada.

Past Reviewer Participants

Shawn Abbott, College of the Siskiyous
Linda Abernathy, Kirkwood Community College
Sol Ahiarah, SUNY College at Buffalo (Buffalo State)
M. J. Albin, University of Southern Mississippi
Gary Ames, Brigham Young University, Idaho
Elizabeth Ammann, Lindenwood University
Brenda Anderson, Brandeis University
Kim Anderson, Indiana University of Pennsylvania
Florence Atiase, University of Texas at Austin
Walter Austin, Mercer University, Macon
Brad Badertscher, University of Iowa
Sandra Bailey, Oregon Institute of Technology
Patrick Bauer, DeVry University, Kansas City
Barbara A. Beltrand, Metropolitan State University
Jerry Bennett, University of South Carolina–Spartanburg
Peg Beresewski, Robert Morris College
Lucille Berry, Webster University
John Bildersee, New York University, Stern School
Brenda Bindschatel, Green River Community College
Candace Blankenship, Belmont University
Charlie Bokemeier, Michigan State University
Patrick Bouker, North Seattle Community College
Amy Bourne, Oregon State University
Scott Boylan, Washington and Lee University
Robert Braun, Southeastern Louisiana University
Linda Bressler, University of Houston–Downtown
Michael Broihahn, Barry University
Rada Brooks, University of California, Berkeley
Carol Brown, Oregon State University
Elizabeth Brown, Keene State College
Helen Brubeck, San Jose State University
Scott Bryant, Baylor University
Marcus Butler, University of Rochester
Marci Butterfield, University of Utah
Mark Camma, Atlantic Cape Community College
Kay Carnes, Gonzaga University
Brian Carpenter, University of Scranton
Sandra Cereola, James Madison University
Kam Chan, Pace University
Hong Chen, Northeastern Illinois University
C. Catherine Chiang, Elon University
Freddy Choo, San Francisco State University
Charles Christy, Delaware Tech and Community College, Stanton Campus
Lawrence Chui, Opus College of Business, University of St. Thomas
Shifei Chung, Rowan University
Bryan Church, Georgia Tech at Atlanta
Carolyn Clark, Saint Joseph's University
Dr. Paul Clikeman, University of Richmond
Charles Coate, St. Bonaventure University
Dianne Conry, University of California State College Extension–Cupertino
Ellen D. Cook, University of Louisiana at Lafayette
John Coulter, Western New England College
Sue Counte, Saint Louis Community College–Meramec
Julia Creighton, American University
Sue Cullers, Buena Vista University
Donald Curfman, McHenry County College
Alan Czyzewski, Indiana State University
Laurie Dahlin, Worcester State College
Bonita Daly, University of Southern Maine
Kreag Danvers, Clarion University
Betty David, Francis Marion University
Patricia Derrick, George Washington University
Peter DiCarlo, Boston College
Charles Dick, Miami University
Barbara Doughty, New Hampshire Community Technical College
Allan Drebin, Northwestern University
Carolyn Dreher, Southern Methodist University
Emily Drogt, Grand Valley State University
Carol Dutton, South Florida Community College
James Emig, Villanova University
Ellen Engel, University of Chicago
Mary Ewanechko, Monroe Community College
Alan Falcon, Loyola Marymount University
Janet Farler, Pima Community College
Dr. Andrew Felo, Penn State Great Valley
Ken Ferris, Thunderbird College
Dr. Mary Fischer, The University of Texas at Tyler
Dr. Caroline Ford, Baylor University
Clayton Forester, University of Minnesota
Lou Fowler, Missouri Western State College
Timothy Gagnon, Northeastern University
Terrie Gehman, Elizabethtown College
Lucille Genduso, Nova Southeastern University
Frank Gersich, Monmouth College
Bradley Gillespie, Saddleback College
Lisa Gillespie, Loyola University, Chicago
Marvin Gordon, University of Illinois at Chicago
Brian Green, University of Michigan at Dearborn
Anthony Greig, Purdue University
Ronald Guidry, University of Louisiana at Monroe
Konrad Gunderson, Missouri Western State College
Dr. Geoffrey J. Gurka, Colorado Mesa University
William Hahn, Southeastern College
Jack Hall, Western Kentucky University
Gloria Halpern, Montgomery College
Penny Hanes, Mercyhurst College
Dr. Heidi Hansel, Kirkwood Community College
Kenneth Hart, Brigham Young University, Idaho
Al Hartgraves, Emory University
Michael Haselkorn, Bentley University
Thomas Hayes, University of North Texas
Larry Hegstad, Pacific Lutheran University
Candy Heino, Anoka-Ramsey Community College
Mary Hollars, Vincennes University

Anit Hope, Tarrant County College
Thomas Huse, Boston College
Fred R. Jex, Macomb Community College
Grace Johnson, Marietta College
Celina Jozsi, University of South Florida
John Karayan, Woodbury University
Beth Kern, Indiana University, South Bend
Irene Kim, The George Washington University
Hans E. Klein, Babson College
Robert Kollar, Duquesne University
Willem Koole, North Carolina State University
Emil Koren, Hillsborough Community College
Dennis Kovach, Community College of Allegheny County–North Campus
Maria U. Ku, Ohlone College & Diablo Valley College
Ellen Landgraf, Loyola University Chicago
Howard Lawrence, Christian Brothers University
Barry Leffkov, Regis College
Elliott Levy, Bentley University
Chao-Shin Liu, Notre Dame
Barbara Lougee, University of California, Irvine
Heidemarie Lundblad, California State University, Northridge
Joseph Lupino, Saint Mary's College of California
Anna Lusher, West Liberty State College
Harriet Maccracken, Arizona State University
Constance Malone Hylton, George Mason University
Carol Mannino, Milwaukee School of Engineering
Herb Martin, Hope College
Aziz Martinez, Harvard University, Harvard Business School
Anthony Masino, Queens University/NC Central
Lizbeth Matz, University of Pittsburgh, Bradford
Bruce Maule, College of San Mateo
Michelle McEacharn, University of Louisiana at Monroe
Molly McFadden-May, Tulsa Community College
Nick McGaughey, San Jose State University
Allison McLeod, University of North Texas
Cathleen Miller, University of Michigan–Flint
Cynthia J. Miller, Gatton College of Business & Economics, University of Kentucky
Mark Miller, University of San Francisco
Mary Miller, University of New Haven
Scott Miller, Gannon University
Frank Mioni, Madonna University
Dr. Birendra (Barry) K. Mishra, University of California, Riverside
Theodore D. Morrison III, Wingate University
Lisa Nash, Vincennes University
Rosemary Nurre, College of San Mateo
Bruce L. Oliver, Rochester Institute of Technology
Stephen Owen, Hamilton College
Charles Pedersen, Quinsigamond Community College
Richard J. Pettit, Mountain View College
George Plesko, Massachusetts Institute of Technology
David Plumlee, University of Utah
Gregory Prescott, University of South Alabama
Rama Ramamurthy, College of William and Mary
Craig Reeder, Florida A&M University
Barb Reeves, Cleary University
Bettye Rogers-Desselle, Prairie View A&M University
Darren Roulstone, University of Chicago
Norlin Rueschhoff, Notre Dame
Anwar Salimi, California State Polytechnic University, Pomona
Philippe Sammour, Eastern Michigan University
Angela Sandberg, Jacksonville State University
George Sanders, Western Washington University
Betty Saunders, University of North Florida
Albert A Schepanski, University of Iowa
William Schmul, Notre Dame
Arnie Schnieder, Georgia Tech at Atlanta
Gim Seow, University of Connecticut
Itzhak Sharav, CUNY–Lehman Graduate School of Business
Allan Sheets, International Business College
Lily Sieux, California State University, East Bay
Alvin Gerald Smith, University of Northern Iowa
James Smith, Community College of Philadelphia
Virginia Smith, Saint Mary's College of California
Beverly Soriano, Framingham State College
Vic Stanton, Stanford University
Carolyn R. Stokes, Frances Marion University
J. B. Stroud, Nicholls State University
Gloria J. Stuart, Georgia Southern University
Al Taccone, Cuyamaca College
Diane Tanner, University of North Florida
Martin Taylor, University of Texas at Arlington
Howard Toole, San Diego State University
Vincent Turner, California State Polytechnic University, Pomona
Sue Van Boven, Paradise Valley Community College
Marcia Veit, University of Central Florida
Bruce Wampler, Louisiana State University, Shreveport
Suzanne Ward, University of Louisiana at Lafayette
Craig Weaver, University of California, Riverside
Frederick Weis, Claremont McKenna College
Frederick Weiss, Virginia Wesleyan College
Betsy Willis, Baylor University
Ronald Woan, Indiana University of Pennsylvania
Allen Wright, Hillsborough Community College
Dr. Jia Wu, University of Massachusetts, Dartmouth
Yanfeng Xue, George Washington University
Barbara Yahvah, University of Montana–Helena
Myung Yoon, Northeastern Illinois University
Lin Zeng, Northeastern Illinois University
Tony Zordan, University of St. Francis

ACCOUNTING CAREERS: MUCH MORE THAN COUNTING THINGS

What kind of career can you have in accounting? Almost any kind you want. A career in accounting lets you use your analytical skills in a variety of ways, and it brings both monetary and personal rewards.

Today's accountants obtain years of formal education at the college level which, for most, culminates in taking a very rigorous professional exam that qualifies them to hold the designation of Certified Public Accountant (CPA) or chartered accountant (CA). There are other professional designations that accountants may obtain as well, each with its own professional exam and set of professional standards. Examples are Certified Management Accountant (CMA), certified internal auditor (CIA), and Certified Fraud Examiner (CFE).

WHERE ACCOUNTANTS WORK

Where can you work as an accountant? There are four kinds of employers.

Public Practice

You can work for public accounting firm, which could be a large international firm or a variety of medium to small-sized firms. Within a CPA firm, you can specialize in areas such as audit, tax, or consulting. In this capacity, you'll be serving as an external accountant to many clients. At present, the six largest international firms are Deloitte, Ernst & Young (E&Y), KPMG, PricewaterhouseCoopers (PwC), Grant Thornton, and RSM McGladrey. However, there are many other firms with an international or national scope of practice. Most CPAs start their career at a large CPA firm. From there, they move on to obtain positions of leadership in the corporate finance world or just about anywhere with a demand for people who like solving complex problems.

Managerial Accounting

Instead of working for various clients, you can work in one corporation or nonprofit enterprise. Your role may be to analyze financial information and communicate that information to managers, who would use it to strategize and make decisions. You may be asked to help allocate corporate resources or make recommendations to improve financial performance. For example, you might do a cost-benefit analysis to help decide whether to acquire a company or build a factory. Or you might describe the financial implications of choosing one strategy over another. You might work in areas such as internal auditing, financial management, financial reporting, treasury management, and tax planning. The highest position in management accounting is the chief financial officer (CFO) position, with some CFOs rising to become chief executive officers (CEOs).

Government and Not-for-Profit Entities

As an accountant, you might work for the government—central, state, or local. Similar to corporate or private accounting roles, a government accountant's role includes responsibilities in the areas of auditing, financial reporting, and management accounting. You will be expected to evaluate how government agencies are managed. You may advise decision makers on how to allocate resources to improve efficiency. Many countries have agencies that hire CPAs to investigate the financial aspects of white-collar crime. You might find yourself working for tax authorities, national accounting or audit agencies, security commissions or stock exchanges, the ministry of finance or the treasury, or even the parliament.

As an accountant, you might also decide to work in the nonprofit sector. Colleges, universities, primary and secondary schools, hospitals, and charitable organizations all have accounting functions. Accountants for these types of entities prepare financial statements as well as budgets and projections. Most have special training in accounting standards that are specially designed for the nonprofit sector.

Education

You can work at a college or university, advancing the thought and theory of accounting and teaching future generations of new accountants. On the research side, you might study how companies use accounting information. You might develop new ways of categorizing financial data, or study accounting practices in different countries. You can then publish your ideas in journals and books and present them to colleagues at meetings around the world. On the education side, you can help others learn about accounting and give them the tools they need to be their best.

CPA: THREE LETTERS THAT SPEAK VOLUMES

When employers see the CPA designation, they know what to expect about your education, knowledge, abilities, and personal attributes. They value your analytical skills and extensive training. Your CPA credential gives you a distinct advantage in the job market and credibility in the workplace. It's a plus when dealing with other professionals such as bankers, attorneys, auditors, and government regulators. In addition, your colleagues in the private industry would tend to defer to you when dealing with complex business matters, particularly those involving financial management.

THE HOTTEST GROWTH AREAS IN ACCOUNTING

Recent legislations, such as the Sarbanes-Oxley Act of 2002 (SOX), around the world have increased the demand for accountants of all kinds. In addition to a strong overall demand, the following areas* of accounting are especially popular:

Sustainability Reporting

Sustainability reporting involves reporting on an organization's performance with respect to health, safety, and environmental issues (HSE). As businesses take a greater interest in environmental issues, CPAs are getting involved in reporting on matters like employee health, on-the-job accident rates, emissions of certain pollutants, spills, volumes of waste generated, and initiatives to minimize such incidents. Utilities, manufacturers, and chemical companies are particularly affected by environmental issues. As a result, they approach CPAs to set up a preventive system to ensure compliance and avoid future disputes or to provide assistance once legal complications arise.

*Refer to the Pearson Series in Accounting to identify the textbooks that will help you prepare for various branches of accounting.

Corporate social responsibility (CSR) reporting is similar to HSE reporting, but with a broader emphasis on social matters, such as ethical labor practices, training, education, diversity of workforce, and corporate philanthropic initiatives. Most of the world's largest corporations have extensive CSR initiatives.

Assurance Services

Assurance services are provided by a CPA to improve the quality of information, or its context, for decision makers. Such information can be financial or non-financial, and can be about past events or ongoing processes and systems. This broad concept includes audit and attestation services and is distinct from consulting because it focuses primarily on improving information rather than on providing advice or installing systems. You can use your analytical and information-processing expertise to provide assurance services in areas ranging from e-commerce to elder care, comprehensive risk assessment, business valuation, entity performance measurement, and information systems quality assessment.

Information Technology Services

Companies can't compete effectively if their information technology systems don't have the power or flexibility to perform essential functions. Companies need accountants with strong computer skills who can design and implement advanced systems to fit a company's specific needs and to find ways to protect and insulate data. CPAs skilled in software research and development (including multimedia technology) are also highly valued.

International Accounting

Globalization means that cross-border transactions have become commonplace. Countries in Eastern Europe and Latin America, which previously had closed economies, have open trade relations and are doing business with new trading partners. The passage of the North American Free Trade Agreement (NAFTA) and the General Agreement on Tariffs and Trade (GATT) facilitates trade, and the economic growth in areas such as the Pacific Rim further brings greater volumes of trade and financial flows. Organizations need accountants who understand international trade rules, accords, and laws; cross-border merger and acquisition issues; and foreign business customs, languages, cultures, and procedures.

Forensic Accounting

Forensic accounting is in growing demand after scandals such as the collapse of Enron and WorldCom, which are featured in this text. Forensic accountants look at a company's financial records for evidence of criminal activity. This could be anything from securities fraud to overvaluation of inventory; from money laundering to improper capitalization of expenses.

Whether you seek a career in a business, government, or nonprofit sector, accounting has a career for you. Every organization, from the smallest mom-and-pop music retailer to the biggest government agency in the world, needs accountants to help manage its resources.

International Financial Reporting Standards

1 Conceptual Framework and Financial Statements

SPOTLIGHT | Alibaba Group www.alibabagroup.com

In 1998, Jack Ma, a former English teacher from Hangzhou, China, started Alibaba with 18 other people. Alibaba was established to champion small businesses, in the belief that the Internet would level the playing field by enabling small enterprises to leverage innovation and technology to grow and compete more effectively in the domestic and global economies. Fast-forward 20 years. Alibaba is now a global Internet e-commerce giant with businesses ranging from marketplaces such as alibaba.com and taobao.com to financial services (AliPay), cloud computing, and even motion pictures (Alibaba Pictures). Alibaba's Initial Public Offering (IPO) on the New York Stock Exchange in 2014 is currently the largest IPO to date, having raised over US$20 billion.

In the financial year ended March 31, 2016, Alibaba earned a total revenue in excess of 100 billion Renminbi (¥), which is equivalent to about US$15.7 billion. After deducting the cost of sales and other expenses, Alibaba's 2016 net income was about ¥71 billion. From its operating activities, Alibaba generated cash flows of about ¥57 billion. Its assets grew from ¥255 billion the year before to ¥364 billion in 2016. ●

Renminbi Chinese currency, abbreviated RMB or CNY for Chinese Yuan, ¥

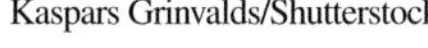

Kaspars Grinvalds/Shutterstock

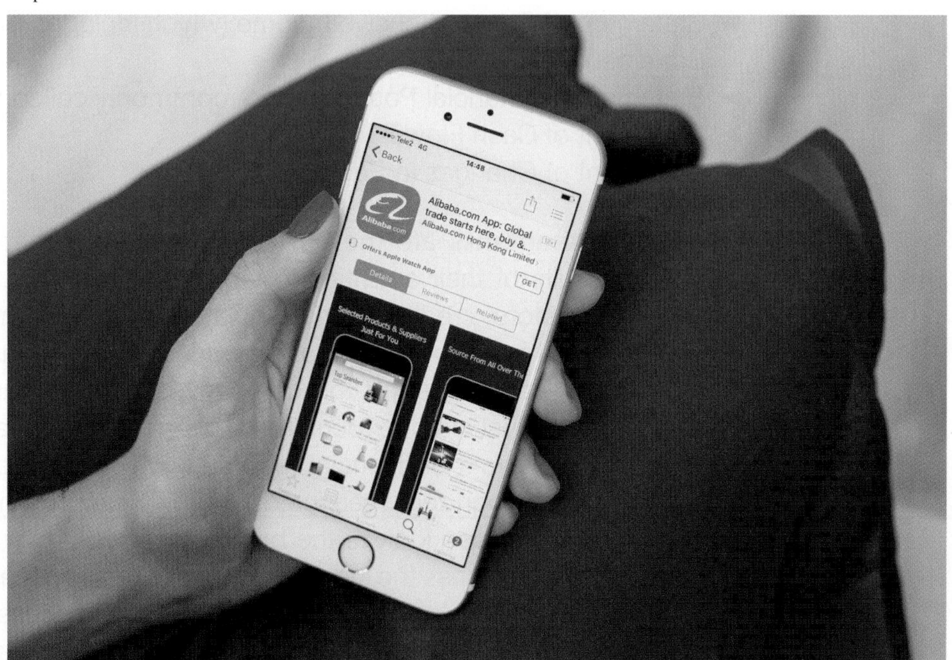

Alibaba Group Holdings Limited Consolidated Income Statement	Year Ended March 31		
(Adapted, in millions of ¥ and US$)	**Mar. 31, 2015**	**Mar. 31, 2016**	**Mar. 31, 2016**
Revenue	¥ 76,204	¥ 101,143	$ 15,686
Cost of revenue	(23,834)	(34,355)	(5,328)
Product development expenses	(10,658)	(13,788)	(2,138)
Sales and marketing expenses	(8,513)	(11,307)	(1,753)
General and administrative expenses	(7,800)	(9,205)	(1,428)
Amortization of intangible assets	(2,089)	(2,931)	(455)
Impairment of goodwill	(175)	(455)	(71)
Income from operations	23,135	29,102	4,513
Other income	2,486	2,058	319
Interest and investment income	9,455	52,254	8,104
Interest expense	(2,750)	(1,946)	(301)
Share of results of equity investees	(1,590)	(1,730)	(269)
Income tax expenses	(6,416)	(8,449)	(1,310)
Net income	¥ 24,320	¥ 71,289	$ 11,056

The terms *revenue, net income,* etc. may be foreign to you now, but after you read this chapter, you will gain a greater understanding of financial statements. Welcome to the world of accounting!

Each chapter of this text begins with adapted extracts of an actual financial statement. In this chapter, our reference is the Consolidated Income Statements of Alibaba, for the two years ended March 31, 2015, and March 31, 2016. We will continue to explore various examples of financial statements (and their notes to the accounts) throughout this text, so you can relate the theories and concepts to actual financial accounting practices and disclosures.

The core of financial accounting revolves around the following financial statements:

- Statement of Comprehensive Income (which includes the above Income Statement)
- Statement of Financial Position (more commonly called Balance Sheet)
- Statement of Cash Flows
- Statement of Changes in Equity

Financial statements are the business documents that companies use to report the results of their activities to various user groups, which can include managers, investors, creditors, and regulatory agencies. In turn, these parties use the reported information to make a variety of decisions, such as whether to invest in or loan money to the company, amongst many others. To learn accounting, you must learn to focus on decisions. In this chapter we explain the *Conceptual Framework* of financial reporting, which underpins how a financial phenomenon is recognized, measured, and disclosed to the users of financial statements. We will also look at the bodies responsible for issuing accounting standards. We will discuss the judgment process that is necessary to make good accounting decisions. In addition to this, we will also discuss the contents of the four basic financial statements that report the results of those decisions. In later chapters, we will explain in more detail how to construct financial statements as well as how user groups typically use the information contained in these statements to make business decisions.

LEARNING OBJECTIVES

1. **Understand** the role of accounting in communicating financial information
2. **Understand** the underlying accounting concepts in the IFRS *Conceptual Framework*
3. **Obtain** insights into business operations through financial statements
4. **Identify** financial statements and their inter-relationships
5. **Understand** the role of ethics in accounting

UNDERSTAND THE ROLE OF ACCOUNTING IN COMMUNICATING FINANCIAL INFORMATION

Business Decisions

1 **Understand the role** of accounting in communicating financial information

Alibaba's shareholders and potential investors make many financial decisions. They decide when to buy, hold, or sell their investment. They assess the stewardship and accountability of the company's management. They assess the profitability, efficiency, liquidity, and cash flows of the company. Alibaba's management also uses financial information to help the company decide on its sources of funding and capital; they make costing and pricing decisions and analyze the performance of various business groups within the company. Accounting helps companies, their shareholders, and management make these decisions.

Take a look again at Alibaba's Consolidated Income Statement. Let us start with its "bottom line" on line 16. Alibaba calls it "net income" but other businesses may use terms such as "net profit" or "Income for the year." Net income is the excess of revenues over expenses. We can see that Alibaba earned a net income of ¥71 billion for the financial year ended March 31, 2016. That's good news because it means that Alibaba had ¥71 billion more in revenues than its expenses for the year, despite the challenging economic conditions and subdued economic growth since the global financial crisis of 2008. What is amazing is that Alibaba's growth in revenue is at 33%, but its net income has almost doubled!

Suppose you have some money to invest. What information would you need before deciding to invest in Alibaba? How would you know if the information appropriately reflects Alibaba's actual financial performance and financial position? Let's see how accounting gives you all this information.

Accounting Is the Language of Business

Italian merchants in Genoa, Florence, and Venice were at the epicenter of trade between Europe and the Middle East in the 13th and the 14th centuries. As trading ventures grew, individual merchants were not able to provide the capital necessary to conduct business ventures on their own. Thus, the concept of "shareholders" and "capital" was born, and along with it the need to report on the venture's financial status to investors. Father Luca Pacioli, a contemporary of Leonardo da Vinci, documented the so-called "Venetian Method" of bookkeeping in his book titled *Summa de Arithmetica, Geometria, Proportioni et Proportionalita* (*Everything About Arithmetic, Geometry and Proportion*), published on November 10, 1494. As commerce grew in Europe, it quickly spread, and today we know it as the **double-entry system** of bookkeeping, which forms the basis of financial reporting to shareholders. In fact, November 10 is celebrated as International Accounting Day!

Accounting today is clearly more complex and sophisticated than what was prescribed by Pacioli, but at its heart, **accounting** is an information system. It records and measures business activities, processes data into information, and communicates this information to decision makers who make decisions that will have an impact on business activities. Indeed, accounting is "the language of business."

Exhibit 1-1 shows how business activities are recorded in the accounting system, which, in turn, produces financial reports that help decision making in business activities.

Exhibit 1-1 | The Flow of Accounting Information

So, who needs to be familiar with this language? Those who run a business? Shareholders? Well anyone who makes any business decision needs to be familiar with accounting. Accounting is the language of communication in all businesses. The better our understanding of this language, the better we can understand our finances, our businesses, or our investments!

Two Perspectives of Accounting: Financial Accounting and Management Accounting

Both *external* and *internal users* of financial information exist. Therefore, we can classify accounting into two branches. **Financial accounting** provides information to decision makers outside the **reporting entity**. These are investors, creditors, government agencies, and the public. This text focuses on financial accounting.

Management accounting provides information for Alibaba's managers. Examples of management accounting information include budgets, forecasts, and projections that are used in making strategic decisions for the entity. Managers of Alibaba have the ability to determine the form and content of financial information in order to meet their own needs. Internal information must still be reliable and relevant for their decision needs.

You may be doing this course as an accounting student or a non-accounting student. Regardless of your eventual career ambitions, knowledge of accounting will help you understand how organizations operate. Many accounting graduates work in professional accounting services, typically with public accounting firms. These firms offer various services to business and government sectors, such as audit and assurance, taxation advice, consultancy, and advisory. Those who venture into the corporate world may work in various accounting functions, from treasury and finance, to internal audit and risk management. Even if you are not an accounting student, in almost all lines of work and across industries, you will have to make decisions in your day-to-day activities, most of which will require you to understand, prepare, or work with some form of financial reporting and budgeting. On an personal level, you may also find that accounting helps you manage your own finances and investments better.

Organizing a Business

Accounting is used in every type of business. A business generally takes one of the following forms:

- Proprietorship
- Partnership
- Corporation

Exhibit 1-2 compares ways to organize a business.

Exhibit 1-2 The Various Forms of Business Organization

	Proprietorship	Partnership	Corporation
1. *Owner(s)*	Proprietor—one owner	Partners—two or more owners	Shareholders—generally many owners
2. *Personal liability of owner(s) for business debts*	Proprietor is personally liable	General partners are personally liable; limited partners are not	Shareholders are *not* personally liable

Proprietorship. A **proprietorship** has a single owner, called the proprietor. Mark Zuckerburg's Facebook started out in a dormitory room at Harvard University; it was originally designed to serve as an intra-university software to help students recognize faces on campus. Steve Jobs and Steve Wozniak started Apple in the garage of Jobs' childhood home. Jack Ma started Alibaba in his apartment in Hangzhou. Almost every single big company you see today started just like Facebook, Apple, and Alibaba. Proprietorships tend to be small retail stores or individual providers of professional services—physicians, attorneys, software programmers, or accountants. Legally, the business *is* the proprietor, and the proprietor is personally liable for all the business's debts. But for accounting purposes, a proprietorship is a distinct entity, separate from its proprietor. Thus, the business records should not include the proprietor's personal finances.

Partnership. A **partnership** has two or more parties as co-owners, and each owner is a partner. Individuals, corporations, partnerships, or other types of entities can be partners. Income and loss of the partnership "flows through" to the partners and they recognize it based on their agreed-upon percentage interest in the business. In general, a partnership is not a taxpaying entity. Instead, each partner takes a proportionate share of the entity's taxable income and pays tax according to that partner's individual or corporate rate. Many retail establishments, professional service firms (law, accounting, etc.), real estate, and oil and gas exploration companies operate as partnerships. Many partnerships are small or medium-sized, but some are very large, with thousands of partners. Partnerships are governed by agreement, usually spelled out in writing in the form of a contract between the partners. General partnerships have mutual agency and unlimited liability, meaning that each partner may conduct business in the name of the entity and can make agreements that legally bind all partners without limit for the partnership's debts. Therefore, partnerships are quite risky because an irresponsible partner can create large debts for the other general partners without their knowledge or authorization. This feature of general partnerships has spawned the creation of limited-liability partnerships (LLPs).

A *limited-liability partnership* is one in which a wayward partner cannot create a large liability for the other partners. In LLPs, each partner is liable for partnership debts only up to the extent of his or her investment in the partnership, plus his or her proportionate share of the liabilities. Each LLP, however, must have one general partner with unlimited liability for all partnership debts. Many of the accounting firms, such as the "Big 4" accounting firms (Deloitte, E&Y, KPMG, and PricewaterhouseCooopers) are now organized as LLPs.

Corporation. A **corporation** is a business owned by the **shareholders**, who own shares representing ownership in the corporation. One of the major advantages of doing business in the corporate form is the ability to raise capital from issuance of shares to the public. In 1999, Jack Ma founded Alibaba with a mere US$60,000—this was an initial investment from friends and close ones. Mark Zuckerberg and other Facebook founders incorporated their company in late 2004 and received initial investments from a group of people, including Peter Thiel, the co-founder of PayPal. All types of entities (individuals, partnerships, corporations, or other types) may be shareholders in a corporation. Even though proprietorships and partnerships are more numerous, corporations transact much more business and are larger in terms of assets, income, and number of employees. Most well-known companies, such as the Samsung Group, Starbucks, Google,

Toyota, and LEGO, are corporations. Their full names usually indicate that they are structured as a company. The most common labels include *Corporation*, *Incorporated*, or simply *Company*. This depends very much on the local and legal practices in the country of incorporation. For example, in Australia you often see *Pty Ltd* (*Proprietary Limited*), in the United Kingdom you will see *PLC* (*Public Limited Company*), in Germany *AG* (*Aktiengesellschaft*), in Italy *SpA* (*Società per Azioni*), in Malaysia *Sdn Bhd* (*Sendirian Berhad*), in Singapore *Pte Ltd* (*Private Limited*), in Belgium *SA* (*Société Anonyme*), in Brazil *Ltda* (*Sociedade Limitada*), etc.

A corporation is formed under the relevant legislations extant in the country of incorporation. Unlike proprietorships and partnerships, a corporation is legally distinct from its owners. The corporation is like an artificial person and possesses many of the same rights that a person has. The shareholders have no personal obligation for the corporation's debts and have limited liability. Ultimate control of a corporation rests with the shareholders, who generally get one vote for each share they own. In general, shareholders elect the board of directors, which sets policy and appoints management officers, such as the chief executive officer (CEO), chief operating officer (COO), and chief financial officer (CFO), and other key functions as necessary.

Role of Accounting Standards

In science, we assign numerals to represent the properties of material systems according to the scientific laws that govern those properties. For example, we can measure the size of an object, the temperature of a room, the speed of a car, and so on. Similarly, in accounting, we assign monetary amounts to represent elements of financial statements in accordance to some accounting standards. Accounting standards are necessary because without them, users of financial statements would have to learn the basis of accounting for each company, making comparisons to other companies' financial statements difficult.

Unfortunately, unlike scientific laws, accounting rules tend to vary in different jurisdictions. Until recently, one of the major challenges in conducting global business has been the fact that different countries have adopted different accounting standards for business transactions. Developed countries like the United States, the United Kingdom, Japan, Germany, Australia, etc., follow their own professional frameworks for measurement and disclosure of financial information, usually called **generally accepted accounting principles (GAAP)**. As investors seek to compare financial results across entities from different countries, they have had to restate and convert accounting data from one country to the next in order to make them comparable. This takes time and can be expensive, especially in a globalized world with multinationals operating across many countries.

Alibaba's financial statements were prepared under U.S. GAAP (more on the role of accounting standards later in this chapter). For our discussions in this introductory chapter, there is no discernible difference in the presentation of items on the financial statements.

The potential solution to this problem lies with the **International Accounting Standards Board (IASB)** and its **International Financial Reporting Standards (IFRS)**. The IASB was formed in 2001 to replace the International Accounting Standards Committee (IASC) with the objective of developing a single set of high-quality, understandable, and enforceable accounting standards to help participants in the world's capital markets and other users make economic decisions. While IASB now sets IFRS, the previously issued International Accounting Standards (IAS) by the IASC continue to remain effective. This is why, in our study of accounting, we will see some standards labeled IAS or IFRS. Collectively, they can simply be referred to as IFRS. These standards may also be relabeled differently in different countries. For example, in Singapore, they are called Financial Reporting Standards (FRS), in Australia, they are labeled AASB after its national Australian Accounting Standards Board, in South Africa, they are called Generally Recognized Accounting Principles (GRAP), and so forth. Throughout this book, we will make references to accounting standards by their original IAS and IFRS numbers and titles. You can access IFRS from the IASB website at www.ifrs.org after completing a free registration process. If you are interested in comparisons between your local accounting standards and IFRS, you can refer to Appendix D which contains a listing of IFRS and some other useful resources.

These standards are now being used by most countries around the world. According to the IFRS Foundation, 84% of 150 jurisdictions (countries and territories) around the world either require or permit the use of IFRS for financial reporting, especially for listed companies. Other major economies, including the United States, Japan, India, and China, are working towards IFRS convergence. As this exercise gains momentum, you can expect to hear more about the adoption and use of IFRS, as well as global harmonization of accounting standards. When you do, the most important things to remember will be that these changes will be beneficial for financial statement users in the long run, and that most of what you learn in this accounting course will strongly apply.

A Closer Look

For a while, there was talk about the possibility of a full convergence between U.S. GAAP and IFRS. The signing of a Memorandum of Understanding (MoU) in September 2002 between the U.S. Financial Accounting Standards Board (FASB) and the International Accounting Standards Board (IASB) opened the way for various joint projects and joint pronouncements. Since 2007, non-U.S. companies listed in the United States are able to report using IFRS without reconciliation to GAAP. In 2008, an updated MoU further placed a set of common priorities and milestones for both IASB and FASB. Despite progress (and successes) in many joint projects between the FASB and the IASB, including the new joint standard on Revenue (see Chapter 3), the appetite for full convergence has diminished. The two boards have agreed to disagree on a number of key standards such as leasing, financial instruments, etc.

Outside of the United States, however, convergence is continuing with increasing jurisdiction, either mandating or allowing the use of IFRS for listed companies. In fact, the vision of global accounting standards has been publicly supported by many governments and international organizations, including the G20 (group of twenty major economies in the world), the World Bank, the International Monetary Fund (IMF), the International Committee of Securities Commissions (IOSCO), and the International Federation of Accountants (IFAC).

	Number of Jurisdictions				
Region	**Jurisdictions in the region**	**Jurisdictions that require IFRS Standards for all or most domestic publicly accountable entities**	**Jurisdictions that require IFRS Standards as % of total jurisdictions in the region**	**Jurisdictions that permit or require IFRS Standards for at least some (but not all or most) domestic publicly accountable entities**	**Jurisdictions that neither require nor permit IFRS Standards for any domestic publicly accountable entities**
Europe	44	43	98%	1	0
Africa	23	19	83%	1	3
Middle East	13	13	100%	0	0
Asia-Oceania	33	24	73%	3	6
Americas	37	27	73%	8	2
Totals	150	126	84%	13	11
As % of 150	100%	84%		9%	7%

For more information about individual jurisdiction profile, visit http://www.ifrs.org/Use-around-the-world/Pages/Jurisdiction-profiles.aspx.

The advantages of adopting one common set of standards are clear. Companies in jurisdictions that have mandated or allowed the use of IFRS, such as Australia, Hong Kong, the United Arab Emirates, Europe, Japan, and the United States, will have financial statements that are more comparable with each other. It will be far easier for investors and other financial statement users to evaluate the information of various companies across the globe, and companies will only have to prepare one set of financial statements, instead of multiple versions. Thus, in the long run, the global use of IFRS should reduce the costs of doing business globally.

UNDERSTAND THE UNDERLYING ACCOUNTING CONCEPTS IN THE IFRS *CONCEPTUAL FRAMEWORK*

The *Conceptual Framework*

2 **Understand** the underlying accounting concepts in the IFRS *Conceptual Framework*

The ***Conceptual Framework*** lays the foundation for resolving the big issues in accounting. You can think of it as the "Why, Who, What, How" of financial reporting. The *Conceptual Framework for Financial Reporting* (we will refer to it as the *Conceptual Framework*) prescribes the nature, function, and boundaries within which financial accounting and reporting operate. The existing *Conceptual Framework* (last updated in 2010) is a joint publication by the IASB and the FASB, used as a foundation for reviewing existing and developing new accounting standards. The revised *Conceptual Framework* is expected to be released toward the end of 2017. You can access the *Conceptual Framework* on the IASB website. Your instructor may alternatively direct you to a copy of the *Conceptual Framework* as applicable in your jurisdiction.

The *Conceptual Framework's* focus is on **general purpose financial statements**, which are prepared and presented annually and are directed toward the common information needs of a wide range of financial statement users. Many of these users rely on the financial statements as their major source of financial information. Special purpose financial reports, such as computations for taxation purposes or other regulatory reporting requirements, are outside the scope of the *Conceptual Framework*. Exhibit 1-3 gives an overview of the *Conceptual Framework*.

Exhibit 1-3 | *Conceptual Framework* of Financial Reporting

Objective	To provide financial information that is useful to existing and potential investors, lenders, and other creditors in making decisions about providing resources to the entity				
Financial Information	General purpose financial reports which provide information on the entity's economic resources, claims, and changes in resources and claims				
Qualitative Characteristics	Fundamental: Relevance and Faithful Representation Enhancing: Comparability, Verifiability, Timeliness, Understandability				
Constraint and Assumptions	Cost Constraint		Accrual Accounting		Going Concern
Elements	Assets	Liabilities	Equity	Income	Expenses
	Definition, Recognition, Measurement, Presentation, and Disclosure				

Why Is Financial Reporting Important?

The *Conceptual Framework* states that the objective of financial reporting is to provide financial information about the reporting entity that is useful to existing and potential investors, lenders, and other creditors. This includes information about the entity's resources and claims to those resources, and the effects of transactions and other events and conditions that change those resources and claims. Users evaluate financial statements to make decisions like whether or not to make additional investments into the entity, provide credit and financing, or assess the management's efficiency and effectiveness in its use of the entity's resources.

While financial statements can be used to help users assess the financial health of an entity, as well as its strengths and weaknesses, they are not designed to show the "value" of an entity; that depends on many other factors besides financial statements, such as general economic conditions and expectations, political events and climate, and industry and company outlook.

Who Are the Users of Financial Reports?

Different users make different types of economic decisions based on their relationship with the entity. In your personal and professional life, you are very likely to assume any of these user roles. Here are some examples of users who may be interested in Alibaba's financial statements (and other parts of a company's annual report, which we will discuss in Chapter 4):

- Investors in Alibaba would want to know if they are getting adequate returns for the risks they are taking when they invest in the company. They may decide to increase, hold, or decrease their ownership of Alibaba by buying or selling their shares on the stock exchange.
- Employees of Alibaba may be interested in its financial information for many reasons. Job security, salary increments, and compensation bonuses are usually worse off when a company has declining profits or is experiencing losses.
- Creditors, such as bankers or other financial institutions, may need to decide if they will grant Alibaba additional loans for expansion plans. They would want to know if Alibaba has the ability to service interest payments and whether it will be able to repay the loan principal.
- Suppliers and trade creditors often grant credit terms to their customers. They would want to know that Alibaba will be able to pay their invoices as and when they become due.
- It is unlikely that retail customers would demand financial information before buying merchandise from Alibaba. However, if you know that Alibaba is experiencing financial difficulties or suffering losses, you may be worried that it will not be able to offer warranty support or repair services for its products.
- The government and its agencies are interested in various aspects of a business, for example, tax collection and allocation of grants or subsidies. Listed companies would also need to comply with the stock exchange's disclosure requirements or "listing rules."
- With increasing expectations of corporate social responsibility, members of the public may be interested in Alibaba executive remuneration, health and safety issues, or even the environmental impact of its business operations.

It is important to note that the *Conceptual Framework* specifically states that general purpose financial reports do not satisfy all the potential information needs of financial statement users. The *Conceptual Framework* focuses on primary users of financial statements, which includes existing and potential investors, lenders, and creditors. The IASB uses the *Conceptual Framework* in setting accounting standards that provide an information set to meet the needs of the maximum number of primary users. Other non-primary users, such as government regulators, may find financial statements useful, but the financial statements are not primarily directed towards them.

What Makes Financial Information Useful?

The *Conceptual Framework* uses the term **qualitative characteristics** to describe the attributes that will most likely make the information provided in financial statements useful to users. The *Conceptual Framework* suggests that if financial information is to be useful, it must first be relevant and it must faithfully represent what it purports to represent—these are the "fundamental qualitative characteristics." Information that is relevant and faithfully represented may be further enhanced if it is comparable, verifiable, timely, and understandable—these are the "enhancing qualitative characteristics." Enhancing qualitative characteristics will never make information that is not relevant become relevant, and similarly, will not make information that is not faithfully representative be so.

Fundamental Characteristic: Relevance

To be relevant, information must be capable of making a difference to the decision maker. Typically, this happens when financial information is used to help users in making their own predictions of future outcomes (predictive value) or in assessing previous evaluations (confirmatory value). Information that has predictive value often also has confirmatory value. For example, Alibaba's revenue for 2016, ¥101 billion, can be used as the basis for predicting revenue for 2017 and compared against the revenue of previous years.

The degree of relevance may be influenced by the **materiality** of the information. Materiality means that the information must be important enough to the user to make a difference to his or her decision if it were omitted or erroneously declared. Only the information that is material needs to be separately disclosed, listed, or discussed in financial statements. An item may be material due to its nature or magnitude, or both. For example, all entities are required to disclose financial expenses (borrowing costs, interest expenses) regardless of their magnitude. Immaterial items are not required to be disclosed separately and may be combined with other information. Thus, materiality depends on the size of the item or the scale and impact of the error in the particular circumstances of its omission or misstatement. The *Conceptual Framework* did not prescribe a fixed level of materiality since it is entity-specific—what is material for one entity may not be material for another.

Fundamental Characteristic: Faithful Representation

Financial statements represent **economic phenomena**, i.e., resources, claims to resources, and changes in resources and claims, in words and numbers. Such depiction should reflect the substance of an economic phenomenon rather than its legal form. Information that faithfully represents the underlying economic phenomenon should be complete, neutral, and free from error. Completeness means that the financial reports should include all necessary information for a user to understand the economic phenomenon being depicted, including all necessary descriptions and explanations. Neutrality means that the information must be depicted without bias. It is supported by the concept of prudence, i.e., the exercise of caution when making judgments under conditions of uncertainty. Freedom from error means that there are no erroneous depictions of economic phenomenon nor any omission. If you were to discover that Alibaba's total expenses in 2016 were not complete or were riddled with errors, you would not rely on its financial statements.

Enhancing Characteristic: Comparability

Users usually compare financial statements of an entity over a period to identify trends in its financial position and performance. Thus, it is important that the basis of preparation and presentation remains comparable over time. For example, the comparison between Alibaba's sales in 2016 and 2015 only makes sense if you know that there has been no material change in the way sales are recognized in the financial statements. Similarly, you may want to compare Alibaba's performance to another retailer, and before drawing any conclusions you would want to be sure that net sales are derived in the same way for both companies. To be comparable, "like things must look alike, and different things must look different." Comparability does not force an entity to continue using the same accounting principles, policies, or estimates when more relevant and newer information surfaces.

Enhancing Characteristic: Verifiability

Verifiability helps assure users that information faithfully represents the economic phenomenon it purports to represent. It means that given the same economic phenomenon and its depiction, two different knowledgeable and independent parties can come to a consensus that the depiction is a faithful representation of the economic phenomenon.

Enhancing Characteristic: Timeliness

Timeliness means that the information must be made available to users early enough to help them make decisions, thus, making the information more relevant to their needs. By providing information about its financial position and performance to the users of the financial statement in a timely manner, Alibaba allows investors to readily make decisions about their investments in the company. Normally, the stock exchange on which a company is listed will determine how often and how quickly a company must publish its financial results.

Enhancing Characteristic: Understandability

We discussed earlier that accounting is the language of business. And just like any language, you will need some basic knowledge before you can converse, read, or write about it. Understandability means that financial information must be classified, characterized, and presented clearly and concisely. The framework assumes that users have a reasonable knowledge of business, economic activities and accounting, and a willingness to study the information with reasonable diligence. Thus, whilst you may not have the knowledge right now, by the end of this course you will be able to understand the accounting vocabulary and use financial information for decision making.

What Constraints Do We Face in Providing Useful Information?

In providing information that can be useful to our users, a pervasive constraint we face is cost. Financial information is not produced without costs; for example, cost of data collection, cost of data processing, and cost of verifying and disseminating the information. Naturally, higher costs result in lower returns to shareholders. Businesses will need to assess whether the benefits of reporting particular information are likely to outweigh the costs incurred in providing or using the information.

What Are Our Assumptions in Financial Reporting?

The *Conceptual Framework* states that in order to meet the objectives of financial reporting, there are assumptions that we need to make. Firstly, we prepare our financial statements on an **accrual basis**. In short, this means that transactions and other events are recognized when they occur and not when cash is received or paid. We will explore more about accrual accounting in Chapter 3.

In measuring and reporting financial information, we also assume that the entity will continue to operate long enough to use existing assets like land, buildings, equipment, and supplies for its intended purposes. In other words, the business has neither the intention nor the need to liquidate or curtail the scale of its operations. This is called the **going concern** assumption that would normally apply to most entities. This is how a business can buy assets with expectations to derive benefits from the use of the assets beyond the current financial period. An entity that is not continuing would be accounted for very differently from one that is a going concern.

What Exactly Are We Accounting For?

Alibaba's financial statements tell us how the business is performing and where it stands. But how do we arrive at the financial statements? Let's examine the elements of the financial statements, which are the building blocks on which these statements rest:

- **Assets** are economic resources controlled by the entity that are expected to produce a benefit in the future. Examples of assets include cash, inventory, account receivables (money owed to the entity by its debtors), machinery, equipment, and properties.
- **Liabilities** are present obligations of the entity that are expected to result in an outflow of economic benefits from the entity, i.e., something the company owes (to a party outside the company). Examples of liabilities include bank loans, accounts payable (money owed by the entity to its creditors), and other obligations.
- **Equity** is what's left of the assets after deducting liabilities; it represents shareholder's residual claim to the entity's assets. You will find two major sub-parts in the equity section: **share capital** and **retained earnings**. Share capital is the amount shareholders have invested in the entity (by purchasing shares or stock), and retained earnings is the amount earned by income-producing activities and kept for use in the business.
- **Income** refers to increases in economic benefits during an accounting period, i.e., increases in assets or decreases in liabilities that result in an increase in equity, other than those related to transactions with shareholders. The *Conceptual Framework* further separates

income into **revenue** and **gains**. Revenue arises from the ordinary course of business (such as sales revenue), whereas gains are typically outside the ordinary course of business (such as gain on disposal of a subsidiary).

- **Expenses** are decreases in economic benefits during an accounting period, i.e., decreases in assets or increases in liabilities that result in a decrease in equity, other than those related to transactions with shareholders. Similarly, expenses can be incurred in the ordinary course of business (such as salaries and wages, rent, and other expenses), whereas **losses** may or may not be in the ordinary course of business, such as loss on disposal of a long-term asset). Similar to gains, losses are reported on a net basis.

The *Conceptual Framework* essentially provides guidance on how and when to recognize items on financial statements. An item is recognizable if (a) it is probable that any future economic benefit associated with the item will flow to or from the entity; and (b) the item has a cost or value that can be measured with reliability.

Information about financial position (assets, liabilities, and equity) is primarily provided in a **Balance Sheet**, whereas information about financial performance (income and expenses) is primarily provided in an **Income Statement**. We will examine financial statements later in this chapter.

Now that you have a basic understanding of the *Conceptual Framework*, let's see how the elements of financial statements are interconnected and reported.

Accounting Equations

The basic **accounting equation** shows the relationship that exists among assets, liabilities, and equity. Assets appear on the left side, and liabilities and owners' equity appear on the right. The accounting equation can be written as Assets = Liabilities + Equity, or alternatively, Assets − Liabilities = Equity. As Exhibit 1-4 shows, the two sides must be equal. This is the underlying premise of the double-entry system of bookkeeping where total debits will always equal total credits. In this example, the entity's assets of $1,000 are financed by liabilities of $600 and equity of $400. We refer to equity as owner's equity or shareholders' equity.

Exhibit 1-4 The Accounting Equation (1)

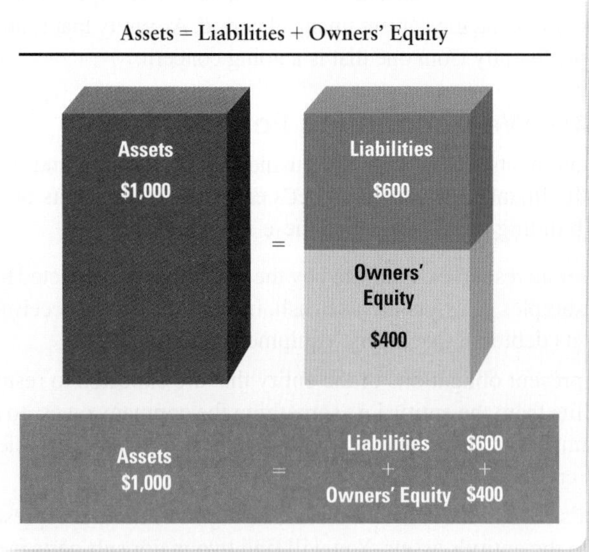

A second accounting equation relates to the calculation of profits earned by an entity during a financial period. Profit is simply Income (Revenue and Gains) less Expenses (Expenses and Losses). Exhibit 1-5 shows that a profit of $200 resulted from a total revenue of $500 and expenses of $300. When total revenues exceed total expenses, the result is called **net income**, or

net profit. When expenses exceed revenues, the result is called **net loss**. In accounting, the word net refers to an amount after a subtraction. Net income is, thus, the profit left over after subtracting expenses and losses from revenues and gains.

Exhibit 1-5 | The Accounting Equation (2)

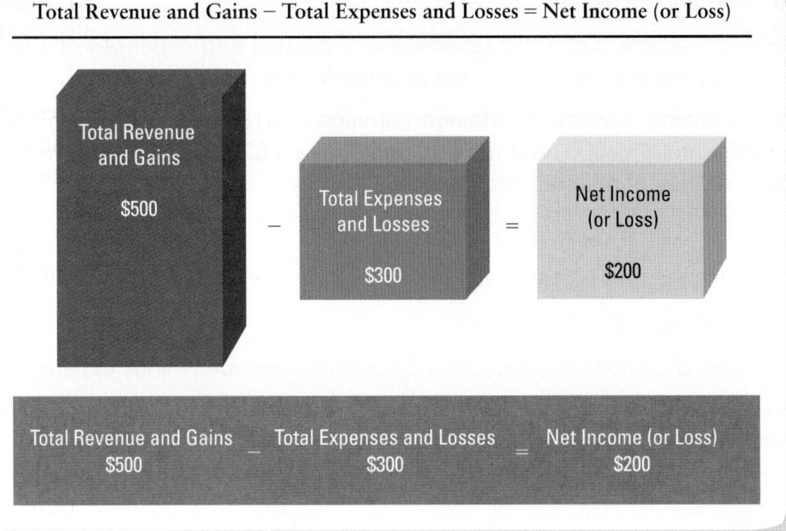

Recall that the *Conceptual Framework* states that income increases equity, whereas expenses decrease equity. This is usually shown as an increase in *retained earnings* for net income or a decrease in retained earnings for net loss. **Retained earnings** are a percentage of net income and are *retained* by the company for reinvestment or debt payment. A successful business usually pays **dividends** to shareholders (when there is an increase in retained earnings) as a return on their investments, usually in the form of cash. Dividends are recorded as direct reductions of retained earnings. Remember that just as capital contribution from shareholders to the company is not income, dividend distribution is not an expense and will never affect net income. Exhibit 1-6 shows the movement in retained earnings over an accounting period.

Exhibit 1-6 | The Components of Retained Earnings

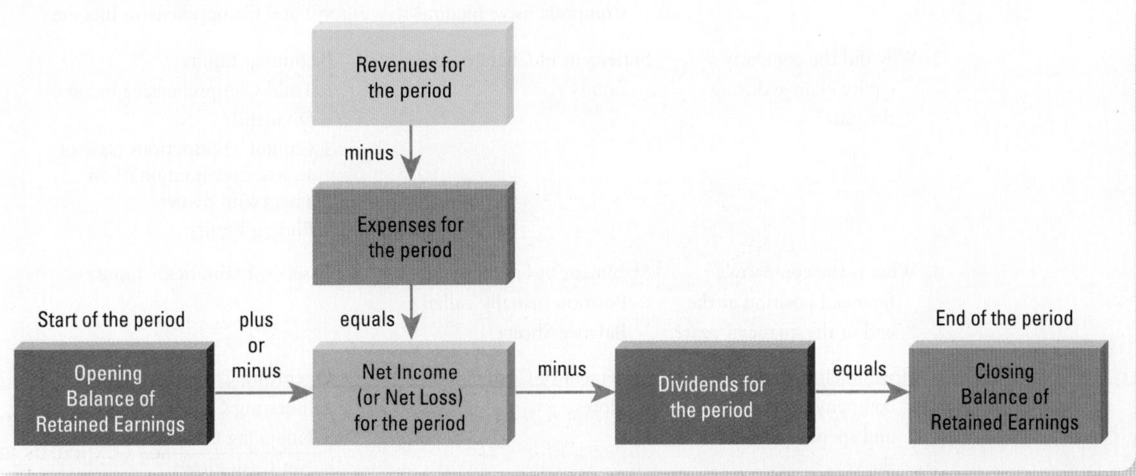

Stop & Think

(1) If the assets of a business are $480,000 and the liabilities are $160,000, how much is the owners' equity?

(2) If the owners' equity in a business is $160,000 and the liabilities are $100,000, how much are the assets?

(3) A company reported monthly revenues of $365,000 and expenses of $225,000. What is the result of operations (net income) for the month?

(4) If the beginning balance of retained earnings is $180,000, revenue is $85,000, expenses total $35,000, and the company pays a $20,000 dividend, what is the ending balance of retained earnings?

Answers:

(1) $320,000 ($480,000 – $160,000)

(2) $260,000 ($160,000 + $100,000)

(3) Net income of $140,000 ($365,000 – $225,000); revenues minus expenses

(4) $210,000 [$180,000 beginning balance + net income $50,000 ($85,000 – $35,000) – dividends $20,000]

OBTAIN INSIGHTS INTO BUSINESS OPERATIONS THROUGH FINANCIAL STATEMENTS

3 **Obtain** insights into business operations through financial statements

Financial statements present an entity to the public in financial terms. Each financial statement relates to a specific date or time period. Now, what would investors want to know about Alibaba at the end of its financial year? Exhibit 1-7 lists four questions decision makers may ask. Each answer comes from one of the financial statements.

Exhibit 1-7 Questions from Decision Makers

Question	Financial Statement	Answer
1. How well did the company perform during the year?	Statement of Comprehensive Income (which consists of two parts: Income Statement and Other Comprehensive Income)	Revenues – Expenses Net income (or Net loss) ± Other Comprehensive Income = Total Comprehensive Income
2. Why did the company's equity change during the year?	Statement of Changes in Equity	Beginning Equity + Total Comprehensive Income – Dividends ± Capital Transactions (sale of an asset/revaluation of an asset) with owners = Ending Equity
3. What is the company's financial position at the end of the financial year?	Statement of Financial Position (usually called Balance Sheet)	Assets = Liabilities + Equity
4. How much cash did the company generate and spend during the year?	Statement of Cash Flows	Operating Cash Flows ± Investing Cash Flows ± Financing Cash Flows = Net Cash Flows

To learn how to use financial statements, let's work through Alibaba's statements for the 2016 financial year (ended March 31, 2016). For your first reading of financial statements, we have simplified some of the items in the financial statements. You will get to see more detailed disclosures as you progress in your study of financial accounting. Exhibit 1-8 shows how the financial information flows from one financial statement to the next. The order is important.

Exhibit 1-8 Flow of Financial Information

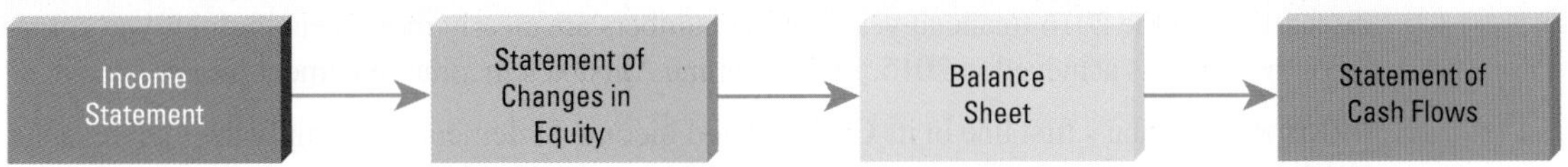

We begin with the Income Statement, shown at the beginning of this chapter, duplicated as Exhibit 1-9.

Exhibit 1-9 Alibaba's Income Statement

	A	B	C	D
1	**Alibaba Group Holdings Limited Consolidated Income Statement**	**Year Ended March 31**		
2	**(Adapted, in millions of ¥ and US$)**	**Mar. 31, 2015**	**Mar. 31, 2016**	**Mar. 31, 2016**
3	**Revenue**	¥ 76,204	¥ 101,143	$ 15,686
4	Cost of revenue	(23,834)	(34,355)	(5,328)
5	Product development expenses	(10,658)	(13,788)	(2,138)
6	Sales and marketing expenses	(8,513)	(11,307)	(1,753)
7	General and administrative expenses	(7,800)	(9,205)	(1,428)
8	Amortization of intangible assets	(2,089)	(2,931)	(455)
9	Impairment of goodwill	(175)	(455)	(71)
10	**Income from operations**	23,135	29,102	4,513
11	Other income	2,486	2,058	319
12	Interest and investment income	9,455	52,254	8,104
13	Interest expense	(2,750)	(1,946)	(301)
14	Share of results of equity investees	(1,590)	(1,730)	(269)
15	Income tax expenses	(6,416)	(8,449)	(1,310)
16	**Net income**	¥ 24,320	¥ 71,289	$ 11,056
17				

The Income Statement Shows a Company's Financial Performance

The Income Statement, which is part of the **Statement of Comprehensive Income**, reports revenues and expenses for the period. The bottom line is net income or net loss for the period. At the top of Exhibit 1-9 is the company's name, Alibaba Group Holdings Limited. On the second line is the term "Consolidated Income Statement." Alibaba is actually made up of several corporations that are owned by a common group of shareholders. Commonly controlled corporations like this are required to combine, or consolidate, all of their revenues, expenses, assets, liabilities, and shareholders' equity, and to report them all as if they were one combined entity.

The dates of Alibaba's Consolidated Income Statement are for the (financial/fiscal) "Year Ended March 31, 2016 and 2015." In this case, Alibaba's financial year (April 1, 2015, to March 31, 2016) is not the same as the calendar year (which would have been January 1, 2016, to December 31, 2016). You will see other companies using different year-end dates. For example, many companies such as Samsung Electronics, SAP, and Jollibee use the same calendar and fiscal year, and thus have a December 31 year-end. Other companies may use other dates, Wal-Mart uses January 31 as its fiscal year-end, FedEx uses May 31, and Steinhoff uses June 30. Some companies use a 52- or 53-week financial period ending nearest to a particular date. For example, Ahold NV uses the Sunday nearest to December 31 and Walt Disney uses the Saturday nearest to September 30 as their respective year-end dates. Usually, companies attempt to end their fiscal year in their least busy period. Don't fret too much about the different dates, what is more important is that all the financial statements are prepared on an annual basis.

You will also notice that Alibaba presented its accounts in billions of Renminbi as well as the U.S. dollar equivalent for additional information. It also presented two years of information, 2016 and 2015, to show comparable figures for revenues, expenses, and net income. We shall focus our discussions on the 2016 financial year, but the numbers are clearly more meaningful if you compare them to what was achieved in 2015. Let's examine Alibaba's Income Statement in more detail.

Income. Alibaba's first line in its Consolidated Income Statement was simply the total revenue of ¥101,143 million for the financial year ended March 31, 2016. Alibaba's revenue has increased from ¥76,204 to ¥101,143. Revenues do not always carry the word "revenue" in their titles. For example, net sales revenue is often abbreviated as net sales. Net sales means sales revenue after subtracting all the goods customers have returned to the company.

Other income items may consist of peripheral income generation activities, such as financial and travel services, rental income, and royalty fees. You can't quite figure this out from the Income Statement, but additional information is usually disclosed in the reporting entity's Notes to the Accounts, which gives additional information about accounting policies, breakdown of totals, etc. You will see examples of Notes to the Accounts in later chapters. Alibaba's Income Statement (lines 11 and 12) showed "Other income" of ¥2,058 million, and "Interest and investment income" of ¥52,254 million for 2016.

Expenses. Similarly, not all expenses have the word "expense" in their title. For example, Alibaba's expenses in lines 4, 8, and 9 do not have the word expense in them, but the expense nature is implied. Alibaba's biggest expense item is "cost of revenue." For the more traditional merchandisers, you may see the title Cost of Sales, Cost of Goods Sold, or Cost of Merchandise, which represents the costs of items sold. For example, a company like Toys-R-Us sells a plush toy costing $30 for $75. The sales revenue will be $75, and the cost of goods sold will be $30. Therefore, we can say that the **gross profit** is $45 ($75 less $30).

In general, you may see companies report the following expenses:

- Selling, general, and administrative expenses are the costs of everyday operations that are not directly related to merchandise purchases. Many expenses may be included in this category, including labor costs, property rentals, maintenance and repairs, fees, advertising, consumables, and other general expenses.
- Interest expenses (also labeled as borrowing costs or finance costs) represent the cost of borrowing money via bank loans or other debt instruments.
- For companies that do research and development (R&D) work, you may see R&D expenses listed. Microsoft spends about 13% of its revenue on R&D, Samsung about 6%, and Apple about 3%.
- Companies may also have other operating expenses that consist of other aggregated expenses, such as losses from disposing its assets and donations.
- Income tax expense is the expense levied on a company's income by the tax authorities. Taxation rules can be complicated, especially for a global corporation with businesses around the world, and the amount of income subject to taxation (called taxable income) is not always equal to net income. (Chapter 9 covers this aspect in more detail.)

Profits. Income Statements may show a few variations of profit. Many retailers would report a gross profit, which is basically sales revenue less cost of sales. After subtracting other operating expenses (and sometimes other lines of income), a company may report an **operating profit**. Alibaba's operating profit is shown on line 10 at ¥29,102 million. Non-operating income and expenses come next—typically interest expense and income, share of results of equity investees (more on this in Chapter 8), and tax expenses. The "bottom line" here would be the net profit, i.e., profit after subtracting all expenses from all income items. Alibaba's net profit, or net income, is shown on line 16, at ¥71,289 million.

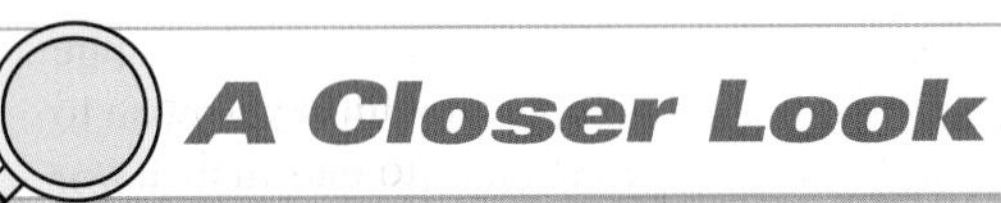

Names of Financial Statements

The official terminologies are Statement of Financial Position, Statement of Comprehensive Income, Statement of Changes in Equity, and Statement of Cash Flows. However, the Standard allows other titles to be used. You may find that some companies will continue to use the more common names such as Balance Sheet.

Statement of Comprehensive Income and Statement of Changes in Equity

IAS 1—Presentation of Financial Statements requires that only transactions with owners (in their capacity as owners) are presented in the Statement of Changes in Equity. All other non-owner changes in equity are now presented in the Statement of Comprehensive Income, which can be shown as a single statement (i.e., Statement of Comprehensive Income) or two statements (Income Statement, followed by Statement of Comprehensive Income, which will begin with the net profit or loss from the Income Statement).

For simplicity, we shall continue to use the term Balance Sheet for Statement of Financial Position and Income Statement to refer to the first portion of the Statement of Comprehensive Income. We shall discuss more of this distinction later in Chapter 4.

Now, let's examine the Statement of Changes in Equity.

The Statement of Changes in Equity Shows a Company's Transactions with its Owners

Recall that the equity is the owner's residual interest in the entity after deducting liabilities. Profits that a company generates ultimately belong to the owners of the company. Shareholders are happy when their wealth in the company increases. In 2016, Alibaba generated a profit of ¥71,289 million. Let's see how this is reflected in its **Statement of Changes in Equity** (see Exhibit 1-10).

Exhibit 1-10 Alibaba's Changes in Equity

A1

	A	B	C	D
1	**Alibaba Group Holdings Limited Consolidated Statement of Changes in Equity**	**Financial Year Ended March 31**		
2	**(Adapted, in millions of ¥ and $)**	**2015**	**2016**	**2016**
3	Balance as of 1 April preceeding year	¥ 30,417	¥ 158,071	$ 25,393
4	Issuance of shares (Initial Public Offering)	61,536	-	-
5	Net income for the year	24,320	71,289	11,056
6	Other equity movements	41,798	20,529	2,305
7	Balance as of 31 March	¥ 158,071	¥ 249,889	$ 38,754
8				

Alibaba started the 2016 financial year with the 2015 ending balance of total equity: ¥158,071 million. You can see that the same number appears at the end of 2015 and at the start of 2016. Net income or net loss flows from the Income Statement to the Statement of Changes in Equity (line 5). Take a moment to trace these two amounts from the Statement of Changes in Equity to the Income Statement (see line 16 in Exhibit 1-9). You can see that net income increases total equity, and if you have any net losses, it will decrease total equity.

Line 4 was Alibaba's record-setting Initial Public Offering on the New York Stock Exchange in 2015. We simplify a few things into line 6 for now. It included a number of items that relate to the impact of fluctuations of foreign currency, fair value changes in financial instruments, and/or other transactions with shareholders.

After a company earns its net income, its board of directors decides if the company should pay a dividend to the shareholders. Corporations are not obligated to pay dividends unless their boards decide to pay (i.e., declare) them. Usually, companies that are in development stages or growth mode elect not to pay dividends, opting instead to plough the money back into the company to expand operations or to purchase property, plant, and equipment. Established companies usually have regular earnings (and cash) to pay dividends. Dividends decrease retained earnings because they represent a distribution of a company's assets (usually cash) to its shareholders. Alibaba has stated that it will not be paying any dividends for now, so you do not see any dividends going out from its equity.

The Balance Sheet Shows a Company's Financial Position

A company's Balance Sheet, also called the **Statement of Financial Position**, reports three groups of items: in Exhibit 1-11, assets (lines 3–14), liabilities (lines 15–25), and shareholders' equity (lines 26–30). Alibaba's Consolidated Balance Sheet, in Exhibit 1-11, is dated March 31, 2016 and 2015, as financial position is always for a specific point in time, unlike an Income Statement, which covers a period of time.

Exhibit 1-11 Alibaba's Balance Sheet

A1	A	B	C	D
1	**Alibaba Group Holdings Limited Consolidated Balance Sheets**	**As of March 31**		
2	**(Adapted, in millions of ¥ and US$)**	**2015**	**2016**	**2016**
3	**Assets:**			
4	Cash and cash equivalents	¥ 108,193	¥ 106,818	$ 16,566
5	Short-term investments	17,806	8,878	1,377
6	Accounts receivable	1,067	1,209	188
7	Other current assets	15,043	17,165	2,661
8	**Total current assets**	142,109	134,070	20,792
9	Property, plant and equipment	12,244	16,505	2,560
10	Long-term investments	48,488	120,853	18,742
11	Intangible assets	48,508	87,015	13,495
12	Other non-current assets	4,085	6,007	932
13	**Total non-current assets**	113,325	230,380	35,729
14	**Total assets**	255,434	364,450	56,521
15	**Liabilities:**			
16	Accounts payable and accruals	19,834	27,334	4,240
17	Short-term bank borrowings	1,990	4,304	667
18	Income tax payable	2,733	2,790	433
19	Customer deposits and advances	15,115	17,611	2,731
20	**Total current liabilities**	39,672	52,039	8,071
21	Long-term bank borrowings	1,609	1,871	290
22	Other borrowings	48,994	51,596	8,002
23	Other non-current liabilities	7,088	9,055	1,404
24	**Total non-current liabilities**	57,691	62,522	9,696
25	**Total liabilities**	97,363	114,561	17,767
26	**Equity:**			
27	Share capital	117,143	132,207	20,504
28	Retained earnings	24,842	78,752	12,213
29	Other equity items	16,086	38,930	6,037
30	**Total equity**	158,071	249,889	38,754
31	**Total liabilities and equity**	¥ 255,434	¥ 364,450	$ 56,521
32				

Before we proceed, let's just make sure Alibaba's accounting equation is correct. At March 31, 2016, it has total assets of ¥364,450 million (line 14), which is financed by total liabilities of ¥114,561 million (line 25) and equity of ¥249,889 million (line 30). So we can prove that Alibaba's Assets = Liabilities + Equity. Alternatively, we can say that Alibaba's shareholders have a net claim of ¥249,889 million to the total assets of ¥364,450 million after deducting liabilities of ¥114,561 million. This relationship will always remain true at all times. You can do the same for the previous year's assets, liabilities, and equity.

Assets. There are two main categories of assets: current and non-current (sometimes referred to as long-term) assets. **Current assets** are assets that are expected to be converted to cash, sold, or consumed during the next 12 months. Current assets typically include cash, short-term investments, receivables (also called debtors), inventory, and prepaid expenses. Alibaba's total current assets at March 31, 2016, were ¥134,070 million (line 8). Let's have a quick look at Alibaba's current assets:

- All companies have (and need) cash. **Cash** is the most liquid asset that's a medium of exchange, and cash equivalents include money-market accounts or other financial instruments that are easily convertible to cash. Alibaba owns ¥106,818 million in cash and cash equivalents at March 31, 2016 (line 4).
- Alibaba has a number of short-term investments that we have summarized in line 5 amounting to ¥8,878 million. This includes its investments in fixed deposits, money market funds, or other investments.
- Accounts receivable refer to the amount of cash the company expects to collect from its debtors. Alibaba has trade and other receivables totaling ¥1,209 million (line 6). Sometimes you may see certain companies use the term "debtors" to describe account receivables. Often, companies will also distinguish between trade and other receivables. Trade receivables are usually amounts due from customers, in the context of trading activities. We'll discuss accounts receivable further in Chapter 5. You may also often come across the term notes receivable, which is the amount a company expects to collect from a party who has signed a promissory note to that company and, therefore, owes it money. Alibaba doesn't own any notes receivable.
- For simplicity, we have summarized other current assets into one line as "other current assets" (line 7) amounting to ¥17,165 million. Typically, this could include items such as prepaid expenses and deposits placed with a landlord or business. Prepaid expenses or prepayments represent amounts paid in advance for advertisements, rent, insurance, and supplies. Prepaid expenses are current assets because Alibaba will benefit from these expenditures in the next financial year. We will discuss more about prepayments in Chapter 3.

The main categories of long-term or non-current assets are **property, plant and equipment (PPE)** (line 9), long-term investments (line 10), intangible assets (line 11), and other non-current assets. We will examine PPE and intangibles in greater detail later (in Chapter 7), and also investments (in Chapter 8). Let's have a quick look at what non-current assets Alibaba has on its Balance Sheet:

- Property, plant and equipment (PPE, or sometimes referred to as fixed assets) of ¥16,505 million includes Alibaba's land use rights, buildings, equipment, fixtures, and fittings and installations. PPE conveys economic benefits over the useful lives of its components, and their acquisition costs are allocated systematically throughout their useful lives. This process is called depreciation. The cumulative amounts that have been previously allocated are called accumulated depreciation. On the Balance Sheet, it is shown net at ¥16,505 million.
- Long-term investments include Alibaba's investments in its affiliates and associates, as well as investments in other forms of financial assets. This amounts to ¥120,853 million. We discuss investments (both short-term and long-term) in Chapter 8.
- Intangibles are assets with no physical form, such as patents, trademarks, and goodwill. Alibaba has ¥87,015 million of intangibles, mostly in the form of intellectual property rights and goodwill on acquisitions of subsidiaries.

- Again, for simplicity, we have combined various other non-current assets into one account (line 12). These include long-term prepayments, deferred tax assets, and other non-current financial assets.

Overall, Alibaba reports total assets of ¥364,450 million at March 31, 2016.

Liabilities. Liabilities are also divided into current and non-current categories. Current liabilities (lines 20–23) are obligations or debts payable within one year. **Current liabilities** typically include accounts such as accounts payable, taxes payable, and other liabilities like short-term notes payable and salaries/wages payable. Non-current liabilities are obligations that are likely to require an outflow of economic benefits after one financial year:

- Accounts payables and accruals (line 16) are the amount due to Alibaba's creditors, including its suppliers and other service providers. This amounts to ¥27,334 million, clearly Alibaba's largest current liability. Similar to receivables, sometimes you will see companies further classifying payables into trade payables (or Creditors), notes payable, and other payables.
- Alibaba has total bank borrowings of ¥6,175 million, of which ¥4,304 million is due within the next financial year (line 17) and ¥1,871 million of long-term debt due beyond the next financial year (line 21). While you see two line items on this Balance Sheet, it does not necessarily mean that Alibaba has two (and only two) distinct loans. Even if Alibaba only has one financing arrangement, as long as there is some amount due in the next financial year, it will disclose the current portion separately from the non-current portion. Similarly, Alibaba may have a number of long-term loans, and the figures on the Balance Sheet are the aggregate amounts of the various long-term loans it has.
- Income tax payable (lines 18) of ¥2,790 million is the amount due to various tax authorities.
- Customer deposits and advances (line 19) are funds paid in advance by customers. In Chapter 3, we will see how accrual accounting works, but for now, just remember that until Alibaba has performed its obligations (either supplying goods or providing services) to its customers, this amount remains as a liability because it is a form of financial obligation. When the goods or services are delivered, Alibaba would then earn the money.
- Other liabilities (lines 19, 22, and 23) comprise provisions, pre-collected revenue (or unearned revenue) resulting from customer deposits and advances, and other long-term liabilities. We will discuss unearned revenue in Chapter 3 and look at provisions and other long-term liabilities in Chapter 9.

Overall, Alibaba reports total liabilities of ¥114,561 million as of March 31, 2016 (line 25). You may recall earlier that the total assets were ¥364,450 million. This means that almost 31% of Alibaba's assets are financed by liabilities.

Shareholders' Equity. Earlier you have seen the reconciliation of movement in total equity in the last two financial years (Exhibit 1-10). You can check that the total equity figures at the end of 2015 and 2016 financial year (line 30 of Exhibit 1-11) tally with line 7 of Exhibit 1-10. Alibaba's equity consists of:

- Capital. **Paid-in capital** (sometimes labeled share capital or simply capital) of ¥132,207 million (line 27). This is the amount raised as capital contributions from Alibaba's shareholders. Some companies may have different types of share capital, and would label them as ordinary share capital or preference shares (also called "preferred stock" and "common stock," respectively). We will examine equity items and transactions later (in Chapter 10).
- Retained earnings totaled ¥78,752 million (line 28). Recall our earlier discussions on retained earnings (see Exhibit 1-6). Retained earnings records the cumulative earnings of the entity less the dividends it has paid out.
- In Alibaba's Balance Sheet, we have combined a number of items under the headings "Other equity items" (which includes various reserves and non-controlling interests). The

detailed breakdown of the other items is beyond what we want to cover for now. We will explore more in Chapter 10.

On the whole, the Balance Sheet summarizes the following elements of accounting: assets, liabilities, and equity (net income or loss, i.e., income and expenses for the period).

The Statement of Cash Flows Shows a Company's Cash Receipts and Payments

Finally, the Statement of Cash Flows is the fourth, required financial statement. Alibaba's cash flow statement is shown in Exhibit 1-12. We will examine the components of various cash flow activities in detail later (in Chapter 11). For now, we will discuss the overall concept.

Exhibit 1-12 Alibaba's Statement of Cash Flows

	A	B	C	D
1	**Alibaba Group Holdings Limited Consolidated Statement of Cash Flows**	**Year Ended March 31**		
2	**(Adapted, in millions of ¥ and US$)**	**2015**	**2016**	**2016**
3	Net income	¥ 24,320	¥ 71,289	$ 11,056
4	Adjustments and changes in working capital	16,897	(14,453)	(2,241)
5	Net cash provided by operating activities	41,217	56,836	8,815
6	Net cash used by investing activities	(53,454)	(42,831)	(6,643)
7	Net cash provided/used by financing activities	87,497	(15,846)	(2,457)
8	Effect of exchange rate changes	(112)	466	72
9	Net cash flows for the period	75,148	(1,375)	(213)
10	Cash and cash equivalents at beginning of the year	33,045	108,193	16,779
11	Cash and cash equivalents at end of the year	¥ 108,193	¥ 106,818	$ 16,566
12				

Companies engage in three basic types of activities: **operating activities**, **investing activities**, and **financing activities**. The **statement of cash flows** reports cash flows under each of these activities. In this statement, the use of parentheses around figures indicates money going out, and the absence of parentheses indicates money coming in. Think about the cash flows (receipts and payments) in each category:

- Companies operate by selling goods and services to customers; these are called operating activities. Operating activities either increase or decrease cash. The Income Statement tells us whether the company is profitable, but this does not necessarily mean the company has been able to generate cash from operations. Sooner or later, to be successful, a company will need to bring in cash from its operations. For now, we will calculate cash flow from operating activities as an adjustment (line 4) to net income (line 3). Alibaba generated cash from operations totaling ¥56,836 million in the financial year ended March 31, 2016.
- Companies also invest in non-current assets such as property, plant and equipment, or make other long-term investments. Both purchases and sales of long-term assets are investing cash flows. Cash flows from investing activities show a company's investments into its production capacity. Alibaba used ¥42,831 million in its investing activities.
- Companies need to raise money from financing. Financing comes from both equity owners and borrowings. Alibaba's cash flows from financing activities would include any issuance of shares, repurchase of shares, as well as proceeds and repayments of borrowings.

For companies that pay dividends, you will also see dividend payments included as a cash flow from financing. Alibaba's net cash used by financing activities amounted to ¥15,846 million.

- Overall, Alibaba's cash decreased by about ¥1,375 million in financial year ended March 31, 2016, compared to a significant increase of ¥75,148 million the previous year when it went for its initial public offering (IPO).
- The cash flow statement also provides a reconciliation back to the cash and cash equivalent balances at the beginning and end of the year. You can trace lines 10 and 11 in Exhibit 1-12 back to line 4 in Exhibit 1-11. You can see that because net cash flow saw a decrease of ¥1,375 million, ending cash and cash equivalents is now less than the beginning balance (from ¥108,193 to ¥106,818 million).

Let's now summarize the relationships that link the financial statements.

IDENTIFY FINANCIAL STATEMENTS AND THEIR INTER-RELATIONSHIPS

4 **Identify** financial statements and their inter-relationships

Exhibit 1-13 summarizes the relationships among the financial statements of Alibaba for the financial year ended March 31, 2016. These statements are condensed, so the details of Exhibits 1-9 through 1-12 are omitted. Study the exhibit carefully because these relationships apply to all organizations. Specifically, note the following:

1. The Income Statement for the 12 months ended March 31, 2016
   a. Reports total income and expenses of the year. Income and expenses are reported only on the Income Statement.
   b. Reports net income if total revenues exceed total expenses. If expenses exceed income, there will be a net loss.
2. The Statement of Changes in Equity for the 12 months ended March 31, 2016
   a. Begins with the total equity at the start of the financial year (which is the ending balance of the previous financial year).
   b. Adds net income (or subtracts net loss). Net income comes directly from the Income Statement (arrow ① in Exhibit 1-13).
   c. Adds and subtracts any transactions with owners, as appropriate. For example, if there is new capital issued during the year, or if there are dividends paid during the year.
   d. Ends with the total equity at the end of the financial year (which will be the beginning balance for the next financial year).
3. The Balance Sheet at March 31, 2016
   a. Reports assets, liabilities, and shareholders' equity at the end of the year. Only the Balance Sheet reports assets and liabilities.
   b. Reports that assets equal the sum of liabilities plus equity (or alternatively, assets less liabilities equal equity). This balancing feature follows the basic accounting equation and gives the Balance Sheet its name.
   c. Reports total equity, which comes from the Statement of Changes in Equity (arrow ② in Exhibit 1-13).
4. The Statement of Cash Flows for the year ended March 31, 2016
   a. Reports cash flows from operating, investing, and financing activities. Each category results in net cash provided (an increase) or net cash used (a decrease).
   b. Reports whether cash has increased (or decreased) during the year.
   c. When the net cash increase (or decrease) is added to the beginning cash and cash equivalent balance, it will show the cash and cash equivalents at the end of the year, as reported in the Balance Sheet (arrow ③ in Exhibit 1-13).

Exhibit 1-13 | Relationships Among the Financial Statements

Alibaba Group Holdings Limited
Consolidated Income Statement

	A	B	C	D
1		Financial Year Ended March 31		
2	**(Adapted, in millions of ¥ and US$)**	**2015**	**2016**	**2016**
3	Total income	¥ 88,145	¥ 155,455	$ 24,109
4	Total expenses	(63,825)	(84,166)	(13,053)
5	**Net income**	¥ 24,320	¥ 71,289	$ 11,056
6				

①

Alibaba Group Holdings Limited
Consolidated Statement of Changes in Equity

	A	B	C	D
1		Financial Year Ended March 31		
2	**(Adapted, in millions of ¥ and US$)**	**2015**	**2016**	**2016**
3	Balance as of 1 April preceeding year	¥ 30,417	¥ 158,071	$ 25,393
4	Issuance of shares (Initial Public Offering)	61,536	–	–
5	Net income for the year	24,320	71,289	11,056
6	Other equity movements	41,798	20,529	2,305
7	Balance as of 31 March	¥ 158,071	¥ 249,889	$ 38,754
8				

②

Alibaba Group Holdings Limited
Consolidated Balance Sheets

	A	B	C	D
1		As of March 31		
2	**(Adapted, in millions of ¥ and US$)**	**2015**	**2016**	**2016**
3	**Assets:**			
4	Cash and cash equivalents	¥ 108,193	¥ 106,818	$ 16,566
5	All other assets	147,241	257,632	39,955
6	**Total assets**	255,434	364,450	56,521
7	Total liabilities	97,363	114,561	17,767
8	Total equity	158,071	249,889	38,754
9	Total liabilities and equity	¥ 255,434	¥ 364,450	$ 56,521
10				

③

Alibaba Group Holdings Limited
Consolidated Statement of Cash Flows

	A	B	C	D
1		Financial Year Ended March 31		
2	**(Adapted, in millions of ¥ and US$)**	**2015**	**2016**	**2016**
3	Net cash provided by operating activities	¥ 41,217	¥ 56,836	$ 8,815
4	Net cash used by investing activities	(53,454)	(42,831)	(6,643)
5	Net cash provided/used by financing activities	87,497	(15,846)	(2,457)
6	Effect of exchange rate changes	(112)	466	72
7	Net cash flows for the period	75,148	(1,375)	(213)
8	Cash and cash equivalents at beginning of the year	33,045	108,193	16,779
9	Cash and cash equivalents at end of the year	¥ 108,193	¥ 106,818	$ 16,566
10				

DECISION GUIDELINES

IN EVALUATING A COMPANY, WHAT DO DECISION MAKERS LOOK FOR?

These Decision Guidelines illustrate how people use financial statements. Decision Guidelines appear throughout the text to show how accounting information aids decision making.

Suppose you are considering an investment in Alibaba. How do you proceed? Where do you get the information you need? What do you look for?

Decision	Guidelines
1. Can the company sell its products?	**1.** Sales revenue on the Income Statement. Are sales growing or falling?
2. What are the main income measures to watch for trends?	**2.** a. Gross profit (Sales – Cost of goods sold) b. Operating income (Gross profit – Operating expenses) c. Net income (bottom line of the Income Statement) All three income measures should be increasing over time.
3. What percentage of sales revenue ends up as profit?	**3.** Divide net income by sales revenue. Examine the trend of the net income percentage from year to year.
4. Can the company collect its receivables?	**4.** From the Balance Sheet, compare the percentage increase in accounts receivable to the percentage increase in sales. If receivables are growing much faster than sales, collections may be too slow, and the risk of defaults increases.
5. Can the company pay its a. Current liabilities? b. Current and long-term liabilities?	**5.** From the Balance Sheet, compare a. Current assets to current liabilities. Current assets should be somewhat greater than current liabilities. b. Total assets to total liabilities. Total assets must be somewhat greater than total liabilities.
6. Where is the company's cash coming from? How is cash being used?	**6.** On the cash flow statement, operating activities should provide the bulk of the company's cash during most years. Otherwise, the business will fail. Examine investing cash flows to see if the company is purchasing long-term assets—property, plant, and equipment, and intangibles (this usually signals potential growth).

UNDERSTAND THE ROLE OF ETHICS IN ACCOUNTING

5 **Understand** the role of ethics in accounting

Good business requires decision making, which in turn requires the exercise of good judgment, both at the individual and corporate levels. For example, you may work for or eventually run a company like Starbucks that has decided to devote 5 cents from every cup of coffee sold to helping save the lives of AIDS victims in Africa. Can that be profitable in the long run?

As an accountant, you may have to decide whether to record a $50,000 expenditure for a piece of equipment as an asset on the Balance Sheet or an expense on the Income Statement. Alternatively, as a sales manager for a company like SAP, you may have to decide whether $25 million of goods and services delivered to customers in 2018 would be more appropriately recorded as revenue in 2018 or 2019.

IFRS are "principles-based," as opposed to U.S. GAAP, which are largely more "rules-based." This puts greater emphasis on the importance of judgment in determining the appropriate accounting recognition, measurement, and presentation. Depending on the type of business, the facts and circumstances surrounding accounting decisions may not always make them clear cut, and yet the decision may determine whether the company shows a profit or a loss in a particular period. What are the factors that influence business and accounting decisions, and how should these factors be weighed? Generally, three factors influence accounting decisions: economic, legal, and ethical.

The *economic* factor states that the decision being made should benefit the decision maker economically. Based on most economic theories, every rational person faced with a decision will choose the course of action that maximizes his or her own welfare, without regard to how that decision impacts others. In summary, the combined outcome of each person acting in his or her own self-interest will maximize the benefits to society as a whole.

The *legal* factor is based on the proposition that free societies are governed by laws. Laws are written to provide clarity and to prevent the abuse of the rights of individuals or society. Democratically enacted laws both contain and express society's collective moral standards. Legal analysis involves applying the relevant laws to each decision and then choosing the action that complies with those laws. A complicating factor for a global business may be that what is legal in one country might not be legal in another. In that case, it is usually best to abide by the laws of the most restrictive country.

The *ethical* factor states that while certain actions might be both economically profitable and legal, they may still not be right. Therefore, most companies, and many individuals, have established standards for themselves to enforce a higher level of conduct than that imposed by law. These standards govern how we treat others and the way in which we restrain our selfish desires. This behavior and its underlying beliefs are the essence of ethics. **Ethics** are shaped by our cultural, socioeconomic, and religious backgrounds. An *ethical analysis* is needed to guide judgment for making decisions.

The decision rule in an ethical analysis is to choose the action that fulfills ethical duties—responsibilities of the members of society to each other. The challenge in an ethical analysis is to identify specific ethical duties and stakeholders to whom you owe these duties. As with legal issues, a complicating factor in making global ethical decisions may be that what is considered ethical in one country is not considered ethical in another.

The questions you may ask in making an ethical analysis include:

- *Which options are most honest, open, and truthful?*
- *Which options are most kind and compassionate and build a sense of community?*
- *Which options create the greatest good for the greatest number of stakeholders?*
- *Which options result in treating others as I would want to be treated?*

Ethical training starts at home and continues throughout our lives. It is reinforced by the teaching that we receive in our churches, temples, synagogues, or mosques; by the schools we attend; and by the persons we associate with and the company we keep. A thorough understanding of ethics requires more study than we can accomplish in this book. However, remember that while making accounting decisions, do not leave your ethics at the door.

In business settings, ethics work best when modeled from the top. Ethisphere Institute (www.ethisphere.com) has recently established the Business Ethics Leadership Alliance (BELA), aimed at "reestablishing ethics as the foundation of everyday business practices." BELA members agree to embrace and uphold four core values that incorporate ethics and integrity into all their practices: (1) Legal compliance; (2) Transparency; (3) Conflict identification; and (4) Accountability. Each year, Ethisphere Institute publishes a list of the World's Most Ethical Companies. The 2016 list includes corporations like L'Oréal, Accenture, H&M, 3M, Marks and Spencer, Cisco, Colgate-Palmolive Company, Dell Inc., GE, Tata Steel, LinkedIn, and UPS. As you begin to make your decisions about future employers, put these companies on your list! It's easier to act ethically when those you work for recognize the importance of ethics in business practices. These companies have learned from experience that, in the long run, ethical conduct pays big rewards, not only socially, morally, and spiritually, but economically as well.

DECISION GUIDELINES

DECISION FRAMEWORK FOR MAKING ETHICAL JUDGMENTS

Weighing tough ethical judgments in business and accounting requires a decision framework. Answering the following four elements will guide you through tough decisions:

Decision	Guidelines
1. What is the issue?	**1.** The issue will usually deal with making a judgment about an accounting measurement or disclosure that results in economic consequences, often to numerous parties.
2. Who are the stakeholders, and what are the consequences of the decision to each?	**2.** Stakeholders are anyone who might be impacted by the decision—you, your company, and potential users of the information (investors, creditors, regulatory agencies). Consequences can be economic, legal, or ethical in nature.
3. Weigh the alternatives.	**3.** Analyze the impact of the decision on all stakeholders, using economic, legal, and ethical criteria. Ask "Who will be helped or hurt, whose rights will be exercised or denied, and in what way?"
4. Make the decision and be prepared to deal with the consequences.	**4.** Exercise the courage to either defend the decision or to change it, depending on its positive or negative impact. How does your decision make you feel afterward?

To simplify, we might ask three questions:

1. Is the action legal? If not, steer clear, unless you want to go to jail or pay monetary damages to injured parties. If the action is legal, go on to questions (2) and (3).

2. Who will be affected by the decision and how? Be as thorough about this analysis as possible, and analyze it from all three standpoints (economic, legal, and ethical).

3. How will this decision make me feel afterward? How would it make me feel if my family were to read about it in the newspaper?

In later chapters throughout the text, we will apply this model to different accounting decisions.

Code of Ethics for Professional Accountants

The decision framework for making ethical judgments provides general guidance for everyone, regardless of the profession or industry. Many professional organizations, businesses, and other entities adopt their own ethical guidelines or codes of conduct so that their employees have specific guidelines. One day you might become a member of a professional body like the national professional accounting body in your country of residence or any other international professional bodies. All professional accounting bodies have a Code of Ethics, which is almost universally based on the *Code of Ethics for Professional Accountants* as issued by the *International Ethics Standards Board for Accountants* (IESBA).

This code provides guidance to all members in the performance of their professional duties and is composed of several principles that form the basic building blocks of ethical and professional conduct. Even though you may not be an accounting major and may never be a member of a professional accounting body, the basic principles contained in its code can be applied to a wide range of professions and organizations. In your future career, you may also interact with Chartered Accountants (CAs) or Certified Public Accountants (CPAs), and it is helpful to understand the code of conduct that accountants are expected to adhere to.

An excerpt from the Code is provided below as an introduction to the fundamental principles for ethical behavior.

A professional accountant shall comply with the following fundamental principles:

(a) Integrity

The principle of integrity imposes an obligation on all professional accountants to be straightforward and honest in all professional and business relationships. Integrity also implies fair dealing and truthfulness.

(b) Objectivity

The principle of objectivity imposes an obligation on all professional accountants not to compromise their professional or business judgment because of bias, conflict of interest, or the undue influence of others.

(c) Professional Competence and Due Care

The principle of professional competence and due care imposes an obligation on all professional accountants to maintain professional knowledge and skill at the level required to ensure that clients or employers receive competent professional service and to act diligently in accordance with applicable technical and professional standards when performing professional activities or providing professional services.

(d) Confidentiality

The principle of confidentiality imposes an obligation on all professional accountants to refrain from disclosing or employing confidential information, acquired as a result of professional and business relationships, outside the firm without proper and specific authority, or unless there is a legal or professional right or duty to disclose the information. They should also refrain from using the confidential information acquired as a result of professional and business relationships to their personal advantage or the advantage of third parties.

(e) Professional Behavior

The principle of professional behavior imposes an obligation on all professional accountants to comply with relevant laws and regulations and avoid any action that the professional accountant knows or should know may discredit the profession. This includes actions that a reasonable and informed third party, after weighing all the facts and circumstances available to the professional accountant at that time, would be likely to conclude adversely affects the good reputation of the profession.

End-of-Chapter Summary Problem

Starr Williams started RedLotus Travel, Inc., on April 1, 20X8. Through April, the business provided services for customers. It is now April 30, and investors wonder how well RedLotus, Inc., performed during its first month. The investors also want to know the company's financial position at the end of April and its cash flows during the month.

The following data are listed in alphabetical order. Prepare the RedLotus, Inc., financial statements at the end of April 20X8.

Accounts payable	$ 1,800	Land	$20,000
Accounts receivable	2,000	Payments of cash:	
Adjustments to reconcile net income to net cash provided by operating activities	(5,900)	Acquisition of land	40,000
		Dividends	2,100
		Rent expense	1,100
Cash balance at beginning of April	0	Retained earnings at beginning of April	0
Cash balance at end of April	?	Retained earnings at end of April	?
Cash receipts:		Salary expense	1,200
Issuance (sale) of shares to owners	50,000	Service revenue	10,000
Sale of land	22,000	Supplies	3,700
Share capital	50,000	Utilities expense	400
Gain on sale of land	2,000		

Requirements

1. Prepare the Income Statement, the Statement of Changes in Equity, and the Statement of Cash Flows for the month ended April 30, 20X8, and the Balance Sheet at April 30, 20X8. Draw arrows linking the statements.
2. Answer the following questions:
   a. How well did RedLotus perform during its first month of operations?
   b. Where does RedLotus stand financially at the end of April?

Answers

Requirement 1

Financial Statements of RedLotus Travel, Inc.

	A	B	C	D
1	**RedLotus Travel, Inc.** **Income Statement** **Month Ended April 30, 20X8**			
2	**Revenue:**			
3	Service revenue		$ 10,000	
4	Gain on sale of land		$ 2,000	
5	**Expenses:**			
6	Salary expense	$ 1,200		
7	Rent expense	1,100		
8	Utilities expense	400		
9	Total expenses		2,900	
10	Net Income		$ 9,300	
11				

①

	A	B	C	D
1	**RedLotus Travel, Inc.** **Statement of Changes in Equity** **Month Ended April 30, 20X8**			
2	Total equity, April 1, 20X8		$ 0	
3	Add: Issuance of share capital		50,000	
4	Add: Net income for the month		9,300	
5			$ 59,300	
6	Less: Dividends		(2,100)	
7	Total equity, April 30, 20X8		$ 57,200	
8				

	A		B	C		D
1			**RedLotus Travel, Inc.** **Balance Sheet** **April 30, 20X8**			
2	**Assets**			**Liabilities**		
3	Cash	$	33,300	Accounts payable	$	1,800
4	Accounts receivable		2,000	**Shareholders' equity**		
5	Supplies		3,700	Share capital		50,000
6	Land		20,000	Retained earnings		7,200
7				Total shareholders' equity		57,200
8				Total liabilities and		
9	Total assets	$	59,000	shareholders' equity	$	59,000
10						

② (Total shareholders' equity, row 7)

	A	B	C
1	**RedLotus Travel, Inc.** **Statement of Cash Flows** **Month Ended April 30, 20X8**		
2	**Cash flows from operating activities:**		
3	Net income		$ 9,300
4	Adjustments to reconcile net income to net cash provided by operating activities		(5,900)
5	Net cash provided by operating activities		3,400
6	**Cash flows from investing activities:**		
7	Acquisition of land	$ (40,000)	
8	Sale of land	22,000	
9	Net cash used for investing activities		(18,000)
10	**Cash flows from financing activities:**		
11	Issuance (sale) of shares	$ 50,000	
12	Payment of dividends	(2,100)	
13	Net cash provided by financing activities		47,900
14	Net increase in cash		$ 33,300
15	Cash balance, April 1, 20X8		0
16	Cash balance, April 30, 20X8		$ 33,300
17			

③ (Cash balance, row 16 → Cash, balance sheet row 3)

Requirement 2

a. RedLotus, Inc., performed rather well in April. Net income was $9,300—very good in relation to service revenue of $10,000. The company was able to pay cash dividends of $2,100.

b. RedLotus, Inc., ended April with cash of $33,300. Total assets of $59,000 far exceed total liabilities of $1,800. Shareholders' equity of $57,200 provides a good cushion for borrowing. The business's financial position at April 30, 20X8, is strong.

REVIEW | *Conceptual Framework and Financial Statements*

Quick Check (Answers are given at the end of the chapter.)

1. All of the following statements are true except one. Which statement is false?

a. The organization that formulates IFRS is the International Accounting Standards Board.
b. Users of financial information are limited to shareholders of the company.
c. Professional accountants are held to a high standard of ethical conduct.
d. Bookkeeping is only a part of accounting.

2. Which of the following items are fundamental qualitative characteristics of financial information?

a. Going concern and accrual accounting
b. Relevance and faithful representation
c. Materiality and Cost-benefits
d. Assets and Liabilities

3. The accounting equation can be expressed as:

a. Assets = Liabilities – Owners' Equity
b. Assets + Liabilities = Owners' Equity
c. Assets – Liabilities = Owners' Equity
d. Owners' Equity – Assets = Liabilities

4. The nature of an asset is best described as:

a. an economic resource that's expected to benefit future operations
b. something with physical form that's valued at cost in the accounting records
c. something owned by a business that has a ready market value
d. an economic resource representing cash or the right to receive cash in the future

5. Which financial statement covers a period of time?

a. Balance Sheet
b. Income Statement
c. Statement of cash flows
d. Both b and c

6. How would net income be most likely to affect the accounting equation?

a. Increase assets and increase liabilities
b. Decrease assets and decrease liabilities
c. Increase liabilities and decrease shareholders' equity
d. Increase assets and increase shareholders' equity

7. During the year, EcoWash has \$120,000 in revenues, \$50,000 in expenses, and \$4,000 in dividend payments. Shareholders' equity changed by:

a. +\$66,000
b. +\$70,000
d. +\$74,000
c. –\$66,000

8. EcoWash in question 7 had a:

a. net loss of \$50,000
b. net income of \$70,000
c. net income of \$66,000
d. net income of \$120,000

9. Rochester Corporation holds cash of \$11,000 and owes \$27,000 in accounts payable. Rochester has accounts receivable of \$40,000, inventory of \$34,000, and land that cost \$55,000. How much are Rochester's total assets and liabilities?

	Total assets	*Liabilities*
a.	\$129,000	\$27,000
b.	\$27,000	\$140,000
c.	\$140,000	\$27,000
d.	\$140,000	\$93,000

10. Which item(s) is (are) reported on the Balance Sheet?

a. Inventory
b. Accounts payable
c. Retained earnings
d. All of the above

11. During the year, McKenna Company's shareholders' equity increased from $38,000 to $50,000. McKenna earned net income of $18,000. How much in dividends did McKenna declare and paid during the year?

a. $0 (no dividends were paid)
b. $6,000
c. $12,000
d. $7,000

12. Javis Company had total assets of $340,000 and total shareholders' equity of $130,000 at the beginning of the year. During the year assets increased by $70,000 and liabilities increased by $25,000. Shareholders' equity at the end of the year is:

a. $95,000
b. $175,000
c. $200,000
d. $155,000

13. Which of the following is a true statement about International Financial Reporting Standards?

a. They are newer than US financial reporting standards.
b. They require less judgement than other accounting standards.
c. They have been adopted (or allowed as an alternative) by many countries and territories around the world.
d. They are worse than local accounting standards as they do not understand local business conditions and practices.

14. Which of the following is the most accurate statement regarding ethics as applied to decision making in accounting?

a. Ethics involves making difficult choices under pressure, and should be kept in mind in making every decision, including those involving accounting.
b. Ethics has no place in accounting, since accounting deals purely with numbers.
c. It is impossible to learn ethical decision making, since it is just something you decide to do or not to do.
d. Ethics is becoming less and less important as a field of study in business.

Accounting Vocabulary

accounting (p. 3) The information system that measures business activities, processes that information into reports and financial statements, and communicates the results to decision makers.

accounting equation (p. 12) The most basic relationship in accounting: Assets = Liabilities + Equity, or Assets − Liabilities = Equity. Also Revenue − Expenses = Profit (Loss).

accrual basis (p. 11) Business transactions and other events are recognized when they occur and not when cash is received or paid.

asset (p. 11) A resource controlled by an entity as a result of past events and from which future economic benefits are expected to flow to the entity.

Balance Sheet (p. 12) List of an entity's assets, liabilities, and owners' equity at a specific date. Also called the Statement of Financial Position.

cash (p. 19) Money or any medium of exchange that a bank accepts at face value.

Conceptual Framework (p. 8) The basic objective, principles and assumptions guiding the presentation and preparation of general purpose financial statements.

corporation (p. 5) A business owned by shareholders. A corporation is a legal entity, an "artificial person" in the eye of the law.

current asset (p. 19) An asset that is expected to be converted to cash, sold, or consumed during the next 12 months.

current liability (p. 20) A debt due to be paid within one year.

dividends (p. 13) Distributions (usually in the form of cash) by a corporation to its shareholders.

double-entry system (p. 3) A system of recording business transactions where every financial transaction has equal amounts of debits and credits recorded in at least two accounts.

economic phenomena (p. 10) Information about the reporting entity's economic resources, claims against the reporting entity, and the effects of transactions and other events and conditions that change those resources and claims.

equity (p. 11) The residual interest in the assets of an entity after deducting all its liabilities. Also called owners' or shareholders' equity or net assets.

ethics (p. 25) Standards of right and wrong that transcend economic and legal boundaries. Ethical standards deal with the way we treat others and restrain our own actions because of the desires, expectations, or rights of others, or with our obligations to them.

expenses (p. 12) Decrease in equity that results from operations; the cost of doing business; opposite of revenues.

financial accounting (p. 4) The branch of accounting that provides information to people outside the firm.

financial statements (p. 2) Business documents that report financial information about a business entity to decision makers.

financing activities (p. 21) Activities that obtain from investors and creditors the cash needed to launch and sustain the business; a section of the statement of cash flows.

gains (p. 12) Usually separated from revenues. Part of income and result in an increase in equity.

general purpose financial statements (p. 8) The common set of financial statements prepared for all users of financial statements.

Generally Accepted Accounting Principles (GAAP) (p. 6) Accounting guidelines, usually in reference to U.S. standards as formulated by the Financial Accounting Standards Board. By 2014, U.S. GAAP is expected to converge with IFRS.

going concern (p. 11) An assumption that an entity will remain in operation for the foreseeable future.

gross profit (p. 16) Revenue from a particular activity minus the direct costs associated with earning that revenue.

income (p. 11) Increases in equity from revenue and gains.

Income Statement (p. 12) A financial statement listing an entity's revenues, expenses, and net income or net loss for a specific period. Part of the Statement of Comprehensive Income.

International Accounting Standards Board (IASB) (p. 6) A board formed to replace the International Accounting Standards Committee (IASC).

International Financial Reporting Standards (IFRS) (p. 6) Accounting guidelines, formulated by the International Accounting Standards Board (IASB).

inventory (p. 22) The merchandise that a company holds for sale to customers.

investing activities (p. 21) Activities that increase or decrease the long-term assets available to the business; a section of the statement of cash flows.

liability (p. 11) A present obligation of an entity arising from past events, the settlement of which is expected to result in an outflow from the entity of resources embodying economic benefits.

losses (p. 12) Usually separated from expenses; result in a reduction in equity.

management accounting (p. 4) The branch of accounting that generates information for the internal decision makers of a business, such as top executives.

materiality (p. 10) The importance or significance of information that may change the user's final assessment of a situation.

net income (p. 12) Excess of total revenues over total expenses. Also called net earnings or net profit.

net loss (p. 13) Excess of total expenses over total revenues.

net profit (p. 13) Another name for net income.

operating activities (p. 21) Activities that create revenue or expense in the entity's major line of business; a section of the statement of cash flows.

paid-in capital (p. 20) The amount of shareholders' equity that shareholders have contributed to the corporation.

partnership (p. 5) An association of two or more persons who co-own a business for profit.

property, plant and equipment or PPE (p. 19) Long-lived assets, such as land, buildings, and equipment, used in the operation of the business. Also called fixed assets.

proprietorship (p. 5) A business with a single owner.

qualitative characteristics (p. 9) The attributes that are most likely to make the information provided in financial statements useful to users.

reporting entity (p. 4) An organization or a section of an organization that, for accounting purposes, stands apart from other organizations and individuals as a separate economic unit.

retained earnings (p. 11) The amount of shareholders' equity that the corporation has earned through profitable operation that has been retained in the business (not distributed back to shareholders).

revenue (p. 12) Increase in retained earnings from delivering goods or services to customers or clients.

share capital (p. 11) Proof of ownership in a company. Amount invested by owners into the business through share ownership.

shareholder (p. 5) A person who owns shares in a corporation.

Statement of Cash Flows (p. 21) Reports cash receipts and cash payments classified according to the entity's major activities: operating, investing, and financing.

Statement of Changes in Equity (p. 17) Provides a reconciliation of the movement of equity items during a financial period. Affected share issuance, share cancellation, net income (or net loss), and dividends paid.

Statement of Comprehensive Income (p. 15) Net profit (loss) for the period plus other comprehensive income.

Statement of Financial Position (p. 18) Another name for the Balance Sheet.

ASSESS YOUR PROGRESS

Short Exercises

S1-1. ***(Learning Objective 1: Organizing a business)*** Keyboard Warrior needs funds, and Mary Barry, the president, has asked you to consider investing in the business. Answer the following questions about the different ways that Barry might organize the business. Explain each answer. LO 1

a. What forms of organization will enable the owners of Keyboard Warrior to limit their risk of loss to the amounts they have invested in the business?

b. What form of business organization will give Mary Barry the most freedom to manage the business as she wishes?

c. What form of organization will give creditors the maximum protection in the event that Keyboard Warrior fails and cannot pay its debts?

S1-2. ***(Learning Objective 1, 2: Defining key accounting terms)*** Accounting definitions are precise, and you must understand the vocabulary to be able to properly use accounting. Sharpen your understanding of key terms by answering the following questions: LO 1 2

1. How do the assets and owners' equity of Volkswagen Corporation differ from each other? Which one (assets or owners' equity) must be at least as large as the other? Which one can be smaller than the other?
2. How are Volkswagen's liabilities and owners' equity similar or different?

S1-3. ***(Learning Objective 1, 2: Classifying assets, liabilities, and owners' equity)*** Consider Carrefour, a large retailer. Classify the following items as Asset (A), Liability (L), or Shareholders' Equity (S) for Carrefour: LO 1 2

a.	____ Accounts receivable	**g.**	____ Accounts payable
b.	____ Long-term debt	**h.**	____ Share capital
c.	____ Merchandise inventory	**i.**	____ Supplies
d.	____ Notes payable	**j.**	____ Retained earnings
e.	____ Expenses payable	**k.**	____ Land
f.	____ Equipment	**l.**	____ Prepaid expenses

S1-4. ***(Learning Objective 2: Using accounting vocabulary)*** LO 2

1. Identify the two accounting elements you would find on an Income Statement.
2. What do we call the bottom line of the Income Statement?

S1-5. ***(Learning Objective 2: Applying accounting assumptions)*** Daniel Newman is the chair of the board of Quality Food Brands, Inc. Suppose Mr. Newman has just founded Quality Food Brands, and assume that he treats his home and other personal assets as part of Quality Food Brands. Answer these questions about the evaluation of Quality Food Brands, Inc. LO 2

1. Which accounting principle governs this situation?
2. How can the proper application of this accounting concept give Newman and others a realistic view of Quality Food Brands, Inc.? Explain in detail.

S1-6. ***(Learning Objective 2: Understanding the Conceptual Framework)*** Identify the accounting assumption, principle, or qualitative characteristic that best applies to each of the following situations: LO 2

a. At the height of the financial crisis, there were speculations that Lehman Brothers would not be able to meet its obligations before it eventually filed for bankruptcy on September 15, 2008.

b. ComfortDelgro, a transportation company, has been using an eight-year lifespan on the roadworthiness of its fleet of buses. Better maintenance and servicing have allowed the company to use its buses for a period of 12 years.

c. F&N is the parent company of Asia Pacific Breweries and Boncafé Beverages, and wishes to evaluate which subsidiary has performed better.

d. You are about to report your net income for the year. It looks like a record-breaking year, and sales are expected to top the $10 million mark for the first time. However, you are uncertain if you have actually delivered the goods ordered by one customer on December 30, 20X6, totaling $500,000.

LO 2 **S1-7.** ***(Learning Objective 2: Using the accounting equation)*** Identify the missing amount for each situation:

	Total Assets	=	Total Liabilities	+	Shareholders' Equity
a.	$?		$50,200		$160,800
b.	270,000		50,290		?
c.	172,800		?		76,800

LO 2 **S1-8.** ***(Learning Objective 2: Using the accounting equation)***

1. Use the accounting equation to show how to determine the amount of a company's owners' equity. How would your answer change if you were analyzing your own household or a single Burger King outlet?
2. If you know the assets and the owners' equity of a business, how can you measure its liabilities? Give the equation.

LO 3 **S1-9.** ***(Learning Objective 3: Preparing an Income Statement)*** Barbed Wires began 20X6 with total assets of $160 million and ended 20X6 with assets of $190 million. During 20X6 Barbed Wires earned revenues of $131 million and had expenses of $54 million. Barbed Wires paid dividends of $13 million in 20X6. Prepare the company's Income Statement for the year ended December 31, 20X6, complete with an appropriate heading.

LO 3 **S1-10.** ***(Learning Objective 3: Preparing a statement of changes in equity)*** Roam Corp. began 20X6 with retained earnings of $300 million and share capital of $125 million. Revenues during the year were $510 million and expenses totaled $325 million. Roam declared and paid dividends of $15 million. What was the company's ending balance of retained earnings? To answer this question, prepare Roam's statement of changes in equity for the year ended December 31, 20X6, complete with its proper heading.

LO 3 **S1-11.** ***(Learning Objective 3: Preparing a Balance Sheet)*** At December 31, 20X6, Grande Products has cash of $15,000, receivables of $22,000, and inventory of $20,000. The company's equipment totals $49,000. Grande owes accounts payable of $21,000, and long-term notes payable of $50,000. Share capital amounts to $35,000.

Prepare Grande's Balance Sheet at December 31, 20X6, complete with its proper heading. Use the accounting equation to compute retained earnings.

LO 3 **S1-12.** ***(Learning Objective 3: Preparing a statement of cash flows)*** Lanos Medical, Inc., ended 20X5 with cash of $30,000. During 20X6, Lanos earned net income of $72,100 and had adjustments to reconcile net income to net cash provided by operations totaling $22,000 (this is a negative amount).

Lanos paid $45,000 to purchase equipment during 20X6. During 20X6, the company paid dividends of $10,700.

Prepare Lanos' statement of cash flows for the year ended December 31, 20X6, complete with its proper heading.

LO 3 4 **S1-13.** ***(Learning Objectives 3, 4: Using accounting vocabulary; identifying items with the appropriate financial statement)*** Suppose you are analyzing the financial statements of Murphy Radiology, Inc. Identify each item with its appropriate financial statement, using the following abbreviations: Income Statement (IS), Statement of Changes in Equity (SCE), Balance Sheet (BS), and Statement of cash flows (SCF). Three items appear on two financial statements, and one item shows up on three statements.

a. ____ Cash
b. ____ Net cash used for financing activities
c. ____ Accounts payable
d. ____ Share capital
e. ____ Interest revenue
f. ____ Long-term debt
g. ____ Increase or decrease in cash
h. ____ Dividends
i. ____ Salary expense
j. ____ Inventory
k. ____ Sales revenue
l. ____ Retained earnings
m. ____ Net cash provided by operating activities
n. ____ Net income

S1-14. ***(Learning Objectives 2, 4: Applying accounting concepts, assumptions, and principles to explain business activity)*** Apply your understanding of the relationships among the financial statements to answer these questions.

a. How can a business earn large profits but have a small balance of retained earnings?
b. Give two reasons why a business can have a steady stream of net income over a six-year period and still experience a cash shortage.
c. If you could pick a single source of cash for your business, what would it be? Why?
d. How can a business lose money several years in a row and still have plenty of cash?

S1-15. ***(Learning Objective 5: Making ethical judgments)*** Good business and accounting practices require the exercise of good judgment. How should ethics be incorporated into making accounting judgments? Why is ethics important?

Exercises MyLab Accounting

Select A and B exercises can be found within MyLab Accounting, an online homework and practice environment. Your instructor may ask you to complete select exercises using MyLab Accounting.

Group A

LO 2 3

E1-16A. ***(Learning Objectives 2, 3: Using the accounting equation; evaluating business operations)*** Compute the missing amount in the accounting equation for each company (amounts in thousands):

	Assets	Liabilities	Owners' Equity
Alpha	$?	$12	$20
Bravo	21	?	5
Charlie	44	21	?

Which company appears to have the strongest financial position? Explain your reasoning.

E1-17A. ***(Learning Objectives 2, 3: Using the accounting equation; evaluating business operations)*** Double Doughnuts has current assets of $250 million; property, plant and equipment of $440 million; and other assets totaling $100 million. Current liabilities are $120 million and long-term liabilities total $300 million.

Requirements

1. Use the data to write Double Doughnuts' accounting equation.
2. How much in resources does Double Doughnuts' have to work with?
3. How much does Double Doughnuts' owe creditors?
4. How much of the company's assets do the Double Doughnuts' shareholders actually own?

E1-18A. ***(Learning Objectives 2, 3: Using the accounting equation; evaluating business operations)*** Spicer, Inc.'s comparative Balance Sheet at January 31, 20X7 and 20X6, reports (in millions):

	20X7	20X6
Total assets	$37	$30
Total liabilities	8	6

Requirements

Three independent scenarios about Spicer's issuance of shares and payment of dividends during the year ended January 31, 20X7, are provided below. For each scenario, use the accounting equation and the statement of changes in equity to compute the amount of Spicer's net income or net loss during the year ended January 31, 20X7.

1. Spicer issued $8 million of shares and paid no dividends.
2. Spicer issued no shares but paid dividends of $8 million.
3. Spicer issued $2 million of shares and paid dividends of $6 million.

LO 3

E1-19A. ***(Learning Objective 3: Using the accounting equation)*** Answer these questions about the following companies:

1. Delta Cruises began the year with total liabilities of $60,000 and total shareholders' equity of $90,000. During the year, total assets increased by 20%. How much are total assets at the end of the year?
2. Carnival Airlines Ltd. began the year with total assets of $120,000 and total liabilities of $15,000. Net income for the year was $20,000, and dividends were $4,000. How much is shareholders' equity at the end of the year?

LO 3 4

E1-20A. ***(Learning Objectives 3, 4: Evaluating business operations; making business decisions)*** Assume LINE is expanding into Ireland. The company must decide where to locate and how to finance the expansion. Identify the financial statement where these decision makers can find the following information about LINE. In some cases, more than one statement will report the needed data.

a. Cash spent to acquire the building
b. Selling, general, and administrative expenses
c. Adjustments to reconcile net income to net cash provided by operations
d. Ending cash balance
e. Current liabilities
f. Net income
g. Share capital
h. Income tax payable
i. Dividends
j. Income tax expense
k. Ending balance of retained earnings
l. Total assets
m. Long-term debt
n. Revenue

LO 3 4
■ spreadsheet

E1-21A. ***(Learning Objectives 3, 4: Using the accounting equation; preparing a Balance Sheet)*** Amounts of the assets and liabilities of Angelababy Company, as of January 31, 20X6, are given as follows. The revenue and expense figures for the year ended on that date (amounts in millions) are also included:

Total revenue	$38.8	Investments	$15.0
Receivables	0.8	Property and equipment, net	16.6
Current liabilities	2.0	Other expenses	6.7
Share capital	14.3	Retained earnings, beginning	8.2
Interest expense	0.7	Retained earnings, ending	?
Salary and other employee expenses	17.5	Cash	2.5
Long-term liabilities	3.0	Other assets	5.0

Requirement

1. Prepare the Balance Sheet of Angelababy Company at January 31, 20X6. Use the accounting equation to compute ending retained earnings.

LO 3 4

E1-22A. ***(Learning Objective 3, 4: Preparing an Income Statement and a Statement of Changes in Equity)*** This exercise should be used with Exercise 1-21A. Refer to the data of Angelababy Company in Exercise 1-21A.

Requirements

1. Prepare the Income Statement of Angelababy Company, for the year ended January 31, 20X6.
2. What amount of dividends did Angelababy declare during the year ended January 31, 20X6? Hint: Prepare a statement of changes in equity.

E1-23A. ***(Learning Objective 3, 4: Preparing a statement of cash flows)*** Gravity began 20X6 with $88,000 in cash. During 20X6, Gravity earned net income of $420,000, and adjustments to reconcile net income to net cash provided by operations totaled $60,000, a positive amount. Investing activities used cash of $400,000, and financing activities provided cash of $68,000. Gravity ended 20X6 with total assets of $260,000 and total liabilities of $115,000.

Requirement

1. Prepare Gravity's statement of cash flows for the year ended December 31, 20X6. Identify the data items given that do not appear on the statement of cash flows. Also identify the financial statement that reports the unused items.

LO 3 4

E1-24A. ***(Learning Objective 3, 4: Preparing an Income Statement and a statement of changes in equity)*** Assume Fast Copy Center ended the month of July 20X6 with this data:

Payments of cash:		Cash balance, June 30, 20X6	$ 0
Acquisition of equipment	$480,000	Cash balance, July 31, 20X6	10,000
Dividends	4,200	Cash receipts:	
Retained earnings June 30, 20X6	0	Issuance of shares to owners	69,500
Retained earnings July 31, 20X6	?	Rent expense	2,300
Utilities expense	12,000	Share capital	69,500
Adjustments to reconcile net income to net cash provided by operations	2,300	Equipment	41,000
Salary expense	168,000	Office supplies	13,700
		Accounts payable	16,000
		Service revenue	604,500

Requirement

1. Prepare the Income Statement and the Statement of Changes in Equity of Fast Copy Center, for the month ended July 31, 20X6.

LO 3 4

E1-25A. ***(Learning Objective 3, 4: Preparing a Balance Sheet)*** Refer to the data in Exercise 1-24A.

Requirement

1. Prepare the Balance Sheet of Fast Copy Center, Inc., for July 31, 20X6.

E1-26A. ***(Learning Objective 3, 4: Preparing a Statement of Cash Flows)*** Refer to the data in Exercises 1-24A and 1-25A.

Requirement

1. Prepare the statement of cash flows of Fast Copy Center, for the month ended July 31, 20X6. Also explain the relationship among Income Statement, statement of changes in equity, Balance Sheet, and statement of cash flows.

LO 3 4

writing assignment

E1-27A. ***(Learning Objectives 3, 4: Evaluating a business; advising a business)*** This exercise should be used in conjunction with Exercises 1-24A through 1-26A.

The owner of Fast Copy Center seeks your advice as to whether he should cease operations or continue the business. Complete the report giving him your opinion of net income, dividends, financial position, and cash flows during his first month of operations. Cite specifics from the financial statements to support your opinion. Conclude your memo with advice on whether to stay in business or cease operations.

Group B

E1-28B. ***(Learning Objectives 2, 3: Using the accounting equation; evaluating business operations)*** Compute the missing amount in the accounting equation for each company (amounts in thousands):

	Assets	Liabilities	Owners' Equity
Delta video rentals	$?	$ 9	$19
Echo entertainment	35	?	5
Portal gifts and cards	33	16	?

Which company appears to have the strongest financial position? Explain your reasoning.

LO 2 3

E1-29B. ***(Learning Objectives 2, 3: Using the accounting equation; evaluating business operations)*** Tripple Doughnuts has current assets of €250 million; property, plant and equipment of €420 million; and other assets totaling €100 million. Current liabilities are €100 million and long-term liabilities total €320 million.

Requirements

1. Use this data to write Tripple's accounting equation.
2. How much in resources does Tripple have to work with?
3. How much does Tripple owe creditors?
4. How much of the company's assets do the Tripple shareholders actually own?

LO 2 3

E1-30B. ***(Learning Objectives 2, 3: Using the accounting equation; evaluating business operations)*** Sprinkler, Inc.'s comparative Balance Sheet at January 31, 20X7 and 20X6, reports (in millions):

	20X7	20X6
Total assets	€39	€20
Total liabilities	12	3

Requirements

Three independent scenarios about Sprinkler's issuance of shares and payment of dividends during the year ended January 31, 20X7, follow. For each situation, use the accounting equation and the statement of changes in equity to compute the amount of Sprinkler's net income or net loss during the year ended January 31, 20X7.

1. Sprinkler issued €10 million of shares and paid no dividends.
2. Sprinkler issued no shares but paid dividends of €10 million.
3. Sprinkler issued €6 million of shares and paid dividends of €2 million.

LO 3

E1-31B. ***(Learning Objective 3: Applying the accounting equation)*** Answer these questions about two companies.

1. Emerald Cruises began the year with total liabilities of €80,000 and total shareholders' equity of €45,000. During the year, total assets increased by 25%. How much are total assets at the end of the year?
2. Starjet Airlines Ltd. began the year with total assets of €75,000 and total liabilities of €50,000. Net income for the year was €24,000, and dividends were €6,000. How much is shareholders' equity at the end of the year?

LO 3 4

E1-32B. ***(Learning Objectives 3, 4: Evaluating business operations; making business decisions)*** Assume Lesley, Inc., is expanding into Sweden. The company must decide where to locate and how to finance the expansion. Identify the financial statement where these decision makers can find the following information about Lesley, Inc. In some cases, more than one statement will report the needed data.

a. Dividends
b. Total assets
c. Long-term debt
d. Selling, general, and administrative expenses
e. Cash spent to acquire the building
f. Adjustments to reconcile net income to net cash provided by operations
g. Share capital
h. Net income

i. Current liabilities
j. Share capital
k. Income tax payable
l. Ending balance of retained earnings
m. Revenue
n. Ending cash balance

E1-33B. ***(Learning Objectives 3, 4: Using the accounting equation; preparing a Balance Sheet)*** Amounts of the assets and liabilities of Bobbyboy Company, as of May 31, 20X6, are given as follows. Also included are revenue and expense figures for the year ended on that date (amounts in millions):

Total revenue	€34.0	Investments	€16.1
Receivables	0.2	Property and equipment, net	18.0
Current liabilities	6.0	Other expenses	6.8
Share capital	15.9	Retained earnings, beginning	9.3
Interest expense	0.2	Retained earnings, ending	?
Salary and other employee expenses	15.5	Cash	2.5
Long-term liabilities	2.3	Other assets	5.0

Requirement

1. Prepare the Balance Sheet of Bobbyboy Company at May 31, 20X6. Use the accounting equation to compute ending retained earnings.

E1-34B. ***(Learning Objective 3, 4: Preparing an Income Statement and a Statement of Changes in Equity)*** This exercise should be used with Exercise 1-33B.

Requirements

1. Prepare the Income Statement of Bobbyboy Company, for the year ended May 31, 20X6.
2. What amount of dividends did Bobbyboy declare during the year ended May 31, 20X6? Hint: Prepare a statement of changes in equity.

E1-35B. ***(Learning Objective 3, 4: Preparing a Statement of Cash Flows)*** Lucky began 20X6 with €80,000 in cash. During 20X6, Lucky earned net income of €442,000, and adjustments to reconcile net income to net cash provided by operations totaled €58,000, a positive amount. Investing activities used cash of €390,000, and financing activities provided cash of €72,000. Lucky ended 20X6 with total assets of €380,000 and total liabilities of €150,000.

Requirement

1. Prepare Lucky's Statement of Cash Flows for the year ended December 31, 20X6. Identify the data items given that do not appear on the Statement of Cash Flows. Also identify the financial statement that reports each unused item.

LO 4

E1-36B. ***(Learning Objective 4: Preparing an Income Statement and a Statement of Changes in Equity)*** Assume Express Copy Center ended the month of July 20X7 with this data:

Payments of cash:		Cash balance, June 30, 20X7	€ 0
Acquisition of equipment	€411,000	Cash balance, July 31, 20X7	9,500
Dividends	3,100	Cash receipts:	
Retained earnings June 30, 20X7	0	Issuance of shares to owners	54,000
Retained earnings July 31, 20X7	?	Rent expense	5,750
Utilities expense	11,000	Share capital	54,000
Adjustments to reconcile net income to net cash provided by operations	2,800	Equipment	411,000
		Office supplies	14,200
		Accounts payable	17,000
Salary expense	161,800	Service revenue	544,450

Requirement

1. Prepare the Income Statement and the Statement of Changes in Equity of Express Copy Center, for the month ended July 31, 20X7.

LO 3 4

E1-37B. ***(Learning Objective 3, 4: Preparing a Balance Sheet)*** Refer to the data in Exercise 1-36B.

Requirement

1. Prepare the Balance Sheet of Express Copy Center, at July 31, 20X7.

LO 3 4

E1-38B. ***(Learning Objective 3, 4: Preparing a Statement of Cash Flows)*** Refer to the data in Exercises 1-36B and 1-37B.

Requirement

1. Prepare the Statement of Cash Flows of Express Copy Center, for the month ended July 31, 20X7. Also explain the relationship among Income Statement, Statement of Changes in Equity, Balance Sheet, and Statement of Cash Flows.

LO 3 4

■ **writing assignment**

E1-39B. ***(Learning Objectives 3, 4: Evaluating a business; advising a business)*** This exercise should be used in conjunction with Exercises 1-36B through 1-38B.

The owner of Express Copy Center now seeks your advice as to whether he should cease operations or continue the business. Complete the report giving him your opinion of net income, dividends, financial position, and cash flows during his first month of operations. Cite specifics from the financial statements to support your opinion. Conclude your memo with advice on whether to stay in business or cease operations.

Quiz

Test your understanding of the financial statements by answering the following questions. Select the best choice from among the possible answers given.

Q1-40. The *primary* objective of financial reporting is to provide information

- **a.** to the federal government.
- **b.** useful for making investment and credit decisions.
- **c.** about the profitability of the enterprise.
- **d.** on the cash flows of the company.

Q1-41. Which type of business organization provides the least amount of protection for bankers and other creditors of the company?

- **a.** Corporation
- **b.** Partnership
- **c.** Proprietorship
- **d.** Both a and b

Q1-42. Assets are usually reported at their

- **a.** appraised value.
- **b.** historical cost.
- **c.** current market value.
- **d.** assumed value.

Q1-43. During March, assets increased by $18,000 and liabilities increased by $5,000. Shareholders' equity must have

- **a.** increased by $23,000.
- **b.** decreased by $23,000.
- **c.** increased by $13,000.
- **d.** decreased by $13,000.

Q1-44. The amount a company expects to collect from customers appears on the

- **a.** statement of cash flows.
- **b.** Income Statement in the expenses section.
- **c.** Balance Sheet in the shareholders' equity section.
- **d.** Balance Sheet in the current assets section.

Q1-45. All of the following are current assets except

- **a.** cash.
- **b.** accounts receivable.
- **c.** inventory.
- **d.** sales revenue.

Q1-46. Revenue is

a. an increase in paid-in capital resulting from the owners investing in the business.
b. a decrease in liabilities resulting from paying off loans.
c. an increase in retained earnings resulting from selling products or performing services.
d. all of the above.

Q1-47. The financial statement that reports revenues and expenses is called the

a. Balance Sheet.
b. statement of cash flows.
c. Income Statement.
d. statement of changes in equity.

Q1-48. Another name for the Balance Sheet is the

a. statement of earnings.
b. statement of financial position.
c. statement of operations.
d. statement of profit and loss.

Q1-49. Rainbow Corporation began the year with cash of $32,000 and other assets that totalled $22,000. During the year Rainbow earned sales revenue of $133,000 and had the following expenses: salaries: $56,000; rent: $10,000; and utilities: $5,000. At year-end Rainbow's cash balance was down to $20,000. How much net income (or net loss) did Rainbow experience for the year?

a. ($62,000)
b. $12,000
c. $20,000
d. $43,200

Q1-50. Advanced Instruments had retained earnings of $150,000 at December 31, 20X5. Net income for 20X6 totaled $120,000, and dividends for 20X6 were $20,000. How much retained earnings should Advanced Instruments report at December 31, 20X6?

a. $150,000
b. $250,000
c. $130,000
d. $290,000

Q1-51. Which of the following is not an enhancing qualitative characteristic?

a. Materiality
b. Understandability
c. Verifiability
d. Comparability

Q1-52. Cash paid to purchase a building appears on the statement of cash flows among the

a. financing activities.
b. investing activities.
c. shareholders' equity.
d. operating activities.

Q1-53. The shareholders' equity of Diakovsky Company at the beginning and end of 20X6 totaled $16,000 and $21,000, respectively. Assets at the beginning of 20X6 were $25,000. If Diakovsky Company's liabilities increased by $8,000 in 20X6, how much were total assets at the end of 20X6? Use the accounting equation.

a. $41,000
b. $46,000
c. $35,000
d. $38,000

Q1-54. Ribbon Company had the following on the dates indicated:

	Dec. 31, 20X6	Dec. 31, 20X5
Total assets	$750,000	$520,000
Total liabilities	280,000	180,000

Ribbon had no share issuance in 20X6, and thus the change in shareholders' equity for 20X6 was due to net income and dividends. If dividends were $50,000, how much was Ribbon's net income for 20X6? Use the accounting equation and the statement of changes in equity.

a. $290,000
b. $180,000
c. $180,000
d. $260,000

Problems MyLab Accounting

Select A and B problems can be found within MyLab Accounting, an online homework and practice environment. Your instructor may ask you to complete these problems using MyLab Accounting.

Group A

P1-55A. ***(Learning Objectives 1, 2, 4: Applying accounting vocabulary, concepts, and principles; evaluating business operations)*** Assume that Division A of Smith Corporation experienced the following transactions during the year ended December 31, 20X7:

a. Suppose Division A supplied copy products to a customer at a discounted price of $250,000. Under normal conditions they would have provided these services for $305,000.

b. The customer paid $102,000 in December 20X7, and the balance was paid in full in January 20X8.

c. During the period, Division A also sold some products to Division B amounting to $55,000 at a cost of $32,000.

d. Division A discovered that the remaining useful life of its equipment is three years instead of two years. This resulted in a lower depreciation expense of $3,000 for the year (instead of $5,000).

e. All other expenses totaled $245,000 for the year, but only $217,000 was paid to employees and suppliers.

Requirements

1. Prepare the Division A's Income Statement for the year ended December 31, 20X7.
2. For items **a** through **e**, identify the accounting concept, assumption, or principle that provides guidance in accounting for the item. State how you have applied the concept or principle in preparing the Income Statement.

P1-56A. ***(Learning Objectives 3, 4: Using the accounting equation; evaluating business operations)*** Compute the missing amount (?) for each company, amounts in millions.

	Gilbert Corp.	Mandy Co.	Gurbir Inc.
Beginning			
Assets	$ 80	$ 40	$?
Liabilities	43	25	1
Share capital	9	3	2
Retained earnings	?	12	5
Ending			
Assets	$?	$ 42	$ 8
Liabilities	48	24	?
Share capital	3	?	1
Retained earnings	33	?	?
Income Statement			
Revenues	$ 218	$?	$ 12
Expenses	210	152	?
Net income	?	?	?
Retained Earnings			
Beginning retained earnings	$ 28	$ 12	$ 5
+ Net income	?	9	4
− Dividends	(3)	(5)	(2)
= Ending retained earnings	$ 33	$ 22	$ 7

At the end of the year, which company has the:

- Highest net income?
- Highest percentage of net income to revenues?

P1-57A. ***(Learning Objectives 3, 4: Using the accounting equation; preparing a Balance Sheet; making decisions)*** The manager of Headlines, Inc., prepared the company's Balance Sheet while the accountant was ill. The Balance Sheet contains numerous errors. In particular, the manager knew that the Balance Sheet should balance, so he plugged in the shareholders' equity amount needed to achieve this balance. The shareholders' equity amount is *not* correct. All other amounts are accurate.

	A	B	C	D
1	**Headlines, Inc.** **Balance Sheet**		**For the Month Ended June 30, 20X6**	
2	**Assets**		**Liabilities**	
3	Cash	$ 7,000	Notes receivable	$ 1,500
4	Equipment	40,000	Interest expense	1,500
5	Accounts payable	7,500	Office supplies	1,200
6	Utilities expense	1,300	Accounts receivable	2,750
7	Advertising expense	650	Notes payable	55,000
8	Land	78,000	Total	75,450
9	Salary expense	3,000	**Shareholders' Equity**	
10			Shareholders' equity	62,000
11	Total assets	$ 137,450	Total liabilities	$ 137,450
12				

Requirements

1. Prepare the correct Balance Sheet and date it properly. Compute total assets, total liabilities, and shareholders' equity.
2. Is Headlines actually in a better (or worse) financial position than the erroneous Balance Sheet reports? Give reasons for your answer.
3. Identify the accounts listed on the incorrect Balance Sheet that should not be reported on the Balance Sheet. State why you excluded them from the correct Balance Sheet you prepared for Requirement 1. On which financial statement should these accounts appear?

LO 2 4

P1-58A. ***(Learning Objectives 2, 4: Preparing a Balance Sheet; applying the entity assumption; making business decisions)*** Sandy Healey is a realtor. She organized the business as a corporation on April 16, 20X7. The business received $85,000 cash from Healey and issued shares to Healey. Consider the following facts as of April 30, 20X7.

a. Healey has $15,000 in her personal bank account and $70,000 in the business bank account.
b. Healey owes $2,000 on a personal charge account with a department store.
c. Healey acquired business furniture for $38,000 on April 25. Of this amount, the business owes $32,000 on accounts payable at April 30.
d. Office supplies on hand at the real estate office total $13,000.
e. Healey's business owes $36,000 on a note payable for some land acquired for a total price of $112,000.
f. Healey's business spent $22,000 for a Realty Universe franchise, which entitles her to represent herself as an agent. Realty Universe is a national affiliation of independent real estate agents. This franchise is a business asset.
g. Healey owes $142,000 in mortgage on her personal residence, which she acquired in 20X1 for a total price of $360,000.

Requirements

1. Prepare the Balance Sheet of the real estate business of Sandy Healey Realtor, Inc., at April 30, 20X7.
2. Does it appear that the realty business can pay its debts? How can you tell?
3. Identify the personal items given in the facts that should not be reported on the Balance Sheet of the business.

■ spreadsheet

P1-59A. ***(Learning Objectives 3, 4: Preparing an Income Statement, a Statement of Changes in Equity and a Balance Sheet; using accounting information to make decisions)*** The assets and liabilities of California Rollers, as of December 31, 20X6, and revenues and expenses for the year ended on that date follow.

Land	$ 8,000	Equipment	$ 31,700
Note payable	27,500	Interest expense	4,000
Property tax expense	1,600	Interest payable	1,800
Rent expense	13,000	Accounts payable	10,000
Accounts receivable	22,000	Salary expense	33,200
Service revenue	144,000	Building	125,400
Supplies	2,300	Cash	14,000
Utilities expense	3,700	Share capital	1,200

Beginning retained earnings was $116,000, and dividends totaled $41,600 for the year.

Requirements

1. Prepare the Income Statement of California Rollers for the year ended December 31, 20X6.
2. Prepare the company's statement of changes in equity for the year.
3. Prepare the company's Balance Sheet at December 31, 20X6.
4. Analyze California Rollers by answering these questions:
   a. Was California Rollers profitable during 20X6? By how much?
   b. Did retained earnings increase or decrease? By how much?
   c. Which is greater, total liabilities or total equity? Who owns more of California Rollers' assets, creditors of the company or the company's shareholders?

P1-60A. ***(Learning Objective 4: Preparing a Statement of Cash Flows)*** The following data is derived from the financial statements of the Water Fountain Company for the year ended May 31, 20X7 (in thousands):

Purchases of property, plant and equipment	$ 3,500	Other investing cash payments	$ 320
Net income	3,000	Accounts receivable	750
Adjustments to reconcile net income to net cash provided by operating activities	2,250	Payment of dividends	300
Revenues	58,700	Share capital	5,000
Cash, beginning of year	300	Issuance of shares	200
end of year	1,680	Sales of property, plant and equipment	50
Cost of goods sold	40,800	Retained earnings	13,100

Requirements

1. Prepare a Statement of Cash Flows for the year ended May 31, 20X7. Not all items given appear on the Statement of Cash Flows.
2. What activities provided the largest source amount of cash? Is this a sign of financial strength or weakness?

P1-61A. ***(Learning Objective 4: Analyzing a company's financial statements)*** Summarized versions of Carlos Corporation's financial statements are given for two recent years. 

	A	B	C
1			
2		**20X6**	**20X5**
3	**Income Statement**	**(In thousands)**	
4	Revenues	$ k	$ 16,020
5	Cost of goods sold	11,000	a
6	Other expenses	1,250	1,200
7	Income before income taxes	1,600	1,920
8	Income taxes (35% tax rate)	l	672
9	Net income	$ m	$ b
10	**Statement of Changes in Equity**		
11	Beginning balance	$ n	$ 2,826
12	Shares bought back	(30)	0
13	Net income	o	c
14	Dividends	(96)	(200)
15	Ending balance	$ p	$ d
16	**Balance Sheet**		
17	**Assets**		
18	Cash	$ q	$ e
19	Property, plant and equipment	1,680	1,725
20	Other assets	r	10,184
21	Total assets	$ s	$ 13,069
22	**Liabilities**		
23	Current liabilities	$ t	$ 5,725
24	Notes payable and long-term debt	4,250	3,400
25	Other liabilities	60	70
26	Total liabilities	$ 9,600	$ f
27	**Shareholders' equity:**		
28	Share capital	$ 400	$ 410
29	Retained earnings	u	g
30	Total shareholders' equity	v	3,874
31	Total liabilities and shareholders' equity	$ w	$ h
32	**Cash Flow Statement**		
33	Net cash provided by operating activities	$ x	$ 850
34	Net cash used in investing activities	(220)	(320)
35	Net cash used in financing activities	(575)	(570)
36	Increase (decrease) in cash	(80)	i
37	Cash at beginning of year	y	1,200
38	Cash at end of year	$ z	$ j
39			

Requirement

1. Determine the missing amounts as denoted by the letters.

Group B

P1-62B. ***(Learning Objectives 1, 2, 4: Applying accounting vocabulary, concepts, and principles to the Income Statement; evaluating business operations)*** Assume that Division X of Paris Corporation experienced the following transactions during the year ended December 31, 20X7: 

a. Suppose Division X supplied copy products for a customer for the discounted price of €262,000. Under normal conditions they would have provided these services for €290,000.

b. The customer paid €125,000 in December 20X7, and the balance was paid in full in January 20X8.

c. During the period, Division X also sold some products to Division Y amounting to €20,000 at a cost of €17,000.

d. Division X discovered that the remaining useful life of its equipment is three years instead of two years. This resulted in a lower depreciation expense of €7,000 for the year (instead of €12,000).

e. All other expenses totaled €230,000 for the year, but only €215,000 was paid to employees and suppliers.

Requirements

1. Prepare Division X's Income Statement for the year ended December 31, 20X7.
2. For items **a** through **e**, identify the accounting concept or principle that provides guidance in accounting for the item described. State how you have applied the concept or principle in preparing the Income Statement.

P1-63B. ***(Learning Objectives 3, 4: Using the accounting equation; evaluating business operations)*** Compute the missing amounts (?) for each company—amounts in millions. Which company has the:

- Highest net income?
- Highest percent of net income to revenues?

	Daphne Corp.	Joshua Co.	Eugene
Beginning			
Assets	€ 80	€ 40	€ ?
Liabilities	43	25	1
Share capital	9	3	2
Retained earnings	?	12	5
Ending			
Assets	€ ?	€ 42	€ 8
Liabilities	48	24	?
Share capital	3	?	1
Retained earnings	33	?	?
Income Statement			
Revenues	€218	€ ?	€12
Expenses	210	152	?
Net income	?	?	?
Retained Earnings			
Beginning retained earnings	€ 28	€ 12	€ 5
+ Net income	?	9	4
− Dividends	(3)	(5)	(2)
= Ending retained earnings	€ 33	€ 22	€ 7

P1-64B. ***(Learning Objectives 3, 4: Using the accounting equation; preparing a Balance Sheet; making decisions)*** The manager of News Maker, Inc., prepared the company's Balance Sheet while the accountant was ill. The Balance Sheet contains numerous errors. In particular, the manager knew that the Balance Sheet should balance, so he plugged in the shareholders' equity amount needed to achieve this balance. The shareholders' equity amount is not correct. All other amounts are accurate.

	A	B	C	D
1	**News Maker, Inc.** **Balance Sheet**	**Month Ended November 30, 20X6**		
2	**Assets**		**Liabilities**	
3	Cash	€ 7,200	Notes receivable	€ 14,600
4	Equipment	38,200	Interest expense	2,000
5	Accounts payable	5,000	Office supplies	700
6	Utilities expense	1,200	Accounts receivable	3,200
7	Advertising expense	200	Note payable	56,000
8	Land	81,000	Total	95,900
9	Salary expense	55,000	**Shareholders' Equity**	
10			Shareholders' equity	62,400
11	**Total assets**	€ 138,300	Total liabilities	€ 138,300
12				

Requirements

1. Prepare the correct Balance Sheet and date it properly. Compute total assets, total liabilities, and shareholders' equity.
2. Is News Maker in better (or worse) financial position than the erroneous Balance Sheet reports? Give the reason for your answer.
3. Identify the accounts that should not be reported on the Balance Sheet. State why you excluded them from the correct Balance Sheet you prepared for Requirement 1. On which financial statement should these accounts appear?

LO 2 4

P1-65B. ***(Learning Objectives 2, 4: Preparing a Balance Sheet; applying the entity assumption; making business decisions)*** Jeana Hart is a realtor. She organized her business as a corporation on September 16, 20X7. The business received €80,000 from Hart and issued shares to Hart. Consider these facts as of September 30, 20X7.

a. Hart has €11,000 in her personal bank account and €31,000 in the business bank account.

b. Hart owes €1,000 on a personal charge account with a department store.

c. Hart acquired business furniture for €40,000 on September 25. Of this amount, the business owes €30,000 on accounts payable at September 30.

d. Office supplies on hand at the real estate office total €5,000.

e. Hart's business owes €35,000 on a note payable for some land acquired for a total price of €115,000.

f. Hart's business spent €28,000 for a Realty Region franchise, which entitles her to represent herself as an agent. Realty Region is a national affiliation of independent real estate agents. This franchise is a business asset.

g. Hart owes €141,000 in mortgage on her personal residence, which she acquired in 20X1 for a total price of €375,000.

Requirements

1. Prepare the Balance Sheet of the real estate business of Jeana Hart Realtor, Inc., at September 30, 20X7.
2. Does it appear that the realty business can pay its debts? How can you tell?
3. Identify the personal items given in the preceding facts that should not be reported on the Balance Sheet of the business.

■ spreadsheet

P1-66B. ***(Learning Objectives 4, 5: Preparing an Income Statement, a Statement of Changes in Equity, and a Balance Sheet; using accounting information to make decisions)*** The assets and liabilities of Post Shrub as of December 31, 20X6, and revenues and expenses for the year ended on that date follow.

Land	€ 8,000	Equipment	€ 36,300
Note payable	32,500	Interest expense	4,850
Property tax expense	1,500	Interest payable	1,000
Rent expense	13,200	Accounts payable	13,500
Accounts receivable	27,000	Salary expense	37,000
Service revenue	143,000	Building	129,200
Supplies	1,700	Cash	15,000
Utilities expense	3,000	Share capital	16,250

Beginning retained earnings were €116,500, and dividends totaled €46,100 for the year.

Requirements

1. Prepare the Income Statement of Post Shrub, Inc., for the year ended December 31, 20X6.
2. Prepare the company's statement of changes in equity for the year.
3. Prepare the company's Balance Sheet at December 31, 20X6.
4. Analyze Post Shrub, Inc., by answering these questions:
   a. Was Post Shrub profitable during 20X6? By how much?
   b. Did retained earnings increase or decrease? By how much?
   c. Which is greater, total liabilities or total equity? Who owns more of Post Shrub's assets, creditors of the company or Post Shrub's shareholders?

LO 4

P1-67B. ***(Learning Objective 4: Preparing a Statement of Cash Flows)*** The following data is derived from the financial statements of The High Tide Company at the year ended May 31, 20X7 (in thousands).

Purchases of property, plant and equipment	€ 3,500	Other investing cash payments	€ 180
Net income	3,000	Accounts receivable	510
Adjustments to reconcile net income to net cash provided by operating activities	2,420	Payment of dividends	290
Revenues	59,200	Share capital	4,900
Cash, beginning of year	150	Issuance of shares	175
end of year	1,825	Sales of property, plant and equipment	50
Cost of goods sold	36,250	Retained earnings	12,000

Requirements

1. Prepare a Statement of Cash Flows for the year ended May 31, 20X7. Not all the items given appear on the Statement of Cash Flows.
2. Which activities provided the largest amount of cash? Is this a sign of financial strength or weakness?

P1-68B. ***(Learning Objective 4: Analyzing a company's financial statements)*** Summarized versions of Espinola Corporation's financial statements for two recent years follow.

	A	B	C
1			
2		**20X7**	**20X6**
3	**Income Statement**	**(in thousands)**	
4	Revenues	€ k	€ 15,300
5	Cost of goods sold	11,010	a
6	Other expenses	1,300	1,200
7	Income before income taxes	1,600	1,800
8	Income taxes (35% tax rate)	l	630
9	Net income	€ m	€ b
10	**Statement of Changes in Equity**		
11	Beginning balance	€ n	€ 3,430
12	Shares bought back	(100)	0
13	Net income	o	c
14	Dividends	(121)	(200)
15	Ending balance	€ p	€ d
16	**Balance Sheet**		
17	**Assets**		
18	Cash	€ q	€ e
19	Property, plant and equipment	2,006	1,830
20	Other assets	r	10,500
21	Total assets	€ s	€ 13,565
22	**Liabilities**		
23	Current liabilities	€ t	€ 5,800
24	Notes payable and long-term debt	4,600	3,300
25	Other liabilities	60	65
26	Total liabilities	€ 8,986	€ f
27	**Shareholders' Equity:**		
28	Share capital	€ 479	€ 556
29	Retained earnings	u	g
30	Total shareholders' equity	v	4,400
31	Total liabilities and shareholders' equity	€ w	€ h
32	**Cash Flows Statement**		
33	Net cash provided by operating activities	€ x	€ 840
34	Net cash used in investing activities	(230)	(330)
35	Net cash used in financing activities	(480)	(475)
36	Increase (decrease) in cash	(80)	i
37	Cash at beginning of year	y	1,200
38	Cash at end of year	€ z	€ j
39			

Requirement

1. Complete Espinola Corporation's financial statements by determining the missing amounts as denoted by the letters.

APPLY YOUR KNOWLEDGE

Decision Cases

LO 1 2 4

Case 1. ***(Learning Objectives 1, 2, 4: Using financial statements to evaluate a loan request)*** Two businesses, Blue Skies Corp. and Open Road, Inc., have sought business loans from you. To decide whether to make the loans, you have requested their Balance Sheets.

	A	B	C	D
1	**Blue Skies Corp. Balance Sheet**		**August 31, 20X7**	
2	**Assets**		**Liabilities**	
3	Cash	$ 6,000	Accounts payable	$ 40,000
4	Accounts receivable	11,000	Notes payable	90,000
5	Furniture	12,000	Total liabilities	130,000
6	Land	76,000	**Owners' Equity**	
7	Equipment	45,000	Owners' equity	20,000
8			Total liabilities and	
9	Total assets	$ 150,000	owners' equity	$ 150,000
10				

	A	B	C	D
1	**Open Road, Inc. Balance Sheet**		**August 31, 20X7**	
2	**Assets**		**Liabilities**	
3	Cash	$ 3,000	Accounts payable	$ 5,000
4	Accounts receivable	12,000	Note payable	10,000
5	Merchandise inventory	12,500	Total liabilities	15,000
6	Building	37,500	**Shareholders' Equity**	
7			Shareholders' equity	50,000
8			Total liabilities and	
9	Total assets	$ 65,000	shareholders' equity	$ 65,000
10				

Requirement

1. Using only these Balance Sheets, to which entity would you be more comfortable lending money? Explain fully, citing specific items and amounts from the respective Balance Sheets. (Challenge)

Case 2. ***(Learning Objectives 2, 5: Analyzing a company as an investment)*** A year out of college, you have $10,000 to invest. A friend has started GrandPrize Unlimited, Inc., and she asks you to invest in her company. You obtain the company's financial statements, which are summarized at the end of the first year as follows:

	A	B	C
1	**Grand Prize Unlimited, Inc. Income Statement**	**Year Ended Dec. 31, 20X6**	
2	Revenues		$ 120,000
3	Expenses		75,000
4	Net income		$ 45,000
5			

A1			
Grand Prize Unlimited, Inc. Balance Sheet	**December 31, 20X6**		
Cash	$ 7,000	Liabilities	$ 56,000
Other assets	99,000	Equity	50,000
Total assets	$ 106,000	Total liabilities and equity	$ 106,000

Conversations with your friend turn up the following facts:

a. Revenues and receivables of $25,000 were overlooked and omitted.

b. Advertising costs of $45,000 were recorded as assets. These costs should have been expenses. GrandPrize Unlimited paid cash for these expenses and recorded the cash payment correctly.

c. The company owes an additional $10,000 for accounts payable.

Requirements

1. Prepare corrected financial statements.
2. Use your corrected statements to evaluate GrandPrize Unlimited's results of operations and financial position. (Challenge)
3. Will you invest in Grand Prize Unlimited? Give your reason. (Challenge)

Ethical Issue

You are studying frantically for a mid-term exam due tomorrow. You are having difficulty with the course, and the grade you obtain for this exam can make the difference between receiving a final grade of B or C. If you receive a C, it will lower your grade point average to the point that you could lose your academic scholarship. An hour ago, a friend, who is also enrolled in the course, but in a different section under the same professor, sent you an email telling you how she found the mid-term exam very challenging. Her class is on Tuesdays and yours is on Fridays. She accidentally took an extra copy of the mid-term exam question paper when she was packing her bags and asks if you would like it.

You glance at your course syllabus and find the following: "You are expected to do your own work in this class. Although you may study with others, giving, receiving, or obtaining information pertaining to an examination is considered an act of academic dishonesty, unless such action is authorized by the instructor administering the examination. Also, divulging the contents of an essay or objective examination designated by the instructor is considered an act of academic dishonesty. Academic dishonesty is considered a violation of the student honor code, and will subject the student to disciplinary procedures, which can include suspension from the University."

It is now close to midnight on Tuesday evening. You have been staring at your friend's email for the last hour. You click on the reply button, and start to type. . . .

Requirements

1. What is the ethical issue in this situation?
2. Who are the stakeholders? What are the possible consequences for each stakeholder?
3. Analyze the alternatives from the following standpoints: (a) economic, (b) legal, and (c) ethical.
4. What would you do? How would you justify your decision? How would your decision make you feel afterward?
5. How is this similar to a business situation?

Focus on Financials: | Nestlé

This case spans all 12 chapters and is based on the consolidated financial statements of Nestlé. As you work with Nestlé throughout this course, you will develop the confidence and ability to use the financial statements of other companies as well.

Refer to Nestlé's consolidated financial statements in Appendix A. If you wish, you can obtain the full annual report from www.nestle.com/investors. You may find the information overwhelming for now, but try to spot the key principles that we have discussed in this chapter. It will get progressively easier as you gain familiarity with the elements of the financial statements.

Requirements

1. Suppose you are a Nestlé shareholder. If you could pick one item on the company's Consolidated Income Statement to increase year after year, what would it be and why? Did this item increase or decrease during 2016? What does this mean for Nestlé?
2. What was Nestlé's largest expense for 2016? In your own words, explain what you understand by this item.
3. Investors are keenly interested not just in a company's sales and profits for a given year, but in trends in its sales and profits over time. Consider Nestlé's sales and net income during the period from 2014 through 2016. Can you offer a possible explanation for these changes?
4. Use the Consolidated Balance Sheets of Nestlé in Appendix A to answer these questions:
   a. At the end of 2016, how much in total resources did Nestlé have to work with?
   b. How much of these resources did the company owe to external parties?
   c. How much of these resources did the company's shareholders actually own? Use these amounts to write Nestlé's accounting equation at December 31, 2016.
5. Examine retained earnings in the Statement of Changes in Equity. Did retained earnings increase or decrease from 2015 to 2016? Also state how much in dividends the company paid out in 2016.
6. How much cash did Nestlé have at the beginning of the most recent year? How much cash did Nestlé have at the end of the year? Why is it important that a firm maintains a healthy cash balance?

Group Projects

Project 1. As instructed by your professor, obtain the annual report of a well-known company.

Requirements

1. Take the role of a loan committee of ABN-Amro, a large banking company headquartered in Amsterdam. Assume the company has requested a loan from ABN-Amro. Analyze the company's financial statements and any other information that you need to reach a decision regarding the maximum amount of money that you would be willing to lend. Go as deeply into the analysis and the related decision as you can. Specify the following:
   a. The length of the loan period; that is, over what period will you allow the company to pay you back?
   b. The interest rate you will charge on the loan. Will you charge the prevailing interest rate, a lower rate, or a higher rate? Why?
   c. Any restrictions you will impose on the borrower as a condition for giving the loan. *Note:* The long-term debt note to the financial statements gives details of the company's existing liabilities.
2. Write your group decision in a report addressed to the bank's board of directors. Limit your report to 500 words.
3. If your professor directs, present your decision and analysis to the class. Limit your presentation to 10–15 minutes.

Project 2. You are the owner of a company that is about to "go public," i.e., issue its shares to outside investors. You wish to make your company look as attractive as possible in order to raise $1 million in cash and expand the business. At the same time, you want to give potential investors a realistic picture of your company.

Requirements

1. Design a booklet (not more that 1,300 words or five pages) to portray your company in a way that will enable outsiders to reach an informed decision as to whether they should buy some of your shares. The booklet should include the following:
   a. Name and location of your company.
   b. Nature of the company's business (be as detailed as possible).
   c. How you plan to spend the money you raise.
   d. The company's comparative Income Statement, statement of changes in equity, Balance Sheet, and statement of cash flows for two years: the current year and the preceding year. Make the data as realistic as possible with the intent of receiving $1 million.
2. If directed by your professor, make a copy of the booklet for each member of your class. Distribute copies to the class and present your case with the intent of interesting your classmates in investing in the company. Limit your presentation to 10–15 minutes.

Quick Check Answers

1. *b*
2. *b*
3. *c*
4. *a*
5. *d*
6. *d*
7. *a* ($120,000 – $50,000 – $4,000 = $66,000)
8. *b* ($120,000 – $50,000 = $70,000)
9. *c* Total assets = $140,000 ($11,000 + $40,000 + $34,000 + $55,000). Liabilities = $27,000.
10. *d*
11. *b* $38,000 + Net income ($18,000) – Dividends = $50,000; Dividends = $6,000
12. *b*

	Assets	=	Liabilities	+	Equity
Beginning	$340,000	=	$210,000*	+	$130,000
Increase	70,000	=	25,000	+	45,000*
Ending	$410,000*	=	$235,000*	+	$175,000*

*Must solve for these amounts.

13. *c*
14. *a*

MyLab Accounting

For online homework, exercises, and problems that provide you with immediate feedback, please visit www.myaccountinglab.com.

Demo Doc

The Accounting Equation and Financial Statement Preparation

To make sure you understand this material, work through the following demonstration "Demo Doc" with detailed comments to help you see the concept within the framework of a worked-through problem.

Learning Objectives 3, 4, 5

David Richardson is the only shareholder of DR Painting, Inc., a painting business near a historical housing district. At March 31, 20X6, DR Painting had the following information:

Cash	$27,300
Accounts receivable	1,400
Supplies	1,800
Truck	20,000
Accounts payable	1,000
Share capital	40,000
Retained earnings (March 1)	5,000
Retained earnings (March 31)	?
Dividends	1,500
Service revenue	7,000
Salary expense	1,000

➤ Requirements

1. Prepare the Income Statement (the first part of the statement of comprehensive income) and statement of changes in equity for the month of March 20X6 and the Balance Sheet of the business at March 31, 20X6. Use Exhibits 1-8, 1-9, and 1-10 in the text as a guide.
2. Write the accounting equation of the business.

Demo Doc Solutions

➤ Requirement 1

Prepare the Income Statement (the first part of the statement of comprehensive Income), Statement of changes in equity, and Balance Sheet of the business. Use Exhibits 1-8, 1-9, and 1-10 in the text as a guide.

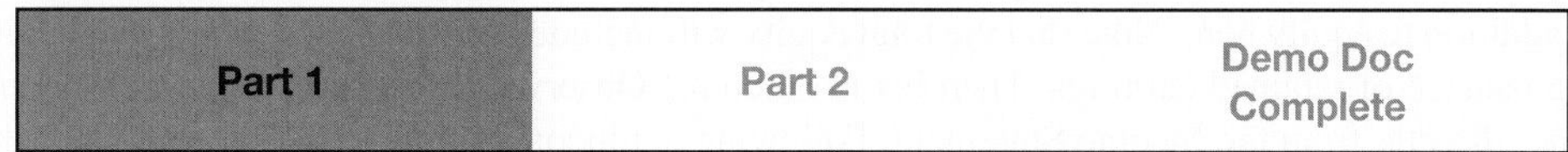

Part 1	Part 2	Demo Doc Complete

Income Statement

The Income Statement shows the changes in assets and liabilities that increase and decrease equity, i.e., income and expenses for the period. It is usually the first statement prepared because it contains the smallest subset of information, and the resulting profit or loss will flow to other financial statements.

The Income Statement reports the profitability of the business. To prepare an Income Statement, begin with the proper heading. A proper heading includes the name of the company (DR Painting, Inc.), the name of the statement (Income Statement), and the time period covered (Month Ended March 31, 20X6). Notice that we are reporting income for a period of time, rather than at a single date.

The Income Statement lists all revenues and expenses. It uses the following formula to calculate net income:

Revenues − Expenses = Net income

First, you should list revenues. Second, list the expenses. After you have listed and totaled the revenues and expenses, subtract the total expenses from total revenues to determine net income or net loss. A positive number means you earned net income (revenues exceeded expenses). A negative number indicates that expenses exceeded revenues, and this is a net loss.

DR Painting's total Service Revenue for the month was $7,000. The only expense is Salary Expense of $1,000. On the Income Statement, these would be reported as follows:

	A	B	C
1	**DR Painting, Inc.** **Income Statement**	**Month Ended** **March 31, 20X6**	
2	**Revenue:**		
3	Service revenue		$ 7,000
4	**Expenses:**		
5	Salary expense	$ 1,000	
6	Total expenses		1,000
7	Net Income		$ 6,000
8			

Note that the result is a net income of $6,000 ($7,000 − $1,000 = $6,000). You will also report net income on the statement of changes in equity, which comes next.

Statement of Changes in Equity

The statement of changes in equity shows the changes in total equity of the entity for a period of time. To prepare a statement of changes in equity, begin with the proper heading. A proper heading includes the name of the company (DR Painting, Inc.), the name of the statement (Statement of Changes in Equity), and the time period covered (Month Ended March 31, 20X6). As with the Income Statement, we are reporting the changes in equity for a period of time, rather than at a single date.

Start the body of the statement of changes in equity with the total equity at the beginning of the period (March 1). If there is any additional capital contributed by the owners, we would list the addition to equity here. Note that the total equity will include both the share capital and beginning balance of retained earnings. Then list net income. Observe that the amount of net income comes directly from the Income Statement. Following net income you will list the dividends declared and paid, which reduce total equity. Finally, total all amounts and compute the total equity at the end of the period.

The share capital of $40,000 was given in the question, and since there is no additional information on any additional issuance of capital, we can assume that both the beginning and ending share capital is $40,000. Beginning Retained Earnings of $5,000 was given in the problem. Net income of $6,000 comes from the Income Statement and is added. Dividends of $1,500 are deducted. On the statement of changes in equity, these amounts are reported as follows:

	A	B
1	**DR Painting, Inc.** **Statement of Changes in Equity**	**Month Ended** **March 31, 20X6**
2	Beginning total equity, March 1, 20X6	$ 45,000
3	Add: Net income	6,000
4		$ 51,000
5	Less: Dividends	(1,500)
6	Ending total equity, March 31, 20X6	$ 49,500
7		

Note that Retained Earnings has a balance of $9,500 ($5,000 plus net income of $6,000 less dividends of $1,500) at March 31, 20X6. You will also report Retained Earnings' ending balance on the Balance Sheet, which you prepare last because it has the biggest information set.

Balance Sheet

The Balance Sheet reports the financial position of the business at a moment in time. To prepare a Balance Sheet, begin with the proper heading. A proper heading includes the name of the company (DR Painting, Inc.), the name of the statement (Balance Sheet), and the time of the ending balances (March 31, 20X6). Unlike the Income Statement and statement of changes in equity, we are reporting the financial position of the company at a specific date rather than for a period of time.

The Balance Sheet lists all assets, liabilities, and equity of the business, with the accounting equation verified at the bottom.

To prepare the body of the Balance Sheet, begin by listing assets. Then list all the liabilities and shareholders' equity. Notice that the Balance Sheet is organized in the same order as the accounting equation. The amount of Retained Earnings comes directly from the ending balance on your statement of changes in equity. You should then total both sides of the Balance Sheet to make sure that they are equal. If they are not equal, then you must correct an error.

In this case, assets include cash of $27,300, accounts receivable of $1,400, $1,800 worth of supplies, and the truck, valued at $20,000. The only liability is accounts payable of $1,000. Shareholders' equity consists of share capital of $40,000, and the updated retained earnings of $9,500, for a total of $49,500, which was calculated in the statement of changes of equity.

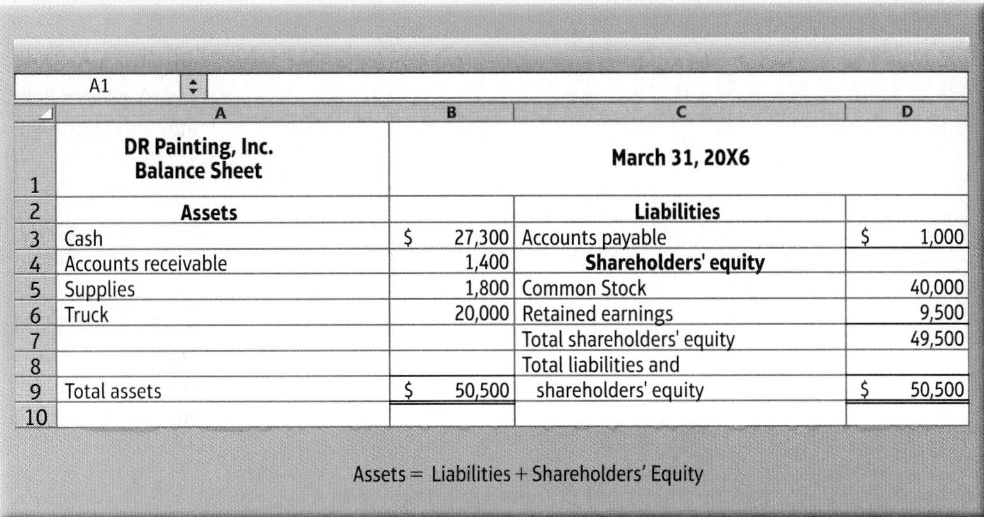

	A	B	C	D
1	**DR Painting, Inc. Balance Sheet**		**March 31, 20X6**	
2	**Assets**		**Liabilities**	
3	Cash	$ 27,300	Accounts payable	$ 1,000
4	Accounts receivable	1,400	**Shareholders' equity**	
5	Supplies	1,800	Common Stock	40,000
6	Truck	20,000	Retained earnings	9,500
7			Total shareholders' equity	49,500
8			Total liabilities and	
9	Total assets	$ 50,500	shareholders' equity	$ 50,500
10				

Assets = Liabilities + Shareholders' Equity

➤ Requirement 2

Write the accounting equation of the business.

Part 1	Part 2	Demo Doc Complete

In this case, asset accounts total $50,500. Liabilities total $1,000—the balance of Accounts Payable—and shareholder's equity is $49,500. This gives us a total for liabilities and equity of $50,500 ($1,000 + $49,500).

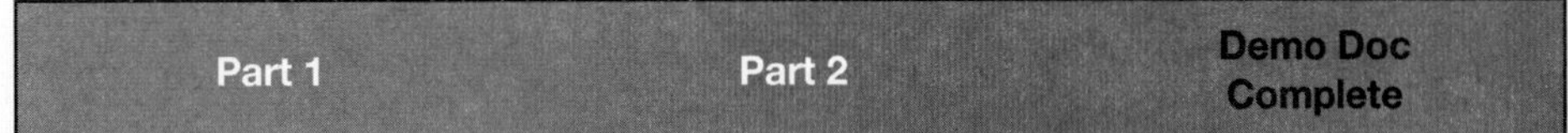

Assets of $50,500 = Liabilities of $1,000 + Shareholders' Equity of $49,500

Part 1	Part 2	Demo Doc Complete

2 Recording Business Transactions

SPOTLIGHT | Daimler AG www.daimler.com/en/

Daimler AG is a German multinational automotive company and one of the world's most successful ones. The Daimler Group ranks among the biggest producers of premium cars (with its Mercedes-Benz cars, including Maybach and AMG variants) and commercial vehicles (with Daimler Trucks, Mercedes-Benz Vans, Daimler Buses, and others). It also provides various financing, leasing, insurance, and financial investments services through Daimler Financial Services. ●

Pajor Pawel/Shutterstock

How does Daimler determine the amount of its revenues, expenses, and net income? The numbers can't possibly be random. Like all other companies, Daimler has a comprehensive accounting system. Daimler's Income Statement shows that during the financial year ended December 31, 2015, it made just under €150,000 million of sales and earned a net income of €8,711 million.

	A	B	C
1	**Daimler AG Consolidated Income Statement**	**Year Ended December 31**	
2	**(Adapted, in millions of €)**	**2015**	**2014**
3	**Revenue**	€ 149,467	€ 129,872
4	Cost of revenue	(117,670)	(101,688)
5	Gross profit	31,797	28,184
6	Selling expenses	(12,147)	(11,534)
7	General administrative expense	(3,710)	(3,329)
8	Research expenditures	(4,760)	(4,532)
9	Other operating income	2,114	1,759
10	Other operating expense	(555)	(1,160)
11	Operating income	12,739	9,388
12	Income from equity investments	464	897
13	Other financial income/expense	(27)	458
14	Interest income	170	145
15	Interest expense	(602)	(715)
16	Income taxes	(4,033)	(2,883)
17	**Net profit**	€ 8,711	€ 7,290
18			

You can also see below that Daimler has assets totaling under €217.2 billion, funded by liabilities of €162.5 billion and total equity of €54.6 billion.

	A	B	C
1	**Daimler AG Consolidated Balance Sheet**	**As at December 31**	
2	**(Adapted, in millions of €)**	**2015**	**2014**
3	Cash and cash equivalents	9,936	9,667
4	Inventories	23,760	20,864
5	Trade receivables	9,054	8,634
6	All other current assets	49,097	37,980
7	Total current assets	91,847	77,145
8	Property, plant and equipment	24,322	23,182
9	Intangible assets	10,069	9,367
10	All other non-current assets	90,928	79,941
11	Total non-current assets	125,319	112,490
12	Total assets	217,166	189,635
13	Trade payables	10,548	10,178
14	Loans and borrowings	41,311	36,290
15	All other current liabilities	25,222	20,506
16	Total current liabilities	77,081	66,974
17	Loans and borrowings	59,831	50,399
18	All other non-current liabilities	25,630	27,678
19	Total non-current liabilities	85,461	78,077
20	Total liabilities	162,542	145,051
21	Share capital	3,070	3,070
22	Retained earnings	36,991	28,487
23	Other equity items	14,563	13,027
24	Total equity	54,624	44,584
25	Total liabilities and equity	217,166	189,635
26			

How does Daimler know the amount of assets, liabilities, and equity it has? This chapter will show you how companies, large and small, actually record the transactions that eventually become part of the financial statements. We will discover that all companies, including Daimler, record their transactions based on a double-entry accounting system.

LEARNING OBJECTIVES

1. **Explain** what a business transaction is
2. **Keep** track of financial statement items
3. **Analyze** the impact of business transactions on accounts
4. **Record** (journalize and post) transactions in the books
5. **Construct** and use a trial balance

EXPLAIN WHAT A BUSINESS TRANSACTION IS

1 **Explain** what a business transaction is

Financial statements summarize the effects of economic phenomena in words and numbers. They show the resources of an entity and claims to those resources. To be able to do this, an entity must be able to capture information about its economic resources and claims against these resources as well as the effects of transactions, other events, and conditions that change those resources and claims. A **transaction** is any event that has a financial impact on the business and can be measured reliably. For example, Daimler sells cars, borrows money, pays for materials, pays salaries and taxes, and buys equipment—these are all separate transactions.

But not all events qualify as transactions. Daimler may apply for a bank loan, but no transaction will be recorded until it has utilized the loan facility. Automotive retailers may place an order with Daimler and it will not be recorded as a transaction until Daimler delivers the cars to its customers. A transaction, i.e., a change in the organization's resources and claims to those resources, must occur before Daimler records anything.

Transactions provide objective information about the financial impact of an exchange on an entity. Transactions reflect increases and/or decreases to financial statement elements. While the financial impact of a transaction is generally measurable, usually reflected by a quantifiable monetary amount—the price charged/paid and the amount of cash collected/paid—in certain situations, some estimation based on observable data or assumptions may be necessary. In accounting, we always record these effects so that the eventual financial statements are relevant and faithfully represent the economic phenomenon that transpired during the reporting period.

KEEP TRACK OF FINANCIAL STATEMENT ITEMS

2 **Keep** track of financial statement items

As we saw in Chapter 1, we account for the five elements of financial statements: assets, liabilities, equity, income, and expenses. Income increases equity and expense decreases equity. Thus, we can think of income and expenses as a component of equity for our initial study on how business transactions are recorded.

Businesses need a sufficient level of information from an accounting system. Daimler would not be able to operate if its accounting system only captured total assets, total liabilities, total equity, total income, and total expenses. It would want to know what comprises the totals. In accounting, we call this "item of interest" an account. An **account** is the record of all the changes in a particular asset, liability, or shareholders' equity during a period. The account is the basic summary device of accounting. Obviously, the *more details* you desire, the *more accounts* you will need to keep track of. A multinational corporation's accounting system may utilize millions of accounts!

In the next section, we will discuss some accounts that entities keep track of within their accounting systems. Different entities may use slightly different names to represent these accounts, due to historical and cultural factors and preference. For example, while many entities now use the term "Property, Plant and Equipment" (or PPE), U. S. companies tend to label them "Plant Assets," and others prefer the label them "Fixed Assets." Americans uses the term "stock" for both inventory and shares. For example, a statement like "I have sold all my Apple stocks" may mean Apple products or Apple shares. Similarly, many non-American entities will use the term "shareholders" as opposed to "stockholders." In our discussions, we will give you some synonyms or alternative account names so you can have a wider understanding of what different entities use in practice.

Let's review some of the accounts that a company such as Daimler would use in recording business transactions.

Assets

Assets are economic resources that provide a future benefit for a business. Most firms use the following asset accounts:

Cash. Cash is money and any medium of exchange including bank account balances, paper currency, coins, certificates of deposit, and checks.

Accounts Receivable. Daimler, like most other companies, sells its goods and services and receives a promise for future collection of cash. The Accounts Receivable account holds these amounts. Some entities prefer to use the label Debtors or Receivables for this account.

Notes Receivable. Daimler may receive a notes receivable from a customer, who signed the note promising to pay Daimler. A notes receivable is similar to an accounts receivable, but it is usually more binding because the customer signed the promissory note to pay on a certain day (or after a certain period). Notes receivable usually specify an interest rate.

Inventory. Daimler's most important asset is its inventory—the cars it sells to its customers. Other titles for this account include *Stocks* and *Merchandise Inventory*.

Prepaid Expenses. Don't be misled by the word "expenses" in this account title. **A prepaid expense** or prepayment is an asset because the payment provides a *future* economic benefit for the business. Businesses like Daimler can often be asked to pay early for rental charges and insurance premiums. Such businesses could also be asked to place deposits for services required.

Property, Plant and Equipment (PPE). This is a summary account for Daimler's assets that are expected to be used for more than one period for the purposes of production or supply of goods or services or for administrative purposes. Some of the more common **PPE** items are described below:

- **Land.** The Land account shows the cost of the land Daimler uses in its operations.
- **Buildings.** The costs of Daimler's office building, manufacturing plant, and the like appear in the Buildings account.
- **Equipment, Furniture, and Fixtures.** Daimler has a separate asset account for each type of equipment, for example, Manufacturing Equipment and Office Equipment. The Equipment, Furniture, and Fixtures account shows the cost of these assets, which are similar to equipment.

Liabilities

Recall that a *liability* is an obligation to pay an individual or organization. A payable is always a liability. The most common types of liabilities include:

Accounts Payable. The Accounts Payable account is the direct opposite of Accounts Receivable. Daimler's promise to pay a debt arising from a credit purchase of inventory or from a utility bill appears in the Accounts Payable account. Similarly, some businesses prefer to label the accounts payable as Creditors or Payables.

Notes Payable. A notes payable is the opposite of a notes receivable. The Notes Payable account includes the amounts Daimler must *pay* because it signed notes promising to pay a future amount. Notes payable, like notes receivable, usually carry interest.

Accrued Liabilities. An **accrued liability** is a liability for an expense you have not yet incurred. Interest Payable and Salary Payable are accrued liability accounts for most companies.

Equity

The owners' claims to the assets of a corporation are called *shareholders' equity*, *owners' equity*, or simply *equity*. A corporation such as Daimler uses Share Capital, Retained Earnings, and Dividends accounts to record the various components of shareholders' equity. In a proprietorship, there is a single capital account. For a partnership, each partner has a separate capital account.

Share Capital. The Share Capital account shows the owners' investment in the corporation. Daimler receives cash and issues shares to its shareholders. A company's common share capital is its most basic element of equity. All corporations have ordinary shares. We will examine other forms of share capital later in Chapter 10.

Retained Earnings. The Retained Earnings account shows the cumulative net income earned by Daimler over the company's lifetime, minus its cumulative net losses and dividends.

Dividends. Dividends are optional; they are *declared* by the board of directors (may require shareholders' approval at the corporation's annual general meeting). After profitable operations, the board of directors of Daimler may declare and pay dividends. The corporation usually keeps a separate account titled *Dividends*, which indicates a decrease in retained earnings for the financial year.

Stop & Think

Name two things that (1) increase Daimler's shareholders' equity and (2) decrease Daimler's shareholders' equity.

Answer:

(1) Increases in equity: Issuance of share capital and net income (revenues greater than expenses).

(2) Decreases in equity: Dividends and net loss (expenses greater than revenues).

Income. The increase in shareholders' equity from delivering goods or services to customers is usually called *revenue* or *sales revenue*. The company uses as many income accounts as needed. Daimler uses a Sales Revenue account for revenue earned by selling its products. An accountant provides accountancy services for clients and uses a Service Revenue account. A business that loans money to an outsider needs an Interest Income account. If the business rents a building to a tenant, the business needs a Rent Revenue or Rental Income account.

Expenses. The cost of operating a business is called *expense*. Expenses *decrease* shareholders' equity, the opposite effect of revenues. A business needs a separate account for each type of expense, such as cost of goods sold, salary expense, rent expense, advertising expense, insurance expense, utilities expense, and income tax expense. The more it wants to keep track of an item of interest, the more detailed its accounts will be. Thus, the level of details captured in the accounting system depends on the information required by the business. Businesses with less total expenses than total income will report a net profit, and those with more total expenses than total income will report a net loss. Again, there is no fixed number of expense accounts a business needs to maintain.

ANALYZE THE IMPACT OF BUSINESS TRANSACTIONS ON ACCOUNTS

Example: RedLotus, Inc.

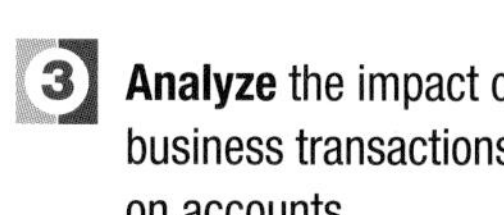
3 **Analyze** the impact of business transactions on accounts

To illustrate the accounting for transactions, let's return to RedLotus Travel, Inc. In the Chapter 1 End-of-Chapter problem, Starr Williams opened RedLotus Travel, Inc., in April 20X8.

We will consider 11 events and analyze each in terms of its effect on RedLotus Travel. We will begin by using the accounting equation. Income and expense transactions are taken directly to equity for this illustration. In the second half of the chapter, we will record transactions using the journal and ledger of the business.

Try It in Excel®

As you review the 11 transactions, build an Excel template. Use the accounting equation (Assets = Liabilities + Shareholders' Equity) as a model. Remember that each transaction has either an equal effect on both the left- and right-hand sides of the accounting equation, or an offsetting effect (both positive and negative) on the same side of the equation.

Re-create the spreadsheet in Exhibit 2-1, Panel B (page 68), step by step, as you go along. In Excel, open a new blank spreadsheet.

Step 1 Format the worksheet. Label cell A2 "Trans." You will put transaction numbers corresponding to the transactions below in the cells in column A. Row 1 will contain the elements of the accounting equation. Enter "Assets" in cell D1. Enter an "=" sign in cell F1. Enter "Liabilities + Shareholders' Equity" in cell G1. Enter "Type of SE Transaction" (abbreviation for shareholders' equity) in cell J1. Highlight cells B1 through E1 and click "merge and center" on the top toolbar. Highlight cells G1 through I1 and click "merge and center." Now you will have a spreadsheet organized around the elements of the accounting equation: "Assets = Liabilities + Shareholders' Equity" and, for all transactions impacting shareholders' equity, you will be able to enter the type (capital share, revenue, expense, or dividends). This will be important later when you construct the financial statements (Exhibit 2-2, page 69).

Step 2 Continue formatting. In cells B2 through E2, enter the asset account titles that transactions 1–11 deal with. B2: Cash; C2: AR (an abbreviation for accounts receivable); D2: Supplies; E2: Land. In cells G2 through I2, enter the liability and stockholders' equity account titles that RedLotus Travel, Inc.'s, transactions deal with: G2: AP (an abbreviation for accounts payable); H2: SC (an abbreviation for share capital); and I2: RE (abbreviation for retained earnings; this is where all transactions impacting revenue, expenses, and dividends will go for now).

Step 3 In Row 15, enter the formula to sum each column from B through E and G through I. For example, the formula in cell B15 should be "=sum(B3:B14)." In cell A15, enter "Bal." This will allow you to keep a running sum of the accounts in the Balance Sheet as you enter each transaction.

Step 4 In cell A16, enter "Totals." In cell C16, enter "=sum(B15:E15)." In cell H16, enter "=sum(G15:I15)." You can use the short cut symbol "∑" followed by highlighting the respective cells. Excel allows you to keep a running sum of the column totals on each side of the equation. You should find that the running sum of the column totals on the left-hand side of the equation always equals the running sum of the column totals on the right-hand side, so the accounting equation always stays in balance. As a final formatting step, highlight cells B3 through I16. Using the "number" tab on the toolbar at the top of the spreadsheet, select "Accounting" for format with no $ sign, and select "decrease decimal" to zero places. Now you're ready to process the transactions.

Transaction 1. Starr and a few friends invest $50,000 to open RedLotus Travel, Inc., and the business issues ordinary share capital to the shareholders. The effect of this transaction on the accounting equation of RedLotus Travel, Inc., is a receipt of cash and issuance of ordinary share capital:

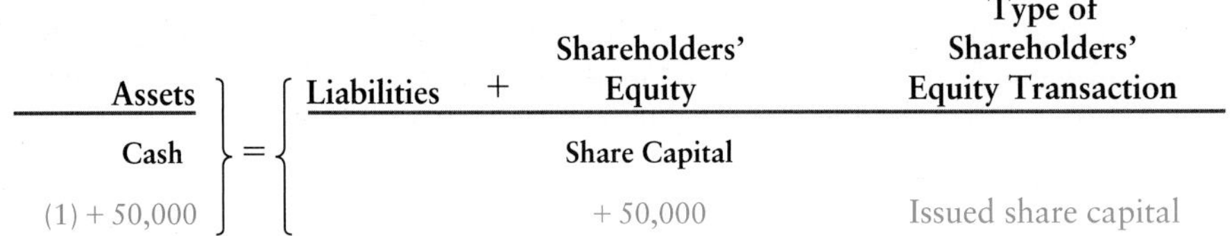

Assets		Liabilities	+	Shareholders' Equity	Type of Shareholders' Equity Transaction
Cash	=			Share Capital	
(1) + 50,000				+ 50,000	Issued share capital

Every transaction's net amount on the left side of the accounting equation must equal the net amount on the right side. The first transaction increases both the cash and the share capital of the business. If you're following along in Excel, enter 1 in cell A3 of the spreadsheet you are creating. Enter 50000 in cell B3 (under Cash) and 50000 in cell H3 (under Share Capital). To the right of the transaction in cell J3, write "Issued share capital" to show the reason for the increase in stockholders' equity. You don't have to enter commas; Excel will do that for you. Notice that the sum of Cash (cell B15) is now 50,000, and the sum of Common Stock (cell H15) is also 50,000. The total of accounts on the left side of the accounting equation is 50,000 (cell C16), and it equals the total of accounts on the right side of the accounting equation (cell H16).

Every transaction affects the financial statements of the business, and we can prepare financial statements after one, two, or any number of transactions. For example, RedLotus Travel, Inc., could report the company's Balance Sheet after its first transaction, shown as follows.

This Balance Sheet shows that the business holds cash of $50,000 and owes no liabilities. The shareholders' equity is recorded as *share capital* on the Balance Sheet. A bank would look favorably on this Balance Sheet because the business has $50,000 cash and no debt—a strong financial position.

A1

	A	B	C	D
1	**RedLotus Travel, Inc.** **Balance Sheet** **April 1, 20X8**			
2	**Assets**		**Liabilities**	
3	Cash	$ 50,000	None	
4				
5			**Shareholders' Equity**	
6			Share capital	$ 50,000
7			Total shareholders' equity	50,000
8			Total liabilities and	
9	Total assets	$ 50,000	shareholders' equity	$ 50,000
10				

In this example, we are going to show you how each business transaction is reflected in the financial statements immediately. However, as a practical matter, most entities report their financial statements at the end of the accounting period, not after each transaction. But an accounting system can produce statements whenever managers need to know where the business stands.

Transaction 2. RedLotus purchases land and pays cash of $40,000. The effect of this transaction on the accounting equation is:

	Assets			Liabilities + Shareholders' Equity	Type of Shareholders' Equity Transaction
	Cash	+	Land	Share Capital	
(1)	50,000			50,000	Issued share capital
(2)	− 40,000		+ 40,000		
Bal.	10,000		40,000	50,000	
		50,000	=	50,000	

The purchase increases one asset (Land) and decreases another asset (Cash) by the same amount. If you're following along in Excel, enter a 2 in cell A4. Enter –40000 in cell B4 and 40000 in cell E4. The spreadsheet automatically updates, showing that after the transaction is completed, RedLotus has cash of $10,000, land of $40,000, and no liabilities. Shareholders' equity is unchanged at $50,000. Note that total assets must always equal total liabilities plus equity. Alternatively, you can say equity is always the residual of assets less liabilities.

Transaction 3. The business buys supplies on account, agreeing to pay $3,700 within 30 days. This transaction increases both the assets and the liabilities of the business. Its effect on the accounting equation follows:

	Assets					Liabilities	+	Shareholders' Equity
	Cash	+	Supplies	+	Land	Accounts Payable	+	Share Capital
Bal.	10,000				40,000			50,000
(3)			+ 3,700			+ 3,700		
Bal.	10,000		3,700		40,000	3,700		50,000
			53,700		=		53,700	

The new asset is Supplies, and the liability is an account payable. RedLotus signs no formal promissory note, so the liability is an account payable, not a note payable.

Transaction 4. RedLotus earns $7,000 of service revenue by providing services for customers. The business collects the cash. The effect on the accounting equation is an increase in the asset Cash and an increase in equity (via the Retained Earnings account), as follows:

	Assets					Liabilities +	Shareholders' Equity				Type of Shareholders' Equity Transaction
	Cash	+	Supplies	+	Land	Accounts Payable	+	Share Capital	+	Retained Earnings	
Bal.	10,000		3,700		40,000	3,700		50,000			
(4)	+ 7,000									+ 7,000	Service revenue
Bal.	17,000		3,700		40,000	3,700		50,000		7,000	
			60,700		=			60,700			

In the Excel spreadsheet on line 6, we enter 7000 under Cash (cell B6) and 7000 under Retained Earnings (cell I6). In cell J6, we enter "Service revenue" to show where the $7,000 of increase in retained earnings came from. Our grand totals on the bottom of the spreadsheet now show $60,700 for total assets as well as $60,700 for total liabilities and shareholders' equity.

Transaction 5. RedLotus performs service on account, which means that RedLotus lets some customers pay later. RedLotus earns revenue but doesn't receive the cash immediately. In Transaction 5, RedLotus cleans a fleet of UPS delivery trucks, and UPS promises to pay RedLotus $3,000 within one month. This promise is an account receivable—an asset—of RedLotus, Inc. The transaction record follows:

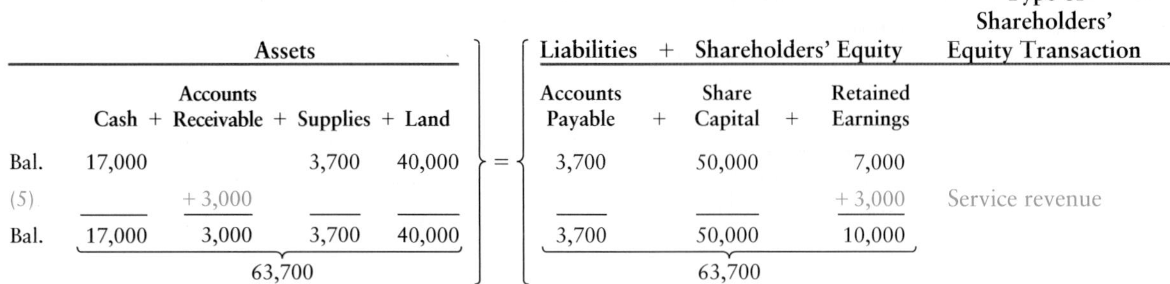

	Assets					Liabilities +	Shareholders' Equity		Type of Shareholders' Equity Transaction
	Cash +	Accounts Receivable +	Supplies +	Land		Accounts Payable +	Share Capital +	Retained Earnings	
Bal.	17,000		3,700	40,000	=	3,700	50,000	7,000	
(5)		+ 3,000						+ 3,000	Service revenue
Bal.	17,000	3,000	3,700	40,000		3,700	50,000	10,000	
		63,700					63,700		

Remember, performing the service is what earns RedLotus the revenue—not collecting the cash. Therefore, RedLotus records revenue when it performs the service—regardless of whether RedLotus receives cash now or later. In your Excel spreadsheet, enter 3000 under Accounts Receivable on the left-hand side (cell C7) and 3000 under Retained Earnings on the right-hand side (cell I7). Also enter "Service revenue" in cell J7 to keep a record of the type of transaction (revenue) that affects shareholders' equity (SE). (This is an application of accrual accounting you read about earlier in Chapter 1. We will explore accrual accounting in greater detail in Chapter 3.)

Transaction 6. During the month, RedLotus, Inc., pays $2,700 for the following expenses: equipment rent, $1,100; employee salaries, $1,200; and utilities, $400. The effect on the accounting equation is:

	Assets					Liabilities +	Shareholders' Equity		Type of Shareholders' Equity Transaction
	Cash +	Accounts Receivable +	Supplies +	Land		Accounts Payable +	Share Capital +	Retained Earnings	
Bal.	17,000	3,000	3,700	40,000		3,700	50,000	10,000	
(6)	− 1,100				=			− 1,100	Rent expense
	− 1,200							− 1,200	Salary expense
	− 400							− 400	Utilities expense
Bal.	14,300	3,000	3,700	40,000		3,700	50,000	7,300	
		61,000					61,000		

The expenses decrease RedLotus Travel's Cash and Retained Earnings accounts. List each expense separately to keep track of its amount.

Transaction 7. RedLotus Travel pays $1,900 on account, which means to pay off an account payable. In this transaction RedLotus pays the store from which it purchased supplies in Transaction 3. The transaction decreases Cash (cell B11 on the Excel spreadsheet) and also decreases Accounts Payable (cell G11):

	Assets					Liabilities +	Shareholders' Equity	
	Cash +	Accounts Receivable +	Supplies +	Land		Accounts Payable +	Share Capital +	Retained Earnings
Bal.	14,300	3,000	3,700	40,000	=	3,700	50,000	7,300
(7)	− 1,900					− 1,900		
Bal.	12,400	3,000	3,700	40,000		1,800	50,000	7,300
		59,100					59,100	

Transaction 8. Starr Williams, the major shareholder of RedLotus Travel, Inc., paid $30,000 to remodel his home. This event is a personal transaction of the Williams family. It is not recorded by RedLotus. We focus solely on the business entity, not on its owners. This transaction illustrates the reporting entity concept from Chapter 1.

Transaction 9. In Transaction 5, RedLotus performed services for UPS on account. The business now collects $1,000 from UPS. We say that RedLotus *collects the cash on account*, which means that RedLotus Travel will record an increase in Cash and a decrease in Accounts Receivable. This is not service revenue because RedLotus Travel already recorded the revenue in Transaction 5. This transaction is entered on line 12 of the Excel spreadsheet as an increase in Cash (cell B12) and a decrease in AR (cell C12). The effect of collecting cash on account is:

	Assets					Liabilities	+ Shareholders' Equity	
	Cash	+ Accounts Receivable	+ Supplies	+ Land		Accounts Payable	+ Share Capital	+ Retained Earnings
Bal.	12,400	3,000	3,700	40,000	=	1,800	50,000	7,300
(9)	+1,000	−1,000						
Bal.	13,400	2,000	3,700	40,000		1,800	50,000	7,300
	59,100					59,100		

Transaction 10. RedLotus Travel sells half of the land it bought for $20,000. RedLotus receives $22,000 cash and makes a $2,000 gain on the sale of the land. The effect on the accounting equation is as follows:

	Assets					Liabilities	+ Shareholders' Equity		Type of Shareholders' Equity Transaction
	Cash	+ Accounts Receivable	+ Supplies	+ Land		Accounts Payable	+ Share Capital	+ Retained Earnings	
Bal.	13,400	2,000	3,700	40,000	=	1,800	50,000	7,300	
(10)	+22,000			−20,000				+2,000	Gain from Sale of Land
Bal.	35,400	2,000	3,700	20,000		1,800	50,000	9,300	
	61,100					61,100			

Note that the company did not sell all its land; RedLotus Travel still owns $20,000 worth of land. This transaction is entered in the Excel spreadsheet as an increase in Cash (cell B13) and a decrease in Land (cell E13).

A Closer Look

You may be wondering why we treat gains from disposal of land differently from sales revenue. Both are incomes, i.e., they ultimately increase equity. We will discuss this further in Chapters 3 and 4, but for now it is sufficient to note that revenue is generally used to record income from ordinary business activities. RedLotus Travel's ordinary business activity is providing travel services, not the buying and selling land; thus, the sale of land is more appropriately shown as a gain rather than as a revenue. Gains are reported net on the Income Statement.

Transaction 11. RedLotus Travel, Inc., declares a dividend and pays the shareholders $2,100 cash. The effect on the accounting equation is as follows:

	Assets					Liabilities	+ Shareholders' Equity		Type of Shareholders' Equity Transaction
	Cash	+ Accounts Receivable	+ Supplies	+ Land		Accounts Payable	+ Share Capital	+ Retained Earnings	
Bal.	35,400	2,000	3,700	20,000	=	1,800	50,000	9,300	
(11)	−2,100							−2,100	Dividends
Bal.	33,300	2,000	3,700	20,000		1,800	50,000	7,200	
	59,000					59,000			

The dividend decreases both the Cash (cell B14) and the Retained Earnings (cell I14) accounts of the business. *But dividends are not an expense*, because they are transactions with owners of the business. Therefore, enter "Dividend" in cell J14.

Transactions and Financial Statements

Exhibit 2-1 summarizes the 11 preceding transactions. Panel A gives the details of the transactions, and Panel B shows the transaction analysis.

Exhibit 2-1 | Transaction Analysis: RedLotus Travel, Inc.

PANEL A—Transaction Details

(1) Received $50,000 cash and issued shares to the owners
(2) Paid $40,000 cash for land
(3) Bought $3,700 of supplies on account
(4) Received $7,000 cash from customers for service revenue earned
(5) Performed services for a customer on account, $3,000
(6) Paid cash expenses: rent, $1,100; employee salary, $1,200; utilities, $400
(7) Paid $1,900 on the account payable created in Transaction 3
(8) Major shareholder paid personal funds to remodel home, *not* a transaction of the business
(9) Received $1,000 on account
(10) Sold half of the land for $22,000 cash
(11) Declared and paid a dividend of $2,100 to the shareholders

PANEL B—Transaction Analysis

A1

	A	B	C	D	E	F	G	H	I	J
1		Assets				=	Liabilities + Equity			Type of Equity Transaction
2	Trans	Cash	Accounts Receivable	Supplies	Land		Accounts Payable	Share Capital	Retained Earnings	
3	1	50,000						50,000		Issued share capital
4	2	(40,000)			40,000					
5	3			3,700			3,700			
6	4	7,000							7,000	Service revenue
7	5		3,000						3,000	Service revenue
8	6	(1,100)							(1,100)	Rent expense
9		(1,200)							(1,200)	Salary expense
10		(400)							(400)	Utilities expense
11	7	(1,900)					(1,900)			
12	9	1,000	(1,000)							
13	10	22,000			(20,000)				2,000	Gain from sale of land
14	11	(2,100)							(2,100)	Dividend
15	Bal	33,300	2,000	3,700	20,000		1,800	50,000	7,200	
16	Totals		59,000					59,000		
17										

Statement of Cash Flows Data (rows 3–12)

Income Statement Data (rows 6–13)

Statement of Changes in Equity Data (rows 3–14)

Balance Sheet Data

If you prepared an Excel spreadsheet, it should look very similar to Panel B. As you study the exhibit, note that every transaction maintains the equality of the accounting equation: Assets = Liabilities + Equity. Exhibit 2-1 provides the data for RedLotus Travel's financial statements:

- *Income Statement* data appear as revenues and expenses under Retained Earnings. The revenues increase retained earnings; the expenses decrease retained earnings.
- The *Balance Sheet* data are composed of the ending balances of the assets, liabilities, and shareholders' equities shown at the bottom of the exhibit. The accounting equation shows that total assets ($59,000) equal total liabilities plus shareholders' equity ($59,000).
- The *Statement of Changes in Equity* reconciles the movements in equity for the period. Issuance of share capital and net income increases total equity, whereas dividends decrease equity. Ending equity is the final result.
- Data for the *Statement of Cash Flows* are aligned under the Cash account. Cash receipts increase cash, and cash payments decrease cash.

Exhibit 2-2 shows the RedLotus Travel financial statements at the end of April 20X8, the company's first month of operations. Follow the flow of financial information to observe the following:

1. The Income Statement reports revenues, expenses, and either a net income or a net loss for the period. During April, RedLotus Travel earned net income of $9,300. Compare RedLotus Travel's Income Statement with that of Daimler, at the beginning of the chapter. Notice both Income Statements show income and expenses for the period.
2. The Statement of Changes in Equity starts with the beginning balance of equity, which is zero for a new business. Add share capital contribution and net income for the period (arrow ①), subtract dividends, and compute the ending balance of equity ($57,200).
3. The Balance Sheet lists the assets, liabilities, and shareholders' equity of the business at the end of the period. Included in shareholders' equity is retained earnings (net profit of $9,300 less dividend paid of $2,100). The ending equity balance from the Statement of Changes in Equity is shown on the Balance Sheet (arrow ②).

Try It in Excel®

If you are familiar with Excel, a quick look at Exhibit 2-2 should convince you of how easy it is to prepare the Income Statement, statement of retained earnings, and Balance Sheet in Excel. If you have not already prepared them earlier, prepare three simple templates for each of these financial statements for RedLotus Travel, Inc. You may use these templates again, and add to them, in Chapter 3 as you learn the adjusting entry process.

Selected problems in MyLab Accounting have already prepared these templates for you. The mid-chapter summary problem will illustrate this with another small company.

Let's put into practice what you have learned so far.

Exhibit 2-2 Financial Statements of RedLotus Travel, Inc.

	A	B	C	D
1	**RedLotus Travel, Inc.** **Income Statement** **Month Ended April 30, 20X8**			
2	**Income**			
3	Service revenue ($7,000 + $3,000)	$ 10,000		
4	Gain from sale of land	2,000	$ 12,000	
5	**Expenses**			
6	Salary expense	1,200		
7	Rent expense	1,100		
8	Utilities expense	400	2,700	
9	Net Income		$ 9,300	
10				

①

	A	B	C	D
1	**RedLotus Travel, Inc.** **Statement of Changes in Equity** **Month Ended April 30, 20X8**			
2	Total equity, April 1, 20X*		$ 0	
3	Add: Issuance of share capital		50,000	
4	Add: Net income for the month		9,300	
5			$ 59,300	
6	Less: Dividends		(2,100)	
7	Total equity, April 30, 20X*		$ 57,200	
8				

②

	A	B	C	D
1	**RedLotus Travel, Inc.** **Balance Sheet** **April 30, 20X8**			
2	**Assets**		**Liabilities**	
3	Cash	$ 33,300	Accounts payable	$ 1,800
4	Accounts receivable	2,000	**Shareholders' equity**	
5	Supplies	3,700	Share capital	50,000
6	Land	20,000	Retained earnings	7,200
7			Total shareholders' equity	57,200
8			Total liabilities and	
9	Total assets	$ 59,000	shareholders' equity	$ 59,000
10				

Mid-Chapter Summary Problem

Shelly Richmond opens a research service near a college campus. She names the corporation Richmond Researchers Ltd. During the first month of operations, July 20X6, the business engages in the following transactions:

a. Richmond Researchers Ltd. issues its ordinary shares to Shelly Richmond, who invests $25,000 to open the business.

b. The company purchases on account office supplies costing $350.

c. Richmond Researchers pays cash of $20,000 to acquire a lot next to the campus. The company intends to use the land as a building site for a business office.

d. Richmond Researchers performs research for clients and receives cash of $1,900.

e. Richmond Researchers pays $100 on the account payable it created in transaction b.

f. Richmond pays $2,000 of personal funds for a vacation.

g. Richmond Researchers pays cash expenses for office rent ($400) and utilities ($100).

h. The business sells a quarter of its land parcel for $6,000.

i. The business declares and pays a cash dividend of $1,200.

Requirements

1. Analyze the preceding transactions in terms of their effects on the accounting equation of Richmond Researchers Ltd. Use Exhibit 2-1, Panel B as a guide.
2. Prepare the Income Statement, Statement of Changes in Equity, and Balance Sheet of Richmond Researchers Ltd., after recording the transactions. Draw arrows linking the statements. Use Exhibit 2-2 as a guide.

Answers

Requirement 1

Panel B—Analysis of Transactions

	A	B	C	D	E	F	G	H	I
1		Assets			=	Liabilities + Equity			Type of Equity Transaction
2		Cash	Office Supplies	Land		Accounts Payable	Share Capital	Retained Earnings	
3	a	25,000					25,000		Issued share capital
4	b		350			350			
5	c	(20,000)		20,000					
6	d	1,900						1,900	Service revenue
7	e	(100)				(100)			
8	f	Not a transaction of the business							
9	g	(400)						(400)	Rent expense
10		(100)						(100)	Utilities expense
11	h	6,000		(5,000)				1,000	Gain on sale of land
12	i	(1,200)						(1,200)	Dividends
13	Bal	11,100	350	15,000		250	25,000	1,200	
14	Totals		26,450				26,450		
15									

Requirement 2

	A	B	C	D
1	**Richmond Researchers, Ltd** **Income Statement** **Month Ended May 31, 20X6**			
2	**Income**			
3	Service revenue	$ 1,900		
4	Gain on sale of land	1,000	$ 2,900	
5	**Expenses**			
6	Rent expense	$ 400		
7	Utilities expense	100	500	
8	Net income		$ 2,400	
9				

①

	A	B	C	D
1	**Richmond Researchers, Ltd** **Statement of Changes in Equity** **Month Ended May 31, 20X6**			
2	Total equity, July 1, 20X6		$ 0	
3	Add: Issuance of share capital		25,000	
4	Add: Net income for the month		2,400	
5			27,400	
6	Less: Dividends		(1,200)	
7	Total equity, July 31, 20X6		$ 26,200	
8				

②

	A	B	C	D	E	F
1	**Richmond Researchers, Ltd** **Balance Sheet** **July 31, 20X6**					
2	**Assets**			**Liabilities**		
3	Cash		$ 11,100	Accounts payable	$ 250	
4	Office supplies		350	**Shareholders' Equity**		
5	Land		15,000	Share capital	25,000	
6				Retained earnings	1,200	
7				Total shareholders' equity	26,200	
8				Total liabilities and		
9	Total assets		$ 26,450	shareholders' equity	$ 26,450	
10						

The analysis in the first half of this chapter can be used, but it is cumbersome even in Excel. Daimler has hundreds of accounts and millions of transactions. If we were using a spreadsheet to account for Daimler's transactions, it would be a very huge spreadsheet! In the second half of this chapter we discuss double-entry accounting as it is actually used in business.

Double-Entry Accounting

All business transactions include at least two effects on an entity's financial statement elements. And at all times, the accounting equation (assets = liabilities + equity) must remain in balance. A simple way to help you start understanding this concept is to think about "giving" something and "receiving" something.

Accounting is, therefore, based on a double-entry system, which records the *dual effects* on the entity. *Each transaction affects at least two accounts*. For example, RedLotus Travel's receipt of $50,000 cash and issuance of ordinary shares increased both Cash and Share Capital. It would be incomplete to record only the increase in Cash or only the increase in Share Capital.

The T-Account

Earlier we introduced you to the concept of an account. It is where we keep track of increases and decreases (and, thus, the balance) of items of interests to a business. The account can be represented by the letter T and we call them *T-accounts*. The vertical line in the letter divides the account into its two sides: left and right. The account title appears at the top of the T. For example, the Cash account can appear as follows:

Cash	
(Left side)	(Right side)
Debit	*Credit*

The left side of each account is called the **debit** side, and the right side is called the **credit** side. Often, students are confused by the words *debit* and *credit*. To become comfortable using these terms, remember that for every account, Debit is on the left, Credit is on the right.

Every business transaction involves both a debit and a credit. The total debits and credits for every business transaction must be equal. This is the cornerstone of the double-entry accounting system.

Increases and Decreases in the Accounts: The Rules of Debit and Credit

The type of account determines how we record increases and decreases. *The rules of debit and credit* follow in Exhibit 2-3.

Exhibit 2-3 | Accounting Equation and the Rules of Debit and Credit

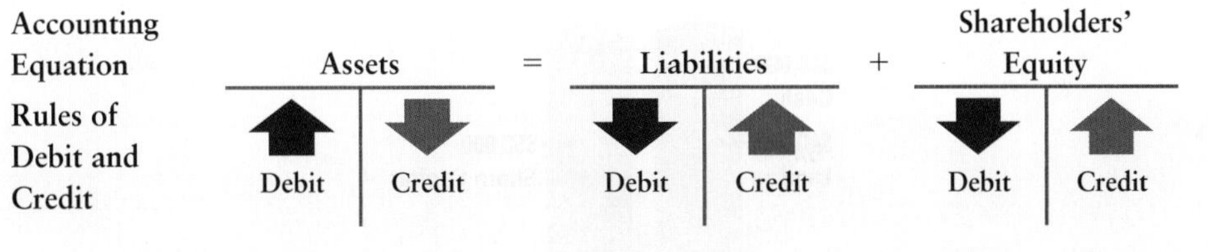

- Increases in *assets* are recorded on the left (debit) side of the account. Decreases in *assets* are recorded on the right (credit) side. You receive cash and debit the Cash account. You pay cash and credit the Cash account.
- Conversely, increases in *liabilities* and *shareholders' equity* are recorded by credits. Decreases in *liabilities* and *shareholders' equity* are recorded by debits.

To illustrate the ideas displayed in Exhibit 2-3, let's review the first transaction. RedLotus Travel received $50,000 and issued ordinary shares. Which accounts are affected? The Cash account and the Share Capital account will hold these amounts:

Exhibit 2-4 | The Accounting Equation after RedLotus Travel's First Transaction

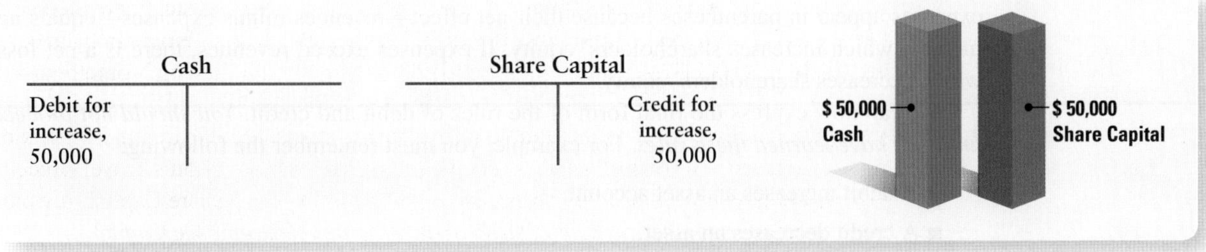

The amount remaining in an account, after netting the sum of the left-hand side with the sum of the right-hand side of the T account, is called its *balance*. This first transaction gives Cash a $50,000 debit balance and Share Capital a $50,000 credit balance. Exhibit 2-4 shows this relationship.

RedLotus Travel's second transaction is a $40,000 cash purchase of land. This transaction decreases Cash with a credit and increases Land with a debit, as shown in the following T-accounts (focus on Cash and Land):

Cash			
Bal.	50,000	Credit for decrease, 40,000	
Bal.	10,000		

Share Capital			
		Bal.	50,000

Land			
Debit for increase, 40,000			
Bal.	40,000		

After this transaction, Cash has a $10,000 debit balance, Land has a debit balance of $40,000, and Share Capital has a $50,000 credit balance, as shown in Exhibit 2-5.

Exhibit 2-5 The Accounting Equation after RedLotus Travel's First Two Transactions

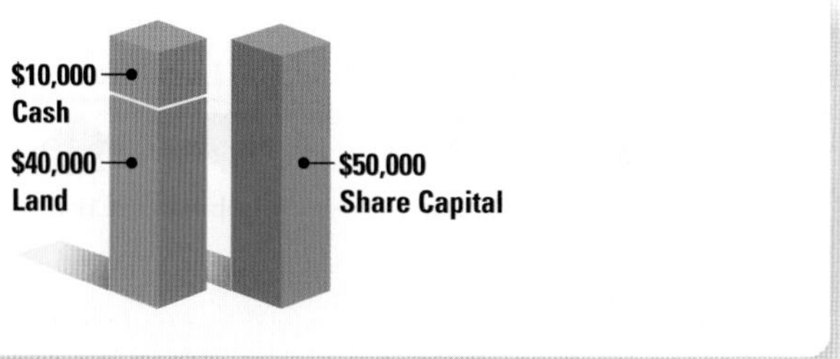

Additional Shareholders' Equity Accounts: Income and Expenses

Shareholders' equity also includes the two categories of Income Statement accounts, Income and Expenses:

- *Income (revenue and gains)* includes increases in shareholders' equity that result from delivering goods or services to customers, or from other activities.
- *Expenses and losses* are decreases in shareholders' equity due to the cost of operating the business.

Therefore, the accounting equation may be expanded as shown in Exhibit 2-6. Revenues and expenses appear in parentheses because their net effect—revenues minus expenses—equals net income, which increases shareholders' equity. If expenses exceed revenues, there is a net loss, which decreases shareholders' equity.

We can now express the final form of the rules of debit and credit. *You should not proceed until you have learned these rules.* For example, you must remember the following:

- A debit increases an asset account.
- A credit decreases an asset.

Exhibit 2-6 | Expansion of the Accounting Equation

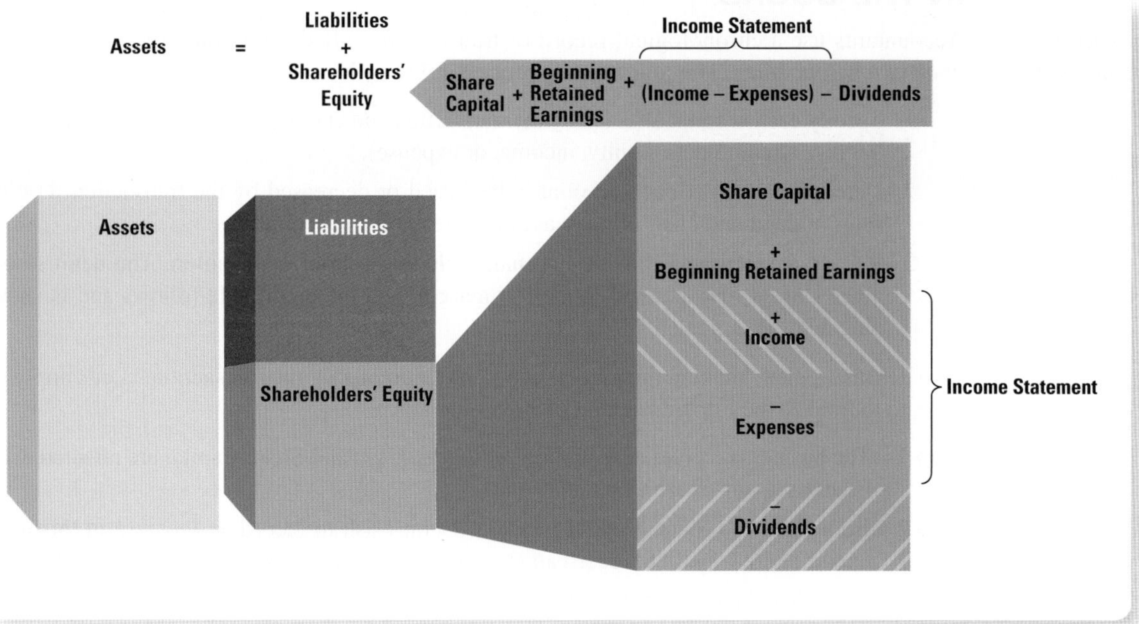

Liabilities and shareholders' equity are the opposite.

- A credit increases a liability, as well as a shareholders' equity account.
- A debit decreases a liability, as well as a shareholders' equity account.

If you look at the components of equity in Exhibit 2-6, you will notice that Dividends and Expense accounts are "contra" accounts, i.e., the bigger they are, the smaller the total equity will be. Thus, increases in dividends and expenses are recorded as debits because they will ultimately reduce equity. Remember:

- A credit increases income, which will ultimately increase equity.
- A debit decreases income, which will ultimately reduce equity.
- A debit increases dividend and expense, which will ultimately reduce equity.
- A credit decreases dividend and expense, which will ultimately increase equity.

Exhibit 2-7 shows the final form of the debit and credit rules.

Exhibit 2-7 | Final Form of the Rules of Debit and Credit

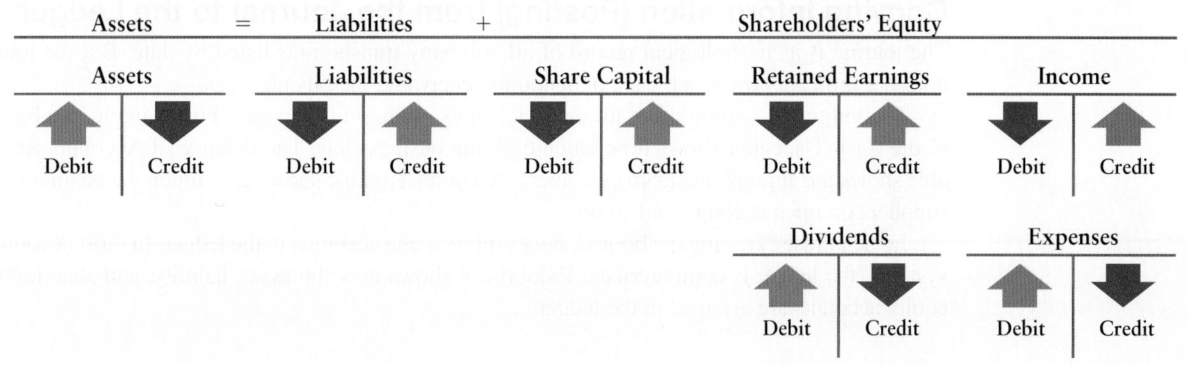

RECORD (JOURNALIZE AND POST) TRANSACTIONS IN THE BOOKS

4 Record (journalize and post) transactions in the books

Accountants use a chronological record of transactions called a **journal**, also known as the *book of original entry*. The journalizing process follows three steps:

1. Specify each account affected by the transaction and classify each account by type (asset, liability, shareholders' equity, income, or expense).
2. Determine whether each account is increased or decreased by the transaction. Use the rules of debit and credit to increase or decrease each account.
3. Record the transaction in the journal, including a brief explanation. The debit side is always listed first, entered in the left margin, and the credit side follows and is shown indented to the right.

Step 3 is also called "making the journal entry" or "journalizing the transaction." Let's apply the steps to journalize the first transaction of RedLotus Travel.

Step 1 The business receives cash and issues shares. Cash and Share Capital are affected. Cash is an asset, and Share Capital is equity.

Step 2 Both Cash and Share Capital increase. Debit Cash to record an increase in this asset. Credit Share Capital to record an increase in this equity account.

Step 3 Journalize the transaction as follows:

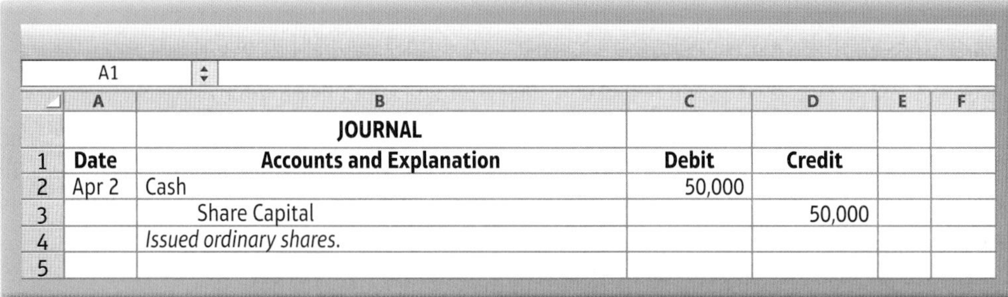

A1

	A	B	C	D	E	F
		JOURNAL				
1	**Date**	**Accounts and Explanation**	**Debit**	**Credit**		
2	Apr 2	Cash	50,000			
3		Share Capital		50,000		
4		*Issued ordinary shares.*				
5						

Typically, it is easiest to identify cash effects. When analyzing a transaction, first pinpoint the effects (if any) on cash. Did cash increase or decrease? If cash increased as a result of the transaction, that's your Debit entry. If cash decreased, then it needs a Credit entry. Then identify the effects on the other accounts.

Copying Information (Posting) from the Journal to the Ledger

The journal is a chronological record of all company transactions listed by date. But the journal does not indicate how much cash or accounts receivable the business has.

The **ledger** is a grouping of all the T-accounts, with their balances. For example, the balance of the Cash T-account shows how much cash the business has. The balance of Accounts Receivable shows the amount due from customers. Accounts Payable shows how much the business owes suppliers on open account, and so on.

In the phrase "keeping the books," *books* refers to the accounts in the ledger. In most accounting systems, the ledger is computerized. Exhibit 2-8 shows how the asset, liability, and shareholders' equity accounts are grouped in the ledger.

Exhibit 2-8 The Ledger (Asset, Liability, and Shareholders' Equity Accounts)

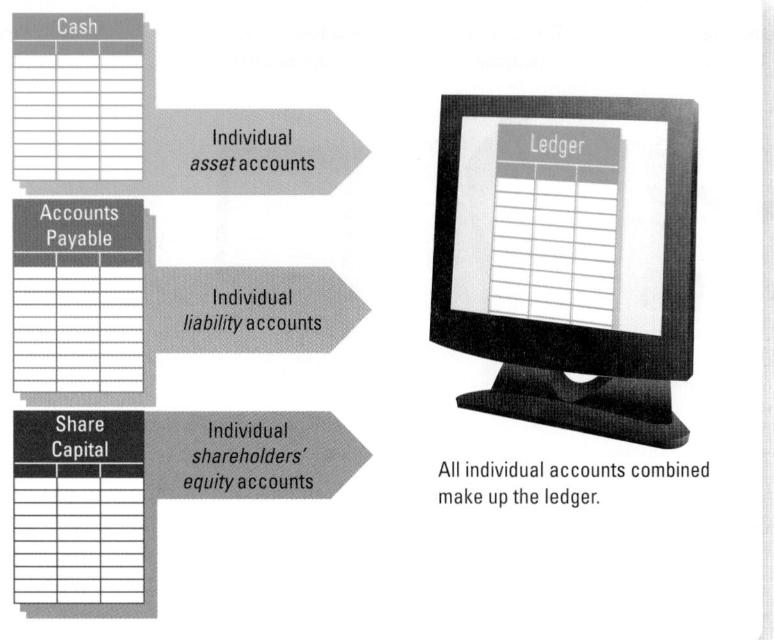

Entering a transaction in the journal does not get the data into the ledger. Data must be copied to the ledger—a process called **posting**. Debits in the journal are always posted as debits in the accounts, and likewise for credits. Exhibit 2-9 shows how ShineBrite Car Wash's share issuance transaction is posted to the accounts.

Exhibit 2-9 Journal Entry and Posting to the Accounts

PANEL A—Journal Entry

A1

	A	B	C
1	**Accounts and Explanation**	**Debit**	**Credit**
2	Cash	50,000	
3	Share Capital		50,000
4	*Issued ordinary shares.*		
5			

PANEL B—Posting to the Accounts

Cash
50,000 |

Share Capital
| 50,000

The Flow of Accounting Data

Exhibit 2-10 summarizes the flow of accounting data from the business transaction to the ledger.

Exhibit 2-10 | Flow of Accounting Data

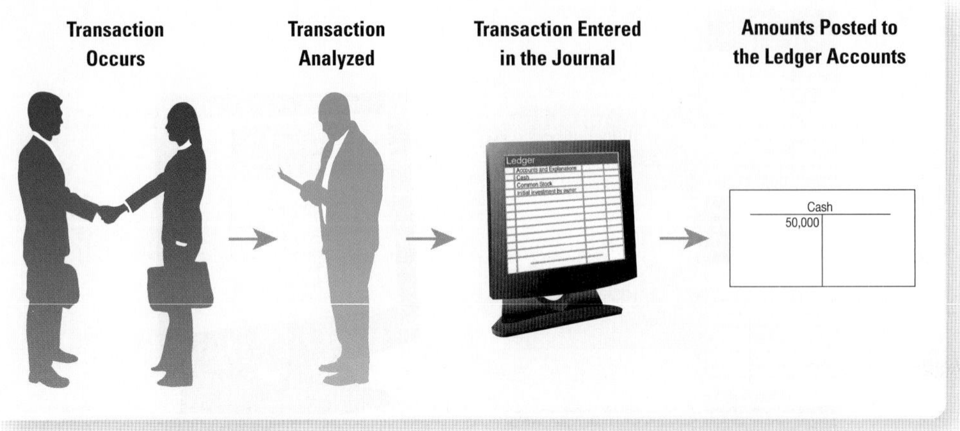

Let's continue the example of RedLotus Travel, Inc., and account for the same 11 transactions we illustrated earlier. Here we use the journal and the accounts. Each journal entry posted to the accounts is referenced by date or by transaction number. This cross-reference is important so you can trace back the entry you see in the accounts, and it allows you to locate any information you may need.

Transaction 1 Analysis. RedLotus Travel, Inc., received $50,000 cash from the shareholders and in turn issued ordinary shares to them. The journal entry, accounting equation, and ledger accounts follow.

	A	B	C	D	E
1	Cash	50,000			
2	Share capital		50,000		
3	*Issued ordinary shares.*				
4					

	Assets	=	Liabilities	+	Shareholders' Equity
Accounting equation	+50,000	=	0	+	50,000

The ledger accounts

Cash		Share Capital	
(1) 50,000			(1) 50,000

Transaction 2 Analysis. The business paid $40,000 cash for land. The purchase decreased Cash; therefore, credit Cash. The purchase increased the asset Land; to record this increase, debit Land.

	A	B	C	D	E
1	Land	40,000			
2	Cash		40,000		
3	*Paid cash for land.*				
4					

	Assets	=	Liabilities	+	Shareholders' Equity
Accounting equation	+ 40,000	=	0	+	0
	− 40,000				

The ledger accounts

Cash				Land			
(1)	50,000	(2)	40,000	(2)	40,000		

Transaction 3 Analysis. The business purchased supplies for $3,700 on accounts payable. The purchase increased Supplies, an asset, and Accounts Payable, a liability.

	A	B	C	D	E
1	Supplies	3,700			
2	Accounts Payable		3,700		
3	*Purchased office supplies on account.*				
4					

	Assets	=	Liabilities	+	Shareholders' Equity
Accounting equation	+ 3,700	=	+ 3,700	+	0

The ledger accounts

Supplies				Accounts Payable			
(3)	3,700					(3)	3,700

Transaction 4 Analysis. The business performed services for clients and received cash of $7,000. The transaction increased Cash and Service Revenue. To record the revenue, credit Service Revenue. Remember that all revenue accounts eventually increase total shareholders' equity.

	A	B	C	D	E
1	Cash	7,000			
2	Service Revenue		7,000		
3	*Performed services for cash.*				
4					

	Assets	=	Liabilities	+	Shareholders' Equity
Accounting equation	+ 7,000	=	0	+	7,000 (Service revenue)

The ledger accounts

Cash				Service Revenue			
(1)	50,000	(2)	40,000			(4)	7,000
(4)	7,000						

Transaction 5 Analysis. RedLotus Travel performed services for UPS on account. UPS did not pay immediately, so RedLotus Travel billed UPS for $3,000. The transaction increased accounts receivable; therefore, debit Accounts Receivable. Service revenue also increased, so credit the Service Revenue account.

	A	B	C	D	E
1	Accounts Receivable	3,000			
2	Service Revenue		3,000		
3	*Performed services on account.*				
4					

	Assets	=	Liabilities	+	Shareholders' Equity
Accounting equation	+ 3,000	=	0	+	3,000 (Service revenues)

The ledger accounts

Accounts Receivable			
(5)	3,000		

Service Revenue			
		(4)	7,000
		(5)	3,000

Transaction 6 Analysis. The business paid $2,700 for the following expenses: equipment rent, $1,100; employee salary, $1,200; and utilities, $400. Credit Cash for the sum of the expense amounts. The expenses increased, so debit each expense account separately.

	A	B	C	D	E
1	Rent Expense	1,100			
2	Salary Expense	1,200			
3	Utilities Expense	400			
4	Cash		2,700		
5	*Paid expenses.*				
6					

	Assets	=	Liabilities	+	Shareholders' Equity
Accounting equation	− 2,700	=	0	−	2,700 (Various expenses)

The ledger accounts

Cash			
(1)	50,000	(2)	40,000
(4)	7,000	(6)	2,700

Rent Expense			
(6)	1,100		

Salary Expense			
(6)	1,200		

Utilities Expense			
(6)	400		

Transaction 7 Analysis. The business paid $1,900 on the account payable created in Transaction 3. Credit Cash for the payment. The payment decreased a liability, so debit Accounts Payable.

	A	B	C	D	E
1	Accounts Payable	1,900			
2	Cash		1,900		
3	*Paid cash on account.*				
4					

	Assets	=	Liabilities	+	Shareholders' Equity
Accounting equation	− 1,900	=	− 1,900	+	0

The ledger accounts

Cash				Accounts Payable			
(1)	50,000	(2)	40,000	(7)	1,900	(3)	3,700
(4)	7,000	(6)	2,700				
		(7)	1,900				

Transaction 8 Analysis. Starr Williams, the major shareholder of RedLotus Travel, remodeled his personal residence. This is not a transaction of the business, so the business does not record the transaction.

Transaction 9 Analysis. The business collected $1,000 cash on account from the clients in Transaction 5. Cash increased so debit Cash. The asset accounts receivable decreased; therefore, credit Accounts Receivable.

A1

	A	B	C	D	E
1	Cash	1,000			
2	Accounts Receivable		1,000		
3	*Collected cash on account.*				
4					

Accounting equation

Assets	=	Liabilities	+	Shareholders' Equity
+ 1,000	=	0	+	0
− 1,000				

The ledger accounts

Cash				Accounts Receivable			
(1)	50,000	(2)	40,000	(5)	3,000	(9)	1,000
(4)	7,000	(6)	2,700				
(9)	1,000	(7)	1,900				

Transaction 10 Analysis. The business sold half of its land for $22,000, receiving cash. The asset Cash increased; debit Cash by the amount received. The asset Land decreased; credit Land by $20,000 (half of $40,000) and a gain of $2,000 is recognized. Note that the total debits always equal total credits, even when you have more than one debit or more than one credit entry for the journal.

A1

	A	B	C	D	E
1	Cash	22,000			
2	Land		20,000		
3	Gain on sale of land		2,000		
4	*Sold land costing $20,000 for $22,000.*				

Accounting equation

Assets	=	Liabilities	+	Shareholders' Equity
+ 22,000	=	0	+	2,000 (gain on sale)
− 20,000				

The ledger accounts

Cash				Land				Gain on sale of land			
(1)	50,000	(2)	40,000	(2)	40,000	(10)	22,000			(10)	2,000
(4)	7,000	(6)	2,700								
(9)	1,000	(7)	1,900								
(10)	22,000										

Transaction 11 Analysis. RedLotus Travel paid its shareholders cash dividends of $2,100. Credit Cash for the payment. The transaction also decreased shareholders' equity and requires a debit to an equity account. Therefore, debit Dividends.

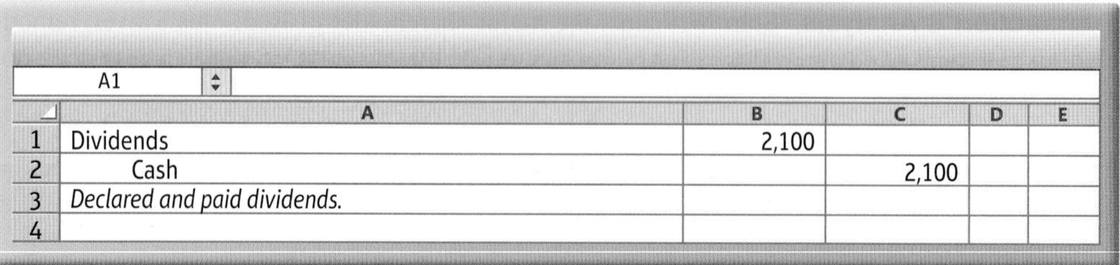

	A	B	C	D	E
1	Dividends	2,100			
2	Cash		2,100		
3	*Declared and paid dividends.*				
4					

	Assets	=	Liabilities	+	Shareholders' Equity
Accounting equation	− 2,100	=	0	−	2,100 (Dividends)

The ledger accounts

Cash

(1)	50,000	(2)	40,000
(4)	7,000	(6)	2,700
(9)	1,000	(7)	1,900
(10)	22,000	(11)	2,100

Dividends

(11)	2,100		

Accounts after Posting to the Ledger

Exhibit 2-11 shows the accounts after all transactions have been posted to the ledger. Group the accounts under assets, liabilities, and equity.

Exhibit 2-11 RedLotus Travel's Ledger Accounts after Posting

Assets = Liabilities + Shareholders' Equity

Assets

Cash

(1)	50,000	(2)	40,000
(4)	7,000	(6)	2,700
(9)	1,000	(7)	1,900
(10)	22,000	(11)	2,100
Bal.	33,300		

Accounts Receivable

(5)	3,000	(9)	1,000
Bal.	2,000		

Supplies

(3)	3,700		
Bal.	3,700		

Land

(2)	40,000	(10)	20,000
Bal.	20,000		

Liabilities

Accounts Payable

(7)	1,900	(3)	3,700
		Bal.	1,800

Shareholders' Equity

Share Capital

		(1)	50,000
		Bal.	50,000

Dividends

(11)	2,100		
Bal.	2,100		

Income

Service Revenue

		(4)	7,000
		(5)	3,000
		Bal.	10,000

Gain on sale of land

		(10)	2,000
		Bal.	2,000

Expenses

Rent Expense

(6)	1,100		
Bal.	1,100		

Salary Expense

(6)	1,200		
Bal.	1,200		

Utilities Expense

(6)	400		
Bal.	400		

Each account has a balance, denoted by "Bal.," which is the difference between the account's total debits and its total credits. For example, the Accounts Payable's balance of $1,800 is the difference between the credit ($3,700) and the debit ($1,900). Cash has a debit balance of $33,300.

A horizontal line separates the transaction amounts from the account balance. If an account's debits exceed its total credits, that account has a debit balance, as for Cash. If the sum of the credits is greater, the account has a credit balance, as for Accounts Payable.

CONSTRUCT AND USE A TRIAL BALANCE

5
Construct and use a trial balance

A **trial balance** lists all accounts with their balances—assets first, then liabilities and shareholders' equity. The trial balance summarizes all the account balances for the financial statements and *shows whether total debits equal total credits*. A trial balance may be constructed at any time, but the most common time is at the end of the period. Exhibit 2-12 is the trial balance of RedLotus Travel, Inc., after all transactions have been journalized and posted at the end of April.

Exhibit 2-12 | Trial Balance

	A	B	C	D	E
1	**RedLotus Travel, Inc. Trial Balance April 30, 20X8**				
2		**Balance**			
3	**Account Title**	**Debit**	**Credit**		
4	Cash	$ 33,300			
5	Accounts receivable	2,000			
6	Supplies	3,700			
7	Land	20,000			
8	Accounts payable		$ 1,800		
9	Share capital		50,000		
10	Dividends	2,100			
11	Service revenue		10,000		
12	Gain on sale of land		2,000		
13	Rent expense	1,100			
14	Salary expense	1,200			
15	Utilities expense	400			
16	Total	$ 63,800	$ 63,800		
17					

Note that the last line of the trial balance provides proof of the equality of debits and credits we have entered into the accounting records.

Analyzing Accounts

You can often tell what a company did by analyzing its accounts. This is a powerful tool for a manager who knows accounting. For example, if you know the beginning and ending balances of Cash, and if you know total cash receipts, you can compute your total cash payments during the period.

In our chapter example, RedLotus Travel will start the month of May with a cash balance of $33,000. Suppose during May RedLotus Travel received cash of $8,000 and ended the month with a cash balance of $35,000. You can compute total cash payments by analyzing RedLotus Travel's Cash account as follows:

Cash			
Beginning balance	33,000		
Cash receipts	8,000	Cash payments	$x = 6,000$
Ending balance	35,000		

Or, if you know the Cash account's beginning and ending balances and total payments, you can compute cash receipts during the period—for any company!

Similary, you can compute either sales on account or cash collections from receivables by analyzing the Accounts Receivable account as follows (using assumed amounts):

Accounts Receivable			
Beginning balance	6,000		
Sales on account	10,000	Collections from receivables	$x = 11,000$
Ending balance	5,000		

Also, you can determine how much you paid on account by analyzing Accounts Payable as follows (using assumed amounts):

Accounts Payable			
		Beginning balance	9,000
Payments on creditors	$x = 4,000$	Purchases on account	6,000
		Ending balance	11,000

Please master this powerful technique. It works for any company and for your own personal finances! You will find this tool very helpful when you become a manager.

Correcting Accounting Errors

Accounting errors can occur even in computerized systems. Input data may be wrong, or they may be entered twice or not at all. A debit may be entered as a credit, and vice versa. You can detect the reason or reasons behind many out-of-balance conditions by computing the difference between total debits and total credits. Then perform one or more of the following actions:

1. Search the records for a missing account. Trace each account back and forth from the journal to the ledger. A $200 transaction may have been recorded incorrectly in the journal or posted incorrectly to the ledger. Search the journal for a $200 transaction.
2. Divide the out-of-balance amount by 2. A debit treated as a credit, or vice versa, doubles the amount of the error. Suppose RedLotus, Inc., added $300 to Cash instead of subtracting $300. The out-of-balance amount is $600, and dividing by 2 identifies $300 as the amount of the transaction. Search the journal for the $300 transaction and trace to the account affected.
3. Divide the out-of-balance amount by 9. If the result is an integer (no decimals), the error may be

   - ***a slide*** (e.g., writing $400 as $40). The accounts would be out of balance by $360 ($400 − $40 = $360). Dividing $360 by 9 yields $40. Scan the trial balance in

Exhibit 2-12 for an amount similar to $40. Utilities Expense (balance of $400) is the misstated account.

- *a transposition* (e.g., writing $2,100 as $1,200). The accounts would be out of balance by $900 ($2,100 – $1,200 = $900). Dividing $900 by 9 yields $100. Trace all amounts on the trial balance back to the T-accounts. Dividends (balance of $2,100) is the misstated account.

Chart of Accounts

As you know, the ledger contains the accounts grouped under these headings:

1. Balance Sheet accounts: Assets, Liabilities, and Shareholders' Equity
2. Income Statement accounts: Income and Expenses

Organizations use a **chart of accounts** to list all their accounts and account numbers. Account numbers usually have two or more digits. Asset account numbers may begin with 1, liabilities with 2, shareholders' equity with 3, revenues with 4, and expenses with 5. The second, third, and higher digits in an account number indicate the position of the individual account within the category. For example, Cash may be account number 101, which is the first asset account. Accounts Payable may be number 201, the first liability. All accounts are numbered by using this system.

Organizations with many accounts use lengthy account numbers. For example, the chart of accounts of Daimler may use 10-digit account numbers. The chart of accounts for RedLotus Travel appears in Exhibit 2-13. The gap between account numbers 111 and 141 leaves room to add another category of receivables, for example, Notes Receivable, which may be numbered 121. A good chart of accounts has structure and proper categorization of accounts, and there's always room for creation of additional accounts when the need arises.

Exhibit 2-13 Chart of Accounts: RedLotus Travel, Inc.

Balance Sheet Accounts

Assets		Liabilities		Shareholders' Equity	
101	Cash	201	Accounts Payable	301	Share Capital
111	Accounts Receivable	231	Notes Payable	311	Dividends
141	Office Supplies			312	Retained Earnings
151	Office Furniture				
191	Land				

Income Statement Accounts (Part of Shareholders' Equity)

Income		Expenses	
401	Service Revenue	501	Rent Expense
402	Gain on Sale of Land	502	Salary Expense
		503	Utilities Expense

Appendix C gives two expanded charts of accounts that you will find helpful as you work through this course. The first chart lists the typical accounts that a *service* corporation, such as RedLotus Travel, would have after a period of growth. The second chart is for a *merchandizing* corporation, one that sells a product instead of a service.

The Normal Balance of an Account

An account's *normal balance* falls on the side of the account—debit or credit—where increases are recorded. The normal balance of assets is on the debit side, so assets are *debit-balance accounts*. Conversely, liabilities and shareholders' equity usually have a credit balance, so these are *credit-balance accounts*. Exhibit 2-14 illustrates the normal balances of all the assets, liabilities, and shareholders' equities, including revenues and expenses.

Exhibit 2-14 Normal Balances of the Accounts

Assets	Debit	
Liabilities		Credit
Shareholders' Equity—overall		Credit
Share capital		Credit
Retained earnings		Credit
Dividends	Debit	
Income (revenue and gains)		Credit
Expenses (including losses)	Debit	

As explained earlier, shareholders' equity usually contains several accounts. Dividends and expenses carry debit balances because they represent decreases in shareholders' equity. In total, the equity accounts show a normal credit balance.

Account Formats

So far we have illustrated accounts in a two-column T-account format, with the debit column on the left and the credit column on the right. Another style of representing accounts is called the columnar format. It has three or four *amount* columns, as illustrated for the Cash account in Exhibit 2-15. The first pair of amount columns are for the debit and credit amounts of individual transactions. The last two columns are for the account balance (they may be combined into one column). This columnar format keeps a running balance for every account. In computerized accounting systems, you will see accounts printed in columnar formats rather than T-accounts.

Exhibit 2-15 Account in Four-Column Format

Account: Cash — **Account No. 101**

				Balance	
Date	Item	Debit	Credit	Debit	Credit
20X8					
Apr 2	Share Capital	50,000		50,000	
3	Land		40,000	10,000	

Analyzing Transactions Using Only T-Accounts

Businesspeople must often make decisions without the benefit of a complete accounting system. For example, the managers of Daimler may consider borrowing $100,000 to buy equipment. To see how the two transactions [(a) borrowing cash and (b) buying equipment] affect Daimler, the manager can go directly to T-accounts, as follows:

T-accounts:

Cash				Note Payable			
(a)	100,000					(a)	100,000

T-accounts:

Cash				Equipment				Note Payable			
(a)	100,000	(b)	100,000	(b)	100,000					(a)	100,000

This informal analysis shows immediately that Daimler will add $100,000 of equipment and a $100,000 note payable. Assuming that Daimler began with zero balances, the equipment and note payable transactions would result in the following Balance Sheet (date assumed for illustration only):

	A	B	C	D
1	**Daimler's Balance Sheet September 12, 2019**			
2	**Assets**		**Liabilities**	
3	Cash	$ 0	Note payable	$ 100,000
4	Equipment	100,000		
5			**Shareholders' Equity**	0
6			Total liabilities and	
7	Total assets	$ 100,000	shareholders' equity	$ 100,000
8				

Companies don't actually keep records in this shortcut fashion. But a decision maker who needs information quickly may not have time to journalize, post to the accounts, take a trial balance, and prepare the financial statements. A manager who knows accounting can analyze the transaction and make the decision quickly. Now apply what you've learned. Study the Decision Guidelines, which summarize the chapter.

DECISION GUIDELINES

HOW TO MEASURE RESULTS OF OPERATIONS AND FINANCIAL POSITION

Any entrepreneur must determine whether the venture is profitable. To do this, he or she needs to know its results of operations and financial position. If Daimler wants to know whether the business is making money, the guidelines that follow will help them.

Decision	Guidelines
Has a transaction occurred?	If the event affects the entity's financial position and can be reliably recorded—Yes. If either condition is absent—No.
Where to record the transaction?	In the *journal*, the chronological record of transactions
How to record an increase or decrease in the following accounts?	Rules of *debit* and *credit*:

	Increase	Decrease
Assets	Debit	Credit
Liabilities	Credit	Debit
Shareholders' equity	Credit	Debit
Income	Credit	Debit
Expenses	Debit	Credit
Dividends	Debit	Credit

Decision	Guidelines
Where to store all the information for each account?	In the *ledger*, the book of accounts
Where to list all the accounts and their balances?	In the *trial balance*
Where to report the:	In the *Income Statement*
Results of operations?	(Revenues – Expenses = Net income or net loss)
	In the *Balance Sheet*
Financial position?	(Assets = Liabilities + Shareholders' equity)

End-of-Chapter Summary Problem

The trial balance of Calderon Service Center, Inc., on March 1, 20X6, lists the entity's assets, liabilities, and shareholders' equity on that date.

	Balance	
Account Title	Debit	Credit
Cash	$ 26,000	
Accounts receivable	4,500	
Accounts payable		$ 2,000
Share capital		10,000
Retained earnings		18,500
Total	$ 30,500	$ 30,500

During March, the business completed the following transactions:

a. Borrowed $45,000 from the bank, with Calderon signing a note payable in the name of the business.

b. Paid cash of $40,000 to a real estate company to acquire land.

c. Performed service for a customer and received cash of $5,000.

d. Purchased supplies on credit, $300.

e. Performed customer service and earned revenue on account, $2,600.

f. Paid $1,200 on account.

g. Paid the following cash expenses: salaries, $3,000; rent, $1,500; and interest, $400.

h. Received $3,100 on account.

i. Received a $200 utility bill that will be paid next week.

j. Declared and paid dividends of $1,800.

Requirements

1. Make the following accounts, with the balances indicated, in the ledger of Calderon Service Center, Inc. Use the T-account format.
   - Assets—Cash, $26,000; Accounts Receivable, $4,500; Supplies, no balance; Land, no balance
   - Liabilities—Accounts Payable, $2,000; Note Payable, no balance
   - Shareholders' Equity—Share Capital, $10,000; Retained Earnings, $18,500; Dividends, no balance
   - Revenues—Service Revenue, no balance
   - Expenses—(none have balances) Salary Expense, Rent Expense, Interest Expense, Utilities Expense
2. Journalize the preceding transactions. Key journal entries by transaction letter.
3. Post to the ledger and show the balance in each account after all the transactions have been posted.

4. Prepare the trial balance of Calderon Service Center, Inc., at March 31, 20X6.
5. To determine the net income or net loss of the entity during the month of March, prepare the Income Statement for the month ended March 31, 20X6. List expenses in order from the largest to the smallest.

Answers

Requirement 1

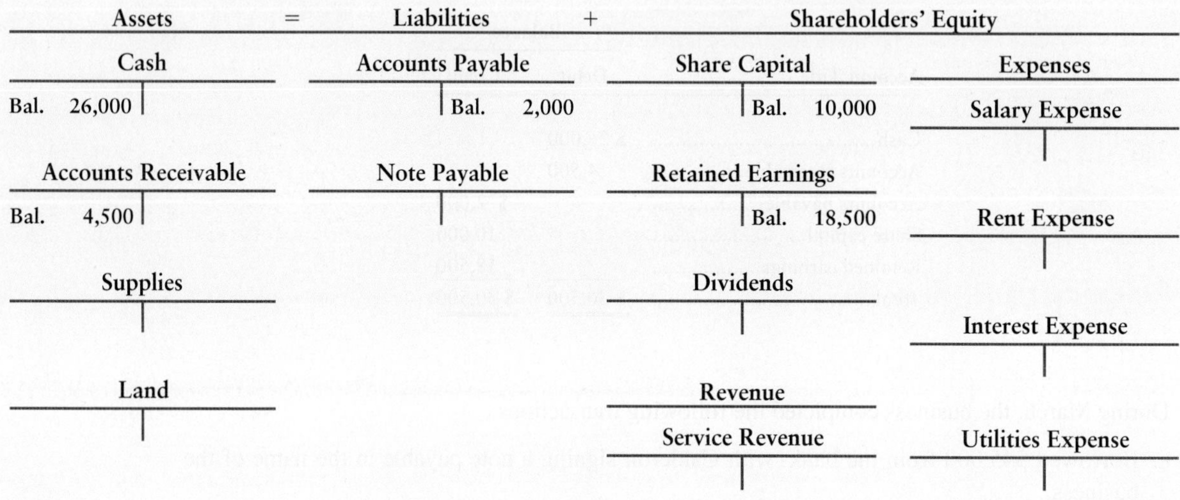

Requirement 2

Accounts and Explanation	Debit	Credit	Accounts and Explanation	Debit	Credit
a. Cash	45,000		g. Salary Expense	3,000	
Note Payable		45,000	Rent Expense	1,500	
Borrowed cash on note payable.			Interest Expense	400	
b. Land	40,000		Cash		4,900
Cash		40,000	Paid cash expenses.		
Purchased land for cash.			h. Cash	3,100	
c. Cash	5,000		Accounts Receivable		3,100
Service Revenue		5,000	Received on account.		
Performed service and received cash.			i. Utilities Expense	200	
d. Supplies	300		Accounts Payable		200
Accounts Payable		300	Received utility bill.		
Purchased supplies on account.			j. Dividends	1,800	
e. Accounts Receivable	2,600		Cash		1,800
Service Revenue		2,600	Declared and paid dividends.		
Performed service on account.					
f. Accounts Payable	1,200				
Cash		1,200			
Paid on account.					

Requirement 3

Assets = Liabilities + Shareholders' Equity

Assets

Cash

Bal.	26,000	(b)	40,000
(a)	45,000	(f)	1,200
(c)	5,000	(g)	4,900
(h)	3,100	(j)	1,800
Bal.	31,200		

Accounts Receivable

Bal.	4,500	(h)	3,100
(e)	2,600		
Bal.	4,000		

Supplies

(d)	300		
Bal.	300		

Land

(b)	40,000		
Bal.	40,000		

Liabilities

Accounts Payable

(f)	1,200	Bal.	2,000
		(d)	300
		(i)	200
		Bal.	1,300

Note Payable

		(a)	45,000
		Bal.	45,000

Shareholders' Equity

Share Capital

		Bal.	10,000

Retained Earnings

		Bal.	18,500

Dividends

(j)	1,800		
Bal.	1,800		

Revenue

Service Revenue

		(c)	5,000
		(e)	2,600
		Bal.	7,600

Expenses

Salary Expense

(g)	3,000		
Bal.	3,000		

Rent Expense

(g)	1,500		
Bal.	1,500		

Interest Expense

(g)	400		
Bal.	400		

Utilities Expense

(i)	200		
Bal.	200		

Requirement 4

A1

	A	B	C	D	E
1	**Calderon Service Center, Inc.** **Trial Balance** **March 31, 20X6**				
2		**Balance**			
3	**Account Title**	**Debit**	**Credit**		
4	Cash	$ 31,200			
5	Accounts receivable	4,000			
6	Supplies	300			
7	Land	40,000			
8	Accounts payable		$ 1,300		
9	Notes payable		45,000		
10	Share capital		10,000		
11	Retained earnings		18,500		
12	Dividends	1,800			
13	Service revenue		7,600		
14	Salary expense	3,000			
15	Rent expense	1,500			
16	Interest expense	400			
17	Utilities expense	200			
18	Total	$ 82,400	$ 82,400		
19					

Requirement 5

	A	B	C	D	E
1	**Calderon Service Center, Inc.** **Income Statement** **Month Ended March 31, 20X6**				
2	**Revenues**				
3	Service revenue		$ 7,600		
4					
5	**Expenses**				
6	Salary expense	$ 3,000			
7	Rent expense	1,500			
8	Interest expense	400			
9	Utilities expense	200			
10	Total expenses		5,100		
11	Net income		$ 2,500		
12					

REVIEW | Recording Business Transactions

Quick Check (Answers are given at the end of the chapter.)

1. A debit entry to an account

a. increases shareholders' equity.
b. increases liabilities.
c. increases assets.
d. both a and c.

2. Which account types normally have a debit balance?

a. Revenues **b.** Expenses **c.** Liabilities **d.** Both a and b

3. An attorney performs services of $800 for a client and receives $200 cash with the remainder on account. The journal entry for this transaction would

a. debit Cash, credit Service Revenue.
b. debit Cash, debit Accounts Receivable, credit Service Revenue.
c. debit Cash, debit Service Revenue, credit Accounts Receivable.
d. debit Cash, credit Accounts Receivable, credit Service Revenue.

4. Accounts Payable had a normal beginning balance of $1,700. During the period, there were debit postings of $200 and credit postings of $700. What was the ending balance?

a. $2,200 credit **b.** $2,200 debit **c.** $1,000 debit **d.** $1,000 credit

5. The list of all accounts with their balances is the

a. Balance Sheet. **b.** chart of accounts. **c.** trial balance. **d.** journal.

6. The basic summary device of business transactions is the

a. journal. **b.** ledger. **c.** trial balance. **d.** account.

7. The beginning Cash balance was $8,000. At the end of the period, the balance was $12,000. If total cash paid out during the period was $24,000, the amount of cash receipts was

a. $32,000. **b.** $28,000. **c.** $44,000. **d.** $36,000.

8. In a double-entry accounting system

a. a debit entry is recorded on the left side of a T-account.
b. liabilities, owners' equity, and revenue accounts all have normal debit balances.
c. half of all the accounts have a credit balance, and the other half have a debit balance.
d. both a and c are correct.

9. Which accounts appear on which financial statement?

	Balance Sheet	*Income Statement*
a.	Cash, receivables, payables	Revenues, expenses
b.	Receivables, land, payables	Revenues, supplies
c.	Cash, revenues, land	Expenses, payables
d.	Expenses, payables, cash	Revenues, receivables, land

10. A doctor purchases medical supplies of $740 and pays $320 cash with the remainder on account. The journal entry for this transaction would be which of the following?
   a. Debit Supplies
   Credit Accounts Payable
   Credit Cash
   b. Debit Supplies
   Debit Accounts Payable
   Credit Cash
   c. Debit Supplies
   Credit Accounts Receivable
   Credit Cash
   d. Debit Supplies
   Debit Cash
   Credit Accounts Payable

11. Which is the correct sequence for recording transactions and preparing financial statements?
   a. Journal, ledger, trial balance, financial statements
   b. Ledger, journal, trial balance, financial statements
   c. Ledger, trial balance, journal, financial statements
   d. Financial statements, trial balance, ledger, journal

12. The error of posting $300 as $30 can be detected by
   a. dividing the out-of-balance amount by 2.
   b. dividing the out-of-balance amount by 9.
   c. examining the chart of accounts.
   d. totaling each account's balance in the ledger.

Accounting Vocabulary

account (p. 60) The record of the changes that have occurred in a particular asset, liability, or shareholders' equity during a period. The basic summary device of accounting.

accrued liability (p. 62) A liability for an expense that has not yet been paid by the company.

chart of accounts (p. 85) List of a company's accounts and their account numbers.

credit (p. 73) The right side of an account.

debit (p. 73) The left side of an account.

journal (p. 76) The chronological accounting record of an entity's transactions.

ledger (p. 76) The book of accounts and their balances.

posting (p. 77) Copying amounts from the journal to the respective ledger accounts.

prepaid expenses (p. 61). Paying expenses in advance before actual consumption. Also called prepayments.

property, plant and equipment, PPE (p. 61) Assets that are expected to be used for more than one period for the purposes of production or supply of goods or services or for administrative purposes.

transaction (p. 60) Any event that has a financial impact on the business and can be measured reliably.

trial balance (p. 83) A list of all the ledger accounts with their balances.

ASSESS YOUR PROGRESS

Short Exercises

S2-1. ***(Learning Objective 1: Explaining an asset versus an expense)*** Brian Norton opened a software consulting firm that immediately bought and paid $2,000 for a computer. Was Norton's computer an expense of the business? If not, explain. LO 1

S2-2. ***(Learning Objective 1, 2: Analyzing the effects of transactions)*** Young Software began with cash of $12,500. Young then bought supplies for $1,500 on account. Separately, Young paid $3,000 for a computer. Answer these questions. LO 1 2
   a. How much in total assets does Young have?
   b. How much in liabilities does Young owe?

LO 1 2

S2-3. ***(Learning Objectives 1, 2: Analyzing transactions; understanding how accounting works)*** Hannah Lyle, a medical doctor, opened a medical practice. The business completed the following transactions:

Aug 1	Lyle invested $20,000 cash to start her medical practice. The business issued ordinary shares to Lyle.
1	Purchased medical supplies on account totaling $8,100.
2	Paid monthly office rent of $2,500.
3	Recorded $15,000 revenue for service rendered to patients, received cash of $4,000, and sent bills to patients for the remainder.

After these transactions, how much cash does the business have to work with? Use a T-account to show your answer.

LO 1

S2-4. ***(Learning Objective 1: Analyzing transactions)*** Refer to Short Exercise 2-3. Which of the transactions of Hannah Lyle increased the total assets of the business? For each transaction, identify the asset that was increased.

LO 1

S2-5. ***(Learning Objective 1: Analyzing transactions)*** Capri Design specializes in imported clothing. During May, Capri completed a series of transactions. For each of the following items, give an example of a transaction that has the described effect on the accounting equation of Capri Design.

a. Increase one asset and decrease another asset.
b. Decrease an asset and decrease owners' equity.
c. Decrease an asset and decrease a liability.
d. Increase an asset and increase owners' equity.
e. Increase an asset and increase a liability.

LO 2 3

S2-6. ***(Learning Objectives 2, 3: Understanding how accounting works; journalizing transactions)*** After operating for several months, architect Gwen Markum completed the following transactions during the latter part of July:

Jul 15	Borrowed $35,000 from the bank, signing a note payable.
22	Performed service for clients on account totaling $9,200.
28	Received $6,300 cash on account from clients.
29	Received a utility bill of $500, an account payable that will be paid during August.
31	Paid monthly salary of $3,200 to employee.

Journalize the transactions of Gwen Markum. Include an explanation with each journal entry.

LO 2 3

S2-7. ***(Learning Objectives 2, 3: Understanding how accounting works; journalizing transactions; posting)*** David Delorme purchased supplies on account for $3,000. Later Delorme paid $550 on account.

1. Journalize the two transactions on the books of David Delorme. Include an explanation for each transaction.
2. Open a T-account for Accounts Payable and post to Accounts Payable. Compute the balance and denote it as Bal.
3. How much does the Delorme business owe after both transactions? In which account does this amount appear?

LO 2 3

S2-8. ***(Learning Objectives 2, 3: Understanding how accounting works; journalizing transactions; posting)*** Orman performed services for a client who could not pay immediately. Orman expected to collect the $5,200 the following month. A month later, Orman received $2,400 cash from the client.

1. Record the two transactions on the books of Orman. Include an explanation for each transaction.
2. Post to these T-accounts: Cash, Accounts Receivable, and Service Revenue. Compute each account balance and denote it as Bal.

S2-9. ***(Learning Objective 5: Preparing and using a trial balance)*** Assume that Old Boardwalk reported the following summarized data at December 31, 20X6. Accounts appear in no particular order; dollar amounts are in millions. LO 5

Other liabilities	$ 4	Revenues	$ 33
Cash	7	Other assets	14
Expenses	20	Accounts payable	2
Shareholders' equity	2		

Prepare the trial balance of Old Boardwalk at December 31, 20X6. List the accounts in their proper order. How much was Old Boardwalk's net income or net loss?

S2-10. ***(Learning Objective 5: Using a trial balance)*** Redberry's trial balance follows: LO 5

	A	B	C	D	E
1	**Redberry, Inc.** **Trial Balance** **December 31, 20X6**				
2		**Balance**			
3	**Account Title**	**Debit**	**Credit**		
4	Cash	$ 5,000			
5	Accounts receivable	12,000			
6	Supplies	2,000			
7	Equipment	26,000			
8	Land	50,000			
9	Accounts payable		$ 20,000		
10	Note payable		31,000		
11	Share capital		8,000		
12	Retained earnings		7,000		
13	Service revenue		62,500		
14	Salary expense	27,000			
15	Rent expense	4,500			
16	Utilities expense	2,000			
17	Total	$ 128,500	$ 128,500		
18					

Compute these amounts for the business:

1. Total assets
2. Total liabilities
3. Net income or net loss during December

S2-11. ***(Learning Objective 5: Using a trial balance)*** Refer to Redberry's trial balance in Short Exercise 2-10. The purpose of this exercise is to help you learn how to correct three common accounting errors. LO 5

Error 1. Slide. Suppose the trial balance lists Land as $5,000 instead of $50,000. Recompute column totals, take the difference, and divide by 9. The result is an integer (no decimals), which suggests that the error is either a transposition or a slide.

Error 2. Transposition. Assume the trial balance lists Accounts Receivable as $21,000 instead of $12,000. Recompute column totals, take the difference, and divide by 9. The result is an integer (no decimals), which suggests that the error is either a transposition or a slide.

Error 3. Mislabeling an item. Assume that Redberry accidentally listed Accounts Receivable as a credit balance instead of a debit. Recompute the trial balance totals for debits and credits. Then take the difference between total debits and total credits, and divide the difference by 2. You get back to the original amount of Accounts Receivable.

LO 2

S2-12. ***(Learning Objective 2: Using key accounting terms)*** Accounting has its own vocabulary and basic relationships. Match the accounting terms at left with the corresponding definition or meaning at right.

____	**1.** Normal balance	**A.** Record of transactions
____	**2.** Payable	**B.** Always an asset
____	**3.** Journal	**C.** Left side of an account
____	**4.** Receivable	**D.** Side of an account where increases are recorded
____	**5.** Owners' equity	**E.** Copying data from the journal to the ledger
____	**6.** Debit	**F.** A decrease in shareholders' equity
____	**7.** Expense	**G.** Always a liability
____	**8.** Net income	**H.** Revenues – Expenses
____	**9.** Ledger	**I.** Collection of accounts used in a business
____	**10.** Posting	**J.** Assets – Liabilities

LO 5

S2-13. ***(Learning Objective 5: Analyzing transactions without a journal)*** Seventh Investments, Inc., began by issuing ordinary shares for cash of $200,000. The company immediately purchased computer equipment on account for $120,000.

1. Set up the following T-accounts of Seventh Investments, Inc.: Cash, Computer Equipment, Accounts Payable, Share Capital.
2. Record the first two transactions of the business directly in the T-accounts without using a journal.
3. Show that total debits equal total credits.

Exercises MyLab Accounting

Select A and B exercises can be found within MyLab Accounting, an online homework and practice environment. Your instructor may ask you to complete these select exercises using MyLab Accounting.

Group A

LO 1
■ **writing assignment**

E2-14A. ***(Learning Objective 1: Analyzing transactions)*** Assume M. Crew opened a store in Hong Kong, starting with cash and ordinary shares of $81,000. Melissa Lim, the store manager, then signed a note payable to purchase land for $75,000 and a building for $101,000. Lim also paid $60,000 for equipment and $7,000 for supplies to use in the business.

Suppose the home office of M. Crew requires a weekly report from store managers. Write Lim's memo to the home office to report on her purchases. Include the store's Balance Sheet as the final part of your memo. Prepare a T-account to compute the balance for Cash.

LO 1 3

E2-15A. ***(Learning Objective 1, 3: Analyzing transactions)*** The following selected events were experienced by either Solution Seekers, Inc., a corporation, or Paul Flynn, the major shareholder. State whether each event (1) increased, (2) decreased, or (3) had no effect on the total assets of the business. Identify any specific asset affected.

a. Received $9,100 cash from customers on account.
b. Flynn used personal funds to purchase a theater system for his home.
c. Sold land and received cash of $55,000 (the land was carried on the company's books at $55,000).
d. Borrowed $75,000.
e. Made cash purchase of land for a building site, $85,000.
f. Received $20,000 cash and issued shares to a shareholder.
g. Paid $65,000 cash on accounts payable.
h. Purchased equipment and signed a $103,500 promissory note in payment.
i. Purchased merchandise inventory on account for $10,000.
j. The business paid Flynn a cash dividend of $4,500.

LO 1 2

E2-16A. ***(Learning Objective 1, 2: Analyzing transactions; using the accounting equation)*** Harry Samson opened a medical practice specializing in surgery. During the first month of operation (March), the business, titled Harry Samson, Professional Corporation (P.C.), experienced the following events:

Mar	6	Samson invested $40,000 in the business, which in turn issued its ordinary shares to him.
	9	The business paid cash for land costing $22,000. Samson plans to build an office building on the land.
	12	The business purchased medical supplies for $15,000 on account.
	15	Harry Samson, P.C., officially opened for business.
	15–31	During the rest of the month, Samson treated patients and earned service revenue of $8,500, receiving cash for half the revenue earned.
	15–31	The business paid cash expenses: employee salaries, $750; office rent, $700; utilities, $300.
	31	The business sold supplies to another physician for cost of $300.
	31	The business borrowed $17,000, signing a note payable to the bank.
	31	The business paid $1,200 on account.

Requirements

1. Analyze the effects of these events on the accounting equation of the medical practice of Harry Samson, P.C.
2. After completing the analysis, answer these questions about the business.
   a. How much are total assets?
   b. How much does the business expect to collect from patients?
   c. How much does the business owe in total?
   d. How much of the business's assets does Samson really own?
   e. How much net income or net loss did the business experience during its first month of operations?

LO 2 3

E2-17A. ***(Learning Objectives 2, 3: Understanding how accounting works; journalizing transactions)*** Refer to Exercise 2-16A.

Requirement

1. Record the transactions in the journal of Harry Samson, P.C. List the transactions by date and give an explanation for each transaction.

E2-18A. ***(Learning Objectives 2, 3: Understanding how accounting works; journalizing transactions)*** Harris Tree Cellular, Inc., completed the following transactions during April 20X6, its first month of operations:

Apr	1	Received $18,200 and issued ordinary shares.
	2	Purchased $200 of office supplies on account.
	4	Paid $15,200 cash for land to use as a building site.
	6	Performed service for customers and received cash of $3,300.
	9	Paid $100 on accounts payable.
	17	Performed service for ShipEx on account totaling $2,100.
	23	Collected $1,000 from ShipEx on account.
	30	Paid the following expenses: salary, $1,200; rent, $600.

Requirement

1. Record the transactions in the journal of Harris Tree Cellular, Inc. Key transactions by date and include an explanation for each entry.

LO 3 4

E2-19A. ***(Learning Objectives 3, 4: Posting to the ledger; preparing and using a trial balance)*** Refer to Exercise 2-18A.

Requirements

1. After journalizing the transactions of Exercise 2-18A, post the entries to the ledger, using T-accounts. Key transactions by date. Date the ending balance of each account April 30.

2. Prepare the trial balance of Harris Tree Cellular, Inc., at April 30, 20X6.
3. How much are total assets, total liabilities, and total shareholders' equity on April 30?

LO 2 3

E2-20A. ***(Learning Objectives 2, 3: Understanding how accounting works; journalizing transactions)*** The first seven transactions of Fournier Advertising, Inc., have been posted to the company's accounts as follows:

Cash

	Debit		Credit
(1)	9,200	(3)	10,000
(2)	7,500	(6)	3,200
(5)	200	(7)	200

Supplies

	Debit		Credit
(4)	600	(5)	200

Equipment

	Debit		Credit
(6)	3,200		

Land

	Debit		Credit
(3)	40,000		

Accounts Payable

	Debit		Credit
(7)	200	(4)	600

Note Payable

	Debit		Credit
		(2)	7,500
		(3)	30,000

Share Capital

	Debit		Credit
		(1)	9,200

Requirement

1. Prepare the journal entries that served as the sources for the seven transactions. Include an explanation for each entry. As Fournier moves into the next period, how much cash does the business have? How much does Fournier owe in total liabilities?

LO 4

E2-21A. ***(Learning Objective 4: Preparing and using a trial balance)*** The accounts of Deluxe Deck Service, Inc., follow with their normal balances at June 30, 20X6. The accounts are listed in no particular order.

Account	Balance	Account	Balance
Share Capital	$ 8,500	Dividends	$ 6,100
Accounts payable	4,200	Utilities expense	3,000
Service revenue	21,200	Accounts receivable	16,000
Land	27,900	Delivery expense	600
Note payable	11,600	Retained earnings	26,100
Cash	9,000	Salary expense	8,100

Requirements

1. Prepare the company's trial balance at June 30, 20X6, listing accounts in proper sequence, as illustrated in the chapter. For example, Accounts Receivable comes before Land. List the expense with the largest balance first, the expense with the next largest balance second, and so on.
2. Prepare the financial statement for the month ended June 30, 20X6, which will tell the company the results of operations for the month.

LO 5

E2-22A. ***(Learning Objective 5: Correcting errors in a trial balance)*** The trial balance of Carver, Inc., at September 30, 20X6, does not balance:

Cash	$ 4,200	
Accounts receivable	13,200	
Inventory	16,700	
Supplies	100	
Land	52,100	
Accounts payable		$ 11,800
Share capital		45,000
Service revenue		32,500
Salary expense	1,200	
Rent expense	1,400	
Utilities expense	500	
Total	$ 89,400	$ 89,300

The accounting records hold the following errors:

- **a.** Recorded a $500 cash revenue transaction by debiting Accounts Receivable. The credit entry was correct.
- **b.** Posted a $2,000 credit to Accounts Payable as $200.
- **c.** Did not record utilities expense or the related account payable in the amount of $1,000.
- **d.** Understated Share Capital by $1,400.
- **e.** Omitted Insurance Expense of $4,000 from the trial balance.

Requirement

1. Prepare the correct trial balance at September 30, 20X6, complete with a heading. Journal entries are not required.

E2-23A. ***(Learning Objective 5: Recording transactions without a journal)*** Set up the following T-accounts: Cash, Accounts Receivable, Office Supplies, Office Furniture, Accounts Payable, Share Capital, Dividends, Service Revenue, Salary Expense, and Rent Expense. Record the following transactions directly in the T-accounts without using a journal. Use the letters to identify the transactions.

LO 5

- **a.** Linda Oxford opened a law firm by investing $13,000 cash and office furniture valued at $7,500. Organized as a corporation, the business issued ordinary shares to Oxford.
- **b.** Paid monthly rent of $1,200.
- **c.** Purchased office supplies on account, $600.
- **d.** Paid employees' salaries of $1,700.
- **e.** Paid $200 of the account payable created in Transaction c.
- **f.** Performed legal service on account, $8,200.
- **g.** Declared and paid dividends of $3,300.

E2-24A. ***(Learning Objective 4: Preparing and using a trial balance)*** Refer to Exercise 2-23A.

LO 4
■ **writing assignment**

1. After recording the transactions in Exercise 2-23A, prepare the trial balance of Linda Oxford, Attorney, at May 31, 20X6. Use the T-accounts that have been prepared for the business.
2. How well did the business perform during its first month? Compute net income (or net loss) for the month.

Group B

E2-25B. ***(Learning Objective 1: Analyzing transactions)*** Assume T. Crew opened a store in Frankfurt, Germany, starting with cash and ordinary shares of €85,000. Barbara Breen, the store manager, then signed a note payable to purchase land for €87,000 and a building for €123,000. Breen also paid €59,000 for equipment and €12,000 for supplies to use in the business.

LO 1
■ **writing assignment**

Suppose the home office of T. Crew requires a weekly report from store managers. Write Breen's memo to the head office to report on her purchases. Include the store's Balance Sheet as the final part of your memo. Prepare a T-account to compute the balance for Cash.

E2-26B. ***(Learning Objective 1: Analyzing transactions)*** The following selected events were experienced by either Simple Solutions, Inc., a corporation, or Bob Gallagher, the major shareholder. State whether each event (1) increased, (2) decreased, or (3) had no effect on the total assets of the business. Identify any specific asset affected.

LO 1

- **a.** Received €25,000 cash and issued shares to a shareholder.
- **b.** Purchased equipment for €62,000 cash.
- **c.** Paid €11,000 cash on accounts payable.
- **d.** Gallagher used personal funds to purchase a flat screen TV for his home.
- **e.** Purchased land for a building site and signed a €95,000 promissory note to the bank.
- **f.** Received €18,000 cash from customers for services performed.
- **g.** Sold land and received a note receivable of €45,000 (the land was carried on the company's books at €45,000).
- **h.** Earned €32,000 in revenue for services performed. The customer promises to pay Simple Solutions in one month.
- **i.** Purchased supplies on account for €4,500.
- **j.** The business paid Gallagher a cash dividend of €5,000.

LO 1 2

E2-27B. *(Learning Objective 1, 2: Analyzing transactions; using the accounting equation)* Kyle Cohen opened a medical practice specializing in surgery. During the first month of operation (July), the business, titled Kyle Cohen, Professional Corporation (P.C.), experienced the following events:

Jul	6	Cohen invested €54,000 in the business, which in turn issued its ordinary shares to him.
	9	The business paid cash for land costing €21,000. Cohen plans to build an office building on the land.
	12	The business purchased medical supplies for €3,200 on account.
	15	Kyle Cohen, P.C., officially opened for business.
	15–31	During the rest of the month, Cohen treated patients and earned service revenue of €8,400, receiving cash for half the revenue earned.
	15–31	The business paid cash expenses: employee salaries, €700; office rent, €750; utilities, €500.
	31	The business sold supplies to another physician for cost of €500.
	31	The business borrowed €17,000, signing a note payable to the bank.
	31	The business paid €800 on account.

Requirements

1. Analyze the effects of these events on the accounting equation of the medical practice of Kyle Cohen, P.C.
2. After completing the analysis, answer these questions about the business.
   - **a.** How much are total assets?
   - **b.** How much does the business expect to collect from patients?
   - **c.** How much does the business owe in total?
   - **d.** How much of the business's assets does Cohen really own?
   - **e.** How much net income or net loss did the business experience during its first month of operations?

LO 2 3

E2-28B. *(Learning Objectives 2, 3: Understanding how accounting works; journalizing transactions)* Refer to Exercise 2-27B.

Requirement

1. Record the transactions in the journal of Kyle Cohen, P.C. List the transactions by date and give an explanation for each transaction.

LO 2 3

E2-29B. *(Learning Objectives 2, 3: Understanding how accounting works; journalizing transactions)* Green Tree Cellular, Inc., completed the following transactions during April 20X6, its first month of operations:

Apr	1	Received €20,100 and issued ordinary shares.
	2	Purchased €700 of office supplies on account.
	4	Paid €15,200 cash for land to use as a building site.
	6	Performed service for customers and received cash of €2,300.
	9	Paid €150 on accounts payable.
	17	Performed service for UPS on account totaling €1,100.
	23	Collected €850 from UPS on account.
	30	Paid the following expenses: salary, €1,700; rent, €1,300.

Requirement

1. Record the transactions in the journal of Green Tree Cellular, Inc. Key transactions by date and include an explanation for each entry.

LO 3 4

E2-30B. *(Learning Objectives 3, 4: Posting to the ledger; preparing and using a trial balance)* Refer to Exercise 2-29B.

Requirements

1. Post the entries to the ledger, using T-accounts. Key transactions by date. Date the ending balance of each account April 30.
2. Prepare the trial balance of Green Tree Cellular, Inc., at April 30, 20X6.
3. From the trial balance, determine total assets, total liabilities, and total shareholders' equity on April 30?

LO 2 3

E2-31B. ***(Learning Objectives 2, 3: Understanding how accounting works; journalizing transactions)*** The first seven transactions of Portman Advertising, Inc., have been posted to the company's accounts as follows:

Cash

	Debit		Credit
(1)	9,000	(3)	6,500
(2)	6,300	(6)	7,000
(5)	90	(7)	70

Supplies

	Debit		Credit
(4)	750	(5)	90

Equipment

	Debit		Credit
(6)	7,000		

Land

	Debit		Credit
(3)	28,500		

Accounts Payable

	Debit		Credit
(7)	70	(4)	750

Note Payable

	Debit		Credit
		(2)	6,300
		(3)	22,000

Share Capital

	Debit		Credit
		(1)	9,000

Requirement

1. Prepare the journal entries that served as the sources for the seven transactions. Include an explanation for each entry. As Portman moves into the next period, how much cash does the business have? How much does Portman owe in total liabilities?

E2-32B. ***(Learning Objective 5: Preparing and using a trial balance)*** The accounts of Grand Pool Service, Inc., follow with their normal balances at June 30, 20X6. The accounts are listed in no particular order.

Account	Balance	Account	Balance
Share Capital....................	€ 7,000	Dividends..........................	€ 8,100
Accounts payable	5,700	Utilities expense	2,000
Service revenue.................	23,100	Accounts receivable...........	15,900
Land................................	25,100	Delivery expense	500
Note payable.....................	7,200	Retained earnings.............	25,300
Cash................................	9,200	Salary expense..................	750

Requirements

1. Prepare the company's trial balance at June 30, 20X6, listing accounts in proper sequence, as illustrated in the chapter. For example, Accounts Receivable comes before Land. List the expense with the largest balance first, the expense with the next largest balance second, and so on.
2. Prepare the financial statement for the month ended June 30, 20X6, that will tell the company the results of operations for the month.

LO 5

E2-33B. ***(Learning Objective 5: Correcting errors in a trial balance)*** The trial balance of Farris, Inc., at June 30, 20X6, does not balance.

Cash....................................	€ 4,000	
Accounts receivable..............	12,800	
Inventory..............................	17,000	
Supplies................................	500	
Land.....................................	50,100	
Accounts payable		€ 14,200
Share capital.........................		45,300
Service revenue.....................		30,300
Salary expense......................	2,100	
Rent expense........................	800	
Utilities expense	500	
Total	€ 87,800	€ 89,800

The accounting records hold the following errors:

a. Recorded a €300 cash revenue transaction by debiting Accounts Receivable. The credit entry was correct.
b. Posted a €1,000 credit to Accounts Payable as €100.
c. Did not record utilities expense or the related account payable in the amount of €200.
d. Understated Share Capital by €200.
e. Omitted Insurance Expense of €3,100 from the trial balance.

Requirement

1. Prepare the correct trial balance at June 30, 20X6, complete with a heading. Journal entries are not required.

LO 5

E2-34B. ***(Learning Objective 5: Recording transactions without a journal)*** Set up the following T-accounts: Cash, Accounts Receivable, Office Supplies, Office Furniture, Accounts Payable, Share Capital, Dividends, Service Revenue, Salary Expense, and Rent Expense. Record the following transactions directly in the T-accounts without using a journal. Use the letters to identify the transactions.

a. Linda Conway opened a law firm by investing €12,000 cash and office furniture valued at €8,900. Organized as a corporation, the business issued ordinary shares to Conway.
b. Paid monthly rent of €1,500.
c. Purchased office supplies on account, €600.
d. Paid employee salaries of €2,100.
e. Paid €400 of the accounts payable created in Transaction c.
f. Performed legal service on account, €9,100.
g. Declared and paid dividends of €2,000.

LO 4

E2-35B. ***(Learning Objective 4: Preparing and using a trial balance)*** Refer to Exercise 2-34B.

Requirements

1. Prepare the trial balance of Linda Conway, Attorney, at January 31, 20X6. Use the T-accounts that have been prepared for the business.
2. How well did the business perform during its first month? Compute net income (or net loss) for the month.

Serial Exercise

Exercise 2-36 begins an accounting cycle exercise that will be completed in Chapter 3.

LO 2 3 4

E2-36. ***(Learning Objectives 2, 3, 4: Recording transactions; preparing a trial balance)*** Jerome Smith, Certified Public Accountant, operates as a professional corporation (P.C.). The business completed these transactions during the first part of March, 20X6:

Mar	2	Received $6,500 cash from Smith, and issued ordinary shares to him.
	2	Paid monthly office rent, $500.
	3	Paid cash for a Dell computer, $2,500, with the computer expected to remain in service for five years.
	4	Purchased office furniture on account, $7,200, with the furniture projected to last for five years.
	5	Purchased supplies on account, $400.
	9	Performed tax service for a client and received cash for the full amount of $1,500.
	12	Paid utility expenses, $400.
	18	Performed consulting service for a client on account, $1,900.

Requirements

1. Journalize the transactions. Explanations are not required.
2. Post to the T-accounts. Key all items by date and denote an account balance on March 18, 20X6, as Bal.
3. Prepare a trial balance at March 18, 20X6. In the Serial Exercise of Chapter 3, we add transactions for the remainder of March and will require a trial balance at March 31.

Challenge Exercises

E2-37. ***(Learning Objective 5: Computing financial statement amounts)*** The manager of Pierce Furniture needs to compute the following amounts: LO 5

a. Total cash paid during October.
b. Cash collections from customers during October. Analyze Accounts Receivable.
c. Cash paid on a note payable during October. Analyze Notes Payable.

Here's the additional data you need to analyze the accounts:

Account	Balance Sep 30	Balance Oct 31	Additional Information for the Month of October
1. Cash..............................	$ 12,000	$ 6,000	Cash receipts, $ 85,000
2. Accounts Receivable.......	27,500	26,000	Sales on account, $ 50,000
3. Notes Payable	16,100	23,000	New borrowing, $ 15,000

Requirement

1. Prepare a T-account to compute each amount, ***a*** through ***c***.

E2-38. ***(Learning Objectives 1, 4: Analyzing transactions; using a trial balance)*** The trial balance of Circle 360, Inc., at October 31, 20X6, does not balance. LO 1 4

Cash....................................	$ 4,200	Share capital.......................	$ 20,800
Accounts receivable............	6,900	Retained earnings................	7,900
Land....................................	35,100	Service revenue....................	9,100
Accounts payable	6,200	Salary expense.....................	3,000
Note payable.......................	5,100	Advertising expense............	1,100

Requirements

1. How much out of balance is the trial balance? Determine the out-of-balance amount. The error lies in the Accounts Receivable account. Add the out-of-balance amount to, or subtract it from, Accounts Receivable to determine the correct balance of Accounts Receivable.
2. After correcting Accounts receivable, advise the top management of Circle 360, Inc., on the company's
   a. total assets
   b. total liabilities
   c. net income or net loss for October

E2-39. ***(Learning Objective 1: Analyzing transactions)*** This question concerns the items and the amounts that two entities, Nashua Co. and Ditka Hospital, should report in their financial statements. LO 1

During September, Ditka provided Nashua with medical exams for Nashua employees and sent a bill for $3,000. On October 7, Nashua sent a check to Ditka for $24,000. Nashua began September with a cash balance of $43,000; Ditka began with cash of $0.

Requirements

1. For this situation, show everything that both Nashua and Ditka will report on their September and October Income Statements and on their Balance Sheets at September 30 and October 31.
2. After showing what each company should report, briefly explain how the Nashua and Ditka data relate to each other.

Quiz

Test your understanding of recording business transactions by answering the following questions. Select the best choice from among the possible answers.

Q2-40. A shareholder's investment of cash into the business will

a. decrease total assets.
b. decrease total liabilities.
c. increase shareholders' equity.
d. have no effect on total assets.

Q2-41. Purchasing a laptop computer on account will

a. increase total assets.
b. have no effect on shareholders' equity.
c. increase total liabilities.
d. all of the above.

Q2-42. Performing a service on account will

a. increase total liabilities.
b. increase shareholders' equity.
c. increase total assets.
d. both b and c.

Q2-43. Receiving cash from a customer on account will

a. increase total assets.
b. decrease liabilities.
c. increase shareholders' equity.
d. have no effect on total assets.

Q2-44. Purchasing computer equipment for cash will

a. decrease both total assets and shareholders' equity.
b. decrease both total liabilities and shareholders' equity.
c. have no effect on total assets, total liabilities, or shareholders' equity.
d. increase both total assets and total liabilities.

Q2-45. Purchasing a building for $110,000 by paying cash of $15,000 and signing a note payable for $95,000 will

a. decrease total assets and increase total liabilities by $15,000.
b. increase both total assets and total liabilities by $95,000.
c. increase both total assets and total liabilities by $110,000.
d. decrease both total assets and total liabilities by $15,000.

Q2-46. What is the effect on total assets and shareholders' equity of paying the telephone bill as soon as it is received each month?

Total assets	**Shareholders' equity**
a. Decrease	Decrease
b. No effect	Decrease
c. No effect	No effect
d. Decrease	No effect

Q2-47. Which of the following transactions will increase an asset and increase a liability?

a. Purchasing office equipment for cash
b. Paying an account payable
c. Buying equipment on account
d. Issuing shares

Q2-48. Which of the following transactions will increase an asset and increase shareholders' equity?

a. Performing a service on account for a customer
b. Borrowing money from a bank
c. Purchasing supplies on account
d. Collecting cash from a customer on an account receivable

Q2-49. Where do we first record a transaction?

a. Journal
b. Account
c. Ledger
d. Trial balance

Q2-50. Which of the following is not an asset account?

a. Service Revenue
b. Share Capital
c. Salary Expense
d. None of the above accounts is an asset.

Q2-51. Which statement is false?

a. Dividends are increased by credits.
b. Assets are increased by debits.
c. Revenues are increased by credits.
d. Liabilities are decreased by debits.

Q2-52. The journal entry to record the receipt of land and a building and issuance of ordinary shares

a. debits Share Capital and credits Land and Building.
b. debits Land and Building and credits Share Capital.
c. debits Land and credits Share Capital.
d. debits Land, Building, and Share Capital.

Q2-53. The journal entry to record the purchase of supplies on account

a. debits Supplies Expense and credits Supplies.
b. debits Supplies and credits Accounts Payable.
c. credits Supplies and debits Cash.
d. credits Supplies and debits Accounts Payable.

Q2-54. If the credit to record the purchase of supplies on account is not posted,

a. liabilities will be understated.
b. expenses will be overstated.
c. assets will be understated.
d. shareholders' equity will be understated.

Q2-55. The journal entry to record a payment on account will

a. debit Expenses and credit Cash.
b. debit Cash and credit Expenses.
c. debit Accounts Payable and credit Retained Earnings.
d. debit Accounts Payable and credit Cash.

Q2-56. If the credit to record the payment of an account payable is not posted,

a. cash will be overstated.
b. liabilities will be understated.
c. expenses will be understated.
d. cash will be understated.

Q2-57. Which statement is false?

a. A trial balance lists all the accounts with their current balances.
b. A trial balance can be taken at any time.
c. A trial balance can verify the equality of debits and credits.
d. A trial balance is the same as a Balance Sheet.

Q2-58. A business's receipt of a $105,000 building, with a $65,000 mortgage payable and issuance of $40,000 of ordinary shares, will

a. increase shareholders' equity by $40,000.
b. increase assets by $65,000.
c. decrease assets by $65,000.
d. increase shareholders' equity by $105,000.

Q2-59. Gartex, a new company, completed these transactions.

1. Shareholders invested $45,000 cash and inventory worth $28,000.
2. Sales on account, $20,000.

What will Gartex's total assets equal?

a. $93,000
b. $73,000
c. $65,000
d. $53,000

Problems MyLab Accounting

Select A and B problems can be found within MyLab Accounting, an online homework and practice environment. Your instructor may ask you to complete these select problems using MyLab Accounting.

Group A

LO 4
■ writing assignment

P2-60A. ***(Learning Objective 4: Analyzing a trial balance)*** The trial balance of Luxury Specialties, Inc., follows.

	A	B	C	D	E
1	**Luxury Specialties** **Trial Balance** **December 31, 20X6**				
2	Cash	$ 12,000			
3	Accounts receivable	46,000			
4	Prepaid expenses	3,000			
5	Equipment	245,000			
6	Building	101,000			
7	Accounts payable		$ 107,000		
8	Note payable		95,000		
9	Share capital		32,000		
10	Retained earnings		35,000		
11	Dividends	19,000			
12	Service revenue		255,000		
13	Rent expense	308,000			
14	Advertising expense	5,000			
15	Wage expense	58,000			
16	Supplies expense	7,000			
17	Total	$ 524,000	$ 524,000		
18					

Ashley Richards, your best friend, is considering investing in Luxury Specialties, Inc. Ashley seeks your advice in interpreting this information. Specifically, she asks how to use this trial balance to compute the company's total assets, total liabilities, and net income or net loss for the year.

Requirement

1. Write a short note to answer Ashley's questions. In your note, state the amounts of Luxury Specialties' total assets, total liabilities, and net income or net loss for the year. Also show how you computed each amount.

LO 1

P2-61A. ***(Learning Objective 1: Analyzing transactions with the accounting equation; preparing the financial statements)*** The following amounts summarize the financial position of Mason Resources, Inc., on May 31, 20X6:

	Assets							=	Liabilities	+	Shareholders' Equity		
	Cash	+	Accounts Receivable	+	Supplies	+	Land	=	Accounts Payable	+	Share Capital	+	Retained Earnings
Bal.	1,350		1,250				11,500		7,200		4,500		2,400

During June 20X6, Mason Resources completed these transactions:

- **a.** The business received cash of $8,100 and issued ordinary shares.
- **b.** Performed services for a customer and received cash of $7,200.
- **c.** Paid $5,100 on accounts payable.
- **d.** Purchased supplies on account, $700.

e. Collected cash from a customer on account, $1,000.
f. Consulted on the design of a computer system and billed the customer for services rendered, $2,400.
g. Recorded the following business expenses for the month: (1) paid office rent—$1,200; (2) paid advertising—$900.
h. Declared and paid a cash dividend of $1,400.

Requirements

1. Analyze the effects of the preceding transactions on the accounting equation of Mason Resources, Inc.
2. Prepare the Income Statement of Mason Resources, Inc., for the month ended June 30, 20X6. List expenses in decreasing order by amount.
3. Prepare the entity's statement of changes in equity for the month ended June 30, 20X6.
4. Prepare the Balance Sheet of Mason Resources, Inc., at June 30, 20X6.

P2-62A. ***(Learning Objectives 2, 3: Recording transactions; posting)*** This problem can be used in conjunction with Problem 2-61A.

Requirements

1. Journalize the June transactions of Mason Resources, Inc. Explanations are not required.
2. Prepare T-Accounts for each account. Insert in each T-account its May 31 balance as given (example: Cash $1,150). Then, post the June transactions to the T-accounts.
3. Compute the balance in each account.

P2-63A. ***(Learning Objectives 1, 2, 3: Analyzing transactions; understanding how accounting works; journalizing transactions)*** Demers Real Estate Co. experienced the following events during the organizing phase and its first month of operations. Some of the events were personal for the shareholders and did not affect the business. Others were transactions of the business.

Nov	4	David Demers, the major shareholder of a real estate company, received $75,000 cash from an inheritance.
	5	Demers deposited $45,000 cash in a new business bank account titled Demers Real Estate Co. The business issued ordinary shares to Demers.
	6	The business paid $700 cash for letterhead stationery for the new office.
	7	The business purchased office equipment. The company paid cash of $13,000 and agreed to pay the account payable for the remainder, $7,000, within three months.
	10	Demers sold EVN shares, which he had owned for several years, receiving $74,500 cash from his stockbroker.
	11	Demers deposited the $74,500 cash from sale of the EVN shares in his personal bank account.
	12	A representative of a large company telephoned Demers and told him of the company's intention to transfer $16,000 of business to Demers.
	18	Demers finished a real estate deal for a client and submitted his bill for services, $4,000. Demers expects to collect from the client within two weeks.
	21	The business paid half its account payable on the equipment purchased on November 7.
	25	The business paid office rent of $1,500.
	30	The business declared and paid a cash dividend of $2,100.

Requirements

1. Classify each of the preceding events as one of the following:
   a. A business-related event but not a transaction to be recorded by Demers Real Estate Co.
   b. A business transaction for a shareholder, not to be recorded by Demers Real Estate Co.
   c. A business transaction to be recorded by Demers Real Estate Co.
2. Analyze the effects of the preceding events on the accounting equation of Demers Real Estate Co.
3. Record the transactions of the business in its journal. Include an explanation for each entry.

P2-64A. ***(Learning Objectives 2, 3: Understanding how accounting works; analyzing and recording transactions)*** During December, Smith Auction Co. completed the following transactions:

Dec 1	Smith received $25,000 cash and issued ordinary shares to the shareholders.
5	Paid monthly rent, $1,200.
9	Paid $7,200 cash and signed a $31,000 note payable to purchase land for an office site.
10	Purchased supplies on account, $1,500.
19	Paid $700 on account.
22	Borrowed $21,000 from the bank for business use. Smith signed a note payable to the bank in the name of the business.
31	Service revenue earned during the month included $13,000 cash and $7,000 on account.
31	Paid employees' salaries ($2,200), advertising expense ($1,600), and utilities expense ($1,500).
31	Declared and paid a cash dividend of $6,200.

Smith's business uses the following accounts: Cash, Accounts Receivable, Supplies, Land, Accounts Payable, Notes Payable, Share Capital, Dividends, Service Revenue, Salary Expense, Advertising Expense, and Utilities Expense.

Requirements

1. Journalize each transaction of Smith Auction Co. Explanations are not required.
2. Post to these T-accounts: Cash, Accounts Payable, and Notes Payable.
3. After these transactions, how much cash does the business have? How much in total liabilities does it owe?

P2-65A. ***(Learning Objectives 2, 3, 4: Understanding how accounting works; journalizing transactions; posting; preparing and using a trial balance)*** During the first month of operations, Simmons Heating and Air Conditioning, Inc., completed the following transactions:

Jan 2	Simmons received $45,000 cash and issued ordinary shares to the shareholders.
3	Purchased supplies, $300, and equipment, $5,200, on account.
4	Performed services for a customer and received cash, $2,400.
7	Paid cash to acquire land, $25,000.
11	Performed services for a customer and billed the customer, $1,100. We expect to collect within one month.
16	Paid for the equipment purchased January 3 on account.
17	Paid the telephone bill, $200.
18	Received partial payment from customer on account, $540.
22	Paid the water and electricity bills, $130.
29	Received $1,500 cash for servicing the heating unit of a customer.
31	Paid employee salary, $2,800.
31	Declared and paid dividends of $2,500.

Requirements

1. Record each transaction in the journal. Key each transaction by date. Explanations are not required.
2. Post the transactions to the T-accounts, using transaction dates as posting references. Label the ending balance of each account Bal., as shown in the chapter.
3. Prepare the trial balance of Simmons Heating and Air Conditioning, Inc., at January 31 of the current year.
4. The manager asks you how much in total resources the business has to work with, how much it owes, and whether January was profitable (and by how much).

P2-66A. ***(Learning Objectives 4, 5: Recording transactions directly in T-accounts; preparing and using a trial balance)*** During the first month of operations (November 20X6), Stein Services Corporation completed the following selected transactions:

- **a.** The business received cash of \$32,000 and a building valued at \$51,000. The corporation issued ordinary shares to the shareholders.
- **b.** Borrowed \$35,000 from the bank; signed a note payable.
- **c.** Paid \$33,000 for music equipment.
- **d.** Purchased supplies on account, \$400.
- **e.** Paid employees' salaries, \$1,500.
- **f.** Received \$2,300 for music service performed for customers.
- **g.** Performed service for customers on account, \$300.
- **h.** Paid \$200 of the account payable created in Transaction d.
- **i.** Received a \$550 bill for utility expense that will be paid in the near future.
- **j.** Received cash on account, \$2,100.
- **k.** Paid the following cash expenses: (1) rent, \$1,100; (2) advertising, \$600.

Requirements

1. Record each transaction directly in the T-accounts without using a journal. Use the letters to identify the transactions.
2. Prepare the trial balance of Stein Services Corporation at November 30, 20X6.

Group B

LO 4
■ writing assignment

P2-67B. ***(Learning Objective 4: Analyzing a trial balance)*** The trial balance of Advantage Specialties, Inc., follows:

A1

	A	B	C	D	E
1	**Advantage Specialties, Inc.** **Trial Balance** **December 31, 20X6**				
2	Cash	€ 12,100			
3	Accounts receivable	48,000			
4	Prepaid expenses	6,000			
5	Equipment	225,000			
6	Building	95,000			
7	Accounts payable		€ 105,000		
8	Note payable		87,500		
9	Share capital		35,000		
10	Retained earnings		37,000		
11	Dividends	22,000			
12	Service revenue		244,600		
13	Rent expense	23,000			
14	Advertising expense	5,000			
15	Wage expense	67,000			
16	Supplies expense	6,000			
17	Total	€ 509,100	€ 509,100		
18					

Rebecca Smith, your best friend, is considering making an investment in Advantage Specialties, Inc. Rebecca seeks your advice in interpreting the company's information. Specifically, she asks how to use this trial balance to compute the company's total assets, total liabilities, and net income or net loss for the year.

Requirement

1. Write a short note to answer Rebecca's questions. In your note, state the amounts of Advantage Specialties' total assets, total liabilities, and net income or net loss for the year. Also show how you computed each amount.

LO 1

P2-68B. ***(Learning Objective 1: Analyzing transactions with the accounting equation; preparing the financial statements)*** The following amounts summarize the financial position of Rodriguez Resources on May 31, 20X6:

	Assets							=	Liabilities	+	Shareholders' Equity		
	Cash	+	Accounts Receivable	+	Supplies	+	Land	=	Accounts Payable	+	Share Capital	+	Retained Earnings
Bal.	1,200		1,500				12,500		6,300		5,200		3,700

During June, 20X6, the business completed these transactions:

a. Rodriguez Resources received cash of €7,500 and issued shares.
b. Performed services for a customer and received cash of €6,300.
c. Paid €5,200 on accounts payable.
d. Purchased supplies on account, €500.
e. Collected cash from a customer on account, €300.
f. Consulted on the design of a computer system and billed the customer for services rendered, €3,100.
g. Recorded the following expenses for the month: (1) paid office rent, €700; (2) paid advertising, €900.
h. Declared and paid a cash dividend of €2,200.

Requirements

1. Analyze the effects of the preceding transactions on the accounting equation of Rodriguez Resources, Inc.
2. Prepare the Income Statement of Rodriguez Resources, Inc., for the month ended June 30, 20X6. List expenses in decreasing order by amount.
3. Prepare the statement of changes in equity of Rodriguez Resources, Inc., for the month ended June 30, 20X6.
4. Prepare the Balance Sheet of Rodriguez Resources, Inc., at June 30, 20X6.

LO 2 3

P2-69B. ***(Learning Objectives 2, 3: Understanding how accounting works; journalizing transactions; posting)*** This problem can be used in conjunction with Problem 2-68B. Refer to Problem 2-68B.

Requirements

1. Journalize the transactions of Rodriguez Resources, Inc. Explanations are not required.
2. Prepare T-accounts for each account. Insert in each T-account its May 31 balance as given (example: Cash €1,450). Then, post the June transactions to the T-accounts.
3. Compute the balance in each account.

LO 1 2 3

P2-70B. ***(Learning Objectives 1, 2, 3: Analyzing transactions; understanding how accounting works; journalizing transactions)*** Smith Real Estate Co. experienced the following events during the organizing phase and its first month of operations. Some of the events were personal for the shareholders and did not affect the business. Others were transactions of the business.

Nov 4	John Smith, the major shareholder of real estate company, received €121,000 cash from an inheritance.
5	Smith deposited €61,000 cash in a new business bank account titled Smith Real Estate Co. The business issued ordinary shares to Smith.
6	The business paid €700 cash for letterhead stationery for the new office.
7	The business purchased office equipment. The company paid cash of €13,500 and agreed to pay the account payable for the remainder, €7,500, within three months.
10	Smith sold DLD shares, which he owned for several years, receiving €68,000 cash from his stockbroker.
11	Smith deposited the €68,000 cash from sale of the DLD shares in his personal bank account.
12	A representative of a large company telephoned Smith and told him of the company's intention to transfer €13,000 of business to Smith.
18	Smith finished a real estate deal for a client and submitted his bill for services, €5,000. Smith expects to collect from the client within two weeks.
21	The business paid half its account payable for the equipment purchased on November 7.
25	The business paid office rent of €700.
30	The business declared and paid a cash dividend of €2,000.

Requirements

1. Classify each of the preceding events as one of the following:
   a. A business-related event but not a transaction to be recorded by Smith Real Estate Co.
   b. A business transaction for a shareholder, not to be recorded by Smith Real Estate Co.
   c. A business transaction to be recorded by the Smith Real Estate Co.
2. Analyze the effects of the preceding events on the accounting equation of Smith Real Estate Co.
3. Record the transactions of the business in its journal. Include an explanation for each entry.

P2-71B. ***(Learning Objectives 2, 3: Analyzing and recording transactions)*** During December, Swanson Auction Co. completed the following transactions:

Dec 1	Swanson received €27,000 cash and issued ordinary shares to the shareholders.
5	Paid monthly rent, €3,000.
9	Paid €12,100 cash and signed a €32,000 note payable to purchase land for an office site.
10	Purchased supplies on account, €1,600.
19	Paid €500 on account.
22	Borrowed €19,000 from the bank for business use. Swanson signed a note payable to the bank in the name of the business.
31	Service revenue earned during the month included €15,200 cash and €5,000 on account.
31	Paid employees' salaries (€2,200), advertising expense (€900), and utilities expense (€1,300).
31	Declared and paid a cash dividend of €3,000.

Swanson's business uses the following accounts: Cash, Accounts Receivable, Supplies, Land, Accounts Payable, Notes Payable, Share Capital, Dividends, Service Revenue, Salary Expense, Rent Expense, Advertising Expense, and Utilities Expense.

Requirements

1. Journalize each transaction of Swanson Auction Co. Explanations are not required.
2. Post to these T-accounts: Cash, Accounts Payable, and Notes Payable.
3. After these transactions, how much cash does the business have? How much does it owe in total liabilities?

LO 2 3 4

P2-72B. ***(Learning Objectives 2, 3, 4: Understanding how accounting works; journalizing transactions; posting; preparing and using a trial balance)*** During the first month of operations, O'Shea Plumbing, Inc., completed the following transactions:

Jan 2	O'Shea received €28,000 cash and issued ordinary shares to the shareholders.
3	Purchased supplies, €500, and equipment, €3,100, on account.
4	Performed service for a client and received cash, €3,000.
7	Paid cash to acquire land, €20,000.
11	Performed service for a customer and billed the customer, €1,200. We expect to collect within one month.
16	Paid for the equipment purchased January 3 on account.
17	Paid the telephone bill, €120.
18	Received partial payment from customer on account, €570.
22	Paid the water and electricity bills, €120.
29	Received €1,300 cash for servicing the heating unit of a customer.
31	Paid employee salaries, €1,800.
31	Declared and paid dividends of €2,500.

Requirements

1. Record each transaction in the journal. Key each transaction by date. Explanations are not required.
2. Post the transactions to the T-accounts, using transaction dates as posting references.
3. Prepare the trial balance of O'Shea Plumbing, Inc., at January 31 of the current year.
4. The manager asks you how much in total resources the business has to work with, how much it owes, and whether January was profitable (and by how much).

P2-73B. ***(Learning Objectives, 4, 5: Recording transactions directly in T-accounts; preparing and using a trial balance)*** During the first month of operations (March 20X6), Silver Entertainment Corporation completed the following selected transactions:

- **a.** The business received cash of €35,000 and a building valued at €55,000. The corporation issued ordinary shares to the shareholders.
- **b.** Borrowed €32,300 from the bank; signed a note payable.
- **c.** Paid €31,500 for music equipment.
- **d.** Purchased supplies on account, €300.
- **e.** Paid employees' salaries, €2,100.
- **f.** Received €1,800 for music service performed for customers.
- **g.** Performed service for customers on account, €2,700.
- **h.** Paid €200 of the account payable created in Transaction d.
- **i.** Received a €700 bill for advertising expense that will be paid in the near future.
- **j.** Received cash on account, €1,500.
- **k.** Paid the following cash expenses: (1) rent, €1,000; (2) advertising, €700.

Requirements

1. Record each transaction directly in the T-accounts without using a journal. Use the letters to identify the transactions.
2. Prepare the trial balance of Silver Entertainment Corporation, at March 31, 20X6.

APPLY YOUR KNOWLEDGE

Decision Cases

Case 1. ***(Learning Objectives 4, 5: Recording transactions directly in T-accounts; preparing a trial balance; measuring net income or loss)*** A friend named Jay Barlow has asked what effect certain transactions will have on his company. Time is short, so you cannot apply the detailed procedures of journalizing and posting. Instead, you must analyze the transactions without the use of

a journal. Barlow will continue the business only if he can expect to earn monthly net income of at least $5,000. The following transactions occurred this month:

a. Barlow deposited $5,000 cash in a business bank account, and the corporation issued ordinary shares to him.
b. Borrowed $5,000 cash from the bank and signed a note payable due within 1 year.
c. Paid $1,300 cash for supplies.
d. Purchased advertising in the local newspaper for cash, $1,800.
e. Purchased office furniture on account, $4,400.
f. Paid the following cash expenses for 1 month: employee salary, $2,000; office rent, $1,200.
g. Earned revenue on account, $7,000.
h. Earned revenue and received $2,500 cash.
i. Collected cash from customers on account, $1,200.
j. Paid on account, $1,000.

Requirements

1. Set up the following T-accounts: Cash, Accounts Receivable, Supplies, Furniture, Accounts Payable, Notes Payable, Share Capital, Service Revenue, Salary Expense, Advertising Expense, and Rent Expense.
2. Record the transactions directly in the accounts without using a journal. Key each transaction by letter.
3. Prepare a trial balance for Barlow Networks, Inc., at the current date. List expenses with the largest amount first, the next largest amount second, and so on.
4. Compute the amount of net income or net loss for this first month of operations. Why would you recommend (or not) that Barlow continue in business?

Case 2. *(Learning Objective 2: Correcting financial statements; deciding whether to expand a business)* Gianna Loren opened an Italian restaurant. Business has been good, and Gianna is considering expanding the restaurant. Gianna, who knows little accounting, produced the following financial statements for Little Italy, Inc., at December 31, 20X7, the end of the first month of operations: LO 2

A1

	A	B	C
1	**Little Italy, Inc. Income Statement Month Ended December 31, 20X7**		
2	Sales revenue		$ 42,000
3	Share capital		10,000
4	Total revenue		52,000
5			
6	Accounts payable		$ 8,000
7	Advertising expense		5,000
8	Rent expense		6,000
9	Total expenses		19,000
10	Net income		$ 33,000
11			

A1

	A	B	C
1	**Little Italy, Inc. Balance Sheet December 31, 20X7**		
2	Assets		
3	Cash		$ 12,000
4	Cost of goods sold (expense)		22,000
5	Food inventory		5,000
6	Furniture		10,000
7	Total Assets		$ 49,000
8	Liabilities		
9	None		
10	Owners' Equity		$ 49,000
11			

In these financial statements all *amounts* are correct, except for Owners' Equity. Gianna heard that total assets should equal total liabilities plus owners' equity, so she plugged in the amount of owners' equity at $49,000 to make the Balance Sheet come out even.

Requirement

1. Gianna Loren has asked whether she should expand the restaurant. Her banker says she may be wise to expand if (a) net income for the first month reached $10,000 and (b) total assets are at least $35,000. It appears that the business has reached these milestones, but Gianna doubts whether her financial statements tell the true story. She needs your help in making this decision. Prepare a corrected Income Statement and Balance Sheet. (Remember that Retained Earnings, which was omitted from the Balance Sheet, should equal net income for the first month; there were no dividends.) After preparing the statements, give Gianna Loren your recommendation as to whether she should expand the restaurant.

Ethical Issues

Issue 1. Scruffy Murphy is the president and principal shareholder of Scruffy's Bar & Grill, Inc. To expand, the business is applying for a $250,000 bank loan. To get the loan, Murphy is considering two options for beefing up the owners' equity of the business:

Option 1. Issue $100,000 of ordinary shares for cash. A friend has been wanting to invest in the company. This may be the right time to extend the offer.
Option 2. Transfer $100,000 of Murphy's personal land to the business, and issue ordinary shares to Murphy. Then, after obtaining the loan, Murphy can transfer the land back to himself and zero out the ordinary shares.

Requirements

Use the ethical decision model (in Chapter 1) to answer the following questions:

1. What is the ethical issue?
2. Who are the stakeholders? What are the possible consequences to each?
3. Analyze the alternatives from the following standpoints: (a) economic, (b) legal, and (c) ethical.
4. What would you do? How would you justify your decision? How would your decision make you feel afterward?

Issue 2. Part a. You have received your grade in your first accounting course, and to your amazement, it is an A. You feel the instructor must have made a big mistake. Your grade was a B going into the final, but you are sure that you really "bombed" the exam, which is worth 30% of the final grade. In fact, you walked out after finishing only 50% of the exam, and the grade report says you made 99% on the exam!

Requirements

1. What is the ethical issue?
2. Who are the stakeholders? What are the possible consequences to each?
3. Analyze the alternatives from the following standpoints: (a) economic, (b) legal, and (c) ethical.
4. What would you do? How would you justify your decision? How would it make you feel afterward?

Part b. Now assume the same facts as above, except that you have received your final grade for the course and the grade is a B. You are confident that you "aced" the final. In fact, you stayed to the very end of the period, and checked every figure twice! You are confident that the instructor must have made a mistake grading the final.

Requirements

1. What is the ethical issue?
2. Who are the stakeholders and what are the consequences to each?
3. Analyze the alternatives from the following standpoints: (a) economic, (b) legal, and (c) ethical.
4. What would you do? How would you justify your decision? How would it make you feel?

Part c. How is this situation like a financial accounting misstatement? How is it different?

Focus on Financials: | Nestlé

This case spans all 12 chapters and is based on the consolidated financial statements of Nestlé. As you work with Nestlé throughout this course, you will develop the confidence and ability to use the financial statements of other companies as well. Refer to Nestlé's financial statements in Appendix A. Alternatively, you may choose to obtain the full annual report from www.nestle.com/investors. You may find the information overwhelming for now, but try to spot the key principles that we have discussed in this chapter. It will get progressively easier as you gain familiarity with the elements of the financial statements.

Assume that Nestlé completed the following transactions during 2016:

a. Made company sales (revenue) of CHF 89,310 million, all on account.
b. Collected cash on trade receivable CHF 89,310 million.
c. Purchased inventories, paying cash of CHF 44,447 million.
d. Incurred cost of sales in the amount of CHF 44,199 million (debit Cost of Goods Sold [Expense] and credit Inventory).
e. Paid in cash distribution expenses of CHF 8,059 million.
f. Paid in cash marketing and administrative expenses of CHF 21,485 million.
g. Collected other income of CHF 99 million in cash.
h. Paid income tax expenses of CHF 4,413 million in cash.
i. Incurred other non-cash expenses of CHF 713 million, to be recorded as "accrued expenses."
j. Purchased other assets in cash for £6,982 million.

Requirements

1. Set up T-accounts for Cash (beginning debit balance of CHF 4,884 million); Trade Receivables, (debit balance of CHF 12,252 million); Inventories (debit balance CHF 8,153 million); Sales (CHF 0 balance); Cost of Sales (CHF 0 balance); Distribution expenses (CHF 0 balance); Marketing and administrative expenses (CHF 0 balance); Other income (CHF 0 balance); Income tax expense (CHF 0 balance); and Other non-cash expenses (CHF 0 balance).
2. Journalize Nestlé's transactions a–j. Explanations are not required.
3. Post to the T-accounts, and compute the balance for each account. Key postings by transaction letters a–j.
4. For each of the following accounts, compare your computed balance to Nestlé's actual balances as shown on its 2016 Income Statement or Balance Sheet in Appendix A. Note that in this question, "Other expenses" include Nestlé's other trading expenses, research and development costs, other operating expenses, financial expenses, and profit attributable to non-controlling interests. "Other income" includes Nestlé's other revenue, other trading income, other operating income, financial income, and income from associates and joint ventures. Your amounts should agree with the actual figures in Nestlé's financial statements.
   a. Cash
   b. Trade Receivable
   c. Inventories
   d. Sales
   e. Cost of Sales
   f. Selling and distribution expenses
   g. Administrative expenses
   h. Other income
   i. Income tax expense
   j. Other assets
5. Use the relevant accounts from requirement 4 to prepare a summary Income Statement for Nestlé for 2016. Compare the net income you computed to Nestlé's actual net income. The two amounts should be equal.

Group Projects

Project 1. You are promoting a rock concert in your area. Your purpose is to earn a profit, so you need to establish the formal structure of a business entity. Assume you organize as a corporation.

Requirements

1. Make a detailed list of 10 factors you must consider as you establish the business.
2. Describe 10 of the items your business must arrange to promote and stage the rock concert.
3. Identify the transactions that your business can undertake to organize, promote, and stage the concert. Journalize the transactions, and post to the relevant T-accounts. Set up the accounts you need for your business ledger. Refer to Appendix D if needed.
4. Prepare the Income Statement, statement of changes in equity, and Balance Sheet immediately after the rock concert, that is, before you have had time to pay all the business bills and to collect all receivables.
5. Assume that you will continue to promote rock concerts if the venture is successful. If it is unsuccessful, you will terminate the business within three months after the concert. Discuss how to evaluate the success of your venture and how to decide whether to continue in business.

Project 2. Contact a local business and arrange with the owner to learn what accounts the business uses.

Requirements

1. Obtain a copy of the business's chart of accounts.
2. Prepare the company's financial statements for the most recent month, quarter, or year. You may use either made-up account balances or balances supplied by the owner.

If the business has a large number of accounts within a category, combine related accounts and report a single amount on the financial statements. For example, the company may have several cash accounts. Combine all cash amounts and report a single Cash amount on the Balance Sheet.

You will probably encounter numerous accounts that you have not yet learned. Deal with these as best you can. The charts of accounts given in Appendix D can be helpful.

Quick Check Answers

1. *c*
2. *b*
3. *b*
4. *a* ($1,700 + 700 – 200)
5. *c*
6. *d*
7. *b* ($8,000 + x – 24,000 = 12,000; x = 28,000)
8. *a*
9. *a*
10. *a*
11. *a*
12. *b*

MyLab Accounting

For online homework, exercises, and problems that provide you with immediate feedback, please visit www.myaccountinglab.com.

Demo Doc

Debit/Credit Transaction Analysis

To make sure you understand this material, work through the following demonstration "Demo Doc" with detailed comments to help you see the concept within the framework of a worked-through problem.

Learning Objectives 1, 2, 3, 4

On September 1, 20X6, Michael Moe incorporated Moe's Mowing, Inc., a company that provides mowing and landscaping services. During the month of September, the business incurred the following transactions:

a. To begin operations, Michael deposited $10,000 cash in the business's bank account. The business received the cash and issued shares to Michael.

b. The business purchased equipment for $3,500 on account.

c. The business purchased office supplies for $800 cash.

d. The business provided $2,600 of landscaping works to a customer on account.

e. The business paid $500 cash toward the equipment previously purchased on account in transaction b.

f. The business received $2,000 in cash for services provided to a new customer.

g. The business paid $200 cash to repair equipment.

h. The business paid $900 cash for September's salary expense.

i. The business received a utilities bill amounting to $150; it has not paid this bill.

j. The business received $2,100 cash from a customer on account.

k. The business paid cash dividends of $1,500.

➤ Requirements

1. Create blank T-accounts for the following accounts: Cash, Accounts Receivable, Supplies, Equipment, Accounts Payable, Utilities Payable, Share Capital, Dividends, Service Revenue, Salary Expense, Repair Expense.
2. Journalize the transactions and then post to the T-accounts. Use the table in Exhibit 2-16 to help with the journal entries.

Exhibit 2-16 | The Rules of Debit and Credit

	Increase	Decrease
Assets	debit	credit
Liabilities	credit	debit
Shareholders' Equity	credit	debit
Revenues	credit	debit
Expenses	debit	credit
Dividends	debit	credit

3. Total each T-account to determine its balance at the end of the month.
4. Prepare the trial balance of Moe's Mowing, Inc., at September 30, 20X6.

Demo Doc Solutions

➤ Requirement 1

Create blank T-accounts for the following accounts: Cash, Accounts Receivable, Supplies, Equipment, Accounts Payable, Share Capital, Dividends, Service Revenue, Salary Expense, Repair Expense.

Part 1	Part 2	Part 3	Part 4	Demo Doc Complete

ASSETS = LIABILITIES + SHAREHOLDERS' EQUITY

Cash

Accounts Payable

Share Capital

Utilities Payable

Dividends

REVENUE

Service Revenue

Accounts Receivable

EXPENSES

Supplies

Salary Expense

Equipment

Repair Expense

Utilities Expense

Opening a T-account means drawing a blank account that looks like a capital "T" and putting the account title across the top. T-accounts show the additions and subtractions made to each account. For easy reference, the accounts are grouped into assets, liabilities, shareholders' equity, revenue, and expenses (in that order).

➤ Requirement 2

Journalize the transactions and show how they are recorded in T-accounts.

Part 1	Part 2	Part 3	Part 4	Demo Doc Complete

a. To begin operations, Michael deposited $10,000 cash in the business's bank account. The business received the cash and issued shares to Michael.

First, we must determine which accounts are affected by the transaction.

The business received $10,000 cash from its principal shareholder (Michael Moe). In exchange, the business issued shares to Michael. So, the accounts involved are Cash and Share Capital.

Remember that we are recording the transactions of Moe's Mowing, Inc., not the transactions of Michael Moe, the person. Michael and his business are two entirely separate accounting entities.

The next step is to determine what type of accounts these are. Cash is an asset; share capital is part of equity.

Next, we must determine if these accounts increased or decreased. From the business's point of view, Cash (an asset) has increased. Share Capital (equity) has also increased.

Now we must determine if these accounts should be debited or credited. According to the rules of debit and credit (see Exhibit 2-16), an increase in assets is a debit, while an increase in equity is a credit.

So, Cash (an asset) increases, which requires a debit. Share Capital (equity) also increases, which requires a credit.

The journal entry follows ordinary shares.

A1

		A	B	C	D	E
1	a	Cash (Asset ↑; debit)	10,000			
2		Share Capital (Equity ↑; credit)		10,000		
3		*Issued ordinary shares.*				
4						

The total dollar amounts of debits must always equal the total dollar amounts of credits.

Remember to use the transaction letters as references. This will help as we post entries to the T-accounts.

Each T-account has two sides—one for recording debits and the other for recording credits. To post the transaction to a T-account, simply transfer the amount of each debit to the correct account as a debit (left-side) entry, and transfer the amount of each credit to the correct account as a credit (right-side) entry.

This transaction includes a debit of $10,000 to cash. This means that $10,000 is posted to the left side of the Cash T-account. The transaction also includes a credit of $10,000 to Share Capital. This means that $10,000 is posted to the right side of the Share Capital account, as follows:

Cash	
a. 10,000	

Share Capital	
	a. 10,000

Now the first transaction has been journalized and posted. We repeat this process for every journal entry. Let's proceed to the next transaction.

b. The business purchased equipment for $3,500 on account.

The business received equipment in exchange for a promise to pay for the $3,500 cost at a future date. So the accounts involved in the transaction are Equipment and Accounts Payable.

Equipment is an asset and Accounts Payable is a liability.

The asset Equipment has increased. The liability Accounts Payable has also increased.

Looking at Exhibit 2-16, an increase in assets (in this case, the increase in Equipment) is a debit, while an increase in liabilities (in this case, Accounts Payable) is a credit.

The journal entry follows.

A1

		A	B	C	D	E
1	b	Equipment (Asset↑; debit)	3,500			
2		Accounts Payable (Liability↑; credit)		3,500		
3		*Purchased equipment on account.*				
4						

$3,500 is then posted to the debit (left) side of the Equipment T-account. $3,500 is posted to the credit (right) side of Accounts Payable, as follows:

Equipment	
b. 3,500	

Accounts Payable	
	b. 3,500

c. The business purchased office supplies for $800 cash.

The business purchased supplies, paying cash of $800. So the accounts involved in the transaction are Supplies and Cash.

Supplies and Cash are both assets.

Supplies (an asset) has increased. Cash (an asset) has decreased.

Looking at Exhibit 2-16, an increase in assets is a debit, while a decrease in assets is a credit.

So the increase to Supplies (an asset) is a debit, while the decrease to Cash (an asset) is a credit.

The journal entry follows:

A1

		A	B	C	D	E
1	c	Supplies (Asset↑; debit)	800			
2		Cash (Asset↓; credit)		800		
3		*Purchased supplies for cash.*				
4						

$800 is then posted to the debit (left) side of the Supplies T-account. $800 is posted to the credit (right) side of the Cash account, as follows:

Cash				Supplies			
a.	10,000	c.	800	c.	800		

Notice the $10,000 already on the debit side of the Cash account. This came from transaction a.

d. The business provided $2,600 of landscaping work to a customer on account.

The business rendered landscaping services to a customer and received a promise from the customer to pay $2,600 cash next month. So the accounts involved in the transaction are Accounts Receivable and Service Revenue.

Accounts Receivable is an asset and Service Revenue is revenue.

Accounts Receivable (an asset) has increased. Service Revenue (revenue) has also increased.

Looking at Exhibit 2-16, an increase in assets is a debit, while an increase in revenue is a credit.

So the increase to Accounts Receivable (an asset) is a debit, while the increase to Service Revenue (revenue) is a credit.

The journal entry follows.

A1

		A	B	C	D	E
1	d	Accounts Receivable (Asset ↑; debit)	2,600			
2		Service Revenue (Revenue ↑; credit)		2,600		
3		*Provided services on account.*				
4						

$2,600 is posted to the debit (left) side of the Accounts Receivable T-account. $2,600 is posted to the credit (right) side of the Service Revenue account, as follows:

Accounts Receivable				Service Revenue			
d.	2,600					d.	2,600

e. The business paid $500 cash toward the equipment previously purchased on account in transaction b.

The business paid some of the money that it owed on the purchase of equipment in transaction b. The accounts involved in the transaction are Accounts Payable and Cash.

Accounts Payable is a liability that has decreased. Cash is an asset that has also decreased.

Remember that Accounts Payable shows the amount the business must pay in the future (a liability). When the business pays these creditors, Accounts Payable will decrease because the business will then owe less (in this case, Accounts Payable drops from $3,500—in transaction b—to $3,000).

Looking at Exhibit 2-16, a decrease in liabilities is a debit, while a decrease in assets is a credit.

So Accounts Payable (a liability) decreases, which is a debit. Cash (an asset) decreases, which is a credit.

		A	B	C	D	E
1	e	Accounts Payable (Liability↓; debit)	500			
2		Cash (Asset↓; credit)		500		
3		*Partial payment on account.*				
4						

$500 is posted to the debit (left) side of the Accounts Payable T-account. $500 is posted to the credit (right) side of the Cash account, as follows:

Cash

a.	10,000	c.	800
		e.	500

Accounts Payable

e.	500	b.	3,500

Again notice the amounts already in the T-accounts from previous transactions. The reference letters show which transaction caused each amount to appear in the T-account.

f. The business received $2,000 in cash for services provided to a new customer.

The business received $2,000 cash in exchange for mowing and landscaping services rendered to a customer. The accounts involved in the transaction are Cash and Service Revenue.

Cash is an asset that has increased, and Service Revenue is revenue, which has also increased.

Looking at Exhibit 2-16, an increase in assets is a debit, while an increase in revenue is a credit.

So the increase to Cash (an asset) is a debit. The increase to Service Revenue (revenue) is a credit.

		A	B	C	D	E
1	f	Cash (Asset↑; debit)	2,000			
2		Service Revenue (Revenue↑; credit)		2,000		
3		*Provided services for cash.*				
4						

$2,000 is then posted to the debit (left) side of the Cash T-account. $2,000 is posted to the credit (right) side of the Service Revenue account, as follows:

Cash

a.	10,000	c.	800
f.	2,000	e.	500

Service Revenue

d.	2,600
f.	2,000

Notice how we keep adding onto the T-accounts. The values from previous transactions remain in their places.

g. The business paid $200 cash to repair equipment.

The business paid $200 cash to have equipment repaired. Because the benefit of the repairs has already been used, the repairs are recorded as Repair Expense. Because the repairs were paid in cash, the Cash account is also involved.

Repair Expense is an expense that has increased, and Cash is an asset that has decreased.

Looking at Exhibit 2-16, an increase in expenses calls for a debit, while a decrease in an asset requires a credit.

		A	B	C	D	E
1	g	Repair Expense (Expense ↑; debit)	200			
2		Cash (Asset ↓; credit)		200		
3		*Paid for repairs.*				
4						

So Repair Expense (an expense) increases, which is a debit. Cash (an asset) decreases, which is a credit.

$200 is then posted to the debit (left) side of the Repair Expense T-account. $200 is posted to the credit (right) side of the Cash account, as follows:

Cash

	Debit		Credit
a.	10,000	c.	800
f.	2,000	e.	500
		g.	200

Repair Expense

	Debit		Credit
g.	200		

h. The business paid $900 cash for September's salary expense.

The business paid employees $900 in cash. Because the benefit of the employees' work has already been used, their salaries are recorded as Salary Expense. Because the salaries were paid in cash, the Cash account is also involved.

Salary Expense is an expense that has increased, and Cash is an asset that has decreased.

Looking at Exhibit 2-16, an increase in expenses is a debit, while a decrease in an asset is a credit.

In this case, Salary Expense (an expense) increases, which is a debit. Cash (an asset) decreases, which is a credit.

		A	B	C	D	E
1	h	Salary Expense (Expense ↑; debit)	900			
2		Cash (Asset ↓; credit)		900		
3		*Paid salary.*				
4						

$900 is posted to the debit (left) side of the Salary Expense T-account. $900 is posted to the credit (right) side of the Cash account, as follows:

Cash

	Debit		Credit
a.	10,000	c.	800
f.	2,000	e.	500
		g.	200
		h.	900

Salary Expense

	Debit		Credit
h.	900		

i. The business received a utilities bill amounting to $150; it has not paid this bill.

The business received a bill for benefits consumed during the period but has not paid this bill as of September 30, 20X6. This amount owed is a liability and it decreases equity, and thus must be recognized as an expense. We will discuss the accrual accounting concept in more detail later (see Chapter 3).

The accounts affected by this transaction are Utilities Payable and Utilities Expense. The liability account Utilities Payable has increased, and the expense Utilities Expense has increased. Note that we use a different liability account ("Utility Payable" as opposed to the general "Accounts Payable") to signify the specific liability. Accounts Payable is typically used when we purchase assets or services on account. Looking at Exhibit 2-16, an increase in expense is a debit, and an increase in liability is a credit.

A1

		A	B	C	D	E
1	i	Utilities Expense (Expense ↑; debit)	150			
2		Utilities Payable (Liability ↑; credit)		150		
3		*Received utilities bill (unpaid).*				
4						

$150 is posted to the debit (left) side of the Utilities Expense T-account, and the other $150 is posted to the credit (right) side of the Utilities Payable account, as follows:

Utilities Payable		Utilities Expense	
	i. 150	i. 150	

j. The business received $2,100 cash from a customer on account.

The business received cash of $2,100 from a customer for services previously provided in transaction d. The accounts affected by this transaction are Cash and Accounts Receivable.

Cash and Accounts Receivable are both assets.

The asset Cash has increased, and the asset Accounts Receivable has decreased.

Remember, Accounts Receivable shows the amount of cash the business has coming from customers. When the business receives cash from these customers, Accounts Receivable will decrease, because the business will have less to receive in the future (in this case, it reduces from $2,600—in transaction d—to $500).

Looking at Exhibit 2-16, an increase in assets is a debit, while a decrease in assets is a credit.

So Cash (an asset) increases, which is a debit. Accounts Receivable (an asset) decreases, which is a credit.

A1

		A	B	C	D	E
1	j	Cash (Asset ↑; debit)	2,100			
2		Accounts Receivable (Asset ↓; credit)		2,100		
3		*Received cash on account.*				
4						

$2,100 is posted to the debit (left) side of the Cash T-account. $2,100 is posted to the credit (right) side of the Accounts Receivable account, as follows:

Cash			
a.	10,000	c.	800
f.	2,000	e.	500
i.	2,100	g.	200
		h.	900

Accounts Receivable			
d.	2,600	j.	2,100

k. The business declared and paid cash dividends of $1,500.

The business paid Michael dividends from the earnings it had retained on his behalf. This caused Michael's ownership interest (equity) to decrease. The accounts involved in this transaction are Dividends and Cash.

Dividends have increased and Cash is an asset that has decreased.

Looking at Exhibit 2-16, an increase in dividends is a debit, while a decrease in an asset is a credit.

Remember that Dividends are a negative element of shareholders' equity. Therefore, when Dividends increase, shareholders' equity decreases. So in this case, Dividends decrease equity with a debit. Cash (an asset) decreases with a credit.

A1

		A	B	C	D	E
1	k	Dividends (Dividends ↑; debit) ↓ SE	1,500			
2		Cash (Asset ↓; credit)		1,500		
3		*Paid dividends.*				
4						

$1,500 is posted to the debit (left) side of the Dividends T-account. $1,500 is posted to the credit (right) side of the Cash account, as follows:

Cash			
a.	10,000	c.	800
f.	2,000	e.	500
i.	2,100	g.	200
		h.	900
		k.	1,500

Dividends			
k.	1,500		

Now we can summarize all of the journal entries during the month.

	A	B	C	D
1	**Ref.**	**Accounts and Explanation**	**Debit**	**Credit**
2	a	Cash	10,000	
3		Share capital		10,000
4		*Issued share capital.*		
5				
6	b	Equipment	3,500	
7		Accounts payable		3,500
8		*Purchased equipment on account.*		
9				
10	c	Supplies	800	
11		Cash		800
12		*Purchased supplies for cash.*		
13				
14	d	Accounts receivable	2,600	
15		Service revenue		2,600
16		*Provided services on account.*		
17				
18	e	Account payable	500	
19		Cash		500
20		*Partial payment on account.*		
21				
22	f	Cash	2,000	
23		Service revenue		2,000
24		*Provided services for cash.*		
25				
26	g	Repair expense	200	
27		Cash		200
28		*Paid for repairs.*		
29				
30	h	Salary expense	900	
31				900
32		*Paid salary.*		
33				
34	i	DR utilities expense	150	
35		Utilities payable		150
36		*Received utilities bill (not paid).*		
37				
38	j	Cash	2,100	
39		Accounts receivable		2,100
40		*Received cash on account.*		
41				
42	k	Dividends	1,500	
43		Cash		1,500
44		*Paid dividends.*		
45				

➤ Requirement 3

Total each T-account to determine its balance at the end of the month.

Part 1	Part 2	**Part 3**	Part 4	Demo Doc Complete

To compute the balance in a T-account (total the T-account), add up the numbers on the debit/left side of the account and (separately) add the credit/right side of the account. The difference between the total debits and the total credits is the account's balance, which is placed on the side that holds the larger total. This gives the balance in the T-account.

For example, for the Cash account, the numbers on the debit/left side total \$10,000 + \$2,000 + \$2,100 = \$14,100. The credit/right side = \$800 + \$500 + \$200 + \$900 + \$1,500 = \$3,900. The difference is \$14,100 – \$3,900 = \$10,200. At the end of the period Cash has a debit balance of \$10,200. We put the \$10,200 at the bottom of the debit side because that was the side that showed the bigger total (\$14,100). This is called a debit balance.

An easy way to think of totaling T-accounts is:

Beginning balance in a T-account
+ Increases to the T-account
– Decreases to the T-account
T-account balance (net total)

T-accounts after posting all transactions and totaling each account are as follows:

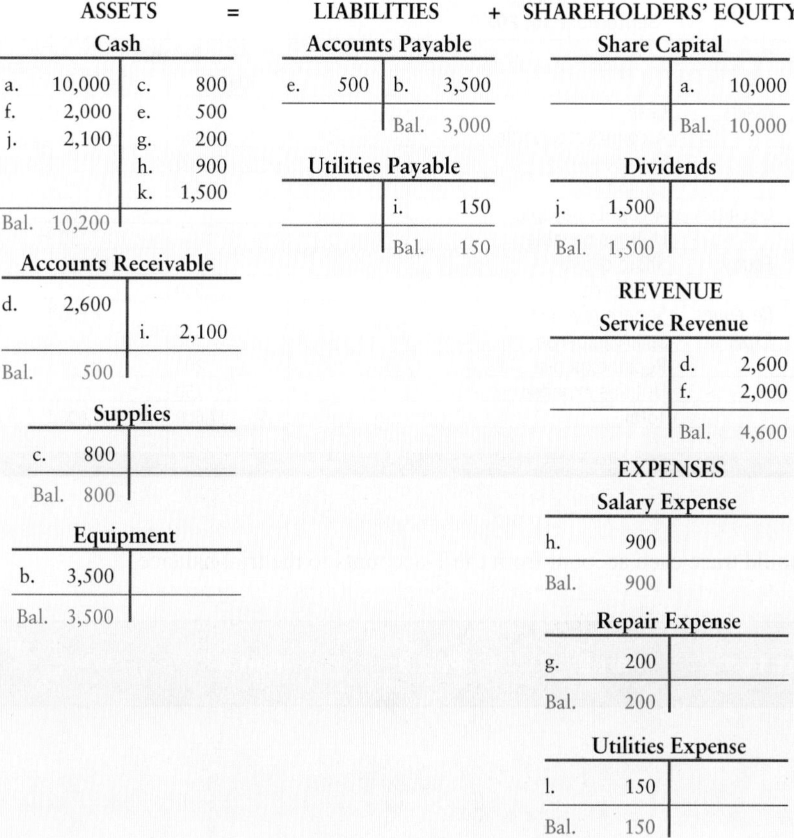

➤ Requirement 4

Part 1	Part 2	Part 3	Part 4	Demo Doc Complete

The trial balance lists all the accounts along with their balances. This listing is helpful because it summarizes all the accounts in one place. Otherwise one must plow through all the T-accounts to find the balance of Accounts Payable, Salary Expense, or any other account.

The trial balance is an *internal* accounting document that accountants and managers use to prepare the financial statements. It's not like the Income Statement and Balance Sheet, which are presented to the public.

Data for the trial balance come directly from the T-accounts that we prepared in Requirement 3. A debit balance in a T-account remains a debit in the trial balance, and likewise for credits. For example, the T-account for Cash shows a debit balance of $10,200, and the trial balance lists Cash the same way. The Accounts Payable T-account shows a $3,000 credit balance, and the trial balance lists Accounts Payable correctly.

The trial balance for Moe's Mowing at September 30, 20X6, appears as follows. Notice that we list the accounts in their proper order—assets, liabilities, shareholder's equity, revenues, and expenses.

	A		B	C	D	E
1	**Moe's Mowing, Inc.** **Trial Balance** **September 30, 20X6**					
2			**Balance**			
3			**Debit**	**Credit**		
4	*Assets*	Cash	$ 10,200			
5		Accounts receivable	500			
6		Supplies	800			
7		Equipment	3,500			
8	*Liabilities*	Accounts payable		$ 3,000		
9		Utilities payable		150		
10	*Equity*	Share capital		10,000		
11		Dividends	1,500			
12	*Revenues*	Service revenue		4,600		
13	*Expenses*	Salary expense	900			
14		Repair expense	200			
15		Utilities expense	150			
16		Total	$ 17,600	$ 17,600		
17						

You should trace each account from the T-accounts to the trial balance.

3 Accrual Accounting

 SPOTLIGHT | Richemont www.richemont.com

You may not have heard of Richemont, but its products and brands are among the most recognized in the world. From jewelry (Cartier), to watches (Montblanc, Jaeger-LeCoultre, Piaget, Baume & Mercier), to Alfred Dunhill, Shanghai Tang, Chloé, and net-a-porter.com (the world's premier online luxury fashion retailer), these are all products and brands of Richemont. Founded in 1988, Richemont is a spin-off of the Rembrandt Group, South Africa, and it is the second largest luxury goods company in the world. Richemont is listed on the SIX (Swiss) and JSE (South African) stock exchanges. ●

Peter Horree/Alamy Stock Photo

At the beginning of the 2016 fiscal year, Richemont started with cash (and cash equivalents) of €5,654 million. During the fiscal year, Richemont made a net profit of €2,227 million from sales of €11,076 million. However, it ended the fiscal year with less cash and cash equivalents at €4,569 million. How is this possible?

Cash and profits are not the same thing. You may have used part of your profits to pay for new assets; you may have collected cash in advance from your customers; you may have expenses that you have not paid or prepaid some expenses ahead of utilizing them.

We use accrual accounting in financial reporting because it is a better measure of performance than cash payments and receipts. Let's find out more about accrual accounting!

A1

	A	B	C
1	**Compagnie Financière Richemont Consolidated Income Statement**	**Financial Year Ended March 31**	
2	**(Adapted, in millions of €)**	**March 31, 2016**	**March 31, 2015**
3	**Sales**	€ 11,076	€ 10,410
4	Cost of sales	(3,958)	(3,534)
5	Gross profit	7,118	6,876
6	Selling and distribution expenses	(2,950)	(2,554)
7	Communication expenses	(1,093)	(1,010)
8	Administrative expenses	(992)	(874)
9	Other operating income/(expense)	(22)	232
10	Operating profit	2,061	2,670
11	Finance costs	(166)	(972)
12	Finance income	168	19
13	Other income/(expenses)	534	(14)
14	Income taxes	(370)	(369)
15	**Profit for the year**	€ 2,227	€ 1,334
16			

	A	B	C
1	**Compagnie Financière Richemont Consolidated Statement of Financial Position**	**At March 31**	
2	**(Adapted, in millions of €)**	**March 31, 2016**	**March 31, 2015**
3	Cash and cash equivalents	€ 4,569	€ 5,654
4	Inventories	5,345	5,438
5	Trade and other receivables	1,021	1,071
6	Prepayments	135	140
7	All other current assets	3,288	3,625
8	Total current assets	14,358	15,928
9	Property, plant and equipment	2,476	2,446
10	Intangible assets	712	781
11	Investment property	191	70
12	All other non-current assets	2,388	1,225
13	Total non-current assets	5,767	4,522
14	Total assets	€ 20,125	€ 20,450
15	Trade and other payables	1,526	1,514
16	Provisions	211	277
17	Loans and borrowings	2,098	2,688
18	All other current liabilities	361	609
19	Total current liabilities	4,196	5,088
20	Loans and borrowings	379	405
21	All other non-current liabilities	503	537
22	Total non-current liabilities	882	942
23	Total liabilities	5,078	6,030
24	Share capital	334	334
25	Retained earnings	12,111	10,854
26	Other equity items	2,602	3,232
27	Total equity	15,047	14,420
28	Total liabilities and equity	€ 20,125	€ 20,450
29			

	A	B	C
1	**Compagnie Financière Richemont Consolidated Statement of Cash Flows**	**Financial Year Ended March 31**	
2	**(Adapted, in millions of €)**	**Dec. 31, 2016**	**Dec. 31, 2015**
3	Net cash from operating activities	€ 1,964	€ 1,704
4	Net cash used in investing activities	(1,287)	(343)
5	Net cash used in financing activities	(1,201)	(642)
6	Net cash flows	(524)	719
7	Effect of exchange rates	(80)	219
8	Beginning cash and cash equivalents	3,152	2,214
9	Ending cash and cash equivalents	€ 2,548	€ 3,152
10			

This chapter will complete our coverage of the accounting cycle. It will provide the basics of what you need before tackling individual topics such as receivables, inventory, PPEs, and liabilities.

LEARNING OBJECTIVES

1 **Explain** how accrual accounting differs from cash-basis accounting

2 **Apply** the revenue and expense recognition principles

3 **Adjust** the accounts

4 **Prepare** updated financial statements

5 **Close** the books

EXPLAIN HOW ACCRUAL ACCOUNTING DIFFERS FROM CASH-BASIS ACCOUNTING

1 **Explain** how accrual accounting differs from cash-basis accounting

Shareholders want to earn a profit. Investors search for companies whose share prices will increase. Banks seek borrowers who will pay their debts. Accounting provides the information these people or institutions use for decision making. Accounting can be based on one of the following:

- Accrual basis
- Cash basis

Accrual accounting records the impact of business transactions and events on an entity's assets and liabilities over the period in which they occur, even if the resulting cash receipts or payments occur in a past or future period. For example, when a business performs a service, makes a sale, or incurs an expense, the accountant records the transaction even if it receives or pays no cash at the time of the transaction.

Cash-basis accounting records only cash transactions—cash receipts and cash payments. Cash receipts are treated as revenues, and cash payments are handled as expenses. Profits are earned when cash receipts are greater than cash payments, and similarly, losses are incurred when cash receipts are less than cash payments.

To illustrate the difference between the two bases of accounting, consider the following example. Richemont sells inventory produced at the cost of €500 to a customer for €800 on account. The customer promises to pay in 60 days' time. Accrual accounting would recognize the €800 as income because making the sale increases Richemont's wealth and Richemont now has the right to some future economic benefits (in the form of receivables, an asset). The eventual payment is merely an exchange of one asset (receivable) for another (cash) and has no impact on Richemont's income. Cash accounting, on the other hand, will not record a sale as there was no exchange of cash at the time of the sale. Only when cash is received (60 days later) will cash basis accounting record the transaction.

Cash accounting fails to capture the underlying economic phenomenon. First, the €800 receivable represents a claim to receive cash in the future, which is an asset, and it should appear on the Balance Sheet. Without it, assets are understated. Second, the increase in assets also results in an increase in equity and should be recognized as income. Without it, income is understated.

Suppose Richemont paid a portion of the office rent prior to the actual occupation. Cash may have been paid, but has Richemont actually incurred the expense? Obviously not. If you look at Richemont's Balance Sheet at the start of this chapter, you will see on line 6, prepayments totaling €135 million. These are monies paid to various parties that continue to represent future economic benefits to Richemont, and are thus accounted for as an asset. As the prepayments are consumed, Richemont will recognize a reduction of assets and an increase in expense. Cash accounting would have treated all payments as expenses, i.e., understating assets and overstating expenses.

On the other hand, Richemont may have consumed economic benefits without paying for them. It will "accrue" (more on this later) these obligations as liabilities. Richemont also collected money in advance of selling its merchandise.

The take-away lessons from this discussion are as follows:

- Virtually all businesses use the accrual basis of accounting as required by financial reporting standards.

- Entities that use the cash basis of accounting do not follow accounting standards. Their financial statements omit important information and thus are less relevant to users of financial statements.

We are not saying that cash flows are not important, they are! However, in measuring financial performance and financial position, accrual accounting gives us a better understanding of how businesses actually perform during a financial period. We will look at cash flows in more detail later (in Chapter 11).

Accrual Accounting and Cash Flows

Accrual accounting is a more faithful representation of economic reality than cash-basis accounting. To be sure, accrual accounting records cash transactions, such as the following:

- Collecting cash from customers
- Receiving cash from interest earned
- Paying salaries, rent, and other expenses
- Borrowing money
- Paying off loans
- Issuing shares

But accrual accounting also records *noncash* transactions, such as the following:

- Sales on account
- Purchases of inventory on account
- Accrual of expenses incurred but not yet paid
- Depreciation expense
- Usage of prepaid rent, insurance, and supplies
- Earning of revenue when cash was collected in advance

Remember that the *Conceptual Framework* tells us that profit is determined by income and expense. Excluding transactions with owners (such as additional capital contributions or dividend payments), income is further defined as increases in equity in the form of inflows, enhancements of assets, or decreases in liabilities, and expense is defined as a decrease in equity in the form of outflows, depletion of assets, or incurrence of liabilities.

To use accrual accounting, we need to understand a few more concepts. We turn now to the time-period concept, the revenue recognition principle, and the expense recognition principle.

The Time-Period Concept

The only way for a business to know for certain how well it has performed is to shut down, sell the assets, pay the liabilities, and return any leftover cash to the owners. This process, called liquidation, means going out of business. Ongoing companies cannot close down operations just to measure income! Instead, they need regular progress reports. Accountants, therefore, prepare financial statements for specific periods. The **time-period concept** ensures that accounting information is reported at regular intervals.

IAS 1 – Presentation of Financial Statements requires an entity to present a complete set of financial statements (including comparative information, as appropriate) at least annually. This is why you have been looking at extracts of *annual* reports of companies at the start of every chapter.

Companies also prepare financial statements for interim periods of less than a year, such as a month, a quarter (three months), or a half-yearly period (six months). Usually, this is a requirement of the stock exchange where the company is listed. In general, as a company gets larger, it may be subjected to more frequent reporting requirements. Most of the discussions in this text are based on an annual accounting period.

APPLY THE REVENUE AND EXPENSE RECOGNITION PRINCIPLES

The Revenue Recognition Principle

2 **Apply** the revenue and expense recognition principles

When should you recognize, i.e., record, revenue? In short, when you "earn" revenue. It sounds simple, but revenue recognition can be a very contentious topic. Think about the things you buy (music DVDs, electronic gadgets, and clothes), the services you consume (a magazine, a World of Warcraft or Netflix subscription, and your tuition fees), and ask yourself when do the companies that provide you with these goods and/or services actually earn your money?

The basic guidance for the **revenue recognition principle** comes from *IAS 18 – Revenue*. In general, for the sale of goods, revenue is recognized when:

- the entity has transferred to the buyer the significant risks and rewards of ownership of the goods;
- the entity retains neither continuing managerial involvement to the degree usually associated with ownership nor effective control over the goods sold;
- the amount of revenue can be measured reliably;
- it is probable that the economic benefits associated with the transaction will flow to the entity; and
- the costs incurred or to be incurred in respect of the transaction can be measured reliably.

Thus, for consumer sales transactions, it is usually at the point of sale when you hand over your hard-earned cash in return for the goods you wish to purchase. Think about how such over-the-counter purchases would meet the *IAS 18* criteria above.

For services, similar principles apply. The only difference is that the services you engage may not be consumed at the same time. Revenue is, thus, earned by reference to a "stage of completion" of the transaction at the Balance Sheet date. For example, suppose you engaged Maersk, the world's biggest container-ship operator, to make 12 shipments of your goods and you paid the entire shipping fee, in advance, on November 1, 20X6. Should Maersk recognize the entire revenue for the 12 shipments when you sign the contract? No, it shouldn't. Maersk only earns the relevant shipping revenue when services are provided. Suppose by the end of the financial year on December 31, 20X6, Maersk shipped a total of eight consignments. Maersk's obligation has been partially satisfied. It now only owes you four more shipments. This reduction in liability increases equity. Maersk will report the remaining four shipments as its obligations on its Balance Sheet and the revenue for the eight shipments in its Income Statement. Stage of completion can also be estimated using time period, milestones (such as engineering estimates), or percentage of cost incurred in relation to total costs.

The *amount* of revenue to record is the fair value of the consideration received or receivable taking into account the amount of any trade discounts and volume rebates allowed by the entity. If the shipment fees for your 12 shipments totaled $10,000 and you were given a discount of 10%, Maersk should recognize a total of $6,000 at year ended December 31, 20X6, and a further $3,000 when the remaining shipments have been performed, say in February 20X7.

This revenue recognition example is depicted in Exhibit 3-1.

Exhibit 3-1 | When to Record Revenue

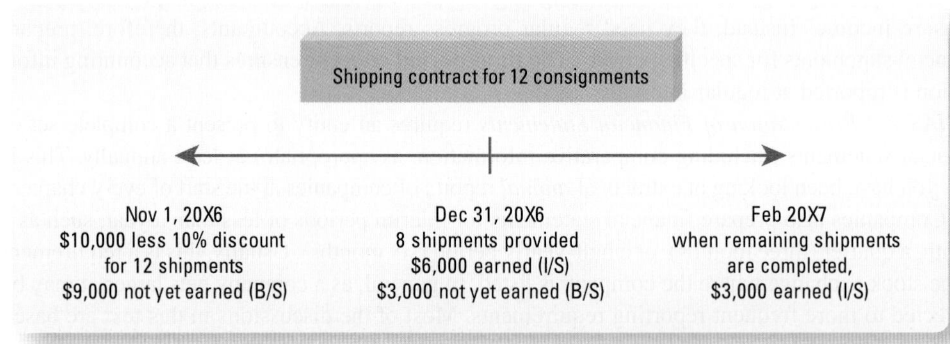

So, to conclude, when should you record revenue? After it has been earned—and not before. Revenue is earned when there is an increase in asset or reduction in liability that results in an increase in equity (excluding transactions with owners). In most cases, revenue is earned when a business delivers goods or services to its customer.

A Closer Look

A new accounting standard, *IFRS 15—Revenue from Contract from Customers*, will be effective for financial statements beginning January 1, 2018 (actual dates may vary in different jurisdictions). This is a major standard, jointly developed by the International Accounting Standards Board (IASB) and the Financial Accounting Standards Board (FASB). This new standard provides a single, joint revenue standard to be applied across all industries and capital markets.

The new standard is based on the core principle of "revenue is recognized to depict transfer of goods or services," which could be satisfied over time or at a point in time. The new standard proposes five steps of revenue recognition:

Step 1—Identify the contract with the customers
Step 2—Identify the performance obligations in the contract
Step 3—Determine the transaction price
Step 4—Allocate the transaction price
Step 5—Recognize revenue when (or as) a performance obligation is satisfied

While this standard will impact revenue recognition on some more complicated revenue transactions (such as multi-elements contracts), our discussions in this chapter will still be relevant under the new standards.

Every reporting entity must disclose its revenue recognition policy. You would find this in the notes to the accounts that accompany the financial statements. Here is Richemont's revenue recognition policy.

ADAPTED EXCERPTS FROM RICHEMONT'S NOTES TO THE FINANCIAL STATEMENTS

2.19. Revenue Recognition

(a) Goods

Sales revenue is measured at the fair value of the consideration received from the sale of goods, net of value-added tax, duties, other sales taxes, rebates and trade discounts, and after eliminating sales within the Group. Revenue is recognized when significant risks and rewards of ownership of the goods are transferred to the buyer. Where there is a practice of agreeing to customer returns, accumulated experience is used to estimate and provide for such returns at the time of sale.

(b) Interest income

Interest income is recognized on a time-proportion basis using the effective interest method.

(c) Royalty income

Royalty income is recognized on the accruals basis in accordance with the substance of the relevant agreements.

(d) Dividend income

Dividend income is recognized when the right to receive payment is established.

The Expense Recognition Principle

The **expense recognition principle** is the basis for recording expenses. Expenses are the costs of assets used up or liabilities incurred in earning income. Expenses have no future benefit to the business. Once you have identified and measured all the expenses, we match the expenses incurred to the associated revenue earned during the same period in order to obtain profit or loss.

The Matching Concept

The **matching concept** is used to explain the relationship between expenses and revenues. The *Conceptual Framework* states that expenses are recognized in the Income Statement on the basis of a direct association between the costs incurred and the earning of specific items of income. This process is commonly referred to as the "matching of costs with revenues." Unlike assets, expenses offer no future benefits to the company. Matching includes two steps:

1. Identify decreases in assets or increases in liabilities that result in a reduction in equity (excluding transactions with owners) during the period. These are expenses.
2. Measure these expenses, and subtract expenses from revenues to compute profit or loss.

Remember that the change in assets and liabilities determines profit or loss, not the application of a matching concept. You should not let the matching concept result in assets and liabilities (on the statement of financial position) that do not meet the definition of assets and liabilities as stated in the *Conceptual Framework*. Exhibit 3-2 illustrates the matching concept.

Exhibit 3-2 | The Matching Concept

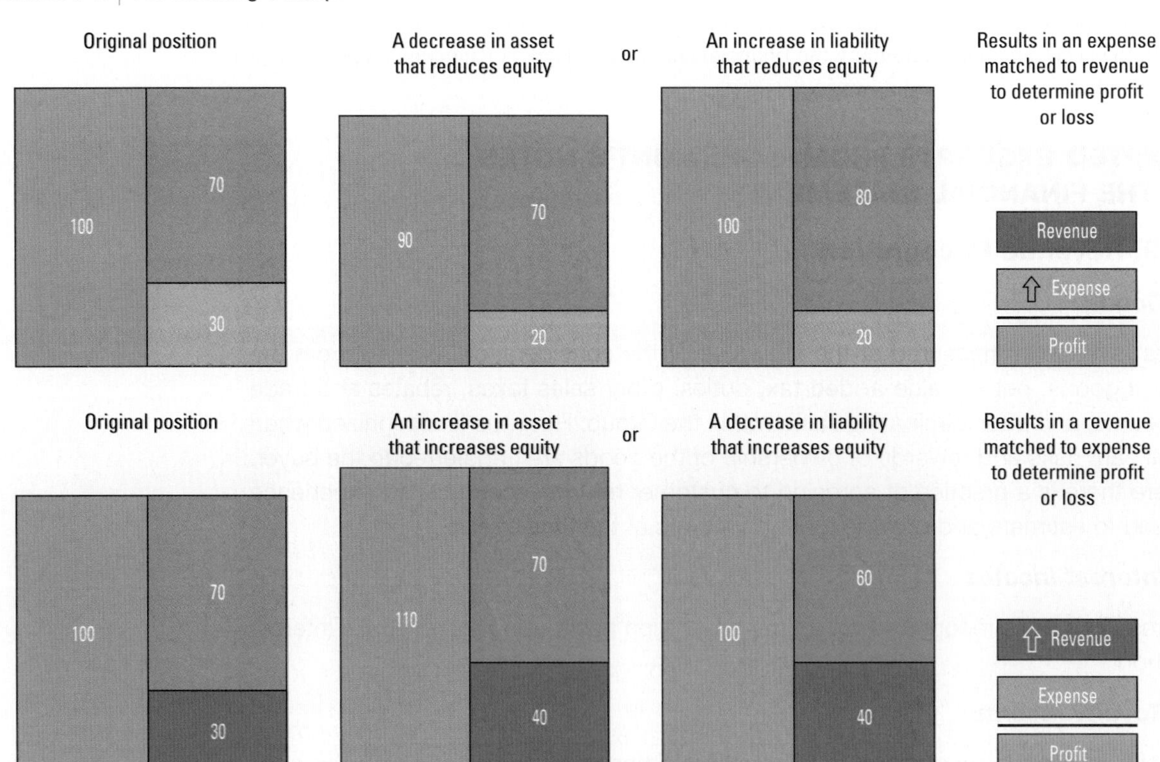

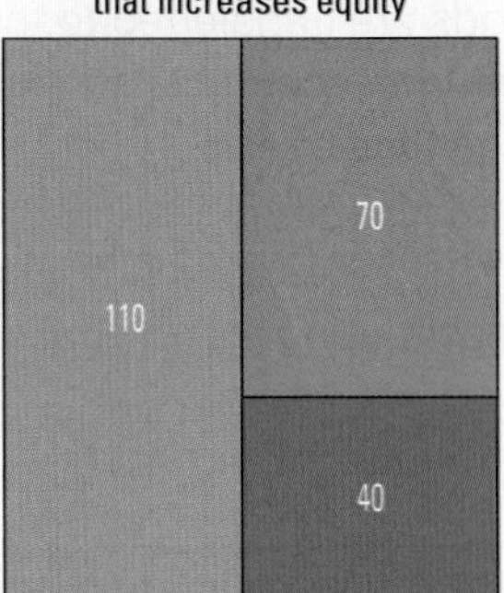

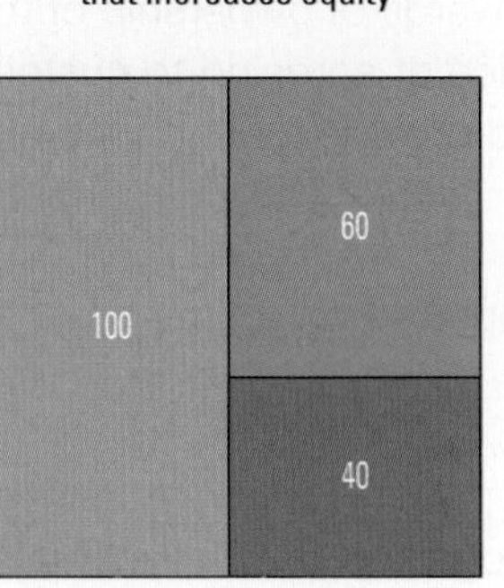

The authors thank Professor Mary Barth for her guidance on this topic.

Stop & Think

(1) A customer pays Maersk $1,000 on March 15 for a shipment in April. Has Maersk earned revenue on March 15? When will Maersk earn the revenue?

(2) Maersk pays $4,500 on July 1 for office rent for the next three months. Has Maersk incurred an expense on July 1?

Answers:

(1) No. Maersk has received the cash but will not perform the shipping services until later. Maersk earns the revenue when it has completed the service for the customer.

(2) No. Maersk has paid cash for rent in advance. There is no expense. This prepaid rent is an asset because Maersk has some future economic benefits (i.e., the use of an office space).

Some expenses are paid in cash. Other expenses arise from using up an asset such as supplies. When expenses are incurred but not yet paid, a company has a liability. For example, Richemont incurs salary expense when employees work for the company. Richemont may pay the salary expense immediately, or it may record a liability for the salary to be paid later. In either case, Richemont incurs salary expense. The critical event for recording an expense is the record of employees working for the company, not the payment of cash. We will discuss other issues related to expense capitalization later (in Chapter 7 on PPE and Intangibles).

Ethics in Business and Accounting Decisions

Accrual accounting provides some ethical challenges that cash accounting avoids. For example, suppose that on January 15, 20X6, Richemont pays €3 million for an advertising campaign to be conducted by an advertising agency. The advertisements are scheduled to run during February to April of 20X6. At the time of payment, Richemont is buying an asset, a prepaid expense. Under accrual accounting, Richemont should record two-thirds of the expense (€2 million) during its fiscal year ended March 31, 20X6, and one-third (€1 million) for April 20X6, which is part of fiscal year 20X7.

Now, let's say fiscal year 20X6 is a great year for Richemont—net income is better than expected. Richemont's top managers believe that fiscal year 20X7 will not be as profitable. In this case, the company may be motivated to expense the full €3 million during fiscal year 20X6 in order to report all the advertising expense in the 20X6 Income Statement. This questionable action would keep €1 million of advertising expense off the 20X7 Income Statement and make 20X7's net income look €1 million better.

Deloitte Forensic Center

The Deloitte Forensic Center[1] published a report on financial statement fraud schemes alleged by the United States' Securities and Exchange Commission (SEC) in enforcement releases issued from 2000 to 2008. Revenue recognition was the most susceptible area of fraud, accounting for almost 40% of the financial statement frauds alleged during the period. The two most common alleged methods of cheating on revenue recognition identified in the SEC enforcement releases were recording fictitious revenue and recognition of revenue when products or services are not yet delivered or are delivered without customer acceptance, or when delivery is incomplete.

[1] The Deloitte Forensic Center is a think tank aimed at exploring new approaches for mitigating the costs, risks, and effects of fraud, corruption, and other issues facing the global business community. The Center aims to advance the state of thinking in areas such as fraud and corruption by exploring issues from the perspective of forensic accountants, corporate leaders, and other professionals involved in forensic matters. The Deloitte Forensic Center is sponsored by Deloitte Financial Advisory Services LLP. For more information, visit www.deloitte.com/forensiccenter.

Proportion of financial statement fraud schemes represented by each alleged fraud scheme in SEC enforcement releases from 2000–2008	Percentage
Revenue Recognition	38
Manipulation of Expense	12
Improper Disclosures	12
Manipulation of Liabilities	8
Manipulation of Assets	7
Manipulation of Reserves	7
Bribery & Kickbacks	4
Asset Misappropriation	3
Manipulation of A/R	3
Investments	2
Aiding and Abetting	2
Goodwill	2
Total	100

Source: Adapted from *Ten Things about Financial Statement Fraud*—3rd Edition, A review of SEC enforcement releases, 2000–2008. Deloitte Forensic Center, 2009.

Mid-Chapter Summary Problem

Requirements

Think about the following independent revenue scenarios, identify the key revenue issue, and propose the appropriate revenue recognition policy. Support your arguments with revenue recognition policies used by similar businesses.

1. Stamps sold by a post office
2. Concert tickets sold by a ticketing agency
3. Course fees paid to universities
4. Gift vouchers sold by a retailer
5. Computer games with options for Internet gaming

Answers

Requirement 1

The key revenue issue is whether or not stamps sold are recognized as revenue upon sale or upon usage by customers. When stamps are sold, there is a performance obligation (liability) and this obligation is only satisfied when the stamps are actually used by customers. The post office will probably rely on some estimates of unused stamps and defer the revenue until such time as they have been used or deemed earned. Examples of revenue recognition policies are as follows:

ADAPTED EXCERPTS FROM UPS'S NOTES TO THE FINANCIAL STATEMENTS

Revenue Recognition

Revenue is recognized upon delivery of a letter or package.

Source: UPS Incorporated, *Annual Report 2016*, page 66

ADAPTED EXCERPTS FROM SINGPOST'S NOTES TO THE FINANCIAL STATEMENTS

Revenue recognition for sales of goods and services—Mail and Logistics related
Accrual for unearned revenue is made for stamps that have been sold, but for those for which services have not been rendered as at the Balance Sheet date. This accrual is classified as advanced billings under trade and other payables.

Source: Singapore Post Limited, *Annual Report 2016*, pages 99–100

ADAPTED EXCERPTS FROM HONG KONG POST'S NOTES TO THE FINANCIAL STATEMENTS

Revenue Recognition

Revenue for postal services is recognized as the services are provided. Allowance for a measured share of stamp income for the amount of revenue from postage stamps sold in respect of which postal services has not yet been provided is made at the end of the reporting period.

Source: Hong Kong Post, *Annual Report 2016*, page 71

Requirement 2

The key revenue issues are the amount and the timing of revenue. Some concert tickets may be sold on an "agency" basis, which means the revenue to be recognized should only be the booking fee/commission amount. For example, you paid Ticketmaster $105 for a Lady Gaga concert ticket, where $5 was the booking fee on top of the $100 concert ticket. Ticketmaster will recognize ticket processing fee revenue of $5 at the time of sale. On the other hand, if Ticketmaster's parent company, Live Nation Entertainment, was responsible for staging the concert, Ticketmaster wouldn't recognize the $5 processing fee immediately but would have to defer it until the concert takes place, which is the same time as when Live Nation Entertainment also would recognize the $100 from the concert ticket revenue. Live Nation Entertainment is the parent company of Ticketmaster and its revenue recognition policy states the following:

ADAPTED EXCERPTS FROM LIVE NATION ENTERTAINMENT INC.'S NOTES TO THE FINANCIAL STATEMENTS

Revenue Recognition

Revenue from our ticketing operations primarily consists of convenience and order processing fees charged at the time a ticket for an event is sold and is recorded on a net basis (net of the face value of the ticket). For tickets sold for events at our owned or operated venues in the United States, and where we control the tickets internationally, revenue is recognized after the performance occurs. Revenue for these ticket service charges collected in advance of the event is recorded as deferred revenue until the event occurs, and these service charges will be shared between our Ticketing segment and our Concerts segment.

Source: Live Nation Entertainment Inc., *Annual Report 2016*, page 52

ADAPTED EXCERPTS FROM NINE ENTERTAINMENT CO.'S NOTES TO THE FINANCIAL STATEMENTS

Revenue

Revenue from ticketing operations primarily consists of booking and service/delivery fees charged at the time a ticket for an event is sold and is recorded on a net basis (net of the face value of the ticket). This revenue is recognized at the time of sale.

Revenue from the promotion and production of an event is recognized in the month the performance occurs.

Source: Nine Entertainment Co., *Annual Report 2014*, page 67

Requirement 3

The key revenue issue is timing of the revenue recognition. The consideration paid is usually fixed and easily determinable. For example, is the tuition earned at the start of the semester/term and earned progressively, or earned in its entirety at the start of each term? What happens when the school term does not coincide with the financial period? For example, the University of Cambridge has this revenue recognition policy:

ADAPTED EXCERPTS FROM UNIVERSITY OF CAMBRIDGE'S NOTES TO THE FINANCIAL STATEMENTS

Recognition of Income: Academic Fees

Tuition fees for degree courses are charged to students by academic term. Income is recognized for academic terms falling within the period. For short courses, fees are charged in advance for the entire course and income is recognized to the extent that the course duration falls within the period.

Source: University of Cambridge, *Annual Report 2015*, page 50

ADAPTED EXCERPTS FROM NATIONAL UNIVERSITY OF SINGAPORE'S NOTES TO THE FINANCIAL STATEMENTS

Revenue Recognition

Tuition and other related fees for the academic year and all other income (including course and conference fees, and clinical and consultancy fees) are recognized in the period in which the services are rendered.

Source: National University of Singapore, *Annual Report 2016*, page 23

Requirement 4

The key revenue question is timing of the revenue recognition. Is revenue earned when the gift voucher is sold or used? Gift vouchers are similar in principle to prepayments made by customers, i.e., a liability for the business. Thus, a business should not recognize gift vouchers as revenue upon the sale of gift vouchers. For example, Amazon.com provides the following information about its gift vouchers.

ADAPTED EXCERPTS FROM AMAZON INC.'S NOTES TO THE FINANCIAL STATEMENTS

Revenue Recognition

As of December 31, 2015 and 2014, our liabilities for unredeemed gift cards was $2.0 billion and $1.7 billion. We reduce the liability for a gift card when redeemed by a customer. If a gift certificate is not redeemed, we recognize revenue when it expires or when the likelihood of its redemption becomes remote, generally two years from the date of issuance.

Source: Amazon.com, *Annual Reports 2015*, page 49

Requirement 5

The key revenue issues are amount and timing of revenue. Whilst the sale price may be easily determined, a computer game that offers an Internet gaming option may mean that the game developer will continue to have an obligation to ensure that the Internet platform is available to customers, long after the sale. It may be difficult to "cost" the obligation to do so. For example, Vivendi (parent company of Activision Blizzard, the maker of *World of Warcraft* games) states:

ADAPTED EXCERPTS FROM ACTIVISION BLIZZARD INC.'S NOTES TO THE FINANCIAL STATEMENTS

Subscription Revenues

Subscription revenues are mostly derived from *World of Warcraft*. *World of Warcraft* is a game that is playable through Blizzard's servers and is generally sold on a subscription-only basis.

For *World of Warcraft*, after the first month of free usage that is included with the boxed software, the *World of Warcraft* end user may enter into a subscription agreement for additional future access. Revenues associated with the sales of subscriptions via boxed software and prepaid subscription cards, as well as prepaid subscriptions sales, are deferred until the subscription service is activated by the consumer and are then recognized ratably over the subscription period.

Source: Activision Blizzard Inc., *Annual Report 2016*, page 49

ADJUST THE ACCOUNTS

At the end of the period, a reporting entity presents its financial statements to its users. This process begins with the trial balance introduced earlier (in Chapter 2). We refer to this trial balance as unadjusted because the accounts are not yet ready for the financial statements. We shall continue with our RedLotus Travel, Inc., example in the following discussions.

Which Accounts Need to Be Updated (Adjusted)?

The shareholders and management need to know how well RedLotus Travel, Inc., is performing. The financial statements report this information, and all accounts must be up-to-date. That means we need to make sure all necessary adjustments and updates are reflected in the accounts before the financial statements are prepared.

Exhibit 3-3 gives the unadjusted trial balance of RedLotus Travel, Inc., at June 30, 20X8. It reflects the same accounts as those in Chapter 2 (Exhibit 2-12), except for two additional months of transaction activities (i.e., May and June). However, the trial balance remains unadjusted. Let's see what we need to do to prepare the accounts before financial statements can be produced.

Exhibit 3-3 | Unadjusted Trial Balance

	A	B	C
1	**RedLotus Travel, Inc.** **Unadjusted Trial Balance** **June 30, 2018**	**Debit**	**Credit**
2	Cash	$ 34,800	
3	Accounts receivable	2,200	
4	Supplies	700	
5	Prepaid rent	3,000	
6	Land	20,000	
7	Equipment	24,000	
8	Accounts payable		$ 13,100
9	Unearned service revenue		400
10	Share capital		50,000
11	Retained earnings		18,800
12	Dividends	3,200	
13	Service revenue		7,000
14	Salary expense	900	
15	Utilities expense	500	
16	Total	$ 89,300	$ 89,300
17			

Cash, Equipment, Accounts Payable, Share Capital, and Dividends are up-to-date and need no adjustment at the end of the period. Why? Because the day-to-day transactions provide all the data for these accounts.

Accounts Receivable, Supplies, Prepaid Rent, and the other accounts are a different story. These accounts are not yet up-to-date on June 30. Why? Because certain transactions have not yet been recorded. Let's consider Supplies. During June, RedLotus used supplies in their operations. But RedLotus didn't make a journal entry for every supply item used each time it used them. That would be inefficient, wasting time and money. Instead, RedLotus waits until the end of the period and then records the supplies used up during the entire month.

The cost of supplies used up is an expense. An adjusting entry at the end of June updates both Supplies (an asset) and Supplies Expense. We must adjust all accounts whose balances are not yet up-to-date.

Categories of Adjusting Entries

Accounting end-of-period adjustments fall into three basic categories: deferrals, depreciation, and accruals. Deferral adjustments include deferred expenses (or prepaid expenses) and deferred income (or unearned revenue). Accrual adjustments include accrued expenses and accrual revenue. As you move forward with this textbook, you may see additional end-of-period adjustments for other items on the Balance Sheet.

Deferrals. A **deferral** is an adjustment for an item for which the business paid or received cash in advance. Richemont purchases supplies for use in its operations. During the period, some supplies (assets) are used up and become expenses. At the end of the period, an adjustment is needed to decrease the supplies account for the supplies used up and to record the supplies expense. Prepaid rent, prepaid insurance, and all other prepaid expenses require deferral adjustments.

There are also deferral adjustments for liabilities. Companies like Richemont may collect cash from its customers in advance of earning the revenue. When Richemont receives cash up front, it has an obligation (i.e., a liability) to provide goods and services for its customer. This liability is called Unearned Revenue or Deferred Income. Then, when Richemont delivers the goods to the customer, the obligation is reduced and it recognizes an increase in Sales Revenue. This earning process requires an adjustment at the end of the period. The adjustment decreases the liability and increases the revenue for the amount earned. Publishers of magazines, such as

Fortune, and your cell phone company usually collect cash in advance from their subscribers. They too must make adjusting entries for revenues earned after initial receipt of cash.

Accruals. An **accrual** is the opposite of a deferral. For an accrued *expense*, Richemont records the expense before (eventually) paying for it. For an accrued *revenue*, Richemont records the revenue before (eventually) collecting cash.

Salary Expense is an example of an accrual adjustment. As employees work for Richemont, the company's salary expense accrues with the passage of time. At the end of its fiscal year, Richemont owed employees some salaries to be paid after year-end, so Richemont recorded Salary Expense and Salary Payable for the amount owed. Other examples of expense accruals include interest expense and income tax expense.

An accrued revenue is a revenue that the business has earned and will collect next year. At year-end, Richemont must accrue such revenue. The adjustment debits a receivable and credits a revenue. For example, accrual of interest revenue debits Interest Receivable and credits Interest Revenue.

Depreciation. Depreciation allocates the cost of an item of Property, Plant and Equipment (PPE) to expense over the asset's useful life. Depreciation is the most common long-term deferral. Richemont buys buildings, equipment, and other fixed assets to use in its operations. As Richemont uses the assets, it allocates the cost of the PPE over its useful life. The accounting adjustment records Depreciation Expense and decreases the asset's carrying amount over its life. The process is identical to a deferral-type adjustment; the only difference is the type of asset involved. We will look at other issues related to PPE and depreciation later (in Chapter 7).

Let's see how the adjusting process actually works for RedLotus on June 30. We start with prepaid expenses.

Prepaid Expenses

A **prepaid expense (or prepayment)** is an expense paid in advance. Therefore, prepaid expenses are assets because they provide a future benefit for the owner. Let's make the adjustments for prepaid rent and supplies.

Prepaid Rent. Companies pay rent in advance. This prepayment creates an asset for the renter, who can then use the rented item in the future. Suppose RedLotus prepays three months' store rent ($3,000) on June 1. The entry for the prepayment of three months' rent debits Prepaid Rent as follows:

A1

	A	B	C	D	E	F
1	Jun. 1	Prepaid Rent ($1,000 × 3)	3,000			
2		Cash		3,000		
3		*Paid three months' rent in advance.*				
4						

The accounting equation shows that one asset increases and another decreases. Total assets are unchanged. Again, we show the impact of revenue and expense transactions directly to equity.

Assets	=	Liabilities	+	Shareholders' Equity
3,000	=	0	+	0
− 3,000				

After posting, the Prepaid Rent account appears as follows:

	Prepaid Rent	
Jun. 1	3,000	

Throughout June, the Prepaid Rent account carries this beginning balance, as shown in Exhibit 3-3. The adjustment transfers $1,000 from Prepaid Rent to Rent Expense as follows:[2]

Adjusting entry a

	A	B	C	D	E	F
1	Jun. 30	Rent Expense ($3,000 × 1/3)	1,000			
2		Prepaid Rent		1,000		
3		*To record rent expense.*				
4						

Both assets and shareholders' equity decrease.

Assets	=	Liabilities	+	Shareholders' Equity	
− 1,000	=	0	+	− 1,000	(rent expense)

After posting, Prepaid Rent and Rent Expense appear as follows:

Prepaid Rent

Jun. 1	3,000	Jun. 30	1,000
Bal.	2,000		

→

Rent Expense

Jun. 30	1,000		
Bal.	1,000		

This expense illustrates the matching concept. The decrease in future economic benefits of "prepaid rent" results in an increase in expenses (and reduces equity).

Supplies. Supplies are another type of prepaid expense. On June 2, RedLotus paid cash of $700 for cleaning supplies:

	A	B	C	D	E	F
1	Jun. 2	Supplies	700			
2		Cash		700		
3		*Paid cash for supplies.*				
4						

Assets	=	Liabilities	+	Shareholders' Equity
+ 700	=	0	+	0
− 700				

The cost of the supplies RedLotus used is Supplies Expense. To measure June's supplies expense, the business counts the supplies on hand at the end of the month. The count shows that $400 of supplies remains. Subtracting the $400 of supplies on hand from the supplies available ($700) measures the supplies expense for the month ($300):

Asset Available During the Period	−	Asset on Hand at the End of the Period	=	Asset Used (Expense) During the Period
$700	−	$400	=	$300

[2] See Exhibit 3-8 for a summary of adjustments a–g.

The June 30 adjusting entry debits the expense and credits the asset, as follows:

Adjusting entry b

	A	B	C	D	E	F
1	Jun. 30	Supplies Expense ($700 – $400)	300			
2		Supplies		300		
3		*To record supplies expense.*				
4						

Assets	=	Liabilities	+	Shareholders' Equity	
– 300	=	0	+	– 300	(supplies expense)

After posting, the Supplies and Supplies Expense accounts appear as follows. The adjustment is highlighted for emphasis.

Supplies

Jun. 2	700	Jun. 30	300
Bal.	400		

Supplies Expense

Jun. 30	300		
Bal.	300		

At the start of July, Supplies has this $400 balance, and the adjustment process is repeated each month.

Stop & Think

At the beginning of the month, supplies were $5,000. During the month, $7,000 of supplies were purchased. At month's end, $3,000 of supplies are still on hand. What is the

- adjusting entry?
- ending balance in the Supplies account?

Answer:

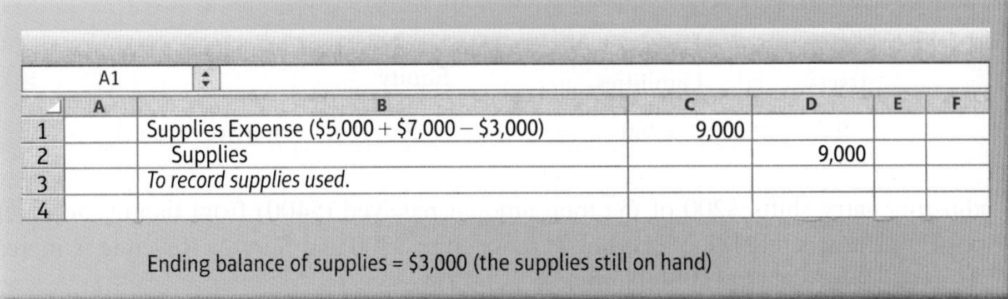

	A	B	C	D	E	F
1		Supplies Expense ($5,000 + $7,000 – $3,000)	9,000			
2		Supplies		9,000		
3		*To record supplies used.*				
4						

Ending balance of supplies = $3,000 (the supplies still on hand)

Unearned Revenues

Some businesses collect cash from customers before earning the revenue. This creates a liability or performance obligation called **unearned revenue** (also known as deferred income or revenue collected in advance). The business only earns the income when the goods are delivered or services are performed. Suppose another hotel chain engages RedLotus Travel, Inc., along with other travel agents, on a special incentive scheme where travel agents will be paid in advance

$400 if the agents undertake to make 10 bookings within 30 days. If RedLotus collects the $400 on 15 June, it will record this transaction as follows:

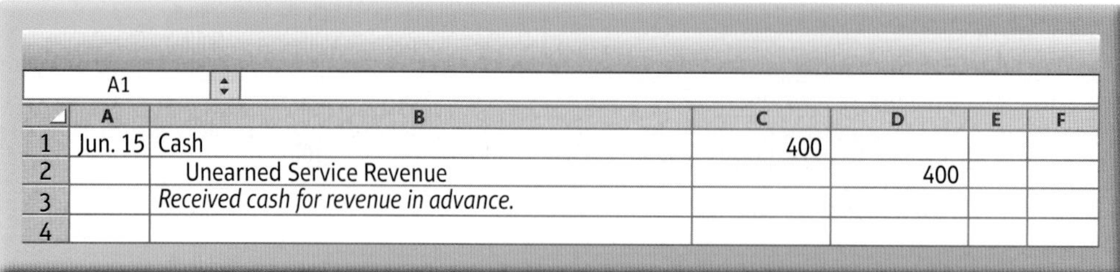

	A	B	C	D	E	F
1	Jun. 15	Cash	400			
2		Unearned Service Revenue		400		
3		*Received cash for revenue in advance.*				
4						

Assets	=	Liabilities	+	Shareholders' Equity
+ 400	=	+ 400	+	0

After posting, the liability account appears as follows:

Unearned Service Revenue			
		Jun. 15	400

Unearned Service Revenue is a liability because RedLotus is obligated to perform services for the hotel chain. The unadjusted trial balance lists Unearned Service Revenue with a $400 credit balance. Let's say RedLotus was able to make five bookings by the end of June, RedLotus would have satisfied half (i.e., 5 out of 10) of its performance obligation. On 30 June, RedLotus, Inc., makes the following adjustment:

Adjusting entry c

	A	B	C	D	E	F
1	Jun. 30	Unearned Service Revenue ($400 × 1/2)	200			
2		Service Revenue		200		
3		*To record unearned service revenue that has been earned.*				
4						
5						

Assets	=	Liabilities	+	Shareholders' Equity	
0	=	− 200	+	+ 200	(service revenue)

This adjusting entry shifts $200 of the total amount received ($400) from liability to revenue. After posting, Unearned Service Revenue is reduced to $200 and Service Revenue is increased by $200, as follows (adjustment highlighted):

Unearned Service Revenue			
Jun. 30	200	Jun. 15	400
		Bal.	200

Service Revenue			
			7,000
		Jun. 30	300
		Jun. 30	200
		Bal.	7,500

All revenues collected in advance are accounted for this way. An unearned revenue represents an obligation to perform and, as such, is a liability, not a revenue.

One company's prepaid expense is the other company's unearned revenue. For example, the hotel's prepaid expense is RedLotus Travel, Inc.'s liability for unearned revenue.

Accrued Expenses

Businesses incur expenses before they pay cash. Consider an employee's salary. Richemont's salary expense and payable will grow as the employee works, so the liability is said to accrue. Another example is interest expense on a note payable. Interest accrues as the clock ticks. The term **accrued expense** refers to a liability that arises from an expense that has not yet been paid.

Businesses do not record accrued expenses daily or weekly. Instead, they wait until the end of the period and use an adjusting entry to update each expense (and related liability) for the financial statements. Let's look at salary expense.

Most companies pay their employees at set times. Suppose RedLotus pays its employee a monthly salary of $1,800, half on the 15th and half on the last day of the month. The following calendar for June has the paydays highlighted:

June						
Sun.	Mon.	Tue.	Wed.	Thur.	Fri.	Sat.
						1
2	3	4	5	6	7	8
9	10	11	12	13	14	(15)
16	17	18	19	20	21	22
23	24	25	26	27	28	29
(30)						

Assume that if a payday falls on a Sunday, RedLotus pays the employee the following Monday. During June, RedLotus paid its employees the first half-month salary of $900 and made the following entry:

A1

	A	B	C	D	E	F
1	Jun. 15	Salary Expense	900			
2		Cash		900		
3		*To pay salary.*				
4						

Assets	=	Liabilities	+	Shareholders' Equity	
− 900	=	0	+	− 900	(salary expense)

After posting, the Salary Expense account is

Salary Expense		
Jun. 15	900	

The trial balance at June 30 (Exhibit 3-3) includes Salary Expense with its debit balance of $900. Because June 30, the second payday of the month, falls on a Sunday, the second half-month amount of $900 will be paid on Monday, July 1. At June 30, therefore, RedLotus adjusts for additional salary expense and salary payable of $900 as follows:

Adjusting entry d

A1

	A	B	C	D	E	F
1	Jun. 30	Salary Expense	900			
2		Salary Payable		900		
3		*To accrue salary expense.*				
4						

An accrued expense increases liabilities and decreases shareholders' equity:

Assets	=	Liabilities	+	Shareholders' Equity	
0	=	+ 900	+	− 900	(salary expense)

After posting, the Salary Payable and Salary Expense accounts appear as follows (adjustment highlighted):

Salary Payable

		Jun. 30	900
		Bal.	900

Salary Expense

Jun. 15	900		
Jun. 30	900		
Bal.	1,800		

The accounts now hold all of June's salary information. Salary Expense has a full month's salary, and Salary Payable shows the amount owed at June 30. All accrued expenses are recorded this way—debit the expense and credit the liability.

Computerized systems usually contain a payroll module. Accrued salaries can be automatically journalized and posted at the end of each period.

Accrued Revenues

Businesses may earn revenue before they receive the cash. A revenue that has been earned but not yet collected is called an **accrued revenue**.

Assume that on June 15, a hotel chain agrees to pay RedLotus a commision of $30 per booking made into its hotels over the next 30 days, payable at the end of July. RedLotus books 10 clients for the hotel chain in June and earns the agreed $300 commision for work done in June. Note that the commision is not yet paid to RedLotus at end of June. On June 30, RedLotus will make the following adjusting entry:

Adjusting entry e

A1

	A	B	C	D	E	F
1	Jun. 30	Accounts Receivable ($30 × 10 bookings)	300			
2		Service Revenue		300		
3		*To accrue service revenue.*				
4						

Revenue increases both total assets and shareholders' equity:

Assets	=	Liabilities	+	Shareholders' Equity	
+300	=	0	+	+ 300	(service revenue)

Recall that Accounts Receivable has an unadjusted balance of $2,200, and Service Revenue's unadjusted balance is $7,000 (Exhibit 3-3). This June 30 adjusting entry has the following effects (adjustment highlighted):

Unearned Service Revenue

Jun. 30	200	Jun. 15	400
		Bal.	200

Service Revenue

			7,000
		Jun. 30	300
		Jun. 30	200
		Bal.	7,500

All accrued revenues are accounted for similarly—debit a receivable and credit a revenue.

Stop & Think

Suppose RedLotus holds a note receivable as an investment. At the end of June, $100 of interest revenue has been earned but not yet received. Journalize the accrued revenue adjustment at June 30.

Answer:

	A	B	C	D	E	F
1	Jun. 30	Interest Receivable	100			
2		Interest Revenue		100		
3		*To accrue interest revenue.*				
4						

Exhibit 3-4 Prepaid and Accruals Adjustments

PREPAIDS—Cash First	First			Later		
Prepaid expenses	*Pay cash and record an asset:*			*Record an expense and decrease the asset:*		
	Prepaid Expense......	XXX		Expense..............................	XXX	
	Cash...............		XXX	Prepaid Expense.........		XXX
Unearned revenues	*Receive cash and record unearned revenue:*			*Record revenue and decrease unearned revenue:*		
	Cash........................	XXX		Unearned Revenue	XXX	
	Unearned Revenue		XXX	Revenue		XXX
ACCRUALS—Cash Later	**First**			**Later**		
Accrued expenses	*Accrue expense and a payable:*			*Pay cash and decrease the payable:*		
	Expense...................	XXX		Payable..............................	XXX	
	Payable...........		XXX	Cash..........................		XXX
Accrued revenues	*Accrue revenue and a receivable:*			*Receive cash and decrease the receivable:*		
	Receivable...............	XXX		Cash..................................	XXX	
	Revenue		XXX	Receivable..................		XXX

The authors thank Professors Darrel Davis and Alfonso Oddo for suggesting this exhibit.

Depreciation of Property, Plant, and Equipment

Property, Plant and Equipment (PPE) are long-lived tangible assets, such as land, buildings, furniture, and equipment. Sometimes you may see them referred to as fixed assets or plant assets. All PPE (except for freehold land) has finite useful lives, and the passage of time reduces their usefulness, and this decline is an expense. Accountants allocate the cost of each PPE item over its useful life. Depreciation is the process of allocating cost to expense for PPE. Note that in some countries, land titles are not issued in perpetuity, so in such cases you may see "leasehold land" (as opposed to freehold land) that is depreciated over the period of the leasehold.

To illustrate depreciation, consider RedLotus. Suppose that on June 2, RedLotus purchased an equipment on account for $24,000:

	A	B	C	D	E	F
1	Jun. 2	Equipment	24,000			
2		Accounts Payable		24,000		
3		*Purchased equipment on account.*				
4						

Assets	=	Liabilities	+	Shareholders' Equity
+24,000	=	+24,000	+	0

After posting, the Equipment account appears as follows:

Equipment	
Jun. 2 24,000	

RedLotus records an asset when it purchases equipment. Then, as the asset is used, a portion of the asset's cost is transferred to Depreciation Expense. This is an example of the application of the matching concept. Computerized accounting systems program the depreciation for automatic entry of each period.

RedLotus estimates that equipment will remain useful for five years. One simple way to allocate the amount of depreciation for each year is to divide the cost of the asset ($24,000 in our example) by its expected useful life (five years). This procedure—called the straight-line depreciation method—gives annual depreciation of $4,800. (Chapter 7 covers PPE and depreciation in more detail.)

Annual Depreciation = $24,000/5 years = $4,800 per year

Depreciation for June is $400.

Monthly Depreciation = $4,800/12 months = $400 per month

The Accumulated Depreciation Account. Depreciation expense for June is recorded as follows:

Adjusting entry f

	A	B	C	D	E	F
1	Jun. 30	Depreciation Expense—Equipment	400			
2		Accumulated Depreciation—Equipment		400		
3		*To record depreciation.*				
4						

Total assets decrease by the amount of the expense:

Assets	=	Liabilities	+	Shareholders' Equity	
−400	=	0	+	−400	(depreciation expense)

The Accumulated Depreciation—Equipment account (not Equipment) is credited to preserve the original cost of the asset in the Equipment account. Managers can then refer to the Equipment account if they ever need to know how much the asset cost.

The **Accumulated Depreciation** account shows the sum of all depreciation expense from using the asset. Therefore, the balance in the Accumulated Depreciation account increases over the asset's life.

Accumulated Depreciation is a contra asset account—an asset account with a normal credit balance. A **contra account** has two distinguishing characteristics:

1. It always has a companion account.
2. Its normal balance is the opposite of the companion account.

In this case, Accumulated Depreciation—Equipment is the contra account to Equipment, so it appears directly after Equipment on the Balance Sheet. A business carries an accumulated depreciation account for each class of depreciable asset, for example, Accumulated Depreciation—Building and Accumulated Depreciation—Equipment.

After posting, the PPE accounts of RedLotus are as follows—with the adjustment highlighted:

Equipment			
Jun. 3	24,000		
Bal.	24,000		

Accumulated Depreciation—Equipment			
		Jun. 30	400
		Bal.	400

Depreciation Expense—Equipment			
Jun. 30	400		
Bal.	400		

Carrying amount. The net amount of a PPE (cost minus accumulated depreciation) is called that asset's **carrying amount (of a PPE)**. Sometimes carrying amount is also referred to as book value, but this is less appropriate because it has nothing to do with value of the asset. Exhibit 3-5 shows how RedLotus would report the carrying amount of its equipment and building at June 30.

Exhibit 3-5 PPE on the Balance Sheet of RedLotus Travel, Inc.

A1

	A	B	C	D	E
1	**RedLotus Travel, Inc., PPE at June 30**				
2	Equipment	$ 24,000			
3	Less: Accumulated Depreciation	(400)	$ 23,600		
4	Land		20,000		
5	Carrying amount of PPE		$ 43,600		
6					

At June 30, the carrying amount of equipment is $23,600; the carrying amount of the building is $49,800.

Stop & Think

What will be the carrying amount of RedLotus' equipment at the end of July?

Answer:

$24,000 – $400 – $400 = $23,200.

Exhibit 3-6 shows how Richemont reports its PPE in its annual report. As you can see, Richemont reports four categories of PPE. You will find that different companies categorize their PPE differently. Lines 3 to 6 list the four asset categories and their costs, accumulated depreciation, and carrying amounts. Line 7 shows that the total cost of PPE is €4,817 million, with accumulated depreciation of €2,341 million, resulting in a carrying amount of €2,476 million. Note that assets under construction are also not depreciated until they are ready for use.

Exhibit 3-6 Richemont's PPE (Adapted)

	A	B	C	D
1	**As at March 31, 2015**			
2		**Cost**	**Acc. Depn.**	**Carrying amount**
3	Land and buildings	€ 1,299	€ (369)	€ 930
4	Plant and machinery	830	(523)	307
5	Fixtures, fittings, tools, and equipment	2,494	(1,449)	1,045
6	Assets under construction	194	–	194
7	Total PPE	€ 4,817	€ (2,341)	€ 2,476
8				

Like individual taxpayers, corporations are subject to income tax. They typically accrue income tax expense and the related income tax payable as the final adjusting entry of the period. Obviously, taxation systems vary from country to country, and we are simplifying tax for now and assuming that income tax payable is $600. We will treat income tax expense like an accrued expense. RedLotus, Inc., accrues income tax expense with adjusting entry g:

Adjusting entry g

	A	B	C	D	E	F
1	Jun. 30	Income Tax Expense	600			
2		Income Tax Payable		600		
3		*To accrue income tax expense.*				
4						

The income tax accrual follows the pattern for accrued expenses.

Summary of the Adjusting Process

Two purposes of the adjusting process are: Update the Balance Sheet and Measure income; therefore, every adjusting entry affects at least one of the following: Asset or liability, to update the Balance Sheet; or Revenue or expense, to measure income.

Exhibit 3-7 summarizes the basic accounting adjustments at the end of an accounting period.

Exhibit 3-7 Summary of Adjusting Entries

	Type of Account	
Category of Adjusting Entry	**Debit**	**Credit**
Prepaid expense..................	Expense	Asset
Unearned revenue...............	Liability	Revenue
Accrued expense.................	Expense	Liability
Accrued revenue..................	Asset	Revenue
Depreciation.......................	Expense	Contra asset

Source: Adapted from material provided by Beverly Terry.

Exhibit 3-8 summarizes the adjustments of RedLotus, at June 30—the adjusting entries we've examined over the past few pages. Panel A repeats the data for each adjustment; Panel B gives the adjusting entries; and Panel C shows the accounts after posting the adjusting entries. The adjustments are keyed by letter. It includes an additional adjusting entry—the accrual of income tax expense.

Exhibit 3-8 | The Adjusting Process of RedLotus, Inc.

PANEL A—Information for Adjustments at June 30, 2016	PANEL B—Adjusting Entries		
(a) Prepaid rent expired, $1,000.	(a) Rent Expense	1,000	
	Prepaid Rent		1,000
	To record rent expense.		
(b) Supplies used, $300.	(b) Supplies Expense	300	
	Supplies		300
	To record supplies used.		
(c) Amount of unearned service revenue that has been earned, $200.	(c) Unearned Service Revenue	200	
	Service Revenue		200
	To record unearned revenue that has been earned.		
(d) Accrued salary expense, $900.	(d) Salary Expense	900	
	Salary Payable		900
	To accrue salary expense.		
(e) Accrued service revenue, $300.	(e) Accounts Receivable	300	
	Service Revenue		300
	To accrue service revenue.		
(f) Depreciation on equipment, $400.	(f) Depreciation Expense—Equipment	400	
	Accumulated Depreciation—Equipment		400
	To record depreciation.		
(g) Accrued income tax expense, $600.	(g) Income Tax Expense	600	
	Income Tax Payable		600
	To accrue income tax expense.		

PANEL C—Ledger Accounts

Assets

Cash

Debit	Credit
Bal. 34,800	

Accounts Receivable

Debit	Credit
2,200	
(e) 300	
Bal. 2,500	

Supplies

Debit	Credit
700	(b) 300
Bal. 400	

Prepaid Rent

Debit	Credit
3,000	(a) 1,000
Bal. 2,000	

Equipment

Debit	Credit
Bal. 24,000	

Accumulated Depreciation—Equipment

Debit	Credit
	(h) 400
	Bal. 400

Liabilities

Accounts Payable

Debit	Credit
	Bal. 13,100

Salary Payable

Debit	Credit
	(d) 900
	Bal. 900

Unearned Service Revenue

Debit	Credit
(c) 200	400
	Bal. 200

Income Tax Payable

Debit	Credit
	(g) 600
	Bal. 600

Shareholders' Equity

Share Capital

Debit	Credit
	Bal. 50,000

Retained Earnings

Debit	Credit
	Bal. 18,800

Dividends

Debit	Credit
Bal. 3,200	

Revenue

Service Revenue

Debit	Credit
	7,000
	(e) 300
	(c) 200
	Bal. 7,500

Expenses

Rent Expense

Debit	Credit
(a) 1,000	
Bal. 1,000	

Salary Expense

Debit	Credit
900	
(d) 900	
Bal. 1,800	

Supplies Expense

Debit	Credit
(b) 300	
Bal. 300	

Depreciation Expense—Equipment

Debit	Credit
(f) 400	
Bal. 400	

Utilities Expense

Debit	Credit
Bal. 500	

Income Tax Expense

Debit	Credit
(g) 600	
Bal. 600	

The Adjusted Trial Balance

This chapter began with the unadjusted trial balance (see Exhibit 3-3). After the adjustments are journalized and posted, the accounts appear as shown in Exhibit 3-8, Panel C. A useful step in preparing the financial statements is to list the accounts, along with their adjusted balances, on an **adjusted trial balance**. This document lists all the accounts and their final balances in a single place. Exhibit 3-9 shows the adjusted trial balance of RedLotus, Inc.

Exhibit 3-9 | Adjusted Trial Balance

	A	B	C	D	E	F	G	H
1	**RedLotus Travel, Inc. Preparation of Adjusted Trial Balance June 30, 20X8**							
2		**Trial Balance**		**Adjustments**		**Adjusted Trial Balance**		
3	**Account Title**	**Debit**	**Credit**	**Debit**	**Credit**	**Debit**	**Credit**	
4	Cash	34,800				34,800		
5	Accounts receivable	2,200		(e) 300		2,500		
6	Supplies	700			(a) 300	400		
7	Prepaid rent	3,000			(a) 1,000	2,000		
8	Land	20,000				20,000		
9	Equipment	24,000				24,000		
10	Accumulated depreciation—equipment				(c) 400		400	Balance Sheet (Exhibit 3-12)
11	Accounts payable		13,100				13,100	
12	Salary payable				(d) 900		900	
13	Unearned service revenue		400	(f) 200			200	
14	Income tax payable				(g) 600		600	
15	Share capital		50,000				50,000	Statement of
16	Retained earnings		18,800				18,800	Changes in Equity
17	Dividends	3,200				3,200		(Exhibit 3-11)
18	Service revenue		7,000		(e) 300		7,500	
19					(f) 200			
20	Rent expense			(a) 1,000		1,000		
21	Salary expense	900		(c) 900		1,800		Income Statement
22	Supplies expense			(b) 300		300		(Exhibit 3-10)
23	Depreciation expense			(c) 400		400		
24	Utilities expense	500				500		
25	Income tax expense			(g) 600		600		
26		89,300	89,300	3,700	3,700	91,500	91,500	
27								

Note how clearly the adjusted trial balance presents the data. The Account Title and the Trial Balance data come from the trial balance. The two Adjustments columns summarize the adjusting entries. The Adjusted Trial Balance columns then give the final account balances. Each adjusted amount in Exhibit 3-9 is the unadjusted balance plus or minus the adjustments. For example, Accounts Receivable starts with a balance of $2,200. Add the $300 debit adjustment to get Accounts Receivable's ending balance of $2,500. Spreadsheets are very useful for this type of analysis.

PREPARE UPDATED FINANCIAL STATEMENTS

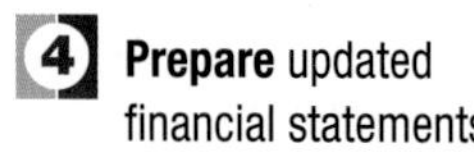

Prepare updated financial statements

The June financial statements of RedLotus can be prepared from the adjusted trial balance. At the far right, Exhibit 3-9 shows how the accounts are distributed to the financial statements:

- The Income Statement (Exhibit 3-10) lists the revenue and expense accounts.
- The statement of changes in equity (Exhibit 3-11) shows the changes in various components of equity during the period.
- The Balance Sheet (Exhibit 3-12) reports assets, liabilities, and shareholders' equity.

Exhibit 3-10 | Income Statement

	A	B	C
1	**RedLotus Travel, Inc. Income Statement**	**Month Ended June 30, 20X8**	
2	Revenue:		
3	Service revenue		$ 7,500
4	Expenses:		
5	Salary expense	$ 1,800	
6	Rent expense	1,000	
7	Utilities expense	500	
8	Depreciation expense	400	
9	Supplies expenses	300	4,000
10	Income before tax		3,500
11	Income tax expense		600
12	Net income		$ 2,900
13			

Exhibit 3-11 | Statement of Changes in Equity

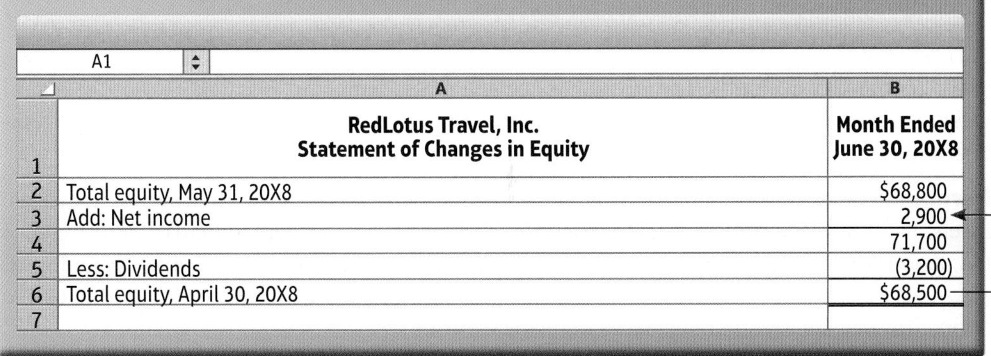

	A	B
1	**RedLotus Travel, Inc. Statement of Changes in Equity**	**Month Ended June 30, 20X8**
2	Total equity, May 31, 20X8	$68,800
3	Add: Net income	2,900
4		71,700
5	Less: Dividends	(3,200)
6	Total equity, April 30, 20X8	$68,500
7		

②

Exhibit 3-12 | Balance Sheet

	A	B	C	D	E
1	**RedLotus Travel, Inc. Balance Sheet**	**As at June 30, 20X8**			
2	**Assets**			**Liabilities**	
3	Cash		$ 34,800	Accounts payable	$ 13,100
4	Accounts receivable		2,500	Salary payable	900
5	Supplies		400	Unearned service revenue	200
6	Prepaid rent		2,000	Income tax payable	600
7	Land		20,000	Total liabilities	14,800
8	Equipment	$ 24,000			
9	Less: Accumulated				
10	depreciation	(400)	23,600	**Shareholders' Equity**	
11				Share capital	$ 50,000
12				Retained earnings	18,500
13				Total shareholders' equity	68,500
14				Total liabilities and	
15	Total assets		$ 83,300	shareholders' equity	$ 83,300
17					

②

The arrows in Exhibits 3-10, 3-11, and 3-12 show the flow of data from one statement to the next. Why is the Income Statement prepared first and the Balance Sheet last?

1. The Income Statement reports net income or net loss, the result of revenues minus expenses. Revenues and expenses will affect shareholders' equity, hence net income is then transferred to retained earnings. The first arrow tracks net income.
2. The statement of changes in equity reflects the increase in retained earnings from the Income Statement and records the payment of dividends. If there was any additional capital contribution from owners, it would also be reflected in this statement. The ending balance of equity from Exhibit 3-11 is carried to the Balance Sheet in Exhibit 3-12 as shown by the second arrow.

CLOSE THE BOOKS

Close the books

It is now June 30, the end of the month. Starr Williams, the manager, will continue RedLotus into July, August, and beyond. But wait—the revenue and the expense accounts still hold amounts for June. At the end of each accounting period, it is necessary to close the books in order to make an accurate measurement of revenue, expenses, and dividends for the period before proceeding to the next.

Closing the books means to prepare the accounts for the next period's transactions. The **closing entries** set the revenue, expense, and dividends balances back to zero at the end of the period. The idea is the same as setting the scoreboard back to zero after a game.

Closing is easily handled by computers. Recall that the Income Statement for a particular year reports only one year's income. For example, the net income for Richemont in 2016 relates exclusively to the year ended March 31, 2016. At each year-end, Richemont's accountants close the company's revenues and expenses for that year.

Temporary Accounts. Because income and expenses relate to a limited period, they are called **temporary accounts**. The Dividends account is also temporary because it is used to record the amount of distributions to owners during the period. The closing process applies only to temporary accounts (income, expenses, and dividends).

Permanent Accounts. Let's contrast the temporary accounts with the **permanent accounts**: assets, liabilities, and shareholders' equity. The permanent accounts are not closed at the end of the period because they carry over to the next period. Consider Cash, Receivables, Equipment, Accounts Payable, Share Capital, and Retained Earnings. Their ending balances at the end of one period become the beginning balances of the next period.

Closing entries transfer the revenue, expense, and dividends balances to Retained Earnings. Here are the steps to close the books of a company such as Richemont or RedLotus, Inc.:

1. Debit each income account for the amount of its credit balance. Credit Retained Earnings for the sum of the revenues. Now the sum of the revenues is in Retained Earnings.
2. Credit each expense account for the amount of its debit balance. Debit Retained Earnings for the sum of the expenses. The sum of the expenses is now in Retained Earnings.
3. Credit the Dividends account for the amount of its debit balance. Debit Retained Earnings. This entry places the dividends amount in the debit side of Retained Earnings. Remember that dividends are not expenses. Dividends never affect net income.

After closing the books, the Retained Earnings account of RedLotus appears as follows (data from Exhibits 3-10 to 3-12):

Retained Earnings

		Beginning balance	18,800
Expenses	4,600	Revenues	7,500
Dividends	3,200		
		Ending balance	18,500

Assume that RedLotus closes the books at the end of June. Exhibit 3-13 presents the complete closing process for the business. Panel A gives the closing journal entries, and Panel B shows the accounts after closing.

Exhibit 3-13 | Journalizing and Posting the Closing Entries

PANEL A—Journalizing the Closing Entries

		Closing Entries		
①	Jun. 30	Service Revenue	7,500	
		Retained Earnings		7,500
②	Jun. 30	Retained Earnings	4,600	
		Rent Expense		1,000
		Salary Expense		1,800
		Supplies Expense		300
		Depreciation Expense		400
		Utilities Expense		500
		Income Tax Expense		600
③	Jun. 30	Retained Earnings	3,200	
		Dividends		3,200

PANEL B—Posting to the Accounts

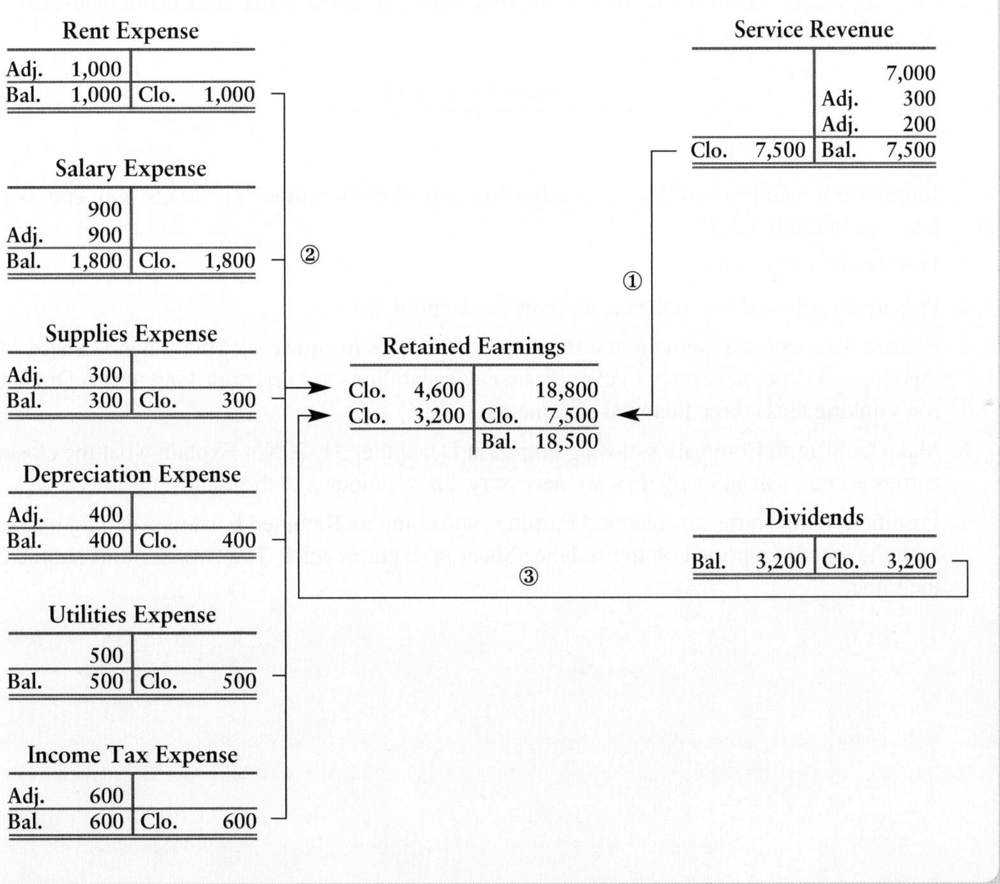

Adj. = Amount posted from an adjusting entry
Clo. = Amount posted from a closing entry
Bal. = Balance
As arrow ② in Panel B shows, we can make a compound closing entry for all the expenses.

Instead of closing the revenue and expense account directly to retained earnings, some accountants prefer to use a temporary account (usually called Income Summary). After closing all income and expense accounts to the Income Summary account, the balance of Income Summary (i.e., the profit or loss for the period) is, in turn, closed to the retained earnings account.

End-of-Chapter Summary Problem

The trial balance of Goldsmith Company shown below pertains to December 31, 20X6, which is the end of its year-long accounting period. Data needed for the adjusting entries include the following:

a. Supplies on hand at year-end, $2,000.

b. Depreciation on furniture and fixtures, $20,000.

c. Depreciation on building, $10,000.

d. Salaries owed but not yet paid, $5,000.

e. Accrued service revenue, $12,000.

f. Of the $45,000 balance of unearned service revenue, $32,000 was earned during the year.

g. Accrued income tax expense, $35,000.

Requirements

1. Open the ledger accounts with their unadjusted balances. Show dollar amounts in thousands, as shown for Accounts Receivable:

Accounts Receivable	
370	

2. Journalize the Goldsmith Company adjusting entries at December 31, 20X6. Key entries by letter, as in Exhibit 3-8.
3. Post the adjusting entries.
4. Prepare an adjusted trial balance, as shown in Exhibit 3-9.
5. Prepare the Income Statement, the statement of changes in equity, and the Balance Sheet. (At this stage, it is not necessary to classify assets or liabilities as current or long term.) Draw arrows linking these three financial statements.
6. Make Goldsmith Company's closing entries at December 31, 20X6. Explain what the closing entries accomplish and why they are necessary. Show amounts in thousands.
7. Post the closing entries to Retained Earnings and compare Retained Earnings' ending balance with the amount reported on the Balance Sheet in requirement 5. The two amounts should be the same.

	A	B	C
1	**Goldsmith Company Trial Balance**	**December 31, 20X6**	
2	Cash	$ 198,000	
3	Accounts receivable	370,000	
4	Supplies	6,000	
5	Furniture and fixtures	100,000	
6	Accumulated depreciation—furniture and fixtures		$ 40,000
7	Building	250,000	
8	Accumulated depreciation—building		130,000
9	Accounts payable		380,000
10	Salary payable		
11	Unearned service revenue		45,000
12	Income tax payable		
13	Share capital		100,000
14	Retained earnings		193,000
15	Dividends	65,000	
16	Service revenue		286,000
17	Salary expense	172,000	
18	Supplies expense		
19	Depreciation expense—furniture and fixtures		
20	Depreciation expense—building		
21	Income tax expense		
22	Miscellaneous expense	13,000	
23	Total	$1,174,000	$ 1,174,000
24			

Answers

Requirements 1 and 3

(Amounts in thousands)

Assets

Cash

Debit	Credit
Bal. 198	

Accounts Receivable

Debit	Credit
370	
(e) 12	
Bal. 382	

Supplies

Debit	Credit
6	(a) 4
Bal. 2	

Furniture and Fixtures

Debit	Credit
Bal. 100	

Accumulated Depreciation—Furniture and Fixtures

Debit	Credit
	40
	(b) 20
	Bal. 60

Building

Debit	Credit
Bal. 250	

Accumulated Depreciation—Building

Debit	Credit
	130
	(c) 10
	Bal. 140

Liabilities

Accounts Payable

Debit	Credit
	Bal. 380

Salary Payable

Debit	Credit
	(d) 5
	Bal. 5

Unearned Service Revenue

Debit	Credit
(f) 32	45
	Bal. 13

Income Tax Payable

Debit	Credit
	(g) 35
	Bal. 35

Shareholders' Equity

Share Capital

Debit	Credit
	Bal. 100

Retained Earnings

Debit	Credit
	Bal. 193

Dividends

Debit	Credit
Bal. 65	

Revenues

Service Revenue

Debit	Credit
	286
	(e) 12
	(f) 32
	Bal. 330

Expenses

Salary Expense

Debit	Credit
172	
(d) 5	
Bal. 177	

Supplies Expense

Debit	Credit
(a) 4	
Bal. 4	

Depreciation Expense—Furniture and Fixtures

Debit	Credit
(b) 20	
Bal. 20	

Depreciation Expense—Building

Debit	Credit
(c) 10	
Bal. 10	

Income Tax Expense

Debit	Credit
(g) 35	
Bal. 35	

Miscellaneous Expense

Debit	Credit
Bal. 13	

Requirement 2

A1

	A	B	C	D	E
1	(a)	Dec. 31	Supplies Expense ($6,000 − $2,000)	4,000	
2			Supplies		4,000
3			*To record supplies used.*		
4					
5	(b)	31	Depreciation Expense—Furniture and Fixtures	20,000	
6			Accumulated Depreciation—Furniture and Fixtures		20,000
7			*To record depreciation expense on furniture and fixtures.*		
8					
9	(c)	31	Depreciation Expense—Building	10,000	
10			Accumulated Depreciation—Building		10,000
11			*To record depreciation expense on building.*		
12					
13	(d)	31	Salary Expense	5,000	
14			Salary Payable		5,000
15			*To accrue salary expense.*		
16					
17	(e)	31	Accounts Receivable	12,000	
18			Service Revenue		12,000
19			*To accrue service revenue.*		
20					
21	(f)	31	Unearned Service Revenue	32,000	
22			Service Revenue		32,000
23			*To record unearned service revenue that has been earned.*		
24					
25	(g)	31	Income Tax Expense	35,000	
26			Income Tax Payable		35,000
27			*To accrue income tax expense.*		
28					

Requirement 4

A1

	A	B	C	D	E	F	G
1	**Goldsmith Company Adjusted Trial Balance**	**December 31, 20X6**					
2	**(Amounts in thousands)**	**Trial Balance**		**Adjustments**		**Adjusted Trial Balance**	
3	**Account title**	**Debit**	**Credit**	**Debit**	**Credit**	**Debit**	**Credit**
4	Cash	198				198	
5	Accounts receivable	370		(e) 12		382	
6	Supplies	6			(a) 4	2	
7	Furniture and fixtures	100				100	
8	Accumulated depreciation—furniture and fixtures		40		(b) 20		60
9	Building	250				250	
10	Accumulated depreciation—building		130		(c) 10		140
11	Accounts payable		380				380
12	Salary payable				(d) 5		5
13	Unearned service revenue		45	(f) 32			13
14	Income tax payable				(g) 35		35
15	Share capital		100				100
16	Retained earnings		193				193
17	Dividends	65				65	
18	Service revenue		286		(e) 12		330
19					(f) 32		
20	Salary expense	172		(d) 5		177	
21	Supplies expense			(a) 4		4	
22	Depreciation expense—furniture and fixtures			(b) 20		20	
23	Depreciation expense—building			(c) 10		10	
24	Income tax expense			(g) 35		35	
25	Miscellaneous expense	13				13	
26		1,174	1,174	118	118	1,256	1,256
27							

Requirement 5

	A	B	C
1	**Goldsmith Company Income Statement**	**Year Ended December 31, 20X6**	
2	**(Amounts in thousands)**		
3	Revenue:		
4	Service revenue		$ 330
5	Expenses:		
6	Salary expense	$ 177	
7	Depreciation expense—furniture and fixtures	20	
8	Depreciation expense—building	10	
9	Supplies expense	4	
10	Miscellaneous expenses	13	224
11	Income before tax		106
12	Income tax expense		35
13	Net income		$ 71

①

	A	B
1	**Goldsmith Company Statement of Changes in Equity**	**Year Ended December 31, 20X6**
2	**(Amounts in thousands)**	
3	Total equity, December 31, 20X5	$293
4	Add: Net income	71
5		264
6	Less: Dividends	(65)
7	Total equity, December 31, 20X6	$299
8		

②

	A	B	C	D	E	F
1	**Goldsmith Company Balance Sheet**			**As at December 31, 20X6**		
2	**(Amounts in thousands)**					
3	**Assets**			**Liabilities**		
4	Cash		$ 198	Accounts payable	$ 380	
5	Accounts receivable		382	Salary payable	5	
6	Supplies		2	Unearned service revenue	13	
7	Furniture and fixtures	$100		Income tax payable	35	
8	Less: Accumulated			Total liabilities	433	
9	depreciation	(60)	40			
10				**Shareholders' Equity**		
11	Building	$250		Share capital	100	
12	Less: Accumulated			Retained earnings	199	
13	depreciation	(140)	110	Total shareholders' equity	299	
14				Total liabilities and		
15	Total assets		$ 732	shareholders' equity	$ 732	
16						

Requirement 6

20X6		(In thousands)	
Dec. 31	Service Revenue	330	
	Retained Earnings		330
31	Retained Earnings	259	
	Salary Expense		177
	Depreciation Expense—Furniture and Fixtures		20
	Depreciation Expense—Building		10
	Supplies Expense		4
	Income Tax Expense		35
	Miscellaneous Expense		13
31	Retained Earnings	65	
	Dividends		65

Explanation of Closing Entries

The closing entries set the balance of Revenue, Expense, and Dividends accounts back to zero for the start of the next accounting period. We must close these accounts because their balances relate only to one accounting period.

Requirement 7

The balance in the Retained Earnings account agrees with the amount reported on the Balance Sheet, as it should.

Retained Earnings

			193
Clo.	259	Clo.	330
Clo.	65		
		Bal.	199

REVIEW | Accrual Accounting

Quick Check (Answers are given at the end of the chapter.)

1. On October 1, Seaview Apartments received $6,000 from a tenant for four months' rent. The receipt was credited to Unearned Rent Revenue. What adjusting entry is needed on December 31?

a. Unearned Rent Revenue	1,500	
Rent Revenue		1,500
b. Cash	4,500	
Rent Revenue		4,500
c. Rent Revenue	1,500	
Unearned Rent Revenue		1,500
d. Unearned Rent Revenue	4,500	
Rent Revenue		4,500

2. The following normal balances appear on the *adjusted* trial balance of Parks National Company:

Equipment	$150,000
Accumulated depreciation, equipment	22,500
Depreciation expense, equipment	7,500

The carrying amount of the equipment is

a. $120,000.
b. $127,500.
c. $142,500.
d. $150,000.

3. Pisces, Inc., purchased supplies for $1,300 during 20X6. At year-end, Pisces had $800 of supplies left. The adjusting entry should

a. credit Supplies $800.
b. debit Supplies $500.
c. debit Supplies Expense $500.
d. debit Supplies Expense $800.

4. The accountant for Starter Corp. failed to make the adjusting entry to record depreciation for the current year. The effect of this error is which of the following?

a. Assets are overstated; shareholders' equity and net income are understated.
b. Assets, net income, and shareholders' equity are all overstated.
c. Assets and expenses are understated; net income is understated.
d. Net income is overstated and liabilities are understated.

5. Interest earned on a note receivable at December 31 equals $400. What adjusting entry is required to accrue this interest?

a. Interest Receivable	400	
Interest Revenue		400
b. Interest Expense	400	
Cash		400
c. Interest Expense	400	
Interest Payable		400
d. Interest Payable	400	
Interest Expense		400

6. If a real estate company fails to accrue commission revenue,

a. revenues are understated and net income is overstated.
b. net income is understated and shareholders' equity is overstated.
c. liabilities are overstated and owners' equity is understated.
d. assets are understated and net income is understated.

7. All of the following statements are true except one. Which statement is false?

a. Accrual-basis accounting produces better information than cash-basis accounting.
b. Adjusting entries are required for a business that uses the cash-basis accounting.
c. The matching concept directs accountants to identify and measure all expenses incurred and deduct them from revenues earned during the same period.
d. A fiscal year is not always the same as a calendar year.

8. The account Unearned Revenue is a(n)

a. revenue.
b. asset.
c. liability.
d. expense.

9. Adjusting entries
   a. are needed to measure the period's net income or net loss accounts.
   b. usually do not debit or credit the cash account.
   c. update the accounts.
   d. apply to all of the above.

10. An adjusting entry that debits an expense and credits a liability is which type of expense?
   a. Accrued expense
   b. Cash expense
   c. Prepaid expense
   d. Depreciation expense

11. On a trial balance, which of the following would indicate that an error has been made?
   a. Accumulated Depreciation has a credit balance.
   b. Service Revenue has a debit balance.
   c. Salary Expense has a debit balance.
   d. All of the above indicate errors.

12. The entry to close Management Fee Revenue would be which of the following?
   a. Retained Earnings
   b. Management Fee Revenue
   c. Retained Earnings
   d. Dividend does not need to be closed.

13. Which of the following accounts is not closed?
   a. Accumulated Depreciation
   b. Dividends
   c. Interest Revenue
   d. Depreciation Expense

Accounting Vocabulary

accrual (p. 143) An expense or a revenue that occurs before the business pays or receives cash. An accrual is the opposite of a deferral.

accrual accounting (p. 132) Accounting that records the impact of a business event as it occurs, regardless of whether the transaction affected cash.

accrued expense (p. 147) An expense incurred but not yet paid in cash.

accrued revenue (p. 148) A revenue that has been earned but not yet received in cash.

accumulated depreciation (p. 151) The cumulative sum of all depreciation expense from the date of acquiring a PPE.

adjusted trial balance (p. 154) A list of all the ledger accounts with their adjusted balances.

carrying amount (of a PPE) (p. 151) The asset's cost minus accumulated depreciation.

cash-basis accounting (p. 132) Accounting that records only transactions in which cash is received or paid.

closing the books (p. 156) The process of preparing the accounts to begin recording the next period's transactions. Closing the accounts consists of journalizing and posting the closing entries to set the balances of the revenue, expense, and dividends accounts to zero. Also called closing the accounts.

closing entries (p. 156) Entries that transfer the income, expense, and dividends balances from these respective accounts to the Retained Earnings account.

contra account (p. 151) An account that always has a companion account and whose normal balance is opposite that of the companion account.

deferral (p. 142) An adjustment for which the business paid or received cash in advance. Examples include prepaid rent, prepaid insurance, and supplies.

depreciation (p. 143) Allocation of the cost of a PPE to expense over its useful life.

matching concept (p. 136) A concept for matching expenses to revenue. Directs accountants to identify all expenses incurred during the period, to measure the expenses, and to match them against the revenues earned during that same period.

permanent accounts (p. 156) Asset, liability, and shareholders' equity accounts that are not closed at the end of the period.

prepaid expense (p. 143) A category of miscellaneous assets that typically expire or get used up in the near future. Examples include prepaid rent, prepaid insurance, and supplies.

property, plant and equipment or PPE (p. 149) Long-lived assets, such as land, buildings, and equipment, used in the operation of the business. Sometimes referred to as fixed assets or plant assets.

revenue recognition principle (p. 134) The basis for recording and measurement of revenues; tells accountants when to record revenue and the amount of revenue to record.

temporary accounts (p. 156) The revenue and expense accounts that relate to a limited period and are closed at the end of the period are temporary accounts. For a corporation, the Dividends account is also temporary.

time-period concept (p. 133) Ensures that accounting information is reported at regular intervals.

unearned revenue (p. 145) A liability created when a business collects cash from customers in advance of earning the revenue. The obligation is to provide a product or a service in the future.

ASSESS YOUR PROGRESS

Short Exercises

LO 1

S3-1. ***(Learning Objective 1: Linking accrual accounting and cash flows)*** Patrick Corporation made sales of $850 million during 20X6. Of this amount, Patrick collected cash for all but $30 million. The company's cost of goods sold was $225 million, and all other expenses for the year totaled $355 million. Also during 20X6, Patrick paid $320 million for its inventory and $265 million for everything else. Beginning cash was $140 million. Patrick's top management is interviewing you for a job and they ask two questions:

a. How much was Patrick's net income for 20X6?
b. How much was Patrick's cash balance at the end of 20X6?

You will get the job only if you answer both questions correctly.

LO 1

S3-2. ***(Learning Objective 1: Explaining how accrual accounting differs from cash-basis accounting)*** County Corporation began 20X6 owing notes payable of $4.2 million. During 20X6, County borrowed $2.8 million on notes payable and paid off $2.4 million of notes payable from prior years. Interest expense for the year was $1.5 million, including $0.3 million of interest payable accrued at December 31, 20X6.

Show what County should report for these facts on the following financial statements:

1. Income Statement
   a. Interest expense
2. Balance Sheet
   a. Notes payable
   b. Interest payable

LO 1 2
■ writing assignment

S3-3. ***(Learning Objectives 1, 2: Linking accrual accounting and cash flows; applying accounting principles)*** As the controller of Apple Consulting, you have hired a new employee, whom you must train. She objects to making an adjusting entry for accrued salaries at the end of the period. She reasons, "We will pay the salaries soon. Why not wait until payment to record the expense? In the end, the result will be the same." Write a reply to explain to the employee why the adjusting entry is needed for accrued salary expense.

LO 2
■ writing assignment

S3-4. ***(Learning Objective 2: Applying the revenue and expense recognition principles)*** A large auto manufacturer sells large fleets of vehicles to auto rental companies, such as Lewis and Clark. Suppose Lewis is negotiating with the auto manufacturer to purchase 80 vehicles. Write a short paragraph to explain to the auto manufacturer when the company should, and should not, record this sales revenue and the related expense for cost of goods sold. Mention the accounting principles that provide the basis for your explanation.

LO 2

S3-5. ***(Learning Objective 2: Applying accounting concepts and principles)*** Write a short paragraph in your own words to explain the concept of depreciation as used in accounting.

LO 2 **S3-6.** ***(Learning Objective 2: Applying accounting concepts and principles)*** Identify the accounting concept or principle that gives the most direction on how to account for each of the following situations:

- **a.** A physician performs a surgical operation and bills the patient's insurance company. It may take four months to collect the payment from the insurance company. Should the physician record revenue now or wait until cash is collected?
- **b.** May has been a particularly slow month, and the business will have a net loss for the second quarter of the year. Management is considering not following its customary practice of reporting quarterly earnings to the public.
- **c.** Salary expense of $2,835,000 is accrued at the end of the period to measure income properly.
- **d.** A utility bill is received on December 28 and will be paid next year. When should the company record this utility expense?
- **e.** A construction company is building a highway system, and construction will take five years. When should the company record the revenue it earns?

LO 3 **S3-7.** ***(Learning Objective 3: Adjusting prepaid expenses)*** Answer the following questions about prepaid expenses:

- **a.** On March 1, Sunshine Travel prepaid $5,400 for six months' rent. Provide the adjusting entry to record rent expense at March 31. Include the date of the entry and an explanation. Then post all amounts to the two accounts involved and show their balances at March 31. Sunshine Travel adjusts the accounts only at March 31, the end of its fiscal year.
- **b.** On December 1, Sunshine Travel paid $980 for supplies. At March 31, Sunshine has $750 of supplies on hand. Make the required journal entry at March 31. Then post all amounts to the accounts and show their balances at March 31.

LO 1 3 **S3-8.** ***(Learning Objectives 1, 3: Recording depreciation; linking accrual accounting and cash flows)*** Suppose that on January 1 Gulfstream Golf Company paid cash of $60,000 for computers that are expected to remain useful for four years. At the end of four years, the value of the computers are expected to be zero.

1. Make journal entries to record (a) the purchase of the computers on January 1, and (b) annual depreciation on December 31. Include dates and explanations, and use the following accounts: Computer Equipment; Accumulated Depreciation—Computer Equipment; and Depreciation Expense—Computer Equipment.
2. Post to the accounts and show their balances at December 31.
3. What is the computer equipment's carrying amount at December 31?

LO 2 **S3-9.** ***(Learning Objective 2: Applying the revenue recognition principles and matching concept)*** During 20X6, Litblue Airlines paid salary expenses of €39.7 million. At December 31, 20X6, Litblue accrued salary expenses of €3.1 million. Litblue then paid €2.3 million to its employees on January 3, 20X7, the company's next payday after the end of the 20X6 year. For this sequence of transactions, show what Litblue would report on its 20X6 Income Statement and on its Balance Sheet at the end of 20X6.

LO 3 **S3-10.** ***(Learning Objective 3: Accruing and paying interest expense)*** Leisure Travel borrowed $100,000 on October 1 by signing a note payable to First State Bank. The interest expense for each month is $800. The loan agreement requires Leisure to pay interest on December 31.

1. Make Leisure's adjusting entry to accrue monthly interest expense at October 31, at November 30, and at December 31. Date each entry and include its explanation.
2. Post all three entries to the Interest Payable account. You need not take the balance of the account at the end of each month.
3. Record the payment of three months' interest at December 31.

LO 3 **S3-11.** ***(Learning Objective 3: Accruing and receiving cash from interest revenue)*** Return to the situation in Short Exercise 3-10. Here you are accounting for the same transactions on the books of First State Bank, which lent the money to Leisure Travel.

1. Make First State Bank's adjusting entry to accrue monthly interest revenue at October 31, at November 30, and at December 31. Date each entry and include its explanation.

2. Post all three entries to the Interest Receivable account. You need not take the balance of the account at the end of each month.
3. Record the receipt of three months' interest at December 31.

LO 1 3
■ writing assignment

S3-12. ***(Learning Objectives 1, 3: Relating accrual accounting to cash flows; adjusting the accounts)*** Write a paragraph to explain why unearned revenues are liabilities instead of revenues. In your explanation, use the following example: *The Asahi Shimbun*, a Japanese national newspaper, collects cash from subscribers in advance and later delivers newspapers to subscribers over a one-year period. Explain what happens to the unearned revenue over the course of a year as *The Asahi Shimbun* delivers papers to subscribers. Into what account does the earned subscription revenue go as *The Asahi Shimbun* delivers papers? Give the journal entries that *The Asahi Shimbun* would make to (a) collect ¥5 million of subscription revenue in advance, and (b) record earning ¥5 million of subscription revenue. Include an explanation for each entry, as illustrated in the chapter.

LO 3 4

S3-13. ***(Learning Objectives 3, 4: Adjusting the accounts; reporting prepaid expenses)*** Eagle Express Co. prepaid four years' rent ($24,000) on January 1, 20X6. At December 31, 20X6, Eagle prepared a trial balance and then made the necessary adjusting entry at the end of the year. Eagle adjusts its accounts once each year—on December 31.

What amount appears for Prepaid Rent on

a. Eagle's *unadjusted* trial balance at December 31, 20X6?
b. Eagle's *adjusted* trial balance at December 31, 20X6?

What amount appears for Rent Expense on

a. Eagle's *unadjusted* trial balance at December 31, 20X6?
b. Eagle's *adjusted* trial balance at December 31, 20X6?

S3-14. ***(Learning Objective 3: Adjusting the accounts)*** Richmond, Inc., collects cash from customers two ways:

a. Accrued revenue. Some customers pay Richmond after Richmond has performed services for the customer. During 20X6, Richmond performed services worth $75,000 on account and later received cash of $50,000 on account from these customers.
b. Unearned revenue. A few customers pay Richmond in advance, and Richmond later performs the service for the customer. During 20X6, Richmond collected $8,000 cash in advance and later earned $3,600 of this amount.

Journalize for Richmond

a. Earning service revenue of $75,000 on account and then collecting $45,000 on account.
b. Receiving $8,000 in advance and then earning $3,600 as service revenue.

LO 4

S3-15. ***(Learning Objective 4: Preparing the financial statements)*** Suppose Hawk Sporting Goods Company reported the following data at March 31, 20X8, with amounts in thousands:

Retained earnings, March 31, 20X7	$ 4,000	Cost of goods sold................	$142,500
Accounts receivable.......	37,800	Cash....................................	1,700
Net revenues	188,000	Property and equipment, net ...	7,500
Total current liabilities..	48,000	Share capital.........................	30,000
All other expenses	24,300	Inventories	25,000
Other current assets	6,400	Long-term liabilities	8,000
Other assets...................	31,600	Dividends.............................	1,200

Use these data to prepare Hawk Sporting Goods Company's Income Statement for the year ended March 31, 20X8; statement of changes in equity for the year ended March 31, 20X8; and classified Balance Sheet at March 31, 20X8. Use the report format for the Balance Sheet. Draw arrows linking the three statements.

LO 5

S3-16. ***(Learning Objective 5: Making closing entries)*** Use the Hawk Sporting Goods Company data in Short Exercise 3-15 to make the company's closing entries at March 31, 20X8.

Then set up a T-account for Retained Earnings and post to that account. Compare Retained Earnings' ending balance to the amount reported on Hawk's statement of changes in equity and Balance Sheet. What do you find?

Exercises MyLab Accounting

Select A and B exercises can be found within MyLab Accounting, an online homework and practice environment. Your instructor may ask you to complete select exercises using MyLab Accounting.

Group A

LO 1

E3-17A. ***(Learning Objective 1: Linking accrual accounting and cash flows)*** During 20X7, Milky Way Corporation made sales of $4,600 (assume all on account) and collected cash of $4,800 from customers. Operating expenses totaled $1,100, all paid in cash. At year-end, 20X7, Milky Way customers owed the company $500. Milky Way owed creditors $1,200 on account. All amounts are in thousands.

1. For these facts, show what Milky Way reported on the following financial statements:
   a. Income Statement
   b. Balance Sheet
2. Suppose Milky Way had used the cash basis of accounting. What would Milky Way have reported for these facts?

LO 1

E3-18A. ***(Learning Objective 1: Linking accrual accounting and cash flows)*** During 20X7, Plateau Sales, Inc., earned revenues of $590,000 on account. Plateau collected $610,000 from customers during the year. Expenses totaled $450,000, and the related cash payments were $460,000. Show what Plateau would report on its 20X7 Income Statement under the

a. cash basis.
b. accrual basis.

Compute net income under both bases of accounting. Which basis measures net income better? Explain your answer.

LO 1 2

E3-19A. ***(Learning Objectives 1, 2: Using accrual accounting; applying accounting principles)*** During 20X8, Carson Network, Inc., which designs network servers, earned revenues of $850 million. Expenses totaled $560 million. Carson collected all but $30 million of the revenues and paid $610 million on its expenses. Carson's top managers are evaluating 20X8, and they ask you the following questions:

a. Under accrual accounting, what amount of revenue should Carson Network report for 20X8? Is the revenue the $850 million earned or is it the amount of cash actually collected? How does the revenue principle help to answer these questions?
b. Under accrual accounting, what amount of total expense should Carson Network report for 20X8—$560 million or $610 million? Which accounting principle helps answer this question?
c. Which financial statement reports revenues and expenses? Which statement reports cash receipts and cash payments?

LO 1 3

E3-20A. ***(Learning Objectives 1, 3: Journalizing adjusting entries and analyzing their effects on net income; comparing accrual and cash basis)*** An accountant made the following adjustments at December 31, the end of the accounting period:

a. Prepaid insurance, beginning, $600. Payments for insurance during the period, $1,800. Prepaid insurance, ending, $1,000.
b. Interest revenue accrued, $1,500.

c. Unearned service revenue, beginning, $1,200. Unearned service revenue, ending, $800.
d. Depreciation, $4,400.
e. Employees' salaries owed for three days of a five-day work week; weekly payroll, $20,000.
f. Income before income tax, $24,000. Income tax rate is 25%.

Requirements

1. Journalize the adjusting entries.
2. Suppose the adjustments were not made. Compute the overall overstatement or understatement of net income as a result of the omission of these adjustments.

E3-21A. ***(Learning Objectives 2, 3: Applying the matching concept; allocating supplies cost between the asset and the expense)*** Blue Buttons, Inc., experienced four situations for its supplies. Compute the amounts that have been left blank for each situation. For situations 1 and 2, journalize the needed transaction. Consider each situation separately.

	Situation			
	1	2	3	4
Beginning supplies	$ 200	$ 900	$ 1,500	$ 800
Payments for supplies during the year	?	600	?	700
Total amount to account for	1,600	?	?	1,500
Ending supplies	(500)	(200)	(1,200)	?
Supplies expense	$1,100	$?	$ 1,500	$1,200

E3-22A. ***(Learning Objective 3: Journalizing adjusting entries)*** Jose Motor Company faced the following situations. Journalize the adjusting entry needed at December 31, 20X7, for each situation. Consider each fact separately.

a. The business has an interest expense of $8,400 that it must pay by early January 20X8.
b. Interest revenue of $5,000 has been earned but not yet received.
c. On July 1, when $12,800 for rent was collected in advance, Cash was debited and Unearned Rent Revenue was credited. The tenant was paying two years' rent.
d. Salary expense is $1,600 per day—Monday through Friday—and the business pays employees each Friday. This year, December 31 falls on a Wednesday.
e. The unadjusted balance of the Supplies account is $3,500. The total cost of supplies on hand is $1,300.
f. Equipment was purchased at the beginning of this year at a cost of $110,000. The equipment's useful life is five years. There is no residual value. Record depreciation for this year and then determine the equipment's carrying amount.

LO 3

E3-23A. ***(Learning Objective 3: Making adjustments in T-accounts)*** The accounting records of Fiona Publishing Company include the following unadjusted balances at May 31: Accounts Receivable, $1,500; Supplies, $900; Salary Payable, $0; Unearned Service Revenue, $700; Service Revenue, $5,000; Salary Expense, $2,500; Supplies Expense, $0.

Fiona's accountant develops the following data for the May 31 adjusting entries:

a. Supplies on hand, $200
b. Salary owed to employees, $500
c. Service revenue accrued, $600
d. Unearned service revenue that has been earned, $400

Open the foregoing T-accounts with their beginning balances. Then record the adjustments directly in the accounts, keying each adjustment amount by letter. Show each account's adjusted balance. Journal entries are not required.

LO 4

E3-24A. ***(Learning Objective 4: Preparing the financial statements)*** The adjusted trial balance of Tasty Food, Inc., follows.

	A	B	C
1	**Tasty Food, Inc.** **Adjusted Trial Balance**	**December 31, 20X8**	
2	**(Amounts in thousands)**		
3	**Account**	**Debit**	**Credit**
4	Cash	$ 3,900	
5	Accounts receivable	1,600	
6	Inventories	1,200	
7	Prepaid expenses	1,800	
8	Property, plant, and equipment	6,600	
9	Accumulated depreciation		$ 2,200
10	Other assets	9,500	
11	Accounts payable		7,700
12	Income tax payable		500
13	Other liabilities		2,300
14	Share capital		4,800
15	Retained earnings (beginning, December 31, 20X7)		4,700
16	Dividends	1,500	
17	Sales revenue		41,800
18	Cost of goods sold	26,300	
19	Selling, administrative, and general expenses	10,200	
20	Income tax expense	1,400	
21			
22	Total	$64,000	$64,000
23			

Requirement

1. Prepare Tasty Food, Inc.'s Income Statement and statement of changes in equity for the year ended December 31, 20X8, and its Balance Sheet on that date.

LO 3 4

E3-25A. ***(Learning Objectives 3, 4: Measuring financial statement amounts; preparing financial statement amounts)*** The adjusted trial balances of Doyle Corporation at March 31, 20X8, and March 31, 20X7, include these amounts (in millions):

	20X8	20X7
Receivables	$370	$290
Prepaid insurance	160	190
Accrued liabilities payable (for other operating expenses)	710	630

Doyle completed these transactions (in millions) during the year ended March 31, 20X8.

Collections from customers	$20,400
Payment of prepaid insurance	450
Cash payments for other operating expenses	4,100

Compute the amount of sales revenue, insurance expense, and other operating expenses to report on the Income Statement for the year ended March 31, 20X8.

E3-26A. ***(Learning Objective 4: Reporting on the financial statements)*** This question deals with the items and the amounts that two entities, Mother Catherine Hospital (Mother Catherine) and City of Cologne (Cologne), should report in their financial statements. Fill in the blanks.

Requirements

1. On July 1, 20X6, Mother Catherine collected $6,000 in advance from Cologne, a client. Under the contract, Mother Catherine is obligated to perform medical exams for City of Cologne employees evenly during the 12 months ending June 30, 20X7. Assume you are Mother Catherine.

   Mother Catherine's Income Statement for the year ended December 31, 20X6, will report _____ of $ _____.

   Mother Catherine's Balance Sheet at December 31, 20X6, will report _____ of $ _____.
2. Cologne's Income Statement for the year ended December 31, 20X6, will report _____ of $ _____.

   Cologne's Balance Sheet at December 31, 20X6, will report _____ of $ _____.

E3-27A. ***(Learning Objectives 1, 3: Linking deferrals and cash flows)*** New Age Mobile, the British wireless phone service provider, collects cash in advance from customers. All amounts are in millions of pound sterling (£). Assume New Age Mobile collected £410 in advance during 20X7 and at year-end still owed customers phone service worth £160.

Requirements

1. Show what New Age Mobile will report for 20X7 on its Income Statement and Balance Sheet.
2. Use the same facts for New Age Mobile as in Requirement 1. Further, assume New Age Mobile reported unearned service revenue of £65 back at the end of 20X6. Show what New Age Mobile will report for 20X7 on the same financial statements. Explain why your answer here differs from your answer to Requirement 1.

LO 5

E3-28A. ***(Learning Objective 5: Closing the accounts)*** Prepare the closing entries from the following selected accounts from the records of Sunnyside Corporation at December 31, 20X8:

Cost of services sold	$11,500	Service revenue	$24,900
Accumulated depreciation	42,800	Depreciation expense	4,800
Selling, general, and administrative expenses	6,200	Other revenue	800
		Dividends	900
Retained earnings, December 31, 20X5	2,600	Income tax expense	500
		Income tax payable	700

How much net income did Sunnyside earn during 20X8? Prepare a T-account for Retained Earnings to show the December 31, 20X8, balance of Retained Earnings.

E3-29A. ***(Learning Objectives 3, 5: Identifying and recording adjusting and closing entries)*** The unadjusted trial balance and Income Statement amounts from the December 31 adjusted trial balance of Tape Production Company follow.

	A	B	C	D	E	F
1	**Tape Production Company**					
2	**Account**	**Unadjusted Trial Balance**		**From the Adjusted Trial Balance**		
3	Cash	14,800				
4	Prepaid rent	1,200				
5	Equipment	45,000				
6	Accumulated depreciation		3,300			
7	Accounts payable		5,300			
8	Salary payable					
9	Unearned service revenue		9,400			
10	Income tax payable					
11	Notes payable, long term		13,500			
12	Share capital		8,600			
13	Retained earnings		14,200			
14	Dividends	1,300				
15	Service revenue		13,600		20,400	
16	Salary expense	4,600		5,200		
17	Rent expense	1,000		1,400		
18	Depreciation expense			500		
19	Income tax expense			1,000		
20	Total	67,900	67,900	8,100	20,400	
21						

Requirement

1. Journalize the adjusting and closing entries of Tape Production Company at December 31. There was only one adjustment to Service Revenue.

Group B

LO 1

E3-30B. ***(Learning Objective 1: Linking accrual accounting and cash flows)*** During 20X7, Andromeda Corporation made sales of €4,200 (assume all on account) and collected cash of €4,800 from customers. Operating expenses totaled €1,400, all paid in cash. At year-end, 20X7, Andromeda customers owed the company €400. Andromeda owed creditors €800 on account. All amounts are in thousands.

1. For these facts, show what Andromeda reported on the following financial statements:
   - **a.** Income Statement
   - **b.** Balance Sheet
2. Suppose Andromeda had used the cash basis of accounting. What would Andromeda have reported for these facts?

LO 1

E3-31B. ***(Learning Objective 1: Linking accrual accounting and cash flows)*** During 20X7, Valley Sales, Inc., earned revenues of €690,000 on account. Valley collected €650,000 from customers during the year. Expenses totaled €500,000, and the related cash payments were €440,000. Show what Valley would report on its 20X7 Income Statement under the

- **a.** cash basis.
- **b.** accrual basis.

Compute net income under both bases of accounting. Which basis measures net income better? Explain your answer.

LO 1 2

E3-32B. ***(Learning Objectives 1, 2: Using the accrual basis of accounting; applying accounting principles)*** During 20X8, Carlton Network, Inc., which designs network servers, earned revenues of €800 million. Expenses totaled €590 million. Carlton collected all but €25 million of the revenues and paid €570 million on its expenses. Carlton's top managers are evaluating 20X8, and they ask you the following questions:

a. Under accrual accounting, what amount of revenue should Carlton Network report for 20X8? Is it the revenue of €800 million earned or is it the amount of cash actually collected? How does the revenue principle help to answer these questions?
b. Under accrual accounting, what amount of total expense should Carlton report for 20X8—€590 million or €570 million? Which accounting principle helps to answer this question?
c. Which financial statement reports revenues and expenses? Which statement reports cash receipts and cash payments?

E3-33B. ***(Learning Objectives 1, 3: Journalizing adjusting entries and analyzing their effects on net income; comparing accrual and cash basis)*** An accountant made the following adjustments at December 31, the end of the accounting period: LO 1 3

a. Prepaid insurance, beginning, €800. Payments for insurance during the period, €2,500. Prepaid insurance, ending, €1,400.
b. Interest revenue accrued, €1,200.
c. Unearned service revenue, beginning, €1,500. Unearned service revenue, ending, €600.
d. Depreciation, €4,700.
e. Employees' salaries owed for three days of a five-day work week; weekly payroll, €24,000.
f. Income before income tax, €21,000. Income tax rate is 25%.

Requirements

1. Journalize the adjusting entries.
2. Suppose the adjustments were not made. Compute the overall overstatement or understatement of net income as a result of the omission of these adjustments.

E3-34B. ***(Learning Objectives 2, 3: Applying the revenue recognition principles; allocating supplies cost between the asset and the expense)*** Mega Minds, Inc., experienced four situations for its supplies. Compute the amounts that have been left blank for each situation. For situations 1 and 2, journalize the needed transaction. Consider each situation separately. LO 2 3

	Situation			
	1	2	3	4
Beginning supplies	$ 100	$ 600	$1,100	$ 700
Payments for supplies during the year	?	1,000	?	600
Total amount to account for	1,600	?	?	1,300
Ending supplies	(400)	(200)	(800)	?
Supplies expense	$1,200	$?	$1,000	$ 800

E3-35B. ***(Learning Objective 3: Journalizing adjusting entries)*** Felipe Motor Company faced the following situations. Journalize the adjusting entry needed at December 31, 20X7, for each situation. Consider each fact separately. LO 3

a. The business has an interest expense of €9,000 that it must pay early in January 20X8.
b. Interest revenue of €4,800 has been earned but not yet received.
c. On July 1, €13,200 rent in advance was collected; Cash was debited and Unearned Rent Revenue was credited. The tenant was paying two years' rent.
d. Salary expense is €1,800 per day—Monday through Friday—and the business pays employees each Friday. This year, December 31 falls on a Wednesday.
e. The unadjusted balance of the Supplies account is €3,300. The total cost of supplies on hand is €1,200.
f. Equipment was purchased at the beginning of this year at a cost of €150,000. The equipment's useful life is five years. There is no residual value. Record depreciation for this year and then determine the equipment's carrying amount.

LO 3

E3-36B. *(Learning Objective 3: Making adjustments in T-accounts)* The accounting records of Harry Publishing Company include the following unadjusted balances at May 31: Accounts Receivable, €1,400; Supplies, €500; Salary Payable, €0; Unearned Service Revenue, €600; Service Revenue, €4,900; Salary Expense, €1,700; Supplies Expense, €0.

Harry's accountant develops the following data for the May 31 adjusting entries:

a. Supplies on hand, €300
b. Salary owed to employees, €800
c. Service revenue accrued, €200
d. Unearned service revenue that has been earned, €100

Open the foregoing T-accounts with their beginning balances. Then record the adjustments directly in the accounts, keying each adjustment amount by letter. Show each account's adjusted balance. Journal entries are not required.

LO 4

E3-37B. *(Learning Objective 4: Preparing the financial statements)* The adjusted trial balance of Sweet Hut, Inc., is as follows.

	A	B	C
1	**Sweet Hut, Inc.** **Adjusted Trial Balance**	**December 31, 20X8**	
2	**(Amounts in thousands)**	**Adjusted Trial Balance**	
3	**Account**	**Debit**	**Credit**
4	Cash	$ 3,600	
5	Accounts receivable	1,600	
6	Inventories	1,300	
7	Prepaid expenses	1,700	
8	Property, plant, and equipment	6,800	
9	Accumulated depreciation		$ 2,800
10	Other assets	9,600	
11	Accounts payable		7,900
12	Income tax payable		1,000
13	Other liabilities		2,800
14	Share capital		4,900
15	Retained earnings (beginning, December 31, 20X7)		4,800
16	Dividends	1,200	
17	Sales revenue		40,900
18	Cost of goods sold	26,400	
19	Selling, administrative, and general expenses	10,500	
20	Income tax expense	2,400	
21			
22	Total	$ 65,100	$ 65,100
23			

Requirement

1. Prepare Sweet Hut, Inc.'s Income Statement and statement of changes in equity for the year ended December 31, 20X8, and its Balance Sheet on that date. Draw arrows linking the three statements.

LO 3 4

E3-38B. ***(Learning Objectives 3, 4: Measuring financial statement amounts; preparing financial statement amounts)*** The adjusted trial balances of Austen Corporation at March 31, 20X8, and March 31, 20X7, include these amounts (in millions):

	20X8	20X7
Receivables	€350	€230
Prepaid insurance	130	140
Accrued liabilities payable (for other operating expenses)	700	660

Austen completed these transactions during the year ended March 31, 20X8.

Collections from customers	$20,500
Payment of prepaid insurance	420
Cash payments for other operating expenses	4,300

Compute the amount of sales revenue, insurance expense, and other operating expenses to report on the Income Statement for the year ended March 31, 20X8.

LO 4

E3-39B. ***(Learning Objective 4: Reporting on the financial statements)*** This question deals with the items and the amounts that two entities, Mother Claire Hospital (Mother Claire) and City of Murcia (Murcia), should report in their financial statements. Fill in the blanks.

Requirements

1. On July 1, 20X6, Mother Claire collected €8,600 in advance from Murcia, a client. Under the contract, Mother Claire is obligated to perform medical exams for Murcia employees evenly during the 12 months ending June 30, 20X7.
   Mother Claire's Income Statement for the year ended December 31, 20X6, will report ___ of € ___.
   Mother Claire's Balance Sheet at December 31, 20X6, will report ___ of € ___.
2. Murcia's Income Statement for the year ended December 31, 20X6, will report ___ of € ___.
   Murcia's Balance Sheet at December 31, 20X6, will report ___ of € ___.

LO 1 3

E3-40B. ***(Learning Objectives 1, 3: Linking deferrals and cash flows)*** GTel, the British wireless phone service provider, collects cash in advance from customers. All amounts are in millions of pounds sterling (£). Assume GTel collected £500 in advance during 20X7 and at year-end still owed customers phone service worth £125.

Requirements

1. Show what GTel will report for 20X7 on its Income Statement Balance Sheet.
2. Use the same facts for GTel as in Requirement 1. Further, assume GTel reported unearned service revenue of £85 back at the end of 20X6. Show what GTel will report for 20X7 on the same financial statements. Explain why your answer here differs from your answer to Requirement 1.

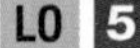

E3-41B. ***(Learning Objective 5: Closing the accounts)*** Prepare the closing entries from the following selected accounts from the records of North Shore Corporation at December 31, 20X8:

Cost of services sold	$11,600	Service revenue	$24,800
Accumulated depreciation ...	42,800	Depreciation expense	4,700
Selling, general, and administrative expenses	6,400	Other revenue	900
		Dividends	800
Retained earnings, December 31, 20X7	2,500	Income tax expense	700
		Income tax payable	500

How much net income did North Shore earn during 20X8? Prepare a T-account for Retained Earnings to show the December 31, 20X8, balance of Retained Earnings.

E3-42B. ***(Learning Objectives 3, 5: Identifying and recording adjusting and closing entries)*** The unadjusted trial balance and Income Statement amounts from the December 31 adjusted trial balance of Cassette Production Company follow.

	A	B	C	D	E
1	**Cassette Production Company**				
2	**Account**	**Unadjusted Trial Balance**		**From the Adjusted Trial Balance**	
3	Cash	14,500			
4	Prepaid rent	1,200			
5	Equipment	46,000			
6	Accumulated depreciation		3,300		
7	Accounts payable		5,100		
8	Salary payable				
9	Unearned service revenue		9,400		
10	Income tax payable				
11	Notes payable, long term		13,500		
12	Share capital		8,500		
13	Retained earnings		15,000		
14	Dividends	1,100			
15	Service revenue		13,300		19,600
16	Salary expense	4,500		5,200	
17	Rent expense	800		1,500	
18	Depreciation expense			600	
19	Income tax expense			900	
20	Total	68,100	68,100	8,200	19,600
21					

Requirement

1. Journalize the adjusting and closing entries of Cassette Production Company at December 31. There was only one adjustment to Service Revenue.

Serial Exercise

Exercise 3-43 continues the Jerome Smith, Certified Public Accountant, P.C., situation begun in Exercise 2-36.

E3-43. ***(Learning Objectives 3, 4, 5: Adjusting the accounts; preparing the financial statements; closing the accounts)*** Refer to Exercise 2-36. Start from the trial balance and the posted T-accounts that Jerome Smith, Certified Public Accountant, Professional Corporation (P.C.), prepared for his accounting practice at March 18. A professional corporation is not subject to income tax. Later in March, the business completed these transactions:

Mar 21	Received $2,000 in advance for tax work to be performed over the next 30 days.
21	Hired a secretary to be paid on the 15th day of each month.
26	Paid $800 for the supplies purchased on March 5.
28	Collected $1,900 from the client on March 18.
31	Declared and paid dividends of $1,600.

Requirements

1. Journalize the transactions of March 21 through 31.
2. Post the March 21 to 31 transactions to the T-accounts, keying all items by date.
3. Prepare a trial balance at March 31.
4. At March 31, gather the following information for the adjusting entries:
   a. Accrued service revenue, $1,800
   b. Earned $600 of the service revenue collected in advance on March 21
   c. Supplies on hand, $300
   d. Depreciation expense equipment, $70; furniture, $125
   e. Accrued expense for secretary's salary, $620

   Make these adjustments in the adjustments columns and complete the adjusted trial balance at March 31.
5. Journalize and post the adjusting entries. Denote each adjusting amount as Adj. and an account balance as Bal.
6. Prepare the Income Statement and statement of changes in equity of Jerome Smith Certified Public Accountant, P.C., for the month ended March 31 and the classified Balance Sheet at that date.
7. Journalize and post the closing entries at March 31. Denote each closing amount as Clo. and an account balance as Bal.

Challenge Exercises

E3-44. ***(Learning Objectives 3, 4: Computing financial statement amounts)*** The accounts of Gretel Company prior to the year-end adjustments follow.

Cash	$ 16,700	Share capital	$ 14,500
Accounts receivable	7,200	Retained earnings	45,000
Supplies	4,100	Dividends	13,000
Prepaid insurance	3,500	Service revenue	165,000
Building	110,000	Salary expense	38,000
Accumulated depreciation—building	15,000	Depreciation expense—building	
Land	50,000	Supplies expense	
Accounts payable	7,700	Insurance expense	
Salary payable		Advertising expense	7,700
Unearned service revenue	5,400	Utilities expense	2,400

Adjusting data at the end of the year include which of the following?

a. Unearned service revenue that has been earned, $1,820
b. Accrued service revenue, $34,000
c. Supplies used in operations, $3,400
d. Accrued salary expense, $3,300
e. Prepaid insurance expired, $1,400
f. Depreciation expense—building, $2,500

Hansel Lacourse, the principal shareholder, has received an offer to sell Gretel Company. He needs to know the following information within one hour:

a. Net income for the year covered by these data
b. Total assets
c. Total liabilities
d. Total shareholders' equity
e. Proof that Total assets = Total liabilities + Total shareholders' equity after all items are updated.

Requirement

1. Without opening any accounts, making any journal entries, or using a work sheet, provide Mr. Lacourse with the requested information. The business is not subject to income tax.

Quiz

Test your understanding of accrual accounting by answering the following questions. Select the best choice from among the possible answers given.

Questions 45–47 are based on the following facts:
Denise Kelly began a cleaning supplies business in January 20X8. Kelly prepares monthly financial statements and uses the accrual basis of accounting. The following transactions are Kelly Company's only activities during January through April:

Jan. 14	Bought cleaning supplies on account for $28, with payment to the supplier due in 90 days.
Feb. 3	Performed a job on account for Jodi Jetson for $35, collectible from Jetson in 30 days. Used up all the cleaning supplies purchased on Jan. 14.
Mar. 16	Collected the $35 receivable from Jetson.
Apr. 22	Paid the $28 owed to the supplier from the January 14 transaction.

Q3-45. In which month should Kelly record the cost of the cleaning supplies as an expense?

a. January
b. February
c. March
d. April

Q3-46. In which month should Kelly report the $35 revenue on the company's Income Statement?

a. January
b. February
c. March
d. April

Q3-47. If Kelly Company uses the *cash* basis of accounting instead of the accrual basis, in which month will it report revenue and in which month will it report expense?

Revenue	**Expense**
a. February	February
b. March	April
c. February	April
d. March	February

Q3-48. In which month should revenue be recorded?

a. In the month that goods are ordered by the customer
b. In the month that cash is collected from the customer
c. In the month that the invoice is mailed to the customer
d. In the month that goods are shipped to the customer

Q3-49. On January 1 of the current year, Dumbo Company paid $1,200 rent to cover six months (January–June). Dumbo recorded this transaction as follows:

	A	B	C	D	E	F
1		Journal Entry				
2	Date	Accounts	Debit	Credit		
3	Jan. 1	Prepaid Rent	1,200			
4		Cash		1,200		
5						

Dumbo adjusts the accounts at the end of each month. Based on these facts, the adjusting entry at the end of January should include:

a. a debit to Prepaid Rent for $1,000.
b. a debit to Prepaid Rent for $200.
c. a credit to Prepaid Rent for $1,000.
d. a credit to Prepaid Rent for $200.

Q3-50. Assume the same facts as in question 3-49. Dumbo's adjusting entry at the end of February should include a debit to Rent Expense in the amount of

a. $400.
b. $0.
c. $200.
d. $1,000.

Q3-51. What effect does the adjusting entry in question 3-50 have on Dumbo's net income for February?

a. Increase by $200
b. Increase by $400
c. Decrease by $200
d. Decrease by $400

Q3-52. An adjusting entry recorded April salary expense that will be paid in May. Which statement best describes the effect of this adjusting entry on the company's accounting equation?

a. Assets are not affected, liabilities are increased, and shareholders' equity is decreased.
b. Assets are not affected, liabilities are increased, and shareholders' equity is increased.
c. Assets are decreased, liabilities are increased, and shareholders' equity is decreased.
d. Assets are decreased, liabilities are not affected, and shareholders' equity is decreased.

Q3-53. On April 1, 20X7, Royal Insurance Company sold a one-year insurance policy covering the year ended April 1, 20X8. Royal collected the full $3,200 on April 1, 20X7. Royal made the following journal entry to record the receipt of cash in advance:

	A	B	C	D
1		Journal Entry		
2	Date	Accounts	Debit	Credit
3	Apr. 1	Cash	3,200	
4		Unearned Revenue		3,200
5				

Nine months have passed, and Royal has made no adjusting entries. Based on these facts, the adjusting entry needed by Royal at December 31, 20X7, is:

	A	B	C	D
1	a.	Unearned Revenue	2,400	
2		Insurance Revenue		2,400
3	b.	Insurance Revenue	800	
4		Unearned Revenue		800
5	c.	Unearned Revenue	800	
6		Insurance Revenue		800
7	d.	Insurance Revenue	2,400	
8		Unearned Revenue		2,400
9				

Q3-54. The Unearned Revenue account of Genius Incorporated began 20X6 with a normal balance of $3,000 and ended 20X6 with a normal balance of $18,000. During 20X6, the Unearned Revenue account was credited for $27,000 that Genius will earn later. Based on these facts, how much revenue did Genius earn in 20X6?

a. $6,000
b. $12,000
c. $15,000
d. $27,000

Q3-55. What is the effect on the financial statements of *recording* depreciation on equipment?

a. Assets are decreased, but net income and shareholders' equity are not affected.
b. Net income and assets are decreased, but shareholders' equity is not affected.
c. Net income is not affected, but assets and shareholders' equity are decreased.
d. Net income, assets, and shareholders' equity are all decreased.

Q3-56. For 20X6, Martin Company had revenues in excess of expenses. Which statement describes Martin's closing entries at the end of 20X6?

a. Revenues will be debited, expenses will be credited, and retained earnings will be debited.
b. Revenues will be credited, expenses will be debited, and retained earnings will be debited.
c. Revenues will be debited, expenses will be credited, and retained earnings will be credited.
d. Revenues will be credited, expenses will be debited, and retained earnings will be credited.

Q3-57. Which of the following accounts would *not* be included in the closing entries?

a. Accumulated Depreciation
b. Depreciation Expense
c. Service Revenue
d. Retained Earnings

Q3-58. A major purpose of preparing closing entries is to

a. update the Retained Earnings account.
b. adjust the asset accounts to their correct current balances.
c. close out the Supplies account.
d. zero out the liability accounts.

Q3-59. Unadjusted net income equals $7,800. Calculate net income after the following adjustments: Salaries payable to employees, $680; Interest due on note payable at the bank, $120; Unearned revenue that has been earned, $940; Supplies used, $360

a. $8,020
b. $7,800
c. $7,580
d. $7,820

Q3-60. Salary Payable at the beginning of the month totals $27,000. During the month, salaries of $132,000 were accrued as expense. If ending Salary Payable is $18,000, what amount of cash did the company pay for salaries during the month?

a. $123,000
b. $132,000
c. $141,000
d. $159,000

Problems MyLab Accounting

Select A and B problems can be found within MyLab Accounting, an online homework and practice environment. Your instructor may ask you to complete select problems using MyLab Accounting.

Group A

LO 1

P3-61A. ***(Learning Objective 1: Linking accrual accounting and cash flows)*** Catdog Corporation earned revenues of $45 million during 20X7 and ended the year with net income of $8 million. During 20X7, Catdog collected $25 million from customers and paid cash for all of its expenses plus an additional $5 million for amounts payable at December 31, 20X6. Answer these questions about Catdog's operating results, financial position, and cash flows during 20X7:

Requirements

1. How much were Catdog's total expenses? Show your work.
2. Identify all the items that Catdog will report on its 20X7 Income Statement. Show each amount.

3. Catdog began 20X7 with receivables of $6 million. All sales are on account. What was the company's receivables balance at the end of 20X7? Identify the appropriate financial statement, and show how Catdog will report ending receivables in its 20X7 annual report.
4. Catdog began 20X7 owing accounts payable of $8 million. All expenses are incurred on account. During 20X7, Catdog paid $41 million on account. How much in accounts payable did the company owe at the end of 20X7? Identify the appropriate financial statement and show how Catdog will report accounts payable in its 20X7 annual report.

P3-62A. ***(Learning Objective 1: Comparing cash basis and accrual basis)*** Ethan Consulting had the following transactions in May: LO 1

May 1	Prepaid insurance for May through September, $400.
4	Purchased software for cash, $700.
5	Performed services and received cash, $800.
8	Paid advertising expense, $500.
11	Performed service on account, $3,600.
19	Purchased computer on account, $1,300.
24	Collected for May 11 service.
26	Paid account payable from May 19.
29	Paid salary expense, $600.
31	Adjusted for May insurance expense (see May 1).
31	Earned revenue of $400 that was collected in advance back in April.

Requirements

1. Show how each transaction would be handled using the cash basis and the accrual basis.
2. Compute May income (loss) before tax under each accounting method.
3. Indicate which measure of net income or net loss is preferable. Use the transactions on May 11 and May 24 to explain.

P3-63A. ***(Learning Objective 3: Making accounting adjustments)*** Journalize the adjusting entry needed on December 31, the end of the current accounting period, for each of the following independent cases affecting Speedy Corp. Include an explanation for each entry. LO 3 ■ **writing assignment**

a. Details of Prepaid Insurance are shown in the account:

Prepaid Insurance		
Jan. 1 Bal.	900	
Mar. 31	3,600	

Speedy prepays insurance on March 31 each year. At December 31, $1,700 is still prepaid.

b. Speedy pays employees each Friday. The amount of the weekly payroll is $6,200 for a five-day work week. The current accounting period ends on Tuesday.

c. Speedy has a note receivable. During the current year, Speedy has earned accrued interest revenue of $500 that it will collect next year.

d. The beginning balance of supplies was $2,500. During the year, Speedy purchased supplies costing $6,300, and at December 31 supplies on hand total $2,100.

e. Speedy is providing services for Gold Investments, and the owner of Gold paid Speedy $15,000 as the annual service fee. Speedy recorded this amount as Unearned Service Revenue. Speedy estimates that it has earned 70% of the total fee during the current year.

f. Depreciation for the current year includes Office Furniture worth $3,200 and Equipment worth $5,000. Make a combined entry.

P3-64A. ***(Learning Objectives 3, 4: Preparing an adjusted trial balance and the financial statements)*** Consider the unadjusted trial balance of Moscow, Inc., at December 31, 20X6, and the related month-end adjustment data.

	A	B	C	D	E	F	G
1	**Moscow, Inc. Trial Balance Worksheet December 31, 20X6**						
2		**Trial Balance**		**Adjustments**		**Adjusted Trial Balance**	
3	**Account**	**Debit**	**Credit**	**Debit**	**Credit**	**Debit**	**Credit**
4	Cash	8,900					
5	Accounts receivable	1,300					
6	Prepaid rent	2,400					
7	Supplies	2,600					
8	Furniture	72,000					
9	Accumulated depreciation		4,000				
10	Accounts payable		3,400				
11	Salary payable						
12	Share capital		12,000				
13	Retained earnings		63,250				
14	Dividends	3,600					
15	Service revenue		11,200				
16	Salary expense	2,400					
17	Rent expense						
18	Utilities expense	650					
19	Depreciation expense						
20	Supplies expense						
21	Total	93,850	93,850				
22							

Adjustment data December 31, 20X6:

a. Accrued service revenue at December 31, $2,200.

b. Prepaid rent expired during the month. The unadjusted prepaid balance of $2,400 relates to the period December 1, 20X6, through February, 20X7.

c. Supplies used during December, $2,100.

d. Depreciation on furniture for the month. The estimated useful life of the furniture is three years.

e. Accrued salary expense at December 31 for Monday, Tuesday, and Wednesday. The five-day weekly payroll of $5,000 will be paid on Friday.

Requirements

1. Using Exhibit 3-9 as an example, prepare the adjusted trial balance of Moscow, Inc., at December 31, 20X6. Key each adjusting entry by letter.
2. Prepare the monthly Income Statement, the statement of changes in equity, and the classified Balance Sheet. Draw arrows linking the three statements.

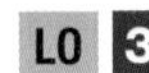

P3-65A. ***(Learning Objective 3: Analyzing and recording adjustments)*** Cherrytree Apartments, Inc.'s unadjusted and adjusted trial balances at April 30, 20X6, follow.

A1

	A	B	C	D	E
1	**Cherrytree Apartments, Inc. Adjusted Trial Balance**	**April 30, 20X6**			
2		**Trial Balance**		**Adjusted Trial Balance**	
3	**Account**	**Debit**	**Credit**	**Debit**	**Credit**
4	Cash	$ 8,900		$ 8,900	
5	Accounts receivable	5,900		7,580	
6	Interest receivable			400	
7	Note receivable	4,400		4,400	
8	Supplies	1,800		800	
9	Prepaid insurance	2,300		500	
10	Building	70,000		70,000	
11	Accumulated depreciation		$ 7,400		$ 8,900
12	Accounts payable		6,700		6,700
13	Wages payable				1,100
14	Unearned rental revenue		2,100		1,400
15	Share capital		17,000		17,000
16	Retained earnings		40,000		40,000
17	Dividends	3,300		3,300	
18	Rental revenue		25,100		27,480
19	Interest revenue		400		600
20	Depreciation expense			1,500	
21	Supplies expense			1,000	
22	Utilities expense	400		400	
23	Wage expense	1,300		2,400	
24	Property tax expense	400		400	
25	Insurance expense			1,800	
26	Total	$ 98,700	$ 98,700	$ 103,380	$ 103,380
27					

Requirements

1. Make the adjusting entries that account for the differences between the two trial balances.
2. Compute Cherrytree's total assets, total liabilities, total equity, and net income.

LO 4

■ spreadsheet

P3-66A. ***(Learning Objectives 4: Preparing the financial statements)*** The adjusted trial balance of Seinfield Corporation at September 30, 20X6, follows.

	A	B	C
1	**Seinfield Corporation Adjusted Trial Balance**	**September 30, 20X6**	
2	**Account**	**Debit**	**Credit**
3	Cash	$ 2,200	
4	Accounts receivable	9,500	
5	Supplies	2,600	
6	Prepaid rent	1,300	
7	Equipment	38,800	
8	Accumulated depreciation		$ 4,400
9	Accounts payable		3,500
10	Interest payable		300
11	Unearned service revenue		900
12	Income tax payable		2,000
13	Note payable		19,800
14	Share capital		4,000
15	Retained earnings		5,200
16	Dividends	20,000	
17	Service revenue		102,600
18	Depreciation expense	1,800	
19	Salary expense	39,800	
20	Rent expense	10,400	
21	Interest expense	3,400	
22	Insurance expense	3,500	
23	Supplies expense	2,900	
24	Income tax expense	6,500	
25	Total	$ 142,700	$ 142,700
26			

Requirements

1. Prepare Seinfield Corporation's 20X6 Income Statement, statement of changes in equity, and Balance Sheet. List expenses (except for income tax) in decreasing order on the Income Statement and show total liabilities on the Balance Sheet. Draw arrows linking the three financial statements.

LO 5

P3-67A. ***(Learning Objective 5: Closing the books; evaluating retained earnings)*** The accounts of Bay View Services, Inc., at June 30, 20X6, are listed in alphabetical order.

Accounts payable	$ 14,400	Note payable, long term	$ 6,000
Accounts receivable	16,100	Other assets	14,400
Accumulated depreciation-equipment	6,900	Prepaid expenses	6,000
Advertising expense	10,500	Retained earnings, June 30, 20X5	21,000
Cash	7,900	Salary expense	17,600
Current portion of note payable	1,000	Salary payable	2,700
Depreciation expense	1,800	Service revenue	95,400
Dividends	21,200	Share capital	6,600
Equipment	51,600	Supplies	3,900
Interest expense	800	Supplies expense	4,500
		Unearned service revenue	2,800

Requirements

1. All adjustments have been journalized and posted, but the closing entries have not yet been made. Journalize Bay View's closing entries at June 30, 20X6.
2. Set up a T-account for Retained Earnings and post to that account. Then compute Bay View's net income for the year ended June 30, 20X6. What is the ending balance of Retained Earnings?
3. Did Retained Earnings increase or decrease during the year? What caused the increase or the decrease?

Group B

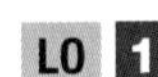

P3-68B. ***(Learning Objective 1: Linking accrual accounting and cash flows)*** Garage Corporation earned revenues of €38 million during 20X6 and ended the year with net income of €4 million. During 20X6, Garage collected cash of €27 million from customers and paid cash for all of its expenses plus an additional €1 million on account for amounts payable at December 31, 20X5. Answer the following questions about Garage's operating results, financial position, and cash flows during 20X6.

Requirements

1. How much were Garage's total expenses? Show your analysis.
2. Identify all the items that Garage will report on its 20X6 Income Statement. Show each amount.
3. Garage began 20X6 with receivables of €9 million. All sales are on account. What was Garage's receivables balance at the end of 20X6? Identify the appropriate financial statement and show how Garage will report its ending receivables balance in its 20X6 annual report.
4. Garage began 20X6 owing accounts payable of €10 million. All expenses are incurred on account. During 20X6, Garage paid €28 million on account. How much in accounts payable did Garage owe at the end of 20X6? Identify the appropriate financial statement and show how Garage will report accounts payable in its 20X6 annual report.

LO 1

P3-69B. ***(Learning Objective 1: Comparing cash basis and accrual basis)*** Queen Consulting had the following selected transactions in August:

Aug.	1	Prepaid insurance for August through December, $500.
	4	Purchased software for cash, $800.
	5	Performed services and received cash, $600.
	8	Paid advertising expense, $700.
	11	Performed service on account, $3,200.
	19	Purchased computer on account, $1,100.
	24	Collected for August 11 service.
	26	Paid account payable from August 19.
	29	Paid salary expense, $500.
	31	Adjusted for August insurance expense (see August 1).
	31	Earned revenue of $300 that was collected in advance back in July.

Requirements

1. Show how each transaction would be handled using the cash basis and the accrual basis.
2. Compute August income (loss) before tax under each accounting method.
3. Indicate which measure of net income or net loss is preferable. Use the transactions on August 11 and August 24 to explain.

LO 3

P3-70B. ***(Learning Objective 3: Making accounting adjustments)*** Journalize the adjusting entry needed on December 31, the end of the current accounting period, for each of the following independent cases affecting Sawyer Corp. Include an explanation for each entry.

a. Details of Prepaid Insurance are shown in the account:

Prepaid Insurance		
Jan. 1 Bal.	500	
Mar. 31	3,800	

Sawyer prepays insurance on March 31 each year. At December 31, €700 is still prepaid.

b. Sawyer pays employees each Friday. The amount of the weekly payroll is €5,400 for a five-day work week. The current accounting period ends on Wednesday.

c. Sawyer has a note receivable. During the current year, Sawyer has earned accrued interest revenue of €800 that it will collect next year.

d. The beginning balance of supplies was €2,900. During the year, Sawyer purchased supplies costing €6,200, and at December 31 supplies on hand total €2,300.

e. Sawyer is providing services for Orca Investments, and the owner of Orca paid Sawyer €12,500 as the annual service fee. Sawyer recorded this amount as Unearned Service Revenue. Sawyer estimates that it has earned 60% of the total fee during the current year.

f. Depreciation for the current year includes office furniture, €3,500, and equipment, €5,400. Make a combined entry.

LO 3 4

P3-71B. ***(Learning Objectives 3, 4: Preparing an adjusted trial balance and the financial statements)*** Consider the unadjusted trial balance of Glasgow, Inc., at August 31, 20X6, and the related month-end adjustment data.

A1

	A	B	C	D	E	F	G
1	**Glasgow, Inc.** **Trial Balance Worksheet** **August 31, 20X6**						
2		**Trial Balance**		**Adjustments**		**Adjusted Trial Balance**	
3	**Account**	**Debit**	**Credit**	**Debit**	**Credit**	**Debit**	**Credit**
4	Cash	9,300					
5	Accounts receivable	1,600					
6	Prepaid rent	2,400					
7	Supplies	2,200					
8	Furniture	81,000					
9	Accumulated depreciation		4,000				
10	Accounts payable		3,500				
11	Salary payable						
12	Share capital		15,200				
13	Retained earnings		71,000				
14	Dividends	3,800					
15	Service revenue		10,400				
16	Salary expense	3,200					
17	Rent expense						
18	Utilities expense	600					
19	Depreciation expense						
20	Supplies expense						
21	Total	104,100	104,100				
22							

Adjustment data at August 31, 20X6, include the following:

a. Accrued advertising revenue at August 31, €2,200

b. Prepaid rent expired during the month. The unadjusted prepaid balance of €2,400 relates to the period August 20X6 through October 20X6.

c. Supplies used during August, €1,900

d. Depreciation on furniture for the month. The furniture's expected useful life is five years.

e. Accrued salary expense at August 31 for Monday, Tuesday, and Wednesday. The five-day weekly payroll is €5,500 and will be paid on Friday.

Requirements

1. Using Exhibit 3-9 as an example, prepare the adjusted trial balance of Glasgow, Inc., at August 31, 20X6. Key each adjusting entry by letter.
2. Prepare the monthly Income Statement, the statement of changes in equity, and the classified Balance Sheet. Draw arrows linking the three statements.

P3-72B. ***(Learning Objective 3: Analyzing and recording adjustments)*** Greenfield Apartments, Inc.'s unadjusted and adjusted trial balances at April 30, 20X6, follow:

	A	B	C	D	E
1	**Greenfield Apartments, Inc. Adjusted Trial Balance**	**April 30, 20X6**			
2		**Trial Balance**		**Adjusted Trial Balance**	
3	**Account**	**Debit**	**Credit**	**Debit**	**Credit**
4	Cash	€ 7,900		€ 7,900	
5	Accounts receivable	6,000		7,850	
6	Interest receivable			750	
7	Note receivable	5,000		5,000	
8	Supplies	1,500		800	
9	Prepaid insurance	2,500		600	
10	Building	67,000		67,000	
11	Accumulated depreciation		€ 8,800		€ 10,300
12	Accounts payable		6,500		6,500
13	Wages payable				1,100
14	Unearned rental revenue		1,500		1,200
15	Share capital		17,000		17,000
16	Retained earnings		43,300		43,300
17	Dividends	3,200		3,200	
18	Rental revenue		18,300		20,450
19	Interest revenue		200		950
20	Depreciation expense			1,500	
21	Supplies expense			700	
22	Utilities expense	300		300	
23	Wage expense	1,900		3,000	
24	Property tax expense	300		300	
25	Insurance expense			1,900	
26	Total	€ 95,600	€ 95,600	€ 100,800	€ 100,800
27					

Requirements

1. Make the adjusting entries that account for the differences between the two trial balances.
2. Compute Greenfield's total assets, total liabilities, total equity, and net income.

LO 4

■ spreadsheet

P3-73B. ***(Learning Objectives 4: Preparing the financial statements)*** The adjusted trial balance of Murray Corporation at December 31, 20X6, follows:

	A	B	C
1	**Murray Corporation Adjusted Trial Balance**	**December 31, 20X6**	
2	**Account**	**Debit**	**Credit**
3	Cash	$ 1,700	
4	Accounts receivable	8,900	
5	Supplies	2,300	
6	Prepaid rent	1,200	
7	Equipment	38,700	
8	Accumulated depreciation		$ 4,500
9	Accounts payable		3,900
10	Interest payable		500
11	Unearned service revenue		700
12	Income tax payable		2,600
13	Note payable		18,800
14	Share capital		8,000
15	Retained earnings		4,500
16	Dividends	25,000	
17	Service revenue		103,800
18	Depreciation expense	1,200	
19	Salary expense	40,600	
20	Rent expense	10,300	
21	Interest expense	3,300	
22	Insurance expense	3,700	
23	Supplies expense	2,800	
24	Income tax expense	7,600	
25	Total	$ 147,300	$ 147,300
26			

Requirements

1. Prepare Murray's 20X6 Income Statement, statement of changes in equity, and Balance Sheet. List expenses (except for income tax) in decreasing order on the Income Statement and show total liabilities on the Balance Sheet.

LO 5

P3-74B. ***(Learning Objective 5: Making closing entries; evaluating retained earnings)*** The accounts of Silent Stream Service, Inc., at March 31, 20X6, are listed in alphabetical order.

Accounts payable	$ 14,800	Note payable, long term	$ 5,900
Accounts receivable	16,900	Other assets	14,000
Accumulated depreciation— equipment	7,200	Prepaid expenses	5,800
Advertising expense	11,200	Retained earnings, March 31, 20X5	22,500
Cash	7,200	Salary expense	18,200
Current portion of note payable	500	Salary payable	2,600
Depreciation expense	2,200	Service revenue	95,600
Dividends	30,000	Share capital	6,200
Equipment	44,000	Supplies	3,300
Interest expense	900	Supplies expense	4,500
		Unearned service revenue	2,900

Requirements

1. All adjustments have been journalized and posted, but the closing entries have not yet been made. Journalize Silent Stream's closing entries at March 31, 20X6.
2. Set up a T-account for Retained Earnings and post to that account. Then compute Silent Stream's net income for 20X6. What is the ending balance of Retained Earnings?
3. Did Retained Earnings increase or decrease during the year? What caused the increase or decrease?

APPLY YOUR KNOWLEDGE

Decision Cases

Case 1. *(Learning Objective 3: Adjusting and correcting the accounts)* The unadjusted trial balance of Good Times, Inc., at January 31, 20X6, does not balance. In addition, the trial balance needs to be adjusted before the financial statements at January 31, 20X6, can be prepared. LO 3

Cash	8,200
Accounts receivable	4,300
Supplies	900
Prepaid rent	1,200
Land	43,000
Accounts payable	12,100
Salary payable	0
Unearned service revenue	500
Note payable, due in three years	23,400
Share capital	5,000
Retained earnings	9,500
Service revenue	9,900
Salary expense	3,600
Rent expense	0
Advertising expense	800
Supplies expense	0

Requirements

1. How much *out of balance* is the trial balance? Notes Payable (the only error) is understated.
2. Good Times needs to make the following adjustments at January 31:
   a. Supplies of $600 were used during January.
   b. The balance of Prepaid rent was paid on January 1 and covers the whole year 20X6. No adjustment was made on January 31.
   c. At January 31, Good Times owed employees $1,200.
   d. Unearned service revenue of $300 was earned during January.

Prepare a corrected, adjusted trial balance. Give Notes Payable its correct balance.

Case 2. *(Learning Objective 4: Preparing financial statements; deciding to continue or shut down the business)* On October 1, Lou Clark opened Tiger Restaurant, Inc. Clark is now at a crossroads. The October financial statements paint a glowing picture of the business, and Clark has asked you whether he should expand the business. To expand the business, Clark wants to be earning net income of $10,000 per month and have total assets of $50,000. Clark believes he is meeting both goals. LO 4

To start the business, Clark invested $25,000, not the $15,500 amount reported as "Share capital" on the Balance Sheet. The business issued $25,000 of shares to Clark. The bookkeeper plugged the $15,500 "Share capital" amount into the Balance Sheet to make it balance. The bookkeeper made some other errors too. Clark shows you the following financial statements that the bookkeeper prepared:

	A	B	C
1	**Tiger Restaurant, Inc.** **Income Statement**	**Month Ended** **October 31, 20X7**	
2	**Revenues:**		
3	Investments by owner	$ 25,000	
4	Unearned banquet sales revenue	5,000	
5			$ 30,000
6	**Expenses:**		
7	Wages expense	$ 6,000	
8	Rent expense	4,500	
9	Dividends	3,000	
10	Depreciation expense-fixtures	1,000	
11			14,500
12	**Net income**		$ 15,500
13			

	A	B	C	D	E
1		**Tiger Restaurant, Inc.** **Balance Sheet** **October 31, 20X7**			
2	**Assets**		**Liabilities**		
3	Cash	$ 8,000	Accounts payable	$ 9,000	
4	Prepaid insurance	2,000	Sales revenue	33,000	
5	Insurance expense	1,000	Accumulated depreciation—		
6	Food inventory	6,000	fixtures	1,000	
7	Cost of goods sold (expense)	12,500			
8	Fixtures (tables, chairs, etc.)	25,000	**Owners' equity**		
9	Dishes and silverware	4,000	Share capital	15,500	
10		$ 58,500		$ 58,500	
11					

Requirement

1. Prepare corrected financial statements for Tiger Restaurant, Inc.: Income Statement, Statement of Changes in Equity, and Balance Sheet. Then, based on Clark's goals and your corrected statements, recommend to Clark whether he should expand the restaurant.

Case 3. ***(Learning Objectives 3, 4: Valuing a business on the basis of its net income)*** Stanley Williams has owned and operated SW Advertising, Inc., since its beginning, 10 years ago. Recently, Williams mentioned that he would consider selling the company for the right price.

Assume that you are interested in buying this business. You obtain its most recent monthly trial balance. Revenues and expenses vary little from month to month, and June is a typical month. Your investigation reveals that the trial balance does not include the effects of monthly revenues of $5,000 and expenses totaling $1,200. If you were to buy SW Advertising, you would hire a manager so you could devote your time to other duties. Assume that your manager would require a monthly salary of $5,000.

	A	B	C
1	**SW Advertising, Inc.** **Trial Balance**	**June 30, 20X6**	
2	Cash	$ 12,000	
3	Accounts receivable	7,000	
4	Prepaid expenses	3,200	
5	Property, plant and equipment	125,000	
6	Accumulated depreciation		$ 81,500
7	Land	155,000	
8	Accounts payable		13,800
9	Salary payable		
10	Unearned advertising revenue		58,700
11	Share capital		60,000
12	Retained earnings		82,000
13	Dividends	9,000	
14	Advertising revenue		20,000
15	Rent expense		
16	Salary expense	4,000	
17	Utilities expense	800	
18	Depreciation expense		
19	Supplies expense		
20	Total	$ 316,000	$ 316,000
21			

Requirements

1. Assume that the most you would pay for the business is 16 times the amount of monthly net income *you could expect to earn* from it. Compute this possible price.
2. Williams states that the least he will take for selling the business is two times its shareholders' equity on June 30. Compute this amount.
3. Under these conditions, how much should you offer Williams? Give your reason. (Challenge)

Ethical Issues

Issue 1. Cross Timbers Energy Co. is in its third year of operations, and the company has grown to be the major producer of compressed natural gas (CNG) in the region. To expand the business, Cross Timbers borrowed $15 million from Bank of Fort Worth. As a condition for making this loan, the bank required that Cross Timbers maintain a net profit of at least $5 million per year.

Business recently has been worse than expected. Lower revenue and higher expenses have brought net profit down to $4.5 million at December 27. Lane Collins, the general manager, is considering what would happen when the bank receives reports of its lower than required profit. Collins is considering the $3 million deferred income that's sitting on his Balance Sheet. It represents cash collected ahead of delivery of CNG next month. He told himself, "This money is as good as earned, I have the money in the bank account, I can deliver the goods anytime, so why did the accountant insist that they must be shown as a liability? I think I will just say I have earned $1 million by the end of the year and everyone will be happy."

Requirements

1. Journalize the revenue transaction, and indicate how recording this revenue in December would affect the company's net profit.
2. Analyze this transaction according to the decision framework for making ethical judgments (in Chapter 1):
   a. What is the issue?
   b. Who are the stakeholders and what are the alternatives? Weigh them from the standpoint of economic, legal, and ethical implications.
   c. What decision would you make?
3. Propose for Cross Timbers a course of action that is ethical.

Issue 2. The net income of Solas Photography Company decreased sharply during 20X6. Lisa Almond, owner of the company, anticipates the need for a bank loan in 20X7. Late in 20X6, Almond instructed Brad Lail, the accountant and a personal friend of yours, to record a $10,000 sale of portraits to the Almond family, even though the photos will not be shot until January 20X7. Almond also told Lail *not* to make the following December 31, 20X6, adjusting entries:

Salaries owed to employees $10,000
Prepaid insurance that has expired 1,000

Requirements

1. Compute the overall effect of these transactions on the company's reported income for 20X6. Is reported net income overstated or understated?
2. Why did Almond take these actions? Are they ethical? Give your reason, identifying the parties helped and the parties harmed by Almond's action. Consult the Decision Framework for Making Ethical Judgments in Chapter 1. Which factor (economic, legal, or ethical) seems to be taking precedence? Identify the stakeholders and the potential consequences to each.
3. As a personal friend of Brad's, what advice would you give him?

Focus on Financials: | Nestlé

This case spans all 12 chapters and is based on the consolidated financial statements of Nestlé. As you work with Nestlé throughout this course, you will develop the confidence and ability to use the financial statements of other companies as well.

Refer to Nestlé's financial statements in Appendix A. Alternatively, you may obtain the full annual report from Nestlé's website at www.nestle.com/investors. You may find the information overwhelming for now, but try to spot the key principles that we have discussed in this chapter. It will get progressively easier as you gain familiarity with the elements of the financial statements.

Nestlé—like all other businesses—adjusts accounts prior to year-end to get correct amounts for the financial statements. Examine Nestlé's Balance Sheets in Appendix A, and pay particular attention to Note 11 on provisions.

Requirements

1. Open a T-account for "provisions." Insert Nestlé's balance of CHF 3,165 million at December 31, 2015. What four items does this total consist of? (Hint: for further details refer to the notes to the financial statements.)
2. For simplicity's sake, assume that there is only one provisions account, provisions for warranties, with an opening balance of CHF 3,165 million at December 31, 2015. Journalize the following transactions for the year ended December 31, 2016. Key entries by letter, and show amounts in millions.
   a. Made warranty payments of CHF 464 million to consumers.
   b. Charged CHF 895 million to the Income Statement as its best estimate of future warranty needs.
   c. Misc. adjustments to the provisions account to the tune of a CHF 336 million debit due to exchange movements and reversal of previous over-estimation (credit retained earnings).
3. Post these entries to "provisions" and show that the ending balance of the account agrees with the corresponding amount reported in Nestlé's December 31, 2016, Balance Sheets.
4. Examine Note 8—Property, plant and equipment. Notice that accumulated depreciation and impairment stood at CHF 26,323 million at December 31, 2015, and at CHF 28,376 million at December 31, 2016. Assume depreciation and impairment expense for 2016 was CHF 2,795 million in total. Explain what must have happened to account for the remainder of the change in the accumulated depreciation and impairment account during 2016.

Group Project

Mark Davis formed a lawn service company as a summer job. To start the business on May 1, he deposited $2,000 in a new bank account in the name of the corporation. The $2,000 consisted of a $1,600 loan from his father and $400 of his own money. The corporation issued 200 shares of share capital to Davis.

Davis rented lawn equipment, purchased supplies, and hired high school students to mow and trim his customers' lawns. At the end of each month, Davis mailed bills to his customers. On August 31, Davis was ready to dissolve the business and return to Rutgers University for the fall semester. Because he had been so busy, he had kept few records other than his checkbook and a list of amounts owed by customers.

At August 31, Davis' checkbook shows a balance of $2,040, and his customers still owe him $600. During the summer, he collected $5,600 from customers. His checkbook lists payments for supplies totaling $400, and he still has gasoline, weedeater cord, and other supplies that cost a total of $50. He paid his employees wages of $1,900, and he still owes them $200 for the final week of the summer.

Davis rented some equipment from Ludwig Tool Company. On May 1, he signed a six-month lease on mowers and paid $600 for the full lease period. Ludwig will refund the unused portion of the prepayment if the equipment is in good shape. To get the refund, Davis has kept the mowers in excellent condition. In fact, he had to pay $300 to repair a mower that ran over a hidden tree stump.

To transport employees and equipment to jobs, Davis used a trailer that he bought for $300. He figures that the summer's work used up one-third of the trailer's service potential. The business checkbook lists an expenditure of $460 for dividends paid to Davis during the summer. Also, Davis paid his father back during the summer.

Requirements

1. Prepare the Income Statement of Davis Lawn Service, Inc., for the four months May through August. The business is not subject to income tax.
2. Prepare the classified Balance Sheet of Davis Lawn Service, Inc., at August 31.

Quick Check Answers

1. *d*	6. *d*	11. *b*
2. *b*	7. *b*	12. *b*
3. *c*	8. *c*	13. *a*
4. *b*	9. *d*	
5. *b*	10. *a*	

MyLab Accounting

For online homework, exercises, and problems that provide you with immediate feedback, please visit www.myaccountinglab.com.

Demo Doc

Preparation of Adjusting Entries, Closing Entries, and Financial Statements

To make sure you understand this material, work through the following demonstration "Demo Doc" with detailed comments to help you see the concept within the framework of a worked-through problem.

Learning Objectives 2–5

Cloud Break Consulting, Inc., has the following information at June 30, 20X6:

	A	B	C
1	**Cloud Break Consulting, Inc.** **Unadjusted Trial Balance** **June 30, 20X6**	**Balance**	
2	**Account Title**	**Debit**	**Credit**
3	Cash	$ 131,000	
4	Accounts receivable	104,000	
5	Supplies	4,000	
6	Prepaid rent	27,000	
7	Land	45,000	
8	Building	300,000	
9	Accumulated depreciation—building		$ 155,000
10	Accounts payable		159,000
11	Unearned service revenue		40,000
12	Share capital		50,000
13	Retained earnings		52,000
14	Dividends	7,000	
15	Service revenue		450,000
16	Salary expense	255,000	
17	Rent expense	25,000	
18	Miscellaneous expense	8,000	
19	Total	$ 906,000	$ 906,000
20			

June 30 is Cloud Break's fiscal year-end; accordingly, it must make adjusting entries for the following items:

a. Supplies on hand at year-end, $1,000.
b. Nine months of rent totaling $27,000 were paid in advance on April 1, 20X6. Cloud Break has recorded no rent expense yet.
c. Depreciation expense has not been recorded on the building for the 20X6 fiscal year. The building has a useful life of 25 years.
d. Employees work Monday through Friday. The weekly payroll is $5,000 and is paid every Friday. June 30, 20X6, falls on a Thursday.
e. Service revenue of $15,000 must be accrued.
f. Cloud Break received $40,000 in advance for consulting services to be provided evenly from January 1, 20X6, through August 31, 20X6. Cloud Break has recorded none of this revenue.

➤ Requirements

1. Open the T-accounts with their unadjusted balances.
2. Journalize Cloud Break's adjusting entries at June 30, 20X6, and post the entries to the T-accounts.
3. Total each T-account in the ledger.
4. Journalize and post Cloud Break's closing entries.
5. Prepare Cloud Break's Income Statement and statement of changes in equity for the year ended June 30, 20X6, and the Balance Sheet at June 30, 20X6. Draw arrows linking the three financial statements.

Demo Doc Solutions

➤ Requirement 1

Open the T-accounts with their unadjusted balances.

Part 1	Part 2	Part 3	Part 4	Part 5	Demo Doc Complete

Remember from Chapter 2 that opening a T-account means drawing a blank account that looks like a capital "T" and putting the account title across the top. To help find the accounts later, they are grouped into assets, liabilities, shareholders' equity, revenues, and expenses (in that order). If the account has a starting balance, it ***must*** appear on the correct side.

Remember that debits are always on the left side of the T-account and credits are always on the right side. This is true for *every* account.

The correct side to enter each account's starting balance is the side of *increase* in the account. This is because we expect all accounts to have a *positive* balance (that is, more increases than decreases).

For assets, an increase is a debit, so we would expect all assets (except contra assets such as Accumulated Depreciation) to have a debit balance. For liabilities and shareholders' equity, an increase is a credit, so we would expect all liabilities and equities (except Dividends) to have a credit balance. By the same reasoning, we expect revenues to have credit balances and expenses and dividends to have debit balances.

The unadjusted balances appearing in the T-accounts are simply the amounts from the starting trial balance.

Assets = Liabilities + Shareholders' Equity

Assets

Account	Debit	Credit
Cash	Bal. 131,000	
Accounts Receivable	Bal. 104,000	
Supplies	Bal. 4,000	
Prepaid Rent	Bal. 27,000	
Land	Bal. 45,000	
Building	Bal. 300,000	
Accumulated Depreciation—Building		Bal. 155,000

Liabilities

Account	Debit	Credit
Accounts Payable		Bal. 159,000
Unearned Service Revenue		Bal. 40,000

Shareholders' Equity

Account	Debit	Credit
Share Capital		Bal. 50,000
Retained Earnings		Bal. 52,000
Dividends	Bal. 7,000	

Revenue

Account	Debit	Credit
Service Revenue		Bal. 450,000

Expenses

Account	Debit	Credit
Salary Expense	Bal. 255,000	
Rent Expense	Bal. 25,000	
Miscellaneous Expense	Bal. 8,000	

➤ Requirement 2

Journalize Cloud Break's adjusting entries at June 30, 20X6, and post the entries to the T-accounts.

Part 1	Part 2	Part 3	Part 4	Part 5	Demo Doc Complete

a. Supplies on hand at year-end, $1,000.

On June 30, 20X6, the unadjusted balance in the Supplies account was $4,000. However, a count shows that only $1,000 of supplies actually remains on hand. The supplies that are no longer there have been used. When assets/benefits are used, an expense is created.

Cloud Break will need to make an adjusting journal entry in order to report the correct amount of supplies on the Balance Sheet.

Looking at the Supplies T-account:

Supplies

	Debit		Credit
	4,000	Used up	X
Bal.	1,000		

The supplies have decreased because they have been used up. The amount of the decrease is X. X = $4,000 – $1,000 = $3,000.

$3,000 of supplies expense must be recorded to show the value of supplies that have been used.

	A	B	C	D	E	F
1	(a)	Jun. 30	Supplies Expense ($4,000 – $1,000) (Expense↑; debit)	3,000		
2			Supplies (Asset↓; credit)		3,000	
3			*To record supplies expense.*			
4						

After posting, Supplies and Supplies Expense hold their correct ending balances:

ASSETS

Supplies

	Debit		Credit
	4,000	a.	3,000
Bal.	1,000		

EXPENSES

Supplies Expense

	Debit	
a.	3,000	
Bal.	3,000	

b. Nine months of rent (totaling $27,000) were paid in advance on April 1, 20X6. Cloud Break has recorded no rent expense yet.

A prepayment for something, such as for rent or insurance, creates a *future* benefit (an asset) because the business is now entitled to receive the prepaid goods or services. Once those goods or services are received (in this case, once Cloud Break has occupied the building being rented), the benefit expires, and the prepaid cost becomes an expense.

Cloud Break prepaid $27,000 for nine months of rent on April 1. This means that Cloud Break pays $27,000/9 = $3,000 a month for rent. At June 30, Prepaid Rent is adjusted for the amount of the asset that has been used up. Because Cloud Break has occupied the building being rented for three months (April, May, and June), three months of the prepayment have been used. The amount of rent used is 3 × $3,000 = $9,000. Because that portion of the past benefit (asset) has expired, it becomes an expense (in this case, the adjustment transfers $9,000 from Prepaid Rent to Rent Expense).

This means that Rent Expense must be increased (a debit) and Prepaid Rent (an asset) must be decreased (a credit), with the following journal entry:

	A	B	C	D	E	F
1	(b)	Jun. 30	Rent Expense (Expense ↑; debit)	9,000		
2			Prepaid Rent (Asset ↓; credit)		9,000	
3			*To record rent expense.*			
4						

Posting places $9,000 in each account, as follows:

ASSETS

Prepaid Rent

	27,000	b.	9,000
Bal.	18,000		

EXPENSES

Rent Expense

	25,000	
b.	9,000	
Bal.	34,000	

c. Depreciation expense has not been recorded on the building for the 20X6 fiscal year. The building has a useful life of 25 years.

Depreciation expense per year is calculated as:

$$\text{Depreciation expense per year} = \frac{\text{Original cost of asset}}{\text{Useful life of asset (in years)}}$$

The cost principle compels us to keep the original cost of a PPE in that asset account. Because there is $300,000 in the Building account, we know that this is the original cost of the building. We are told in the question that the building's useful life is 25 years.

$$\text{Depreciation expense per year} = \$300{,}000/25 \text{ years} = \$12{,}000 \text{ per year}$$

We will record depreciation of $12,000 in an adjusting journal entry. The journal entry for depreciation expense is *always* the same. Only the dollar amount changes. There is always an increase to Depreciation Expense (a debit) and an increase to the contra asset account of Accumulated Depreciation (a credit).

	A	B	C	D	E	F
1	(c)	Jun. 30	Depreciation Expense—Building (Expense ↑; debit)	12,000		
2			Accumulated Depreciation—Building			
3			(Contra Asset ↑; credit)		12,000	
4			*To record depreciation on building.*			
5						

ASSETS						EXPENSES	
ASSET		CONTRA ASSET					
Building		Accumulated Depreciation—Building				Depreciation Expense—Building	
300,000					155,000	c.	12,000
				c.	12,000		
Bal.	300,000			Bal.	167,000	Bal.	12,000

The carrying amount of the building is its original cost (the amount in the Building T-account) minus the accumulated depreciation on the building.

Carrying amount of PPE:	
Building..	$ 300,000
Less: Accumulated depreciation	(167,000)
Carrying amount of the building............	$ 133,000

d. Employees work Monday through Friday. The weekly payroll is $5,000 and is paid every Friday. June 30, 20X6, falls on a Thursday.

Salary is an accrued expense. That is, it's a liability that comes from an *expense* that hasn't been paid yet. Most employers pay their employees *after* the work has been done, so the work is a past benefit to the employer. This expense (Salary Expense, in this case) grows until payday.

Cloud Break's employees are paid $5,000 for five days of work. That means they earn $5,000/5 = $1,000 per day. By the end of the day on Thursday, June 30, they have earned $1,000/day × 4 days = $4,000 of salary.

If the salaries have not been paid, then they are pay*able* (or in other words, they are *owed*) and must be recorded as some kind of payable account. You might be tempted to use Accounts Payable, but this account is usually reserved for *bills* received. But employees don't bill employers for their paychecks. The appropriate payable account for salaries is Salary Payable.

The accrual of salary expense creates an increase to Salary Expense (a debit) and an increase to the liability Salary Payable (a credit) of $4,000.

A1

	A	B	C	D	E	F
1	(d)	Jun. 30	Salary Expense (Expense ↑; debit)	4,000		
2			Salary Payable (Liability ↑; credit)		4,000	
3			*To accrue salary expense.*			
4						
5						

EXPENSES			LIABILITIES	
Salary Expense			Salary Payable	
	255,000		d.	4,000
d.	4,000			
Bal.	259,000		Bal.	4,000

e. Service revenue of $15,000 must be accrued.

Accrued revenue is another way of saying "accounts receivable" (or receipt in the future). When *accrued* revenue is recorded, it means that accounts receivable are also recorded (that is, the business gave goods or services to customers, but the business has not yet received the cash). The business is entitled to these receivables because the revenue has been earned.

Service Revenue must be increased by $15,000 (a credit) and the Accounts Receivable asset must be increased by $15,000 (a debit).

	A	B	C	D	E	F
1	(e)	Jun. 30	Accounts Receivable (Asset ↑; debit)	15,000		
2			Service Revenue (Revenue ↑; credit)		15,000	
3			*To accrue service revenue.*			
4						
5						

ASSETS

Accounts Receivable		
	104,000	
e.	15,000	
Bal.	119,000	

REVENUES

Service Revenue		
		450,000
	e.	15,000
	Bal.	465,000

f. Cloud Break received $40,000 in advance for consulting services to be provided evenly from January 1, 20X6, through August 31, 20X6. Cloud Break has recorded none of this revenue.

Cloud Break received cash in advance for work to be performed in the future. By accepting the cash, Cloud Break also accepted the obligation to perform that work (or provide a refund). In accounting, an obligation is a liability. We call this liability "unearned revenue" because it *will* be revenue (after the work is performed), but it is not revenue *yet*.

The $40,000 collected in advance is still in the Unearned Service Revenue account. However, some of the revenue has been earned as of June 30. Six months of the earnings period have passed (January through June), so Cloud Break has earned six months of the revenue.

The entire revenue-earning period is eight months (January through August), so the revenue earned per month is $40,000/8 = $5,000. The six months of revenue that Cloud Break has earned through the end of June totals $30,000 (6 × $5,000).

So Unearned Service Revenue, a liability, must be decreased by $30,000 (a debit). Because that portion of the revenue is now earned, Service Revenue is increased by $30,000 (a credit).

	A	B	C	D	E	F
1	f	Jun. 30	Unearned Service Revenue (Liability ↓; debit)	30,000		
2			Service Revenue (Revenue ↑; credit)		30,000	
3			*To record the earning of service revenue that was*			
4			*collected in advance.*			
5						

Essentially, the $30,000 has been shifted from "unearned revenue" to "earned" revenue.

LIABILITIES

Unearned Service Revenue

	Debit		Credit
f.	30,000		40,000
		Bal.	10,000

REVENUES

Service Revenue

Debit		Credit
		450,000
	e.	15,000
	f.	30,000
	Bal.	495,000

Now we can summarize all of the adjusting journal entries:

	A	B	C	D	E	F
1	**Ref.**	**Date**	**Accounts and Explanation**	**Debit**	**Credit**	
2		20X6				
3	a.	Jun 30	Supplies Expense ($4,000 – $1,000)	3,000		
4			Supplies		3,000	
5			*To record supplies expense.*			
6						
7	b.	30	Rent Expense	9,000		
8			Prepaid Rent		9,000	
9			*To record rent expense.*			
10						
11	c.	30	Depreciation Expense—Building	12,000		
12			Accumulated Depreciation—Building		12,000	
13			*To record depreciation on building.*			
14						
15	d.	30	Salary Expense	4,000		
16			Salary Payable		4,000	
17			*To accrue salary expense.*			
18						
19	e.	30	Accounts Receivable	15,000		
20			Service Revenue		15,000	
21			*To accrue service revenue.*			
22						
23	f.	30	Unearned Service Revenue	30,000		
24			Service Revenue		30,000	
25			*To record the earning of service revenue that was*			
26			*collected in advance.*			
27						
28						

➤ Requirement 3

Total each T-account in the ledger.

After posting all of these entries and totaling all of the T-accounts, we have:

Assets = Liabilities + Shareholders' Equity

Assets

Cash	
Bal. 131,000	

Accounts Receivable	
104,000	
e. 15,000	
Bal. 119,000	

Supplies	
4,000	a. 3,000
Bal. 1,000	

Prepaid Rent	
27,000	b. 9,000
Bal. 18,000	

Land	
Bal. 45,000	

Building	
Bal. 300,000	

Accumulated Depreciation—Building	
	155,000
	c. 12,000
	Bal. 167,000

Liabilities

Accounts Payable	
	Bal. 159,000

Salary Payable	
	d. 4,000
	Bal. 4,000

Unearned Service Revenue	
	40,000
f. 30,000	
	Bal. 10,000

Shareholders' Equity

Share Capital	
	Bal. 50,000

Retained Earnings	
	Bal. 52,000

Dividends	
Bal. 7,000	

Revenue

Service Revenue	
	450,000
	e. 15,000
	f. 30,000
	Bal. 495,000

Expenses

Salary Expense	
255,000	
d. 4,000	
Bal. 259,000	

Supplies Expense	
a. 3,000	
Bal. 3,000	

Rent Expense	
25,000	
b. 9,000	
Bal. 34,000	

Depreciation Expense—Building	
c. 12,000	
Bal. 12,000	

Miscellaneous Expense	
Bal. 8,000	

➤ Requirement 4

Journalize and post Cloud Break's closing entries.

Part 1 | Part 2 | Part 3 | Part 4 | Part 5 | Demo Doc Complete

We prepare closing entries to (1) clear out or "reset" the revenue, expense, and dividends accounts to a zero balance in order to get them ready for the next period. They must begin the next period empty so that we can evaluate each period's income separately from all other periods. We also need to (2) update the Retained Earnings account by transferring all revenues, expenses, and dividends into it.

The Retained Earnings balance is calculated each year using the following formula:

Beginning retained earnings
+ Net income (or − Net loss)
− Dividends paid
= Ending retained earnings

You can see this in the Retained Earnings T-account as well:

Retained Earnings	
Dividends	Beginning retained earnings
	Net income
	Ending retained earnings

This formula is the key to preparing the closing entries. We will use this formula, but we will do it *inside* the Retained Earnings T-account.

From the trial balance given in the problem, we know that beginning Retained Earnings is $52,000. The first component of the formula is already in the T-account.

The next component is net income, which is *not* yet in the Retained Earnings account. We can place all the components of net income into the Retained Earnings account and come out with the net income number at the bottom. Remember:

Revenues − Expenses = Net income

This means that we need to get all of the revenues and expenses into the Retained Earnings account.

a. We start with our revenue T-account (service revenue as shown)

Service Revenue	
	Bal. 495,000

In order to clear out or reset all the Income Statement accounts so that they are empty to begin the next year, the first step is to *debit* each revenue account for the amount of its *credit* balance. Service Revenue has a *credit* balance of $495,000, so to bring that to zero, we need to *debit* Service Revenue for $495,000.

This means that we have part of our first closing entry:

A1

	A	B	C	D	E	F
1	1.	Service Revenue	495,000			
2		???		495,000		
3						

What is the credit side of this entry? The reason we started with Service Revenue was to help calculate net income in the Retained Earnings account. So the other side of the entry must go to Retained Earnings:

A1

	A	B	C	D	E	F
1	1.	Service Revenue	495,000			
2		Retained Earnings		495,000		
3						

b. The second step is to *credit* each expense account for the amount of its *debit* balance to bring each expense account to zero.

In this case, we have five different expenses:

Salary Expense

Bal. 259,000	

Supplies Expense

Bal. 3,000	

Rent Expense

Bal. 34,000	

Depreciation Expense—Building

Bal. 12,000	

Miscellaneous Expense

Bal. 8,000	

The sum of all the expenses will go to the debit side of the Retained Earnings account:

	A	B	C	D	E	F
1	2.	Retained Earnings	316,000			
2		Salary Expense		259,000		
3		Supplies Expense		3,000		
4		Rent Expense		34,000		
5		Depreciation Expense—Building		12,000		
6		Miscellaneous Expense		8,000		
7						

The last component of the Retained Earnings formula is dividends. There is a Dividends account:

Dividends

Bal. 7,000	

c. The final step in the closing process is to transfer Dividends to the debit site of the Retained Earnings account.

The Dividends account has a *debit* balance of $7,000, so to bring that to zero, we need to *credit* Dividends by $7,000. The balancing debit will go to Retained Earnings:

	A	B	C	D	E	F
1	3.	Retained Earnings	7,000			
2		Dividends		7,000		
3						

This entry subtracts Dividends from Retained Earnings. Retained Earnings now holds the following data:

Retained Earnings

	Debit		Credit	
Expenses	2. 316,000		52,000	Beginning retained earnings
Dividends	3. 7,000	1.	495,000	Revenue Net income
		Bal.	224,000	Ending retained earnings

The formula to update Retained Earnings has now been re-created inside the Retained Earnings T-account.

The following accounts are included in the closing process:

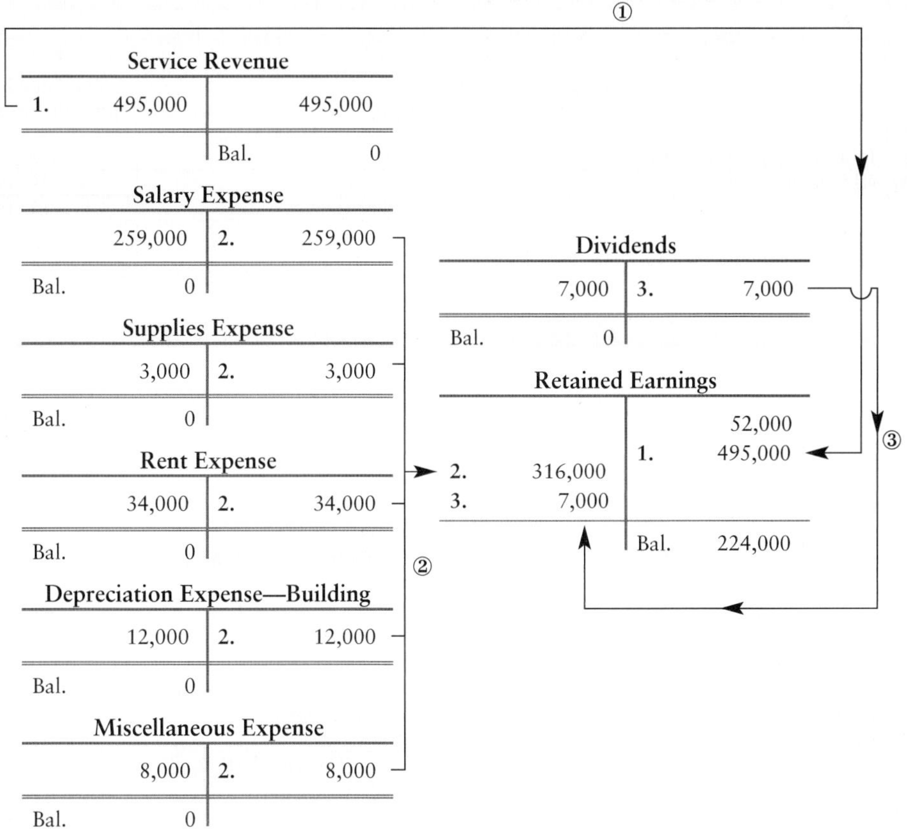

Notice that each temporary account (the Revenues, the Expenses, and Dividends), now has a zero balance.

➤ Requirement 5

Prepare Cloud Break's Income Statement and the Statement of Changes in Equity for the year ended June 30, 20X6, and the Balance Sheet at June 30, 20X6. Draw arrows linking the three financial statements.

Part 1	Part 2	Part 3	Part 4	Part 5	Demo Doc Complete

	A	B	C
1	**Cloud Break Consulting, Inc.** **Income Statement**	**Year Ended** **June 30, 20X6**	
2	**Revenue:**		
3	Service revenue		$ 495,000
4	**Expenses:**		
5	Salary expense	$ 259,000	
6	Rent expense	34,000	
7	Depreciation expense—building	12,000	
8	Supplies expense	3,000	
9	Miscellaneous expense	8,000	
10	Total expenses		316,000
11	**Net income**		$ 179,000
12			
13			

	A	B
1	**Cloud Break Consulting, Inc.** **Statement of Changes in Equity**	**Year Ended** **June 30, 20X6**
2	Total equity, June 30, 20X5	$ 102,000
3	Add: Net income	179,000
4		281,000
5	Less: Dividends	(7,000)
6	Retained earnings, June 30, 20X6	$ 274,000
7		
8		

	A	B	C	D	E
1	**Cloud Break Consulting, Inc.** **Balance Sheet**			**As at June 30, 20X6**	
2	**Assets**			**Liabilities**	
3	Cash		$ 131,000	Accounts payable	$ 159,000
4	Accounts receivable		119,000	Salary payable	4,000
5	Supplies		1,000	Unearned service revenue	10,000
6	Prepaid rent		18,000	Total liabilities	173,000
7	Land		45,000		
8	Building	$ 300,000)		**Shareholders' Equity**	
9	Less: Accumulated			Share capital	50,000
10	depreciation	(167,000)	133,000	Retained earnings	224,000
11				Total Shareholders' equity	274,000
12				Total liabilities and	
13	Total assets		$ 447,000	Shareholders' equity	$ 447,000
14					
15					

RELATIONSHIPS AMONG THE FINANCIAL STATEMENTS

The arrows in these statements show how the financial statements relate to each other. Follow the arrow that takes the ending balance of total equity to the Balance Sheet.

1. Net income from the Income Statements is reported as an increase to retained earnings (equity) on the statement of changes in equity. A net loss would be reported as a decrease to retained earnings (equity). Any dividends paid will also reduce retained earnings (equity).
2. The new total equity (and Ending Retained Earnings) from the statement of changes in equity is transferred to the Balance Sheet.

4 Presentation of Financial Statements

SPOTLIGHT | BASF www.basf.com

BASF is the world's leading chemical company, with more than 112,000 employees and about 350 production sites worldwide, including six *verbund,* integrated or linked, production sites. Its portfolio ranges from chemicals, plastics, and performance products to crop protection products, oil, and gas. Through science and innovation, BASF enables its customers across industries to meet the current and future needs of society. Its products and system solutions contribute to conserving resources, ensuring healthy food and nutrition, and helping to improve the quality of life. BASF has summed up this contribution in its corporate purpose: "We create chemistry for a sustainable future." ●

Mihai Simonia/Shutterstock

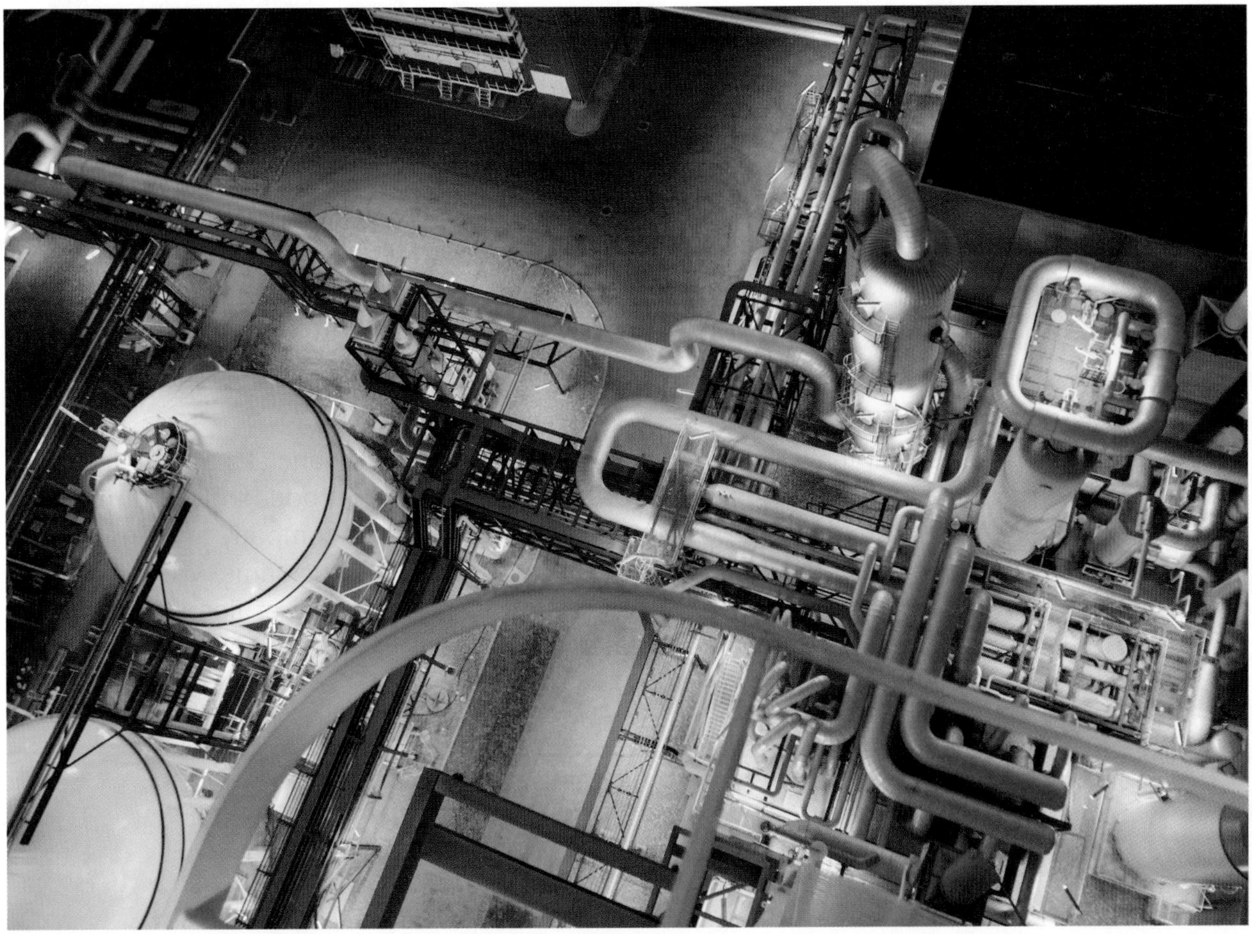

For the last 20 years, the Report Watch (www.reportwatch.net) has been running an annual competition to select the best annual reports. Annual reports are rated from a "D" (uncompetitive) to "A+" (first rate). BASF's annual reports have consistently received an "A" rating, and in fact was judged to have the Best Annual Report in 2011. It scored well on a number of criteria including overall package, highlights, strategy and communications, and financial and accounting disclosures.

BASF's annual reports, together with other disclosures on its investors' relations website, communicate important financial information and management reviews of the business to over 500,000 BASF shareholders around the world. In the first three chapters you have seen extracts of financial statements contained in the annual reports of Alibaba, Daimler, and Richemont.

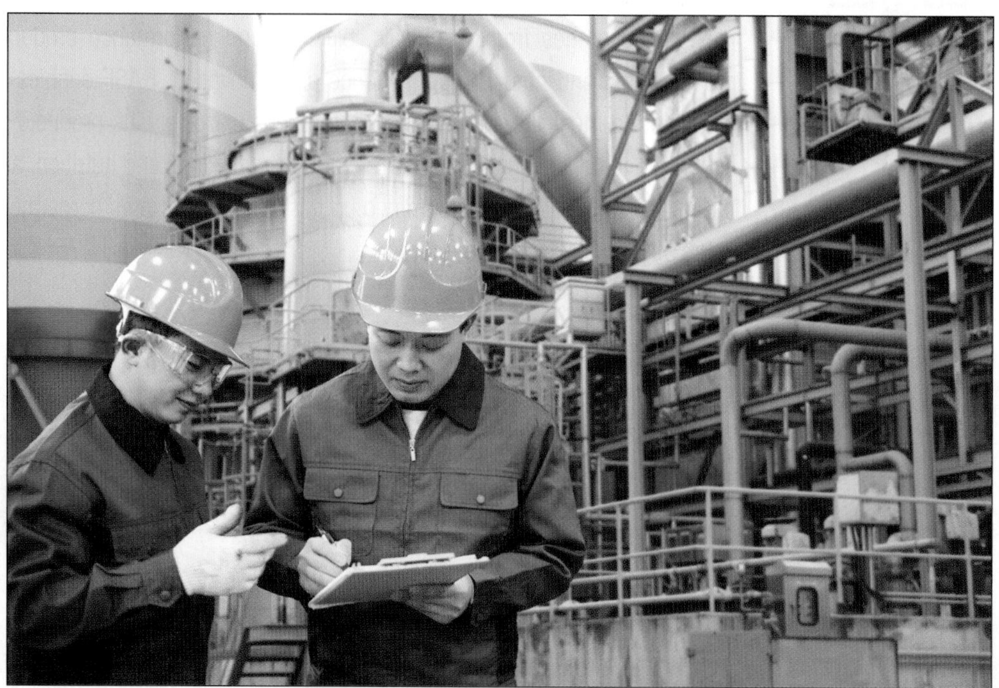

Ndoeljindoel/Shutterstock

This chapter will give you an appreciation of how financial statements are presented and communicated to users. You will be introduced to the major sections of an annual report. Annual reports vary from company to company, year to year, but their overall structure remains largely the same. We will also cover some of the key principles related to presentation of financial statements (with the exception of Statement of Cash Flows, which is covered in Chapter 11).

LEARNING OBJECTIVES

1. **Appreciate** the role of annual reports as a communication tool
2. **Know** the general presentation requirements of financial statements
3. **Understand** presentation requirements for Statement of Financial Position
4. **Understand** presentation requirements for Statement of Comprehensive Income
5. **Understand** presentation requirements for Statement of Changes in Equity
6. **Evaluate** a company's short-term liquidity

APPRECIATE THE ROLE OF ANNUAL REPORTS AS A COMMUNICATION TOOL

1 **Appreciate** the role of annual reports as a communication tool

A search on Google for "annual report" yields over a billion entries. In the world of electronic information and communication, **annual reports** are the top source of information for shareholders, lenders, potential investors, and many other stakeholders. Annual reports are used to project and share a vision, and with the ease of distribution via the Internet, they serve as an important element of any entity's communication with all its stakeholders. Annual reports provide readers with information on a company, ranging from company visions, goals, and strategies, to its financial statements and other required or compulsory disclosures (depending on jurisdictions). If you read a series of the same company's annual reports, you can often construct a story about how a particular business venture is doing, how the company has grown or declined, or how its management team and strategy have changed throughout the years.

Annual reports are not limited to commercial entities. Many nonprofit organizations, charities, and other welfare organizations also publish some form of annual publications to connect with their various stakeholders. As these entities do not have shareholders or investors that you would normally associate with commercial entities, their annual reports may differ slightly from corporate annual reports. For example, Médecins Sans Frontières (www.doctorswithoutbordersorg), CARE (www.care.org), and Oxfam (www.oxfam.org) all publish annual reports with financial statements. In many countries, even governments, including their ministries and regulatory authorities, publish annual reports.

Sometimes companies will highlight a particular creative theme for one financial year and, thus, will structure their report to fit this theme. For example, Podravka, a food and beverage company headquartered in Croatia, included a cookbook with its 2006 annual report that had to be baked (at 150°C for 25 minutes) to make the thermoreactive ink permanently readable. Austria Solar, an association for the promotion of thermal solar energy in Austria, created a big buzz online for its 2011 annual report that must be read in sunlight. Exhibit 4-12 is an example of a cover template used for creating Annual Reports for various organizations.

Substance Over Style

You should not judge a company by the artistic value of its annual report, and it clearly should not be the basis for deciding whether or not you would invest in a particular company. This would be like saying you will invest in companies that have impressive websites. No matter how slick and impressive an annual report may look, you must remember that it is the substance that matters. The audited financial statements are the substance of annual reports. This, not attractive pictures or glossy prints, should be the basis of your decision making.

For an example of the minimalist approach, look no further than Berkshire Hathaway, Warren Buffett's investment holding company. Its corporate annual report is the basic Form 10K (see A

Exhibit 4-1 | Annual Report Cover Template

Kolonko/Shutterstock

Closer Look on page 212), which you can download from its even more minimalist website (www.berkshirehathaway.com). No pictures, no fancy animation or videos, just straightforward company information.

Obtaining Annual Reports

Traditionally, annual reports are hard copy reports that are only sent to shareholders (and those who request them directly from the company). With advances in information technology and connectivity of the Internet, virtually everyone now can obtain an electronic copy of annual

You may find some companies talk about their "Integrated Report" instead of an annual report. Integrated reporting is a recent move towards a "concise communication about how an organization's strategy, governance, performance, and prospects lead to creation of value over the short, medium, and long term" (as defined by the Integrated Reporting Council, www.integratedreporting.org). An integrated report seeks to bring together how firms create values from its various capitals (not only financial capital but also manufactured, human [social and relationship], intellectual, and natural capital). You can think of it as an annual report that tries to show you a bigger, more complete picture, instead of just focusing on financial reporting.

You can find out more about integrated reporting from the website mentioned earlier, including a quick animated explanation of integrated reporting at http://integratedreporting.org/wp-content/uploads/2016/12/ACCA-Integrated-Reporting-M4V.m4v.

The following image is an example of what an integrated report may look like and how companies, like BASF, articulate their value creation process.

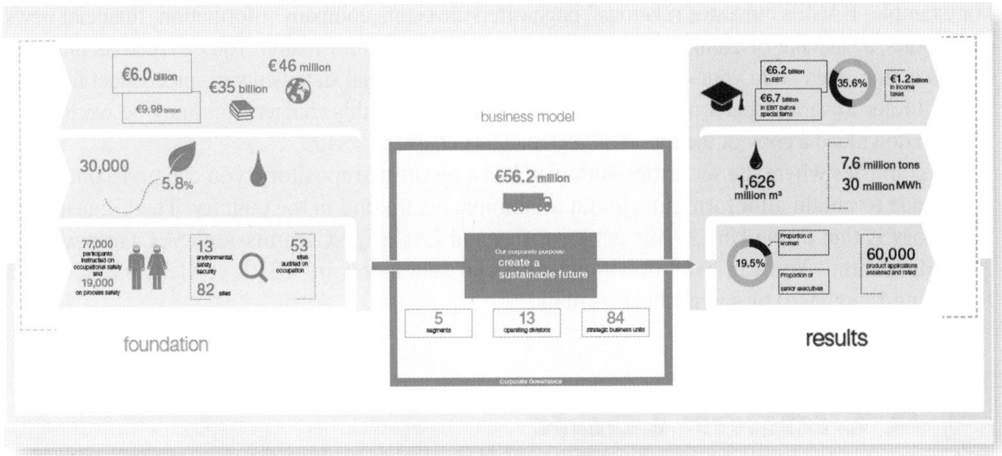

reports of any public companies online. With search engines such as Google or Bing, it is usually easy to find the websites of the companies you are interested in. Many companies have now developed "web versions" of their annual report, which allows for better navigation, use of digital media, and interactivity.

Note that some businesses separate their "corporate website" from their "consumer website." The corporate website is where you will find company and financial information pertinent to you, the investor or potential investor, whereas the consumer website is where the company showcases its product and services offerings to the consumer. With many websites now making use of location-based data, sometimes you may be redirected to your local, country, or region consumer website by default. You will have to specifically navigate to the company's corporate website in order to obtain financial statements. For example, for Sony Corporation, if you go to www.sony.com, you will arrive at the consumer side (either a global or local site, depending on your physical location), whereas www.sony.net will direct you to Sony's corporate website.

Many companies are now dedicating more resources to connect with their shareholders through a specific section of their websites, typically labeled "Investors" or "Investor Relations" (see Exhibit 4-2).

Exhibit 4-2 | An Investor Relations Landing Page

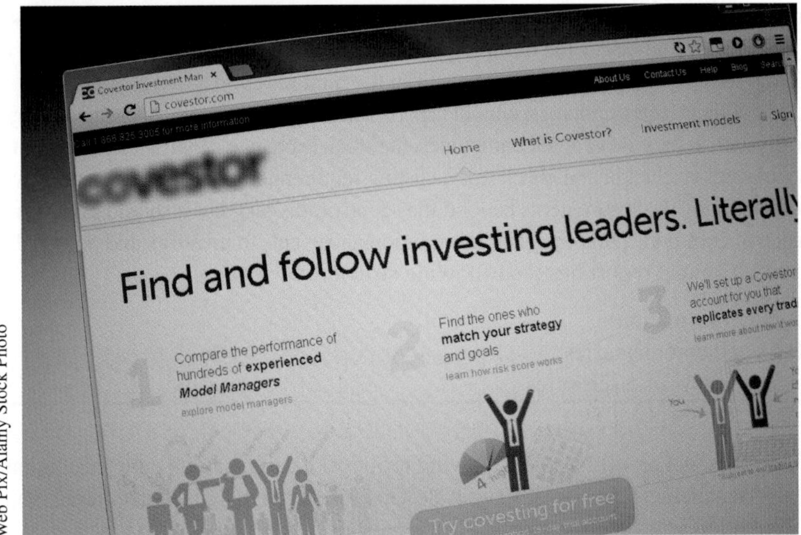

Web Pix/Alamy Stock Photo

For example, BASF's "investor relations" page offers investors company information, financial news and reports, a calendar of events, and other share holder-related information. You can read its financial reports online, even build your own charts, and download financial statements in spreadsheet formats. We will refer to various parts of BASF's 2015 annual report in this chapter, so it may be worth your while to download a copy of the report as you read this chapter.

In countries where the securities authority has a reporting repository, you can go to one common place to obtain all information about all companies trading in the country. The biggest such repository is that of the United States' Securities and Exchange Commission (SEC) at www.sec.gov/edgar.shtml. You can even download financial statements in XBRL (eXtensible Business Reporting Language) or spreadsheet formats.

A Closer Look

For SEC registrants, financial filings are referred to by their form numbers. For example, "Form 10-K" and "Form 10-Q" refer to annual and quarter filings, respectively. There are many others, such as:

- Form 1 for the offering of securities, typically for initial public offerings or additional securities issuances
- Form 4 for material changes in the holding of company securities by "insiders" (major shareholders, company executives)
- Form 8-K for important material events or corporate changes of high importance such as major asset acquisition or disposal, appointment or resignation of directors, etc.
- Form S-4 for important events related to mergers and acquisitions.

While these forms contain significant financial information, they are highly structured and largely dictated by the SEC's regulatory requirements. They are quite different from the typical annual reports that you will see in other parts of the world. Many U.S. companies produce annual reports in addition to their regulatory filings.

As filing requirements may differ from one country to another, your instructor may direct you to specific issues related to corporate reporting in your jurisdiction.

Typical Structure of an Annual Report

For some companies, the primary purpose of an annual report is to meet legal requirements. Consequently, they only focus on compliance and do not invest much in corporate reporting. Small private companies' annual reports, for example, primarily consist of financial statements and their accompanying notes. The larger the company and the more investors (or in some cases, creditors) it has, the more likely you will see more content in the annual report.

Regardless of their creative themes, annual reports must meet requirements as dictated by the regulatory authority and, in the case of listed companies, the stock exchange's **listing requirements**. You can visit your local stock exchange and check out its listing requirements or listing manual. It would most probably contain many disclosure items beyond the scope of this text, but it should give you an idea of the importance of communicating financial information and events to investors and potential investors.

Typically, an annual report has the following structure:

- corporate information
- analysis and commentaries
- other statements or disclosures
- financial statements

The BASF 2015 annual report has the following top-level headings in its table of contents: To our shareholders, Management Analysis, Corporate Governance, Financial Statements, and Supplementary Information.

Corporate Information

Companies provide various kinds of corporate information to their shareholders. For example, they could include information related to the history of the company, members of the board of directors and key management personnel, organizational structure of key subsidiaries or affiliates (more on this in Chapter 8), key markets and products, major events during the financial period (such as mergers and acquisitions, or disposal of business units), awards and accolades received, operating statistics, financial highlights, and any other general information about the company that may be useful to a reader's understanding of the company. You will not find all these examples in one single section, and different companies might present different items. For example, companies like BASF provide an introduction to its various business segments, as illustrated in Exhibit 4-3.

Exhibit 4-3 | Segment Information

	**Chemicals** The Chemicals segment comprises our business with basic chemicals and intermediates. Its portfolio ranges from solvents, plasticizers, and high-volume monomers to glues and electronic chemicals as well as raw materials for detergents, plastics, textile fibers, paints and coatings, crop protection, and medicines. In addition to supplying customers in the chemical industry and numerous other sectors, we also ensure that other BASF segments are supplied with chemicals for producing downstream products.
	**Performance Products** Our Performance Products lend stability, color, and better application properties to many everyday products. Our product portfolio includes vitamins and other food additives in addition to ingredients for pharmaceuticals, personal care and cosmetics, as well as hygiene and household products. Other products from this segment improve processes in the paper industry, in oil, gas, and ore extraction, and in water treatment. They furthermore enhance the efficiency of fuels and lubricants, the effectiveness of adhesives and coatings, and the stability of plastics.
	**Functional Materials and Solutions** In the Functional Materials and Solutions segment we bundle system solutions, services, and innovative products for specific sectors and customers, especially the automotive, electrical, chemical, and construction industries, as well as for household applications, and sports and leisure. Our portfolio comprises catalysts, battery materials, engineering plastics, polyurethane systems, automotive and industrial coatings, and concrete admixtures as well as construction systems like tile adhesives and decorative paints.
	**Agricultural Solutions** The Agricultural Solutions segment provides innovative solutions in the areas of chemical and biological crop protection, seed treatment and water management as well as solutions for nutrient supply and plant stress. Our research in plant biotechnology concentrates on plants for greater efficiency in agriculture, better nutrition, and use as renewable raw materials.
	**Oil and Gas** We focus on exploration and production in oil and gas-rich regions in Europe, North Africa, Russia, South America, and the Middle East. Together with our Russian partner Gazprom, we are active in the transport of natural gas in Europe. At the end of the third quarter in 2015, we exited the natural gas trading and storage business, which we previously operated together with Gazprom, and, in exchange, we are expanding our oil and gas production in western Serbia.

Zenphotography/Shutterstock; Michal Ludwiczak/Shutterstock; Olivier Le Queinec/Shutterstock; Redhen/Shutterstock; Trevor Clifford/Pearson Education Ltd

Analysis and Commentaries

Like many other annual reports, the BASF 2015 annual report's first major item is the "Letter from the Chairman of the Board of Executive Directors." Depending on the organizational structure (and local practice), you may see the title President used in place of **Chairman**. You can read Dr. Kurt Block's (BASF's chairman of the board of directors) letter to shareholders on pages 9–11 of the BASF 2015 annual report. It talks about achievements in the financial year, returns to shareholders, and the key focus or goals for the future.

ADAPTED EXCERPTS FROM BASF'S ANNUAL REPORT

Excerpt from the Letter from the Chairman of the Board of Executive Directors

Dear Shareholder,

As this report goes to print, we are looking back at one of the most turbulent starts to the year for decades. At times, oil prices fell to below $27 per barrel—the lowest level since 2003. In 2015, oil prices averaged $52 per barrel, almost half the previous year's figure. This price slump reflects not only an oil surplus but also a slowdown in global economic growth, especially in emerging markets. Our share price has also suffered from these developments. Since the beginning of the year it has fallen significantly to below €60 and is thus substantially lower than the peak of nearly €97 in April 2015.

These figures underline the level of uncertainty about the future performance of the global economy. This raises some legitimate questions: How will demand for chemical products develop? What will be the impact if oil prices remain low for any length of time? How does one steer a company like BASF in such turbulent and challenging times?

[and so on]

Yours,

Kurt Block

Source: BASF, Annual Report 2015, page 9

The next set of commentaries is from the company's management. Before we go further, perhaps it is useful to explain how corporations, especially public or listed companies, structure themselves organizationally. The ultimate control of the company rests with shareholders, who appoint a **board of directors** to provide oversight of the company. The board, in turn, hires a management team to run the company. Of course, in many instances, an individual may be a shareholder, a member of the board of directors, and a CEO of the company. We discuss corporate structure later in more detail (in Chapter 10, for example, see Exhibit 10-2). For now, let's just take it that a board of directors means shareholders' representatives overseeing a management team that runs the company.

The objective of such commentaries is to provide users with an understanding of the company via an analysis of the company's businesses as seen through the eyes of the directors and management. These commentaries serve to facilitate assessment of the company's business and business objectives, its principal drivers of performance, the dynamics of the business, and the financial performance and condition of the company.

Thus, the management analysis and commentaries are basically management's explanations to shareholders of how the company has performed during the year. In some parts of the world, this set of commentaries may be known as "MD&A" (Management Discussions and Analysis) or "OFR" (Operating and Financial Review), or something similar. Typically, management would explain the performance of various products or segments of the company, the status of the company's strategic initiatives or projects, and plans or goals for the upcoming financial year.

BASF's management analysis is extremely comprehensive (see pages 21 to 126 of its 2015 annual report). It describes its view of the trends in the global economy and the industries it operates in, the performance of its business segments (chemicals, plastics, performance products, functional solutions, agricultural solutions, and oil and gas), and geographical regions. It also describes BASF's corporate social responsibility to its employees and the society, and its commitment to the environment and overall safety. It even provides the management's outlook for the future.

ADAPTED EXCERPTS FROM BASF'S ANNUAL REPORT

Management's Report: Results of Operations

In 2015, the market environment continued to be volatile and challenging. Growth rates for the global economy, industrial production, and the chemical industry all lagged considerably behind our expectations. The economic environment deteriorated in important emerging markets, especially China. The sharp drop in the price of oil led to falling prices for basic chemicals in particular. The divestitures completed in 2015 also put a strain on both sales and income from operations (EBIT) before special items. Impairments in the Oil & Gas segment resulting from the reduced forecast for oil and gas prices led to considerably lower EBIT. In light of these factors, our overall business development remained behind our expectations.

Source: BASF, Annual Report 2015, page 52

Other Statements and Disclosures

This varies from one jurisdiction to another, but you will always find disclosures related to corporate governance. **Corporate governance** refers broadly to a set of principles adopted or practiced by organizations in order to ensure a clear corporate direction, responsibility, and accountability of those managing the organization. Typically, it prescribes matters such as the composition, duties, and responsibilities of the board of directors, oversights of management, and its dealings with shareholders.

BASF's corporate governance disclosures are on pages 129 to 147 of its 2015 annual report. The introduction to that section is shown below.

ADAPTED EXCERPTS FROM BASF'S ANNUAL REPORT

Corporate Governance Report

Corporate governance refers to the entire system for managing and supervising a company. This includes the organization values, corporate principles and guidelines, as well as all internal and external regulatory and monitoring mechanisms. Effective and transparent corporate governance guarantees that BASF is managed and monitored in a responsible manner focused on value creation. This fosters the confidence of our domestic and international investors, the financial markets, our customers, other business partners, employees, and the public in BASF.

Source: BASF, Annual Report 2015, page 129

A key part of any corporate governance framework is internal control. We will provide an introduction to internal control in Chapter 5.

Other statements and disclosures may include a compensation report for directors and the senior management team, economic-value added or EVA statements (more on this in Chapter 12), and sustainability and/or environmental reporting (often referred to as corporate social responsibility). An example of BASF's extensive "Safety, Security, Health and the Environment" disclosure is shown in the following adapted excerpt.

ADAPTED EXCERPTS FROM BASF'S ANNUAL REPORT

Safety, Security, Health and the Environment

Safety Security and Health		**2015**	**2014**	**Change in %**
Transportation incidents with significant impact on the environment		0	1	(100)
Process safety incidents	per one million working hours	2.1	2.2	(4.5)
Lost-time injuries	per one million working hours	1.4	1.5	(6.7)
Health Performance Index[1]		0.97	0.91	6.6
Environment				
Primary energy use[2]	million MWh	57.3	59.0	(2.9)
Energy efficiency in production processes	kilograms of sales product/MWh	599	588	1.9
Total water withdrawal	million cubic meters	1,686	1,877	(10.2)
Withdrawal of drinking water	million cubic meters	22.1	22.7	(2.6)
Emissions of organic substances to water[3]	thousand metric tons	17.3	18.7	(7.5)
Emissions of nitrogen to water[3]	thousand metric tons	3.0	3.2	(6.3)
Emissions of heavy metals to water[3]	metric tons	25.1	21.5	16.7
Emissions of greenhouse gases	million metric tons of CO_2 equivalents	22.2	22.4	(0.9)
Emissions to air (air pollutants)[3]	thousand metric tons	28.6	31.5	(9.2)
Waste	million metric tons	2.0	2.1	(4.8)
Operating costs for environmental protection	million €	962	897	7.2
Investments in environmental protection plants and facilities	million €	346	349	(0.9)

[1] For more information, see Production. http://bericht.basf.com/2015/en/managements-report/responsibility-along-the-value-chain/safety-security-health-and-environment/production.html

[2] Primary energy used in BASF's plants as well as in the plants of our energy suppliers to cover energy demand for production processes

[3] Excluding emissions from oil and gas production

Source: BASF, Annual Report 2015, http://berich.basf.com/2015/en/shareholders/key-data.html

Financial Statements

Typically the financial statement section starts with an acknowledgement by directors and management that they are responsible for the financial statements, followed by an auditor's report and the full set of financial statements.

ADAPTED EXCERPTS FROM BASF'S ANNUAL REPORT

Statement by the Board of Executive Directors and Assurance Pursuant to Sections 297(2), Section 315(1) of the German Commercial Code (HGB)

The Board of Executive Directors of BASF SE is responsible for preparing the Consolidated Financial Statements and Management's Report of the BASF Group.

The Consolidated Financial Statements for 2015 were prepared according to the International Financial Reporting Standards (IFRS), which are published by the International Accounting Standards Board (IASB), London, and have been endorsed by the European Union.

We have established effective internal control and steering systems in order to ensure that the BASF Group's Consolidated Financial Statements and Management's Report comply with applicable accounting rules and to ensure proper corporate reporting.

The risk management system we have set up is designed to identify material risks early on and take appropriate defensive measures as necessary. The reliability and effectiveness of the internal control and risk management system are continually audited throughout the Group by our internal audit department.

To the best of our knowledge, and in accordance with the applicable reporting principles, the Consolidated Financial Statements of the BASF Group give a true and fair view of the net assets, financial position, and results of operations of the Group, and the Management's Report includes a fair review of the development and performance of the business and the position of the BASF Group, together with a description of the principal opportunities and risks associated with the expected development of the BASF Group.

Source: BASF, Annual Report 2015, page 155

A statement of responsibility, such as the one you just saw, is also an important element of corporate governance. It clearly spells out that preparation of financial statements is not just the job of the chief financial officer or the accounting or finance department. As financial statements (and their integrity) are crucial to all stakeholders in a company, it is of utmost importance that everyone in the company, regardless of job functions, lives up to their responsibility.

Another key element of ensuring the integrity of financial statements is the audit requirement imposed on all listed companies. The requirement for an audit of financial statements is legally imposed by the respective jurisdiction's corporation or company law. Companies engage *external auditors*, who are completely independent of the business. They are hired to determine whether or not the company's financial statements are in compliance with generally accepted accounting principles. Auditors examine the client's financial statements and the underlying transactions in order to form a professional opinion on the accuracy and reliability of the company's financial statements. This opinion is contained in an **auditor's report**, which provides an independent professional opinion to the company's shareholders that the company's financial statements were prepared in accordance with stipulated standards and represent a true and fair reflection of the company's performance. An audit report is usually addressed to the board of directors and shareholders of a company. A partner of the auditing firm signs the firm's name to the report.

KPMG, one of the "Big 4" accounting firms, is the auditor for BASF. The other members of the "Big 4" are Deloitte, Ernst & Young (EY), and PricewaterhouseCoopers. Together, they command a large share of the audit market, especially those of larger, listed multinational companies. KPMG arrives at an opinion after conducting its audit procedures in accordance to required auditing standards. Let's have a look at KPMG's audit report on BASF's financial statements.

ADAPTED EXCERPTS FROM BASF'S ANNUAL REPORT

Auditor's Report

We have audited the Consolidated Financial Statements prepared by BASF SE, Ludwigshafen am Rhein, Germany, comprising the statement of Income, Statement of income and expense recognized in equity, Balance Sheet, statement of cash flows, statement of equity and the notes to the Consolidated Financial Statements, together with the Group Management's Report for the business year from January 1 to December 31, 2015. The preparation of the Consolidated Financial Statements and the Group Management's Report in accordance with IFRS as adopted by the European Union (EU), and the additional requirements of German commercial law pursuant to Section 315a(1) of the German Commercial Code (HGB) are the responsibility of the parent company's management. Our responsibility is to express an opinion on the Consolidated Financial Statements and on the Group Management's Report based on our audit. In addition, we have been instructed to express an opinion as to whether the Consolidated Financial Statements comply with full IFRS.

We conducted our audit of the Consolidated Financial Statements in accordance with Section 317 HGB and the German generally accepted standards for the audit of financial statements promulgated by the Institute of Public Auditors in Germany (Institut

continued on the following page

der Wirtschaftsprüfer, IDW). Those standards require that we plan and perform the audit such that misstatements materially affecting the presentation of the net assets, financial position, and results of operations in the Consolidated Financial Statements in accordance with the applicable financial reporting framework and in the Group Management's Report are detected with reasonable assurance. Knowledge of the business activities and the economic and legal environment of the Group and expectations as to possible misstatements are taken into account in the determination of audit procedures. The effectiveness of the accounting-related internal control system and the evidence supporting the disclosures in the Consolidated Financial Statements and the Group Management's Report are examined primarily on a test basis within the framework of the audit. The audit includes assessing the annual financial statements of those entities included in consolidation, the determination of entities to be included in consolidation, the accounting and consolidation principles used, and significant estimates made by the Board of Executive Directors, as well as evaluating the overall presentation of the Consolidated Financial Statements and the Group Management's Report. We believe that our audit provides a reasonable basis for our opinion.

Our audit has not led to any reservations.

In our opinion, based on the findings of our audit, the Consolidated Financial Statements comply with IFRS as adopted by the EU, the additional requirements of German commercial law pursuant to Section 315a(1) HGB and full IFRS and give a true and fair view of the net assets, financial position, and results of operations of the Group in accordance with these requirements. The Group Management's Report is consistent with the Consolidated Financial Statements and as a whole provides a suitable view of the Group's position and suitably presents the opportunities and risks of future development.

Frankfurt am Main, February 23, 2016

KPMG AG

Source: BASF, Annual Report 2015, page 155

The audit report on financial statements typically contains four sections:

- The first section identifies the audited financial statements as well as the company being audited.
- The second section outlines the respective responsibilities of the company's management as well as the auditor's responsibilities.
- The third section describes how the audit was performed in accordance with the generally accepted auditing standards of the jurisdiction. These are the standards used by auditors as the benchmark for evaluating audit quality (in this case, auditing standards as promulgated by the Institute of Public Auditors in Germany).
- The last section expresses the auditor's combined opinion about the entity's financial statements, remuneration report, and director's report. This may be different in different jurisdictions, depending on the local requirements.

A Closer Look

From 2017, you may see enhanced auditor reports instead of the typical one-page auditor report (similar to the BASF excerpts shown earlier). This enhanced report will provide more disclosure on what the auditors judged as "key audit matters" and how they addressed them during the audit. These matters may include elements such as choice of accounting policies, significant use of accounting estimates, or potential weaknesses in internal controls. There are other changes in the new auditor report, but they are beyond our scope of discussion in this introductory text.

As you can see, KPMG's opinion is that the Consolidated Financial Statements provide a "true and fair view of the net assets, financial position and results of the Group." This is what we call an **unqualified opinion**. It is the highest statement of assurance that an independent auditing firm can express. An unqualified opinion is one that is made without reservation or qualification. In other words, unqualified means the auditors did not qualify the opinion with matters that would require the readers' attention.

A **qualified opinion**, on the other hand, may be issued if, as a whole, the financial statements are fairly presented, except for disagreement on how to treat a particular transaction. Another situation could be where the auditors were not able to complete their planned audit procedures on a particular item or transaction. If the issue is beyond a single item or single transaction, an auditor may issue an **adverse opinion**. This opinion is the opposite of an unqualified opinion, i.e., the financial statements, as a whole, do not fairly represent the company's financial position. In very rare cases, auditors may not even be able to express an opinion due to their inability to complete the audit procedures as required.

If you are an accounting major student, you will learn more about various aspects of auditing in your audit course. Reliable audits are a crucial element of the stability of the financial market. If no one trusts audited financial statements, there will be chaos because you would never buy from, invest in, or loan money to any business.

After an audit report ends, you will find pages containing financial statements and accompanying notes. We will discuss the principles of presentation of these financial statements in the next few sections. Presentation requirements for Statement of Cash Flows will be discussed in Chapter 11.

KNOW THE GENERAL PRESENTATION REQUIREMENTS OF FINANCIAL STATEMENTS

Know the general presentation requirements of financial statements

The *Conceptual Framework* (discussed in Chapter 1) states that the objective of financial reporting is to provide financial information, in the form of general purpose financial statements, which is useful to existing and potential investors, lenders, and other creditors when making decisions about providing resources to an entity. Thus, how financial statements are presented is of great importance. For example, how should an entity decide what items to show on its statement of comprehensive income? Is it allowed to combine different types of assets into one account on a Balance Sheet? Can it offset a receivable from and payable to the same counterparty? These general presentation requirements are addressed in *IAS 1—Presentation of Financial Statements*. Let's have a brief look at *IAS 1*.

Complete Set of Financial Statements

A complete set of financial statements comprises:

- a statement of financial position at the end of the period
- a statement of comprehensive income for the period
- a statement of changes in equity for the period
- a statement of cash flows for the period
- notes, comprising a summary of significant accounting policies and other explanatory information

Entities are allowed to use alternative names for the financial statements. For example, the Statement of Financial Position is usually called a Balance Sheet. The first part of a Statement of Comprehensive Income is usually called an Income Statement or a Profit and Loss Statement. The Statement of Comprehensive Income itself is sometimes called a Statement of Recognized Income and Expenses.

These financial statements must be displayed with equal prominence. In practice, this means the financial statements are presented together, one after another. The standard does not prescribe the exact order of how the financial statements should appear. Most companies usually start with either the statement of financial position or statement of comprehensive income, followed by either the statement of changes in equity or the statement of cash flows, and then the notes to the financial statements. The BASF 2015 financial statements (pages 157 to 161) were in the following order: Statement of Income, Statement of Income and Expense recognized in Equity, Balance Sheet, Statement of Cash flows, and Statement of Equity. Note that BASF uses slightly different names.

In addition, the financial statements must be properly labeled. *IAS 1* requires an entity to clearly identify:

- the name of the reporting entity
- if it is a consolidated or an individual entity's account (see Chapter 8)
- the date of the end of the reporting period or the period covered by the financial statements
- the presentation currency used
- the level of rounding used in presenting the amounts in the financial statements

Fair Presentation and Compliance with IFRS

You saw earlier that BASF and its auditor made references to how the financial statements fairly present the net assets, financial position, and results of operations of the company. Fair presentation requires the faithful representation of the effects of transactions, other events, and conditions in accordance with the definitions and recognition criteria for assets, liabilities, income, and expenses set out in the *Conceptual Framework*. When an entity applies IFRS, with additional disclosure when necessary, it is presumed to result in financial statements that achieve a fair presentation. It cannot selectively apply the standards it likes (and not apply the ones it doesn't like) and proclaim compliance with IFRS.

An entity cannot rectify inappropriate accounting policies either by disclosure of the accounting policies used or by notes or explanatory material. For example, it cannot say it applies a policy that is not compliant with accounting standards, and then offer an explanation as to how the alternative treatment is better than the one under accounting standards, or how the alternative result is not materially different from one that is prepared under proper accounting standards.

Going Concern

We mentioned the going concern assumption earlier (in Chapter 1). Going concern means the entity intends to, and has the ability to, operate into the foreseeable future. When an entity does not have a going concern, financial statements can no longer assume such an ability to operate into the future. The basis for accounting will be completely different from what we would normally do. For example, you can no longer depreciate an item of property, plant and equipment (PPE) because useful lives are no longer relevant if the entity ceases operations.

Accrual Basis of Accounting

We discussed earlier (in Chapter 3) how accrual accounting is better because it properly reflects changes in net assets of an entity, rather than how much cash has gone in and out of an entity. *IAS 1* requires that an entity prepare its financial statements, except for cash flow information, using the accrual basis of accounting.

Materiality and Aggregation

How many accounts do you think a business would utilize in its accounting system? The RedLotus, Inc., example you have worked on earlier (in Chapters 1 to 3) used about 20 accounts (see Exhibit 3-9). It would be easy just to show all these 20 accounts in the financial statements of RedLotus, Inc.

In real life, however, companies use thousands, millions, and even billions of accounts. For every inventory, receivable, and payable, companies will keep track of individual account balances rather than just the total. If a company has 100,000 customers, it will have 100,000 customer accounts in Accounts Receivable. Add another 20,000 suppliers and another 10,000 items on inventory, and you can see how the number of accounts quickly racks up.

A Closer Look

While we have used a single accounts receivable and a single accounts payable in our examples, in real life this is not going to be good enough. Think about it. If you have 100 customers, can you use a single, combined, receivable account to track each customer's credit purchases, returns, and subsequent payments? You clearly need an account for each customer. But if each customer has an account, how big will your chart of accounts be? How are you going show them all on the trial balance?

Accounting systems make use of two levels of accounts: the control or summary account in the general ledger and its subsidiary accounts (also called subsidiary ledger, or sub-ledger for short). For example, you can see how the accounts receivable below is the control (or summary) account and that it represents the total of all the individual debtors' account balances.

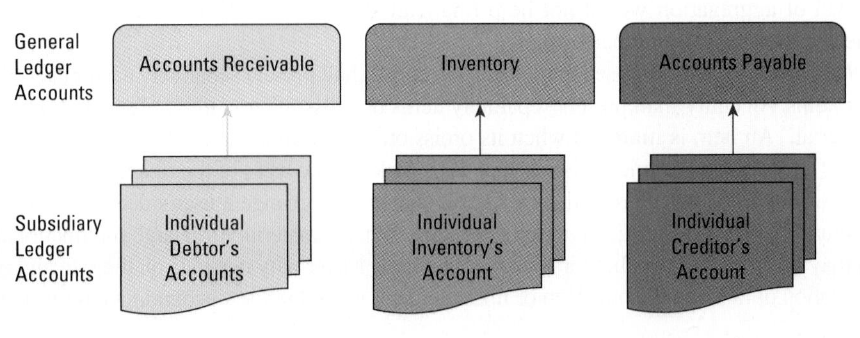

When transactions are processed, the accounting system will record at the individual level. For example, when M&R Ltd, one of your customers, paid the amount it owes to you, the balance is updated at the individual debtor's account (otherwise, you would still be chasing M&R for payments). The summary account is updated periodically with the totals of all the individual debtors' accounts.

Even beyond these sub-ledger accounts, a company may keep a very detailed record of all its expenses, each account perhaps further sub-categorized by location, line of business, etc. For example, a business may keep track of the following accounts related to motor vehicle expenditures:

- Motor Vehicles—Fuel
- Motor Vehicles—Registration fees
- Motor Vehicles—Insurance
- Motor Vehicles—Repairs and maintenance
- Motor Vehicles—Other.

It may even sub-categorize the accounts further by types of motor vehicle: corporate office vehicles, delivery trucks, etc. When presenting financial statements to external users, companies will most probably aggregate these accounts. They may even be aggregated further with other expenses, such as telecommunication expenses, subscription expenses, and supplies expenses, as "other operating expenses."

So how many accounts do companies use? A recent survey of 1,400 companies shows that this is largely dependent on the size and complexity of the business (Exhibit 4-4).

Exhibit 4-4 Number of General Ledger Accounts by Revenue Size

	Less than $25M	$25M–$99M	$100M–$499M	$500M–$999M	$1B–$4.9B	$5B and over
100–500	86%	60%	50%	43%	41%	27%
501–1,000	9%	23%	28%	29%	23%	18%
1,001–3,000	4%	11%	13%	17%	15%	18%
3,001–5,000	0%	3%	3%	9%	8%	27%
5,001–10,000	0%	2%	3%	3%	8%	2%
More than 10,000	1%	2%	3%	0%	5%	9%

How much should a company aggregate before it loses meaning? What if a company aggregates everything to one total revenue and one total expenses account without additional details? Surely, such a level of aggregation would not help financial statement users make informed decisions about the company's financial performance.

IAS 1 provides a principle-based guideline: "An entity shall present separately each material class of similar items. An entity shall present separately items of a dissimilar nature or function unless they are immaterial." An item is **material** when its omission or misstatement could, individually or collectively, influence the economic decisions that users make on the basis of the financial statements. In other words, something is material when it has the potential to change a user's decision. It does not need to actually result in a change in a user's decision. What is material for a large multinational corporation may be different from that for a smaller business. Materiality depends on the size and nature (or combination of both) of the omission or misstatement, judged in the surrounding circumstances.

Offsetting

In general, unless required or permitted by an accounting standard, an entity is not allowed to offset assets and liabilities, or income and expenses. For example, if you have a receivable of €100 from BASF and a payable to BASF amounting to €80, you cannot offset the amounts and only show a receivable of €20. Such offsetting practices reduce the financial statement user's ability to understand the two separate business phenomena.

Note that offsetting is not the same as netting. For example, you can net off Accumulated Depreciation from a Property, Plant and Equipment (PPE) cost to arrive at a carrying amount. Similarly, netting receivables with allowances for uncollectible accounts (see Chapter 5) is perfectly fine and, in fact, done to provide the entity's net position on the Balance Sheet.

A Closer Look

Generally, when you sell something, you would show cost of goods sold as an expense item and the sales proceeds as revenue (more on this in Chapter 6). They are shown separately and not netted off. However, income outside ordinary activities, such as one generated from *incidental transactions* from disposal of a PPE is shown net (the difference between the sales proceeds and the carrying amount of the PPE). This netting reflects the substance of the business phenomenon. We will discuss disposals of PPE again later (in Chapter 7).

Frequency of Reporting

Entities are required to present a complete set of financial information at least annually. Some entities do not use fixed date year-ends but use a 52-week period instead (see Chapter 1). Larger entities, depending on stock exchange requirements, are often required to report on a half-yearly or even quarterly basis. These are usually referred to as **interim reports**. Interim reports do not have the same amount of detail as annual reports and are not audited.

Comparative Information

From the extracts of companies' financial statements you have seen thus far in this text, you would have noticed that each financial statement has **comparative information**, i.e., numbers from previous period(s). This allows readers to make better sense of the financial information. *IAS 1* requires entities to disclose, at a minimum, two years of information, i.e., the current financial period and the previous financial period. Under certain situations, entities may be required to provide three years of Balance Sheet information (as at the end of the current period, as at the end of the previous period, and at the beginning of previous period). Comparatives must also be made in the narrative and descriptive information.

Consistency of Presentation

Further, entities are expected to maintain the presentation and classification of items in the financial statements from one period to another. For example, if an entity has always included and presented a particular income item under the heading "other income," it should continue to do so, unless presenting it otherwise is required by an accounting standard or results in more relevant and reliable information to the financial statement users. If a new presentation is carried out, then naturally the comparative amounts have to be adjusted accordingly.

For example, suppose that for 20X5 and 20X4, your sales and marketing expenses were $20,000 and $30,000, respectively. Prior to issuing the financial statements, you decided that a particular other operating expense amounting to $2,000 is more appropriately disclosed as a sales and marketing expense. If you only reflect this new classification for 20X5, you will show:

	20X5	20X4
Sales and marketing expenses	$22,000	$20,000
Other operating expenses	$28,000	$30,000

This gives an impression that you have incurred more sales and marketing expenses and fewer other operating expenses in 20X5 compared to 20X4. This obviously would mislead readers as the expenses were exactly the same for 20X5 and 20X4. The change was caused by a reclassification. If this new classification is adopted, you would have to adjust your 20X4 comparative as well, and show:

	20X5	20X4
Sales and marketing expenses	$22,000	$22,000
Other operating expenses	$28,000	$28,000

Earlier (in Chapter 1), we saw how comparability enhances the quality of financial information. When presented with comparatives, the information must be presented on the same basis ("like things must look alike, different things must look different"). Otherwise, you will be looking at different ways of grouping items that may distort your view of the financial statements.

Notes to the Accounts

Recall that a complete set of financial statements include notes to the accounts. Notes to the accounts are an integral part of financial statements and contain additional information beyond the items presented on the face of financial statements. The notes are presented in a systematic manner, with appropriate cross-references from each item on the financial statements. While there is no specific order of items disclosed in the notes to the accounts, typically you will find it starts with a summary of significant accounting policies, estimates, and assumptions used in the preparation of financial statements, followed by additional supporting information for items on the financial statements, and lastly other disclosure requirements that are not based on items shown on the financial statements.

You have seen various examples of accounting policy disclosures on revenue recognition earlier (in Chapter 3). You will see other examples as we discuss various topics throughout this text. Here's an example from BASF's notes to the financial statements on its revenue recognition policies.

ADAPTED EXCERPTS FROM BASF'S NOTES TO THE FINANCIAL STATEMENTS

Revenue Recognition (partial)

Revenues from the sale of goods or the rendering of services are recognized upon the transfer of ownership and risk to the buyer. They are measured at the fair value of the consideration received. Sales revenues are reported without sales tax. Expected rebates and other trade discounts are accrued or deducted. Provisions are recognized according to the principle of individual measurement to cover probable risks related to the return of products, future warranty obligations and other claims.

Source: BASF, Annual Report 2015, page 166

In preparing financial statements, you have also seen that many accounting policies require the use of estimates and reliance on some assumptions. This is a critical understanding that anyone who studies accounting should realize. The numbers are meaningless until you know the accounting policies, estimates, and assumptions used to determine how transactions are recorded, measured, and eventually reported on the financial statements. For example, BASF provided this disclosure in its notes:

ADAPTED EXCERPTS FROM BASF'S NOTES TO THE FINANCIAL STATEMENTS

Use of estimates and assumptions in the preparation of the Consolidated Financial Statements

The carrying amount of assets, liabilities and provisions, contingent liabilities and other financial obligations in the Consolidated Financial Statements depends on the use of estimates, assumptions and use of discretionary scope. Specific estimates or assumptions used in individual accounting or valuation methods are disclosed in their respective sections. They are based on the circumstances and estimates on the Balance Sheet date and affect the reported amounts of income and expenses during the reporting periods. These assumptions particularly concern discounted cash flows in the context of impairment tests and purchase price allocations; the determination of useful lives of property, plant and equipment and intangible assets; the carrying amount of investments; and the measurement of provisions for such things as employee benefits, warranties, trade discounts, environmental protection and taxes. Although uncertainty is appropriately incorporated in the valuation factors, actual results can differ from these estimates.

Source: BASF, Annual Report 2015, page 172

Many other notes simply provide an additional breakdown of the numbers on the financial statements. For example, you can reconcile the Inventories balance of €9,693 million (line 9 on Exhibit 4-7) with Note 17.

ADAPTED EXCERPTS FROM BASF'S NOTES TO THE FINANCIAL STATEMENTS

Note 17: Inventory (partial)

Million €	**December 31, 2015**	**December 31, 2014**
Raw materials and factory supplies	2,944	2,814
Work-in-process, finished goods and merchandise	6,680	8,358
Advance payments and service-in-process	69	94
Inventories	**9,693**	**11,266**

Source: BASF, Annual Report 2015, page 198

Mid-Chapter Summary Problem

Nora, the owner of a small business, came to you for help in reviewing the business's financial statements. She passed you a (rather disorganized) file containing many separate pieces of papers collated by her assistant. The first thing you noticed when you open the file was this document:

A1

	A	B	C
1	**20X6 Balance Sheet**[1]		
2	All other assets less accumulated depreciation	58,000	
3	Cash	3,000	
4	Equity	2,500	
5	Loans[2]	80,000	
6	Payables[3]	1,170	
7	Prepayments	2,470	
8	Receivables[3]	15,920	
9	Supplies	4,280	
10	Total Balance Sheet this year[4]	167,340	
11			

Notes to the Balance Sheet:
1 Prepared on accrual basis unless immaterial
2 Consists of loans from Citibank (due 20X7) and HSBC (due 20X8)
3 Receivables of $50 from Marcus Ltd was netted off with payables of $200 to Marcus
4 Total Balance Sheet last year $140,010

Requirements

1. Explain to Nora how the above Balance Sheet does not follow the general presentation requirement of financial statements.
2. What else do you expect to find in the file Nora passed to you?

Answers

Requirement 1: The general presentation requirements of financial statements include the following:

- **Identification**: The Balance Sheet should be labeled appropriately. For example, the name of the entity, the date of the end of the reporting period, the currency used, and any rounding (if any).
- **Fair presentation, compliance to accounting standards, and accrual accounting**: Compliance with accounting standards is presumed to result in fair presentation of the financial statements. Nora has selectively applied the accrual basis of accounting, unless immaterial. This is not allowed under *IAS 1*.

- **Going concern**: The notes to the account should contain a reference to the appropriateness of the going concern assumption. From the Balance Sheet alone, it appears the going concern may be an issue as Nora has outstanding loans within the next two years, with very little resources to settle the obligations.
- **Materiality and aggregation**: There is not enough information to determine the level of materiality, but it appears that line items of the Balance Sheet are highly aggregated.
- **Offsetting**: Nora deducted a receivable of $50 from a payable of $200 to Marcus Ltd. This is not allowed under *IAS 1*.
- **Frequency, comparative information, and consistency of presentation**: There was no information on the financial statements that they are prepared at least annually. Furthermore, there was no comparative information provided and thus consistency of presentation cannot be assured. The only comparative was a "total" of all numbers at the bottom of the Balance Sheet, which does not convey any meaning.

Requirement 2: IAS 1 specifies that a complete set of financial statements consists of the statement of financial position, statement of comprehensive Income, Statement of changes in equity, statement of cash flows, and notes to the account. The file should contain these items.

UNDERSTAND THE PRESENTATION REQUIREMENTS FOR STATEMENT OF FINANCIAL POSITION

Understand presentation requirements for Statement of Financial Position

The statement of financial position shows an entity's assets and claims to these assets. You saw earlier that this could be kept in thousands of accounts and some form of aggregation would be necessary before presenting the assets, liabilities, and equity on the statement of financial position.

IAS 1 specifies that, at a minimum, these line items should be displayed on the Balance Sheet, as they are sufficiently different in nature or function to warrant separate presentation in the statement of financial position (Exhibit 4-5). Obviously, if you do not have these items, you do not need to show them with zero balances. Many of these accounts may be foreign to you right now, but we will discuss them throughout this text.

Exhibit 4-5 | Line Items on the Balance Sheet

ASSETS

- Cash and cash equivalents
- Trade and other receivables
- Inventories
- Investment (under equity method)
- Other financial assets
- Current and deferred tax assets
- Property, plant and equipment
- Biological assets
- Investment properties
- Intangible assets
- Assets held for sale and discontinued operations

LIABILITIES

- Trade and other payable
- Provisions
- Other financial liabilities
- Current and deferred tax liabilities
- Liabilities held for sale and discontinued operations

EQUITY

- Issued capital
- Reserves
- Non-controlling interests

In addition, entities shall present additional line items, headings, and subtotals in the statement of financial position when such presentation is relevant to an understanding of the entity's financial position. This is an assessment that each reporting entity has to make, taking into consideration the nature and liquidity of the assets, the functions of the assets within the entity, and the amount, timing, and nature of liabilities.

Information on the liquidity of an entity's financial resources and obligations is important to the investors. **Liquidity** basically means how quickly an item can be readily converted to cash. This is typically done by grouping its assets into **current assets** and non-current assets, and grouping liabilities into **current liabilities** and non-current liabilities. The basic principle in determining whether an asset (or liability) is current or non-current is whether or not the amount is expected to be recovered (or settled) within 12 months.

IAS 1 specifies that assets are current if any of the following apply:

(a) the asset is cash or a cash equivalent;

(b) the entity expects to realize the asset within 12 months after the reporting period;

(c) it holds the asset primarily for the purpose of trading; or

(d) it expects to realize the asset, or intends to sell or consume it, in its normal operating cycle.

All other assets would be considered non-current.

The operating cycle of an entity is the time between the acquisition of assets for processing and their realization in cash or cash equivalents. When the entity's normal operating cycle is not clearly identifiable, it is assumed to be 12 months.

Conversely, liabilities are considered current if any of the following apply:

(a) the entity expects to settle the liability in its normal operating cycle;

(b) it holds the liability primarily for the purpose of trading;

(c) the liability is due to be settled within 12 months after the reporting period; or

(d) it does not have an unconditional right to defer settlement of the liability for at least 12 months after the reporting period.

All other liabilities would be considered non-current.

IAS 1 does not prescribe a fixed format for Balance Sheets. For smaller companies, you may find that the Balance Sheet is presented in an **account format**. The account format lists the assets on the left and the liabilities and shareholders' equity on the right in the same way that a T-account appears, with assets (debits) on the left and liabilities and equity (credits) on the right. In Chapter 3, Exhibit 3-12 shows an account-format Balance Sheet for RedLotus Travel, Inc.

Most of the time, you will not see Balance Sheets presented this way in an annual report. It is more likely that they will be shown in a **report format**, which typically lists assets first, followed by liabilities, and then shareholders' equity. A global survey of 170 IFRS companies around the world shows a wide variety of practices on how items are ordered in Balance Sheets (see Exhibit 4-6).

Exhibit 4-6 | Order of Presentation in Balance Sheets

A1

	A	B	C
1		**No. of Companies**	**%**
2	**Classified into current and non-current:**		
3	Current assets, non-current assets, current liabilities, non-current	51	30
4	liabilities, equity		
5	Non-current assets, current assets, equity, non-current liabilities,	67	39
6	current liabilities		
7	Non-current assets, current assets, current liabilities, non-current	30	18
8	liabilities, equity		
9	Non-current assets, current assets, non-current liabilities, current	5	3
10	liabilities, equity		
11			
12	**Classified by other order of liquidity:**		
13	Most current to least current	14	8
14	Least current to most current	3	2
15	Total companies surveyed	170	100
16			

BASF's consolidated statement of financial position (shown in Exhibit 4-7) illustrates the report format. The emphasis is on proving that the accounting equation balances, i.e., total assets equal total liabilities plus total equity. BASF reports its non-current assets first, followed by current assets, equity, non-current liabilities, and finally, current liabilities. Other companies may present their Balance Sheet sections differently. You may see some accounts that are not familiar right now. As we go through the remainder of this text, you will learn more about the specific elements of financial statements.

Exhibit 4-7 BASF's Statement of Financial Position

	A	B	C	D
1	**BASF Group Balance Sheet**	**As at December 31**		
2	**(Adapted, in millions of €)**	**Note**	**2015**	**2014**
3	Intangible assets	14	12,537	12,967
4	Property, plant and equipment	15	25,260	23,496
5	Investments accounting for using the equity method	16	4,436	3,245
6	Other financial assets	16	526	540
7	All other non-current assets	11, 18	3,511	3,691
8	Total non-current assets		46,270	43,939
9	Inventories	17	9,693	11,266
10	Accounts receivables	18	9,516	10,385
11	Cash and cash equivalents	1	2,241	1,718
12	All other current assets	18	3,116	4,051
13	Total current assets		24,566	27,420
14	Total assets		70,836	71,359
15	Subscribed capital	19	1,176	1,176
16	Capital surplus	19	3,141	3,143
17	Retained earnings	19	30,120	28,777
18	Other equity items	20	(3,521)	(5,482)
19	Minority interests	21	629	581
20	Total equity		31,545	28,195
21	Long-term provisions	22, 23	9,682	10,815
22	Financial indebtedness	24	11,123	11,839
23	All other non-current liabilities	11, 24	4,250	4,617
24	Total non-current liabilities		25,055	27,271
25	Accounts payable		4,020	4,861
26	Provisions	23	2,540	2,844
27	Financial indebtedness	24	4,074	3,545
28	All other current liabilities	11, 24	3,602	4,643
29	Total current liabilities		14,236	15,893
30	Total liabilities and equity		70,836	71,359
31				

The Balance Sheet also shows cross-references to notes to the accounts, which provide additional breakdown and information on the numbers on the financial statement. We will discuss notes to the accounts later in this chapter, and you will continue to see many examples of companies' notes to the accounts throughout this book.

UNDERSTAND PRESENTATION REQUIREMENTS FOR STATEMENT OF COMPREHENSIVE INCOME

Understand presentation requirements for Statement of Comprehensive Income

IAS 1 requires an entity to present all items of income and expense recognized in a period in one of the following formats:

- in a single Statement of Comprehensive Income
- in two statements: (1) an Income Statement and (2) a Statement of Comprehensive Income that starts with the profit or loss from the Income Statement and continues with other comprehensive income to arrive at total comprehensive income (see Exhibit 4-8)

Exhibit 4-8 | Statement of Comprehensive Income Formats

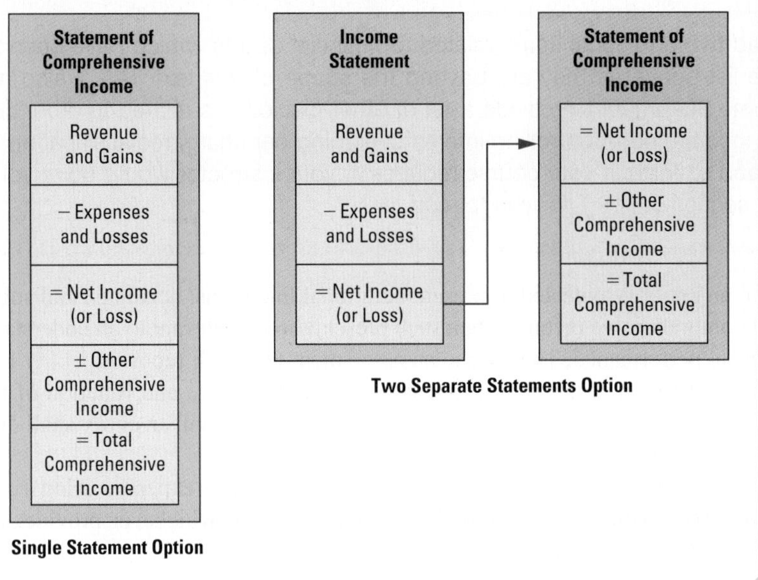

A Closer Look

Other comprehensive income includes items that we would normally not cover in an introductory financial accounting course. They include:

- changes in revaluation surplus for PPE and intangible assets
- some actuarial gains and losses on defined benefit plans
- gains and losses arising from translating the financial statements of a foreign operation
- gains and losses from investments in equity instruments measured at fair value through other comprehensive income
- the effective portion of gains and losses on hedging instruments in a cash flow hedge
- for some liabilities designated as at fair value through profit or loss, the changes in fair value attributable to changes in credit risks

If you are pursuing an accounting major, these items will be covered in your advanced accounting courses. For our current coverage, you can assume that other comprehensive income equals zero. This means the Income Statement shows all the revenue and expenses recognized in a financial period and is equivalent to a statement of comprehensive income (when other comprehensive income is zero).

In Exhibit 4-5 we showed the items to be displayed on the face of a Balance Sheet as required by *IAS 1*. For the Income Statement, *IAS 1* simply states, in addition to items required by other accounting standards, that the Income Statement should present the following amounts for the period:

- revenue
- finance costs
- share of profits of associates (under equity method)
- tax expense

A Closer Look

IAS 1 had two additional items related to financial assets, which have been left out from the list above as they are beyond the scope of this text. *IAS 1* also requires the Income Statement to provide a list of other disclosures related to other comprehensive income, non-controlling interests, earning per share, reclassification adjustments, and so forth. If your course requires it, your instructor would point you to the relevant section of *IAS 1* for you to read.

However, an entity is expected to present additional line items, headings, and subtotals in its statement of comprehensive income when such presentation is relevant to an understanding of the entity's financial performance. This is also an assessment that each reporting entity has to make, taking into consideration issues such as materiality and the nature and function of the items of income and expense. When items of income or expense are material, an entity shall disclose their nature and amount separately.

IAS 1 also requires that an entity shall present an analysis of its expenses using a classification based on either their nature or their function within the entity, whichever provides information that is reliable and more relevant.

Categorizing **expenses by nature** means the reporting entity aggregates expenses according to their nature (for example, depreciation, purchases of materials, transport costs, employee compensation, and advertising costs), and does not reallocate them among functions within the entity. This method may be simple to apply because no allocations of expenses to functional classifications are necessary.

On the other hand, **expenses by function** means the reporting entity classifies expenses into functional categories such as cost of sales, cost of distribution, cost of administration, and so forth. At a minimum, an entity must disclose its cost of sales under this method separately from other expenses. This method can provide more relevant information to users than the classification of expenses by nature, but allocating costs to functions may require arbitrary allocations and involve some judgement.

Let's have a look at BASF's consolidated statement of income, shown in Exhibit 4-9.

Exhibit 4-9 | BASF's Consolidated Statement of Income

A1

	A	B	C	D
1	**BASF Group Statement of Income (Adapted)**	**As at December 31**		
2	**(In millions of Euros)**	**Note**	**2015**	**2014**
3	Sales Revenue	4	70,449	74,326
4	Cost of sales	6	(51,372)	(55,839)
5	Gross profit on sales		19,077	18,487
6	Selling expenses	6	(8,062)	(7,493)
7	General administrative expenses	6	(1,429)	(1,359)
8	Research expenses	6	(1,953)	(1,884)
9	Other operating income	7	2,004	2,231
10	Other operating expenses	8	(3,640)	(2,629)
11	Income from companies accounted for using equity method	9	251	273
12	Income from operations	4	6,248	7,626
13	Interest income		213	207
14	Interest expenses		(638)	(711)
15	All other income and expenses		(275)	81
16	Income before taxes		5,548	7,203
17	Income taxes	11	(1,247)	(1,711)
18	Net income		4,301	5,492
19				

Note that whilst BASF has used negative figures (in parentheses) to denote expenses, not all companies present their expenses as negative figures. Some may simply use the word "less" followed by a list of expenses, or present expenses in a colored or shaded box to signify reductions.

BASF's expenses are presented by function. As you can see, there is a cost of sales, and the expenses are grouped under these functional categories: selling expenses, general administrative expenses, and research expenses.

Here's an example of a nature format. Cathay Pacific is one of the leading airlines of the world. Its Income Statement below presents a list of expenses organized by nature. You can see that there is no cost of sales, and no functional grouping of expenses.

Exhibit 4-10 Cathay Pacific's Consolidated Income Statement

The Hong Kong dollar is the official currency of the Hong Kong Special Administrative Region, abbreviated HKD or HK$.

	A	B	C	D
1	**Cathay Pacific** **Statement of Income** **Financial year ended 31 December**			
2	**(Adapted, in millions of HK$)**	**2015**	**2014**	
3	**Revenue**	102,342	105,991	
4	**Expenses:**			
5	Staff	(18,990)	(18,101)	
6	Inflight service and passenger expenses	(4,713)	(4,438)	
7	Landing, parking and route expenses	(14,675)	(14,196)	
8	Fuel, including hedging losses	(32,968)	(40,299)	
9	Aircraft maintenance	(7,504)	(7,077)	
10	Aircraft depreciation and operating leases	(10,883)	(10,411)	
11	Other depreciation, amortization and operating leases	(2,310)	(2,116)	
12	Commissions	(798)	(799)	
13	Others	(2,837)	(4,119)	
14	**Total operating expenses**	(95,678)	(101,556)	
15	**Operating profit**	6,664	4,435	
16	**Net profit**	6,308	3,450	
17				

A Closer Look

Which analysis of expenses do you think is more informative? Is an analysis of expenses by function better than an analysis of expenses by nature?

IAS 1 states that both methods are acceptable and provides information on expenses that may vary, directly or indirectly, with the level of sales or production of the entity. The choice between the two depends on the historical context, industry, and the nature of the entity. Management has to select the presentation that it believes will result in information that is more reliable and relevant.

IAS 1 requires entities using the function format to disclose total staff costs, depreciation, and amortization in the notes to the account.

A global survey of 170 IFRS companies showed that 92 (55%) use analysis of expenses by function and the remaining 78 (or 45%) use analysis of expenses by nature.

IAS 1 specifically prohibits the use of the label "extraordinary" to describe items of income and expenses. This term was historically used to describe income or expenses that arise from events or transactions that are clearly distinct from the ordinary activities of the enterprise and therefore are not expected to recur frequently or regularly. They were also reported separately after net profit after tax. The prohibition stems from the idea that these "extraordinary" items are actually not so special after all, and that they result from normal business risks and should not be used to send signals to readers to ignore these items.

UNDERSTAND PRESENTATION REQUIREMENTS FOR STATEMENT OF CHANGES IN EQUITY

5 Understand presentation requirements for Statement of Changes in Equity

The statement of changes in equity reconciles the movement in total equity, from the beginning to the end of its financial period. What may cause a change in total equity from one period to another? Exhibit 4-11 summarizes the key reconciling items for the statement of changes in equity.

Exhibit 4-11 Key Reconciling Items for Statement of Changes in Equity

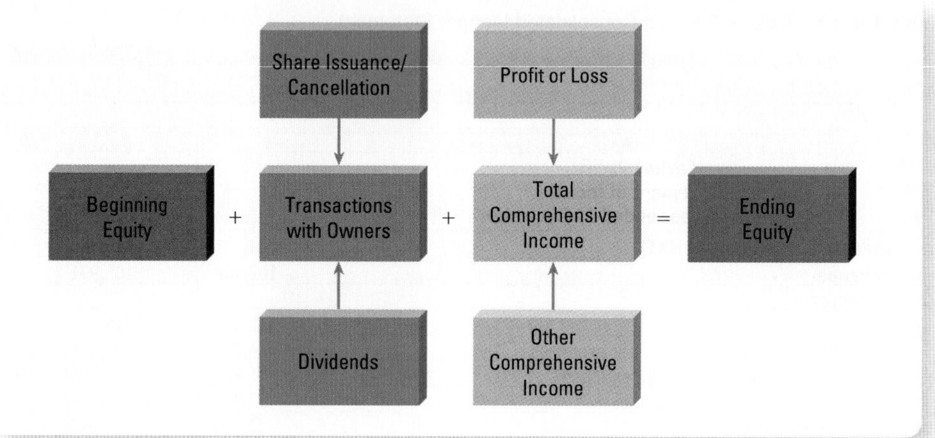

The changes may come from transactions with owners (in their capacity as shareholders) such as additional capital contribution, capital withdrawals (or share buyback and cancellation), and dividend payments. We will discuss equity-related transactions in more detail later (in Chapter 10). Another reason why equity would change from one period to another is, of course, the resulting total comprehensive income (or loss) for the period.

IAS 1 requires such reconciliation be done for each component of equity. This is why you often see a statement of changes in equity with many columns. Many companies also resorted to showing the statement on a landscape format to fit the various components of equity it maintains. A simplified version of BASF's statement of changes in equity is shown in Exhibit 4-12.

Exhibit 4-12 BASF's Statement of Changes in Equity

BASF Group
Statement of Changes in Equity
Financial Year Ended December 31, 2015

(Adapted, in millions of euros)	Subscribed capital	Capital surplus	Retained earnings	Other equity items	Minority interests	Total equity
Balance at January 1, 2014	1,176	3,165	26,102	(3,400)	630	27,673
Net income			5,155		337	5,492
Dividends paid			(2,480)		(286)	(2,766)
Other movements (summarized)		(22)		(2,082)	(100)	(2,204)
Balance at December 31, 2014 and January 1, 2015	1,176	3,143	28,777	(5,482)	581	28,195
Net income			3,987		314	4,301
Dividends paid			(2,572)		(234)	(2,806)
Other movements (summarized)		(2)	(72)	1,961	(32)	1,855
Balance at December 31, 2015	1,176	3,141	30,120	(3,521)	629	31,545

IAS 1 also requires entities to report on information on share capital, such as number of shares, par value, and so forth. This is typically done in the notes to the accounts. We will explain the concept of share and capital structure further later in the text (see Chapter 10).

Occasionally, you may see equity adjusted due to an accounting policy change. The primary source of authority for accounting changes is *IAS 8—Accounting Policies, Changes in Accounting Estimates and Errors*. **Accounting policies** are defined as the specific principles, bases, conventions, rules, and practices applied by an entity in preparing and presenting financial statements. There are three types of accounting changes relevant to us:

1. **Changes due to new accounting standards or pronouncements.** Accounting standards do evolve, so from time to time, an entity would need to apply new or updated accounting standards. Such changes should be done in accordance with the specific transitional provisions in the new IFRS.
2. **Changes in accounting estimates.** We use estimates in much of our accounting work. You saw earlier (in Chapter 3) that the process of allocating the costs of PPE involves estimates such as useful life of the asset. For these types of changes, companies report amounts for the current and future periods on the new basis, i.e., *prospectively*. There is no looking back to the past, but a disclosure of the impact of the change is required (we will discuss this further in Chapter 7).
3. **Changes in accounting policies.** Entities sometimes change from one accounting policy to another. For example, an entity may have accounted for a particular asset under one policy and then decided that it is more reliable and relevant to account and present the asset using another policy. Such accounting changes make it difficult to compare one period with preceding periods. Without detailed information, investors can be misled into thinking that the current year is better or worse than the preceding year, when in fact the only difference is a change in accounting method. Thus, for these changes, the entity would report figures for all periods presented in the Income Statement, past as well as current, on the new basis. The company *retrospectively* applies (looks back and reapplies) all prior-period amounts that are presented for comparative purposes with the current year, as though the new accounting method had been in effect all along. This lets investors compare all periods that are presented on the same accounting basis. If an accounting policy change impacts periods prior to the earliest one presented in the current Income Statement, an adjustment to equity (via retained earnings) must be made. *IAS 8* contains additional provisions when the retrospective application is "impractical." For our purpose, prior period adjustments can be made to beginning retained earnings.

You would expect financial statements to contain no factual errors. However, sometimes errors are only discovered after the financial statements have been issued. How do you deal with these errors? *IAS 8* refers to these as **prior-period errors**, which may be caused by omissions from, and mis-statements in, the entity's financial statements for one or more prior-periods arising from a failure to use, or misuse of, reliable information. These errors include the effects of arithmetic mistakes, mistakes in applying accounting policies, oversights or misinterpretations of facts, and fraud.

All material prior-period errors require retrospective restatement, either by restating the opening balances of assets, liabilities, and equity for the earliest prior-period presented in a set of financial statements, or, if impractical, through a "prior-period adjustment" to the beginning retained earnings in the statement of changes in equity.

Let's use an example. Assume that MWS Corporation incorrectly recorded an expense as \$30,000, but the correct amount was \$40,000. This error understated expenses by \$10,000 and overstated net income by \$10,000. Let's also assume we will correct this accounting error using a prior-period adjustment. Prior-period adjustments are not reported on the Income Statement because they relate to an earlier accounting period. This prior-period adjustment would appear on the statement of changes in equity earnings, as shown in Exhibit 4-13, with all amounts assumed.

Exhibit 4-13 | Reporting a Prior Period Adjustment

	A	B	C
1	**MWS Corporation** **Statement of Changes in Equity** **Year Ended December 31, 20X6**		
2	Total shareholder equity, December 31, 20X5		$ 490,000
3	Share capital	$ 100,000	
4	Retained earnings balance, December 31, 20X5, as reported	390,000	
5	Prior-period adjustment—to correct error in recording expense	(10,000)	
6	Retained earnings balance, December 31, 20X5, as adjusted	380,000	
7	Net income for 20X6	110,000	
8	Dividends for 20X6	(40,000)	
9	Retained earnings balance, December 31, 20X6	450,000	
10	Total shareholder equity, December 31, 20X6		$ 550,000
11			

EVALUATE A COMPANY'S SHORT-TERM LIQUIDITY

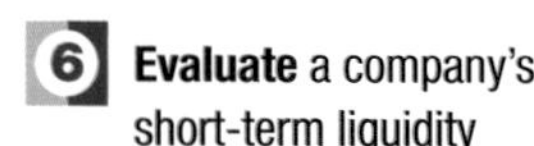

Evaluate a company's short-term liquidity

As you've seen, accounting provides information for decision making. A bank considering lending money must make an assessment as to whether the borrower can repay the loan. If the borrower already has a lot of debt, the probability of repayment will be lower than otherwise. To analyze a company's financial position, decision makers use ratios computed from various items in the financial statements. We will begin introducing financial ratios to you from this chapter onwards. Let's start with current ratio, which helps investors measure the short-term liquidity of a company.

Current Ratio

One of the most widely used financial ratios is the **current ratio**, which divides total current assets by total current liabilities, taken from the Balance Sheet.

$$\text{Current ratio} = \frac{\text{Total current assets}}{\text{Total current liabilities}}$$

Refer to BASF's Balance Sheet in Exhibit 4-7 on page 228. For BASF, the current ratio for 2015 is line 13 divided by line 29:

Current ratio	BASF 2015	BASF 2014
$\frac{\text{Current assets}}{\text{Current liabilities}}$	$\frac{24{,}566}{14{,}236} = 1.73$	$\frac{27{,}420}{15{,}893} = 1.73$

The current ratio measures the company's ability to pay current liabilities with current assets. A company prefers a high current ratio, which means that the business has plenty of current assets to pay current liabilities. An increasing current ratio from period to period indicates improvement in financial position.

BASF's 2015 current ratio is 1.73. Is this current ratio good or bad? Well, any number or ratio is meaningful unless you give it context. For example, we can compare the 2015 current ratio to that of the previous year. It seems that BASF's current ratio is unchanged from 2014, both at 1.73. Another way to make sense of the 1.73 current ratio is to compare it to similar companies in the same (broadly classified) industry as BASF, for example Dow Chemicals (2015 current ratio of 2.18) or DuPont (2015 current ratio of 1.72). We can say that BASF's short-term liquidity, as measured by current ratio, is comparable to that of DuPont but below that of Dow Chemicals. Refer to Exhibit 4-14 for a comparison of current ratios for BASF, DuPont, and Dow Chemicals.

Exhibit 4-14 | Current Ratio Comparisons

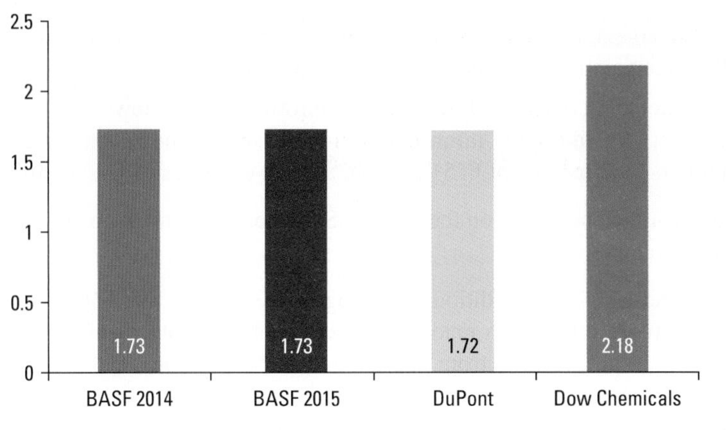

As a rule of thumb, a strong current ratio is 1.50, which indicates that the company has $1.50 in current assets for every $1.00 in current liabilities. A company with a current ratio of 1.50 would probably have little trouble paying its current liabilities. Most successful businesses operate with current ratios between 1.20 and 1.80. A current ratio of less than 1.00 is considered low, but it has to be seen in the context of the business operations and cash flows.

End-of-Chapter Summary Problem

Refer to the BASF financial statements presented in Exhibits 4-7 and 4-9.

Requirements

1. Examine BASF's statement of financial position in Exhibit 4-7. What are its current and non-current assets, and current and non-current liabilities? Does it appear to meet the presentation requirements of a statement of financial position?
2. Examine BASF's consolidated statement of income in Exhibit 4-9. Does it appear to meet the presentation requirements of an Income Statement? Do you find sufficient details on the face of the Income Statement to make a judgment about BASF's financial performance in 2015?

Answers

Requirement 1

BASF uses a short-term versus long-term classification to denote current and non-current assets/liabilities, respectively. Total currents assets are €24,566 million, total non-current assets are €46,270 million, total current liabilities are €14,236 million, and total non-current liabilities are €25,055 million. BASF's statement of financial position appears to meet the requirements in *IAS 1*, for example:

a. The financial statement title, date of end of reporting period, presentation currency, and rounding, as well as comparative information, are all clearly displayed.

b. The Balance Sheet appears to display the minimum line items shown in Exhibit 4-6 (BASF is unlikely to have assets such as biological assets). If BASF has any investment properties, this should be presented separately on the Balance Sheet. BASF uses an older term for non-controlling interest (labeled "minority interests").

Requirement 2

BASF's Income Statement appears to meet the requirements in *IAS 1*, for example:

a. The financial statement title, date of end of reporting period, presentation currency, and rounding, as well as comparative information, are all clearly displayed.

b. The Income Statement contains all the required information. It shows total sales revenue of €70,449 million (with additional information in Notes 4, not shown), finance costs of €638 million, equity method income of €251 million, and tax expenses of €1,247 million.

BASF also offered sufficient details on the Income Statement for readers to evaluate its financial performance. For example:

a. The Income Statement shows additional headings and subtotals that BASF felt would make the information more relevant to readers. For example, it displays subtotals such as gross profit (€18,077 million), income from operations (€6,248 million), and income before taxes (€5,548 million).

b. BASF provides additional explanation for a number of items on the Income Statement. There is, however, a practical limit of how much you can expect a company to disclose. For example, cost of sales is a total number without specific information on the actual cost of every product that BASF sells. Notes 7 and 8, explaining breakdown of other operating income and other operating expenses (not shown), provide additional details of disclosure as well.

REVIEW | Presentation of Financial Statements

Quick Check (Answers are given at the end of the chapter.)

1. Which statement is true?

a. Chairman's letters are part of a financial statement.
b. Corporate annual reports are part of a financial statement.
c. Management discussions and analysis are part of notes to the accounts.
d. Financial statements are part of corporate annual reports.

2. Corporate annual reports typically appear in this order:

a. Corporate information, other statements and disclosures, analysis and commentaries, and financial statements
b. Financial statements, analysis and commentaries, other statements and disclosures, and corporate information
c. Corporate information, analysis and commentaries, other statements and disclosures, and financial statements
d. Financial statements, other statement and disclosures, analysis and commentaries, and corporate information

3. The first item in the analysis and commentaries section of an annual report is typically:

a. Management analysis and discussions
b. Chairman's message/letter to shareholders
c. Auditor's report on the company's financial position and performance
d. Segment performance

4. Who is responsible for the preparation of financial statements?

a. Auditor
b. Management
c. Chief Financial Officer (CFO) and the accounting staff
d. Chairman of the Board

5. Materiality means:

a. The amount in question had the potential to result in a different decision had it been known to financial statement users.
b. The amount in question is greater than 10% of total assets.
c. The amount in question is greater than 10% of revenue.
d. The amount in question would have resulted in a different decision had it been known to financial statement users.

6. *IAS 1* does not require the following item to be displayed on the statement of financial position:

a. Provisions
b. Cash and cash equivalents
c. Accumulated depreciation
d. Intangible assets

7. Which of the following is correct?

a. A statement of financial position contains information about how components of equity change during a period.
b. An entity is not allowed to aggregate its revenue into one single line on the Income Statement.
c. Entities must present their statement of comprehensive income, followed by the statement of financial position, statement of changes in equity, and, lastly, statement of cash flows.
d. Other comprehensive income items may turn a "loss" on the Income Statement into a "profit" on the statement of comprehensive income.

8. An entity has the following balances: Cash $15,000, Inventory $10,000, Receivables $22,000, PPE $50,000, and Intangible assets $40,000. Its total current assets are:

a. $25,000
b. $37,000
c. $47,000
d. $97,000

9. All of the following may explain changes in equity from one period to another, except for:

a. Additional share issuance during the period
b. Payment of dividend during the period
c. Increase in the entity's share price during the year
d. Total comprehensive income

10. Which of the following statements best describes notes to the financial statements?

a. They are part of a complete set of financial statements.
b. They are used to explain how the company has performed during the financial year.
c. They provide a breakdown of all the numbers that appear on financial statements.
d. The more important numbers are shown on the financial statements and the less important ones are shown in the notes to the financial statements.

Accounting Vocabulary

account format (p. 227) A Balance-Sheet format that lists assets on the left and liabilities and shareholders' equity on the right.

accounting policies (p. 233) Specific principles, bases, conventions, rules, and practices applied by an entity in preparing and presenting financial statements.

adverse opinion (p. 219) An auditor's opinion that the financial statements, as a whole, do not fairly represent the financial position and performance of the audited entity.

annual reports (p. 209) Reports prepared by entities for their shareholders, potential investors, and stakeholders.

auditor's report (p. 217) A report from the external auditor expressing an opinion on the financial statement, after conducting an audit in accordance with applicable auditing standards.

board of directors (p. 214) Shareholder representatives elected to oversee the company and its management team.

chairman (p. 214) Head of a board of directors.

comparative information (p. 223) Corresponding figures from previous financial period(s) that must be displayed on the same presentation basis as the current year's financial period.

corporate governance (p. 215) The broad guidelines regulating how a company should be governed and managed, to ensure accountability to shareholders.

current asset (p. 226) An asset that is expected to be converted to cash, sold, or consumed during the next 12 months.

current liability (p. 226) A financial obligation that is due to be paid within 12 months.

current ratio (p. 234) Current assets divided by current liabilities. Measures a company's ability to pay current liabilities with current assets.

expenses by function (p. 230) One alternative in presenting expenses of a company, where expenses are categorized into major functions, such as cost of sales, selling and administration expenses, and so forth.

expenses by nature (p. 230) One alternative in presenting expenses of a company, where expenses are reported as they are (e.g. depreciation, purchases of materials, staff costs, etc.) without allocation to functional areas.

interim reports (p. 223) Quarterly or half-yearly financial reports that are usually not audited and are less detailed than an annual report.

liquidity (p. 226) A measure of an entity's ability to convert an asset to cash (if it is not already cash) or settle an obligation. Typically grouped into current and non-current assets and liabilities.

listing requirements (p. 212) The rules stipulated by a stock exchange, or a bourse, for all listed companies.

material (p. 222) An item is material when its omission or misstatement could, individually or collectively, influence the economic decisions that users make on the basis of the financial statements.

prior-period errors (p. 233) Errors arising from arithmetic mistakes, mistakes in applying accounting policies, oversights or misinterpretations of facts, and fraud, that are discovered in a subsequent accounting period.

qualified opinion (p. 219) An auditor's opinion that the financial statements, as a whole, fairly represent the financial position and performance of the audited entity, with exception in one or two areas.

report format (p. 227) A Balance-Sheet format that lists assets at the top, followed by liabilities and shareholders' equity below.

unqualified opinion (p. 219) An auditor's opinion that the financial statements fairly represent the financial position and performance of the audited entity.

ASSESS YOUR PROGRESS

Short Exercises

LO 1
■ writing assignments

S4-1. *(Learning Objective 1: Understanding annual reports as a communication tool)* You were discussing corporate annual reports with your friends. One of them said "Annual reports are no different from a marketing brochure." How would you react to this statement?

LO 1
■ writing assignments

S4-2. *(Learning Objective 1: Understanding annual reports as a communication tool)* Bobby Young is one of the many investors in your company. He demands to see your accounting records because he wants to have a "complete picture of the company's operations." Write a short email in response to Bobby's request.

LO 2

S4-3. *(Learning Objective 2: Identifying financial statements)* What are the *IAS 1* requirements in terms of the ordering of financial statements in an annual report? What additional labels must each financial statement display?

S4-4. ***(Learning Objective 2: Using accounts to keep track of information)*** What is the difference between keeping track of customer accounts using subsidiary ledger accounts versus using general ledger accounts?

LO 2

S4-5. ***(Learning Objective 2: Understanding general reporting requirements)*** Write a short paragraph explaining how corporate governance is important for the integrity of financial reporting.

LO 2
■ writing assignments

S4-6. ***(Learning Objectives 2, 3: Aggregating information for presentation on the Balance Sheet)*** Trivago has the following account balances:

LO 2 3

RECEIVABLES	
• Amsterdam Supplies	$1,200
• Bangkok Groceries	$1,800
• Doha Markets	$2,500
• Frankfurt Museum	$3,900
• Geneva Tours	$4,100

PAYABLES	
• Doha Markets	$1,200
• Jakarta Leisure Group	$1,900
• London Bridge Souvenirs	$2,200
• Penang Kitchen	$3,300

What amount of total receivables and total payables should Trivago report on its Balance Sheet? Is it allowed to net off the balances to and from Doha Markets?

S4-7. ***(Learning Objective 3: Distinguishing current assets from non-current assets)*** Wayne Enterprises has the following assets: Cash and cash equivalents $35,200, Inventory $18,200, Receivables $32,900, Prepayments $12,000, Long-term interest-free loan to employees $20,000, Equipment $40,000, Accumulated depreciation—equipment $4,200, Motor vehicle $78,000, Accumulated depreciation—motor vehicle $22,800, Intangible assets $21,000.

What are Wayne's total current assets and total non-current assets?

LO 3

S4-8. ***(Learning Objective 3: Distinguishing current assets from non-current assets)*** Wayne Enterprises has the following liabilities: Accounts payable $24,000, Accrued staff wages $3,100, Accrued interest $2,600, Commission payable $2,800, Tax payable $6,000, Loan $110,000 (half of which is due in the coming financial period).

What are Wayne's total current liabilities and total non-current liabilities?

LO 3

S4-9. ***(Learning Objective 4: Assessing net income versus comprehensive income)*** Company Nile reported a net profit of $2 million on its Income Statement and a $2 million loss in other comprehensive income. Company Thames reported a net loss of $2 million on its Income Statement and $2 million other comprehensive income. Both Nile and Thames, thus, report zero total comprehensive income.

If you have to pick one company, which company would you pick? Why?

LO 4
■ writing assignments

S4-10. ***(Learning Objective 4: Knowing components of other comprehensive income)*** List the items that could appear as other comprehensive items.

LO 4

S4-11. ***(Learning Objectives 2, 4: Understanding reporting requirements for Income Statements)*** You were reading a posting in a local small business discussion forum online. Someone with the nickname "Goblin" has just posted a message that says: "I am applying for a bank loan for my flower shop, and the bank has asked for an audited set of financial statements. I don't understand why they need to do so. My credit history is impeccable!"

Write a short reply to the discussion forum on why the bank would require financial statements to be audited.

LO 2 4

LO 5 **S4-12.** ***(Learning Objective 5: Understanding major items that change equity)*** Dynamite Corp. reported total equity of £183,528 at the end of its 20X5 financial year. At the end of its 20X6 financial year, total equity grew to £394,418. List the major items that caused this change.

Exercises MyLab Accounting

Select A and B exercises can be found within MyLab Accounting, an online homework and practice environment. Your instructor may ask you to complete the select exercises using MyLab Accounting.

Group A

LO 1 **E4-13A.** ***(Learning Objective 1: Identifying key elements of an annual report)*** For each of the following items, identify which section they would typically appear in on an annual report. Use (1) for corporate information, (2) for analysis and commentaries, (3) for other statements and disclosures, and (4) for financial statements.

a. Revenue recognition policy ______
b. Company history ______
c. Listing of company's subsidiaries and associated entities ______
d. Review of segment performance ______
e. New upcoming product launches ______
f. Breakdown of trade and other payables ______
g. Chairman's letter to shareholders ______

LO 2 **E4-14A.** ***(Learning Objective 2: Identifying financial statements)*** Gant Corp. is a large multinational company with many subsidiaries and associated companies. It is headquartered in Manchester, United Kingdom, and is listed on both the London Stock Exchange and the Hong Kong Stock Exchange. Its Income Statement heading is shown below. Identify any deficiencies in relation to requirements of *IAS 1*.

A1

	A	B	C	D	E
1	**Gant Corporation**				
2		**20X5**	**20X4**		
3					

LO 2 **E4-15A.** ***(Learning Objective 2: Understanding materiality)*** Insignia is a company with total assets of $500,000, total revenue of $800,000, gross profit of $300,000, and net profit of $100,000 in its last financial year, 20X5. Which of the following items are likely to be material for Insignia?

a. There was an error in the calculation of commission payable to employees amounting to $2,200 in 20X4. The additional payments were made in 20X5, but the 20X4 comparatives on the financial statement were not adjusted for this error.
b. Insignia has erroneously recognized revenue for items that have not yet been shipped to customers at the end of 20X5, amounting to $28,000.
c. Insignia suffered a major flood in one of its largest warehouses in September 20X5. Insignia did not recognize or disclose the losses it suffered because it was in the process of making claims to its insurance company. In early 20X6, before the issuance of the annual report, the insurance company paid the claims in full.
d. Insignia sold an old factory to another company. The buyer was going to demolish the factory and build a hostel on the site. However, the buyer failed to secure permission to build the hostel because the grounds showed higher levels of toxicity than allowed. The buyer claimed this is due to Insignia's failure to meet environmental regulations on disposal of industrial waste in the past. The buyer is now suing Insignia for damages, expected to be in the millions. Insignia believes this lawsuit is baseless and would vigorously defend the case in court. It did not mention this lawsuit in its annual report.

E4-16A. ***(Learning Objectives 2 and 3: Aggregating assets on the Balance Sheet)*** Travis Ltd. has the following assets. Assuming that each account is not material, what is the highest level of aggregation allowed under *IAS 1*? LO 2 3

Trade receivables	Building	Inventory—raw materials
Other receivables	Plantation	Inventory—work-in-progress
Notes receivables	Intellectual property rights	Inventory—finished goods
Cash on hand	Equipment	Short-term share investments
Deposits at banks	Furniture and fixtures	Investment under equity method
Prepayments and deposits	Motor vehicles	Goodwill

E4-17A. ***(Learning Objective 3: Classifying assets based on liquidity)*** A thorough review of GE Broadcasting assets at the end of December 31, 20X5, resulted in the following information: LO 3

- Cash on hand and cash at bank totaling $484,000
- Fixed-term deposits with banks totaling $142,000 (matures July 1, 20X7)
- Inventories totaling $324,000
- Trade receivables totaling $245,000
- Loans to employees of $120,000, 30% of which is due by the end of 20X6
- PPE with a historical cost of $129,000 and accumulated depreciation of $12,000
- Investment in associate companies using equity method at $35,000
- Short-term investment in publicly traded shares of listed companies at $10,000

What are GE Broadcasting's current and non-current assets?

E4-18A. ***(Learning Objective 3: Classifying liabilities based on liquidity)*** The same review in E4-17A resulted in the following information on GE Broadcasting's liabilities at the end of December 31, 20X5: LO 3

- Trade payable of $317,000
- Note payable of $245,000 due July 1, 20X7
- Interest accrued for note payable $8,000 (payable every quarter, the next payment being on April 1, 20X6)
- Provisions for unbilled expenses of $40,000
- Provision for employee benefit of $248,000 (first employee retirement expected in 20X9)
- Interest-free loan from a shareholder, totaling $400,000, payable in eight equal quarterly installments, first payment due on March 1, 20X6.

What are GE Broadcasting's current and non-current liabilities?

E4-19A. ***(Learning Objective 4: Preparing Statement of Comprehensive Income)*** Logan Enterprise reported the following balances. LO 4

A1

	A	B	C	D	E
1	**Logan Enterprises** **Partial Account Listing and Balances** **As of December 31, 20X5 and 20X4**				
2		**20X5**	**20X4**		
3	Sales revenue	$ 37,800	$ 22,900		
4	Other income	5,300	4,700		
5	Cost of goods sold	12,200	9,300		
6	Distribution expenses	2,300	2,200		
7	Marketing expenses	3,700	3,000		
8	Administrative expenses	2,800	2,400		
9	Finance expense	600	500		
10	Tax expense	1,500	1,000		
11	Other comprehensive income	$ 4,400	$ 3,600		
12					

Prepare Logan's Statement of Comprehensive Income in a single statement format and a two separate statements format.

LO 4

E4-20A. ***(Learning Objective 4: Reporting expenses by function and nature)*** Potomac's accountant has just prepared an analysis of its expenses for the year, by nature and by functions. The company earned service revenue totaling $480,000 during the year.

A1

	A	B	C	D	E	F
1	**Expense by Nature and Function**	**Cost of Sales**	**Sales and Marketing**	**Distribution and Logistics**	**Administrative Expenses**	**Unallocated**
2	Wages and Salaries	44,000	31,000	38,000	26,000	
3	Depreciation	5,000	3,000	9,000	1,000	
4	Advertising expense		32,000			
5	Motor vehicle expense		12,000	35,000	28,000	
6	Utilities expense	8,000	2,000	11,000	6,000	
7	Interest expense					
8	Tax expense					7,800
9						3,200
10						

1. Prepare Potomac's Income Statement using analysis of expenses by nature.
2. Prepare Potomac's Income Statement using analysis of expenses by function.
3. Looking at your answers to parts 1 and 2 above, which one do you prefer as a user of financial statements?

Group B

LO 1

E4-21B. ***(Learning Objective 1: Identifying key elements of an annual report)*** For each of the following items, identify which section they would typically appear in on an annual report. Use (1) for corporate information, (2) for analysis and commentaries, (3) for other statements and disclosures, and (4) for financial statements.

a. Auditor's opinion ______
b. Members of the board of directors ______
c. CEO's letter to shareholders ______
d. Information on the company's latest business acquisitions ______
e. Report on environmental impact ______
f. Estimates used in depreciation allocation ______
g. Awards and accolades received ______

LO 2

E4-22B. ***(Learning Objective 2: Identifying financial statements)*** Hoffman Enterprises Ltd. is a large multinational company with many subsidiaries and associated companies. It is headquartered in Luxembourg and is listed on both the Frankfurt Stock Exchange and the Taiwan Stock Exchange. Its Balance Sheet heading is shown below. Identify any deficiencies in relation to requirements of *IAS 1*.

A1

	A	B	C	D	E
	Hoffman Enterprises Ltd.				
1		**20X5**	**20X4**		
2					

LO 2

E4-23B. ***(Learning Objective 2: Understanding materiality)*** Indie is a company with total assets of €500,000, total revenue of €800,000, gross profit of €300,000, and net profit of €100,000 in its last financial year, 20X5. Which of the following items are likely to be material for Indie?

a. There was an error in the calculation of commission payable to employees amounting to €2,100 in 20X4. The additional payments were made in 20X5, but the 20X4 comparatives on the financial statement were not adjusted for this error.

b. Indie has erroneously recognized revenue for items that have not yet been shipped to customers at the end of 20X5, amounting to €26,000.

c. Indie suffered a major flood in one of its largest warehouses in September 20X5. Indie did not recognize or disclose the losses it suffered because it was in the process of making claims to its insurance company. In early 20X6, before the issuance of the annual report, the insurance company paid the claims in full.

d. Indie sold an old factory to another company. The buyer was going to demolish the factory and build a hostel on the site. However, the buyer failed to secure permission to build the hostel because the grounds showed higher levels of toxicity than allowed. The buyer claimed this was due to Indie's failure to meet environmental regulations on disposal of industrial waste in the past. The buyer is now suing Indie for damages, expected to be in the millions. Indie believes this lawsuit is baseless and would vigorously defend the case in court. It did not mention this lawsuit in its annual report.

LO 2 3

E4-24B. ***(Learning Objectives 2 and 3: Aggregating assets on the Balance Sheet)*** Marvis Ltd. has the following assets. Assuming that each account is not material, what is the highest level of aggregation allowed under *IAS 1*?

Short-term share investments	Cash	Machinery and equipment
Investment under equity method	Term deposits	Furniture and fittings
Goodwill	Prepayments and deposits	Trucks
Inventory—raw materials	Accounts receivables	Factory
Inventory—work-in-progress	Other receivables	Plantation
Inventory—finished goods	Notes receivables	Intellectual property rights

LO 3

E4-25B. ***(Learning Objective 3: Classifying assets based on liquidity)*** A thorough review of PG Broadcasting assets at the end of December 31, 20X5, resulted in the following information:

- Cash on hand and cash at bank totaling €241,000
- Fixed-term deposits with banks totaling €180,000 (matures July 1, 20X7)
- Inventories totaling €127,000
- Trade receivables totaling €158,000
- Loans to employees of €40,000, 30% of which is due by the end of 20X6
- PPE with a historical cost of €128,000 and accumulated depreciation of €48,000
- Investment in associate companies using equity method at €55,000
- Short-term investment in publicly traded shares of listed companies at €24,000

What are PG Broadcasting's current and non-current assets?

E4-26B. ***(Learning Objective 3: Classifying liabilities based on liquidity)*** The same review in E4-25B resulted in the following information on PG Broadcasting's liabilities at the end of December 31, 20X5:

- Trade payable of €117,000
- Note payable of €180,000 due July 1, 20X7
- Interest accrued for note payable €4,200 (payable every quarter, the next payment being on April 1, 20X6)
- Provisions for unbilled expenses of €22,400
- Provision for employee benefit of €198,500 (first employee retirement expected in 20X9)
- Interest-free loan from a shareholder, totaling €200,000, repayable in eight equal quarterly installments, first payment due on March 1, 20X6.

What are PG Broadcasting's current and non-current liabilities?

LO 4

E4-27B. *(Learning Objective 4: Preparing Statement of Comprehensive Income)* Victor Limited reported the following balances.

	A	B	C	D	E
1	**Victor Limited** **Partial Account Listing and Balances** **As of December 31, 20X5 and 20X4**				
2		**20X5**	**20X4**		
3	Sales revenue	€ 27,800	€ 32,900		
4	Other income	4,300	5,700		
5	Cost of goods sold	9,200	12,300		
6	Distribution expenses	2,300	2,200		
7	Marketing expenses	3,700	4,000		
8	Administrative expenses	2,800	3,400		
9	Finance expense	600	800		
10	Tax expense	1,500	1,800		
11	Other comprehensive income	3,400	4,600		
12					

Prepare Victor's Statement of Comprehensive Income in a single statement format and a two separate statement format.

LO 4

E4-28B. *(Learning Objective 4: Reporting expenses function and nature)* Maryland's accountant has just prepared an analysis of its expenses for the year, by nature and by functions. The company earned service revenue totaling €450,000 during the year.

	A	B	C	D	E	F
1	**Expense by Nature and Function**	**Cost of Sales**	**Sales and Marketing**	**Distribution and Logistics**	**Administrative Expenses**	**Unallocated**
2	Wages and Salaries	32,000	36,000	29,000	16,000	
3	Depreciation	4,200	3,800	7,000	2,000	
4	Advertising expense		27,000			
5	Motor vehicle expense		21,000	32,000	23,000	
6	Utilities expense	12,000	5,000	11,000	3,000	
7	Interest expense					
8	Tax expense					8,700
9						4,300
10						

1. Prepare Maryland's Income Statement using analysis of expenses by nature.
2. Prepare Maryland's Income Statement using analysis of expenses by function.
3. Looking at your answers to parts 1 and 2 above, which one do you prefer as a user of financial statements?

Quiz

Test your understanding of presentation of financial statements by answering the following questions. Answer each question by selecting the best choice from among the answers given.

Q4-29. An entity shall present:

- **a.** The statement of changes in equity following the statement of financial position.
- **b.** The statement of comprehensive income first and the statement of changes in equity last.
- **c.** If presented in two-statement format, the Income Statement immediately followed by the statement of comprehensive income.
- **d.** The statement of financial position more prominently than the other statements.

Q4-30. In accordance with *IAS 1*, which of the following statements is correct?

a. For the purpose of classifying assets and liabilities into current and non-current components, the entity's operating cycle can be more than 12 months.
b. Intangible assets must be presented separately in the statement of financial position.
c. Assets and liabilities can be offset if they arise from the same transaction or event.
d. Assets and liabilities must be presented in the order of decreasing liquidity.

Q4-31. Which of the following entities appears not to be a going concern?

a. Company M's management is unable to extend its long-term loan, and, given its losses in recent years, it is unlikely that it will be able to raise funds through other means to pay for the loan.
b. Company K's management intends to liquidate the entity.
c. Company L's management is being forced to cease the entity's operations due to a major change in government policies.
d. None of the three companies is likely to be a going concern.

Q4-32. When the classification of items in its financial statements is changed, the entity:

a. Must not reclassify the comparative amounts unless absolutely necessary.
b. Must reclassify comparative amounts, unless it is impractical to do so.
c. Has an unrestricted choice whether to reclassify the comparative amount or not.
d. Must preserve consistency in reporting, and no new reclassification should be allowed.

Q4-33. The information which must be provided so as to properly identify each component of a set of financial statements does not include:

a. The name of the reporting entity.
b. The presentation currency and level of rounding used.
c. The country in which the entity operates.
d. The date of the end of the reporting period or the period covered by the financial statements.

Q4-34. Items of dissimilar nature or function:

a. Must be presented separately if they are material.
b. May be aggregated if accompanied by a note to the account explaining the breakdown.
c. Must always be presented separately in financial statements.
d. Must be aggregated until they are material.

Q4-35. Materiality depends on:

a. The nature of the omission or misstatement.
b. The size of the omission or misstatement.
c. Both the nature and size of the omission or misstatement.
d. The higher of 10% of total assets and 10% of total revenue.

Q4-36. An entity must disclose comparative information for:

a. Only the immediate past financial period.
b. Only for material items on the financial statements.
c. The previous comparable period for all amounts reported in the financial statements.
d. The previous comparable period for all amounts reported in the financial statements, as well as any narrative and descriptive information.

Q4-37. An entity's equity may decrease during a financial period because:

a. Other comprehensive income was lower than net profit.
b. There was a new share issuance.
c. Total comprehensive income was higher than net profit.
d. Prior-period errors resulted from overstatement of the previous year's profits.

Q4-38. The notes to the accounts can be used for the following, except for:

a. Explaining why a certain accounting standard was not followed.
b. Providing disclosures of items not shown on the face of financial statements.
c. Providing additional breakdown of line items on the face of financial statements.
d. Explaining the accounting policies used.

Problems MyLab Accounting

All of the Group A and Group B problems can be found within MyLab Accounting, an online homework and practice environment. Your instructor may ask you to complete these problems using MyLab Accounting.

LO 1

P4-39A. ***(Learning Objective 1: Expressing an audit opinion)*** You have just completed the audit of four companies: Summer, Autumn, Winter, and Spring. The conclusions of the audits are summarized below for each company.

- Summer: Its financial statements fairly represent the company's financial position and performance, but the audit team disagreed with management's use of a particular estimate.
- Autumn: Its financial statements are wrought with errors, as the accountant has completely messed up the translation of various foreign currencies in numerous accounts. As a result, the Balance Sheet, whilst still balanced, is not a faithful representation of the economic phenomenon during the financial period.
- Winter: The accountant was not able to explain numerous discrepancies. One of the major problems was that the receivable, inventory, and payable control accounts do not tally with their respective sub-ledger, making it impossible to audit.
- Spring: The audit highlighted a number of immaterial differences in the calculation of depreciation for the year.

Requirements

Propose the most appropriate type of audit opinion for Summer, Autumn, Winter, and Spring based on the audit notes above.

LO 3

P4-40A. ***(Learning Objective 3: Preparing a classified Balance Sheet)*** The accounts of Bay View Services Ltd. as of June 30, 20X5, are listed below in alphabetical order.

Accounts payable	$ 14,400	Note payable, long term	$ 6,000
Accounts receivable	16,600	Other assets	14,400
Accumulated depreciation—equipment	6,900	Prepaid expenses	6,000
Advertising expense	10,500	Retained earnings, June 30, 20X5	21,000
Cash	7,900	Salary expense	17,600
Current portion of note payable	1,000	Salary payable	2,700
Depreciation expense	1,800	Service revenue	95,400
Dividends	21,200	Share capital	6,600
Equipment	51,600	Supplies	3,900
Interest expense	800	Supplies expense	4,500
		Unearned service revenue	2,800

Requirements

Prepare the Bay View Services' classified Balance Sheet at June 30, 20X5. Show necessary captions. Note that for this question, you do not need to show comparative amounts.

LO 2 4

P4-41A. ***(Learning Objectives 2, 4: Aggregating information for presentation on the Income Statement)*** Robert's Home Repair Services had the following balances at the end of 20X4 and 20X5.

A1					
	A	B	C	D	E
1	**Robert's Home Repair Services Partial Account Listing and Balances As of December 31, 20X5 and 20X4**				
2		**20X5**	**20X4**		
3	Sales revenue	$ 40,800	$ 32,900		
4	Service revenue	21,300	17,700		
5	Interest income	3,300	2,900		
6	Cost of goods sold	17,200	13,400		
7	Wages and salaries	12,300	10,200		
8	Depreciation	2,700	2,700		
9	Supplies expense	8,800	7,400		
10	Interest expense	600	500		
11	Motor vehicle expense	4,500	3,100		
12	Fuel expense	2,600	1,400		
13	Utilities expense	1,100	2,500		
14	Advertising expense	3,700	3,100		
15	Tax expense	2,400	1,000		
16					

Requirements

1. Assuming that Robert would like to disclose no more than what is required by accounting standards, with the maximum level of aggregation possible, prepare an Income Statement to such effect.
2. Why would it not be possible for Robert to simply show a three-line Income Statement, one that simply lists total revenue, total expenses, and net profit?
3. How should Robert decide which line items are important enough to be shown separately on the Income Statement and which ones to aggregate?

LO 2 4

P4-42A. ***(Learning Objectives 2, 4: Reporting comparative amounts on the Income Statement)*** Refer to Robert's Home Repair Services account balances for 20X4 and 20X5 in P4-41A. Suppose Robert decided to show all the accounts on its Income Statement. In addition, Robert discovered that:

- Supplies expense in 20X4 and 20X5 contained an item amounting to $500 in each year that is more appropriately classified as advertising expense.
- Other expenses in 20X4 and 20X5 contained an item amounting to $400 in each year that is more appropriately classified as motor vehicle expense.

Requirements

Prepare Robert's Income Statement for 20X5 with the appropriate 20X4 comparative amounts.

P4-43A. ***(Learning Objectives 3, 5: Preparing a note to the financial statement)*** Musashi Ltd. commenced operations on January 1, 20X6. On that day, it bought:

- Equipment costing ¥3.6 million, with a useful life of 3 years.
- Furniture and fittings costing ¥2.4 million, with a useful life of 4 years.
- Motor vehicles costing ¥4.5 million, with a useful life of 10 years.

No other PPE was purchased or disposed of during the year.

Requirements

What would Musashi report as PPE on its Balance Sheet? Prepare the notes to the accounts related to PPE. Note that you may need to look at how BASF provided a similar note on its PPE.

P4-44A. ***(Learning Objectives 2, 5: Understanding materiality, correction of prior period profits)*** In December 20X8, just before the financial statements were finalized, James & Jones discovered that a programming error in the calculation of depreciation of specialized, expensive machinery has caused the annual depreciation charge to be erroneously calculated. The error started from the date the machinery was purchased on January 1, 20X2. The error resulted in a lower depreciation of $120,000 per year. Due to a large dividend payment in the previous year, J&J's total equity balance stands at $1,200,000 at the end of 20X8.

Requirements

In your opinion, is this error material or not material? Why? How should this be rectified in the 20X8 financial statements, if needed?

LO 2 5
■ writing assignment

P4-45A. ***(Learning Objectives 2, 5: Understanding annual reports and financial statements reporting requirements)*** Manuel Young, the new accountant of Raffles Place Ltd., was preparing the company's financial statements ending 20X6. During the year, the company:

- Changed the useful life estimates of some assets from 3 to 5 years.
- Had to account for its investment differently due to the publication of a new IFRS.
- Changed its accounting policy on revenue recognition.
- Discovered an error in the 20X5 financial statement.

Manuel is somewhat unsure of what to do next. He has emailed you, his former accounting professor, for advice.

Requirement

Write a reply to Manuel and offer your guidance on the appropriate treatment of the items.

Group B

LO 1

P4-46B. ***(Learning Objective 1: Expressing an audit opinion)*** You have just completed the audit of four companies: North, East, West, and South. The conclusions of the audits are summarized below for each company.

- North: The audit highlighted a number of immaterial differences in the calculation of commission expenses for the year.
- East: The accountant was not able to explain numerous discrepancies. One of the major problems was that many customer orders and invoices were missing, making it impossible to audit.
- West: Its financial statements fairly represent the company's financial position and performance, but the audit team disagreed with management's use of a particular accounting policy.
- South: Its financial statements are wrought with errors, as the accountant has completely messed up the translation of the process of consolidating South's subsidiaries. As a result, none of the financial statements faithfully represent the economic phenomenon during the financial period.

Requirements

Propose the most appropriate type of audit opinion for North, East, West, and South based on the audit notes above.

LO 3

P4-47B. ***(Learning Objective 3: Preparing a classified Balance Sheet)*** The accounts of Sunny Laundry Services Ltd. as of March 31, 20X5, are listed below in alphabetical order.

Accounts payable	$ 14,800	Note payable, long term	$ 5,900
Accounts receivable	16,900	Other assets	14,000
Accumulated depreciation—equipment	7,300	Prepaid expenses	5,800
Advertising expense	11,200	Retained earnings, March 31, 2009	22,500
Cash	7,300	Salary expense	18,200
Current portion of note payable	500	Salary payable	2,600
Depreciation expense	2,200	Service revenue	95,600
Dividends	30,000	Share capital	6,200
Equipment	44,000	Supplies	3,300
Interest expense	900	Supplies expense	4,500
		Unearned service revenue	2,900

Requirements

Prepare the Sunny Laundry Services' classified Balance Sheet at March 31, 20X5. Show necessary captions. Note that for this question, you do not need to show comparative amounts.

P4-48B. ***(Learning Objectives 2, 4: Aggregating information for presentation on the Income Statement)*** Rupert's Home Repair Services had the following balances at the end of 20X4 and 20X5.

	A	B	C	D	E
	Rupert's Home Repair Services **Partial Account Listing and Balances** **As of December 31, 20X5 and 20X4**				
1		**20X5**	**20X4**		
2	Sales revenue	$ 39,800	$ 42,900		
3	Service revenue	11,300	27,700		
4	Interest income	2,300	3,900		
5	Cost of goods sold	13,200	17,400		
6	Wages and salaries	10,300	12,200		
7	Depreciation	2,900	2,900		
8	Supplies expense	7,800	8,400		
9	Interest expense	400	600		
10	Motor vehicle expense	3,500	4,100		
11	Fuel expense	1,600	2,400		
12	Utilities expense	2,100	1,500		
13	Advertising expense	2,700	3,200		
14	Tax expense	1,400	2,000		
15					

Requirements

1. Assuming that Rupert would like to disclose no more than what is required by accounting standards, with the maximum level of aggregation possible, prepare an Income Statement to such effect.
2. Why would it not be possible for Rupert to simply show a three-line Income Statement, one that simply lists total revenue, total expenses, and net profit?
3. How should Rupert decide which line items are important enough to be shown separately on the Income Statement and which ones to aggregate?

P4-49B. ***(Learning Objectives 2, 4: Reporting comparative amounts on the Income Statement)*** Refer to Rupert's Home Repair Services account balances for 20X4 and 20X5 in P4-48B. Suppose Rupert decided to show all the accounts on its Income Statement. In addition, Rupert discovered that:

- Supplies expense in 20X4 and 20X5 contained an item amounting to €800 in each year that is more appropriately classified as advertising expense.
- Other expenses in 20X4 and 20X5 contained an item amounting to €300 in each year that is more appropriately classified as motor vehicle expense.

Requirements

Prepare Rupert's Income Statement for 20X5 with the appropriate 20X4 comparative amounts.

P4-50B. ***(Learning Objectives 3, 5: Preparing a note to the financial statement)*** Knight Ltd. commenced operations on January 1, 20X6. On that day, it bought:

- Equipment costing €500,000 million, with a useful life of 5 years.
- Furniture and fittings costing €160,000, with a useful life of 4 years.
- Motor vehicles costing €300,000, with a useful life of 10 years.

Knight depreciates all PPE on a straight-line basis with no residual value. No other PPE was purchased or disposed of during the year.

Requirements

What would Knight report as PPE on its Balance Sheet? Prepare the notes to the accounts related to PPE. Note that you may need to look at how BASF provided a similar note on its PPE.

LO 2 5

P4-51B. ***(Learning Objectives 2, 5: Understanding materiality, correction of prior period profits)*** In December 20X8, just before the financial statements were finalized, Kit & Kat discovered that a programming error in the calculation of depreciation of specialized, expensive machinery had caused the annual depreciation charge to be erroneously calculated. The error started from the date the machinery was purchased on January 1, 20X2. The error resulted in a lower depreciation of €100,000 per year. Due to a large dividend payment in the previous year, Kit & Kat's total equity balance stands at €1,000,000 at the end of 20X8.

Requirements

In your opinion, is this error material or not material? Why? How should this be rectified in the 20X8 financial statements, if needed?

LO 2 5
■ **writing assignment**

P4-52B. ***(Learning Objectives 2, 5: Understanding annual reports and financial statements reporting requirements)*** Melvyn Smith, the new accountant of Stamford Place Ltd., was preparing the company's financial statements ending 20X6. During the year, the company:

- Changed the useful life estimates of some assets from 5 to 3 years.
- Had to account for its investment differently due to the publication of a new IFRS.
- Changed its accounting policy on expense capitalization.
- Discovered an error in the 20X5 financial statement.

Melvyn is somewhat unsure of what to do next. He has emailed you, his former accounting professor, for advice.

Requirement

Write a reply to Melvyn and offer your guidance on the appropriate treatment of the items.

APPLY YOUR KNOWLEDGE

Decision Cases

LO 3 4 5

Case 1. ***(Learning Objectives 3, 4, 5: Preparing financial statements)*** You are the accountant of Majestic Limited, headquartered in Zurich, Switzerland, and have just completed the accounting cycle for the period ended December 31, 20X5. You have performed all necessary adjustments and closing entries to the accounts. The adjusted trial balance (after allocation to function expense categories) is shown as follows, along with comparative figures from the last financial year.

A1

	A	B		C	
1	(in CHF)	Dec 31, 20X5		Dec 31, 20X4	
2	Account balances	Debits	Credits	Debits	Credits
3	Cash on hand	68,900		51,200	
4	Bank account balances	76,000		55,000	
5	Prepaid insurance	25,800		24,300	
6	Prepaid subscriptions	3,500		2,300	
7	Prepaid rent	10,200		24,300	
8	Trade receivables	80,300		47,000	
9	Advances to employees	43,600		49,400	
10	Interest receivable	26,100		25,300	
11	Other receivables	46,000		60,300	
12	Inventory	50,300		47,000	
13	Vehicles and trucks	60,000		60,000	
14	Acc Depn—Vehicles and trucks		35,000		30,000
15	Furniture and fixtures	43,000		43,000	
16	Acc Depn—Furniture and fixtures		13,500		12,000
17	Office equipment	47,000		47,000	
18	Acc Depn—Office equipment		16,000		14,000
19	Store equipment	36,000		36,000	
20	Acc Depn—Store equipment		15,000		12,000
21	Trade payables		39,900		34,900
22	Dues to employees		27,200		17,700
23	Unearned revenue		22,900		29,100
24	Deferred income		25,000		24,000
25	Accrued liabilities		8,300		13,600
26	Bank loan (due 20X8)		120,000		120,000
27	Notes payable (due 20X6)		40,000		40,000
28	Share capital		169,500		150,000
29	Retained earnings (beginning)		74,800		87,400
30	Dividends paid	80,000		45,000	
31	Sales revenue		166,700		151,100
32	Commission revenue		32,900		26,500
33	Dividend income		49,300		53,800
34	Cost of sales	41,600		39,800	
35	Logistics and distribution expenses	26,900		34,200	
36	Sales and marketing expenses	16,300		35,700	
37	Finance expenses	21,700		22,200	
38	Other administrative expenses	29,100		46,300	
39	Tax expense	23,700		20,800	
40		856,000	856,000	816,100	816,100
41					

Requirement

Prepare the statement of financial position, statement of comprehensive income, and statement of changes in equity in good form, with any relevant accompanying notes to the financial statements. Before aggregating line items, you should consider the key principles outlined in *IAS 1*.

Ethical Issues

Issue 1. James Hardie, the CEO of PAS Software, is having a tough time. The company that he has built over the past 10 years has suffered badly in the global financial crisis. In order to show "acceptable" financial statements to the creditors and investors, James undertook the following:

- Losses from the online advertising division were shown as "extraordinary loss" below net profit, and he explained it away by saying the loss is a one-time occurrence and prospects for a strong rebound are good next year.
- He aggregated many large expenses into a category called "Other operating expenses" and did not provide limited information on the breakdown of this expense.

- A large bank loan is due next year, but in order to show increased liquidity, he has insisted on classifying it as a non-current liability because he believed the bank would be willing to extend the term of the loan.
- He doubled the useful life estimates of almost all his property, plant and equipment items, arguing that the original useful lives were not representative of the assets' usage patterns. He did not provide any information on how much reduction in depreciation expense resulted from this action.

Requirements

Examine James' actions in relation to the presentation requirements for financial statements. How do you think readers of the financial statements would react if they came to know of James' actions?

Focus on Financials: | Nestlé

This case spans all 12 chapters and is based on the consolidated financial statements of Nestlé Corporation. As you work with Nestlé throughout this course, you will develop the confidence and ability to use the financial statements of other companies as well. Refer to Nestlé's consolidated financial statements in Appendix A. If you wish, you can obtain the full annual report from www.nestle.com/investors. You may find the information overwhelming for now, but try to spot the key principles that we have discussed in this chapter. It will get progressively easier as you gain familiarity with the elements of the financial statements.

Requirements

1. Do Nestlé's Balance Sheet and Income Statement conform to requirements of *IAS 1*?
2. Did Nestlé use a single statement or a two separate statements option for its statement of comprehensive income?
3. Why would trade and receivables appear under both current assets and non-current assets? Similarly, why would trade and other payables, provisions, and taxation liabilities appear on both current and non-current liabilities?
4. *IAS 1* does not require three years of Income Statement information. Why do you think Nestlé would go beyond the requirements of an accounting standard?

Group Project

Project 1. You are a member of the selection panel for the "best annual report" competition in your country. Outline the selection criteria you would use in deciding on the winner of the competition.

Project 2. Select three listed companies, visit their websites and, in particular, their "investor relation" sections. Compare the amount of information and resources provided by the three companies. Which company has done the most to meet the information needs of its shareholders and stakeholders?

Quick Check Answers

1. *d*	4. *b*	7. *d*	9. *c*
2. *c*	5. *a*	8. *c* (cash, inventory, and receivable)	10. *a*
3. *b*	6. *c*		

MyLab Accounting

For online homework, exercises, and problems that provide you with immediate feedback, please visit www.myaccountinglab.com.

5 Internal Control, Cash, and Receivables

SPOTLIGHT | LEGO www.lego.com

Founded in 1932 in Denmark, the name LEGO was a mash up of the Danish words "leg godt," meaning "play well." Started with wooden toys and then the classic interlocking plastic bricks, it is now one of the most recognizable toys in the world. Many of us have grown up playing with LEGOs at one point in our life. LEGO has launched many new product lines, and more recently we have seen LEGOLAND (theme parks) in a number of countries and even watched LEGO movies. LEGO has its ups and downs, but with sales over $5 billion and profit of over $1.3 billion, LEGO is clearly enjoying a surge in popularity despite challenges from digital toys and games. ●

Tpfeller/Shutterstock

The Danish Krone, abbreviated kr, is the official currency of Denmark, Greenland, and the Faroe Islands.

LEGO's total current assets at the end of 2015 were 16,653 million kr. Given LEGO's wide product range, you might think that inventories are the company's largest current asset. Actually, as you can see from its Balance Sheet below, LEGO's largest current asset is its receivables (6,410 and 5,852 million kr). LEGO's cash and receivables total 13,473 kr and represent over 80% of its total current assets. How does LEGO protect and account for these important assets?

	A	B		C	
1	**LEGO Group Consolidated Balance Sheet**	**At December 31**			
2	**(Adapted, in millions of kr)**		**2015**		**2014**
3	Cash at banks	kr	1,211	kr	482
4	Inventories		2,747		2,182
5	Trade receivables		6,410		5,891
6	Other receivables		5,852		3,281
7	Prepayments		179		149
8	All other current assets		254		48
9	Total current assets		16,653		12,033
10	Total non-current assets		11,224		9,386
11	Total assets	kr	27,877	kr	21,419
12	Total liabilities		10,126		8,587
13	Total equity		17,751		12,832
14	Total liabilities and equity	kr	27,877	kr	21,419
15					

This chapter begins with a discussion of fraud, its types, and common characteristics. All companies are concerned with the risk of fraud. A basic understanding of what it is would be useful in helping companies safeguard against fraud.

We then discuss internal controls, which are the primary means by which fraud as well as unintentional financial statement errors are prevented. We also discuss how to account for cash and receivables. As cash is probably the asset that is most susceptible to misappropriation through fraud, we will apply internal control concepts on cash receipt and cash disbursement processes.

LEARNING OBJECTIVES

1. **Understand** the role of internal controls and corporate governance
2. **Apply** internal controls over cash receipts and cash payments
3. **Prepare and use** a bank reconciliation
4. **Account** for receivables and its potential impairment
5. **Evaluate** a company's ability to collect receivables

UNDERSTAND THE ROLE OF INTERNAL CONTROLS AND CORPORATE GOVERNANCE

Fraud and Its Impact

Understand the role of internal controls and corporate governance

Fraud is an intentional misrepresentation of facts, made for the purpose of persuading another party to act in a way that causes injury or damage to that party. You may have also heard of other "famous" frauds in the last decade: WorldCom, Enron, Parmalat, Toshiba, Olympus, and unfortunately, the list seem to goes on. A more recent financial statement fraud was that of Satyam Computer Services. Headquartered in Hyderabad (India), Satyam was one of the biggest players in the information technology consultancy, integration, and outsourcing business in the world with clients across the globe, including Nestlé, General Motors, and General Electric. In fact, about 185 Fortune 500 companies were clients of Satyam, which employed over 53,000 people. Ramalinga Raju, former Chairman of Satyam Computer, intentionally misstated cash, revenue, receivables, and payables in Satyam's financial statements. His actions caused shareholders of Satyam Computer Services to lose billions of dollars. In early 2009, Ramalinga Raju's resignation letter (and admission of wrongdoing) shocked the business world. An excerpt is reproduced below, with references to Indian numerical conventions of *crores* (units of ten millions) and *lakhs* (units of one hundred thousands) converted to millions or billions as appropriate.

The Indian rupee is the official currency of the Republic of India, abbreviated ₹.

January 7, 2009
To the Board of Directors
Satyam Computer Services Ltd.

Dear Board Members,

It is with deep regret, and tremendous burden that I am carrying on my conscience, that I would like to bring the following facts to your notice:

1. The Balance Sheet carries as of September 30, 2008:
   a. Inflated (non-existent) cash and bank balances of ₹50.40 billion (about $1.04 billion) as against ₹53.61 billion reflected in the books.
   b. An accrued interest of ₹3.76 billion which is non-existent.
   c. An understated liability of ₹12.30 billion on account of funds arranged by me.
   d. An overstated debtors' position of ₹4.90 billion (as against ₹26.51 billion reflected in the books).
2. For the September quarter (Q2) we reported a revenue of ₹27.00 billion and an operating margin of ₹6.49 billion (24% of revenues) as against the actual revenues of ₹21.12 billion and an actual operating margin of 610 million rupees (3% of revenues). This has resulted in artificial cash and bank balances going up by ₹5.88 billion in Q2 alone.

The gap in the Balance Sheet has arisen purely on account of inflated profits over a period of last several years (limited only to Satyam standalone, books of subsidiaries reflecting true performance). What started as a marginal gap between actual operating profit and the one reflected in the books of accounts continued to grow over the years. It has attained unmanageable proportions as the size of company operations grew significantly (annualized revenue run rate of ₹112.76 billion in the September quarter, 2008, and official reserves of ₹83.92 billion). The differential in the real

continued on the following page

profits and the one reflected in the books was further accentuated by the fact that the company had to carry additional resources and assets to justify higher level of operations—thereby significantly increasing the costs.

Every attempt made to eliminate the gap failed. As the promoters held a small percentage of equity, the concern was that poor performance would result in a take-over, thereby exposing the gap. It was like riding a tiger, not knowing how to get off without being eaten. Having put these facts before you, I leave it to the wisdom of the board to take the matters forward.

Under the circumstances, I am tendering my resignation as the chairman of Satyam and shall continue in this position only till such time the current board is expanded. My continuance is just to ensure enhancement of the board over the next several days or as early as possible.

I am now prepared to subject myself to the laws of the land and face consequences thereof.

B. Ramalinga Raju
Chairman, Satyam Computer Services Ltd.

Source: Satyam Computer Services Ltd.

What Ramalinga Raju admitted can be summarized as follows.

	A	B	C
1	**Satyam Computer Services** **Selected Financial Statement Data** **Income Statement for Quarter Ended September 30, 2008**		
2	**(Adapted, in crores/ten million ₹)**	Reported	Admitted
3	Sales	₹ 2,701	₹ 2,112
4	Gross profit	724	
5	Operating profit	649	61
6			
7	Balance Sheet at Sept. 30, 2008	Reported	Admitted
8	Cash	5,361	321
9	Accounts receivable net	2,651	490
10	Other receivables	676	300
11	Total current assets	9,065	
12	Property, plant, and equipment net	1,434	
13	Goodwill	446	
14	Total non-current assets	1,996	
15	Total assets	11,062	
16	Accounts payable	1,379	
17	Other current liabilities	823	₹ 2,053
18	Total current liabilities	2,202	
19	Long-term debt	488	
20	Total non-current liabilities	488	
21	Total liabilities	2,690	
22	Total equity	8,372	
23	Total liabilities and equity	₹ 11,062	
24			

*Adapted from various sources by the author.

How can a company with such a supposedly sterling reputation commit such a fraud? One billion U.S. dollars in cash unaccounted for, operating profit inflated by over 10 times, receivables overstated by over 500%. Satyam's shares went into freefall immediately following the news, dropping by about 80%, as investors around the world thrashed the company's shares. *Reuters* called it "India's Enron."

Fraud can happen to any business, and businesses spend much time and effort in preventing, detecting, and correcting fraudulent activities. PricewaterhouseCooper's Global Economic Crime Survey 2016 showed that fraud is a global problem, not confined to just developing countries. Globally, more than one-third of the respondents reported that they have experienced some form of frauds.

In its 2016 survey titled *Report to the Nations on Occupational Fraud and Abuse,*[1] the Association for Certified Fraud Examiners (ACFE) revealed the following:

- A typical organization loses 5% of its revenue each year to fraud. Applied to the 2011 gross world product, this translates to a projected annual fraud loss of over $3.7 trillion. If you apply this 5% to your national GDP, you can imagine potentially how much is lost due to fraudulent activities.
- The median loss in occupational fraud case is $150,000, with 23.2% of reported cases causing losses of $1 million or more.
- Asset misappropriation was by far the most common form of occupational fraud, followed by corruption cases and financial statement fraud. In terms of impact, it is the reverse, i.e., financial fraud cases, on average, caused the greatest amount of losses.
- The longer a fraud lasted, the greater the financial damage it caused. A majority of fraudsters try to conceal their illegal activities by creating fake documents or altering physical documents.
- Close to 80% of fraudsters exhibit one or more behavioral red flags, including (a) living beyond one's means, (b) experiencing financial difficulties, (c) having unusually close associations with vendors or customers, or (d) a general "wheeler-dealer" attitude involving unscrupulous behavior.

What are the most common types of fraud? What causes fraud? What can be done to prevent it? There are many types of fraud. Some of the most common types are insurance fraud, forgery, credit card fraud, and identity theft. The two most common types of fraud that impact businesses' financial statements are

1. **Misappropriation of assets.** *This type of fraud is committed by employees of an entity who steal money from the company and cover it up* through erroneous entries in the books. Other examples of asset misappropriation include employee theft of inventory, bribery or kickback schemes in the purchasing function, or employee overstatement of expense reimbursement requests.
2. **Fraudulent financial reporting.** *This type of fraud is committed by company managers who make false and misleading entries in the books*, making financial results of the company appear to be better than they actually are. This may be done through aggressive revenue recognition or fictitious sales, using inappropriate accounting treatment and estimates that do not represent the underlying economic phenomenon. The purpose of this type of fraud is to deceive investors and creditors into investing or loaning money to the company that they might not otherwise have invested in or loaned money to.

Both of these types of fraud involve making false or misleading entries in the books of the company. We call this *cooking the books*. Of these two types, asset misappropriation is the most common, but fraudulent financial reporting is by far the most expensive. The two most notorious financial reporting frauds involved Enron Corporation in 2001 and WorldCom, Inc., in 2002. These two scandals alone rocked the U.S. economy and impacted financial markets across the world. Enron (discussed in Chapter 8) committed fraudulent financial reporting by overstating profits through bogus sales of non-existent assets with inflated values. When Enron's banks found out, they stopped loaning the company money to operate, causing it to go out of business almost overnight.

WorldCom (discussed in Chapter 7) reported expenses as assets and overstated both profits and assets. The company's internal auditor blew the whistle on WorldCom, resulting in the company's eventual collapse. Waste Management (also in Chapter 7) manipulated accounting

[1]Association for Certified Fraud Examiners. *Report to the Nations on Occupational Fraud and Abuse.* Austin, TX: ACFE, 2016. http://www.acfe.com/rttn2016/docs/2016-report-to-the-nations.pdf.

estimates to meet earning projections. Sadly, the same international accounting firm, Arthur Andersen, had audited both companies' financial statements. Because of these and other failed audits, the once mighty firm of Arthur Andersen was forced to close its doors in 2002.

More recently, in one of the biggest ever accounting scandals in Japanese corporate history, Toshiba senior management overstated operating profits by over $1.2 billion. This was committed over a number of years, by a corporate culture that perpetuates the achievement of sales and revenue targets above ethics (and accounting standards). Employees were pressured by top management into unethical accounting practices, including the deferment of expenses into future years to meet revenue targets.

Each of these frauds, from WorldCom, Waste Management, and Enron to Satyam, involved losses of billions of dollars and thousands of jobs when the companies went out of business or were bought out by other companies. Widespread media coverage sparked adverse market reaction, loss of confidence in the financial reporting system, and losses through declines in share values that ran in the trillions of dollars! We will discuss some of these cases throughout the text as examples of how accounting principles were deliberately misapplied, through cooking the books, in environments characterized by *weak internal controls*.

Exhibit 5-1 explains in graphic form the elements that make up virtually every fraud. We call it the **fraud triangle**.

Exhibit 5-1 | The Fraud Triangle

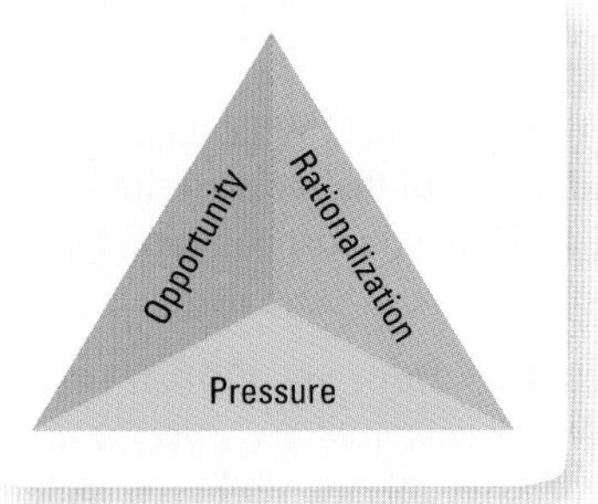

The first element in the fraud triangle is *pressure*. This usually results from either financial or personal pressure. Being saddled with debts, living beyond one's means, being greedy, and having unreasonable expectations to consistently top a previous year's results create pressure to commit fraud (by the perpetrator). Sometimes it is a matter of just never having enough (because some people who commit fraud are already rich by most people's standards). Sometimes it is more about psychological satisfaction, proving that one can "beat the system." Other times, the perpetrator of the fraud might have a legitimate financial need, such as a medical emergency, but he or she uses illegitimate means to meet that need. A recent article in the *Wall Street Journal* indicated that theft by employees was on the rise due to economic hard times. In any case, the prevailing attitude on the part of the perpetrator is, "I need it, I want it, so I'm going to do whatever I have to do to get it."

The second element in the fraud triangle is *opportunity*. Opportunities to commit fraud usually arise through weak internal controls. It might be a breakdown in a key element of controls, such as *improper segregation of duties* and/or *improper access to assets or computer systems*. Or it might result from a weak *control environment*, such as a domineering CEO, a weak or conflicted board of directors, or lax ethical practices, allowing top management to override whatever controls the company has placed in operation for other transactions.

The third element in the triangle is *rationalization*. The perpetrator engages in self-justification for his or her actions through distorted thinking, such as: "I deserve this because I have done so much for the company"; "Nobody treats me fairly"; "No one will ever know"; "Just this once, I won't let it happen again"; or "Everyone else is doing it."

All three elements of the fraud triangle must be present and take over your decision-making process for fraud to occur. Thieves and robbers have no problems with rationalization or with motives; all they need is opportunity. You, on the other hand, may have the opportunity to steal money or property without people knowing, you may even have a great need for them, but if your moral and ethical values are strong, you will not rationalize the action and will walk away from the opportunity to steal.

Ethics in Business and Accounting Decisions

As we pointed out in our decision model for making ethical accounting and business judgments (introduced in Chapter 1), the decision to engage in fraud is an act with economic, legal, and ethical implications. The perpetrators of fraud usually do so for their own short-term *economic gain*, while others incur *economic losses* that may far outstrip the gains of the fraudsters. Moreover, fraud is defined by state, federal, and international law as *illegal*. Those who are caught and found guilty of fraud ultimately face penalties which include imprisonment, fines, and monetary damages. Finally, from an *ethical* standpoint, fraud violates the rights of many for the temporary betterment of a few, and for the ultimate betterment of no one. At the end of the day, everyone loses! **Fraud is the ultimate unethical act in business!**

Internal Control

The primary way that fraud, as well as unintentional errors, are prevented, detected, or corrected in an organization is through a proper system of internal control. **Internal control** is a plan of organization and a system of procedures, implemented by company management and the board of directors, designed to accomplish the following five objectives:

1. *Safeguard assets.* A company must safeguard its assets against waste, inefficiency, and fraud. If management fails to safeguard assets such as cash or inventory, those assets will slip away. Most retailers would put in some physical control over their merchandise inventory to prevent shoplifting or employee theft.
2. *Encourage employees to follow company policy.* Everyone in an organization—managers and employees—needs to work toward the same goals. A proper system of controls provides clear policies that result in fair treatment of both customers and employees.
3. *Promote operational efficiency.* Companies cannot afford to waste resources. They work hard to make a sale, and they don't want to waste any of the benefits. If the company can buy something for $30, why pay $35? Effective controls minimize waste, which lowers costs and increases profits.
4. *Ensure accurate, reliable accounting records.* Accurate records are essential. Without proper controls, records may be unreliable, making it impossible to tell which part of the business is profitable and which part needs improvement. A business could be losing money on every product it sells—unless it keeps accurate records for the cost of its products.
5. *Comply with legal requirements.* Companies, like people, are subject to laws, such as those of regulatory agencies like the Securities and Exchange Commission or SEC (in the United States); stock exchanges; tax authorities; and state, local, and international governing bodies. When companies disobey the law, they are subject to fines, or, in extreme cases, their top executives may even go to prison. Effective internal controls help ensure compliance with the law and help avoid legal difficulties.

How critical are internal controls? They're so important that in some jurisdictions, boards of directors and/or auditors are required to examine and assess the effectiveness of internal controls of publicly listed companies. For example, BASF, our spotlight company in Chapter 4, has this to say about internal controls (emphasis added):

ADAPTED EXCERPTS FROM BASF'S ANNUAL REPORT

Statement of the Board of Executive Directors (partial):

We have established effective internal control and steering systems in order to ensure that the BASF Group's Consolidated Financial Statements and Management's Report comply with applicable accounting rules and to ensure proper corporate

continued on the following page

reporting. The risk management system we have set up is designed such that the Board of Executive Directors can identify material risks early on and take appropriate defensive measures as necessary. The reliability and effectiveness of the internal control and risk management system are continually audited throughout the Group by our internal audit department.

Management Report on Internal Control System (Partial):

Employees involved in the accounting and reporting process meet the qualitative requirements and participate in training on a regular basis. There is a clear assignment of responsibilities between the specialist units, companies and regional service units involved. We strictly adhere to the principles of segregation of duties and dual control, or the "four-eyes principle." Complex actuarial reports and evaluations are produced by specialized service providers or specially qualified employees.

An internal control system for financial reporting continuously monitors these principles. To this end, methods are provided for the structured and Group-wide uniform evaluation of the internal control system in financial reporting. The significant risks for the BASF Group regarding a reliable control environment for proper financial reporting are reviewed and updated on an annual basis.

Source: BASF 2015 Annual Report, pages 155 and 115

One of the most well-known examples of this requirement is the Sarbanes-Oxley Act (SOX) in the United States. While this is a U.S. regulation, as you will read later, many jurisdictions around the world have enacted similar requirements.

The Sarbanes-Oxley Act (SOX)

As the Enron and WorldCom scandals unfolded, many people asked, "How can these things happen? If such large companies that we have trusted commit such acts, how can we trust any company to be telling the truth in its financial statements? Where were the auditors?" To address public concerns, the U.S. Congress passed the Sarbanes-Oxley Act of 2002 (SOX). SOX revamped corporate governance in the United States and profoundly affected the way that accounting and auditing are done in public companies. Here are some of the SOX provisions:

1. Public companies must issue an internal control report, and the outside auditor must evaluate and report on the soundness of the company's internal controls.
2. A new body, the Public Company Accounting Oversight Board, has been created to oversee the audits of public companies.
3. An accounting firm may not both audit a public client and also provide certain consulting services for the same client.
4. Stiff penalties await violators: 25 years in prison for securities fraud; 20 years for an executive making false-sworn statements.

In many other parts of the world, responses to corporate failures, frauds, and scandals resulted in similar increased regulatory requirements. In Japan, "J-SOX" (an unofficial term for parts of the Japan's Financial Instruments and Exchange Law) was passed in response to corporate scandals such as Kanebo, Livedoor, and Murakami Fund. In China, the China Securities Regulatory Commission, the National Audit Office, the China Banking Regulatory Commission, and the China Insurance Regulatory Commission jointly announced the Basic Standard for Enterprise Internal Control (also nicknamed "Chinese SOX"). Many other countries have also raised the bar in terms of corporate governance practices. The United Kingdom's Financial Reporting Council recently revised its Combined Code on Corporate Governance. In the European Union, there are various Company Law Directives that regulate company audits, disclosure, and governance.

You may be wondering what all of these internal controls, governance, and risk issues have to do with accounting. Simple, accounting matters! The financial information that an accounting system produces is crucial information to capital market participants. Accountants (and auditors) thus have a clear role to play to ensure that the financial information is prepared in accordance with applicable rules, regulations, and ethics!

Exhibit 5-2 shows the shield that internal controls provide for an organization. Protected by this shield, which provides protection from fraud, waste, and inefficiency, companies can do business in a trustworthy manner that ensures public confidence, an extremely important element in maintaining the stability of financial markets around the world.

Exhibit 5-2 | The Shield of Internal Control

How does a business achieve good internal controls? The next section will discuss common internal control procedures deployed by business entities. To help you understand the discussion better, we will use the story about EPIC Products, adapted from a case study on a real company, shown in Exhibit 5-3.

Exhibit 5-3 | Cooking the Books: EPIC Products

The following is adapted from a true story:

"I've never been so shocked in my life!" exclaimed Lee Riffe, manager of the EPIC Products office in Palo Alto, California.

"I never thought this could happen to us. We are such a close-knit organization where everyone trusts everyone else. Why, people at EPIC feel like family! I feel betrayed, violated."

Riffe had just returned from the trial of Melissa Price, who had been convicted of embezzling over $600,000 from EPIC over a six-year period. Price had been one of EPIC's most trusted employees for 10 years. A single mom with two teenage daughters, Price had pulled herself up by her own bootstraps, putting herself through community college where she had obtained an associate's degree in accounting. Riffe had hired her as a part-time bookkeeper at EPIC while Price was in college to help her out. She had done such a good job that when she completed her degree, Riffe asked her to stay on and assigned her the additional role of cashier, in charge of accumulating the daily cash receipts from customers and taking them to the night depository at the bank each day after work. Through the years, he also awarded her what he considered good raises, compensating her at a rate that was generally higher than other employees with her education and experience levels.

Price rapidly became the company's "go-to" financial employee. She was eager to learn, dependable, responsible. In 10 years she never took a day of vacation, choosing instead to take advantage of the company's policy that allowed employees to draw additional compensation for vacation accrued but not taken at the end of each year. Riffe grew to depend on Price more and more each month, as the business grew to serve over 1,000 customers. Price's increased involvement on the financial side of the business freed Riffe to spend his time working on new business, spending less and less time on financial matters. Riffe had noticed that in the past few years, Price had begun to wear better clothes and drive a shiny late-model convertible around town. Both of her teenagers also drove late-model automobiles, and the family had recently moved into a new home in an upscale subdivision of the city. Riffe had been pleased that he had contributed to Price's success. But in recent months, Riffe was becoming worried because, in spite of increasing revenues, the cash balances and cash flows from operations at EPIC had been steadily deteriorating, sometimes causing the company difficulty in paying its bills on time.

Price, on the other hand, had felt underappreciated and underpaid for all of her hard work. Having learned the system well, and observing that no one was monitoring her, Price fell into a simple but deadly trap. As cashier, she was in charge of receiving customer payments that came in by mail. Unknown to Riffe, Price had been lapping accounts receivable, an embezzlement scheme nicknamed "robbing Peter to pay Paul." Price began by misappropriating (stealing) some of the customers' checks, endorsing them, and depositing them to her own bank account. To cover up the shortage in a particular customer's account, Price would apply the collections received later from another customer's account. She would do this just before the monthly statements were mailed to the first customer, so that the customer wouldn't notice when he or she received the statement that someone else's payment was being applied to the amount owed to EPIC. Of course, this left the second customer's account short, so Price had to misapply the collection from a third customer to straighten out the discrepancy in the second customer's account. She did this for many customers, over a period of many months, boldly stealing more and more each month. With unlimited access to both cash and customer accounts, and with careful planning and constant diligence, Price became very proficient at juggling entries in the books to keep anyone from discovering her scheme. This embezzlement went on for six years, allowing Price to misappropriate $622,000 from the company. The customer accounts that were misstated due to the fraud eventually had to be written off.

What tipped off Riffe to the embezzlement? Price was involved in an automobile accident and couldn't work for two weeks. The employee covering for Price was swamped with telephone calls from customers wanting to discuss unexplained differences in their billing statements for amounts they could prove had been paid. The ensuing investigation pointed straight to Price, and Riffe turned the case over to the authorities.

Due to Price's scheme, the company had been cheated of $622,000 over several years that it could have used to buy new equipment, expand operations, or pay off debts. EPIC Products has now revamped its internal controls. The company has hired a separate person, with no access to cash, to keep customer accounts receivable records. The company now uses a lock-box system for all checks received by mail. They are sent to EPIC's bank lock box, where they are gathered by a bank employee and immediately deposited. The remittance advices accompanying the checks are electronically scanned and forwarded to EPIC's accounts receivable bookkeeper where they are used as the source documents for posting amounts collected from customers. A summary of cash received goes to Riffe, who reviews it for reasonableness and compares it with the daily bank deposit total. Another employee, who has neither cash handling nor customer bookkeeping responsibilities, reconciles EPIC's monthly bank statement, and reconciles the total cash deposited per the daily listings with the total credits to customer accounts receivable. Now Riffe requires every employee to take time off for earned vacation, and he rotates other employees through those positions while those employees are away.

Internal Control Procedures

Whether it is Alibaba, Daimler, Richemont, BASF, or LEGO, every major class of transactions needs to be protected by the following *internal control procedures.*

Smart Hiring Practices and Separation of Duties. In a business with good internal controls, no important duty is overlooked. Each person in the information chain is important. The chain should start with hiring. Background checks should be conducted on job applicants. Proper training and supervision, as well as paying competitive salaries, help ensure that all employees are sufficiently competent for their jobs. Employee responsibilities should be clearly laid out in position descriptions. For example, the **treasurer**'s department should be in charge of cash handling, as well as signing and approving checks. Warehouse personnel should be in charge of storing and keeping track of inventory. With clearly assigned responsibilities, all important jobs get done.

In processing transactions, smart management *separates three key duties: asset handling, record keeping, and transaction approval.* For example, in the case of EPIC Products, separation of the duties of cash handling from record keeping for customer accounts receivable would have removed Melissa Price's incentive to engage in fraud, because it would have made it impossible for her to have lapped accounts receivable if another employee had been keeping the books. Ideally, someone else should also review customer accounts for collectability and be in charge of writing them off if they become completely uncollectible.

The accounting department should be completely separate from the operating departments, such as production and sales. What would happen if sales personnel, who were compensated based on a percentage of the amount of sales they made, approved the company's sales transactions to customers? Sales figures could be inflated and might not reflect the eventual amount collected from customers.

At all costs, accountants must not handle cash, and cash handlers must not have access to the accounting records. If one employee has both cash-handling and accounting duties, that person can steal cash and conceal the theft. This is what happened at EPIC Products.

For companies that are *too small* to hire separate persons to do all of these functions, the key to good internal control is *getting the owner involved*, usually by approving all large transactions, making bank deposits, or reconciling the monthly bank account.

Comparisons and Compliance Monitoring. No person or department should be able to completely process a transaction from beginning to end without being cross-checked by another person or department. For example, separate divisions of the treasurer's department should be responsible for depositing daily cash receipts in the bank. The **controller**'s department should be responsible for recording customer collections to individual customer accounts receivable. A third employee (perhaps the person in the controller's department who reconciles the bank statement) should compare the treasurer department's daily records of cash deposited with the total collections posted to individual customer accounts by the accounting department.

One of the most effective tools for monitoring compliance with management's policies is the use of **operating budgets** and **cash budgets**. A **budget** is a quantitative financial plan that helps control day-to-day management activities. Management may prepare these budgets on a yearly, quarterly, monthly, or on a more frequent basis. Operating budgets are budgets of future periods' net income. They are prepared by line item of the Income Statement. Cash budgets, discussed in depth later in this chapter, are budgets of future periods' cash receipts and cash disbursements. Often these budgets are "rolling," being constantly updated by adding a time period a year away while dropping the time period that has just passed. Computer systems are programmed to prepare exception reports for data that are out of line with expectations. This data can include variances for each account from budgeted amounts. Department managers are required to explain the variances, and to take corrective actions in their operating plans to keep the budgets in line with expectations. This is an example of the use of **exception reporting**.

To validate the accounting records and monitor compliance with company policies, most companies have an audit. An **audit** is an examination of the company's financial statements and its accounting system, including its controls.

Audits can be internal or external. *Internal auditors* are employees of the business. They ensure that employees are following company policies and operations are running efficiently. Internal auditors also determine whether the company is following legal requirements.

External auditors are completely independent of the business. They are hired to determine whether or not the company's financial statements agree with generally accepted accounting principles. Auditors examine the client's financial statements and the underlying transactions in order to form a professional opinion on the accuracy and reliability of the company's financial statements.

Adequate Records. *Accounting records* provide the details of business transactions. The general rule is that all major groups of transactions should be supported by either hard copy documents or electronic records. Examples of documents include sales invoices, shipping records, customer remittance advices, purchase orders, vendor invoices, receiving reports, and canceled (i.e., paid) checks. Documents should be prenumbered to assure completeness of processing and proper transaction cutoff, and to prevent theft and inefficiency. A gap in the numbered document sequence draws attention to the possibility that transactions might have been omitted from processing.

Limited Access. To complement segregation of duties, company policy should limit access to assets only to those persons or departments that have custodial responsibilities. For example, access to cash should be limited to persons in the treasurer's department. Cash receipts might be processed through a **lock-box system**. Access to inventory should be limited to persons in the company warehouse where inventories are stored, or to persons in the shipping and receiving functions. Likewise, the company should limit access to records to those persons who have record-keeping responsibilities. All manual records of the business should be protected by lock and key, and electronic records should be protected by passwords. Only authorized persons should have access to certain records. Individual computers in the business should be protected by user identification and password. Electronic data files should be encrypted (processed through a special code) to prevent their recognition if accessed by a "hacker" or other unauthorized person.

Proper Approvals. No transaction should be processed without management's general or specific approval. The bigger the transaction, the more specific approval it should have. For individual small transactions, management might delegate approval to a specific department. For example:

- Sales to customers on account should all be approved by a separate *credit department* that reviews all customers for creditworthiness before goods are shipped to customers on credit. This helps assure that the company doesn't make sales to customers who cannot afford to pay their bills.
- Purchases of all items on credit should be approved by a separate *purchasing department* that specializes in that function. Among other things, a purchasing department should only buy from approved vendors, on the basis of competitive bids, to assure that the company gets the highest quality products for the most competitive prices.
- All personnel decisions, including hiring, firing, and adjusting pay, should be handled by a separate *human resources (HR) department* that specializes in personnel-related matters.

Very large (material) transactions should generally be approved by top management, and may even require the board of directors' approval.

Information Technology. Accounting systems are relying less on manual procedures and more on information technology (IT) than ever before for record keeping, asset handling, approval, and monitoring, as well as physically safeguarding the assets. For example, retailers such as Marks and Spencer and Woolworths control inventory by attaching an *electronic sensor* to merchandise. The cashier must remove the sensor before the customer can walk out of the store. If a customer tries to leave the store with the sensor attached, an alarm sounds. According to *Checkpoint Systems*, these devices reduce theft by as much as 50%. *Bar codes* speed checkout at retail stores, performing multiple operations in a single step (see Exhibit 5-4). When the sales associate scans the merchandise at the register, the computer records the sale, removes the item from inventory, and computes the amount of cash tendered.

When a company employs sophisticated IT, the basic attributes of internal control do not change, but the procedures by which these attributes are implemented change substantially. For example, segregation of duties is often accomplished by separating mainframe computer departments from other user departments (i.e., controller, sales, purchasing, receiving, credit, HR, treasurer) and restricting access to the IT department only to authorized personnel. Within the computer department, programmers should be separated from computer operators and data librarians. Access to sensitive data files is protected by password and data encryption. Electronic

Exhibit 5-4 | Bar Codes Speed Up the Checkout Process

Vartanov Anatoly/Shutterstock

records must be saved routinely, or they might be written over or erased. Comparisons of data (such as cash receipts with total credits to customer accounts) that might otherwise be done by hand are performed by the computer. Computers can help monitor inventory levels by item, generating a purchase order for the inventory when it reaches a certain level.

The use of computers has the advantage of speed and accuracy (when programmed correctly). However, a computer that is *not* programmed correctly can corrupt *all* the data, making it unusable. It is, therefore, important to hire experienced and competent people to run the IT department, to restrict access to sensitive data and the IT department only to authorized personnel, to check data entered into and retrieved from the computer for accuracy and completeness, and to test and retest programs on a regular basis to assure data integrity and accuracy.

Internal Controls for e-Commerce. As businesses and consumers conduct more transactions over the Internet, e-commerce creates its own risks. Hackers may gain access to confidential information such as account numbers and passwords, resulting in loss of confidence in the business. E-commerce pitfalls include the following:

- **Stolen Credit Card Numbers.** Suppose you buy music from iTunes. To make the purchase, your credit card number must travel through cyberspace. Wireless networks (Wi-Fi) are creating new security hazards. Amateur hacker Carlos Salgado, Jr., used his home computer to steal 100,000 credit card numbers with a combined limit exceeding $1 billion. Salgado was caught when he tried to sell the numbers to an undercover FBI agent.
- **Computer Viruses and Trojan Horses.** A **computer virus** is a malicious program that (1) enters program code without consent and (2) performs destructive actions in the victim's computer files or programs. A Trojan horse is a malicious computer program that hides inside a legitimate program and works like a virus. Viruses can destroy or alter data, make bogus calculations, and infect files. Most firms have found a virus in their system at some point.
- **Phishing Expeditions.** Thieves phish by creating bogus websites that sound very similar to the original websites to spoof and trick visitors, usually via spam emails, such as ebay-uk.com and BankAmerica.com. The "almost-right" sounding websites attract lots of visitors, and the thieves obtain account numbers and passwords from unsuspecting people. The thieves then use the data for illicit purposes.

The Limitations of Internal Control—Costs and Benefits

Unfortunately, most internal controls can be overcome. Collusion—two or more people working together—can beat internal controls. Consider EPIC Products, discussed in Exhibit 5-3. Even if Riffe were to hire a new person to keep the books, if that person had a relationship with Price and if they conspired with each other, they could design a scheme to lap accounts receivable, the same as Price did, and split the take. Other ways to circumvent a good system of internal controls include management override, human limitations such as fatigue and negligence, and gradual deterioration over time due to neglect. Because of the cost/benefit principle, discussed in the next paragraph, internal controls are not generally designed to detect these types of breakdowns. The best a company can do in this regard is to exercise care in hiring honest persons who have no conflicts of interest with existing employees, and to exercise constant diligence in monitoring the system to assure it continues to work properly.

The stricter the internal control system, the more it costs. An overly complex system of internal control can strangle the business with red tape. How tight should the controls be? Internal controls must be judged in light of their costs and benefits. The following is an example of a good cost/benefit relationship. A part-time security guard at a WalMart store costs about $28,000 a year. If we can show that, on average, each part-time guard prevents about $50,000 of theft, then the net saving to WalMart is $22,000. Most people would say the extra guard is well worth the cost!

APPLY INTERNAL CONTROLS OVER CASH RECEIPTS AND CASH PAYMENTS

Internal Control over Cash Receipts

2 **Apply** internal controls over cash receipts and cash payments

Cash requires some specific internal controls because cash is relatively easy to steal and it's easy to convert to other forms of wealth. Moreover, all transactions ultimately affect cash. Let's see how to control cash receipts.

All cash receipts should be deposited for safekeeping in the bank—quickly. Companies receive cash over the counter and through the mail. Each source of cash has its own security measures.

Cash Receipts over the Counter. Exhibit 5-5 illustrates the purchase of products in a grocery store. The point-of-sale terminal provides control over the cash receipts, while also recording the sale and relieving inventory for the appropriate cost of the goods sold. Consider a Whole Foods Market store. For each transaction, the Whole Foods sales associate issues a receipt to the customer as proof of purchase. The cash drawer opens when the sales associate enters a transaction, and the machine electronically transmits a record of the sale to the store's main computer. At the end of each shift, the sales associate delivers his or her cash drawer to the office, where it is combined with cash from all other terminals and delivered by armored car to the bank for deposit, as explained in the next section. Later, a separate employee in the accounting department reconciles the electronic record of the sales per terminal to the record of the cash turned in. These measures, coupled with oversight by a manager, discourage theft.

Exhibit 5-5 | Cash Receipts Over the Counter

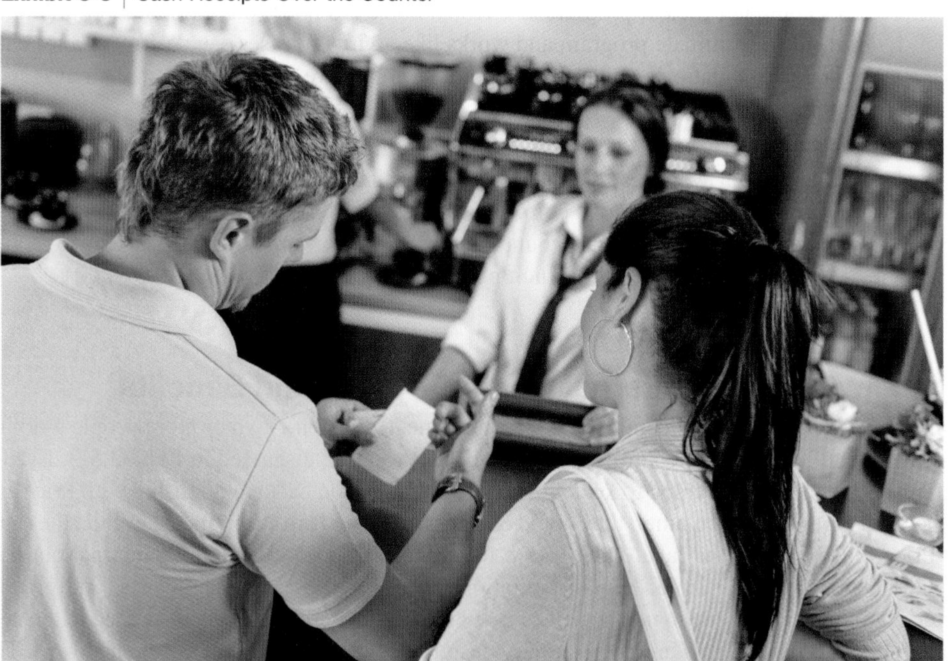

CandyBox Images/Shutterstock

Point-of-sale terminals also provide effective control over inventory. For example, in a restaurant, these devices track sales by menu item and total sales by cash, type of credit card, gift card redeemed, etc. They create the daily sales journal for that store, which, in turn, interfaces with the general ledger. Managers can use records produced by point-of-sale terminals to check inventory levels and compare them against sales records for accuracy. For example, in a restaurant, an effective way to monitor sales of expensive wine is for a manager to perform a quick count of the bottles on hand at the end of the day and compare it with the count at the end of the previous day, plus the record of any purchased. The count at the end of the previous day, plus the record of bottles purchased, minus the count at the end of the current day should equal the amount sold as recorded by the point-of-sale terminals in the restaurant.

An effective control for many chain retail businesses, such as restaurants, grocery stores, or clothing stores, to prevent unauthorized access to cash as well as to allow for more efficient management of cash, is the use of "depository bank accounts." Cash receipts for an individual store are deposited into a local bank account (preferably delivered by armored car for security reasons) on a daily basis. The corporate headquarters arranges for its centralized bank to draft the local depository accounts on a frequent (perhaps daily) basis to get the money concentrated into the company's centralized account, where it can be used to pay the corporation's bills. Depository accounts are "one-way" accounts where the local management may only make deposits. They have no authority to write checks on the account or take money out of the store's account.

Cash Receipts by Mail. Many companies receive cash (in the form of checks or bank orders) by mail, usually from corporate customers and sometimes from retail customers. Exhibit 5-6 shows how companies control cash received by mail. All incoming mail is opened by a mailroom employee. The mailroom then sends all customer checks to the treasurer, who has the cashier deposit the money in the bank. The remittance advices go to the accounting department for journal entries to Cash and customer accounts receivable. As a final step, the controller compares the following records for the day:

- Bank deposit amount from the treasurer
- Debit to Cash from the accounting department

Exhibit 5-6 | Cash Receipts by Mail

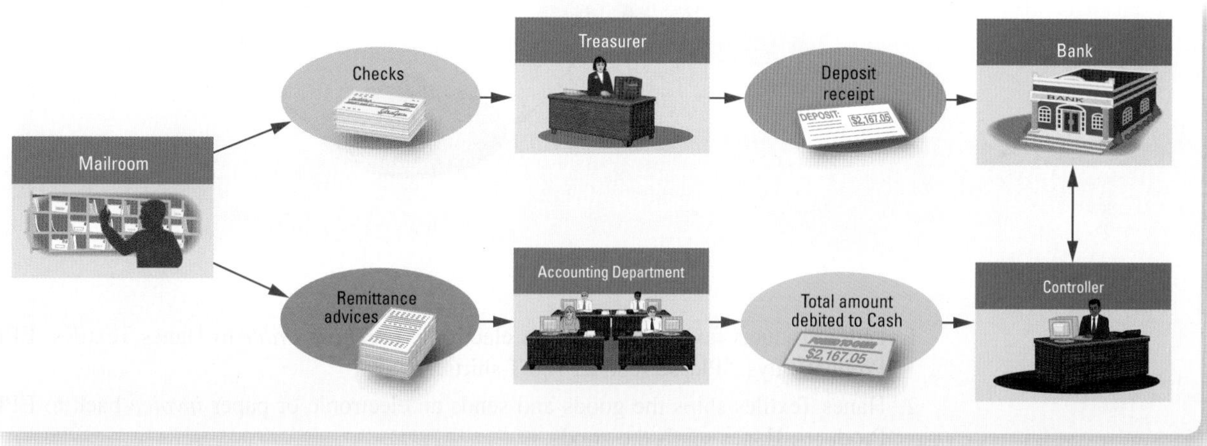

The debit to Cash should equal the amount deposited in the bank. All cash receipts are safe in the bank, and the company books are up-to-date.

To prevent unauthorized access to cash, many companies use a bank lock-box system, rather than risk processing checks through the mailroom. Customers send their checks by return mail directly to a post office box controlled by the company's bank. The bank sends a detailed record of cash received, by customer, to the company for use in posting collections to Accounts Receivable. Internal control is tight because company personnel never touch incoming cash. The lock-box system also gets the cash to the bank in a more timely manner, allowing the company to put the cash to work faster than would be possible if it were processed by the company's mailroom.

Internal Control over Cash Payments

Companies make most payments by check. Let's see how cash payments by check can be controlled.

Controls over Payments by Check. As we have seen, you need a good separation of duties between (1) operations and (2) writing checks for cash payments. Payment by check is an important internal control, as follows:

- The check provides a record of the payment.
- The check must be signed by an authorized official.
- Before signing the check, the official should study the evidence supporting the payment.

Controls over Purchase and Payment. To illustrate the internal control over cash payments by check, suppose EPIC Products buys some of its inventory from Hanes Textiles. The purchasing and payment process follows these steps, as shown in Exhibit 5-7. Start with the box for EPIC Products on the left side.

Exhibit 5-7 | Cash Payments by Check

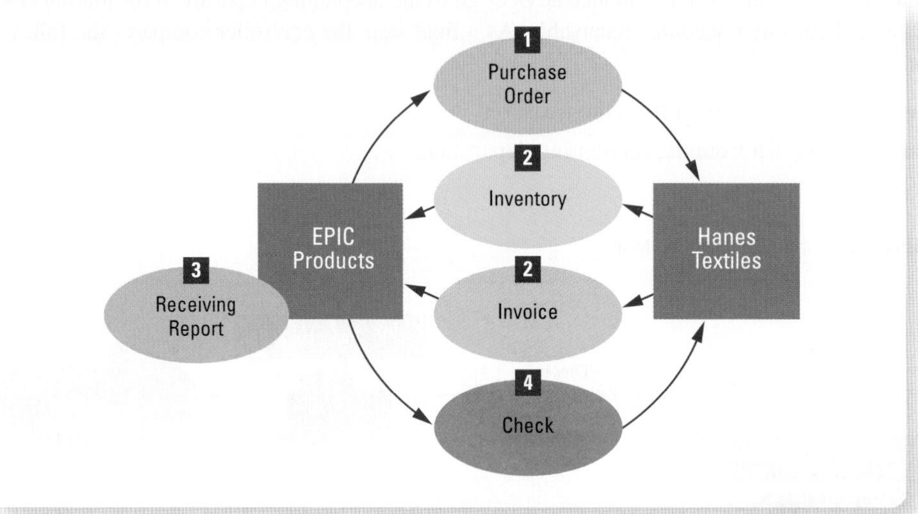

1. EPIC Products faxes or e-mails an electronic *purchase order* to Hanes Textiles. EPIC Products says, "Please send us 100 T-shirts."
2. Hanes Textiles ships the goods and sends an electronic or paper *invoice* back to EPIC Products. Hanes sends the goods.
3. EPIC Products receives the *inventory* and prepares a *receiving report* to list the goods received. EPIC Products receives its T-shirts.
4. After approving all documents, EPIC Products sends a *check* to Hanes, or authorizes an electronic funds transfer (EFT) directly from its bank to Hanes' bank. By this action, EPIC Products says, "Okay, we'll pay you."

For good internal control, the purchasing agent should neither receive the goods nor approve the payment. If these duties aren't separated, a purchasing agent can buy goods and have them shipped to his or her home. Or a purchasing agent can spend too much on purchases, approve the payment, and split the excess with the supplier. To avoid these problems, companies split the following duties among different employees:

- Purchasing goods
- Receiving goods
- Approving and paying for goods

Exhibit 5-8 shows EPIC Products' payment packet of documents. Before signing the check or approving the EFT, the treasurer's department should examine the packet to prove that all the documents agree. Only then does the company know that

1. it received the goods ordered.
2. it is paying only for the goods received.

Exhibit 5-8 | Payment Packet

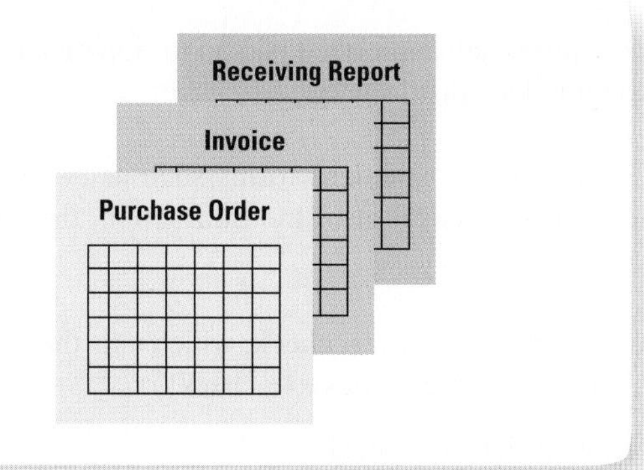

After payment, the person in the treasurer's department who has authorized the disbursement stamps the payment packet "paid" or punches a hole through it to prevent it from being submitted a second time. Dishonest people have tried to run a bill through twice for payment. The stamp or hole shows that the bill has been paid. If checks are used, they should then be mailed directly to the payee without being allowed to return to the department that prepared them. To do so would violate separation of the duties of cash handling and record keeping, as well as unauthorized access to cash.

Petty Cash. It would be wasteful to write separate checks for an executive's taxi fare, name tags needed right away, or delivery of a package across town. Therefore, companies keep a **petty cash** fund on hand to pay such minor amounts. The word "petty" means small. That's what petty cash is—a small cash fund kept by a single employee for the purpose of making such on-the-spot minor purchases or reimbursements.

The petty cash fund is opened with a particular amount of cash. A check for that amount is then issued to the custodian of the petty cash fund, who is solely responsible for accounting for it. Assume that on February 28, Cisco Systems, the worldwide leader in networks for the Internet, establishes a petty cash fund of $500 in a sales department by writing a check to the designated custodian. The custodian of the petty cash fund cashes the check and places $500 in the fund, which may be a cash box or other device.

For each petty cash payment, the custodian prepares a petty cash voucher to list the item purchased. The sum of the cash in the petty cash fund plus the total of the paid vouchers in the cash box should equal the opening balance at all times—in this case, $500. The Petty Cash account keeps its $500 balance at all times. Maintaining the Petty Cash account at this balance, supported by the fund (cash plus vouchers), is how an **imprest system** works. The control feature is that it clearly identifies the amount for which the custodian is responsible.

PREPARE AND USE A BANK RECONCILIATION

Cash is the most liquid asset because it is the medium of exchange for all economies in the world. Cash is easy to conceal and relatively easy to steal. As a result, most businesses create specific controls for cash.

Keeping cash in a bank account helps control cash because banks have established practices for safeguarding customers' money. The documents used to control a bank account include the following:

- signature card
- deposit ticket
- check
- bank statement
- bank reconciliation

Signature Card. Banks require each authorized person to sign on an account to provide a *signature card*. This helps safeguard against forgery.

Deposit Ticket/Slip. Banks supply standard forms such as *deposit tickets*. The customer fills in the amount of each deposit. As proof of the transaction, the customer keeps a deposit receipt.

Check. To pay cash, the depositor can write a **check**, which tells the bank to pay the designated party a specified amount. There are three parties to a check:

- the maker, or drawer, who signs the check
- the payee, to whom the check is paid
- the bank on which the check is drawn

Exhibit 5-9 shows a check drawn by EPIC Products, the maker. The check has two parts, the check itself and the **remittance advice** below. This optional attachment, which may often be scanned electronically, tells the payee the reason for the payment and is used as the source document for posting to proper accounts.

Exhibit 5-9 | Check with Remittance Advice

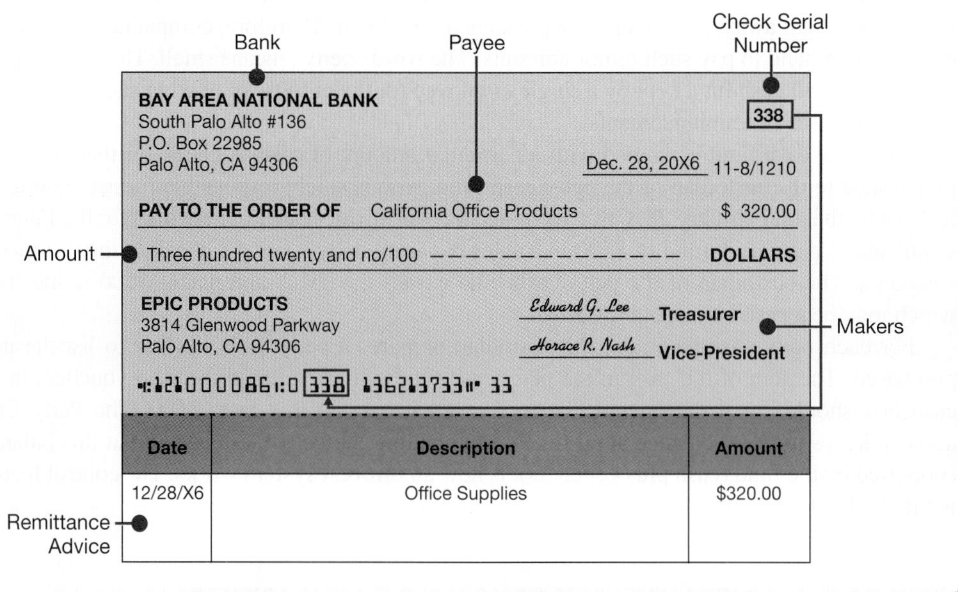

Bank Statement. Banks send monthly statements to customers. A **bank statement** reports what the bank did with the customer's cash. The statement shows the account's beginning and ending balances, cash receipts, and payments. Exhibit 5-10 is the December bank statement of the Palo Alto office of EPIC Products.

Exhibit 5-10 | Bank Statement

BANK STATEMENT

BAY AREA NATIONAL BANK
SOUTH PALO ALTO #136 P.O. BOX 22985 PALO ALTO, CA 94306

EPIC Products
3814 Glenwood Parkway
Palo Alto, CA 94306

ACCOUNT 136–213733

DECEMBER 31, 20X6

BEGINNING BALANCE	TOTAL DEPOSITS	TOTAL WITHDRAWALS	SERVICE CHARGES	ENDING BALANCE
6,550	4,370	5,000	20	5,900

TRANSACTIONS

DEPOSITS	DATE	AMOUNT
Deposit	12/04	1,150
Deposit	12/08	190
EFT—Receipt of cash dividend	12/17	900
Bank Collection	12/26	2,100
Interest	12/31	30

CHARGES	DATE	AMOUNT
Service Charge	12/31	20

CHECKS

Number	Amount	Number	Amount	Number	Amount
307	100	333	150	335	100
332	3,000	334	100	336	1,100

OTHER DEDUCTIONS	DATE	AMOUNT
NSF	12/04	50
EFT—Insurance	12/20	400

Electronic funds transfer (EFT) moves cash by electronic communication. It is cheaper to pay without having to mail a check, so many people pay their mortgage, rent, utilities, and insurance by EFT.

Bank Reconciliation. There are two records of a business's cash:

1. The bank statement, which shows the cash receipts and payments transacted through the bank. In Exhibit 5-10 the bank shows an ending balance of $5,900 for EPIC Products.
2. The Cash account in the company's general ledger. Exhibit 5-11 shows that EPIC Products' ending cash balance is $3,340.

Exhibit 5-11 | Cash Records of EPIC Products

General Ledger:

ACCOUNT Cash

Date	Item	Debit	Credit	Balance
20X6				
Dec 1	Balance			6,550
2	Cash receipt	1,150		7,700
7	Cash receipt	190		7,890
31	Cash payments		6,150	1,740
31	Cash receipt	1,600		3,340

Cash Payments:

	A	B	C	D
1	**Check No.**	**Amount**	**Check No.**	**Amount**
2	332	$ 3,000	337	$ 280
3	333	510*	338	320
4	334	100	339	250
5	335	100	340	490
6	336	1,100	Total	$ 6,150
7				

*Correct amount of check #333 is $150. See bank reconciliation in Exhibit 5-12 for correction.

The books and the bank statement usually show different cash balances. Differences arise because of a time lag in recording transactions—two examples follow:

- When you write a check, you immediately deduct it in your checkbook. But the bank does not subtract the check from your account until the bank pays the check a few days later, after your payee presents the check to his or her own bank (which may be different from your bank). And you immediately add the cash receipt for all your deposits. But it may take a day or two for the bank to add deposits to your balance.
- Your EFT payments and cash receipts may be directly deposited by your customers and recorded by the bank before you learn of them.

To ensure accurate cash records, you need to update your cash record—either online or after you receive your bank statement. The result of this updating process creates a **bank reconciliation**, which you must prepare. The bank reconciliation explains all differences between your cash records and your bank balance. The person who prepares the bank reconciliation should have no other cash duties. Otherwise, he or she can steal cash and manipulate the reconciliation to conceal the theft.

Preparing the Bank Reconciliation

Here are the items that appear on a bank reconciliation. They all cause differences between the bank balance and the book balance. We call your cash record the "Books."

Bank Side of the Reconciliation

1. Items to show on the *Bank* side of the bank reconciliation include the following:
   a. **Deposits in transit** (outstanding deposits). You have recorded these deposits, but the bank has not. Add **deposits in transit** on the bank reconciliation.
   b. **Outstanding checks.** You have recorded these checks, but the bank has not yet paid them. Subtract outstanding checks.
   c. **Bank errors.** Correct all bank errors on the Bank side of the reconciliation. For example, the bank may erroneously subtract from your account a check written by someone else.

Book Side of the Reconciliation

2. Items to show on the Book side of the bank reconciliation include the following:
   a. **Bank collections.** Bank collections are cash receipts that the bank has recorded for your account. But you haven't recorded the cash receipt yet. Many businesses have their customers pay directly to their bank. This is called a *lock-box system* and reduces theft. An example is a bank collecting an account receivable for you. Add bank collections on the bank reconciliation.
   b. **Electronic funds transfers.** The bank may receive or pay cash on your behalf. An EFT may be a cash receipt or a cash payment. Add EFT receipts and subtract EFT payments.
   c. **Service charge.** This cash payment is the bank's fee for processing your transactions. Subtract service charges.
   d. **Interest revenue on your check account.** On certain types of bank accounts, you earn **interest** if you keep enough cash in your account. The bank statement tells you of this cash receipt. Add interest revenue.
   e. **Non-sufficient funds (NSF) checks.** These are cash receipts from customers for which there are not sufficient funds in their bank to cover the amount. The NSF checks (sometimes called "bounced" checks) are treated as cash payments on your bank reconciliation. Subtract NSF checks.
   f. **The cost of printed checks.** This is usually deducted automatically by the bank and is handled like a service charge. Subtract this cost.
   g. **Book errors.** Correct all book errors on the Book side of the reconciliation. For example, you may have recorded a $150 check that you wrote as $510 on your books.

Bank Reconciliation Illustrated. The bank statement in Exhibit 5-10 shows that the December 31 bank balance of EPIC Products is $5,900 (upper-right corner). However, the company's Cash account has a balance of $3,340, as shown in Exhibit 5-11. This situation calls for a bank reconciliation. Exhibit 5-12, panel A, lists the reconciling items for easy reference, and panel B shows the completed reconciliation.

Exhibit 5-12 | Bank Reconciliation

PANEL A—Reconciling Items

Bank side:

1. Deposit in transit, $1,600.
2. Bank error: The bank deducted $100 for a check written by another company. Add $100 to the bank balance.
3. Outstanding checks—total of $1,340.

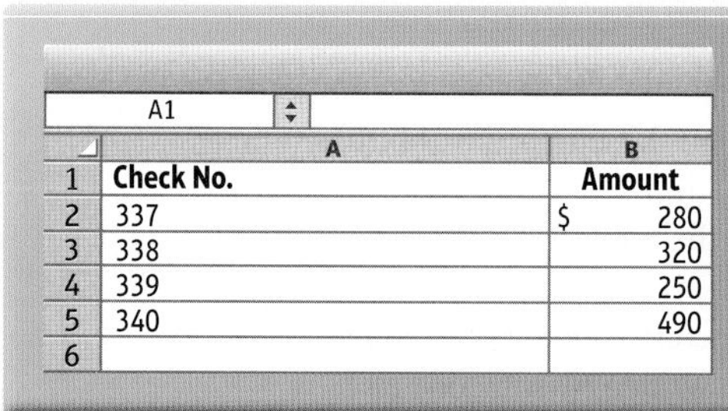

	A	B
1	Check No.	Amount
2	337	$ 280
3	338	320
4	339	250
5	340	490
6		

Book side:

4. EFT receipt of your dividend revenue earned on an investment, $900.
5. Bank collection of your account receivable, $2,100.
6. Interest revenue earned on your bank balance, $30.
7. Book error: You recorded check no. 333 for $510. The amount you actually paid on account was $150. Add $360 to your book balance.
8. Bank service charge, $20.
9. The NSF check from a customer, $50. Subtract $50 from your book balance.
10. The EFT payment of insurance expense, $400.

PANEL B—Bank Reconciliation

	A	B	C	D	E	F
1	**EPIC Products Bank Reconciliation December 31, 20X6**					
2	**Bank**			**Books**		
3	**Balance, December 31**		**$ 5,900**	**Balance, December 31**		**$ 3,340**
4	Add:			Add:		
5	1. Deposit in transit		1,600	4. EFT receipt of dividend revenue		900
6	2. Correction of bank error		100	5. Bank collection of account		
7			7,600	receivable		2,100
8				6. Interest revenue earned on		
9				bank balance		30
10				7. Correction of book error—		
11				overstated our check no. 333		360
12	Less:					6,730
13	3. Outstanding checks					
14	No. 337	$ 280		Less:		
15	No. 338	320		8. Service charge	$ 20	
16	No. 339	250		9. NSF check	50	
17	No. 340	490	(1,340)	10. EFT payment of insurance expense	400	(470)
18	**Adjusted bank balance**		$ 6,260	**Adjusted book balance**		$ 6,260
19						

These amounts should agree.

SUMMARY OF THE VARIOUS RECONCILING ITEMS:

BANK BALANCE

- *Add* deposits in transit.
- *Subtract* outstanding checks.
- *Add* or *subtract* corrections of bank errors.

BOOK BALANCE

- *Add* bank collections, interest revenue, and EFT receipts.
- *Subtract* service charges, NSF checks, and EFT payments.
- *Add* or *subtract* corrections of book errors.

Journalizing Transactions from the Bank Reconciliation. The bank reconciliation is an accountant's tool separate from the journals and ledgers. It does *not* account for transactions in the journal. To get the transactions into the accounts, we must make journal entries and post to the ledger. All items on the Book side of the bank reconciliation require journal entries. The bank reconciliation in Exhibit 5-12 requires EPIC Products to make journal entries to bring the Cash account up to date. The numbers in red correspond to the reconciling items listed in Exhibit 5-12, Panel A.

	A	B	C	D	E
1	4.	Dec. 31	Cash	900	
2			Dividend Revenue		900
3			*Receipt of dividend revenue earned on investment.*		
4					
5	5.	31	Cash	2,100	
6			Accounts Receivable		2,100
7			*Account receivable collected by bank.*		
8					
9	6.	31	Cash	30	
10			Interest Revenue		30
11			*Interest earned on bank balance.*		
12					
13	7.	31	Cash	360	
14			Accounts Payable		360
15			*Correction of check no. 333.*		
16					
17	8.	31	Bank Service Charges	20	
18			Cash		20
19			*Bank service charge.*		
20					
21	9.	31	Accounts Receivable	50	
22			Cash		50
23			*NSF check returned by bank.*		
24					
25	10.	31	Insurance Expense	400	
26			Cash		400
27			*Payment of monthly insurance.*		
28					

The entry for the NSF check (entry 9) deserves additional explanation. Upon learning that a customer's $50 check was not honored (i.e., declined) by the customer's bank, Cash must be credited to update the Cash account. This typically happens when there are insufficient funds for the check issued, an unauthorized signature, or other reasons. Unfortunately, there is still a receivable from the customer, so Accounts Receivable must be debited to reinstate the receivable.

Online Banking

Online banking allows you to pay bills and view your account electronically. You don't have to wait until the end of the month to get a bank statement. With online banking, you can reconcile transactions at any time and keep your account current whenever you wish. Exhibit 5-13 shows a sample page from the account history of a bank account.

Exhibit 5-13 | Online Banking: Account History

Transaction History for Account # 5401-632-9
as of Close of Business 07/27/20X6

Account Details
Current Balance $4,136.08

Date ↓	Description	Withdrawals	Deposits	Balance
	Current Balance			**$4,136.08**
07/27/X6	DEPOSIT		1,170.35	
07/26/X6	28 DAYS INTEREST		2.26	
07/25/X6	Check #6131 View Image	443.83		
07/24/X6	Check #6130 View Image	401.52		
07/23/X6	EFT PYMT CINGULAR	61.15		
07/22/X6	EFT PYMT CITICARD PAYMENT	3,172.85		
07/20/X6	Check #6127 View Image	550.00		
07/19/X6	Check #6122 View Image	50.00		
07/16/X6	Check #6116 View Image	2,056.75		
07/15/X6	Check #6123 View Image	830.00		
07/13/X6	Check #6124 View Image	150.00		
07/11/X6	ATM 4900 SANGER AVE	200.00		
07/09/X6	Check #6119 View Image	30.00		
07/05/X6	Check #6125 View Image	2,500.00		
07/04/X6	ATM 4900 SANGER AVE	100.00		
07/01/X6	DEPOSIT		9,026.37	

From Federal Deposit Insurance Corporation. Published by Federal Deposit Insurance Corporation.

The account history—like a bank statement—lists deposits, checks, EFT payments, ATM withdrawals, and interest earned on your bank balance. But depending on the bank's online system, the account history may not show your beginning balance, so you can't work from your beginning balance to your ending balance.

Stop & Think

The bank statement balance is $4,500 and shows a service charge of $15, interest earned of $5, and an NSF check for $300. Deposits in transit total $1,200; outstanding checks are $575. The bookkeeper recorded as $152 a check of $125 in payment of an account payable. This created a book error of $27 (positive amount to correct the error).

(1) What is the adjusted bank balance?

(2) What was the book balance of cash before the reconciliation?

Answers:

(1) $5,125 ($4,500 + $1,200 − $575).

(2) $5,408 ($5,125 + $15 − $5 + $300 − $27). The adjusted book and bank balances are the same. The answer can be determined by working backward from the adjusted balance.

Whether it is conventional banking or online banking, the discussions we had earlier are still applicable. Organizations that pay their bills electronically would also need to ensure that there are proper authorization processes and adequate internal control measures in place. Payments from customers are received directly to our bank accounts, minimizing risks of misappropriation. Bank reconciliations would still be needed to ensure that the bank balances agree with our records.

Using the Bank Reconciliation to Control Cash. The bank reconciliation can be a powerful control device. Jonathan Leong is a CPA in Hong Kong. He owns several apartments that are managed by one of his nephews, Alex. Alex signs up tenants, collects the monthly rents, arranges maintenance work, hires and fires employees, writes the checks, and performs the bank reconciliation. In short, he does it all. This concentration of duties in one person is evidence of weak internal control. Alex could be stealing from him, and as a CPA, Jonathan is aware of this possibility.

Jonathan trusts Alex because he is a member of the family. Nevertheless, Jonathan exercises some controls over Alex's management of his apartments. Jonathan periodically drops by the apartments to see whether the maintenance staff are keeping the property in good condition. To control cash, Jonathan occasionally examines the bank reconciliation that Alex has performed. Jonathan would know immediately if Alex were writing checks to himself. By examining the copy of each check issued, Jonathan establishes control over cash payments.

Jonathan has a simple method for controlling cash receipts. He knows the occupancy level of his apartments. He also knows the monthly rent he charges. Jonathan multiplies the number of apartments—say five—by the monthly rent (which averages $5,000 per unit) to arrive at expected monthly rent revenue of $25,000. By tracing the $25,000 revenue to the bank statement, Jonathan can tell if all his rent money went into his bank account. To keep Alex on his toes, Jonathan lets him know that he periodically audits his work.

Control activities such as these are critical. If there are only a few employees, separation of duties may not be feasible. The manager must control operations, or the assets may slip away.

Using a Budget to Manage Cash

As mentioned earlier in the chapter, a budget is a financial plan that helps coordinate business activities. Managers control operations with an operating budget. They also control cash receipts and cash payments, as well as ending cash balances, through use of a cash budget.

For example, how does EPIC Products decide when to invest in new inventory tracking technology? How will EPIC Products decide how much to spend? Will borrowing be needed, or can EPIC Products finance the purchase with internally generated cash? What do ending cash balances need to be in order to provide a "safety margin" so the company won't unexpectedly run out of cash? A cash budget for a business works on roughly the same concept as a personal budget. By what process do you decide how much to spend on your education? On an automobile? On a house? All these decisions depend to some degree on the information that a cash budget provides.

A *cash budget helps a company or an individual manage cash by planning receipts and payments during a future period.* The company must determine how much cash it will need and then decide whether or not operations will bring in the needed cash. Managers proceed as follows:

1. Start with the entity's cash balance at the beginning of the period. This is the amount left over from the preceding period.
2. Add the budgeted cash receipts and subtract the budgeted cash payments.
3. The beginning balance plus receipts and minus payments equals the expected cash balance at the end of the period.
4. Compare the cash available before new financing to the budgeted cash balance at the end of the period. Managers know the minimum amount of cash they need (the budgeted balance). If the budget shows excess cash, managers can invest the excess. But if the cash available falls below the budgeted balance, the company will need additional financing. The company may need to borrow the shortfall amount. The budget is a valuable tool for helping the company plan for the future.

The budget period can span any length of time—a day, a week, a month, or a year. Exhibit 5-14 shows a cash budget for EPIC Products, Inc., for the year ended December 31, 20X7. Study it carefully, because at some point you will use a cash budget.

Exhibit 5-14 Cash Budget

	A	B	C
1	**EPIC Products** **Cash Budget** **For the Year Ended December 31, 20X7**		
2	Cash balance, December 31, 20X6		$ 6,260
3	Budgeted cash receipts:		
4	Collections from customers		55,990
5	Dividends on investments		1,200
6	Sale of store fixtures		5,700
7			69,150
8	Budgeted cash payments:		
9	Purchases of inventory	$ 33,720	
10	Operating expenses	11,530	
11	Expansion of store	12,000	
12	Payment of long-term debt	5,000	
13	Payment of dividends	3,000	65,250
14	Cash available (needed) before new financing		$ 3,900
15	Budgeted cash balance, December 31, 20X7		(5,000)
16	Cash available for additional investments, or		
17	(New financing needed)		$ (1,100)
18			

EPIC Products' cash budget in Exhibit 5-14 begins with $6,260 of cash at the end of the previous year (Line 1). Then add budgeted cash receipts and subtract budgeted payments for the current year. In this case, EPIC Products expects to have $3,900 of cash available at year-end (Line 10). EPIC Products managers need to maintain a cash balance of at least $5,000 (line 11). Line 12 shows that EPIC Products must arrange $1,100 of financing in order to achieve its goals for 20X7.

Reporting Cash on the Balance Sheet

Most companies have numerous bank accounts, but they usually combine all cash amounts into a single total called "Cash and Cash Equivalents." You saw at the start of this chapter LEGO reports cash and cash equivalent of 1,211 million kr on its Balance Sheet. **Cash equivalents** include highly liquid assets such as time deposits, certificates of deposit, and high-grade government securities that are not subjected to any significant change of value. Slightly less liquid than cash, cash equivalents are sufficiently similar to be reported along with cash. We will discuss cash and cash equivalents further in Chapter 11.

Mid-Chapter Summary Problem

The cash account of Baylor Associates at February 28, 20X7, follows.

Cash				
Feb. 1	Bal. 3,995	Feb. 3	400
6	800	12	3,100
15	1,800	19	1,100
23	1,100	25	500
28	2,400	27	900
Feb. 28	Bal. 4,095		

Baylor Associates received the bank statement on February 28, 20X7 (negative amounts are in parentheses):

	A	B	C
1	**Bank Statement for February 20X7**		
2	Beginning balance		$ 3,995
3	Deposits:		
4	Feb. 7	$ 800	
5	15	1,800	
6	24	1,100	3,700
7	Checks (total per day):		
8	Feb. 8	$ 400	
9	16	3,100	
10	23	1,100	(4,600)
11	Other items:		
12	Service charge		(10)
13	NSF check from M. E. Crown		(700)
14	Bank collection of note receivable for the company		1,000
15	EFT—monthly rent expense		(330)
16	Interest revenue earned on account balance		15
17	Ending balance		$ 3,070
18			

Additional data:
Baylor deposits all cash receipts in the bank and makes all payments by check.

Requirements

1. Prepare the bank reconciliation of Baylor Associates at February 28, 20X7.
2. Journalize the entries based on the bank reconciliation.

Answers

Requirement 1

	A	B	C
1	**Baylor Associates** **Bank Reconciliation** **February 28, 20X7**		
2	**Bank:**		
3	Balance, February 28, 20X7		$ 3,070
4	Add: Deposit of February 28 in transit		2,400
5			5,470
6			
7	Less: Outstanding checks issued on Feb. 25 ($500)		
8	and Feb. 27 ($900)		(1,400)
9	Adjusted bank balance, February 28, 20X7		$ 4,070
10			
11	**Books:**		
12	Balance, February 28, 20X7		$ 4,095
13	Add: Bank collection of note receivable		1,000
14	Interest revenue earned on bank balance		15
15			5,110
16	Less: Service charge	$ 10	
17	NSF check	700	
18	EFT—Rent expense	330	(1,040)
19	Adjusted book balance, February 28, 20X7		$ 4,070
20			

equal

Requirement 2

	A	B	C	D
1	Feb 28	Cash	1,000	
2		Note Receivable		1,000
3		*Note receivable collected by bank.*		
4				
5	28	Cash	15	
6		Interest Revenue		15
7		*Interest earned on bank balance.*		
8				
9	28	Miscellaneous Expense	10	
10		Cash		10
11		*Bank service charge.*		
12				
13	28	Accounts Receivable	700	
14		Cash		700
15		*NSF check returned by bank.*		
16				
17	28	Rent Expense	330	
18		Cash		330
19		*Monthly rent expense.*		
20				

ACCOUNT FOR RECEIVABLES AND ITS POTENTIAL IMPAIRMENT

Types of Receivables

Account for receivables and its potential impairment

Receivables are monetary claims against others. Receivables are acquired mainly by selling goods and services (accounts receivable) and by lending money (notes receivable). The journal entries to record the receivables can be shown as follows:

Performing a Service on Account			Lending Money on a Note Receivable		
Accounts Receivable....................	XXX		Note Receivable	XXX	
Service Revenue.......................		XXX	Cash.......................................		XXX
Performed a service on account.			*Loaned money to another company.*		

The two major types of receivables are accounts receivable and notes receivable. A business's *accounts receivables* are the amounts collectible from customers from the sale of goods and services. Accounts receivable, which are typically classified as *current assets*, are sometimes called *trade receivables, debtors*, or sometimes just *receivables*. The use of the word "trade" is usually to separate receivables (and payables) arising from the selling of goods or provision of services to customers (and buying of goods or services from suppliers) as opposed to non-trade receivables. LEGO's Balance Sheet at the start of this chapter showed trade and other receivables as one item (line 5) but there is additional information in the notes to the financial statement on the breakdown between trade versus non-trade receivables.

When items are sold on account, the amount recognized as receivable is the fair value of the consideration to be received (recall our discussion in Chapter 3 on revenue recognition). This receivable meets the definition of an asset because it represents future economic benefits the selling entity expects to collect, and it can be measured reliably through contract, invoice, or some other form of sales documentation.

The Accounts Receivable account in the general ledger serves as a *control account* that summarizes the total amount receivable from all customers. Companies also keep a *subsidiary record* of accounts receivable with a separate account for each customer, illustrated as follows:

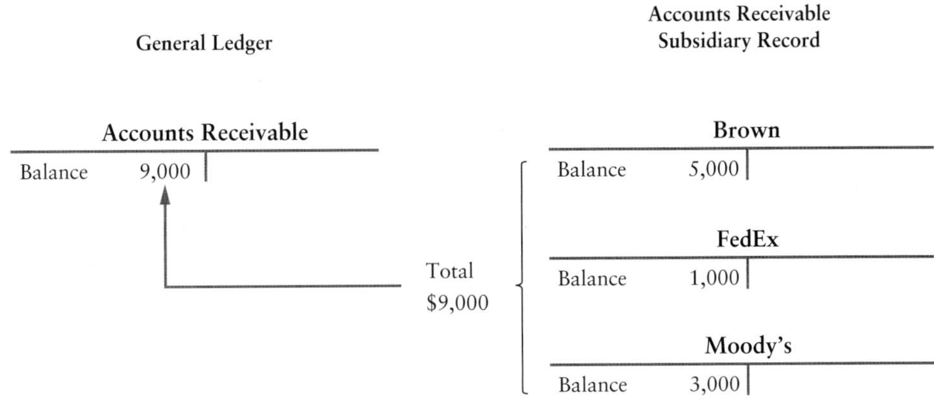

Notes receivable are more formal contracts than accounts receivable. For a note, the borrower signs a written promise to pay the lender a definite sum at a future date, plus interest. This is why notes are also called promissory notes. The note may require the borrower to pledge *security* for the loan. This means that the borrower gives the lender permission to claim certain assets, called *collateral*, if the borrower fails to pay the amount due. We cover the details of notes receivable later in this chapter.

Other than trade and other receivables, an entity may also have *other receivables*, which include various advances and loans to employees and other parties.

Internal Controls over Cash Collections on Account

Businesses that sell on credit receive most of their cash receipts from collections of accounts receivable. Internal control over collections on account is just as important as cash collection at point of sale. Earlier we discussed control procedures for cash receipts, but another element of internal control deserves emphasis here—the separation of cash-handling and cash-accounting duties. Consider the following case:

> Central Paint Company is a small, family-owned business that takes pride in the loyalty of its workers. Most employees have been with Central for 10 or more years. The company makes 90% of its sales on account and receives most of its cash (in the form of checks) by mail.
>
> The office staff consists of a bookkeeper and an office supervisor. The bookkeeper maintains the general ledger and a subsidiary record of individual customer accounts receivable. The bookkeeper also makes the daily bank deposit.
>
> The supervisor prepares monthly financial statements and any special reports the company needs. The supervisor also takes sales orders from customers and serves as office manager.

Can you identify the internal control weakness here? The problem is that the bookkeeper makes the bank deposit. Remember the EPIC Products case (see Exhibit 5-3)? With this cash-handling duty, the bookkeeper could lap accounts receivable. Alternatively, he or she could steal an incoming customer check and write off the customer's account as uncollectible. The customer doesn't complain because the bookkeeper wrote off the customer's account, and Central, therefore, stops pursuing collection.

How can this weakness be corrected? The supervisor—not the bookkeeper—could open incoming mail and make the daily bank deposit. The bookkeeper should *not* be allowed to handle cash. Only the remittance advices should be forwarded to the bookkeeper to credit customer accounts receivable. Removing cash handling from the bookkeeper and keeping the accounts away from the supervisor separate duties and strengthen internal control.

Using a bank lock box achieves the same separation of duties. Customers send their payments directly to Central Paint Company's bank, which records cash as the cash goes into Central's bank account. The bank then forwards the remittance advice to Central's bookkeeper, who credits the customer account. No Central Paint employee even touches incoming cash.

How Do We Manage the Risk of Not Collecting?

In Chapters 1 to 4, we used many different companies to illustrate how to account for a business. All of them hold substantial amounts of receivables from selling goods or providing services on credit.

Selling on credit creates both a benefit and a cost:

- *Benefit*: Customers who cannot pay cash immediately can buy on credit, so sales and profits increase.
- *Cost*: The company cannot collect from some customers. Accountants label this cost **uncollectible-account expense**, **doubtful-account expense**, or **bad-debt expense**.

By selling on credit, companies run the risk of not collecting some receivables. Unfortunately, some customers don't pay their debts. The prospect of failing to collect from a customer provides the biggest challenge in accounting for receivables. The Decision Guidelines address this challenge.

DECISION GUIDELINES

MANAGING AND ACCOUNTING FOR RECEIVABLES

Here are the management and accounting issues a business faces when the company extends credit to customers. For each issue, the Decision Guidelines propose a plan of action. Let's look at a business situation: Suppose you open a health club near your college. Assume you will let customers use the club and bill them for their monthly dues. What challenges will you encounter by extending credit to customers? The main issues in managing receivables, along with plans of action, are:

Issues	Plans of Action
1. What are the benefits and costs of extending credit to customers?	1. Benefit: Increase in sales. Cost: Risk of not collecting.
2. Extend credit only to creditworthy customers.	2. Run a credit check on prospective customers.
3. Separate cash-handling and accounting duties to keep employees from stealing the cash collected from customers.	3. Design the internal control system to separate duties.
4. Pursue collection from customers to maximize cash flow.	4. Keep a close eye on customer pay habits. Send second and third statements to slow-paying customers, if necessary.

The main issues in accounting for receivables, and the related plans of action, are (amounts are assumed):

Issues	Plans of Action	
1. Measure and report receivables on the Balance Sheet at their net carrying amount, the amount we expect to collect. This is the appropriate amount to report for receivables.	Report receivables at their net carrying amount:	
	Balance Sheet	
	Receivables	$1,000
	Less: Allowance for uncollectibles	(80)
	Receivables, net	$ 920
2. Measure and report the expense associated with failure to collect receivables. This expense is called uncollectible-account expense and is reported on the Income Statement.	Measure the expense of not collecting from customers:	
	Income Statement	
	Sales (or service) revenue	$8,000
	Expenses:	
	Uncollectible-account expense	190

These guidelines lead to our next topic, Accounting for Uncollectible Receivables.

Accounting for Uncollectible Receivables

A company gets an account receivable only when it sells its product or service on credit (on account). You'll recall that the entry to record the earning of revenue on account is (amount assumed):

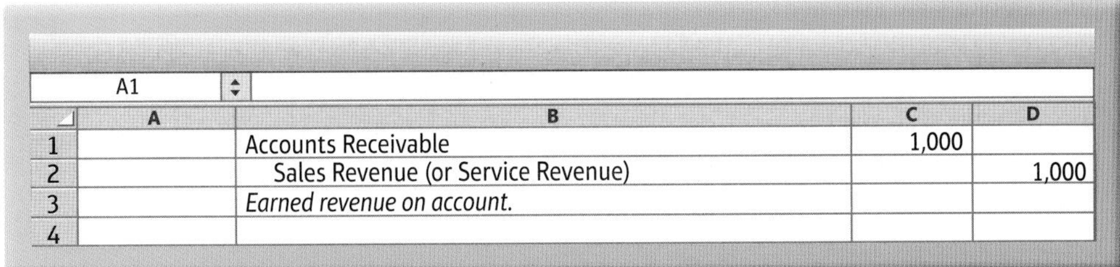

	A	B	C	D
1		Accounts Receivable	1,000	
2		Sales Revenue (or Service Revenue)		1,000
3		*Earned revenue on account.*		
4				

Ideally, the company would collect cash for all of its receivables. But unfortunately, this does not happen all the time. How do we account for uncollectible receivables? Uncollectible-account expense is an operating expense along with salaries, depreciation, rent, and utilities. You may also see companies label this as *bad debt expense, impairment of receivables expense*, or something similar. To measure uncollectible-account expense, accountants use the allowance method or, in certain limited cases, the direct write-off method (see later in this chapter).

Allowance Method

The best way to provide for bad debts is by the allowance method. *IAS 39—Financial Instruments: Recognition and Measurement* stipulates that loans and receivables, like other financial assets, are impaired if, and only if, there is objective evidence of impairment as a result of one or more "loss events" that occurred after their initial recognition. This includes observable data that comes to the attention of the holder of the loans and receivables about the following loss events:

- Significant financial difficulty of a specific debtor, including the possibility of becoming bankrupt.
- A breach of contract by a specific debtor, such as default or inability to make interest and/or principal payments.
- Adverse changes in the number of delayed payments by debtors in general.
- National or local economic conditions that correlate with defaults by debtors in general (e.g., increase in unemployment rates and other adverse changes in industry conditions that affect debtors).

A Closer Look

IAS 39 is being replaced by *IFRS 9 – Financial Instruments* effective for annual periods beginning January 1, 2018. Some jurisdictions may have a different effective date for the implementation of IFRS 9. With IFRS 9, a new "expected loss impairment model" will result in more timely recognition of impairment losses. Non-financial institutions are allowed to use a simplified matrix model for trade receivables. This model will look similar to the aging of customer balances that will be shown later in this chapter. The specifics of IFRS 9 is beyond the scope of this introductory text, but the basic impairment concepts we discuss here will still be relevant, whether under IAS 39 or IFRS 9.

The allowance method thus records collection losses based on estimates developed from the company's collection experience and information about debtors. LEGO doesn't wait to see which customers will not pay. Instead, LEGO records the estimated amount as Uncollectible-Account Expense and also sets up an *Allowance for Uncollectible Receivables* account. Other titles for this account are *Allowance for Doubtful Receivables* and *Allowance for Receivables Impairment*. This is a contra account to Accounts Receivable. The allowance shows the amount of the receivables the business expects not to collect.

In Chapter 3 we used the Accumulated Depreciation account to show the amount of a PPE's cost that has been expensed—the portion of the asset whose benefits have been allocated to prior periods. Allowance for Doubtful Debt serves a similar purpose for Accounts Receivable. The allowance shows how much of the receivable is unlikely to be collected. You'll find this diagram helpful (amounts are assumed):

Equipment..........................	$100,000	Accounts receivable....................	$10,000
Less: Accumulated depreciation	(40,000)	Less: Allowance for uncollectible receivables	(900)
Equipment, net....................	60,000	Accounts receivable, net.............	9,100

Focus on Accounts Receivable. Customers owe this company $10,000, but it expects to collect only $9,100. The net receivables is therefore $9,100. Another way to report these receivables is

Accounts receivable, less allowance of $900.................	$9,100

You can work backward to determine the full amount of the receivable, $10,000 (net receivables of $9,100 plus the allowance of $900). The Income Statement reports Uncollectible-Account Expense (or receivables impairment expense, bad debt expense, or something similar) among the operating expenses, as follows (using assumed figures):

Equipment..........................	$100,000	Accounts receivable....................	$10,000
Less: Accumulated depreciation	(40,000)	Less: Allowance for uncollectible accounts	(900)
Equipment, net....................	60,000	Accounts receivable, net.............	9,100

Income Statement (partial):	
Expenses:	
Uncollectible-account expense.......................	$2,000

The best way to estimate uncollectibles uses the company's history of collections from customers and information on "loss events" as suggested by *IAS 39* (see earlier). In practice, a popular method for estimating uncollectibles is called aging-of-receivables. The aging method is a Balance-Sheet approach because it focuses on what should be the most relevant and faithful representation of accounts receivable as of the Balance Sheet date. In the aging method, individual receivables from specific customers are analyzed based on how long they have been outstanding. A simplified version of the aging method would simply list the status or age of the receivables, typically classified into age groups such as "Not yet due," "1–30 days overdue," "31–60 days overdue," and "over 60 days overdue." A business entity may estimate that accounts that are not yet due only have a 1% chance of not being collectible, and those that have been overdue for 1–30 days are more likely to be uncollectible, say 5%, and so forth. The allowance for each age group is thus determined *vertically*, and the totals of these allowances will be what the business will need to provide at the year-end. Exhibit 5-15 illustrates a simplified aging method of calculating allowance for uncollectible receivables.

As you can see, the total desired amount of allowance based on our aging analysis is $1,200 for receivables totaling $20,000. Whilst we can express this allowance as a percentage of the receivables, i.e., 6% ($1,200 of $20,000) of the receivables are expected to be impaired or uncollectible, you don't decide on the 6% first and then calculate the $1,200. The actual calculation depends on the age groups and the individual percentage uncollectible assigned to each age group.

What is the limitation of this simplified aging method? Well, have a look at Customer C in Exhibit 5-15. Let's say you are now aware of a "loss event" about Customer C, who is very likely to enter bankruptcy. The aging method disregards this fact and only provides an allowance of $123 (300 × 1% + 200 × 5% + 600 × 15% + 100 × 20%) when it is possible that all $1,200 is impaired! If you have assessed each customer's receivable row by row (i.e., *horizontally* rather than by age group *vertically*), you would have taken into account specific information about each customer in your

Exhibit 5-15 Age of Accounts Receivables

Age of Account Receivables					
Receivables	Not yet due	1–30 Days	31–60 Days	Over 60 Days	Total
Customer A	$400				$400
Customer B	$100	$100			$200
Customer C	$300	$200	$600	$100	$1,200
...	...	...	...	...	...
Totals	$10,000	$5,000	$3,000	$2,000	$20,000
Percentage uncollectible	1.0%	5.0%	15.0%	20.0%	
Required allowance	$100	$250	$450	$400	$1,200

assessment of receivables impairment. For example, you may decide that Customer C's likelihood to be a "loss event" is 80%. You would then set an allowance amounting to $960 ($1,200 × 80%) specifically for Customer C. In practice, a combination of aging and specific customer credit information may be used to determine the required allowance of uncollectible accounts at year-end.

LEGO's accounting policies and notes on receivables are shown below. In total, customers owe LEGO 6,770 million kr. After examining the potential impairment of these receivables, LEGO

ADAPTED EXCERPTS FROM LEGO'S NOTES TO THE FINANCIAL STATEMENTS

Receivables

Trade receivables are initially recognized at fair value and subsequently measured at amortized cost less write down for losses. Allowance for doubtful receivables are made on basis of an objective indication if an individual receivable or a portfolio of receivables are impaired.

Management makes allowance for doubtful trade receivables in anticipation of estimated losses resulting from the subsequent inability of customers to make required payments. Management analyses trade receivables and examines historical bad debt, customer concentrations, customer creditworthiness, and payment history and changes in customer payment terms.

The age distribution of gross trade receivable is as follows:	2015	2014
Not overdue	6,234	5,329
0–60 days overdue	449	577
61–120 days overdue	13	23
121–180 days overdue	21	9
More than 180 days overdue	53	32
Total gross receivables	6,770	5,970
Less allowance for doubtful receivables	(360)	(79)
Net trade receivables	6,410	5,891

Movement of allowance for bad debt:	2015	2014
Balance as at January 1	(79)	(48)
Realized losses for the year*	10	13
Charged to Income Statement as expense	(291)	(44)
Balance as at December 31	(360)	(79)

*for simplicity, including exchange rates translations and adjustments

Source: LEGO 2015 Annual Report, pages 24, 26, and 36

estimates that 360 million kr is doubtful. Thus, the amount that LEGO expects to collect is DKK 6,410 million. This is called the net receivables because it is the amount of cash LEGO expects to realize in cash receipts eventually. This is also the number reported on the face of LEGO's Balance Sheet (Line 4 on Balance Sheet at the start of this chapter). We could say that as a percentage of total receivables, LEGO provided 5.32% allowance for doubtful receivables. But remember, LEGO does not predetermine this percentage and then apply it to total receivables to get the allowance.

Now, let's look at the last portion of LEGO's excerpt. It shows the movements of the allowance account: the beginning balance (which is equal to last year's ending balance), the amount used, the desired ending balance, and the necessary allowance for the year.

To recap, allowance was 79 million kr at the start of the year, and 10 million kr was used for receivable write-offs (more on this later). The total allowance after write-offs was 69 million kr (79 – 10), but a total of 360 is required based on LEGO's assessment of its customers' credit risks. Thus, the necessary allowance "top up" (and thus bad debt expense for the year) is 291 kr, calculated as 360 – 69 million kr.

You can think of the following formula to help you better understand the relationship between uncollectible-account expense, write-offs of receivables, and allowance for doubtful receivables accounts.

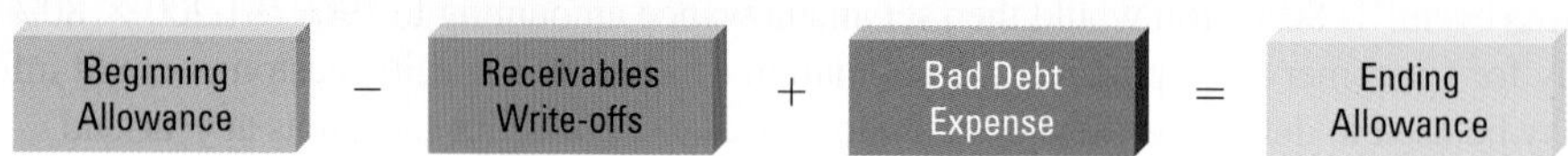

Suppose it is December 31, 2015, and LEGO's receivables show the following before the year-end adjustment (amounts in millions). The allowance account has a balance of 69 kr after receivable write-offs during the year.

Accounts Receivable		Allowance for Doubtful Receivables	
6,770		10	79

These accounts are not yet ready for the financial statements because the allowance balance has not been adjusted to reflect LEGO's year-end assessment of the collectability of its receivables. You saw from earlier that the required ending balance of the allowance for doubtful receivables was 360 kr. To update the allowance, LEGO would make this adjusting entry at year-end:

	A	B	C	D
1	2015			
2	Dec. 31	Uncollectible-Account Expense	291	
3		Allowance for Doubtful Receivables		291
4		*Recorded bad debt expense for the year.*		
5				

The expense decreases LEGO's assets and net income, as shown by the accounting equation.

Assets	=	Liabilities	+	Shareholders' Equity
–291	=	0	+	–291 (uncollectible account expense)

Now the Balance Sheet can report the amount that LEGO expects to collect from customers: 6,410 kr (6,770 kr less allowance of 360 kr).

Accounts Receivable		Allowance for Doubtful Receivables				Uncollectible-Account Expense	
6,770		Write-off	10	Beg. Bal.	79	291	
				Adj.	291		
				End. Bal.	360		

Net receivable, $6,410

Writing Off Uncollectible Accounts. Let's use a more specific example with customer balances to illustrate how businesses handle uncollectible receivables. Let's assume that at the beginning of 20X7 a Singapore division of LEGO had these accounts receivable (amounts in thousands):

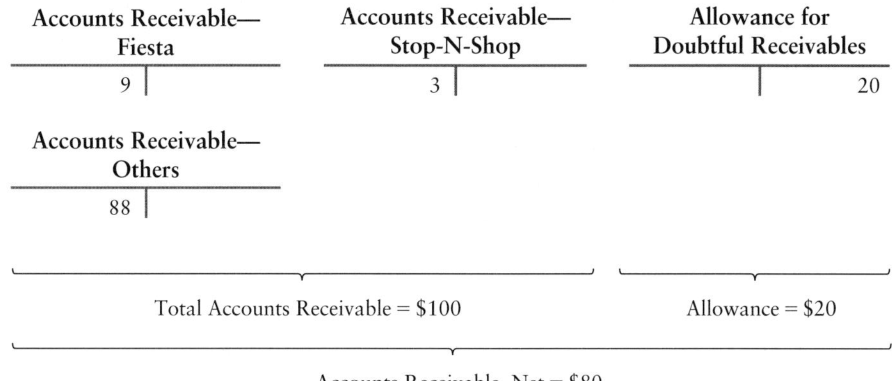

Suppose that early in 20X7, LEGO's credit department determines that LEGO cannot collect from customers of Toys Kingdom and Hamleys. LEGO then writes off the receivables from these customers with the following entry:

	A	B	C	D
1	20X7			
2	Jan. 31	Allowance for Doubtful Receivables	12	
3		Accounts Receivable—Toys Kingdom		9
4		Accounts Receivable—Hamleys		3
5		*Wrote off uncollectible receivables.*		
6				

After the write-off, LEGO's accounts show these amounts:

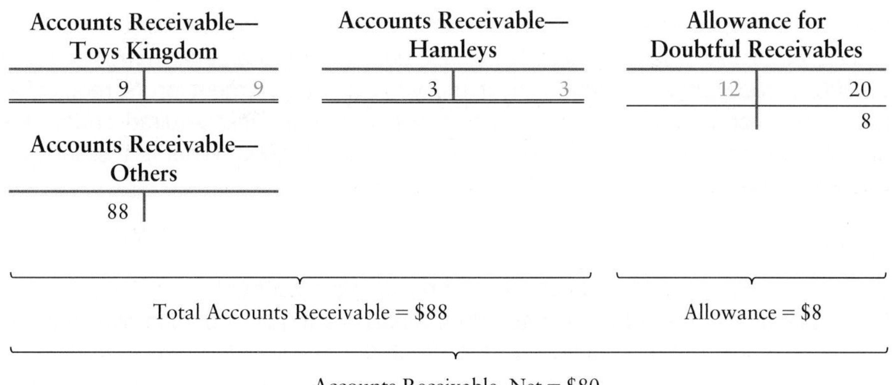

The receivables are reduced because it is now clear that these amounts will not be collected, and the allowance previously set aside is now "used" by the write-off.

Assets	=	Liabilities	+	Shareholders' Equity
+ 12 − 12	=	0	+	0

The accounting equation shows that the write-off of uncollectibles has no effect on LEGO's total assets, no effect on current assets, and no effect on net accounts receivable. Notice that Accounts Receivable, Net is still $80. There is no effect on net income either. Why is there no effect on net income? Net income is unaffected because the write-off of uncollectibles affects no expense account. It is merely a realization of the allowance of uncollectible receivables that has been provided in previous accounting periods. Naturally, at the year-end, when LEGO makes an adjustment for the required amount of allowance of uncollectible receivables, it may recognize more expenses as some of the allowance has been used by the earlier write-offs for Toys Kingdom and Hamleys.

Adjusting Ending Allowance for Doubtful Receivables. Let's continue with this example. Suppose by the end of 20X7, LEGO has receivables totaling $200, and the balance of allowance for uncollectible receivables was the original $20 less the write-offs of $12 = $8. The division also estimated that an appropriate level of allowance for the $200 ending receivables is $30. It will then adjust the allowance for uncollectible receivables to the desired ending balance by recording the following, and at the same time recognize an uncollectible receivables expense:

A1

	A	B	C	D
1	20X7			
2	Dec. 31	Uncollectible Receivables Expense	22	
3		Allowance for Doubtful Receivables		
4		($30 − $8)		22
5		*Recorded bad debt expense for the year.*		
6				

Recovery of Previously Written-off Receivables. Sometimes, accounts that have been written off may be partially recovered. This may take place after liquidation of the customer's business. Such recovery can be treated in one of two ways: (1) reverse the write-off entry or (2) decrease bad debt expense by the amount recovered. Both methods will eventually result in the same bad debt expense at the end of the period when new allowance (and expense) is calculated.

Stop & Think

Suppose Mustafa Confectionery had beginning allowance for uncollectible account receivables of SAR (Saudi Arabia Riyal) 600,000. During the year, it wrote off SAR 200,000 of receivables. At the end of the year, an assessment of its receivables shows that credit quality has improved, and accordingly, the required ending balance for allowance for uncollectible account is SAR 300,000. What is the bad debt expense for the year?

Answer:

The current balance of the allowance for uncollectible account receivables account after receivable write-offs is SAR 400,000. Since the required ending allowance for uncollectible account receivables is SAR 300,000, i.e., lower than the current allowance, Mustafa will record a "negative" expense of SAR 100,000. This negative expense will result in an increase in profit for the year.

Direct Write-Off Method

There is another, less preferable, way to account for uncollectible receivables. Under the **direct write-off method**, the company waits until a specific customer's receivable proves uncollectible. Then the accountant writes off the customer's account and records Uncollectible-Account Expense, as follows (using assumed data):

	A	B	C	D
1	20X7			
2	Jan. 31	Uncollectible-Account Expense	12	
3		Accounts Receivable—Fiesta		9
4		Accounts Receivable—Stop-N-Shop		3
5		*Wrote off bad debts by direct write-off method.*		
6				

The direct write-off method is not considered an accepted accounting practice for financial statement purposes. It is considered defective because it fails to take into account the possibility of impairment of the receivables at Balance Sheet date. As a result, receivables are always reported at their full amount, which is more than the business expects to collect. *Assets on the Balance Sheet may be overstated.* Because of these deficiencies, LEGO and virtually all companies use the allowance method for preparing their financial statements.

Sometimes you may see the concept of the direct write-off method being used for income tax purposes. It is one of several sources of temporary differences that may arise between net income for financial reporting purposes and net income for income tax purposes. We will discuss other differences between book and taxable income in later chapters.

Computing Cash Collections from Customers

CASH FLOW

A company earns revenue and then collects the cash from customers. For LEGO and most other companies, there is a time lag between earning the revenue and collecting the cash. Collections from customers are the single most important source of cash for any business. You can compute a company's collections from customers by analyzing its Accounts Receivable account. Receivables typically hold only three types of transactions, as reflected in the five elements of the following Accounts Receivable account balance (amounts assumed):

Accounts Receivable

Beg. Bal. (left over from last period)	200	Write-offs of uncollectibles	100[b]
Sales (or service) revenue	1,800[a]	Collections from customers	X = 1,500[c]
End. Bal. (carries over to next period)	400		

[a]The journal entry that places revenue into the accounts receivable account is

	A	B	C
1	Accounts Receivable	1,800	
2	Sales (or Service) Revenue		1,800
3			

[b]The journal entry for write-offs is

	A	B	C
1	Allowance for Uncollectibles	100	
2	Accounts Receivable		100
3			

[c] The journal entry that places collections into the receivable account is

	A	B	C
1	Cash	1,500	
2	Accounts Receivable		1,500
3			

Suppose you know all these amounts *except* collections from customers. You can compute collections by solving for *x* in the T-account. The following diagram may help you link the numbers. Collections from customers, *x*, is therefore $1,500.

Often write-offs are unknown and may be omitted. Then the computation of collections becomes an approximation.

Accounting for Notes Receivable

As stated earlier, notes receivable are more formal than accounts receivable. Notes receivable due within one year or less are current assets. Notes due beyond one year are *long-term receivables* and are reported as long-term assets. Some notes receivable are collected in installments. The portion due within one year is a current asset and the remainder is long term. LEGO may hold a $20,000 note receivable from a customer, but only the $6,000 the customer must pay within one year is a current asset of LEGO.

Before launching into the accounting for notes receivable, let's define some key terms:

Creditor. The party to whom money is owed. The **creditor** is also called the *lender*.
Debtor. The party that borrowed and owes money on the note. The **debtor** is also called the *maker* of the note or the *borrower*.
Interest. Interest is the cost of borrowing money. The interest is stated as an annual percentage rate.
Maturity date. The date on which the debtor must pay the note.
Maturity value. The sum of principal and interest on the note payable on maturity.
Principal. The amount of money borrowed by the debtor.
Term. The length of time from when the note was signed by the debtor to when the debtor must pay the note.

There are two parties to a note:

- The *creditor* has a note receivable.
- The *debtor* has a note payable.

Exhibit 5-16 is a typical promissory note.

Exhibit 5-16 | A Promissory Note

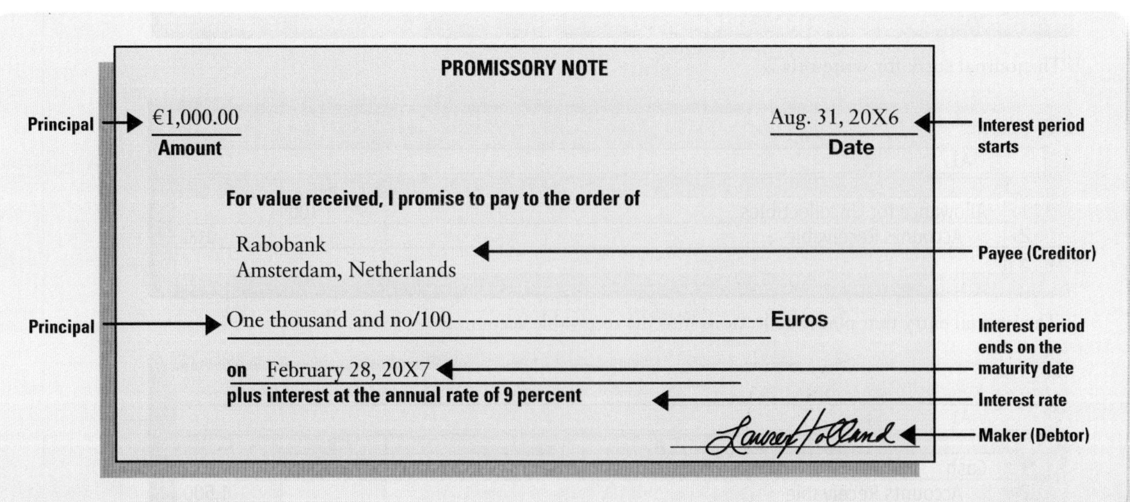
PROMISSORY NOTE

€1,000.00
Amount

Aug. 31, 20X6
Date

For value received, I promise to pay to the order of

Rabobank
Amsterdam, Netherlands

One thousand and no/100------------------------------------ Euros

on February 28, 20X7
plus interest at the annual rate of 9 percent

The **principal** amount of the note (€1,000) is the amount borrowed by the debtor, lent by the creditor. This six-month note receivable runs from August 31, 20X6, to February 28, 20X7, when Lauren Holland (the maker) promises to pay Rabobank (the creditor) the principal of €1,000 plus 9% annual interest. Interest is revenue to the creditor (Rabobank, in this case).

Consider the promissory note in Exhibit 5-16. After Lauren Holland signs the note, Rabobank gives her €1,000 cash. The bank's entries follow, assuming a December 31 year-end for Rabobank:

	A	B	C	D
1	20X6			
2	Aug. 31	Note Receivable—L. Holland	1,000	
3		Cash		1,000
4		*Made a loan.*		
5				

Note Receivable—
L. Holland

Debit	Credit
1,000	

The bank gave one asset, cash, in return for another asset, a note receivable, so total assets did not change.

Rabobank earns interest revenue during September, October, November, and December. At December 31, the bank accrues 9% interest revenue for four months as follows:

	A	B	C	D
1	20X6			
2	Dec. 31	Interest Receivable (€1,000 × 0.09 × 4/12)	30	
3		Interest Revenue		30
4		*Accrued interest revenue.*		
5				

The bank's assets and revenues increase. Rabobank reports these amounts in its financial statements at December 31, 20X7:

Balance Sheet	
Current assets:	
Note receivable	€1,000
Interest receivable................	30
Income Statement	
Interest revenue	€ 30

The bank collects the note on February 28, 20X7, and records:

	A	B	C	D
1	20X7			
2	Feb. 28	Cash	1,045	
3		Note Receivable—L. Holland		1,000
4		Interest Receivable		30
5		Interest Revenue (€1,000 × 0.09 × 2/12)		15
6		*Collected note at maturity.*		
7				

This entry zeroes out Note Receivable and Interest Receivable and also records the interest revenue earned in 20X7.

Note Receivable— L. Holland	
1,000	1,000

In its 20X7 financial statements, the only item that Rabobank will report is the interest revenue of €15 that was earned in 20X7. There's no note receivable or interest receivable on the Balance Sheet because those items were zeroed out when the bank collected the note at maturity.

Three aspects of the interest computation deserve further mention:

1. Interest rates are always for an annual period, unless stated otherwise. In this example, the annual interest rate is 9%. At December 31, 20X6, Rabobank accrues interest revenue for four months. The interest computation is

Principal	×	Interest Rate	×	Time	=	Amount of Interest
€1,000	×	0.09	×	4/12	=	€30

2. The time element (4/12) is the fraction of the year that the note has been in force during 20X6.
3. Interest is often computed for a number of days. For example, suppose you loaned out €10,000 on April 10. The note receivable runs for 90 days and specifies interest at 8%.
   a. Interest starts accruing on April 11 and runs for 90 days, ending on the due date, July 9, as follows:

Month	Number of Days That Interest Accrues
April	20
May	31
June	30
July	9
Total	90

   b. The interest computation is $10,000 × 0.08 × 90/365 = $197

Some companies sell goods and services on notes receivable (versus selling on accounts receivable). This often occurs when the payment term extends beyond the customary accounts receivable period of 30 to 60 days.

Suppose that on March 20, 20X7, LEGO sells a large amount of merchandise to Robinson Department Store. LEGO gets Robinson's three-month promissory note plus 10% annual interest. On initial recognition, Nestlé would debit Notes Receivable and credit Sales Revenue.

A company may also accept a note receivable from a trade customer whose account receivable is past due. The company then debits Notes Receivable and credits Accounts Receivable. We would say the company "received a note receivable on account." Now let's examine some strategies to speed up cash flow.

How to Speed Up Cash Flow

All companies want speedy cash receipts. Rapid cash flow finances new products, research, and development. Thus, companies such as LEGO find ways to collect cash quickly. Two common strategies generate cash quickly.

Credit Card or Bankcard Sales. The merchant sells merchandise and lets the customer pay with credit cards such as American Express, VISA, or MasterCard. This strategy may increase sales, but the added revenue comes at a cost, which is typically about 2% to 3% of the total amount of the sale. Let's see how credit cards and bankcards work from the seller's perspective.

Suppose Fujitsu sells computers for $2,000, and the customer pays with a VISA card. Fujitsu records the sale as follows:

	A	B	C
1	Cash	1,960	
2	Credit Card Processing Fee	40	
3	Sales Revenue		2,000
4	*Recorded bankcard sales.*		
5			

Assets	=	Liabilities	+	Shareholders' Equity	
+ 1,960	=	0	+	+ 2,000	(sales revenue)
				− 40	(credit card fees)

Fujitsu enters the transaction in the credit card machine. The machine, linked to a VISA server, automatically credits Fujitsu's account for a discounted portion, say $1,960, of the $2,000 sale amount. Two percent ($40) goes to VISA. To Fujitsu, the credit card processing fee is an operating expense that reduces Fujitsu's net profit for the year.

Selling (Factoring) Receivables. LEGO makes some large sales to toy stores on account, debiting Accounts Receivable and crediting Sales Revenue. LEGO might then sell these accounts receivable to another business, called a *factor*. The factor earns revenue by paying a discounted price for the receivable and then hopefully collecting the full amount from the customer. The benefit to LEGO is the immediate receipt of cash. The biggest disadvantage of factoring is that it is often quite expensive, when compared to the costs of retaining the receivable on the books and ultimately collecting the full amount. In addition, the company that factors its receivables may lose control over the collection process and yet be responsible for any bad debts that may arise after the factoring. For these reasons, factoring is often not used by companies who have other less costly means to raise cash, such as short-term borrowing from banks. Factoring may be used by start-up companies with insufficient credit history to obtain loans at a reasonable cost, by companies with weaker credit history, or by companies that are already saddled with a significant amount of debt.

To illustrate selling, or *factoring*, accounts receivable, suppose a company wishes to speed up cash flow and therefore sells $100,000 of accounts receivables, receiving cash of $95,000. The company would record the sale of the receivables as follows:

	A	B	C
1	Cash	95,000	
2	Financing Expense	5,000	
3	Accounting Receivable		100,000
4	*Sold accounts receivable.*		
5			

Again, Financing Expense is an operating expense, with the same effect as Interest Expense. Discounting a note receivable is similar to selling an account receivable. However, the credit is to Notes Receivable (instead of Accounts Receivable).

Notice the high price (5% of the face amount, or $5,000) the company has had to sacrifice in order to collect the cash immediately, as opposed to waiting 30 to 60 days to collect the full amount. Therefore, if the company can afford to wait, it will probably not engage in factoring in order to collect the full amount of the receivables.

EVALUATE A COMPANY'S ABILITY TO COLLECT RECEIVABLES

5 **Evaluate** a company's ability to collect receivables

After a business makes a credit sale, the next step is collecting the receivable. **Receivable collection period**, also called the *days' sales in receivables*, or *days sales outstanding*, tells a company how long it takes to collect its average level of receivables. Shorter is better because cash is coming in more quickly. The longer the collection period, the less cash is available to pay bills and expand.

The receivable collection period can be computed in two logical steps. First, we can calculate the **receivables turnover**. The receivable turnover is the number of times average receivables are converted into cash in a year. This is calculated as Sales Revenue divided by Average Receivables. Second, we can convert this number of times into days by dividing 365 by the receivable turnover. Net sales come from the Income Statement, and the receivables amounts are taken from the Balance Sheet. Average receivables is the simple average of the beginning and ending balances.

Receivable turnover and resident period	LEGO 2015	LEGO 2014
$\frac{\text{Sales}}{\text{Average receivables*}}$	$\frac{35{,}780}{6{,}150.5} = 5.82$ times	$\frac{28{,}578}{5{,}380.5} = 5.31$ times
365/Receivable turnover	365/5.82 = 63 days	365/5.31 = 69 days

**Average = (beginning + ending balance)/2, which is (6,410 + 5981)/2 for 2015*

It takes LEGO an average of 63 days to collect its receivables in 2015 (compared to 69 days in 2014). It appears that LEGO is more effective in collecting its receivables in 2015. To evaluate LEGO's collection period of 69 days, we can also compare it to the credit terms that LEGO offers customers when the company makes a sale, as well as the number of days on average that creditors typically allow LEGO to pay them without penalty. Suppose LEGO makes sales on "net 30" terms, which means that customers should pay LEGO within 30 days of the sale. LEGO's collection period of 69 days is longer than the credit terms it gives to its customers. After all, some customers do drag out their payments. And, as we've seen, some customers don't pay at all. On the other hand, if LEGO's short-term creditors expect payment of their accounts payable within 30 days, LEGO may need to borrow cash in order to pay its creditors on time, if it doesn't have enough cash on hand.

Remember that it is a good practice to compare a company's performance to some other benchmarks or industry average. Let's compare LEGO's receivable collection period to other big names in the toy industry, as shown in Exhibit 5-17. Mattel and Hasbro have receivable collection periods of 72 days and 95 days, respectively. We can conclude that LEGO's receivable collection period is much better than Mattel and Hasbro.

Exhibit 5-17 Receivable Collection Period Comparisons

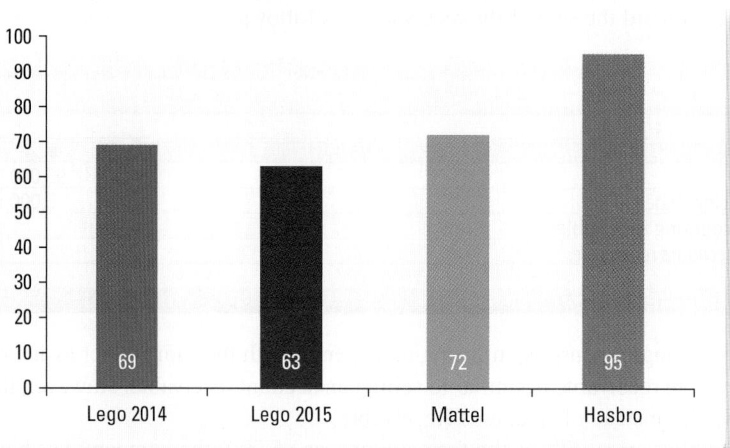

Companies watch their collection periods closely. Whenever collections slow down, the business must find other sources of financing, such as borrowing or selling receivables. During recessions, customers may take an even longer time to pay, and a longer collection period may be unavoidable.

End-of-Chapter Summary Problem

Superior Technical Resources' (STR's) Balance Sheet at December 31, 20X6, reported STR uses the aging method to account for uncollectible receivables.

	(In millions)
Accounts receivable....................................	$382
Allowance for doubtful accounts................	(92)

Requirements

1. How much of the December 31, 20X6, balance of accounts receivables did STR expect to collect? Stated differently, what was the net realizable value of STR's receivables?
2. Journalize, without explanations, 20X7 entries for STR:
   a. Write-offs of uncollectible accounts receivable totaling $58 million. Prepare a T-account for Allowance for Doubtful Accounts and post to this account. Show its unadjusted balance at December 31, 20X7.
   b. December 31, 20X7, aging of receivables, which indicates that $47 million of the total receivables of $409 million is uncollectible at year-end. Post to Allowance for Doubtful Accounts, and show its adjusted balance at December 31, 20X7.
3. Show how STR's receivables and the related allowance will appear on the December 31, 20X7, Balance Sheet.
4. Show how STR's Income Statement will report for the foregoing transactions.

Answers

Requirement 1

	(In millions)
Net realizable value of receivables ($382 − $92)	$290

Requirement 2

	A	B	C	D
1			(In millions)	
2	a.	Allowance for Doubtful Accounts	58	
3		Accounts Receivable		58
4				

Allowance for Doubtful Accounts

		Dec. 31, 20X6	92
20X7 Write-offs	58		
		Unadjusted balance at Dec. 31, 20X7	34

	A	B	C	D
1	c.	Doubtful-Account Expense ($47 – $34)	13	
2		Allowance for Doubtful Accounts		13
3				

Allowance for Doubtful Accounts

	Dec. 31, 20X7 Unadj. bal. 34
	2011 Expense 13
	Dec. 31, 20X7 Adj. bal. 47

Requirement 3

	(In millions)
Accounts receivable	$409
Allowance for doubtful accounts	(47)

Requirement 4

	(In millions)
Expenses: Doubtful-account expense for 20X7 ($40 + $13)	$53

REVIEW | Internal Control, Cash, and Receivables

Quick Check (Answers are given at the end of the chapter.)

1. Each of the following is an example of a control procedure, *except*

a. a sound marketing plan.
b. sound personnel procedures.
c. limited access to assets.
d. separation of duties.

Laurie Corporation has asked you to prepare its bank reconciliation at the end of the current month. Answer **questions 2–6** using the following code letters to indicate how the item described would be reported on the bank reconciliation.

a. Add to the book balance
b. Deduct from the book balance
c. Add to the bank balance
d. Deduct from the bank balance
e. Does not belong on the bank reconciliation

2. A check for $925 written by Laurie during the current month was erroneously recorded as a $952 payment.

3. A $400 deposit made on the last day of the current month did not appear on this month's bank statement.

4. The bank statement showed interest earned of $75.

5. The bank statement included a check from a customer that was marked NSF.

6. The bank statement showed the bank had credited Laurie's account for a $750 deposit made by Lawrence Company.

7. Which of the following reconciling items does not require a journal entry?
   a. NSF check
   b. Deposit in transit
   c. Bank service charge
   d. Bank collection of note receivable

8. A cash budget helps control cash by
   a. helping to determine whether additional cash is available for investments or new financing is needed.
   b. ensuring accurate cash records.
   c. developing a plan for increasing sales.
   d. all of the above.

9. Accounts Receivable has a debit balance of $2,400, and the Allowance for Uncollectible Accounts has a credit balance of $400. A $90 account receivable is written off. What is the amount of net receivables (net realizable value) after the write-off?
   a. $1,910 **c.** $2,090
   b. $2,000 **d.** $2,310

10. Aurora Company received a four-month, 6% per annum, $2,800 note receivable on December 1. The adjusting entry on December 31 will
    a. debit Interest Receivable $14. **c.** both a and b.
    b. credit Interest Revenue $14. **d.** credit Interest Revenue $168.

11. If the adjusting entry to accrue interest on a note receivable is omitted, then
    a. assets, net income, and shareholders' equity are overstated.
    b. assets, net income, and shareholders' equity are understated.
    c. assets are overstated, net income is understated, and shareholders' equity is understated.
    d. liabilities are understated, net income is overstated, and shareholders' equity is overstated.

12. Net sales total $803,000. Beginning and ending accounts receivable are $80,000 and $74,000, respectively. Calculate receivables collection period.
    a. 10 days **c.** 34 days
    b. 35 days **d.** 36 days

Accounting Vocabulary

audit (p. 263) A periodic examination of a company's financial statements and the accounting systems, controls, and records that produce them. Audits may be either external or internal. External audits are usually performed by certified public accountants (CPAs).

bank collection (p. 273) Collection of money by the bank on behalf of a depositor.

bank reconciliation (p. 273) A document explaining the reasons for the difference between a depositor's records and the bank's records about the depositor's cash.

bank statement (p. 271) Document showing the beginning and ending balances of a particular bank account listing the month's transactions that affected the account.

budget (p. 263) A quantitative expression of a plan that helps managers coordinate the entity's activities.

cash budget (p. 263) A budget that projects the entity's future cash receipts and cash disbursements.

cash equivalent (p. 278) Investments such as time deposits, certificates of deposit, or high-grade government securities that are considered so similar to cash that they are combined with cash for financial disclosure purposes on the Balance Sheet and cash flow statement.

check (p. 270) Document instructing a bank to pay the designated person or business the specified amount of money.

computer virus (p. 265) A malicious program that enters a company's computer system by e-mail or other means and destroys program and data files.

controller (p. 263) The chief accounting officer of a business.

creditor (p. 290) The party to whom money is owed; also called the lender.

debtor (p. 290) The party that borrowed and owes money on the note; also called the maker of the note or the borrower.

deposits in transit (p. 273) A deposit recorded by the company but not yet by its bank.

direct write-off method (p. 288) A method of accounting for bad debts.

doubtful-account expense (p. 282) Another name for *uncollectible-account expense.*

electronic fund transfer (EFT) (p. 272) System that transfers cash by electronic communication rather than by paper documents.

exception reporting (p. 263) Identifying data that is not within "normal limits" so that managers can follow up and take corrective action. Exception reporting is used in operating and cash budgets to keep company profits and cash flow in line with management's plans.

fraud (p. 255) An intentional misrepresentation of facts, made for the purpose of persuading another party to act in a way that causes injury or damage to that party.

fraud triangle (p. 258) The three elements that are present in almost all cases of fraud. These elements are pressure, opportunity, and rationalization on the part of the perpetrator.

fraudulent financial reporting (p. 257) Fraud perpetrated by management by preparing misleading financial statements.

imprest system (p. 269) A way to account for petty cash by maintaining a constant balance in the petty cash account, supported by the fund (cash plus payment tickets) totaling the same amount.

interest (p. 290) The borrower's cost of renting money from a lender. Interest is revenue for the lender and expense for the borrower.

internal control (p. 259) Organizational plan and related measures adopted by an entity to safeguard assets, encourage adherence to company policies, promote operational efficiency, and ensure accurate and reliable accounting records.

lapping (p. 262) A fraudulent scheme to steal cash through misappropriating certain customer payments and posting payments from other customers to the affected accounts to cover it up. Lapping is caused by weak internal controls (i.e., not segregating the duties of cash handling and accounts receivable bookkeeping, allowing the bookkeeper improper access to cash, and not appropriately monitoring the activities of those who handle cash).

lock-box system (p. 263) A system of handling cash receipts by mail whereby customers remit payment directly to the bank, rather than through the entity's mail system.

maturity date (p. 290) The date on which the debtor must pay the note.

maturity value (p. 290) The sum of principal and interest on the note.

misappropriation of assets (p. 257) Fraud committed by employees by stealing assets from the company.

non-sufficient funds (NSF) cheque (p. 273) A "hot" cheque, one for which the payer's bank account has insufficient money to pay the cheque. NSF cheques are cash receipts that turn out to be worthless.

operating budget (p. 263) A budget of future net income. The operating budget projects a company's future revenue and expenses. It is usually prepared by line item of the company's Income Statement.

outstanding cheques (p. 273) A cheque issued by the company and recorded on its books but not yet paid by its bank.

petty cash (p. 269) Fund containing a small amount of cash that is used to pay minor amounts.

phishing (p. 265) Creating bogus websites for the purpose of stealing unauthorized data, such as names, addresses, social security numbers, bank account, and credit card numbers.

principal (p. 291) The amount borrowed by a debtor and lent by a creditor.

receivable collection period (p. 294) the average number of days to collect receivables from customers, calculated by dividing 365 by receivable turnover. Also called days' *sales in receivables* or *days sales outstanding*.

receivable turnover (p. 294) the number of times receivables are collected during the year, approximated by taking total sales divided by average receivables. Used in calculating *receivable collection period.*

receivables (p. 280) Monetary claims against a business or an individual, acquired mainly by selling goods or services and by lending money.

remittance advice (p. 270) An optional attachment to a cheque (sometimes a perforated tear-off document and sometimes capable of being electronically scanned) that indicates the payer, date, and purpose of the cash payment. The remittance advice is often used as the source documents for posting cash receipts or payments.

term (p. 290) The length of time from when the note was signed by the debtor to when the debtor must pay the note.

treasurer (p. 262) In a large company, the department that has total responsibility for cash handling and cash management. This includes cash budgeting, cash collections, writing cheques, investing excess funds, and making proposals for raising additional cash when needed.

Trojan horse (p. 265) A malicious program that hides within legitimate programs and acts like a computer virus.

uncollectible-account expense (p. 282) Cost to the seller of extending credit. Arises from the failure to collect from credit customers. Also called doubtful-account expense, or bad-debt expense.

ASSESS YOUR PROGRESS

Short Exercises

LO 1 ■ writing assignment

S5-1. ***(Learning Objective 1: Defining fraud)*** Define "fraud." List and briefly discuss the three major components of the fraud triangle.

LO 1

S5-2. ***(Learning Objective 1: Explaining and describing characteristics of an effective system of internal control)*** Explain why separation of duties is often described as the cornerstone of internal control for safeguarding assets. Describe what can happen if the same person has custody of an asset and also accounts for the asset.

LO 1

S5-3. ***(Learning Objective 1: Explaining the role of internal control)*** Cash may be a small item on the financial statements. Nevertheless, internal control over cash is very important. Why is this true?

LO 2

S5-4. ***(Learning Objective 2: Applying internal controls over cash receipts)*** Candice Cassidy sells memberships to the Phoenix Symphony Association in Vienna, Austria. The Symphony's procedure requires Cassidy to write a patron receipt for all memberships sold. The receipt forms are prenumbered. Cassidy is having personal financial problems and she stole $600 received from a customer. To hide her theft, Cassidy destroyed the company copy of the receipt that she gave the patron. What will alert manager Stephanie Stevens that something is wrong?

LO 2

S5-5. ***(Learning Objective 2: Applying internal control over cash payments by check)*** Answer the following questions about internal control over cash payments:

1. Payment by check carries three controls over cash. What are they?
2. Suppose a purchasing agent receives the goods that he purchases and also approves payment for the goods. How could a dishonest purchasing agent cheat his company? How do companies avoid this internal control weakness?

LO 3

S5-6. ***(Learning Objective 3: Preparing a bank reconciliation)*** The Cash account of Randell Corp. reported a balance of $2,500 at October 31. Included were outstanding checks totaling $600 and an October 31 deposit of $350 that did not appear on the bank statement. The bank statement, which came from Park Bank, listed an October 31 balance of $3,280. Included in the bank balance was an October 30 collection of $560 on account from a customer who pays the bank directly. The bank statement also shows a $20 service charge, $30 of interest revenue that Randell earned on its bank balance, and an NSF check for $40.

Prepare a bank reconciliation to determine how much cash Randell actually has at October 31.

LO 3 ■ writing assignment

S5-7. ***(Learning Objective 3: Recording transactions from a bank reconciliation)*** After preparing Randell Corp.'s bank reconciliation in Short Exercise 5-6, make the company's journal entries for transactions that arise from the bank reconciliation. Date each transaction October 31, and include an explanation with each entry.

LO 3

S5-8. ***(Learning Objective 3: Using a bank reconciliation as a control device)*** Jessica Smith manages Jones Advertising. Smith fears that a trusted employee has been stealing from the company. This employee receives cash from clients and also prepares the monthly bank reconciliation. To check up on the employee, Smith prepares her own bank reconciliation, as follows:

	A	B	C	D
1	**Jones Advertising Bank Reconciliation October 31, 20X7**			
2	**Bank**		**Books**	
3	Balance, October 31	$ 4,600	Balance, October 31	$ 3,920
4	Add:		Add:	
5	Deposit in transit	800	Bank collections	1,100
6			Interest revenue	20
7	Less:		Less:	
8	Outstanding checks	(900)	Service charge	(40)
9	Adjusted bank balance	$ 4,500	Adjusted book balance	$ 5,000
10				

Does it appear that the employee has stolen from the company? If so, how much? Explain your answer. Which side of the bank reconciliation shows the company's true cash balance?

LO 3 **S5-9.** ***(Learning Objective 3: Preparing a cash budget)*** Crescent Artichoke Growers (CAG) is a major food cooperative. Suppose CAG begins 20X6 with cash of $14 million. CAG estimates cash receipts during 20X6 will total $124 million. Planned payments will total $106 million. To meet daily cash needs next year, CAG must maintain a cash balance of at least $22 million. Prepare the organization's cash budget for 20X6.

LO 4 **S5-10.** ***(Learning Objective 4: Applying the allowance method to account for uncollectibles)*** Use the information from the following journal entries of Green Leaves Furniture Restoration to answer the questions below:

	A	B	C	D
1		**Journal Entry**		
2		**Accounts**	**Debit**	**Credit**
3	**1.**	Accounts Receivable	1,200,000	
4		Sales Revenue		1,200,000
5				
6	**2.**	Cash	980,000	
7		Accounts Receivable		980,000
8				
9	**3.**	Allowance for Uncollectible Accounts	18,000	
10		Accounts Receivable		18,000
11				
12	**4.**	Uncollectible-Account Expense	40,000	
13		Allowance for Uncollectible Accounts		40,000
14				

Requirements

1. Start with Accounts Receivable's beginning balance ($48,000) and then post to the Accounts Receivable T-account. How much do Green Leaves Furniture Restoration's customers owe the company at December 31?
2. Start with the Allowance account's beginning credit balance ($10,480) and then post to the Allowance for Uncollectible Accounts T-account. How much of the receivables at December 31 does Green Leaves Furniture Restoration expect *not* to collect?
3. At December 31, how much cash does Green Leaves Furniture Restoration expect to collect on its accounts receivable?

LO 4 **S5-11.** ***(Learning Objective 4: Applying the allowance method to account for uncollectibles)*** Goode and Devlin, a law firm, started 20X6 with accounts receivable of $31,000 and an allowance for uncollectible accounts of $4,200. The 20X6 service revenues on account totaled $157,000, and cash collections on account totaled $121,000. During 20X6, Goode and Devlin wrote off uncollectible accounts receivable of $3,200. At December 31, 20X6, the aging of accounts receivable indicated that Goode and Devlin will not collect $1,850 of its accounts receivable.

Journalize Goode and Devlin's (a) service revenue, (b) cash collections on account, (c) write-offs of uncollectible receivables, and (d) uncollectible-account expense for the year. Explanations are not required. Prepare a T-account for Allowance for Uncollectible Accounts to show your computation of uncollectible-account expense for the year.

LO 4 **S5-12.** ***(Learning Objective 4: Applying the allowance method to account for uncollectibles)*** Perform the following accounting for the receivables of Robbins and Williams, a law firm, at December 31, 20X6.

Requirements

1. Start with the beginning balances for these T-accounts:
   - Accounts Receivable, $89,000
   - Allowance for Uncollectible Accounts, $6,000

   Post the following 20X6 transactions to the T-accounts:

   a. Service revenue of $753,000, all on account
   b. Collections on account, $774,000
   c. Write-offs of uncollectible accounts, $8,000
   d. Uncollectible-account expense (allowance method), $12,000
2. What are the ending balances of Accounts Receivable and Allowance for Uncollectible Accounts?
3. Show how Robbins and Williams will report accounts receivable on its Balance Sheet at December 31, 20X6.

S5-13. ***(Learning Objectives 4: Answering practical questions about receivables)*** Answer these questions about receivables and uncollectibles. For the true-false questions, explain any answers that turn out to be false. LO 4

1. True or false? The direct write-off method of accounting for uncollectibles understates assets.
2. California Bank lent $240,000 to Sacramento Company on a six-month, 8% note. Which party has interest receivable? Which party has interest payable? Interest expense? Interest revenue? How much interest will these organizations record one month after Sacramento Company signs the note?
3. When California Bank accrues interest on the Sacramento Company note, show the directional effects on the bank's assets, liabilities, and equity (increase, decrease, or no effect).
4. True or false? Credit sales increase receivables. Collections and write-offs decrease receivables.
5. Which receivables figure (the *total* amount that customers *owe* the company, or the *net* amount the company expects to collect) is more interesting to investors as they consider buying the company's shares? Give your reason.
6. Show how to determine net accounts receivable.

S5-14. ***(Learning Objective 4: Accruing interest receivable and collecting a note receivable)*** On August 31, 20X6, Nancy Thompson borrowed $2,200 from Yellow Interstate Bank. Thompson signed a note payable, promising to pay the bank principal plus interest on August 31, 20X7. The interest rate on the note is 9%. The accounting year of Yellow Interstate Bank ends on June 30, 20X7. Journalize Yellow Interstate Bank's (a) lending money on the note receivable at August 31, 20X6, (b) accrual of interest at June 30, 20X7, and (c) collection of principal and interest at August 31, 20X7, the maturity date of the note. LO 4

S5-15. ***(Learning Objective 5: Evaluating the current ratio and days' sales in receivables)*** West Highland Clothiers reported the following amounts in its 20X7 financial statements. The 20X6 amounts are given for comparison. LO 5

	20X7		20X6	
Current assets:				
Cash		$ 10,200		$ 9,700
Short-term investments		19,000		14,000
Accounts receivable	$86,000		$77,000	
Less: Allowance for uncollectibles	(6,400)	79,600	(6,100)	70,900
Inventory		189,000		190,500
Prepaid insurance		2,400		2,300
Total current assets		300,200		287,400
Total current liabilities		103,000		111,000
Net sales		852,000		736,000

Requirements

1. Compute West Highland's current ratio at the end of 20X7. Round to two decimal places.
2. Compute West Highland's receivables collection period for 20X7.

Exercises MyLab Accounting

Select Group A and Group B exercises can be found within MyLab Accounting, an online homework and practice environment. Your instructor may ask you to complete select exercises using MyLab Accounting.

Group A

LO 1 2
■ writing assignment

E5-16A. *(Learning Objectives 1, 2: Learning about fraud; identifying internal control weaknesses)* Identify the internal control weakness in the following situations. State how the person can hurt the company.

- **a.** Jim Morris works as a security guard at SAFETY parking in Budapest. Morris has a master key to the cash box where customers pay for parking. Each night Morris prepares the cash report that shows (a) the number of cars that parked on the lot and (b) the day's cash receipts. Lucy Carrols, the SAFETY treasurer, checks Morris's figures by multiplying the number of cars by the parking fee per car. Carrington then deposits the cash in the bank.
- **b.** Cecilia Albom is the purchasing agent for Marshfield Golf Equipment. Albom prepares purchase orders based on requests from division managers of the company. Albom faxes the purchase order to suppliers who then ship the goods to Marshfield. Albom receives each incoming shipment and checks it for agreement with the purchase order and the related invoice. She then routes the goods to the respective division managers and sends the receiving report and the invoice to the accounting department for payment.

LO 2

E5-17A. *(Learning Objective 2: Identifying internal control strengths and weaknesses)* The following situations describe two cash payment situations and two cash receipt situations. In each pair, one set of internal controls is better than the other. Evaluate the internal controls in each situation as strong or weak, and give the reason for your answer.

Cash payments:

- **a.** Stone & Grain, Inc., policy calls for project supervisors to purchase the equipment needed for jobs. The supervisors then submit the paid receipts to the home office for reimbursement. This policy enables supervisors to get the equipment quickly and keep construction jobs moving.
- **b.** Tony McGraw Construction policy calls for construction supervisors to request the equipment needed for their jobs. The home office then purchases the equipment and has it shipped to the construction site.

Cash receipts:

- **a.** Cash received by mail at Wright Orthopedic Clinic goes to the mail room, where a mail clerk opens envelopes and totals the cash receipts for the day. The mail clerk forwards customer checks to the cashier for deposit in the bank and forwards the remittance advices to the accounting department for posting credits to customer accounts.
- **b.** At Cristy Auto Parts, cash received by mail goes straight to the accountant, who debits Cash and credits Accounts Receivable to record the collections from customers. The Cristy accountant then deposits the cash in the bank.

LO 1 2
■ writing assignment

E5-18A. *(Learning Objectives 1, 2: Learning about fraud; correcting an internal control weakness)* Barry Floyd served as executive director of Downtown Kalamazoo, an organization created to revitalize Kalamazoo. Over the course of 13 years, Floyd embezzled $348,000. How did Floyd do it? By depositing subscriber cash receipts in his own bank account, writing Downtown Kalamazoo checks to himself, and creating phony entities to which Downtown Kalamazoo wrote checks.

Downtown Kalamazoo was led by a board of directors comprised of civic leaders. Floyd's embezzlement went undetected until Downtown Kalamazoo couldn't pay its bills. Give four ways in which Floyd's embezzlement could have been prevented.

LO 2

E5-19A. *(Learning Objective 2: Evaluating internal control over cash receipts)* McKinley stores use point-of-sale terminals as cash registers. The register shows the amount of each sale, the cash received from the customer, and any change returned to the customer. The machine also produces a customer receipt but keeps no record of transactions. At the end of the day, the clerk counts the cash in the register and gives it to the cashier for deposit in the company's bank account.

Write a memo to convince the store manager that there is an internal control weakness over cash receipts. Identify the weakness that gives an employee the best opportunity to steal cash, and state how to prevent such a theft.

E5-20A. *(Learning Objective 2: Evaluating internal control over cash payments)* New Pastures Golf Company manufactures a popular line of golf clubs. New Pastures Golf employs 176 workers and keeps their employment records on time sheets that show how many hours the employee works each week. On Friday the shop foreman collects the time sheets, checks them for accuracy, and delivers them to the payroll department for preparation of paychecks. The treasurer signs the paychecks and returns the checks to the payroll department for distribution to the employees. LO 2

Identify the main internal control weakness in this situation, state how the weakness can hurt New Pastures Golf, and propose a way to correct the weakness.

E5-21A. *(Learning Objective 3: Classifying bank reconciliation items)* The following items appear on a bank reconciliation: LO 3

1. ___ Service charge
2. ___ Deposits in transit
3. ___ Outstanding checks
4. ___ Bank error: The bank credited our account for a deposit made by another bank customer.
5. ___ Book error: We debited Cash for $200. The correct debit was $2,000.
6. ___ NSF check
7. ___ Bank collection of a note receivable on our behalf

Classify each item as (a) an addition to the bank balance, (b) a subtraction from the bank balance, (c) an addition to the book balance, or (d) a subtraction from the book balance.

E5-22A. *(Learning Objective 3: Preparing a bank reconciliation)* D.J. Holt's checkbook lists the following: LO 3

Date	Check No.	Item	Check	Deposit	Balance
8/1					$ 675
4	852	Art Cafe	$ 40		635
9		Dividends received		$ 120	755
13	853	General Tire Co.	45		710
14	854	QuickMobil	58		652
18	855	Cash	65		587
26	856	Woodway Baptist Church	95		492
28	857	Bent Tree Apartments	275		217
31		Paycheck		1,010	1,227

The August bank statement shows

Balance				$675
Add: Deposits				120
Debit checks:	No.	Amount		
	852	$40		
	853	45		
	854	85*		
	855	65		(235)
Other charges:				
NSF check			$20	
Service charge			10	(30)
Balance				$530

*This is the correct amount for check number 854.

Requirement

1. Prepare Holt's bank reconciliation at August 31, 20X7.

LO 3

E5-23A. ***(Learning Objective 3: Preparing a bank reconciliation)*** Evan Stephens operates a bowling alley. He has just received the monthly bank statement at April 30 from City National Bank, and the statement shows an ending balance of $585. Listed on the statement are an EFT rent collection of $330, a service charge of $8, two NSF checks totaling $135, and a $10 charge for printed checks. In reviewing his cash records, Stephens identifies outstanding checks totaling $622 and an April 30 deposit in transit of $1,898. During April, he recorded a $280 check for the salary of a part-time employee as $28. Stephens's Cash account shows an April 30 cash balance of $1,936. How much cash does Stephens actually have at April 30?

LO 3

■ writing assignment

E5-24A. ***(Learning Objective 3: Making journal entries from a bank reconciliation)*** Use the data from Exercise 5-23A to make the journal entries that Stephens should record on April 30 to update his Cash account. Include an explanation for each entry.

LO 3

■ spreadsheet

E5-25A. ***(Learning Objective 3: Preparing a cash budget)*** Chad Communications, Inc., is preparing its cash budget for 20X7. Chad ended 20X6 with cash of $82 million, and managers need to keep a cash balance of at least $86 million for operations.

Collections from customers are expected to total $11,308 million during 20X7, and payments for the cost of services and products should reach $6,165 million. Operating expense payments are budgeted at $2,543 million.

During 20X7, Chad expects to invest $1,816 million in new equipment and sell older assets for $116 million. Debt payments scheduled for 20X7 will total $604 million. The company forecasts net income of $895 million for 20X7 and plans to pay dividends of $33 million.

Prepare Chad Communications' cash budget for 20X7. Will the budgeted level of cash receipts leave Chad with the desired ending cash balance of $86 million, or will the company need additional financing? If so, how much?

LO 4

E5-26A. ***(Learning Objective 4: Reporting bad debts by the allowance method)*** On December 31, Darla's Travel has an accounts receivable balance of $85,000. Allowance for Doubtful Accounts has a credit balance of $680 before the year-end adjustment. Darla's Travel estimates that doubtful-account expense for the year is equal to 8% of ending receivables. Make the year-end entry to record doubtful-account expense. Show how the accounts receivable and the allowance for doubtful accounts are reported on the Balance Sheet.

LO 4

E5-27A. ***(Learning Objective 4: Using the allowance method for bad debts)*** On September 30, Hilly Mountain Party Planners had a $35,000 balance in Accounts Receivable and a $2,300 credit balance in Allowance for Uncollectible Accounts. During October, the store made credit sales of $163,000. October collections on account were $142,000, and write-offs of uncollectible receivables totaled $3,200. The required allowance at year-end is calculated to be $4,500.

Requirements

1. Journalize sales, collections, write-offs of uncollectibles, and uncollectible-account expense by the allowance method during October. Explanations are not required.
2. Show the ending balances in Accounts Receivable, Allowance for Uncollectible Accounts, and *Net* Accounts Receivable at October 31. How much does the store expect to collect?
3. Show how the store will report Accounts Receivable on its October 31 Balance Sheet.

LO 4

E5-28A. ***(Learning Objective 4: Using the aging approach to estimate bad debts)*** On December 31, before any year-end adjustments, the Accounts Receivable balance of Athens Company is $260,000. The Allowance for Doubtful Accounts has a $12,500 credit balance. Athens Company prepares the following aging schedule for Accounts Receivable:

	Age of Accounts			
Total Balance	1–30 Days	31–60 Days	61–90 Days	Over 90 Days
$210,000	$100,000	$80,000	$50,000	$30,000
Estimated uncollectible	0.5%	2.0%	5.0%	50.0%

■ spreadsheet

Requirements

1. Based on the aging of accounts receivable, is the unadjusted balance of the allowance account adequate? Too high? Too low?
2. Make the entry required by the aging schedule. Prepare a T-account for the allowance.
3. Show how Athens Company will report Accounts Receivable on its December 31 Balance Sheet.

E5-29A. ***(Learning Objective 4: Recording notes receivable and accruing interest revenue)*** Record the following note receivable transactions in the journal of Aegean Realty. How much interest revenue did Aegean earn this year? Use a 365-day year for interest computations, and round interest amounts to the nearest dollar.

Sept.	1	Loaned $12,000 cash to Cristy Rocker on a one-year, 8% note.
Nov.	6	Performed service for Top Masters, receiving a 90-day, 6% note for $10,000.
	16	Received a $5,000, six-month, 12% note on account from Veron, Inc.
	30	Accrued interest revenue for the year.

LO 5

E5-30A. ***(Learning Objective 5: Using the current ratio and days' sales in receivables to evaluate a company)*** Champi, Inc., reported the following items at December 31, 20X8 and 20X7:

A1

	A	B	C	D	E	F
1	**Balance Sheets (Summarized)**					
2		**Year End**			**Year End**	
3		**20X8**	**20X7**		**20X8**	**20X7**
4	**Current assets:**			**Current liabilities:**		
5	Cash	$ 3,000	$ 9,000	Accounts payable	$ 18,000	$ 22,000
6	Marketable securities	20,000	10,000	Other current liabilities	105,000	105,000
7	Accounts receivable, net	58,000	72,000	Long-term liabilities	15,000	19,000
8	Inventory	90,000	88,000			
9	Other current assets	2,000	2,000	Shareholders' equity	145,000	145,000
10	Long-term assets	110,000	110,000			
11	Total assets	$283,000	$291,000	Total liabilities and equity	$283,000	$291,000
12						
13	**Income Statement (partial):**	**20X8**				
14	Sales Revenue	$750,000				
15						

Requirement

1. Compute Champi's (a) current ratio and (b) days' sales in average receivables for 20X8. Evaluate each ratio value as strong or weak. Champi sells on terms of net 30 days.

E5-31A. ***(Learning Objective 5: Analyzing a company's financial statements)*** Modern Limited, the electronics and appliance chain, reported these figures in millions of dollars:

	20X7	20X6
Net sales	$578,000	$607,000
Receivables at end of year	3,750	4,920

Requirements

1. Compute Modern's average collection period during 20X7.
2. Is Modern's collection period long or short? Viflex Networks takes 25 days to collect its average level of receivables. Domarko, the overnight shipper, takes 35 days. What causes Modern's collection period to be so different?

Group B

LO 1 2
■ writing assignment

E5-32B. *(Learning Objectives 1, 2: Learning about fraud; identifying internal control weaknesses)* Identify the internal control weakness in the following situations. State how the person can hurt the company.

a. Josh Michaels works as a security guard at CITY parking in Cologne, Germany. Michaels has a master key to the cash box where customers pay for parking. Each night Michaels prepares the cash report that shows (a) the number of cars that parked on the lot and (b) the day's cash receipts. Lily Cooper, the CITY treasurer, checks Michaels's figures by multiplying the number of cars by the parking fee per car. Cooper then deposits the cash in the bank.

b. Ara Ahern is the purchasing agent for Superior Golf Equipment. Ahern prepares purchase orders based on requests from division managers of the company. Ahern faxes the purchase order to suppliers who then ship the goods to Superior. Ahern receives each incoming shipment and checks it for agreement with the purchase order and the related invoice. She then routes the goods to the respective division managers and sends the receiving report and the invoice to the accounting department for payment.

LO 2

E5-33B. *(Learning Objective 2: Identifying internal control strengths and weaknesses)* The following situations describe two cash payment situations and two cash receipt situations. In each pair, one set of internal controls is better than the other. Evaluate the internal controls in each situation as strong or weak, and give the reason for your answer.

Cash payments:

a. Sturdy Structures, Inc., policy calls for project supervisors to purchase the equipment needed for jobs. The supervisors then submit the paid receipts to the home office for reimbursement. This policy enables supervisors to get the equipment quickly and keep construction jobs moving.

b. Milton Malcolm Construction policy calls for construction supervisors to request the equipment needed for their jobs. The home office then purchases the equipment and has it shipped to the construction site.

Cash receipts:

a. At Carl Auto Parts, cash received by mail goes straight to the accountant, who debits Cash and credits Accounts Receivable to record the collections from customers. The Cramer accountant then deposits the cash in the bank.

b. Cash received by mail at Clear Vision Eye Clinic goes to the mail room, where a mail clerk opens envelopes and totals the cash receipts for the day. The mail clerk forwards customer checks to the cashier for deposit in the bank and forwards the remittance slips to the accounting department for posting credits to customer accounts.

LO 1 2
■ writing assignment

E5-34B. *(Learning Objectives 1, 2: Learning about fraud; correcting an internal control weakness)* Simon Stuart served as executive director of Downtown Scanlon, an organization created to revitalize Scanlon. Over the course of 11 years Stuart embezzled €273,000. How did Stuart do it? He did it by depositing subscriber cash receipts in his own bank account, writing Downtown Scanlon checks to himself, and creating phony entities that Downtown Scanlon wrote checks to.

Downtown Scanlon was led by a board of directors comprised of civic leaders. Stuart's embezzlement went undetected until Downtown Scanlon couldn't pay its bills.

Give four ways Stuart's embezzlement could have been prevented.

E5-35B. ***(Learning Objective 2: Evaluating internal control over cash receipts)*** Ripley stores use point-of-sale terminals as cash registers. The register shows the amount of each sale, the cash received from the customer, and any change returned to the customer. The machine also produces a customer receipt but keeps no record of transactions. At the end of the day, the clerk counts the cash in the register and gives it to the cashier for deposit in the company bank account. LO 2

Write a memo to convince the store manager that there is an internal control weakness over cash receipts. Identify the weakness that gives an employee the best opportunity to steal cash and state how to prevent such a theft.

E5-36B. ***(Learning Objective 2, 4: Evaluating internal control over cash payments)*** Long Range Golf Company manufactures a popular line of golf clubs. Long Range Golf employs 167 workers and keeps their employment records on time sheets that show how many hours the employee works each week. On Friday the shop foreman collects the time sheets, checks them for accuracy, and delivers them to the payroll department for preparation of paychecks. The treasurer signs the paychecks and returns the checks to the payroll department for distribution to the employees. LO 2 4

Identify the main internal control weakness in this situation, state how the weakness can hurt Long Range Golf, and propose a way to correct the weakness.

E5-37B. ***(Learning Objective 3: Classifying bank reconciliation items)*** The following items appear on a bank reconciliation. LO 3

Classify each item as (a) an addition to the book balance, (b) a subtraction from the book balance, (c) an addition to the bank balance, or (d) a subtraction from the bank balance.

1. ___ Outstanding checks
2. ___ Bank error: The bank credited our account for a deposit made by another bank customer.
3. ___ Service charge
4. ___ Deposits in transit
5. ___ NSF check
6. ___ Bank collection of a note receivable on our behalf
7. ___ Book error: We debited Cash for €300. The correct debit was €3,000.

E5-38B. ***(Learning Objective 3: Preparing a bank reconciliation)*** D.J. Hilton's checkbook and March bank statement show the following: LO 3

Date	Check No.	Item	Check	Deposit	Balance
3/1					$ 575
4	852	Art Cafe	$ 30		545
9		Dividends received		$ 135	680
13	853	General Tire Co.	35		645
14	854	QuickMobil	56		589
18	855	Cash	60		529
26	856	Woodway Baptist Church	80		449
28	857	Bent Tree Apartments	255		194
31		Paycheck		1,120	1,314

Balance				$575
Add: Deposits				135
Debit checks:	No.	Amount		
	852	$30		
	853	35		
	854	65*		
	855	60		(190)
Other charges:				
NSF check			$20	
Service charge			10	(30)
Balance				490

*This is the correct amount for check number 854.

Requirement

1. Prepare Hilton's bank reconciliation at March 31.

LO 3

E5-39B. ***(Learning Objective 3: Preparing a bank reconciliation)*** Harry Sparks operates a bowling alley. He has just received the monthly bank statement at September 30 from City National Bank, and the statement shows an ending balance of €565. Listed on the statement are an EFT rent collection of €345, a service charge of €9, two NSF checks totaling €135, and a €12 charge for printed checks. In reviewing his cash records, Sparks identifies outstanding checks totaling €639 and a September 30 deposit in transit of €1,970. During September, he recorded a €320 check for the salary of a part-time employee as €32. Sparks's Cash account shows a September 30 cash balance of €1,995. How much cash does Sparks actually have at September 30?

LO 3
■ writing assignment

E5-40B. ***(Learning Objective 3: Making journal entries from a bank reconciliation)*** Use the data from Exercise 5-39B to make the journal entries that Sparks should record on September 30 to update his Cash account. Include an explanation for each entry.

LO 3
■ spreadsheet

E5-41B. ***(Learning Objective 3: Preparing a cash budget)*** Fellow Communications, Inc., is preparing its cash budget for 20X7. Fellow ended 20X6 with cash of €85 million, and managers need to keep a cash balance of at least €82 million for operations.

Collections from customers are expected to total €11,317 million during 20X7, and payments for the cost of services and products should reach €6,184 million. Operating expense payments are budgeted at €2,546 million.

During 20X7, Fellow expects to invest €1,841 million in new equipment and sell older assets for €125 million. Debt payments scheduled for 20X7 will total €602 million. The company forecasts net income of €883 million for 20X7 and plans to pay dividends of €321 million.

Prepare Fellow Communications' cash budget for 20X7. Will the budgeted level of cash receipts leave Fellow with the desired ending cash balance of €82 million, or will the company need additional financing? If so, how much?

LO 4

E5-42B. ***(Learning Objective 4: Reporting bad debts by the allowance method)*** At December 31, Will's Travel has an accounts receivable balance of €90,000. Allowance for Doubtful Accounts has a credit balance of €700 before the year-end adjustment. Will's Travel estimates that doubtful-account expense for the year is equal to 8% of ending receivables. Make the December 31 entry to record doubtful-account expense. Show how the Accounts Receivable and the Allowance for Doubtful Accounts are reported on the Balance Sheet.

LO 4

E5-43B. ***(Learning Objective 4: Using the allowance method for bad debts)*** On April 30, Hilltop Party Planners had a €38,000 balance in Accounts Receivable and a €4,500 credit balance in Allowance for Uncollectible Accounts. During May, the store made credit sales of €146,000. May collections on account were €123,000, and write-offs of uncollectible receivables totaled €2,300. Hilltop Party Planners estimates the required allowance for uncollectible accounts for the year is €4,000.

Requirements

1. Journalize sales, collections, write-offs of uncollectibles, and uncollectible-account expense by the allowance method during May. Explanations are not required.
2. Show the ending balances in Accounts Receivable, Allowance for Uncollectible Accounts, and *Net* Accounts Receivable at May 31. How much does the store expect to collect?
3. Show how the store will report Accounts Receivable on its May 31 Balance Sheet.

LO 4
■ spreadsheet

E5-44B. ***(Learning Objective 4: Using the aging approach to estimate bad debts)*** At December 31, before any year-end adjustments, the accounts receivable balance of Delta Electronics Company is €180,000. The allowance for doubtful accounts has a €6,500 credit balance. Delta Electronics Company prepares the following aging schedule for accounts receivable:

Total Balance	Age of Accounts			
	1–30 Days	31–60 Days	61–90 Days	Over 90 Days
$180,000	€80,000	€50,000	€30,000	€10,000
Estimated uncollectible	0.5%	3.0%	7.0%	40.0%

Requirements

1. Based on the aging of accounts receivable, is the unadjusted balance of the allowance account adequate? Too high? Too low?
2. Make the entry required by the aging schedule. Prepare a T-account for the allowance.
3. Show how Delta Electronics Company will report Accounts Receivable on its December 31 Balance Sheet.

E5-45B. *(Learning Objective 4: Recording notes receivable and accruing interest revenue)* Record the following note receivable transactions in the journal of Celtic Realty. How much interest revenue did Celtic earn this year? Use a 365-day year for interest computations, and round interest amounts to the nearest dollar.

Apr. 1	Loaned $18,000 cash to Boyle Denvers on a one-year 10% note.
Jun. 6	Performed service for Pot Masters, receiving a 90-day, 8% note for $15,000.
16	Received a $4,000, six-month, 12% note on account from Veron, Inc.
30	Accrued interest revenue for the year.

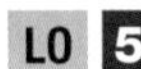

E5-46B. *(Learning Objective 5: Using the current ratio and days' sales in receivables to evaluate a company)* Navajo, Inc., reported the following items at December 31, 20X8 and 20X7:

	A	B	C	D	E	F
1	**Balance Sheets (Summarized)**					
2		**Year End**			**Year End**	
3		**20X8**	**20X7**		**20X8**	**20X7**
4	**Current assets:**			**Current liabilities:**		
5	Cash	$ 4,000	$ 10,000	Accounts payable	$ 17,000	$ 18,000
6	Marketable securities	24,000	13,000	Other current liabilities	106,000	109,000
7	Accounts receivable, net	58,000	75,000	Long-term liabilities	15,000	19,000
8	Inventory	92,000	88,000			
9	Other current assets	6,000	6,000	Stockholders' equity	146,000	146,500
10	Long-term assets	100,000	100,000			
11	Total assets	$284,000	$292,000	Total liabilities and equity	$284,000	$292,000
12						
13	**Income Statement (partial):**	**20X8**				
14	Sales Revenue	$730,000				
15						

Requirement

1. Compute Navajo's (a) current ratio and (b) days' sales in average receivables for 20X8. Evaluate each ratio value as strong or weak. Navajo sells on terms of net 30 days.

E5-47B. *(Learning Objective 5: Analyzing a company's financial statements)* Contemporary Limited, the electronics and appliance chain, reported these figures in millions of dollars:

	20X7	20X6
Net sales	€574,000	€603,000
Receivables at end of year	3,670	4,380

Requirements

1. Compute Contemporary's average collection period during 20X7.
2. Is Contemporary's collection period long or short? Kurzwel Networks takes 40 days to collect its average level of receivables. Damascus, the overnight shipper, takes 25 days. What causes Contemporary's collection period to be so different?

Challenge Exercises

E5-48. ***(Learning Objectives 1, 2: Learning about fraud; evaluating internal controls over cash payments; focusing on ethical considerations)*** Shirley Hopper, the owner of Shirley's Perfect Presents, has delegated management of the business to Leslie Temple, a friend. Hopper drops by to meet customers and check up on cash receipts, but Temple buys the merchandise and handles cash payments. Business has been very good lately, and cash receipts have kept pace with the apparent level of sales. However, for a year or so, the amount of cash on hand has been too low. When asked about this, Temple explains that suppliers are charging more for goods than in the past. During the past year, Temple has taken two expensive vacations, and Hopper wonders how Temple can afford these trips on her $60,000 annual salary and commissions.

List at least three ways Temple could be defrauding Hopper of cash. In each instance also identify how Hopper can determine whether Temple's actions are ethical. Limit your answers to the store's cash payments. The business pays all suppliers by check (no EFTs).

LO 3

E5-49. ***(Learning Objective 3: Preparing and using a cash budget)*** Dexter Dunne, the chief financial officer, is responsible for The Furniture Mart's cash budget for 20X6. The budget will help Dunne determine the amount of long-term borrowing needed to end the year with a cash balance of $160,000. Dunne's assistants have assembled budget data for 20X6, which the computer printed in alphabetical order. Not all the data items reproduced below are used in preparing the cash budget.

(Assumed Data)	(In thousands)
Actual cash balance, December 31, 20X5	$ 150
Budgeted total assets	24,377
Budgeted total current assets	7,769
Budgeted total current liabilities	4,620
Budgeted total liabilities	12,088
Budgeted total shareholders' equity	12,289
Collections from customers	22,100
Dividend payments	371
Issuance of shares	647
Net income	1,183
Payment of long-term and short-term debt	984
Payment of operating expenses	2,438
Purchases of inventory items	14,655
Purchase of property and equipment	1,257

Requirements

1. Prepare the cash budget of The Furniture Mart, Inc.
2. Compute The Furniture Mart's budgeted current ratio at December 31, 20X6. Based on the current ratio and on the cash budget, would you lend $100,000 to The Furniture Mart? Give the reason for your decision.

E5-50. ***(Learning Objective 4: Reconstructing receivables and bad-debt amounts)*** Suppose Hearts, Inc., reported net receivables of $2,856 million and $2,628 million at January 31, 20X7 and 20X6, after subtracting allowances of $74 million and $69 million on these respective dates. Hearts earned total revenue of $54,333 million (all on account) and recorded doubtful-account expense of $18 million for the year ended January 31, 20X7. LO 4

Requirement

1. Use this information to measure the following amounts for the year ended January 31, 20X7:
   a. Write-offs of uncollectible receivables.
   b. Collections from customers.

Quiz

Test your understanding of internal control and cash by answering the following questions. Answer each question by selecting the best choice from among the answers given.

Q5-51. All of the following are objectives of internal control *except*

a. to safeguard assets.
b. to maximize net income.
c. to comply with legal requirements.
d. to ensure accurate and reliable accounting records.

Q5-52. Requiring that an employee with no access to cash do the accounting is an example of which characteristic of internal control?

a. Competent and reliable personnel
b. Assignment of responsibility
c. Separation of duties
d. Monitoring of controls

Q5-53. All of the following are controls for cash received over the counter *except*

a. the cash drawer should open only when the sales clerk enters an amount on the keys.
b. the customer should be able to see the amounts entered into the cash register.
c. the sales clerk must have access to the cash register tape.
d. a printed receipt must be given to the customer.

Q5-54. If a bookkeeper mistakenly recorded a $45 deposit as $54, the error would be shown on the bank reconciliation as a

a. $9 deduction from the book balance.
b. $9 addition to the book balance.
c. $54 deduction from the book balance.
d. $54 addition to the book balance.

Q5-55. If a bank reconciliation included a deposit in transit of $780, the entry to record this reconciling item would include

a. a debit to cash for $780.
b. a credit to cash for $780.
c. a credit to prepaid insurance for $780.
d. Nothing, as no entry is required.

Q5-56. Before paying an invoice for goods received on account, the controller or treasurer should ensure that

a. the company is paying for the goods it ordered.
b. the company has not already paid this invoice.
c. the company is paying for the goods it actually received.
d. all of the above are taken into account.

Q5-57. Under the allowance method for uncollectible receivables, the entry to record uncollectible-account expense has what effect on the financial statements?

a. Decreases assets and has no effect on net income
b. Decreases net income and decreases assets
c. Decreases owners' equity and increases liabilities
d. Increases expenses and increases owners' equity

Q5-58. Van Gogh Company uses the aging method to adjust the allowance for uncollectible accounts at the end of the period. At December 31, the balance of accounts receivable is $240,000 and the allowance for uncollectible accounts has a credit balance of $5,000 (before adjustment). An analysis of accounts receivable produced the following age groups:

Current	$180,000
60 days past due	50,000
Over 60 days past due	10,000
	$240,000

Based on past experience, Van Gogh estimates that the percentage of accounts that will prove to be uncollectible within the three age groups is 2%, 8%, and 20%, respectively. Based on these facts, the adjusting entry for uncollectible accounts should be made in the amount of

a. $9,600.
b. $5,000.
c. $4,600.
d. $14,600.

Q5-59. Refer to Question 5-58. The net receivables on the Balance Sheet is

a. $230,400.
b. $235,000.
c. $235,400.
d. $225,400.

Q5-60. Gordon Company uses the aging method in setting its allowance for doubtful receivables. Allowance for doubtful accounts prior to adjustment has a credit balance of $2,900. Management estimates that due to the economic crisis, a higher level of allowance is necessary and decides that a $5,600 allowance is an appropriate amount at the year-end. The amount of expense to report on the Income Statement will be

a. $2,700.
b. $5,600.
c. $8,500.
d. $2,900.

Problems MyLab Accounting

Select Group A and Group B problems can be found within MyLab Accounting, an online homework and practice environment. Your instructor may ask you to complete select problems using MyLab Accounting.

Group A

■ writing assignment

P5-61A. ***(Learning Objectives 1, 2: Learning about fraud; identifying internal control weakness)*** Each of the following situations reveals an internal control weakness:

a. In evaluating the internal control over cash payments of Bermingham Manufacturing, an auditor learns that the purchasing agent is responsible for purchasing diamonds for use in the company's manufacturing process, approving the invoices for payment, and signing the checks. No supervisor reviews the purchasing agent's work.

b. Mary Angela owns an architectural firm. Angela's staff consists of 20 professional architects, and Angela manages the office. Often, Angela's work requires her to travel to meet with clients. During the past six months, Angela has observed that when she returns from a business trip, the architecture jobs in the office have not progressed satisfactorily. Angela learns that when she is away, three of her senior architects take over office management and neglect their normal duties. One employee could manage the office.

c. J. T. Derby has been an employee of the City of Maron for many years. Because the city is small, Derby performs all accounting duties, plus opening the mail, preparing the bank deposit, and preparing the bank reconciliation.

Requirements

1. Identify the missing internal control characteristic in each situation.
2. Identify each firm's possible problem.
3. Propose a solution to the problem.

■ writing assignment

P5-62A. ***(Learning Objective 3: Using the bank reconciliation as a control device)*** The cash data of Dursley Automotive for July 20X6 follow:

Cash					Account No. 101
Date	Item	Jrnl. Ref.	Debit	Credit	Balance
Jul. 1	Balance				7,900
31		CR6	9,154		17,054
31		CP11		9,097	7,957

Cash Receipts (CR)		Cash Payments (CP)	
Date	Cash Debit	Check No.	Cash Credit
Jul. 2	$2,771	3113	$1,503
8	516	3114	1,149
10	1,682	3115	1,620
16	871	3116	19
22	352	3117	825
29	934	3118	91
30	2,028	3119	450
Total	$9,154	3120	975
		3121	215
		3122	2,250
		Total	$9,097

Dursley received the following bank statement on July 31, 20X6:

spreadsheet

	A	B		C
1	**Bank Statement for July 20X6**			
2	Beginning balance			$ 7,900
3	Deposits and other additions:			
4	July 1	$ 760	EFT	
5	4	2,771		
6	9	516		
7	12	1,682		
8	17	871		
9	22	352		
10	23	1,270	BC	8,222
11	Checks and other deductions:			
12	July 7	$1,503		
13	13	1,260		
14	14	417	US	
15	15	1,149		
16	18	19		
17	21	343	EFT	
18	26	825		
19	30	91		
20	30	28	SC	(5,635)
21	Ending balance			$10,487
22				

Explanation: BC—bank collection, EFT—electronic funds transfer, US—unauthorized signature, SC—service charge

Additional data for the bank reconciliation include the following:

a. The EFT deposit was a receipt of monthly rent. The EFT debit was a monthly insurance payment.

b. The unauthorized signature check was received from a customer.

c. The correct amount of check number 3115, a payment on account, is $1,260. (Dursley's accountant mistakenly recorded the check for $1,620.)

Requirements

1. Prepare the Dursley Automotive bank reconciliation at July 31, 20X6.
2. Describe how a bank account and the bank reconciliation help the general manager control Dursley's cash.

LO 2

■ spreadsheet

P5-63A. ***(Learning Objective 2: Identifying internal control weakness in sales and cash receipts)*** Smooth Skin Care makes all sales on credit. Cash receipts arrive by mail, usually within 30 days of the sale. Kate Marco opens envelopes and separates the checks from the accompanying remittance advices. Marco forwards the checks to another employee, who makes the daily bank deposit but has no access to the accounting records. Marco sends the remittance advices, which show the amount of cash received, to the accounting department for entry in the accounts receivable. Marco's only other duty is to grant allowances to customers. (An allowance decreases the amount that the customer must pay.) When Marco receives a customer check for less than the full amount of the invoice, she records the allowance in the accounting records and forwards the document to the accounting department.

Requirement

1. You are a new employee of Smooth Skin Care. Write a memo to the company president identifying the internal control weakness in this situation. State how to correct the weakness.

LO 3

■ writing assignment

P5-64A. ***(Learning Objective 3: Preparing a bank reconciliation and the related journal entries)*** The August 31 bank statement of Grayson Engineering Associates has just arrived from Carolina First Bank. To prepare the Grayson bank reconciliation, you gather the following data:

a. Grayson's Cash account shows a balance of $8,158.71 on August 31.
b. The August 31 bank balance is $8,789.23.
c. The bank statement shows that Grayson earned $18.58 of interest on its bank balance during August. This amount was added to Grayson's bank balance.
d. Grayson pays utilities ($740) and insurance ($290) by EFT.
e. The following Grayson checks did not clear the bank by August 31:

Check No.	Amount
237	$401.00
288	74.82
291	33.25
293	165.55
294	236.00
295	47.75
296	107.85

f. The bank statement includes a deposit of $895.15, collected on account by the bank on behalf of Grayson.
g. The bank statement lists a $7.50 bank service charge.
h. On August 31, the Grayson treasurer deposited $354.38, which will appear on the September bank statement.
i. The bank statement includes a $268.40 deposit that Grayson did not make. The bank added $268.40 to Grayson's account for another company's deposit.
j. The bank statement includes two charges for returned checks from customers. One is a $158.50 check received from a customer with the imprint "Unauthorized Signature." The other is a nonsufficient funds check in the amount of $67.45 received from another customer.

Requirements

1. Prepare the bank reconciliation for Grayson Engineering Associates.
2. Journalize the August 31 transactions needed to update Grayson's Cash account. Include an explanation for each entry.

P5-65A. ***(Learning Objective 3: Preparing a cash budget and using cash-flow information)*** John Watson, chief financial officer of Scott Wireless, is responsible for the company's budgeting process. Watson's staff is preparing the Scott cash budget for 20X7. A key input to the budgeting process is last year's statement of cash flows, which follows (amounts in thousands): LO 3

	A	B
1	**Scott Wireless Statement of Cash Flows 20X6**	
2	**(In thousands)**	
3	**Cash Flows from Operating Activities**	
4	Collections from customers	$ 64,000
5	Interest received	300
6	Purchases of inventory	(49,000)
7	Operating expenses	(13,500)
8	Net cash provided by operating activities	1,800
9	**Cash Flows from Investing Activities**	
10	Purchases of equipment	(4,800)
11	Purchases of investments	(400)
12	Sales of investments	500
13	Net cash used for investing activities	(4,700)
14	**Cash Flows from Financing Activities**	
15	Payment of long-term debt	(400)
16	Issuance of shares	1,700
17	Payment of cash dividends	(300)
18	Net cash provided by financing activities	1,000
19	**Cash**	
20	Increase (decrease) in Cash	(1,900)
21	Cash, beginning of year	3,400
22	Cash, end of year	$ 1,500
23		

Requirements

1. Prepare the Scott Wireless cash budget for 20X7. Date the budget simply "20X7" and denote the beginning and ending cash balances as "beginning" and "ending." Assume the company expects 20X7 to be the same as 20X6, but with the following changes:
   a. In 20X7, the company expects a 12% increase in collections from customers and a 25% increase in purchases of inventory.
   b. There will be no sales of investments in 20X7.
   c. Scott plans to issue no shares in 20X7.
   d. Scott plans to end the year with a cash balance of $3,500 (thousand).
2. Does the company's cash budget for 20X7 suggest that Scott is growing, holding steady, or decreasing in size? (Challenge)

P5-66A. ***(Learning Objective 4: Accounting for revenue, collections, and uncollectibles)*** This problem takes you through the accounting for sales, receivables, and uncollectibles for Mail Time Corp., the overnight shipper. By selling on credit, the company cannot expect to collect 100% of its accounts receivable. At May 31, 20X6 and 20X7, respectively, Mail Time Corp. reported the following on its Balance Sheet (in millions of dollars): LO 4 ■ **writing assignment**

	May 31	
	20X7	20X6
Accounts receivable	$3,703	$3,345
Less: Allowance for uncollectible accounts	(139)	(166)
Accounts receivable, net	$3,564	$3,179

During the year ended May 31, 20X7, Mail Time Corp. earned service revenue and collected cash from customers. Assume that Mail Time wrote off uncollectible receivables. At year-end Mail Time ended with the foregoing May 31, 20X7, balances.

Requirements

1. Prepare T-accounts for Accounts Receivable and Allowance for Uncollectibles and insert the May 31, 20X6, balances as given.
2. Journalize the following assumed transactions of Mail Time Corp. for the year ended May 31, 20X7 (explanations are not required):
   a. Service revenue on account, $32,491 million
   b. Collections from customers on account, $31,779 million
   c. Write-offs of uncollectible accounts receivable, $354 million
   d. Uncollectible-account expense, $327 million
3. Post your entries to the Accounts Receivable and the Allowance for Uncollectibles T-accounts.
4. Compute the ending balances for the two T-accounts and compare your balances to the actual May 31, 20X7, amounts. They should be the same.
5. Show what Mail Time would report on its Income Statement for the year ended May 31, 20X7.

LO 4

P5-67A. ***(Learning Objective 4: Using the aging approach for uncollectibles)*** The September 30, 20X7, records of Effective Communications include these accounts:

Accounts Receivable	$270,000
Allowance for Doubtful Accounts	(9,100)

At year-end (December 31), the company ages its receivables and adjusts the balance in Allowance for Doubtful Accounts to correspond to the aging schedule. During the last quarter of 20X7, the company completed the following selected transactions:

Nov. 30	Wrote off as uncollectible the $1,100 account receivable from Black Carpets and the $500 account receivable from Old Timer Antiques.
Dec. 31	Adjusted the Allowance for Doubtful Accounts and recorded doubtful-account expense at year-end, based on the aging of receivables, which follows.

	Age of Accounts			
Accounts Receivable	1–30 Days	31–60 Days	61–90 Days	Over 90 Days
$235,000	$150,000	$35,000	$20,000	$30,000
Estimated percent uncollectible	0.2%	2.0%	8.0%	40.0%

Requirements

1. Record the transactions in the journal. Explanations are not required.
2. Prepare a T-account for Allowance for Doubtful Accounts and post to that account.
3. Show how Effective Communications will report its accounts receivable on its Balance Sheet at December 31, 20X7.

LO 4

P5-68A. ***(Learning Objective 4: Accounting for notes receivable and accrued interest revenue)*** Healthy Meal completed the following selected transactions.

20X6	
Oct. 31	Sold goods to Buy Low Foods, receiving a $36,000, three-month, 6.50% note.
Dec. 31	Made an adjusting entry to accrue interest on the Buy Low Foods note.
20X7	
Jan. 31	Collected the Buy Low Foods note.
Feb. 18	Received a 90-day, 8.25%, $7,400 note from Dutton Market on account.
19	Sold the Dutton Market note to Amherst Bank, receiving cash of $7,300. (Debit the difference to financing expense.)
Nov. 11	Lent $16,400 cash to Street Provisions, receiving a 90-day, 9.50% note.
Dec. 31	Accrued the interest on the Street Provisions note.

Requirements

1. Record the transactions in Healthy Meal's journal. Round interest amounts to the nearest dollar. Explanations are not required.
2. Show what Healthy Meal will report on its comparative classified Balance Sheet at December 31, 20X7, and December 31, 20X6.

P5-69A. ***(Learning Objective 5: Using ratio data to evaluate a company's financial position)*** The comparative financial statements of Highland Pools, Inc., for 20X7, 20X6, and 20X5 included the following select data:

	(In millions)		
	20X7	20X6	20X5
Balance Sheet			
Current assets:			
Cash	$ 80	$ 70	$ 60
Short-term investments	145	170	120
Receivables, net of allowance for doubtful accounts of $7, $6, and $4, respectively	290	260	250
Inventories	355	345	300
Prepaid expenses	60	30	55
Total current assets	$ 930	$ 875	$ 785
Total current liabilities	$ 590	$ 640	$ 690
Income Statement			
Net sales	$5,900	$5,150	$4,230

Requirements

1. Compute current ratio and days' sales in receivables for 20X7 and 20X6:
2. Which ratio(s) improved from 20X6 to 20X7 and which ratio(s) deteriorated? Is this trend favorable or unfavorable?

Group B

P5-70B. ***(Learning Objectives 1, 2: Learning about fraud; identifying internal control weakness)*** Each of the following situations reveals an internal control weakness:

Situation a. In evaluating the internal control over cash payments of Chester Manufacturing, an auditor learns that the purchasing agent is responsible for purchasing diamonds for use in the company's manufacturing process, approving the invoices for payment, and signing the checks. No supervisor reviews the purchasing agent's work.

Situation b. Rose White owns an architectural firm. White's staff consists of 15 professional architects, and White manages the office. Often, White's work requires her to travel to meet with clients. During the past six months, White has observed that when she returns from a business trip, the architecture jobs in the office have not progressed satisfactorily. White learns that when she is away, two of her senior architects take over office management and neglect their normal duties. One employee could manage the office.

Situation c. M. J. Davis has been an employee of the City of Northport for many years. Because the city is small, Davis performs all accounting duties, plus opening the mail, preparing the bank deposit, and preparing the bank reconciliation.

Requirements

1. Identify the missing internal control characteristic in each situation.
2. Identify each firm's possible problem.
3. Propose a solution to the problem.

LO 3

■ writing assignment

■ spreadsheet

P5-71B. ***(Learning Objective 3: Using the bank reconciliation as a control device)*** The cash data of Dudley Automotive for January 20X6 follow:

Cash — Account No. 101

Date	Item	Jrnl. Ref.	Debit	Credit	Balance
Jan. 1	Balance				7,200
31		CR 6	9,156		16,356
31		CP 11		10,023	6,333

Cash Receipts (CR)		Cash Payments (CP)	
Date	Cash Debit	Check No.	Cash Credit
Jan. 2	$2,726	3113	$ 1,475
8	572	3114	1,925
10	1,647	3115	1,530
16	837	3116	32
22	436	3117	870
29	865	3118	132
30	2,073	3119	483
Total	$9,156	3120	995
		3121	249
		3122	2,332
		Total	$10,023

Dudley received the following bank statement on January 31, 20X6:

	A	B		C
1	**Bank Statement for January 20X6**			
2	Beginning balance			€ 7,200
3	Deposits and other additions:			
4	Jan. 1	$ 680	EFT	
5	4	2,726		
6	9	572		
7	12	1,647		
8	17	837		
9	22	436		
10	23	1,340	BC	8,238
11	Checks and other deductions:			
12	Jan. 7	€1,475		
13	13	1,350		
14	14	436	US	
15	15	1,925		
16	18	32		
17	21	313	EFT	
18	26	870		
19	30	132		
20	30	22	SC	(6,555)
21	Ending balance			€ 8,883
22				

Explanation: BC—bank collection, EFT—electronic funds transfer, US—unauthorized signature, SC—service charge

Additional data for the bank reconciliation include the following:

a. The EFT deposit was a receipt of monthly rent. The EFT debit was a monthly insurance expense.

b. The unauthorized signature check was received from a customer.

c. The correct amount of check number 3115, a payment on account, is €1,350. (Dudley's accountant mistakenly recorded the check for €1,530.)

Requirements

1. Prepare the Dudley Automotive bank reconciliation at January 31, 20X6.
2. Describe how a bank account and the bank reconciliation help the general manager control Dudley's cash.

LO 2 ■ **writing assignment**

P5-72B. ***(Learning Objective 2: Identifying internal control weakness in sales and cash receipts)*** Glowing Skin Care makes all sales on credit. Cash receipts arrive by mail, usually within 30 days of the sale. Emily Nolan opens envelopes and separates the checks from the accompanying remittance advices. Nolan forwards the checks to another employee, who makes the daily bank deposit but has no access to the accounting records. Nolan sends the remittance advices, which show the amount of cash received, to the accounting department for entry in the accounts receivable. Nolan's only other duty is to grant allowances to customers. (An *allowance* decreases the amount that the customer must pay.) When Nolan receives a customer check for less than the full amount of the invoice, she records the allowance in the accounting records and forwards the document to the accounting department.

Requirement

1. You are a new employee of Glowing Skin Care. Write a memo to the company president identifying the internal control weakness in this situation. State how to correct the weakness.

LO 3

■ spreadsheet

P5-73B. ***(Learning Objective 3: Preparing a bank reconciliation and the related journal entries)*** The October 31 bank statement of Drake Engineering Associates has just arrived from Carolina First Bank. To prepare the Drake bank reconciliation, you gather the following data:

a. Drake's Cash account shows a balance of €7,506.86 on October 31.
b. The October 31 bank balance is €8,353.87.
c. The bank statement shows that Drake earned €15.65 of interest on its bank balance during October. This amount was added to Drake's bank balance.
d. Drake pays utilities (€780) and insurance (€260) by EFT.
e. The following Drake checks did not clear the bank by October 31:

Check No.	Amount
237	€403.15
288	78.98
291	36.39
293	155.45
294	234.00
295	47.50
296	106.79

f. The bank statement includes a deposit of €925.20, collected on account by the bank on behalf of Drake.
g. The bank statement lists a €8.25 bank service charge.
h. On October 31, the Drake treasurer deposited €350.80, which will appear on the November bank statement.
i. The bank statement includes a €496.10 deposit that Drake did not make. The bank added €496.10 to Drake's account for another company's deposit.
j. The bank statement includes two charges for returned checks from customers. One is a €185.50 check received from a customer with the imprint "Unauthorized Signature." The other is a nonsufficient funds check in the amount of €67.65 received from another customer.

Requirements

1. Prepare the bank reconciliation for Drake Engineering Associates.
2. Journalize the October 31 transactions needed to update Drake's Cash account. Include an explanation for each entry.

LO 3

P5-74B. ***(Learning Objective 3: Preparing a cash budget and using cash-flow information)*** Don Beecher, chief financial officer of Carlisle Wireless, is responsible for the company's budgeting process. Beecher's staff is preparing the Carlisle cash budget for 20X7. A key input to the budgeting process is last year's statement of cash flows, which follows (amount in thousands):

	A	B
1	**Carlisle Wireless** **Statement of Cash Flows** **20X6**	
2	**(In thousands)**	
3	**Cash Flows from Operating Activities**	
4	Collections from customers	€ 62,000
5	Interest received	700
6	Purchases of inventory	(47,000)
7	Operating expenses	(13,700)
8	Net cash provided by operating activities	2,000
9	**Cash Flows from Investing Activities**	
10	Purchases of equipment	(4,100)
11	Purchases of investments	(300)
12	Sales of investments	900
13	Net cash used for investing activities	(3,500)
14	**Cash Flows from Financing Activities**	
15	Payment of long-term debt	(500)
16	Issuance of shares	1,500
17	Payment of cash dividends	(400)
18	Net cash provided by financing activities	600
19	**Cash**	
20	Increase (decrease) in Cash	(900)
21	Cash, beginning of year	2,800
22	Cash, end of year	€ 1,900
23		

Requirements

1. Prepare the Carlisle Wireless cash budget for 20X7. Date the budget simply "20X7" and denote the beginning and ending cash balances as "beginning" and "ending." Assume the company expects 20X7 to be the same as 2010, but with the following changes:
   a. In 20X7, the company expects a 15% increase in collections from customers and a 22% increase in purchases of inventory.
   b. There will be no sales of investments in 20X7.
   c. Carlisle plans to issue no shares in 20X7.
   d. Carlisle plans to end the year with a cash balance of €3,650 (thousand).
2. Does the company's cash budget for 20X7 suggest that Carlisle is growing, holding steady, or decreasing in size?

P5-75B. *(Learning Objective 4: Accounting for revenue, collections, and uncollectibles)* This problem takes you through the accounting for sales, receivables, and uncollectibles for On-time Delivery Corp, the overnight shipper. By selling on credit, the company cannot expect to collect 100% of its accounts receivable. At May 31, 20X6 and 20X7, respectively, On-time Delivery Corp. reported the following on its Balance Sheet (in millions of euros): LO 4

	May 31	
	20X7	20X6
Accounts receivable	€3,693	€3,435
Less: Allowance for uncollectible accounts	(129)	(156)
Accounts receivable, net	€3,564	€3,279

During the year ended May 31, 20X7, On-time Delivery Corp. earned sales revenue and collected cash from customers. Assume that On-time Delivery Corp. wrote off uncollectible receivables. At year-end, On-time Delivery Corp. ended with the foregoing May 31, 20X7, balances.

Requirements

1. Prepare T-accounts for Accounts Receivable and Allowance for Uncollectibles, and insert the May 31, 20X6, balances as given.
2. Journalize the following transactions of On-time Delivery for the year ended May 31, 20X7. (Explanations are not required.)
   a. Service revenue on account, €32,587 million.
   b. Collections from customers on account, €31,979 million.
   c. Write-offs of uncollectible accounts receivable, €350 million.
   d. Uncollectible-account expense, €323 million.
3. Post to the Accounts Receivable and Allowance for Uncollectibles T-accounts.
4. Compute the ending balances for the two T-accounts and compare your balances to the actual May 31, 20X7, amounts. They should be the same.
5. Show what On-time Delivery should report on its Income Statement for the year ended May 31, 20X7.

LO 4 **P5-76B.** ***(Learning Objective 4: Using the aging approach for uncollectibles)*** The September 30, 20X7, records of Image Communications include these accounts:

Accounts receivable	€290,000
Allowance for doubtful accounts	(9,700)

At year-end, the company ages its receivables and adjusts the balance in Allowance for Doubtful Accounts to correspond to the aging schedule. During the last quarter of 20X7, the company completed the following selected transactions:

Dec. 28	Wrote off as uncollectible the €1,300 account receivable from Blue Carpets and the €700 account receivable from Show-N-Tell Antiques.
Dec. 31	Adjusted the Allowance for Doubtful Accounts and recorded doubtful-account expense at year-end, based on the aging of receivables, which follows.

	Age of Accounts			
Total Balance	1–30 Days	31–60 Days	61–90 Days	Over 90 Days
€238,000	€160,000	€40,000	€18,000	€20,000
Estimated uncollectible	0.5%	1.0%	10.0%	50.0%

Requirements

1. Record the transactions in the journal. Explanations are not required.
2. Prepare a T-account for Allowance for Doubtful Accounts and post to that account.
3. Show how Image Communications will report its accounts receivable on its Balance Sheet at December 31, 20X7.

LO 4 **P5-77B.** ***(Learning Objective 4: Accounting for notes receivable and accrued interest revenue)*** Organic Meals completed the following selected transactions:

20X6	
Nov. 30	Sold goods to Bragg Market, receiving a €30,000, three-month, 4.25% note.
Dec. 31	Made an adjusting entry to accrue interest on the Bragg Market note.
20X7	
Feb. 28	Collected the Bragg Market note.
Mar. 1	Received a 90-day, 8.50%, €7,500 note from Don's Market on account.
1	Sold the Don's Market note to Chelmsford Bank, receiving cash of €7,400. (Debit the difference to financing expense.)
Dec. 16	Lent €14,400 cash to Stratford Provisions, receiving a 90-day, 10.00% note.
Dec. 31	Accrued the interest on the Stratford Provisions note.

Requirements

1. Record the transactions in Organic Meals' journal. Round all amounts to the nearest dollar. Explanations are not required.
2. Show what Organic Meals will report on its comparative classified Balance Sheet at December 31, 20X7, and December 31, 20X6.

P5-78B. *(Learning Objective 5: Using ratio data to evaluate a company's financial position)* The comparative financial statements of Gold Pools, Inc., for 20X7, 20X6, and 20X5 included the following select data:

	(In millions)		
	20X7	20X6	20X5
Balance Sheet			
Current assets:			
Cash	€ 70	€ 80	€ 50
Short-term investments	145	160	110
Receivables, net of allowance for doubtful accounts of €7, €6, and €4, respectively	260	230	200
Inventories	360	345	310
Prepaid expenses	70	10	40
Total current assets	€ 905	€ 825	€ 710
Total current liabilities	€ 550	€ 600	€ 660
Income Statement			
Net sales	€5,890	€5,120	€4,210

Requirements

1. Compute current ratio and days' sales in receivables for 20X7 and 20X6.
2. Which ratio(s) improved from 20X6 to 20X7 and which ratio(s) deteriorated? Is this trend favorable or unfavorable?

APPLY YOUR KNOWLEDGE

Decision Cases

Case 1. *(Learning Objectives 1, 2, 3: Learning about fraud; using a bank reconciliation to detect a theft)* Environmental Concerns, Inc., has poor internal control. Recently, Oscar Benz, the manager, has suspected the bookkeeper of stealing. Details of the business's cash position at September 30 follow.

a. The Cash account shows a balance of $10,912. This amount includes a September 30 deposit of $3,994 that does not appear on the September 30 bank statement.

b. The September 30 bank statement shows a balance of $8,324. The bank statement lists a $200 bank collection, a $13 service charge, and a $41 NSF check. The accountant has not recorded any of these items.

c. At September 30, the following checks are outstanding:

Check No.	Amount
154	$116
256	150
278	853
291	990
292	206
293	145

d. The bookkeeper receives all incoming cash and makes the bank deposits. He also reconciles the monthly bank statement. Here is his September 30 reconciliation:

Balance per books, September 30		$10,912
Add: Outstanding check		1,260
Bank collection		200
Subtotal		12,372
Less: Deposits in transit	$3,994	
Service charge	13	
NSF check	41	(4,048)
Balance per bank, September 30		$ 8,324

Requirement

1. Benz has requested that you determine whether the bookkeeper has stolen cash from the business and, if so, how much. He also asks you to explain how the bookkeeper attempted to conceal the theft. To make this determination, you perform a proper bank reconciliation. There are no bank or book errors. Benz also asks you to evaluate the internal controls and to recommend any changes needed to improve them.

LO 1 2 **Case 2.** ***(Learning Objectives 1, 2: Learning about fraud; correcting an internal control weakness)*** This case is based on an actual situation experienced by one of the authors. Gilead Construction, headquartered in Topeka, Kansas, built a motel in Kansas City. The construction foreman, Slim Pickins, hired the workers for the project. Pickins had his workers fill out the necessary tax forms and sent the employment documents to the home office.

Work on the motel began on May 1 and ended in December. Each Thursday evening, Pickins filled out a time card that listed the hours worked by each employee during the five-day work-week ended at 5 p.m. on Thursday. Pickins faxed the time sheets to the home office, which prepared the payroll checks on Friday mornings. Pickins drove to the home office after lunch every Friday, picked up the payroll checks, and returned to the construction site. At 5 p.m. on Fridays, Pickins distributed the paychecks to the workers.

a. Describe in detail the internal control weakness in this situation. Specify what negative result could occur because of the internal control weakness.

b. Describe what you would do to correct the internal control weakness.

LO 3 **Case 3.** ***(Learning Objective 3: Determining allowance for doubtful receivables using the aging method, with and without additional information about loss events)*** Two accounting interns, Serene and Joel, were tasked by you, their supervisor, to propose the required amount of allowance at December 31, 20X7, for Alyssa Candy Empire (ACE), a distributor of specialty confectionery. Data provided to the two interns include an aging schedule below:

Age of Account Receivables

Receivables	Not Yet Due	1–30 Days	31–60 Days	Over 60 Days	Total
Customer A	400				400
Customer B	100	100			200
Customer C	300	200	600	100	1,200
...	...	...	...	...	...
Totals	11,060	1,363	370	1,093	13,886
Percentage uncollectible	1.0%	5.0%	12.5%	20.0%	
Required allowance	111	68	46	219	444

Serene evaluated ACE's historical records of customer defaults and concluded that the likelihood of a receivable becoming bad is correlated to the age of the receivable. She assigned a 1%, 5%, 10%, and 20% likelihood for each age group of receivables.

Joel took another approach and evaluated the likelihood of receivable impairment customer by customer. His research shows that Customer A is a new customer and since it is not yet overdue, there is only a 1% chance that it will not be collected. Customer B and Customer D are long-time customers, and whilst they may pay a little later than the usual credit term of 30 days, the likelihood of not being able to collect their receivables is only 10%. Joel has read that Customer C was not able to make its loan repayments last month. Newspaper articles also point to some worry about Customer C's ability to continue as a growing concern. Joel estimated that it is almost certain that the amount owing would be uncollectible. Customer E, located in another country, has also experienced significant decline in business due to a severe recession in the country. Joel believes that there is a 20% chance that the receivables may be impaired.

Joel and Serene performed their analysis and reported back to you with their recommendations. Whose recommendation will you accept? Why?

Ethical Issue

For each of the following situations, answer the following questions:

1. What is the ethical issue in this situation?
2. What are the alternatives?
3. Who are the stakeholders? What are the possible consequences to each? Analyze from the following standpoints: (a) economic, (b) legal, and (c) ethical.
4. Place yourself in the role of the decision maker. What would you do? How would you justify your decision?

Issue 1. Sunrise Bank recently appointed the accounting firm of Smith, Godfroy, and Hannaford as the bank's auditor. Sunrise quickly became one of Smith, Godfroy, and Hannaford's largest clients. Subject to banking regulations, Sunrise must provide for any expected losses on notes receivable that Sunrise may not collect in full.

During the course of the audit, Smith, Godfroy, and Hannaford determined that three large notes receivable of Sunrise seem questionable. Smith, Godfroy, and Hannaford discussed these loans with Susan Carter, controller of Sunrise. Carter assured the auditors that these notes were good and that the makers of the notes will be able to pay their notes after the economy improves.

Smith, Godfroy, and Hannaford stated that Sunrise must record a loss for a portion of these notes receivable to account for the likelihood that Sunrise may never collect their full amount. Carter objected and threatened to dismiss Smith, Godfroy, and Hannaford if the auditor demands that the bank record the loss. Smith, Godfroy, and Hannaford want to keep Sunrise as a client. In fact, Smith, Godfroy, and Hannaford were counting on the revenue from the Sunrise audit to finance an expansion of the firm.

Issue 2. Barry Galvin is executive vice president of Community Bank. Active in community affairs, Galvin serves on the board of directors of The Salvation Army. The Salvation Army is expanding rapidly and is considering relocating. At a recent meeting, The Salvation Army decided to buy 250 acres of land on the edge of town. The owner of the property is Olga Nadar, a major depositor in Community Bank. Nadar is completing a bitter divorce, and Galvin knows that Nadar is eager to sell her property. In view of Nadar's difficult situation, Galvin believes Nadar would accept a low offer for the land. Realtors have appraised the property at $3.6 million.

Issue 3. Community Bank has a loan receivable from IMS Chocolates. IMS is six months late in making payments to the bank, and Jan French, a Community Bank vice president, is assisting IMS to restructure its debt.

French learns that IMS is depending on landing a contract with Snicker Foods, another Community Bank client. French also serves as Snicker Foods' loan officer at the bank. In this capacity, French is aware that Snicker is considering bankruptcy. No one else outside Snicker Foods knows this. French has been a great help to IMS, and IMS's owner is counting on French's expertise in loan workouts to advise the company through this difficult process. To help the bank collect on this large loan, French has a strong motivation to alert IMS of Snicker's financial difficulties.

Issue 4. Sunnyvale Loan Company is in the consumer loan business. Sunnyvale borrows from banks and loans out the money at higher interest rates. Sunnyvale's bank requires Sunnyvale to submit quarterly financial statements to keep its line of credit. Sunnyvale's main asset is Accounts Receivable. Therefore, Uncollectible-Account Expense and Allowance for Uncollectible Accounts are important accounts for the company.

	20X7	20X6	20X5
	(In thousands)		
Sales	$1,475	$1,001	$902
Cost of goods sold	876	647	605
Gross profit	599	354	297
Other expenses	518	287	253
Net profit or (loss) before taxes	$ 81	$ 67	$ 44
Accounts receivable	$ 128	$ 107	$ 94
Allowance for doubtful accounts	13	11	9

Kimberly Burnham, the company's owner, prefers that net income reflect a steady increase in a smooth pattern, rather than increase in some periods and decrease in other periods. To report smoothly increasing net income, Burnham underestimates Uncollectible-Account Expense in some periods. In other periods, Burnham overestimates the expense. She reasons that the income overstatements roughly offset the income understatements over time.

Focus on Financials: | Nestlé

This case spans all 12 chapters and is based on the consolidated financial statements of Nestlé. As you work with Nestlé throughout this course, you will develop the confidence and ability to use the financial statements of other companies as well. Refer to Nestlé's financial statements in Appendix A. If you wish, you can obtain the full annual report from www.nestle.com/investors. You may find the information overwhelming for now, but try to spot the key principles that we have discussed in this chapter. It will get progressively easier as you gain familiarity with the elements of the financial statements.

Requirements

1. The bank and cash section of the Balance Sheet shows a balance of CHF 7,990 million as of December 31, 2016, and is made up of many different bank accounts, as well as time deposits, certificates of deposit, and perhaps government securities that are equivalent to cash. Suppose one of Nestlé's year-end bank statements, dated December 31, 2016, has just arrived at company headquarters. Further assume the bank statement shows Nestlé's cash balance at CHF 7,990 million and that Nestlé's record for this bank account has a balance of CHF 8,070 million on the books. You must determine the correct balance for cash in this bank account on December 31, 2016. Suppose you uncover the following reconciling items (all amounts are assumed and are stated in millions):
   a. Interest earned on bank balance, CHF 10 million
   b. Outstanding checks, CHF 80 million
   c. Bank collections of various items, CHF 20 million
   d. Deposits in transit, CHF 30 million
   Prepare a bank reconciliation to show how Nestlé arrived at the correct amount of cash in this bank account at December 31, 2016. Journal entries are not required.
2. Refer to the account in Nestlé's Balance Sheet entitled "trade and other receivables." This amount is typically shown net of allowances for doubtful accounts. What does "net" mean? How does Nestlé determine its allowance for doubtful accounts? You may refer to Note 7.
3. How much is the allowance for bad and doubtful accounts in 2016 and 2015? Assume that the allowance utilized in 2016 was CHF 100 million? Do the journal entries for the writing off of uncollectible accounts and the allowance for bad debts in 2016.

Group Project

You are promoting a rock concert in your area. Assume you organize as a corporation, with each member of your group purchasing $10,000 of the corporation's shares. Therefore, each of you is risking some hard-earned money on this venture. Assume it is April 1 and that the concert will be performed on June 30. Your promotional activities begin immediately, and ticket sales start on May 1. You expect to sell all of the firm's assets, pay all the liabilities, and distribute all remaining cash to the group members by July 31.

Requirements

Write an internal control manual that will help to safeguard the assets of the business. The manual should address the following aspects of internal control:

1. Assign responsibilities among the group members.
2. Authorize individuals, including group members and any outsiders that you need to hire, to perform specific jobs.
3. Separate duties among the group and any employees.
4. Describe all documents needed to account for and safeguard the business's assets.

Quick Check Answers

1. *a*	7. *b*
2. *b*	8. *a*
3. *c*	9. *b* ($2,400 − $90) − ($400 − $90)
4 *a*	10. *c* ($2,800 × 0.06 × 4/12 × 1/4)
5. *b*	11. *b*
6. *d*	12. *b* (365 × [($80,000 + $74,000)/2] ÷ $803,000)

MyLab Accounting

For online homework, exercises, and problems that provide you with immediate feedback, please visit www.myaccountinglab.com.

6 Inventory and Merchandising Operations

SPOTLIGHT | Fast Retailing www.fastretailing.com

Fast Retailing (FR), a public Japanese retail holding company, is the company responsible for the very successful UNIQLO brand, as well as others such as GU, Theory, Comptoir des Cotonniers, Princesse tam.tam, and J Brand. Since the inauguration of its first store in Hiroshima in 1984, UNIQLO's growth in Japan, and later regionally and globally, has been the envy of many retailers. Now Asia's biggest clothing retailer with sales of about US $15 billion, FR is only behind Inditex (Zara) and H&M. FR's Chief Executive, Tadashi Yanai, has set a lofty goal of making the company the world's top apparel retailer by 2020.

As a retailer, inventory is an important part of FR's operations. Its Balance Sheet showed that inventories (at ¥260 billion, about US $2.2 billion) comprise the second largest current asset after cash at ¥355 billion. In FR's inventory policy, on the next page, certain terms, such as *purchase allowance* and *consignment*, may be new to you now, but as you go through the chapter, you will understand how FR determines the amount it reports as inventory on its Balance Sheet.

Sorbis/Shutterstock

ADAPTED EXCERPTS FROM FAST RETAILING'S NOTES TO THE ACCOUNTS

Inventories

Inventories are valued at the lower of cost and net realizable value; the weighted average method is principally used to determine cost. Net realizable value is based on the estimated selling price in the ordinary course of business less any estimated costs to be incurred to sell the goods.

Source: From Fast Retailing, Annual Report, 2015, page 10.

	A	B	C
1	**Fast Retailing Consolidated Balance Sheet**	**At August 31**	
2	**(Adapted, in billions of ¥)**	**2015**	**2014**
3	Cash at banks	¥ 355.2	¥ 314.0
4	Trade and other receivables	44.8	47.4
5	Inventories	260.0	223.2
6	All other current assets	214.4	132.3
7	Total current assets	874.4	717.0
8	Total non-current assets	289.3	275.3
9	Total assets	1,163.7	992.3
10	Total liabilities	388.9	356.3
11	Total equity	774.8	636.0
12	Total liabilities and equity	¥ 1,163.7	¥ 992.3
13			

In addition to this, cost of sales (¥833 billion) was the biggest expense, on net sales of around ¥1,682 billion, on FR's Consolidated Income Statement for the financial year ended August 31, 2015. How was this cost of sales arrived at?

	A	B	C
1	**Fast Retailing Consolidated Income Statement**	**12 Months Ended Aug. 31**	
2	**(Adapted, in billions of ¥)**	**2015**	**2014**
3	Revenue	¥ 1,681.8	¥ 1,382.9
4	Cost of sales	(833.2)	(683.2)
5	Gross profit	848.6	699.7
6	Selling, general, and administrative expenses	(671.9)	(549.2)
7	Other income	8.8	7.0
8	Other expenses	(21.0)	(27.2)
9	Operating profit	164.5	130.3
10	Finance income	17.4	6.0
11	Finance costs	(1.1)	(0.9)
12	Income taxes	(63.3)	(56.1)
13	Profit for the year	¥ 117.5	¥ 79.3
14			

You can see that cost of sales is by far FR's largest expense item. The title *Cost of Merchandise*, *Cost of Sales,* or *Cost of Goods Sold* perfectly describes that expense. In short:

- Fast Retailing buys (or manufactures) inventory, an asset carried on the books at cost.
- Once sold, the inventory is no longer FR's assets. The cost of inventory sold gets shifted into the expense account, called Cost of Sales or Cost of Goods Sold (usually abbreviated COGS). We will use both terms interchangeably.

Inventory is the heart of a merchandising business, and cost of goods sold is the most important expense item for a retailer. Gross profit (or gross margin, line 5 in FR's Consolidated Income Statement) is the difference between net sales and cost of goods sold. This chapter covers the accounting for inventory and cost of goods sold. It also shows you how to further analyze financial statements. Here we focus on inventory, cost of goods sold, and gross profit.

LEARNING OBJECTIVES

1. **Understand** the nature of inventory and retailing operations
2. **Record** inventory-related transactions
3. **Understand and apply** different inventory cost assumptions
4. **Analyze** effects of inventory errors
5. **Evaluate** a company's retailing operations

UNDERSTAND THE NATURE OF INVENTORY AND RETAILING OPERATIONS

1 **Understand** the nature of inventory and retailing operations

We begin by showing how the financial statements of merchandisers or retailers, such as Fast Retailing or Muji, differ from those of service entities, such as Qatar Airways, and accounting firms. The financial statements in Exhibit 6-1 highlight how service entities differ from merchandisers (dollar amounts are assumed).

The basic concept of accounting for merchandise inventory can be illustrated with an example. Suppose a retailer has in stock three shirts that cost $30 each. The retailer sells two shirts for $50 each:

- The Balance Sheet reports the one shirt that the company still holds in inventory.
- The Income Statement reports the cost of the two shirts sold, as shown in Exhibit 6-2.

This is the basic concept of how we identify **inventory**, the asset, from **cost of goods sold** (COGS) or **cost of sales**, the expense. The cost of the inventory sold shifts from asset to expense when the seller delivers the goods to the buyer. We discussed this in Chapter 3, and looked at the revenue recognition criteria stipulated in *IAS 18—Revenue*. For manufacturers, inventory is handled in much the same way as merchandisers, the difference being that manufacturers buy raw materials (accounted for as "raw materials inventory") that they work on (as "work-in-progress, or WIP inventory") until they are ready for sale ("finished goods inventory"). Whatever costs (and overheads) they incur during the production process is added (or allocated) to the WIP inventory. Finished goods that are sold are shown in the Income Statement, and those that remain on hand are shown in the Balance Sheet (Exhibit 6-3).

Exhibit 6-1 | Contrasting a Service Company with a Merchandiser

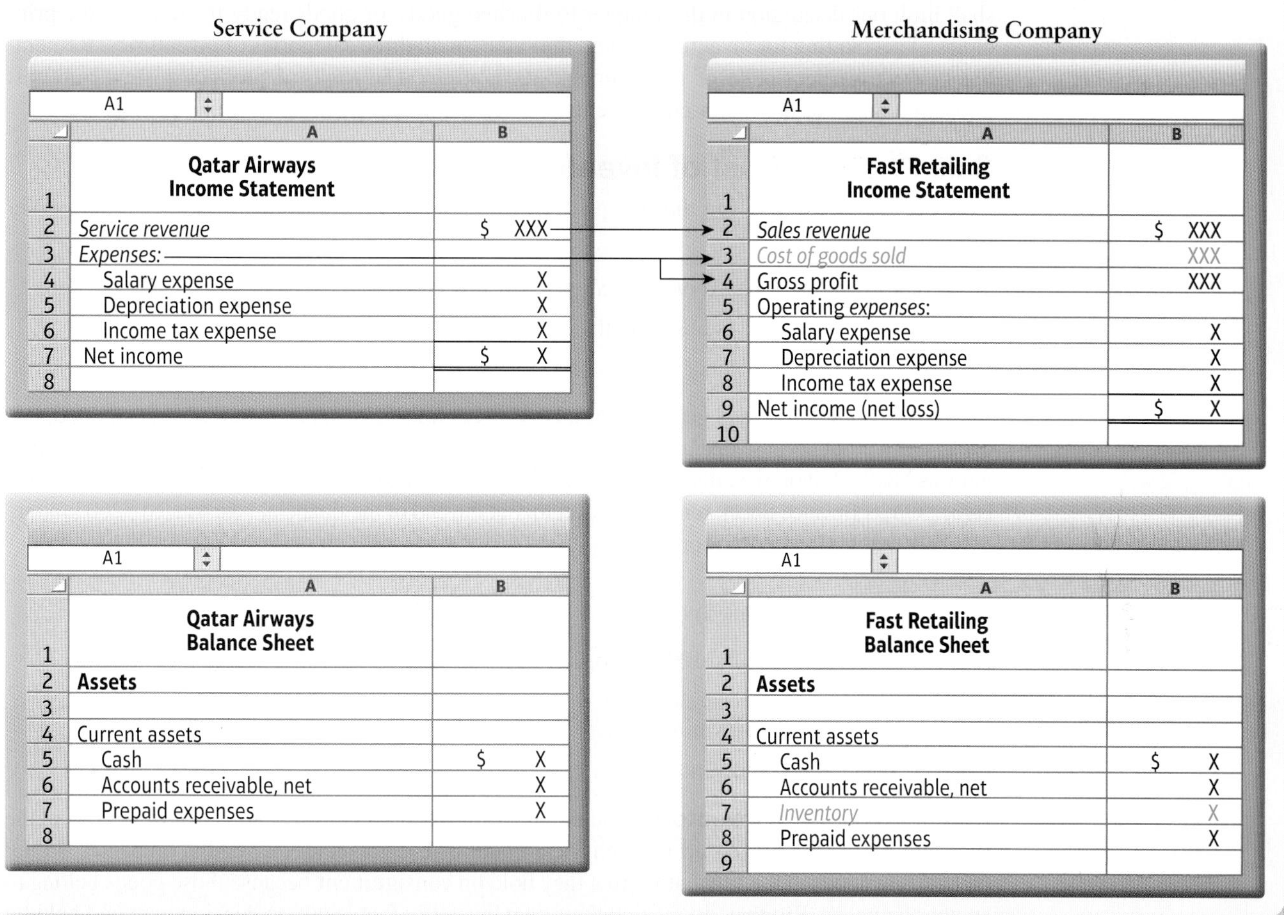

Service Company

	A	B
1	**Qatar Airways Income Statement**	
2	*Service revenue*	$ XXX
3	*Expenses:*	
4	Salary expense	X
5	Depreciation expense	X
6	Income tax expense	X
7	Net income	$ X
8		

	A	B
1	**Qatar Airways Balance Sheet**	
2	**Assets**	
3		
4	Current assets	
5	Cash	$ X
6	Accounts receivable, net	X
7	Prepaid expenses	X
8		

Merchandising Company

	A	B
1	**Fast Retailing Income Statement**	
2	*Sales revenue*	$ XXX
3	*Cost of goods sold*	XXX
4	Gross profit	XXX
5	Operating *expenses:*	
6	Salary expense	X
7	Depreciation expense	X
8	Income tax expense	X
9	Net income (net loss)	$ X
10		

	A	B
1	**Fast Retailing Balance Sheet**	
2	**Assets**	
3		
4	Current assets	
5	Cash	$ X
6	Accounts receivable, net	X
7	*Inventory*	X
8	Prepaid expenses	X
9		

Exhibit 6-2 | Inventory and Cost of Goods Sold When Inventory Cost Is Constant

Balance Sheet (partial)		Income Statement (partial)	
Current assets		Sales revenue	
Cash	$XXX	(2 shirts @ sale price of $50 each)	$100
Short-term investments	XXX	Cost of goods sold	
Accounts receivable	XXX	(2 shirts @ cost of $30 each)	60
Inventory (1 shirt @ cost of $30)	30	Gross profit	$ 40
Prepaid expenses	XXX		

Exhibit 6-3 | Overview of Inventory for Manufacturers

Balance Sheet | Income Statement

Labor Costs → Work in Progress → Finished Goods → Cost of Goods Sold (when sold)

Raw Materials → Work in Progress

Production Overheads → Work in Progress

A retailer is more likely to have only finished goods in its inventory, whereas a manufacturer may have inventories at various stages of completion (from raw materials to finished goods). We shall limit our discussion in this chapter to finished goods, or goods ready for sale, but the principles of accounting for inventory remain the same for all three categories of inventories. Remember how we earlier spoke of management accounting? The topic of product costing and cost allocation methods are major components of a typical management accounting course.

Sale Price vs. Cost of Inventory

Note the difference between the sale price of inventory and the cost of inventory. In our earlier example:

- Sales revenue is based on the *sale price* of inventory sold ($50 per shirt).
- Cost of goods sold is based on the *cost* of inventory sold ($30 per shirt).
- Inventory on the Balance Sheet is based on the *cost* of inventory still on hand ($30 per shirt).

Gross profit, also called **gross margin**, is the excess of sales revenue over cost of goods sold. It is called *gross* profit because operating expenses have not yet been subtracted. Fast Retailing's gross margin was ¥848.6 billion (i.e., net sales of ¥1,681.8 billion less cost of sales of ¥833.2 billion) as shown earlier. On its Balance Sheet, remaining inventory at the end of the financial year totaled ¥260 billion.

This ending inventory represents:

Inventory (Balance Sheet)	=	Number of units of inventory *on hand*	×	Cost per unit of inventory

And the cost of goods sold of ¥833.2 billion represents:

Cost of goods sold (Income Statement)	=	Number of units of inventory *sold*	×	Cost per unit of inventory

Let's see what "units of inventory" and "cost per unit" mean.

Number of Units of Inventory. The number of inventory units on hand is determined from the accounting records, backed up by a physical count of the goods at year-end. Companies do not include any goods in their inventory that they hold on **consignment** because those goods belong to another company. But they do include their own inventory that is out on consignment and held by another company. Companies include inventory in transit from suppliers or in transit to customers that, according to shipping terms, legally belong to them as of the year-end. Shipping terms, otherwise known as *FOB terms*, indicate who owns the goods at a particular time and, therefore, who must pay for the shipping costs. The term **FOB** stands for *free on board* (or *freight on board*). When the vendor invoice specifies *FOB shipping point* (the most common business practice), legal title to the goods passes from the seller to the purchaser when inventory leaves the seller's place of business. The purchaser, therefore, owns the goods while they are in transit and must pay the transportation costs. In the case of goods purchased FOB shipping point, the company purchasing the goods must include goods in transit from suppliers as units in inventory as of the year-end. In the case of goods purchased *FOB destination*, title to the goods does not pass from the seller to the purchaser until the goods arrive at the purchaser's receiving dock. Therefore, these goods are not counted in year-end inventory of the purchasing company. Rather, the cost of these goods is included in inventory of the seller until the goods reach their destination.

This summary may help you understand the difference between FOB shipping point and FOB destination.

Shipping Terms	
FOB Shipping Point	**FOB Destination**
• Ownership of goods changes hands at the shipping point (i.e., the seller's place of business) • The buyer pays for shipping • The buyer includes the goods in its inventory while the goods are in transit	• Ownership of goods changes hands at the destination (i.e., the buyer's place of business) • The seller pays for shipping • The seller includes the goods in its inventory while the goods are in transit

Cost per Unit of Inventory. The cost per unit of inventory poses a challenge because companies purchase goods at different prices throughout the year. Which unit costs go into ending inventory? Which unit costs go to cost of goods sold?

For most inventory, it will be impossible to track the exact cost of items being sold and the exact cost of those that remain at the end of the financial year. Companies make use of inventory cost flow assumptions to help them determine cost of inventory. We will discuss these later, after we understand the basic inventory relationship.

Basic Inventory Relationship

The basic inventory principle will hold regardless of the inventory systems or cost assumptions you use (more on these two concepts later in this chapter). The model is extremely useful because it captures all inventory information for an entire accounting period. Study this model carefully (note that all amounts are assumed). Exhibit 6-4 presents this basic inventory principle.

Exhibit 6-4 | Basic Inventory Relationship

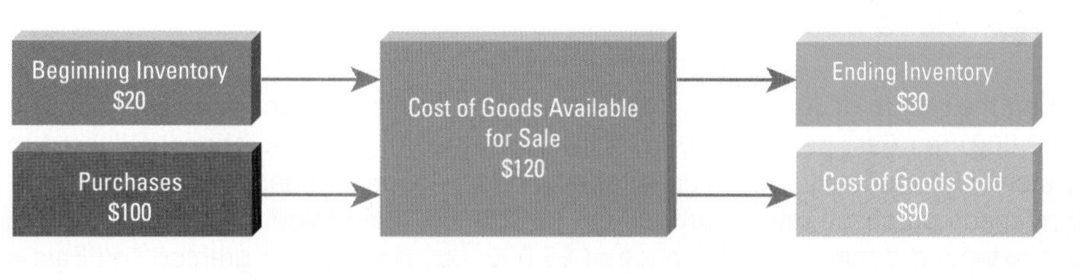

This relationship reinforces what we already know about accounts, ending inventory, and cost of goods sold. If the beginning inventory is $20 and we buy (or produce) $100 worth of goods during a period, we can say that the total goods available for sale is $120. Now, this does not mean that the entire $120 worth of inventory is present all at once in a warehouse somewhere. There may be multiple purchases and sales during the period. Suppose we know that the ending inventory is $30; we can say that cost of goods sold must have been $90. Similarly, if we know cost of goods sold is $90, we must have $30 of inventory left on our Balance Sheet.

Stop & Think

Zerillo & Sons started and ended the financial year with inventory totaling $15,000 and $28,000, respectively. Its cost of goods sold for the period totaled $168,000. How much was the total inventory purchased during the period?

Answer:

Beginning Inventory + Purchases − Ending Inventory = Cost of Goods Sold
$15,000 + Purchases − $28,000 = $168,000
So, Purchases = $168,000 − $15,000 + $28,000 = $181,000

You can rearrange the basic inventory relationship any way you wish in order to find the missing information.

A Closer Look

The cost of inventory on the Balance Sheet represents all the costs that the entity incurred to make its inventory ready for sale. *IAS 2—Inventories* states that the cost of inventories shall comprise all costs of purchase, costs of conversion, and other costs incurred in bringing the inventories to their present location and condition. The costs of purchase of inventories, thus, comprise the purchase price, import duties and other taxes, transport, handling, and other costs directly attributable to the acquisition of finished goods, materials, and services. If an entity receives trade discounts, rebates, and other similar items, they are deducted when determining the costs of purchase. Once the goods are ready for resale, other costs, such as advertising and sales commissions, are *not* included as the cost of inventory. Advertising, sales commissions, and delivery costs are selling expenses that go in the Income Statement, rather than in the Balance Sheet.

Stop & Think

During the month of June 20X4, Ten East, a shoe retailer, bought purchases totaling $600,000. Ten East paid $4,000 in delivery charges to get some shoes delivered to its store. Unfortunately, due to unsuitable goods or incorrect specifications, the company made purchase returns amounting to $25,000. In addition, one of its suppliers also extended a purchase allowance of $5,000, i.e., the supplier granted Ten East a subtraction from the amount owed. Ten East took advantage of early settlement discount schemes offered by its suppliers, and enjoyed a total of $14,000 in discounts. What is Ten East's net cost of inventory purchases?

Purchase price of inventory	$600,000
+ **Freight-in** (the cost to transport the goods from the seller to the buyer)	4,000
− **Purchase returns** for unsuitable goods returned to the seller	(25,000)
− **Purchase allowances** granted by the seller	(5,000)
− **Purchase discounts** for early payment by the buyer	(14,000)
= Net purchases of inventory (Cost to the buyer)	$560,000

The next section shows how different accounting methods determine amounts reported on the Balance Sheet and the Income Statement. First, however, you need to understand how Inventory Accounting systems work.

RECORD INVENTORY-RELATED TRANSACTIONS

Inventory Systems

2 **Record** inventory-related transactions

There are two main types of Inventory Accounting systems: the periodic system and the perpetual system. The **periodic inventory system**, discussed in more detail in Appendix 6A, is typically used for inexpensive goods. A fabric store or a lumber yard won't keep a running record of every bolt of fabric or every piece of wood. Instead, these stores count their inventory periodically to determine the quantities on hand. Other businesses, such as restaurants and florists, may also use the periodic system because it does not make sense to keep track of the exact amount of meat, vegetables, cooking oil, and other ingredients that are used in producing the food items. This is an example of applying the "cost-benefit constraints" of the *Conceptual Framework*. The difference between quantity on hand and accounting records is simply considered used or sold.

A **perpetual inventory system**, on the other hand, tracks all inventory movements and typically uses a computer system to keep a running record of inventory on hand and what has been sold. This system provides better information and control over inventory for companies such as FR, Carrefour, Nestlé, and a majority of other retailers. In fact, every time you see a retailer scanning bar codes of the products you are buying, it is more likely that the business is using a perpetual inventory system. The bar code on the product label holds lots of information. The optical scanner reads the bar code, and the computer system automatically records the sale and updates the inventory records.

Even with a perpetual system, a business must still count inventory on hand annually. The physical count establishes the correct amount of ending inventory for the financial statements and also serves as a check on the perpetual records. Any discrepancy may signal the possibility of inventory theft that we should be aware of. Here is a quick summary of the two main Inventory Accounting systems.

Perpetual Inventory System	Periodic Inventory System
• Used for all types of goods • Keeps a running record of all goods bought, sold, and on hand • Inventory counted at least once a year to determine any discrepancies between accounting records and inventory on hand	• Used for inexpensive goods • Does *not* keep a running record of all goods bought, sold, and on hand • Inventory counted at least once a year to determine ending inventory with any difference assumed to be used or sold

Recording Transactions in the Perpetual System

In a perpetual inventory system, all inventory transactions are tracked and accounting records are updated. At any point in time, the Inventory Account and cost of sales account are always up-to-date. Let's walk through a typical set of transactions related to the purchase and sale of inventory.

On January 1, 20X1, Natalie Quah started an online shop called We Love Baby Stuff to sell clothes for babies. She sources various manufacturers of baby clothing, orders select styles in bulk, and then sells the clothes to customers via her "blog shop."

Recording Inventory Purchases. Natalie selected and ordered a number of clothing items from a manufacturer. She was also able to negotiate a bulk **purchase discount** of 10% and a payment period of 30 days. When the goods arrived, they were accompanied by an invoice that also showed a total purchase price of $2,000 (after deducting the bulk purchase discount) and a freight-in wards, delivery, or shipping charge of $50. Freight-in is the transportation cost paid by the buyer to move goods from the seller to the buyer. Freight-in is accounted for as part of the cost of inventory, but some businesses may choose to keep track of it separately before adding it to the cost of inventory at a later point. Doing this will allow a business to track and monitor how much shipping charges it incurs. For example, Natalie could record either of the following journal entries:

Option 1

A1

	A	B	C	D
1	Jan 1			
2	20X1	Inventory	2,050	
3		Accounts Payable		2,050
4		*Purchase of inventory, including $50 freight costs*		
5				

Option 2

A1

	A	B	C	D
1	Jan 1			
2	20X1	Inventory	2,000	
3		Freight-inwards	50	
4		Accounts Payable		2,050
5		*Purchase of inventory, including $50 freight costs*		
6				

If Natalie uses Option 2, at the end of the accounting period, the freight-inwards should be transferred to the Inventory Account as part of the closing entry process (as discussed in Chapter 3).

A1			
A	**B**	**C**	**D**
Jan 31			
20X1	Inventory	50	
	Freight-inwards		50
	Transfer of freight-inwards to inventory cost		

Recording Purchase Returns. Sometimes, businesses may receive goods that fail to meet their specifications. For example, Natalie might have ordered 10 units of blue rompers, but green ones were delivered instead, or in the wrong sizes, or perhaps the items were defective. Depending on the purchase contract or terms of sales, Natalie may be able to ask for either a refund or a further discount. A **purchase return** is a decrease in the cost of inventory because the buyer returned the goods to the vendor. A **purchase allowance** also decreases the cost of inventory because the buyer got an allowance (a deduction) from the amount owed. To document approval of purchase returns, the vendor issues a **debit memorandum** (or debit memo), meaning that accounts payable are reduced (debited) for the amount of the return. The offsetting credit is to inventory as the goods are shipped back to the seller (vendor). Purchase discounts and allowances are usually documented on a revised invoice from the vendor. Suppose Natalie returned $100 worth of products to her supplier and the vendor agreed to deduct this amount from the amount due. Natalie would record the following entry:

A1			
A	**B**	**C**	**D**
Jan XX			
20X1	Accounts Payable	100	
	Inventory		100
	Returned defective inventory to vendor		

The amount due to the vendor is now reduced by $100 to $1,950, called net purchases after deducting purchase returns and/or allowances. Throughout this book, we often refer to net purchases simply as *Purchases*.

Recording Inventory Sales. When Natalie's blog shop makes a sale, two things happen, in accordance with the *Conceptual Framework*.

- First, it now has an increase in assets, either in the form of cash or rights to receive cash (i.e., accounts receivable),which results in an increase in the business's net worth (via revenue).
- Second, it gave up some assets (i.e., inventory sold), which results in a reduction in the business's net worth (via expense).

For example, if Natalie sold a romper suit that costs $15 for $25, she would record the following journal entry:

A1			
A	**B**	**C**	**D**
Jan XX			
20X1	Cash	25	
	Sales Revenue		25
	Cost of Sales	15	
	Inventory		15
	Sold inventory costing $15 for $25 cash		

If Natalie incurs freight-out, delivery, or shipping costs in transporting her goods to the customers (i.e., under a FOB destination), such an expense is recorded as an operating expense, and not as part of cost of goods sold.

Recording Settlement Discount. We mentioned earlier that Natalie purchased her inventory from suppliers on credit. Usually, you may see the term "net 30," which tells the buyer to pay the full amount within 30 days. Occasionally, you may see payment terms such as "2/10, n/30." This means the buyer can take a 2% discount for early payments made within 10 days, otherwise the invoiced amount is due within 30 days. The discount is applied to the amount owed from goods purchased and excludes other charges such as shipping and handling costs. Of course, other suppliers may offer different payment terms, such as 1/15, n/45.

Suppose Natalie ordered another line of baby clothing from a different vendor, totaling $1,000. This particular vendor offers a "2/10, n/30" with free shipping and handling. Upon receipt of inventory from the supplier, Natalie recorded the following.

	A	B	C	D
1	Jan XX			
2	20X1	Inventory	1,000	
3		Accounts Payable		1,000
4		*Purchase of inventory on 2/10, n/30 terms*		
5				

If Natalie decides to take advantage of the early settlement discount, she would pay $980 to settle the $1,000 obligation with the following journal entry.

	A	B	C	D
1	Jan XX			
2	20X1	Accounts Payable	1,000	
3		Cash		980
4		Discounts Received (or Inventory)		20
5		*Payment for inventory with 2/10 settlement discount*		
6				

Discount received is a reduction in the cost of inventory purchased. Similar to our earlier discussion on freight-inwards, if Natalie wants to keep track of the various settlement discounts she has received, she can use a specific account to keep track of it. At the end of the accounting period, discount received is closed to the Inventory Account. Alternatively, she can reduce the cost of inventory directly. Naturally, if Natalie does not act on the early settlement discount, the account payable will be paid in full by cash ($1,000) when payment is made.

UNDERSTAND AND APPLY DIFFERENT INVENTORY COST ASSUMPTIONS

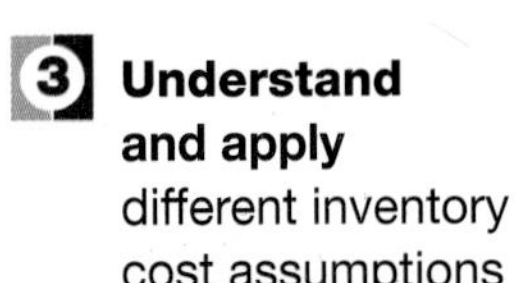
3
Understand and apply different inventory cost assumptions

Inventory is an example of an asset for which a manager can decide which accounting method to use. The accounting method selected affects the profits to be reported, the amount of income tax to be paid, and the values of the financial ratios derived from the financial statements.

Determining the cost of inventory is easy when the unit cost remains constant, as in Exhibit 6-2. But the unit cost usually changes. For example, prices often rise. The trousers that cost UNIQLO $10 in January may cost $14 in June and $18 in October. Suppose UNIQLO sells 1,000 pairs of trousers in November. How many of those cost $10, how many cost $14, and how many cost $18?

To compute cost of goods sold and the cost of ending inventory still on hand, we must assign unit cost to the items. *IAS 2—Inventories* prescribes that cost of inventory items that are not ordinarily interchangeable (and goods or services produced and segregated for specific projects) shall be assigned by using **specific identification** of their individual costs. Cost of other inventories that are ordinarily interchangeable shall be determined using **cost formulas**. The common cost formulas (also known as **inventory costing methods**) include **first-in, first-out (FIFO)**; **last-in, first-out (LIFO)**; and **weighted average cost method**.

A Closer Look

IAS 2—Inventories prohibits the use of the last-in, first-out (LIFO) cost formula. This is one of the major differences between the U.S. and International GAAP. For the purpose of this chapter, we will continue to elaborate on LIFO because it provides a good contrast to FIFO, one of the cost formulas allowed under IFRS.

IAS 2—Inventories also allows the *retail inventory method* to be used, as long as it approximates the cost. This method is used by certain retailers for measuring inventories of large numbers of rapidly changing items with similar margins. The cost of inventory is determined by reducing the sales value of the inventory by the appropriate percentage gross margin. The percentage used takes into consideration inventory that has been marked down to below its original selling price. As this is an industry-specific cost formula, we will not be discussing this method in detail. If you want to find out more, you can visit https://www.accountingtools.com/articles/2017/5/13/retail-inventory-method.

The inventory costing methods can have very different effects on reported profits in the Income Statement and inventory on the Balance Sheet. Therefore, companies select their inventory method with great care. *IAS 2* requires an entity to use the same cost formula for all inventories having a similar nature and use to the entity. It is possible to use different cost formulas for inventories with a different nature or use. For example, Chow Tai Fook, a leading jeweler in Asia, uses different inventory methods for different inventory items.

ADAPTED EXCERPTS FROM CHOW TAI FOOK'S NOTES TO THE ACCOUNTS

Inventories

Inventories are stated at the lower of cost and net realizable value. Cost is calculated using *specific identification* basis for gem-set jewelry and watches, and weighted average for other inventories.

Source: From Chow Tai Fook, Annual Report, 2016, page 154.

Exhibit 6-5, based on a survey of 170 IFRS companies in 2010, indicates that weighted average is the most popular inventory costing method. The same survey also shows that 30 out of the 170 companies employ more than one inventory costing method, like Chow Tai Fook.

Let's start with looking at Exhibit 6-6, a diagrammatic overview of how specific identification and the other cost formulas work. Boxes 1, 2, 3, and 4 are units purchased at different prices in a chronological order. For now, just look at how the different inventory costing methods will result in different costs being reported on the Balance Sheet as ending inventory and on the Income Statement as cost of goods sold.

Specific Identification. Some businesses deal in unique inventory items, such as automobiles, antique furniture, jewelry, and real estate. These businesses cost their inventories at the specific cost of the particular unit. For instance, a Toyota dealer may have four vehicles in the showroom—(1) a Camry, (2) a Corolla, (3) a Prius, and (4) a Lexus. If the dealer sells the Camry, Prius, and Lexus, the cost of goods sold is the cost of the three vehicles (1, 3, and 4) sold. The only item remaining on its Balance Sheet will be the (2) Corolla.

Exhibit 6-5 | Use of the Various Inventory Methods

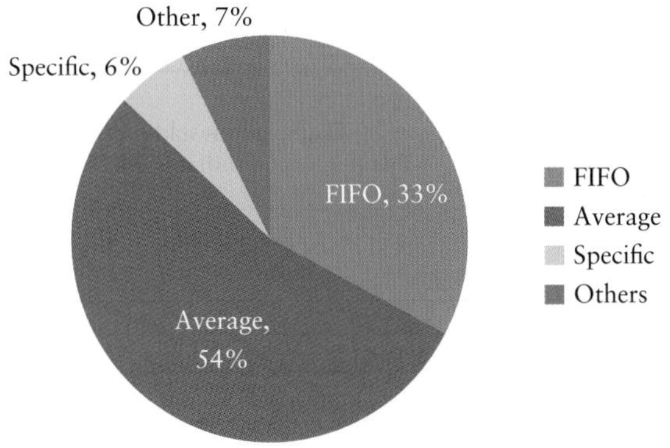

Other, 7%
Specific, 6%
FIFO, 33%
Average, 54%

FIFO
Average
Specific
Others

Source: Exhibit created from source data found in IFRS Financial Statements – Best Practices in Presentation and Disclosure, 2012/13, AICPA.

The specific identification method is also called the specific-unit-cost method. For most businesses, this method is too expensive to use for inventory items that have common characteristics, such as bushels of wheat, gallons of paint, or the casual apparel that UNIQLO sells.

The other inventory costing methods, or cost formulas (FIFO, LIFO, and weighted average), are fundamentally different. These other methods do not use the specific cost of a particular unit. Instead, they assume different flows of inventory costs. Remember that the goods are interchangeable, and cost formulas are not the same as the physical units. Businesses will always try to sell older units first (to prevent spoilage, obsolescence, etc.) before selling newer units. This is independent of the cost formulas used.

To illustrate FIFO, LIFO, and average inventory costing methods, we use a common set of data, given in Exhibit 6-7.

For Exhibit 6-7, let's assume UNIQLO began the period with 10 khakis that cost $10 each; thus, the beginning inventory was $100. During the period, UNIQLO bought 50 more khakis (at different prices), sold 40 khakis, and ended the period with 20 khakis. These have been summarized in Exhibit 6-7.

Exhibit 6-6 | Overview of Costing Methods

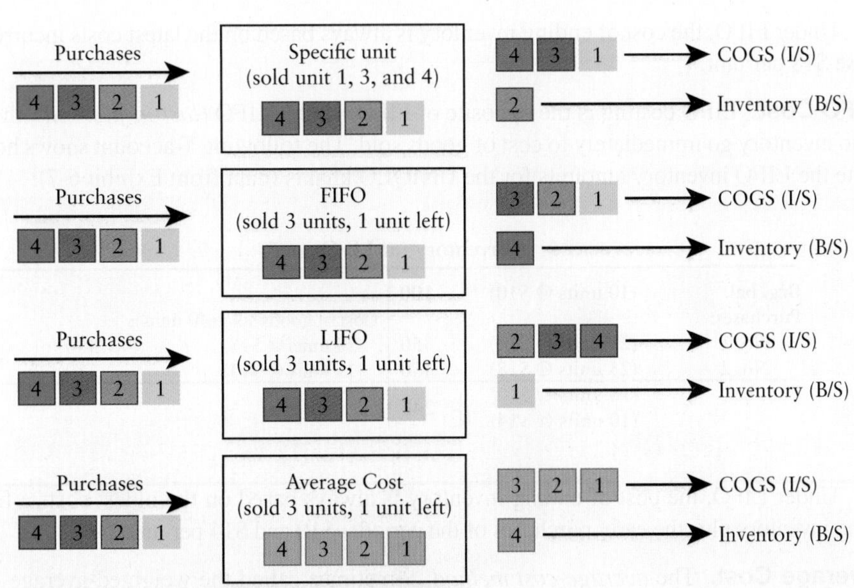

Exhibit 6-7 | Inventory Data Used to Illustrate the Various Inventory Costing Methods

Inventory					
Beg. bal.	(10 units @ $10)	100			
Purchases:			Cost of goods sold		
No. 1	(25 units @ $14)	350	(40 units @ ?)		?
No. 2	(25 units @ $18)	450			
End. bal.	(20 units @ ?)	?			

Goods Available		Number of Units	Total Cost
Goods available	=	10 + 25 + 25 = 60 units	$100 + $350 + $450 = $900
Cost of goods sold	=	40 units	?
Ending inventory	=	20 units	?

The big accounting questions are:

1. What is the cost of goods sold for the Income Statement?
2. What is the cost of the ending inventory for the Balance Sheet?

It all depends on which inventory method UNIQLO uses. Let's look at FIFO costing first.

FIFO Cost. Under the FIFO method, the first costs into inventory are the first costs assigned to cost of goods sold—hence, the name *first-in, first-out*. The following T-account shows how to compute FIFO cost of goods sold and ending inventory for the UNIQLO khakis (data from Exhibit 6-7):

Inventory (at FIFO cost)					
Beg. bal.	(10 units @ $10)	100			
Purchases:			Cost of goods sold (40 units):		
No. 1	(25 units @ $14)	350	(10 units @ $10)	100	
No. 2	(25 units @ $18)	450	(25 units @ $14)	350	540
			(5 units @ $18)	90	
End. bal.	(20 units @ $18)	360			

Under FIFO, the cost of ending inventory is always based on the latest costs incurred—in this case $18 per unit.

LIFO Cost. LIFO costing is the opposite of FIFO. Under LIFO *(last-in-first-out)*, the last costs into inventory go immediately to cost of goods sold. The following T-account shows how to compute the LIFO inventory amounts for the UNIQLO khakis (data from Exhibit 6-7):

Inventory (at LIFO cost)					
Beg. bal.	(10 units @ $10)	100			
Purchases:			Cost of goods sold (40 units):		
No. 1	(25 units @ $14)	350	(25 units @ $18)	450	660
No. 2	(25 units @ $18)	450	(15 units @ $14)	210	
End. bal.	(10 units @ $10)	240			
	(10 units @ $14)				

Under LIFO, the cost of ending inventory is always based on the oldest costs—from beginning inventory plus the early purchases of the period—$10 and $14 per unit.

Average Cost. The *average-cost method*, sometimes called the weighted-average method, is based on the average cost of inventory during the period. Unlike LIFO and FIFO, the individual inventory costs are no longer relevant when inventory is sold. Average cost per unit is determined as follows (data from Exhibit 6-7):

$$\text{Average cost per unit} = \frac{\text{Cost of goods available*}}{\text{Number of units available*}} = \frac{\$900}{60} = \$15$$

$$\begin{aligned}\text{Cost of goods sold} &= \text{Number of units sold} \times \text{Average cost per unit}\\ &= 40 \text{ units} \times \$15 = \$600\end{aligned}$$

$$\begin{aligned}\text{Ending inventory} &= \text{Number of units on hand} \times \text{Average cost per unit}\\ &= 20 \text{ units} \times \$15 = \$300\end{aligned}$$

The following T-account shows the effects of average costing:

Inventory (at Average Cost)

Beg. bal.	**(10 units @ $10)**	**100**		
Purchases:				
No. 1	**(25 units @ $14)**	**350**		
No. 2	**(25 units @ $18)**	**450**	Cost of goods sold (40 units @ average cost of $15 per unit)	600
End. bal.	(20 units @ average cost of $15 per unit)	300		

Effects of FIFO, LIFO, and Average Cost on Cost of Goods Sold, Gross Profit, and Ending Inventory

In our UNIQLO trousers example, the cost of inventory rose from $10 to $14 to $18. When inventory unit costs change this way, the various inventory methods produce different cost-of-goods sold figures. Exhibit 6-8 summarizes the income effects (sales – cost of goods sold = gross profit) of the three inventory methods (remember that prices are rising). Study Exhibit 6-8 carefully, focusing on cost of goods sold and gross profit.

Exhibit 6-8 | Financial Statement Effects of the FIFO, LIFO, and Average Cost Inventory Methods

	FIFO	LIFO	Average
Sales revenue (assumed)	$1,000	$1,000	$1,000
Cost of goods sold.........................	540 (lowest)	660 (highest)	600
Gross profit..................................	$ 460 (highest)	$ 340 (lowest)	$ 400
Inventory (on Balance Sheet)	$ 360 (highest)	$ 240 (lowest)	$ 300

Exhibit 6-9 shows the impact of both FIFO and LIFO costing methods on cost of goods sold and inventories during both increasing costs (Panel A) and decreasing costs (Panel B). Study this exhibit carefully; it will help you *really* understand FIFO and LIFO.

*Goods available = Beginning inventory + Purchases

Exhibit 6-9 Cost of Goods Sold and Ending Inventory: FIFO and LIFO; Increasing and Decreasing Costs

Panel A—When Inventory Costs Are Increasing

	Cost of Goods Sold (COGS)	Ending Inventory
FIFO	FIFO COGS is lowest because it's based on the oldest costs, which are low. Gross profit is, therefore, the highest.	FIFO ending inventory is highest because it's based on the most recent costs, which are high.
LIFO	LIFO COGS is highest because it's based on the most recent costs, which are high. Gross profit is, therefore, the lowest.	LIFO ending inventory is lowest because it's based on the oldest costs, which are low.

Panel B—When Inventory Costs Are Decreasing

	Cost of Goods Sold (COGS)	Ending Inventory
FIFO	FIFO COGS is highest because it's based on the oldest costs, which are high. Gross profit is, therefore, the lowest.	FIFO ending inventory is lowest because it's based on the most recent costs, which are low.
LIFO	LIFO COGS is lowest because it's based on the most recent costs, which are low. Gross profit is, therefore, the highest.	LIFO ending inventory is highest because it's based on the oldest costs, which are high.

Comparison of the Inventory Methods

Let's compare the average, FIFO, and LIFO inventory methods.

1. Measuring Cost of Goods Sold. How well does each method match inventory expense—cost of goods sold—against revenue? LIFO results in the most realistic net income figure because LIFO assigns the most recent inventory costs to expense. In contrast, FIFO matches older inventory costs against revenue—a poor measure of expense. FIFO income is, therefore, less realistic than LIFO income.
2. Measuring Ending Inventory. Which method reports the most up-to-date inventory cost on the Balance Sheet? FIFO. LIFO can value inventory at very old costs because LIFO leaves the oldest prices in ending inventory.

A Closer Look

How would the method of recording inventory transactions and cost flow assumptions interact with each other? The frequency of recording inventory transactions (perpetual versus periodic) affects how we calculate weighted average and LIFO. For example, let's consider the following simple illustration.

Suppose Natalie's We Love Baby Stuff has an opening inventory balance of \$1,000 (100 units) on July 1, 20X2. Natalie sold 30 units of inventory for \$400 on July 10 and bought an additional 50 units of inventory totaling \$575 on July 20. Under the "periodic average," the average inventory cost is \$10.50 (\$1,000 + \$575 for 150 units), resulting in ending inventory of \$1,260 (120 units × \$10.50) and cost of sales of \$315 (30 units × \$10.50).

However, if a "perpetual average" is used, we will calculate a new weighted average cost every time we make a purchase. In this example, at the time of the sale on July 10, the average cost per inventory item was still \$10 (based on 100 units of opening inventory for \$1,000), so the cost of sales is \$300 (30 units × \$10 per unit). After the additional inventory purchase on July 20, the "new" average cost per unit is now \$10.63 (\$700 + \$575 for 120 units). Any sales Natalie makes after July 20 will use this \$10.63 as the average cost (until new purchases that will produce a newer average cost). A similar concept applies to "periodic LIFO" verus "perpetual LIFO."

As perpetual inventory systems use computerized accounting systems, these calculations are usually automated. Unless you are given specific dates and quantities of inventory purchases and sales, you will not be able to work out the perpetual variations of LIFO or weighted average. In such cases, for simplicity, you can assume that the cost of sales and ending inventory are calculated at the end of the period.

Mid-Chapter Summary Problem

Suppose a division of HH Precision Industry that sells computer microchips has these inventory records for January 20X7:

Date		Item	Quantity	Unit Cost	Total Cost
Jan	1	Beginning inventory	100 units	\$ 8	\$ 800
	6	Purchase	60 units	9	540
	21	Purchase	150 units	9	1,350
	27	Purchase	90 units	10	900

Company accounting records show sales of 310 units for revenue of \$6,770. Operating expense for January was \$1,900.

Requirements

1. Prepare the January Income Statement, showing the amounts for LIFO, average, and FIFO cost. Label the bottom line "Operating income." Round the average cost per unit to three decimal places and all other figures to whole-dollar amounts. Show your computations.
2. Suppose you are the financial vice president of HH Precision Industry. Which inventory method will you use if your motive is to
   a. minimize income taxes?
   b. report the highest operating income?

c. report operating income between the extremes of FIFO and LIFO?
d. report inventory on the Balance Sheet at the most current cost?
e. attain the best measure of net income for the Income Statement?

State the reason for each of your answers.

Answers

Requirement 1

	A	B	C	D
1	**HH Precision Industry** **Income Statement for Microchip** **Month Ended January 31, 20X7**			
2		**LIFO**	**Average**	**FIFO**
3	Sales revenue	$ 6,770	$ 6,770	$ 6,770
4	Cost of goods sold	2,870	2,782	2,690
5	Gross profit	3,900	3,988	4,080
6	Operating expenses	1,900	1,900	1,900
7	Operating income	$ 2,000	$ 2,088	$ 2,180
8				

Cost of goods sold computations:

LIFO: (90 @ $10) + (150 @ $9) + (60 @ $9) + (10 @ $8) = $2,870

Average: 310 × $8.975* = $2,782

FIFO: (100 @ $8) + (60 @ $9) + (150 @ $9) = $2,690

$$^*\frac{(\$800 + \$540 + \$1{,}350 + \$900)}{(100 + 60 + 150 + 90)} = \$8.975$$

Requirement 2

a. Use LIFO to minimize income taxes. Operating income under LIFO is lowest when inventory unit costs are increasing, as they are in this case (from $8 to $10). (If inventory costs were decreasing, income under FIFO would be lowest.)

b. Use FIFO to report the highest operating income. Income under FIFO is highest when inventory unit costs are increasing, as in this situation.

c. Use the **average-cost method** to report an operating income amount between the FIFO and LIFO extremes. This is true in this situation and in others when inventory unit costs are increasing or decreasing.

d. Use FIFO to report inventory on the Balance Sheet at the most current cost. The oldest inventory costs are expensed as cost of goods sold, leaving in ending inventory the most recent (most current) costs of the period.

e. Use LIFO to attain the best measure of net income. LIFO produces the best matching of current expense with current revenue. The most recent (most current) inventory costs are expensed as cost of goods sold.

Other Inventory Issues

Comparability as an Enhancing Qualitative Characteristic. The **comparability** qualitative characteristic states that businesses should use the same accounting methods and procedures from period to period. Consistency enables investors to compare a company's financial statements from one period to the next.

Suppose you are analyzing a company's net income pattern, which showed an increase over a two-year period. However, you also noted that the company switched from LIFO to FIFO during that time. Its net income increased dramatically but only because of the change in inventory method. If you did not know of the accounting change, you might believe that the company's income increased due to improved operations, but that's not the case.

The comparability qualitative characteristic does not mean that a company is not permitted to change its accounting methods. As long as the change reflects a more relevant and faithful representation of an underlying economic phenomenon, the lack of (short-term) comparability should not prevent the accounting method change. Typically, a reporting entity that makes an accounting change must disclose the effect of the change on net income or restate the previous year's figures for comparative purposes.

For example, HollyFrontier Corporation changed its inventory cost method from FIFO to LIFO in 2009. In its press release on the accounting policy change, HollyFrontier stated that its pre-tax income would decrease by $180 million.

On the other hand, Pactiv Corporation changed its inventory cost method from a combination of LIFO and FIFO to exclusively FIFO. It claimed that this change would better reflect the current value of inventories, provide better matching of sales and expenses, provide uniformity across all operations with respect to the method of Inventory Accounting, and enhance comparability with peers. Another reason cited for the switch was that the convergence of U.S. and International GAAP would likely eliminate LIFO because IFRS does not allow the use of LIFO.

Clearly, the choice of inventory method is an important one for all companies that deal with inventory.

Why is LIFO not allowed under IFRS? In the introduction section of *IAS 2—Inventories*, IASB simply states: "The Standard does not permit the use of the last-in, first-out (LIFO) formula to measure the cost of inventories." So why does IASB prohibit the use of LIFO?

We said earlier that using the latest costs is a better measure of income, and, on the other hand, using older costs results in more appropriate inventory values on the Balance Sheet. The *Conceptual Framework* favors a Balance Sheet primacy. Changes in assets and liabilities determine income and net worth of a business. LIFO prioritizes income measurements over that of assets and liabilities and results in inventories being recognized on the Balance Sheet at amounts that bear little relationship to cost level of inventories. In its basis for conclusions for *IAS 2*, the IASB stated: "It is not appropriate to allow an approach that results in a measurement of profit or loss for the period that is inconsistent with the measurement of inventories for Balance Sheet purposes."

In fact, LIFO can also distort income when inventory is depleted to a very low level, as much older costs (that could have been in the inventory for years) are used, creating unrealistic profits. Furthermore, IASB explained that the concept of selling newer items first before older ones is "generally not a reliable representation of actual inventory flows," and that LIFO lacks "representation faithfulness of inventory flows."

What is interesting is how the accounting standard is determined at the highest level. The IASB uses the *Conceptual Framework* to determine what should be the most appropriate accounting treatment for items on the financial statements.

Net Realizable Value. All our previous discussions have focused on the cost aspect of inventory. Regardless of which cost method you are using, there is one additional aspect that is equally important. *IAS 2* requires inventories to be measured at the lower of cost and net realizable value

(NRV). In other words, once you have determined cost (using specific identification, FIFO, or average cost method), you will need to compare the inventory to its NRV. The lower of the two shall be what is reported on the Balance Sheet. **Net realizable value** is the estimated selling price in the ordinary course of business less the estimated costs of completion and the estimated costs necessary to make the sale.

This evaluation of cost versus NRV is necessary because an entity may not be able to recover the cost of inventory if the goods are damaged or obsolete, or if their selling price has declined below costs. If an inventory is written down to an NRV below cost, the write-down is recognized as an expense in the period of the write-down. Any subsequent reversal is recognized as a reduction in COGS during the period in which the reversal occurs. The exact determination of NRV is not within the scope of this textbook, but the example below demonstrates the concept of lower of cost and NRV.

Suppose UNIQLO paid $3,000 for inventory on September 26. By January 31, its financial year-end, $2,000 of the inventory has been sold, and the cost of the remaining inventory is $1,000. Let's further assume that some of these inventories are damaged and no longer suitable for normal sale. UNIQLO estimates the net realizable value of these goods to be $400. UNIQLO's year-end Balance Sheet must report this inventory at NRV of $400. Exhibit 6-10 presents the effects of NRV on the Balance Sheet and the Income Statement. Before any NRV effect, cost of goods sold is $2,000. An NRV write-down decreases inventory and increases cost of goods sold, as follows:

	A	B	C
1	Cost of Goods Sold	600	
2	Inventory		600
3	*Wrote inventory down to realizable value.*		
4			

If the NRV of UNIQLO's inventory had been above cost, it would have made no adjustment for NRV. In that case, simply report inventory at cost, which is the lower of cost and NRV.

Exhibit 6-10 Net Realizable Value (NRV) Effects on Inventory and Cost of Goods Sold

Balance Sheet	
Current assets:	
Cash	$ XXX
Short-term investments	XXX
Accounts receivable	XXX
Inventories, net realizable value (which is lower than $1,000 cost)	400
Prepaid expenses	XXX
Total current assets	$X,XXX

Income Statement	
Sales revenue	$ XXX
Cost of goods sold ($2,000 + $600)	2,600
Gross profit	$X,XXX

Let's have a look at how Bossini, another clothing retailer, provides disclosure on its determination of NRV (adapted).

ADAPTED EXCERPTS FROM BOSSINI'S NOTES TO THE ACCOUNTS

Inventories

Management reviews the aged analysis of inventories of the Group at the end of each reporting period, and makes allowance for obsolete and slow-moving inventory items identified that are no longer suitable for sale. The assessment of allowance amount required involves management judgements and estimates. When the actual outcome or expectation in future is different from the original estimate, such differences will have an impact on the carrying value of the inventories and allowance charge/write-back of allowance in the period in which such estimate has been changed. In addition, physical counts on all inventories are carried out on a periodical basis in order to determine whether allowance needs to be made in respect of any obsolete inventories identified. The Group carries out an inventory review at the end of each reporting period and makes provision against obsolete and slow-moving items. Management reassesses the estimation at the end of each reporting period. The Group is satisfied that sufficient allowance for obsolete and slow-moving inventories has been made in the consolidated financial statements.

Source: From Bossini, Annual Report, 2015, page 112–119.

As mentioned in the excerpt, Bossini uses an allowance for inventory obsolescence account. The concept is similar to the allowance for uncollectible account we saw in Chapter 5 for receivables.

Let's take another look at FR's inventory excerpt that we saw at the start of this chapter.

ADAPTED EXCERPTS FROM FAST RETAILING'S NOTES TO THE ACCOUNTS

Inventories

Inventories are valued at the lower of cost and net realizable value; the weighted average method is principally used to determine cost. Net realizable value is based on the estimated selling price in the ordinary course of business less any estimated costs to be incurred to sell the goods.

Source: From Fast Retailing, Annual Report, 2015 page 10.

You should have a better understanding of the policy now. Notice FR is using the weighted average method, and it makes sure inventory is valued at the lower of cost and net realizable value.

ANALYZE EFFECTS OF INVENTORY ERRORS

Inventory errors sometimes occur. An error in ending inventory creates errors for two accounting periods. For example, if ending inventory has been *overstated* by $5,000, cost of goods sold will thus be *understated* by the same amount, resulting in an *overstated* gross profit. In addition, the error in ending inventory in period 1 will also impact the beginning inventory in period 2. In the absence of any further errors, inventory errors counterbalance in two consecutive periods. Why? Period 1's ending inventory becomes period 2's beginning amount. Thus, the period 1 error carries over into period 2, resulting in an *overstated* cost of goods sold, and an *understated* gross profit in period 2.

In Exhibit 6-11, we show the effect of the above inventory errors over a three-year period, with constant sales and purchases. Had there been no error in period 1, the figures under period 3 are the correct ones. You can compare the figures in period 1 and 2 to those in period 3 for a better understanding of the impact of the inventory errors.

Exhibit 6-11 Inventory Errors: An Example

	Period 1 Ending Inventory Overstated by $5,000		Period 2 Beginning Inventory Overstated by $5,000		Period 3 Correct	
Sales revenue		$ 100,000		$ 100,000		$ 100,000
Cost of goods sold:						
Beginning inventory	$ 10,000		$ 15,000		$ 10,000	
Purchases	50,000		50,000		50,000	
Cost of goods available	60,000		65,000		60,000	
Ending inventory	(15,000)		(10,000)		(10,000)	
Cost of goods sold		45,000		55,000		50,000
Gross profit		$ 55,000		$ 45,000		$ 50,000
			100,000			

The authors thank Professor Carl High for this example.

Beginning inventory and ending inventory have opposite effects on cost of goods sold (beginning inventory is added; ending inventory is subtracted). Therefore, after two periods, an inventory error washes out (counterbalances). Notice that total gross profit is correct for periods 1 and 2 combined ($100,000) even though each year's gross profit is off by $5,000. The correct gross profit is $50,000 for each period, as shown in period 3.

We must have accurate information for all periods. Exhibit 6-12 summarizes the effects of Inventory Accounting errors.

Exhibit 6-12 Effects of Inventory Errors

	Period 1		Period 2	
Inventory Error	**Cost of Goods Sold**	**Gross Profit and Net Income**	**Cost of Goods Sold**	**Gross Profit and Net Income**
Period 1				
Ending inventory **overstated**	Understated	Overstated	Overstated	Understated
Period 1				
Ending inventory **understated**	Overstated	Understated	Understated	Overstated

Crazy Eddie

It is one thing to make honest mistakes in accounting for inventory, but quite another to use inventory to commit fraud. The two most common ways to "cook the books" with inventory are as follows:

1. Inserting fictitious inventory, thus overstating quantities
2. Deliberately overstating unit prices used in the computation of ending inventory amounts

Either one of these tricks has exactly the same effect on income as inventory errors, discussed in the previous section. The difference is that honest inventory errors are often corrected as soon as they are detected, thus minimizing their impact on income. In contrast, deliberate overstatement of inventories tends to be repeated over and over again throughout the course of months, or even years, thus causing the misstatement to grow ever higher until it is discovered. By that time, it can be too late for the company.

Crazy Eddie, Inc.,[1] was a retail consumer electronics store in 1987, operating 43 retail outlets in the New York City area, with $350 million in reported sales and reported profits of $10.5 million. Its stock was a Wall Street "darling," with a collective market value of $600 million. The only problem was that the company's reported profits had been grossly overstated since 1984, the year that the company went public.

Eddie Antar, the company's founder and major shareholder, became preoccupied with the price of his company's shares in 1984. Antar realized that the company, in an extremely competitive retail market in the largest city in the United States, had to keep posting impressive operating profits in order to maintain the upward trend in the company's share price.

Within the first six months, Antar ordered a subordinate to double count about $2 million of inventory in the company's stores and warehouses. Using Exhibits 6-14 and 6-15, you can see that the impact of this inventory overstatement went straight to the "bottom line," overstating profits by the same amount. Unfortunately, the company's auditors failed to detect the inventory overstatement. The following year, emboldened by the audit error, Antar ordered subordinates (now accomplices) to bump the overstatement to $9 million. In addition, he ordered employees to destroy incriminating documents to conceal the inventory shortage. When auditors asked for these documents, employees told them they had been lost. Antar also ordered that the company scrap its sophisticated computerized perpetual inventory system and return to an outdated manual system that was easier to manipulate. The auditors made the mistake of telling Antar which company stores and warehouses they were going to visit in order to observe the year-end physical count of inventory. Antar shifted sufficient inventory to those locations just before the counts to conceal the shortages. By 1988, when the fraud was discovered, the inventory shortage (overstatement) was larger than the total profits the company had reported since it went public in 1984.

In June 1989, Crazy Eddie, Inc., filed for Chapter 11 bankruptcy protection. Later that year, the company closed its stores and sold off its assets. Eddie Antar became a fugitive from justice, moved to Israel, and took an assumed name. He was arrested in 1992, extradited to the United States, and convicted on 17 counts of fraudulent financial reporting in 1993. He was ordered to pay $121 million in restitution to former shareholders and creditors.

A series of missteps by the courts led to a plea bargain agreement in 1996, a condition of which Antar admitted, for the first time, that he had defrauded investors by manipulating the company's accounting records. One of the prosecuting attorneys was quoted as saying, "Crazy Eddie wasn't crazy, just crooked."

EVALUATE A COMPANY'S RETAILING OPERATIONS

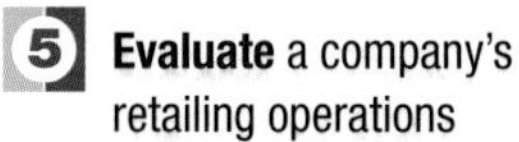
5
Evaluate a company's retailing operations

Owners, managers, and investors use ratios to evaluate a business. Two ratios relate directly to inventory: gross profit percentage and the rate of inventory turnover.

Gross Profit Percentage. Gross profit (sales − cost of goods sold) is a key indicator of a company's ability to sell inventory at a profit. Merchandisers strive to increase **gross profit percentage**, also called the **gross margin percentage**. Gross profit percentage is mark-up stated as a percentage of sales. Gross profit percentage is computed as follows for FR. Data (in billions of ¥) for 2015 was taken from FR's financial statements at the start of this chapter.

Gross Profit Margin	Fast Retailing 2015	Fast Retailing 2014
$\frac{\text{Gross profit}}{\text{Sales}}$	$\frac{848.6}{1{,}681.8} = 51\%$	$\frac{699.7}{1{,}382.9} = 51\%$

[1] Michael C. Knapp, *Contemporary Auditing: Real Issues and Cases*, 6th edition, Mason, Ohio: Thomson Southwestern, 2009.

The gross profit percentage is watched carefully by managers and investors. A 50% gross margin means that each dollar of sales generates 50 cents of gross profit. In other words, cost of goods sold consumes 50 cents of each sales dollar for FR. You can see that FR's gross profit margin has declined slightly from 51% the year before. Many firms do not enjoy such a high gross profit margin as FR. But the top apparel retailers are doing well. Inditex (Zara and other brands) and H&M have gross profit margins of 58% and 57%, respectively.

You may also find that fashion retailers generally have higher gross profit margins than, say, supermarkets and department stores. Carrefour, for example, usually has gross profit margins of around 20%. For most merchandising firms, the gross profit percentage changes little from year to year, but a small change may have a big impact on the bottom line. Exhibit 6-13 graphs the gross profit percentages for these companies. We will further discuss how to evaluate a company's performance in comparison with its peers later (in Chapter 12).

Exhibit 6-13 | Gross Profit Percentages of Selected Retailers

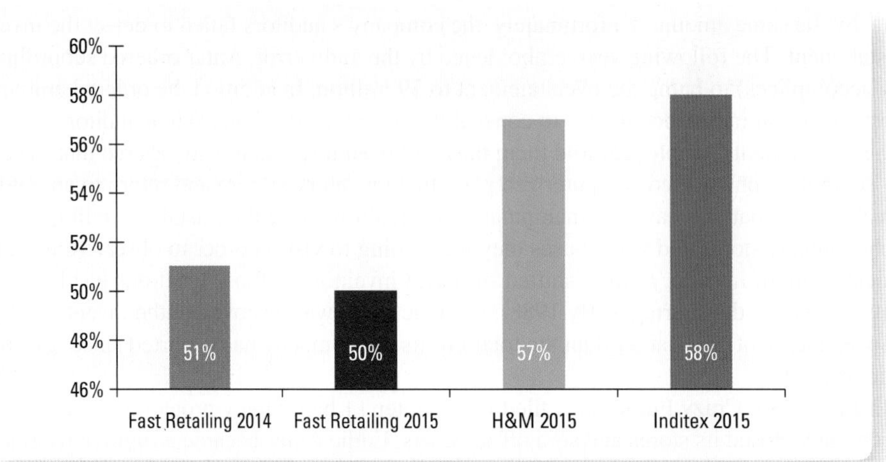

Inventory Turnover and Resident Period. Fast Retailing strives to sell its inventory as quickly as possible because the goods generate no profit until they're sold. The faster the sales, the higher the income; on the other hand, slow-moving goods generate fewer sales and lower income. Ideally, a business should operate with as little inventory as possible, but most businesses, especially retailers, must keep some goods on hand. **Inventory turnover**, the ratio of cost of goods sold to average inventory, indicates how rapidly inventory is sold. The 2015 computation for FR follows (data in billions of ¥) from FR's financial statements at the start of this chapter:

Inventory Turnover and Resident Period	Fast Retailing 2015	Fast Retailing 2014
$\frac{\text{Cost of goods sold}}{\text{Average inventory*}}$	$\frac{833.2}{241.6} = 3.45$ times	$\frac{683.2}{195.4} = 3.50$ times
365 / Inventory turnover	365 / 3.45 = 106 days	365 / 3.50 = 104 days

Average inventory = (beginning balance + ending balance)/2, which is (260 + 223.2)/2 = 241.6 for 2015

The inventory turnover ratio shows how many times the company sold (or turned over) its average level of inventory during the year. The turnover can also be expressed in days, called **inventory resident period** or days inventory on hand, by dividing 365 by the turnover (365/3.45 = 106 days). Inventory turnover varies from industry to industry.

Exhibit 6-14 charts the rates of inventory turnover for the top three apparel retail companies in the world. You saw earlier that FR's inventory days were 106 days in 2015 and 105 days in 2014. Inditex and H&M inventory days are 104 days and 84 days, respectively. You can see that Inditex has the highest gross margin and has the fastest inventory turnover. That's one reason Inditex is the top apparel company in the world, at least in financial performance terms.

Exhibit 6-14 | Inventory Resident Period of Selected Retailers

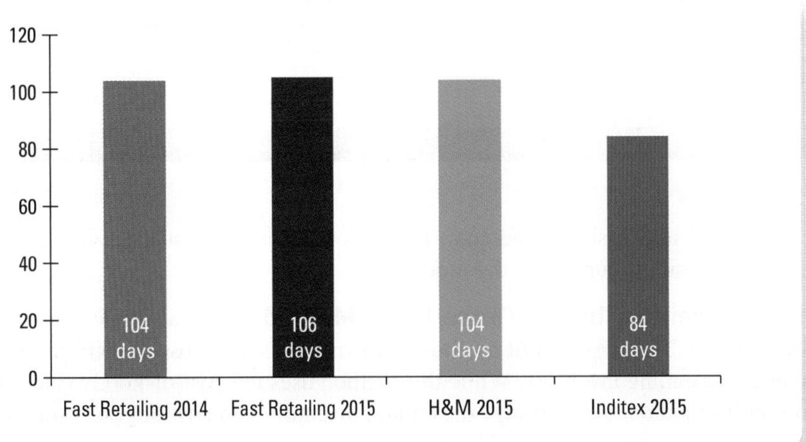

Stop & Think

Beginning inventory is $70,000, net purchases total $365,000, and net sales are $500,000. With a normal gross profit ratio of 40% of sales (i.e., cost of goods sold is 60% of sales revenue), how much is ending inventory?

Answer:

Beginning Inventory + Purchases − Ending Inventory = Cost of Goods Sold
$70,000 + $365,000 − Ending Inventory = 60% of $500,000
Ending Inventory = $70,000 + $365,000 − $300,000 = $135,000

The following Decision Guidelines summarize the situations that call for (a) a particular inventory system and (b) the motivation for using each costing method.

Analyzing Financial Statements

Using the Cost-of-Goods-Sold Model. While some may view this model as related to the periodic entry system, the **cost-of-goods-sold model** is used by all companies, regardless of their accounting system. The model is extremely powerful because it captures all the inventory information for an entire accounting period.

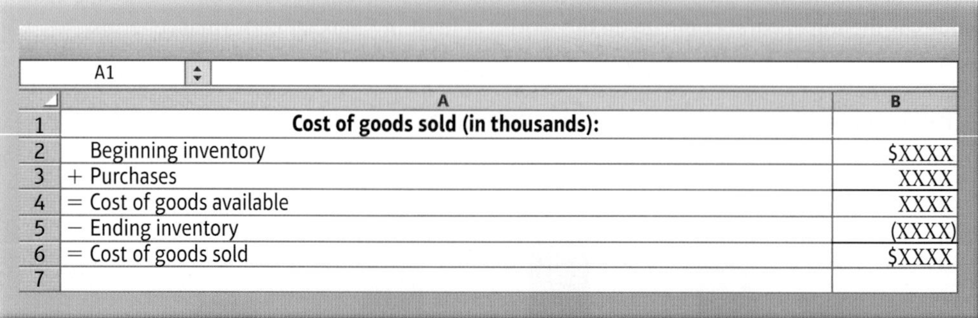

	A	B
1	**Cost of goods sold (in thousands):**	
2	Beginning inventory	$XXXX
3	+ Purchases	XXXX
4	= Cost of goods available	XXXX
5	− Ending inventory	(XXXX)
6	= Cost of goods sold	$XXXX
7		

While the model above shows the cost of goods sold on the last line, you can rework it to calculate any missing figure from the model.

Estimating Inventory by the Gross Profit Method. Often a business must *estimate* the value of its goods. The **gross profit method**, also known as the **gross margin method**, is widely used to estimate ending inventory. While this method uses the cost-of-goods-sold model, but for the gross-profit method, we rearrange the ending inventory and cost of goods sold as follows:

Beginning inventory	$ XXXX
+ Purchases	XXXX
= Cost of goods available	XXXX
− Cost of goods sold	(XXXX)
= Ending inventory	$ XXXX

Suppose a fire destroys some store's inventory as well as the computer system on which its records are kept, which prevents the manager from physically reconstructing the records of the inventory lost. To collect insurance, the store must estimate the cost of the ending inventory lost. Let's assume the store uses a *gross profit percentage* of 35%. We can estimate the store's cost of goods sold. Then subtract cost of goods sold from cost of goods available to estimate the amount of ending inventory. The calculations for the gross profit method are shown below, with new amounts assumed for the illustration.

You can also use the gross profit method to test the overall reasonableness of an ending inventory amount. This method also helps to detect large errors.

	A	B	C
1	Beginning inventory		$ XXXX
2	Purchases		XXXX
3	Cost of goods available		XXXX
4	Estimated cost of goods sold:		
5	Net sales revenue	$ XXXX	
6	Less estimated gross profit of 35%	XXXX	
7	Estimated cost of goods sold		XXXX
8	Estimated cost of ending inventory lost		$ XXXX
9			

DECISION GUIDELINES

ACCOUNTING FOR INVENTORY

Suppose Franc Franc, a furniture store, stocks two basic categories of merchandise:

- furniture pieces, such as tables and chairs
- small items of low value, near the checkout stations, such as cupholders and coasters

Jacob Stiles, the store manager, is considering how accounting will affect the business. Let's examine several decisions Stiles must make to properly account for the store's inventory.

Decision	Guidelines	System or Method
Which inventory system to use?	• Expensive merchandise • Cannot control inventory by visual inspection	Perpetual system for the furniture
	• Can control inventory by visual inspection	Periodic system for the small, low-value items
Which costing method to use?	• Unique inventory items	Specific unit cost for designer furniture because they are unique
	• Most current cost of ending inventory • Maximizes reported income when costs are rising	FIFO
	• Most current measure of cost of goods sold and net income • Minimizes income tax when costs are rising	LIFO (not allowed under IFRS)
	• Middle-of-the-road approach for income tax and reported income	Average

End-of-Chapter Summary Problem

Town & Country Gift Ideas began 20X6 with 60,000 units of inventory that cost $36,000. During 20X6, Town & Country purchased merchandise on account for $352,500 as follows:

Purchase 1	(100,000 units costing)	$ 65,000
Purchase 2	(270,000 units costing)	175,500
Purchase 3	(160,000 units costing)	112,000

Cash payments on account totaled $326,000 during the year.

Town & Country's sales during 20X6 consisted of 520,000 units of inventory for $660,000, all on account. The company uses the FIFO inventory method.

Cash collections from customers were $630,000. Operating expenses totaled $240,500, of which Town & Country paid $211,000 in cash. Town & Country credited Accrued Liabilities for the remainder. At December 31, Town & Country accrued income tax expense at the rate of 35% of income before tax.

Requirements

1. Make summary journal entries to record Town & Country's transactions for the year, assuming the company uses a perpetual inventory system.
2. Determine the FIFO cost of Town & Country's ending inventory at December 31, 20X6, in two ways:
   a. Use a T-account.
   b. Multiply the number of units on hand by the unit cost.
3. Show how Town & Country would compute cost of goods sold for 20X6. Follow the FIFO example on page 339.
4. Prepare Town & Country's Income Statement for 20X6. Show totals for the gross profit and income before tax.
5. Determine Town & Country's gross profit percentage, rate of inventory turnover, and net income as a percentage of sales for the year. In Town & Country's industry, a gross profit percentage of 40%, an inventory turnover of six times per year, and a net income percentage of 7% are considered excellent. How well does Town & Country compare to these industry averages?

Answers

Requirement 1

A1

	A	B	C
1	Inventory ($65,000 + $175,500 + $112,000)	352,500	
2	Accounts Payable		352,500
3			
4	Accounts Payable	326,000	
5	Cash		326,000
6			
7	Accounts Receivable	660,000	
8	Sales Revenue		660,000
9			
10	Cost of Goods Sold (see Requirement 3)	339,500	
11	Inventory		339,500
12			
13	Cash	630,000	
14	Accounts Receivable		630,000
15			
16	Operating Expenses	240,500	
17	Cash		211,000
18	Accrued Liabilities		29,500
19			
20	Income Tax Expense (see Requirement 4)	28,000	
21	Income Tax Payable		28,000
22			

Requirement 2

Inventory			
Beg. bal.	36,000		
Purchases	352,500	Cost of goods sold	339,500
End. bal.	49,000		

Number of units in ending inventory (60,000 + 100,000 + 270,000 + 160,000 − 520,000).............	70,000
Unit cost of ending inventory at FIFO ($112,000 ÷ 160,000 from Purchase 3).....	× $ 0.70
FIFO cost of ending inventory......................	$49,000

Requirement 3

Cost of goods sold (520,000 units):	
60,000 units costing..	$ 36,000
100,000 units costing..	65,000
270,000 units costing..	175,500
90,000 units costing $0.70 each*	63,000
Cost of goods sold...	$339,500

*From Purchase 3: $112,000/160,000 units = $0.70 per unit.

Requirement 4

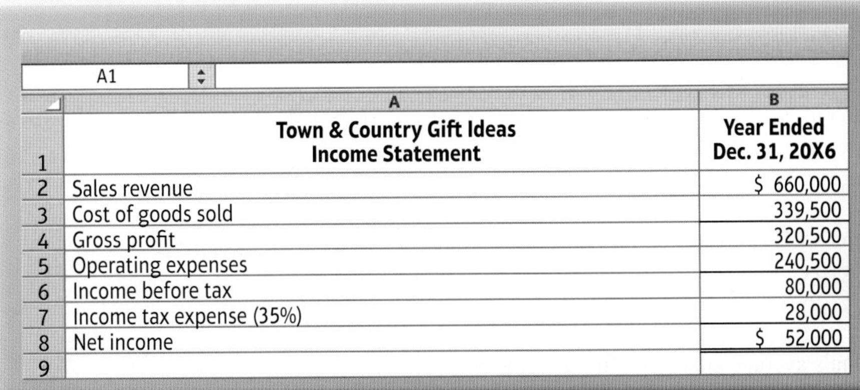

	A	B
1	Town & Country Gift Ideas Income Statement	Year Ended Dec. 31, 20X6
2	Sales revenue	$ 660,000
3	Cost of goods sold	339,500
4	Gross profit	320,500
5	Operating expenses	240,500
6	Income before tax	80,000
7	Income tax expense (35%)	28,000
8	Net income	$ 52,000
9		

Requirement 5

		Industry Average
Gross profit percentage:	$\$320{,}500 \div \$660{,}000 = 48.6\%$	40%
Inventory turnover:	$\dfrac{\$339{,}500}{(\$36{,}000 + \$49{,}000)/2} = 8 \text{ times}$	6 times
Net income as a percent of sales:	$\$52{,}000 \div \$660{,}000 = 7.9\%$	7%

Town & Country's statistics are better than the industry averages.

REVIEW | Inventory and Merchandising Operations

Quick Check (Answers are given at the end of the chapter.)

1. Which statement is true?

a. The invoice is the purchaser's request for collection from the customer.
b. A service company purchases products from suppliers and then sells them.
c. Gross profit is the excess of sales revenue over cost of goods sold.
d. The Sales account is used to record only sales on account.

2. Sales discounts should appear in the financial statements

a. as an addition to inventory.
b. as a deduction from sales.
c. among the current liabilities.
d. as an addition to sales.
e. as an operating expense.

3. How is inventory classified in the financial statements?

a. As a liability
b. As a contra account to Cost of Goods Sold
c. As an expense
d. As an asset
e. As a revenue

Questions 4–6 use the following data of Dana, Inc.

	Units	Unit Cost	Total Cost	Units Sold
Beginning inventory	15	$6	$ 90	
Purchase on Apr 25	40	7	280	
Purchase on Nov 13	10	9	90	
Sales	40	?	?	

4. Dana uses a FIFO inventory system. Cost of goods sold for the period is

a. $300.
b. $283.
c. $265.
d. $195.

5. Dana's LIFO cost of ending inventory would be

a. $195.
b. $160.
c. $177.
d. $175.

6. Dana's average cost of ending inventory is

a. $195.
b. $160.
c. $177.
d. $175.

7. When applying the lower of cost or net realizable value, NRV means

a. selling price less discounts.
b. original cost plus profit margin.
c. selling price less cost to sell.
d. original cost less physical deterioration.

8. During a period of rising prices, the inventory method that will yield the highest net income and asset value is

a. LIFO.
b. FIFO.
c. specific identification.
d. average cost.

9. Which statement is true?

a. The inventory method that best matches current expense with current revenue is FIFO.
b. When prices are rising, the inventory method that results in the lowest ending inventory value is FIFO.
c. An error overstating ending inventory in 2010 will understate 2010 net income.
d. Application of the inventory valuation rule may result in a lower inventory value than the cost of inventory.

10. The ending inventory of Misty Harbor Co. is $75,000. If beginning inventory was $86,000 and goods available totaled $127,000, the cost of goods sold is

a. $41,000.
b. $52,000.
c. $86,000.
d. $138,000.
e. none of the above.

11. Lantern Company had cost of goods sold of $148,000. The beginning and ending inventories were $16,000 and $28,000, respectively. Purchases for the period must have been

a. $136,000.
b. $160,000.
c. $164,000.
d. $176,000.
e. $192,000.

Use the following information for questions 12–14.
Highway Company had a $28,000 beginning inventory and a $35,000 ending inventory. Net sales were $184,000; purchases, $93,000; purchase returns and allowances, $7,000; and freight-in, $3,000.

12. Cost of goods sold for the period is

a. $96,000.
b. $98,000.
c. $82,000.
d. $81,000.
e. none of the above.

13. What is Highway's gross profit percentage (rounded to the nearest percentage)?

a. 50%
b. 55%
c. 45%
d. None of the above

14. What is Highway's rate of inventory turnover?

a. 2.6 times
b. 5.3 times
c. 3.0 times
d. 2.3 times

15. Beginning inventory is $120,000, purchases are $270,000, and sales total $460,000. The normal gross profit is 40%. Using the gross profit method, how much is ending inventory?

a. $206,000
b. $132,000
c. $114,000
d. $88,000
e. None of the above

16. An overstatement of ending inventory in one period results in

a. an understatement of the beginning inventory of the next period.
b. an understatement of net income of the next period.
c. an overstatement of net income of the next period.
d. no effect on net income of the next period.

Accounting Vocabulary

average-cost method (p. 344) Inventory costing method based on the average cost of inventory during the period. Average cost is determined by dividing the cost of goods available by the number of units available. Also called the *weighted-average method*.

consignment (p. 332) An inventory arrangement where the seller sells inventory that belongs to another party. The seller does not include consigned merchandise on hand in its Balance Sheet, because the seller does not own this inventory.

comparability (p. 345) A business must use the same accounting methods and procedures from period to period. Comparability is an enhancing qualitative characteristic of financial statements.

cost formulas (p. 338) Cost assumptions (e.g., LIFO, FIFO, or weighted-average) used in the measurement of inventory and cost of goods sold when goods are ordinarily interchangeable. Also called *inventory costing method.*

cost of goods sold (p. 330) Cost of the inventory the business has sold to customers. Also known as cost of sales.

cost-of-goods-sold model (p. 352) Formula that brings together all the inventory data for the entire accounting period: Beginning inventory + Purchases = Goods available. Then, Goods available – Ending inventory = Cost of goods sold.

cost of sales (p. 330). A synonym for *cost of goods sold.*

debit memorandum (p. 336) A document issued to the seller (vendor) when an item of inventory that is unwanted or damaged is returned. This document authorizes a reduction (debit) to accounts payable for the amount of the goods returned.

first-in, first-out (FIFO) cost (method) (p. 338) Inventory costing method by which the first costs into inventory are the first costs out to cost of goods sold. Ending inventory is based on the costs of the most recent purchases.

FOB (p. 332) Stands for *free on board* (or *freight on board*), a legal term that designates the point at which title passes for goods sold. FOB shipping point means that the buyer owns, and therefore is legally obligated to pay for, goods at the point of shipment, including transportation costs. In this case, the buyer owns the goods while they are in transit from the seller and must include their costs, including freight, in inventory at that point. FOB destination means that the seller pays the transportation costs, so the goods do not belong to the buyer until they reach the buyer's place of business.

gross margin (p. 332) Another name for *gross profit.*

gross margin percentage (p. 349) Another name for the *gross profit percentage.*

gross profit (p. 332) Sales revenue minus cost of goods sold. Also called *gross margin.*

gross profit method (p. 352) A way to estimate inventory based on a rearrangement of the cost-of-goods-sold model: Beginning inventory + Net purchases = Goods available – Cost of goods sold = Ending inventory. Also called the *gross margin method.*

gross profit percentage (p. 349) Gross profit divided by net sales revenue. Also called the *gross margin percentage.*

inventory (p. 330) The merchandise that a company sells to customers.

inventory costing method (p. 338) Cost assumptions (e.g. LIFO, FIFO, or weighted-average) used in the measurement of inventory and cost of goods sold when goods are ordinarily interchangeable. Also called *cost formulas.*

inventory resident period (p. 351) The average number of days to sell inventory to customers, calculated by dividing 365 by inventory turnover. Also called *days inventory on hand.*

inventory turnover (p. 350) The number of times inventories are sold during the year, approximated by taking total cost of goods sold divided by average inventory. Used in calculating *inventory resident period.*

last-in, first-out (LIFO) cost (method) (p. 338) Inventory costing method by which the last costs into inventory are the first costs out to cost of goods sold. This method leaves the oldest costs—those of beginning inventory and the earliest purchases of the period—in ending inventory.

net realizable value (NRV) (p. 346) The estimated selling price in the ordinary course of business less the estimated costs of completion and the estimated costs necessary to make the sale.

periodic inventory system (p. 334) An inventory system in which the business does not keep a continuous record of the inventory on hand. Instead, at the end of the period, the business makes a physical count of the inventory on hand and applies the appropriate unit costs to determine the cost of the ending inventory.

perpetual inventory system (p. 334) An inventory system in which the business keeps a continuous record for each inventory item to show the inventory on hand at all times.

purchase allowance (p. 336) A decrease in the cost of purchases because the seller has granted the buyer a subtraction (an allowance) from the amount owed.

purchase discount (p. 335) A decrease in the cost of purchases earned by making an early payment to the vendor.

purchase return (p. 336) A decrease in the cost of purchases because the buyer returned the goods to the seller.

specific identification (p. 338) When goods are ordinarily not interchangeable, cost of goods sold and on-hand are determined by specifically identifying which units have been sold and which units remain on-hand, respectively.

weighted-average cost method (p. 338) Another name for the *average-cost method.*

ASSESS YOUR PROGRESS

Short Exercises

S6-1. ***(Learning Objective 2: Accounting for inventory transactions)*** Journalize the following assumed transactions for The Debson Company. Show amounts in millions. LO 2

a. Cash purchases of inventory, $3.6 million
b. Sales on account, $19.5 million
c. Cost of goods sold (perpetual inventory system), $4.8 million
d. Collections on account, $19.1 million

S6-2. ***(Learning Objective 2: Accounting for inventory transactions)*** Summer Kluxon, Inc., purchased inventory costing $150,000 and sold 75% of the goods for $180,000. All purchases and sales were on account. Kluxon later collected 40% of the accounts receivable. LO 2

1. Journalize these transactions for Kluxon, which uses the perpetual inventory system.
2. For these transactions, show what Kluxon will report for inventory, revenues, and expenses on its financial statements. Report gross profit on the appropriate statement.

S6-3. ***(Learning Objective 3: Applying the average, FIFO, and LIFO methods)*** Coastal Sporting Goods started April with an inventory of nine sets of golf clubs that cost a total of $1,620. During April, Coastal purchased 25 sets of clubs for $4,750. At the end of the month, Coastal had eight sets of golf clubs on hand. The store manager must select an inventory costing method, and he asks you to tell him both cost of goods sold and ending inventory under these three accounting methods: LO 3

a. Average cost (round average unit cost to the nearest cent)
b. FIFO
c. LIFO

S6-4. ***(Learning Objective 2: Applying the average, FIFO, and LIFO methods)*** Jackson's Copy Center uses laser printers. Assume Jackson started the year with 92 containers of ink (average cost of $9.20 each, FIFO cost of $8.75 each, LIFO cost of $8.30 each). During the year, Jackson purchased 680 containers of ink at $10.30 and sold 580 units for $22.50 each. Jackson paid operating expenses throughout the year, a total of $3,570. Jackson is not subject to income tax. LO 2

Prepare Jackson's Income Statement for the current year ended December 31 under the average, FIFO, and LIFO inventory costing methods. Include a complete statement heading.

S6-5. ***(Learning Objective 3: Computing income tax effects of the inventory costing methods)*** This exercise should be used in conjunction with Short Exercise 6-4. Jackson is a corporation subject to a 35% income tax. Compute Jackson's income tax expense under the average, FIFO, and LIFO inventory costing methods. Which method would you select to (a) maximize income before tax and (b) minimize income tax expense? LO 3

S6-6. ***(Learning Objective 3: Computing income and income tax effects of LIFO)*** Macrodata.com uses the LIFO method to account for inventory. Macrodata is having an unusually good year, with net income well above expectations. The company's inventory costs are rising rapidly. What can Macrodata do immediately before the end of the year to decrease net income? Explain how this action decreases reported income, and also why Macrodata might want to decrease its net income. LO 3 ■ **writing assignment**

S6-7. ***(Learning Objective 3: Applying the Net Realizable Value to inventory)*** It is December 31, end of the year, and the controller of Grass Corporation is applying the Net Realizable Value (NRV) to inventories. Before any year-end adjustments, Grass reports the following data: LO 3

Cost of goods sold	$470,000
Historical cost of ending inventory, as determined by a physical count	54,000

Grass determines that the NRV of ending inventory is $48,000. Show what Grass should report for ending inventory and for cost of goods sold. Identify the financial statement where each item appears.

LO 3
■ **writing assignment**

S6-8. ***(Learning Objective 3: Managing income taxes under the LIFO method)*** Stone Saxophone Company is nearing the end of its worst year ever. With two weeks until year-end, it appears that net income for the year will have decreased by 25% from last year. Jason Stone, the president and principal shareholder, is distressed with the year's results. Stone asks you, the financial vice president, to come up with a way to increase the business's net income. Inventory quantities are a little higher than normal because sales have been slow during the last few months. Stone uses the LIFO inventory method, and inventory costs have risen dramatically during the latter part of the year.

Complete the memorandum to Jason Stone to explain how the company can increase its net income for the year. Explain your reasoning in detail. Stone is a man of integrity, so your plan must be completely ethical.

LO 3

S6-9. ***(Learning Objective 3: Identifying income, tax, and other effects of the inventory methods)*** This exercise tests your understanding of the four inventory methods. List the name of the inventory method that best fits the description. Assume that the cost of inventory is rising.

1. Matches the most current cost of goods sold against sales revenue.
2. Results in an old measure of the cost of ending inventory.
3. Writes inventory down when replacement cost drops below historical cost.
4. Enables a company to buy high-cost inventory at year-end and thereby decrease reported income and income tax.
5. Enables a company to keep reported income from dropping lower by liquidating older layers of inventory.
6. Is generally associated with saving income taxes.
7. Results in a cost of ending inventory that is close to the current cost of replacing the inventory.
8. Is used to account for automobiles, jewelry, and art objects.
9. Provides a middle-ground measure of ending inventory and cost of goods sold.
10. Maximizes reported income.

LO 4

S6-10. ***(Learning Objective 4: Using ratio data to evaluate operations)*** Mountain Company made sales of $38,542 million during 20X6. Cost of goods sold for the year totaled $16,543 million. At the end of 20X5, Mountain's inventory stood at $1,461 million, and Mountain ended 20X6 with inventory of $2,045 million.

Compute Mountain's gross profit percentage and rate of inventory turnover for 20X6.

LO 4

S6-11. ***(Learning Objective 4: Estimating ending inventory by the gross profit method)*** Meteor Technology began the year with inventory of $254,000 and purchased $1,580,000 of goods during the year. Sales for the year are $4,200,000, and Meteor's gross profit percentage is 60% of sales. Compute Meteor's estimated cost of ending inventory by using the gross profit method.

LO 5

S6-12. ***(Learning Objective 5: Assessing the effect of an inventory error—one year only)*** XYZ, Inc., reported these figures for its fiscal year (amounts in millions):

Net sales	$ 2,100
Cost of goods sold	1,150
Ending inventory	480

Suppose XYZ later learns that ending inventory was overstated by $14 million. What are the correct amounts for (a) net sales, (b) ending inventory, (c) cost of goods sold, and (d) gross profit?

LO 5

S6-13. ***(Learning Objective 5: Assessing the effect of an inventory error on 2 years)*** Kinder's $5.8 million cost of inventory at the end of last year was understated by $1.9 million.

1. Was last year's reported gross profit of $3.2 million overstated, understated, or correct? What was the correct amount of gross profit last year?
2. Is this year's gross profit of $5.6 million overstated, understated, or correct? What is the correct amount of gross profit for the current year?

S6-14. *(Learning Objectives 2, 4: Considering ethical implications of inventory actions)* Determine whether each of the following actions in buying, selling, and accounting for inventories is ethical or unethical. Give your reason for each answer.

LO 2 4

1. Wellness Pharmaceuticals purchased lots of inventory shortly before year-end to increase the LIFO cost of goods sold and decrease reported income for the year.
2. In applying the net realizable value to inventories, Rich Financial Industries recorded an excessively low market value for ending inventory. This allowed the company to pay less income tax for the year.
3. Geller Corporation deliberately overstated purchases to produce a high figure for cost of goods sold (low amount of net income). The real reason was to decrease the company's income tax payments to the government.
4. Ditto Sales Company deliberately overstated ending inventory in order to report higher profits (net income).
5. Blueberry, Inc., delayed the purchase of inventory until after December 31, 20X6, to keep 20X6's cost of goods sold from growing too large. The delay in purchasing inventory helped net income of 20X6 to reach the level of profit demanded by the company's investors.

Exercises MyLab Accounting

Select A and B exercises can be found within MyLab Accounting, an online homework and practice environment. Your instructor may ask you to complete select exercises using MyLab Accounting.

Group A

E6-15A. *(Learning Objectives 1, 2: Accounting for inventory transactions under FIFO costing)* Accounting records for Richard Corporation yield the following data for the year ended December 31, 20X6:

LO 1 2

Inventory, December 31, 20X5	$ 9,000
Purchases of inventory (on account)	48,000
Sales of inventory—79% on account; 21% for cash (cost $41,000)	77,000
Inventory at FIFO, December 31, 20X6	16,000

Requirements

1. Journalize Richard's inventory transactions for the year under the perpetual system.
2. Report ending inventory, sales, cost of goods sold, and gross profit on the appropriate financial statement.

E6-16A. *(Learning Objectives 2, 3: Analyzing inventory transactions under FIFO costing)* Kurt's, Inc.'s inventory records for a particular development program show the following at December 31:

LO 2 3
■ spreadsheet

Dec 1	Beginning inventory	5 units @ $160	=	$ 800
15	Purchase	4 units @ $165	=	$ 660
26	Purchase	12 units @ $180	=	$ 2,160

At December 31, nine of these programs are on hand. Journalize for Kurt's:

1. Total December purchases in one summary entry. All purchases were on credit.
2. Total December sales and cost of goods sold in two summary entries. The selling price was $520 per unit, and all sales were on credit. Assume that Kurt's uses the FIFO inventory method and the sale took place on December 28.
3. Under FIFO, how much gross profit would Kurt's earn on these transactions? What is the FIFO cost of Kurt's ending inventory?

LO 2 3

E6-17A. ***(Learning Objective 2, 3: Determining ending inventory and cost of goods sold by four methods)*** Use the data for Kurt's in Exercise 6-16A to answer the following:

Requirements

1. Compute cost of goods sold and ending inventory, using each of the following methods:
   a. Specific unit cost, with three $160 units and six $180 units still on hand at the end.
   b. Average cost.
   c. First-in, first-out.
   d. Last-in, first-out.
2. Which method produces the highest cost of goods sold? Which method produces the lowest cost of goods sold? What causes the difference in cost of goods sold?

LO 2 3

E6-18A. ***(Learning Objective 2, 3: Computing the tax advantage of LIFO over FIFO)*** Use the data for Kurt's in Exercise 6-16A to illustrate Kurt's income tax advantage from using LIFO over FIFO. Sales revenue is $6,800, operating expenses are $1,200, and the income tax rate is 35%. How much in taxes would Kurt's save by using the LIFO method versus FIFO?

LO 2 3

E6-19A. ***(Learning Objective 2, 3: Determining ending inventory and cost of goods sold—FIFO vs. LIFO)*** MusicSheet.net specializes in sound equipment. Because each inventory item is expensive, MusicSheet uses a perpetual inventory system. Company records indicate the following data for a line of speakers:

Date	Item	Quantity	Unit Cost	Sale Price
Apr 1	Balance..................	18	$34	
Apr 2	Purchase................	6	65	
Apr 7	Sale	9		$122
Apr 13	Sale	6		122

Requirements

1. Determine the amounts that MusicSheet should report for cost of goods sold and ending inventory in two ways:
   a. FIFO
   b. LIFO
2. MusicSheet uses the FIFO method. Prepare MusicSheet's Income Statement for the month ended April 30, reporting gross profit. Operating expenses totaled $280, and the income tax rate was 32%.

LO 3

E6-20A. ***(Learning Objective 3: Measuring gross profit—FIFO vs. LIFO; Falling prices)*** Suppose a Waldorf store in Atlanta, Georgia, ended November 20X6 with 800,000 units of merchandise that cost an average of $5 each. Suppose the store then sold 600,000 units for $5.2 million during December. Further, assume the store made two large purchases during December as follows:

Dec 11	200,000 units @ $4.00 =	$ 800,000
24	500,000 units @ $3.00 =	$1,500,000

Requirements

1. At December 31, the store manager needs to know the store's gross profit under both FIFO and LIFO. Supply this information.
2. What caused the FIFO and LIFO gross profit figures to differ?
3. Assume that the store uses FIFO to value inventories, and that the store manager, whose bonus is based on profits, decides to change the unit cost on inventory to $5 for all units. What impact will this have on gross profit and net income? Should this be allowed?

E6-21A. ***(Learning Objective 3: Applying the net realizable value to inventories)*** Lush Garden Supplies uses a perpetual inventory system. Lush Garden Supplies has these account balances at July 31, 20X6, prior to making the year-end adjustments:

Inventory	
Beg. bal. 11,500	
End. bal. 18,000	

Cost of Goods Sold	
Bal. 76,000	

Sales Revenue	
	Bal. 161,000

A year ago, the NRV cost of ending inventory was $12,000, which exceeded cost of $11,500. Lush Garden Supplies has determined that the NRV cost of the July 31, 20X6, ending inventory is $14,800.

Requirement

1. Prepare Lush Garden Supplies' 20X6 Income Statement through gross profit to show how the company would apply the net realizable value to its inventories.

LO 4

E6-22A. ***(Learning Objective 4: Using the cost-of-goods-sold model)*** Supply the missing Income Statement amounts for each of the following companies:

Company	Net Sales	Beginning Inventory	Net Purchases	Ending Inventory	Cost of Goods Sold	Gross Profit
Chris	$125,000	$21,000	$65,000	$19,000	(a)	(b)
Ford	138,000	26,000	(c)	27,000	(d)	44,000
Arthur	(e)	(f)	65,000	32,000	60,000	38,000
Michaels	94,000	11,000	32,000	(g)	38,000	(h)

Requirement

1. Prepare the Income Statement for Chris Company, for the year ended December 31. Use the cost-of-goods-sold model to compute cost of goods sold. Chris's operating and other expenses, as adapted, for the year were $42,000. Ignore income tax.

LO 4

E6-23A. ***(Learning Objective 4: Measuring profitability)*** Refer to the data in Exercise 6-22A. Compute all ratio values to answer the following questions:

- Which company has the highest, and which company has the lowest, gross profit percentage?
- Which company has the highest, and which the lowest, rate of inventory turnover? Based on your figures, which company appears to be the most profitable?

E6-24A. ***(Learning Objective 4: Computing gross profit percentage and inventory turnover)*** Thick & Thin, a partnership, had the following inventory data:

	20X5	20X6
Ending inventory at:		
FIFO Cost..............	$22,000	$ 24,000
LIFO Cost..............	10,000	16,000
Cost of goods sold at:		
FIFO Cost..............		$ 82,500
LIFO Cost..............		98,200
Sales revenue..............		148,000

Thick & Thin need to know the company's gross profit percentage and rate of inventory turnover for 20X6 under:

1. FIFO
2. LIFO

Which method makes the business look better on:

3. Gross profit percentage?
4. Inventory turnover?

LO 4

E6-25A. ***(Learning Objective 4: Budgeting inventory purchases)*** Toys Plus prepares budgets to help manage the company. Toys Plus is budgeting for the fiscal year ended January 31, 20X6. During the preceding year ended January 31, 20X5, sales totaled $9,400 million and cost of goods sold was $6,700 million. At January 31, 20X5, inventory stood at $2,200 million. During the upcoming 20X6 year, suppose Toys Plus expects cost of goods sold to increase by 10%. The company budgets next year's ending inventory at $2,500 million.

Requirement

1. One of the most important decisions a manager makes is how much inventory to buy. How much inventory should Toys Plus purchase during the upcoming year to reach its budgeted figures?

LO 4 ■ spreadsheet

E6-26A. ***(Learning Objective 4: Estimating inventory by the gross profit method)*** J C Company began May with inventory of $48,500. The business made net purchases of $32,900 and had net sales of $64,000 before a fire destroyed the company's inventory. For the past several years, J C's gross profit percentage has been 35%. Estimate the cost of the inventory destroyed by the fire. Identify another reason owners and managers use the gross profit method to estimate inventory.

LO 5

E6-27A. ***(Learning Objective 5: Correcting an inventory error)*** Mighty Sea Marine Supply reported the following comparative Income Statement for the years ended September 30, 20X6 and 20X5:

A1

	A	B	C	D	E
1	**Mighty Sea Marine Supply Income Statements**	**Year Ended September 30**			
2		**20X6**		**20X5**	
3	Sales revenue		$ 143,000		$ 120,000
4	Cost of goods sold:				
5	Beginning inventory	$ 14,500		$ 9,000	
6	Net purchases	74,000		67,000	
7	Cost of goods available	88,500		76,000	
8	Ending inventory	(19,000)		(14,500)	
9	Cost of goods sold		69,500		61,500
10	Gross profit		73,500		58,500
11	Operating expenses		28,000		24,000
12	Net income		$ 45,500		$ 34,500
13					

Mighty Sea's president and shareholders are thrilled by the company's boost in sales and net income during 20X6. Then the accountants for the company discover that ending 20X5 inventory was understated by $7,500. Prepare the corrected comparative Income Statement for the two-year period, complete with a heading for the statement. How well did Mighty Sea really perform in 20X6, as compared with 20X5?

Group B

LO 1 2

E6-28B. ***(Learning Objectives 1, 2: Accounting for inventory transactions under FIFO costing)*** Accounting records for Rockfeller Corporation yield the following data for the year ended December 31, 20X6:

Inventory, December 31, 20X5	€ 7,000
Purchases of inventory (on account)	45,000
Sales of inventory—76% on account; 24% for cash (cost $40,000)	72,000
Inventory at FIFO, December 31, 20X6	19,000

Requirements

1. Journalize Rockfeller's inventory transactions for the year under the perpetual system.
2. Report ending inventory, sales, cost of goods sold, and gross profit on the appropriate financial statement.

E6-29B. ***(Learning Objectives 2, 3: Analyzing inventory transactions under FIFO costing)*** Riva's, Inc.'s inventory records for a particular development program show the following at May 31:

May 1	Beginning inventory	8 units @ $150	=	$1,200
15	Purchase	5 units @ $150	=	750
26	Purchase	13 units @ $160	=	2,080

At May 31, 10 of these programs are on hand. Journalize for Riva's:

1. Total May purchases in one summary entry. All purchases were on credit.
2. Total May sales and cost of goods sold in two summary entries. The selling price was $640 per unit and all sales were on credit. Assume that Riva's uses the FIFO inventory method and the sale took place on May 28.
3. Under FIFO, how much gross profit would Riva's earn on these transactions? What is the FIFO cost of Riva's, Inc.'s ending inventory?

E6-30B. ***(Learning Objective 2, 3: Determining ending inventory and cost of goods sold by four methods)*** Use the data for Riva's, Inc., in Exercise 6-29B to answer the following.

Requirements

1. Compute cost of goods sold and ending inventory using each of the following methods:
   a. Specific unit cost, with four $150 units and six $160 units still on hand at the end
   b. Average cost
   c. FIFO
   d. LIFO
2. Which method produces the highest cost of goods sold? Which method produces the lowest cost of goods sold? What causes the difference in cost of goods sold?

LO 2 3

E6-31B. ***(Learning Objectives 2, 3: Computing the tax advantage of LIFO over FIFO)*** Use the data for Riva's, Inc., in Exercise 6-29B to illustrate Riva's income tax advantage from using LIFO over FIFO. Sales revenue is $8,570, operating expenses are $2,300, and the income tax rate is 38%. How much in taxes would Riva's save by using the LIFO method versus FIFO?

LO 2 3

E6-32B. ***(Learning Objectives 2, 3: Determining ending inventory and cost of goods sold—FIFO vs. LIFO)*** MusicNotes.net specializes in sound equipment. Because each inventory item is expensive, MusicNotes uses a perpetual inventory system. Company records indicate the following data for a line of speakers:

Date	Item	Quantity	Unit Cost	Sale Price
Apr 1	Balance..................	17	$38	
Apr 2	Purchase................	5	68	
Apr 7	Sale	9		$106
Apr 13	Sale	5		92

Requirements

1. Determine the amounts that MusicNotes should report for cost of goods sold and ending inventory two ways:
   a. FIFO
   b. LIFO
2. MusicNotes uses the FIFO method. Prepare MusicNotes' Income Statement for the month ended April 30, reporting gross profit. Operating expenses totaled $430, and the income tax rate was 30%.

LO 3

E6-33B. ***(Learning Objective 3: Measuring gross profit—FIFO vs. LIFO; Falling prices)*** Suppose a store in Milan ended September with 1,500,000 units of merchandise that cost an average of €9.00 each. Suppose the store then sold 1,300,000 units for €14.1 million during October. Further, assume the store made two large purchases during October as follows:

Oct 12	100,000 units @ $8.00	=	€ 800,000
24	600,000 units @ $7.00	=	€4,200,000

Requirements

1. At October 31, the store manager needs to know the store's gross profit under both FIFO and LIFO. Supply this information.
2. What caused the FIFO and LIFO gross profit figures to differ?
3. Assume that the store uses FIFO, and that the store manager, whose bonus is based on profits, decides to value all units in ending inventory at €9 per unit. What impact will this action have on gross profit and net income? Should this be allowed?

LO 3

E6-34B. ***(Learning Objective 3: Applying the net realizable value to inventories)*** Secret Garden Supplies uses a perpetual inventory system. Secret Garden Supplies has these account balances at May 31, 20X6, prior to making the year-end adjustments:

Inventory		Cost of Goods Sold		Sales Revenue	
Beg. bal. 12,500					
End. bal. 15,300		Bal. 63,000			Bal. 152,000

A year ago, the NRV cost of ending inventory was €14,600, which exceeded the cost of €12,500. Secret Garden Supplies has determined that the NRV cost of the May 31, 20X6, ending inventory is €13,400.

Requirement

1. Prepare Secret Garden Supplies' 20X6 Income Statement through gross profit to show how the company would apply the net realizable value to its inventories.

LO 4

E6-35B. ***(Learning Objective 4: Using the cost-of-goods-sold model)*** Supply the missing amounts for each of the following companies:

Company	Net Sales	Beginning Inventory	Net Purchases	Ending Inventory	Cost of Goods Sold	Gross Profit
Frank	€121,000	€18,000	€64,000	€17,000	(a)	(b)
Hill	135,000	26,000	(c)	28,000	(d)	48,000
Fort	(e)	(f)	56,000	22,000	61,000	32,000
Orville	89,000	8,000	33,000	(g)	36,000	(h)

Requirement

1. Prepare the Income Statement for Frank Company, for the year ended December 31. Use the cost-of-goods-sold model to compute cost of goods sold. Frank's operating and other expenses for the year were €48,000. Ignore income tax.

E6-36B. ***(Learning Objective 3: Measuring profitability)*** Refer to the data in Exercise 6-35B. Compute all ratio values to answer the following questions: LO 3

- Which company has the highest, and which company has the lowest, gross profit percentage?
- Which company has the highest, and which the lowest, rate of inventory turnover? Based on your figures, which company appears to be the most profitable?

E6-37B. ***(Learning Objective 3: Computing gross profit percentage and inventory turnover)*** Dunk & Dive, a partnership, had these inventory data: LO 3

	20X5	20X6
Ending inventory at:		
FIFO Cost	$19,000	$ 22,000
LIFO Cost	16,000	23,000
Cost of goods sold at:		
FIFO Cost		$ 87,500
LIFO Cost		95,200
Sales revenue		145,000

Dunk & Dive need to know the company's gross profit percentage and rate of inventory turnover for 20X6 under

1. FIFO
2. LIFO

Which method makes the business look better on

3. Gross profit percentage?
4. Inventory turnover?

E6-38B. ***(Learning Objective 4: Budgeting inventory purchases)*** Toyland prepares budgets to help manage the company. Toyland is budgeting for the fiscal year ended January 31, 20X6. During the preceding year ended January 31, 20X5, sales totaled €9,500 million and cost of goods sold was €6,400 million. At January 31, 20X5, inventory stood at €1,900 million. During the upcoming 20X6 year, suppose Toyland expects cost of goods sold to increase by 10%. The company budgets next year's inventory at €2,200 million. LO 4

Requirement

1. One of the most important decisions a manager makes is how much inventory to buy. How much inventory should Toyland purchase during the upcoming year to reach its budgeted figures?

LO 4

spreadsheet

E6-39B. ***(Learning Objective 4: Estimating inventory by the gross profit method)*** R T Company began June with inventory of €45,700. The business made net purchases of €39,100 and had net sales of €68,400 before a fire destroyed the company's inventory. For the past several years, R T's gross profit percentage has been 40%. Estimate the cost of the inventory destroyed by the fire. Identify another reason owners and managers use the gross profit method to estimate inventory.

LO 5

E6-40B. ***(Learning Objective 5: Correcting an inventory error)*** Friendly Harbor Marine Supply reported the following comparative Income Statement for the years ended September 30, 20X6 and 20X5:

	A	B	C	D	E
1	**Friendly Harbor Marine Supply Income Statements**	**12 Months Ended September 30**			
2		**20X6**		**20X5**	
3	Sales revenue		€ 139,000		€ 121,000
4	Cost of goods sold:				
5	Beginning inventory	€ 13,000		€ 12,000	
6	Net purchases	74,000		69,000	
7	Cost of goods available	87,000		81,000	
8	Ending inventory	(18,500)		(13,000)	
9	Cost of goods sold		68,500		68,000
10	Gross profit		70,500		53,000
11	Operating expenses		26,000		19,000
12	Net income		€ 44,500		€ 34,000
13					

Friendly Harbor's president and shareholders are thrilled by the company's boost in sales and net income during 20X6. Then the accountants for the company discover that ending 20X5 inventory was understated by €6,800. Prepare the corrected comparative Income Statement for the two-year period, complete with a heading for the statement. How well did Friendly Harbor really perform in 20X6, as compared with 20X5?

Challenge Exercises

LO 1 3

E6-41. ***(Learning Objectives 1, 3: Making inventory policy decisions)*** For each of the following situations, identify the inventory method that you would use, or, given the use of a particular method, state the strategy that you would follow to accomplish your goal:

a. Company management, like that of IBM and Esplanade Imports, prefers a middle-of-the-road inventory policy that avoids extremes.

b. Inventory costs are *decreasing*, and your company's board of directors wants to minimize income taxes.

c. Inventory costs are *increasing*, and the company prefers to report high income.

d. Inventory costs have been stable for several years, and you expect costs to remain stable for the indefinite future. (Give the reason for your choice of method.)

e. Inventory costs are increasing. Your company uses LIFO and is having an unexpectedly good year. It is near year-end, and you need to keep net income from increasing too much in order to save on income tax.

f. Suppliers of your inventory are threatening a labor strike, and it may be difficult for your company to obtain inventory. This situation could increase your income taxes.

LO 3

E6-42. ***(Learning Objective 3: Evaluating a company's profitability)*** L Mart, Inc., declared bankruptcy. Let's see why. L Mart reported these figures:

	A	B	C	D	E
1	L Mart, Inc. Statement of Income	12 Months Ended Dec. 31			
2	(In millions of $)	20X6	20X5	20X4	20X3
3	Sales	$ 36.2	$ 35.8	$ 34.3	
4	Cost of sales	28.6	27.7	26.8	
5	Selling expenses	7.8	6.9	6.0	
6	Other expenses	0.2	1.0	0.8	
7	Net income (net loss)	$ (0.4)	$ 0.2	$ 0.7	
8	Additional data:				
9	Ending inventory	$ 8.9	$ 7.3	$ 7.8	$ 6.4
10					

Requirement

1. Evaluate the trend of L Mart's results of operations during 20X4 through 20X6. Consider the trends of sales, gross profit, and net income. Track the gross profit percentage (to three decimal places) and the rate of inventory turnover (to one decimal place) in each year. Also discuss the role that selling expenses must have played in L Mart's difficulties.

Quiz

Test your understanding of accounting for inventory by answering the following questions. Select the best choice from among the possible answers given.

The next two questions use the following facts. Oceanview Software began January with $3,500 of merchandise inventory. During January, Oceanview made the following entries for its inventory transactions:

	A	B	C	D
1		Inventory	6,300	
2		Accounts Payable		6,300
3				
4		Accounts Receivable	7,600	
5		Sales Revenue		7,600
6				
7		Cost of Goods Sold	5,400	
8		Inventory		5,400
9				

Q6-43. How much was Oceanview's inventory at the end of January?

a. $5,400
b. Zero
c. $4,400
d. $2,200

Q6-44. What was Oceanview's gross profit for January?

a. Zero
b. $7,600
c. $5,400
d. $2,200

Q6-45. When does the cost of inventory become an expense?

a. When inventory is delivered to a customer.
b. When inventory is purchased from the supplier.
c. When cash is collected from the customer.
d. When payment is made to the supplier.

The next two questions use the following facts. Marble Frame Shop wants to know the effect of different inventory costing methods on its financial statements. Inventory and purchases data for April follow:

		Units	Unit Cost	Total Cost
Apr 1	Beginning inventory	2,600	$15.00	$39,000
4	Purchase	1,300	15.20	19,760
9	Sale	(1,500)		

Q6-46. If Marble Frame uses the FIFO method, the cost of the ending inventory will be
a. $39,000.
b. $36,160.
c. $36,260.
d. $36,000.

Q6-47. If Marble Frame uses the LIFO method, cost of goods sold will be
a. $22,600.
b. $22,760.
c. $22,500.
d. $19,760.

Q6-48. In a period of rising prices,
a. Gross profit under FIFO will be higher than under LIFO.
b. LIFO inventory will be greater than FIFO inventory.
c. Net income under LIFO will be higher than under FIFO.
d. Cost of goods sold under LIFO will be less than under FIFO.

Q6-49. The Income Statement for Feel Good Health Foods shows gross profit of $154,000, operating expenses of $128,000, and cost of goods sold of $213,000. What is the amount of net sales revenue?
a. $367,000
b. $341,000
c. $495,000
d. $341,000

Q6-50. When the inventory cost is lower than NRV, the inventory should be reported at
a. market price of inventory.
b. replacement of inventory.
c. selling price of inventory less cost to sell.
d. acquisition cost of inventory.

Q6-51. The sum of (a) ending inventory and (b) cost of goods sold is
a. goods available.
b. beginning inventory.
c. gross profit.
d. net purchases.

Q6-52. The following data come from the inventory records of Draper Company:

Net sales revenue	$632,000
Beginning inventory	68,000
Ending inventory	45,000
Net purchases	480,000

Based on these facts, the gross profit for Dapper Company is
a. $152,000.
b. $175,000.
c. $129,000.
d. Some other amount.

Q6-53. Ellen Braun Cosmetics ended the month of May with inventory of $26,000. Ellen Braun expects to end June with inventory of $14,000 after cost of goods sold of $103,000. How much inventory must Ellen Braun purchase during June in order to accomplish these results?
a. $89,000
b. $91,000
c. $115,000
d. Cannot be determined from the data given

Q6-54. Two financial ratios that clearly distinguish a discount chain such as Kmart from a high-end retailer such as Saks Fifth Avenue are the gross profit percentage and the rate of inventory turnover. Which set of relationships is most likely for Saks Fifth Avenue?

Gross profit percentage	Inventory turnover
a. Low	Low
b. Low	High
c. High	Low
d. High	High

Q6-55. Sales are $540,000 and cost of goods sold is $330,000. Beginning and ending inventories are $29,000 and $34,000, respectively. How many times did the company turn its inventory over during this period?

a. 17.1 times
b. 6.7 times
c. 7.2 times
d. 10.5 times

Q6-56. Kruger, Inc., reported the following data:

Freight in....................	$ 24,000	Sales returns.............	$ 7,000
Purchases	215,000	Purchase returns........	6,200
Beginning inventory	57,000	Sales revenue............	460,000
Purchase discounts	4,800	Ending inventory.......	48,000

Kruger's gross profit percentage is

a. 46.1.
b. 51.7.
c. 47.7.
d. 50.0.

Q6-57. Shailene Wood Company had the following beginning inventory, net purchases, net sales, and gross profit percentage for the first quarter of 20X6:

Beginning inventory, $50,000	Net purchases, $74,000
Net sales revenue, $96,000	Gross profit rate, 50%

By the gross profit method, the ending inventory should be

a. $74,000.
b. $76,000.
c. $81,000.
d. $79,000.

Q6-58. An error understated Regan Corporation's December 31, 20X6, ending inventory by $42,000. What effect will this error have on total assets and net income for 20X6?

Assets	Net income
a. Understate	Understate
b. No effect	Overstate
c. Understate	No effect
d. No effect	No effect

Q6-59. An error understated Regan Corporation's December 31, 20X6, ending inventory by $42,000. What effect will this error have on net income for 20X7?

a. Understate
b. Overstate
c. No effect

Problems MyLab Accounting

Select A and B problems can be found within MyLab Accounting, an online homework and practice environment. Your instructor may ask you to complete select problems using MyLab Accounting

Group A

P6-60A. ***(Learning Objectives 1, 2: Accounting for inventory in a perpetual system using average costing method)*** Nice Buy purchases inventory in crates of merchandise; each crate of inventory is a unit. The fiscal year of Nice Buy ends each February 28. Assume you are dealing with a single Nice Buy store in Taipei, Taiwan. The Taiwan store began 20X6 with an inventory of 23,000 units that cost a total of $1,150,000. During the year, the store purchased merchandise on account as follows:

April (31,000 units at $51)	$1,581,000
August (51,000 units at $55)	2,805,000
November (61,000 units at $61)	3,721,000
Total purchases	$8,107,000

Cash payments on account totaled $7,907,000. During fiscal year 20X6, the store sold 150,000 units of merchandise for $14,700,000, of which $4,800,000 was for cash and the balance was on account. Nice Buy uses the average cost method for inventories. Operating expenses for the year were $3,550,000. Nice Buy paid 70% in cash and accrued the rest as accrued liabilities. The store accrued income tax at the rate of 30%.

Requirements

1. Make summary journal entries to record the store's transactions for the year ended February 28, 20X6. Nice Buy uses a perpetual inventory system.
2. Prepare a T-account to show the activity in the Inventory Account.
3. Prepare the store's Income Statement for the year ended February 28, 20X6. Show totals for gross profit, income before tax, and net income.

P6-61A. ***(Learning Objective 1, 2: Measuring cost of goods sold and ending inventory—perpetual system)*** Assume a Jaguar Sports outlet store began October 20X6 with 52 pairs of running shoes that cost the store $35 each. The sale price of these shoes was $70. During October, the store completed these inventory transactions:

		Units	Unit Cost	Unit Sales Price
Oct 3	Sale	13	$35	$70
8	Purchase	84	36	
11	Sale	39	35	70
19	Sale	5	36	71
24	Sale	40	36	71
30	Purchase	24	37	

Requirements

1. The preceding data are taken from the store's perpetual inventory records. Which cost method does the store use? Explain how you arrived at your answer.
2. Determine the store's cost of goods sold for October. Also compute gross profit for October.
3. What is the cost of the store's October 31 inventory of running shoes?

LO 2 3

P6-62A. ***(Learning Objectives 2, 3: Computing inventory by three methods—perpetual system)*** Fatigues Surplus began October with 78 tents that cost $19 each. During the month, Fatigues Surplus made the following purchases at cost:

Oct 4	99 tents @ $20 =	$1,980
19	155 tents @ $21 =	3,410
25	48 tents @ $23 =	1,104

Fatigues Surplus sold 334 tents, and at October 31 the ending inventory consisted of 46 tents. The sale price of each tent was $52.

Requirements

1. Determine the cost of goods sold and ending inventory amounts for October under the average cost, FIFO cost, and LIFO cost. Round average cost per unit to four decimal places, and round all other amounts to the nearest dollar.
2. Explain why cost of goods sold is highest under LIFO. Be specific.
3. Prepare Fatigues Surplus' Income Statement for October. Report gross profit. Operating expenses totaled $5,400. Fatigues Surplus uses average costing for inventory. The income tax rate is 40%.

P6-63A. ***(Learning Objective 2, 3: Applying the different inventory costing methods—perpetual system)*** The records of Byron Aviation include the following accounts for inventory of aviation fuel at December 31 of the current year:

LO 2 3
■ **writing assignment**

Inventory

Date		Description	Amount	
Jan	1	Balance 780 units @ $7.80	$ 6,084	
Mar	6	Purchase 310 units @ $7.90	2,449	
Jun	22	Purchase 8,360 units @ $8.10	67,716	
Oct	4	Purchase 540 units @ $9.20	4,968	

Sales Revenue

	Date	Description	Amount
	Dec 31	9,010 units	$132,447

Requirements

1. Prepare a partial Income Statement through gross profit under the average, FIFO, and LIFO methods. Round average cost per unit to four decimal places and all other amounts to the nearest dollar.
2. Which inventory method would you use to minimize income tax? Explain why this method causes income tax to be the lowest.

P6-64A. ***(Learning Objective 3: Applying the net realizable value to inventories—perpetual system)*** Everything Trade Mart has recently had lackluster sales. The rate of inventory turnover has dropped, and the merchandise is gathering dust. It is now December 31, 20X6, and the current NRV cost of Everything's ending inventory is $78,000 below what Everything actually paid for the goods, which was $210,000. Before any adjustments at the end of the period, the Cost of Goods Sold account has a balance of $750,000.

LO 3
■ **writing assignment**

a. What accounting action should Everything take in this situation?
b. Give any journal entry required.
c. At what amount should Everything report Inventory on the Balance Sheet?
d. At what amount should the company report Cost of Goods Sold on the Income Statement?
e. Discuss the accounting principle or concept that is most relevant to this situation.

LO 4

P6-65A. ***(Learning Objective 4: Using gross profit percentage and inventory turnover to evaluate two companies)*** Sprinkle Top and Coffee Shop are both specialty food chains. The two companies reported these figures, in millions:

	A	B	C
1	**Sprinkle Top, Inc.** **Income Statement**	**12 Months** **Ended Dec. 31**	
2	**(Adapted, in millions of $)**	**20X6**	**20X5**
3	**Revenues:**		
4	Net sales	$ 554	$ 727
5			
6	**Costs and Expenses:**		
7	Cost of goods sold	487	598
8	Selling, general, and administrative expenses	63	59
9			

	A	B	C
1	**Sprinkle Top, Inc.** **Balance Sheet**	**December 31**	
2	**(Adapted, in millions of $)**	**20X6**	**20X5**
3	**Assets**		
4	Current assets:		
5	Cash and cash equivalents	$ 15	$ 29
6	Receivables	31	42
7	Inventories	29	38
8			

	A	B	C
1	**Coffee Shop Corporation** **Income Statement**	**12 Months** **Ended Dec. 31**	
2	**(Adapted, in millions of $)**	**20X6**	**20X5**
3	**Net sales**	$ 7,720	$ 6,310
4	Cost of goods sold	3,170	2,614
5	Selling, general, and administrative expenses	2,930	2,350
6			

	A	B	C
1	**Coffee Shop Corporation** **Balance Sheet**	**December 31**	
2	**(Adapted, in millions of $)**	**20X6**	**20X5**
3	**Assets**		
4	Current assets:		
5	Cash and temporary investments	$ 318	$ 173
6	Receivables, net	232	185
7	Inventories	629	547
8			

Requirements

1. Compute the gross profit percentage and the rate of inventory turnover for Sprinkle Top and Coffee Shop for 20X6.
2. Based on these statistics, which company looks more profitable? Why? What other expense category should we consider in evaluating these two companies?

P6-66A. ***(Learning Objectives 1, 4: Estimating inventory by the gross profit method; preparing the Income Statement)*** Assume Theon Company, a copy center, lost some inventory in a fire. To file an insurance claim, Theon Company must estimate its inventory by the gross profit method. Assume that for the past two years Theon Company's gross profit has averaged 40% of net sales. Suppose the Theon Company's inventory records reveal the following data:

Inventory, October 1	$ 57,200
Transactions during October:	
Purchases	490,400
Purchase discounts	11,100
Purchase returns	70,800
Sales	668,000
Sales returns	11,500

Requirements

1. Estimate the cost of the lost inventory, using the gross profit method.
2. Prepare the October Income Statement for this product through gross profit. Show the detailed computations of cost of goods sold in a separate schedule.

P6-67A. ***(Learning Objective 3: Determining the amount of inventory to purchase)*** Grammy's Convenience Store's Income Statement and Balance Sheet reported the following:

	A	B
1	**Grammy's Convenience Stores Income Statement Year Ended December 31, 20X5**	
2	Sales	$ 957,000
3	Cost of sales	720,000
4	Gross profit	237,000
5	Operating expenses	114,000
6	Net income	$ 123,000
7		

	A	B	C	D
1	**Grammy's Convenience Stores Balance Sheet December 31, 20X5**			
2	**Assets**		**Liabilities**	
3	Cash	$ 44,000	Accounts payable	$ 31,000
4	Inventories	68,000	Note payable	187,000
5	Land and buildings, net	273,000	Total liabilities	218,000
6			Owner, capital	167,000
7	Total assets	$ 385,000	Total liabilities and capital	$ 385,000
8				

The business is organized as a proprietorship, so it pays no corporate income tax. The owner is budgeting for 20X6. He expects sales and cost of goods sold to increase by 8%. To meet customer demand, ending inventory will need to be $78,000 at December 31, 20X6. The owner hopes to earn a net income of $158,000 next year.

Requirements

1. One of the most important decisions a manager makes is the amount of inventory to purchase. Show how to determine the amount of inventory to purchase in 20X6.
2. Prepare the store's budgeted Income Statement for 20X6 to reach the target net income of $158,000. To reach this goal, operating expenses must decrease by $16,040.

LO 5

P6-68A. ***(Learning Objective 5: Correcting inventory errors over a three-year period)*** The accounting records of R.B. Video Sales show the data betow (in millions). The shareholders are very happy with R.B.'s steady increase in net income.

Auditors discovered that the ending inventory for 20X4 was understated by \$3 million and that the ending inventory for 20X5 was also understated by \$3 million. The ending inventory at December 31, 20X6, was correct.

	20X6		20X5		20X4	
Net sales revenue		\$43		\$40		\$37
Cost of goods sold:						
Beginning inventory	\$ 6		\$ 5		\$ 4	
Net purchases	29		27		25	
Cost of goods available	35		32		29	
Less ending inventory	(7)		(6)		(5)	
Cost of goods sold		28		26		24
Gross profit		15		14		13
Operating expenses		7		7		7
Net income		\$ 8		\$ 7		\$ 6

Requirements

1. Show corrected Income Statements for each of the three years.
2. How much did these assumed corrections add to or take away from R.B.'s total net income over the three-year period? How did the corrections affect the trend of net income?
3. Will R.B.'s shareholders still be happy with the company's trend of net income? Give the reason for your answer.

Group B

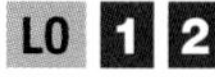

P6-69B. ***(Learning Objectives 1, 2: Accounting for inventory in a perpetual system using average costing method)*** Best Guy purchases inventory in crates of merchandise; each crate of inventory is a unit. The fiscal year of Best Guy ends each February 28. Assume you are dealing with a single Best Guy store in Paris, France. The Paris store began 20X6 with an inventory of 18,000 units that cost a total of €990,000. During the year, the store purchased merchandise on account as follows:

April (33,000 units at €60)	€1,980,000
August (53,000 units at €64)	3,392,000
November (63,000 units at €70)	4,410,000
Total purchases	€9,782,000

Cash payments on account totaled €9,492,000. During fiscal 20X6, the store sold 158,000 units of merchandise for €15,484,000, of which €5,400,000 was for cash and the balance was on account. Best Guy uses the average cost method for inventories. Operating expenses for the year were €2,860,000. Best Guy paid 70% in cash and accrued the rest as accrued liabilities. The store accrued income tax at the rate of 35%.

Requirements

1. Make summary journal entries to record the store's transactions for the year ended February 28, 20X6. Best Guy uses a perpetual inventory system.
2. Prepare a T-account to show the activity in the Inventory Account.
3. Prepare the store's Income Statement for the year ended February 28, 20X6. Show totals for gross profit, income before tax, and net income.

P6-70B. ***(Learning Objective 1, 2: Measuring cost of goods sold and ending inventory—perpetual system)*** Assume a Championship Sports outlet store began March with 48 pairs of running shoes that cost the store $38 each. The sale price of these shoes was $66. During March the store completed these inventory transactions:

		Units	Unit Cost	Unit Sale Price
Mar 3	Sale	18	$38	$66
8	Purchase......	77	39	
11	Sale	30	38	66
19	Sale	12	39	69
24	Sale	37	39	69
30	Purchase......	17	40	

Requirements

1. The preceding data are taken from the store's perpetual inventory records. Which cost method does the store use? Explain how you arrived at your answer.
2. Determine the store's cost of goods sold for March. Also compute gross profit for March.
3. What is the cost of the store's March 31 inventory of running shoes?

P6-71B. ***(Learning Objectives 2, 3: Computing inventory by three methods—perpetual system)*** SWAT Team Surplus began July with 69 tents that cost €24 each. During the month, SWAT Team Surplus made the following purchases at cost:

Jul 4	108 tents @ €26 = €2,808
19	153 tents @ €28 = 4,284
25	38 tents @ €29 = 1,102

SWAT Team Surplus sold 316 tents, and at July 31 the ending inventory consists of 52 tents. The sale price of each tent was €55.

Requirements

1. Determine the cost of goods sold and ending inventory amounts for July under the average cost, FIFO cost, and LIFO cost. Round average cost per unit four decimal places, and round all other amounts to the nearest dollar.
2. Explain why cost of goods sold is highest under LIFO. Be specific.
3. Prepare a SWAT Team Surplus Income Statement for July. Report gross profit. Operating expenses totaled €3,500. SWAT Team Surplus uses average costing for inventory. The income tax rate is 32%.

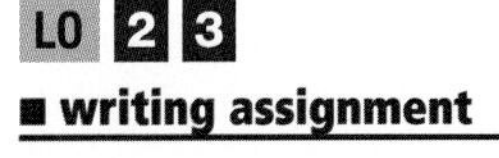

P6-72B. ***(Learning Objectives 2, 3: Applying the different inventory costing methods—perpetual system)*** The records of Bryan Aviation include the following accounts for inventory of aviation fuel at December 31 of the current year:

Inventory

Jan 1	Balance 740 units @ €7.50	€ 5,550	
Mar 6	Purchase 320 units @ €7.80	2,496	
Jun 22	Purchase 8,380 units @ €8.10	67,878	
Oct 4	Purchase 530 units @ €9.10	4,823	

Sales Revenue

	Dec 31	9,030 units	€128,226

Requirements

1. Prepare a partial Income Statement through gross profit under the average, FIFO, and LIFO methods. Round average cost per unit to four decimal places and all other amounts to the nearest whole dollar.
2. Which inventory method would you use to minimize income tax? Explain why this method causes income tax to be the lowest.

LO 3
■ writing assignment

P6-73B. ***(Learning Objective 3: Applying the net realizable value to inventories—perpetual system)*** Ariel Trade Mart has recently had lackluster sales. The rate of inventory turnover has dropped, and the merchandise is gathering dust. It is now December 31, 20X6, and the current NRV cost of Ariel's ending inventory is €72,000 below what Ariel actually paid for the goods, which was €270,000. Before any adjustments at the end of the period, the Cost of Goods Sold account has a balance of €830,000.

a. What accounting action should Ariel take in this situation?
b. Give any journal entry required.
c. At what amount should Ariel report Inventory on the Balance Sheet?
d. At what amount should the company report Cost of Goods Sold on the Income Statement?
e. Discuss the accounting principle or concept that is most relevant to this situation.

LO 4

P6-74B. ***(Learning Objective 4: Using gross profit percentage and inventory turnover to evaluate two companies)*** Pastry People and Coffee Grind are both specialty food chains. The two companies reported these figures, in millions:

A1

	A	B	C
1	**Pastry People, Inc.** **Income Statement**	**12 Months** **Ended Dec. 31**	
2	**(Adapted, in millions of $)**	**20X6**	**20X5**
3	**Revenues:**		
4	Net sales	$ 558	$ 711
5			
6	**Costs and Expenses:**		
7	Cost of goods sold	486	595
8	Selling, general, and administrative expenses	62	56
9			

	A	B	C
1	**Pastry People, Inc. Balance Sheet**	**December 31**	
2	**(Adapted, in millions of $)**	**20X6**	**20X5**
3	**Assets**		
4	Current assets:		
5	Cash and cash equivalents	$ 18	$ 26
6	Receivables	23	38
7	Inventories	18	31
8			

	A	B	C
1	**Coffee Grind Corporation Income Statement**	**12 Months Ended Dec. 31**	
2	**(Adapted, in millions of $)**	**20X6**	**20X5**
3	**Net sales**	$ 7,270	$ 6,460
4	Cost of goods sold	3,290	2,702
5	Selling, general, and administrative expenses	2,965	2,380
6			

	A	B	C
1	**Coffee Grind Corporation Balance Sheet**	**December 31**	
2	**(Adapted, in millions of $)**	**20X6**	**20X5**
3	**Assets**		
4	Current assets:		
5	Cash and temporary investments	$ 311	$ 178
6	Receivables, net	222	196
7	Inventories	632	548
8			

Requirements

1. Compute the gross profit percentage and the rate of inventory turnover for Pastry People and Coffee Grind for 20X6.
2. Based on these statistics, which company looks more profitable? Why? What other expense category should we consider in evaluating these two companies?

■ spreadsheet

P6-75B. ***(Learning Objectives 1, 4: Estimating inventory by the gross profit method; preparing the Income Statement)*** Assume Joey Company, a sporting goods store, lost some inventory in a fire. To file an insurance claim, Joey Company must estimate its ending inventory by the gross profit method. Assume that for the past two years, Joey Company's gross profit has averaged 45% of net sales. Suppose Joey Company's inventory records reveal the following data:

Inventory, January 1	€ 57,700
Transactions during January:	
Purchases	490,800
Purchase discounts	12,200
Purchase returns	70,200
Sales	665,000
Sales returns	16,500

Requirements

1. Estimate the cost of the lost inventory, using the gross profit method.
2. Prepare the January Income Statement for this product through gross profit. Show the detailed computation of cost of goods sold in a separate schedule.

LO 3

P6-76B. ***(Learning Objective 3: Determining the amount of inventory to purchase)*** Chris' Convenience Store's Income Statement and Balance Sheet reported the following. The business is organized as a proprietorship, so it pays no corporate income tax. The owner is budgeting for 20X6. He expects sales and cost of goods sold to increase by 10%. To meet customer demand, ending inventory will need to be €76,000 at December 31, 20X6. The owner hopes to earn a net income of €161,000 next year.

	A	B
1	**Chris' Convenience Stores Income Statement Year Ended December 31, 20X5**	
2	Sales	€ 964,000
3	Cost of sales	722,000
4	Gross profit	242,000
5	Operating expenses	110,000
6	Net income	€ 132,000
7		

	A	B	C	D
1	**Chris' Convenience Stores Balance Sheet December 31, 20X5**			
2	**Assets**		**Liabilities**	
3	Cash	€ 35,000	Accounts payable	€ 28,000
4	Inventories	65,000	Note payable	193,000
5	Land and buildings, net	268,000	Total liabilities	221,000
6			Owner, capital	147,000
7	Total assets	€ 368,000	Total liabilities and capital	€ 368,000
8				

Requirements

1. One of the most important decisions a manager makes is the amount of inventory to purchase. Show how to determine the amount of inventory to purchase in 20X6.
2. Prepare the store's budgeted Income Statement for 20X6 to reach the target net income of €161,000. To reach this goal, operating expenses must decrease by €4,800.

LO 5

P6-77B. ***(Learning Objective 5: Correcting inventory errors over a three-year period)*** The accounting records of Waterville Video Sales show the data betow (in millions). The shareholders are very happy with Waterville's steady increase in net income.

	20X6		20X5		20X4	
Net sales revenue		€38		€35		€32
Cost of goods sold:						
Beginning inventory	€ 9		€ 8		€ 7	
Net purchases	32		30		28	
Cost of goods available	41		38		35	
Less ending inventory	(10)		(9)		(8)	
Cost of goods sold		31		29		27
Gross profit		7		6		5
Operating expenses		3		3		3
Net income		$ 4		$ 3		$ 2

Auditors discovered that the ending inventory for 20X4 was understated by €2 million and that the ending inventory for 20X5 was also understated by €2 million. The ending inventory at December 31, 20X6, was correct.

Requirements

1. Show corrected Income Statements for each of the three years.
2. How much did these assumed corrections add to or take away from Waterville's total net income over the three-year period? How did the corrections affect the trend of net income?
3. Will Waterville's shareholders still be happy with the company's trend of net income? Give the reason for your answer.

APPLY YOUR KNOWLEDGE

Decision Cases

Case 1. *(Learning Objectives 1, 2: Assessing the impact of a year-end purchase of inventory)* Duracraft Corporation is nearing the end of its first year of operations. Duracraft made inventory purchases of $745,000 during the year, as follows:

LO 1 2
■ writing assignment

January	1,000 units @	$100.00 =	$100,000
July	4,000	121.25	485,000
November	1,000	160.00	160,000
Totals	6,000		$745,000

Sales for the year are 5,000 units for $1,200,000 of revenue. Expenses other than cost of goods sold and income taxes total $200,000. The president of the company is undecided about whether to adopt the FIFO method or the LIFO method for inventories. The income tax rate is 40%.

Requirements

1. To aid company decision making, prepare Income Statements under FIFO and under LIFO.
2. Compare the net income under FIFO with net income under LIFO. Which method produces the higher net income? What causes this difference? Be specific.

Case 2. *(Learning Objective 3: Assessing the impact of the inventory costing method on the financial statements)* The inventory costing method a company chooses can affect the financial statements and thus the decisions of the people who use those statements.

LO 3
■ writing assignment

Requirements

1. Company A uses the LIFO inventory method and discloses its use of the LIFO method in notes to the financial statements. Company B uses the FIFO method to account for its inventory. Company B does *not* disclose which inventory method it uses. Company B reports a higher net income than Company A. In which company would you prefer to invest? Give your reason.
2. Conservatism is an accepted accounting concept. Would you want management to be conservative in accounting for inventory if you were a shareholder or a creditor of a company? Give your reason.

Ethical Issue

During 20X6, Vanguard, Inc., changed to the LIFO method of accounting for inventory. Suppose that during 20X7, Vanguard changes back to the FIFO method and the following year Vanguard switches back to LIFO again.

Requirements

1. What would you think of a company's ethics if it changed accounting methods every year?
2. What accounting principle would changing methods every year violate?
3. Who can be harmed when a company changes its accounting methods too often? How?

Focus on Financials: | Nestlé

This case spans all 12 chapters and is based on the consolidated financial statements of Nestlé. As you work with Nestlé throughout this course, you will develop the confidence and ability to use the financial statements of other companies as well.

Refer to Nestlé financial statements in Appendix A. Alternatively, you may choose to obtain the full annual report from Nestlé's website at www.nestle.com/investors. You may find the information overwhelming for now, but try to spot the key principles that we have discussed in this chapter. It will get progressively easier as you gain familiarity with the elements of the financial statements.

Requirements

1. What method does Nestlé use to measure its inventories?
2. What would be the effect of Nestlé adopting FIFO to measure the value of its sundry supplies (previously measured under weighted average method) assuming rising inventory prices?
3. Three important pieces of inventory information are the cost of inventory on hand, (a) the cost of goods sold, and (b) the cost of inventory purchases. Assume that the actual cost of inventory is equal to the fair value of the inventory, at CHF 8,401 million and CHF 8,153 million at December 31, 2016 and 2015, respectively. Identify or compute items (a) and (b) for Nestlé for the year ended December 31, 2016.
4. Did Nestlé's gross profit margin percentage (use sales and cost of goods sold) on company sales improve or deteriorate in the year ended December 31, 2016, compared to the previous year?
5. Calculate Nestlé's inventory turnover for the years ended December 31, 2015, and December 31, 2016. Did inventory turnover rise or fall? How does this affect your analysis of Nestlé? What additional information would help you make a better judgment on Nestlé's inventory management practices? (Assume that the value of inventory at December 31, 2014, is CHF 9,170 million.)

Group Project

■ **writing assignment**

(Learning Objective 4: Comparing companies' inventory turnover ratios) Obtain the annual reports of 10 companies, two from each of five different industries. Most companies' financial statements can be downloaded from their websites.

1. Compute each company's gross profit percentage and rate of inventory turnover for the most recent two years. If annual reports are unavailable or do not provide enough data for multiple-year computations, you can gather financial statement data from *Moody's Industrial Manual.*

2. How well does each of your companies compare to the other company in its industry? What insight about your companies can you glean from these ratios?
3. Write a memo to summarize your findings, stating whether your group would invest in each of the companies it has analyzed.

Quick Check Answers

1. *c*
2. *b*
3. *d*
4. *c* [(15 × $6) + (25 × $7)]
5. *b* (15 × $6) + ($10 × $7)
6. *c* 25 × [($90 + $280 + $90) ÷ 65]
7. *c*
8. *b*
9. *d*
10. *b* ($127,000 – $75,000)
11. *b* ($148,000 + $28,000 – $16,000)
12. *c* ($28,000 + $93,000 + $3,000 – $7,000 – $35,000)
13. *b* ($184,000 – $82,000)/$184,000
14. *a* [$82,000 ÷ ($28,000 + $35,000)/2]
15. *c* $120,000 + $270,000 – [$460,000 × (1 – 0.40)]
16. *b*

MyLab Accounting

For online homework, exercises, and problems that provide you with immediate feedback, please visit www.myaccountinglab.com.

APPENDIX 6A

ACCOUNTING FOR INVENTORY IN THE PERIODIC SYSTEM

In the periodic inventory system, the business keeps no running record of the merchandise. Instead, at the end of the period, the business counts inventory on hand and applies the unit costs to determine the cost of ending inventory. This inventory figure appears on the Balance Sheet and is used directly to calculate cost of goods sold.

Recording Transactions in the Periodic System

In the periodic system, throughout the period, the Inventory Account carries the beginning balance left over from the preceding period. During the period, the business records purchases of inventory in the *Purchases* account (an expense account). For inventory sales, only the revenue and considerations received (or receivable) are recorded.

At the end of the period, the purchases are added to the Inventory Account. A stocktake is then performed to determine the ending inventory balance. Any stock that is not present is *assumed* to be sold and charged to the cost of goods sold account. These end-of-period entries can be made during the closing process (see Chapter 3).

Exhibit 6A-1 illustrates the Inventory Accounting in a periodic system. Let's assume Jean-Luc Products (JLP) started the period with a beginning inventory balance of $100,000. During the year, JLP made purchases on credit, totaling $560,000. JLP's total sales for the year were $900,000, all on credit. A stocktake at the end of the period revealed that JLP has an inventory ending balance of $120,000.

Exhibit 6-A1 Recording and Reporting Inventories: Periodic System

PANEL A—Recording Transactions and the T-accounts

	A	B	C	D
1	1.	Purchases	560,000	
2		Accounts Payable		560,000
3		*Purchased inventory on account.*		
4				
5	2.	Accounts Receivable	900,000	
6		Sales Revenue		900,000
7		*Sold inventory on account.*		
8				
9	3.	End-of-period entries to update Inventory and record Cost of Goods Sold:		
10	a.	Inventory	560,000	
11		Purchases		560,000
12		*Transferred purchases to inventory.*		
13				
14	b.	Cost of Goods Sold	540,000	
15		Inventory		540,000
16		*Set up ending inventory based on physical count.*		
17				

The T-accounts show the following:

Purchases

Purchases 560,000	Inventory 560,000
End. Bal. 0	

Inventory

Beg. bal. 100,000	COGS 540,000
Purchases 560,000	
End. Bal. 120,000	

Cost of Goods Sold

Inventory 540,000	

PANEL B—Reporting in the Financial Statements

Income Statement (Partial)

Sales revenue		$900,000
Cost of goods sold:		
Beginning inventory	$ 100,000	
Purchases	560,000	
Goods available	660,000	
Ending inventory	(120,000)	
Cost of goods sold		540,000
Gross profit		$360,000

Ending Balance Sheet (Partial)

Current assets:	
Cash	$ XXX
Short-term investments	XXX
Accounts receivable	XXX
Inventory	120,000
Prepaid expenses	XXX

APPENDIX ASSIGNMENTS

Short Exercises

S6A-1. ***(Recording inventory transactions in the periodic system)*** Paxton Technologies began the year with inventory of $460. During the year, Paxton purchased inventory costing $1,270 and sold goods for $3,400, with all transactions on account. Paxton ended the year with inventory of $630. Journalize all the necessary transactions under the periodic inventory system.

S6A-2. ***(Computing cost of goods sold and preparing the Income Statement—periodic system)*** Use the data in Short Exercise 6A-1 to do the following for Paxton Technologies:

➤ Requirements

1. Post to the Inventory and Cost of Goods Sold accounts.
2. Compute cost of goods sold by using the cost-of-goods-sold model.
3. Prepare the Income Statement of Paxton Technologies through gross profit.

Exercises MyLab Accounting

Select exercises can be found within MyLab Accounting, an online homework and practice environment. Your instructor may ask you to complete select exercises using MyLab Accounting.

Group A

E6A-3A. ***(Computing amounts for various inventory methods—periodic system)*** Suppose Haley Corporation's inventory records for a particular computer chip indicate the following at July 31:

Jul 1	Beginning inventory	6 units @ $60 = $360
8	Purchase................................	3 units @ $60 = 180
15	Purchase................................	14 units @ $70 = 980
26	Purchase................................	2 units @ $80 = 160

The physical count of inventory at July 31 indicates that seven units of inventory are on hand.

➤ Requirements

Compute ending inventory and cost of goods sold, using each of the following methods:

1. Specific unit cost, assuming two $60 units and five $70 units are on hand
2. Average cost (round average unit cost to the nearest cent)
3. First-in, first-out
4. Last-in, first-out

E6A-4A. ***(Journalizing inventory transactions in the periodic system; computing cost of goods sold)*** Use the data in Exercise 6A-3A.

➤ Requirements

Journalize the following for the periodic system:

1. Total July purchases in one summary entry. All purchases were on credit.
2. Total July sales in a summary entry. Assume that the selling price was $298 per unit and that all sales were on credit.
3. July 31 entries for inventory. Haley uses LIFO. Post to the Cost of Goods Sold T-account to show how this amount is determined. Label each item in the account.
4. Show the computation of cost of goods sold by the cost-of-goods-sold model.

Group B

E6A-5B. ***(Computing amounts for various inventory methods—periodic system)*** Suppose Daxton Corporation's inventory records for a particular computer chip indicate the following at December 31:

Dec 1	Beginning inventory	7 units @ €62 = € 434
8	Purchase................................	5 units @ €62 = 310
15	Purchase................................	14 units @ €72 = 1,008
26	Purchase................................	3 units @ €82 = 246

The physical count of inventory at December 31 indicates that nine units of inventory are on hand.

➤ Requirements

Compute ending inventory and cost of goods sold, using each of the following methods:

1. Specific unit cost, assuming four €62 units and five €72 units are on hand
2. Average cost (round average unit cost to the nearest cent)
3. First-in, first-out
4. Last-in, first-out

E6A-6B. ***(Journalizing inventory transactions in the periodic system; computing cost of goods sold)*** Use the data in Exercise 6A-5B.

➤ Requirements

Journalize the following for the periodic system:

1. Total December purchases in one summary entry. All purchases were on credit.
2. Total December sales in a summary entry. Assume that the selling price was €318 per unit and that all sales were on credit.
3. December 31 entries for inventory. Daxton uses LIFO. Post to the Cost of Goods Sold T-account to show how this amount is determined. Label each item in the account.
4. Show the computation of cost of goods sold by the cost-of-goods-sold model.

Problems MyLab Accounting

Select problems can be found within MyLab Accounting, an online homework and practice environment. Your instructor may ask you to complete select problems using MyLab Accounting.

Group A

P6A-7A. ***(Computing cost of goods sold and gross profit on sales—periodic system)*** Assume a Watercrest outlet store began July 20X6 with 50 units of inventory that cost $16 each. The sale price of these units was $70. During July, the store completed the following inventory transactions:

		Units	Unit Cost	Unit Sale Price
Jul 3	Sale	18	$18	$70
8	Purchase......	80	19	71
11	Sale	32	18	70
19	Sale	4	19	72
24	Sale	36	19	72
30	Purchase......	21	20	72
31	Sale	5	19	72

➤ Requirements

1. Determine the store's cost of goods sold for July under the periodic inventory system. Assume the FIFO method.
2. Compute gross profit for July.

P6A-8A. ***(Recording transactions in the periodic system; reporting inventory items in the financial statements)*** Accounting records for Decadent Desserts, Inc., yield the following data for the year ended December 31, 20X6 (amounts in thousands):

Inventory, December 31, 20X5	$ 580
Purchases of inventory (on account)............	2,240
Sales of inventory—70% on account; 30% for cash............	3,600
Inventory at the lower of FIFO cost or NRV, December 31, 20X6	700

➤ Requirements

1. Journalize Decadent Desserts' inventory transactions for the year under the periodic system. Show all amounts in thousands.
2. Report ending inventory, sales, cost of goods sold, and gross profit on the appropriate financial statement (amounts in thousands). Show the computation of cost of goods sold.

Group B

P6A-9B. ***(Computing cost of goods sold and gross profit on sales—periodic system)*** Assume a Championship outlet store began January 20X6 with 52 units of inventory that cost €20 each. The sale price of these units was €75. During January the store completed these inventory transactions:

		Units	Unit Cost	Unit Sale Price
Jan 3	Sale	19	€20	€75
8	Purchase......	75	21	73
11	Sale	33	20	75
19	Sale	3	21	77
24	Sale	40	21	77
30	Purchase......	20	22	74
31	Sale	7	21	77

➤ Requirements

1. Determine the store's cost of goods sold for January under the periodic inventory system. Assume the FIFO method.
2. Compute gross profit for January.

P6A-10B. ***(Recording transactions in the periodic system; reporting inventory items in the financial statements)*** Accounting records for Sinful Desserts, Inc., yield the following data for the year ended December 31, 20X6 (amounts in thousands):

Inventory, December 31, 20X5	€ 520
Purchases of inventory (on account)..	2,100
Sales of inventory—75% on account, 25% for cash........................	4,000
Inventory at the lower of FIFO cost or market, December 31, 20X6..............	680

➤ Requirements

1. Journalize Sinful Desserts' inventory transactions for the year under the periodic system. Show all amounts in thousands.
2. Report ending inventory, sales, cost of goods sold, and gross profit on the appropriate financial statement (amounts in thousands). Show the computation of cost of goods sold.

7 PPE and Intangibles

SPOTLIGHT | Airbus Group www.airbusgroup.com

The International Air Traffic Association (IATA) reported 3.7 billion commercial airline passenger departures in 2016. That averaged out to be more than 10 million passengers flying each day! Many of them traveled on Airbus planes, from the A320 family of aircrafts to the world's largest commercial aircraft, the A380. Airbus delivers almost 700 aircrafts a year to its customers. What does it take to manufacture those aircrafts?

Alexey Y. Petrov/Shutterstock

To be able to operate on such a scale, Airbus has to decide where to allocate its assets, from cash and receivables (Chapter 5), inventory (Chapter 6), to long-term assets such as Property, Plant and Equipment (PPE), as well as intangible assets. Airbus Group's consolidated Balance Sheet and extracts of its PPE and intangible assets are shown below. Property, Plant, and Equipment and intangible assets form about 30% of Airbus Group's total assets.

	A	B	C	D
1	**Airbus Group** **Consolidated Balance Sheet (Adapted)** **At December 31**			
2	**(In millions of Euro)**	**2015**	**2014**	
3	Current assets	53,243	47,682	
4	Property, plant and equipment	17,127	16,321	
5	Intangible assets	12,555	12,758	
6	All other non-current assets	23,756	19,341	
7	Total assets	106,681	96,102	
8	Total liabilities	100,708	89,023	
9	Total equity	5,973	7,079	
10	Total liabilities and equity	106,681	96,102	
11				
12	**Notes to the accounts:**			
13	Propery, plant and equipment (line 4) 31 Dec 2015	Cost	ADI*	Carrying Amount
14	Land, leasehold improvements and buildings	9,518	(4,349)	5,169
15	Technical equipment and machinery	20,296	(11,946)	8,350
16	Other equipment, factory and office equipment	4,324	(3,290)	1,034
17	Construction in progress	2,574	–	2,574
18	Total property, plant, and equipment	36,712	(19,585)	17,127
19				
20	Intangible assets (line 5) 31 Dec 2015	Cost	AAI*	Carrying Amount
21	Goodwill	10,995	(1,088)	9,907
22	Capitalized development costs	2,686	(1,027)	1,659
23	Other intangible assets	3,375	(2,386)	989
24	Total intangible assets	17,056	(4,501)	12,555
25				

ADI* = Accumulated Depreciation and Impairment; AAI* = Accumulated Amortization and Impairment

PPE and intangibles are long-term assets because they provide economic benefits that extend beyond a single financial period. The allocation of their costs over their useful lives is called depreciation (for PPE) or amortization (for intangible assets). This chapter will start with an overview of various types of long-term assets that businesses have in their operations before proceeding to discuss the specific accounting treatments for long-term assets. As different companies have different types of long-term assets, we will use a few companies as illustrations during our discussions.

LEARNING OBJECTIVES

1. **Understand** the different types of long-term assets
2. **Determine** the cost of PPE on initial recognition
3. **Understand** when to capitalize or expense subsequent costs
4. **Measure** and **record** depreciation
5. **Account** for PPE disposals
6. **Understand** the recognition and subsequent measurement of intangible assets
7. **Evaluate** a company's performance based on its assets

UNDERSTAND THE DIFFERENT TYPES OF LONG-TERM ASSETS

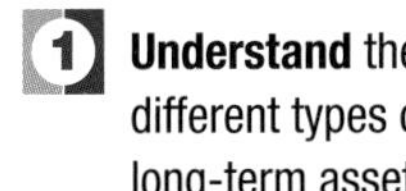

1 **Understand** the different types of long-term assets

Property, Plant and Equipment (PPE)

Property, Plant and Equipment **(PPE)**, sometimes called *fixed assets*, are long-term, non-current or long-lived assets that are tangible—for instance, land, buildings, and equipment. They may be held for use in the production or supply of goods or services, for rental to others, or for administrative purposes, and they are expected to be used during more than one period. The allocation of a PPE's cost over its useful life is called *depreciation*. The amount that has been allocated over the years is called *accumulated depreciation*. The primary source of guidance for accounting for PPE is *IAS 16—Property, Plant and Equipment*.

Businesses use several types of PPE, as shown in Airbus's Balance Sheet. It has PPE totaling €17,127 million (line 4), which is further detailed in its notes to the accounts (lines 13–17) into (1) land, leasehold improvements and buildings; (2) technical equipment and machinery; (3) other equipment, factory and office equipment; and (4) construction in progress, each with its own costs and accumulated depreciation and **impairment**. The difference between a PPE's cost and its accumulated depreciation is called the "carrying amount" (or net book value). Note that the carrying amount on the Balance Sheet tallies with the details provided in the notes to the accounts (line 4 and line 18).

Different entities may classify their PPE items into somewhat different categories that are suitable (and meaningful) for their business and financial statement users. An airline company, such as Singapore Airlines, would typically use additional PPE categories such as "Aircraft" and "Aircraft spare parts." Hutchison Whampoa, a Hong Kong-based diversified company with interests in the telecommunication industry amongst many others, uses a PPE category called "telecommunication network assets." Sinopec (China's largest oil producer and refiner) uses a PPE category "Oil depots, storage tanks, and service stations."

A recent survey of 170 IFRS companies showed the following top 10 PPE headings reported by these companies, as shown in Exhibit 7-1.

Exhibit 7-1 | Top 10 PPE Categories

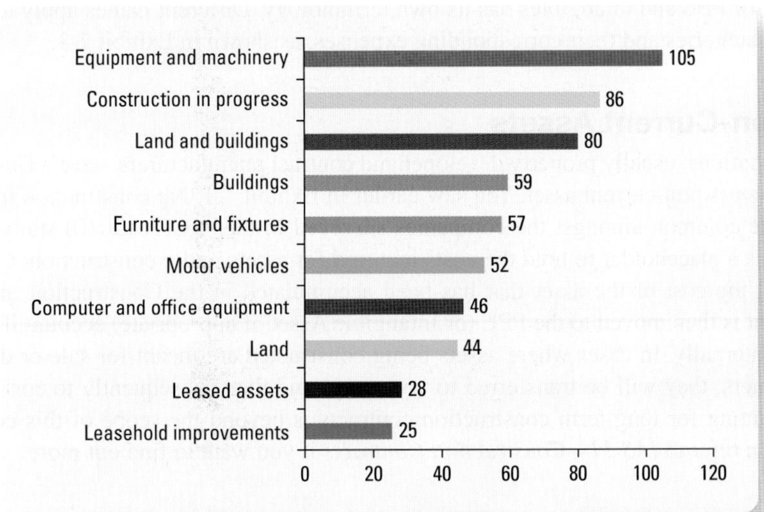

Intangible Assets

Intangible assets are identifiable non-monetary assets without physical substance. Non-monetary simply means that the asset is not expressed in fixed or determinable amounts of money. These intangible assets are unique because they do not have any physical form. Airbus reports a total of €12,555 million of net intangible assets (line 5), comprising (1) goodwill, (2) capitalized development costs, and (3) other intangible assets (lines 21–23). You can check that line 5 tallies with line 24, too. Accounting for intangibles is similar in nature to accounting for PPE assets. With the exception of goodwill (and other intangible assets with indefinite useful lives, more on this later), the costs of intangible assets are also allocated over the assets' respective useful lives. We usually refer to this as amortization. The primary source of guidance for intangible assets is *IAS 38—Intangible Assets*.

Similarly, the categories of intangible assets differ between entities depending on what an entity actually has. For example, Lenovo, the world's second largest computer vendor, categorizes its \$2.1 billion intangible assets into (1) goodwill, (2) trademarks and trade names, (3) internal use software, (4) customer relationships, and (5) patent and technology.

A recent survey of 170 IFRS companies showed that the majority of them (77%) have goodwill on their Balance Sheets (AICPA, 2010). Other intangible assets reported include software, patents, licenses, trademarks, development costs, customer lists and relationships, and many others. Exhibit 7-2 shows the top 10 intangible assets reported by these companies.

Exhibit 7-2 Top 10 Intangible Asset Categories

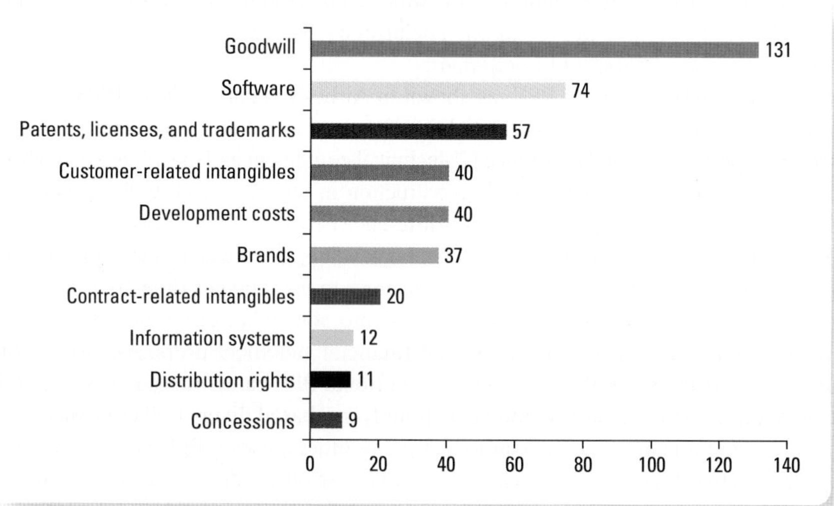

Both PPE and intangibles are subject to impairment tests (*IAS 36—Impairment of Assets*) to ensure that the values reported on the Balance Sheet do not exceed the fair value of the assets. Accounting for PPE and intangibles has its own terminology. Different names apply to the individual PPE categories and their corresponding expenses, as shown in Exhibit 7-3.

Other Non-Current Assets

- Some entities, usually property developer and contract manufacturers, have a *Construction in Progress* non-current asset. You saw earlier in Exhibit 7-1 that construction in progress is quite common amongst the companies surveyed in the AICPA (2010) study. This account is a placeholder to hold the costs incurred for assets under construction. Once completed, the cost of the asset that has been accumulated in the Construction in Progress account is then moved to the PPE (or Intangible Asset, if appropriate) account if it is to be used internally. In cases where assets being constructed are meant for sale or delivery to customers, they will be transferred to inventory (and then subsequently to cost of sales). Accounting for long-term construction contracts is beyond the scope of this course, but you can refer to *IAS 11—Construction Contracts* if you want to find out more.

Exhibit 7-3 | PPE and Intangibles Terminology

Asset Account (Balance Sheet)	Related Expense Account (Income Statement)
Property, Plant, and Equipment	
Freehold Land	None
Leasehold Land	Depreciation
Buildings, Machinery and Equipment	Depreciation
Furniture and Fixtures	Depreciation
Land Improvements	Depreciation
Natural Resources	Depletion
Intangibles	
Intangibles with finite useful lives	Amortization
Intangibles with indefinite useful lives	None

- Sometimes, you may also see entities, such as real estate companies or hotels, with *Investment Properties* as a non-current asset. These are a specially designated class of properties (land and/or buildings) held to earn rentals or for capital appreciation or both, rather than for usage associated with sales, production, or general administrative functions. Investment properties are beyond the scope of this course, but you can refer to *IAS 40—Investment Properties* for additional information.
- You may also see companies reporting "Lease Asset" on their Balance Sheets, as well as a corresponding "Lease Liabilities." These are assets and liabilities that are recognized on the financial statement in relation to lease arrangements. We will discuss these later in Chapter 9.
- For certain companies in the agriculture industry, you may also see a category labeled "biological assets." For example, Qian Hu (an ornamental fish-breeder headquartered in Singapore) has biological assets that are for sale (as inventory) as well as biological assets that are for breeding purposes (and thus depreciated!). Illovo, Africa's biggest sugar producer, has cane roots and growing cane as their agriculture assets. JBS Group (the world's largest meat producer, headquartered in São Paulo, Brazil) has "cattle, hogs and lamb, poultry and plants for harvests" as its biological assets. Agriculture and biological assets are accounted for under *IAS 41—Agriculture*.

Now that you have been introduced to common types of PPE and intangibles, let's see how we can recognize and measure them.

DETERMINE THE COST OF PPE ON INITIAL RECOGNITION

Recognition of PPE and Intangible Assets

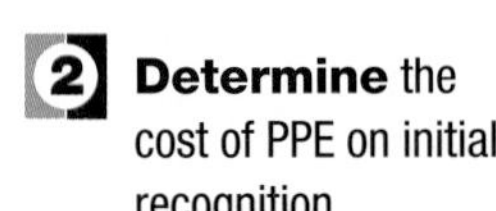
2 **Determine** the cost of PPE on initial recognition

Property, Plant, and Equipment and intangible assets are recognized in financial statements using the same way as other assets, when (1) it is probable that future economic benefits associated with the item will flow to the entity and (2) the cost of the item can be measured reliably. We will start our discussion with PPE for now and discuss intangible assets later.

Measurement of PPE on Initial Recognition

Here is a basic working rule for determining the cost of an asset: *The cost of any asset is the sum of all the costs incurred to bring the asset to its intended use.* Specifically, *IAS 16* requires that the cost of an item of PPE includes the following:

- Its purchase price, including import duties and non-refundable purchase taxes, after deducting trade discounts and rebates.
- Any costs directly attributable to bringing the asset to the location and condition necessary for it to be capable of operating in the manner intended by management.

A Closer Look

There is a third cost element in *IAS 16* that is seldom applicable to the majority of PPE items. *IAS 16* requires that the cost of an item of PPE also includes an initial estimate of the costs of dismantling and removing the item and restoring the site on which it is located, the obligation for which an entity incurs when the item is acquired. For example, a company may have rented an empty retail space in a local mall and proceeded to extensively renovate the space. It is very likely that the rental agreement will require the company to return the space to the landlord in its original state at the end of the rental period. Similarly, mining and oil exploration companies would typically have some form of environmental remediation obligation. The corresponding obligation component of the dismantling cost is accounted as a provision per *IAS 37—Provisions, Contingent Liabilities and Contingent Assets*. As this is a more advanced element of measurement of PPE on initial recognition, for our understanding, we can assume that there is no such dismantling obligations in subsequent discussions.

IAS 16 provides some examples of "directly attributable cost:"

- costs of employee benefits, like staff wages and salaries, arising directly from the construction or acquisition of the item of PPE
- costs of site preparation
- initial delivery and handling costs
- installation and assembly costs
- costs of testing whether the asset is functioning properly, after deducting the net proceeds from selling any items produced while bringing the asset to that location and condition (such as samples produced when testing equipment)
- professional fees

Similarly, *IAS 16* also provides examples of what should *not* be included in the cost of an item of PPE:

- costs of opening a new facility
- costs of introducing a new product or service (including costs of advertising and promotional activities)
- costs of conducting business in a new location or with a new class of customer (including costs of staff training)
- administration and other general overhead costs

Let's apply this recognition and measurement criteria to a number of PPE items.

Land and Land Improvements

The cost of land includes its purchase price (cash plus any note payable given), brokerage commission, survey fees, legal fees, and any property taxes that the purchaser pays. Land cost also includes expenditures for grading and clearing the land and for removing unwanted buildings.

The cost of land does not include the cost of fencing, paving, security systems, lighting, and other similar items. These are separate PPE—called land improvements—and they are subject to depreciation. You saw earlier that Airbus's PPE included a "land, leasehold improvements, and buildings" category. Whilst it is presented as a single category with a carrying amount of €5,169 million, Airbus's accounts would have the specific breakdown of these items.

Suppose Airbus signs a €300,000 note payable to purchase a parcel of land for a new logistic site. Airbus also pays €10,000 for real estate commission, €13,000 of stamp duty, a €1,000 land survey fee, and €16,000 to pave the parking lot—all in cash. What should Airbus recognize as the cost of this land?

Purchase price of land		€300,000
Add related costs:		
Real estate commission	€10,000	
Stamp duty	13,000	
Survey fee	1,000	
Total related costs		24,000
Total cost of land		€324,000

Note that the cost to pave the parking lot, €16,000, is *not* included in the land's cost, because the pavement is a land improvement. Airbus would record the purchase of this land as follows:

	A	B	C	D
1		Land	324,000	
2		Note Payable		300,000
3		Cash		24,000
4				

Assets	=	Liabilities	+	Shareholders' Equity
+ 324,000 − 24,000	=	+ 300,000	+	0

This purchase of land increases both assets and liabilities. There is no effect on equity.[1]

The cost to pave a parking lot (€16,000) would be recorded in a separate account entitled Land Improvements (or Leasehold Improvements if the land title is not in perpetuity). This account includes costs for such other items as driveways, signs, fences, and sprinkler systems. Although these assets are located on the land, they are subject to wear and tear and have a limited useful life, and their cost should therefore be depreciated over the term of the lease. Some companies call the depreciation on leasehold improvements *amortization*, which is the same concept as *depreciation*.

Buildings, Machinery, and Equipment

The cost of constructing a building includes architectural fees, building permits, contractors' charges, and payments for material, labor, and overhead. If the company constructs its own building, the cost will also include the cost of interest on money borrowed to finance the construction (if the recognition criteria in *IAS 23—Borrowing Costs* are met).

When an existing building (new or old) is purchased, its cost includes the purchase price, brokerage commission, sales and other taxes paid, and all expenditures to repair and renovate the building for its intended purpose.

The cost of Airbus's equipment includes its purchase price (less any discounts), plus transportation from the seller to Airbus, insurance while in transit, sales and other taxes, purchase commission, installation costs, and any expenditures to test the asset before it's placed in service. The equipment cost may also include the cost of any special platform necessary to place the equipment or other necessary safety measures. After the asset is up and running, insurance, taxes, and regular maintenance costs are recorded as expenses, not as part of the asset's cost.

[1] We show the accounting equation along with each journal entry—where the accounting equation aids your understanding of the transaction. Impact of revenue and expense transactions are taken directly to equity.

Is a building sitting on a piece of land one asset or two? *IAS 16* suggests that these are separate assets that are to be accounted for separately, even when they are acquired together. Buildings have limited useful life and are always depreciated. On the other hand, land may be "freehold" (an estate owned for perpetuity) and not depreciated because it has an infinite useful life.

In many countries, however, land titles are not issued in perpetuity and usually have a limited tenure (for example, 30 years, 99 years, or even 999 years!), after which the title is returned to the leaseholder. This type of land is usually called "leasehold land." Even for leasehold properties, the useful life of the building is usually not the same as the length of the leasehold tenure. That's why we account for a building on a piece of land as two separate assets.

Lump-Sum (or Basket) Purchases of Assets

Businesses often purchase several assets as a group, or a "basket," for a single lump-sum amount. For example, Airbus may pay one price for land and a building, but the company must first identify the cost of each asset. The total cost is then divided among the assets according to their relative sales (or market) values. This technique is called the *relative-sales-value method.*

Suppose Airbus purchases land and a building in Luxemburg. The building sits on two acres of land, and the combined purchase price of land and building is €2.7 million. An appraisal indicates that the land's fair value is €1 million and the building's fair value is €2 million. Airbus first figures the ratio of each asset's fair value to the total fair value. The total appraised value is €1 + €2 million = €3 million. Thus, the land, valued at €1 million, is one-third of the total fair value. The building's appraised value is two-thirds of the total. These percentages are then used to determine the cost of each asset, as follows:

Asset	Fair Value		Total Fair Value		Percentage of Total Fair Value		Total Cost	Cost of Each Asset
Land	€1,000,000	÷	€3,000,000	=	33.3%	×	€2,700,000	€ 900,000
Building	2,000,000	÷	3,000,000	=	66.6%	×	€2,700,000	1,800,000
Total	€3,000,000				100%			€2,700,000

If Airbus pays cash, the entry to record the purchase of the land and building is

	A	B	C	D
1		Land	900,000	
2		Building	1,800,000	
3		Cash		2,700,000
4				

Assets	=	Liabilities	+	Shareholders' Equity
+ 900,000	=			
+ 1,800,000	=	0	+	0
− 2,700,000	=			

Total assets don't change—only the makeup of Airbus's assets will change.

Stop & Think

How would Airbus divide a €120,000 lump-sum purchase price for land, building, and equipment with estimated market values of €40,000, €95,000, and €15,000, respectively?

Answer:

	Estimated Market Value	Percentage of Total Market Value	×	Total Cost	=	Cost of Each Asset
Land..................	€ 40,000	26.7%*	×	€120,000	=	€ 32,040
Building............	95,000	63.3%	×	120,000	=	75,960
Equipment.........	15,000	10.0%	×	120,000	=	12,000
Total.................	€150,000	100.0%				€120,000

*€40,000/€150,000 = 0.267, and so on

UNDERSTAND WHEN TO CAPITALIZE OR EXPENSE SUBSEQUENT COSTS

Subsequent Costs

3 **Understand** when to capitalize or expense subsequent costs

The PPE recognition criteria in *IAS 16* helps us in determining whether an expenditure should be recognized as an asset in the Balance Sheet or expensed immediately to the Income Statement. The same criteria also help us with expenditures subsequent to the initial recognition. Specifically, *IAS 16* states that an entity should *not* recognize the costs of the day-to-day servicing (which typically comprises the costs of labor and consumables, or small parts of the item) in the carrying amount of an item of PPE. These costs are expensed or charged to the Income Statement as incurred. The purpose of these expenditures is often described as for the "repairs and maintenance" of the PPE. For example, Airbus may perform regular maintenance of its motor vehicles. The costs of repainting an Airbus delivery truck, repairing its dented bumper, or replacing worn tires are also expensed immediately.

On the other hand, expenditures that increase the asset's capacity or extend its useful life are called **capital expenditures**. For example, the cost of a major overhaul that extends the useful life of a Airbus truck is a capital expenditure. Capital expenditures are said to be "capitalized," which means the cost is added to an asset account and not expensed immediately. Thus, a major decision in accounting for PPE is whether to capitalize or to expense a certain cost.

Continuing with our delivery truck example, Exhibit 7-4 shows the distinction between recognizing the capital expenditures as an asset and immediate charging the expenditure as an expense for the period.

Exhibit 7-4 Capital Expenditure or Immediate Expense for Costs Associated with a Delivery Truck

Record an Asset for Capital Expenditures	Record Repair and Maintenance Asset Expense
Significant or major repairs:	Ordinary repairs:
Major engine overhaul	Repair of transmission or other mechanism
Addition to storage capacity of truck	Oil change, lubrication, and so on
Modification of body for new use of truck	Replacement of tires and windshield, or a paint job

For certain industries, it is possible that certain "repairs and maintenance" may be a necessary precondition to continue to operate the asset. For example, you would want to be sure that any airline you fly with has complied with all the required safety and maintenance checks. These are probably regular major inspections at certain points of the asset's useful life or at preset usage intervals. *IAS 16* allows for the capitalization of these major inspections as part of the carrying amount of the item of property and allocated over the period (until the next inspection).

For example, Air France-KLM's 2015 annual report states that: "Maintenance costs are recorded as expenses during the period when incurred, with the exception of programs that extend the useful life of the asset or increase its value, which are then capitalized (e.g., maintenance on airframes and engines, excluding parts with limited useful lives)." And similarly, Qantas's 2016 annual report states: "The costs of subsequent major cyclical maintenance checks for owned and leased aircraft are recognized and depreciated over the shorter of the scheduled usage period to the next major inspection event or the remaining life of the aircraft or lease term (as appropriate) . . . All other maintenance costs are expensed as incurred."

The distinction between a capital expenditure and an expense requires judgment: Does the cost extend the asset's usefulness or its useful life? If so, record an asset. If the cost merely repairs the asset or returns it to its prior condition, then record an expense.

Most entities expense all expenditures below a certain threshold, say, $1,000. Remember that there are always cost constraints in producing financial information. If the resulting information does not increase fundamental and enhancing qualitative characteristics, why incur unnecessary costs to produce the information? For higher costs, they follow the rule we gave earlier: capitalize costs that extend the asset's usefulness or its useful life, and allocate the capitalized amount over the expected useful life of the asset.

Accounting errors sometimes occur for PPE costs. For example, a company may:

- Expense a cost that should have been capitalized. This error overstates expenses and understates net income in the year of the error.
- Capitalize a cost that should have been expensed. This error understates expenses and overstates net income in the year of the error.

WorldCom

It is one thing to accidentally capitalize an expense as PPE but quite another to do it intentionally, thus deliberately overstating assets, understating expenses, and overstating net income. One well-known company committed one of the biggest financial statement frauds in U.S. history in this way.

In 2002, WorldCom, Inc., was one of the largest telecommunications service providers in the world. The company had grown rapidly from a small, regional telephone company in 1983 to a giant corporation in 2002 by acquiring an ever-increasing number of other such companies. But 2002 was a bad year for WorldCom, as well as for many others in the "telecom" industry. The United States was reeling from the effects of a deep economic recession spawned by the "bursting dot-com bubble" in 2000 and intensified by the terrorist attacks on U.S. soil in 2001. Wall Street was looking high and low for positive signs, pressuring public companies to keep profits trending upward in order to support share prices, without much success, at least for the honest companies.

Bernard J. ("Bernie") Ebbers, WorldCom's chief executive officer, was worried. He began to press his chief financial officer, Scott Sullivan, to find a way to make the company's Income

Statement look healthier. After all legitimate attempts to improve earnings failed, Sullivan concocted a scheme to cook the books.

Like all telecommunications companies, WorldCom had signed contracts with other telephone companies, paying them fees so that WorldCom customers could use their lines for telephone calls and Internet usage. Accounting standards require such fees to be expensed as incurred, rather than capitalized. Overestimating the growth of its business, WorldCom had incurred billions of dollars in such costs, about 15% more than its customers would ever use.

In direct violation of accounting standards, Sullivan rationalized that the excessive amounts WorldCom had spent on line costs would eventually lead to the company's recognizing revenue in future years (thus extending their usefulness and justifying, in his mind, their classification as assets). Sullivan directed the accountants working under him to reclassify line costs as property, plant, and equipment assets, rather than as expenses, and to amortize (spread) the costs over several years rather than to expense them in the periods in which they were incurred. Over several quarters, Sullivan and his assistants transferred a total of $3.1 billion in such charges from operating expense accounts to PPE, resulting in the transformation of what would have been a net loss for all of 2001 and the first quarter of 2002 into a sizeable profit. It was the largest single fraud in U.S. history to that point.

Sullivan's fraudulent scheme was discovered by the company's internal audit staff during a routine spot-check of the company's records for capital expenditures. The staff members reported Sullivan's (and his staff's) fraudulent activities to the head of the company's audit committee and its external auditor, setting in motion a chain of events that resulted in Ebbers's and Sullivan's firing, and the company's eventual bankruptcy. Ebbers, Sullivan, and several of their assistants went to prison for their participation in this fraudulent scheme.

Shareholders of WorldCom lost billions of dollars in share value when the company went down, and more than 500,000 people lost their jobs. The WorldCom scandal rocked the financial world, causing global stock markets to plummet from lack of confidence. This scandal (as well as others such as Enron) eventually led to the passage of the U.S. Sarbanes-Oxley Act (see Chapter 5).

Stop & Think

Ivana Low is the CFO of SMOO, an online retailing company. At the end of the fiscal year, the net profit before tax was $100,000 (total revenue of $300,000 and expenses of $200,000). This was below the profit target set by the board of directors. Ivana noted that there was an expense of $30,000 recorded at the end of the year for advertising during the year. Ivana decided to classify the expense as an asset with a useful life of 4 years in order to meet the profit target. What is the impact of this alternative accounting treatment on SMOO's pre-tax profit?

Answer:

The reclassification of an expense incurred at the end of the fiscal year as an asset will reduce expense, increase profit, and increase assets. The SMOO's pre-tax profit would now be (incorrectly) reported as: $300,000 – $170,000 = $130,000.

MEASURE AND RECORD DEPRECIATION

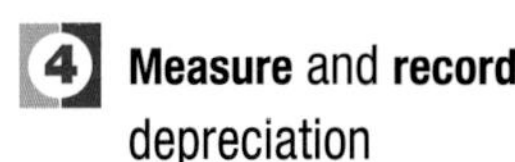
4 Measure and record depreciation

As we've seen in previous chapters, PPE items are reported on the Balance Sheet at their carrying amounts or book values, which is:

Carrying amount of an item PPE = Cost − Accumulated Depreciation

Depreciation is the systematic allocation of the cost of a long-term asset over its useful life. As the cost of an item of PPE is allocated to its useful lives, its carrying amounts are reduced and the corresponding depreciation expense results in a reduction in equity. Exhibit 7-5 illustrates this concept with an example of an Airbus A330 owned by Brussels Airlines.

Exhibit 7-5 | Allocating Cost of Assets Over Useful Life

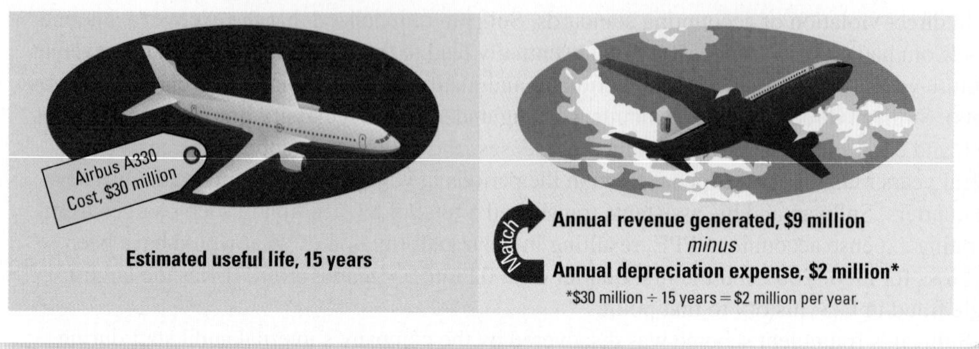

Recall that depreciation expense is charged periodically to the Income Statement. The cumulative amount of depreciation charged since the initial recognition and measurement of an asset is called **accumulated depreciation**, which you will find on the Balance Sheet (or in the notes to the accounts). At the start of this chapter, you saw the accumulated depreciation for all of Airbus's PPE (second column of lines 14–17).

You've just seen what depreciation is. Let's see what depreciation is *not*.

1. ***Depreciation is not a process of valuation.*** Businesses do *not* record depreciation based on changes in the market value of their PPEs.
2. ***Depreciation does not mean setting aside cash to replace assets as they wear out.*** Any cash fund set aside to purchase a new asset is entirely separate from depreciation.

How to Allocate Depreciation

Before we move to the specific depreciation methods, let's make sure we understand the basic concepts and terminologies related to depreciation. To allocate depreciation for a PPE item, we must know three things about the asset:

1. Cost
2. Estimated useful life
3. Estimated residual value

We have discussed cost earlier, which is a known amount. The other two factors must be estimated.

The economic benefit from owning a PPE is consumed by an entity primarily through the use of the PPE in the ordinary course of business over the PPE's useful life. As the allocation of expenses is usually predetermined in advance (we will discuss methods of depreciation in the next section), an entity such as Airbus would have to make an estimate of the useful lives of its buildings, leasehold improvements, plant and machinery, furniture and fixtures, office equipment, and motor vehicles. *IAS 16* indicates that the following factors ought to be considered in determining an asset's useful life:

- expected usage of the asset
- expected physical wear and tear, including the necessary repair and maintenance program
- technical or commercial obsolescence, including a change in the market demand for the product or service output of the asset

■ legal or similar limits on the use of the asset, such as the expiry dates of Airbus's leasehold land

Estimated useful life is thus the length of service expected from using the asset. Useful life may be expressed in years, units of output, miles, or some other measure. For example, the useful life of Airbus's buildings, furniture and fixtures, and office equipment can be stated in years. Some of its specialized machinery may have its useful life expressed in number of units or usage or capacity. Occasionally, you may see this useful life expressed as a percentage, for example, a depreciation rate of 10% per year is equal to 10 years' useful life, 20% is equal to 5 years', etc. Companies base estimates on their experiences and trade publications. Useful life is not necessarily the same as the physical or economic life of the asset. An airplane may physically last over 30 years, but if the management's intention is to use it over a shorter time period, its useful life may be shorter. Singapore Airlines and Emirates Airline, for example, depreciate their passenger airplanes over 15 years' useful life, whereas Cathay Pacific and Thai Airways use 20 years' useful life, and British Airways uses 18–25 years.

Estimated residual value—also sometimes called *scrap value* or *salvage value*—of an asset is the estimated amount that an entity would currently obtain from disposal of the asset, after deducting the estimated costs of disposal, if the asset were already of the age and in the condition expected at the end of its useful life. For example, Airbus may believe that a package-handling machine will be useful for seven years. After that time, Airbus may expect to sell the machine as scrap metal. The amount Airbus believes it can get for the machine is the estimated residual value. In computing depreciation, the estimated residual value is not depreciated because Airbus expects to receive this amount from selling the asset. If there's no expected residual value, the full cost of the asset is depreciated. The residual value may be expressed as an absolute amount or as a percentage of the asset's cost. For example, Singapore Airlines uses a "10% residual value" in its depreciation allocation. A PPE's depreciable amount or **depreciable cost** is therefore:

Depreciable Amount = Asset's cost − Estimated residual value

Depreciation Methods

There are three main depreciation methods:

- constant allocation, i.e., straight-line
- by actual usages, i.e., units-of-production
- accelerated allocation, i.e., double-declining-balance

These methods allocate different amounts of depreciation to each period. However, they all result in the same total amount of depreciation, which is the asset's depreciable amount, over the life of the asset. Exhibit 7-6 presents the data we use to illustrate depreciation computations for an Airbus delivery truck.

Exhibit 7-6 | Data for Depreciation Computations: Example

Data Item	Amount
Cost of truck	€41,000
Less: Estimated residual value	(1,000)
Depreciable cost	€40,000
Estimated useful life:	
Years	5 years
Units of production	100,000 units [miles]

Straight-Line Method. In the **straight-line (SL) method**, an equal amount of depreciation is assigned to each year (or period) of asset use. Depreciable cost is divided by useful life in years to determine the annual depreciation expense. Applied to the truck data from Exhibit 7-6, SL depreciation is

$$\text{Straight-line depreciation per year} = \frac{\text{Cost} - \text{Residual value}}{\text{Useful life, in years}}$$
$$= \frac{€41{,}000 - €1{,}000}{5}$$
$$= €8{,}000$$

The entry to record depreciation is:

	A	B	C	D
1		Depreciation Expense	8,000	
2		Accumulated Depreciation		8,000
3				

Assets	=	Liabilities	+	Shareholders' Equity	
− 8,000	=	0	+	− 8,000	(depreciation expense)

Observe that depreciation decreases the asset (through Accumulated Depreciation) and also decreases equity (through Depreciation Expense). Let's assume that Airbus purchased this truck on January 1, 20X5. Exhibit 7-7 gives a *straight-line depreciation schedule* for the truck. The final column of the exhibit shows the asset's *carrying amount* or *net book value*, which is cost less accumulated depreciation. Note that we can develop this depreciation schedule before we have even bought the truck! Such schedules help us understand the impact of our purchase decisions on financial statements over the years.

Exhibit 7-7 Straight-Line Depreciation Schedule

	A	B	C					D	E
1			Depreciation for the Year						
2–4	Date	Asset Cost	Depreciation Rate*		Depreciable Amount		Depreciation Expense	Accumulated Depreciation	Asset Carrying Amount
5	1/1/20X5	€ 41,000							€ 41,000
6	12/31/20X5		0.20	×	€40,000	=	€8,000	€ 8,000	33,000
7	12/31/20X6		0.20	×	40,000	=	8,000	16,000	25,000
8	12/31/20X7		0.20	×	40,000	=	8,000	24,000	17,000
9	12/31/20X8		0.20	×	40,000	=	8,000	32,000	9,000
10	12/31/20X9		0.20	×	40,000	=	8,000	40,000	1,000
11									

*5 years' useful life = 20% (0.2) depreciation rate per year.

As an asset is used in operations:

- the accumulated depreciation increases.
- the carrying amount of the asset decreases.

An asset's final book value is its *residual value* (€1,000 in Exhibit 7-7). At the end of its useful life, the asset is said to be *fully depreciated*.

Stop & Think

An item of Airbus office equipment that cost €10,000, has a useful life of three years, and has a residual value of €1,000 was purchased on January 1. What is its straight-line depreciation for each year?

Answer:

€3,000 = (€10,000 − €1,000)/3

Units-of-Production Method. In the **units-of-production (UOP) method**, a fixed amount of depreciation is assigned to each unit of output or service produced by the asset. Depreciable cost is divided by useful life—in units of production—to determine this amount. This per-unit depreciation expense is then multiplied by the number of units produced each period to compute depreciation. Obviously, the Dairy Farm delivery truck will not stop working just because it has been driven to 100,000 miles. We continue with the same delivery truck as an illustration, but in real life, this method is more likely to be used with assets with technical capacity or unit limitations rather than a delivery truck. The UOP depreciation for the Airbus truck data in Exhibit 7-6 is

$$\text{Units-of-production depreciation per unit of output} = \frac{\text{Cost} - \text{Residual value}}{\text{Useful life, in units of production}}$$

$$= \frac{€41{,}000 - €1{,}000}{100{,}000 \text{ miles}} = €0.40 \text{ per mile}$$

Assume that Airbus expects to drive the truck 20,000 miles during the first year, 30,000 during the second, 25,000 during the third, 15,000 during the fourth, and 10,000 during the fifth. Exhibit 7-8 shows the UOP depreciation schedule.

Exhibit 7-8 | Units-of-Production Depreciation Schedule

	A	B	C					D	E
1			Depreciation for the Year						
2–4	Date	Asset Cost	Depreciation Per Unit*		Number of Units		Depreciation Expense	Accumulated Depreciation	Asset Carrying Amount
5	1/1/20X5	€ 41,000							€ 41,000
6	12/31/20X5		€0.40*	×	€20,000	=	€ 8,000	€ 8,000	33,000
7	12/31/20X6		0.40	×	30,000	=	12,000	20,000	21,000
8	12/31/20X7		0.40	×	25,000	=	10,000	30,000	11,000
9	12/31/20X8		0.40	×	15,000	=	6,000	36,000	5,000
10	12/31/20X9		0.40	×	10,000	=	4,000	40,000	1,000
11									

*(€41,000 − €1,000)/100,000 miles = €0.40 per mile.

The amount of UOP depreciation varies with the number of units the asset produces in a year. In our example above, we have estimated the usage pattern, but the actual depreciation charge each year will be based on the actual outputs for the year. Thus, the amount charged each year may differ from what was originally planned.

For example, if the actual miles driven in 20X5 were 21,000, the depreciation charge for the year would have been €0.40 × 21,000 = €8,400. The UOP depreciation does not depend directly on passage of time, as do the other methods.

Double-Declining-Balance Method. An **accelerated depreciation method** (or using *IAS 16*'s terminology, "diminishing balance method") writes off a larger amount of the asset's cost near the start of its useful life than the straight-line method does.

Double-declining-balance (DDB) is the main accelerated depreciation method and computes annual depreciation by multiplying the asset's declining book value by a constant percentage, which is double (or two times) the straight-line depreciation rate. DDB amounts are computed as follows:

- *First*, compute the straight-line depreciation rate per year. A five-year truck has a straight-line depreciation rate of 1/5, or 20% each year. A 10-year asset has a straight-line rate of 1/10, or 10%, and so on.
- *Second*, multiply the straight-line rate by 2 to compute the DDB rate. For a five-year asset, the DDB rate is 40% (20% × 2). A 10-year asset has a DDB rate of 20% (10% × 2). The DDB rate for the delivery truck in Exhibit 7-6 is:

$$\text{DDB depreciation rate per year} = \frac{1}{\text{Useful life, in years}} \times 2$$

$$= \frac{1}{5\text{ years}} \times 2$$

$$= 20\% \times 2 = 40\%$$

- *Third*, multiply the DDB rate by the period's beginning asset book value (cost less accumulated depreciation). Under the DDB method, ignore the residual value of the asset in computing depreciation, except during the last year.
- *Fourth*, determine the final year's depreciation amount—that is, the amount needed to reduce asset book value to its residual value. In Exhibit 7-9, the fifth and final year's DDB depreciation is €4,314—book value of €5,314 less the €1,000 residual value. *The residual value should not be depreciated* but should remain on the books until the asset is disposed of.

Exhibit 7-9 Double-Declining-Balance Depreciation Schedule

	A	B	C					D	E
1			Depreciation for the Year						
2–4	Date	Asset Cost	DDB Rate		Asset Carrying Amount		Depreciation Expense	Accumulated Depreciation	Asset Carrying Amount
5	1/1/20X5	€ 41,000							€ 41,000
6	12/31/20X5		0.40	×	€41,000	=	€16,400	€ 16,400	24,600
7	12/31/20X6		0.40	×	24,600	=	9,840	26,240	14,760
8	12/31/20X7		0.40	×	14,760	=	5,904	32,144	8,856
9	12/31/20X8		0.40	×	8,856	=	3,542	35,686	5,314
10	12/31/20X9						4,314*	40,000	1,000
11									

*Last-year depreciation is the "plug" amount needed to reduce asset book value (far right column) to the residual amount (€5,314 − €1,000 = €4,314).

The DDB method differs from the other methods in three ways:

1. It is an accelerated depreciation method, so depreciation expenses in the early years are significantly more than in later years.
2. Residual value is ignored initially; first-year depreciation is computed on the asset's full cost.
3. Depreciation expense in the final year is the "plug" amount needed to reduce the asset's book value to the residual amount.

What is the DDB depreciation each year for the asset in the Stop & Think on page 401?

Answers:

Yr. 1: €4,000 (€10,000 × 40%)
Yr. 2: €2,400 (€6,000 × 40%)
Yr. 3: €1,440 (€3,600 × 40%)
Yr. 4: €160 (€10,000 – €4,000 – €2,400 – €1,440 – €2,000 = €160)*
Yr. 5: €0

*The asset is not depreciated below residual value of €2,000.

Comparing Depreciation Methods

Let's compare the three methods in terms of the yearly amount of depreciation. The yearly amount varies by method, but the total €40,000 depreciable cost, i.e., the total accumulated depreciation at the end of the asset's life, is the same under all methods.

	Amount of Depreciation Expense per Year		
Year	Straight-Line	Estimated Units-of-Production	Accelerated Method Double-Declining Balance
1	€ 8,000	€ 8,000	€16,400
2	8,000	12,000	9,840
3	8,000	10,000	5,904
4	8,000	6,000	3,542
5	8,000	4,000	4,314
Total	€40,000	€40,000	€40,000

Exhibit 7-10 graphs annual depreciation amounts for the straight-line, units-of-production, and accelerated depreciation (DDB) methods. The graph of straight-line depreciation is flat through time because annual depreciation is the same in all periods.

Units-of-production depreciation follows no particular pattern because annual depreciation depends on the actual use of the asset during the year. Accelerated depreciation is greatest in the first year and less in the later years.

Exhibit 7-10 | Depreciation Patterns Through Time

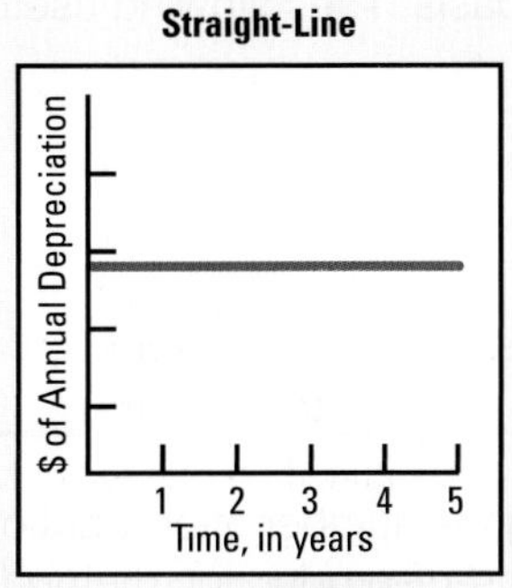

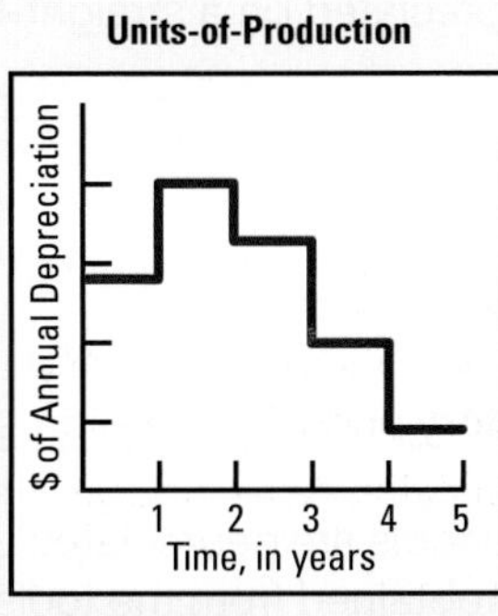

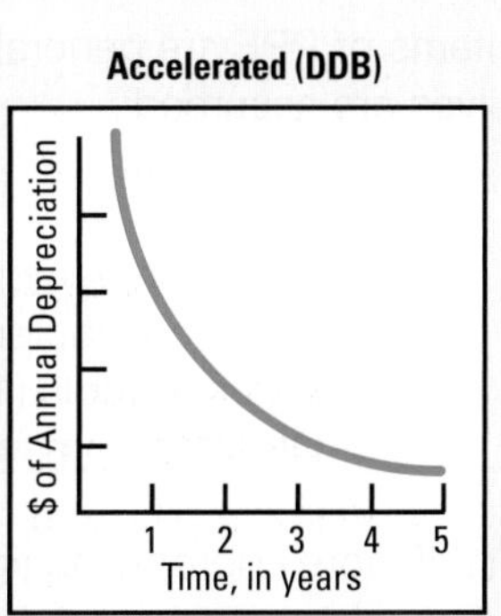

Choosing a Depreciation Method

Clearly, the choice of a depreciation method will impact the profit of any entity. How should an entity choose the "right" depreciation method? *IAS 16* requires that the depreciation method chosen ought to reflect the *pattern of consumption* of the economic benefits embodied in the asset. At every financial year-end, an entity should review the depreciation method, and unless there is a significant change in the pattern of consumption, it should continue to apply the method consistently from period to period.

For PPE assets with a reasonably constant pattern of consumption, the allocation basis should be done using the straight-line method. The units-of-production method best fits those assets that wear out because of physical use rather than obsolescence.

An accelerated method (such as DDB) applies best to assets that generate more revenue earlier in their useful lives and less in later years. Exhibit 7-11 shows a recent study of 170 IFRS companies and their depreciation method (AICPA 2010). It is clear that a very significant majority of the survey companies use the straight-line method of depreciation. About 20 companies in the survey use more than one method of depreciation.

Exhibit 7-11 | Depreciation Methods Used by 170 Companies

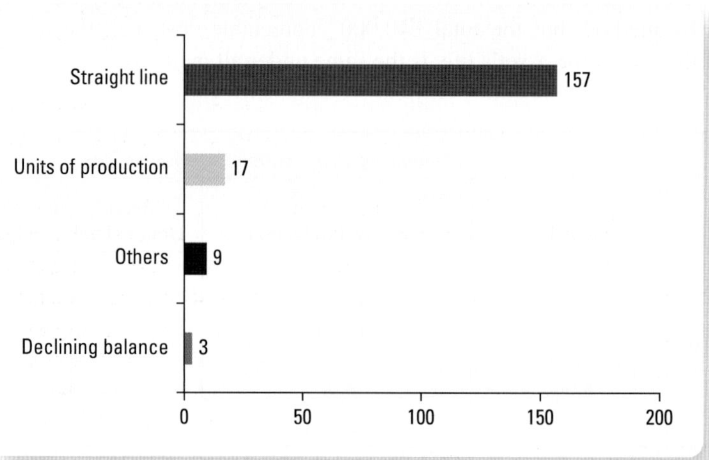

Airbus uses the following useful lives for its assets, and the primary method used for depreciation is the straight-line method.

ADAPTED EXCERPTS FROM AIRBUS GROUP'S NOTES TO THE ACCOUNTS

Property, Plant, and Equipment

Items of PPE are generally depreciated on a straight-line basis. The following useful lives are assumed:

Buildings	10 to 50 years
Site improvements	6 to 30 years
Technical equipment and machinery	3 to 20 years
Jigs and tools (1)	5 years
Other equipment, factory and office equipment	2 to 10 years

(1) If more appropriate, jigs and tools are depreciated using the number of production or similar units expected to be obtained from the tools (units-of-production method).

Source: Airbus Group's 2015 Financial Statements, page 36

Mid-Chapter Summary Problem

Suppose Airbus purchased equipment on January 1, 20X6, for €44,000. The expected useful life of the equipment is 10 years or 100,000 units of production, and its residual value is €4,000. Under three depreciation methods, the annual depreciation expense and the balance of accumulated depreciation at the end of 20X6 and 20X7 are as follows:

	Method A		*Method B*		*Method C*	
Year	Annual Depreciation Expense	Accumulated Depreciation	Annual Depreciation Expense	Accumulated Depreciation	Annual Depreciation Expense	Accumulated Depreciation
20X6	€4,000	€4,000	€8,800	€ 8,800	€1,200	€1,200
20X7	4,000	8,000	7,040	15,840	5,600	6,800

Requirements

1. Identify the depreciation method used in each instance, and show the equation and computation for each. (Round to the nearest euro.)
2. Assume continued use of the same method through year 20X8. Determine the annual depreciation expense, accumulated depreciation, and carrying amount (or book value) of the equipment for 20X6 through 20X8 under each method, assuming 12,000 units of production in 20X8.

Answers

Requirement 1

Method A: Straight-Line

Depreciable amount = €40,000 (€44,000 − €4,000)

Each year: €40,000/10 years = €4,000

Method B: Double-Declining-Balance

$$\text{Rate} = \frac{1}{10\text{ years}} \times 2 = 10\% \times 2 = 20\%$$

20X6: 0.20 × €44,000 = €8,800

20X7: 0.20 × (€44,000 − €8,800) = €7,040

Method C: Units-of-Production

$$\text{Depreciation per unit} = \frac{€44{,}000 - €4{,}000}{100{,}000\text{ units}} = €0.40$$

20X6: €0.40 × 3,000 units = €1,200

20X7: €0.40 × 14,000 units = €5,600

Requirement 2

Method A: Straight-Line

Year	Annual Depreciation Expense	Accumulated Depreciation	Book Value
Start			€44,000
20X6	€4,000	€ 4,000	40,000
20X7	4,000	8,000	36,000
20X8	4,000	12,000	32,000

Method B: Double-Declining-Balance

Year	Annual Depreciation Expense	Accumulated Depreciation	Book Value
Start			€44,000
20X6	€8,800	€ 8,800	35,200
20X7	7,040	15,840	28,160
20X8	5,632	21,472	22,528

Method C: Units-of-Production

Year	Annual Depreciation Expense	Accumulated Depreciation	Book Value
Start			€44,000
20X6	€1,200	€ 1,200	42,800
20X7	5,600	6,800	37,200
20X8	4,800	11,600	32,400

Computations for 20X8

Straight-line	€40,000/10 years = €4,000
Double-declining-balance	€28,160 × 0.20 = €5,632
Units-of-production	12,000 units × €0.40 = €4,800

Other Issues in Accounting for PPE

Accounting for PPE may also need to handle additional issues related to:

- choice of depreciation method, which may affect income taxes; a different depreciation method may be used for financial reporting versus tax purposes
- depreciation for partial years
- the fact that PPE have long lives; subsequently, better information may change estimates of useful life of assets and residual values
- alternative models for measurement of PPE subsequent to initial recognition
- companies that have gains or losses when they sell PPE

Let's take a brief look at some of these issues.

Depreciation for Tax Purposes

Airbus and most other companies use straight-line depreciation for reporting to shareholders and creditors on their financial statements. But for tax purposes, they may keep a separate set of depreciation records, depending on the specific tax regulations in various jurisdictions. There are two primary reasons why this is the case.

First, certain jurisdictions may mandate a specific treatment for specific assets. For example, in Singapore, the depreciation of Airbus's commercial vehicles, such as its delivery trucks, may be used to claim capital allowances (i.e., deductions from taxable income), but the depreciation of non-commercial vehicles, such as motor vehicles for its senior management staff, would not be allowed as a deduction. In other countries, there may be a maximum cap on the depreciable amount allowed for certain assets. Clearly, in order to comply with taxation rules, a different set of depreciation records will be required.

Second, tax regulations could provide alternative depreciation methods or schedules that are more favorable than what is being used for financial reporting. For example, investment in "green technologies" may be granted a double tax deduction to encourage businesses to make headway in the fight against climate change. You may have spent $1 million on such equipment, but you are entitled to claim $2 million as deductions in your tax forms. In other instances, you may be using the straight-line method for financial reporting, but the tax regulations may allow you to use an accelerated method such as DDB for tax reporting.

Suppose you are an Airbus country manager, and your local tax authority allows an accelerated depreciation method. Why would you prefer accelerated over straight-line depreciation for income tax purposes? This choice is easy. Accelerated depreciation provides the fastest tax deductions, thus decreasing immediate tax payments. Airbus can reinvest the tax savings back into the business or pay off interest-bearing debts (see Exhibit 7-12).

To understand the relationships between cash flow, depreciation, and income tax, recall our depreciation example of an Airbus delivery truck:

- First-year depreciation is €8,000 under straight-line and €16,400 under double-declining balance (DDB).
- DDB is permitted for income tax purposes, and headline corporate tax rate is 30%.

Exhibit 7-12 | The Cash-Flow Advantage of Accelerated Depreciation over Straight-Line Depreciation for Income Tax Purposes

		SL	Accelerated
1	Cash revenue	€400,000	€400,000
2	Cash operating expenses	300,000	300,000
3	Cash provided by operations before income tax	100,000	100,000
4	Depreciation expense (a noncash expense)	8,000	16,400
5	Income before income tax	€ 92,000	€ 83,600
6	Income tax expense (30%)	€ 27,600	€ 25,080
	Cash-flow analysis:		
7	Cash provided by operations before tax	€100,000	€100,000
8	Income tax expense	27,600	25,080
9	Cash provided by operations	€ 72,400	€ 74,920
10	Extra cash available for investment or debt repayment if DDB is used (€74,920 – €72,400)		€ 2,520

You can see that, for income tax purposes, accelerated depreciation helps conserve cash for the business. That's why virtually all companies will choose accelerated depreciation to compute their income tax, if allowed.

A Closer Look

Remember that there are two different "profits": one is the net profit in your financial statements, which are prepared in accordance with the applicable financial standards, and the other is taxable income on your tax filings, which are prepared in accordance with the applicable taxation rules. To understand more about taxation for accounting purposes, you may cover *IAS 12—Income Taxes* in your future courses, but if your interest is on the tax reporting side, you will need to read the various taxation rules and regulations. *IAS 12* is beyond our course coverage, but it results in some accounts that you may encounter in many companies: *deferred tax assets* and *deferred tax liabilities*. These accounts arise due to the difference between net profit (in financial reporting) and taxable income (in tax reporting). This does not mean that we are "keeping two sets of books," which is usually associated with unscrupulous behavior and cheating. We need to maintain two separate schedules because the rules are different, not because we are trying to hide income from the tax authorities!

Depreciation for Partial Years

Companies purchase PPE whenever they need them, not just at the beginning of the year. Therefore, companies must compute depreciation for partial years or whenever they need to report to shareholders (e.g., quarterly or half-yearly reports). Suppose Airbus purchases a warehouse building on April 1 for €500,000. The building's estimated life is 20 years, and its estimated residual value is €80,000. Airbus's fiscal year-end is December 31. Let's consider how Airbus computes depreciation for April through December:

- First, compute depreciation for a full year.
- Second, multiply full-year depreciation by the fraction of the year that you held the asset—in this case, 9/12. Assuming the straight-line method, the year's depreciation for this Airbus building is €15,750, as follows:

$$\text{Full-year depreciation} \quad \frac{€500{,}000 - €80{,}000}{20} = €21{,}000$$

$$\text{Partial year depreciation} \quad €21{,}000 \times 9/12 = €15{,}750$$

What if Airbus bought the asset on April 18? Many businesses record no monthly depreciation on assets purchased after the 15th of the month, and they record a full month's depreciation on an asset bought on or before the 15th. Actual practices may vary from company to company, but in the overall scheme of things, a difference of a few days is not likely to be material for long-lived assets. Most companies use computerized systems to account for fixed assets. Each depreciable asset has a unique identification number, and the system will automatically calculate the asset's depreciation expense. Accumulated Depreciation will then be automatically updated.

Changes in Estimates of Useful Lives or Residual Values

After an asset is in use, managers may change its useful life on the basis of experience and new information. This is not something that would happen often. Here's an example from Lenovo in 2008:

EXCERPTS (ADAPTED) FROM LENOVO'S 2008 NOTES TO THE FINANCIAL STATEMENTS

During the year, the estimated useful life of tooling equipment was reviewed and changed from 10–20 years to two years as it reflects the current product life cycle. This change has resulted in an accelerated depreciation charge of approximately $37 million.

As you can see from the disclosure above, the change to a shorter useful life increased the depreciation charge for the year. This is called a change in accounting estimates (*IAS 8—Accounting Policies, Changes in Accounting Estimates and Errors*). Changes in estimates are accounted for *prospectively*, which means "from now on." Lenovo recalculated depreciation on the basis of revised useful lives of its tooling equipment. Changes in estimates may also occur for residual values and are accounted for similarly.

Assume that Lenovo bought equipment costing \$50,000 and that the company originally believed the asset had a 10-year useful life with no residual value. Using the straight-line method, the company would record \$5,000 depreciation each year (\$50,000/10 years = \$5,000). Suppose Lenovo used the asset for four years. Accumulated depreciation reached \$20,000, leaving a remaining depreciable book value (cost less accumulated depreciation less residual value) of \$30,000 (\$50,000 – \$20,000). Based on the asset's conditions at the end of year four, management believes the asset will remain useful for eight more years. The company would spread the remaining depreciable book value over the asset's remaining life as follows:

Asset's remaining depreciable book value	÷	(New) Estimated useful life remaining	=	(New) Annual depreciation
\$30,000	÷	8 years	=	\$3,750

The yearly depreciation entry based on the new estimated useful life is

	A	B	C	D
1		Depreciation Expense—Equipment	3,750	
2		Accumulated Depreciation—Equipment		3,750
3				

Depreciation decreases both assets and equity.

Assets	=	Liabilities	+	Shareholders' Equity	
– 3,750	=	0	+	– 3,750	(depreciation expense)

COOKING THE BOOKS
Through Depreciation

Waste Management

Since PPEs usually involve relatively large amounts and relatively large numbers of assets, sometimes a seemingly subtle change in the way they are accounted for can have a tremendous impact on the financial statements. When these changes are made in order to cook the books, the results can be devastating.

Waste Management, Inc., is North America's largest integrated waste service company, providing collection, transfer, recycling, disposal, and waste-to-energy services for commercial, industrial, municipal, and residential customers from coast to coast.

Starting in 1992, six top executives of the company, including its founder and chairman of the board, its chief financial officer, its corporate controller, its top lawyer, and its vice president of finance, decided that the company's profits were not growing fast enough to meet "earnings targets," which were tied to their executive bonuses. Among several fraudulent financial tactics these top executives employed to cook the books were: (1) assigning unsupported and inflated salvage values to garbage trucks; (2) unjustifiably extending the estimated useful lives of their garbage trucks; and (3) assigning arbitrary salvage values to other fixed assets that previously had no salvage values. All of these tactics had the effect of decreasing the amount of depreciation expense in the Income Statements and increasing net income by a corresponding amount. While practices like this might seem relatively subtle and even insignificant when performed on an individual asset, remember that there were thousands of trash trucks and dumpsters involved, so the dollar amount grew huge in a short time. In addition, the company continued these practices for five years, overstating earnings by \$1.7 billion.

The Waste Management fraud was the largest of its kind in history until the WorldCom scandal, discussed earlier in this chapter. In 1997, the company fired the officers involved and hired a new CEO who ordered a review of these practices, which uncovered the fraud. In the meantime, these dishonest executives had profited handsomely, receiving performance-based bonuses based on the company's inflated earnings, retaining their high-paying jobs, and receiving enhanced retirement benefits. One of the executives took the fraud to another level. Just 10 days before the fraud was disclosed, he enriched himself with a tax benefit by donating inflated company shares to his alma mater to fund a building in his name! Although the men involved were sued for monetary damages, none of them ever went to jail.

When the fraud was disclosed, Waste Management shareholders lost over $6 billion in the market value of their investments when the share price plummeted by more than 33%. The company and these officers eventually settled civil lawsuits for approximately $700 million because of the fraud.

You might ask, "Where were the auditors while this was occurring?" The company's auditor was Arthur Andersen, LLP, whose partners involved on the audit engagement were eventually found to be complicit in the scheme. In fact, a few of the Waste Management officers who perpetrated the scheme had been ex-partners of the audit firm. As it turns out, the auditors actually identified many of the improper accounting practices of Waste Management. However, rather than insisting that the company fix the errors, or risk exposure, they merely "persuaded" management to agree not to repeat these practices in the future, and entered into an agreement with them to write off the accumulated Balance Sheet overstatement over a period of 10 years. In June 2001, the SEC fined Arthur Andersen $7 million for "knowingly and recklessly issuing false and misleading audit reports" for Waste Management from 1993 through 1996.

In October 2001, immediately on the heels of these disclosures, the notorious Enron scandal broke. Enron, as well as WorldCom, were Arthur Andersen clients at the time. The Enron scandal (discussed in Chapter 10) finally put the firm out of business. Many people felt that, had it not been for Andersen's involvement in the Waste Management affair, the SEC might have been more lenient toward the company in the Enron scandal.

Impairment of PPE

As you probably know, the fight for the next generation format was won by Sony's Blu-ray when Toshiba abandoned the HD DVD format in February 2008. Prior to this, Toshiba had experienced significant difficulties over a period of time. Warner Brothers, Wal-Mart, Best-Buy, and many others had started to stop the sales of HD DVD, causing a severe drop in demand for it. Suppose that at the start of the format war, Toshiba had a dedicated factory costing $1 billion that produced HD DVD, which was being depreciated over its estimated useful life of 10 years on a straight-line basis. After three years, the carrying amount of the equipment would have been $700 million. In this scenario, should Toshiba have continued depreciating the factory over 10 years, in light of the significant changes in the market for the outputs of its factory?

This is an example of how an asset may be impaired. *IAS 36—Impairment of Assets* provides guidance on this matter. An asset is impaired when its carrying amount is higher than its recoverable amount. **Recoverable amount** is the higher of fair value less cost to sell and value-in-use. The exact determination of the recoverable amount, and many other aspects of impairment of assets, is beyond an introductory accounting course. However, it is important for you to know the basic concepts of impairment. Many companies in the financial crisis have reported billions of impairment losses.

Suppose that when the carrying amount of the factory was $700 million, the fair value less cost to sell was $300 million and the value-in-use was $100 million. First, we determine that the recoverable amount was $300 million (higher of the two amounts). Toshiba would then recognize an impairment loss of $400 million (from $700 to $300 million) with the following journal entry (in millions):

A1

	A	B	C	D
1	Year 3	Impairment Loss on Factory ($700 – $300)	400	
2		Accumulated Depreciation and Impairment Loss		400
3				

Both assets (Factory) and equity decrease (through the Loss account). Under IFRS, reversal of impairment losses may be permitted under certain limited circumstances.

Assets	=	Liabilities	+	Shareholders' Equity	
−400	=	0	+	−400	(impairment loss)

Measurement Subsequent to Initial Recognition

Under *IAS 16*, an entity elects one out of two measurement models for each class of property, which is defined as a grouping of assets of similar nature and use in an entity's operations. For example, Airbus uses five classes of PPE: Freehold properties, Leasehold properties, Leasehold improvements, Plant and machinery, and Furniture, equipment and motor vehicles.

- **Cost model:** An item of PPE shall be carried at its cost, less any accumulated depreciation and any accumulated impairment losses. This is similar to what we have discussed in this chapter thus far.
- **Revaluation model:** An item of PPE whose fair value can be measured reliably shall be carried at a revalued amount, being its fair value at the date of the revaluation less any subsequent accumulated depreciation and subsequent accumulated impairment losses. Revaluations shall be made with sufficient regularity to ensure that the carrying amount does not differ materially from that which would be determined using fair value at the Balance Sheet dates.

A Closer Look

The revaluation model is a little more complicated than the cost model. *IAS 16* provides additional guidelines on the determination of fair values, the frequency of revaluations, the treatment of revaluation gains and losses, and adjustments to accumulated depreciation. Your instructor may refer you to *IAS 16* if additional coverage of the operations of revaluation model is required for your course.

Suppose you have a PPE item with a carrying amount of $100,000 (cost of $150,000 less $50,000 accumulated depreciation) and elected to use the revaluation model for this class of PPE. The fair value amount is reliably determined to be $120,000. One common way to handle the revaluation is to "restate" the asset at the new amount with zero depreciation. Using this approach, the following journal entry is entered.

A1

	A	B	C	D
1	Jan. XX	Accumulated depreciation	50,000	
2	20X1	PPE revalued (150,000 – 120,000)		30,000
3		Revaluation adjustment		20,000
4		*Revalued PPE from $150,000–$50,000 to $120,000*		
5				

After posting this entry, the accumulated depreciation is now zero, and the PPE is carried at the new fair value of $120,000. The revaluation adjustment is an equity account and will be shown as other comprehensive income in the Statement of Comprehensive Income.

Using Fully Depreciated Assets

A *fully depreciated asset* is one that has reached the end of its estimated useful life. Suppose Airbus has fully depreciated equipment with zero residual value (cost was $60,000). Airbus's accounts will appear as follows:

Equipment		−	Accumulated Depreciation		=	Book value
60,000				60,000	=	$0

The equipment's book value is zero, but that doesn't mean the equipment is worthless. Airbus may use the equipment for a few more years, but Airbus will not record any more depreciation on a fully depreciated asset.

When Airbus disposes of the equipment, Airbus will remove both the asset's cost ($60,000) and its accumulated depreciation ($60,000) from the books. The next section shows how PPE disposals are accounted.

ACCOUNT FOR PPE DISPOSALS

5 **Analyze** the effects of a PPE disposal

Eventually, a PPE will cease to serve a company's needs. The asset may wear out or become obsolete. Before accounting for the disposal of the asset, the business should bring depreciation up-to-date to:

- Update the asset's final book value.
- Record the expense up to the date of disposal.

To account for disposal, remove the asset and its related accumulated depreciation from the books. Suppose the final year's depreciation expense has just been recorded for a machine that cost $60,000 and is estimated to have zero residual value. The machine's accumulated depreciation thus totals $60,000. Assuming that this asset is junked or scrapped, the entry to record its disposal is:

A1

	A	B	C	D
1		Accumulated Depreciation—Machinery	60,000	
2		Machinery		60,000
3		*To dispose of a fully depreciated machine.*		
4				

Assets	=	Liabilities	+	Shareholders' Equity
+ 60,000 − 60,000	=	0	+	0

There is no gain or loss on this disposal, and there's no effect on total assets, liabilities, or equity. If assets are junked, scrapped, or disposed of before being fully depreciated, the company incurs a loss on the disposal. Suppose the company disposes of equipment that cost $60,000. This asset's accumulated depreciation is $50,000, and its book value is, therefore, $10,000. Scrapping this equipment results in a loss equal to the carrying amount of the asset, as follows:

A1

	A	B	C	D
1		Accumulated Depreciation—Equipment	50,000	
2		Loss on Disposal of Equipment	10,000	
3		Equipment		60,000
4		*To dispose of equipment.*		
5				

Assets	=	Liabilities	+	Shareholders' Equity	
+ 50,000 − 60,000	=	0	+	− 10,000	(loss on disposal of PPE)

The company disposed of an asset with a $10,000 book value and received nothing. The result is a $10,000 loss, which decreases both total assets and equity. The (gain) loss on disposal of equipment is typically reported as other income (expense) on the Income Statement. Losses decrease net income exactly as expenses do. Gains increase net income in the same way as revenues.

Selling a PPE. Suppose Zar Zar Trading sells equipment on September 30, 20X8, for $7,300 cash. The equipment cost $10,000 when purchased on January 1, 20X5, and has been depreciated straight-line. Zar Zar estimated a 10-year useful life and no residual value. Prior to recording the sale, Zar Zar's accountants must update the asset's depreciation. Partial-year depreciation must be recorded for the asset's depreciation from January 1, 20X8, to the sale date. The straight-line depreciation entry at September 30, 20X8, is

	A	B	C	D
1	Sept. 30	Depreciation Expense ($10,000/10 years × 9/12)	750	
2		Accumulated Depreciation—Equipment		750
3		*To update depreciation.*		
4				

The Equipment account and the Accumulated Depreciation account appear as follows. Observe that the equipment's book value is $6,250 ($10,000 – $3,750).

Equipment

Jan. 1, 20X5	10,000	

−

Accumulated Depreciation

	Dec. 31, 20X5	1,000
	Dec. 31, 20X6	1,000
	Dec. 31, 20X7	1,000
	Sept. 30, 20X8	750
	Balance	3,750

= Book value $6,250

The gain on the sale of the equipment for $7,300 is $1,050, computed as follows:

Cash received from sale of the asset		$7,300
Book value of asset sold:		
Cost	$10,000	
Less: Accumulated depreciation	(3,750)	6,250
Gain on sale of the asset		$1,050

The entry to record sale of the equipment is:

	A	B	C	D
1	Sept. 30	Cash	7,300	
2		Accumulated Depreciation—Equipment	3,750	
3		Equipment		10,000
4		Gain on Sale of Equipment		1,050
5		*To sell equipment.*		
6				

This shows that the total assets will increase along with equity—by the amount of the gain.

Assets	=	Liabilities	+	Shareholders' Equity
+ 7,300 + 3,750 − 10,000	=	0	+	1,050 (gain from sale of equipment)

Gains are recorded as credits. Gains and losses on asset disposals appear on the Income Statement as Other income (expense) or Other gains (losses). What if Zar Zar sold the same asset on September 30, 20X8, for $5,000? Recall that the book value on the date of the sale was $6,250. Thus, a loss of $1,250 on disposal of PPE would be recognized.

	A	B	C	D
1	Sept. 30	Cash	5,000	
2		Accumulated Depreciation—Equipment	3,750	
3		Loss on Sale of PPE	1,250	
4		Equipment		10,000
5		*To sell equipment.*		
6				

Total assets decrease, and equity decreases—by the amount of the loss.

Assets	=	Liabilities	+	Shareholders' Equity
+ 5,000 + 3,750 − 10,000	=	0	+	− 1,250 (loss on sale of equipment)

Exchanging PPE. Managers often trade in old assets for new ones. This is called a *non-monetary exchange*. The accounting for non-monetary exchanges is based on the *fair values of the assets involved*. Thus, the cost of an asset like plant and equipment received in a non-monetary exchange is equal to the fair values of the assets given up (including the old asset and any cash paid). Any difference between the fair value of the old asset from its book value is recognized as a gain (fair value of old asset exceeds book value) or a loss (book value of old asset exceeds fair value) on the exchange.

For example, assume Zar Zar has an old delivery car that cost $9,000 and has accumulated depreciation of $8,000. Thus, the old car's book value is $1,000. Zar Zar trades in the old automobile for a new one with a fair market value of $15,000 and pays cash of $10,000. Thus, the implied fair value of the old car is $5,000 ($15,000 – $10,000). This amount is treated as cash paid by the seller for the old vehicle. The cost of the new delivery car is $15,000 (fair value of the old asset, $5,000, plus cash paid, $10,000). Zar Zar would record the exchange transaction as follows:

	A	B	C	D
1		Delivery Auto (new)	15,000	
2		Accumulated Depreciation (old)	8,000	
3		Delivery Auto (old)		9,000
4		Cash		10,000
5		Gain on Exchange of Delivery Auto		4,000
6		*Traded in old delivery car for new auto.*		
7				

Assets	=	Liabilities	+	Shareholders' Equity	
+ 15,000 + 8,000 − 9,000 − 10,000	=	0	+	4,000	(gain on exchange of assets)

There was a net increase in total assets of $4,000 and a corresponding increase in shareholders' equity, to reflect the gain on the exchange. Notice that this amount represents the excess of the fair value of the old asset over its book value. Some other special rules may apply here, but they are covered in more advanced courses.

T-Accounts for Analyzing PPE Transactions

You can perform quite a bit of analysis if you know how transactions affect the PPE accounts. Here are the accounts with descriptions of the activity in each account.

PPE	
Beg. bal. Cost of assets purchased	Cost of assets disposed of
End. bal.	

Accumulated Depreciation	
Acc. depn. of assets disposed of	Beg. bal. Depreciation expense for the current period
	End. bal.

Depreciation Expense	
Depreciation expense for the current period	

Gain on Sale of PPE	
	Gain on sale

OR

Loss on Sale of PPE	
Loss on sale	

Example: Suppose you started the year with buildings that cost $100,000. During the year you bought another building for $150,000 and ended the year with buildings that cost $180,000. What was the cost of the building you sold?

Building			
Beg. bal.	100,000		
Cost of assets purchased	150,000	Cost of assets sold	? = $70,000*
End. bal.	180,000		

*100,000 + 150,000 − $180,000

You can perform similar analyses to answer other interesting questions about what the business did during the period.

Accounting for Natural Resources

Natural resources are PPE of a special type, such as iron ore, petroleum (oil), and timber. As PPE are expensed through depreciation, natural resource assets are expensed through *depletion*. **Depletion expense** is that portion of the cost of a natural resource that is used up in a particular period. Depletion expense is computed in the same way as units-of-production depreciation.

An oil lease may cost Royal Dutch Shell $100,000 and contain an estimated 10,000 barrels of oil. The depletion rate would be $10 per barrel ($100,000/10,000 barrels). If 3,000 barrels are extracted, depletion expense is $30,000 (3,000 barrels × $10 per barrel). The depletion entry is:

	A	B	C	D
1		Depletion Expense (3,000 barrels × $10)	30,000	
2		Accumulated Depletion—Oil		30,000
3				

This entry is almost identical to a depreciation entry using the units-of-production method. If 4,500 barrels are removed the next year, that period's depletion is $45,000 (4,500 barrels × $10 per barrel). Accumulated Depletion is a contra account similar to Accumulated Depreciation.

Natural resource assets can be reported on Shell's Balance Sheet as follows (amounts assumed):

Property, Plant, and Equipment:		
Equipment	$960,000	
Less: Accumulated depreciation	(410,000)	$550,000
Oil	$340,000	
Less: Accumulated depletion	(140,000)	200,000
Total property, plant, and equipment		$750,000

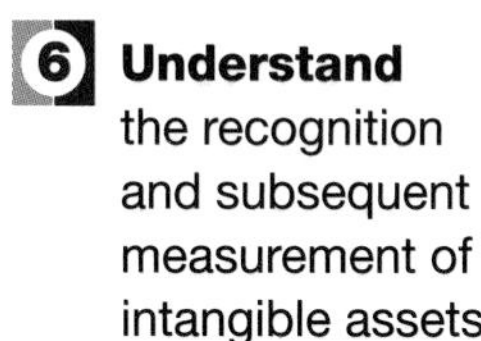
Understand the recognition and subsequent measurement of intangible assets

UNDERSTAND THE RECOGNITION AND SUBSEQUENT MEASUREMENT OF INTANGIBLE ASSETS

As we have discussed at the start of this chapter, *intangible assets* are identifiable, long-lived assets without physical substance. Intangibles are valuable because they carry special rights from patents, copyrights, trademarks, franchises, leaseholds, and goodwill. If you look back at Airbus's Balance Sheet at the start of this chapter, you may notice that its intangible assets (line 6) amounted to €12,555 million, about 12% of total non-current assets. Intangibles are the most valuable assets for high-tech companies and those that depend on research and development. For example, many companies are now fighting over patents and copyrights on various smartphone and mobile technologies.

Like buildings and equipment, an intangible asset is recorded at its acquisition cost. However, unlike PPE, *IAS 38—Intangible Assets* states that it is unlikely that any subsequent expenditure will be recognized in the carrying amount of an intangible asset. The choice of cost model or revaluation model is also available for intangible assets, but *IAS 38* made it clear that it will be very rare for an entity to be able to use the revaluation model. In our discussions, we will assume that the intangibles will be measured at cost subsequent to acquisition.

The accounting for intangible assets can be a little more abstract. After all, it's definitely harder to account for things that have no physical form than those with physical form! We will cover the basics here, but you will likely revisit this topic in greater detail in more advanced accounting courses. Let's see what *IAS 38* says. Intangible assets fall into two categories:

- Intangibles with *finite lives* that can be measured reliably—we record **amortization** for these intangibles. Amortization works like depreciation and is usually computed on a straight-line basis. The residual value of most intangibles is zero. Intangibles with finite lives are also subjected to impairment tests.
- Intangibles with *indefinite lives*—because they have indefinite lives, we will not be able to allocate any amortization, so these intangibles are not amortized. Instead, they are tested for impairment for any loss in value, and, if any, a loss is recorded when it occurs. Goodwill is the most prominent example of an intangible asset with an indefinite life.

As far as intangible assets are concerned, remember that the opposite of *finite lives* is *indefinite lives*, and not *infinite lives*! Both categories of intangibles are subject to impairment tests. Impairment was previously explained in relation to PPE, but the same principles apply. For more details, if required by your course coverage, you instructor may refer you to *IAS 36—Impairment of Assets*. In the following discussions, we illustrate the accounting for both categories of intangibles.

This is what Airbus says about its intangible assets:

ADAPTED EXCERPTS FROM AIRBUS GROUP'S NOTES TO THE ACCOUNTS

Intangible Assets

Intangible assets comprise (1) goodwill, (2) capitalized development costs, and (3) other intangible assets, e.g., internally developed software and acquired intangible assets. Intangible assets with finite useful lives are generally amortized on a straight-line basis over their respective estimated useful lives (3 to 10 years) to their estimated residual values.

Source: Airbus Group's 2015 Financial Statements, page 34.

In the following discussions, we will look at some specific examples of intangible assets.

Accounting for Specific Intangibles

Each type of intangible asset is unique, and the accounting can vary from one asset to another. How the asset is acquired, for example, through purchase, a business combination (i.e., merger or acquisition of another company), or internal development, may also impact how the intangible asset is recognized and measured.

Patents. **Patents** are granted by a government to give the holder the exclusive right for a certain number of years to produce and sell an invention. The invention may be a specific product or process—for example, Apple's iPad and the Dolby noise-reduction process. Like any other asset, a patent may be purchased. Suppose Yamaha pays 15 million JPY (Japanese yen), or about \$170,000, to acquire a patent on January 1, and the business believes the expected useful life of the patent is five years (not necessarily the entire legal enforceability of the patent). Amortization expense is \$34,000 per year (\$170,000/5 years). Yamaha records the acquisition and amortization for this patent as follows:

	A	B	C	D
1	Jan. 1	Patents	170,000	
2		Cash		170,000
3		*To acquire a patent.*		
4				

	A	B	C	D
1	Dec. 31	Amortization Expense—Patents (\$170,000/5)	34,000	
2		Accumulated Amortization—Patents		34,000
3		*To amortize the cost of a patent.*		
4				

Alternatively, we can credit the patents account directly (not using an Accumulated Amortization account). Either way, the impact on the accounting equation is the same.

Assets	=	Liabilities	+	Shareholders' Equity	
− 34,000	=	0	+	− 34,000	(amortization expense)

Amortization for an intangible decreases both assets and equity exactly as depreciation does for equipment or a building.

Copyrights. **Copyrights** are exclusive rights to reproduce and sell a book, musical composition, film, or other work of art. Copyrights also protect computer software programs, such as Microsoft's Windows® and Excel. Issued by governments, copyrights in certain jurisdictions can extend up to 70 years beyond the author's (composer's, artist's, or programmer's) life. The cost of obtaining a copyright from the government is low, but a company may pay a large sum to purchase an existing copyright from the owner or to buy a company for its copyrights. For example, Zynga (one of the biggest social network game companies) has been buying game developers such as Newtoy (publisher of "Words with Friends") and OMGPOP (publisher of "Draw Something").

Trademarks and Trade Names. **Trademarks** and **trade names** (or *brand names*) are distinctive identification of a product or service. The "swoosh" symbol is the trademark of Nike, a symbol that has become synonymous with the company itself. Similarly, other logos such as Coca-Cola's "Dynamic Ribbon" and McDonald's golden arches and its *I'm lovin' it!* slogan are all registered trademarks. Often, you see distinctive identifications of products or services, marked with the symbol ™ or ®. Some trademarks may have a definite useful life set by contract. Again, useful life for the purpose of amortization may be shorter than the legal useful life. This is similar to how the useful lives of a PPE, as intended by management, may be shorter than its actual capability.

Franchises and Licenses. **Franchises and licenses** are privileges granted by a private business or a government to sell a product or service in accordance with specified conditions. Many franchises are in the food or retail industry (Subway, Pizza Hut, Dunkin' Donuts, 7-Eleven, and thousands more), but there are also franchises in the service industry (H&R Block, Kumon Maths & Reading Centers, Days Inn, etc.). The useful lives of many franchises and licenses are usually indefinite (as the management is able to continue renewing the agreement) and, therefore, are not amortized.

Goodwill. In accounting, **goodwill** has a very specific meaning. Goodwill is defined as the excess of the cost of purchasing another company over the sum of the fair values of the acquired company's net assets (assets minus liabilities). For example, a purchaser is willing to pay for goodwill when the purchaser buys another company that has abnormal earning power to bring about a comparative advantage in the market. *IAS 38* prohibits the recognition of internally generated goodwill. Thus, the only goodwill you will see in financial statements is goodwill that results from business combinations or mergers and acquisitions as outlined in *IFRS 3—Business Combinations.*

Airbus operates in many countries across Asia. Suppose Airbus acquires Europa Company at a cost of $10 million. Europa's assets have a market value of $9 million, and its liabilities total $2 million, so Europa's net assets total $7 million at current market value. Note that the assets and liabilities may include new identifiable intangible assets that were previously not recorded in Europa's books, for example brand names, trademarks, customer relationships, etc. In this case, Europa paid $3 million for goodwill, computed as follows:

Purchase price paid for Europa Company		$10 million
Sum of the fair values of Europa Company's assets	$9 million	
Less: Europa Company's liabilities	(2 million)	
Market value of Europa Company's net assets		7 million
Excess is called *goodwill*		$ 3 million

Airbus's entry to record the acquisition of Europa Company, including its goodwill, would be:

	A	B	C	D
1		Assets (Cash, Receivables, Inventories, PPE,		
2		all at fair value)	9,000,000	
3		Goodwill	3,000,000	
4		Liabilities		2,000,000
5		Cash		10,000,000
6				

Goodwill in accounting has special features, as follows:

1. Goodwill is recorded only when it is purchased in the acquisition of another company. A purchase transaction provides objective evidence of the value of goodwill as the excess of purchase consideration over the net fair value of identifiable assets and liabilities. Companies are not allowed to record internally generated goodwill that they create for their own business.
2. Unlike other intangibles with finite useful lives, goodwill is not amortized and is subjected to strict impairment tests.

Is it possible to acquire a company for a consideration that is less than the fair value of its identifiable assets and liabilities? A "negative goodwill?" Yes! This is what *IFRS 3—Business Combinations* calls "bargain purchase." Any resulting gain, subject to a number of caveats, may be recognized by the acquirer as a gain in the Income Statement on the acquisition date.

Accounting for Research and Development Costs

In a company with significant research and development (R&D) activities, such as Lenovo or Samsung, should the expenditures be treated as assets or expenses? Under *IAS 38*, the accounting treatment for R&D expenditures is literally split in the middle between research and development. Under IFRS, costs associated with the creation of intangible assets are classified into *research phase* costs and *development phase* costs. Costs in the research phase are always expensed. However, costs in the development phase are capitalized if the company can demonstrate meeting all of the following six criteria:

- the technical feasibility of completing the intangible asset
- the intention to complete the intangible asset
- the ability to use or sell the intangible asset
- the future economic benefits (e.g., the existence of a market or, if for internal use, the usefulness of the intangible asset)
- the availability of adequate resources to complete development of the asset
- the ability to reliably measure the expenditure attributable to the intangible asset during its development

Like many accounting standards, the separation between research and development is one that requires judgment, supported by objective evidence.

You saw earlier at the start of this chapter that one of Airbus's intangible assets was "Capitalized Development Costs" (line 22), with a gross amount of €2,686 million, an accumulated amortization and impairment of €1,027, million, and, thus, a net carrying amount of €1,659 million. Its accounting policies reflect the discussion we had earlier about accounting for research and development costs.

ADAPTED EXCERPTS FROM AIRBUS GROUP'S NOTES TO THE ACCOUNTS

Research and Development

The costs for self-initiated research are expensed when incurred. The costs for self-initiated development are capitalized when:

- the product or process is technically feasible and clearly defined (i.e., the critical design review is finalized)

- adequate resources are available to successfully complete the development
- the benefits from the assets are demonstrated (a market exists or the internal usefulness is demonstrated), and the costs attributable to the projects are reliably measured
- the Group intends to produce and market or use the developed product or process and can demonstrate its profitability

Development costs which are capitalized are recognized either as intangible assets or, when the related development activities lead to the construction, of specialized tooling for production ("jigs and tools"), or involve the design, construction, and testing of prototypes and models, as property, plant, and equipment. Capitalized development costs are generally amortized over the estimated number of units produced. If the number of units produced cannot be estimated reliably, capitalized development costs are amortized over the estimated useful life of the internally generated intangible asset. Amortization of capitalized development costs is recognized in cost of sales.

Source: Airbus Group's 2015 Financial Statements, page 15

Accounting for the Impairment of an Intangible Asset

Impairment testing applies to intangible assets as it does to PPE (as described earlier). Some intangibles—such as goodwill, licenses, and some trademarks—have indefinite lives and therefore are not subject to amortization. But all intangibles are subject to a write-down when their value decreases. Recall that such a decline in value of an asset is called impairment.

Let's look at our hypothetical purchase of Europa Company by Airbus. After a couple of years, market conditions indicate that the goodwill paid during the acquisition of Europa Company is impaired. The recoverable amount of the goodwill is calculated to be $1,000,000. Airbus would then record a $2 million impairment loss and write down the book value of the goodwill, as follows:

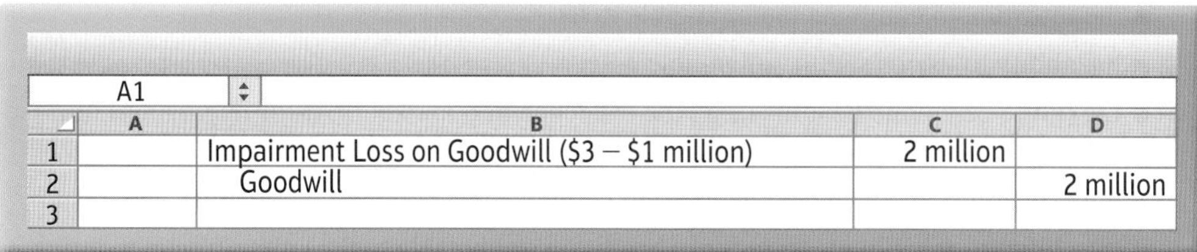

	A	B	C	D
1		Impairment Loss on Goodwill ($3 – $1 million)	2 million	
2		Goodwill		2 million
3				

Both assets (goodwill) and equity decrease (through the Loss account). Unlike tangible assets, once goodwill is impaired, IFRS prohibit any reversal of the impairment. Airbus's financial statements will report the following (in millions):

Assets	=	Liabilities	+	Shareholders' Equity	
– 2 million	=	0	+	– 2 million	(impairment loss)

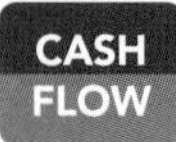

Reporting Long-Term Assets Transactions on the Statement of Cash Flows

Three main types of long-term asset transactions appear on the statement of cash flows: their acquisitions and disposals that are settled in cash. Specifically, acquisitions and disposal of long-term assets are cash flows from investing activities. Have a look Exhibit 7-13, which shows extracts of Airbus's statements of cash flows for 2015 and 2014. Acquisitions and disposals of PPE, intangibles, assets, and investment property are denoted in color (lines 6 to 7).

Exhibit 7-13 | Airbus's Statement of Cash Flows

	A	B	C
1 2	**Airbus Group Consolidated Statement of Cash Flows (Adapted) For year ended December 31**		
3	**(In millions of Euro)**	**2015**	**2014**
4	Cash flows from operating activities	3,600	2,560
5	Cash flows from investing activities		
6	Purchase of intangible assets, PPE and investment property	(2,924)	(2,548)
7	Process from disposal of intangible assets, PPE and investment property	78	232
8	Other cash flows from investing activities	(613)	(907)
9	Cash flows from investing activities	(3,459)	(3,223)
10	Cash flows from financing activities	(25)	495
11	Net cash flows (excluding foreign exchange rate changes)	116	(168)
12			

As you can see, the cash components of long-term asset transactions will be reflected in the statement of cash flows. We will look into cash flows later in Chapter 11, but for now, just remember that the cash elements of PPE and intangibles transactions will be reported in the cash flow statement.

EVALUATE A COMPANY'S PERFORMANCE BASED ON ITS ASSETS

7
Evaluate a company's performance based on its assets

Owners, managers, and investors use ratios to evaluate a business. Two ratios relate directly to non-current assets: asset turnover ratio and return on asset. The ability of a business to generate sales and profit from its asset is an important indication of effectiveness. Non-productive assets will hurt asset turnover and return on assets.

Asset Turnover and Return on Assets. **Asset turnover** is how many sales a business can generate from its assets. Similarly, **return on assets** is how much profit a business can generate from its assets. The higher the turnover or the return, the more effective the business is at utilizing its assets. Let's have a look at how Airbus performs on these two ratios and compare it to two other aircraft manufacturers, Boeing and General Dynamics (makers of the Gulfstream aircrafts, but also a defense contractor).

Asset Turnover and Return on Assets	Airbus 2015	Airbus 2014
$\frac{\text{Sales}}{\text{Average assets*}}$	$\frac{64{,}450}{101{,}392} = 0.64$ times	$\frac{60{,}713}{93{,}188} = 0.65$
$\frac{\text{Net profit}}{\text{Average assets*}}$	$\frac{2{,}698}{101{,}392} = 2.66\%$	$\frac{2{,}350}{93{,}188} = 2.52$

**Average = (beginning + ending balance)/2*

Airbus's asset turnover declined slightly (from 0.65 to 0.64 times), but its return on assets showed marginal improvements (from 2.52% to 2.66%) in 2015 compared to 2014. Exhibits 7-14 and 7-15 plot the two ratios for the three aircaraft manufacturers. You can see that Airbus is behind Boeing and General Dynamics in terms of utilization of assets to generate revenue, and its returns are half that of Boeing's and one-third that of General Dynamics.

Exhibit 7-14 | Asset Turnover Comparisons

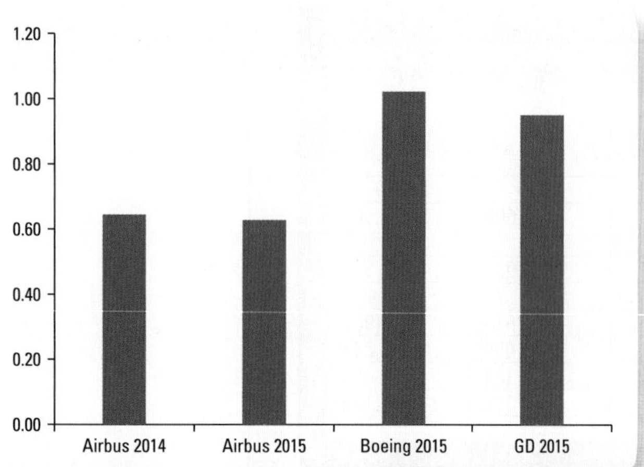

Exhibit 7-15 | Return on Assets Comparisons

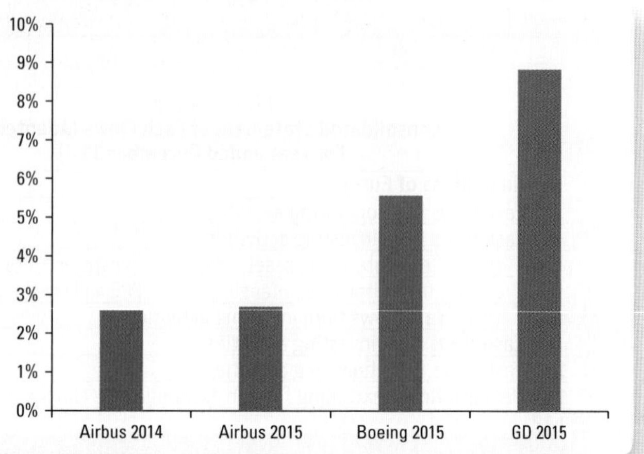

DECISION GUIDELINES

PPE AND RELATED EXPENSES

Airbus, like all other companies, must make some decisions about how to account for its property, plant, and equipment (PPE) and intangibles. Let's review some of these decisions.

Decision	Guidelines
Capitalize or expense a cost?	General rule: Capitalize all costs that provide future benefit for the business such as a new package-handling system. Expense all costs that provide no future benefit, such as ordinary repairs to a delivery vehicle.
Capitalize or expense:	
■ Cost associated with a new asset?	Capitalize all costs that bring the asset to its intended use, including asset purchase price, transportation charges, and taxes paid to acquire the asset.
■ Cost associated with an existing asset?	Capitalize only those costs that add to the asset's usefulness or to its useful life. Expense all other costs as maintenance or repairs.
Which depreciation method to use:	
■ For financial reporting?	Use the method that best matches depreciation expense against the revenues produced by the asset. Most companies use the straight-line method.
■ For income tax?	Use the method that produces the fastest tax deductions. Depending on the applicable tax regulations, a company may be able to apply different depreciation methods for financial reporting and for income-tax purposes.
■ How to account for natural resources?	Capitalize the asset's acquisition cost and all later costs that add to the natural resource's future benefit. Then record depletion expense, as computed by the units-of-production method.
■ How to account for intangibles?	Capitalize acquisition cost for intangibles that meet the definition, recognition, and measurement criteria. For intangibles with finite lives, record amortization expense. For intangibles with indefinite lives, do not record amortization. All intangible assets are subject to impairment tests.

End-of-Chapter Summary Problem

The figures that follow appear in the *Answers to the Mid-Chapter Summary Problem*, Requirement 2.

	Method A: Straight-Line			*Method B: Double-Declining-Balance*		
Financial Year	Annual Depreciation Expense	Accumulated Depreciation	Book Value	Annual Depreciation Expense	Accumulated Depreciation	Book Value
Start			$44,000			$44,000
20X6	$4,000	$ 4,000	40,000	$8,800	$ 8,800	35,200
20X7	4,000	8,000	36,000	7,040	15,840	28,160
20X8	4,000	12,000	32,000	5,632	21,472	22,528

Requirements

1. Suppose the income tax authorities permitted a choice between these two depreciation methods. Which method would Airbus select for income-tax purposes? Why?
2. Suppose Airbus purchased the equipment described earlier (€44,000 cost, €4,000 residual value, and 10 years' useful life) on January 1, 20X6. Management has depreciated the equipment by using the double-declining-balance method. On June 30, 20X8, Airbus sold the equipment for €27,000 cash.

Record depreciation for 20X7 and the sale of the equipment on June 30, 20X8.

Answers

Requirement 1

For tax purposes, most companies select the accelerated method because it results in the greatest depreciation in the earliest years of the asset's life. Accelerated depreciation minimizes income tax payments in the early years of the asset's life. That maximizes the business's cash at the earliest possible time.

Requirement 2

Entries to record depreciation to date of sale, and then the sale of the equipment, follow:

A1

	A	B	C	D
1	20X8			
2	Jun 30	Depreciation Expense—Equipment ($5,632 X 1/2 year)	2,816	
3		Accumulated Depreciation—Equipment		2,816
4		*To update depreciation.*		
5				
6		Cash	27,000	
7	Jun 30	Accumulated Depreciation—Equipment ($15,840 + $2,816)	18,656	
8		Equipment		44,000
9		Gain on Sale of Equipment		1,656
10		*To record sale of equipment.*		
11				

REVIEW | PPES and Intangibles

Quick Check (Answers are given at the end of the chapter.)

1. Bretman, Inc., purchased a tract of land, a small office building, and some equipment for \$1,800,000. The appraised value of the land was \$1,420,000, the building \$650,000, and the equipment \$430,000. What is the cost of the land?

   a. \$600,000
   b. \$1,022,400
   c. \$1,420,000
   d. None of the above

2. Which statement is false?

   a. Depreciation is based on the matching principle because it matches the cost of the asset with the revenue generated over the asset's useful life.
   b. Depreciation is a process of allocating the cost of a PPE over its useful life.
   c. Depreciation creates a fund to replace the asset at the end of its useful life.
   d. The cost of a PPE minus accumulated depreciation equals the asset's book value.

Use the following data for questions 3–6.
On July 1, 20X6, Amir Communications purchased a new piece of equipment that cost \$65,000. The estimated useful life is 10 years and estimated residual value is \$5,000.

3. What is the depreciation expense for 20X6 if Amir uses the straight-line method?

   a. \$3,000
   b. \$6,000
   c. \$3,250
   d. \$6,500

4. Assume Amir Communications purchased the equipment on January 1, 20X6. If Amir uses the straight-line method for depreciation, what is the asset's book value at the end of 20X7?

   a. \$54,000
   b. \$59,000
   c. \$48,000
   d. \$53,000

5. Assume Amir Communications purchased the equipment on January 1, 20X6. If Amir uses the double-declining-balance method, what is the depreciation for 20X7?

   a. \$13,000
   b. \$10,400
   c. \$12,000
   d. \$9,600

6. Return to Amir's original purchase date of July 1, 20X5. Assume that Amir uses the straight-line method of depreciation and sells the equipment for \$44,500 on July 1, 20X9. The result of the sale of the equipment is a gain (loss) of

   a. \$3,500.
   b. \$8,500.
   c. \$ (15,500).
   d. \$0.

7. A company bought a new machine for \$30,000 on January 1. The machine is expected to last five years and has a residual value of \$6,000. If the company uses the double-declining-balance method, accumulated depreciation at the end of year 2 will be

   a. \$12,000.
   b. \$9,600.
   c. \$19,200.
   d. \$15,360.

8. Which of the following is *not* a capital expenditure?

   a. A complete overhaul of an air-conditioning system
   b. Replacement of an old motor with a new one in a piece of equipment
   c. The cost of installing a piece of equipment
   d. The addition of a building wing
   e. A tune-up of a company vehicle

9. Which of the following assets is *not* subject to a decreasing book value through depreciation, depletion, or amortization?

a. Goodwill
b. Land improvements
c. Natural resources
d. Intangibles

10. Why would a business select an accelerated method of depreciation for tax purposes?

a. Accelerated depreciation will result in higher gain on disposal of PPE than straight-line depreciation.
b. Accelerated depreciation generates a greater amount of depreciation over the life of the asset than does straight-line depreciation.
c. Accelerated depreciation is easier to calculate because salvage value is ignored.
d. Accelerated depreciation generates higher depreciation expense immediately, and therefore lowers tax payments in the early years of the asset's life.

11. A company purchased an oil well for $270,000. It estimates that the well contains 100,000 barrels, has an eight-year life, and has no salvage value. If the company extracts and sells 20,000 barrels of oil in the first year, how much depletion expense should be recorded?

a. $33,750
b. $54,000
c. $27,000
d. $67,500

12. Which item among the following is not an intangible asset?

a. A copyright
b. A patent
c. A trademark
d. Goodwill
e. All of the above are intangible assets.

Accounting Vocabulary

accelerated depreciation method (p. 404) A depreciation method that writes off a relatively larger amount of the asset's cost nearer the start of its useful life than does the straight-line method.

accumulated depreciation (p. 400) The cumulative sum of all depreciation expense from the date of acquiring PPE.

amortization (p. 418) The systematic reduction of a lump-sum amount. Expense that applies to intangible assets in the same way depreciation applies to PPE and depletion applies to natural resources.

asset turnover (p. 423) A measure of efficiency on the use of assets to generate sales.

capital expenditure (p. 397) An expenditure that increases an asset's capacity or efficiency or extends its useful life. Capital expenditures are debited to an asset account.

copyright (p. 420) Exclusive right to reproduce and sell a book, musical composition, film, other work of art, or computer program. Issued by the government, copyrights may extend many years beyond the author's life.

depletion expense (p. 417) That portion of a natural resource's cost that is used up in a particular period. Depletion expense is computed in the same way as units-of-production depreciation.

depreciation (p. 399) The systematic allocation of the cost of a long-term asset over its useful life.

depreciable cost (p. 401) The cost of a PPE minus its estimated residual value.

double-declining-balance (DDB) method (p. 404) An accelerated depreciation method that computes annual depreciation by multiplying the asset's decreasing book value by a constant percentage, which is two times the straight-line rate.

estimated residual value (p. 401) Expected cash value of an asset at the end of its useful life. Also called *residual value, scrap value*, or *salvage value*.

estimated useful life (p. 401) Length of service that a business expects to get from an asset. May be expressed in years, units of output, miles, or other measures.

franchises and licenses (p. 420) Privileges granted by a private business or a government to sell a product or service in accordance with specified conditions.

goodwill (p. 420) Excess of the cost of an acquired company over the sum of the market values of its net assets (assets minus liabilities).

impairment (p. 391) The condition that exists when the carrying amount of an asset exceeds its recoverable amount.

intangible assets (p. 392) A non-monetary asset with no physical form that conveys future economic benefits to the entity.

patent (p. 419) A government grant giving the holder the exclusive right for a certain number of years to produce and sell an invention.

property, plant and equipment (PPE) (p. 391) Long-lived assets, such as land, buildings, and equipment, used in the operation of the business. Also called *fixed assets* or *plant assets*.

recoverable amount (p. 412) The higher of fair value less cost to sell and value-in-use. Used in impairment tests.

return on assets (p. 423) A measure of the level of returns or profit generated from assets.

straight-line (SL) method (p. 402) Depreciation method in which an equal amount of depreciation expense is assigned to each year of asset use.

trademark, trade name (p. 420) A distinctive identification of a product or service. Also called a *brand name*.

units-of-production (UOP) method (p. 403) Depreciation method by which a fixed amount of depreciation is assigned to each unit of output produced by the PPE.

ASSESS YOUR PROGRESS

Short Exercises

LO 2

S7-1. *(Learning Objective 2: Determining cost and book value of a company's PPEs)* Examine Round Rock's assets.

	A	B	C
1	**Hard Stone Corporation Consolidated Balance Sheets (Partial, Adapted)**		
2	**(In millions)**	**May 31, 20X7**	**May 31, 20X6**
3	Assets		
4	Current assets		
5	Cash and cash equivalents	$ 2,098	$ 246
6	Receivables, less allowances of $144 and $125	2,772	2,610
7	Spare parts, supplies and fuel	4,670	4,510
8	Prepaid expenses and other	468	411
9	Total current assets	10,008	7,777
10	Property and equipment, at cost		
11	Aircraft	2,394	2,394
12	Package handling and ground support equipment	12,225	12,139
13	Computer and electronic equipment	28,165	26,115
14	Vehicles	586	453
15	Facilities and other	1,435	1,594
16	Total cost	44,805	42,695
17	Less: Accumulated depreciation	(14,903)	(12,942)
18	Net property and equipment	29,902	29,753
19	Other long-term assets		
20	Goodwill	724	724
21	Prepaid pension cost	1,341	1,275
22	Intangible and other assets	324	329
23	Total other long-term assets	2,389	2,328
24	Total assets	$ 42,299	$ 39,858
25			

1. What is Hard Stone's largest category of assets? List all 20X7 assets in the largest category and their amounts as reported by Hard Stone.
2. What was Hard Stone's cost of property and equipment at May 31, 20X7? What was the book value of property and equipment on this date? Why is book value less than cost?

LO 2

S7-2. *(Learning Objective 2: Measuring the cost of a PPE)* The costs included for the acquisition of land are listed in the "Land and Land Improvements" section of this chapter. First is the purchase price of the land, which is obviously included in the cost of the land. The reasons for including the other costs are not so obvious. For example, property tax is ordinarily an expense, not part of the cost of an asset. State why the other costs listed are included as part of the cost of the land. After the land is ready for use, will these related costs be capitalized or expensed?

S7-3. ***(Learning Objective 2: Determining the cost of individual assets in a lump-sum purchase of assets)*** Farah Distribution Service pays $110,000 for a group purchase of land, building, and equipment. At the time of acquisition, the land has a current market value of $75,000, the building's current market value is $45,000, and the equipment's current market value is $30,000. Journalize the lump-sum purchase of the three assets for a total cost of $110,000. You sign a note payable for this amount. LO 2

S7-4. ***(Learning Objective 2: Capitalizing versus expensing PPE costs)*** Assume Speed Car Rentals changed the tires for its entire fleet of cars at a cost of $1.8 million, which Speed paid in cash. Further, assume the Speed accountant erroneously capitalized this expense as part of the cost of the fleet. LO 2

Show the effects of the accounting error on Speed Car Rentals' Income Statement. To answer this question, determine whether revenues, total expenses, and net income were overstated or understated by the accounting error.

S7-5. ***(Learning Objective 4: Computing depreciation by three methods—first year only)*** Assume that at the beginning of 20X6, AirAsia, a regional airline operating predominantly in Southeast Asia, purchased a used Boeing 737 aircraft at a cost of $55,000,000. AirAsia expects the plane to remain useful for five years (7 million miles) and to have a residual value of $6,000,000. AirAsia expects to fly the plane 875,000 miles the first year; 1,475,000 miles each year during the second, third, and fourth years; and 1,700,000 miles the last year. LO 4

1. Compute AirAsia's first-year depreciation on the plane using the following methods:
   a. Straight-line
   b. Units-of-production
   c. Double-declining-balance
2. Show the airplane's book value at the end of the first year under each depreciation method.

S7-6. ***(Learning Objective 4: Computing depreciation by three methods—third year only)*** Use the AirAsia data in Short Exercise 7-5 to compute AirAsia's third-year depreciation on the plane using the following methods: LO 4

a. Straight-line
b. Units-of-production
c. Double-declining-balance

S7-7. ***(Learning Objective 4: Selecting the best depreciation method for income tax purposes)*** This exercise uses the assumed AirAsia data from Short Exercise 7-5. Assume AirAsia is trying to decide which depreciation method to use for income tax purposes. The company can choose from among the following methods: (a) straight-line, (b) units of production, or (c) double-declining-balance. LO 4

1. Which depreciation method offers the tax advantage for the first year? Describe the nature of the tax advantage.
2. How much income tax will AirAsia save for the first year of the airplane's use under the method you selected above as compared with using the straight-line depreciation method? Assume the tax rate is 30%. Ignore any earnings from investing the extra cash.

S7-8. ***(Learning Objectives 3, 4: Computing partial year depreciation; selecting the best depreciation method)*** Assume that on September 30, 20X6, LoganAir, the national airline of Switzerland, purchased an Airbus aircraft at a cost of €48,000,000. LoganAir expects the plane to remain useful for six years (4,500,000 miles) and to have a residual value of €6,000,000. LoganAir will fly the plane 420,000 miles during the remainder of 20X6. Compute LoganAir's depreciation on the plane for the year ended December 31, 20X6, using the following methods: LO 3 4

a. Straight-line
b. Units-of-production
c. Double-declining-balance

Which method would produce the highest net income for 20X6? Which method produces the lowest net income?

LO 3 4

S7-9. ***(Learning Objectives 3, 4: Computing and recording depreciation after a change in useful life of the asset)*** Ten Flags over Georgia paid $120,000 for a concession stand. Ten Flags started out depreciating the building using the straight-line method over 20 years with zero residual value. After using the concession stand for three years, Ten Flags determines that the building will remain useful for only six more years. Record Ten Flags' depreciation on the concession stand for year 4 by the straight-line method.

LO 3 4

S7-10. ***(Learning Objectives 3, 4: Computing depreciation; recording a gain or loss on disposal)*** On January 1, 20X6, Scoot Airline purchased an airplane for $38,700,000. Scoot Airline expects the plane to remain useful for six years and to have a residual value of $3,500,000. Scoot Airline uses the straight-line method to depreciate its airplanes. Scoot Airline flew the plane for three years and sold it on January 1, 20X9, for $9,300,000.

1. Compute accumulated depreciation on the airplane at January 1, 20X9 (same as December 31, 20X8).
2. Record the sale of the plane on January 1, 20X9.

LO 5

S7-11. ***(Learning Objective 5: Accounting for the depletion of a company's natural resources)*** Abundant Petroleum, the giant oil company, holds reserves of oil and gas assets. At the end of 20X6, assume the cost of Abundant Petroleum's mineral assets totaled $160 billion, representing 10 billion barrels of oil in the ground.

1. Which depreciation method is similar to the depletion method that Abundant Petroleum and other oil companies use to compute their annual depletion expense for the minerals removed from the ground?
2. Suppose Abundant Petroleum removed 0.4 billion barrels of oil during 20X7. Record depletion expense for the year. Show amounts in billions.
3. At December 31, 20X6, Abundant Petroleum's Accumulated Depletion account stood at $58 billion. Report Mineral Assets and Accumulated Depletion at December 31, 20X7. Do Abundant Petroleum's Mineral Assets appear to be plentiful or mostly used up? Give your reason.

LO 1 6

S7-12. ***(Learning Objectives 1, 6: Measuring and recording goodwill; Reporting cash flows)*** Hector, Inc., dominates the snack-food industry with its Tasty-Chip brand. Assume that Hector, Inc., purchased Crunchy Snacks, Inc., for $10.8 million cash. The market value of Concord Snacks' assets is $18 million, and Concord Snacks has liabilities of $12 million.

1. Compute the cost of the goodwill purchased by Hector.
2. Explain how Hector will account for goodwill in future years.

LO 5

S7-13. ***(Learning Objective 5: Accounting for patents and research and development costs)*** This exercise summarizes the accounting for patents, which, like copyrights, trademarks, and franchises, provide the owner with a special right or privilege. It also covers research and development costs.

Suppose Solar Automobiles Limited paid $700,000 to research and develop a new global positioning system. Solar also paid $420,000 to acquire a patent on a new motor. After readying the motor for production, Solar's sales revenue for the first year totaled $5,600,000. Cost of goods sold was $3,900,000, and selling expenses totaled $580,000. All these transactions occurred during 20X6. Solar expects the patent to have a useful life of seven years.

Prepare Solar Automobiles' Income Statement for the year ended December 31, 20X6, complete with a heading. Ignore income tax.

LO 7

S7-14. ***(Learning Objective 7: Reporting investing activities on the statement of cash flows)*** During 20X6, Orion Satellite Systems, Inc., purchased two other companies for $18 million. Also during 20X6, Orion made capital expenditures of $8 million to expand its market share. During the year, Orion sold its North American operations, receiving cash of $16 million. Overall, Orion reported a net income of $3 million during 20X6.

Show what Orion would report for cash flows from investing activities on its statement of cash flows for 20X6. Report a total amount for net cash provided by (used in) investing activities.

Exercises MyLab Accounting

Select A and B exercises can be found within MyLab Accounting, an online homework and practice environment. Your instructor may ask you to complete select exercises using MyLab Accounting.

Group A

E7-15A. *(Learning Objective 1: Determining the cost of PPE)* Ariana Self Storage purchased land, paying $185,000 cash as a downpayment and signing a $200,000 note payable for the balance. Ariana also had to pay delinquent property tax of $4,500, title insurance costing $3,000, and $10,000 to level the land and remove an unwanted building. The company paid $63,000 to add soil for the foundation and then constructed an office building at a cost of $640,000. It also paid $57,000 for a fence around the property, $15,000 for the company sign near the property entrance, and $9,000 for lighting of the grounds. Determine the cost of Ariana's land, land improvements, and building.

E7-16A. *(Learning Objectives 1, 2: Allocating costs to assets acquired in a lump-sum purchase; disposing of a PPE)* Goodwood Manufacturing bought three used machines in a $154,000 lump-sum purchase. An independent appraiser valued the machines as shown in the table.

Machine No.	Appraised Value
1	$38,250
2	73,100
3	58,650

What is each machine's individual cost? Immediately after making this purchase, Goodwood sold machine 2 for its appraised value. What is the result of the sale? (Round decimals to three places when calculating proportions, and use your computed percentages throughout.)

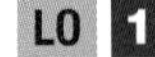

E7-17A. *(Learning Objective 1: Distinguishing capital expenditures from expenses)* Assume Sweets Emporium, Inc., purchased conveyor-belt machinery. Classify each of the following expenditures as a capital expenditure or an immediate expense related to machinery:

- **a.** Income tax paid on income earned from the sale of products manufactured by the machinery
- **b.** Major overhaul to extend the machinery's useful life by three years
- **c.** Ordinary repairs to keep the machinery in good working order
- **d.** Lubrication of the machinery before it is placed in service
- **e.** Periodic lubrication after the machinery is placed in service
- **f.** Sales tax paid on the purchase price
- **g.** Transportation and insurance while machinery is in transit from seller to buyer
- **h.** Purchase price
- **i.** Installation
- **j.** Training of personnel for initial operation of the machinery
- **k.** Special reinforcement to the machinery platform

E7-18A. *(Learning Objective 4: Measuring, depreciating, and reporting PPE)* During 20X6, Cho Book Store paid $485,000 for land and built a store in Akron. Prior to construction, the city of Akron charged Cho $1,500 for a building permit, which Cho paid. Cho also paid $15,200 for architect's fees. The construction cost of $670,000 was financed by a long-term note payable, with interest cost of $27,300 paid at completion of the project. The building was completed September 30, 20X6. Cho depreciates the building by the straight-line method over 35 years, with estimated residual value of $338,000.

1. Journalize transactions for:
   a. Purchase of the land
   b. All the costs chargeable to the building in a single entry
   c. Depreciation on the building
   Explanations are not required.
2. Report Cho Book Store's PPE on the company's Balance Sheet at December 31, 20X6.
3. What will Cho's Income Statement for the year ended December 31, 20X6, report for this situation?

LO 3 4
■ writing assignment
■ spreadsheet

E7-19A. ***(Learning Objectives 3, 4: Determining depreciation amounts by three methods; depreciation)*** West Side Pizza bought a used Nissan delivery van on January 2, 20X6, for $19,200. The van was expected to remain in service for four years (32,000 miles). At the end of its useful life, West Side's officials estimated that the van's residual value would be $3,200. The van traveled 10,000 miles the first year, 12,000 miles the second year, 4,000 miles the third year, and 6,000 miles the fourth year. Prepare a schedule of *depreciation expense* per year for the van under the three depreciation methods. (For units-of-production and double-declining-balance, round to the nearest two decimals after each step of the calculation.)

Which method best tracks the wear and tear on the van? Which method would West Side prefer to use for income tax purposes? Explain in detail why West Side prefers this method.

LO 1 4 7

E7-20A. ***(Learning Objectives 1, 4, 7: Reporting PPE; depreciation; and investing cash flows)*** Assume that in January 20X6, an Hotcake House restaurant purchased a building, paying $57,000 cash and signing a $108,000 note payable. The restaurant paid another $60,000 to remodel the building. Furniture and fixtures cost $54,000, and dishes and supplies—a current asset—were obtained for $10,200.

Hotcake House is depreciating the building over 20 years by the straight-line method, with estimated residual value of $55,000. The furniture and fixtures will be replaced at the end of five years and are being depreciated by the double-declining-balance method, with zero residual value. At the end of the first year, the restaurant still has dishes and supplies worth $1,900.

Show what the restaurant will report for supplies, PPE, and cash flows at the end of the first year on its:

- Income Statement
- Balance Sheet
- Statement of cash flows (investing only)

Note: The purchase of dishes and supplies is an operating cash flow because supplies are a current asset.

LO 2

E7-21A. ***(Learning Objective 2: Selecting the best depreciation method for income tax purposes)*** On June 30, 20X6, Rafa Corp. paid $260,000 for equipment that is expected to have an eight-year life. In this industry, the residual value of equipment is approximately 10% of the asset's cost. Rafa's cash revenues for the year are $125,000, and cash expenses total $75,000.

Assume Rafa has a choice of straight-line or DDB depreciation for taxation purposes. Select the depreciation method for income tax purposes. Then determine the extra amount of cash that Rafa can invest by using DDB depreciation, versus straight-line, for the year ended December 31, 20X6. The income tax rate is 40%.

LO 2

E7-22A. ***(Learning Objective 2: Changing a PPE's useful life)*** Assume G-1 Designing Consultants purchased a building for $420,000 and depreciated it on a straight-line basis over 40 years. The estimated residual value was $56,000. After using the building for 20 years, G-1 realized that the building will remain useful for only 15 more years. Starting with the 21st year, G-1 began depreciating the building over a revised total life of 35 years and decreased the residual value to $13,000. Record depreciation expense on the building for years 20 and 21.

LO 2 3

E7-23A. ***(Learning Objectives 2, 3: Analyzing the effect of a sale of a PPE; DDB depreciation)*** Assume that on January 2, 20X6, Maxwell of Michigan purchased fixtures for $8,900 cash, expecting the fixtures to remain in service for five years. Maxwell has depreciated the fixtures on a double-declining-balance basis, with $1,400 estimated residual value. On August 31, 20X7, Maxwell sold the fixtures for $2,800 cash. Record both the depreciation expense on the fixtures for 20X7 and the sale of the fixtures. Apart from your journal entry, also show how to compute the gain or loss on Maxwell's disposal of these fixtures.

E7-24A. ***(Learning Objectives 1, 2, 3: Measuring a PPE's cost; using UOP depreciation; trading in a used asset)*** Prompt Truck Company is a large trucking company that operates throughout the United States. Prompt Truck Company uses the units-of-production (UOP) method to depreciate its trucks. LO 1 2 3

Prompt Truck Company trades in trucks often to keep driver morale high and to maximize fuel economy. Consider these facts about one Mack truck in the company's fleet. When acquired in 20X6, the tractor-trailer rig cost $390,000 and was expected to remain in service for 10 years or 1,000,000 miles. Estimated residual value was $100,000. During 20X6, the truck was driven 78,000 miles; during 20X7, 118,000 miles; and during 20X8, 156,000 miles. After 38,000 miles in 20X9, the company traded in the Mack truck for a less expensive Freightliner with a sticker price of $300,000. Prompt Truck Company paid cash of $27,000. Determine Prompt's gain or loss on the transaction. Prepare the journal entry to record the trade-in of the old truck for the new one.

E7-25A. ***(Learning Objective 4: Recording natural resource assets and depletion)*** Rich Mines paid $428,000 for the right to extract ore from a 275,000-ton mineral deposit. In addition to the purchase price, Rich Mines also paid a $180 filing fee, a $2,120 license fee to the state of Colorado, and $65,000 for a geologic survey of the property. Because the company purchased the rights to the minerals only, it expects the asset to have zero residual value when fully depleted. During the first year of production, Rich Mines removed 45,000 tons of ore. Make journal entries to record (a) purchase of the mineral rights, (b) payment of fees and other costs, and (c) depletion for first-year production. What is the mineral asset's book value at the end of the year? LO 4

E7-26A. ***(Learning Objectives 3, 5: Recording intangibles, amortization, and a change in the asset's useful life)*** LO 3 5

1. Master Printers purchased for $920,000 a patent for a new laser printer. Although the patent gives legal protection for 20 years, it is expected to provide Master Printers with a competitive advantage for only 10 years. Assuming the straight-line method of amortization, make journal entries to record (a) the purchase of the patent and (b) amortization for year 1.
2. After using the patent for five years, Master Printers learns at an industry trade show that Super Printers is designing a more efficient printer. On the basis of this new information, Master Printers determines that the patent's total useful life is only seven years. Record amortization for year 6.

E7-27A. ***(Learning Objective 5: Computing and accounting for goodwill)*** Assume Holden paid $15 million to purchase Northshore.com. Assume further that Northshore had the following summarized data at the time of the Holden acquisition (amounts in millions): LO 5

Northshore.com			
Assets		**Liabilities and Equity**	
Current assets	$13	Total liabilities	$25
Long-term assets	23	Shareholders' equity	11
	$36		$36

Northshore's long-term assets had a current market value of only $20 million.

Requirements

1. Compute the cost of goodwill purchased by Holden.
2. Journalize Holden's purchase of Northshore.
3. Explain how Holden will account for goodwill in the future.

LO 6

E7-28A. ***(Learning Objective 6: Reporting cash flows for property and equipment)*** Assume Shoe Warehouse Corporation completed the following transactions:

a. Sold a store building for $680,000. The building had cost Shoe Warehouse $1,800,000, and at the time of the sale its accumulated depreciation totaled $1,100,000.
b. Lost a store building in a fire. The building cost $390,000 and had accumulated depreciation of $180,000. The insurance proceeds received by Shoe Warehouse totaled $140,000.
c. Renovated a store at a cost of $170,000.
d. Purchased store fixtures for $80,000. The fixtures are expected to remain in service for 10 years and then be sold for $10,000. Shoe Warehouse uses the straight-line depreciation method.

For each transaction, show what Shoe Warehouse would report for investing activities on its statement of cash flows. Show negative amounts in parentheses.

Group B

LO 1

E7-29B. ***(Learning Objective 1: Determining the cost of PPE)*** Deville Self Storage purchased land, paying €165,000 cash as a downpayment and signing a €192,000 note payable for the balance. Deville also had to pay delinquent property tax of €4,500, title insurance costing €3,000, and €6,000 to level the land and remove an unwanted building. The company paid €58,000 to add soil for the foundation and then constructed an office building at a cost of €620,000. It also paid €48,000 for a fence around the property, €22,000 for the company sign near the property entrance, and €2,000 for lighting of the grounds. Determine the cost of Deville's land, land improvements, and building.

LO 1 2

E7-30B. ***(Learning Objectives 1, 2: Allocating costs to assets acquired in a lump-sum purchase; disposing of a PPE)*** Clintwood Manufacturing bought three used machines in a €226,000 lump-sum purchase. An independent appraiser valued the machines as shown in the table.

Machine No.	Appraised Value
1	€ 84,000
2	127,200
3	28,800

What is each machine's individual cost? Immediately after making this purchase, Clintwood sold machine 2 for its appraised value. What is the result of the sale? (Round decimals to three places when calculating proportions, and use your computed percentages throughout.)

LO 1

E7-31B. ***(Learning Objective 1: Distinguishing capital expenditures from expenses)*** Assume Desserts Galore, Inc., purchased conveyor-belt machinery. Classify each of the following expenditures as a capital expenditure or an immediate expense related to machinery:

a. Training of personnel for initial operation of the machinery
b. Special reinforcement to the machinery platform
c. Income tax paid on income earned from the sale of products manufactured by the machinery
d. Major overhaul to extend the machinery's useful life by three years
e. Sales tax paid on the purchase price
f. Transportation and insurance while machinery is in transit from seller to buyer
g. Purchase price
h. Installation
i. Lubrication of the machinery before it is placed in service
j. Ordinary repairs to keep the machinery in good working order
k. Periodic lubrication after the machinery is placed in service

E7-32B. *(Learning Objectives 1, 2: Measuring, depreciating, and reporting PPE)* During 20X6, Lao Book Store paid €489,000 for land and built a store in Lisbon. Prior to construction, the city of Lisbon charged Tao €1,600 for a building permit, which Lao paid. Lao also paid €15,700 for architect's fees. The construction cost of €210,000 was financed by a long-term note payable, with interest cost of €30,100 paid at completion of the project. The building was completed on September 30, 20X6. Lao depreciates the building by the straight-line method over 35 years, with estimated residual value of €344,000.

LO 1 2

1. Journalize transactions for:
   a. Purchase of the land
   b. All the costs chargeable to the building in a single entry
   c. Depreciation on the building

   Explanations are not required.
2. Report Lao Book Store's PPE on the company's Balance Sheet at December 31, 20X6.
3. What will Lao's Income Statement for the year ended December 31, 20X6, report for this situation?

E7-33B. *(Learning Objectives 2, 3: Determining depreciation amounts by three methods)* Southern's Pizza bought a used Nissan delivery van on January 2, 20X6, for €19,500. The van was expected to remain in service four years (30,000 miles). At the end of its useful life, Southern's officials estimated that the van's residual value would be €2,700. The van traveled 7,000 miles the first year, 9,500 miles the second year, 4,500 miles the third year, and 9,000 miles the fourth year. Prepare a schedule of *depreciation expense* per year for the van under the three depreciation methods. (For units-of-production and double-declining-balance, round to the nearest two decimals after each step of the calculation.)

LO 2 3
■ **writing assignment**
■ spreadsheet

Which method best tracks the wear and tear on the van? Which method would Southern's prefer to use for income tax purposes? Explain in detail why Southern's prefers this method.

E7-34B. *(Learning Objectives 1, 2, 6: Reporting PPE; depreciation; and investing cash flows)* Assume that in January 20X6, an Exquisite Eatery restaurant purchased a building, paying €53,000 cash and signing a €106,000 note payable. The restaurant paid another €65,000 to remodel the building. Furniture and fixtures cost €59,000, and dishes and supplies—a current asset—were obtained for €9,800.

LO 1 2 6

Exquisite Eatery is depreciating the building over 20 years by the straight-line method, with estimated residual value of €52,000. The furniture and fixtures will be replaced at the end of five years and are being depreciated by the double-declining-balance method, with zero residual value. At the end of the first year, the restaurant still has dishes and supplies worth €1,500.

Show what the restaurant will report for supplies, PPE, and cash flows at the end of the first year on its:

- Income Statement
- Balance Sheet
- Statement of cash flows (investing only)

Note: The purchase of dishes and supplies is an operating cash flow because supplies are a current asset.

E7-35B. *(Learning Objective 2: Selecting the best depreciation method for income tax purposes)* On June 30, 20X6, Reel Corp. paid €240,000 for equipment that is expected to have an eight-year life. In this industry, the residual value is approximately 10% of the asset's cost. Reel's cash revenues for the year are €160,000 and cash expenses total €120,000.

LO 2

Assume Reel has a choice of straight-line or DDB depreciation for taxation purposes. Select the depreciation method for income tax purposes. Then determine the extra amount of cash that Reel can invest by using DDB depreciation, versus straight-line, for the year ended December 31, 20X6. The income tax rate is 40%.

E7-36B. *(Learning Objective 2: Changing a PPE's useful life)* Assume B–1 Accounting Consultants purchased a building for €438,000 and depreciated it on a straight-line basis over 40 years. The estimated residual value was €72,000. After using the building for 20 years, B–1 realized that the building will remain useful for only 15 more years. Starting with the 21st year,

LO 2

B–1 began depreciating the building over the newly revised total life of 35 years and decreased the estimated residual value to €13,800. Record depreciation expense on the building for years 20 and 21.

LO 2 3

E7-37B. ***(Learning Objectives 2, 3: Analyzing the effect of a sale of a PPE; DDB depreciation)*** Assume that on January 2, 20X6, LaSalle of Lyon purchased fixtures for €8,400 cash, expecting the fixtures to remain in service for five years. LaSalle has depreciated the fixtures on a double-declining-balance basis, with €1,800 estimated residual value. On September 30, 20X7, LaSalle sold the fixtures for €2,200 cash. Record both the depreciation expense on the fixtures for 20X7 and then the sale of the fixtures. Apart from your journal entry, also show how to compute the gain or loss on LaSalle's disposal of these fixtures.

LO 1 2 3

E7-38B. ***(Learning Objectives 1, 2, 3: Measuring a PPE's cost; using UOP depreciation; trading in a used asset)*** EasyTruck Company is a large trucking company that operates throughout the EU. EasyTruck Company uses the units-of-production (UOP) method to depreciate its trucks.

EasyTruck Company trades in trucks often to keep driver morale high and to maximize fuel economy. Consider these facts about one Mack truck in the company's fleet. When acquired in 20X6, the rig cost €360,000 and was expected to remain in service for 10 years or 1,000,000 miles. Estimated residual value was €100,000. During 20X6, the truck was driven 79,000 miles; during 20X7, 119,000 miles; and during 20X8, 158,000 miles. After 44,000 miles in 20X9, the company traded in the Mack truck for a less expensive Freightliner with a sticker price of €300,000. EasyTruck Company paid cash of €24,000. Determine EasyTruck's gain or loss on the transaction. Prepare the journal entry to record the trade-in of the old truck on the new one.

LO 4

E7-39B. ***(Learning Objective 4: Recording natural resource assets and depletion)*** Gold Mines paid €435,000 for the right to extract ore from a 400,000-ton mineral deposit. In addition to the purchase price, Gold Mines also paid a €170 filing fee, a €2,600 license fee, and €92,230 for a geologic survey of the property. Because the company purchased the rights to the minerals only, it expected the asset to have zero residual value when fully depleted. During the first year of production, Gold Mines removed 80,000 tons of ore. Make journal entries to record (a) the purchase of the mineral rights, (b) the payment of fees and other costs, and (c) the depletion for first-year production. What is the mineral asset's book value at the end of the year?

LO 3 5

E7-40B. ***(Learning Objectives 3, 5: Recording intangibles; amortization, and a change in the asset's useful life)***

1. Royal Printers purchased for €780,000 a patent for a new laser printer. Although the patent gives legal protection for 20 years, it is expected to provide Royal Printers with a competitive advantage for only eight years. Assuming the straight-line method of amortization, make journal entries to record (a) the purchase of the patent and (b) amortization for year 1.
2. After using the patent for four years, Royal Printers learns at an industry trade show that Speedy Printers is designing a more efficient printer. On the basis of this new information, Royal Printers determines that the patent's total useful life is only six years. Record amortization for year 5.

LO 5

E7-41B. ***(Learning Objective 5: Computing and accounting for goodwill)*** Assume Golden paid €20 million to purchase Southwest.com. Assume further that Southwest had the following summarized data at the time of the Golden acquisition (amounts in millions):

Southwest.com			
Assets		**Liabilities and Equity**	
Current assets	€10	Total liabilities	€25
Long-term assets	22	Shareholders' equity	7
	€32		€32

Southwest's long-term assets had a current market value of only €18 million.

Requirements

1. Compute the cost of goodwill purchased by Golden.
2. Journalize Golden's purchase of Southwest.
3. Explain how Golden will account for goodwill in the future.

E7-42B. ***(Learning Objective 6: Reporting cash flows for property and equipment)*** Assume Shoes-R-Us Corporation completed the following transactions: LO 6

- **a.** Sold a store building for €640,000. The building had cost Shoes-R-Us €1,400,000, and at the time of the sale its accumulated depreciation totaled €780,000.
- **b.** Lost a store building in a fire. The building cost €360,000 and had accumulated depreciation of €160,000. The insurance proceeds received by Shoes-R-Us totaled €120,000.
- **c.** Renovated a store at a cost of €140,000.
- **d.** Purchased store fixtures for €100,000. The fixtures are expected to remain in service for 10 years and then be sold for €20,000. Shoes-R-Us uses the straight-line depreciation method.

For each transaction, show what Shoes-R-Us would report for investing activities on its statement of cash flows. Show negative amounts in parentheses.

Challenge Exercises

E7-43. ***(Learning Objective 2: Computing units-of-production depreciation)*** Buff Gym purchased exercise equipment at a cost of $116,000. In addition, Buff paid $4,000 for a special platform on which to stabilize the equipment for use. Freight costs of $1,800 to ship the equipment were borne by the seller. Buff will depreciate the equipment by the units-of-production method, based on an expected useful life of 60,000 hours of exercise. The estimated residual value of the equipment is $12,000. How many hours did Buff Gym use the machine if depreciation expense is $4,680? LO 2

E7-44. ***(Learning Objective 4: Determining the sale price of property and equipment)*** Willis Corporation reported the following for property and equipment (in millions, adapted): LO 4

	Year End	
	20X7	20X6
Property and equipment	$24,073	$22,011
Accumulated depreciation	(13,306)	(12,087)

During 20X7, Willis paid $2,580 million for new property and equipment. Depreciation for the year totaled $1,595 million. During 20X7, Willis sold property and equipment for cash of $45 million. How much was Willis's gain or loss on the sale of property and equipment during 20X7?

E7-45. ***(Learning Objectives 2, 3: Determining net income after a change in depreciation method)*** Norzani, Inc., has a popular line of sunglasses. Norzani reported net income of $68 million for 20X6. Depreciation expense for the year totaled $36 million. Norzani, Inc., depreciated PPE over eight years using the straight-line method and no residual value. LO 2 3

Norzani Inc., paid $288 million for PPE at the beginning of 20X6. Then at the start of 20X7, Norzani switched over to double-declining-balance (DDB) depreciation. 20X7 is expected to be the same as 20X6 except for the change in depreciation method. If Norzani had been using DDB depreciation all along, how much net income can Norzani, Inc., expect to earn during 20X7? Ignore income tax.

E7-46. ***(Learning Objective 1: Capitalizing versus expensing; measuring the effect of an error)*** All French Press (AFP) is a major French telecommunication conglomerate. Assume that early in year 1, AFP purchased equipment at a cost of €8.4 million. Management expects the equipment to remain in service for four years and the estimated residual value to be LO 1 negligible. AFP uses the straight-line depreciation method. *Through an accounting error, AFP expensed the entire cost of the equipment at the time of purchase.* Because AFP is operated as a partnership, it pays no income tax.

Requirements

Prepare a schedule to show the overstatement or understatement in the following items at the end of each year over the four-year life of the equipment:

1. Total current assets
2. Equipment, net
3. Net income

Quiz

Test your understanding of accounting for PPE, natural resources, and intangibles by answering the following questions. Select the best choice from among the possible answers given.

Q7-47. A capital expenditure

a. is expensed immediately.
b. adds to an asset.
c. records additional capital.
d. is a credit like capital (owners' equity).

Q7-48. Which of the following items should be accounted for as a capital expenditure?

a. Costs incurred to repair leaks in the building roof.
b. Maintenance fees paid with funds provided by the company's capital.
c. Taxes paid in conjunction with the purchase of office equipment.
d. The monthly rental cost of an office building.

Q7-49. Suppose you buy land for $3,200,000 and spend $1,300,000 to develop the property. You then divide the land into lots as follows:

Category	Sale Price per Lot
10 hilltop lots................	$525,000
10 valley lots.................	350,000

How much did each hilltop lot cost you?

a. $270,000
b. $192,000
c. $128,000
d. $180,000

Q7-50. Which statement about depreciation is false?

a. Obsolescence as well as physical wear and tear should be considered when determining the period over which an asset should be depreciated.
b. Depreciation is a process of allocating the cost of an asset to expense over its useful life.
c. A major objective of depreciation accounting is to match the cost of using an asset with the revenues it helps to generate.
d. Depreciation should not be recorded in years that the market value of the asset has increased.

Q7-51. Cleveland Corporation acquired a machine for $42,000 and has recorded depreciation for two years using the straight-line method over a five-year life and $7,000 residual value. At the start of the third year of use, Cleveland revised the estimated useful life to a total of 10 years. Estimated residual value declined to $0.

What is the book value of the machine at the end of two full years of use?

a. $21,000
b. $22,000
c. $14,000
d. $28,000

Q7-52. Cleveland Corporation acquired a machine for $42,000 and has recorded depreciation for two years using the straight-line method over a five-year life and $7,000 residual value. At the start of the third year of use, Cleveland revised the estimated useful life to a total of 10 years. Estimated residual value declined to $0.

How much depreciation should Cleveland record in each of the asset's last eight years (that is, year 3 through year 10), following the revision?

a. $9,333
b. $2,800
c. $3,500
d. Some other amount

Q7-53. King Company failed to record depreciation of equipment. How does this omission affect King's financial statements?

a. Net income is understated, and assets are overstated.
b. Net income is overstated, and assets are understated.
c. Net income is understated, and assets are understated.
d. Net income is overstated, and assets are overstated.

Q7-54. Jimmy's DVD, Inc., uses the double-declining-balance method for depreciation on its computers. Which item is not needed to compute depreciation for the first year?

a. Original cost
b. Estimated residual value
c. Expected useful life in years
d. All the above are needed.

Q7-55. Which of the following costs is reported on a company's Income Statement?

a. Accumulated depreciation
b. Land
c. Accounts payable
d. Depreciation expense

Q7-56. Which of the following items is reported on the Balance Sheet?

a. Accumulated depreciation
b. Gain on disposal of equipment
c. Cost of goods sold
d. Net sales revenue

Use the following information to answer questions 7-57 through 7-59.
Hal Company purchased a machine for $9,500 on January 1, 20X6. The machine has been depreciated using the straight-line method over a 10-year life and $500 residual value. Hal sold the machine on January 1, 20X8, for $8,200.

Q7-57. What gain or loss should Hal record on the sale?

a. Gain, $500
b. Loss, $400
c. Gain, $1,000
d. Gain, $100

Q7-58. Journalize Hal's sale of the machine.

Q7-59. What is straight-line depreciation for the year ended December 31, 20X6, and what is the book value on December 31, 20X7?

Q7-60. A company purchased mineral assets costing $960,000, with an estimated residual value of $40,000, holding approximately 400,000 tons of ore. During the first year, 48,000 tons are extracted and sold. What is the amount of depletion for the first year?

a. $110,400
b. $96,000
c. $115,200
d. Cannot be determined from the data given

Q7-61. Suppose Smooth Delivery pays $68 million to buy Guaranteed Overnight. Guaranteed's assets are valued at $74 million, and its liabilities total $16 million. How much goodwill did Timely Delivery purchase in its acquisition of Guaranteed Overnight?

a. $22 million
b. $16 million
c. $10 million
d. $6 million

Problems MyLab Accounting

Select A and B problems can be found within MyLab Accounting, an online homework and practice environment. Your instructor may ask you to complete select problems using MyLab Accounting.

Group A

P7-62A. ***(Learning Objectives 1, 2: Identifying the elements of a PPE's cost; depreciation)*** Assume Online, Inc., opened an office in Durban, South Africa. Further assume that Online 

incurred the following costs in acquiring land, making land improvements, and constructing and furnishing the new building:

a. Purchase price of land, including an old building that will be used for a garage (land market value is $315,000; building market value is $85,000)	$380,000
b. Landscaping (additional dirt and earth moving)	8,700
c. Fence around the land	31,600
d. Attorney fee for title search on the land	900
e. Delinquent real estate taxes on the land to be paid by Online	5,700
f. Company signs at entrance to the property	1,300
g. Building permit for the sales building	500
h. Architect fee for the design of the sales building	19,700
i. Masonry, carpentry, and roofing of the sales building	525,000
j. Renovation of the garage building	41,300
k. Interest cost on construction loan for sales building	9,200
l. Landscaping (trees and shrubs)	6,700
m. Parking lot and concrete walks on the property	53,100
n. Lights for the parking lot and walkways	7,600
o. Salary of construction supervisor (86% to sales building; 11% to land improvements; and 3% to garage building renovations)	45,000
p. Office furniture for the sales building	79,900
q. Transportation and installation of furniture	1,800

Assume Online depreciates buildings over 40 years, land improvements over 20 years, and furniture over 10 years, all on a straight-line basis with zero residual value.

Requirements

1. Show how to account for each of Online's costs by listing the cost under the correct account. Determine the total cost of each asset.
2. All construction was complete and the assets were placed in service on May 2. Record depreciation for the year ended December 31. Round to the nearest dollar.
3. How will what you learned in this problem help you manage a business?

LO 1 2

P7-63A. ***(Learning Objectives 1, 2: Recording PPE transactions; reporting on the Balance Sheet)*** Rocco Lakes Resort reported the following on its Balance Sheet at December 31, 20X6:

Property, plant, and equipment, at cost:	
Land	$ 146,000
Buildings	709,000
Less: Accumulated depreciation	(342,000)
Equipment	405,000)
Less: Accumulated depreciation	(265,000)

In early July 20X7, the resort expanded operations and purchased additional equipment at a cost of $108,000. The company depreciates buildings by the straight-line method over 20 years with residual value of $84,000. Due to obsolescence, the equipment has a useful life of only 10 years and is being depreciated by the double-declining-balance method with zero residual value.

Requirements

1. Journalize Rocco Lakes Resort's PPE purchase and depreciation transactions for 20X7.
2. Report PPEs on the December 31, 20X7, Balance Sheet.

P7-64A. ***(Learning Objectives 1, 2, 3: Recording PPE transactions; exchanges; and changes in useful life)*** Carr, Inc., has the following PPE accounts: Land, Buildings, and Equipment, with a separate accumulated depreciation account for each of these except land. Carr completed the following transactions:

Jan 2	Traded in equipment with accumulated depreciation of $65,000 (cost of $136,000) for similar new equipment with a cash cost of $175,000. Received a trade-in allowance of $75,000 on the old equipment and paid $100,000 in cash.
Jun 30	Sold a building that had a cost of $655,000 and had accumulated depreciation of $130,000 through December 31 of the preceding year. Depreciation is computed on a straight-line basis. The building has a 40-year useful life and a residual value of $275,000. Carr received $115,000 cash and a $405,250 note receivable.
Oct 29	Purchased land and a building for a single price of $390,000. An independent appraisal valued the land at $221,100 and the building at $180,900.
Dec 31	Recorded depreciation as follows: Equipment has an expected useful life of 5 years and an estimated residual value of 6% of cost. Depreciation is computed on the double-declining-balance method. Depreciation on buildings is computed by the straight-line method. The new building carries a 40-year useful life and a residual value equal to 20% of its cost.

Requirement

1. Record the transactions in Carr, Inc.'s journal.

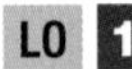

■ **writing assignment**

P7-65A. ***(Learning Objective 1: Explaining the concept of depreciation)*** The board of directors of Crystal Structures, Inc., is reviewing the 20X6 annual report. A new board member—a wealthy woman with little business experience—questions the company accountant about the depreciation amounts. The new board member wonders why depreciation expense has decreased from $240,000 in 20X4 to $224,000 in 20X5 to $216,000 in 20X6. She states that she could understand the decreasing annual amounts if the company had been disposing of properties each year, but that has not occurred. Further, she notes that growth in the city is increasing the values of company properties. Why is the company recording depreciation when the property values are increasing?

■ spreadsheet

P7-66A. ***(Learning Objectives 1, 2, 3: Computing depreciation by three methods; identifying the cash-flow advantage of accelerated depreciation for tax purposes; subsequent costs)*** On January 9, 20X6, J. T. Orlando Co. paid $240,000 for a computer system. In addition to the basic purchase price, the company paid a setup fee of $2,000, $8,000 sales tax, and $30,000 for a special platform on which to place the computer. J. T. Orlando management estimates that the computer will remain in service for five years and have a residual value of $20,000. The computer will process 30,000 documents the first year, with annual processing decreasing by 2,500 documents during each of the next four years (that is, 27,500 documents in year 20X7; 25,000 documents in year 20X8; and so on). In trying to decide which depreciation method to use, the company president has requested a depreciation schedule for each of the three depreciation methods (straight-line, units-of-production, and double-declining-balance).

Requirements

1. For each of the generally accepted depreciation methods, prepare a depreciation schedule showing asset cost, depreciation expense, accumulated depreciation, and asset book value.
2. J. T. Orlando reports to shareholders and creditors in the financial statements using the depreciation method that maximizes reported income in the early years of asset use. For income tax purposes, the company uses the depreciation method that minimizes income tax payments in those early years. Consider the first year J. T. Orlando Co. uses the computer. Identify the depreciation methods that meet Orlando's objectives, assuming the income tax authorities permit the use of any of the methods.

P7-67A. ***(Learning Objectives 2, 3, 6: Depreciation; recording intangibles; analyzing PPE transactions from a company's financial statements)*** Gadgets, Inc., sells electronics and appliances. The excerpts that follow are adapted from Gadgets's financial statements for 20X6 and 20X5.

Balance Sheet (dollars in millions)	February 28 20X6	20X5
Assets		
Total current assets	$7,980	$6,900
Property, plant, and equipment	4,835	4,198
Less: Accumulated depreciation	2,128	1,724
Goodwill	560	520

Statement of Cash Flows (dollars in millions)	Year Ended February 28 20X6	20X5
Operating activities:		
Net income	$1,146	$ 981
Non-cash items affecting net income:		
Depreciation	460	457
Investing activities:		
Additions to property, plant, and equipment	(707)	(615)

Requirements

1. How much was Gadgets's cost of PPE at February 28, 20X6? How much was the book value of PPE? Show computations.
2. The financial statements give three pieces of evidence that Gadgets purchased PPE and goodwill during fiscal year 20X6. What are they?
3. Prepare T-accounts for Property, Plant, and Equipment; Accumulated Depreciation; and Goodwill. Then show all the activity in these accounts during 20X6. Label each increase or decrease and give its dollar amount. During 20X6, Gadgets sold PPE that had cost the company $70 million (accumulated depreciation on these assets was $56 million). Assume there were no losses on goodwill during 20X6.

P7-68A. ***(Learning Objective 4: Accounting for natural resources, and the related expense)*** NorthAtlantic Energy Company's Balance Sheet includes the asset Iron Ore. NorthAtlantic Energy paid $2.8 million cash for a lease giving the firm the right to work a mine that contained an estimated 198,000 tons of ore. The company paid $68,000 to remove unwanted buildings from the land and $72,000 to prepare the surface for mining. NorthAtlantic Energy also signed a $37,300 note payable to a landscaping company to return the land surface to its original condition after the lease ends. During the first year, NorthAtlantic Energy removed 34,500 tons of ore, which it sold on account for $36 per ton. Operating expenses for the first year totaled $250,000, all paid in cash. In addition, the company accrued income tax at the tax rate of 32%.

Requirements

1. Record all of NorthAtlantic Energy's transactions for the year.
2. Prepare the company's Income Statement for its iron ore operations for the first year. Evaluate the profitability of the company's operations.

P7-69A. ***(Learning Objectives 4, 6: Reporting PPE transactions on the statement of cash flows)*** At the end of 20X5, Solving Engineering Associates (SEA) had total assets of $17.1 billion and total liabilities of $9.7 billion. Included among the assets were property, plant, and equipment with a cost of $4.4 billion and accumulated depreciation of $3.2 billion.

LO 4 6

SEA completed the following selected transactions during 20X6. The company earned total revenues of $26.6 billion and incurred total expenses of $21.2 billion, which included depreciation of $1.9 billion. During the year, SEA paid $1.8 billion for new property, plant, and equipment and sold old PPE for $0.4 billion. The cost of the assets sold was $1.2 billion, and their accumulated depreciation was $0.6 billion.

Requirements

1. Explain how to determine whether SEA had a gain or loss on the sale of old PPE during the year. What was the amount of the gain or loss, if any?
2. Show how SEA would report property, plant, and equipment on the Balance Sheet at December 31, 20X6, after all the year's activity. What was the book value of property, plant, and equipment?
3. Show how SEA would report its operating activities and investing activities on its statement of cash flows for 20X6. Ignore gains and losses.

Group B

P7-70B. ***(Learning Objectives 1, 2: Identifying the elements of a PPE's cost)*** Assume Lance Pharmacy, Inc., opened an office in Valencia, Italy. Further assume that Lance Pharmacy incurred the following costs in acquiring land, making land improvements, and constructing and furnishing the new sales building:

LO 1 2

a. Purchase price of land, including an old building that will be used for a garage (land market value is €310,000; building market value is €90,000)	€320,000
b. Landscaping (additional dirt and earth moving)	8,200
c. Fence around the land	32,000
d. Attorney fee for title search on the land	300
e. Delinquent real estate taxes on the land to be paid by Lance Pharmacy	5,800
f. Company signs at entrance to the property	1,500
g. Building permit for the sales building	800
h. Architect fee for the design of the sales building	19,800
i. Masonry, carpentry, and roofing of the sales building	505,000
j. Renovation of the garage building	41,800
k. Interest cost on construction loan for sales building	9,400
l. Landscaping (trees and shrubs)	6,500
m. Parking lot and concrete walks on the property	52,800
n. Lights for the parking lot and walkways	7,100
o. Salary of construction supervisor (86% to sales building; 10% to land improvements; and 4% to garage building renovations)	40,000
p. Office furniture for the sales building	78,200
q. Transportation and installation of furniture	1,200

Assume Lance Pharmacy depreciates buildings over 30 years, land improvements over 15 years, and furniture over eight years, all on a straight-line basis with zero residual value.

Requirements

1. Show how to account for each of Lance Pharmacy's costs by listing the cost under the correct account. Determine the total cost of each asset.
2. All construction was complete and the assets were placed in service on May 2. Record depreciation for the year ended December 31. Round to the nearest dollar.
3. How will what you learned in this problem help you manage a business?

LO 2 3

P7-71B. ***(Learning Objectives 2, 3: Recording PPE transactions; reporting on the Balance Sheet)*** Pokko Lakes Resort reported the following on its Balance Sheet at December 31, 20X6:

Property, plant, and equipment, at cost:	
Land	€ 149,000
Buildings	704,000
Less: Accumulated depreciation	(342,000)
Equipment	401,000
Less: Accumulated depreciation	(268,000)

In early July 20X7, the resort expanded operations and purchased additional equipment at a cost of €104,000. The company depreciates buildings by the straight-line method over 20 years with residual value of €88,000. Due to obsolescence, the equipment has a useful life of only 10 years and is being depreciated by the double-declining-balance method with zero residual value.

Requirements

1. Journalize Pokko Lakes Resort's PPE purchase and depreciation transactions for 20X7.
2. Report PPE on the December 31, 20X7, Balance Sheet.

LO 1 2 3

P7-72B. ***(Learning Objectives 1, 2, 3: Recording PPE transactions, exchanges, and changes in useful life)*** Tarrier, Inc., has the following PPE accounts: Land, Buildings, and Equipment, with a separate accumulated depreciation account for each of these except land. Tarrier completed the following transactions:

Jan 2	Traded in equipment with accumulated depreciation of €64,000 (cost of €138,000) for similar new equipment with a cash cost of €179,000. Received a trade-in allowance of €73,000 on the old equipment and paid €106,000 in cash.
Jun 30	Sold a building that had a cost of €645,000 and had accumulated depreciation of €155,000 through December 31 of the preceding year. Depreciation is computed on a straight-line basis. The building has a 40-year useful life and a residual value of €285,000. Tarrier received €135,000 cash and a €350,500 note receivable.
Oct 29	Purchased land and a building for a single price of €340,000. An independent appraisal valued the land at €108,900 and the building at €254,100.
Dec 31	Recorded depreciation as follows: Equipment has an expected useful life of 4 years and an estimated residual value of 4% of cost. Depreciation is computed on the double-declining-balance method. Depreciation on buildings is computed by the straight-line method. The new building carries a 40-year useful life and a residual value equal to 10% of its cost.

Requirement

1. Record the transactions in Tarrier, Inc.'s journal.

LO 2

■ writing assignment

P7-73B. ***(Learning Objective 2: Explaining the concept of depreciation)*** The board of directors of Looper Structures, Inc., is reviewing the 20X6 annual report. A new board member—a wealthy man with little business experience—questions the company accountant about the depreciation amounts. The new board member wonders why depreciation expense has decreased from €200,000 in 20X4 to €184,000 in 20X5 to €176,000 in 20X6. He states that he could understand the decreasing annual amounts if the company had been disposing of properties each year, but that has not occurred. Further, he notes that growth in the city is increasing the values of company properties. Why is the company recording depreciation when the property values are increasing?

LO 1 2 3

■ spreadsheet

P7-74B. ***(Learning Objectives 1, 2, 3: Computing depreciation by three methods; identifying the cash-flow advantage of accelerated depreciation for tax purposes)*** On January 6, 20X6, K. P. Scott Co. paid €265,000 for a computer system. In addition to the basic purchase price, the company paid a setup fee of €800, €6,400 sales tax, and €27,800 for a special platform on which to place the computer. K. P. Scott management estimates that the computer will remain in service for five years and have a residual value of €30,000. The computer will process 45,000 documents the first year, with annual processing decreasing by 2,500 documents during each of the next four years (that is, 42,500 documents in 20X7; 40,000 documents in 20X8; and so on). In trying to decide which depreciation method to use, the company president has requested a depreciation schedule for each of the three depreciation methods (straight-line, units-of-production, and double-declining-balance).

Requirements

1. For each of the generally accepted depreciation methods, prepare a depreciation schedule showing asset cost, depreciation expense, accumulated depreciation, and asset book value.
2. K. P. Scott reports to shareholders and creditors in the financial statements using the depreciation method that maximizes reported income in the early years of asset use. For income tax purposes, the company uses the depreciation method that minimizes income tax payments in those early years. Consider the first year K. P. Scott Co. uses the computer. Identify the depreciation methods that meet Scott's objectives, assuming the income tax authorities permit the use of any of the methods.

LO 2 3 6

P7-75B. ***(Learning Objectives 2, 3, 6: Depreciation; recording intangibles; analyzing PPE transactions from a company's financial statements)*** Perma, Inc., sells electronics and appliances. The excerpts that follow are adapted from Perma's financial statements for 20X6 and 20X5.

Balance Sheet (Euros in millions)	February 28 20X6	20X5
Assets		
Total current assets	€7,988	€6,905
Property, plant, and equipment	4,830	4,192
Less: Accumulated depreciation	2,129	1,728
Goodwill	552	514

Statement of Cash Flows (Euros in millions)	Year Ended February 28 20X6	20X5
Operating activities:		
Net income	€1,147	€ 989
Non-cash items affecting net income:		
Depreciation	458	460
Investing activities:		
Additions to property, plant, and equipment	(716)	(617)

Requirements

1. How much was Perma's cost of PPE at February 28, 20X6? How much was the book value of PPE? Show computations.
2. The financial statements give three pieces of evidence that Perma purchased PPE and goodwill during fiscal year 20X6. What are they?

3. Prepare T-accounts for Property, Plant, and Equipment; Accumulated Depreciation; and Goodwill. Then show all the activity in these accounts during 20X6. Label each increase or decrease and give its dollar amount. During 20X6, Perma sold PPE that had cost the company €78 million (accumulated depreciation on these assets was €57 million). Assume there were no losses on goodwill during 20X6.

LO 4

P7-76B. ***(Learning Objective 4: Accounting for natural resources and the related expense)*** South Pacific Energy Company's Balance Sheet includes the asset Iron Ore. South Pacific Energy paid €2.2 million cash for a lease giving the firm the right to work a mine that contained an estimated 192,000 tons of ore. The company paid €64,600 to remove unwanted buildings from the land and €71,000 to prepare the surface for mining. South Pacific Energy also signed a €26,000 note payable to a landscaping company to return the land surface to its original condition after the lease ends. During the first year, South Pacific Energy removed 31,500 tons of ore, which it sold on account for €32 per ton. Operating expenses for the first year totaled €242,000, all paid in cash. In addition, the company accrued income tax at the tax rate of 25%.

Requirements

1. Record all of South Pacific Energy's transactions for the year.
2. Prepare the company's Income Statement for its iron ore operations for the first year. Evaluate the profitability of the company's operations.

LO 6

P7-77B. ***(Learning Objective 6: Reporting PPE transactions on the statement of cash flows)*** At the end of 20X5, Great Financial Associates (GFA) had total assets of €17.4 billion and total liabilities of €9.9 billion. Included among the assets were property, plant, and equipment with a cost of €4.6 billion and accumulated depreciation of €3.3 billion.

GFA completed the following selected transactions during 20X6. The company earned total revenues of €26.1 billion and incurred total expenses of €21.0 billion, which included depreciation of €1.9 billion. During the year, GFA paid €1.6 billion for new property, plant, and equipment and sold old PPE for €0.3 billion. The cost of the assets sold was €1.1 billion, and their accumulated depreciation was €0.5 billion.

Requirements

1. Explain how to determine whether GFA had a gain or loss on the sale of old PPE during the year. What was the amount of the gain or loss, if any?
2. Show how GFA would report property, plant, and equipment on the Balance Sheet at December 31, 20X6, after all the year's activity. What was the book value of property, plant, and equipment?
3. Show how GFA would report its operating activities and investing activities on its statement of cash flows for 20X6. Ignore gains and losses.

APPLY YOUR KNOWLEDGE

Decision Cases

LO 2 3

■ writing assignment

Case 1. ***(Learning Objectives 2, 3: Measuring profitability based on different inventory and depreciation methods)*** Suppose you are considering investing in two businesses, La Petite France Bakery and Burgers Ahoy. The two companies are virtually identical, and both began operations at the beginning of the current year. During the year, each company purchased inventory as follows:

Jan 4	10,000 units at $4 =	40,000
Apr 6	5,000 units at $5 =	25,000
Aug 9	7,000 units at $6 =	42,000
Nov 27	10,000 units at $7 =	70,000
Totals	32,000	$177,000

During the first year, both companies sold 28,000 units of inventory.

In early January, both companies purchased equipment costing $180,000 that had a 10-year estimated useful life and a $30,000 residual value. La Petite France uses the inventory and depreciation methods that maximize reported income. By contrast, Burgers uses the inventory and depreciation methods that minimize income tax payments. Assume that both companies' trial balances at December 31 included the following:

Sales revenue	$350,000
Operating expenses	50,000

The income tax rate is 35%.

Requirements

1. Prepare both companies' Income Statements.
2. Write an investment newsletter to address the following questions: Which company appears to be more profitable? Which company has more cash to invest in promising projects? If prices continue rising over the long term, which company would you prefer to invest in? Why? (Challenge)

Case 2. *(Learning Objectives 1, 5: Accounting for PPE and intangible assets)* The following questions are unrelated except that they all apply to PPEs and intangible assets:

■ **writing assignment**

1. The manager of Copper World regularly debits the cost of repairs and maintenance of PPE to Plant and Equipment. Why would she do that, since she knows she is violating GAAP?
2. The manager of Hillion Software regularly buys PPE and debits the cost to Repairs and Maintenance Expense. Why would he do that, since he knows this action violates GAAP?
3. It has been suggested that because many intangible assets have no value except to the company that owns them, they should be valued at $1.00 or zero on the Balance Sheet. Many accountants disagree with this view. Which view do you support? Why?

Ethical Issue

United Jersey Bank of Princeton purchased land and a building for the lump sum of $6.0 million. To get the maximum tax deduction, the bank's managers allocated 80% of the purchase price to the building and only 20% to the land. A more realistic allocation would have been 60% to the building and 40% to the land.

Requirements

1. What is the ethical issue in this situation?
2. Who are the stakeholders? What are the possible consequences to each?
3. Analyze the alternatives from the following standpoints: (a) economic, (b) legal, and (c) ethical.
4. What would you do? How would you justify your decision?

Focus on Financials: | Nestlé

This case spans all 12 chapters and is based on the consolidated financial statements of Nestlé. As you work with Nestlé throughout this course, you will develop the confidence and ability to use the financial statements of other companies as well. Refer to Nestlé's consolidated financial statements in Appendix A. If you wish, you can obtain the full annual report from www.nestle.com/investors. You may find the information overwhelming for now, but try to spot the key principles that we have discussed in this chapter. It will get progressively easier as you gain familiarity with the elements of the financial statements.

Requirements

1. Refer to Note 8—Property, plant and equipment. What kinds of fixed assets does Nestlé have?
2. What depreciation method does Nestlé use for reporting to shareholders and creditors in the financial statements? Assume that Nestlé expects fairly constant net income before

depreciation for the next few years. What type of depreciation method would the company probably use for income tax purposes and why?

3. Depreciation expense is not disclosed separately on Nestlé's Consolidated Income Statement. Instead, it is lumped together with other expenses. Nevertheless, we can find the separate figure from the Consolidated Statements of Cash Flows. What was Nestlé's depreciation and amortization expense during 2016? (You can refer to Note 8.) From that note, what was Nestlé's accumulated depreciation at the end of 2016? Ignore the impairment aspect of this figure and treat it as immaterial. Explain why accumulated depreciation exceeds depreciation expense for the current year.
4. What are Nestlé's intangible assets? Assuming straight line amortization of finite live intangible assets, what are your estimates for Nestlé's intangible assets?
5. Refer to Note 8. How much impairment of PPE did Nestlé record for 2016? What do you understand by "impairment"? Examine Note 8 carefully and describe a typical event that would lead to an impairment of PPE.

Group Project

Visit a local business.

Requirements

1. List all its PPE.
2. If possible, interview the manager. Gain as much information as you can about the business's PPE. For example, try to determine the assets' costs, the depreciation method the company is using, and the estimated useful life of each asset category. If an interview is impossible, then develop your own estimates of the assets' costs, useful lives, and book values, assuming an appropriate depreciation method.
3. Determine whether the business has any intangible assets. If so, list them and gain as much information as possible about their nature, cost, and estimated useful lives.
4. Write a detailed report of your findings and be prepared to present your results to the class.

Quick Check Answers

1. *b* {[$1,420/($1,420 + $650 + $430)] × $1,800 = $1,022.4}
2. *c*
3. *a* ($65,000 − $5,000)/10 × 6/12 = $3,000)
4. *d* [($65,000 − $5,000)/10 × 2 = $12,000; $65,000 − $12,000 = $53,000]
5. *b* [$65,000 × .2 = $13,000; ($65,000 − $13,000) × .2 = $10,400]
6. *a* [($65,000 − $5,000)/10 × 4 = $24,000; $65,000 − $24,000 = $41,000; $44,500 − $41,000 = gain of $3,500]
7. *c* [$30,000 × 2/5 = $12,000; ($30,000 − $12,000) × 2/5 = $7,200; $12,000 + $7,200 = $19,200]
8. *e*
9. *a*
10. *d*
11. *c* [$270,000 × (20,000/100,000) = $54,000]
12. *e*

MyLab Accounting

For online homework, exercises, and problems that provide you with immediate feedback, please visit www.myaccountinglab.com.

8 Investments and International Operations

SPOTLIGHT | Vivendi www.vivendi.com

What do *Universal Music Group* (with artists such as Taylor Swift, Katy Perry, and Justin Bieber), *Canal+* (a pay TV operator and a major film production and distribution company), *Dailymotion* (one of the largest video content aggregators on the Internet), *Ubisoft* and *Gameloft* (prominent video game developers), and event venues such as *L'Olympia* and *Abbey Road Studios* have in common? Believe it or not, they are all related companies! Vivendi is either an owner of, or an investor in, all these companies. ●

PIXA/Shutterstock.

You might still be wondering how all those companies are related to Vivendi. This is why some understanding of intercorporate investments is an important element in your study of accounting. It is a challenging topic, but all the companies you have seen so far, from Alibaba and LEGO, to Airbus, have subsidiaries and investments in other companies. For this chapter, our focus is on financial assets and investments, so let's first have a look at the pertinent accounts of Vivendi's consolidated Balance Sheet.

	A	B	C
1	**Vivendi Group** **Consolidated Balance Sheet**		
2	**(Adapted, in millions of €)**	**Dec. 31, 2015**	**Dec. 31, 2014**
3	Cash and cash equivalents	€ 8,225	€ 6,845
4	Trade and other receivables	2,139	1,983
5	Current financial assets	1,111	49
6	Non-current financial assets	4,132	6,144
7	Investment in equity affiliates	3,435	306
8	Subtotal financial assets and investments	19,042	15,327
9	Total assets	€ 34,946	€ 35,738
10			

This Balance Sheet shows the financial assets and investment-related accounts for the Vivendi group. As you can see, Vivendi has some cash and cash equivalents, trade and other receivables, short-term financial assets, investment in equity affiliates, and non-current financial assets, totaling about €19 billion (line 8), out of total assets of €35 billion (line 9). Actual investment (lines 5–7) totaled only €8.7 billion. How could this relatively small amount of investment be the connecting factor for all of Vivendi's businesses?

The consolidated Balance Sheet is what Vivendi (as a group) collectively has in terms of investments and does not show the investments in its own subsidiaries. Financial performance and financial position of all the companies in a group are consolidated at a group level (we will discuss consolation later). The second Balance Sheet, which follows, is for the Vivendi parent entity only. You can see that the overwhelming majority of the parent entity's €31.5 billion total assets (line 8) are in the form of "long-term investments" of about €20.7 billion (line 6). This is the account that connects all the Vivendi businesses because this is where Vivendi, the parent company, records all its investments in its subsidiaries and affiliates.

	A	B	C
1	**Vivendi Group Parent Company Balance Sheet**		
2	**(Adapted, in millions of €)**	**2015**	**2014**
3	Cash and cash equivalents	€ 1,043	€ 1,426
4	Trade and other receivables	2,208	2,014
5	Marketable securities	7,528	5,426
6	Long-term investments	20,697	21,895
7	Subtotal financial assets and investments	31,476	30,761
8	Total assets	€ 31,499	€ 30,781
9			

One of your learning goals should be to develop the ability to analyze whatever you encounter in real-company statements. This chapter will help you advance toward that goal. The first half of this chapter shows how to account for investments, including a brief overview of consolidated financial statements. The second half of the chapter covers accounting for international operations.

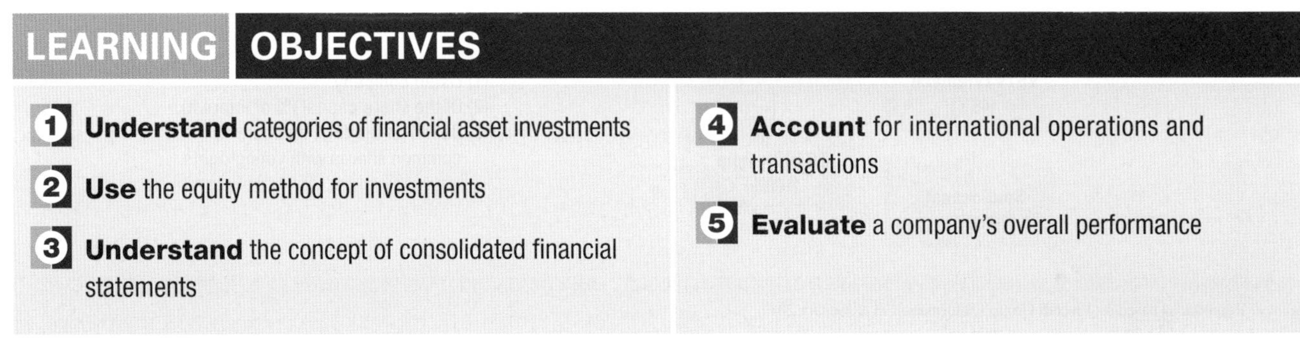

LEARNING OBJECTIVES
1 Understand categories of financial asset investments
2 Use the equity method for investments
3 Understand the concept of consolidated financial statements
4 Account for international operations and transactions
5 Evaluate a company's overall performance

Investments: An Overview

Businesses make investments in many forms, from buying equipment and inventory to investing in **financial assets**. *IAS 32—Financial Instruments: Presentation* defines financial assets as any asset that is (a) cash, (b) an equity instrument in another entity, (c) a contractual right to receive cash or financial assets of another entity, or (d) a contract that will or may be settled in the entity's own equity instruments. In this chapter, we examine various investments that an entity makes, with emphasis on financial asset investments other entities.

Companies invest in debt or equity securities of other companies for a number of reasons, such as:

- They may have excess cash that they do not need immediately that can be put to better use by investing on a short-term basis with the hope to earn additional income (from interest, dividend, or capital appreciation) to benefit operations.
- They may have longer-term strategic objectives, such as obtaining the ability to influence or control another company. For example, a company may move up or down their value chain (a supplier or a distributor) in order to obtain a steady stream of raw materials and a secure distribution channel.

To consider investments, we need to define two key terms. The entity that owns the shares of a corporation is the *investor*. The corporation that issues the shares is the *investee*. If you own Vivendi shares, you are an investor and Vivendi is the investee. Similarly, a company may also own shares of another company. Vivendi, for example, owns 100% of Universal Music Group and Canal+ Group, 90% of Dailymotion, 49% of a TV station in Vietnam, about 30% of Gameloft

Exhibit 8-1 | Vivendi and Its Major Investments

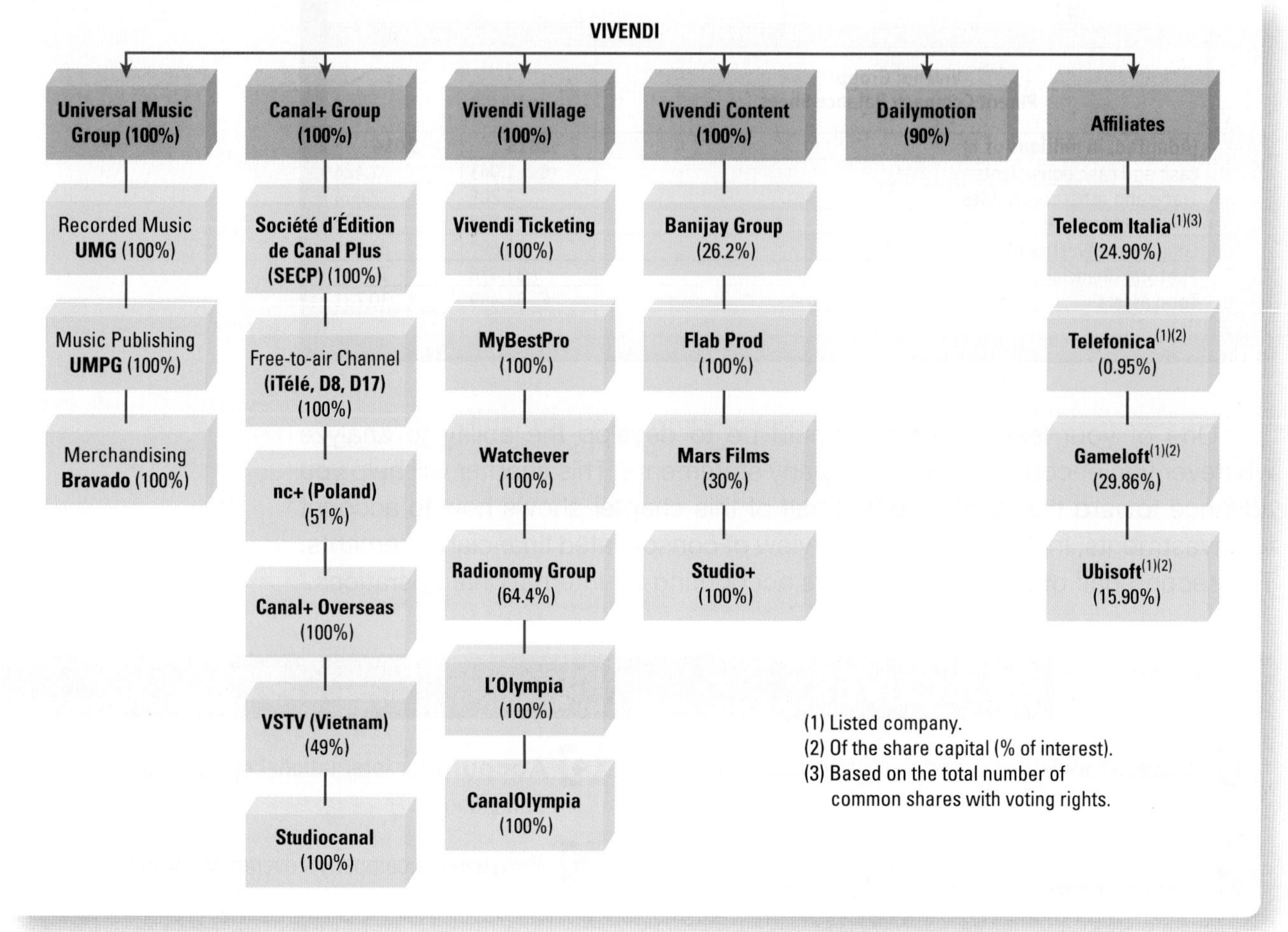

VIVENDI

- **Universal Music Group (100%)**
  - Recorded Music **UMG** (100%)
  - Music Publishing **UMPG** (100%)
  - Merchandising **Bravado** (100%)
- **Canal+ Group (100%)**
  - **Société d'Édition de Canal Plus (SECP)** (100%)
  - Free-to-air Channel **(iTélé, D8, D17)** (100%)
  - **nc+ (Poland)** (51%)
  - **Canal+ Overseas** (100%)
  - **VSTV (Vietnam)** (49%)
  - **Studiocanal** (100%)
- **Vivendi Village (100%)**
  - **Vivendi Ticketing** (100%)
  - **MyBestPro** (100%)
  - **Watchever** (100%)
  - **Radionomy Group** (64.4%)
  - **L'Olympia** (100%)
  - **CanalOlympia** (100%)
- **Vivendi Content (100%)**
  - **Banijay Group** (26.2%)
  - **Flab Prod** (100%)
  - **Mars Films** (30%)
  - **Studio+** (100%)
- **Dailymotion (90%)**
- **Affiliates**
  - **Telecom Italia**(1)(3) (24.90%)
  - **Telefonica**(1)(2) (0.95%)
  - **Gameloft**(1)(2) (29.86%)
  - **Ubisoft**(1)(2) (15.90%)

(1) Listed company.
(2) Of the share capital (% of interest).
(3) Based on the total number of common shares with voting rights.

Source: Reproduced based on Vivendi Group's information as at January 2017.

and others. Exhibit 8-1 shows Vivendi's key subsidiaries and affiliates at March 2016. Prior to 2016, Vivendi was also an investor in GVT and SFR (telecommunication companies in Brazil and France), Activision Blizzard (makers of games such as *World of Warcraft* and *Call of Duty*), and Universal Studios theme parks!

You can check Vivendi's current share price online. Some companies provide share information directly on their websites, but for others, you may have to visit the actual stock exchange where the company is listed to see "live" prices. For Vivendi, you can visit http://www.vivendi.com/investment-analysts/share-price-dividend-and-shareholding-structure/share-price/ and check out its share price information and charts.

Reporting Investments on the Balance Sheet. An investment is an asset to the investor. The investment may be short-term or long-term, as classified by *IAS 1—Presentation of Financial Statements*. **Short-term investments** are investments in financial assets that are expected to be realized within 12 months. They can be classified as either *trading*, *held-to-maturity*, or *available-for-sale*, depending on management's intent and ability to hold them until they mature. Investments that aren't short-term are listed as **long-term investments**, a category of non-current assets. Long-term investments include shares and bonds that the investor expects to hold for longer than one year. Exhibit 8-2 shows where short-term and long-term investments typically appear on the Balance Sheet. In practice, you may see different account names being used.

Exhibit 8-2 | Reporting Investments on the Balance Sheet

	A	B	C
1	**Current Assets:**		
2	Cash	$ X	
3	Short-term investments (or trading / marketable securities)	X	
4	Accounts receivable	X	
5	Inventories	X	
6	Prepaid expenses	X	
7	Total current assets		X
8	**Non-current Assets:**		
9	Long-term investments (or simply Investments)	X	
10	Property, plant and equipment	X	
11	Intangible assets	X	
12	Other assets	X	
13	Total non-current assets		X
14	Total Assets		X
15			

Look at Vivendi's Balance Sheet extracts on p. 448. Vivendi group calls its short-term investments "current financial assets" (line 5) and the long-term investments are further divided into "non-current financial assets" (line 6) and "investment in equity affiliates" (line 7). Vivendi (the parent company) calls its short-term investments "marketable securities" (line 5) and "Long-term investments" (line 6). As of December 31, 2011, approximately 590 entities were consolidated or accounted for using the *equity method* (more on this later) in the Vivendi Group.

UNDERSTAND CATEGORIES OF FINANCIAL ASSET INVESTMENTS

Let's put the various types of investments into the big picture perspective before discussing their accounting treatment. Exhibit 8-3 shows three categories of investments: financial assets, investment in associates (or affiliates), and investment in subsidiaries and their general characteristics.

Exhibit 8-3 | Categories of Investments

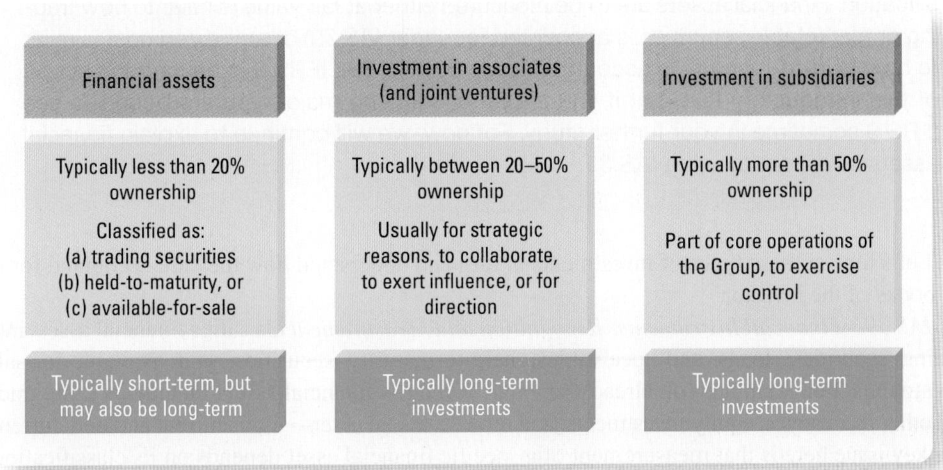

Financial assets
Investment in associates (and joint ventures)
Investment in subsidiaries
Typically less than 20% ownership
Classified as: (a) trading securities (b) held-to-maturity, or (c) available-for-sale
Typically between 20–50% ownership
Usually for strategic reasons, to collaborate, to exert influence, or for direction
Typically more than 50% ownership
Part of core operations of the Group, to exercise control
Typically short-term, but may also be long-term
Typically long-term investments
Typically long-term investments

Financial assets are investments in which an investor does not play any role in the operations of the investee. For example, you can purchase some Vivendi shares from the Euronext Paris stock exchange, but you are unlikely to be able to direct or influence Vivendi to release more sequels of your favorite computer games, or to stop selling records of an artist you don't like. In general, investments below 20% can be termed "passive investments" because the investor does not play an active role or exert much influence on the investee. On the other hand, ownership between 20% and 50% may provide an investor with the opportunity to significantly influence the investee's operating decisions and policies over the long run. These investees are usually called "associates" or "equity affiliates." An investment above 50% would typically allow an investor a great deal of long-term influence and control over the investee company, and these investees are said to be "subsidiaries" of the investor, typically a parent company.

A Closer Look

There is another category of financial assets: "loans and receivables." We have previously discussed the accounting treatment for loans and receivables in Chapter 5. The key thing to remember is that loans and receivables are typically recorded at the original loan or invoiced amount less any impairment for uncollectible loans/receivables. If the loans and receivables contain an interest element (such as notes receivables), the interest component is accounted for using the effective interest rate method. Since our focus is on investments in debt and equity securities, we will not mention loan and receivables as a type as financial asset in this chapter.

Percentage of ownership is a good indicator of this accounting treatment, but the underlying principle is more important than the actual percentage of ownership. *IAS 28—Investment in Associates* states that the equity method is to be used when an entity has "significant influence" over its investee. Significant influence is the power to participate in the financial and operating policy decisions of the investee, but where the investor does not have control or joint control over those policies. While this usually exists when the shareholding exceeds 20%, it is not always the case.

Similarly, consolidation is usually performed when an entity holds more than 50% of an investee. *IFRS—10 Consolidated Financial Statements* states that the primary determinant of whether an entity is consolidated or not is the existence of "control." Control is the power to govern the financial and operating policies of an investee so as to obtain benefits from its activities. For example, even if shareholding is below 50%, if an entity is able to elect a majority of the members of the investee's board of directors and, thus, control the investee, the investee is still considered a subsidiary and will be consolidated.

The new *IFRS 9–Financial Instruments* will be effective from 2018 (but may vary in different jurisdictions). IFRS 9 will effectively remove the "available for sale" classification. Financial assets are to be measured either at fair value (similar to how trading or marketable securities is accounted for under *IAS 39*) or amortized cost (similar to how held-to-maturity is accounted for under *IAS 39*). IFRS 9 is beyond the scope of this introductory text, but if you are an accounting major, you are bound to see IFRS 9 sometime in your further study. For now, we will continue to explain financial assets investments using *IAS 39*.

Let's look at these types of investments in turn and understand how they are accounted for in the books of the investor.

IAS 39—Financial Instruments: Recognition and Measurement classifies financial assets into trading securities, loans and receivables, held-to-maturity securities, and available-for-sale investments. For example, you already saw that Vivendi's financial assets include its cash, trade and other receivables, equity investments, and other financial assets—both current and non-current. The key issue here is that measurement of a specific financial asset depends on its classification. Exhibit 8-4 summarizes the financial classifications under *IAS 39* (i.e., the left-most category in Exhibit 8-3, discussed earlier).

Exhibit 8-4 Financial Classifications under *IAS 39*

Type of Investment	Trading	Available-for-Sale	Held-to-Maturity
Asset classification	Current assets	May be current or non-current asset	May be current or non-current asset
Initial measurement	Cost	Cost	Cost
Subsequent measurement	Fair value	Fair value	Amortized cost
Unrealized gains/losses	Income Statement	Other comprehensive income	Not recognized

Have a look at how Vivendi expressed its financial assets accounting policy. You will notice the characteristics we summarized above in the following excerpts. It may look a little complicated, after all we are dealing with a large, complicated, multinational and diversified company, but we will discuss each classification in turn.

ADAPTED EXCERPTS FROM VIVENDI'S NOTES TO THE ACCOUNTS

Financial Assets

Financial assets consist of *financial assets measured at fair value and financial assets recognized at amortized cost*. Financial assets are initially recognized at fair value corresponding, in general, to the consideration paid, which is best evidenced by the acquisition cost (including associated acquisition costs, if any).

Financial Assets at Fair Value

Financial assets at fair value include (1) available-for-sale securities and other financial assets measured at fair value through profit or loss. Most of these financial assets are actively traded in organized public markets, their fair value being determined by reference to the published market price at period end.

(1) Available-for-sale securities consist of unconsolidated interests and other securities not qualifying for classification in the other financial asset categories described below. Unrealized gains and losses on available-for-sale securities are recognized in charges and income directly recognized in equity until the financial asset is sold.

(2) Other financial assets measured at fair value through profit or loss mainly consist of assets held for trading which Vivendi intends to sell in the near future (primarily marketable securities). Unrealized gains and losses on these assets are recognized in other financial charges and income.

Financial Assets at Amortized Cost

Financial assets at amortized cost consist of loans and receivables and held-to-maturity investments (financial assets with fixed or determinable payments and fixed maturity). At the end of each period, these assets are measured at amortized cost using the effective interest method.

Source: Vivendi's 2015 Financial Statements, pages 41–42

Trading Securities

Trading securities is the common term for short-term investments in marketable securities (such as shares or bonds). The purpose of having trading securities is to hold them for a short time and then sell them for more than their cost; in other words, with the intention of earning a profit. While holding the investments, the investor also collects dividends or interest income paid by the investees. Trading securities allow the company to invest cash for a short period of time and earn a return until the cash is needed. Short-term investments are usually the next-most-liquid asset after cash. This is why we usually report short-term investments immediately after cash and before receivables on the Balance Sheet.

A Closer Look

The official term for trading securities in *IAS 39* is "Fair Value through Profit or Loss," which includes financial assets that are held for trading, which is why they are usually called trading securities. In addition, certain financial assets may also be designated on initial recognition as items to be measured at fair value with fair value changes in profit or loss.

The trading securities category (and later available-for-sale as well) uses a "fair value" as the basis for subsequent measurement on the Balance Sheet. The fair value is the amount that would be received for the securities in an "orderly sale" based on available evidence. *IFRS 13—Fair Value Measurements* offers three levels of fair value hierarchy:

- Level 1: quoted prices in an active market for identical assets.
- Level 2: estimates based on other observable inputs (e.g., quoted prices for similar assets in an active market, or quoted prices for identical assets in an inactive market).
- Level 3: estimates based on unobservable estimates (i.e., the company's own estimates based on certain assumptions, taking into account all information that is reasonably available).

The investor, such as Vivendi, expects to sell a trading security within the coming financial year. Therefore, all trading securities are included in current assets.

Suppose Vivendi purchases Sony Corporation's shares, intending to sell the shares within a few months. If the market value of the Sony shares increases, Vivendi will have a gain; if Sony's share price drops, Vivendi will incur a loss. Along the way, Vivendi will receive dividend income from Sony, like any other Sony shareholder.

Suppose Vivendi buys the Sony shares on November 18, paying $100,000 cash. Vivendi records the purchase of the investment at cost:

A1

	A	B	C	D
1	20X6			
2	Nov 18	Investment in Sony Corp	100,000	
3		Cash		100,000
4		*Purchased investment.*		
5				

Investment in Sony Corp	
100,000	

Assume that Vivendi receives a cash dividend of $4,000 from Sony, on November 27. Vivendi records the dividend income as follows:

A1

	A	B	C	D
1	20X6			
2	Nov 27	Cash	4,000	
3		Dividend Income		4,000
4		*Received cash dividend.*		
5				

Assets	=	Liabilities	+	Shareholders' Equity	
+4,000	=	0	+	4,000	(Dividend Income)

Unrealized gains or losses. Vivendi's fiscal year ends on December 31, and Vivendi prepares its financial statements. The Sony shares have risen in value, and on December 31 Vivendi's investment has a current market value of $102,000. Market value is the amount the owner can sell the securities for. Vivendi has an *unrealized gain* on the investment:

- *Gain* because the market value ($102,000) of the securities is greater than Vivendi's cost of the securities ($100,000). A gain has the same effect as a revenue, i.e., it will increase equity.
- *Unrealized gain* because because Vivendi has not yet sold the securities.

Trading securities are reported on the Balance Sheet at their current **fair market value**, because fair market value is the amount the investor can receive by selling the securities. Prior to preparing financial statements on December 31, Vivendi adjusts the investment in Sony securities to its current market value with this year-end journal entry:

	A	B	C	D
1	20X6			
2	Dec 31	Investment in Sony Corp	2,000	
3		Unrealized Gain on Investments		2,000
4		*Adjusted investment to market value.*		
5				

Investment in Sony Corp	
100,000	
2,000	
102,000	

Unrealized Gain on Investments	
	2,000

After the adjustment, Vivendi's Short-Term Investments account is ready to be reported on the Balance Sheet—at current market value of $102,000.

If, on the other hand, Vivendi's investment in Sony shares had decreased in value, say to $95,000, then Vivendi would have reported an *unrealized loss*. A loss has the same effect as an expense, i.e., it reduces equity. In that case, Vivendi would have made a different entry at December 31. For an unrealized loss of $5,000, the entry would have been as follows:

	A	B	C	D
1		Unrealized Loss on Investments	5,000	
2		Investment in Sony Corp		5,000
3		*Adjusted investment to market value.*		
4				

Investment in Sony Corp	
100,000	5,000
95,000	

Unrealized Loss on Investments	
5,000	

Investments in debt and equity securities earn interest revenue and dividend income. Investments also create gains and losses.

For trading investments, these items may be reported on the Income Statement as Other revenue, gains, and (losses), as shown in Exhibit 8-5.

Exhibit 8-5 Reporting Short-Term Investments and the Related Revenues, Gains, and Losses

Balance Sheet		Income Statement	
Current assets:		Revenues	$ XXX
Cash	$ XXX	Expenses	XXX
Short-term investments, at market value	102,000	Other revenue, gains and (losses):	
Accounts receivable	XXX	Interest revenue	XXX
		Dividend income	4,000
		Unrealized gain on investment	2,000
		Net income	$ XXX

Realized Gains and Losses. A *realized* gain or loss occurs only when the investor sells an investment. This gain or loss is different from the unrealized gain that we reported for Vivendi earlier:

- Realized gain = Sale price is *greater than* the investment carrying amount
- Realized loss = Sale price is *less than* the investment carrying amount

Suppose Vivendi sells its Sony shares during 20X7. Remember that we have already updated the Investment in Sony Corp account to $102,000 on December 31, 20X6. If the sale price is $98,000, Vivendi makes the following journal entry:

	A	B	C	D
1	20X7			
2	Jan 19	Cash	98,000	
3		Loss on Sale of Investments	4,000	
4		Investment in Sony Corp		102,000
5		*Sold investments at a loss.*		
6				

Investment in Sony Corp	
100,000	
2,000	102,000

Loss on Sale of Investments	
4,000	

Accountants rarely use the word "Realized" in the account title. A gain (or a loss) is understood to be a realized gain (or loss) arising from a sale transaction. Unrealized gains and losses are clearly labeled as *unrealized*. Vivendi would report Gain (or Loss) on Sale of Investments among the "Other" items of the Income Statement, as shown in Exhibit 8-5.

Held-to-maturity

IAS 39 defines **held-to-maturity investments** as financial assets with fixed or determinable payments and fixed maturity that an entity has the positive intention and ability to hold to maturity. As shares do not have an expiry date, held-to-maturity financial assets are typically investments in bonds or other fixed income instruments (more on bonds in the next chapter). The major investors in bonds are financial institutions—pension plans, mutual funds, and insurance companies. The relationship between the issuing corporation and the investor (bondholder) may be diagrammed as follows:

Chapter 8 Investor (Bondholder)		Chapter 9 Issuing Corporation
Investment in bonds	←——→	Bonds payable
Interest revenue	←——→	Interest expense

An investment in held-to-maturity securities is classified either as short-term or as long-term, depending on the expected maturity date. Short-term investments in bonds are relatively rare (unless having invested in the bonds for a long time, the bonds are about to mature).

Bond investments are initially recorded at cost. Years later, at maturity, the investor will receive the bonds' face value. Bond investments may be purchased at a premium or a discount (we will discuss bonds from the issuer's perspective in Chapter 9). When there is a premium or discount, held-to-maturity investments are amortized to account for interest revenue and the bonds' carrying amount. Held-to-maturity investments are reported by the *amortized cost method*, which determines the carrying amount on the investor's Balance Sheet.

Suppose Vivendi purchases €10,000 of 6% GlaxoSmithKline (GSK) bonds at a price of €95.2 on April 1, 20X5. Vivendi intends to hold the bonds as a long-term investment until their maturity. Interest payment dates are April 1 and October 1. Because these bonds mature on April 1, 20X9, they will be outstanding for four years (48 months). In this case, the investor paid a discount price for the bonds (95.2% of face value). Vivendi must amortize the bonds' carrying amount from cost of €9,520 up to €10,000 over their term to maturity. For the purpose of illustration, we can use amortization of the bonds by the "quick and dirty" straight-line method (technically, *IAS 39* requires the effective interest amortization method). The following are the entries for this long-term investment:

A1

	A	B	C	D
1	20X5			
2	Apr 1	Long-Term Investment in Bonds (€10,000 × 0.952)	9,520	
3		Cash		9,520
4		*To purchase bond investment.*		
5				
6	Oct 1	Cash (€10,000 × 0.06 × 6/12)	300	
7		Interest Revenue		300
8		*To receive semiannual interest.*		
9				
10	Oct 1	Long-Term Investment in Bonds	60	
11		[(€10,000 – €9,520)/48] × 6		
12		Interest Revenue		60
13		*To amortize bond investment.*		
14				

At December 31, Vivendi's year-end adjustments are:

A1

	A	B	C	D
1	20X5			
2	Dec 31	Interest Receivable (€10,000 × 0.06 × 3/12)	150	
3		Interest Revenue		150
4		*To accrue interest revenue.*		
5				
6	Dec 31	Long-Term Investment in Bonds	30	
7		[(€10,000 – €9,520)/48] × 3		30
8		Interest Revenue		
9		*To amortize bond investment.*		
10				

This amortization entry has two effects:

1. It increases the Long-Term Investment account on its march toward maturity value.
2. It records the interest revenue earned from the increase in the carrying amount of the investment.

The financial statements of Vivendi at December 31, 20X6, would report the following for this investment in bonds:

Balance Sheet at December 31, 20X6:	
Current assets:	
Interest receivable	€ 150
Long-term investments in bonds (€9,520 + €60 + €30)	9,610
Property, plant and equipment	X,XXX
Income Statement for the year ended December 31, 2010:	
Other revenues:	
Interest revenue (€300 + €60 + €150 + €30)	€ 540

Available-for-Sale Investments

Available-for-sale investments are, in effect, a "catch all" category. They are non-derivative financial assets that are designated as available for sale or are not classified as (a) loans and receivables, (b) held-to-maturity investments, or (c) financial assets at fair value through profit or loss. They are classified as current assets if the business expects to sell them within the next year. All other available-for-sale investments are classified as long term.

Available-for-sale investments are accounted for at fair market value on the Balance Sheet, with any change between the fair value and carrying amount recognized as a component of other comprehensive income.

Suppose Vivendi purchases 1,000 Siemens shares at the market price of €44.00 per share. Vivendi intends to hold this investment for longer than a year and classifies it as an available-for-sale investment. Vivendi's entry to record the investment is:

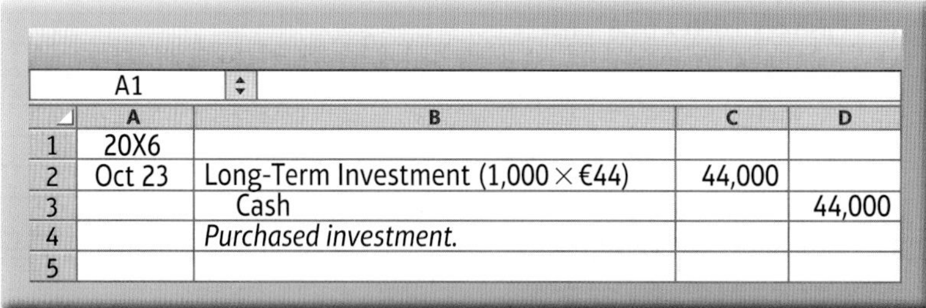

	A	B	C	D
1	20X6			
2	Oct 23	Long-Term Investment (1,000 × €44)	44,000	
3		Cash		44,000
4		*Purchased investment.*		
5				

Assets	=	Liabilities	+	Shareholders' Equity
+44,000 −44,000	=	0	+	0

Assume that Vivendi receives a €0.20 cash dividend on the Siemens shares. Vivendi's entry to record receipt of the dividend is:

	A	B	C	D
1	20X6			
2	Nov 14	Cash (1,000 × €0.20)	200	
3		Dividend Income		200
4		*Received cash dividend.*		
5				

Assets	=	Liabilities	+	Shareholders' Equity	
+200	=	0	+	+200	(Dividend income)

Similar to trading securities, available-for-sale investments are reported on the Balance Sheet at their fair market values. At each reporting date, we adjust available-for-sale investments from their last carrying amount to current fair market value. Assume that the fair market value of the Siemens ordinary shares is €46,500 on December 31, 20X6. Remember that Vivendi bought these shares for €44,000 on October 23, 20X6. In this case, Vivendi makes the following entry to bring the investment to fair market value.

	A	B	C	D
1	20X6			
2	Dec 31	Market Value Adjustments (€46,500 – €44,000)	2,500	
3		Unrealized Gain on Investment		2,500
4		*Adjusted investment to fair market value.*		
5				

The increase in the investment's fair market value creates additional equity for the investor. Available-for-sale differs from trading securities in that the increase in equity is recognized as a component of *other comprehensive income*, net of tax, instead of being recognized in the profit or loss.

Assets	=	Liabilities	+	Shareholders' Equity	
+ 2,500	=	0	+	+ 2,500	(through other comprehensive income)

The following display shows how Vivendi could report its investment and the related unrealized gain in its financial statements at the end of 20X6 (all other figures are assumed for this illustration). Note that the unrealized gain on available-for-sale investments is reported net of tax (assumed 40%) as a component of other comprehensive income.

Balance Sheet:

Assets	
Available for sale investments	€46,500

Equity:

Share capital	€XX,XXX
Retained earnings	€X,XXX
+ Net profit	€20,000
+ Other comprehensive income	€1,500

Income Statement:

Revenue	€50,000
Expenses	€30,000
Net profit	€20,000

Comprehensive income:

Net profit (from Income Statement)	€20,000
Other comprehensive income:	
Unrealized gain on available-for-sale investments net of 40% tax	€1,500
Total comprehensive income	€21,500

A Closer Look

Unrealized gains or losses on available-for-sale investments are recognized in other comprehensive income. What happens when the investment is sold? The resulting gain or loss would be shown as income in the Income Statement, but as previous unrealized gains or losses have been reported as other comprehensive income, we would be double counting total comprehensive income. To avoid this "recycling of gains or losses," the amount of gains or losses that were previously reported as other comprehensive income must be reversed simultaneously with the recognition of the gain or loss in income. This adjustment is beyond the scope of this text.

The preceding example assumes that the investor holds an investment in only one security of another company. Usually companies invest in a portfolio of securities (more than one). In this case, the periodic adjustment to fair market value must be made for the portfolio as a whole. See the following "Stop & Think" exercise for an example.

When eventually sold, the sale of such available-for-sale investments results in a *realized* gain or loss. Realized gains and losses measure the difference between the amount received from the sale and the original cost of the investment. Suppose Vivendi sells its investment in Siemens shares for €43,000 during 20X7 (recall that Vivendi bought them for €44,000). Vivendi would record the sale as follows:

	A	B	C	D
1	20X7	Cash	43,000	
2	May 19	Loss on Sale of Investment	1,000	
3		Long-Term Investment (cost)		44,000
4		*Sold investment.*		
5				

Assets	=	Liabilities	+	Shareholders' Equity	
+43,000 −44,000	=	0	+	−1,000	(loss on sale of investment)

Vivendi would report €1,000 Loss on Sale of Investments on its Income Statement. Vivendi also needs to make further adjusting entries to market value adjustment accounts and prevent double counting of total comprehensive income, as previous unrealized gains and losses were included in other comprehensive income in earlier periods (e.g., the €1,500 in our example at the end of 20X7). These adjustments are covered in intermediate accounting courses.

Stop & Think

Suppose Vivendi holds the following available-for-sale securities as long-term investments at December 31, 20X7:

Available for sale (Investments)	Cost	Current Fair Market Value
Bayer	€85,000	€71,000
Phillips	16,000	12,000
	€101,000	€83,000

Show how Vivendi will report long-term investments on its December 31, 20X7, Balance Sheet.

Answer:

Assets	
Long-term investments, at fair market value	€83,000

Summary of Financial Assets Recognition and Measurements

Exhibit 8-6 summarizes the accounting treatment for the three classifications of financial assets.

Exhibit 8-6 | Accounting Treatment

Financial Asset Category	Balance Sheet Measurement	Income Measurement
Trading securities	Fair market value	Changes in fair value as income
Loans and receivables	Amortized cost	Changes in value due to amortization
Held-to-maturity	Amortized cost	Changes in value due to amortization
Available-for-sale	Fair market value	Changes in fair value as other comprehensive income

Mid-Chapter Summary Problem

During the year 20X6, Win Stone Corp. made the following investments:

- Investment A: trading securities, at a cost of \$20,000 with a current fair value of \$25,000. Dividends received during the year \$1,000.
- Investment B: available-for-sale securities, at a cost of \$10,000 with a current fair value of \$12,000. Dividends received during the year \$500.
- Investment C: \$10,000 held-to-maturity securities at \$95.0, with current fair value of \$96.0. These 5% bonds (semi-annual interest payments on June 30 and December 31 each year) were purchased on July 1 and will mature in 24 months' time.

How would Win Stone Corp. report the investments on its Balance Sheet and Income Statement?

Answer:

Balance Sheet		
Investment A	\$25,000	[at fair value]
Investment B	\$12,000	[at fair value]
Investment C	\$9,625	[at amortized cost, \$9,500 + (500/24 × 6)]

Income Statement		
Dividend income	\$1,500	[\$1,000 + \$500]
Interest revenue (bond amortization)	\$375	[(5% × 10,000 × 6/12) + (500/24 × 6)]
Fair value revaluation income	\$5,000	[\$25,000 − \$20,000]
Other comprehensive income	\$2,000	[AFS at \$12,000 − \$10,000]

USE THE EQUITY METHOD FOR INVESTMENTS

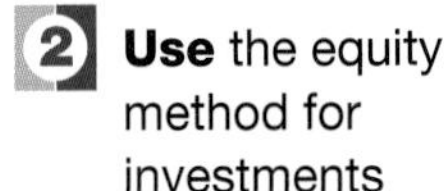
2 Use the equity method for investments

When an investor owns a large portion of an investee, typically between 20% and 50%, the investor is said to have significant influence in the entity's operations. Such an investor can probably affect dividend policy, product lines, and other important matters. *IAS 28—Investment in Associates* refers to these investee entities as associates (but you may see the term "affiliates" used in practice sometimes). We use the **equity method** to account for investment in associated or affiliated entities.

Up to early January 2011, Vivendi holds equity-method investments in NBC Universal. NBC Universal runs television channels such as NBC, CNBC, and MSNBC, and produces TV hits such as *30 Rock*, *The Office*, *The Voice*, and many more. It also produces films under the banner of Universal Pictures, as well as Universal Studios theme parks around the world. As Vivendi had significant influence in shaping the policy and operations of NBC Universal, some measure of NBC Universal's profits and losses should be included in Vivendi's income. At the end of 2015, Vivendi has two primary affiliates: Telecom Italia and VEVO.

ADAPTED EXCERPTS FROM VIVENDI'S NOTES TO THE ACCOUNTS

Equity Accounting

Entities over which Vivendi exercises significant influence as well as joint ventures are accounted for under the equity method.

Significant influence is presumed to exist when Vivendi holds, directly or indirectly, at least 20% of voting rights in an entity unless it can be clearly demonstrated that Vivendi does not exercise significant influence. Significant influence can be evidenced through other criteria, such as representation on the board of directors or the entity's equivalent governing body, participation in policy-making of financial and operational processes, material transactions with the entity or interchange of managerial personnel.

Source: Vivendi's 2015 Financial Statements, page 37

The equity method is a method of accounting whereby the investment is initially recognized at cost and adjusted thereafter for the post-acquisition change in the investor's share of net assets of the investee. The profit or loss of the investor includes the investor's share of the profit or loss of the investee. Let's assume Vivendi is investing €400 million into a fictional company, "YY Entertainment" in exchange for a 20% stake in the company.

Investments accounted for by the equity method are recorded initially at cost. Suppose Vivendi paid €400 million in cash for 20% of the ordinary shares of YY Entertainment. Vivendi's entry to record the purchase of this investment follows (in millions).

	A	B	C	D
1	20X6			
2	Jan 6	Equity Investments in Associate	400	
3		Cash		400
4		*To purchase equity-method investment.*		
5				

Under the equity method, Vivendi, as the investor, applies its percentage of ownership—20%, in our example—in recording its share of the investee's net income and dividends. If YY Entertainment reports net income of €250 million for the year, Vivendi records 20% of this amount as follows (in millions):

	A	B	C	D
1	20X6			
2	Dec 31	Equity Investments in Associate (€250 × 0.20)	50	
3		Income from Associates		50
4		*To record investment revenue.*		
5				

Assets	=	Liabilities	+	Shareholders' Equity	
+ 50	=	0	+	+ 50	(equity-method income)

Because of the close relationship between Vivendi and YY Entertainment, Vivendi (the investor) increases its investment in the associate account and records income from the associate when YY Entertainment (the investee) reports income. In other words, as YY Entertainment's own equity increases because of its own profits, so does the investment account on Vivendi's books. This was what *IAS 28* terms "the investor's share of net assets of the investee." The equity earnings that appear on the investor's Income Statement may be labeled by other terms such as "share of profits of associates." Vivendi uses the term "income from equity affiliates."

If the affiliate made a loss during the financial year, the investor would also have to share the loss of the associate as reduction in income and reduction in its net assets in investment in associates.

Vivendi also records its proportionate part of cash dividends received from YY Entertainment. When YY Entertainment declares and pays a cash dividend of €100 million, Vivendi receives 20% of this dividend and records this entry (in millions):

	A	B	C	D
1	20X6			
2	Dec 31	Cash (€100 × 0.20)	20	
3		Equity Investments in Associate		20
4		*To receive cash dividend on equity-method investment.*		
5				

Assets	=	Liabilities	+	Shareholders' Equity
+20 −20	=	0	+	0

The Investment account is *decreased* for the receipt of a dividend on an equity-method investment. Why? Because the dividend decreases the investee's net assets and thus the investor's investment.

After the preceding entries are posted, Vivendi's Investment account at December 31, 20X6, shows Vivendi's equity in the net assets of YY Entertainment (in millions):

Equity Investments in Associate

Jan 6	Purchase	400	Dec 31	Dividends	20
Dec 31	Net income	50			
Dec 31	Balance	430			

Vivendi would report this investment in associate on the Balance Sheet as a non-current asset and the income from associates on the Income Statement as follows:

	Millions
Balance Sheet (partial):	
Assets	
Total current assets	€XXX
Long-term investments, at equity	430
Property, plant and equipment, net	XXX
Income Statement (partial):	
Income from operations	€XXX
Other revenue:	
Income from associates	50
Net income	€XXX

Gain or loss on the sale of an equity-method investment is measured as the difference between the sale proceeds and the carrying amount of the investment. For example, Vivendi selling all of its 20% holding in YY Entertainment for €425 million would be recorded as follows:

	A	B	C	D
1	20X7			
2	Feb 13	Cash	425	
3		Loss on Sale of Investment	5	
4		Equity Investments in Associates		430
5		*Sold investment in affiliate.*		
6				

Assets	=	Liabilities	+	Shareholders' Equity	
+425 −430	=	0	+	−5	(loss on sale of investment)

Summary of the Equity Method. The following T-account illustrates the accounting for equity-method investments:

Equity-Method Investment	
Original cost	Share of losses
Share of income	Share of dividends
Balance	

UNDERSTAND THE CONCEPT OF CONSOLIDATED FINANCIAL STATEMENTS

Understand the concept of consolidated financial statements

Entities buy a significant stake in another company in order to *influence* the other company's operations. In this section, we cover the situation in which an investor buys enough of an investee's shares to actually *control* that company.

Most large corporations own controlling interests in other companies. A **controlling** (or **majority**) **interest** is typically indicated by the ownership of more than 50% of the investee's voting shares. The investor is called the **"parent company,"** and the investee company is called the **"subsidiary."** For example, Dailymotion, Universal Music Group, and Canal+ are subsidiaries of Vivendi, the parent (see Exhibit 8-1). Therefore, the shareholders of Vivendi control Dailymotion, Universal Music Group, and Canal+ (and many others) as shown in Exhibit 8-7.

Exhibit 8-7 | Ownership Structure of Vivendi and Key Subsidiaries

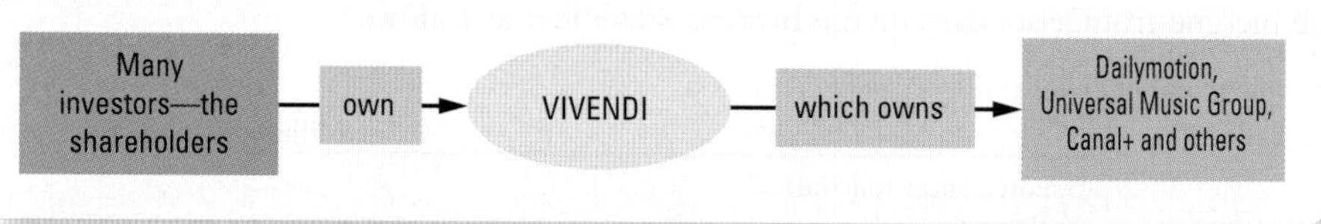

Consolidation Accounting

Consolidation accounting is a method of combining the financial statements of all the companies controlled by the same shareholders. This method reports a single set of financial statements for the consolidated entity, which carries the name of the parent company, usually indicated by the word "consolidated" or "group."

Consolidated financial statements combine the financial statements of the parent company with those of its subsidiaries. The result is a single set of statements as if the parent and its subsidiaries were one entity. If you own shares in Vivendi, the parent company, you want to know the total operations of the group, not just the parent company's own accounts. Consolidated financial statements are presented primarily for the benefit of shareholders, creditors, and other resource providers of the parent.

In consolidated statements, the assets, liabilities, revenues, and expenses of each subsidiary are added to the parent's accounts. For example, the Cash account balances in Dailymotion and Canal+

and all other subsidiaries are added to Vivendi's (the parent company) own Cash balance. The sum of all of the cash amounts is presented as a single amount in Vivendi's consolidated Balance Sheet. Each account balance of a subsidiary, such as UMG or Canal+, loses its identity in the consolidated statements, which bear the name of the parent, Vivendi. In turn, these subsidiaries may even be parents of other subsidiaries! For example, UMG is the parent of Capital Music Group, EMI, Republic Records, and many more. Modern business structures make very complicated family trees!

Exhibit 8-8 demonstrates a corporate structure for a parent corporation that owns controlling interests in five subsidiaries. Together, the dotted line represents the "family of companies under common control." The company may also have investments in affiliates or associates or joint operations, these are not consolidated, i.e., they are shown outside the dotted line.

Exhibit 8-8 | Parent Company with Consolidated Subsidiaries and Unconsolidated Affiliates

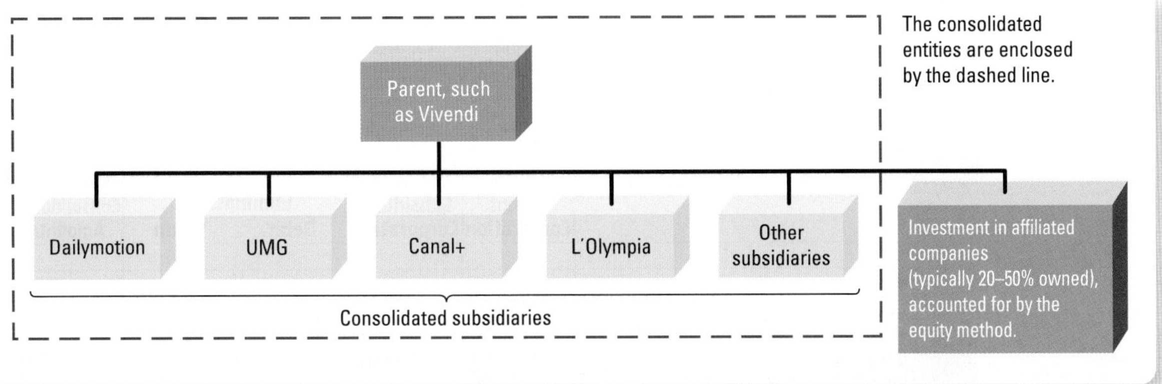

The Consolidated Balance Sheet and the Related Worksheet

Vivendi owns all (100%) the outstanding shares of Universal Music Group (UMG). Both Vivendi and UMG keep their own separate sets of books. Vivendi, the parent company, uses a worksheet to prepare the consolidated statements of Vivendi and its consolidated subsidiaries. Then Vivendi's consolidated Balance Sheet shows the combined assets and liabilities of both Vivendi and all its subsidiaries. Exhibit 8-9 shows how the parent's balances are consolidated with those of the subsidiary, and the resulting consolidated Balance Sheet.

Exhibit 8-9 | Consolidation of a Wholly-Owned Subsidiary

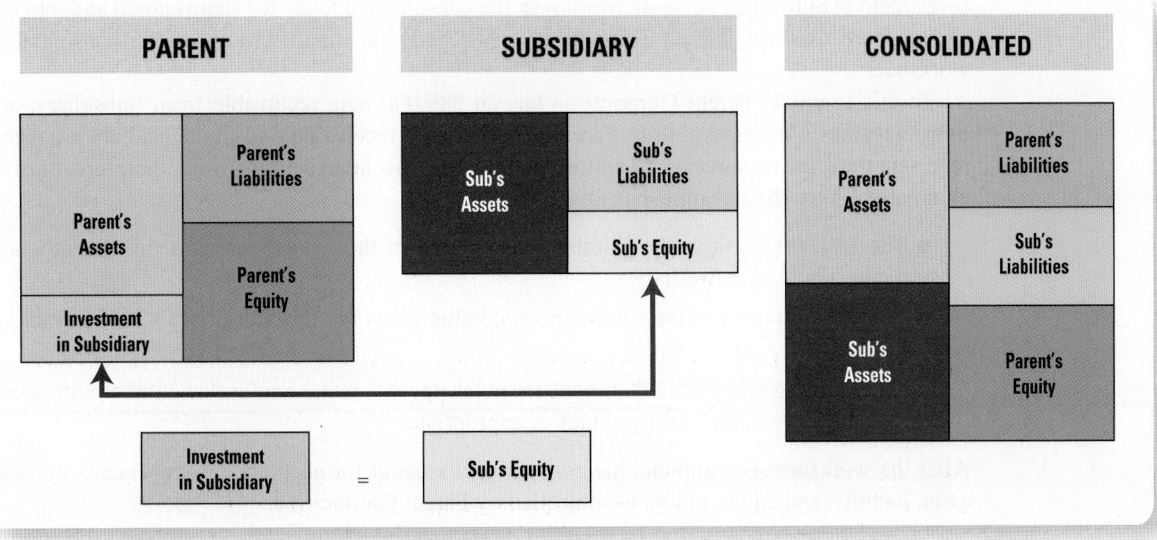

Exhibit 8-10 shows the worksheet for consolidating the Balance Sheets of Parent Corporation and Subsidiary Corporation at the date of acquisition. We use these hypothetical entities to illustrate the consolidation process. Consider elimination entry (a) for the parent-subsidiary ownership accounts. Entry (a) credits the parent's Investment account to eliminate its debit balance. Entry (a) also eliminates the subsidiary's shareholders' equity accounts by debiting the subsidiary's share capital and retained earnings for their full balances. Without this elimination, the consolidated financial statements would include both the parent company's investment in the subsidiary and the subsidiary company's equity. But these accounts represent the same thing—Subsidiary's equity—and so they must be eliminated from the consolidated totals. If they weren't, the same resources would be counted twice.

Exhibit 8-10 | Worksheet for a Consolidated Balance Sheet

	A	B	C	D	E	F
1		Parent Corporation	Subsidiary Corporation	Eliminations Debit	Eliminations Credit	Parent and Subsidiary Consolidated Amounts
2						
3	**Assets**					
4	Cash	12,000	18,000			30,000
5	Note receivable from Subsidiary	80,000	—		(b) 80,000	—
6	Inventory	104,000	91,000			195,000
7	Investment in Subsidiary	150,000	—		(a) 150,000	—
8	Other assets	218,000	138,000			356,000
9	Total	564,000	247,000			581,000
10	**Liabilities and Shareholders' Equity**					
11	Accounts payable	43,000	17,000			60,000
12	Notes payable	190,000	80,000	(b) 80,000		190,000
13	Share capital	176,000	100,000	(a) 100,000		176,000
14	Retained earnings	155,000	50,000	(a) 50,000		155,000
15	Total	564,000	247,000	230,000	230,000	581,000
16						

The resulting Parent and Subsidiary consolidated Balance Sheet (far-right column) reports no Investment in Subsidiary account. Moreover, the consolidated totals for share capital and retained earnings are those of Parent Corporation only. Study the final column of the consolidation worksheet.

In this example, Parent Corporation has an $80,000 note receivable from Subsidiary, and Subsidiary has a note payable to Parent. The parent's receivable and the subsidiary's payable represent the same resources—all entirely within the consolidated entity. Both, therefore, must be eliminated. Entry (b) accomplishes this.

- The $80,000 credit in the Eliminations column of the worksheet zeros out Parent's note receivable from Subsidiary.
- The $80,000 debit in the Eliminations column zeros out the Subsidiary's note payable to Parent.
- The resulting consolidated amount for notes payable is the amount owed to creditors outside the consolidated entity, which is appropriate.

After the worksheet is complete, the consolidated amount for each account represents the total asset, liability, and equity amounts controlled by Parent Corporation.

Stop & Think

Examine Exhibit 8-10. Why does the consolidated shareholders' equity ($176,000 + $155,000) *exclude* the equity of Subsidiary Corporation?

Answer:

The shareholders' equity of the consolidated entity is that of the parent only. To include the shareholders' equity of the subsidiary as well as the investment in the subsidiary on the parent's books would be double counting.

Goodwill and Non-Controlling Interest

Goodwill and Non-Controlling Interest are two accounts that only a consolidated entity can have. Goodwill, which we studied in Chapter 7, arises when a parent company pays more to acquire a subsidiary company than the market value of the subsidiary's net assets. Goodwill is the intangible asset that represents the parent company's excess payment over and above the fair market value of net assets of the subsidiary. Exhibit 8-11 depicts a parent company that owns 80% of a subsidiary, having paid more than its share of the subsidiary's fair value of net assets. You can trace how the assets, liabilities, and equity of the parent and subsidiary's assets and liabilities are eventually shown in the consolidated financial statement.

Exhibit 8-11 | Consolidation of a Partially-Owned Subsidiary

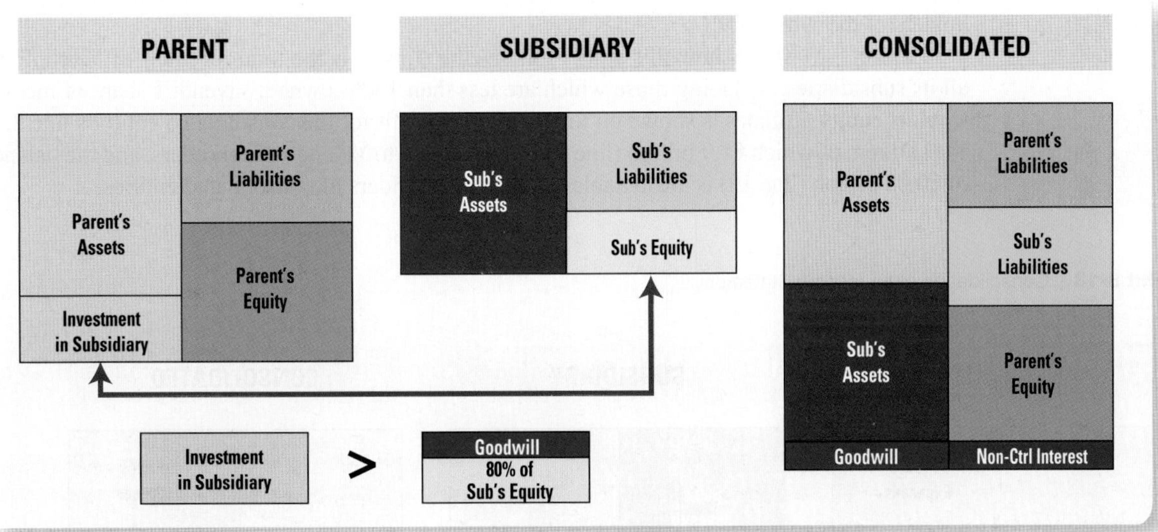

Non-controlling interest arises when a parent company owns less than 100% of the shares of a subsidiary. For example, Vivendi owns less than 100% of some of the companies it controls (such as 51% of NC+ and 64.4% of Radionomy). The remainder of the subsidiaries' shares is non-controlling interest to the Vivendi group. Non-controlling interest is reported as a separate account in the shareholders' equity section of the consolidated Balance Sheet. The amount of non-controlling interest in subsidiaries' shares must be clearly identified and labeled as such. Vivendi reports non-controlling interest (line 6) in the shareholders' equity section on its Balance Sheet as shown in Exhibit 8-12.

Exhibit 8-12 Shareholders' Equity and Non-Controlling Interest

	A	B	C
1	**Vivendi Group Consolidated Balance Sheet**	**As at December 31**	
2	**(Adapted, in millions of euro)**	**2015**	**2014**
3	Total assets	34,946	35,738
4	Total liabilities	13,860	12,750
5	Equity attributable to Vivendi's shareholders	20,854	22,606
6	Non-controlling interests	232	382
7	Total equity	21,086	22,988
8	Total liabilities and equity	34,946	35,738
9			

Income of a Consolidated Entity

The income of a consolidated entity is the net income of the parent plus the parent's proportion of the subsidiaries' net income. If the subsidiary is 100% owned, then all the subsidiary's income belongs to the shareholders of the parent. However, if the ownership is less than 100%, part of the subsidiary's income belongs to non-controlling interests. Have a look at Exhibit 8-13 for an 80% owned subsidiary. Total revenue to the consolidated entity is the revenues of the parent plus subsidiary, and total consolidated expenses is the expenses of the parent plus subsidiary. We include 100% revenue and expenses of the subsidiary, even when we only own 80% of the subsidiary. The total profit attributable to equity holders of the parent company is the total consolidated net income (denoted by red bracket) less the 20% of income that belongs to non-controlling shareholders of the subsidiary.

Exhibit 8-14 shows how this works for Vivendi. Line 3 is the total revenues of Vivendi and all its subsidiaries, including those which are less than 100% owned. Vivendi's share of income from its equity affiliates is shown on line 6. The net profit for the consolidated entity is line 8, at €1.9 billion, of which €1.9 billion (line 9) is attributable to Vivendi shareholders, and the balance of €0.04 billion (line 10) is attributable to other shareholders of consolidated entities.

Exhibit 8-13 Consolidation of an Income Statement

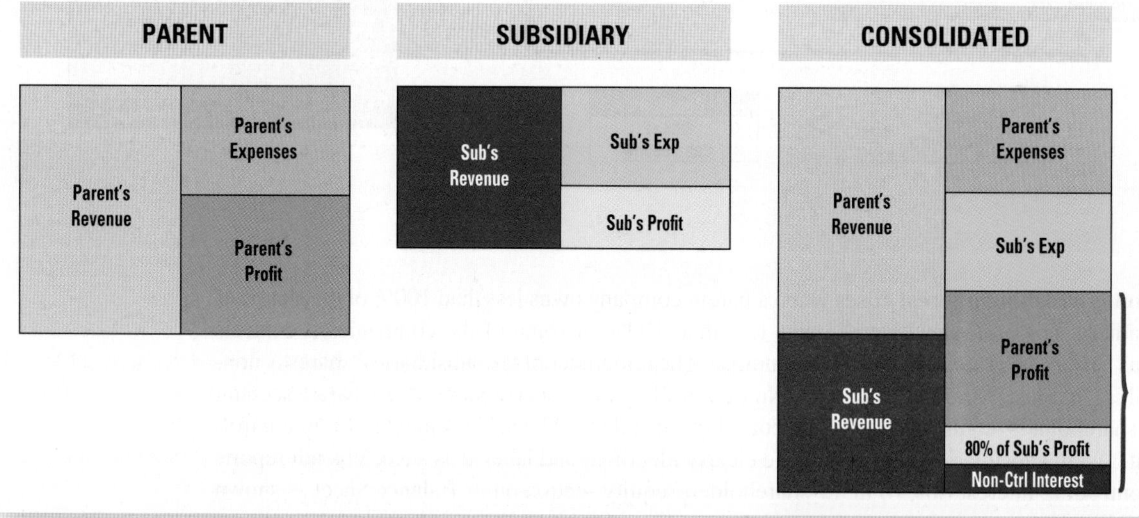

Exhibit 8-14 | Vivendi's Income Statement

	A	B	C
1	**Vivendi Group** **Consolidated Income Statement** **For year ended December 31**		
2	**(Adapted in millions of euro)**	**2015**	**2014**
3	Revenue	10,762	10,089
4	⋮		
5	Operating profit	1,231	736
6	Income (loss) from equity affiliates	(10)	(18)
7	⋮		
8	Net income	1,978	5,025
9	Earning attributable to Vivendi shareowners	1,932	4,744
10	Earning attributable to non-controlling interests	46	280
11			

A Closer Look

Since consolidated financial statements are presented as if the parent and all its subsidiaries are one economic entity, it makes sense that transactions between members of the group need special attention. You have seen in Exhibit 8-10 that any amounts owing to and by members of the group must be eliminated. Similarly, if one member of the consolidated entity sells goods or services to another member of the same entity, this transaction would have to be eliminated as well. For example, if Canal+ licenses some music from UMG for its video games, revenue is earned by UMG and expenses are incurred by Canal+. However, from a consolidated perspective, this transaction should not exist (you can't make money from yourself!) and will be eliminated from the consolidated Income Statement. More complicated transactions would include sale of a PPE from a subsidiary to another subsidiary. As the transaction is deemed non-existent from a consolidated perspective, numerous adjustments would have to be made on the consolidation worksheet. If you are an accounting major, you are likely to cover this topic in your advanced accounting courses.

Enron Corporation

In 2000, Enron Corporation in Houston, Texas, employed approximately 22,000 people and was one of the world's leading electricity, natural gas, pulp and paper, and communications companies, with reported revenues of nearly $101 billion. *Fortune* had named Enron "America's Most Innovative Company" for six consecutive years. To many outside observers, Enron was the model corporation.

Enron's financial statements showed that the company was making a lot of money, but in reality, most of its profits were merely on paper. Rather than from operations, the great majority of the cash Enron needed to operate on a day-to-day basis came from bank loans. It was very important, therefore, that Enron keep its debt ratio (discussed in Chapter 9) as well as its return on assets (ROA, discussed in Chapter 10) at acceptable levels, so the banks would continue to view the company as creditworthy. Enron's Balance Sheets contained large misstatements in the liabilities and shareholders' equity sections over a period of years. Many of the offsetting misstatements were in long-term assets. Specifically, Enron owned numerous long-term investments, including power plants, water, broadband cable, and sophisticated, complex, and somewhat dubious derivative financial instruments in such unusual things as the weather! Many of these investments actually had questionable value, but Enron had abused fair market value accounting to estimate them at grossly inflated values.

To create paper profits, Andrew Fastow, Enron's chief financial officer, created a veritable maze of "special purpose entities" (SPEs), financed with bank debt. He then "sold" the dubious investments to the SPEs to get them off Enron's books. Enron recorded millions of dollars in "profits" from these transactions. Fastow then used Enron shares to collateralize the bank debt of the SPEs, making the transactions entirely circular. Unknown to Enron's board of directors, Fastow or members of his own family owned most of these entities, making them related parties to Enron. Enron was, in fact, the owner of the assets, and was, in fact, obligated for the debts of the SPEs since those debts were collateralized with Enron shares. When Enron's fraud was discovered in late 2001, the company was forced to consolidate the assets of the SPEs, as well as all of their bank debt, into its own financial statements. The end result of the restatement so depressed Enron's debt ratio and ROA that the banks refused to loan the company any more money to operate. Enron's energy trading business virtually dried up overnight, and it was bankrupt within 60 days. An estimated $60 billion in shareholder value, and 22,000 jobs, were lost. Enron's CEO, Jeffrey Skilling, its CFO, Andrew Fastow, and Board Chairman Kenneth Lay were all convicted of fraud. Skilling and Fastow both went to prison. Lay died suddenly of a heart attack before being sentenced.

Enron's audit firm, Arthur Andersen, was accused of trying to cover up its knowledge of Enron's practices by shredding documents. The firm was indicted by the U.S. Justice Department in March 2002. Because of the indictment, Andersen lost all of its public clients and was forced out of business. As a result, over 58,000 people lost their jobs worldwide. A U.S. Supreme Court decision in 2005 eventually led to withdrawal of the indictment, but it came much too late for the once "gold plated" CPA firm. Allegations about the quality of its work on Enron, as well as other well-publicized cases such as Waste Management and WorldCom, who were also clients, doomed Arthur Andersen.

Decision Case 1 in Chapter 9 and Decision Case 3 in Chapter 10 illustrate the financial statement impact of Enron's fraudulent transactions.

DECISION GUIDELINES

ACCOUNTING METHODS FOR INVESTMENTS

These guidelines show which accounting method to use for each type of long-term investment.

Vivendi has all types of investments—shares, bonds, significant interests, and controlling interests. How would Vivendi typically account for its various investments?

Type of Long-Term Investments	Accounting Method
Vivendi owns less than 20% of investee shares	Available-for-sale
Vivendi owns between 20% and 50% of investee/affiliate shares	Equity
Vivendi owns more than 50% of investee shares	Consolidation
Vivendi owns long-term investment in bonds (held-to-maturity investment)	Amortized cost

ACCOUNT FOR INTERNATIONAL OPERATIONS AND TRANSACTIONS

Account for international operations and transactions

In this globalized world, many companies earn revenue beyond their national boundaries. Accounting for business activities across national boundaries involves foreign currencies and exchange rates. Transactions may be expressed in currencies other than the company's local currency. This is the subject of *IAS 21—The Effects of Changes in Foreign Exchange Rates*.

Foreign Currencies and Exchange Rates

Most countries use their own national currency, usually denoted by their three-letter currency codes. For example, the United States uses United States Dollars ($ or USD), South Africa uses South African Rand (ZAR), Bahrain uses Bahraini Dinar (BHD), United Arab Emirates uses Emirati Dirham (AED), Malaysia uses Malaysian Ringgit (MYR), and so forth. An exception is the European Union nations; France, Germany, Italy, Belgium, Netherlands and others use a common currency, the Euro (€ or EUR).

The price of one nation's currency can be stated in terms of another country's monetary unit. This measure of one currency against another is called the **foreign-currency exchange rate**. In Exhibit 8-15, you can see the cross rates of major currencies in the world. You can visit Bloomberg for updated exchange rates.

Exhibit 8-15 | Foreign-Currency Exchange Rates

A1

	A	B	C	D	E	F	G	H	I
1		USD	EUR	JPY	GBP	CHF	CAD	AUD	HKD
2	USD	-	1.0730	0.0087	1.2576	1.0030	0.7615	0.7550	0.1289
3	EUR	0.9320	-	0.0081	1.1720	0.9348	0.7097	0.7036	0.1201
4	JPY	114.4800	122.8370	-	143.9700	114.8245	87.1764	86.4324	14.7554
5	GBP	0.7952	0.8532	0.0069	-	0.7976	0.6055	0.6003	0.1025
6	CHF	0.9970	1.0698	0.0087	1.2538	-	0.7592	0.7527	0.1285
7	CAD	1.3132	1.4091	0.0115	1.6515	1.3172	-	0.9915	0.1693
8	AUD	1.3245	1.4212	0.0116	1.6657	1.3285	1.0086	-	0.1707
9	HKD	7.7585	8.3249	0.0678	9.7571	7.7818	5.9081	5.8577	-
10									

Currency keys: USD = U.S. Dollar; EUR = Euro; JPY = Japanese Yen; GBP = British Pound; CHF = Swiss Franc; CAD = Canadian Dollar; AUD = Australian Dollar; HKD = Hong Kong Dollar; Source: Bloomberg, 27 April 2012.

For example, 1 EUR is equal to 1.0730 USD, 0.8532 GBP, and 8.3249 HKD. Inversely, looking across the second row, 1 USD is worth 0.9320 euro, 1 GBP is worth 1.1720 euro, and 1 HKD is worth 0.1201 euro. Obviously, exchange rates move all the time, so the actual rates at any time may be different from the cross rates table above. We call this conversion a *translation*. Suppose an item costs €400. To compute its cost in Australian dollars (AUD), we multiply the euro amount by the conversion rate: EUR 400 × AUD 1.4212 = AUD 568.48.

There a number of factors that determine foreign currency exchange rates between two currencies. You would typically study this in macroeconomics. These factors include:

- difference in inflation rates (generally, a lower inflation rate means stronger currency);
- difference in interest rates (generally, a higher domestic interest rate means stronger currency);
- current account deficits (the higher the deficit, the weaker the currency);
- public debt (the higher the debt, the weaker the currency);
- political stability (the more unstable, the weaker the currency).

Currencies are often described as "strong" or "weak." The exchange rate of a **strong currency** is rising relative to other nations' currencies. The exchange rate of a **weak currency** is falling relative to other currencies. For example, *Bloomberg* listed the conversion rate for GBP

(£ or British Pounds) to USD at 1.0730 on January 31, 2016. If the rate rose to 1.1000 the next week, we can say that euro has strengthened against the U.S. dollar. If it dropped to 1.0000, we can say that the euro has weakened against the U.S. dollar.

Accounting for Foreign Currency Transactions

International transactions are common. Many businesses buy and sell in currencies other than their local currency. In accounting for transactions involving foreign currencies, *IAS 21—The Effects of Changes in Foreign Exchange Rates* requires the determination of "functional currency," which is the currency of the primary economic environment in which the business operates. In most cases, we can assume that the business's local currency is the functional currency. All foreign currency items are then translated into the functional currency at initial recognition using transaction-date exchange rates.

Let's illustrate foreign currency translation using Qian Hu, an ornamental fish farmer and accessories retailer, as a working example. Qian Hu sells various kinds of ornamental fish and pet accessories from its base in Singapore to over 80 countries around the world. Its sales outside Singapore are about 70% of its total revenue in 2015. Your local pet stores may be selling Qian Hu's fish or aquarium accessories!

Let's be a little more specific in our example. Suppose Qian Hu supplies a pet store in Europe and makes some of its sales in euros and buys some of its breeding equipment from Japan and pays for them in Japanese yen.

Consider Qian Hu's sale of ornamental fish and aquariums to FishyTales, a pet store in Europe, on a 30-day credit term, on June 10, 20X6. The sale can be conducted in Singapore dollars (SGD) or in euros (EUR), or even in other currencies such as U.S. dollars. If FishyTales agrees to pay in SGD, Qian Hu avoids the complication of dealing in a foreign currency, and the transaction is treated the same way as sales of ornamental fish across town in Singapore. But suppose FishyTales orders EUR 1,000 worth of fish and aquariums from Qian Hu. Further suppose FishyTales would like to pay in euros and Qian Hu agrees to receive euros instead of Singapore dollars.

On initial recognition of the sale, Qian Hu would have recorded in its books sales of EUR 1,000 and a receivable of the same amount. This would be entered using transaction date exchange rates. Suppose that the exchange rate on June 10, 20X6, the day of the sale, is 1 EUR for 2.00 SGD. Qian Hu would thus record:

	A	B	C	D
1	20X6			
2	Jun 10	Accounts Receivable—FishyTales	2,000	
3		Sales Revenue		2,000
4		*Sale on account (€1,000 × 2.00).*		
5				

Assets	=	Liabilities	+	Shareholders' Equity	
+ 2,000	=	0	+	2,000	(sales revenue)

When Qian Hu receives payment of EUR 1,000 from FishyTales on July 10, 20X6, it may or may not translate to the amount recognized at initial measurement of SGD 2,000. The prevailing exchange rate on the payment date will determine how much SGD Qian Hu actually receives. If the exchange rate on July 10, 20X6, is 1 EUR for 2.10 SGD (in other words, the euro has strengthened against the Singapore dollar), Qian Hu would collect more in Singapore dollar terms. Qian Hu would collect SGD 2,100 (EUR 1,000 × 2.10), resulting in a "translation gain" of SGD 100.

	A	B	C	D
1	20X6			
2	Jul 10	Cash	2,100	
3		Accounts Receivables—FishyTales		2,000
4		Translation Gain		100
5		*Collection of account (€1,000 × 2.10).*		
6				

Assets	=	Liabilities	+	Shareholders' Equity	
+ 2,100 − 2,000	=	0	+	100	(translation gain)

Conversely, had the euro weakened against the Singapore dollar, Qian Hu would have recognized a translation loss. Suppose the exchange rate on July 10 was 1 EUR = 1.95 SGD instead of 2.10 SGD. The EUR 1,000 payment from FishyTales would translate to SGD 1,950 in settlement of an account receivable of SGD 2,000. Qian Hu would process this journal entry instead:

	A	B	C	D
1	20X6			
2	Jul 10	Cash	1,950	
3		Translation Loss	50	
4		Accounts Receivables—FishyTales		2,000
5		*Collection of account (€1,000 × 1.95).*		
6				

Assets	=	Liabilities	+	Shareholders' Equity	
+ 1,950 − 2,000	=	0	+	− 50	(translation loss)

A Closer Look

What if Qian Hu's financial year-end was June 30, 20X6? How should the transaction be reported on the financial statements?

Subsequent to initial measurement, *IAS 21* requires entities to distinguish between "monetary" and "non-monetary" items. The key distinction between the two categories is whether or not there is a right to receive (or obligation to deliver) a fixed or determinable number of units of currency. For example, FishyTales receivable is a monetary item because it is deliverable in the fixed amount of EUR 1,000. At the end of each reporting period, *IAS 21* requires monetary assets to be retranslated using the closing rate. Non-monetary assets carried at historical costs continue to be measured using historical transaction date exchange rates.

If Qian Hu's financial year-end were June 30, 20X6, it would be required to re-measure the FishyTale receivables using the closing exchange rate on June 30, 20X6. Any gains (or losses) on the Balance Sheet date are recognized in the Income Statement.

Reporting Gains and Losses on the Income Statement

The Foreign-Currency Translation Gain/Loss account holds gains and losses on transactions settled in foreign currencies. The net amount of the gains and losses are reported on the Income Statement as Other Revenues and Gains, or Other Expenses and Losses, as the case may be. For example, Qian Hu may report the net impact of its translation gains and losses as follows:

Other Expenses and Losses:	
Foreign-currency translation loss, net	$2,600

Should We Hedge Our Foreign-Currency Transaction Risk?

One way for companies to avoid foreign-currency transaction losses is to insist that international transactions be settled in the local currency. This requirement puts the burden of currency translation on the foreign party. But this approach may not always work and may even alienate customers and decrease sales. Another way for a company to protect itself is by hedging. **Hedging** means to protect oneself from losing money in one transaction by engaging in a counter-balancing transaction.

A company selling goods to be collected in a foreign currency expects to receive a fixed number of foreign currency units. If the foreign currency weakens, the company would receive the agreed-upon amounts in foreign currency units, but this would translate to a lower local currency, resulting in a foreign currency translation loss.

A company may have accumulated a number of receivables and payables expressed in foreign currencies. Losses on one currency may be offset by gains on another. Most companies do not have equal amounts of receivables and payables in foreign currency. To obtain a more precise hedge, companies can buy futures contracts. These are contracts for foreign currencies to be received in the future. Futures contracts can create a payable to exactly offset a receivable, and vice versa. Many companies that do business internationally use hedging techniques to minimize their foreign currency exposure.

Consolidation of Foreign Subsidiaries

Besides entering into foreign activities directly, an entity may also operate through a "foreign operation." *IAS 21* defines foreign operation as an entity that is a subsidiary, associate, joint venture, or branch of a reporting entity, the activities of which are based or conducted in a country or currency other than those of the reporting entity. Let's look at a simple example on how you would consolidate foreign subsidiaries.

A company with a foreign subsidiary must consolidate the subsidiary's financial statements into its own statements for reporting to the public. The consolidation of a foreign subsidiary poses two special challenges:

1. Some foreign countries may require accounting treatments that differ from the reporting entity's accounting principles. For example, the foreign subsidiary's financial statements might be prepared in accordance with US GAAP, whereas the parent's accounts

are prepared using international financial reporting standards (IFRS). For reporting purposes, if those differences are material, the subsidiary's statements must be adjusted to conform to the parent's accounting policies.

2. The subsidiary's statements may be expressed in a foreign currency different from the parent's currency. We are making an assumption in our discussion here that the parent's functional currency is the parent's local currency. First, we must translate the subsidiary's statements into the parent's currency. Then the two companies' financial statements can be consolidated as illustrated in Exhibit 8-8.

The process of translating a foreign subsidiary's financial statements into the parent's currency usually creates a *foreign-currency translation adjustment.* This item appears in the financial statements of most multinational companies and is reported as part of other comprehensive income on the Income Statement and as part of shareholders' equity on the consolidated Balance Sheet.

A translation adjustment arises due to changes in the foreign exchange rate over time. In general, the foreign operation's:

- monetary *assets* and *liabilities* are translated into the parent's currency at the current exchange rate on the date of the statements;
- non-monetary assets and liabilities carried at historical cost (such as PPE) continue to be measured using the historical transaction-date exchange rates;
- *shareholders' equity* is translated into the parent's currency at older, historical exchange rates. Paid-in capital accounts are translated at the historical exchange rate when the subsidiary was acquired. Retained earnings is translated at the average exchange rates applicable over the period that interest in the subsidiary has been held.

This difference in exchange rates creates an out-of-balance condition on the Balance Sheet. The translation adjustment brings the Balance Sheet back into balance. Let's see how the translation adjustment works.

Suppose Vivendi has an American subsidiary whose financial statements are expressed in U.S. dollars. Vivendi must consolidate the U.S. subsidiary's financials into its own statements. When Vivendi acquired the American company in 20X5, the applicable exchange rate was 1 USD = 0.70 EUR (or 1 EUR = 1.42 USD). When the American firm earned its retained income during 20X5–20X8, the average exchange rate was 1 USD = 0.65 EUR. On the Balance Sheet date in 20X8, 1 USD = 0.60 EUR. Exhibit 8-16 shows how to translate the American company's Balance Sheet into euros.

The **foreign-currency translation adjustment** is the balancing amount that brings the dollar amount of liabilities and equity of a foreign subsidiary into agreement with the dollar amount of total assets (in Exhibit 8-16, total assets equal €540,000). Only after the translation adjustment of €40,000 do total liabilities and equity equal total assets stated in euros.

Exhibit 8-16 | Translation of a Foreign-Currency Balance Sheet in Euros

A1

	A	B	C	D
1	**Balance Sheet Dec 31, 20X8**	**Dollars**	**Exchange Rate**	**Euros**
2	Assets*	800,000	0.60	540,000
3				
4	Liabilities*	500,000	0.60	300,000
5	Shareholders' equity			
6	Share capital	100,000	0.70	70,000
7	Retained earnings	200,000	0.65	130,000
8	Accumulated other comprehensive income:			
9	Foreign-currency translation adjustment			40,000
10		800,000		540,000
11				

**Assume all monetary assets and liabilities.*

What caused the translation adjustment? The euro has strengthened after the acquisition of the U.S. company.

- When Vivendi acquired the foreign subsidiary in 20X6, 1 USD was worth 0.70 EUR (or expressed the other way, 1 EUR was worth USD 1.43).
- When the U.S. company earned its income during 20X6 through 20X8, the average exchange rate was 0.65.
- On the Balance Sheet date in 20X8, 1 USD is worth only €0.60.
- Thus, the U.S. company's equity (assets minus liabilities) is translated into only €240,000 (€540,000 – €300,000).
- To bring shareholders' equity to €240,000 requires a €40,000 adjustment.

In a sense, a translation adjustment is like a profit, reported as an item in the shareholders' equity section of the Balance Sheet, as in Exhibit 8-14. Similarly, had the currency moved the other way, a negative translation adjustment would have resulted, similar to a loss that is reported in the equity section of the Balance Sheet. The U.S. firm's euro figures in Exhibit 8-14 are what Vivendi would include in its consolidated Balance Sheet. The consolidation procedures would follow those illustrated earlier in the chapter.

Impact of Investing Activities on the Statement of Cash Flows

CASH
FLOW

Investing activities include many types of transactions. In Chapter 7, we covered the purchase and sale of long-term assets such as Property, Plant and Equipment (PPE). In this chapter, we examined investments in financial assets, including shares and bonds. The "cash flows from investing activities" section of the Statement of Cash Flows captures the cash movements for these activities. For example, you can see from Exhibit 8-17 that Vivendi has been busy selling and buying companies in the last two years!

Exhibit 8-17 Vivendi's Statement of Cash Flows

	A	B	C
1	**Vivendi Group** **Consolidated Statement of Cash Flows** **For year ended December 31**		
2	**(Adapted, in millions of €)**	**2015**	**2014**
3	Cash flows from operating activities	€ 240	€ 3,593
4	Cash flows from investing activities		
5	Purchase of consolidated companies, after acquired cash	(359)	(100)
6	Investments in equity affiliates	(19)	(87)
7	Proceeds from disposal of consolidated companies, after divested cash	4,032	16,929
8	Disposal of equity affiliates	268	—
9	Dividends received from equity affiliates	5	4
10	Other cash flows from investing activities	665	(2,454)
11	Cash flows from investing activities	4,592	14,292
12	Cash flows from financing activities	(3,495)	(11,884)
13	Net cash flows (excluding foreign exchange rate changes)	€ 1,337	€ 6,001
14			

EVALUATE A COMPANY'S OVERALL PERFORMANCE

5 **Evaluate** a company's overall performance

You may have heard of the term "return on investment." It is a generic way to measure how much you get out of something. For example, if you bought one Vivendi share at €12 and sold it a year later at €15, then you would have made a return of €3 over an investment of €12, or a 25% return on your investment. If you had received dividends during your holding period, your return would be higher.

It is, however, much harder to measure the total returns on all the investments that a company makes. Remember, a company may choose to invest in inventory, equipment, held-to-maturity bonds, and varying degrees of share investments, from trading securities to affiliates and subsidiaries. It may choose to spend its resources through an international expansion, or by venturing into completely different industries. Whatever form of returns the company generates, eventually, they will all be reflected on its bottom line as net profit. Thus, in measuring the profitability of a company's investments, we should look at how much net profit a company generates from its total revenue. This ratio is called the **net profit margin**.

Net profit margin is calculated as a percentage of net profit over the company's revenues. Vivendi, as a group, with all its investments and international operations, made a total of €1,978 million from total revenue of €10,762. Vivendi's net profit margin is thus:

Net Profit Margin	Vivendi 2015	Vivendi 2014
$\frac{\text{Net profit}}{\text{Revenue}}$	$\frac{1,978}{10,762} = 18.4\%$	$\frac{5,025}{10,089} = 49.8\%$

Now obviously, the 2014 net profit margin should be jumping up and down for attention. How can it be so high compared to 2015? In 2014 and 2015, Vivendi sold its stakes in a number of telecommunication companies and entered into a number of mergers and acquisitions. This means a number of companies were deconsolidated or consolidated for the first time in the last two years. This resulted in a much higher net income in 2014. Clearly, the 2014 net income is not out of the ordinary. You will find that when a company has significant change in the scope of consolidation, it reduces comparability from one period to another.

Let's focus on Vivendi's 2015 net profit margin. How does the 18.4% net profit margin compare to its competitors? Well, for a company as diversified as Vivendi, it will be very difficult to find an exact competitor or an exact benchmark. We can look at other diversified media and entertainment companies such as The Walt Disney Company, Time Warner Incorporated, and Sony Corporation (Exhibit 8-18). It looks like Vivendi is well placed amongst these companies!

Exhibit 8-18 | Net Profit Margin Comparisons

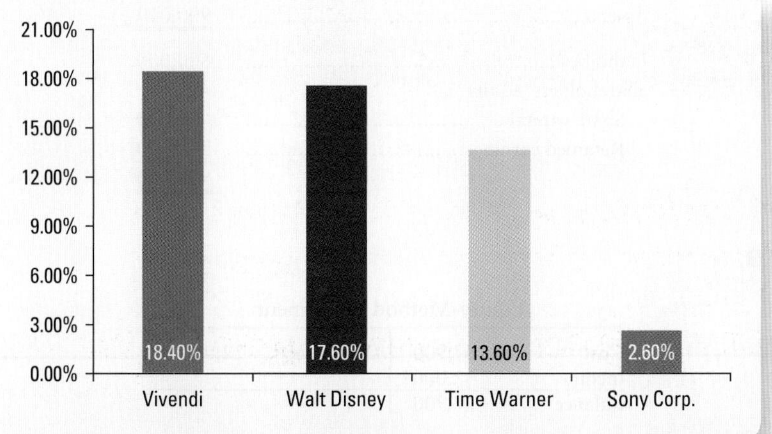

End-of-Chapter Summary Problem

1. Investor paid $67,900 to acquire a 40% equity-method investment in the share capital of Investee. At the end of the first year, Investee's net income was $80,000, and Investee declared and paid cash dividends of $55,000. What is Investor's ending balance in its Equity-Method Investment account? Use a T-account to answer.

2. Parent Company paid $85,000 for all the shares of Subsidiary Company, and Parent owes Subsidiary $20,000 on a note payable. Complete the consolidation worksheet below.

	A	B	C	D	E	F
1		Parent Company	Subsidiary Company	Eliminations Debit	Eliminations Credit	Consolidated Amounts
	Assets					
2	Cash	7,000	4,000			
3	Note receivable from Parent	—	20,000			
4	Investment in Subsidiary	85,000	—			
5	Other assets	108,000	99,000			
6	Total	200,000	123,000			
7	**Liabilities and Shareholders' Equity**					
8	Accounts payable	15,000	8,000			
9	Notes payable	20,000	30,000			
10	Share capital	120,000	60,000			
11	Retained earnings	45,000	25,000			
12	Total	200,000	123,000			
13						

3. Translate the Balance Sheet of the Brazilian subsidiary of Unilever, a European company, into euros. When Unilever acquired this subsidiary, the exchange rate of the Brazilian currency BRL (the real), was €0.40. The average exchange rate applicable to retained earnings is €0.41. The real's current exchange rate is €0.43.

   Before performing the translation, predict whether the translation adjustment will be positive or negative. Does this situation generate a foreign-currency translation gain or loss? Give your reasons.

	Reals
Assets	900,000
Liabilities	600,000
Shareholders' equity:	
Share capital	30,000
Retained earnings	270,000
	900,000

Answers

1.

Equity-Method Investment

Cost	67,900	Dividends	22,000**
Income	32,000*		
Balance	77,900		

*$80,000 × 0.40 = $32,000
**$55,000 × 0.40 = $22,000

2. Consolidation worksheet:

	A	B	C	D	E	F
1		Parent Company	Subsidiary Company	Eliminations Debit	Eliminations Credit	Consolidated Amounts
	Assets					
2	Cash	7,000	4,000			11,000
3	Note receivable from Parent	—	20,000		20,000	—
4	Investment in Subsidiary	85,000	—		85,000	—
5	Other assets	108,000	99,000			207,000
6	Total	200,000	123,000			218,000
7	**Liabilities and Shareholders' Equity**					
8	Accounts payable	15,000	8,000			23,000
9	Notes payable	20,000	30,000	(a) 20,000		30,000
10	Share capital	120,000	60,000	(b) 60,000		120,000
11	Retained earnings	45,000	25,000	(b) 25,000		45,000
12	Total	200,000	123,000	105,000	105,000	218,000
13						

3. Translation of foreign-currency Balance Sheet:

This situation will generate a *positive* translation adjustment, which is like a gain. The gain occurs because the real's current exchange rate, which is used to translate net assets (assets minus liabilities), exceeds the historical exchange rates used for shareholders' equity.

The calculation follows.

	Reals	Exchange Rate	Euros
Assets	900,000	0.43	387,000
Liabilities	600,000	0.43	258,000
Shareholders' equity:			
Share capital	30,000	0.40	12,000
Retained earnings	270,000	0.41	110,700
Accumulated other comprehensive income:			
Foreign-currency translation adjustment	—		6,300
	900,000		387,000

REVIEW | Investments and International Operations

Quick Check (Answers are given at the end of the chapter.)

1. SABIC (Saudi Arabia Basic Industries Company) invests in 100,000 Apple Inc.'s shares. SABIC expects to hold these shares for a medium term and not trade actively. How should SABIC classify this investment?

a. Equity
b. Available-for-sale
c. Trading
d. Consolidation

2. Jacques Corporation purchased an available-for-sale investment in 1,600 shares of Home Central for $25 per share. On the next Balance-Sheet date, Home Central shares are quoted at $28 per share. Jacques' *Balance Sheet* should report

a. a realized gain of $4,800.
b. investments of $44,800.
c. an unrealized loss of $4,800.
d. investments of $40,000.

3. Use the Jacques Corporation data in question 2. Assume a tax rate of 20%. Jacques' should report

a. an unrealized loss of $4,800 on the Income Statement.
b. a realized gain of $4,800 in other comprehensive income.
c. an unrealized gain of $4,800 in other comprehensive income.
d. an unrealized gain of $3,840 in other comprehensive income.

4. Use the Jacques Corporation data in question 2. Jacques sold the Home Central shares for $45,000 two years later. Jacques' *Income Statement* should report

a. investments of $45,000.
b. an unrealized gain of $4,800.
c. a gain on sale of $4,800.
d. a gain on sale of $5,000.

5. Peter Moving & Storage Co. paid $200,000 for 30% of the ordinary shares of McDonough Co. McDonough earned net income of $50,000 and paid dividends of $20,000. The carrying value of Peter's investment in McDonough is

a. $200,000.
b. $250,000.
c. $220,000.
d. $209,000.

6. Stone, Inc., owns 70% of Granite Corporation, and Granite owns 70% of Pebble Company. During 20X6, these companies' net incomes are as follows before any intercorporation income-related consolidations:

- Stone $240,000
- Granite $64,000
- Pebble $56,000

How much net income should Stone report for 20X6?

a. $324,000
b. $240,000
c. $312,240
d. $360,000

7. Riddleston, Inc., holds an investment in Daley bonds that pay interest each October 31. Riddleston's *Balance Sheet* at December 31 should report

a. interest payable.
b. interest receivable.
c. interest expense.
d. interest revenue.

8. You are taking a vacation to Italy, and you buy euros for LC 1.80. LC is your local currency. On your return you cash in your unused euros for LC 1.20. During your vacation

a. your local currency rose against the euro.
b. the euro gained value against your local currency.
c. the euro rose against your local currency.
d. your local currency lost value.

9. Bahrain Development Corporation purchased earth-moving equipment from a Canadian company. The cost was $1,800,000 Canadian (CAD), and the Canadian dollar was quoted at 1 CAD = BHD 0.40. A month later, the corporation paid its debt, and the Canadian dollar was quoted at BHD 0.42. What should the corporation record as the cost of the equipment?

a. BHD 720,000
b. BHD 756,000
c. BHD 4,285,714
d. BHD 4,500,000

10. Insight, a company headquartered in Hong Kong, owns numerous foreign subsidiary companies. When Insight consolidates its subsidiaries, Insight should translate the subsidiary's monetary assets into Hong Kong dollars at the

a. average exchange rate during the period Insight owned the British subsidiary.
b. current exchange rate.
c. historical exchange rate when Insight purchased the British company.
d. none of the above. There's no need to translate the subsidiary's assets into dollars.

Accounting Vocabulary

available-for-sale investments (p. 460) All other financial asset investments not classified as loans and receivables, held-to-maturity, or trading securities.

consolidated statements (p. 466) Financial statements of the parent company plus those of majority-owned subsidiaries as if the combination were a single legal entity.

controlling (majority) interest (p. 466) Ownership of more than 50% of an investee company's voting shares.

equity method (p. 463) The method used to account for investments in which the investor has 20–50% of the investee's voting shares and can significantly influence the decisions of the investee.

fair market value (p. 457) The amount that a seller would receive on the sale of an investment to a willing purchaser on a given date. Securities and available-for-sale securities are valued at fair market values on the Balance Sheet date. Other assets may be recorded at fair market value.

financial asset (p. 451) An asset that arises because of contractual rights to receive items of value, for example, cash, receivables, etc., and similar rights.

foreign-currency exchange rate (p. 473) The measure of one country's currency against another country's currency.

foreign-currency translation adjustment (p. 477) The balancing figure that brings the dollar amount of the total liabilities and shareholders' equity of the foreign subsidiary into agreement with the dollar amount of its total assets.

hedging (p. 476) To protect oneself from losing money in one transaction by engaging in a counterbalancing transaction.

held-to-maturity investments (p. 458) Bonds and notes that an investor intends to hold until maturity.

long-term investment (p. 452) Any investment that does not meet the criteria of a short-term investment; any investment that the investor expects to hold longer than a year or that is not readily marketable.

net profit margin (p. 479) The amount of net profit earned from each currency unit of sale. Also called *return on sales*.

non-controlling interest (p. 469) A subsidiary company's equity that is held by shareholders other than the parent company (i.e., less than 50%).

parent company (p. 466) An investor company that owns more than 50% of the voting shares of a subsidiary company.

short-term investment (p. 452) An investment that a company plans to hold for 1 year or less. Usually in the form of marketable securities.

strong currency (p. 473) A currency whose exchange rate is rising relative to other nations' currencies.

subsidiary (p. 466) An investee company in which a parent company owns more than 50% of the voting shares.

trading securities (p. 455) Investments in financial assets that are primarily for the purpose of trading, with the intent of generating profits on the sale. Also called fair value investments through profit or loss.

weak currency (p. 473) A currency whose exchange rate is falling relative to that of other nations.

ASSESS YOUR PROGRESS

Short Exercises

S8-1. ***(Learning Objective 1: Accounting for an available-for-sale investment; recording unrealized gain or loss)*** Ship Ahoy completed these long-term available-for-sale investment transactions during 20X6:

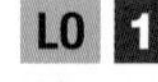

20X6	
Apr 10	Purchased 400 Naradon shares, paying $23 per share. Ship Ahoy intends to hold the investment for the indefinite future.
Jul 22	Received a cash dividend of $1.25 per share on the Naradon investment.
Dec 31	Adjusted the Naradon investment to its current market value of $5,200.

1. Journalize Ship Ahoy's investment transactions. Explanations are not required.
2. Show how to report the investment and any unrealized gain or loss on Ship Ahoy's Balance Sheet at December 31, 20X6. Ignore income tax.

LO 1

S8-2. *(Learning Objective 1: Accounting for the sale of an available-for-sale investment)* Use the data given in Short Exercise 8-1. On May 21, 20X7, Ship Ahoy sold its investment in Naradon for $28 per share.

1. Journalize the sale. No explanation is required.
2. How does the gain or loss that you recorded here differ from the gain or loss that was recorded at December 31, 20X6?

LO 1

S8-3. *(Learning Objective 1: Working with a bond investment)* Hector Kane (HK) owns vast amounts of corporate bonds. Suppose HK buys $1,100,000 of Tetrix bonds at a price of 104. The Tetrix bonds pay cash interest at the annual rate of 6% and mature at the end of five years.

1. How much did HK pay to purchase the bond investment? How much will HK collect when the bond investment matures?
2. How much cash interest will HK receive each year from Tetrix?
3. Will HK's annual interest revenue on the bond investment be more or less than the amount of cash interest received each year? Give your reason.
4. Compute HK's annual interest revenue on this bond investment. Use the straight-line method to amortize the investment.

LO 1

S8-4. *(Learning Objective 1: Recording bond investment transactions)* Return to Short Exercise 8-3, the Hector Kane (HK) investment in Tetrix bonds. Journalize on HK's books:

a. Purchase of the bond investment on June 30, 20X0. HK expects to hold the investment to maturity.
b. Receipt of semi-annual cash interest on December 31, 20X0.
c. Amortization of the bonds on December 31, 20X0. Use the straight-line method.
d. Collection of the investment's face value at the maturity date on June 30, 20X5. (Assume the receipt of 20X5 interest and the amortization of bonds for 20X5 have already been recorded, so ignore these entries.)

LO 2

S8-5. *(Learning Objective 2: Accounting for a 40% investment in another company)* Suppose on February 1, 20X6, Fam Motors paid $400 million for a 40% investment in Yoba Motors. Assume Yoba earned net income of $50 million and paid cash dividends of $35 million during 20X6.

1. What method should Fam Motors use to account for the investment in Yoba? Give your reason.
2. Journalize these three transactions on the books of Fam Motors. Show all amounts in millions of dollars and include an explanation for each entry.
3. Post to the Long-Term Investment T-account. What is its balance after all the transactions are posted?

LO 2

S8-6. *(Learning Objective 2: Accounting for the sale of an equity-method investment)* Use the data given in Short Exercise 8-5. Assume that in November 20X7, Fam Motors sold half its investment in Yoba Motors. The sale price was $145 million. Compute Fam Motors' gain or loss on the sale.

LO 3

S8-7. *(Learning Objective 3: Understanding consolidated financial statements)* Answer these questions about consolidation accounting:

1. Define "parent company." Define "subsidiary company."
2. How do consolidated financial statements differ from the financial statements of a single company?
3. Which company's name appears on the consolidated financial statements? How much of the subsidiary's shares must the parent own before reporting consolidated statements?

LO 3

■ writing assignment

S8-8. *(Learning Objective 3: Understanding goodwill and non-controlling interest)* Two accounts that arise from consolidation accounting are goodwill and non-controlling interest.

1. What is goodwill, and how does it arise? Which company reports goodwill, the parent or the subsidiary? Where is goodwill reported?
2. What is non-controlling interest, and which company reports it, the parent or the subsidiary? Where is non-controlling interest reported?

S8-9. *(Learning Objective 4: Accounting for transactions stated in a foreign currency)* Suppose Poke sells soft drink syrup to a Russian company on September 12. Poke agrees to accept 500,000 Russian rubles. On the date of sale, the ruble is quoted at $0.35. Poke collects half the receivable on October 18, when the ruble is worth $0.32. Then on November 15, when the foreign-exchange rate of the ruble is $0.38, Poke collects the final amount. LO 4

Journalize these three transactions for Poke.

S8-10. *(Learning Objective 4: Accounting for transactions stated in a foreign currency)* Ocean Belting sells goods for 1,100,000 Mexican pesos. The foreign exchange rate for a peso is $0.085 on the date of sale. Ocean Belting then collects cash on April 24, when the exchange rate for a peso is $0.090. Record Ocean's cash collection. LO 4

Ocean Belting buys inventory for 28,000 Swiss francs. A Swiss franc costs $0.82 on the purchase date. Record Ocean Belting's payment of cash on October 25, when the exchange rate for a Swiss Franc is $0.86.

In these two scenarios, which currencies strengthened? Which currencies weakened?

S8-11. *(Learning Objective 5: Reporting cash flows)* Companies divide their cash flows into three categories for reporting on the cash flow statement. LO 5

1. List the three categories of cash flows in the order they appear on the cash flow statement. Which category of cash flow is most closely related to this chapter?
2. Identify two types of transactions that companies report as cash flows from investing activities.

S8-12. *(Learning Objective 5: Using a statement of cash flows)* Excerpts from The ABC Company statement of cash flows, as adapted, appear as follows: LO 5

■ writing assignment

	A	B	C
1	**The ABC Company and Subsidiaries Consolidated Statement of Cash Flows**		
		Years Ended December 31	
2	**(Adapted, in millions)**	**20X7**	**20X6**
3	**Operating Activities**		
4	Net cash provided by operating activities	$ 4,222	$ 1,170
5	**Investing Activities**		
6	Purchases of property, plant and equipment	(782)	(743)
7	Acquisitions and investments, principally trademarks and		
8	bottling companies	(665)	(407)
9	Purchases of investments	(461)	(522)
10	Proceeds from disposals of investments	475	300
11	Proceeds from disposals of property, plant and equipment	100	56
12	Other investing activities	143	139
13	Net cash used in investing activities	(1,190)	(1,177)
14	**Financing Activities**		
15	Issuances of debt (borrowing)	3,021	3,675
16	Payments of debt	(4,017)	(4,279)
17	Issuances of shares	172	342
18	Purchases of shares for treasury	(280)	(145)
19	Dividends	(1,795)	(1,697)
20	Net cash used in financing activities	(2,899)	(2,104)
21			

As the chief executive officer of The ABC Company, your duty is to write the management letter to your shareholders explaining ABC's major investing activities during 20X7. Compare the company's level of investment with previous years and indicate how the company financed its investments during 20X7. Net income for 20X7 was $3,791 million.

Exercises MyLab Accounting

Select A and B exercises can be found within MyLab Accounting, an online homework and practice environment. Your instructor may ask you to complete select exercises using MyLab Accounting.

Group A

LO 1

E8-13A. ***(Learning Objective 1: Journalizing transactions for trading securities)*** Journalize the following trading securities investment transactions of Wesley Brothers Department Stores:

a. Purchased 470 Potter Foods shares at $32 per share, with the intent of holding the shares for the indefinite future.
b. Received cash dividend of $1.80 per share on the Potter investment.
c. At year-end, adjusted the investment account to fair market value of $35 per share.
d. Sold the Potter shares for the market price of $23 per share.

LO 1

E8-14A. ***(Learning Objective 1: Accounting for available-for-sale investments)*** Rand Co. bought 3,400 Stockholm shares at $36; 660 London shares at $47.50; and 1,200 Glasgow shares at $75—all as available-for-sale investments. At December 31, Hoover's Online reports Stockholm shares at $27.375, London at $49.25, and Glasgow at $67.75.

Requirements

1. Determine the cost and the fair market value of the long-term investment portfolio at December 31.
2. Record Rand's adjusting entry at December 31.
3. What would Rand report on its Income Statement and Balance Sheet for the information given? Make the necessary disclosures. Ignore income tax.

LO 1

E8-15A. ***(Learning Objective 1: Recording bond investment transactions)*** Assume that on September 30, 20X0, Pewtex, Inc., paid 98 for 9% bonds of Teal Corporation as a long-term held-to-maturity investment. The maturity value of the bonds will be $30,000 on September 30, 20X5. The bonds pay interest on March 31 and September 30.

Requirements

1. What method should Pewtex use to account for its investment in the Teal bonds?
2. Using the straight-line method of amortizing the bonds, journalize all of Pewtex's transactions on the bonds for 20X0.
3. Show how Pewtex would report everything related to the bond investment on its Balance Sheet at December 31, 20X0.

LO 2

E8-16A. ***(Learning Objective 2: Accounting for transactions under the equity method)*** Pepper Corporation owns equity-method investments in several companies. Suppose Pepper paid $1,600,000 to acquire a 25% investment in Payton Software Company. Payton Software reported net income of $680,000 for the first year and declared and paid cash dividends of $400,000.

Requirements

1. Record the following in Pepper's journal: (a) purchase of the investment, (b) Pepper's proportion of Payton Software's net income, and (c) receipt of the cash dividends.
2. What is the ending balance in Pepper's investment account?

LO 2

E8-17A. ***(Learning Objective 2: Measuring gain or loss on the sale of an equity-method investment)*** Without making journal entries, record the transactions of Exercise 8-16A directly in the Pepper account, Long-Term Investment in Payton Software. Assume that after all the noted transactions took place, Pepper sold its entire investment in Payton Software for $1,800,000 cash. How much is Pepper's gain or loss on the sale of the investment?

LO 2

E8-18A. ***(Learning Objective 2: Applying the appropriate accounting method for a 35% investment)*** Ashcroft Financial paid $580,000 for a 35% investment in the ordinary shares of Sonic, Inc. For the first year, Sonic reported net income of $200,000 and at year-end declared and paid cash dividends of $120,000. On the Balance-Sheet date, the market value of Ashcroft's investment in Sonic shares was $380,000.

Requirements

1. Which method is appropriate for Ashcroft Financial to use in accounting for its investment in Sonic? Why?
2. Show everything that Ashcroft would report for the investment and any investment revenue in its year-end financial statements.

LO 3
■ spreadsheet

E8-19A. ***(Learning Objective 3: Preparing a consolidated Balance Sheet)*** XYZ, Inc., owns Cressida Corp. The two companies' individual Balance Sheets follow:

	A	B	C	D	E
1	XYZ, Inc. Consolidation Worksheet	XYZ, Inc.	Cressida Corp.	Elimination Debit	Elimination Credit
2	**Assets**				
3	Cash	$ 51,000	$ 18,000		
4	Accounts receivable, net	85,000	58,000		
5	Note receivable from XYZ	—	40,000		
6	Inventory	57,000	81,000		
7	Investment in Cressida	103,000	—		
8	PPE, net	291,000	96,000		
9	Other assets	22,000	9,000		
10	Total	$ 609,000	$ 302,000		
11					
12	**Liabilities and Shareholders' Equity**				
13	Accounts payable	$ 46,000	$ 29,000		
14	Notes payable	147,000	35,000		
15	Other liabilities	79,000	135,000		
16	Share capital	113,000	81,000		
17	Retained earnings	224,000	22,000		
18	Total	$ 609,000	$ 302,000		
19					

Requirements

1. Prepare a consolidated Balance Sheet of XYZ, Inc., using the above consolidation worksheet.
2. What is the amount of shareholders' equity for the consolidated entity?

LO 4
■ writing assignment

E8-20A. ***(Learning Objective 4: Managing and accounting for foreign currency transactions)*** Assume that Computer City Stores completed the following foreign currency transactions:

Sep 9	Purchased DVD players as inventory on account from Sona, a Japanese company. The price was 800,000 yen, and the exchange rate of the yen was $0.0088.
Oct 18	Paid Sona when the exchange rate was $0.0085.
22	Sold merchandise on account to CoCo, a French company, at a price of 50,000 euros. The exchange rate was $1.26.
22	Collected from CoCo when the exchange rate was $1.20.

Requirements

1. Journalize these transactions for Computer City. Focus on the gains and losses caused by changes in foreign currency rates. (Round your answers to the nearest whole dollar.)

2. On September 10, immediately after the purchase, and on October 23, immediately after the sale, which currencies did Computer City want to strengthen? Which currencies did in fact strengthen? Explain your reasoning.

LO 4

■ spreadsheet

E8-21A. ***(Learning Objective 4: Translating a foreign-currency Balance Sheet into dollars)*** Translate into dollars the Balance Sheet of Nevada Leather Goods' Spanish subsidiary. When Nevada Leather Goods acquired the foreign subsidiary, a euro was worth $1.02. The current exchange rate is $1.36. During the period when retained earnings were earned, the average exchange rate was $1.15 per euro.

	Euros
Assets	800,000
Liabilities	550,000
Shareholders' equity:	
Share capital	70,000
Retained earnings	180,000
	800,000

During the period covered by this situation, which currency was stronger, the dollar or the euro?

LO 5

E8-22A. ***(Learning Objective 5: Preparing and using the statement of cash flows)*** During fiscal year 20X6, Sweet Land Doughnuts reported net loss of $128.9 million. Sweet Land received $1.4 million from the sale of other businesses. Sweet Land made capital expenditures of $10.0 million and sold property, plant and equipment for $6.8 million. The company purchased long-term investments at a cost of $11.5 million and sold other long-term investments for $2.7 million.

Requirement

1. Prepare the investing activities section of Sweet Land Doughnuts' statement of cash flows. Based solely on Sweet Land Doughnuts' investing activities, does it appear that the company is growing or shrinking? How can you tell?

LO 5

E8-23A. ***(Learning Objective 5: Using the statement of cash flows)*** At the end of the year, Crown King Properties' statement of cash flows reported the following for investment activities:

A1

	A	B
1	**Crown King Properties Consolidated Statement of Cash Flows (Partial)**	
2	Cash flows from Investing Activities:	
3	Notes receivable collected	$ 3,128,000
4	Purchases of short-term investments	(3,475,000)
5	Proceeds from sales of equipment	1,600,000*
6	Proceeds from sales of investments (cost of $470,000)	479,000
7	Expenditures for property and equipment	(1,737,000)
8	Net used by investing activities	$ (5,000)
9		

*Cost $5,400,000; Accumulated depreciation, $3,800,000.

Requirement

1. For each item listed, make the journal entry that placed the item on Crown King's statement of cash flows.

Group B

LO 1

E8-24B. ***(Learning Objective 1: Journalizing transactions for trading securities)*** Journalize the following trading securities investment transactions of Johnson Brothers Department Stores:

a. Purchased 460 Jefferson Foods shares at €31 per share, with the intent of holding the shares for the indefinite future.
b. Received cash dividend of €1.40 per share on the Jefferson investment.
c. At year-end, adjusted the investment account to fair market value of €40 per share.
d. Sold the Jefferson shares for the market price of €20 per share.

E8-25B. ***(Learning Objective 1: Accounting for available-for-sale investments)*** Leroy Co. bought 3,800 Canada shares at €39; 640 Chile shares at €48.25; and 1,500 Milan shares at €78—all as available-for-sale investments. At December 31, Hoover's Online reports Canada shares at €29.125, Chile at €50.25, and Milan at €69.50. LO 1

Requirements

1. Determine the cost and the market value of the long-term investment portfolio at December 31.
2. Record Leroy's adjusting entry at December 31.
3. What would Leroy report on its Income Statement and Balance Sheet for the information given? Make the necessary disclosures. Ignore income tax.

E8-26B. ***(Learning Objective 4: Recording bond investment transactions)*** Assume that on September 30, 20X0, Baytex, Inc., paid 95 for 8.5% bonds of Carly Corporation as a long-term held-to-maturity investment. The maturity value of the bonds will be €40,000 on September 30, 20X5. The bonds pay interest on March 31 and September 30. 

Requirements

1. What method should Baytex use to account for its investment in the Carly bonds?
2. Using the straight-line method of amortizing the bonds, journalize all of Baytex's transactions on the bonds for 20X0.
3. Show how Baytex would report everything related to the bond investment on its Balance Sheet at December 31, 20X0.

E8-27B. ***(Learning Objective 2: Accounting for transactions under the equity method)*** Watson Corporation owns equity-method investments in several companies. Suppose Watson paid €1,200,000 to acquire a 32% investment in Sam Software Company. Sam Software reported net income of €640,000 for the first year and declared and paid cash dividends of €450,000. 

Requirements

1. Record the following in Watson's journal: (a) purchase of the investment, (b) Watson's proportion of Sam Software's net income, and (c) receipt of the cash dividends.
2. What is the ending balance in Watson's investment account?

E8-28B. ***(Learning Objective 2: Measuring gain or loss on the sale of an equity-method investment)*** Without making journal entries, record the transactions of Exercise 8-27B directly in the Watson account, Long-Term Investment in Sam Software. Assume that after all the noted transactions took place, Watson sold its entire investment in Sam Software for cash of €3,200,000. How much is Watson's gain or loss on the sale of the investment? 

E8-29B. ***(Learning Objective 2: Applying the appropriate accounting method for a 20% investment)*** Evaa Financial paid €550,000 for a 20% investment in the ordinary shares of Wally, Inc. For the first year, Wally reported net income of €240,000 and at year-end declared and paid cash dividends of €100,000. On the Balance-Sheet date, the market value of Eva's investment in Wally shares was €420,000. LO 2

Requirements

1. Which method is appropriate for Eva Financial to use in its accounting for its investment in Wally? Why?
2. Show everything that Eva would report for the investment and any investment revenue in its year-end financial statements.

■ spreadsheet

E8-30B. ***(Learning Objective 3: Preparing a consolidated Balance Sheet)*** Gamma, Inc., owns Hamlet Corp. These two companies' individual Balance Sheets follow:

	A	B	C	D	E
1	**Gamma, Inc. Consolidation Worksheet**	**Gamma, Inc.**	**Hamlet Corp.**	**Elimination Debit**	**Credit**
2	**Assets**				
3	Cash	€ 50,000	€ 19,000		
4	Accounts receivable, net	79,000	54,000		
5	Note receivable from Gamma	—	43,000		
6	Inventory	55,000	78,000		
7	Investment in Hamlet	93,000	—		
8	PPE, net	284,000	90,000		
9	Other assets	24,000	5,000		
10	Total	€ 585,000	€ 289,000		
11					
12	**Liabilities and Shareholders' Equity**				
13	Accounts payable	€ 48,000	€ 27,000		
14	Notes payable	154,000	31,000		
15	Other liabilities	80,000	138,000		
16	Share capital	111,000	78,000		
17	Retained earnings	192,000	15,000		
18	Total	€ 585,000	€ 289,000		
19					

Requirements

1. Prepare a consolidated Balance Sheet of Gamma, Inc., using the above consolidation worksheet.
2. What is the amount of shareholders' equity for the consolidated entity?

■ **writing assignment**

E8-31B. ***(Learning Objective 4: Managing and accounting for foreign currency transactions)*** Assume that Tech Know Stores completed the following foreign currency transactions:

Jul 17	Purchased DVD players as inventory on account from Toshikar, a Japanese company. The price was ¥700,000, and the exchange rate of the yen was $0.0086.
Aug 16	Paid Toshikar when the exchange rate was $0.0080.
19	Sold merchandise on account to Magnificent, a French company, at a price of €20,000. The exchange rate was $1.20.
30	Collected from Magnificent when the exchange rate was $1.12.

Requirements

1. Journalize these transactions for Tech Know. Focus on the gains and losses caused by changes in foreign currency rates. (Round your answers to the nearest whole dollar.)
2. On July 18, immediately after the purchase, and on August 20, immediately after the sale, which currencies did Tech Know want to strengthen? Which currencies did in fact strengthen? Explain your reasoning.

E8-32B. ***(Learning Objective 4: Translating a foreign currency Balance Sheet into dollars)*** Translate into dollars the Balance Sheet of Maine Leather Goods' Spanish subsidiary. When Maine Leather Goods acquired the foreign subsidiary, a euro was worth €1.08. The current exchange rate is €1.30. During the period when retained earnings were earned, the average exchange rate was €1.18 per euro.

LO 4
■ spreadsheet

	Euros
Assets	700,000
Liabilities	500,000
Shareholders' equity:	
Share capital	65,000
Retained earnings	135,000
	700,000

During the period covered by this situation, which currency was stronger, the dollar or the euro?

E8-33B. ***(Learning Objective 6: Preparing and using the statement of cash flows)*** During fiscal year 20X5, Glazed Doughnuts reported net loss of €131.3 million. Glazed received €1.8 million from the sale of other businesses. Glazed made capital expenditures of €10.7 million and sold property, plant and equipment for €7.1 million. The company purchased long-term investments at a cost of €11.9 million and sold other long-term investments for €2.2 million.

Requirement

1. Prepare the investing activities section of Glazed Doughnuts' statement of cash flows. Based solely on Glazed Doughnuts' investing activities, does it appear that the company is growing or shrinking? How can you tell?

E8-34B. ***(Learning Objective 5: Using the statement of cash flows)*** At the end of the year, Elite Properties' statement of cash flows reported the following investment activities:

A1

	A	B
1	**Elite Properties** **Consolidated Statement of Cash Flows (Partial)**	
2	Cash flows from Investing Activities:	
3	Notes receivable collected	€ 3,112,000
4	Purchases of short-term investments	(3,454,000)
5	Proceeds from sales of equipment	1,540,000*
6	Proceeds from sales of investments (cost of €490,000)	499,000
7	Expenditures for property and equipment	(1,735,000)
8	Net used for investing activities	€ (38,000)
9		

*Cost €5,200,000; Accumulated depreciation, €3,660,000.

Requirement

1. For each item listed, make the journal entry that placed the item on Elite's statement of cash flows.

Challenge Exercises

E8-35. ***(Learning Objectives 1, 2, 3, 4: Accounting for various types of investments)*** Suppose Heyya owns the following investments at December 31, 20X6:

a. 100% of the ordinary shares of Heyya United Kingdom, which holds assets of £1,500,000 and owes a total of £1,300,000. At December 31, 20X6, the current exchange rate of the pound (£) is £1 = $2.01. The translation rate of the pound applicable to shareholders' equity is £1 = $1.64. During 20X6, Heyya United Kingdom earned net income of £130,000, and the average exchange rate for the year was £1 = $1.92. Heyya United Kingdom paid cash dividends of £30,000 during 20X6.

b. Investments that Heyya is holding to sell. These investments cost $1,600,000 and declined in value by $350,000 during 20X6, but they paid cash dividends of $25,000 to Heyya. One year ago, at December 31, 20X5, the market value of these investments was $1,600,000.

c. 45% of the ordinary shares of Heyya Financing Associates. During 20X6, Heyya Financing earned net income of $500,000 and declared and paid cash dividends of $25,000. The carrying amount of this investment was $500,000 at December 31, 20X5.

Requirements

1. Which method is used to account for each investment?
2. By how much did each of these investments increase or decrease Heyya's net income during 20X6?
3. For investments **b** and **c**, show how Heyya would report these investments on its Balance Sheet at December 31, 20X6.

E8-36. ***(Learning Objectives 1, 4: Explaining and analyzing other comprehensive income)*** Fashion Retail Corporation reported shareholders' equity on its Balance Sheet at December 31, as follows:

	A	B
1	**Fashion Retail Balance Sheet (Partial)**	
2	Shareholders' Equity:	
3	Ordinary shares, $1.00 par value—	
4	600 million shares authorized,	
5	200 shares issued	$ 200
6	Additional paid-in capital	1,100
7	Retained earnings	6,530
8	Accumulated other comprehensive (loss)	(?)
9	Less: Treasury shares, at cost	(80)
10		

Requirements

1. Identify the two components that typically make up other comprehensive income.
2. For each component of accumulated other comprehensive income, describe an example that can cause a *positive* figure and another example that can cause a *negative* figure.

Quiz

Test your understanding of long-term investments and international operations by answering the following questions. Select the best choice from among the possible answers given.

Questions 37–39 use the following data:
Assume that Global Networks owns the following long-term available-for-sale investments:

Company	Number of Shares	Cost per Share	Current Market Value per Share	Dividend per Share
ABC Corp.	1,200	$61	$75	$2.10
Good Food, Inc.	150	12	13	1.40
Lesley Ltd.	700	23	27	0.80

Q8-37. Global's Balance Sheet should report
a. investments of $110,850.
b. unrealized loss of $19,750.
c. investments of $91,100.
d. dividend revenue of $3,290.

Q8-38. Global's Income Statement should report
a. gain on sale of investment of $19,900.
b. unrealized gain of $19,900.
c. dividend revenue of $3,290.
d. investments of $89,050.

Q8-39. Suppose Global sells the ABC shares for $74 per share. Journalize the sale.

Q8-40. Dividends received on an equity-method investment
a. increase the investment account.
b. increase dividend revenue.
c. decrease the investment account.
d. increase owners' equity.

Q8-41. The starting point in accounting for all investments is
a. equity value.
b. cost.
c. market value on the Balance-Sheet date.
d. cost minus dividends.

Q8-42. Consolidation accounting
a. combines the accounts of the parent company and those of the subsidiary companies.
b. eliminates all liabilities.
c. reports the receivables and payables of the parent company only.
d. all of the above.

Q8-43. On January 1, 20X0, Maxspace, Inc., purchased $100,000 face value of the 5% bonds of Mail Frontier, Inc., at 107. The bonds mature on January 1, 20X5. For the year ended December 31, 20X5, Maxspace received cash interest of
a. $2,000.
b. $3,000.
c. $4,000.
d. $5,000.

Q8-44. Return to Maxspace, Inc.'s bond investment in the preceding question. For the year ended December 31, 20X3, Maxspace received cash interest of $5,000. What was the interest revenue that Maxspace earned in this period?
a. $5,000
b. $3,600
c. $7,000
d. $2,000

Q8-45. Providence Systems purchased inventory on account from Megasonic. The price was ¥80,000, and a yen was quoted at $0.0088. Providence paid the debt in yen a month later, when the price of a yen was $0.0093. Providence
a. debited Inventory for $744.
b. recorded a Foreign Currency Transaction Gain of $40.
c. debited Inventory for $704.
d. none of the above.

Q8-46. One way to prevent a foreign currency transaction loss is to
- **a.** offset foreign currency inventory and PPE.
- **b.** pay debts as late as possible.
- **c.** pay in the foreign currency.
- **d.** collect in your currency.

Q8-47. Foreign currency transaction gains and losses are reported on the
- **a.** consolidation worksheet.
- **b.** Income Statement.
- **c.** statement of cash flows.
- **d.** Balance Sheet.

Q8-48. Consolidation of a foreign subsidiary usually results in a
- **a.** gain or loss on consolidation.
- **b.** foreign currency translation adjustment.
- **c.** foreign currency transaction gain or loss.
- **d.** LIFO/FIFO difference.

Problems MyLab Accounting

Select A and B problems can be found within MyLab Accounting, an online homework and practice environment. Your instructor may ask you to complete select problems using MyLab Accounting.

Group A

LO 1

P8-49A. ***(Learning Objective 1: Accounting for a bond investment purchased at a premium)*** Insurance companies and pension plans hold large quantities of bond investments. Secure Insurance Corp. purchased $2,200,000 of 4.0% bonds of Sheehan, Inc., for 112 on January 1, 20X0. These bonds pay interest on January 1 and July 1 each year. They mature on January 1, 20X4. At October 31, 20X0, the market price of the bonds is 108.

Requirements

1. Journalize Secure's purchase of the bonds as a long-term investment on January 1, 20X0 (to be held to maturity), receipt of cash interest, and amortization of the bond investment at July 1, 20X0. The straight-line method is appropriate for amortizing the bond investment.
2. Show all financial statement effects of this long-term bond investment on Secure Insurance Corp.'s Balance Sheet and Income Statement at October 31, 20X0.

LO 1 2

P8-50A. ***(Learning Objectives 1, 2: Reporting investments on the Balance Sheet and the related revenue on the Income Statement)*** Montana Exchange Company completed the following long-term investment transactions during 20X6:

20X6	
May 12	Purchased 20,000 shares, which make up 30% of the ordinary shares of Woburn Corporation at total cost of $380,000.
Jul 9	Received annual cash dividend of $1.28 per share on the Woburn investment.
Sep 16	Purchased 900 shares of Columbus, Inc., ordinary shares as an available-for-sale investment, paying $40.00 per share.
Oct 30	Received cash dividend of $0.38 per share on the Columbus investment.
Dec 31	Received annual report from Woburn Corporation. Net income for the year was $580,000.

At year-end the fair market value of Columbus shares is $30,000. The fair market value of the Woburn shares is $658,000.

Requirements

1. For which investment is fair market value used in the accounting? Why is fair market value used for one investment and not the other?
2. Show what Montana would report on its year-end Balance Sheet and Income Statement for these investment transactions. It is helpful to use a T-account for the Long-Term Investment in Woburn account. Ignore income tax.

P8-51A. ***(Learning Objectives 1, 2: Accounting for available-for-sale and equity-method investments)*** The beginning Balance Sheet of Noram Corporation included the following:

Long-Term Investment in Rockaway Software (equity-method investment)	$612,000

Noram completed the following investment transactions during the year:

Mar 16	Purchased 1,400 shares of Canton, Inc., as a long-term available-for-sale investment, paying $14.00 per share.
May 21	Received cash dividend of $1.85 per share on the Canton investment.
Aug 17	Received cash dividend of $86,000 from Rockaway Software.
Dec 31	Received annual reports from Rockaway Software; net income for the year was $520,000. Of this amount Noram's proportion is 20%.

At year-end, the fair market values of Noram's investments are as follows: Canton, $26,600; Rockaway, $698,000.

Requirements

1. Record the transactions in the journal of Noram Corporation.
2. Post entries to the T-account for Long-Term Investment in Rockaway and determine its balance at December 31.
3. Show how to report the Long-Term Available-for-Sale Investments and the Long-Term Investment in Rockaway accounts on Noram's Balance Sheet at December 31.

P8-52A. ***(Learning Objective 3: Analyzing consolidated financial statements)*** This problem demonstrates the dramatic effect that consolidation accounting can have on a company's ratios. Fixed Motor Company (Fixed) owns 100% of Fixed Motor Credit Corporation (FMCC), its financing subsidiary. Fixed's main operations consist of manufacturing automotive products. FMCC mainly helps people finance the purchase of automobiles from Fixed and its dealers. The two companies' individual Balance Sheets are adapted and summarized as follows (amounts in billions): LO 3

	Fixed (Parent)	FMCC (Subsidiary)
Total assets	$89.7	$170.7
Total liabilities	$65.1	$156.6
Total shareholders' equity	24.6	14.1
Total liabilities and equity	$89.7	$170.7

Assume that FMCC's liabilities include $2.3 billion owed to Fixed, the parent company.

Requirements

1. Compute the debt ratio of Fixed Motor Company considered alone.
2. Determine the consolidated total assets, total liabilities, and shareholders' equity of Fixed Motor Company after consolidating the financial statements of FMCC into the totals of Fixed, the parent company.
3. Recompute the debt ratio of the consolidated entity. Why do companies prefer not to consolidate their financing subsidiaries into their own financial statements?

■ spreadsheet

P8-53A. ***(Learning Objective 3: Consolidating a wholly owned subsidiary)*** Assume Rose, Inc., paid $453,000 to acquire all the share capital of Mountain Corporation, and Mountain owes Rose $175,000 on a note payable. Immediately after the purchase on September 30, 20X6, the two companies' Balance Sheets follow.

	Rose	Mountain
Assets		
Cash	$ 60,000	$ 59,000
Accounts receivable, net	194,000	86,000
Note receivable from Mountain	175,000	—
Inventory	305,000	458,000
Investment in Mountain	453,000	—
PPE, net	403,000	524,000
Total	$1,590,000	$1,127,000
Liabilities and Shareholders' Equity		
Accounts payable	$ 122,000	$ 67,000
Notes payable	410,000	312,000
Other liabilities	216,000	295,000
Share capital	556,000	268,000
Retained earnings	286,000	185,000
Total	$1,590,000	$1,127,000

Requirement

1. Prepare the worksheet for the consolidated Balance Sheet of Rose, Inc.

P8-54A. ***(Learning Objective 4: Recording foreign currency transactions and reporting the transaction gain or loss)*** Suppose Sapphire Corporation completed the following international transactions:

May 1	Sold inventory on account to Fiat, the Italian automaker, for €65,000. The exchange rate of the euro was $1.30, and Fiat demands to pay in euros.
10	Purchased supplies on account from a Canadian company at a price of Canadian $59,000. The exchange rate of the Canadian dollar was $0.78, and the payment will be in Canadian dollars.
17	Sold inventory on account to an English firm for 134,000 British pounds. Payment will be in pounds, and the exchange rate of the pound was $1.98.
22	Collected from Fiat. The exchange rate is €1 = $1.34.
Jun 18	Paid the Canadian company. The exchange rate of the Canadian dollar is $0.76.
24	Collected from the English firm. The exchange rate of the British pound was $1.93.

Requirements

1. Record these transactions in Sapphire's journal and show how to report the transaction gain or loss on the Income Statement.
2. How will what you learned in this problem help you structure international transactions?

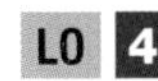

P8-55A. ***(Learning Objective 4: Measuring and explaining the foreign currency translation adjustment)*** Assume that Folgate has a subsidiary company based in Japan.

Requirements

1. Translate into dollars the foreign currency Balance Sheet of the Japanese subsidiary of Folgate.

	Yen
Assets	480,000,000
Liabilities	115,000,000
Shareholders' equity:	
Share capital	40,000,000
Retained earnings	325,000,000
	480,000,000

When Folgate acquired this subsidiary, the Japanese yen was worth $0.0095. The current exchange rate is $0.0120. During the period when the subsidiary earned its income, the average exchange rate was $0.0110 per yen. Before you perform the foreign currency translation calculations, indicate whether Folgate has experienced a positive or a negative translation adjustment. State whether the adjustment is a gain or a loss, and show where it is reported in the financial statements.

2. In which company's financial statements will the translation adjustment be reported?

Group B

P8-56B. ***(Learning Objective 1: Accounting for a bond investment purchased at a premium)*** Insurance companies and pension plans hold large quantities of bond investments. Sound Insurance Corp. purchased €2,800,000 of 9.0% bonds of Sherman, Inc., for 116 on January 1, 20X0. These bonds pay interest on January 1 and July 1 each year. They mature on January 1, 20X4. At October 31, 20X0, the market price of the bonds is 104.

Requirements

1. Journalize Sound's purchase of the bonds as a long-term investment on January 1, 20X0 (to be held to maturity), receipt of cash interest, and amortization of the bond investment at July 1, 20X0. The straight-line method is appropriate for amortizing the bond investment.
2. Show all financial statement effects of this long-term bond investment on Sound Insurance Corp.'s Balance Sheet and Income Statement at October 31, 20X0.

P8-57B. ***(Learning Objectives 1, 2: Reporting investments on the Balance Sheet and the related revenue on the Income Statement)*** Helsinki Exchange Company completed the following long-term investment transactions during 20X6:

20X6	
May 12	Purchased 16,500 shares, which make up 40% of the ordinary shares of Brentwood Corporation at total cost of €330,000.
Jul 9	Received annual cash dividend of €1.22 per share on the Brentwood investment.
Sep 16	Purchased 900 shares of Bangkok, Inc., ordinary shares as an available-for-sale investment, paying €43.00 per share.
Oct 30	Received cash dividend of €0.32 per share on the Bangkok investment.
Dec 31	Received annual report from Brentwood Corporation. Net income for the year was €530,000.

At year-end the fair market value of the Bangkok shares is €30,300. The fair market value of the Brentwood shares is €655,000.

Requirements

1. For which investment is fair market value used in the accounting? Why is fair market value used for one investment and not the other?
2. Show what Helsinki would report on its year-end Balance Sheet and Income Statement for these investment transactions. It is helpful to use a T-account for the Long-Term Investment in Brentwood account. Ignore income tax.

P8-58B. ***(Learning Objectives 1, 2: Accounting for available-for-sale and equity-method investments)*** The beginning Balance Sheet of Segui Corporation included the following:

Long-Term Investment in NEW Software (equity-method investment)	€616,000

Segui completed the following investment transactions during the year:

Mar 16	Purchased 1,500 shares of Hubbardston, Inc., ordinary shares as a long-term available-for-sale investment, paying €12.75 per share.
May 21	Received cash dividend of €1.60 per share on the Hubbardston investment.
Aug 17	Received cash dividend of €85,000 from NEW Software.
Dec 31	Received annual reports from NEW Software; net income for the year was €500,000. Of this amount Segui's proportion is 25%.

At year-end, the fair market values of Segui's investments are as follows: Hubbardston, €26,100; NEW, €701,000.

Requirements

1. Record the transactions in the journal of Segui Corporation.
2. Post entries to the T-account for Long-Term Investment in NEW and determine its balance at December 31.
3. Show how to report the Long-Term Available-for-Sale Investments and the Long-Term Investment in NEW accounts on Segui's Balance Sheet at December 31.

P8-59B. ***(Learning Objective 3: Analyzing consolidated financial statements)*** This problem demonstrates the dramatic effect that consolidation accounting can have on a company's ratios. Space Motor Company (Space) owns 100% of Space Motor Credit Corporation (SMCC), its financing subsidiary. Space's main operations consist of manufacturing automotive products. SMCC mainly helps people finance the purchase of automobiles from Space and its dealers. The two companies' individual Balance Sheets are adapted and summarized as follows (amounts in billions):

	Space (Parent)	SMCC (Subsidiary)
Total assets	€89.5	€170.8
Total liabilities	€65.7	€156.1
Total shareholder's equity	23.8	14.7
Total liabilities and equity	€89.5	€170.8

Assume that SMCC's liabilities include €2.8 billion owed to Space, the parent company.

Requirements

1. Compute the debt ratio of Space Motor Company considered alone.
2. Determine the consolidated total assets, total liabilities, and shareholders' equity of Space Motor Company after consolidating the financial statements of SMCC into the totals of Space, the parent company.
3. Recompute the debt ratio of the consolidated entity. Why do companies prefer not to consolidate their financing subsidiaries into their own financial statements?

P8-60B. ***(Learning Objective 3: Consolidating a wholly owned subsidiary)*** Assume Ronny, Inc., paid €346,000 to acquire all the share capital of Dinette Corporation, and Dinette owes Ronny €192,000 on a note payable. Immediately after the purchase on September 30, 2010, the two companies' Balance Sheets follow.

	Ronny	Dinette
Assets		
Cash	€ 54,000	€ 52,000
Accounts receivable, net	195,000	89,000
Note receivable from Dinette	192,000	—
Inventory	278,000	452,000
Investment in Dinette	346,000	—
PPE, net	397,000	457,000
Total	€1,462,000	€1,050,000
Liabilities and Shareholders' Equity		
Accounts payable	€ 127,000	€ 79,000
Notes payable	399,000	329,000
Other liabilities	249,000	296,000
Share capital	577,000	259,000
Retained earnings	110,000	87,000
Total	€1,462,000	€1,050,000

Requirement

1. Prepare the worksheet for the consolidated Balance Sheet of Ronny, Inc.

P8-61B. ***(Learning Objective 4: Recording foreign currency transactions and reporting the transaction gain or loss)*** Suppose Chamomile Corporation completed the following international transactions:

May 1	Sold inventory on account to Palermo, the Italian automaker, for €60,000. The exchange rate of the euro was $1.37, and Palermo demands to pay in euros.
10	Purchased supplies on account from a Canadian company at a price of Canadian $57,000. The exchange rate of the Canadian dollar was $0.77, and the payment will be in Canadian dollars.
17	Sold inventory on account to an English firm for 148,000 British pounds. Payment will be in pounds, and the exchange rate of the pound was $1.95.
22	Collected from Palermo. The exchange rate is €1 = $1.42.
Jun 18	Paid the Canadian company. The exchange rate of the Canadian dollar is $0.75.
24	Collected from the English firm. The exchange rate of the British pound was $1.91.

Requirements

1. Record these transactions in Chamomile's journal and show how to report the transaction gain or loss on the Income Statement.
2. How will what you learned in this problem help you structure international transactions?

P8-62B. ***(Learning Objective 4: Measuring and explaining the foreign currency translation adjustment)*** Assume that Mason has a subsidiary company based in Japan.

Requirements

1. Translate into dollars the foreign currency Balance Sheet of the Japanese subsidiary of Mason.

	Yen
Assets	410,000,000
Liabilities	100,000,000
Shareholders' equity:	
Share capital	18,000,000
Retained earnings	292,000,000
	410,000,000

When Mason acquired this subsidiary, the Japanese yen was worth €0.0075. The current exchange rate is €0.0100. During the period when the subsidiary earned its income, the average exchange rate was €0.0095 per yen. Before you perform the foreign currency translation calculations, indicate whether Mason has experienced a positive or a negative translation adjustment. State whether the adjustment is a gain or a loss, and show where it is reported in the financial statements.

2. In which company's financial statements will the translation adjustment be reported?

APPLY YOUR KNOWLEDGE

Decision Cases

Case 1. ***(Learning Objectives 1, 5: Making an investment decision)*** Infografix Corporation's consolidated sales for 20X6 were $27.6 billion, and expenses totaled $25.4 billion. Infografix operates worldwide and conducts 38% of its business outside Taiwan, its country of incorporation. During 20X6, Infografix reported the following items in its financial statements (amounts in millions):

Foreign currency translation adjustments	$(202)
Unrealized holding —— on available-for-sale investments	(328)

As you consider an investment in Infografix shares, some concerns arise. Answer each of the following questions:

1. What do the parentheses around the two dollar amounts signify?
2. Are these items reported as assets, liabilities, shareholders' equity, revenues, or expenses? Are they normal-balance accounts, or are they contra accounts?
3. Did Infografix include these items in net income? In retained earnings? In the final analysis, how much net income did Infografix report for 20X6?
4. Should these items scare you away from investing in Infografix shares? Why or why not? (Challenge)

LO 1 2 4

Case 2. ***(Learning Objectives 1, 2, 4: Making an investment sale decision)*** Cathy Talbert is the general manager of Barham Company, which provides data-management services for physicians in the United Arab Emirates area. Barham Company uses USD as its functional currency and accounts for its business transactions in USD. Barham is having a rough year. Net income trails projections for the year by almost $85,000. This shortfall is especially important. Barham plans to issue shares early next year and needs to show investors that the company can meet its earnings targets.

Barham holds several investments purchased a few years ago. Even though investing in shares is outside Barham's core business of data-management services, Talbert thinks these investments may hold the key to helping the company meet its net income goal for the year. She is considering what to do with the following investments:

1. Barham owns 50% of the ordinary shares of Jafar Office Systems, which provides the business forms that Barham uses. Jafar Office Systems has lost money for the past two years but still has a retained earnings balance of $560,000. Talbert thinks she can get Jafar's treasurer to declare a $140,000 cash dividend, half of which would go to Barham.
2. Barham owns a bond investment purchased eight years ago for $270,000. The purchase price represents a discount from the bonds' maturity value of $420,000. These bonds mature two years from now, and their current market value is $400,000. Ms Talbert has checked with a Citibank investment representative, and Talbert is considering selling the bonds. Citibank would charge a 1% commission on the sale transaction.
3. Barham owns 6,000 SABIC's shares valued at $53 per share. One year ago, SABIC's share was worth only $27 per share. Barham purchased the shares for $38 per share. Talbert wonders whether Barham should sell the shares.

Requirement

1. Evaluate all three actions as a way for Barham Company to generate the needed amount of income. Recommend the best way for Barham to achieve its net income goal.

Ethical Issue

Media One owns 18% of the voting shares of Web Talk, Inc. The remainder of the Web Talk shares are held by numerous investors with small holdings. Austin Cohen, president of Media One and a member of Web Talk's board of directors, heavily influences Web Talk's policies.

Under the market value method of accounting for investments, Media One's net income increases as it receives dividend revenue from Web Talk. Media One pays President Cohen a bonus computed as a percentage of Media One's net income. Therefore, Cohen can control his personal bonus to a certain extent by influencing Web Talk's dividends.

A recession occurs in 20X6, and Media One's income is low. Cohen uses his power to have Web Talk pay a large cash dividend. The action requires Web Talk to borrow in order to pay the dividend.

Requirements

1. What are the ethical issues in the Media One case?
2. Who are the stakeholders? What are the possible consequences to each?
3. What are the alternatives for Austin Cohen to consider? Analyze each alternative from the following standpoints: (a) economic, (b) legal, (c) ethical.
4. If you were Cohen, what would you do?
5. Discuss how using the equity method of accounting for investment would decrease Cohen's potential for manipulating his bonus.

Focus on Financials: | Nestlé

This case spans all 12 chapters and is based on the consolidated financial statements of Nestlé. As you work with Nestlé throughout this course, you will develop the confidence and ability to use the financial statements of other companies as well. Refer to Nestlé's consolidated financial statements in Appendix A. If you wish, you can obtain the full annual report from www.nestle.com/investors. You may find the information overwhelming for now, but try to spot the key principles that we have discussed in this chapter. It will get progressively easier as you gain familiarity with the elements of the financial statements.

Requirements

1. How does Nestlé account for its available-for-sale investments? Does it adjust for periodic changes in fair market value of these investments? If so, where do these adjustments appear?

2. Examine Note 12 – Financial Assets and Liabilities. Under liquid assets and non-current assets, Nestlé reports six different classes of assets and lists all of them. Cash at bank and in hand is reported entirely at amortized cost, while commercial paper is reported entirely as an available-for-sale asset. Suggest why that might be the case for Nestlé.
3. What indicates that Nestlé owns foreign subsidiaries? Identify the item that proves your point and the financial statement on which the item appears.
4. Which currency, the Swiss Franc or the currency of foreign countries in which Nestlé did business, was stronger in each fiscal years 2016 and 2015? Give the evidence to support each answer.
5. At December 31, 2016, did Nestlé have a cumulative net gain or a cumulative net loss from translating its foreign subsidiaries' financial statements into dollars? How can you tell?
6. What do you understand by the "equity method?" Under what circumstances would we use it? How much income did Nestlé recognize in 2016 from its associated companies? Assume that Nestlé received CHF 472 million of dividend income and recognized CHF 807 million of income from its holdings of associates. Show the journal entry for recording income from associates. Journalize this transaction from the point of view of the Group.

Group Project

You are a group of investors with $10 million in available funds. You are choosing to make investments in a number of companies.

Requirements

1. Select three entities that you think are appropriate to invest in, as a trading security investment, as an available-for-sale investment, and as a held-to-maturity investment. Briefly explain why you think the companies you selected could be suitable investments.
2. Track the share or bond prices for these three companies for a period specified by your instructor. Over the specified period, keep a daily record of the price of the share to see how well your investment has performed. End the period of your analysis with a month end, such as September 30 or December 31.
3. Journalize all transactions that you have experienced, including the initial purchase, any dividends or interest received, and any year-end adjustment required by the accounting method that is appropriate for your investment.
4. At the end of the period, you will need to report on your selected investments to your own investors. Show what you will report them on your company's Balance Sheet, Income Statement, and statement of cash flows as a result of your investment transactions.

Quick Check Answers

1. *b*
2. *b* (1,600 shares × $28 = $44,800)
3. *d* (unrealized gain less 20% tax, $4,800 – 20% of $4,800 = $3,840)
4. *c* ($45,000 – $40,000 = $5,000)
5. *d* [$200,000 + 0.30 ($50,000 – $20,000) = $209,000]
6. *c* {$240,000 + 0.70 [$64,000 + (0.70 × $56,000)] = $312,240}
7. *b*
8. *a*
9. *d* ($1,800,000 Canadian × 2.5 = $4,500,000)
10. *b*

MyLab Accounting

For online homework, exercises, and problems that provide you with immediate feedback, please visit www.myaccountinglab.com.

9 Liabilities

SPOTLIGHT | Jardine Matheson Holdings Ltd.

www.jardines.com

Jardine Matheson (hereafter "Jardine") may not be a household name, but it is a large diversified conglomerate based in Hong Kong, having been founded in China in 1832. It employs over 440,000 people across varied business interests from motor vehicle and transportation, financial services and insurance, to hotels and restaurants, and even mining and agribusiness. Its subsidiaries include Hong Kong Land, Dairy Farm, Mandarin Oriental, Cycle & Carriage, and Astra International. ●

INTERFOTO/Alamy Stock Photo

In financial year 2015, Jardine made a net profit of $3,982 million. To be able to do this, Jardine required a significant amount of resources, from cash, receivables, and inventory to property, plant and equipment and other assets totaling $66,955 million. These resources are, in turn, funded by shareholders and creditors of Jardine. Shareholders' equity amounted to $45,781 million, and creditors provided liabilities totaling $21,174 million. Most of the liabilities are due within the next financial year, totaling $12,602 million and the rest, $8,572 million, are non-current. Let's see how the various types of liabilities play a role in Jardine's ability to offer goods and services to its customers around the world.

	A	B	C
1	**Jardine Matheson Holdings Ltd. Consolidated Balance Sheet**	**As at December 31**	
2	**(Adapted, in millions of US$)**	**2015**	**2014**
3			
4	Total assets	$ 66,955	$ 66,457
5	Current creditors	8,261	8,244
6	Current borrowings	3,991	4,068
7	Current tax liabilities	266	300
8	Current provisions	84	77
9	Total current liabilities	$ 12,602	$ 12,689
10	Long-term borrowings	6,995	7,416
11	Non-current creditors	430	364
12	Non-current provisions	145	138
13	Pension Liabilities	416	350
14	Other non-current liabilities	586	695
15	Total non-current liabilities	8,572	8,963
16	Total liabilities	21,174	21,652
17	Shareholders' equity	45,781	44,805
18	Total liabilities and shareholders' equity	$ 66,955	$ 66,457
19			

This chapter shows how to account for liabilities—both current and long-term. We begin with a refresher on liabilities and then proceed with our discussions on current liabilities.

LEARNING OBJECTIVES

1. **Understand** the various types of liabilities
2. **Account** for contingent liabilities
3. **Account** for bonds
4. **Account** for leases
5. **Analyze** the advantages and disadvantages of borrowing
6. **Evaluate** a company's debt-paying ability

UNDERSTAND THE VARIOUS TYPES OF LIABILITIES

1 **Understand** the various types of liabilities

You have seen many examples of liability accounts, but let's first recall what a liability is. The *Conceptual Framework* defines liability as a present obligation which will be settled through an outflow of resources embodying economic benefits. Liabilities are recognized on the Balance Sheet when it is probable that such an outflow will occur and the amount of which can be measured reliably. The general principle is for short-term liability to be expressed in nominal amounts and for long-term liability to be expressed in present values, taking into account the time value of money.

Liabilities are classified into current (short-term) and non-current (long-term). Current liabilities are obligations due within one year or within a company's normal operating cycle (see Chapter 4). Obligations due beyond that period of time are classified as non-current or long-term liabilities.

Lines 5 to 8 are Jardine's current liabilities (total at line 9, $12,602 million), and lines 10 to 14 are its non-current liabilities (total at line 15, $8,572 million). Notice that there are many similar account names in both sections, only differentiated with current versus non-current descriptions. For example, there are current and long-term borrowings, and current and long-term provisions. We will discuss liabilities by their most common headings, but remember they can be classified as either current or non-current depending on the timing of expected outflow of economic resources.

Note that Jardine has chosen to label line 5 as "current creditors." Other entities may decide to use different account names and different ways of aggregating its liabilities. For example, some may group "trade" and "other payables" together while others may list them in two separate lines. Let's continue to use Jardine's examples of current creditors in our discussion, and we will add on other types of liabilities you may see disclosed by other companies. Jardine's notes to the accounts provided the following additional information about its trade and other payable balances. We have summarized the list to include only the items we will discuss in this chapter.

ADAPTED EXCERPTS FROM JARDINE MATHESON'S NOTES TO THE ACCOUNTS

Creditors (in $ millions)	**2015**	**2014**
■ Trade creditors	$4,177	$4,171
■ Accruals	1,586	1,626
■ Rental and other refundable deposits	392	420
■ Proceeds from properties sale received in advance	892	697
■ Rental income received in advance	20	26
■ Other income received in advance	204	214
■ All other creditors (summarized)	1,420	1,454
Total	$8,691	$8,608
Current	8,261	8,244
Non-current	430	364
Total	**$8,691**	**$8,608**

Source: Jardine Matheson's 2015 annual report, page 107

Accounts Payable. Amounts owed for products or services purchased on account are called accounts payable or trade payables or trade creditors. You have seen examples of accounts payable in preceding chapters. They are typically short-term, as credit terms are usually between 30 and 90 days. One of a merchandiser's most common transactions is the purchase of inventory, usually on credit. All businesses make the majority of their purchases on account, typically for raw materials, supplies, and inventory, as well as for various services. For example, as you can see from its Balance Sheet, Jardine's trade creditors amounted to $4,177 million on December 31, 2015.

Accrued Liabilities (Accrued Expenses). An **accrued liability** usually results from an expense the business has incurred but not yet paid. Therefore, an **accrued expense** creates a liability, which explains why it is also called an accrued expense. Most accruals are short-term liabilities and will be shown as part of current liabilities. Jardine's accruals include wages and salary payable, and other accruals as relevant. You have seen wages and salary payable and other accruals, such as interest payable, earlier (in Chapter 3).

Deposits. There may be occasions when a business is required to pay a deposit for securing goods, property, or serviced such as power supplies and telephony services. The deposits are refundable once the service is no longer required or when the contract lapses. Obviously, this may go both ways. Jardine may place deposits to secure services from other businesses, and in turn, Jardine's customers may place deposits to secure Jardine's goods or services. The former is an asset and the latter is a liability. In this case, because the deposits are shown as an item of liability, this must be the amount placed by Jardine's customers. In fact, in its Debtors note, Jardine shows the exact same title "Rental and other refundable deposits" of $392 million at December 31, 2015.

Unearned Revenues. Unearned revenues are also called deferred revenues or revenues collected in advance. For all unearned revenue, the business has received cash from customers before earning the revenue. The company has a liability—an obligation to provide goods or services to the customer. Jardine has a number of items related to unearned revenue: proceeds from properties for sale received in advance, rental income received in advance, and other income received in advance, totaling $1,116 million on December 31, 2015. Unearned revenue is typically a current liability. Let's consider another example.

Thai Airways sells tickets and collects cash in advance. Thai Airways therefore reports Unearned Ticket Revenue for airline tickets sold in advance.

Let's consider another example that you may have experienced as an airline customer. You always pay in advance when you buy a ticket. To the airline, this is not an income (until you fly) and is recorded as unearned revenue for tickets sold in advance. Let's see how Thai Airways would account for unearned ticket revenue. Assume that Thai Airways collects $1,000 for a round-trip ticket from Bangkok (Thailand) to Madrid (Spain) and back. Thai Airways records the cash collection and related liability as follows:

	A	B	C	D
1	20X0			
2	Dec 15	Cash	1,000	
3		Unearned Ticket Revenue		1,000
4		*Received cash in advance for ticket sales.*		
5				

Unearned Ticket Revenue	
	1,000

Suppose the customer flies to Madrid late in December. Thai Airways records the revenue earned as follows:

	A	B	C	D
1				
2		Unearned Ticket Revenue	500	
3		Ticket Revenue ($1,000 × 1/2)		500
4		*Earned revenue that was collected in advance.*		
5				

The liability decreases and the revenue goes up.

Unearned Ticket Revenue	
500	1,000
	Bal. 500

Ticket Revenue	
	500

At the year-end, Thai Airways reports:

- $500 of unearned ticket revenue (a liability) on the Balance Sheet; and
- $500 of ticket revenue on the Income Statement.

The customer returns to Bangkok in January 20X1, and Thai Airways records the revenue earned with this journal entry:

	A	B	C	D
1	20X1			
2	Jan 4	Unearned Ticket Revenue	500	
3		Ticket Revenue ($1,000 × 1/2)		500
4		*Earned revenue that was collected in advance.*		
5				

Now the liability balance is zero because Thai Airways has earned all the revenue it collected in advance.

Unearned Ticket Revenue	
500	1,000
500	
	Bal. 0

Payroll-related Liabilities. Payroll, also called employee compensation, is a substantial expense for many companies. For service organizations—such as law firms, real estate companies, and airlines—employee compensation is the major expense, just as cost of goods sold is the largest expense for a merchandising company.

Employee compensation takes many different forms. A salary is employee pay stated at a monthly or yearly rate. A wage is employee pay stated at an hourly rate. Sales employees usually earn a commission, which is a percentage of the sales the employee has made. A bonus is an amount over and above regular compensation. In some jurisdictions, employee's income tax is deducted from employee's salaries as they are paid, or the employer may be required to pay some form of payroll tax. There may also be other kinds of deductions, such as employee's contribution to a provident or superannuation fund. Salary expense thus represents gross pay (that is, employee pay before subtractions for taxes and other deductions). Your instructor may give you additional information about your local payroll regulations. Accounting for all forms of compensation follows the general pattern illustrated in Exhibit 9-1 (using assumed figures). The entries depict payment to a staff member with a monthly salary of $5,000, employee's "pay as you earn" income tax of 20%, and an employer's contribution to superannuation of 10% on top of monthly salary.

Exhibit 9-1 | Accounting for Payroll Expenses and Liabilities

	A	B	C	D
1	20X1			
2	Dec 31	Salary Expense	5,500	
3		Cash (to tax office on behalf of employee)		1,000
4		Cash (to staff)		4,000
5		Cash (to superannuation fund)		500
6		*Salary payment to staff, tax office and fund*		
7				

In countries where businesses provide pension or other post-employment benefits, they must recognize such obligations on each Balance Sheet date and record such expenses for each period. Jardine, for example, has over $416 million of pension liabilities (line 13 on its Balance Sheet at the start of this chapter).

Broadly speaking, there are two basic schemes in relation to employees' post-retirement obligations: defined contributions and defined benefits. In defined contribution schemes, employers contribute a fixed amount of money to an employee's pension (also known as provident, or superannuation) funds. The employer's obligation ends once the contribution has been made. As members of the pension fund, the employees are able to use, invest, or withdraw the contribution accumulated, subject to the fund's rules and regulations.

In a defined benefit plan, the employee is promised some post-retirement benefits, usually referred to as **pensions**. Companies may also provide other post-retirement benefits, such as medical insurance for retired former employees. Because employees earn these benefits by their service, the company records pension and retirement-benefit expenses while employees work for the company.

Pensions are one of the most complex areas of accounting, and beyond the scope of this textbook. As employees earn their pensions and the company pays into the pension plan, the plan's assets grow. The obligation for future pension payments to employees also accumulates. At the end of each period, the company compares the following:

- the fair market value of the assets in the retirement plans—cash and investments
- the plans' accumulated benefit obligation, which is the present value of promised future payments to retirees

If the plan assets exceed the accumulated benefit obligation, the plan is said to be overfunded. In this case, the asset and obligation amounts are to be reported only in the notes to the financial statements. However, if the accumulated benefit obligation (the liability) exceeds plan assets, the plan is underfunded, and the company must report the excess liability amount as a long-term liability on the Balance Sheet.

The accounting for pension and other post-employment benefits requires a significant amount of detailed record keeping and estimates. They are termed "defined benefits plans" because you promise your employees post-employment benefits when they retire. Imagine how you would go about recording an obligation to pay a lifelong pension to a young 25-year-old employee who just started work for you today. You promise him that when he retires at, say, 65, you will pay 25% of his annual salary for life. You don't know exactly how long he will work for you, you don't know exactly what his salary will be when he retires, and you don't know exactly how long he will live after 65! *IAS 19—Employee Benefits* provides guidance on this topic, but it is an area that is clearly beyond an introductory financial accounting textbook.

Sales Tax Payable. Most countries have some form of consumption tax. This tax is usually called Goods and Services Tax (GST), Value-Added Tax (VAT), or simply sales tax. Retailers collect the tax from customers and thus owe the tax authority for sales tax collected. Let's consider IKEA, one of Jardine's subsidiaries. Suppose one Saturday's sales at an IKEA store totaled $200,000. IKEA collected an additional 5% ($10,000) of sales tax. The store would record that day's sales as follows:

A1

	A	B	C	D
1				
2		Cash ($200,000 × 1.05)	210,000	
3		Sales Revenue		200,000
4		Sales Tax Payable ($200,000 × 0.05)		10,000
5		*To record cash sales and the related sales tax.*		
6				

Assets, liabilities, and equity all increase—equity because of the sales.

Assets	=	Liabilities	+	Shareholders' Equity	
+ 210,000	=	+ 10,000	+	+ 200,000	(sales revenue)

When the sales tax payable is remitted to the tax authority, IKEA would perform the following entry. Note that there is no impact on revenue or equity.

	A	B	C	D
1				
2		Sales tax payable	10,000	
3		Cash		10,000
4		*To record payment of sales tax.*		
5				

Assets	=	Liabilities	+	Shareholders' Equity
− 10,000	=	− 10,000	+	0

Tax Payable. Business entities are expected to pay tax on their income. Taxation rules vary from one jurisdiction to another, and in most cases, taxable income may not equal net profit. For example, in Chapter 7 we described how a company may be able to use an accelerated depreciation method for tax purposes while using straight-line depreciation for financial reporting purposes. Ignoring such differences, tax payable can be calculated as the prevailing tax rates multiplied by the profit before tax of the business. For example, Jardine's profit before taxation was $4,591 million, and its tax expense was $609 million, about 13.3% of pre-tax income. Depending on the tax collection schedule, corporate tax may be paid in instalments during the year (or at different times in different tax jurisdictions) and finalized at the tax submission dateline. Jardine showed a current tax payable amount of $266 million on its Balance Sheet.

A Closer Look

Differences in taxable income and profit before tax are caused by differences between tax bases of assets and liabilities and their carrying amounts on the Balance Sheet. The tax base of an asset or liability is the amount attributed to the asset or liability for tax purposes, as opposed to its carrying amount on the Balance Sheet. These differences create deferred tax assets and deferred tax liabilities. If you are an accounting major, you are likely to be studying *IAS 12—Income Taxes* in your future courses.

Provisions. A business may know that a liability exists but not know its exact amount. The business must still report the liability on the Balance Sheet based on the best estimates possible on the reporting date. Estimated liabilities vary among businesses.

The following adapted excerpt shows that Jardine has provisions totaling $229 million on December 31, 2015, of which $84 is current and $145 is non-current. You can tally these totals to its Balance Sheet at the start of this chapter (lines 8 and 12).

ADAPTED EXCERPTS FROM JARDINE MATHESON'S NOTES TO THE ACCOUNTS

Provisions (in $ millions)	**2015 Current**	**2015 Non-current**	**2015 Total**
Motor vehicle warranties	39	-	39
Closure cost provisions	7	1	8
Reinstatement and restoration costs	5	40	45
Others	33	104	137
Total provisions	84	145	229

Source: Jardine Matheson's 2015 annual report, page 108

Provisions are covered under *IAS 37—Provisions, Contingent Assets and Contingent Liabilities*. They are defined as liabilities of uncertain timing and amount. In other words, they meet the definition of a liability. Sometimes you see businesses use the word "provision" to describe an allowance, for example "provision for bad debts" or "provision for inventory obsolescence." This is technically incorrect.

Many businesses, especially manufacturers, guarantee their products under some form of warranty agreement. The warranty period may extend from a short period (e.g., 30 days to 12 months warranty for consumer products) to multiple years for major assets (such as bridges, airplanes, and other infrastructure assets). For example, automobile companies—Peugeot Citroën, BMW, and Toyota—all make provisions for vehicle warranties.

Whatever the warranty's life, businesses need to recognize that they have an obligation to perform services or repairs should the need arise. This increase in liability results in a decrease in equity, and thus an expense (usually called warranty expense) is created and recognized in each reporting period. At the time of the sale, however, the company doesn't know which products are (or will be) defective. The exact amount of warranty expense cannot be known with certainty, so the business must estimate warranty expense and the related liability.

Assume that Black & Decker Corporation, which manufactures power tools, made sales of 100,000 power tools subject to product warranties in a financial year. Black and Decker has information based on product testing and historical experience that 1% of the power tools may require warranty service costing an average of $50 within the warranty period, and a further 0.25% may require warranty service costing an average of $100. Black and Decker could use the "probability-weighted expected value" in *IAS 37* to work out that it has a warranty obligation amounting to $75,000 (1% × 100,000 units × $50 + 0.25% × 100,000 units × $100). In this case, Black and Decker would recognize a warranty expense of $75,000 and make the following entry:

	A	B	C	D
1		Warranty Expense	75,000	
2		Provision for Warranty Repairs		75,000
3		*To accrue warranty expense.*		
4				

Provision for Warranty Repairs	
	75,000

Warranty Expense	
75,000	

If in the following year, Black and Decker actually spent $72,000 repairing these faulty products (assuming it took spare parts or replacement units from its inventory), it would then record the following:

	A	B	C	D
1		Provision for Warranty Repairs	72,000	
2		Inventory		72,000
3		*To replace defective products sold under warranty.*		
4				

Provision for Warranty Repairs

72,000		75,000
	Bal.	3,000

At the end of the year, Black and Decker will repeat the process. It starts by re-estimating the required amount of provision, compares it to the current level of provision, and the difference would be the warranty expense for the year. The Estimated Warranty Payable account probably won't ever zero out. And obviously in real life, product sales (and warranty repairs) often happen within the same period.

Notes Payable. Notes are a common form of borrowing in some parts of the world. Depending on the maturity or term of the note, you may have short-term notes (due within one year) or occasionally medium-term notes, usually up to two or three years but they can be longer as well. We will discuss long-term notes payable together with bonds in the next section.

For example, a business may issue **short-term notes payable** to borrow cash or to purchase assets. On its notes payable, the business must accrue interest expense and interest payable at the end of the period. The following sequence of entries covers the purchase of inventory, accrual of interest expense, and payment of a 10% short-term note payable that's due in one year.

	A	B	C	D
1	20X0			
2	Mar 1	Inventory	8,000	
3		Note Payable, Short-Term		8,000
4		*Purchase of inventory by issuing a note payable.*		
5				

This transaction increases both an asset and a liability.

Assets	=	Liabilities	+	Shareholders' Equity
+ 8,000	=	+ 8,000	+	0

At year-end, the business must accrue interest expense at 10% for March through December:

	A	B	C	D
1	Dec 31	Interest Expense ($8,000 × 0.10 × 9/12)	600	
2		Interest Payable		600
3		*Accrual of interest expense at year-end.*		
4				

Liabilities increase and equity decreases because of the expense.

Assets	=	Liabilities	+	Shareholders' Equity	
0	=	+ 600	+	− 600	(interest expense)

The Balance Sheet at year-end will report the Note Payable of $8,000 and the related Interest Payable of $600 as current liabilities. The Income Statement will report Interest Expense of $600.

The following entry records the note's payment at maturity on March 1, 20X1:

	A	B	C	D
1	20X1			
2	Mar 1	Note Payable, Short-Term	8,000	
3		Interest Payable	600	
4		Interest Expense ($8,000 × 0.10 × 3/12)	200	
5		Cash [$8,000 + ($8,000 × 0.10)]		8,800
6		*Payment of a note payable and interest at maturity.*		
7				

The debits zero out the payables and also record the business's interest expense for January, February, and March 20X1.

Debt. There are many forms of borrowing, from a simple term loan to a complex financing structure. Some long-term debt must be paid in installments. Some only require interest payments during the term of the loan, with payment of the loan amount at a specific time in the future. Whatever the case may be, the part of the loan that is due in the coming financial year is called **current portion of long-term debt** and is shown as a current liability. At the end of each year, an entity reclassifies (from long-term debt to a current liability) the amount of its long-term debt that must be paid the next year.

Jardine's Balance Sheet at the start of this chapter showed that its current or short-term borrowings is at $3,991 million (line 6) and long-term borrowings is at $6,995 million (line 10). Long-term debt refers to long-term notes payable and bonds payable, which we will cover in the later part of this chapter.

You have seen the broad categories of liabilities, both current and non-current. Now, let's look at something that sounds like a liability but is actually not a liability.

ACCOUNT FOR CONTINGENT LIABILITIES

2 Account for contingent liabilities

A contingent liability is *not* an actual liability. A contingent liability is a disclosure item in the notes to the financial statement. *IAS 37* states that a contingent liability arises when:

- there is a possible obligation to be confirmed by a future event that is outside the control of the entity; or
- a present obligation may, but probably will not, require an outflow of resources; or
- a sufficiently reliable estimate of the amount of a present obligation cannot be made.

Note that in each instance, contingent liabilities fail to meet one aspect of the definition of liability. Examples of contingent liabilities include corporate guarantees, lawsuits, tax disputes, or alleged violations of environmental protection laws. If, for example, the probability of a particular contingent liability has risen from possible to probable, the company would have to make a provision (i.e., recognize an expense and a related liability) in anticipation of the settlement of such liability. In some industries, contingent liabilities may be more prevalent than others. Let's look at the contingent liability disclosure of BP, especially in relation to the *Deep Horizon* (Gulf of Mexico) oil spill in 2010.

ADAPTED EXCERPTS FROM BP's NOTES TO THE ACCOUNTS

Contingent liabilities are possible obligations whose existence will only be confirmed by future events not wholly within the control of the group, or present obligations where it is not probable that an outflow of resources will be required or the amount of the obligation cannot be measured with sufficient reliability. Contingent liabilities are not recognized in the financial statements but are disclosed unless the possibility of an outflow of economic resources is considered remote.

Gulf of Mexico Oil Spill

As a consequence of the Gulf of Mexico oil spill in April 2010, BP continues to incur costs and has also recognized liabilities for certain future costs. The cumulative pretax Income Statement charge since the incident amounts to $55.5 billion. The cumulative Income Statement charge does not include amounts for obligations that BP considers are not possible, at this time, to measure reliably. BP has recorded provisions [$16.5 billion] relating to the Gulf of Mexico oil spill in relation to environmental expenditure (including spill response costs), litigation and claims, and Clean Water Act penalties that can be measured reliably at this time.

BP has provided for its best estimate of amounts expected to be paid that can be measured reliably. It is not possible, at this time, to measure reliably other obligations arising from the incident, nor is it practicable to estimate their magnitude or possible timing of payment. Therefore, no amounts have been provided for these obligations at 31 December 2015.

Other Contingent Liabilities

In the normal course of the group's business, legal proceedings are pending or may be brought against BP group entities arising out of current and past operations, including matters related to commercial disputes, product liability, antitrust, commodities trading, premises-liability claims, consumer protection, general environmental claims and allegations of exposures of third parties to toxic substances, such as lead pigment in paint, asbestos and other chemicals. BP believes that the impact of these legal proceedings on the group's results of operations, liquidity or financial position will not be material.

Source: BP's 2015 annual report, pages 114, 117, 119, 120, 159–160

It is important to remember that there is no need to report a contingent loss that is unlikely to occur. Instead, an entity should wait until new information is available to provide further clarity on the situation. For example, suppose Del Monte Foods grows vegetables in a foreign country, where the new president has made threats that it will nationalize (i.e., will confiscate the assets of all foreign companies) Del Monte's plantation. Del Monte will report nothing about the contingency if the probability of such an eventuality is considered remote.

Are All Liabilities Reported on the Balance Sheet?

The big danger with liabilities is that you may fail to report a large debt on your Balance Sheet. What is the consequence of missing a large liability? You will definitely understate your liabilities and your debt ratio (the percentage of your assets financed by liabilities—more on this later in the chapter). By failing to accrue interest on the liability, you'll probably overstate your net income as well. In short, your financial statements will make you look better than you really are. Any such error, if significant, hurts a company's credibility.

Contingent liabilities are very easy to overlook because they aren't actual debts. How would you feel if you owned shares in a company that failed to report a contingency that eventually caused the company to go out of business? If you had known of the contingency, you could have sold the shares and avoided the loss.

COOKING THE BOOKS with Liabilities

Crazy Eddie, Inc.

Accidentally understating liabilities is one thing, but doing it intentionally is quite another. When unethical management decides to cook the books in the area of liabilities, its strategy is to deliberately understate recorded liabilities. This can be done by intentionally under-recording the amount of existing liabilities, or by omitting certain liabilities altogether.

Crazy Eddie, Inc. (first discussed in Chapter 6) used multiple tactics to overstate its financial position from 1984 through 1987. In addition to overstating inventory (thus understating cost of goods sold and overstating income), the management of the company deliberately understated accounts payable by issuing fictitious (false) debit memoranda from suppliers (vendors). A debit memo is issued for goods returned to a vendor, such as Sony. When a debit memorandum is issued, accounts payable are debited (reduced), thus reducing current liabilities and increasing the current ratio. Eventually, expenses are also decreased, and profits are correspondingly increased through reduction of expenses. Crazy Eddie, Inc., issued $3 million of fictitious debit memoranda in 1985, making the company's current ratio and debt ratio look better than they actually were, and eventually overstating profits.

SUMMARY OF CURRENT LIABILITIES

Let's summarize what we've covered thus far. A company can report its current liabilities on the Balance Sheet as follows:

	A	B	C	D
1			**Accounting, Inc.** **Balance Sheet** **December 31, 20X0**	
2	**Assets**		**Liabilities**	
3	Current Assets:		**Current liabilities:**	
4	Cash		Accounts payable	
5	Short-term investments		Salary payable*	
6	Etc.		Interest payable*	
7			Income tax payable*	
8	Non-current Assets:		Unearned revenue	
9	PPE		Provision for warranty repairs*	
10	Intangibles		Notes payable, short-term	
11	Etc.		Current portion of long-term debt	
12			**Total current liabilities**	
13			Long-term liabilities	
14				
15			**Shareholders' Equity**	
16			Share capital	
17			Retained earnings	
18				
19			Total liabilities and	
20	Total assets	$ XXX	shareholders' equity	$ XXX
21				

*These items are often combined and reported in a single total as "Accrued liabilities" or "Accrued expenses payable."

Mid-Chapter Summary Problem

Assume that Estée Lauder faced the following liability situations at June 30, 20X1, the end of the company's fiscal year. Show how Estée Lauder would report these liabilities on its Balance Sheet at June 30, 20X1.

a. Salary expense for the last payroll period of the year was $900,000. Of this amount, employees' withheld income tax totaled $88,000 and employer's payroll taxes were $61,000. These payroll amounts will be paid in early July.

b. In fiscal year 20X1, management estimates a new warranty obligation of $8 million arising from sales in 20X1. One year ago, at June 30, 20X0, provision for warranty stood at $3 million. Warranty payments were $9 million during the year ended June 30, 20X1.

c. The company pays royalties on its purchased trademarks. Royalties for the trademarks are equal to a percentage of Estée Lauder's sales. Assume that sales in 20X1 were $400 million and were subject to a royalty rate of 3%. At June 30, 20X1, Estée Lauder owes two-thirds of the year's royalty, to be paid in July.

d. Long-term debt totals $100 million and is payable in annual installments of $10 million each. The interest rate on the debt is 7%, and the interest is paid each December 31.

Answer

Liabilities at June 30, 20X1:	
a. Current liabilities:	
Salary payable ($900,000 − $88,000 − $61,000)	$ 751,000
Employee income tax payable	88,000
Employer payroll tax payable	61,000
b. Current liabilities:	
Estimated warranty payable	2,000,000
[$3,000,000 − $9,000,000 + $8,000,000]	
c. Current liabilities:	
Royalties payable ($400,000,000 × 0.03 × 2/3)	8,000,000
d. Current liabilities:	
Current installment of long-term debt	10,000,000
Interest payable ($100,000,000 × 0.07 × 6/12)	3,500,000
Long-term debt ($100,000,000 − $10,000,000)	90,000,000

ACCOUNT FOR BONDS

Let's start by having a look at Jardine's non-current borrowings (line 10) on its Balance Sheet at the start of this chapter. The $6,995 non-current borrowings are comprised of the following.

ADAPTED EXCERPTS FROM JARDINE MATHESON'S NOTES TO THE ACCOUNTS

Non-current Borrowings (USD millions)	**2015**	**2014**
■ Bank loans	$2,916	$3,448
■ Bonds and notes	4,009	3,914
■ Finance lease liabilities	65	48
■ Other loans	5	6
	6,995	7,416

Source: Jardine Matheson's 2015 annual report, page 102

The biggest source of Jardine's non-current borrowing is bonds and notes. In fact, Jardine has over 50 bonds and notes outstanding. In this section, we will focus on bonds and notes, and we will look at finance lease later. Here we treat bonds payable and notes payable together because their underlying accounting treatment is similar. The main difference is that bonds tend to be of longer duration than notes, and even this varies from issuer to issuer.

Large companies such as Unilever, Procter & Gamble, and Jardine cannot borrow billions of dollars from a single lender. So how do corporations borrow huge amounts? They issue (sell) bonds to the public. **Bonds payable** are groups of notes payable issued to multiple lenders, called bondholders. Jardine needs financing for its operations and can borrow large amounts by issuing bonds or notes payable to thousands of individual investors, who each lend Jardine a modest amount. Jardine receives the cash it needs, and individual investors limit risk by diversifying their funds.

Don't assume that bonds and notes are limited to companies. In fact, bonds were originally used by governments or public authorities to raise long-term funds well before they were used by companies as a source of funding. The first official government bond was issued by the Bank of England in 1693 to fund a war!

Bonds: An Introduction

Each bond payable is, in effect, a note payable. Bonds payable are debts of the issuing company.

Purchasers of bonds receive a bond's certificate, which carries the issuing company's name. The certificate also states the principal, which is typically stated in units of $1,000; principal is also called the bond's face value, maturity value, or par value. The bond obligates the issuing company to pay the debt at a specific future time called the maturity date.

Interest expense is the rental fee on borrowed money. The bond certificate states the interest rate that the issuer will pay the holder and the dates that the interest payments are due (generally twice a year). Exhibit 9-2 shows an actual bond certificate.

Issuing bonds usually requires the services of a securities firm, such as the Bank of America, to act as the underwriter of the bond issue. The **underwriter** purchases the bonds from the issuing company and resells them to its clients, or it may sell the bonds to its clients and earn a commission on the sale.

Types of Bonds. All the bonds in a particular issue may mature at the same time (**term bonds**) or in installments over a period of time (**serial bonds**). Serial bonds are like installment notes payable. Some long-term debts are serial in nature because they are payable in installments.

Secured, or mortgage, bonds give the bondholder the right to take specified assets of the issuer if the company defaults—that is, fails to pay interest or principal. Unsecured bonds, called **debentures**, are backed only by the good faith of the borrower. Debentures carry a higher rate of interest than secured bonds because debentures are riskier investments.

Bond Prices. Investors may buy and sell bonds through bond markets. Bond prices are quoted at a percentage of their maturity value. For example:

- A $1,000 bond quoted at 100 is bought or sold for $1,000, which is 100% of its face value.
- The same bond quoted at 101.5 has a market price of $1,015 (101.5% of face value = $1,000 × 1.015).
- A $1,000 bond quoted at 88.375 is priced at $883.75 ($1,000 × 0.88375).

While the price of a bond on the market may change, it is important to remember that the face value and interest payments do not change. The accounting for bonds from the issuer perspective ignores fluctuations of market price, but it is disclosed in the notes.

Bond Premium and Bond Discount. A bond issued at a price above its face (par) value is said to be issued at a **premium**, and a bond issued at a price below face (par) value has a **discount**.

Premium on Bonds Payable has a credit balance and Discount on Bonds Payable carries a debit balance. Bond Discount is therefore a contra liability account.

As a bond nears maturity, its market price moves toward par value. Therefore, the price of a bond issued at a:

- premium decreases towards face value;
- discount increases towards face value.

Exhibit 9-2 | Bond Certificate (Adapted)

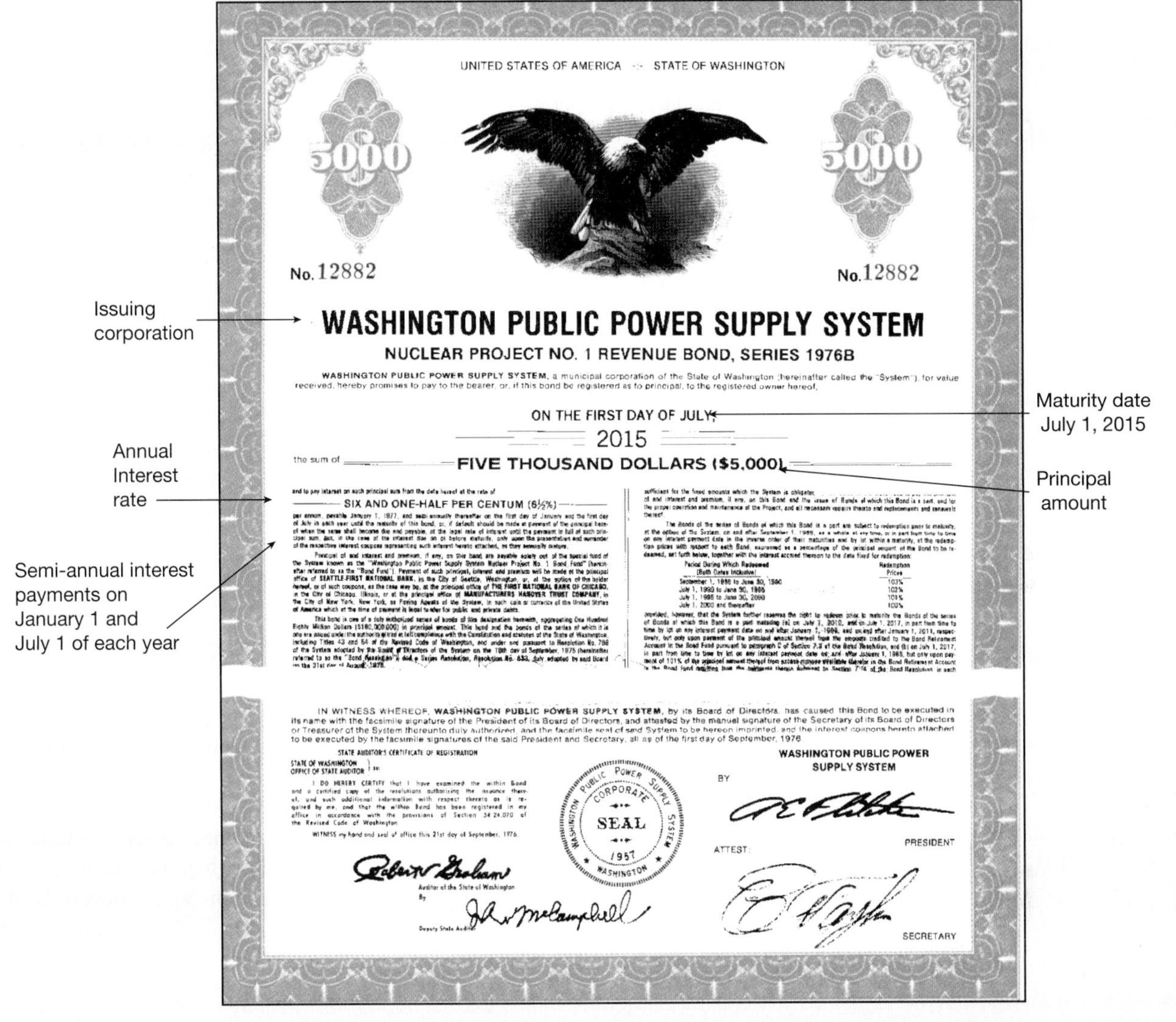

On the maturity date, a bond's market value exactly equals its face value because the company that issued the bond pays that amount to retire the bond.

The Time Value of Money. A dollar received today is worth more than a dollar to be received in the future. You can invest today's dollar immediately and earn income from it. But if you must wait to receive the dollar, you forgo the interest revenue. Money earns income over time; we call this "time value of money" (see Appendix B, available on www.pearsonglobaleditions.com/Harrison). Let's examine how the time value of money affects the pricing of bonds.

Assume that you are looking at a Jardine bond with a face value of $1,000 that reaches maturity three years from today and carries no interest. Would you pay $1,000 today to purchase this bond? No, because the payment of $1,000 today to receive the same amount in the future provides you with no income on the investment. Just how much would you pay today to receive $1,000 at the end of three years? The answer is an amount less than $1,000. Let's suppose that you feel $750 is a good price. By investing $750 now to receive $1,000 later, you earn $250 interest revenue over the three years. The issuing company, such as Jardine, sees the transaction this way: Jardine will pay you $250 interest to use your $750 for three years.

The amount to invest now to receive more later is called the **present value** of a future amount. In our example, $750 is the present value, and $1,000 is the future amount.

Our $750 bond price is a reasonable estimate. The exact present value of any future amount depends on:

- the amount of the future payment ($1,000 in our example);
- the length of time from the investment date to the date when the future amount is to be collected (three years);
- the interest rate during the period (say 10%).

In this case the present value is very close to $750. Present value is always less than the future amount. We discuss how present value is computed in Appendix B (available on www.pearsonglobaleditions.com/Harrison).

Bond Interest Rates Determine Bond Prices. Bonds are always sold at their market price, which is the amount investors will pay for the bond. Market price is the bond's present value, which equals the present value of the principal payment plus the present value of the cash interest payments. Interest is usually paid semi-annually (twice a year). Some companies pay interest annually or quarterly.

Two interest rates work to set the price of a bond:

1. The **stated interest rate**, also called the coupon rate, is the interest rate printed on the bond certificate. The stated interest rate determines the amount of cash interest the borrower pays—and the investor receives—each year. Suppose GSK bonds have a stated interest rate of 9%. GSK would pay $9,000 of interest annually on each $100,000 bond. Each semi-annual payment would be $4,500 ($100,000 × 0.09 × 6/12).
2. The **market interest rate**, or effective interest rate, is the rate that investors demand for loaning their money. The market interest rate can fluctuate after issuance of a bond.

A company may issue bonds with a stated interest rate that differs from the prevailing market interest rate. In fact, the two interest rates often differ.

Exhibit 9-3 shows how the stated interest rate and the market interest rate interact to determine the issue price of a bond payable for three separate cases.

Jardine may issue 9% bonds when the market rate is at 10%. Will Jardine's 9% bonds attract investors in this market? No, because investors can earn 10% on other bonds of similar risk. Therefore, investors will purchase Jardine bonds only at a price less than their face value. The difference between the lower price and face value is a discount (Exhibit 9-3). Conversely, if the

Exhibit 9-3 How the Stated Interest Rate and the Market Interest Rate Interact to Determine the Price of a Bond

Issue Price of Bonds Payable				
Case A:				
Stated interest rate on a bond payable	equals	Market interest rate	Therefore,	Price of face (par, or maturity) value
Example: 9%	=	9%	→	*Par: $1,000 bond issued for $1,000*
Case B:				
Stated interest rate on a bond payable	less than	Market interest rate	Therefore,	Discount price (price below face value)
Example: 9%	<	10%	→	*Discount: $1,000 bond issued for a price below $1,000*
Case C:				
Stated interest rate on a bond payable	greater than	Market interest rate	Therefore,	Premium price (price above face value)
Example: 9%	>	8%	→	*Premium: $1,000 bond issued for a price above $1,000*

market interest rate is 8%, Jardine's 9% bonds will be so attractive that investors will pay more than face value to purchase them. The difference between the higher price and the face value is a premium.

Issuing Bonds Payable at Par (Face Value)

We start with the most straightforward situation—issuing bonds at their par value. There is no premium or discount on these bonds payable.

Suppose Jardine issues $50,000, 9% bonds at par on January 1, 20X1. The bonds pay interests on a semi-annual basis (July 1 and January 1 each year following issuance) and are of five years' duration, i.e., they will mature on January 1, 20X6. The issuance entry is:

	A	B	C	D
1	20X1			
2	Jan 1	Cash	50,000	
3		Bonds Payable		50,000
4		*To issue bonds at par.*		
5				

Bonds Payable	
	50,000

Assets and liabilities increase when a company issues bonds payable.

Assets	=	Liabilities	+	Shareholders' Equity
+ 50,000	=	+ 50,000	+	0

Jardine, the borrower, makes a one-time entry to record the receipt of cash and the issuance of bonds. Afterward, investors buy and sell the bonds through the bond markets. These later buy-and-sell transactions between outside investors do not involve Jardine at all.

Interest payments occur each January 1 and July 1. Jardine's entry to record the first semi-annual interest payment is:

	A	B	C	D
1	20X1			
2	Jul 1	Interest Expense ($50,000 × 0.09 × 6/12)	2,250	
3		Cash		2,250
4		*To pay semi-annual interest.*		
5				

The payment of interest expense decreases assets and equity. Bonds payable are not affected.

Assets	=	Liabilities	+	Shareholders' Equity	
− 2,250	=	0	+	− 2,250	(interest expense)

At its financial year-end, Jardine accrues interest expense and interest payable for six months (July through December), as follows:

	A	B	C	D
1	20X1			
2	Dec 31	Interest Expense ($50,000 × 0.09 × 6/12)	2,250	
3		Interest Payable		2,250
4		*To accrue interest.*		
5				

Liabilities increase, and equity decreases.

Assets	=	Liabilities	+	Shareholders' Equity	
0	=	+2,250	+	− 2,250	(interest expense)

On January 1, Jardine will pay the interest, debiting Interest Payable and crediting Cash. Then, at maturity, Jardine pays off the bonds as follows:

	A	B	C	D
1	20X6			
2	Jan 1	Bonds Payable	50,000	
3		Cash		50,000
4		*To pay bonds payable at maturity.*		
5				

Bonds Payable

50,000		50,000
	Bal.	0

Assets	=	Liabilities	+	Shareholders' Equity
− 50,000	=	− 50,000	+	0

Issuing Bonds Payable at a Discount

Market conditions may force a company to issue bonds at a discount. Suppose Jardine issues $100,000 of 9%, five-year bonds when the market interest rate is 10%. The issuance price of the bonds drops, and Jardine receives $96,139[1] at issuance. The transaction is recorded as follows:

[1] Appendix B (available on www.pearsonglobaleditions.com/Harrison) shows how to determine the price of this bond. If you are using Excel, you can use the PV function, i.e., PV (market rate per period, number of periods, interest payment per period and face value) or "= PV (5%, 10, −4,500, −100,000)" to get $96,139. Any difference from workings using Appendix B is due to rounding of time value factors.

	A	B	C	D
1	20X1			
2	Jan 1	Cash	96,139	
3		Discount on Bonds Payable	3,861	
4		Bonds Payable		100,000
5		*To issue bonds at a discount.*		
6				

The accounting equation shows that Jardine has a net liability of $96,139—not $100,000.

Assets	=	Liabilities	+	Shareholders' Equity
+ 96,139	=	− 3,861	+	0
		+ 100,000		

The bonds payable accounts have a net balance of $96,149 as follows:

Bonds Payable		−	Discount on Bonds Payable		=	Net carrying amount of bonds payable
	100,000		3,861			$96,139

Jardine's Balance Sheet immediately after issuance of the bonds would report the following:

Non-current liabilities:		
Bonds payable, 9%, due 2015....................	$100,000	
Less: Discount on bonds payable................	(3,861)	96,139

Discount on Bonds Payable is a contra account to Bonds Payable, a decrease in the company's liabilities. Subtracting the discount from Bonds Payable yields the carrying amount of the bonds. Thus, Jardine's liability is $96,139, which is the amount the company effectively borrowed.

What Is the Interest Expense on These Bonds Payable?

Jardine pays interest on bonds semi-annually, which is common practice. Each semi-annual interest payment is set by the bond contract and therefore remains the same over the life of the bonds:

$$\text{Semi-annual interest payment} = \$100{,}000 \times 0.09 \times 6/12$$
$$= \$4{,}500$$

But Jardine's interest expense increases as the bonds march toward maturity. Remember: these bonds were issued at a discount.

Panel A of Exhibit 9-4 repeats the Jardine bond example we've been using. Panel B provides an amortization table that does three things:

1. determines the periodic interest expense (column C);
2. shows the amount of bond discount amortization (column E); and
3. shows the bond carrying amount (column G).

Study Exhibit 9-4 carefully because the amounts we'll be using come directly from the amortization table. This exhibit shows the effective-interest method of amortization, which is required by *IAS 39* to measure interest expense.

Exhibit 9-4 | Debt Amortization for a Bond Discount

Panel A – Bond Data

A1	A	B	C	D	E
1	Issue date	1 January 20X1		Maturity date	1 January 20X6
2	Face (or par or maturity) value	$100,000		Number of periods	10 periods
3	Stated interest rate (per year)	9% per year		Market interest rate at issuance (per year)	10% per year
4	Stated interest rate (per period)	4.5% per period		Market interest rate at issuance (per period)	5% per period
5	Issue price	$96,139	=	PV = (market rate, number of periods, interest payment, face value)	

Panel B – Bond Amortization Table

A1	A	B	C	D	E	F	G
1	**Semi-annual Interest Payment Dates**	**Beginning Bond Carrying Amount**	**Interest Expense (Market Rate × B)**	**Interest Payment (Bond Rate × Face Value)**	**Bond Discount Amortization (C – D)**	**Bond Discount Account Balance (Preceeding F – E)**	**Ending Bond Carrying Amount (Face Value – F)**
2	(Issuance) 1 Jan 20X1					$ 3,861	$ 96,139
3	(#1) 1 Jul 20X1	$ 96,139	$ 4,807	$ 4,500	$ 307	3,554	96,446
4	(#2) 1 Jan 20X2	96,446	4,822	4,500	322	3,232	96,768
5	(#3) 1 Jul 20X2	96,768	4,838	4,500	338	2,893	97,107
6	(#4) 1 Jan 20X3	97,107	4,855	4,500	355	2,538	97,462
7	(#5) 1 Jul 20X3	97,462	4,873	4,500	373	2,165	97,835
8	(#6) 1 Jan 20X4	97,835	4,892	4,500	392	1,773	98,227
9	(#7) 1 Jul 20X4	98,227	4,911	4,500	411	1,362	98,638
10	(#8) 1 Jan 20X5	98,638	4,932	4,500	432	930	99,070
11	(#9) 1 Jul 20X5	99,070	4,954	4,500	454	476	99,524
12	(#10) 1 Jan 20X6	99,524	4,976	4,500	476	0	100,000
13							
14	**Notes:**						
15	Column B	Beginning bond carrying amount, which is equal to preceeding Column G					
16		For issuance, carrying amount is the face value of the bond *less* bond discount (Column F)					
17	Column C	Interest expense each period, calculated as market rate per period × the beginning bond carrying amount in Column B					
18	Column D	Fixed interest payment each period, calculated as bond rate per period × the face value of the bond					
19	Column E	Bond discount amortization is the difference between interest expense (Column C) and interest payment (Column D)					
20	Column F	Bond discount balance is the preceeding balance (Column F) adjusted for current period amortization (Column E)					
21	Column G	Ending bond carrying amount, which is face value of the bond *less* the bond discount account balance (Column F)					
22							

Interest Expense on Bonds Issued at a Discount

In Exhibit 9-4, Jardine borrowed $96,139 cash but must pay $100,000 when the bonds mature. What happens to the $3,861 balance of the discount account over the life of the bond issue?

The $3,861 is an additional interest expense to Jardine over and above the stated interest that Jardine pays each six months. Exhibit 9-5 graphs the interest expense and the interest payment on the Jardine bonds over their lifetime. Observe that the semi-annual interest payment is fixed—by contract—at $4,500. But the amount of interest expense increases as the discount bond marches upward towards maturity. These amounts come from Exhibit 9-4 Panel B column C.

Exhibit 9-5 | Interest Expense on Bonds Payable Issued at a Discount

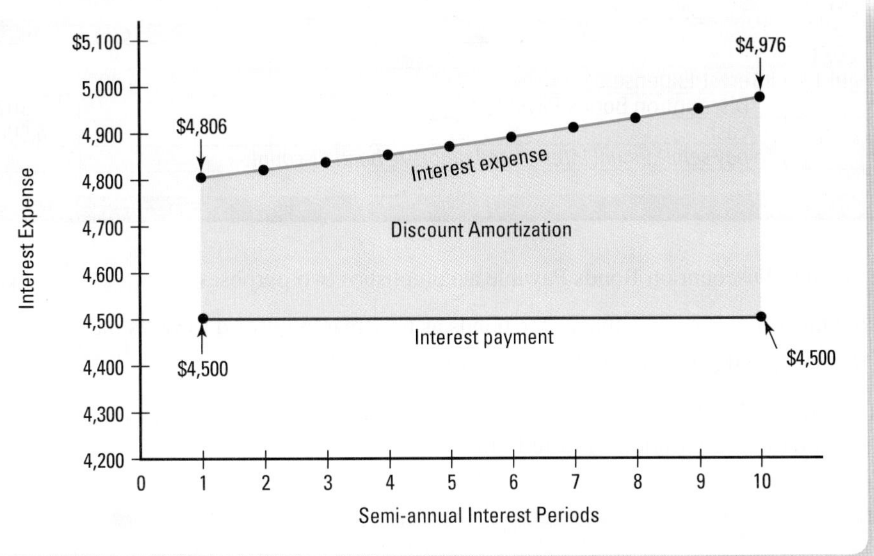

The discount is allocated to interest expense through amortization over the term of the bonds. Exhibit 9-6 illustrates the amortization of the bonds from $96,139 at the start to $100,000 at maturity. These amounts come from Exhibit 9-4, column G.

Exhibit 9-6 | Amortizing Bonds Payable Issued at a Discount

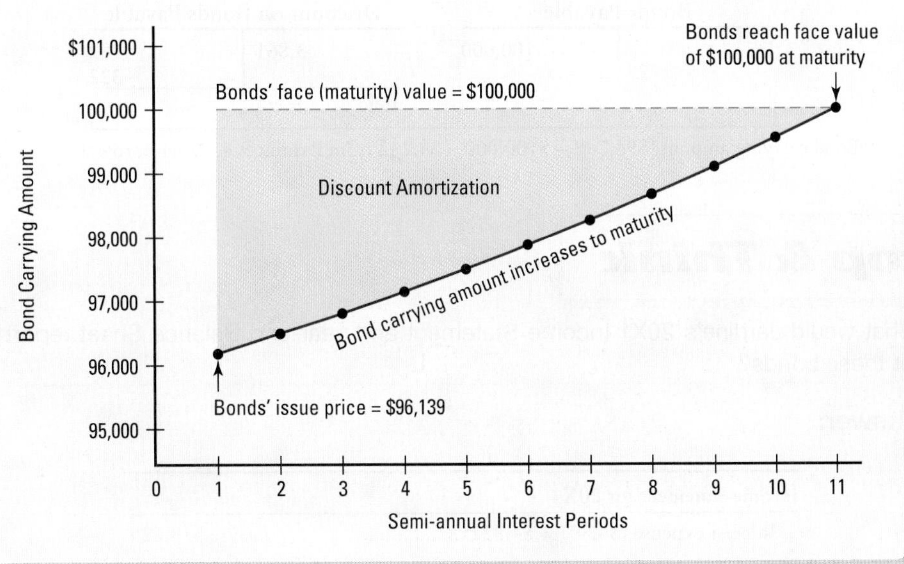

Now let's see how Jardine would account for these bonds issued at a discount. In our example, Jardine issued its bonds on January 1, 20X1. On July 1, Jardine made the first semi-annual interest payment. But Jardine's interest expense is greater than its payment of $4,500. Jardine's journal entry to record interest expense and the interest payment for the first 6 months is as follows (with all amounts taken from Exhibit 9-4):

	A	B	C	D
1	20X1			
2	Jul 1	Interest Expense	4,807	
3		Discount on Bonds Payable		307
4		Cash		4,500
5		*To pay semi-annual interest and amortize bond discount.*		
6				

The credit to Discount on Bonds Payable accomplishes two purposes:

1. It adjusts the carrying value of the bonds as they march upward towards maturity value.
2. It amortizes the discount to interest expense.

At December 31, 20X1, Jardine accrues interest and amortizes the bonds for July through December with this entry (amounts from Exhibit 9-4):

	A	B	C	D
1	20X1			
2	Dec 31	Interest Expense	4,822	
3		Discount on Bonds Payable		322
4		Interest Payable		4,500
5		*To accrue semi-annual interest and amortize bond discount.*		
6				

At December 31, 20X1, Jardine's bond accounts appear as follows:

Bonds Payable		Discount on Bonds Payable	
	100,000	3,861	307
			322
		Bal. 3,232	

Bond carrying amount, $96,768 = $100,000 − $3,232 from Exhibit 9-4, Panel B, row 4.

Stop & Think

What would Jardine's 20X1 Income Statement and year-end Balance Sheet report for these bonds?

Answer:

Income Statement for 20X1		
Interest expense ($4,807 + $4,822)		$ 9,629
Balance Sheet at December 31, 20X1		
Current liabilities:		
Interest payable		$ 4,500
Long-term liabilities:		
Bonds payable	$100,000	
Less: Discount on bonds payable................	(3,232)	96,768

At maturity on January 1, 20X6, the discount will have been amortized to zero, and the bonds' carrying amount will be the face value of $100,000. Jardine will retire the bonds by paying $100,000 to the bondholders.

	A	B	C	D
1	20X6			
2	Jan 1	Bond Payable	100,000	
3		Cash		100,000
4		*To pay bond payable.*		
5				

Issuing Bonds Payable at a Premium

Let's modify the Jardine bond example to illustrate issuance of the bonds at a premium. Assume that Jardine issues $100,000 of five-year, 9% bonds that pay interest semi-annually. If the 9% bonds are issued when the market interest rate is 8%, their issue price is $104,055[2]. The premium on these bonds is $4,055, and Exhibit 9-7 shows how to amortize the bonds by the effective-interest method. In practice, bond premiums are rare because few companies issue their bonds to pay cash interest above the market interest rate. We cover bond premiums for completeness.

Jardine's entries to record issuance of the bonds on January 1, 20X1, is as follows:

	A	B	C	D
1	20X1			
2	Jan 1	Cash	104,055	
3		Bonds Payable		100,000
4		Premium on Bonds Payable		4,055
5		*To issue bonds at a premium.*		
6				

At the beginning, Jardine's liability is $104,055—not $100,000. The accounting equation makes this clear.

Assets	=	Liabilities	+	Shareholders' Equity
+ 104,055	=	+ 100,000	+	0
		+ 4,055		

Immediately after issuing the bonds at a premium on January 1, 20X1, Jardine would report the bonds payable on the Balance Sheet as follows:

Non-current liabilities:		
Bonds payable	$100,000	
Premium on bonds payable	4,055	104,055

[2]Appendix B (available on www.pearsonglobaleditions.com/Harrison) shows how to determine the price of this bond. If you are using Excel, you can use the PV function, i.e., PV (market rate per period, number of periods, interest payment per period, and face value) or "=PV(4%, 10, –4500, –100000)" to get $104,055. Any difference from workings using Appendix B is due to rounding of time value factors.

Exhibit 9-7 is similar in structure to Exhibit 9-4, which you saw earlier. The only difference is in the final column, where the balance of the bond premium account is added to the face value of the bonds to determine the carrying amount.

Exhibit 9-7 Debt Amortization for a Bond Premium

Panel A – Bond Data

A1

	A	B	C	D	E
1	Issue date	1 January 20X1		Maturity date	1 January, 20X6
2	Face (or par or maturity) value	$100,000		Number of periods	10 periods
3	Stated interest rate (per year)	9% per year		Market interest rate at issuance (per year)	8% per year
4	Stated interest rate (per period)	4.5% per period		Market interest rate at issuance (per period)	4% per period
5	Issue price	$104,055	=	PV = (market rate, number of periods, interest payment, face value)	

Panel B – Bond Amortization Table

A1

	A	B	C	D	E	F	G
1	Semi-annual Interest Payment Dates	Beginning Bond Carrying Amount	Interest Expense (Market Rate × B)	Interest Payment (Bond Rate × Face Value)	Bond Premium Amortization (C – D)	Bond Premium Account Balance (Preceeding F – E)	Ending Bond Carrying Amount (Face Value + F)
2	(Issuance) Jan 1 20X1					$ 4,055	$ 104,055
3	(#1) 1 Jul 20X1	$ 104,055	$ 4,162	$ 4,500	$ 338	3,718	103,718
4	(#2) 1 Jan 20X2	103,718	4,149	4,500	351	3,366	103,366
5	(#3) 1 Jul 20X2	103,366	4,135	4,500	365	3,001	103,001
6	(#4) 1 Jan 20X3	103,001	4,120	4,500	380	2,621	102,621
7	(#5) 1 Jul 20X3	102,621	4,105	4,500	395	2,226	102,226
8	(#6) 1 Jan 20X4	102,226	4,089	4,500	411	1,815	101,815
9	(#7) 1 Jul 20X4	101,815	4,073	4,500	427	1,388	101,388
10	(#8) 1 Jan 20X5	101,388	4,056	4,500	444	943	100,943
11	(#9) 1 Jul 20X5	100,943	4,038	4,500	462	481	100,481
12	(#10) 1 Jan 20X6	100,481	4,019	4,500	481	0	100,000
13							
14	**Notes:**						
15	Column B	Beginning bond carrying amount, which is equal to preceeding Column G					
16		For issuance, carrying amount is the face value of the bond *plus* bond premium (Column F)					
17	Column C	Interest expense each period, calculated as market rate per period X the beginning bond carrying amount in Column B					
18	Column D	Fixed interest payment each period, calculated as bond rate per period X the face value of the bond					
19	Column E	Bond premium amortization is the difference between interest expense (Column C) and interest payment (Column D)					
20	Column F	Bond premium balance is the preceeding balance (Column F) adjusted for current period amortization (Column E)					
21	Column G	Ending bond carrying amount, which is face value of the bond *plus* the bond premium account balance (Column F)					
22							

In Exhibit 9-7, Jardine borrowed $104,055 cash but must pay back only $100,000 at maturity. The $4,055 premium is a reduction in Jardine's interest expense over the term of the bonds. Exhibit 9-8 graphs Jardine's interest payments (column D from Exhibit 9-7) and interest expense (column C).

Exhibit 9-8 Interest Expense on Bonds Payable Issued at a Premium

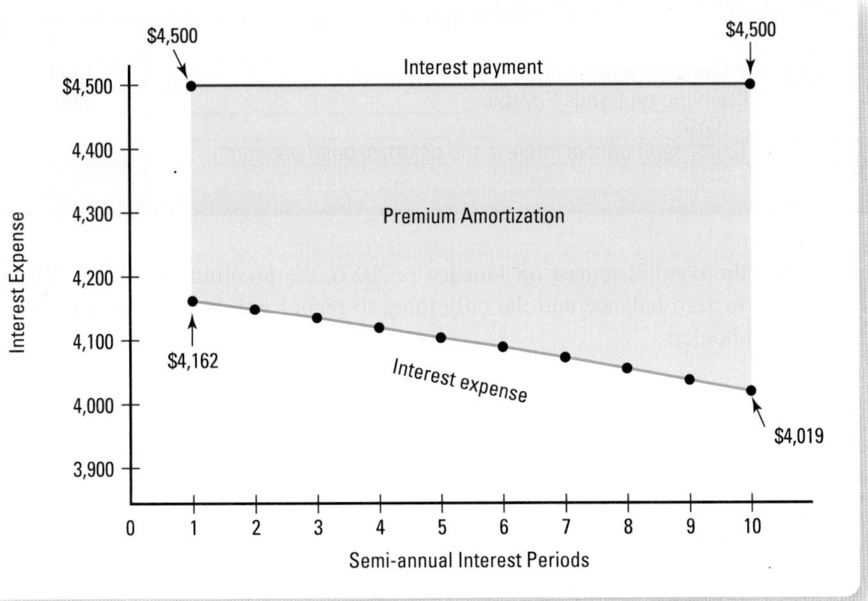

Amortization of the bond's premium decreases interest expense each period over the term of the bonds. Exhibit 9-9 illustrates the amortization of the bonds from the issue price of $104,055 to a maturity value of $100,000. All amounts are taken from Exhibit 9-7.

Exhibit 9-9 Amortizing Bonds Payable Issued at a Premium

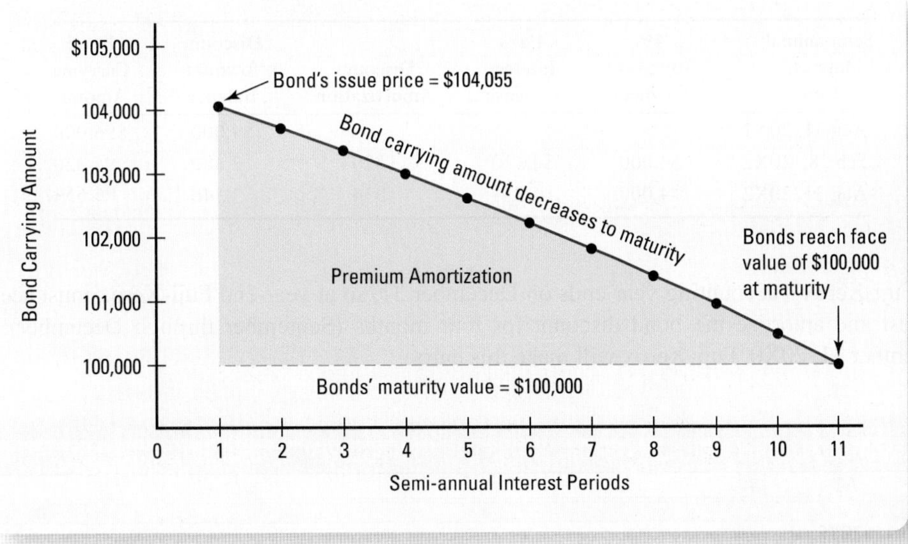

When Jardine makes the first interest payment on July 1, 20X1, the following entry will be recorded, based on row 3 of panel B, Exhibit 9-7.

	A	B	C	D
1	20X1			
2	Jul 1	Interest Expense	4,162	
3		Premium on Bonds Payable	338	
4		Cash		4,500
5		*To pay semi-annual interest and amortize bond premium.*		
6				

Similarly, when the bond is retired on January 1, 20X6, the premium account will have been amortized down to zero balance and the only thing to record will be the payment of the bond principal to bond holders.

	A	B	C	D
1	20X6			
2	Jan 1	Bond Payable	100,000	
3		Cash		100,000
4		*To pay bond payable.*		
5				

Partial-Period Interest Amounts

Companies don't always issue bonds at the beginning or the end of their accounting year. They issue bonds when market conditions are most favorable, and that may be on May 16, August 1, or any other date. To illustrate partial-period interest, assume Fuji-Xerox issues $100,000 of 8% bonds payable at 96 on August 31, 20X0. The market rate of interest was 9%, and these bonds pay semi-annual interest on February 28 and August 31 each year. The first few lines of Fuji-Xerox's amortization table are:

Semi-annual Interest Date	4% Interest Payment	4½% Interest Expense	Discount Amortization	Discount Account Balance	Bond Carrying Amount
Aug 31, 20X1				$4,000	$96,000
Feb 28, 20X2	$4,000	$4,320	$320	3,680	96,320
Aug 31, 20X2	4,000	4,334	334	3,346	96,654

Fuji-Xerox's accounting year ends on December 31, so at year-end Fuji-Xerox must accrue interest and amortize the bond discount for four months (September through December). At December 31, 20X0, Fuji-Xerox will make this entry:

	A	B	C	D
1	20X0			
2	Dec 31	Interest Expense ($4,320 × 4/6)	2,880	
3		Discount on Bonds Payable ($320 × 4/6)		213
4		Interest Payable ($4,000 × 4/6)		2,667
5		*To accrue interest and amortize discount at year-end.*		
6				

The year-end entry at December 31, 20X0, uses 4/6 of the upcoming semi-annual amounts at February 28, 20X1. This example clearly illustrates the benefit of an amortization schedule.

The Straight-line Amortization Method: A Quick Way to Measure Interest Expense

While not allowed by *IAS 39*, there's a less precise way to amortize bond discount or premium. The straight-line amortization method divides a bond discount (or premium) into equal periodic amounts over the bond's term. The amount of interest expense is the same for each interest period. This method is simply a "quick and dirty" way to estimate interest expense when you do not have the tools to use the effective interest rate method as required by *IAS 39*. Unless otherwise stated, you should always use the effective interest method as previously discussed.

Let's apply the effective interest method to the Jardine bonds issued at a discount and illustrated in Exhibit 9-4. Suppose Jardine's Chief Financial Officer is considering issuing the 9% bonds at $96,139. To quickly estimate semi-annual interest expense on the bonds, she can use the straight-line interest amortization method for the bond discount, as an approximation, as follows:

Semi-annual cash interest payment ($100,000 × 0.09 × 6/12)	$4,500
+ Semi-annual amortization of discount ($3,861 ÷ 10)	386
= Estimated semi-annual interest expense	$4,886

The straight-line interest amortization method uses this same amortization amount for every period over the term of the bonds.

Jardine's entry to record interest and amortization of the bond discount under the straight-line interest amortization method would be:

	A	B	C	D
1	20X1			
2	Jul 1	Interest Expense	4,886	
3		Discount on Bonds Payable		386
4		Cash		4,500
5		*To pay semi-annual interest and amortize bond discount.*		
6				

Should We Retire Bonds Payable Before Their Maturity?

Normally, companies wait until maturity to pay off, or retire, their bonds payable. But companies sometimes retire bonds early. The main reason for retiring bonds early is to relieve the pressure of making high interest payments. Also, the company may be able to borrow at a lower interest rate.

Some bonds are **callable**, which means that the issuer may call, or pay off, those bonds at a prearranged price (this is the call price) whenever the issuer chooses. The call price is often a percentage point or two above the par value, perhaps 101 or 102. Callable bonds give the issuer the benefit of being able to pay off the bonds whenever it is most favorable to do so. The alternative to calling the bonds is to purchase them in the open market at their current market price.

Assume that Jardine has $300 million of debenture bonds outstanding and the unamortized discount is $30 million. The bonds are callable at the discretion of the management at 101. Lower interest rates may convince management to pay off these bonds now. If the market price of the bonds is 99, will Jardine call the bonds at 101 or purchase them for 99 in the open market? Market price is the better choice because the market price is lower than the call price. Let's see how to account for an early retirement of bonds payable. Retiring the bonds at 99 results in a loss of $27 million, computed as follows:

	Millions
Par value of bonds being retired...............................	$300
Less: Unamortized discount.....................................	(30)
Carrying amount of the bonds being retired............	270
Market price ($300 × 0.99).......................................	297
Loss on retirement of bonds payable........................	$ 27

Gains and losses on early retirement of bonds payable are usually reported as Other income (loss) on the Income Statement.

Convertible Bonds and Notes

Some corporate bonds may be converted into the issuing company's share capital. These bonds are called **convertible bonds** (or convertible notes). For investors, these bonds combine the safety of (a) assured receipt of interest and principal on the bonds with (b) the opportunity for gains on the shares. The conversion feature can be so attractive that investors are willing to accept a lower interest rate than they would on non-convertible bonds. The lower cash interest payments benefit the issuer. If the market price of the issuing company's shares gets high enough, the bondholders will convert the bonds into shares.

Suppose Jardine has convertible notes payable of $100 million. If Jardine's share price rises high enough, the noteholders will convert the notes into the company's shares. Conversion of the notes payable into shares will decrease Jardine's liabilities and increase its equity.

Assume the noteholders convert the notes into 4 million shares of Jardine shares ($1 par) on May 14. Jardine makes the following entry in its accounting records:

	A	B	C	D
1	May 14	Notes Payable	100,000,000	
2		Share Capital (4,000,000 × $1 par)		4,000,000
3		Capital in Excess of Par		96,000,000
4		*To record conversion of notes payable.*		
5				

The accounting equation shows that liabilities decrease and equity goes up.

Assets	=	Liabilities	+	Shareholders' Equity
0	=	− 100,000,000	+	+ 4,000,000
				+ 96,000,000

The carrying amount of the notes ($100 million) ceases to be debt and becomes shareholders' equity. Share Capital is recorded at its par value, which is a dollar amount assigned to each share. In this case, the credit to Share Capital is $4,000,000 (4,000,000 shares × $1 par value per share). The extra carrying amount of the notes payable ($96,000,000) is credited to another shareholders' equity account, Capital in Excess of Par. We'll be discussing equity transactions in the next chapter.

ACCOUNT FOR LEASES

A **lease** is a rental agreement in which the tenant (**lessee**) agrees to make rent payments to the property owner (**lessor**) in exchange for the use of the asset. Leasing allows the lessee to acquire the use of a needed asset without having to make the large up-front payment that purchase agreements require.

Let's see how Jardine accounts for its leases.

ADAPTED EXCERPTS FROM JARDINE MATHESON'S NOTES TO THE ACCOUNTS

Leases

Leases are classified as *finance leases* when the terms of the lease transfer substantially all the risks and rewards of ownership to the lessee. All other leases are classified as *operating leases*.

Plant and machinery under *finance leases* are capitalized at the commencement of the lease at the lower of the fair value of the leased asset and the present value of the minimum lease payments. Lease payments are allocated between the liability and finance charges so as to achieve a constant rate on the finance balance outstanding.

Payments made under *operating leases* are charged to profit and loss on a straight-line basis over the period of the lease.

Source: Jardine Matheson's 2015 annual report, page 44

Types of Leases

IAS 17—Leases provides for two categories of leases: operating lease and finance lease (sometimes referred to as financing or capital lease). The accounting treatments for the two types of leases are vastly different. It is therefore important to understand the criteria that would make a lease agreement classified as an operating lease or a capital lease. *IAS 17* states that if the terms of the lease meet *any* of the following conditions, it will be recognized as a capital lease:

- The lease transfers substantially all risks and rewards of the asset to the lessee.
- The lease transfers ownership of the asset to the lessee at the end of the lease.
- The lease term represents a substantial part of the asset's useful life.
- The present value of the lease payments represents a substantial part of the fair value of the asset.

A Closer Look

This is a good example of how the overall approaches of IFRSs differ from U.S. GAAPs. Rather than specific rules or "bright lines," IFRSs employs a principle-based approach that focuses on the overall substance of the transaction, rather than on the mechanical form, and that leaves more to the judgment of the preparer of the financial statement. For example, the recognition of a lease as a capital lease under U.S. GAAP would be that the term of the lease exceeds 75% of the asset's useful life, and the present value of the lease payments exceeds 90% of the asset's fair value, as opposed to the use of the "substantial part" principle in IFRS.

The FASB and IASB have recently issued a new replacement standard for Leases, *IFRS 16 – Leases*, which will be effective for financial statements beginning January 1, 2019. The new standard is a very significant departure from what we are using now, *IAS 17 – Leases*. It will substantially change the way we account for leases. The new standard focuses on "rights of use" as the key decision factor in determining the appropriate accounting treatment for leases. This means doing away with the capital versus operating lease classifications. As long as an entity has a rights of use of an asset with an accompanying commitment to make payments, they will be recognized on the books as assets (representing its rights to use the underlying leased asset) and liabilities (representing its obligation to make lease payments), respectively. There will be some "practical expedients" for very short term leases (or leases of items of very low value), which can continue to be paid as an expense.

Operating Leases. These are basically rental agreements between the lessor and lessee. Many operating leases are non-cancellable (or cancellable with substantial penalties), and require the lessee to commit funds to pay the lessor for use of the leased asset for years. They give the lessee the right to use the asset but provide no continuing rights to the asset. Instead, the lessor retains the usual risks and rewards of owning the leased asset. To account for an operating lease, the lessee debits Rent Expense (or Lease Expense) and credits Cash for the amount of the lease payment.

Jardine incurred a total of $1,085 million operating lease expense in the 2015 financial year ended December 31, 2011. Jardine would have performed a journal entry similar to the entry below:

	A	B	C	D
1	31 Dec	Lease expense	1,085 million	
2		Cash		1,085 million
3		*To record operating lease payments*		
4				

Assets	=	Liabilities	+	Shareholders' Equity	
– 154 million	=	0	+	– 154 million	(lease expense)

The properties or equipment being leased (via operating lease) are not reported as Jardine's assets on its Balance Sheet. Similarly, Jardine's non-cancellable future payments for its operating leases are also not recorded as liabilities on its Balance Sheet. Nevertheless, *IAS 17* imposes an additional disclosure requirement on these operating lease commitments. Jardine's operating lease commitments are shown below.

ADAPTED EXCERPTS FROM JARDINE MATHESON'S NOTES TO THE ACCOUNTS

Operating Lease Commitments (USD millions)	**2015**	**2014**
■ Due within one year	$862	$863
■ Due between one and two years	611	605
■ Due between two and three years	376	383
■ Due between three and four years	202	218
■ Due between four and five years	147	146
■ Due beyond five years	610	730
	2,808	**2,945**

Source: Jardine Matheson's 2015 annual report, page 102

Capital Leases (also called **Finance Leases**). Accounting for a **capital lease** is much like accounting for the purchase of an asset. The lessee enters the asset into the lessee's long-term asset accounts and records a long-term lease liability at the beginning of the lease term. Thus, the lessee capitalizes the asset even though the lessee may never take legal title to the asset, because the lease agreement makes the lessee assume the risks and rewards of ownership of the assets and the associated obligations.

When a capital lease is signed, the lessee will record the present value of its lease payments on its books. The original entry is a debit to lease assets and a credit to lease liability. As the asset is being used, it is depreciated in accordance to the entity's usual depreciation policy. When lease payments are made, it is first made against lease interest expense, and the remaining balance reduces the outstanding lease payments.

Let's assume on July 1, 20X1, Jardine signed a capital lease that requires a payment of $10,000 per year for the next five years. The present value of the lease payments is determined to be $43,295 (using a 5% interest rate).[3] On signing this lease agreement, Jardine would record the following:

	A	B	C	D
1	20X1			
2	July 1	Lease Asset	43,295	
3		Lease Liability		43,295
4		*To record capital lease ($10,000 per year for 5 years @5%).*		
5				

When the first payment is made, on June 30, 20X2, the $10,000 payment is first applied to the interest for the lease liability for the period, which is $2,165 ($43,295 × 5%), and the balance of $7,835 ($10,000 less $2,165) reduces the lease liability.

	A	B	C	D
1	20X2			
2	June 30	Lease Liability	7,835	
3		Interest Expense	2,165	
4		Cash		10,000
5		*To record first capital lease payment.*		
6				

The balance of the lease liability is now $43,295 less $7,835, or $35,460. In the subsequent period, less and less interest will be charged, and higher portions of the lease payments will go towards reducing the lease liability. This schedule is called a lease amortization schedule, shown as follows.

	A	B	C	D	E	F
1	**Period**	**Beginning Lease Liability**	**Payment**	**Towards Interest**	**Towards Lease Liability**	**Ending Lease Liability**
2	(#1) 30 Jun 20X2	$ 43,295	$ 10,000	$ 2,165	$ 7,835	$ 35,460
3	(#1) 30 Jun 20X3	35,460	10,000	1,773	8,227	27,233
4	(#2) 30 Jun 20X4	27,233	10,000	1,362	8,638	18,594
5	(#3) 30 Jun 20X5	18,594	10,000	930	9,070	9,524
6	(#4) 30 Jun 20X6	9,524	10,000	476	9,524	0
7						
8	**Notes:**					
9	Column B	At signing of contract, calculated as present value of lease payments, subsequently from ending balance (Column F)				
10	Column C	Payment per period				
11	Column D	Interest expense for the lease, calculated as lease rate X beginning lease liability (Column B)				
12	Column E	Principal payment towards lease liability, difference between payment (Column C) and interest expense (Column D)				
13	Column F	Ending lease liability which is equal to beginning balance (Column B) less principal lease liability payment (Column E)				
14						

[3] Appendix B (available on www.pearsonglobaleditions.com/Harrison) shows the present value calculations for leases. If you are using Excel, you can use the PV function, i.e., PV (market rate per period, number of periods, interest payment per period) or "= PV (5%, 5, −10,000)" to get $43,295. Any difference from workings using Appendix B is due to rounding of time value factors.

ADAPTED EXCERPTS FROM JARDINE MATHESON'S NOTES TO THE ACCOUNTS

Finance Lease Assets (USD millions)	**2015**	**2014**
■ Plant and machinery	$41	$64
■ Motor vehicles	45	3
	$86	$67

Finance Lease Liabilities (USD millions)	**2015**	**2014**
■ Current finance lease liabilities	$31	$36
■ Non-current finance lease liabilities	65	48
	$96	$84

Source: Jardine Matheson's 2015 annual report, pages 70, 102

While lease assets and lease liabilities start as the same amount, they don't always tally afterwards. Leased assets are usually depreciated using a straight-line basis (and may have residual values), while lease liability are amortized using an effective interest rate method. Furthermore, almost all lease arrangements will require payments at the beginning of the period rather than at the end of the period. You can refer to Appendix B (available on www.pearsonglobaleditions.com/Harrison) for further explanation.

Do Lessees Prefer Operating Leases or Capital Leases?

Suppose you were the chief financial officer (CFO) of a company contemplating a lease agreement. Your total assets are now $100, funded by liability of $60 and equity of $40. The leases can be structured either as operating leases or as capital leases, with total lease payments of $25. Which type of lease would you prefer? Why?

Let's use a general measure of indebtedness called *debt ratio* to illustrate the difference between operating and capital lease. We will discuss debt ratio at the end of the chapter, but for now, it is calculated as total liabilities divided by total assets. It shows how much of the operations are funded by non-shareholders. The basic impact of this lease is as follows:

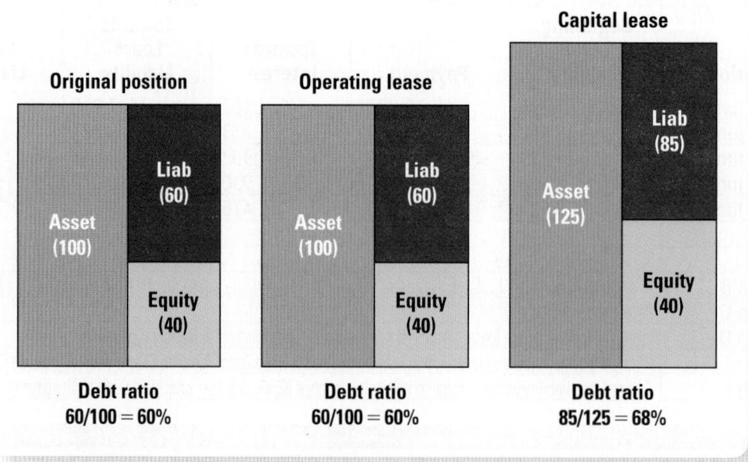

Computing the debt ratio two ways (operating leases versus reclassifying them as capital leases) clearly shows that the addition of assets and liabilities when treated as capital lease will result in a higher debt ratio. You can see that a capital lease increases the debt ratio—by about eight percentage points in this example, but potentially by a lot more for other companies. By contrast, notice that operating leases don't affect the debt ratio. For this reason, many companies prefer operating leases because they allow them to obtain the use of an asset without showing the obligations for the contractual payments.

Another way to think about it is that you will see most businesses having far more operating lease commitments than capital lease obligations. For example, you saw that Jardine has operating lease commitments of $2,808 million and finance lease liabilities of just $96 million. With the new *IFRS 16 – Leases*, most of these "commitments" will be recognized as "liabilities" from 2019 onwards.

ANALYZE THE ADVANTAGES AND DISADVANTAGES OF BORROWING

Financing Operations with Bonds or Shares?

5 **Analyze** the advantages and disadvantages of borrowing

Managers must decide how to get the money they need to pay for assets. There are three main ways to finance operations:

- by retained earnings
- by issuing shares
- by issuing bonds (or notes) payable

Each strategy has its advantages and disadvantages:

1. ***Financed by retained earnings*** means that the company already has enough cash to purchase the needed assets. There's no need to issue more shares or to borrow money. This strategy is low-risk to the company.
2. ***Issuing shares*** creates no liabilities or interest expense and is less risky to the issuing corporation. But issuing shares is more costly, as we shall see.
3. ***Issuing bonds or notes payable*** does not dilute control of the corporation. It often results in higher earnings per share because the earnings on borrowed money can potentially exceed interest expense. But creating more debt increases the risk of the company.

Earnings per share (EPS) is the amount of a company's net income for each of its shares outstanding. EPS is the single most important statistic for evaluating companies because EPS is a standard measure of operating performance that applies to companies of different sizes and from different industries. We will cover EPS in more detail in Chapter 10.

Suppose your business needs $500,000 for expansion. Assume that it has net income of $300,000 and 100,000 shares outstanding. You are considering two financing plans. Plan 1 is to issue $500,000 of 6% bonds payable, and plan 2 is to issue 50,000 shares for $500,000. You believe the new cash can be invested in operations to earn income of $200,000 before interest and taxes.

Exhibit 9-10 shows the earnings-per-share advantage of borrowing. As you can see, your EPS amount is higher if you borrow by issuing bonds (compare lines 10 and 11). You will earn

Exhibit 9-10 Earnings-Per-Share Advantage of Borrowing

A1

	A B C	D	E	F	G
		Plan 1		Plan 2	
1		Borrow $500,000 at 6%		Issue 50,000 Shares of Share Capital for $500,000	
2	Net income before expansion		$ 300,000		$ 300,000
3	Expected project income before interest and income tax	$ 200,000		$200,000	
4	Less interest expense ($500,000 × 0.06)	(30,000)		0	
5	Expected project income before income tax	170,000		200,000	
6	Less income tax expense (40%)	(68,000)		(80,000)	
7	Expected project net income		102,000		120,000
8	Total company net income		$ 402,000		$ 420,000
9	Earnings per share after expansion:				
10	Plan 1 Borrow ($402,000/100,000 shares)		$ 4.02		
11	Plan 2 Issue Shares ($420,000/150,000 shares)				$2.80
12					

DECISION GUIDELINES

FINANCING WITH DEBT OR WITH SHARES

Nando's is the leading chain of Portuguese/Mozambique-themed restaurants, famous for its flame-grilled chicken and "Peri-Peri" sauces. Originated in South Africa, Nando's is now present in over 26 countries and has continued its expansion plan. Suppose Nando's is expanding into a new country or region. Take the role of Fernando Duarte and Robert Brozin, founders of Nando's, and assume you must make some key decisions about how to finance the expansion.

Decision	Guidelines
How will you finance Nando's expansion?	Your financing plan depends on Nando's ability to generate cash flow, your willingness to give up some control of the business, the amount of financing risk you are willing to take, and Nando's credit rating.
Do Nando's operations generate enough cash to meet all its financing needs?	If yes, the business needs little outside financing. There is no need to borrow. If no, the business will need to issue additional shares or borrow the money.
Are you willing to give up some of your control of the business?	If yes, then issue shares to other shareholders, who can vote their shares to elect the company's directors. If no, then borrow from bondholders, or a financial institution, who have no vote in the management of the company.
How much financing risk are you willing to take?	If much, then borrow as much as you can, and you may increase Nando's earnings per share. But this will increase the business's debt ratio and the risk of being unable to pay its debts. If little, then borrow sparingly. This will hold the debt ratio down and reduce the risk of default on borrowing agreements. But Nando's earnings per share may be lower than if you were to borrow.
How good is the business's credit rating?	The better the credit rating, the easier it is to borrow on favorable terms. A good credit rating also makes it easier to issue shares. Neither shareholders nor creditors will entrust their money to a company with a bad credit rating.

more on the investment ($102,000) than the interest it pays on the bonds ($30,000). This is called **trading on the equity**, or using **leverage**. It is widely used to increase earnings per share.

In this case borrowing results in higher earnings per share than issuing new shares. Borrowing has its disadvantages, however. Interest expense may be high enough to eliminate net income and lead to losses. Also, borrowing creates liabilities that must be paid during bad years as well as good years. In contrast, a company that issues shares can omit its dividends during a bad year. The Decision Guidelines provide some help in deciding how to finance operations.

EVALUATE A COMPANY'S DEBT-PAYING ABILITY

Debt Ratio

6 **Evaluate** a company's debt-paying ability

We have just seen how borrowing can increase EPS. But too much debt can lead to bankruptcy if the business cannot pay liabilities as they come due. Many companies in the recent financial crisis fell into the debt trap because they leveraged (borrowed) too much, in anticipation of an unending booming economy, which ran into a crisis eventually.

The **debt ratio** is a general measure of an entity's indebtedness. A simple version of the ratio expresses this indebtedness as the percentage of the assets that are financed by creditors. Jardine's 2015 debt ratio, for example, is its total liabilities ($21,174, line 16 of its Balance Sheet, see start of chapter) divided by its total assets ($66,955, line 4), which is 31.6%. It has decreased slightly from 32.6% ($21,652 over $66,457) in 2014.

Debt Ratio	Jardine 2015	Jardine 2014
$\frac{\text{Total liabilities}}{\text{Total assets}}$	$\frac{21{,}174}{66{,}955} = 31.6\%$	$\frac{21{,}652}{66{,}457} = 32.6\%$

It is difficult to find a company like Jardine. Its business interests span many different sectors and can only be described as a member of a "diversified industry." It may sound counterlogical, but the best comparison to a diversified company is another diversified company even if their businesses are not exactly alike. They all have the power to enter and exit any industry if they wish. Let's use two other Hong Kong-based diversified companies: Swire Pacific (property, aviation, beverages, marine services, and trading and industrial) and Hopewell Holdings (property, expressway, power, and hotel and hospitality) for comparisons to Jardine Matheson (as shown in Exhibit 9-11).

Exhibit 9-11 Debt Ratio Comparisons

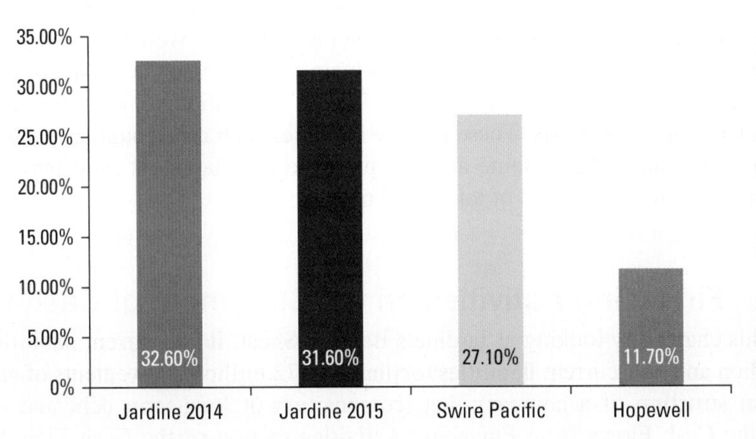

It looks like Jardine is more leveraged, i.e., it has higher debt ratio than the other two companies. However, in general, a debt ratio below 50% is considered low. Different businesses borrow different amounts based on their current needs, expansion plans, and financing model.

The Times-Interest-Earned Ratio

The debt ratio measures the effect of debt on the company's financial position but says nothing about the ability to pay interest expense. Analysts use a second ratio—the **times-interest-earned ratio**—to relate income to interest expense. To compute this ratio, we divide income from operations (also called operating income or operating profit) by interest expense. This ratio measures the number of times that operating income can cover interest expense. The times-interest-earned ratio is also called the **interest-coverage ratio**. A high times-interest-earned ratio indicates ease in paying interest expense; a low value suggests difficulty. As shown in Exhibit 9-12, Jardine's times-interest-earned ratio is at a healthy 13.18 times in 2014 and 14.05 in 2015. These ratios compare favorably to Swire Pacific (at 6.94 times) and Hopewell (at 10.30 times).

Times Interest Earned	Jardine 2015	Jardine 2014
$\frac{\text{Operating income}}{\text{Interest expense}}$	$\frac{3{,}779}{269} = 14.05$ times	$\frac{3{,}676}{279} = 13.18$ times

Exhibit 9-12 | Times-Interest-Earned Ratio Comparisons

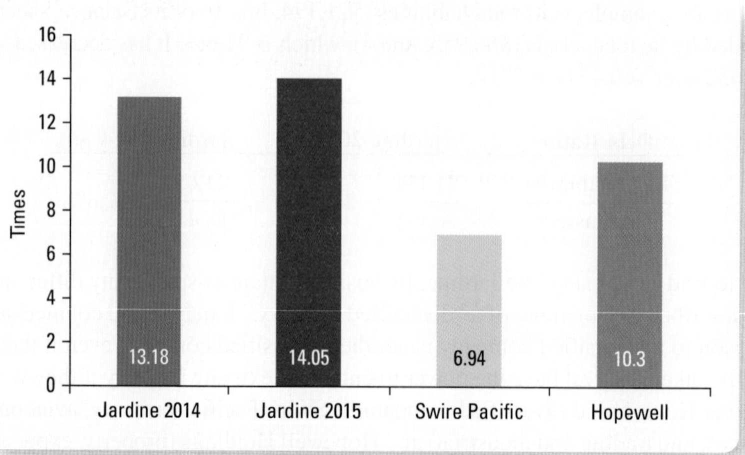

You may be wondering why Jardine's debt ratio is much higher than Swire Pacific and Hopewell, yet its times-interest-earned ratio is much better than the other two. Well, this is why you need to examine more than one financial ratio in order to obtain a more complete picture of the financial position and performance of a company. Much of Jardine's liabilities are non-interest bearing, so they do not incur borrowing costs. These include liabilities such as accounts payable, unearned revenue, provisions, and others. Some analysts prefer to calculate debt ratio purely based on interest-bearing borrowings instead of total liabilities.

Reporting Financing Activities on the Statement of Cash Flows

We started this chapter by looking at Jardine's Balance Sheet. It has current liabilities totaling $12,602 million and non-current liabilities totaling $8,572 million. Movements of cash related to the capital structure of a company, i.e., composition of long-term debt and equity, are reported in the Cash Flows from Financing Activities section of the Cash Flow Statement. We will discuss the Cash Flow Statement fully in Chapter 11, but for now, let's see how these items are reported by Jardine as illustrated in Exhibit 9-13.

Exhibit 9-13 | Jardine Matheson's Consolidated Statement of Cash Flows

	A	B	C
1	**Jardine Matheson Holding Ltd. Consolidated Cash Flow Statement For the Year Ended December 31**		
2	**(Adapted, in millions of US$)**	**2015**	**2014**
3	**Cash flow from operating activities**	$ 4,118	$ 3,354
4	**Cash flow from investing activities**	(3,229)	(2,303)
5	**Cash flow from financing activities**		
6	Issues of shares	2	2
7	Drawdown on borrowings	20,353	20,863
8	Repayment of borrowings	(20,337)	(20,576)
9	Other financing activities	(1,237)	(1,235)
10	Cash flows from financing activities	(1,219)	(946)
11	Net cash flow	$ (330)	$ (105)
12			

End-of-Chapter Summary Problem

The Cessna Aircraft Company has an outstanding issue of 8% convertible bonds that mature in 20X8. Suppose the bonds are issued on October 1, 20X0, and pay interest each April 1 and October 1.

Requirements

1. Complete the following effective-interest amortization table through October 1, 20X2.

   Bond Data

   Maturity (face) value—$100,000

   Stated interest rate—8%

   Interest paid—4% semi-annually, $4,000 ($100,000 × 0.08 × 6/12)

   Market interest rate at the time of issue—9% annually, 4½% semi-annually

   Issue price—93.5 (use this price instead of calculating manually)

Amortization Table

	A	B	C	D	E
Semi-annual Interest Date	Interest Payment (4% of Maturity Amount)	Interest Expense (4½% of Preceding Bond Carrying Amount)	Discount Amortization (B – A)	Discount Account Balance (Preceding D – C)	Bond Carrying Amount ($100,000 – D)
10-1-X0					
4-1-X1					
10-1-X1					
4-1-X2					
10-1-X2					

2. Using the amortization table, record the following transactions:
   a. Issuance of the bonds on October 1, 20X0.
   b. Accrual of interest and amortization of the bonds on December 31, 20X0.
   c. Payment of interest and amortization of the bonds on April 1, 20X1.
   d. Conversion of one-third of the bonds payable into no-par share on October 2, 20X2. For no-par share, transfer the bond carrying amount into the Share Capital account. There is no Additional Paid-in Capital account.
   e. Retirement of two-thirds of the bonds payable on October 2, 20X2. Purchase price of the bonds was based on their call price of 102.

Answers

Requirement 1

Semi-annual Interest Date	A Interest Payment (4% of Maturity Amount)	B Interest Expense (4½% of Preceding Bond Carrying Amount)	C Discount Amortization (B – A)	D Discount Account Balance (Preceding D – C)	E Bond Carrying Amount ($100,000 – D)
10-1-X0				$6,500	$93,500
4-1-X1	$4,000	$4,208	$208	6,292	93,708
10-1-X1	4,000	4,217	217	6,075	93,925
4-1-X2	4,000	4,227	227	5,848	94,152
10-1-X2	4,000	4,237	237	5,611	94,389

Requirement 2

	A	B	C	D	E
1	a.	20X0			
2		Oct 1	Cash ($100,000 × 0.935)	93,500	
3			Discount on Bonds Payable	6,500	
4			Bonds Payable		100,000
5			*To issue bonds at a discount.*		
6					
7	b.	Dec 31	Interest Expense ($4,208 × 3/6)	2,104	
8			Discount on Bonds Payable ($208 × 3/6)		104
9			Interest Payable ($4,000 × 3/6)		2,000
10			*To accrue interest and amortize the bonds.*		
11					
12	c.	20X1			
13		Apr 1	Interest Expense ($4,208 × 3/6)	2,104	
14			Interest Payable	2,000	
15			Discount on Bonds Payable ($208 × 3/6)		104
16			Cash		4,000
17			*To pay semi-annual interest, part of which was*		
18			*accrued, and amortize the bonds.*		
19					
20	d.	20X2			
21		Oct 2	Bonds Payable ($100,000 × 1/3)	33,333	
22			Discount on Bonds Payable ($5,611 × 1/3)		1,870
23			Share Capital ($94,389 × 1/3)		31,463
24			*To record conversion of bonds payable.*		
25					
26	e.	Oct 2	Bonds Payable ($100,000 × 2/3)	66,667	
27			Loss on Retirement of Bonds	5,074	
28			Discount on Bonds Payable ($5,611 × 2/3)		3,741
29			Cash ($100,000 × 2/3 × 1.02)		68,000
30			*To retire bonds payable before maturity.*		
31					

REVIEW | Liabilities

Quick Check (Answers are given at the end of the chapter.)

1. Which of the following is not an estimated liability?
   a. Income taxes paid
   b. Allowance for bad debts
   c. Product warranties
   d. Retirement obligations

2. The estimated warranty obligation at the end of the financial year is best described as which of the following?
   a. Contingent liability
   b. Unrecognized liability
   c. Uncertain liability
   d. Constructive liability
   e. Liability

3. Crank the Volume grants a 120-day warranty on all stereos. Historically, approximately 1% of all units sold prove to be defective, requiring an average repair bill of $100. Sales in March are $472,500 for 4,500 units. In March, $3,900 of defective units are returned for replacement. What entry must Crank the Volume make at the end of March to record the warranty expense?
   a. Debit Warranty Expense and credit Provision for Warranty Repairs, $4,725.
   b. Debit Warranty Expense and credit Provision for Warranty Repairs, $3,900.
   c. Debit Warranty Expense and credit Cash, $4,725.
   d. No entry is needed at March 31.

4. Excursion Camera Co. was organized to sell a single product that carries a 45-day warranty against defects. Engineering estimates indicate that 4% of the units sold will prove defective and require an average repair cost of $25 per unit. During Expedition's first month of operations, total sales were 800 units; by the end of the month, 15 defective units had been repaired. The liability for product warranties at month-end should be
   a. $1,175.
   b. $425.
   c. $375.
   d. $800.
   e. none of these.

5. A contingent liability should be recorded in the accounts
   a. if the amount is due in cash within one year.
   b. if the amount can be reasonably estimated.
   c. if the related future event will probably occur.
   d. Both b and c
   e. Both a and c

6. An unsecured bond is a
   a. serial bond.
   b. term bond.
   c. registered bond.
   d. mortgage bond.
   e. debenture bond.

7. The Discount on Bonds Payable account
   a. is expensed at the bond's maturity.
   b. is a contra account to Bonds Payable.
   c. is an expense account.
   d. is a miscellaneous revenue account.
   e. has a normal credit balance.

8. The discount on a bond payable becomes

a. additional interest expense over the life of the bonds.
b. a liability in the year the bonds are sold.
c. a reduction in interest expense over the life of the bonds.
d. additional interest expense the in year the bonds are sold.
e. a reduction in interest expense in the year the bonds mature.

9. A bond that matures in installments is called a

a. secured bond.
b. term bond.
c. serial bond.
d. callable bond.
e. zero coupon.

10. The carrying value of Bonds Payable equals

a. Bonds Payable + Discount on Bonds Payable.
b. Bonds Payable − Premium on Bonds Payable.
c. Bonds Payable − Discount on Bonds Payable.
d. Bonds Payable + Accrued Interest.

11. A corporation issues bonds that pay interest each May 1 and November 1. The corporation's December 31 adjusting entry may include a

a. credit to Cash.
b. debit to Interest Payable.
c. debit to Cash.
d. credit to Discount on Bonds Payable.
e. credit to Interest Expense.

Use this information to answer questions 12–16.
McCabe Corporation issued $560,000 of 7% 10-year bonds. The bonds are dated and sold on January 1, 20X1. Interest payment dates are January 1 and July 1. The bonds are issued for $521,724 to yield the market interest rate of 8%. Use the effective-interest method for questions 12–16.

12. What is the amount of interest expense that McCabe Corporation will record on July 1, 20X1, the first semi-annual interest payment date? (All amounts rounded to the nearest dollar.)

a. $22,400
b. $39,200
c. $19,600
d. $20,869

13. What is the amount of discount amortization that McCabe Corporation will record on July 1, 20X1, the first semi-annual interest payment date?

a. $0
b. $1,269
c. $2,240
d. $2,538

14. What is the total cash payment for interest for each 12-month period? (All amounts rounded to the nearest dollar.)

a. $22,400
b. $41,789
c. $39,200
d. $44,800

15. What is the total interest expense for the year ended December 31, 20X1?

a. $41,789
b. $41,879
c. $39,200
d. $19,600

16. What is the carrying amount of the bonds on the January 1, 20X2, Balance Sheet?

a. $524,313
b. $521,724
c. $522,993
d. $550,000

Accounting Vocabulary

accrued expense (p. 505) An expense incurred but not yet paid in cash. Also called accrued liability.

accrued liability (p. 505) A liability for an expense that has not yet been paid. Also called accrued expense.

bonds payable (p. 516) Groups of notes payable issued to multiple lenders called bondholders.

callable bond (p. 529) Bonds that are paid off early at a specified price at the option of the issuer.

capital lease (p. 532) Lease agreement in which the lessee assumes, in substance, the risks and rewards of asset ownership.

convertible bonds (or notes) (p. 530) Bonds or notes that may be converted into the issuing company's share capital at the investor's option.

current portion of long-term debt (p. 512) The amount of the principal that is payable within one year.

debentures (p. 516) Unsecured bonds—bonds backed only by the good faith of the borrower.

debt ratio (p. 537). A measure of indebtedness or leverage. Measured by total liabilities divided by total assets.

deposits (p. 506) Sometimes required by businesses before providing goods or services. May be deposits placed (as a customer) or deposits received (as a business).

discount (on a bond) (p. 516) Excess of a bond's face (par) value over its issue price.

earnings per share (EPS) (p. 535) Amount of a company's net income per share of its outstanding share capital.

interest-coverage ratio (p. 537) Another name for the times-interest-earned ratio.

lease (p. 530) Rental agreement in which the tenant (lessee) agrees to make rent payments to the property owner (lessor) in exchange for the use of the asset.

lessee (p. 530) Tenant or recipient of the leased asset in a lease agreement.

lessor (p. 530) Property owner of the leased asset in a lease agreement.

leverage (p. 536) Using borrowed funds to increase the return on equity. Successful use of leverage means earning more income on borrowed money than the related interest expense, thereby increasing the earnings for the owners of the business. Also called trading on the equity.

market interest rate (p. 518) Interest rate that investors demand for loaning their money. Also called effective interest rate.

operating lease (p. 532) A lease in which the lessee does not assume the risks or rewards of asset ownership.

payroll (p. 507) Employee compensation, a major expense of many businesses.

pension (p. 508) Employee compensation that will be paid during the employee's retirement.

premium (on a bond) (p. 516) Excess of a bond's issue price over its face (par) value.

present value (p. 517) Amount a person would invest now to receive a greater amount at a future date.

serial bonds (p. 516) Bonds that mature in installments over a period of time.

short-term notes payable (p. 511) Note payable due within one year.

stated interest rate (p. 518) Interest rate that determines the amount of cash interest the borrower pays and the investor receives each year.

term bonds (p. 516) Bonds that all mature at the same time for a particular issue.

times-interest-earned ratio (p. 537) Ratio of income from operations to interest expense. Measures the number of times that operating income can cover interest expense. Also called the interest-coverage ratio.

trading on the equity (p. 536) Earning more income on borrowed money than the related interest expense, thereby increasing the earnings for the owners of the business. Also called leverage.

underwriter (p. 516) Organization that purchases the bonds from an issuing company and resells them to its clients or sells the bonds for a commission, agreeing to buy all unsold bonds.

ASSESS YOUR PROGRESS

Short Exercises

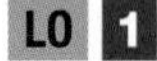

S9-1. ***(Learning Objective 1: Accounting for a note payable)*** Ferdie Sports Authority purchased inventory costing $4,000 by signing an 8% short-term note payable. The purchase occurred on September 30, 20X0. Ferdie pays annual interest each year on September 30. Journalize the company's (a) purchase of inventory, (b) accrual of interest expense on June 30, 20X1, which is the year-end, and (c) payment of the note plus interest on September 30, 20X1. (Round your answers to the nearest whole number.)

LO 1 **S9-2.** ***(Learning Objective 1: Reporting a short-term note payable and the related interest in the financial statements)*** This short exercise works with Short Exercise 9-1.

1. Refer to the data in Short Exercise 9-1. Show what the company would report on its Balance Sheet at June 30, 20X1, and on its Income Statement for the year ended on that date.
2. What single item will the financial statements for the year ended June 30, 20X2, report? Identify the financial statement, the item, and its amount.

LO 1 **S9-3.** ***(Learning Objective 1: Accounting for warranty expense and provision for warranty repairs)*** Lawry guarantees automobiles against defects for five years or 50,000 miles, whichever comes first. Assume that a Lawry dealer in Paris, France, made sales of $485,000 during 20X0. Lawry expects warranty costs during the five-year period to add up to about $29,100. Lawry received cash for 30% of the sales and took notes receivable for the remainder. Payments to satisfy customer warranty claims totaled $18,000 during 20X0.

1. Record the sales, warranty expense, and warranty payments for Lawry.
2. Post to the Provision for Warranty Repairs T-account. The beginning balance was $11,000. At the end of 20X0, how much in provision for warranty repairs does Lawry owe to its customers?

LO 1 **S9-4.** ***(Learning Objective 1: Applying accounting standards; reporting warranties in the financial statements)*** Refer to the data given in Short Exercise 9-3. What amount of warranty expense will Lawry report during 20X0? Which accounting principle addresses this situation? Does the warranty expense for the year equal the year's cash payments for warranties? Explain the relevant accounting principle as it applies to measuring warranty expense.

LO 1 **S9-5.** ***(Learning Objective 1: Interpreting a company's contingent liabilities)*** OC Petroleum Inc., an oil company, included a disclosure in its annual report stating that it was denying a variety of litigations from environmental groups that arose following an incident on one of their rigs in the Gulf of Mexico.

How can a contingency liability become a real liability for the company? What would be the impact on the financial statements if these claims are recognized as a provision instead of contingent liability?

LO 2 **S9-6.** ***(Learning Objective 2: Pricing bonds)*** Compute the cash received from the issuance of the following bonds:

a. $400,000 issued at 75.75
b. $400,000 issued at 102.75
c. $400,000 issued at 94.50
d. $400,000 issued at 104.50

LO 2 **S9-7.** ***(Learning Objective 2: Determining bond prices at par, discount, or premium)*** Determine whether the following bonds payable will be issued at maturity value, at a premium, or at a discount:

a. The market interest rate is 5%. Esme Corp. issues bonds payable with a stated rate of 4.5%.
b. Trinity Corp. issued 5% bonds when the market interest rate was 5%.
c. Ottawa Company issued bonds payable that pay stated interest of 6%. At issuance, the market interest rate was 7.25%.
d. Howler, Inc., issued 7% bonds payable when the market rate was 6.75%.

LO 2 **S9-8.** ***(Learning Objective 2: Journalizing basic bond payable transactions; bonds issued at par)*** Derp Corp. issued 15-year bonds payable with a face amount of $70,000, when the market interest rate was 6.5%. The bonds were issued at par. Assume that the accounting year of Derp ends on December 31. Journalize the following transactions for Derp. Include an explanation for each entry.

a. Issuance of the bonds payable at par on July 1, 20X0.
b. Accrual of interest expense on December 31, 20X0 (rounded to the nearest dollar).
c. Payment of cash interest on January 1, 20X1.
d. Payment of the bonds payable at maturity.

LO 2

S9-9. ***(Learning Objectives 2: Issuing bonds payable; amortizing bonds by the effective-interest method)*** GIT, Inc., issued $60,000 of 5%, 12-year bonds payable on March 31, 20X0. The market interest rate at the date of issuance was 8%, and the GIT bonds pay interest semi-annually.

1. Prepare an effective-interest amortization table for the bonds through the first three interest payments. Round amounts to the nearest dollar.
2. Record GIT, Inc.'s issuance of the bonds on March 31, 20X0, and payment of the first semi-annual interest amount and amortization of the bond discount on September 30, 20X0. Explanations are not required.

LO 2 3

S9-10. ***(Learning Objectives 2, 3: Accounting for bonds payable; analyzing data on long-term debt)*** Use the amortization table that you prepared for GIT's bonds in Short Exercise 9-9 to answer the following questions:

1. How much cash did GIT borrow on March 31, 20X0? How much cash will GIT pay back at maturity on March 31, 20Y2 (i.e., 12 years later).
2. How much cash interest will GIT pay each six months?
3. How much interest expense will GIT report on September 30, 20X0, and on March 31, 20X1? Why does the amount of interest expense increase each period?

S9-11. ***(Learning Objective 2: Issuing bonds payable; accruing interest; amortizing bonds by the effective interest method)*** Villa Drive-Ins Ltd. issued a $520,000, 8%, 10-year bond payable on July 1, 20X0, when the market rate was 10%. Also assume that Villa's accounting year ends on December 31. Journalize the following transactions for Villa Drive-Ins Ltd., including an explanation for each entry:

- **a.** Issuance of the bond payable on July 1, 20X0.
- **b.** Accrual of interest expense and amortization of bonds on December 31, 20X0. (Use the effective interest amortization method, and round amounts to the nearest dollar.)
- **c.** Payment of the first semi-annual interest amount on January 1, 20X1.

S9-12. ***(Learning Objective 3: Recording operating and capital lease)*** Lily Pan Enterprises entered into two lease agreements for 5 years on January 1, 20X0. Both leases require a payment of $15,000 per year at the end of each year. Lease 1 is structured as an operating lease while Lease 2 is structured as a capital lease with an implicit interest rate of 5%. Prepare all relevant journal entries for both leases on:

- **a.** The day of signing the lease contract
- **b.** The day of the first lease payment

LO 4

S9-13. ***(Learning Objective 4: Computing earnings-per-share effects of financing with bonds versus shares)*** Speedtown Marina needs to raise $3.5 million to expand the company. Speedtown Marina is considering the issuance of either:

- $3,500,000 of 8% bonds payable to borrow the money, or
- 100,000 shares of share capital at $35 per share.

Before any new financing, Speedtown Marina expects to earn net income of $300,000, and the company already has 100,000 shares of share capital outstanding. Speedtown Marina believes the expansion will increase income before interest and income tax by $500,000. The income tax rate is 35%.

Prepare an analysis to determine which plan is likely to result in the higher earnings per share. Based solely on the earnings-per-share comparison, which financing plan would you recommend for Speedtown Marina?

LO 4
■ writing assignment

S9-14. ***(Learning Objective 4: Computing the times-interest-earned ratio)*** Kermit Plumbing Products Ltd. reported the following data in 20X0 (in billions):

	20X0
Net operating revenues	$29.8
Operating expenses	24.6
Operating income	5.2
Non-operating items:	
Interest expense	(1.6)
Other	(0.2)
Net income	$ 3.4

Compute Kermit's times-interest-earned ratio, and write a sentence to explain what the ratio value means. Would you be willing to lend Kermit $1 billion? State your reason.

LO 5

S9-15. ***(Learning Objective 5: Reporting liabilities, including capital lease obligations)*** Lovely Home, Inc., includes the following selected accounts in its general ledger at December 31, 20X0:

Bonds payable	$402,000
Equipment	113,000
Current portion of bonds payable	50,000
Notes payable, long-term	320,000
Interest payable (due March 1, 20X1)	2,000
Accounts payable	35,000
Discount on bonds payable (all long-term)	11,000
Accounts receivable	28,000

Prepare the liabilities section of Lovely Home, Inc.'s Balance Sheet at December 31, 20X0, to show how the company would report these items. Report total current liabilities and total liabilities.

Exercises MyLab Accounting

Select A and B exercises can be found within MyLab Accounting, an online homework and practice environment. Your instructor may ask you to complete select exercises using MyLab Accounting.

Group A

LO 1

E9-16A. ***(Learning Objective 1: Accounting for warranty expense and the related liability)*** The accounting records of From the Athena Ceramics included the following balances at the end of the period:

Provision for Warranty Repairs		Warranty Expense	
	Beg. bal. 3,000		

From the Athena has determined that its warranty obligations at the end of the period are equal to $12,000. During 20X0, the business paid $54,000 to satisfy the warranty claims.

Requirements

1. Journalize From the Athena's warranty expense for the period and the company's cash payments to satisfy warranty claims. Explanations are not required.
2. Show what From the Athena will report on its Income Statement and Balance Sheet for this situation.
3. Which data item from Requirement 2 will affect From the Athena's current ratio? Will From the Athena's current ratio increase or decrease as a result of this item?

E9-17A. ***(Learning Objective 1: Recording and reporting current liabilities)*** TransWorld Publishing completed the following transactions for one subscriber during 20X0: LO 1

Oct 1	Sold a one-year subscription, collecting cash of $1,500, plus sales tax of 8%.
Nov 15	Remitted (paid) the sales tax to the TianJin Municipality.
Dec 31	Made the necessary adjustment at year-end.

Requirement

1. Journalize these transactions (explanations not required). Then report any liability on the company's Balance Sheet at December 31, 20X0.

E9-18A. ***(Learning Objective 1: Reporting payroll expense and liabilities)*** Star Talent Search has an annual payroll of $220,000. In addition, the company incurs a payroll tax expense of 8%. At December 31, Star owes salaries of $8,200 and payroll tax of $700. The company will pay these amounts early next year. Show what Star will report for the foregoing on its Income Statement and year-end Balance Sheet. LO 1

E9-19A. ***(Learning Objective 1: Recording note payable transactions)*** Assume that Gretel Company completed the following note-payable transactions. LO 1

20X0	
May 1	Purchased delivery truck costing $85,000 by issuing a one-year, 6% note payable.
Dec 31	Accrued interest on the note payable.
20X1	
May 1	Paid the note payable at maturity.

Requirements

1. How much interest expense must be accrued at December 31, 20X0? (Round your answer to the nearest whole dollar.)
2. Determine the amount of Gretel's final payment on May 1, 20X1.
3. How much interest expense will Gretel report for 20X0 and for 20X1? (Round your answer to the nearest whole dollar.)

E9-20A. ***(Learning Objective 1: Accounting for income tax)*** At December 31, 20X0, Sandara Real Estate reported a current liability for income tax payable of $190,000. During 20X1, Sandara earned income of $1,300,000 before income tax. The company's income tax rate during 20X1 was 36%. Also during 20X1, Sandara paid income taxes of $360,000. LO 1

How much income tax payable did Sandara Real Estate report on its Balance Sheet at December 31, 20X1? How much income tax expense did Sandara report on its 20X1 Income Statement?

E9-21A. ***(Learning Objectives 1, 5: Analyzing liabilities)*** Riverside Manors, Inc., builds environmentally sensitive structures. The company's 20X1 revenues totaled $2,780 million, and at December 31, 20X1, the company had $660 million in current assets. The December 31, 20X1 and 20X0, Balance Sheets reported the liabilities and shareholders' equity as follows: LO 1 5

■ writing assignment

	A	B	C
1	**At year-end (in millions)**	**20X1**	**20X0**
2	Liabilities and Shareholders' Equity		
3	Current Liabilities		
4	Accounts payable	$ 138	$ 179
5	Accrued expenses	155	172
6	Employee compensation and benefits	38	20
7	Current portion of long-term debt	9	24
8	Total Current Liabilities	340	395
9	Long-Term Debt	1,494	1,323
10	Post-Retirement Benefits Payable	122	123
11	Other Liabilities	12	8
12	Shareholders' Equity	2,027	1,784
13	Total Liabilities and Shareholders' Equity	$ 3,995	$ 3,633
14			

Requirements

1. Describe each of Riverside Manors, Inc.'s liabilities and state how the liability arose.
2. What were the company's total assets at December 31, 20X1? Was the company's debt ratio at the end of 20X1 high, low, or in a middle range?

LO 1

E9-22A. ***(Learning Objective 1: Reporting a contingent liability)*** Rupert Security Systems' revenues for 20X0 totaled $7.3 million. As with most companies, Rupert is a defendant in lawsuits related to its products. Note 14 of the Rupert Annual Report for 20X0 explains the company's policy on legal proceedings, stating that they will accrue for amounts related to legal matters if liability is probable and if it is reasonable to estimate an amount.

Requirements

1. Suppose Rupert's lawyers believe that a significant legal judgment against the company is reasonably possible. How should Rupert report this situation in its financial statements?
2. Suppose Rupert's lawyers believe it is probable that a $1.8 million judgment will be rendered against the company. Report this situation in Rupert's financial statements. Journalize any entry requirements by IFRS. Explanations are not required.

LO 1 5

E9-23A. ***(Learning Objectives 1, 5: Reporting current and long-term liabilities)*** Assume that Boni Electronics completed these selected transactions during June 20X0:

- **a.** Sales of $2,400,000 are subject to estimated warranty cost of $168,000. The provision for warranty repairs at the beginning of the year was $35,000, and warranty payments for the year totaled $52,000.
- **b.** On June 1, Boni Electronics signed a $56,000 note payable that requires annual payments of $14,000 plus 6% interest on the unpaid balance each June 2.
- **c.** Music For You, Inc., a chain of music stores, ordered $135,000 worth of CD players. With its order, Music For You, Inc., sent a check for $135,000 in advance, and Boni shipped $75,000 of the goods. Boni will ship the remainder of the goods on July 3, 20X0.
- **d.** The June payroll of $270,000 is subject to employee withheld income tax of $33,000 and payroll tax of 7.65%. On June 30, Boni pays employees their take-home pay and accrues all tax amounts.

Requirement

1. Report these items on Boni Electronics' Balance Sheet at June 30, 20X0.

LO 2

E9-24A. ***(Learning Objective 2: Issuing bonds payable [premium]; paying and accruing interest; amortizing the bonds by the effective interest method)*** On January 31, Driftwood Logistics, Inc., issued 10-year, 6% bonds payable with a face value of $15,000,000. The bonds were issued when the market rate was 5% and pay interest on January 31 and July 31. Driftwood Logistics, Inc., amortizes bonds by the effective interest method.

Requirements

1. Record issuance of the bonds on January 31.
2. Record the semi-annual interest payment and amortization of bond discount on July 31.
3. Record the interest accrual and discount amortization on December 31.

E9-25A. ***(Learning Objectives: Measuring cash amounts for a bond payable [premium]; amortizing the bonds by the straight-line method)*** Federal Bank has $600,000 of 7% debenture bonds outstanding. The bonds were issued at 103 in 20X0 and mature in 20Z0 (20 years later). LO 2

Requirements

1. How much cash did Federal Bank receive when it issued these bonds?
2. How much cash in total will Federal Bank pay the bondholders through the maturity date of the bonds?
3. Take the difference between your answers to Requirements 1 and 2. What does this number represent?
4. Estimate the Federal Bank's interest expense using the straight-line amortization method for the first two interest payments.

E9-26A. ***(Learning Objective 2: Issuing bonds payable [discount]; recording interest payments and the related bond amortization)*** Goal Sports Ltd. is authorized to issue $3,200,000 of 10%, 10-year bonds payable. On December 31, 20X0, when the market interest rate is 12%, the company issues $2,500,000 of the bonds. Goal Sports Ltd. amortizes bond discounts by the effective-interest method. The semi-annual interest dates are June 30 and December 31. LO 2 ■ spreadsheet

Requirements

1. Prepare a bond amortization table for the first four semi-annual interest periods.
2. Record issuance of the bonds payable on December 31, 20X0, the first semi-annual interest payment on June 30, 20X1, and the second payment on December 31, 20X1.

E9-27A. ***(Learning Objective 2: Issuing bonds payable [premium]; recording interest accrual and payment and the related bond amortization)*** On June 30, 20X0, the market interest rate is 4%. Score Sports Ltd. issues $850,000 of 5%, 30-year bonds payable. The bonds pay interest on June 30 and December 31. Score Sports Ltd. amortizes bonds by the effective-interest method. LO 2 ■ spreadsheet

Requirements

1. Prepare a bond amortization table for the first four semi-annual interest periods.
2. Record the issuance of bonds payable on June 30, 20X0, the payment of interest on December 31, 20X0, and the payment of interest on June 30, 20X1.

E9-28A. ***(Learning Objective 2: Creating a bond amortization schedule [discount])*** Dracula Co. issued $110,000 of 8%, 10-year bonds payable on January 1, 20X0, when the market interest rate was 10%. The company pays interest annually at year-end. LO 2 ■ spreadsheet

Requirement

1. Create a spreadsheet model to prepare a schedule to amortize the bonds. Use the effective-interest method of amortization. (Round to the nearest dollar.)

E9-29A. ***(Learning Objective 3: Recording operating and capital lease, preparing lease amortization schedule)*** Big Billy Guff entered into a lease agreement for an asset on the following terms: LO 3

- Lease period = 4 years
- Lease payment = $25,000 at the end of each period
- Lease interest rate = 10%

Requirements

1. Assuming that this lease qualifies as a capital lease, prepare the lease amortization table, starting from the signing of the lease to the final lease payments. Prepare the journal entry for the first lease payment.

2. Assuming that this lease qualifies as an operating lease, prepare the journal entry for the first lease payment.
3. Explain how a lease for the same item may be treated so differently by two companies.

LO 4

E9-30A. *(Learning Objective 4: Measuring the times-interest-earned ratio)* Companies that operate in different industries may have very different financial ratio values. These differences may grow even wider when we compare companies located in different countries.

	A	B	C	D
1	**(Amounts in millions or billions)**	**Company A**	**Company N**	**Company S**
2	**Income data**			
3	Total revenues	$ 9,723	¥ 7,311	€ 136,431
4	Operating income	291	222	5,581
5	Interest expense	42	31	671
6	Net income	27	15	441
7				
8	**Asset and liability data**			
9	**(Amounts in millions or billions)**			
10	Total current assets	430	5,943	170,150
11	Long-term assets	138	48	45,324
12	Total current liabilities	196	2,198	72,420
13	Long-term liabilities	139	2,350	110,757
14	Shareholders' equity	233	1,443	32,297
15				

Compare three leading companies on their current ratio, debt ratio, and times-interest-earned ratio. Compute three ratios for Company A, Company N, and Company S.

Based on your computed ratio values, which company looks the least risky?

LO 4

■ **writing assignment**

E9-31A. *(Learning Objective 4: Analyzing alternative plans for raising money)* First Bank Financial Services is considering two plans for raising $900,000 to expand operations. Plan A is to borrow at 10%, and plan B is to issue 225,000 shares of share capital at $4.00 per share. Before any new financing, First Bank Financial Services has net income of $600,000 and 200,000 shares of share capital outstanding. Assume you own most of First Bank Financial Services' existing shares. Its management believes the company can use the new funds to earn additional income of $800,000 before interest and taxes. First Bank Financial Services' income tax rate is 25%.

Requirements

1. Analyze First Bank Financial Services' situation to determine which plan will result in higher earnings per share.
2. Which plan results in the higher earnings per share? Which plan allows you to retain control of the company? Which plan creates more financial risk for the company? Which plan do you prefer? Why? Present your conclusion in a memo to First Bank Financial Services' board of directors.

Group B

LO 1

E9-32B. *(Learning Objective 1: Accounting for warranty expense and the related liability)* The accounting records of Made of Glass Ceramics included the following balances at the end of the period:

Provision for Warranty Repairs		Warranty Expense	
	Beg. bal. 4,000		

Made of Glass has determined that its warranty obligations at the end of the year are equal to €12,000. During 20X0, the business paid €5,000 to satisfy the warranty claims.

Requirements

1. Journalize Made of Glass's warranty expense for the period and the company's cash payments to satisfy warranty claims. Explanations are not required.
2. Show what Made of Glass will report on its Income Statement and Balance Sheet for this situation.
3. Which data item from Requirement 2 will affect Made of Glass's current ratio? Will Made of Glass's current ratio increase or decrease as a result of this item?

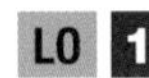

E9-33B. ***(Learning Objective 1: Recording and reporting current liabilities)*** Trevor Publishing completed the following transactions for one subscriber during 20X0:

Oct 1	Sold a one-year subscription, collecting cash of $1,400, plus sales tax of 9%.
Nov 15	Remitted (paid) the sales tax to the Limburg Provincial Office.
Dec 31	Made the necessary adjustment at year-end.

Requirement

1. Journalize these transactions (explanations not required). Then report any liability on the company's Balance Sheet at December 31.

LO 1

E9-34B. ***(Learning Objective 1: Reporting payroll expense and liabilities)*** MV Talent Search has an annual payroll of €180,000. In addition, the company incurs a payroll tax expense of 9%. At December 31, MV owes salaries of €7,800 and payroll tax of €750. The company will pay these amounts early next year.

Show what MV will report for the foregoing on its Income Statement and year-end — Balance Sheet.

LO 1

E9-35B. ***(Learning Objective 1: Recording note payable transactions)*** Assume that Hansel Company completed the following note-payable transactions:

20X0	
Mar 1	Purchased delivery truck costing $80,000 by issuing a one-year, 5% note payable.
Dec 31	Accrued interest on the note payable.
20X1	
Mar 1	Paid the note payable at maturity.

Requirements

1. How much interest expense must be accrued at December 31, 20X0? (Round your answer to the nearest whole dollar.)
2. Determine the amount of Hansel's final payment on March 1, 20X1.
3. How much interest expense will Hansel report for 20X0 and for 20X1? (Round your answer to the nearest whole dollar.)

E9-36B. ***(Learning Objective 1: Accounting for income tax)*** At December 31, 20X0, Sybil Real Estate reported a current liability for income tax payable of €160,000. During 20X1, Sybil earned income of €1,600,000 before income tax. The company's income tax rate during 20X1 was 25%. Also during 20X1, Sybil paid income taxes of €310,000.

How much income tax payable did Sybil Real Estate report on its Balance Sheet at December 31, 20X1? How much income tax expense did Saglio report on its 20X1 Income Statement?

LO 1 5
■ writing assignment

E9-37B. ***(Learning Objectives 1, 5: Analyzing liabilities)*** Green Earth Structures, Inc., builds environmentally sensitive structures. The company's 20X1 revenues totaled €2,852 million, and at December 31, 20X1, the company had €652 million in current assets. The December 31, 20X1 and 20X0, Balance Sheets reported the liabilities and shareholders' equity as follows.

	A	B	C
1	**At year-end (in millions)**	**20X1**	**20X0**
2	Liabilities and Shareholders' Equity		
3	Current Liabilities		
4	Accounts payable	€ 145	€ 183
5	Accrued expenses	161	182
6	Employee compensation and benefits	131	15
7	Current portion of long-term debt	3	9
8	Total Current Liabilities	340	389
9	Long-Term Debt	1,488	1,317
10	Post-Retirement Benefits Payable	129	135
11	Other Liabilities	11	7
12	Shareholders' Equity	2,030	1,776
13	Total Liabilities and Shareholders' Equity	€ 3,998	€ 3,624
14			

Requirements

1. Describe each of Green Earth Structures, Inc.'s liabilities and state how the liability arose.
2. What were the company's total assets at December 31, 20X1? Was the company's debt ratio at the end of 20X1 high, low, or in a middle range?

LO 1

E9-38B. ***(Learning Objective 1: Reporting a contingent liability)*** Edward Security Systems' revenues for 20X0 totaled €26.7 million. As with most companies, Edward is a defendant in lawsuits related to its products. Note 14 of the Edward Annual Report for 20X0 explains the company's policy on legal proceedings, stating that they will accrue for amounts related to legal matters if liability is probable and if it is reasonable to estimate an amount.

Requirements

1. Suppose Edward's lawyers believe that a significant legal judgment against the company is reasonably possible. How should Edward report this situation in its financial statements?
2. Suppose Edward's lawyers believe it is probable that a €2.3 million judgment will be rendered against the company. Report this situation in Edward's financial statements. Journalize any entry required by IFRS. Explanations are not required.

LO 1 5

E9-39B. ***(Learning Objectives 1, 5: Reporting current and long-term liabilities)*** Assume Hi-Tech Electronics completed these transactions during September 20X0.

a. Sales of €2,150,000 are subject to estimated warranty cost of €112,500. The provision for warranty repairs at the beginning of the year was €34,000, and warranty payments for the year totaled €57,000.

b. On September 1, Hi-Tech Electronics signed a €44,000 note payable that requires annual payments of €11,000 plus 4% interest on the unpaid balance each September 2.

c. Music For You, Inc., a chain of music stores, ordered €100,000 worth of CD players. With its order, Music For You, Inc., sent a check for €100,000, and Hi-Tech Electronics shipped €85,000 of the goods. Hi-Tech Electronics will ship the remainder of the goods on October 3, 20X0.

d. The September payroll of €250,000 is subject to employee withheld income tax of €30,000 and payroll tax of 7.65%. On September 30, Hi-Tech Electronics pays employees their take-home pay and accrues all tax amounts.

Requirement

1. Report these items on Hi-Tech Electronics' Balance Sheet at September 30, 20X0.

E9-40B. ***(Learning Objective 2: Issuing bonds payable [discount]; paying and accruing interest; amortizing the bonds by the effective interest method)*** On January 31, Daughtry Logistics, Inc., issued five-year, 5% bonds payable with a face value of €12,000,000. The bonds were issued when the market interest rate was 6% and pay interest on January 31 and July 31. Daughtry Logistics, Inc., amortizes bond discounts by the effective interest method.

Requirements

1. Record issuance of the bonds on January 31.
2. Record the semi-annual interest payment and amortization of bond discount on July 31.
3. Record the interest accrual and discount amortization on December 31.

E9-41B. ***(Learning Objective 2: Measuring cash amounts for a bond payable [premium]; amortizing the bonds using the straight-line method)*** Commonwealth Bank has €400,000 of 9% debenture bonds outstanding. The bonds were issued at 104 in 20X0 and mature in 20Z0 (20 years from now).

Requirements

1. How much cash did Commonwealth Bank receive when it issued these bonds?
2. How much cash in total will Commonwealth Bank pay the bondholders through the maturity date of the bonds?
3. Take the difference between your answers to Requirements 1 and 2. What does this number represent?
4. Estimate Commonwealth Bank's annual interest expense by the effective interest amortization method.

E9-42B. ***(Learning Objective 2: Issuing bonds payable [discount]; recording interest payments and the related bond amortization)*** First Place Sports Ltd. is authorized to issue €1,500,000 of 9%, 10-year bonds payable. On December 31, 20X0, when the market interest rate is 10%, the company issues €840,000 of the bonds. First Place Sports amortizes bonds by the effective-interest method. The semi-annual interest dates are June 30 and December 31.

Requirements

1. Prepare a bond amortization table for the first four semi-annual interest periods.
2. Record issuance of the bonds payable on December 31, 20X0, the first semi-annual interest payment on June 30, 20X1, and the second payment on December 31, 20X1.

E9-43B. ***(Learning Objective 2: Issuing bonds payable [premium]; recording interest accrual and payment and the related bond amortization)*** On June 30, 20X0, the market interest rate is 9%. Team Sports Ltd. issues €3,400,000 of 10%, 10-year bonds payable. The bonds pay interest on June 30 and December 31. Team Sports Ltd. amortizes bonds by the effective-interest method.

Requirements

1. Prepare a bond amortization table for the first four semi-annual interest periods.
2. Record the issuance of bonds payable on June 30, 20X0, the payment of interest on December 31, 20X0, and the payment of interest on June 30, 20X1.

LO 2

■ spreadsheet

E9-44B. ***(Learning Objective 2: Creating a bond amortization schedule [discount])*** Terry Co. issued €750,000 of 11%, 10-year bonds payable on January 1, 20X0, when the market interest rate was 12%. The company pays interest annually at year-end.

Requirement

1. Create a spreadsheet model to prepare a schedule to amortize the bonds. Use the effective-interest method of amortization. (Round to the nearest dollar.)

LO 3

E9-45B. ***(Learning Objective 3: Recording operating and capital lease, preparing lease amortization schedule)*** Small Billy Guff entered into a lease agreement for an asset on the following terms:

- Lease period = 4 years
- Lease payment = €18,000 at the end of each period
- Lease interest rate = 8%

Requirements

1. Assuming that this lease qualifies as a capital lease, prepare the lease amortization table, starting from the signing of the lease to the final lease payments. Prepare the journal entry for the first lease payment.
2. Assuming that this lease qualifies as an operating lease, prepare the journal entry for the first lease payment.
3. Explain how a lease for the same item may be treated so differently by two companies.

LO 4

E9-46B. ***(Learning Objective 4: Measuring the times-interest-earned ratio)*** Companies that operate in different industries may have very different financial ratio values. These differences may grow even wider when we compare companies located in different countries.

Compare three leading companies on their current ratio, debt ratio, and times-interest-earned ratio. Compute three ratios for Company F, Company L, and Company V.
Based on your computed ratio values, which company looks the least risky?

A1

	A	B	C	D
1	**(Amounts in millions or billions)**	**Company F**	**Company L**	**Company V**
2	**Income data**			
3	Total revenues	$ 9,723	¥ 7,312	€ 136,377
4	Operating income	294	229	5,627
5	Interest expense	43	29	687
6	Net income	25	12	443
7				
8	**Asset and liability data**			
9	**(Amounts in millions or billions)**			
10	Total current assets	435	5,422	147,398
11	Long-term assets	135	740	61,173
12	Total current liabilities	227	2,248	72,620
13	Long-term liabilities	109	2,320	110,927
14	Shareholders' equity	234	1,594	25,024
15				

LO 4

■ writing assignment

E9-47B. ***(Learning Objective 4: Analyzing alternative plans for raising money)*** First Federal Financial Services is considering two plans for raising €650,000 to expand operations. Plan A is to borrow at 5%, and plan B is to issue 100,000 shares of share capital at €6.50 per share. Before any new financing, First Federal Financial Services has a net income of €400,000 and 100,000 shares of share capital outstanding. Assume you own most of First Federal Financial Services' existing shares. Its management believes the company can use the new funds to earn additional income of €550,000 before interest and taxes. First Federal Financial Services' income tax rate is 40%.

Requirements

1. Analyze First Federal Financial Services' situation to determine which plan will result in the higher earnings per share.
2. Which plan results in the higher earnings per share? Which plan allows you to retain control of the company? Which plan creates more financial risk for the company? Which plan do you prefer? Why? Present your conclusion in a memo to First Federal Financial Services' board of directors.

Challenge Exercises

E9-48. ***(Learning Objectives 1, 5: Reporting current liabilities)*** The top management of Pratt Marketing Services examines the following company accounting records at August 29, immediately before the end of the year, August 31:

Total current assets	$ 324,700
Non-current assets	1,067,500
	$1,392,200
Total current liabilities	$ 193,400
Non-current liabilities	253,400
Owners' equity	945,400
	$1,392,200

Suppose Pratt's management wants to achieve a current ratio of 2.5. How much in current liabilities should Pratt pay off within the next two days in order to achieve its goal?

LO 2 5

E9-49. ***(Learning Objectives 2, 5: Refinancing old bonds payable with new bonds)*** Great Brands completed one of the most famous debt refinancings in history. A debt refinancing occurs when a company issues new bonds payable to retire old bonds. The company debits the old bonds payable and credits the new bonds payable.

Great Brands had $150 million of 5.75% bonds payable outstanding, with 21 years to maturity. Great retired these old bonds by issuing $85 million of new 11% bonds payable to the holders of the old bonds and paying the bondholders $10 million in cash. Great issued both groups of bonds at face value. At the time of the debt refinancing, Great Brands had total assets of $497 million and total liabilities of $357 million. Net income for the most recent year was $6.2 million on sales of $1 billion.

Requirements

1. Journalize the debt refinancing transaction.
2. Compute annual interest expense for both the old and the new bond issues.
3. Why did Great Brands refinance the old 5.75% bonds with the new 11% bonds? Consider interest expense, net income, and the debt ratio.

LO 2 3
■ **writing assignment**

E9-50. ***(Learning Objectives 2, 3: Analyzing bond transactions)*** This (adapted) advertisement for a 20-year bond appeared in the *Wall Street Chronicle*.

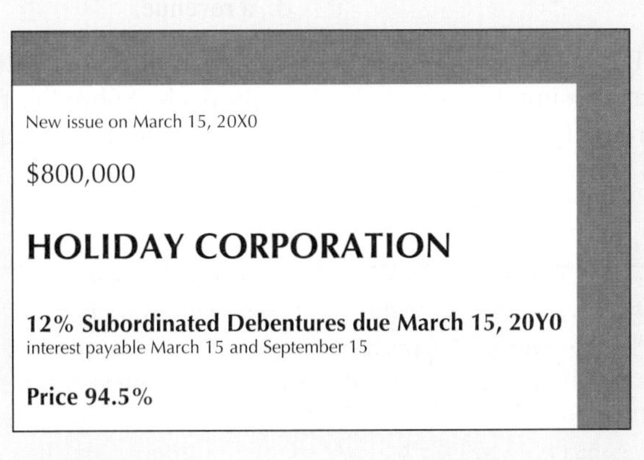

New issue on March 15, 20X0
$800,000
HOLIDAY CORPORATION
12% Subordinated Debentures due March 15, 20Y0
interest payable March 15 and September 15
Price 94.5%

(Note: A *subordinated debenture* is an unsecured bond payable whose rights are less than the rights of other bondholders.)

Requirements

1. Journalize Holiday's issuance of these bonds payable on March 15, 20X0.
2. Compute the semi-annual cash interest payment on the bonds.
3. Compute the semi-annual interest expense under the effective interest amortization method.
4. Compute both the first-year (from March 15, 20X0, to March 15, 20X1) and the second-year (March 15, 20X1, to March 15, 20X2) interest expense under the effective-interest amortization method. The market rate for similar bonds at the date of issuance was 13%. Why is interest expense greater in the second year?

Quiz

Test your understanding of accounting for liabilities by answering the following questions. Select the best choice from among the possible answers given.

Q9-51. For the purpose of classifying liabilities as current or non-current, the term operating cycle refers to

a. the time period between date of sale and the date the related revenue is collected.
b. the average time period between business recessions.
c. a period of one year.
d. the time period between purchase of merchandise and the conversion of this merchandise back to cash.

Q9-52. Failure to accrue interest expense results in

a. an overstatement of net income and an overstatement of liabilities.
b. an understatement of net income and an overstatement of liabilities.
c. an understatement of net income and an understatement of liabilities.
d. an overstatement of net income and an understatement of liabilities.

Q9-53. Feline Warehouse operates in a state with a 5.5% sales tax. For convenience, Feline Warehouse credits Sales Revenue for the total amount (selling price plus sales tax) collected from each customer. If Feline Warehouse fails to make an adjustment for sales taxes,

a. net income will be overstated and liabilities will be overstated.
b. net income will be understated and liabilities will be overstated.
c. net income will be understated and liabilities will be understated.
d. net income will be overstated and liabilities will be understated.

Q9-54. What kind of account is Unearned Revenue?

a. Liability account
b. Asset account
c. Revenue account
d. Expense account

Q9-55. An end-of-period adjusting entry that debits Unearned Revenue most likely will credit

a. a liability.
b. an asset.
c. an expense.
d. a revenue.

Q9-56. Aphrodite, Inc., manufactures and sells computer monitors with a three-year warranty. When calculated using the expected value approach, Aphrodite found that expected warranty costs are roughly equal to about 6% of sales during the warranty period. The following table shows the sales and actual warranty payments during the first two years of operations:

Year	Sales	Warranty Payments
20X0	$450,000	$ 3,150
20X1	750,000	30,000

Based on these facts, what amount of warranty liability should Aphrodite, Inc., report on its Balance Sheet at December 31, 20X1?

a. $30,000
b. $33,150
c. $38,850
d. $72,000

Q9-57. Tomorrow's Fashions has a debt that has been properly reported as a long-term liability up to the present year (20X0). Some of this debt comes due in 20X0. If Tomorrow's Fashions continues to report the current position as a long-term liability, the effect will be to

a. overstate the current ratio.
b. understate total liabilities.
c. overstate net income.
d. understate the debt ratio.

Q9-58. A bond with a face amount of $10,000 has a current price quote of 103.625. What is the bond's price?

a. $1,036.25
b. $10,362.50
c. $10,103.63
d. $1,036,250

Q9-59. Bond carrying value equals Bonds Payable

a. plus Premium on Bonds Payable.
b. plus Discount on Bonds Payable.
c. minus Discount on Bonds Payable.
d. minus Premium on Bonds Payable.
e. Both a and c
f. Both b and d

Q9-60. What type of account is Discount on Bonds Payable and what is its normal balance?

a. Adjusting amount; Credit
b. Reversing account; Debit
c. Contra liability; Debit
d. Contra liability; Credit

Questions 61–64 use the following data:
Spring Company sells $200,000 of 12%, 10-year bonds with $192,000 on April 1, 20X0. The market rate of interest on that day is 12.5%. Interest is paid each year on April 1.

Q9-61. The entry to record the sale of the bonds on April 1 would be

A1

	A	B	C	D
1	a.	Cash	200,000	
2		Bonds Payable		200,000
3				
4	b.	Cash	192,000	
5		Discount on Bonds Payable	8,000	
6		Bonds Payable		200,000
7				
8	c.	Cash	192,000	
9		Bonds Payable		192,000
10				
11	d.	Cash	200,000	
12		Discount on Bonds Payable		8,000
13		Bonds Payable		192,000
14				

Q9-62. Spring Company uses the effective interest amortization method. The amount of interest expense on April 1 of each year will be

a. $24,000.
b. $24,800.
c. $25,000.
d. $32,000.
e. none of these.

Q9-63. Write the adjusting entry required at December 31, 20X0.

Q9-64. Write the journal entry requirements at April 1, 20X1.

Q9-65. McPartlin Corporation issued $350,000 of 10%, 10-year bonds payable on January 1, 20X0, for $275,695. The market interest rate when the bonds were issued was 14%. Interest is paid semi-annually on January 1 and July 1. The first interest payment is July 1, 20X0. Using the effective-interest amortization method, how much interest expense will McPartlin record on July 1, 20X0?

a. $17,500
b. $10,500
c. $24,500
d. $19,425
e. $19,299

Q9-66. Using the facts in the preceding question, McPartlin's journal entry to record the interest expense on July 1, 20X0, will include a

a. credit to Discount on Bonds Payable.
b. debit to Bonds Payable.
c. debit to Premium on Bonds Payable.
d. credit to Interest Expense.

Q9-67. Amortizing the discount on bonds payable

a. is necessary only if the bonds were issued at more than face value.
b. increases the recorded amount of interest expense.
c. reduces the semi-annual cash payment for interest.
d. reduces the carrying value of the bond liability.

Q9-68. The journal entry on the maturity date to record the payment of $600,000 of bonds payable that were issued at a $60,000 discount includes

a. a debit to Discount on Bonds Payable for $60,000.
b. a credit to Cash for $660,000.
c. a debit to Bonds Payable for $600,000.
d. all of the above.

Q9-69. Is the payment of the face amount of a bond on its maturity date regarded as an operating activity, an investing activity, or a financing activity?

a. Operating activity
b. Investing activity
c. Financing activity

Problems MyLab Accounting

Select A and B problems can be found within MyLab Accounting, an online homework and practice environment. Your instructor may ask you to complete select problems using MyLab Accounting.

Group A

LO 1

P9-70A. ***(Learning Objective 1: Measuring current liabilities)*** Deep Waters Marine experienced these events during the current year:

a. Its December revenue totaled $140,000, and Deep Waters collected sales tax of 5%. The tax amount will be sent to the Hanoi Municipality early in January.
b. On August 31, Deep Waters signed a six-month, 4% note payable to purchase a boat costing $87,000. The note requires payment of principal and interest at maturity.
c. On August 31, Deep Waters received cash of $2,700 in advance for service revenue. This revenue will be earned evenly over six months.
d. Revenues of $860,000 were covered by Deep Waters's service warranty. At January 1, provision for warranty repairs was $11,800. During the year, Deep Waters recorded warranty expense of $34,400 and paid warranty claims of $34,800.
e. Deep Waters owes $60,000 on a long-term note payable. At December 31, 12% interest for the year plus $30,000 of this principal are payable within one year.

Requirement

1. For each item, indicate the account and the related amount to be reported as a current liability on the Deep Waters Marine Balance Sheet at December 31.

LO 1

P9-71A. ***(Learning Objective 1: Recording liability-related transactions)*** The following transactions of Sweet Ensemble Music Company occurred during 20X0 and 20X1:

20X0	
May 3	Purchased a piano (inventory) for $72,000, signing a six-month, 4% note payable.
May 31	Borrowed $75,000 on a 5% note payable that calls for annual installment payments of $15,000 principal plus interest. Recorded the short-term note payable in a separate account from the long-term note payable.
Sep 3	Paid the six-month, 4% note at maturity.
Dec 31	Accrued warranty expense, which is estimated at 3.0% of sales of $192,000.
31	Accrued interest on the outstanding note payable.
20X1	
May 31	Paid the first installment and interest for one year on the outstanding note payable.

Requirement

1. Record the transactions in Sweet Ensemble's journal. Explanations are not required.

P9-72A. ***(Learning Objective 2: Recording bond transactions [at par]; reporting bonds payable on the Balance Sheet)*** The board of directors of Displays Plus authorizes the issue of $8,000,000 of 10%, five-year bonds payable. The semi-annual interest dates are May 31 and November 30. The bonds are issued on May 31, 20X0, at par.

Requirements

1. Journalize the following transactions:
   a. Issuance of half of the bonds on May 31, 20X0.
   b. Payment of interest on November 30, 20X0.
   c. Accrual of interest on December 31, 20X0.
   d. Payment of interest on May 31, 20X1.
2. Report interest payable and bonds payable as they would appear on the Displays Plus Balance Sheet at December 31, 20X0.

P9-73A. ***(Learning Objectives 2, 5: Issuing bonds at a premium; amortizing by the effective interest method; reporting bonds payable on the Balance Sheet)*** On February 28, 20X0, Nemo Corp. issues 8%, 10-year bonds payable with a face value of $800,000. The bonds pay interest on February 28 and August 31. Nemo Corp. amortizes bonds by the effective interest method.

Requirements

1. If the market interest rate is 7% when Nemo Corp. issues its bonds, will the bonds be priced at par, at a premium, or at a discount? Explain.
2. If the market interest rate is 9% when Nemo Corp. issues its bonds, will the bonds be priced at par, at a premium, or at a discount? Explain.
3. Assuming that the market rate is 7%, journalize the following bonds payable transactions.
   a. Issuance of the bonds on February 28, 20X0.
   b. Payment of interest and amortization of the bonds on August 31, 20X0.
   c. Accrual of interest and amortization of the bonds on December 31, 20X0.
   d. Payment of interest and amortization of the bonds on February 28, 20X1.
4. Report interest payable and bonds payable as they would appear on the Nemo Corp. Balance Sheet at December 31, 20X0.

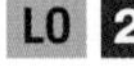

P9-74A. ***(Learning Objective 2: Accounting for bonds payable at a premium; amortizing by the effective interest method)***

Requirements

1. Journalize the following transactions of Dupont Communications, Inc.:

20X0	
Jan 1	Issued $6,000,000 of 9%, 10-year bonds payable when the market rate is 8%.
Jul 1	Paid semi-annual interest and amortized bonds by the effective interest method on the 9% bonds payable.
Dec 31	Accrued semi-annual interest expense and amortized bonds by the effective interest method on the 9% bonds payable.
20X1	
Jan 1	Paid semi-annual interest.
2020	
Jan 1	Paid the 9% bonds at maturity.

2. At December 31, 20X0, after all year-end adjustments, determine the carrying amount of Dupont Communications bonds payable, net.
3. For the six months ended July 1, 20X0, determine for Dupont Communications, Inc.:
   a. Interest expense
   b. Cash interest paid

What causes interest paid for the bonds to be higher than the interest expense?

■ spreadsheet

P9-75A. ***(Learning Objectives 2, 5: Analyzing a company's long-term debt; reporting long-term debt on the Balance Sheet [effective-interest method])*** The notes to the Helping Charities' financial statements reported the following data on December 31, Year 1 (end of the fiscal year):

Note 6. Indebtedness		
Bonds payable, 7% due in Year 7	$3,500,000	
Less: Discount	(162,365)	$3,337,635
Notes payable, 6%, payable in amounts of $55,000 annual installments starting in Year 5		330,000

Helping Charities amortizes bonds by the effective-interest method and pays all interest amounts at December 31.

Requirements

1. Answer the following questions about Helping Charities' long-term liabilities:
   a. What is the maturity value of the 7% bonds?
   b. What are Helping Charities' annual cash interest payments on the 7% bonds?
   c. What is the carrying amount of the 7% bonds at December 31, year 1?
2. Prepare an amortization table through December 31, Year 4, for the 7% bonds. The market interest rate on the bonds was 8%. (Round all amounts to the nearest dollar.) How much is Helping Charities' interest expense on the 7% bonds for the year ended December 31, Year 4?
3. Show how Helping Charities would report the 7% bonds payable and the 6% notes payable at December 31, Year 4.

P9-76A. ***(Learning Objective 3: Determining appropriate lease category, journalizing lease transactions)*** On December 31, 20X0, Meekaboo Corp. entered into the following lease for an asset with six years' useful life and a fair market value of $180,000.

- Lease period = 4 years
- Lease payment of $55,000 per year at the end of each year
- Interest rate implicit in the lease = 10%

Requirements

1. Based on the lease terms, determine if Meekaboo should record an operating or finance lease.
2. Journalize all entries related to the lease between December 31, 20X0 and 20X1.

LO 4
■ writing assignment

P9-77A. ***(Learning Objective 4: Financing operations with debt or with shares)*** Viola Sporting Goods is embarking on a massive expansion. Assume plans call for opening 25 new stores during the next three years. Each store is scheduled to be 30% larger than the company's existing locations, offering more items of inventory, and with more elaborate displays. Its management estimates that company operations will provide $1.5 million of the cash needed for expansion. Viola must raise the remaining $7.5 million from outsiders. The board of directors is considering obtaining the $7.5 million either through borrowing or by issuing share capital.

Requirement

1. Write a memo to Viola's management discussing the advantages and disadvantages of borrowing and of issuing share capital to raise the needed cash. Which method of raising the funds would you recommend?

LO 4 5

P9-78A. ***(Learning Objectives 4, 5: Reporting liabilities on the Balance Sheet; calculating the times-interest-earned ratio)*** The accounting records of Quinzel Foods, Inc., include the following items at December 31, 20X0:

Mortgage note payable, current	$ 94,000	Accumulated depreciation, equipment	$164,000
Accumulated pension benefit obligation	465,000	Discount on bonds payable (all long-term)	27,000
Bonds payable, long-term	1,200,000	Operating income	400,000
Mortgage note payable, long-term	319,000	Equipment	745,000
Bonds payable, current portion	400,000	Pension plan assets (market value)	405,000
Interest expense	222,000	Interest payable	72,000

Requirements

1. Show how each relevant item would be reported on the Quinzel Foods, Inc., classified Balance Sheet, including headings and totals for current liabilities and long-term liabilities.
2. Answer the following questions about Quinzel's financial position at December 31, 20X0:
   a. What is the carrying amount of the bonds payable (combine the current and long-term amounts)?
   b. Why is the interest-payable amount so much less than the amount of interest expense?
3. How many times did Quinzel cover its interest expense during 20X0?

Group B

LO 1

P9-79B. ***(Learning Objective 1: Measuring current liabilities)*** Tropical Shore Marine experienced these events during the current year.

a. December revenue totaled €120,000, and Tropical Shore collected sales tax of 8%. The tax amount will be sent to the Groningen provincial office early in January.
b. On August 31, Tropical Shore signed a six-month, 4% note payable to purchase a boat costing €81,000. The note requires payment of principal and interest at maturity.
c. On August 31, Tropical Shore received cash of €1,500 in advance for service revenue. This revenue will be earned evenly over six months.
d. Revenues of €780,000 were covered by Tropical Shore's service warranty. At January 1, provision for warranty repairs was €11,400. During the year, Tropical Shore recorded warranty expense of €31,200 and paid warranty claims of €34,600.
e. Tropical Shore owes €88,000 on a long-term note payable. At December 31, 10% interest for the year plus €24,000 of this principal are payable within one year.

Requirement

1. For each item, indicate the account and the related amount to be reported as a current liability on the Tropical Shore Marine Balance Sheet at December 31.

LO 1

P9-80B. ***(Learning Objective 1: Recording liability-related transactions)*** The following transactions of Lovely Melody Music Company occurred during 20X0 and 20X1:

20X0	
Mar 3	Purchased a piano (inventory) for €35,000, signing a six-month, 10% note payable.
May 31	Borrowed €75,000 on an 8% note payable that calls for annual installment payments of €15,000 principal plus interest. Recorded the short-term note payable in a separate account from the long-term note payable.
Sep 3	Paid the six-month, 10% note at maturity.
Dec 31	Accrued warranty expense, which is estimated at 1.5% of sales of €198,000.
31	Accrued interest on the outstanding note payable.
20X1	
May 31	Paid the first installment and interest for one year on the outstanding note payable.

Requirement

1. Record the transactions in Lovely Melody Music Company's journal. Explanations are not required.

LO 2

P9-81B. ***(Learning Objective 2: Recording bond transactions [at par]; reporting bonds payable on the Balance Sheet)*** The board of directors of Portraits Plus authorizes the issue of €4,000,000 of 8%, 15-year bonds payable. The semi-annual interest dates are May 31 and November 30. The bonds are issued on May 31, 20X0, at par.

Requirements

1. Journalize the following transactions:
   a. Issuance of half of the bonds on May 31, 20X0.
   b. Payment of interest on November 30, 20X0.
   c. Accrual of interest on December 31, 20X0.
   d. Payment of interest on May 31, 20X1.
2. Report the interest payable and bonds payable as they would appear on the Portraits Plus Balance Sheet at December 31, 20X0.

LO 2 5

P9-82B. ***(Learning Objectives 2, 5: Issuing bonds at a premium; amortizing by the effective interest method; reporting notes payable on the Balance Sheet)*** On February 28, 20X0, Dory Corp. issues 6%, 20-year bonds payable with a face value of €1,500,000. The bonds pay interest on February 28 and August 31. Dory Corp. amortizes bonds by the effective interest method.

Requirements

1. If the market interest rate is 5% when Dory Corp. issues its bonds, will the bonds be priced at par, at a premium, or at a discount? Explain.
2. If the market interest rate is 7% when Dory Corp. issues its bonds, will the bonds be priced at par, at a premium, or at a discount? Explain.
3. Assuming the market rate is 5%, journalize the following bond transactions:
   a. Issuance of the bonds on February 28, 20X0.
   b. Payment of interest and amortization of the bonds on August 31, 20X0.
   c. Accrual of interest and amortization of the bonds on December 31, 20X0, the year-end.
   d. Payment of interest and amortization of the bonds on February 28, 20X1.
4. Report interest payable and bonds payable as they would appear on the Dory Corp. Balance Sheet at December 31, 20X0.

LO 2

P9-83B. ***(Learning Objective 2: Accounting for bonds payable at a premium; amortizing by the effective interest method)***

Requirements

1. Journalize the following transactions of Seville Communications, Inc.:

20X0	
Jan 1	Issued $2,000,000 of 7%, 10-year bonds payable when the market rate is 6%.
Jul 1	Paid semi-annual interest and amortized the bonds by the effective interest method on the 7% bonds payable.
Dec 31	Accrued semi-annual interest expense and amortized the bonds by the effective interest method on the 7% bonds payable.
20X1	
Jan 1	Paid semi-annual interest.
2020	
Jan 1	Paid the 7% bonds at maturity.

2. At December 31, 20X0, after all year-end adjustments, determine the carrying amount of Seville Communications bonds payable, net.
3. For the six months ended July 1, 20X0, determine the following for Seville Communications, Inc:
   a. Interest expense
   b. Cash interest paid

What causes the interest paid for the bonds to be higher than the interest expense?

P9-84B. ***(Learning Objectives 2, 5: Analyzing a company's long-term debt; reporting the long-term debt on the Balance Sheet [effective-interest method])*** The notes to the Helpful Charities financial statements reported the following data on December 31, Year 1 (end of the fiscal year):

Note 6. Indebtedness		
Bonds payable, 4% due in Year 7	€6,500,000	
Less: Discount	(331,240)	€6,168,760
Notes payable, 7%, payable in €60,000 annual installments starting in Year 5		360,000

Helpful Charities amortizes bonds by the effective-interest method and pays all interest amounts at December 31.

Requirements

1. Answer the following questions about Helpful Charities' long-term liabilities:
   a. What is the maturity value of the 4% bonds?
   b. What is Helpful Charities' annual cash interest payment on the 4% bonds?
   c. What is the carrying amount of the 4% bonds at December 31, Year 1?
2. Prepare an amortization table through December 31, Year 4, for the 4% bonds. The market interest rate on the bonds was 5%. Round all amounts to the nearest dollar. How much is Helpful Charities' interest expense on the 4% bonds for the year ended December 31, Year 4?
3. Show how Helpful Charities would report the 4% bonds and the 7% notes payable at December 31, Year 4.

P9-85B. ***(Learning Objective 3: Determining appropriate lease category, journalizing lease transactions)*** On December 31, 20X0, Reekaboo Corp. entered into the following lease for an asset with 8 years useful life and a fair market value of €160,000.

- Lease period = 6 years
- Lease payment of €34,000 per year at the end of each year
- Interest rate implicit in the lease = 8%

Requirements

1. Based on the lease terms, determine if Reekaboo should record an operating or finance lease.
2. Journalize all entries related to the lease between December 31, 20X0 and 20X1.

LO 4
■ writing assignment

P9-86B. *(Learning Objective 4: Financing operations with debt or with shares)* Veronica Sporting Goods is embarking on a massive expansion. Assume plans call for opening 30 new stores during the next four years. Each store is scheduled to be 35% larger than the company's existing locations, offering more items of inventory, and with more elaborate displays. Its management estimates that company operations will provide €1.75 million of the cash needed for expansion. Veronica must raise the remaining €8.25 million from outsiders. The board of directors is considering obtaining the €8.25 million either through borrowing or by issuing share capital.

Requirement

1. Write a memo to Veronica's management discussing the advantages and disadvantages of borrowing and of issuing share capital to raise the needed cash. Which method of raising the funds would you recommend?

LO 4 5

P9-87B. *(Learning Objectives 4, 5: Reporting liabilities on the Balance Sheet; calculating the times-interest-earned ratio)* The accounting records of Isley Foods, Inc., include the following items at December 31, 20X0:

Mortgage note payable, current	€ 95,000	Accumulated depreciation, equipment	€165,000
Accumulated pension benefit obligation	460,000	Discount on bonds payable (all long-term)	23,000
Bonds payable, long-term	200,000	Operating income	360,000
Mortgage note payable, long-term	313,000	Equipment	746,000
Bonds payable, current portion	500,000	Pension plan assets (market value)	410,000
Interest expense	224,000	Interest payable	72,000

Requirements

1. Show how each relevant item would be reported on the Isley Foods, Inc., classified Balance Sheet, including headings and totals for current liabilities and long-term liabilities.
2. Answer the following questions about Isley's financial position at December 31, 20X0:
   a. What is the carrying amount of the bonds payable (combine the current and long-term amounts)?
   b. Why is the interest-payable amount so much less than the amount of interest expense?
3. How many times did Isley cover its interest expense during 20X0?

APPLY YOUR KNOWLEDGE

Decision Cases

Case 1. *(Learning Objective 2: Exploring an actual bankruptcy)* In 2002, Enron Corporation filed for Chapter 11 bankruptcy protection, shocking the business community: How could a company this large and this successful go bankrupt? This case explores the causes and the effects of Enron's bankruptcy.

At December 31, 2000, and for the four years ended on that date, Enron reported the following (amounts in millions):

Balance Sheet (summarized)				
Total assets				$65,503
Total liabilities				54,033
Total shareholders' equity				11,470
Income Statements (excerpts)				
	2000	1999	1998	1997
Net income	$979*	$893	$703	$105

*Operating income = $1,953
Interest expense = $838

Unknown to investors and lenders, Enron also controlled hundreds of partnerships that owed vast amounts of money. These special-purpose entities (SPEs) did not appear on the Enron financial statements. Assume that the SPEs' assets totaled $7,500 million and their liabilities stood at $7,300 million; assume a 10% interest rate on these liabilities.

During the four-year period up to December 31, 2000, Enron's share price shot up from $17.50 to $90.56. Enron used its escalating share price to finance the purchase of the SPEs by guaranteeing lenders that Enron would give them Enron shares if the SPEs could not pay their loans.

In 2001, the SEC launched an investigation into Enron's accounting practices. It was alleged that Enron should have been including the SPEs in its financial statements all along. Enron then restated net income for the years up to 2000, wiping out nearly $800 million of total net income (and total assets) for this four-year period. Enron's share price tumbled, and the guarantees to the SPEs' lenders added millions to Enron's liabilities (assume the full amount of the SPEs' debt). To make matters worse, the assets of the SPEs lost much of their value; assume that their market value is only $500 million.

Requirements

1. Compute the debt ratio that Enron reported at the end of 2000. Recompute this ratio after including the SPEs in Enron's financial statements. Also compute Enron's times-interest-earned ratio both ways for 2000. Assume that the changes to Enron's financial position occurred during 2000.
2. Why does it appear that Enron failed to include the SPEs in its financial statements? How do you view Enron after including the SPEs in the company's financial statements? (Challenge)

Case 2. ***(Learning Objective 4: Analyzing alternative ways of raising $6 million)*** Business is going well for Park 'N Fly, the company that operates remote parking lots near major airports. The board of directors of this family-owned company believes that Park 'N Fly could earn an additional $1.5 million income before interest and taxes by expanding into new markets. However, the $6 million that the business needs for growth cannot be raised within the family. The directors, who strongly wish to retain family control of the company, must consider issuing securities to outsiders. The directors are considering three financing plans.

Plan A is to borrow at 6%. Plan B is to issue 100,000 shares of share capital. Plan C is to issue 100,000 shares of non-voting, $3.75 preference shares ($3.75 is the annual dividend paid on each share of preference shares). Park 'N Fly presently has net income of $3.5 million and 1 million shares of share capital outstanding. The company's income tax rate is 35%.

Requirements

1. Prepare an analysis to determine which plan will result in the highest earnings per share of share capital.
2. Recommend a plan to the board of directors. Give your reasons.

Ethical Issues

Issue 1. Microsoft Corporation is the defendant in numerous lawsuits claiming unfair trade practices. Microsoft has strong incentives not to disclose these contingent liabilities. However, accounting standards require that companies report their contingent liabilities.

Requirements

1. Why would a company prefer not to disclose its contingent liabilities?
2. Identify the parties involved in the decision and the potential consequences to each.
3. Analyze the issue of whether to report contingent liabilities from lawsuits from the following standpoints:
   a. economic
   b. legal
   c. ethical

Issue 2. When is a lease a capital idea? Laurie Gocker, Inc., entered into a lease arrangement with Nathan Morgan Leasing Corporation for an industrial machine. Morgan's primary business is leasing. The cash purchase price of the machine is $1,000,000. Its economic life is six years.

Gocker's Balance Sheet reflects total assets of $10 million and total liabilities of $7.5 million. Among the liabilities is a $2.5 million long-term note outstanding at Last National Bank. The note carries a restrictive covenant that requires the company's debt ratio to be no higher than 75%. The company's revenues have been falling of late and the shareholders are concerned about profitability.

Gocker and Morgan are engaging in negotiations for terms of the lease. Some relevant other facts:

1. Morgan wants to take possession of the machine at the end of the initial lease term.
2. The term may run from four to five years, at Gocker's discretion.
3. Morgan estimates the machine will have no residual value, and Gocker will not purchase it at the end of the lease term.
4. The present value of minimum lease payments on the machine is $890,000.

Requirements

1. What is (are) the ethical issue(s) in this case?
2. Who are the stakeholders? Analyze the consequences for each stakeholder from the following standpoints: (a) economic, (b) legal, and (c) ethical.
3. How should Gocker structure the lease agreement?

Focus on Financials: | Nestlé

This case spans all 12 chapters and is based on the consolidated financial statements of Nestlé Corporation. As you work with Nestlé throughout this course, you will develop the confidence and ability to use the financial statements of other companies as well. Refer to Nestlé's financial statements in Appendix A (available on www.pearsonglobaleditions.com/Harrison). If you wish, you can obtain the full annual report from www.nestle.com/investors. You may find the information overwhelming for now, but try to spot the key principles that we have discussed in this chapter. It will get progressively easier as you gain familiarity with the elements of the financial statements.

Refer to Nestlé's consolidated financial statements in Appendix A.

1. Did trade payables for Nestlé increase or decrease in 2011? What was the amount? What might have caused this change? Refer to note 12.
2. Examine Note 13—Taxation in the Notes to the Consolidated Financial Statements. What was Nestlé's income tax expense in 2016?
3. Did Nestlé borrow more or pay off more long-term debt during 2016? How can you tell?
4. Examine Note 11—Provisions and Contingencies Liabilities in the Notes to Consolidated Financial Statements. Describe some of Nestlé's contingent liabilities as of March 31, 2011.
5. How would you rate Nestlé's overall debt position—risky, safe, or average? Compute the ratio(s) at December 31, 2016, that would help you answer this question. Ratios aside, what qualitative factors would you consider in assessing the riskiness of Nestlé's overall debt?
6. Refer to Note 11—Provisions and Contingencies. What kind of provisions does Nestlé have? Why does it need them? What do you understand by the term "provision," and how is it different from "contingent liabilities?"

Group Projects

Project 1. Consider three different businesses:

1. A bank
2. A magazine publisher
3. A department store

For each business, list all of its liabilities—both current and long-term. Then compare the three lists to identify the liabilities that the three businesses have in common. Also identify the liabilities that are unique to each type of business.

Project 2. Alcenon Corporation leases the majority of the assets that it uses in operations. Alcenon prefers operating leases (versus capital leases) in order to keep the lease liability off its Balance Sheet and maintain a low debt ratio.

Alcenon is negotiating a 10-year lease on an asset with an expected useful life of 15 years. The lease requires Alcenon to make 10 annual lease payments of $20,000 each, with the first payment due at the beginning of the lease term. The leased asset has a market value of $135,180. The lease agreement specifies no transfer of title to the lessee and includes no bargain purchase option.

Write a report for Alcenon's management to explain what conditions must be present for Alcenon to be able to account for this lease as an operating lease.

Quick Check Answers

1. *b*
2. *e*
3. *a* ($472,500 × 0.01 = $4,725)
4. *b* [800 × 0.04 × $25 = warranty expense of $800; repaired $25 × 15 = $375; year-end liability = $425 ($800 – $375)]
5. *d*
6. *e*
7. *b*
8. *a*
9. *c*
10. *c*
11. *d*

12–16.

	Interest Payment	Interest Expense	Discount Amortiz.	Bond Carry Amt.
1/1/2011				$521,724
7/1/2011	$19,600	$20,869	$1,269	522,993
1/1/2012	19,600	20,920	1,320	524,313

12. *d* ($521,724 × 0.08 × 6/12 = $20,869)
13. *b* [Int. exp. = $20,869 Int. payment = $19,600 ($560,000 × 0.07 × 6/12)$20,869 – $19,600 = $1,269]
14. *c* ($560,000 × 0.07 = $39,200)
15. *a* ($20,869 + $20,920 = $41,789)
16. *a* (See Amortization Schedule)

MyLab Accounting

For online homework, exercises, and problems that provide you with immediate feedback, please visit www.myaccountinglab.com.

10 Shareholders' Equity

SPOTLIGHT | L'Occitane www.loccitane.com

Few imagined that a French company would list its shares on an Asian stock exchange. L'Occitane, a company with deep regional roots in Provence, France, did exactly that in May 2010, with its HK$6.1 billion (Hong Kong Dollars, about €618 million) offering. The Initial Public Offering (IPO) saw about 27% of L'Occitane shares floated on the Hong Kong stock exchange. L'Occitane plans to use the proceeds to accelerate its international expansion in high-growth emerging markets such as China, Brazil, and Russia, as well as mature markets such as Japan and the United States.

Boris Popchinskiy/Shutterstock

Earlier in Chapters 5 to 9, we discussed accounting for various assets and liabilities. By this time, you should be familiar with the more common assets and liabilities listed on a company's Balance Sheet. Let's focus now on shareholders' equity. Remember that share capital is the owner's investment into the company, and that retained earnings are profits from prior periods that have not been distributed to owners. You will learn more about equity and equity transactions in this chapter and discuss some of the decisions a company faces when

- paying dividends
- issuing shares
- buying back its shares

Not all companies will have all the various equity transactions we discuss in this chapter, but all equity-related transactions are reported in the statement of changes in equity. L'Occitane's (adapted) statement of changes in equity is shown below. The key transaction in 2010 is the issuance of its shares in May 2011 (line 4). A total of over 405 million shares were floated at the Hong Kong Stock Exchange, with total proceeds of about €618 million. Half of the shares floated were newly issued shares by the company, and the other half were sold by existing shareholders. Thus, from the company's perspective, proceeds from the share issuance was about €300 million (half of the €618 million less costs of issuance).

	A	B	C	D	E	F	G
1	**L'Occitane International S.A. Consolidated Statement of Changes in Equity For the Year Ended March 31, 2011**						
2	**(Adapted, in Thousands of euro)**	**Share Capital**	**Additional Paid-in Capital**	**Retained Earnings**	**Others**	**Non-controlling Interests**	**Total Equity**
3	Balance at March 31, 2010	€ 38,232	€ 48,730	€ 67,774	€ 2,554	€ 3,988	€ 161,278
4	Profit for the year			99,501		3,199	102,700
5	Other comprehensive income				2,194	(437)	1,757
6	Issue of new shares	6,077	294,121				300,198
7	Other equity transactions				1,083	(1,752)	(669)
8	Balance at March 31, 2011	€ 44,309	€ 342,851	€ 167,275	€ 5,831	€ 4,998	€ 565,264
9							

The statement of changes in equity above reconciles the movements in equity accounts from one Balance Sheet to another. You should be able to trace the totals above to L'Occitane's Balance Sheets below.

	A	B	C
1	**L'Occitane International S.A. Consolidated Balance Sheet**	**As at March 31**	
2	**(Adapted, in Thousands of Euro)**	**2011**	**2010**
3	Total assets	€ 785,860	€ 436,590
4	Total liabilities	220,596	275,312
5	Total equity	565,264	161,278
6	Total liabilities and equity	€ 785,860	€ 436,590
7			

Let's begin with our equity discussions with the organization of a corporation.

LEARNING OBJECTIVES

1 **Explain** the features of a corporation
2 **Account** for the issuance of shares
3 **Account** for treasury shares
4 **Account** for other equity transactions
5 **Understand** the different values of shares
6 **Evaluate** a company's return to equity holders

EXPLAIN THE FEATURES OF A CORPORATION

1 **Explain** the features of a corporation

Anyone starting a business must decide how to organize the entity. Corporations differ from proprietorships and partnerships in several ways. Our discussions in this chapter will be based on the general features of these business entities, as actual regulatory requirements will vary from one jurisdiction to another. Your instructor may provide additional information about how to set up companies or corporations in your own country, and any specific rules about corporations relevant for your studies.

Separate Legal Entity. A corporation is a business entity formed under law. It is a distinct entity, an artificial person that exists apart from its owners, the **shareholders**. The corporation has many of the rights that a person has. For example, a corporation may buy, own, and sell property. Assets and liabilities in the business belong to the corporation and not to its owners. The corporation may enter into contracts, sue, and be sued.

Nearly all large companies, such as L'Occitane, Microsoft, and Facebook, are corporations. Their full names usually include the words *Corporation* or *Incorporated* or *Limited* (abbreviated *Corp.*, *Inc.*, and *Ltd*, respectively) to indicate that they are corporations, for example, News Corporation, and Apple Incorporated. This depends very much on the local and legal practices in the country of incorporation. For example, in Australia you often see Pty Ltd (*proprietary limited*), in the UK you will see PLC (public limited company), in Germany, AG (*Aktiengesellschaft*), in Italy, SpA (*società per azioni*), in Malaysia, Sdn Bhd (*Sendirian Berhad*), in Belgium, SA (*Société Anonyme*), in Brazil, Ltda (*Sociedade Limitada*), etc.

Continuous Life and Transferability of Ownership. Corporations have *continuous lives* regardless of changes in their ownership. The shareholders of a corporation may buy more of the **shares**, sell the shares to another person, give them away, or bequeath them in a will. The transfer of the shares from one person to another does not affect the continuity of the corporation. In contrast, proprietorships and partnerships terminate when their ownership changes.

Limited Liability. Shareholders have **limited liability** for the corporation's debts. They have no personal obligation for corporate liabilities. The most that a shareholder can lose on an investment in a corporation's share is the cost of the investment. Limited liability is one of the most attractive features of the corporate form of organization. It enables corporations to raise more capital from a wider group of investors than proprietorships and partnerships can. By contrast, proprietors and partners are personally liable for all the debts of their businesses.[1]

Separation of Ownership and Management. Shareholders own the corporation, but the *board of directors*—elected by the shareholders—appoints officers to manage the business. Thus, shareholders may invest $1,000 or $1 million in the corporation without having to manage it.

The management's goal is to maximize the firm's value for the shareholders. But the separation between owners and managers may create problems. Corporate officers may run the business for their own benefit and not for the shareholders. For example, the CEO of Tyco Corporation was accused of looting Tyco of $600 million. The CFO of Enron Corporation set up outside partnerships and paid himself millions to manage the partnerships—unknown to Enron shareholders. Both men went to prison.

[1] Unless the business is organized as a limited-liability company (LLC) or a limited-liability partnership (LLP).

Corporate Taxation. Proprietorships and partnerships pay no business income tax. Instead, the business's tax falls solely on the owners. On the other hand, corporations are separate taxable entities. Just like individuals, they have to pay taxes, usually referred to as *corporate tax*. In some countries, corporations may be subject to federal and state income taxes. The specific rules on taxation would naturally vary from country to country. In general, not everything on the corporation's Income Statement may be subject to tax, or they may be subject to tax at a different rate. For example, many countries are promoting additional tax deductions for spending on research and development, or allow companies to claim an accelerated method of depreciation for tax purposes for certain assets. Many accounting graduates also work in the area of taxation. If this is an area that is of interest to you, you may find courses on individual and corporate taxation beneficial.

Government Regulation. Because shareholders have only limited liability for corporation debts, outsiders doing business with the corporation can look no further than the corporation if it fails to pay. To protect a corporation's creditors and shareholders, governments monitor corporations. In general, the bigger a company becomes, the more rules and regulations it will have to comply with. For example, a public company (that raises funds from the public) will be subject to more regulatory oversight than a private company with a small number of shareholders. Similarly, a company that is listed on a stock exchange will be expected to follow the exchange's listing rules. The regulations mainly ensure that corporations disclose the information that investors and creditors need to make informed decisions. Accounting provides much of this information. Some jurisdictions may also limit maximum ownership levels for citizens versus non-citizens.

Exhibit 10-1 summarizes the advantages and disadvantages of the corporate form of business organization.

Exhibit 10-1 | Advantages and Disadvantages of the Corporation

Advantages	Disadvantages
1. Can raise more capital than a proprietorship or partnership	1. Separation of ownership and management
2. Continuous life	2. Corporate taxation
3. Ease of transferring ownership	3. Government regulation
4. Limited liability of shareholders	

Organizing a Corporation

The creation of a corporation begins when its organizers apply for registration as a company with the relevant authority. Again, your local requirements may vary from what we discuss here, but would typically require the entity to have a constitution, charter, or memorandum (and articles) of association. The constitution includes the authorization for the corporation to issue a certain number of shares. A share is the basic unit of ownership for a corporation. Once the registration requirements are met, the corporation then comes into existence.

Ultimate control of the corporation rests with the shareholders who elect a **board of directors** that sets company policy and appoints officers. The board elects a **chairperson**, who usually is the most influential person in the organization. The chairperson of the board of directors, or chairman of the board, may be involved in the running of the corporation as the chief executive officer (CEO), or he/she may be an independent chairman who appoints someone else to be the CEO. The board may also designate a chief operating officer (COO) to be in charge of day-to-day operations. Most corporations also have directors or officers in charge of sales, manufacturing, accounting and finance (the chief financial officer, or CFO), and other key areas. Exhibit 10-2 shows the typical authority structure in a corporation. Note that the local practices in your country may use different titles than those listed below.

Shareholders' Rights. Ownership of shares entitles shareholders to four basic rights, unless a specific right is withheld by agreement with the shareholders:

Exhibit 10-2 Authority Structure in a Corporation

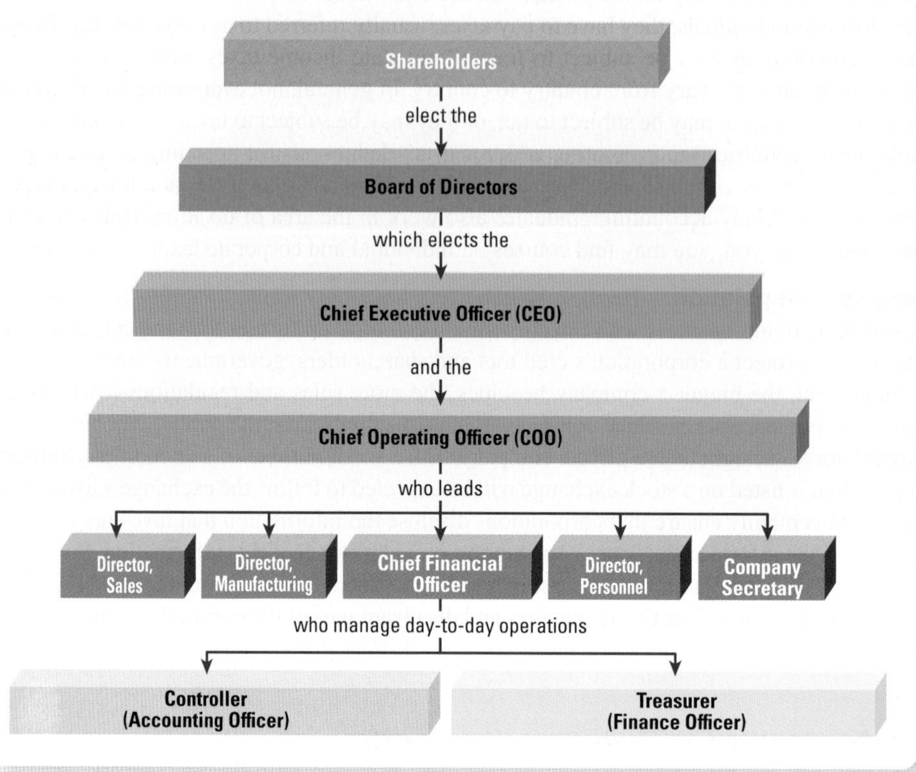

1. *Vote*. The right to participate in management by voting on matters that come before the shareholders, usually in an annual general meeting (AGM). This is the shareholder's sole voice in the management of the corporation. A shareholder gets one vote for each share owned, unless otherwise specified in the company's constitution.
2. *Dividends*. The right to receive a proportionate part of any dividend. Each share in a particular class receives an equal dividend.
3. *Liquidation*. The right to receive a proportionate share of any assets remaining after the corporation pays its liabilities in liquidation. Liquidation means to go out of business, sell the assets, pay all liabilities, and distribute any remaining cash to the owners.
4. *Preemption*. The right to maintain one's proportionate ownership in the corporation. Suppose you own 5% of a corporation's shares. If the corporation issues 100,000 new shares, it must offer you the opportunity to buy 5% (5,000) of the new shares. This right, called the *preemptive right*, may be required by law or incorporated into the company's constitution.

Shareholders' Equity. As we saw in Chapter 1, **shareholders' equity** represents the shareholders' residual ownership interest in the assets of a corporation, i.e., after deducting all liabilities from total assets. Shareholders' equity is divided into two major parts:

1. **Paid-in capital**, also called **contributed capital** or **share capital.** This is the amount of shareholders' equity the shareholders have contributed to the corporation. Paid-in capital includes the share's par values and any additional paid-in capital (more on this later in the chapter).
2. **Retained earnings.** This is the amount of shareholders' equity the corporation has earned through profitable operations and has not used for dividends.

Companies report shareholders' equity by source. They report paid-in capital separately from retained earnings because most jurisdictions prohibit the declaration of cash dividends from paid-in capital. Thus, cash dividends are declared from retained earnings.

A Closer Look

Companies often create further sub-categories of equity accounts. Some would keep separate balances for certain reserves (e.g., revaluation reserves, foreign currency reserves, hedging reserves, and others). You also saw earlier (in Chapter 9) how "non-controlling interests" are used to record the part of consolidated subsidiaries that do not belong to the reporting entity. In this chapter, we have summarized these sub-categories as "others." If you are pursuing further studies in accounting, you will learn more about these accounts.

The owners' equity of a corporation is divided into shares. A corporation issues *share certificates* to its owners when the company receives their investment in the business—usually cash. Many countries have adopted electronic share certificates in favor of physical share certificates that require manual handling and storage. Because shares represent the corporation's capital, it is often called *share capital.* A corporation may issue a share certificate for any number of shares—1,100, or any other number—but the total number of authorized shares is limited by the company's constitution. Exhibit 10-3 shows an example of a share certificate.

Exhibit 10-3 | Hypothetical Corporate Stock (Share) Certificate

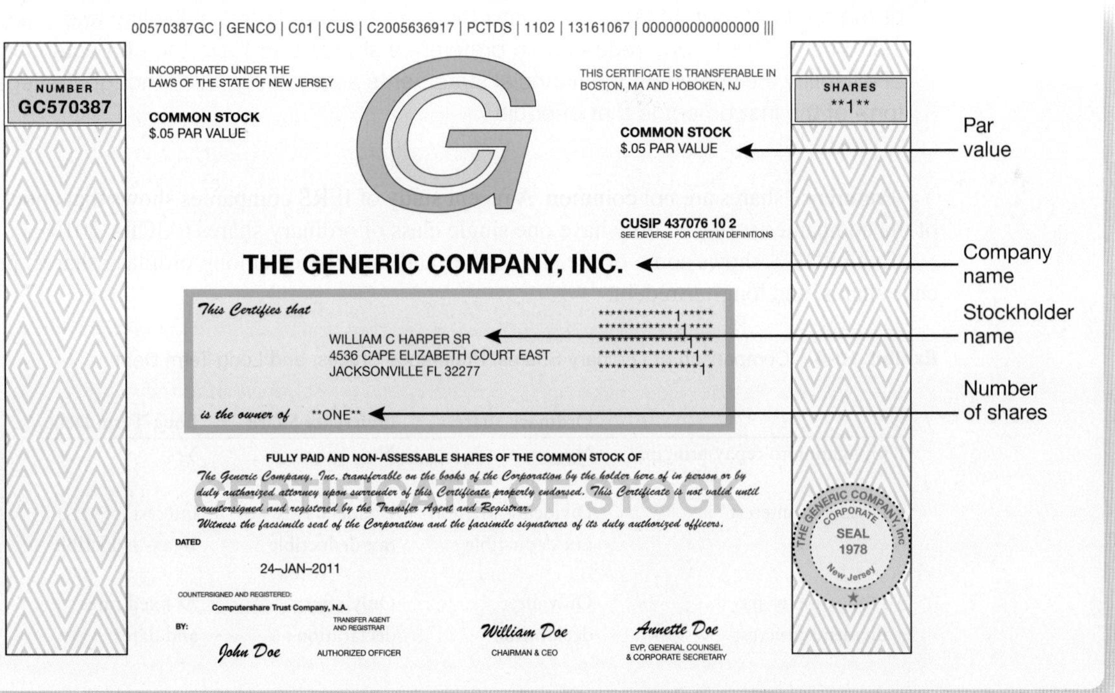

00570387GC | GENCO | C01 | CUS | C2005636917 | PCTDS | 1102 | 13161067 | 000000000000000 |||

NUMBER GC570387

INCORPORATED UNDER THE LAWS OF THE STATE OF NEW JERSEY

COMMON STOCK
$.05 PAR VALUE

THIS CERTIFICATE IS TRANSFERABLE IN BOSTON, MA AND HOBOKEN, NJ

SHARES **1**

COMMON STOCK
$.05 PAR VALUE

CUSIP 437076 10 2
SEE REVERSE FOR CERTAIN DEFINITIONS

THE GENERIC COMPANY, INC.

This Certifies that

WILLIAM C HARPER SR
4536 CAPE ELIZABETH COURT EAST
JACKSONVILLE FL 32277

*************1*****
**************1****
***************1***
****************1**
*****************1*

is the owner of **ONE**

FULLY PAID AND NON-ASSESSABLE SHARES OF THE COMMON STOCK OF

The Generic Company, Inc. transferable on the books of the Corporation by the holder here of in person or by duly authorized attorney upon surrender of this Certificate properly endorsed. This Certificate is not valid until countersigned and registered by the Transfer Agent and Registrar.
Witness the facsimile seal of the Corporation and the facsimile signatures of its duly authorized officers.

DATED 24-JAN-2011

COUNTERSIGNED AND REGISTERED:
Computershare Trust Company, N.A.
TRANSFER AGENT AND REGISTRAR
BY:
John Doe AUTHORIZED OFFICER

William Doe CHAIRMAN & CEO

Annette Doe EVP, GENERAL COUNSEL & CORPORATE SECRETARY

THE GENERIC COMPANY, INC. CORPORATE SEAL 1978 New Jersey

Classes of Shares. Corporations issue different types of shares to appeal to a variety of investors. Some countries use the term "stock" as a synonym for "shares." The shares of a corporation may be either:

- Ordinary shares or preference shares
- With or without par values

Ordinary and Preference Shares. Every corporation issues **ordinary shares**, the basic form of share capital. Unless designated otherwise, the word *share* is understood to mean "ordinary share." Ordinary shareholders have the four basic rights of share ownership, unless a right is specifically withheld. The ordinary shareholders are the owners of the corporation. They stand to benefit the most if the corporation succeeds because they take the most risk by investing in ordinary shares. Sometimes you may see ordinary shares labeled "common stock" in U.S. companies' financial statements.

Preference shares give their owners certain advantages over ordinary shareholders. Preference shareholders receive dividends before the ordinary shareholders, and they also receive assets before the ordinary shareholders if the corporation enters into liquidation. Owners of preference shares also have the four basic shareholder rights, unless a right is specifically denied. Companies may issue different classes of preference shares (Class A and Class B, or Series A and Series B, for example). Each class of preference shares is recorded in a separate account. The preference shareholders expect to earn a fixed dividend on their investments.

A preference share may also have additional features that make it something of a hybrid between ordinary shares and long-term debt. Like interest on debt, preference shares pay a fixed dividend. But unlike interest on debt, the dividend is not required to be paid unless the board of directors declares the dividend. Also, companies have no obligation to pay back true preference shares, unless they are designated as **redeemable preference shares**.

A Closer Look

Consistent with the *IFRS Framework*'s principle of "faithful representation," *IAS 32—Financial Instruments: Presentation* requires financial instruments to be classified as either a financial liability or an equity instrument according to the substance of the contract, not its legal form, and the definitions of financial liability and equity instrument. This is why redeemable preference shares that have the characteristics of a liability are shown on the financial statements as a liability, even though the legal form of the instrument is that of equity.

Preference shares are not common. A recent study of IFRS companies shows that about 80% of the companies surveyed only have one single class of ordinary shares (AICPA 2010).

Exhibit 10-4 shows some of the similarities and differences among ordinary shares, preference shares, and long-term debt.

Exhibit 10-4 | Comparison of Ordinary Shares, Preference Shares, and Long-Term Debt

	Ordinary Share	Preference Share	Long-Term Debt
1 Obligation to repay principal	No	No	Yes
2 Dividends/interest	Dividends are not tax-deductible	Dividends are not tax-deductible	Interest expense is tax-deductible
3 Obligation to pay dividends/interest	Only after declaration	Only after declaration	At fixed rates and dates

Par Value and No-Par Shares. Shares may be par value shares or no-par shares, depending on the applicable regulatory framework. **Par value** is an arbitrary nominal amount assigned by a company to its share. Most companies set the par value of their shares low to avoid legal difficulties from issuing their shares below par. In Exhibit 10-3, you saw that the Generic Company's share has a par value of $0.05 per share. In the same survey of 600 corporations mentioned earlier, less than 9% of the 600 companies use no-par value shares.

Let's have a look now at L'Occitane's share capital. It only has one class of shares, ordinary shares with a par value of €0.03 per share.

EXCERPTS FROM L'OCCITANE's NOTES TO THE 2011 FINANCIAL STATEMENTS

(in thousands €, except for no. of shares)	No. of shares	Share capital	Additional paid-in capital	Total
Balance at March 31, 2010	19,290,674	€ 38,232	€ 48,730	€ 86,962
April 2010, redesignated €0.03 par value	1,255,105,717			
May 2010, issuance of new shares	202,568,500	6,077	294,121	300,198
Balance at March 31, 2011	1,476,964,891	€ 44,309	€ 342,851	€ 387,160

On April 9, 2010, the sole shareholder of the Company, L'Occitane Group S.A., resolved that a value of €0.03 be designated as par value per ordinary share in the share capital of the Company so that the subscribed share capital of the Company amounting to €38,232,000 be represented by 1,274,396,391 shares having a par value of €0.03.

Voting Rights. Companies may have different classes of shares with different voting rights. For example, Berkshire Hathaway has two classes of shares: Common Stock (ordinary share) Class A and Class B. Class A shareholders are entitled to one vote per share and an equal share in dividend and distribution rights. On the other hand, Class B shareholders only have 1/10,000 (one ten-thousandth) of the voting rights of Class A shareholders, and 1/1,500 (one-fifteen-hundredth) of the dividend and distribution rights of Class A shareholders. Similarly, for Chinese companies, you will often see Class A, Class B, and Class H shares. Class A shares are restricted to Chinese residents, whereas Class B shares are open to foreign ownership. H-shares are those of Chinese companies listed on the Hong Kong Stock Exchange.

Sometimes, due to national interests in certain industries of significant importance, you may see "special shares" with very special rights. For example, Singapore Airlines has the following share structure.

EXCERPTS FROM SINGAPORE AIRLINE'S NOTES TO THE 2016 FINANCIAL STATEMENTS

	The Group and the Company			
	Number of shares		Amount (in million SGD)	
	2016	2015	2016	2015
Issued and fully paid share capital				
Ordinary shares				
Balance at March 31	1,199,851,018	1,199,851,018	1,856.1	1,856.1
Special share				
Balance at April 1 and March 31	1	1	*	*

**The value is $0.50*

The Company's ability to operate its existing route network and flight frequency is derived solely from and dependent entirely on the Air Service Agreements ("ASAs") concluded between the Government of Singapore and the governments of other countries. ASAs are therefore critical to the Company's operations. In almost all the ASAs, it is a condition that the Company must at all times be "effectively controlled" and "substantially owned" by Singapore nationals for the tenure of the respective ASAs.

In order to comply with the above requirement, one non-tradable Special Share was issued to the Ministry of Finance. The Special Share enjoys all the rights attached of ordinary shares. In addition, pursuant to Article 3A of the Articles of Association, no resolution may be passed on certain matters without prior written approval of the Special Member.

Source: Singapore Airline, Annual Report 2016, p. 149

ACCOUNT FOR THE ISSUANCE OF SHARES

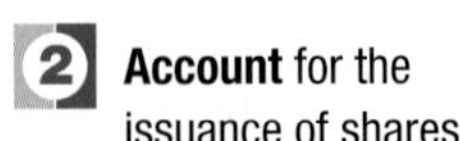
Account for the issuance of shares

Large corporations such as Emirates Airlines, BASF, and SAP need huge quantities of money to operate. Corporations may sell shares directly to the shareholders or use the service of an underwriter, such as the investment banking firms UBS and Goldman Sachs. Companies often advertise the issuance of their shares to attract investors. The *Wall Street Journal* is the most popular medium for such advertisements, especially for IPOs in the United States. These advertisements are colloquially called "tombstones." Exhibit 10-5 is a reproduction of such a tombstone.

Exhibit 10-5 | Hypothetical Tombstone

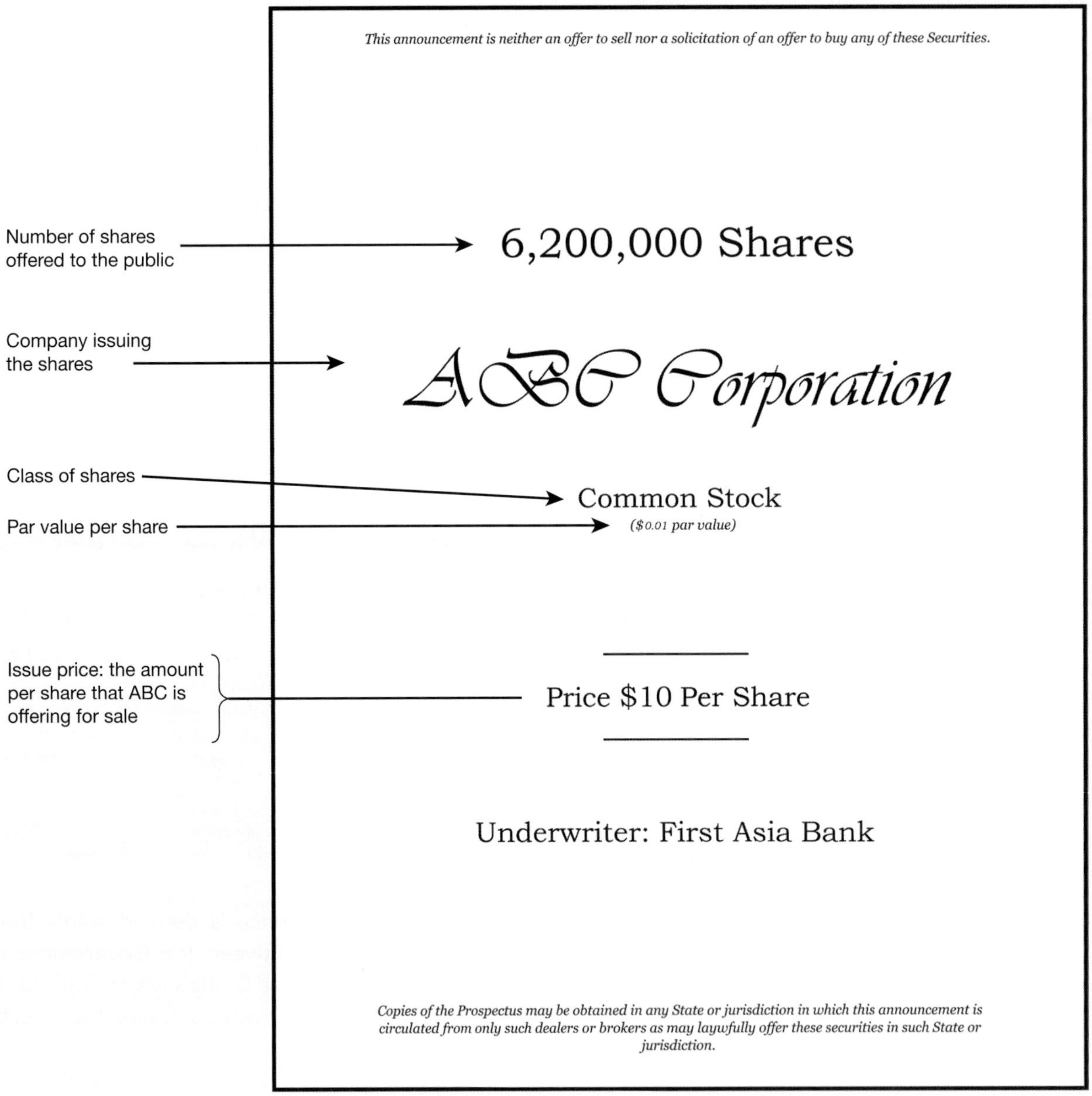

This announcement is neither an offer to sell nor a solicitation of an offer to buy any of these Securities.

Number of shares offered to the public → 6,200,000 Shares

Company issuing the shares → ABC Corporation

Class of shares → Common Stock

Par value per share → *($0.01 par value)*

Issue price: the amount per share that ABC is offering for sale → Price $10 Per Share

Underwriter: First Asia Bank

Copies of the Prospectus may be obtained in any State or jurisdiction in which this announcement is circulated from only such dealers or brokers as may laywfully offer these securities in such State or jurisdiction.

The lead underwriter of ABC's public offering in First Asia Bank. Brokerage firms and investment bankers sold ABC shares to their clients. In its initial public offering, ABC sought to raise $62 million of capital (6.2 million shares at the offering price of $10 per share). Let's see how a shares issuance works using this ABC example.

Ordinary Shares

Ordinary Shares at Par. Suppose ABC's ordinary share had carried a par value equal to its issuance price of $10 per share. The entry for issuance of 6.2 million shares of ordinary shares at par would be:

	A	B	C	D
1	Jul. 23	Cash (6,200,000 × $10)	62,000,000	
2		Ordinary shares		62,000,000
3		*To issue ordinary shares.*		
4				

ABC's assets and shareholders' equity increase by the same amount.

Assets	=	Liabilities	+	Shareholders' Equity
+ 62,000,000	=	0	+	+ 62,000,000

Ordinary Shares above Par. Most corporations set par value low and issue ordinary shares for a price above par. Rather than $10 as in the assumed example above, ABC's ordinary share has a par value of $0.01 (1 cent) per share. You can see this par value stated in the middle of Exhibit 10-5. The $9.99 difference between issue price ($10) and par value ($0.01) is *additional paid-in capital*. You may also see this account labeled *capital in-excess of par* or *share premium*. Both the par value of the share and the additional amount are part of paid-in capital.

Because the entity is dealing with its own shareholders in their capacity as owners of the entity, issuance of shares is not gain, income, or profit to the corporation. This situation illustrates one of the fundamentals of accounting: a company neither earns a profit nor incurs a loss when it sells its shares to, or buys its shares from, its own shareholders.

With par value of $0.01, ABC's actual entry to record the issuance of ordinary shares looked something like this. Again, both assets and equity increase by the same amount.

	A	B	C	D
1	Jul. 23	Cash (6,200,000 × $10)	62,000,000	
2		Ordinary shares (6,200,000 × $0.01)		62,000
3		Paid-in Capital in Excess of Par (6,200,000 × $9.99)		61,938,000
4		*To issue ordinary shares above par.*		
5				

Both assets and equity increase by the same amount.

Assets	=	Liabilities	+	Shareholders' Equity
+ 62,000,000	=	0	+	+ 62,000,000 + 61,938,000

All the transactions in this section include a receipt of cash by the corporation as it issues new shares. The transactions we illustrate are different from those mergers and acquisitions reported in the daily news. In those transactions, one shareholder sold shares to another investor. The corporation doesn't record those transactions because they were between two outside parties.

Stop & Think

Examine L'Occitane's statement of changes in equity at the start of this chapter.

(1) What was L'Occitane's total paid-in capital at March 31, 2011?

(2) Propose the journal entry that L'Occitane would have performed for its IPO share issuance. What is the impact of the issuance on the accounting equation?

Answers:

(1) Total paid-capital includes both the share capital and additional paid in capital. Total paid-in capital at March 31, 2011, is therefore €44,309 + €342,851 = €387,160.

(2) L'Occitane par value per share was €0.03 per share. Its IPO issuance of 202,568,500 new shares equals a total par value of €6,077 and additional paid-up capital of €294,121. L'Occitane would perform the following journal entry in relation to its IPO. Amounts are in thousands of euros.

	A	B	C	D
1	2010			
2	May	Cash	300,198	
3		Share Capital		6,077
4		Share Premium		294,121
5		*To record issuance of shares above par.*		
6				

Assets	=	Liabilities	+	Shareholders' Equity
+ 300,198	=	0	+	+ 6,077 + 294,121

Ordinary Shares with No-Par Values. To record the issuance of no-par shares, the company debits the asset received and credits the share capital for the cash value of the asset received. If L'Occitane shares had been no-par shares, the issuance would be recorded to share capital only.

	A	B	C	D
1	2010			
2	May	Cash	300,198	
3		Share Capital		300,198
4		*To record issuance of no-par shares.*		
5				

Assets	=	Liabilities	+	Shareholders' Equity
+ 300,198	=	0	+	+ 300,198

Shares Issued for Assets Other than Cash. When a corporation issues shares and receives assets other than cash, the company records the assets received at their current market value and credits the share capital and additional paid-in capital accounts accordingly. The assets' prior **book value** isn't relevant because the shareholders will demand shares equal to the market value of the asset contributed. For example, on November 12, Kahn Corporation issued 15,000 shares of its $1 par ordinary shares for equipment worth $4,000 and a building worth $120,000. Kahn's entry is:

	A	B	C	D
1	Nov. 12	Equipment	4,000	
2		Building	120,000	
3		Ordinary Shares (15,000 × $1)		15,000
4		Paid-in Capital in Excess of Par ($124,000 − $15,000)		109,000
5		*To issue no-par shares in exchange for equipment and a building.*		
6				

Assets and equity both increase by $124,000.

Assets	=	Liabilities	+	Shareholders' Equity
+ 4,000	=	0	+	+ 15,000
+ 120,000				+ 109,000

Ordinary Shares Issued for Services. Sometimes a corporation will issue shares in exchange for services rendered, either by employees or outsiders. In this case, no cash is exchanged. However, the transaction should be recognized at fair market value. The corporation would otherwise recognize an expense for the fair market value of the services rendered. Share capital is increased for its par value (if any), and additional paid-in capital is increased for any difference. For example, assume that Kahn Corporation engages a website designer to create the company's website. The website designer would ordinarily charge $25,000 for such services, but agrees to accept shares rather than cash in settlement of the fee. The fair market value of each share at the time of exchange is $10 per share (par value of $1 per share). The journal entry to record the transaction would be:

	A	B	C	D
1		Website development	25,000	
2		Ordinary Shares		2,500
3		Paid-in Capital in Excess of Par ($25,000 − $2,500)		22,500
4				

In this case, retained earnings (shareholders' equity) is eventually decreased by $25,000 (when the net profit is closed to retained earnings account), and paid-in capital (shareholders' equity) is increased for the same amount.

Share Issuance for Other than Cash Can Create an Ethical Challenge

Accounting standards require a company to record its shares at the fair market value of whatever the corporation receives in exchange for the shares. When the corporation receives cash, there is clear evidence of the value of the shares because cash is worth its face amount. But when the corporation receives an asset other than cash, the value of the asset can create an ethical challenge.

A computer whiz may start a new company by investing in computer software. The software may be market-tested or it may be new. The software may be worth millions or worthless. The corporation must record the asset received and the shares exchanged with a journal entry such as the following:

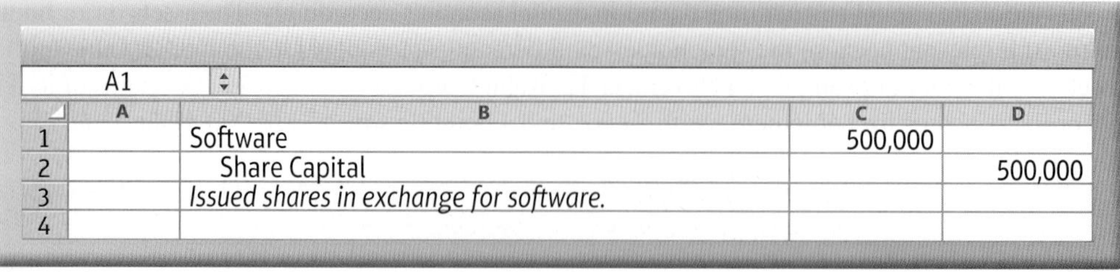

	A	B	C	D
1		Software	500,000	
2		Share Capital		500,000
3		*Issued shares in exchange for software.*		
4				

If the software is really worth \$500,000, the accounting records are okay. But if the software is new and untested, the assets and equity may be overstated. Suppose your computer-whiz friend now invites you to invest in the new business and shows you this Balance Sheet:

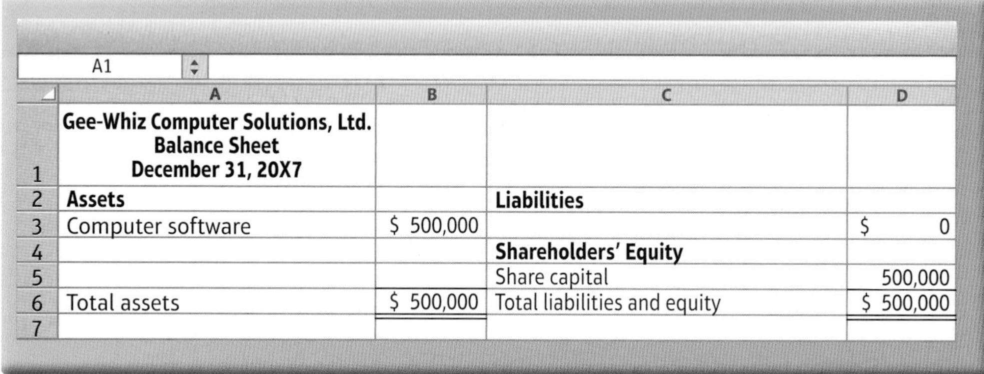

	A	B	C	D
1	**Gee-Whiz Computer Solutions, Ltd.** **Balance Sheet** **December 31, 20X7**			
2	**Assets**		**Liabilities**	
3	Computer software	\$ 500,000		\$ 0
4			**Shareholders' Equity**	
5			Share capital	500,000
6	Total assets	\$ 500,000	Total liabilities and equity	\$ 500,000
7				

Companies like to report large asset and equity amounts on their Balance Sheets. That makes them look prosperous and creditworthy. Gee-Whiz looks debt-free and appears to have a valuable asset. Will you invest in this new business? Here are two takeaway lessons:

1. Some accounting values better represent the underlying economic phenomenon than others.
2. Not all financial statements mean exactly what they say—compliance with accounting standards and an audit by an independent CPA lend more credibility to the financial reporting process.

Preference Shares

Accounting for preference shares follows the same pattern we illustrated for ordinary shares. When a company issues preference shares, it credits the Preference Share account at its par value, with any excess credited to Paid-in Capital in Excess of Par—Preference Shares. There may be separate accounts for paid-in capital in excess of par for preference shares. Many companies combine paid-in capital in excess of par from both preference and ordinary share transactions into one account. Accounting for no-par preference shares follows the pattern for no-par ordinary shares.

Earlier we saw how to account for convertible bonds payable (see Chapter 9). Companies also issue convertible preference shares. The preference shares may be convertible into the company's ordinary shares at the discretion of the preference shareholders.

For example, let's assume that at some time in the future, in November 20X7, L'Occitane issued 30,000 preference shares of €1 par value for €50,000. Each of these preference shares is convertible into 100 L'Occitane ordinary shares. Suppose these preference shares are converted in November 20X9. The journal entries to record this series of transactions would be:

	A	B	C	D
1	20X7			
2	Nov.	Cash	50,000	
3		Preference Share Capital		30,000
4		Share Premium		20,000
5		*To record issuance of preference shares above par.*		
6				

	A	B	C	D
1	20X9			
2	Nov.	Preference Share Capital	30,000	
3		Ordinary Share Capital		30,000
4		*To record conversion of preference shares into ordinary shares.*		
5				

As you can see, we merely remove Preference Share Capital from the books and increase Ordinary Share Capital by the book value of the preference shares.

Mid-Chapter Summary Problem

1. Test your understanding of the first half of this chapter by deciding whether each of the following statements is true or false.
   a. The policy-making body in a corporation is called the board of directors.
   b. The owner of 100 preference shares always has greater voting rights than the owner of 100 ordinary shares.
   c. Par value shares are worth more than no-par shares.
   d. Issuance of 1,000 $5 par value shares at $12 increases contributed capital by $12,000.
   e. A corporation issues its preference shares in exchange for land and a building with a combined market value of $200,000. This transaction increases the corporation's owners' equity by $200,000 regardless of the assets' prior book values.
   f. Preference shares are a riskier investment than ordinary shares.
2. Mustafa Company has two classes of ordinary shares. Only the Class A ordinary shares are entitled to vote. The company's Balance Sheet included the following presentation:

	A	B
1	**Shareholders' Equity**	
2	Share capital:	
3	Class A ordinary share, voting, $1 par value,	
4	authorized and issued 1,260,000 shares	$ 1,260,000
5	Class B ordinary share, non-voting, no par value,	
6	authorized and issued 46,200,000 shares	11,000,000
7		12,260,000
8	Additional paid-in capital	2,011,000
9	Retained earnings	872,403,000
10		$886,674,000
11		

Requirements

a. Record the issuance of the Class A ordinary shares. Use the Mustafa account titles.

b. Record the issuance of the Class B ordinary shares. Use the Mustafa account titles.

c. How much of Mustafa's shareholders' equity was contributed by the shareholders? How much was provided by profitable operations? Does this division of equity suggest that the company has been successful? Why or why not?

d. Write a sentence to describe what Mustafa's shareholders' equity means.

Answers

1. a. True c. False e. True
   b. False d. True f. False

2. a.

	A	B	C	D
1		Cash	3,271,000	
2		Class A Ordinary Shares		1,260,000
3		Additional Paid-in Capital		2,011,000
4		*To record issuance of Class A ordinary shares.*		
5				

b.

	A	B	C	D
1		Cash	11,000,000	
2		Class B Ordinary Shares		11,000,000
3		*To record issuance of Class B ordinary shares.*		
4				

c. Contributed by the shareholders: $14,271,000 ($12,260,000 + $2,011,000). Provided by profitable operations: $872,403,000. This division suggests that the company has been successful because most of its shareholders' equity has come from profitable operations.

d. Mustafa's shareholders' equity of $886,674,000 means that the company's shareholders own $886,674,000 of the business's assets.

Authorized, Issued, and Outstanding Shares

It's important to distinguish among three distinctly different numbers in relation to a company's shares:

1. **Authorized shares capital** is the maximum number of shares the company can issue under its constitution.
2. **Issued shares** is the number of shares the company has issued to its shareholders.
3. **Outstanding shares** are the number of shares that the shareholders own (that is, the number of shares outstanding in the hands of the shareholders). Outstanding shares are issued shares minus shares bought back by the company (more on this later).

Let's have a look at how these three concepts apply with L'Occitane.

EXCERPTS FROM L'OCCITANE'S NOTES TO THE 2011 FINANCIAL STATEMENTS

L'Occitane International S.A. is a corporation incorporated in the Grand Duchy of Luxembourg. The authorized capital of the Company is €1,500,000,000 out of which €44,309,000 is issued at March 31, 2011. All the shares of the Company are fully paid and benefit from the same rights and obligations.

There are no treasury shares held by the Group.

L'Occitane's constitution authorizes it to have up to €1.5 billion share capital (which equals 50 billion shares at €0.03 par value per share). However, L'Occitane has only issued €44,309,000 (about 1,476 million shares) at March 31, 2011. This is the amount of shares issued, as well as the number of shares outstanding at the end of the 2011 financial year as L'Occitane did not have any treasury share.

Stop & Think

What happens if a company has reached its limit of authorized share capital and yet wants to issue more shares?

Answers:

The shares limit (either in total share capital or number of shares) is one that is self-imposed and arbitrary in nature. A company can always ask its members in an Annual General Meeting (AGM) to ratify an increase (or decrease) in the authorized share capital.

This is the reason why some jurisdictions have removed the need for companies to state what their authorized share capital is.

Now, let's learn how treasury shares work.

ACCOUNT FOR TREASURY SHARES

3 **Account** for treasury shares

A company's own shares that it has issued and later reacquired are called **treasury shares**.[2] In effect, the corporation holds these shares in its treasury. Many public companies spend millions of dollars each year to buy back their own shares. Corporations purchase their own shares for several reasons:

1. It offers employee share option compensation or an employee share ownership plan but it does not wish to issue new shares, so it buys the shares from the market and then passes them to employees upon exercise of the share options or purchase of the shares.
2. The management wants to avoid a takeover by an outside party.
3. The management wants to increase its reported earnings per share or EPS (net income/number of shares outstanding). Purchasing shares and holding them as treasury shares reduces outstanding shares, thus decreasing the denominator of this fraction and increasing EPS. More on EPS later in this chapter.

How Are Treasury Shares Recorded?

To understand the way treasury share transactions work, it is helpful to analyze the changes that occur in the treasury share account during the year. L'Occitane did not have any treasury shares in the year it was listed. So let's fast forward a few years and look at L'Occitane in the financial year ended March 31, 2016. This is what L'Occitane says about its treasury shares:

ADAPTED EXCERPTS FROM L'OCCITANE NOTES TO THE ACCOUNTS

Treasury Shares

Where any Group's entity purchases the Group's equity share capital (treasury shares), the consideration paid, including any directly attributable incremental costs (net of income taxes), is deducted from equity attributable to the Group's equity owners. Where such shares are subsequently reissued, any consideration received, net of any directly attributable incremental transaction costs and the related income tax effects, is included in equity.

continued on the following page

[2] In this text, we illustrate the *cost* method of accounting for treasury shares because it is used most widely. Other methods are presented in intermediate accounting courses.

	No. of shares	Amount (EUR)
Treasury shares at start of the financial year (April 1, 2015)	6,655,500	€9,247,000
Use of treasury shares for employee compensation	(933,330)	(1,296,000)
Purchase of treasury shares	2,626,000	4,018,000
Treasury shares at end of financial year (March 31, 2016)	8,348,170	€11,969,000

Source: L'Occitane 2016 Annual Report, page 100

Let's start with purchases of treasury shares. Treasury shares are recorded at cost (the market value of the share on the purchased date) without regard to the share's par value. The treasury share account is a *contra shareholders' equity* account. Therefore, the treasury share account carries a debit balance, the opposite of the other equity accounts. It is reported on the Balance Sheet as a negative amount, as a reduction to share capital or equity. In the fiscal year 2016, L'Occitane bought 2.6 million shares amounting to about €4 million. This would be recorded as below:

A1

	A	B	C	D
1	2016	Treasury Shares	2,626,000	
2		Cash		2,626,000
3		*To record purchases of treasury shared.*		
4				

Notice that treasury shares are recorded at cost, which is the market price of the shares when acquired. The financial statement impact of the transaction is to decrease cash as well as shareholders' equity by $4,018,000.

Assets	=	Liabilities	+	Shareholders' Equity
− 4,018,000	=	0	+	− 4,018,000

In summary, the purchase of treasury shares has the opposite effect of issuing shares:

- Issuing shares *grows* assets and equity.
- Purchasing treasury shares *shrinks* assets and equity.

Resale of Treasury Shares

Reselling treasury shares grows assets and equity exactly as issuing new shares does. The sale increases assets and equity by the full amount of cash received. Notice that the company *never records gains or losses on transactions involving its own treasury shares*. Rather, amounts received in excess of amounts originally paid for treasury shares are recorded as paid-in capital from treasury share transactions, thus bypassing the Income Statement. If the proceeds from the resale of treasury shares were less than the amounts originally paid to acquire them, the difference would be debited to paid-in capital.

L'Occitane did not resell any treasury shares in its fiscal year 2016. Let's assume it actually sold 10,000 treasury shares it bought at €1.50 for €2.00 per share. If this happened, L'Occitane would record:

A1

	A	B	C	D
1	2016	Cash	20,000	
2		Treasury Shares		15,000
3		Share Capital		5,000
4		*To record resale of treasury shares.*		
5				

The impact of this resale would be:

Assets	=	Liabilities	+	Shareholders' Equity
+ 20,000	=	0	+	+ 15,000
				+ 5,000

On the other hand, what if L'Occitane had sold the treasury shares at €1.20 instead of €2.00?

	A	B	C	D
1	2016	Cash	12,000	
2		Share Capital	3,000	
3		Treasury Shares		15,000
4		*To record resale of treasury shares.*		
5				

Assets	=	Liabilities	+	Shareholders' Equity
+ 12,000	=	0	+	− 3,000
				+ 15,000

In both cases, note that any difference is not recognized as a gain or loss on the Income Statement, but is recognized directly in share capital (or additional paid-in capital, if any). This reinforces how we defined income and expenses in the *Conceptual Framework*. As resale of treasury shares represents transactions with owners (in their capacity as owners), any differences are not recognized as income or losses.

Issuing Treasury Shares as Compensation

This is probably the most common use of treasury shares. Many listed companies supplement key employees' salaries (and often also members of the board of directors) by granting them share options. This is covered in *IFRS 2 - Share-based Compensation* which is beyond the scope of this text. For now, we can just note that treasury shares may be reissued as share-based compensation to employees. You saw earlier that L'Occitane used 933,330 treasury shares for employee compensation (costing €1,296,000). L'Occitane would have recorded something similar to this (in aggregate):

	A	B	C	D
1	2016	Share Option Compensation	1,296,000	
2		Treasury Shares		1,296,000
3		*To record reissuance of treasury shares for employee*		
4		*share options.*		
5				

Retiring Treasury Shares

A corporation may purchase its own shares and retire it by canceling the shares. The retired shares cannot be reissued. Suppose L'Occitane canceled 10,000 shares amounting to €15,000 during 2016.

	A	B	C	D
1	2016	Share Capital	15,000	
2		Treasury Shares		15,000
3		*To record cancellation of shares from treasury shares.*		
4				

Note that this cancellation will permanently reduce the amount of outstanding shares.

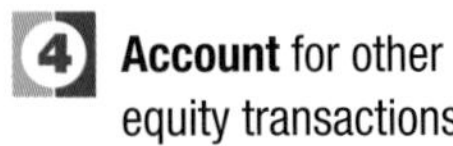
Account for other equity transactions

ACCOUNT FOR OTHER EQUITY TRANSACTIONS

Retained Earnings, Dividends, and Splits

The Retained Earnings account carries the balance of the business's net income, less its net losses and less any declared dividends that have been accumulated over the corporation's lifetime. *Retained* means "held onto." Successful companies grow by reinvesting back into the business the assets they generate through profitable operations.

Let's take another look at L'Occitane's financial statements at the start of this chapter. Notice that the Retained Earnings account grew from €67,774 to €167,275. You would remember that retained earnings are increased by the net profit for the year and decreased by the amount of dividends paid out. L'Occitane's net income for the year was €99,501,700 (plus €3,199 for non-controlling interest), and it didn't pay any dividends for 2011.

The Retained Earnings account is not a reservoir of cash for paying dividends to the shareholders. In fact, the corporation may have a large balance in Retained Earnings but not have enough cash to pay a dividend! Cash and Retained Earnings are two entirely separate accounts with no particular relationship. Retained Earnings says nothing about the company's cash balance. A credit balance in Retained Earnings is normal, indicating that the corporation's lifetime earnings exceed lifetime losses and dividends. The earnings may have been spent on buying more assets or paying off debts. A debit balance in Retained Earnings arises when a corporation's lifetime losses and dividends exceed lifetime earnings. Called a **deficit**, this amount is subtracted to determine total shareholders' equity.

Should the Company Declare and Pay Cash Dividends?

A **dividend** is a distribution by a corporation to its shareholders, usually based on earnings. Dividends usually take one of three forms:

1. Cash
2. Shares
3. Non-cash assets

In this section we focus on cash dividends and share dividends because non-cash dividends are rare. For a non-cash asset dividend, debit Retained Earnings and credit the asset (for example, Long-Term Investment) for the current market value of the asset given.

Cash Dividends

Most dividends are cash dividends. To have cash dividends, a company must have both:

- enough Retained Earnings to *declare* the dividend (as many jurisdictions prohibit distribution of dividends from capital); and
- enough Cash to *pay* the dividend.

A corporation declares a dividend before paying it. A company may pay dividends once a year, twice a year, or sometimes every quarter. Usually, the largest dividend is the one that follows the end of the financial year when financial results are published and the corporation's annual general meeting (AGM) is held. This is called the "final dividend." Other dividends during the financial year are thus called "interim dividends."

Interim dividends are declared by the board of directors and become payable immediately. The final dividend is recommended by the board but requires shareholder approval in an AGM and is not payable until the shareholders vote to do so. Thus, the dividend paid during one financial year typically starts with the prior year's final dividends plus the current year's interim dividends, if any.

There are three relevant dates for dividends (using assumed amounts and dates):

1. ***Declaration date, June 19***. On the declaration date, the board of directors announces the dividend. If it is for an interim dividend, the declaration of the dividend creates a liability for the corporation. If it is for a final dividend, it will have to be approved by shareholders at the AGM. Declaration (or shareholder approval, if it is for a final dividend) is recorded by debiting Retained Earnings and crediting Dividends Payable. Assume a $50,000 dividend was declared and approved.

	A	B	C	D
1	Jun. 19	Retained Earnings[3]	50,000	
2		Dividends Payable		50,000
3		*Declared a cash dividend.*		
4				

Liabilities increase, and equity goes down.

Assets	=	Liabilities	+	Shareholders' Equity
0	=	+ 50,000	+	− 50,000

2. ***Date of record, July 1***. As part of the declaration, the corporation announces the record date (or book closure date), which follows the declaration date by a few weeks. The shareholders on the record date will receive the dividend. You don't need to own shares of a company for a whole period to receive the dividends for the period. You just have to make sure you own the shares at book closure date! There is no journal entry for the date of record.
3. ***Payment date, July 10***. Payment of the dividend usually follows the record date by a week or two. Payment is recorded by debiting Dividends Payable and crediting Cash.

	A	B	C	D
1	Jul. 10	Dividends Payable	50,000	
2		Cash		50,000
3		*Paid cash dividend.*		
4				

Both assets and liabilities decrease.

Assets	=	Liabilities	+	Shareholders' Equity
− 50,000	=	− 50,000	+	0

The net effect of a dividend declaration and its payment, as shown in steps 1, 2, and 3 above, is a decrease in assets and a corresponding decrease in shareholders' equity.

Dividends on Preference Shares

When a company issues both preference and ordinary shares, the preference shareholders receive their dividends first. The ordinary shareholders receive dividends only if the total dividend is large enough to pay the preference shareholders first.

Dividends for preference shares are usually described as a percentage of par value. For example, preference shares may be labeled "6%," which means that owners of the preference shares receive an annual dividend equal to 6% of the preference share's par value. If the preference shares are no-par shares, then it will be based on the share's issuance price.

Consider this example. Avant Garde, Inc., has 100,000 2% preference shares (par value of $100) outstanding in addition to its ordinary shares. The 2% designation means that the preference shareholders receive an annual cash dividend of 2% × $100 par value per share. In 20X6, Avant Garde declares an annual dividend of $500,000. The allocation to preference and ordinary shareholders is:

[3] In the early part of this book, we debited a Dividends account to clearly identify the purpose of the payment. From here on, we follow the more common practice of debiting the Retained Earnings account for dividend declarations.

Preference dividend (100,000 shares × 20% per share)	$200,000
Ordinary dividend (remainder: $500,000 – $200,000)	300,000
Total dividend..	$500,000

If Avant Garde declares only a $250,000 dividend, preference shareholders receive $200,000, and the ordinary shareholders get the remainder, $50,000 ($250,000 – $200,000).

Dividends on Cumulative and Non-Cumulative Preference Shares

Preference shareholders are typically promised a fixed return for their investments. What happens if the company was not able to make payments for the preference dividends? This is not a common occurrence because companies do not want to lose their preference shareholders' faith in them and it would send a negative signal to the market. But it is possible that corporations may fail to pay a dividend to preference shareholders. This is called *passing the dividend*, and the passed dividends are said to be *in arrears*.

In some jurisdictions, preference shares are automatically "cumulative," unless the constitution specifically declares them to be non-cumulative. This means that the owners of **cumulative preference shares** must receive all dividends in arrears plus the current year's dividend before any dividends go to the ordinary shareholders. In this sense, cumulative dividends almost take on the flavor of accrued interest on long-term debt, but not quite. Although cumulative dividends must be paid before other dividends, they must still be declared by the company's board of directors. In contrast, interest on long-term debt doesn't have to go through a formal approval process by the board.

Here's an example of how cumulative dividends work. The preference shares of Avant Garde, Inc., are cumulative. Suppose Avant Garde passed the preference dividend of $200,000 in 20X6. Before paying dividends to ordinary shares in 20X7, Avant Garde must first pay preference dividends of $200,000 for both 20X6 and 20X7, a total of $400,000. On September 6, 20X7, Avant Garde declares a $500,000 dividend. The entry to record the declaration is:

A1

	A	B	C	D
1	20X6	Retained Earnings	500,000	
2		Dividends Payable, Preference ($200,000 × 2)		400,000
3		Dividends Payable, Ordinary ($500,000 – $400,000)		100,000
4		*To declare a cash dividend.*		
5				

If the preference shares are non-cumulative, the corporation is not obligated to pay dividends in arrears—until the board of directors declares such dividends.

Share Dividends

A **share dividend** is a proportional distribution by a corporation of its own shares to its shareholders. Share dividends increase the Share Capital account and decrease Retained Earnings. Total equity is unchanged, and no asset or liability is affected.

The corporation distributes share dividends to shareholders in proportion to the number of shares they already own. If you own 1,000 shares of L'Occitane's ordinary shares and the company distributes a 10% ordinary share dividend, you get 100 (1,000 × 0.10) additional shares. You would then own 1,100 shares. All other shareholders would also receive 10% more shares, leaving all shareholders' ownership unchanged.

In distributing share dividends, the corporation gives up no assets. Why, then, do companies issue share dividends? A corporation may choose to distribute share dividends for these reasons:

- ***To continue dividends but conserve cash.*** A company may need to conserve cash and yet wish to continue dividends in some form. So the corporation may distribute shares as dividends instead.

- ***To reduce the market price of its share.*** Distribution of a share dividend usually causes the share's market price to fall because of the increased number of outstanding shares that result from it. The objective is to make the shares less expensive and therefore attractive to more investors.

Let's continue with our example. Suppose at some time in 20X8, L'Occitane declared the 10% share dividend when the share is trading at €10 per share. Assuming that there are 20,000,000 shares outstanding at the time of the share dividend, L'Occitane.com would record the share dividend as follows:

	A	B	C	D
1	20X8	Retained Earnings[4] (20,000,000 shares		
2		outstanding × 0.10 share dividend × €10		
3		market value per share)	20,000,000	
4		Ordinary Share (20,000,000 × 0.10 × €0.03		
5		par value per share)		60,000
6		Paid-in Capital in Excess of Par		19,940,000
7		*Distributed a 10% share dividend.*		
8				

The accounting equation clearly shows that a share dividend has no effect on total assets, liabilities, or equity. The increases in equity offset the decreases, and the net effect is zero.

Assets	=	Liabilities	+	Shareholders' Equity
				− 20,000,000
0	=	0	+	+ 60,000
				+ 19,940,000

Stock Splits

A **stock split** is an increase in the number of shares authorized, issued, and outstanding, coupled with a proportionate reduction in the share's par value. For example, if the company splits its shares 2 for 1, the number of outstanding shares is doubled and each share's par value is halved. A stock split, like a large share dividend, decreases the market price of the share—with the intention of making the share more attractive in the market. Stock splits are usually undertaken by companies that feel a lower share price would enable more investors to participate in the company's shares. A lower share price also allows a more active or liquid market. Nothing really changes with the company; it still makes the same profit and it still has the same assets. All that changes is the denomination of shares. It is not much different than you changing a $10 note into ten $1 notes or two $5 notes.

Stock splits are more popular with North American companies than companies in other parts of the world. For example, Microsoft, Nike, NVIDIA Corp (makers of computer graphic cards), and Porsche have all carried out some stock splits in recent years.

Suppose the market price of a share of Ryssa Biscuits Factory Ltd. is approximately €0.50. Assume that Ryssa Biscuits Factory Ltd. wishes to decrease the market price to approximately €0.25 per share. Ryssa Biscuits Factory Ltd. can split its shares 2 for 1, and the share price will fall to around €0.25. A 2-for-1 stock split means that:

- the company will have twice as many shares authorized, issued, and outstanding after the split as it had before;
- each share's par value will be cut in half.

[4] Many companies debit Additional Paid-in Capital for their share dividends.

Before the split, Ryssa Biscuits Factory Ltd. had approximately 250 million shares of €0.50 par ordinary shares issued and outstanding. Compare Ryssa Biscuits Factory Ltd.'s shareholders' equity before and after a 2-for-1 stock split:

	A	B	C	D
1	**Ryssa Biscuits Factory Ltd.'s Shareholders' Equity**			
2	**Before 2-for-1 Stock Split**	**(In millions)**	**After 2-for-1 Stock Split**	**(In millions)**
3	Ordinary share, €0.50 par,		Ordinary share, €0.25 par,	
4	500 shares authorized,		1,000 shares authorized,	
5	250 shares issued	€ 125	500 shares issued	€ 125
6	Additional paid-in capital	643	Additional paid-in capital	643
7	Retained earnings	4,304	Retained earnings	4,304
8	Other equity	260	Other	260
9	Total shareholders' equity	€5,332	Total shareholders' equity	€5,332
10				

All account balances are the same after the stock split as before. Only three Ryssa Biscuits Factory Ltd. items are affected:

1. Par value per share drops from €0.50 to €0.25.
2. Shares *authorized* double from 500 to 1,000 (both in millions).
3. Shares *issued* double from 250 to 500 (both in millions).

Total equity doesn't change, nor do any assets or liabilities.

A stock split does not require any journal entry. The record of the split will be a note in the company's corporate action log and share registry.

Summary of the Effects on Assets, Liabilities, and Shareholders' Equity

We've seen how to account for the basic shareholders' equity transactions:

- issuance of shares—ordinary and preference shares
- purchase and sale of treasury shares
- cash dividends
- share dividends and stock splits

How do these transactions affect assets, liabilities, and equity? Exhibit 10-6 provides a helpful summary.

Exhibit 10-6 | Effects on Assets, Liabilities, and Equity

Transaction	Assets	=	Effect on Total Liabilities	+	Shareholders' Equity
Issuance of share—ordinary and preference shares	Increase		No effect		Increase
Purchase of treasury share	Decrease		No effect		Decrease
Sale of treasury share	Increase		No effect		Increase
Declaration of cash dividend	No effect		Increase		Decrease
Payment of cash dividend	Decrease		Decrease		No effect
Share dividend	No effect		No effect		No effect*
Stock split	No effect		No effect		No effect

*The share capital account increases and retained earnings decrease by offsetting amounts that net to zero.

UNDERSTAND THE DIFFERENT VALUES OF SHARES

5 **Understand** the different values of shares

The business community measures *share values* in various ways, depending on the purpose of the measurement. These values include market value, redemption value, liquidation value, and book value.

Market, Redemption, Liquidation, and Book Value

A share's **market value**, or *market price*, is the price at which a person can buy or sell one share. Market value varies with the corporation's net income, financial position, and future prospects, and with general economic conditions. *In almost all cases, shareholders are more concerned about a share's market value than any other share value.*

L'Occitane market price per share is about 15 HKD (about USD 1.93 or €1.82) in May 2012. Multiply this price per share by the shares outstanding (slightly less than 1.5 billion shares), and we can say that L'Occitane's **market capitalization** is about 22.2 billion HKD (or $2.8 billion or €2.7 billion).

Is L'Occitane's HKD 15 per share market value too high, too low, or just about right? Should an investor buy or sell the shares? This is the question that all financial analysts and investors struggle with every day with every stock. There are many reasons why share prices fluctuate. A company's share price may be impacted by its own actions, industry changes, and state of the wider local, regional, or global economy, as well as other psychological reasons driven by emotions and sentiments. Many financial analysts employ stock valuation formulas in an effort to estimate the intrinsic value (or target price) of a share. In other words, they try to see if the market price is at, below, or above this expected value. If market price is higher, then they would recommend a "sell," and if market price is lower, they would recommend a "buy." These valuation techniques use numbers and assumptions based on the company's financial statements.

A preference share that requires the company to redeem the share at a set price is called a redeemable preference share. The company is obligated to redeem (pay to retire) the *preference shares*. The price the corporation agrees to pay for the share, set when the share is issued, is called the **redemption value**. **Liquidation value** is the amount that a company must pay a preference shareholder in the event the company liquidates (sells out) and goes out of business. Not all jurisdictions practice this concept of redemption or liquidation value.

The book value per ordinary share is the amount of owners' equity on the company's books for each ordinary share. If the company has only ordinary shares outstanding, its book value is computed by dividing total equity by the number of shares of ordinary shares *outstanding*. Recall that outstanding shares are equal to issued shares minus treasury shares, if any. For example, a company with shareholders' equity of $150,000 and 5,000 ordinary shares outstanding has a book value of $30 per share ($150,000 ÷ 5,000 shares).

If the company has both preference and ordinary shares outstanding, the preference shareholders have the first claim to owners' equity. Preference shares may have a specified redemption value. The preference component of equity is its redemption value plus any cumulative preference dividends in arrears. The book value per share of ordinary shares is then computed as follows:

$$\text{Book value per ordinary share} = \frac{\text{Total shareholders' equity} - \text{Preference equity}}{\text{Number of ordinary shares outstanding}}$$

Let's consider an example. Crusader Corporation's Balance Sheet reports the following amounts:

	A	B
1	**Shareholders' Equity**	
2	Preference shares, 5%, $100 par, 400 shares issued,	
3	redemption value $130 per share	$ 40,000
4	Ordinary shares, $10 par, 5,500 shares issued	55,000
5	Additional paid-in capital—ordinary shares	72,000
6	Retained earnings	88,000
7	Treasury share, 500 ordinary shares at cost	(15,000)
8	Total shareholders' equity	$ 240,000
9		

Assume Crusader's cumulative preference dividends are in arrears for four years (including the current year). Crusader's preference shares have a redemption value of $130 per share. The book-value-per-share computations for Crusader Corporation are:

Preference Equity	
Redemption value (400 shares × $130)	$52,000
Cumulative dividends ($40,000 × 0.05 × 4 years)	8,000
Preference equity	$60,000*

Ordinary Equity	
Total shareholders' equity	$240,000
Less preference equity	(60,000)
Ordinary equity	$180,000
Book value per share [$180,000 ÷ 5,000 shares outstanding (5,500 shares issued minus 500 treasury shares)]	$ 36

*If the preference share had no redemption value, then preference equity would be $40,000 + preference dividends in arrears.

Some investors search for shares whose market price is below book value. They believe this indicates a good buy. Financial analysts often shy away from companies with a share price at or below book value. To these investors, such a company is in trouble. As you can see, not all investors agree on a share's value. In fact, wise investors base their decisions on more than a single ratio. Later (in Chapter 12), you'll see the full range of financial ratios, plus a few more analytical techniques.

Reporting Shareholders' Equity Transactions

Statement of Cash Flows

Many of the transactions we've covered are reported on the statement of cash flows. Equity transactions are *financing activities* because the company is dealing with its owners. Financing transactions that affect both cash and equity fall into three main categories:

1. issuance of shares
2. treasury shares
3. dividends

Issuances of Shares. During 2011, L'Occitane's IPO generated a significant cash inflow to the company, amounting to over €300 million. This was a financing activity, as shown in Exhibit 10-7.

Exhibit 10-7 L'Occitane's Statement of Cash Flows

	A	B	C
1	**L'Occitane Consolidated Cash Flow Statement**	**For the Year Ended March 31**	
2	**(Adapted, in thousands of euros)**	**2011**	**2010**
3	Cash flow from operating activities	98,911	138,114
4	Cash flow from investing activities	(49,432)	(35,614)
5	Proceeds from share issuance	300,198	206
6	Other financing activities	(86,836)	(88,668)
7	Cash flow from financing activities	213,362	(88,462)
8	Net cash flow	262,841	14,038
9			

Treasury Share. L'Occitane does not hold any treasury shares. If it had purchased (or sold) treasury shares, they would be reported under cash flow from financing activities as well.

Dividends. Most companies pay cash dividends to their shareholders. Dividend payments are a type of financing transaction because the company is paying its shareholders for the use of their money. L'Occitane did not pay any dividends in 2011. Share dividends are not reported in the statement of cash flows because the company pays no cash for them.

In Exhibit 10-7, cash receipts appear as positive amounts and cash payments as negative amounts, denoted by parentheses.

EVALUATE A COMPANY'S RETURN TO EQUITY HOLDERS

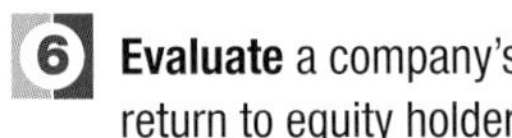
6 Evaluate a company's return to equity holders

Investors search for companies whose shares are likely to increase in value. They're constantly comparing companies. But a comparison of L'Occitane with a new Internet start-up may not be meaningful. L'Occitane's profits run into the millions, which would far exceed a new start-up's net income. Does this automatically make L'Occitane a better investment? Not necessarily. To compare companies of different size, investors use some standard profitability measures, including:

- earnings per share
- return on equity

Earnings Per Share (EPS). Earnings per ordinary share is the company's net income divided by its *outstanding ordinary shares*. The **EPS** is a key measure of a business's success because it shows how much income the company earned for each share. Share prices are quoted at an amount per share, and investors buy a certain number of shares. The EPS is used to help determine the value of a share. The EPS is computed as follows:

$$\text{Earnings per share} = \frac{\text{Net income} - \text{Preferred dividends}}{\text{Average number of ordinary shares outstanding}}$$

IAS 33—Earnings per share requires a reporting entity to disclose its EPS on its Income Statement. Note that two EPS computations are made: one for "basic" (the currently outstanding shares) and one for "diluted" (which takes into account potential increases in outstanding shares). In both cases, companies must first compute a weighted average number of shares outstanding. This computation takes into account the changes that might occur in the number of shares outstanding during the year from such things as treasury share purchases or reissuances and is only possible if you have access to the detailed daily outstanding ordinary shares of the company. L'Occitane reported the following:

EXCERPTS (ADAPTED) FROM L'OCCITANE'S NOTES TO THE 2016 FINANCIAL STATEMENTS

Basic earnings per share are calculated by dividing the profit attributable to equity owners of the Company by the weighted average number of ordinary shares in issue during the year.

Profit for the year attributable to equity holders of the company	€110,343,000
Weighted average number of ordinary shares in issue	1,468,616,721
Basic and Diluted Earnings per share	€0.075

Holders of preference shares have first claim on dividends. Therefore, preference dividends must be subtracted from net income to compute EPS. L'Occitane has only one class of ordinary shares outstanding. Since there are no preference shares, there is no corresponding deduction for preference dividends in L'Occitane's EPS calculation.

Return on Equity. **Rate of return on ordinary equity,** often simply called **return on equity (ROE)**, shows the relationship between net income available and average ordinary shareholders' equity. Return on equity is computed only on ordinary equity because the return to preference shareholders is the specified dividend (for example, 5%). The numerator of return on equity is net income minus preference dividends, if any. The denominator is *average ordinary shareholders' equity*—total *shareholders' equity* minus preference equity. Since L'Occitane does not have any preference shares, we will only use net income and average equity in the calculations that follow.

Return on Equity	L'Occitane 2016	L'Occitane 2015
$\frac{\textit{Net income}}{\textit{Average equity*}}$	$\frac{113{,}555}{857{,}874} = 13.2\%$	$\frac{125{,}578}{811{,}488} = 15.5\%$

**Average* = *(beginning + ending balance)/2, which is (855,557 + 860,191)/2 for 2016.*

As L'Occitane does not have preference shares, we have no preference dividends to subtract from net income on the numerator. Similarly, the denominator is simply average total shareholders' equity. L'Occitane's ROE has dropped from 15.5% in 2015 to 13.2% in 2016. Investors and creditors use ROE to compare companies' performance. The higher the rate of return, the more successful the company. In many industries, an ROE of 15% to 20% is considered a good ROE, depending on the amount of leverage a company takes.

Let's add some context to L'Occitane 13.2% ROE by comparing it to that of L'Oreal (which also owns The Body Shop amongst its many brands) and Estée Lauder. When compared to the other two companies, shown in Exhibit 10-8, we can see that L'Occitane and

Exhibit 10-8 | ROE Comparisons

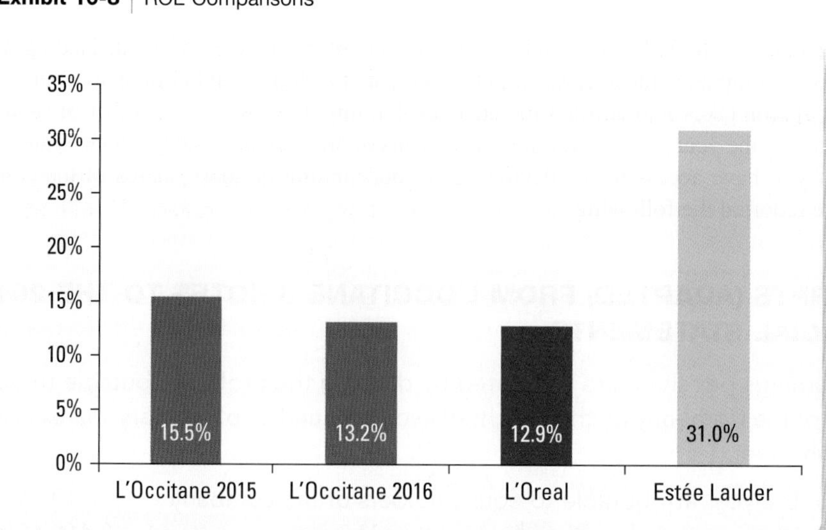

Estée Lauder, with ROE of 31%, on the other hand, seems to be two times better than L'Occitane and L'Oreal.

A word of caution: Remember we said earlier that ROE depends on a company's level of indebtedness. You can increase ROE simply by incurring more debt (and thus a lower equity). L'Occitane, L'Oreal, and Estée Lauder debt ratios are about 28%, 30%, and 61%, respectively. One technique that clearly demonstrates the components of ROE is called the **DuPont Analysis**. We will discuss this later in Chapter 12.

The Decision Guidelines feature offers suggestions for what to consider when investing in shares.

DECISION GUIDELINES

INVESTING IN SHARES

Suppose you've saved $5,000 to invest. You visit a nearby Standard Chartered Bank office, where the financial analyst probes for your risk tolerance. Are you investing mainly for dividends or for growth in the share price? You must make some key decisions.

Investor Decision	Guidelines
Which category of shares to buy for:	
■ A safe investment?	Preference shares are safer than ordinary shares, but for even more safety, invest in high-grade corporate bonds or government securities.
■ Steady dividends?	Cumulative preference shares. However, the company is not obligated to declare preference dividends, and the dividends are unlikely to increase.
■ Increasing dividends?	Ordinary shares, as long as the company's net income is increasing, it has a history of paying regular dividends, and it has sufficient cash flows.
■ Increasing share price?	Ordinary shares, but again only if the company's net income and cash flow are increasing.
How to identify a good share to buy?	There are many ways to pick share investments. One strategy that works reasonably well is to invest in companies that consistently earn higher rates of return on assets and on equity than competing firms in the same industry. Also, select industries that are expected to grow.

End-of-Chapter Summary Problem

1. The Balance Sheet of Trendline Corp. reported the following at December 31, 20X6.

	A	B
1	**Shareholders' Equity**	
2	Preference share, 4%, $10 par, 10,000 shares authorized	
3	and issued (redemption value, $110,000)	$100,000
4	Ordinary share, no-par, $5 stated value, 100,000 shares	
5	authorized, 50,000 shares issued	250,000
6	Paid-in capital in excess of par or stated value:	
7	Ordinary share	239,500
8	Retained earnings	395,000
9	Less: Treasury share, Ordinary (1,000 shares)	(8,000)
10	Total shareholders' equity	$976,500
11		

Requirements

a. Is the preference share cumulative or non-cumulative? How can you tell?

b. What is the total amount of the annual preference dividend?

c. How many ordinary shares are outstanding?

d. Compute the book value per share of the ordinary share. No preference dividends are in arrears, and Trendline has not yet declared the 20X6 dividend.

2. Use the following accounts and related balances to prepare the classified Balance Sheet of Whitehall, Inc., at September 30, 20X7. Use the account format of the Balance Sheet.

Ordinary share, $1 par, 50,000 shares authorized, 20,000 shares issued	20,000	Long-term note payable	80,000
		Inventory	85,000
Dividends payable	4,000	Property, plant and equipment, net	226,000
Cash	9,000	Accounts receivable, net	23,000
Accounts payable	28,000	Preference share, $3.75, no-par, 10,000 shares authorized, 2,000 shares issued	24,000
Paid-in capital in excess of par—Ordinary share	115,000	Accrued liabilities	3,000
Treasury share, Ordinary, 1,000 shares at cost	6,000	Retained earnings	75,000

Answers

1. a. The preference shares are cumulative because they are not specifically labeled otherwise.

b. Total annual preference dividend: $4,000 ($100,000 × 0.04).

c. Ordinary shares outstanding: 49,000 (50,000 issued – 1,000 treasury).

d. Book value per share of ordinary share:

Ordinary:	
Total shareholders' equity	$976,500
Less shareholders' equity allocated to preference	(114,000)*
Shareholders' equity allocated to ordinary	$862,500
Book value per share ($862,500 ÷ 49,000 shares)	$17.60

*Redemption value	$110,000
Cumulative dividend ($100,000 × 0.04)	4,000
Shareholders' equity allocated to preference	$114,000

2.

	A	B	C	D	E
1	**Whitehall, Inc. Balance Sheet September 30, 20X7**				
2	**Assets**		**Liabilities**		
3	Current		Current		
4	Cash	$ 9,000	Account payable		$ 28,000
5	Accounts receivable, net	23,000	Dividends payable		4,000
6	Inventory	85,000	Accrued liabilities		3,000
7	Total current assets	117,000	Total current liabilities		35,000
8	Property, plant and		Long-term note payable		80,000
9	equipment, net	226,000	Total liabilities		115,000
10					
11			**Shareholders' Equity**		
12			Preference share, $3.75, no par,		
13			10,000 shares authorized,		
14			2,000 shares issued	$ 24,000	
15			Ordinary share, $1 par,		
16			50,000 shares authorized,		
17			20,000 shares issued	20,000	
18			Paid-in capital in excess of		
19			par—ordinary shares	115,000	
20			Retained earnings	75,000	
21			Treasury share, ordinary,		
22			1,000 shares at cost	(6,000)	
23			Total shareholders' equity		228,000
24			Total liabilities and		
25	Total assets	$ 343,000	shareholders' equity		$ 343,000
26					

REVIEW | Shareholders' Equity

Quick Check (Answers are given at the end of the chapter.)

1. Harvey Company is authorized to issue 50,000 shares of $25 par ordinary share. On May 30, 20X6, Harvey issued 25,000 shares at $45 per share. Harvey's journal entry to record these facts should include

a. a credit to Paid-in Capital in Excess of Par for $1,125,000.
b. a debit to ordinary shares for $1,125,000.
c. a credit to ordinary shares for $625,000.
d. both a and c.

Questions 2–5 use the following account balances of Machado Co. at August 31, 20X6:

Dividends Payable	$ 12,500	Cash	$111,000
Preference Shares, $150 par	375,000	Ordinary Shares, $5 par	640,000
Paid-in Capital in Excess of Par— Ordinary Shares	60,000	Retained Earnings	325,000

2. How many ordinary shares has Machado issued?

a. 128,000
b. 700,000
c. 375,000
d. Some other amount

3. Machado's total paid-in capital at August 31, 20X6, is

a. $1,387,500.
b. $1,075,000.
c. $1,498,500.
d. $1,400,000.

4. Machado's total shareholders' equity as of August 31, 20X6, is

a. $1,387,500.
b. $1,075,000.
c. $1,498,500.
d. $1,400,000.

5. What would Machado's total shareholders' equity be if Machado had $10,000 of treasury shares?

a. $1,390,000
b. $1,488,500
c. $1,065,000
d. $1,377,500

6. Sycamore Corporation purchased treasury shares in 2010 at a price of $20 per share and resold the treasury shares in 20X7 at a price of $35 per share. What amount should Sycamore report on its Income Statement for 20X7?

a. $20 gain per share
b. $15 gain per share
c. $35 gain per share
d. $0

7. The shareholders' equity section of a corporation's Balance Sheet reports

Discount on Bonds Payable	**Treasury Shares**
a. No	No
b. Yes	Yes
c. No	Yes
d. Yes	No

8. The purchase of treasury shares

a. has no effect on total assets, total liabilities, or total shareholders' equity.
b. decreases total assets and decreases total shareholders' equity.
c. increases one asset and decreases another asset.
d. decreases total assets and increases total shareholders' equity.

9. When does a cash dividend become a legal liability?

a. On date of record.
b. On date of declaration and approval.
c. On date of payment.
d. It never becomes a liability because it is paid.

10. When do dividends increase shareholders' equity?

a. On date of payment.
b. On date of declaration.
c. On date of record.
d. Never.

11. Apple Tree Mall, Inc., has 2,000 shares of 2%, $25 par cumulative preference shares and 125,000 shares of $2 par ordinary shares outstanding. At the beginning of the current year, preference dividends were four years in arrears. Apple Tree's board of directors wants to pay a $2.50 cash dividend on each share of outstanding ordinary shares in the current year. To accomplish this, what total amount of dividends must Apple Tree declare?

a. $312,500
b. $317,500
c. $318,750
d. Some other amount

12. Share dividends

a. have no effect on total shareholders' equity.
b. reduce the total assets of the company.
c. increase the corporation's total liabilities.
d. are distributions of cash to shareholders.

13. What is the effect of a share dividend and a stock split on total assets?

Share dividend	*Stock split*
a. Decrease	Decrease
b. No effect	Decrease
c. Decrease	No effect
d. No effect	No effect

14. A 2-for-1 stock split has the same effect on the number of shares being issued as a

a. 200% share dividend.
b. 50% share dividend.
c. 20% share dividend.
d. 100% share dividend.

15. The denominator for computing earnings per share is

a. weighted average number of ordinary shares outstanding during the year.
b. weighted average number of preference shares outstanding during the year.
c. number of all shares outstanding at year-end.
d. number of ordinary shares outstanding at year-end.

16. The numerator for computing the rate of return on ordinary equity is

a. net income.
b. net income minus interest expense.
c. net income plus preference dividends.
d. net income minus preference dividends.

Accounting Vocabulary

authorized share capital (p. 582) Maximum number of shares a corporation can issue under its constitution.

board of directors (p. 571) Group elected by the shareholders to set policy for a corporation and to appoint its officers.

book value (of a share) (p. 579) Amount of owners' equity on the company's books for each share.

chairperson (p. 571) Elected by a corporation's board of directors, usually the most influential person in the corporation. Usually referred to as chairman.

contributed capital (p. 572) The amount of shareholders' equity that shareholders have contributed to the corporation. Also called *paid-in capital* or *share capital*.

cumulative preference share (p. 588) Preference share whose owners must receive all dividends in arrears before the corporation can pay dividends to the ordinary shareholders.

deficit (p. 586) Retained Earnings account with a debit balance. Also called accumulated losses.

dividend (p. 586) Distribution of assets (usually cash) by a corporation to its shareholders.

DuPont Analysis (p. 595) A method of examining components of Return on Equity (ROE): net profit margin x asset turnover x equity multiplier.

earnings per share (EPS) (p. 593) Amount of a company's net income per share of its outstanding ordinary shares.

issued share (p. 582) Number of shares a corporation has issued to its shareholders.

limited liability (p. 570) No personal obligation of a shareholder for corporation debts. A shareholder can lose no more on an investment in a corporation's share than the cost of the investment.

liquidation value (p. 591) The amount a corporation must pay a preference shareholder in the event the company liquidates and goes out of business, after settling liabilities.

market capitalization (p. 591) A measure of the size of a listed company, equal to the share price multiplied by the number of shares outstanding.

market value (of a share) (p. 591) Price for which a person could buy or sell a share.

ordinary share (p. 574) The most basic form of capital shares. The ordinary shareholders own a corporation.

outstanding share (p. 582) Share in the hands of shareholders calculated as issued shares less treasury shares, if any.

paid-in capital (p. 572) The amount of shareholders' equity that shareholders have contributed to the corporation. Also called *contributed capital* or *share capital*.

par value (p. 574) Arbitrary amount assigned by a company to a share.

preference share (p. 574) Share that gives its owners certain advantages, such as the priority to receive dividends before the ordinary shareholders and the priority to receive assets before the ordinary shareholders if the corporation liquidates.

redeemable preference shares (p. 574) A corporation reserves the right to buy an issue of shares back from its shareholders, with the intent to retire the share.

redemption value (p. 591) The price a corporation agrees to eventually pay for its redeemable preference shares, set when the share is issued.

retained earnings (p. 572) The amount of shareholders' equity that the corporation has earned through profitable operation of the business and has not given back to shareholders.

return on ordinary equity (ROE) (p. 594) Net income minus preference dividends, divided by average ordinary shareholders' equity. A measure of profitability.

share (p. 570) Share into which the owners' equity of a corporation is divided.

share capital (p. 572) The amount of shareholders' equity that shareholders have contributed to the corporation. Also called *contributed capital* or *paid-in capital*.

share dividend (p. 588) A proportional distribution by a corporation of its own shares to its shareholders.

shareholder (p. 570) A person who owns shares in a corporation.

shareholders' equity (p. 572) The shareholders' ownership interest in the assets of a corporation.

stock split (p. 589) An increase in the number of authorized, issued, and outstanding shares coupled with a proportionate reduction in the share's par value and market price per share.

treasury share (p. 583) A corporation's own share that it has issued and later reacquired.

ASSESS YOUR PROGRESS

Short Exercises

LO 1

S10-1. *(Learning Objective 1: Explaining advantages and disadvantages of a corporation)* What are two main advantages that a corporation has over a proprietorship and a partnership? What are two main disadvantages of a corporation?

LO 1

S10-2. *(Learning Objective 1: Describing the authority structure in a corporation)* Consider the authority structure in a corporation, as illustrated in Exhibit 10-2.

1. What group holds the ultimate power in a corporation?
2. Who is the most influential person in the corporation? What's the abbreviation of this person's title?
3. Who's in charge of day-to-day operations? What's the abbreviation of this person's title?
4. Who's in charge of accounting and finance? What's the abbreviation of this person's title?

LO 1

S10-3. *(Learning Objective 1: Describing characteristics of preference and ordinary shares)* Answer the following questions about the characteristics of a corporation's shares:

1. Who are the real owners of a corporation?
2. What privileges do preference shareholders have over ordinary shareholders? What disadvantages do they have?
3. Which class of shareholders reaps greater benefits from a highly profitable corporation? Explain.

S10-4. ***(Learning Objective 1: Organizing a corporation)*** Kitty Page and Jean Scott are opening a Submarine's deli. Page and Scott need outside capital, so they plan to organize the business as a corporation. They come to you for advice. Write a memorandum informing them of the steps in forming a corporation. Identify specific documents used in this process, and name the different parties involved in the ownership and management of a corporation. LO 1

S10-5. ***(Learning Objective 2: Describing the effect of a shares issuance on paid-in capital)*** SHOE received $75,000,000 for the issuance of its shares on April 24. The par value of the SHOE shares was only $75,000. Was the excess amount of $74,925,000 a profit to SHOE? If not, what was it? LO 2

Suppose the par value of the SHOE share had been $2 per share, $12 per share, or $15 per share. Would a change in the par value of the company's share affect SHOE's total paid-in capital? Give the reason for your answer.

S10-6. ***(Learning Objective 2: Issuing shares—par value share and no-par share)*** At fiscal year-end 2010, Harry Printer and Delightful Doughnuts reported these adapted amounts on their Balance Sheets (amounts in millions): LO 2

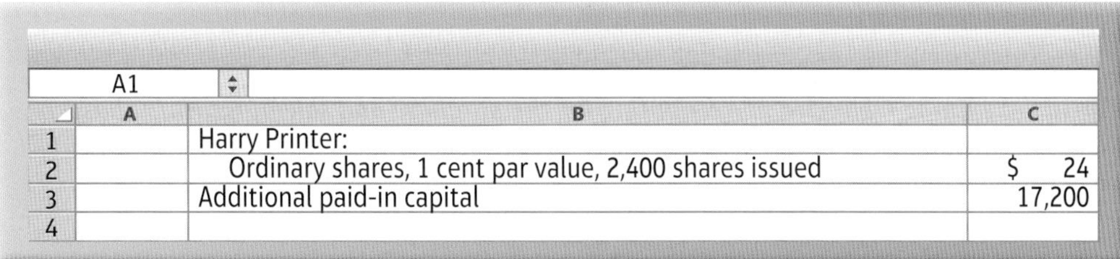

	A	B	C
1		Harry Printer:	
2		Ordinary shares, 1 cent par value, 2,400 shares issued	$ 24
3		Additional paid-in capital	17,200
4			

	A	B	C
1		Delightful Doughnuts:	
2		Ordinary shares, no-par value, 64 shares issued	$ 294
3			

Assume each company issued its shares in a single transaction. Journalize each company's issuance of its shares, using its actual account titles. Explanations are not required.

S10-7. ***(Learning Objective 2: Issuing shares to finance the purchase of assets)*** This short exercise demonstrates the similarity and the difference between two ways to acquire PPE. LO 2

Case A—Issue shares and buy the assets in separate transactions:

Ashley, Inc., issued 10,000 shares of its $20 par ordinary shares for cash of $850,000. In a separate transaction, Ashley used the cash to purchase a building for $620,000 and equipment for $230,000. Journalize the two transactions.

Case B—Issue shares to acquire the assets in a single transaction:

Ashley, Inc., issued 10,000 shares of its $20 par ordinary shares to acquire a building valued at $620,000 and equipment worth $230,000. Journalize this transaction.

Compare the balances in all the accounts after making both sets of entries. Are the account balances similar or different?

LO 2

S10-8. ***(Learning Objective 2: Preparing the shareholders' equity section of a Balance Sheet)*** The financial statements of Green Pastures Employment Services, Inc., reported the following accounts (adapted, with dollar amounts in thousands except for par value):

Paid-in capital in excess of par	$196	Total revenues	$1,430
Other shareholders' equity (negative)	(22)	Accounts payable	450
Ordinary share, $0.01 par		Retained earnings	648
400 shares issued	4	Other current liabilities	2,579
Long-term debt	27	Total expenses	808

Prepare the shareholders' equity section of Green Pastures's Balance Sheet. Net income has already been closed to Retained Earnings.

LO 2

S10-9. ***(Learning Objective 2: Using shareholders' equity data)*** Use the Green Pastures Employment Services data in Short Exercise 10-8 to compute Green Pastures's:

a. Net income.
b. Total liabilities.
c. Total assets (use the accounting equation).

LO 3

S10-10. ***(Learning Objective 3: Accounting for the purchase and sale of treasury shares)*** Newton Marketing Corporation reported the following shareholders' equity at December 31 (adapted and in millions):

Ordinary share	$ 225
Additional paid-in capital	245
Retained earnings	2,149
Treasury share	(621)
Total shareholders' equity	$1,998

During the next year, Newton Marketing purchased treasury shares at a cost of $24 million and resold treasury shares for $6 million (this treasury share had cost Newton Marketing $2 million). Record the purchase and resale of Newton Marketing's treasury shares. Overall, how much did shareholders' equity increase or decrease as a result of the two treasury share transactions?

LO 3

S10-11. ***(Learning Objective 3: Purchasing treasury share to fight off a takeover of the corporation)*** Thi Pham Exports, Inc., is located in Hanoi, Vietnam. TPE is the only company with reliable sources for its specialty gifts that are sold in many department stores around the world. TPE's recent success has made the company a prime target for a takeover. An investment group, PIE Investments, is attempting to buy 51% of TPE's outstanding share against the wishes of TPE's board of directors. TPE board members are convinced that PIE Investments' investors would sell the most desirable pieces of the business and leave little of value.

At the most recent board meeting, several suggestions were advanced to fight off the hostile takeover bid. The suggestion with the most promise is to purchase a huge quantity of treasury shares. PIE has the cash to carry out this plan.

Requirements

1. Suppose you are a significant shareholder of PIE. Write a memorandum to explain to the board how the purchase of treasury shares would make it difficult for the PIE group to take over TPE. Include in your memo a discussion of the effect that purchasing treasury shares would have on shares outstanding and on the size of the corporation.
2. Suppose TPE's management is successful in fighting off the takeover bid and later sells the treasury shares at prices greater than the purchase price. Explain what effect these sales will have on assets, shareholders' equity, and net income. What happens if the prices remained lower than what TPE paid? Will it report a loss?

LO 4

S10-12. ***(Learning Objective 4: Accounting for cash dividends)*** Greentea Corporation earned a net income of $98,000 during the year ended December 31, 20X6. On December 15, Greentea declared the annual cash dividend on its 6% preference shares (10,000 shares with total par value of $100,000) and a $1.00 per share cash dividend on its ordinary shares (50,000 shares with total par value of $500,000). Greentea then paid the dividends on January 4, 20X7.

Journalize for Greentea Corporation:

a. Declaring the cash dividends on December 15, 20X6.

b. Paying the cash dividends on January 4, 20X7.

Did Retained Earnings increase or decrease during 20X6? By how much?

S10-13. ***(Learning Objective 4: Dividing cash dividends between preference and ordinary shares)*** Access Garde, Inc., has 200,000 shares of $1.60 preference shares outstanding in addition to its ordinary shares. The $1.60 designation means that the preference shareholders receive an annual cash dividend of $1.60 per share. In 20X6, Access Garde declares an annual dividend of $450,000. The allocation to preference and ordinary shareholders is:

Preference dividend, (200,000 shares × $1.60 per share)..........	$320,000
Ordinary dividend (remainder: $500,000 – $370,000)	130,000
Total dividend..	$450,000

Answer these questions about Access Garde's cash dividends.

1. How much in dividends must Access Garde declare each year before the ordinary shareholders receive any cash dividends for the year?
2. Suppose Access Garde, Inc., declares cash dividends of $350,000 for 20X6. How much of the dividends goes to preference? How much goes to ordinary?
3. Is Access Garde's preference shares cumulative or non-cumulative? How can you tell?
4. Access Garde, Inc., passed the preference dividend in 20X5 and 20X6. Then in 20X7, Access Garde declared cash dividends of $1,400,000. How much of the dividends goes to preference? How much goes to ordinary?

LO 4

S10-14. ***(Learning Objective 4: Recording a share dividend)*** Centerville Bancshares has 12,000 shares of $3 par ordinary shares outstanding. Suppose Centerville distributes a 15% shares dividend when the market value of its shares is $25 per share.

1. Journalize Centerville's distribution of the share dividend on May 11. An explanation is not required.
2. What was the overall effect of the share dividend on Centerville's total assets? On total liabilities? On total shareholders' equity?

LO 5

S10-15. ***(Learning Objective 5: Computing book value per share)*** Fools Gold, Inc., has the following shareholders' equity:

Preference share, 4%, $5 par,	
34,000 shares authorized and issued..................................	$ 198,000
Ordinary share, $2 par, 100,000 shares authorized	
64,000 shares issued	128,000
Additional paid-in capital..	2,170,000
Retained earnings..	1,700,000
Less treasury share, ordinary share (1,400 shares at cost)	(45,000)
Total shareholders' equity	$4,151,000

The company has passed its preference dividends for three years including the current year. Compute the book value per share of the company's ordinary shares.

LO 6

S10-16. ***(Learning Objective 6: Computing and explaining earning per share and return on equity)*** Give the formula for computing (a) earnings per share (EPS) and (b) rate of return on ordinary shareholders' equity (ROE). Then answer these questions.

1. Why are preference dividends deducted from net income to compute EPS?
2. Why is preference share capital deducted from total equity to compute ROE?

LO 6

S10-17. ***(Learning Objective 6: Computing earnings per share and return on equity for a leading company)*** Sakura Corporation's 20X7 financial statements reported the following items, with the 20X6 figures given for comparison (adapted and in millions).

	A	B	C	D
1			**20X7**	**20X6**
2		**Balance Sheet**		
3		Total assets	¥ 10,624	¥ 9,515
4		Total liabilities	¥ 7,412	¥ 6,637
5		Total shareholders' equity (all ordinary)	3,212	2,878
6		Total liabilities and equity	¥ 10,624	¥ 9,515
7				
8		**Income Statement**		
9		Revenues and other income	¥ 7,633	
10		Operating expense	7,286	
11		Interest expense	31	
12		Other expense	196	
13		Net income	¥ 120	
14				

The weighted average common shares outstanding during 20X7 was 500 million shares. Compute Sakura's earnings per share and return on ordinary equity for 20X7. Evaluate the rates of return as strong or weak.

LO 1 2 5

S10-18. ***(Learning Objectives 1, 2, 5: Explaining the features of a corporation's shares)*** McMillan Corporation is conducting a special meeting of its board of directors to address some concerns raised by the shareholders. Shareholders have submitted the following questions. Answer each question.

1. Why are ordinary shares and retained earnings shown separately in the shareholders' equity section of the Balance Sheet?
2. Lily Lockhart, a McMillan shareholder, proposes to transfer some land she owns to the company in exchange for a share of the company shares. How should McMillan Corporation determine the number of shares to issue for the land?
3. Preference shares generally are preference with respect to dividends and in the event of our liquidation. Why would investors buy our ordinary shares when preference shares are available?
4. What does the redemption value of our preference shares require us to do?
5. One shareholder asked the board why the market value per share is not the same as the book value per share. Explain why this is the case.

LO 7

S10-19. ***(Learning Objective 7: Measuring cash flows from financing activities)*** During 20X6, Dwayne Corporation earned net income of $5.8 billion and paid off $2.5 billion of long-term notes payable. Dwayne raised $1.2 billion by issuing ordinary shares, paid $3.6 billion to purchase treasury shares, and paid cash dividends of $1.6 billion. Report Dwayne's *cash flows from financing* activities on the statement of cash flows for 20X6.

Exercises MyLab Accounting

Select A and B exercises can be found within MyLab Accounting, an online homework and practice environment. Your instructor may ask you to complete select exercises using MyLab Accounting.

Group A

E10-20A. *(Learning Objective 2: Issuing shares and reporting shareholders' equity)* Bread & Butter, Inc., is authorized to issue 120,000 shares of ordinary shares and 7,000 shares of preference shares. During its first year, the business completed the following share issuance transactions:

Jan. 19	Issued 10,000 shares of $2.00 par ordinary shares for cash of $6.00 per share.
Apr. 3	Issued 500 shares of no-par preference shares for $55,000 cash.
11	Received inventory valued at $16,200 and equipment with market value of $9,800 for 3,800 shares of the $2.00 par ordinary share.

Requirements

1. Journalize the transactions. Explanations are not required.
2. Prepare the shareholders' equity section of Bread & Butter's Balance Sheet. The ending balance of retained earnings is a deficit of $45,000.

E10-21A. *(Learning Objective 2: Preparing shareholders' equity section of a Balance Sheet)* Army Navy Sporting Goods is authorized to issue 10,000 preference shares and 20,000 ordinary shares. During a two-month period, Army Navy completed these share-issuance transactions:

Apr. 23	Issued 1,800 shares of $1.50 par ordinary share for cash of $16.50 per share.
May 2	Issued 800 shares of no-par preference share for $24,000 cash.
12	Received inventory valued at $20,000 and equipment with market value of $40,000 for 3,200 shares of the $1.50 par ordinary share.

Requirement

1. Prepare the shareholders' equity section of the Army Navy Sporting Goods' Balance Sheet for the transactions given in this exercise. The Retained Earnings account currently has a balance of $45,000. Journal entries are not required.

E10-22A. *(Learning Objective 2: Measuring the paid-in capital of a corporation)* Travel Publishing was recently organized. The company issued ordinary shares to an attorney who provided legal services worth $22,000 to help organize the corporation. Travel also issued ordinary shares to an inventor in exchange for his patent with a market value of $83,000. In addition, Travel received cash both for the issuance of 3,000 shares of its preference shares at $120 per share and for the issuance of 20,000 of its ordinary shares at $1 per share. During the first year of operations, Travel earned a net income of $50,000 and declared a cash dividend of $29,000. Without making journal entries, determine the total paid-in capital created by these transactions.

E10-23A. *(Learning Objectives 2, 3: Preparing the shareholders' equity section of a Balance Sheet)* Parker Software had the following selected account balances at December 31, 20X6 (in thousands, except par value per share).

Inventory	$ 651	Ordinary share, $0.75 par per share, 800 shares authorized, 320 shares issued	$ 240
Property, plant and equipment, net	900	Retained earnings	2,220
Paid-in capital in excess of par	899	Accounts receivable, net	1,000
Treasury shares, 100 shares at cost	1,150	Notes payable	1,100
Other shareholders' equity	(730)*		

*Debit balance

Requirements

1. Prepare the shareholders' equity section of Parker's Balance Sheet (in thousands).
2. How can Parker have a larger balance of treasury shares than the sum of ordinary shares and Paid-in Capital in Excess of Par?

LO 2 3

E10-24A. ***(Learning Objectives 2, 3: Recording treasury shares transactions and measuring their effects on shareholders' equity)*** Journalize the following transactions of Aliant Productions:

Jan. 17	Issued 2,100 shares of $2.50 par ordinary share at $10 per share.
May 23	Purchased 400 shares of treasury share at $12 per share.
Jul. 11	Sold 300 shares of treasury share at $20 per share.

What was the overall effect of these transactions on Aliant's shareholders' equity?

LO 2 3 4

E10-25A. ***(Learning Objectives 2, 3, 4: Recording share issuance, treasury share, and dividend transactions)*** At December 31, 20X6, Southwest Corporation reported the shareholders' equity accounts shown here (with dollar amounts in millions, except per share amounts).

Ordinary share $2.00 par value per share, 2,100 million shares issued	$ 4,200
Capital in excess of par value	8,400
Retained earnings	250
Treasury share, at cost	(70)
Total shareholders' equity	$12,780

Southwest's 20X7 transactions included the following:

a. Net income, $446 million.
b. Issuance of 9 million shares of ordinary share for $13.50 per share.
c. Purchase of 3 million shares of treasury share for $16 million.
d. Declaration and payment of cash dividends of $32 million.

Requirement

1. Journalize Southwest's transactions in **b**, **c**, and **d**. Explanations are not required.

LO 2 3 4

E10-26A. ***(Learning Objectives 2, 3, 4: Reporting shareholders' equity after a sequence of transactions)*** Use the Southwest Corporation data in Exercise 10-25A to prepare the shareholders' equity section of the company's Balance Sheet at December 31, 20X7.

LO 2 3 4 5

E10-27A. ***(Learning Objectives 2, 3, 4, 5: Inferring transactions from a company's shareholders' equity)*** Theodore Products Company reported the following shareholders' equity on its Balance Sheet:

	A	B	C
	Shareholders' Equity	**December 31**	
1	**(Dollars and shares in millions)**	**20X7**	**20X6**
2	Convertible Preference share—\$0.50 par value; authorized		
3	30 shares; issued and outstanding: 20X7 and 20X6—		
4	6 and 12 shares, respectively	\$ 3	\$ 6
5	Ordinary share—\$2 per share par value; authorized		
6	1,400 shares; issued: 20X7 and 20X6—300		
7	and 200 shares, respectively	600	400
8	Additional paid-in capital	1,950	1,200
9	Retained earnings	6,270	5,066
10	Treasury share, ordinary share—at cost		
11	20X7—52 shares; 20X6—12 shares	(1,144)	(228)
12	Total shareholders' equity	7,679	6,444
13	Total liabilities and shareholders' equity	\$ 48,299	\$ 45,294
14			

Requirements

1. What caused Theodore's preference shares to decrease during 20X7? Cite all possible causes.
2. What caused Theodore's ordinary shares to increase during 20X7? Identify all possible causes.
3. How many shares of Theodore's ordinary shares were outstanding at December 31, 20X7?
4. Theodore's net income during 20X7 was \$1,380 million. How much were Theta's dividends during the year?
5. During 20X7, Theodore sold no treasury shares. What average price per share did Theodore pay for the treasury shares the company purchased during the year?

E10-28A. ***(Learning Objective 4: Computing dividends on preference and ordinary share)*** Huron Manufacturing, Inc., reported the following: LO 4

	A	B
1	**Shareholders' Equity**	
2	Preference share, cumulative, \$0.50 par, 9%, 50,000 shares issued	\$ 25,000
3	Ordinary share, \$0.10 par, 9,180,000 shares issued	918,000
4		

Huron Manufacturing has paid all preference dividends through 20X7.

Requirement

1. Compute the total amounts of dividends to both preference and ordinary shares for 20X6 and 20X7 if total dividends are \$70,000 in 20X6 and \$130,000 in 20X7.

E10-29A. ***(Learning Objective 4: Recording a share dividend and reporting shareholders' equity)*** The shareholders' equity for Heavenly Desserts Drive-Ins (HD) on December 31, 20X6, is as follows: 

	A	B
1	**Shareholders' Equity**	
2	Ordinary share, $0.80 par, 2,600,000 shares	
3	authorized, 400,000 shares issued	$ 320,000
4	Paid-in capital in excess of par—ordinary	307,200
5	Retained earnings	7,122,000
6	Other equity	(200,000)
7	Total shareholders' equity	$ 7,549,200
8		

On May 11, 20X7, the market price of HD's ordinary shares was $19 per share. Assume HD distributed a 15% share dividend on this date.

Requirements

1. Journalize the distribution of the share dividend.
2. Prepare the shareholders' equity section of the Balance Sheet after the share dividend.
3. Why is the total shareholders' equity unchanged by the share dividend?
4. Suppose HD had a cash balance of $580,000 on May 12, 20X7. What is the maximum amount of cash dividends HD can declare?

LO 2 3 4

E10-30A. ***(Learning Objectives 2, 3, 4: Measuring the effects of share issuance, dividends, and treasury shares transactions)*** Identify the effects—both the direction and the dollar amount—of these assumed transactions on the total shareholders' equity of Athol Corporation. Each transaction is independent.

- **a.** Declaration of cash dividends of $75 million.
- **b.** Payment of the cash dividend in **a**.
- **c.** A 25% shares dividend. Before the dividend, 72 million shares of $2.00 par ordinary share were outstanding; the market value was $8.250 at the time of the dividend.
- **d.** Purchase of 1,800 shares of treasury shares (par value $2.00) at $5.25 per share.
- **e.** Sale of 800 shares of the treasury shares for $7.00 per share. Cost of the treasury share was $5.25 per share.
- **f.** A 2-for-1 stock split. Prior to the split, 72 million shares of $2.00 par ordinary shares were outstanding.

LO 4

E10-31A. ***(Learning Objective 4: Reporting shareholders' equity after a stock split)*** Clublink Corp. had the following shareholders' equity at October 31 (dollars in millions, except par value per share):

	A	B
1	**Shareholders' Equity**	
2	Ordinary share, $1.50 par, 750 million shares	
3	authorized, 410,000 million shares issued	$ 615
4	Additional paid-in capital	318
5	Retained earnings	2,399
6	Other equity	(148)
7	Total shareholders' equity	$ 3,184
8		

On December 6, Clublink split its $1.50 par ordinary share 3-for-1.

Requirement

1. Prepare the shareholders' equity section of the Balance Sheet immediately after the split.

E10-32A. ***(Learning Objective 5: Measuring the book value per share of ordinary share)*** The Balance Sheet of Luxury Rug Company reported the following: LO 5

Redeemable preference share, 4%, $60 par value, redemption value $54,000; outstanding 600 shares...............	$36,000
Ordinary shareholders' equity:	
7,000 shares issued and outstanding	77,000
Total shareholders' equity	$113,000

Requirements

1. Compute the book value per share for an ordinary share, assuming all preference dividends are fully paid up (none in arrears).
2. Compute the book value per share of the ordinary shares, assuming that three years' cumulative preference dividends, including the current year, are in arrears.
3. Luxury Rug's ordinary shares recently traded at a market price of $6.00 per share. Does this mean that Luxury Rug's shares are a good buy at $6.00?

E10-33A. ***(Learning Objective 6: Evaluating profitability)*** Luna Inns reported these figures for 20X7 and 20X6 (in millions): LO 6

	A	B	C	D
1			**20X7**	**20X6**
2		**Balance Sheet**		
3		Total assets	$ 15,910	$ 13,710
4		Ordinary share and additional paid-in capital	45	392
5		Retained earnings	11,524	16,493
6		Other equity	(3,019)	(9,045)
7				
8		**Income Statement**		
9		Operating income	$ 4,024	$ 3,815
10		Interest expense	224	268
11		Net income	1,529	1,545
12				

Requirement

1. Compute Luna's return on assets and return on ordinary shareholders' equity for 20X7. Do these rates of return suggest strength or weakness? Give your reason.

E10-34A. ***(Learning Objective 6: Evaluating profitability)*** Littleton Company included the following items in its financial statements for 20X6, the current year (amounts in millions): LO 6

Payment of long-term debt..........	$17,090	Dividends paid.....................	$ 230
Proceeds from issuance		Interest expense:	
of ordinary share.....................	8,600	Current year.....................	1,439
Total liabilities:		Preceding year..................	601
Current year-end.....................	32,325	Net income:	
Preceding year-end	38,035	Current year.....................	1,880
Total shareholders' equity:		Preceding year..................	2,005
Current year-end.....................	23,478	Operating income:	
Preceding year-end	14,034	Current year.....................	4,894
Borrowings................................	6,570	Preceding year..................	4,006

Requirement

1. Compute Littleton's earnings per share and return on ordinary equity during 20X6 (the current year). Littleton has no preference shares outstanding. The weighted average ordinary shares outstanding were 500 million shares. Are the company's returns strong or weak? Give your reason.

LO 7

E10-35A. *(Learning Objective 7: Reporting cash flows from financing activities)* Use the Littleton Company data in Exercise E10-34A to show how the company reported cash flows from financing activities during 20X6 (the current year). List items in descending order from the largest to the smallest dollar amount.

Group B

LO 2

E10-36B. *(Learning Objective 2: Issuing share and reporting shareholders' equity)* Sweet & Sour, Inc., is authorized to issue 120,000 shares of ordinary shares and 8,000 shares of preference shares. During its first year, the business completed the following share issuance transactions:

Apr. 19	Issued 18,000 shares of €3.50 par ordinary share for cash of €7.50 per share.
Nov. 3	Issued 700 shares of no-par preference share for €56,000 cash.
11	Received inventory valued at €18,400 and equipment with market value of €10,600 for 4,000 shares of the €3.50 par ordinary share.

Requirements

1. Journalize the transactions. Explanations are not required.
2. Prepare the shareholders' equity section of Sweet & Sour's Balance Sheet. The ending balance of retained earnings is a deficit of €48,000.

LO 2

E10-37B. *(Learning Objective 2: Preparing shareholders' equity section of a Balance Sheet)* Honcho Sporting Goods is authorized to issue 8,000 preference shares and 16,000 ordinary shares. During a two-month period, Honcho completed these share-issuance transactions:

Jun. 23	Issued 1,400 shares of $2.00 par ordinary share for cash of $17.50 per share.
Jul. 2	Issued 500 shares of $5.50, no-par preference share for $32,000 cash.
12	Received inventory valued at $18,000 and equipment with market value of $42,000 for 3,600 shares of the $2.00 par ordinary share.

Requirement

1. Prepare the shareholders' equity section of the Honcho Sporting Goods Balance Sheet for the transactions given in this exercise. The Retained Earnings account currently has a balance of €45,000. Journal entries are not required.

LO 2

E10-38B. *(Learning Objective 2: Measuring the paid-in capital of a corporation)* Journey Publishing was recently organized. The company issued ordinary shares to a lawyer who provided legal services worth €25,000 to help organize the corporation. Journey also issued ordinary shares to an inventor in exchange for his patent with a market value of €87,000. In addition, Journey received cash both for the issuance of 4,000 shares of its preference shares at €90 per share and for the issuance of 18,000 shares of its ordinary shares at €18 per share. During the first year of operations, Journey earned a net income of €65,000 and declared a cash dividend of €23,000. Without making journal entries, determine the total paid-in capital created by these transactions.

E10-39B. ***(Learning Objectives 2, 3: Shareholders' equity section of a Balance Sheet)*** Baikal Software had the following selected account balances at December 31, 20X6 (in thousands, except par value per share):

Inventory	€ 705	Ordinary share, €0.50 par per share, 900 shares authorized, 300 shares issued	€ 150
Property, plant and equipment, net	903	Retained earnings	2,270
Paid-in capital in excess of par	897	Accounts receivable, net	200
Treasury share, 140 shares at cost	1,610	Notes payable	1,166
Other shareholders' equity	(726)*		

*Debit balance

Requirements

1. Prepare the shareholders' equity section of Baikal Software's Balance Sheet (in thousands).
2. How can Baikal have a larger balance of treasury shares than the sum of ordinary shares and paid-in capital in excess of par?

E10-40B. ***(Learning Objectives 2, 3: Recording treasury share transactions and measuring their effects on shareholders' equity)*** Journalize the following assumed transactions of Applebug Productions:

LO 2 3

Mar. 16	Issued 2,500 shares of $1.50 par ordinary share at $7 per share.
Apr. 20	Purchased 700 shares of treasury share at $16 per share.
Aug. 8	Sold 500 shares of treasury share at $17 per share.

What was the overall effect of these transactions on Applebug's shareholders' equity?

E10-41B. ***(Learning Objectives 2, 3, 4: Recording share issuance, treasury share, and dividend transactions)*** At December 31, 20X6, Western Corporation reported the shareholders' equity accounts shown here (with dollar amounts in millions, except per share amounts).

LO 2 3 4

Ordinary share €1.50 par value per share, 1,700 million shares issued	€ 2,550
Capital in excess of par value	7,650
Retained earnings	260
Treasury share, at cost	(10)
Total shareholders' equity	€10,450

Western's 20X7 transactions included the following:

a. Net income, €447 million.
b. Issuance of 10 million shares of ordinary share for €12.50 per share.
c. Purchase of 4 million shares of treasury share for €15 million.
d. Declaration and payment of cash dividends of €35 million.

Requirement

1. Journalize Western's transactions in **b**, **c**, and **d**. Explanations are not required.

E10-42B. ***(Learning Objectives 2, 3, 4: Reporting shareholders' equity after a sequence of transactions)*** Use the Western Corporation data in Exercise 10-41B to prepare the shareholders' equity section of the company's Balance Sheet at December 31, 20X7.

E10-43B. ***(Learning Objectives 2, 3, 4, 5: Inferring transactions from a company's shareholders' equity)*** Eleanor Products Company reported the following shareholders' equity on its Balance Sheet:

Shareholders' Equity (Dollars and shares in millions)	December 31 20X7	20X6
Convertible preference share—€1.50 par value; authorized 40 shares;		
issued and outstanding:		
20X7 and 20X6—8 and 16 shares, respectively	€ 12	€ 24
Ordinary share—€4 per share par value; authorized		
1,200 shares; issued: 20X7 and 20X6—500		
and 400 shares, respectively	2,000	1,600
Additional paid-in capital	2,750	2,000
Retained earnings	6,300	5,025
Treasury share, ordinary share—at cost		
20X7—54 shares; 20X6—14 shares	(1,242)	(280)
Total shareholders' equity	9,820	8,369
Total liabilities and shareholders' equity	€ 50,320	€ 47,215

Requirements

1. What caused Eleanor's preference shares to decrease during 20X7? Cite all possible causes.
2. What caused Eleanor's ordinary shares to increase during 20X7? Identify all possible causes.
3. How many shares of Eleanor's ordinary shares were outstanding at December 31, 20X7?
4. Eleanor's net income during 20X7 was €1,478 million. How much were Eleanor's dividends during the year?
5. During 20X7, Eleanor sold no treasury shares. What average price per share did Eleanor pay for the treasury shares the company purchased during the year?

LO 4

E10-44B. ***(Learning Objective 4: Computing dividends on preference and ordinary share)*** Eerie Manufacturing, Inc., reported the following:

Shareholders' Equity	
Preference share, cumulative, $1.50 par, 7%, 60,000 shares issued	€ 90,000
Ordinary share, $0.20 par, 9,120,000 shares issued	1,824,000

Eerie Manufacturing has paid all preference dividends through 20X3.

Requirement

1. Compute the total amounts of dividends to both preference and ordinary for 20X6 and 20X7 if total dividends are €110,000 in 20X6 and €220,000 in 20X7.

LO 4

E10-45B. ***(Learning Objective 4: Recording a share dividend and reporting shareholders' equity)*** The shareholders' equity for Icy Pop Drive-Ins (IP) on December 31, 20X6, follows:

Shareholders' Equity	
Ordinary share, €0.30 par, 2,200,000 shares	
authorized, 500,000 shares issued	€ 150,000
Paid-in capital in excess of par—ordinary	409,600
Retained earnings	7,133,000
Other equity	(185,000)
Total shareholders' equity	€ 7,507,600

On August 15, 20X7, the market price of IP's ordinary shares was €15 per share. Assume IP distributed a 20% share dividend on this date.

Requirements

1. Journalize the distribution of the share dividend.
2. Prepare the shareholders' equity section of the Balance Sheet after the share dividend.
3. Why is total shareholders' equity unchanged by the share dividend?
4. Suppose IP had a cash balance of €570,000 on August 16, 20X7. What is the maximum amount of cash dividends IP can declare?

E10-46B. ***(Learning Objectives 2, 3, 4: Measuring the effects of share issuance, dividends, and treasury share transactions)*** Identify the effects—both the direction and the dollar amount—of these assumed transactions on the total shareholders' equity of Dracut Corporation. Each transaction is independent.

- **a.** Declaration of cash dividends of €88 million.
- **b.** Payment of the cash dividend in **a**.
- **c.** A 5% share dividend. Before the dividend, 75 million shares of €3.00 par ordinary shares were outstanding; the market value was €9.185 at the time of the dividend.
- **d.** Purchase of 1,600 shares of treasury shares (par value €3.00) at €6.25 per share.
- **e.** Sale of 800 shares of the treasury shares for €9.00 per share. The cost of the treasury shares was €6.25 per share.
- **f.** A 3-for-1 stock split. Prior to the split, 75 million shares of €3.00 par ordinary share were outstanding.

E10-47B. ***(Learning Objective 4: Reporting shareholders' equity after a stock split)*** Griffin Corp. had the following shareholders' equity at March 31 (dollars in millions, except par value per share):

A1

	A	B
1	**Shareholders' Equity**	
2	Ordinary share, €0.30 par, 500 million shares	
3	authorized, 460 million shares issued	€ 138
4	Additional paid-in capital	315
5	Retained earnings	2,393
6	Other equity	(146)
7	Total shareholders' equity	€ 2,700
8		

On May 3, Griffin split its €0.30 par ordinary share 3-for-1.

Requirement

1. Prepare the shareholders' equity section of the Balance Sheet immediately after the split.

E10-48B. ***(Learning Objective 5: Measuring the book value per share of ordinary share)*** The Balance Sheet of Eclectic Rug Company reported the following:

Redeemable preference share, 10%, €30 par value,	
redemption value €28,500; outstanding 800 shares	€ 21,000
Ordinary shareholders' equity:	
11,000 shares issued and outstanding	110,000
Total shareholders' equity	€134,000

Requirements

1. Compute the book value per share for the ordinary shares, assuming all preference dividends are fully paid up (none in arrears).
2. Compute the book value per share of the ordinary shares, assuming that three years' cumulative preference dividends, including the current year, are in arrears.
3. Eclectic Rug's ordinary shares recently traded at a market price of €7.10 per share. Does this mean that Eclectic Rug's shares are a good buy at €7.10?

LO 6

E10-49B. ***(Learning Objective 6: Evaluating profitability)*** LaSalle Inns reported these figures for 20X7 and 20X6 (in millions):

	A	B	C	D
1			**20X7**	**20X6**
2		**Balance Sheet**		
3		Total assets	€ 16,020	€ 13,760
4		Ordinary share and additional paid-in capital	39	385
5		Retained earnings	11,522	16,534
6		Other equity	(2,961)	(9,119)
7				
8		**Income Statement**		
9		Operating income	€ 4,025	€ 3,818
10		Interest expense	214	274
11		Net income	1,533	1,549
12				

Requirement

1. Compute LaSalle's return on assets and return on ordinary shareholders' equity for 20X7. Do these rates of return suggest strength or weakness? Give your reason.

LO 6

E10-50B. ***(Learning Objective 6: Evaluating profitability)*** Lawrence Company included the following items in its financial statements for 20X6, the current year (amounts in millions):

Payment of long-term debt	€17,120	Dividends paid	€ 225
Proceeds from issuance		Interest expense:	
of ordinary share	8,485	Current year	1,443
Total liabilities:		Preceding year	602
Current year-end	32,315	Net income:	
Preceding year-end	38,033	Current year	1,874
Total shareholders' equity:		Preceding year	1,994
Current year-end	23,472	Operating income:	
Preceding year-end	14,044	Current year	4,876
Borrowings	6,580	Preceding year	3,996

Requirement

1. Compute Lawrence's earnings per share and return on ordinary equity during 20X6 (the current year). Lawrence has no preference shares outstanding. The weighted average ordinary shares outstanding were 500 million shares. Do the company's rates of return look strong or weak? Give your reason.

LO 7

E10-51B. ***(Learning Objective 7: Reporting cash flows from financing activities)*** Use the Lawrence data in Exercise E10-50B to show how the company reported cash flows from financing activities during 20X6 (the current year). List items in descending order from largest to smallest dollar amount.

Challenge Exercises

E10-52. ***(Learning Objectives 2, 3, 4: Reconstructing transactions from the financial statements)*** D-4 Networking Solutions began operations on January 1, 20X6, and immediately issued its shares, receiving cash. D-4's Balance Sheet at December 31, 20X6, reported the following shareholders' equity:

Ordinary share, $1 par	$ 51,000
Additional paid-in capital	102,000
Retained earnings	35,000
Treasury share, 850 shares	(7,650)
Total shareholders' equity	$180,350

During 20X6, D-4

a. Issued shares for $3 per share.
b. Purchased 1,000 shares of treasury shares, paying $9 per share.
c. Resold some of the treasury shares.
d. Earned net income of $60,000 and declared and paid cash dividends. Revenues were $178,000 and expenses totaled $118,000.

Requirement

1. Journalize all of D-4's shareholders' equity transactions during the year. D-4's entry to close net income to Retained Earnings was:

	A	B	C	D
1		Revenues	178,000	
2		Expenses		118,000
3		Retained Earnings		60,000
4				

E10-53. ***(Learning Objective 7: Reporting financing activities on the statement of cash flows)*** Use the D-4 Networking Solutions data in Exercise 10-52 to show how the company reported cash flows from financing activities during 20X6. LO 7

E10-54. ***(Learning Objectives 2, 3, 4: Explaining the changes in shareholders' equity)*** Moon Walk Corporation reported the following shareholders' equity data (all dollars in millions except par value per share): LO 2 3 4

	A	B	C
		December 31	
1		20X6	20X5
2	Preference share	$ 610	$ 740
3	Ordinary share, $1 par value	908	889
4	Additional paid-in capital	1,512	1,482
5	Retained earnings	20,635	19,100
6	Treasury share, ordinary	(2,785)	(2,600)
7			

Moon Walk earned a net income of $2,950 during 20X6. For each account except Retained Earnings, one transaction explains the change from the December 31, 20X5, balance to the December 31, 20X6, balance. Two transactions affected Retained Earnings. Give a full explanation, including the dollar amount, for the change in each account.

E10-55. ***(Learning Objectives 2, 3, 4: Accounting for changes in shareholders' equity)*** Clubhouse, Inc., ended 20X6 with 7 million shares of $1 par ordinary share issued and outstanding. Beginning additional paid-in capital was $10 million, and Retained Earnings totaled $35 million:

- In April 20X7, Clubhouse issued 5 million shares of ordinary shares at a price of $4 per share.
- In June, the company distributed a 10% share dividend at a time when Clubhouse's ordinary shares had a market value of $6 per share.
- Then in September, Clubhouse's share price dropped to $2 per share and the company purchased 4 million shares of treasury share.
- For the year, Clubhouse earned net income of $24 million and declared cash dividends of $13 million.

Requirement

1. Complete the following tabulation to show what Clubhouse should report for shareholders' equity at December 31, 20X7. Journal entries are not required.

(Amounts in millions)	Ordinary Shares	+	Additional Paid-In Capital	+	Retained Earnings	−	Treasury Shares	=	Total Equity
Balance, Dec 31, 20X6	$7		$10		$35		0		$52
Issuance of shares									
Share dividend									
Purchase of treasury shares									
Net income									
Cash dividends									
Balance, Dec 31, 20X7									

Quiz

Test your understanding of shareholders' equity by answering the following questions. Select the best choice from among the possible answers given.

Q10-56. Which of the following is a characteristic of a corporation?

a. Limited life
b. Limited rights of shareholders
c. Limited number of shareholders
d. Limited liability of shareholders

Q10-57. Spirit World, Inc., issues 280,000 shares of no-par ordinary share for $8 per share. The journal entry is:

	A	B	C	D
1	a.	Cash	280,000	
2		Ordinary share		280,000
3				
4	b.	Cash	2,240,000	
5		Ordinary share		280,000
6		Gain on sale of share		1,960,000
7				
8	c.	Cash	2,240,000	
9		Ordinary share		2,240,000
10				
11	d.	Cash	2,240,000	
12		Ordinary share		280,000
13		Paid-in capital in excess of par		1,960,000
14				

Q10-58. Par value
- **a.** represents what a share is worth.
- **b.** represents the original selling price for one share.
- **c.** is established for a portion of share after it is issued.
- **d.** may exist for ordinary share but not for preference share.
- **e.** is an arbitrary amount that establishes the legal capital for each share.

Q10-59. The paid-in capital portion of shareholders' equity does not include
- **a.** Paid-in Capital in Excess of Par Value.
- **b.** Ordinary Share.
- **c.** Preference Share.
- **d.** Retained Earnings.

Q10-60. Preference share is least likely to have which of the following characteristics?
- **a.** The right of the holder to convert to ordinary shares
- **b.** Preference as to assets on liquidation of the corporation
- **c.** Extra liability for the preference shareholders
- **d.** Preference as to dividends

Q10-61. Which of the following classifications represents the most shares of ordinary share?
- **a.** Outstanding shares
- **b.** Authorized shares
- **c.** Unissued shares
- **d.** Issued shares
- **e.** Treasury shares

Use the following information for Questions Q10-62 to Q10-64:
These account balances at December 31 relate to Superworld, Inc.:

Accounts Payable	$ 51,500	Paid-in Capital in Excess of Par—Ordinary Share	$220,000
Accounts Receivable	81,550	Preference share, 10%, $100 Par	85,000
Ordinary Share	317,000	Retained Earnings	71,300
Treasury Share	5,200	Notes Receivable	12,100
Bonds Payable	3,800		

Q10-62. What is total paid-in capital for Superworld, Inc.?
- **a.** $622,000
- **b.** $693,300
- **c.** $641,345
- **d.** $634,445
- **e.** None of the above

Q10-63. What is total shareholders' equity for Superworld, Inc.?
- **a.** $683,300
- **b.** $688,100
- **c.** $641,345
- **d.** $698,500
- **e.** None of the above

Q10-64. Superworld's net income for the period is $119,100 and beginning ordinary shareholders' equity is $681,500. Calculate Superworld's return on ordinary shareholders' equity.
- **a.** 18.2%
- **b.** 16.4%
- **c.** 17.2%
- **d.** 19.3%

Q10-65. A company paid $25 per share to purchase 600 shares of its ordinary shares as treasury shares. The shares were originally issued at $18 per share. The journal entry to record the purchase of the treasury shares is:

	A	B	C	D
1	a.	Treasury shares	15,000	
2		Cash		15,000
3				
4	b.	Ordinary shares	15,000	
5		Cash		15,000
6				
7	c.	Treasury shares	7,500	
8		Paid-in capital in excess of par	7,500	
9		Cash		15,000
10				
11	d.	Treasury shares	10,800	
12		Retained earnings	4,200	
13		Cash		15,000
14				

Q10-66. When treasury shares are sold for less than their cost, the entry should include a debit to:

a. Retained Earnings.
b. Paid-in Capital in Excess of Par.
c. Loss on Sale of Treasury Shares.
d. Gain on Sale of Treasury Shares.

Q10-67. A company purchased 100 shares of its ordinary shares at $50 per share. It then sells 40 of the treasury shares at $56 per share. The entry to sell the treasury shares includes a

a. credit to Cash for $2,240.
b. debit to Retained Earnings for $240.
c. credit to Retained Earnings for $600.
d. credit to Paid-in Capital, Treasury Shares for $240.
e. credit to Treasury Shares for $2,240.

Q10-68. Shareholders are eligible for a dividend if they own the share on the date of

a. issuance.
b. record.
c. payment.
d. declaration.

Q10-69. Loco's Foods has outstanding 600 shares of 8% preference shares, $100 par value, and 1,600 shares of ordinary shares, $35 par value. Loco's declares dividends of $15,800. The correct entry is:

	A	B	C	D
1	a.	Dividends expense	15,800	
2		Cash		15,800
3				
4	b.	Dividends payable, preference	4,800	
5		Dividends payable, ordinary	11,000	
6		Cash		15,800
7				
8	c.	Retained earnings	15,800	
9		Dividends payable, preference		7,900
10		Dividends payable, ordinary		7,900
11				
12	d.	Retained earnings	15,800	
13		Dividends payable, preference		4,800
14		Dividends payable, ordinary		11,000
15				

Q10-70. A corporation has 40,000 shares of 8% preference share outstanding. Also, there are 40,000 shares of ordinary share outstanding. Par value for each is $100. If a $500,000 dividend is paid, how much goes to the preference shareholders?

a. None
b. $400,000
c. $320,000
d. $250,000
e. $500,000

Q10-71. Assume the same facts as in question 70. What is the amount of dividends per share on ordinary share?

a. $1.00
b. $4.50
c. $5.25
d. $11.50
e. None of these

Q10-72. Which of the following is not true about a 10% share dividend?

a. Total shareholders' equity remains the same.
b. Paid-in Capital increases.
c. Retained Earnings decreases.
d. Par value decreases.
e. The market value of the share is needed to record the share dividend.

Q10-73. A company declares a 5% share dividend. The debit to Retained Earnings is an amount equal to

a. the book value of the shares to be issued.
b. the market value of the shares to be issued.
c. the par value of the shares to be issued.
d. the excess of the market price over the original issue price of the shares to be issued.

Q10-74. Which of the following statements is not true about a 3-for-1 stock split?

a. Total shareholders' equity increases.
b. The market price of each share will decrease.
c. Retained Earnings remains the same.
d. A shareholder with 10 shares before the split owns 30 shares after the split.
e. Par value is reduced to one-third of what it was before the split.

Q10-75. Antonio Company's net income for the year was $30,000. Its beginning and ending equity were $540,000 and $660,000, respectively. How much is Antonio's return on equity?

a. 5.0%
b. 4.5%
c. 4.1%
d. 4.0%

Problems MyLab Accounting

Select A and B problems can be found within MyLab Accounting, an online homework and practice environment. Your instructor may ask you to complete select problems using MyLab Accounting.

Group A

P10-76A. ***(Learning Objective 2: Recording corporate transactions and preparing the shareholders' equity section of the Balance Sheet)*** Cullen Canoes' constitution authorizes the corporation to issue 10,000 no-par preference shares and 80,000 shares of $8 par ordinary shares. In its first month, Cullen Canoes completed the following transactions:

May 6	Issued 900 ordinary shares to the promoter for assistance with issuance of the ordinary share. The promotional fee was $22,500. Debit Organization Expense.
9	Issued 10,000 ordinary shares to Ben Cullen and 12,000 shares to Bill Cohen in return for cash equal to the share's market value of $25 per share. The Cullens were partners in Cullen Canoes Co.
10	Issued 800 shares of preference share to acquire a patent with a market value of $20,000.
26	Issued 1,000 shares of ordinary share for $25 cash per share.

Requirements

1. Record the transactions in the journal.
2. Prepare the shareholders' equity section of the Cullen Canoes, Inc., Balance Sheet at May 31. The ending balance of Retained Earnings is $56,000.

LO 2 4

P10-77A. ***(Learning Objectives 2, 4: Preparing the shareholders' equity section of the Balance Sheet)*** Garry Corp. has the following shareholders' equity information: Garry's constitution authorizes the company to issue 8,000 shares of 5% preference shares with par value of $140 and 600,000 shares of no-par ordinary share. The company issued 1,600 shares of the preference share at $140 per share. It issued 120,000 shares of the ordinary share for a total of $540,000. The company's retained earnings balance at the beginning of 20X6 was $75,000, and net income for the year was $94,000. During 20X6, Garry declared the specified dividend on preference shares and a $0.40 per-share dividend on ordinary shares. Preference dividends for 20X5 were in arrears.

Requirement

1. Prepare the shareholders' equity section of Garry Corp.'s Balance Sheet at December 31, 20X6. Show the computation of all amounts. Journal entries are not required.

LO 2 3 4

P10-78A. ***(Learning Objectives 2, 3, 4: Measuring the effects of share issuance, treasury shares, and dividend transactions on shareholders' equity)*** Best Foods, Inc., is authorized to issue 5,500,000 shares of $6.00 par ordinary share.

In its initial public offering during 20X0, Best issued 475,000 shares of its $6.00 par ordinary shares for $8.00 per share. Over the next year, Best's share price increased, and the company issued 380,000 more shares at an average price of $10.00.

During 20X2, the price of Best's ordinary shares dropped to $7.25, and Best purchased 60,000 shares of its ordinary shares for the treasury. After the market price of the ordinary share rose in 20X3, Best sold 40,000 shares of the treasury shares for $10.00 per share.

During the five years from 20X0 to 20X5, Best earned a net income of $1,000,000 and declared and paid cash dividends of $600,000. Share dividends of $641,250 were distributed to the shareholders in 20X1, with $359,100 credited to ordinary shares and $282,150 credited to additional paid-in capital. At December 31, 20X5, total assets of the company are $14,800,000, and liabilities add up to $6,835,000.

Requirement

1. Show the computation of Best's total shareholders' equity at December 31, 20X5. Present a detailed computation of each element of shareholders' equity. Use the end-of chapter summary problem to format your answer.

LO 2 4

P10-79A. ***(Learning Objectives 2, 4: Analyzing the shareholders' equity and dividends of a corporation)*** Carved Outdoor Furniture Company included the following shareholders' equity on its year-end Balance Sheet at February 28, 20X7:

Shareholders' Equity	
Preference share, 6.5% cumulative—par value $35 per share;	
authorized 110,000 shares in each class	
Class A—issued 79,000 shares	$ 2,765,000
Class B—issued 88,000 shares	3,080,000
Ordinary share—$3 par value:	
authorized 1,200,000 shares,	
issued 280,000 shares	840,000
Additional paid-in capital—ordinary	5,542,000
Retained earnings	8,380,000
	$20,407,000

Requirements

1. Identify the different issues of shares that Carved Outdoor Furniture Company has outstanding.
2. Give the summary entries to record issuance of all the Carved shares. Assume that all the shares was issued for cash. Explanations are not required.
3. Suppose Carved passed its preference dividends for three years. Would the company have to pay those dividends in arrears before paying dividends to the ordinary shareholders? Give your reason.
4. What amount of preference dividends must Carved declare and pay each year to avoid having preference dividends in arrears?
5. Assume that preference dividends are in arrears for 20X6. Record the declaration of an $860,000 dividend on February 28, 20X7. An explanation is not required.

P10-80A. ***(Learning Objectives 2, 3, 4: Accounting for shares issuance, dividends, and treasury shares)*** Moscow Jewelry Company reported the following summarized Balance Sheet at December 31, 20X6:

Assets	
Current assets	$ 33,600
Property and equipment, net	74,000
Total assets	$107,600
Liabilities and Equity	
Liabilities	$ 37,300
Shareholders' equity:	
$0.70 cumulative preference share, $5 par, 300 shares issued	1,500
Ordinary share, $4 par, 6,500 shares issued	26,000
Paid-in capital in excess of par	17,800
Retained earnings	25,000
Total liabilities and equity	$107,600

During 20X7, Moscow completed these transactions that affected shareholders' equity:

Feb. 13	Issued 5,400 ordinary shares for $6 per share.
Jun. 7	Declared the regular cash dividend on the preference share.
24	Paid the cash dividend.
Aug. 9	Distributed a 10% share dividend on the ordinary share. Market price of the ordinary share was $7 per share.
Oct. 26	Reacquired 500 shares of ordinary share as treasury share, paying $8 per share.
Nov. 20	Sold 200 shares of the treasury shares for $13 per share.

Requirements

1. Journalize Moscow's transactions. Explanations are not required.
2. Report Moscow's shareholders' equity at December 31, 20X7. Net income for 20X7 was $28,000.

LO 3 4

P10-81A. ***(Learning Objectives 3, 4: Measuring the effects of dividend and treasury share transactions on a company)*** Assume Dessert Destination of Montana, Inc., completed the following transactions during 20X6, the company's fifth year of operations:

Feb. 3	Issued 15,000 ordinary shares ($1.00 par) for cash of $445,000.
Mar. 19	Purchased 2,600 shares of the company's own ordinary share at $25 per share.
Apr. 24	Sold 1,300 shares of treasury share—ordinary for $33 per share.
Aug. 15	Declared a cash dividend on the 18,500 shares of $0.40 no-par preference shares.
Sept. 1	Paid the cash dividends.
Nov. 22	Distributed an 8% share dividend on the 92,000 shares of $1.00 par ordinary share outstanding. The market value of the ordinary share was $27 per share.

Requirement

1. Analyze each transaction in terms of its effect on the accounting equation of Dessert Destination of Montana, Inc.

LO 3 6

P10-82A. ***(Learning Objectives 3, 6: Preparing a corporation's Balance Sheet; measuring profitability)*** The following accounts and related balances of Pelican Designers, Inc., as of December 31, 20X6, are arranged in no particular order.

Cash	$55,000	Interest expense	$ 15,600
Accounts receivable, net	34,000	Property, plant and equipment, net	364,000
Paid-in capital in excess of par—ordinary	20,000	Ordinary share, $2 par, 600,000 shares authorized, 116,000 shares issued	232,000
Accrued liabilities	24,000	Prepaid expenses	13,000
Long-term note payable	99,000	Ordinary shareholders' equity, December 31, 20X6	222,000
Inventory	93,000	Net income	32,000
Dividends payable	6,000	Total assets, December 31, 20X6	493,000
Retained earnings	?	Treasury share, 21,000 shares at cost	24,000
Accounts payable	136,000		
Trademarks, net	4,000		
Preference share, $0.50, no-par, 11,000 shares authorized and issued	29,700		
Goodwill	13,000		

Requirements

1. Prepare Pelican's classified Balance Sheet in the account format at December 31, 20X6.
2. Compute rate of return on ordinary shareholders' equity for the year ended December 31, 20X6.
3. Does the ROE suggest strength or weakness? Give your reason.

LO 7

P10-83A. ***(Learning Objective 7: Analyzing the statement of cash flows)*** The statement of cash flows of Frappe, Inc., reported the following (adapted) for the year ended December 31, 20X6:

Cash flows from financing activities (amounts in millions)	
Cash dividends paid	$(1,850)
Issuance of ordinary shares at par value	1,243
Proceeds from issuance of long-term notes payable	52
Purchases of treasury share	(3,060)
Payments of long-term notes payable	(165)

Requirement

1. Make the journal entry that Frappe would use to record each of these transactions.

Group B

LO 2

P10-84B. ***(Learning Objective 2: Recording corporate transactions and preparing the shareholders' equity section of the Balance Sheet)*** Laurel Canoes' constitution authorizes the corporation to issue 8,000 no-par preference shares and 120,000 shares of €8 par ordinary share. In its first month, Laurel Canoes completed the following transactions:

Jan.	6	Issued 500 ordinary shares to the promoter for assistance with issuance of ordinary shares. The promotional fee was €7,500. Debit Organization Expense.
	9	Issued 9,000 ordinary shares to Lou Laurel and 10,000 shares to Larry Laurel in return for cash equal to the share's market value of €15 per share. The Laurel were partners in Laurel Canoes, Inc.
	10	Issued 600 preference shares to acquire a patent with a market value of €12,000.
	26	Issued 1,400 ordinary shares for €15 cash per share.

Requirements

1. Record the transactions in the journal.
2. Prepare the shareholders' equity section of the Laurel Canoes, Inc., Balance Sheet at January 31. The ending balance of Retained Earnings is €56,000.

P10-85B. ***(Learning Objectives 2, 4: Preparing the shareholders' equity section of the Balance Sheet)*** Harry Corp. has the following shareholders' equity information: Harry's constitution authorizes the company to issue 5,000 shares of 8% preference shares with par value of €120 and 400,000 shares of no-par ordinary shares. The company issued 1,000 shares of the preference shares at €120 per share. It issued 80,000 shares of the ordinary shares for a total of €520,000. The company's retained earnings balance at the beginning of 20X6 was €72,000, and net income for the year was €93,000. During 20X6, Harry declared the specified dividend on preference shares and a €0.70 per-share dividend on ordinary shares. Preference dividends for 20X5 were in arrears.

Requirement

1. Prepare the shareholders' equity section of Harry Corp.'s Balance Sheet at December 31, 20X6. Show the computation of all amounts. Journal entries are not required.

P10-86B. ***(Learning Objectives 2, 3, 4: Measuring the effects of share issuance, treasury share, and dividend transactions on shareholders' equity)*** Rich Foods, Inc., is authorized to issue 5,000,000 shares of €3.00 par ordinary shares.

In its initial public offering during 20X0, Rich issued 500,000 shares of its €3.00 par ordinary shares for €6.00 per share. Over the next year, Rich's share price increased, and the company issued 395,000 more shares at an average price of €9.00.

During 20X2, the price of Rich's ordinary shares dropped to €7.25, and Rich purchased 612,000 shares of its ordinary shares for the treasury. After the market price of the ordinary share rose in 20X3, Rich sold 38,000 shares of the treasury share for €8.00 per share.

During the five years from 20X0 to 20X5, Rich earned a net income of €1,250,000 and declared and paid cash dividends of €800,000. Share dividends of €644,400 were distributed to the shareholders in 20X1, with €214,800 credited to ordinary shares and €429,600 credited to additional paid-in capital. At December 31, 20X5, total assets of the company are €14,300,000, and liabilities add up to €7,440,500.

Requirement

1. Show the computation of Rich's total shareholders' equity at December 31, 20X5. Present a detailed computation of each element of shareholders' equity. Use the end-of-chapter summary problem to format your answer.

LO 2 4

P10-87B. ***(Learning Objectives 2, 4: Analyzing the shareholders' equity and dividends of a corporation)*** Rustic Outdoor Furniture Company included the following shareholders' equity on its year-end Balance Sheet at February 28, 20X7:

Shareholders' Equity	
Preference share, 4.0% cumulative—par value €20 per share	
authorized 100,000 shares in each class	
Class A—issued 77,000 shares	€ 1,540,000
Class B—issued 98,000 shares	1,960,000
Ordinary share—€4 par value:	
authorized 1,500,000 shares,	
issued 240,000 shares	960,000
Additional paid-in capital—ordinary	5,328,000
Retained earnings	8,310,000
	€18,098,000

Requirements

1. Identify the different issues of shares Rustic Outdoor Furniture Company has outstanding.
2. Give the summary entries to record issuance of all the Rustic shares. Assume that all the shares were issued for cash. Explanations are not required.
3. Suppose Rustic passed its preference dividends for three years. Would the company have to pay these dividends in arrears before paying dividends to the ordinary shareholders? Give your reasons.
4. What amount of preference dividends must Rustic declare and pay each year to avoid having preference dividends in arrears?
5. Assume that preference dividends are in arrears for 20X6. Record the declaration of an €840,000 dividend on February 28, 20X7. An explanation is not required.

LO 2 3 4

P10-88B. ***(Learning Objectives 2, 3, 4: Accounting for share issuance, dividends, and treasury share)*** London Gems Company reported the following summarized Balance Sheet at December 31, 20X6:

Assets	
Current assets	€33,500
Property and equipment, net	63,100
Total assets	€96,600
Liabilities and Equity	
Liabilities	€37,600
Shareholders' equity:	
€0.80 cumulative preference share, €15 par, 400 shares issued	6,000
Ordinary share, €2 par, 6,300 shares issued	12,600
Paid-in capital in excess of par	17,400
Retained earnings	23,000
Total liabilities and equity	€96,600

During 20X7, London completed these transactions that affected shareholders' equity:

Feb. 13	Issued 5,200 ordinary shares for €7 per share.
Jun. 7	Declared the regular cash dividend on the preference share.
24	Paid the cash dividend.
Aug. 9	Distributed a 20% share dividend on the ordinary share. Market price of the ordinary share was €8 per share.
Oct. 26	Reacquired 900 ordinary shares as treasury shares, paying €9 per share.
Nov. 20	Sold 600 shares of the treasury shares for €14 per share.

Requirements

1. Journalize London's transactions. Explanations are not required.
2. Report London's shareholders' equity at December 31, 20X7. Net income for 20X7 was €24,000.

P10-89B. ***(Learning Objectives 3, 4: Measuring the effects of dividend and treasury share transactions on a company)*** Assume Cookie Corner completed the following transactions during 20X6, the company's fifth year of operations:

Feb. 4	Issued 14,000 shares (€1.00 par) for cash of €360,000.
Mar. 20	Purchased 2,200 shares of the company's own ordinary share at €22 per share.
Apr. 25	Sold 900 shares of treasury shares—ordinary for €31 per share.
Aug. 17	Declared a cash dividend on the 15,000 shares of €0.80 no-par preference shares.
Sep. 4	Paid the cash dividends.
Nov. 28	Distributed a 5% share dividend on the 99,000 shares of €1.00 par ordinary share outstanding. The market value of the ordinary share was €23 per share.

Requirement

1. Analyze each transaction in terms of its effect on the accounting equation of Cookie Corner of Wisconsin, Inc.

LO 3 6

P10-90B. ***(Learning Objectives 3, 6: Preparing a corporation's Balance Sheet; measuring profitability)*** The following accounts and related balances of Eagle Designers, Inc., as of December 31, 20X6, are arranged in no particular order.

Cash	€43,000	Interest expense	€ 16,000
Accounts receivable, net	22,000	Property, plant and equipment, net	359,000
Paid-in capital in excess of par—ordinary	17,000	Ordinary share, €2 par, 300,000 shares authorized, 117,000 shares issued	234,000
Accrued liabilities	27,000	Prepaid expenses	16,000
Long-term note payable	96,000	Ordinary shareholders' equity, December 31, 20X6	225,000
Inventory	94,000	Net income	30,000
Dividends payable	12,000	Total assets, December 31, 20X6	496,000
Retained earnings	?	Treasury share, ordinary, 19,000 shares at cost	22,000
Accounts payable	133,000		
Trademarks, net	10,000		
Preference share, €.50, no-par, 12,000 shares authorized and issued	32,400		
Goodwill	11,000		

Requirements

1. Prepare Eagle's classified Balance Sheet in the account format at December 31, 20X6.
2. Compute rate of return on ordinary shareholders' equity for the year ended December 31, 20X6.
3. Does the ROE suggest strength or weakness? Give your reason.

LO 7

P10-91B. ***(Learning Objective 7: Analyzing the statement of cash flows)*** The statement of cash flows of Smoothie, Inc., reported the following (adapted) for the year ended December 31, 20X6:

Cash flows from financing activities (amounts in millions)	
Cash dividends paid	€(1,880)
Issuance of common stock at par value	1,236
Proceeds from issuance of long-term notes payable	59
Purchases of treasury stock	(3,084)
Payments of long-term notes payable	(126)

Requirement

1. Make the journal entry that Smoothie would use to record each of these transactions.

APPLY YOUR KNOWLEDGE

Decision Cases

LO 2

writing assignment

Case 1. ***(Learning Objective 2: Evaluating alternative ways of raising capital)*** Nate Santiago and Darla Perez have written a computer program for a video game that may rival PlayStation and Xbox. They need additional capital to market the product, and they plan to incorporate their business. Santiago and Perez are considering alternative capital structures for the corporation. Their primary goal is to raise as much capital as possible without giving up control of the business. Santiago and Perez plan to receive 50,000 of the corporation's ordinary shares in return for the net assets of their old business. After the old company's books are closed and the assets adjusted to current market value, Santiago's and Perez's capital balances will each be $25,000.

The corporation's plans for a constitution include an authorization to issue 10,000 preference shares and 500,000 shares of $1 par ordinary shares. Santiago and Perez are uncertain about the most desirable features for the preference shares. Prior to incorporating, Santiago and Perez are discussing their plans with two investment groups. The corporation can obtain capital from outside investors under either of the following plans:

- *Plan 1.* Group 1 will invest $100,000 to acquire 1,000 shares of 6%, $100 par non-voting, preference shares.
- *Plan 2.* Group 2 will invest $60,000 to acquire 600 shares of $5, no-par preference shares and $50,000 to acquire 50,000 ordinary shares. Each preference share receives 50 votes on matters that come before the shareholders.

Requirements

Assume that the business is now incorporated.

1. Journalize the issuance of ordinary shares to Santiago and Perez. Debit each person's capital account for its balance.
2. Journalize the issuance of shares to the outsiders under both plans.
3. Assume that net income for the first year is $120,000 and total dividends are $30,000. Prepare the shareholders' equity section of the corporation's Balance Sheet under both plans.
4. Recommend one of the plans to Smith and Jones. Give your reasons. (Challenge)

LO 4
■ writing assignment

Case 2. *(Learning Objective 4: Analyzing cash dividends and share dividends)* United Parcel Service (UPS), Inc., had the following shareholders' equity amounts on December 31, 20X6 (adapted, in millions):

Ordinary share and additional paid-in capital; 1,135 shares issued	$ 278
Retained earnings	9,457
Total shareholders' equity	$9,735

During 20X6, UPS paid a cash dividend of $0.825 per share. Assume that, after paying the cash dividends, UPS distributed a 10% share dividend. Assume further that the following year UPS declared and paid a cash dividend of $0.75 per share.

Suppose you own 10,000 shares of UPS ordinary share, acquired three years ago, prior to the 10% share dividend. The market price of UPS shares was $61.05 per share before the share dividend.

Requirements

1. How does the share dividend affect your proportionate ownership in UPS? Explain.
2. What amount of cash dividends did you receive last year? What amount of cash dividends will you receive after the above dividend action?
3. Assume that immediately after the share dividend was distributed, the market value of UPS's share decreased from $61.05 per share to $55.50 per share. Does this decrease represent a loss to you? Explain.
4. Suppose UPS announces at the time of the share dividend that the company will continue to pay the annual $0.825 ***cash*** dividend per share, even after distributing the ***share*** dividend. Would you expect the market price of the share to decrease to $55.50 per share as in Requirement 3? Explain.

LO 2 3 4 5
■ writing assignment

Case 3. *(Learning Objectives 2, 3, 4, 5: Evaluating financial position and profitability)* At December 31, 2000, Enron Corporation reported the following data (condensed in millions):

Total assets	$65,503
Total liabilities	54,033
Shareholders' equity	11,470
Net income, as reported, for 2000	979

During 2001, Enron restated company financial statements for 1997 to 2000, after reporting that some data had been omitted from those prior-year statements. Assume that the startling events of 2001 included the following:

- Several related companies should have been, but were not, included in the Enron statements for 2000. These companies had total assets of $5,700 million, liabilities totaling $5,600 million, and net losses of $130 million.
- In January 2001, Enron's shareholders got the company to give them $2,000 million of 12% long-term notes payable in return for their giving up their ordinary shares. Interest is accrued at year-end.

Take the role of a financial analyst. It is your job to analyze Enron Corporation and rate the company's long-term debt.

Requirements

1. Measure Enron's expected net income for 2001 in two ways:
   a. Assume 2001's net income should be the same as the amount of net income that Enron actually reported for 2000. (Given)
   b. Recompute expected net income for 2001 taking into account the new developments of 2001. (Challenge)
   c. Evaluate Enron's likely trend of net income for the future. Discuss ***why*** this trend is developing. Ignore income tax. (Challenge)
2. Write Enron's accounting equation in two ways:
   a. As actually reported at December 31, 2000.
   b. As adjusted for the events of 2001. (Challenge)
3. Measure Enron's debt ratio as reported at December 31, 2000, and again after making the adjustments for the events of 2001.
4. Based on your analysis, make a recommendation to the Debt-Rating Committee of Moody's Investor Services. Would you recommend upgrading, downgrading, or leaving Enron's debt rating undisturbed (currently, it is "high-grade")? (Challenge)

Ethical Issue

■ **writing assignment**

Ethical Issue 1. *Note:* This case is based on a real situation.

George Campbell paid $50,000 for a franchise that entitled him to market Success Associates' software programs in the countries of the European Union. Campbell intended to sell individual franchises for the major language groups of western Europe—German, French, English, Spanish, and Italian. Naturally, investors considering buying a franchise from Campbell asked to see the financial statements of his business.

Believing the value of the franchise to be greater than $50,000, Campbell sought to capitalize his own franchise at $500,000. The law firm of McDonald & LaDue helped Campbell form a corporation chartered to issue 500,000 ordinary shares with par value of $1 per share. His attorneys suggested the following chain of transactions:

a. A third party borrows $500,000 and purchases the franchise from Campbell.
b. Campbell pays the corporation $500,000 to acquire all its shares.
c. The corporation buys the franchise from the third party, who repays the loan.

In the final analysis, the third party is debt-free and out of the picture. Campbell owns all the corporation's shares, and the corporation owns the franchise. The corporation Balance Sheet lists a franchise acquired at a cost of $500,000. This Balance Sheet is Campbell's most valuable marketing tool.

Requirements

1. What is the ethical issue in this situation?
2. Who are the stakeholders to the suggested transaction?
3. Analyze this case from the following standpoints: (a) economic, (b) legal, (c) ethical. What are the consequences to each stakeholder?
4. How should the transaction be reported?

Ethical Issue 2. St. Genevieve Petroleum Company is an independent oil producer in Baton Parish, Louisiana. In February, company geologists discovered a pool of oil that tripled the company's proven reserves. Prior to disclosing the new oil to the public, St. Genevieve quietly bought most of its shares as treasury shares. After the discovery was announced, the company's share price increased from \$6 to \$27.

■ **writing assignment**

Requirements

1. What is the ethical issue in this situation? What accounting principle is involved?
2. Who are the stakeholders?
3. Analyze the facts from the following standpoints: (a) economic, (b) legal, and (c) ethical. What is the impact to each stakeholder?
4. What decision would you have made?

Focus on Financials: | Nestlé

This case spans all 12 chapters and is based on the consolidated financial statements of Nestlé. As you work with Nestlé throughout this course, you will develop the confidence and ability to use the financial statements of other companies as well.

Refer to Nestlé's financial statements in Appendix A. If you wish, you can obtain the full annual report from www.nestle.com/investors. You may find the information overwhelming for now, but try to spot the key principles that we have discussed in this chapter. It will get progressively easier as you gain familiarity with the elements of the financial statements.

Requirements

1. Describe the class(es) of stocks or shares that Nestlé has authorized. How many shares of each class(es) have been issued? How many are outstanding as of December 31, 2016?
2. Refer to the Consolidated Cash Flow Statement and Note 17 - Equity. How many shares of treasury stock did the company purchase during the year ended December 31, 2015? How much did it pay for it in total? How much per share?
3. Examine Nestlé's consolidated statement of shareholders' equity. Analyze the two biggest changes that occurred in the company's Retained Earnings account during the year ended December 31, 2016. Can you link the changes to any of its other financial statements?
4. Create the T-account for Nestlé's Retained Earnings and show the beginning and ending balances, as well as all related activity for the year ended December 31, 2016. Journalize the transactions relating to profit, dividends, and the cancellation of treasury shares.
5. Compute Nestlé's return on equity for 2016 and 2015 (note that the 2014 ending equity was CHF 70,130 million). Has Nestlé's ROE improved or deteriorated?

Group Project in Ethics

The global financial crisis that started in 2007 has impacted every business, but it was especially hard on banks, automobile manufacturing, and retail companies. Banks were largely responsible for the recession. Some of the biggest banks made excessively risky investments collateralized by real estate mortgages, and many of these investments soured when the real estate markets collapsed. When banks had to write these investments down to market values, the regulatory authorities notified them that they had inadequate capital ratios on their Balance Sheets to operate. Banks stopped loaning money. Because share prices were depressed, companies could not raise capital by selling shares. With both debt and share financing frozen, many businesses had to close their doors.

Fearing collapse of the whole economy, the central governments of the United States and several European nations loaned money to banks to prop up their capital ratios and keep them open. The government also loaned massive amounts to the largest insurance company in the United States (AIG), as well as to General Motors and Chrysler, to help them stay in business. When asked why, many in government replied "these businesses were too important to fail." In several cases, the U.S. government has taken an "equity stake" in some banks and businesses by taking preference shares in exchange for the cash infusion.

Because of the recession, corporate downsizing has occurred on a massive scale throughout the world. While companies in the retail sector provide more jobs than the banking and automobile industry combined, the government has not chosen to "bail out" any retail businesses. Each company or industry mentioned in this book has pared down plant and equipment, laid off employees, or restructured operations. Some companies have been forced out of business altogether.

■ **writing assignment**

Requirements

1. Identify all the stakeholders of a corporation. A stakeholder is a person or a group who has an interest (that is, a stake) in the success of the organization.
2. Do you believe that some entities are "too important to fail?" Should a federal government help certain businesses to stay afloat during economic recessions, and allow others to fail?
3. Identify several measures by which a company may be considered deficient and in need of downsizing. How can downsizing help to solve this problem?
4. Debate the bailout issue. One group of students takes the perspective of the company and its shareholders, and another group of students takes the perspective of the other stakeholders of the company (the community in which the company operates and society at large).
5. What is the problem with the government taking an equity position such as preference shares in a private enterprise?

Quick Check Answers

1. *c* (25,000 shares × $25 = $625,000)
2. *a* ($640,000/$5 par = 128,000 shares)
3. *b* ($375,000 + $60,000 + $640,000 = $1,075,000)
4. *d* ($375,000 + $60,000 + $640,000 + $325,000 = $1,400,000)
5. *a* ($1,400,000 – $10,000 = $1,390,000)
6. *d* [No gain or loss (for the Income Statement) on treasury shares transactions]
7. *c*
8. *b*
9. *b*
10. *d*
11. *b* [First, annual preference dividend = $1,000 (2,000 × $25 × 0.02)]. Five years of preference dividends must be paid (four in arrears plus the current year). [($1,000 × 5) + ($125,000 × $2.50 per share ordinary dividend) = $317,500]
12. *a*
13. *d*
14. *d*
15. *a*
16. *d*

MyLab Accounting

For online homework, exercises, and problems that provide you with immediate feedback, please visit www.myaccountinglab.com.

11 Cash Flows

SPOTLIGHT | Singtel www.singtel.com

Singtel is one of Asia's leading communications groups. Headquartered in Singapore, it has subsidiaries, associates, and joint arrangements around the world—Optus (Australia), Bharti Airtel (India, South Asia, and Africa), Telkomsel (Indonesia), Globe Telecom (the Philippines), and Advanced Info Services (Thailand). Singtel's 2016 fiscal year showed total revenue of S$16,961 million (Singapore Dollars, where S$1 is approximately US $0.7) and a net profit of S$3,871 million. Its cash and cash equivalents, however, decreased from S$563 to S$462 million. ●

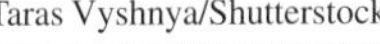

Taras Vyshnya/Shutterstock

	A	B	C	D
1	**Singtel** **Consolidated Statement of Cash Flows**	**12 Months Ended**		
2	**(Adapted, in millions of S$)**	**Dec. 31, 2016**	**Dec. 31, 2015**	**Dec. 31, 2014**
3	Profit before tax	S$ 4,581	S$ 4,463	S$ 4,348
4	Adjustments for:			
5	Depreciation and amortization	2,149	2,161	2,133
6	(Gain)/Loss on sale of PPE	(6)	3	3
7	Changes in working capital	(1,042)	86	(305)
8	All other items (summarized)	(1,034)	(927)	(828)
9	**Net cash inflow from operating activities**	**S$ 4,648**	**S$ 5,787**	**S$ 5,350**
10				
11	Payment for purchase of PPE and intangible assets	(2,103)	(3,204)	(2,378)
12	Payment for investment in associates and subsidiaries	(1,275)	(451)	(451)
13	Purchase of investments	(39)	(23)	(50)
14	Sale of investments	81	75	13
15	Proceeds from sale of PPE and intangible assets	6	16	7
16	All other items (summarized)	590	30	58
17	**Net cash inflow from investing activities**	**S$ (2,740)**	**S$ (3,557)**	**S$ (2,801)**
18				
19	Proceeds from loans and borrowings	7,171	5,215	3,461
20	Repayment of loans	(6,058)	(4,465)	(3,221)
21	Dividends paid	(2,789)	(2,678)	(2,678)
22	All other items (summarized)	(367)	(383)	(387)
23	**Net cash provided by financing activities**	**S$ (2,044)**	**S$ (2,311)**	**S$ (2,825)**
24				
25	**Net cash flows**	**(136)**	**(81)**	**(275)**
26	Effects of exchange rates on cash and cash equivalents	35	21	(13)
27	Cash and cash equivalents at the beginning of the year	563	623	911
28	**Cash and cash equivalents at the end of the year**	**S$ 462**	**S$ 563**	**S$ 623**
29				

In any business, managing cash flows is extremely important. You may have heard the saying that "cash flow is the lifeblood of any business." A profitable company can face bankruptcy if it does not pay adequate attention to how cash is being generated or used. In the preceding chapters, we covered cash flows in relation to various topics: receivables; property, plant and equipment (PPE); liabilities; equity; and so on. In this chapter, we show you how to prepare and use the statement of cash flows.

Singtel's simplified statement of cash flows is shown as follows. For now, pay attention to the key sections and features. In this chapter, we discuss each of them in detail. You should be able to see that the statement of cash flows has three main sections, with some reconciliations at the end of the statement.

For the year ended March 31, 2016, Singtel's cash flows from operating, investing, and financing activities were S$4,648, (S$2,740), and (S$2,044) million, respectively. Net cash flow for the year totaled (S$136) million. In cash flow statements, the numbers in brackets indicate cash outflows, and the numbers without brackets indicate cash inflows. The net cash flows reconcile beginning cash and cash equivalents of S$563 to ending cash and cash equivalents of S$462. These two amounts can be traced to Singtel's Balance Sheet, which has not been presented.

We begin with the statement format used by the vast majority of companies: *indirect method*. Singtel's cash flow from operating activities was prepared using this method. It may look a little complicated for now, but we explain how the indirect method works. We then proceed to discuss the cash flow from operating (using the indirect method), investing, and financing activities. For courses that require materials on the preparation of cash flow from operating activities using the *direct method*, Learning Objective 6 should be assigned. After working through this chapter, you will have a better understanding of the statement of cash flows and will be able to analyze the cash flows of actual companies.

LEARNING OBJECTIVES

1. **Identify** the purposes of the statement of cash flows
2. **Distinguish** among operating, investing, and financing cash flow activities
3. **Prepare** cash flows from operating activities using the indirect method
4. **Prepare** cash flows from investing activities
5. **Prepare** cash flows from financing activities
6. **Prepare** cash flows from operating activities using the direct method
7. **Evaluate** a company's ability to generate cash flows

IDENTIFY THE PURPOSES OF THE STATEMENT OF CASH FLOWS

1 **Identify** the purposes of the statement of cash flows

The Balance Sheet reports financial position, and Balance Sheets from two periods show whether cash increased or decreased. But that doesn't explain *why* the cash balance changed. The Income Statement reports net income and offers clues about cash, but the Income Statement doesn't tell *why* cash increased or decreased. We need a third financial statement.

The **statement of cash flows** reports **cash flows**—cash receipts and cash payments—in other words, where cash came from (receipts) and how it was spent (payments). The statement covers a span of time and, therefore, is labeled "Year Ended December 31, 20X7" or "Month Ended June 30, 20X8."

IAS 7—Cash Flow Statements is the primary accounting standard that provides guidance on this financial statement. The statement of cash flows serves these purposes:

1. *Predicts future cash flows.* Past cash receipts and payments are reasonably good predictors of future cash flows—timing, amount, and certainty. For example, shareholders want dividends on their investments, and creditors demand interest and principal on their loans. The statement of cash flows reports on the ability to make these payments.
2. *Evaluates management decisions.* An entity's ability to adapt to changing circumstances and opportunities depends on its ability to generate funds from operations and raise funds from shareholders and creditors. It also enhances comparability of different entities as it reduces the effects of using different accounting treatments for the same transactions and events.
3. *Shows the relationship of net income to cash flows.* An entity's performance is measured using *accrual accounting*. Under accrual accounting, cash transfers are neither a prerequisite nor evidence of the revenue generation process. Therefore, it is important to understand the relationship between income and cash flows generated over a period of time.

On a statement of cash flows, *cash* means more than just cash in the bank. It includes **cash equivalents**, which are highly liquid short-term investments that can be converted into cash immediately and are not subject to significant risks of changes in value. Examples include money-market accounts and investments in government securities. It may also include bank overdrafts, when used as an integral part of day-to-day cash management of the entity. Throughout this chapter, the term *cash* refers to cash and cash equivalents. Singtel provides this explanation about its cash and cash equivalents.

ADAPTED EXCERPTS FROM SINGTEL'S NOTES TO THE ACCOUNTS

Cash and Cash Equivalents

For the purpose of the consolidated statement of cash flows, cash and cash equivalents comprise: cash on hand, balances with banks, fixed deposits (with original maturity of mainly three months or less), and net of bank overdrafts that are repayable on demand and form an integral part of the Group's cash management. Bank overdrafts are included under borrowings in the statement of financial position.

Source: From Singtel, Annual Report, 2016, page 143.

Have another look at Singtel's consolidated statement of cash flows on page 630. Let's examine some common features of a cash flow statement:

1. It reports inflows and outflows across three categories: operating activities (lines 3–9), investing activities (lines 11–17), and financing activities (lines 19–23). Inflows are shown as positive numbers, and outflows are shown in brackets to indicate negative numbers.
2. The net cash flow from continuing operations (line 25) is the sum of the three cash flow subtotals (lines 9, 17, and 23).
3. Net cash flow (line 25), plus some other adjustment beyond the scope of this text (in Singtel's case, changes in foreign exchange rates on cash and cash equivalents, line 26), explains the changes in cash and cash equivalent at the beginning of the year (line 27) and at the end of the year (line 28).

How's Your Cash Flow? Telltale Signs of Financial Difficulty

Companies want to earn net income because profit measures success. Without net income, a business sinks. There will be no dividends, and the share price suffers. High net income attracts investors, but you can't pay bills with net income. That requires cash.

A company needs both net income and strong cash flow. Income and cash flow usually move together because net income eventually generates cash. Sometimes, however, net income and cash flow take different paths. To illustrate, consider Fastech Company:

	A	B
1	**Fastech Company Income Statement**	**Year Ended December 31, 20X6**
2	Sales revenue	$ 100,000
3	Cost of goods sold	30,000
4	Operating expenses	10,000
5	Net income	$ 60,000
6		

	A	B	C	D
1	**Fastech Company Balance Sheet**	**December 31, 20X6**		
2	Cash	$ 3,000	Total current liabilities	$ 50,000
3	Receivables	37,000	Long-term liabilities	20,000
4	Inventory	40,000		
5	PPE, net	60,000	Shareholders' equity	70,000
6	Total assets	$140,000	Total liabilities and equity	$140,000
7				

What can we glean from Fastech's Income Statement and Balance Sheet?

- Fastech is profitable. Net income is 60% of revenue. Fastech's profitability looks outstanding.
- The current ratio is 1.6, and the debt ratio is only 50%. These measures suggest little trouble in paying bills.
- Fastech is on the verge of bankruptcy. Can you spot the problem? Can you see what is causing the problem? Three trouble spots leap out to a financial analyst.

1. The cash balance is very low. Three thousand dollars isn't enough cash to pay the bills of a company with sales of $100,000.
2. Fastech isn't selling inventory fast enough. Fastech turned over its inventory only 0.75 times during the year. As we saw in Chapter 6, inventory turnover rates of 3–8 times a year are common. A turnover ratio of 0.75 times means it takes Fastech far too long to sell its inventory, and that delays cash collections.
3. Fastech's days' sales in receivables is 135 days (see Chapter 5). Very few companies can wait that long to collect from customers.

The key takeaway lesson from this discussion is that you need both income and strong cash flow to succeed in business. Let's turn now to the different categories of cash flows.

DISTINGUISH AMONG OPERATING, INVESTING AND FINANCING CASH FLOW ACTIVITIES

Operating, Investing, and Financing Activities

2 Distinguish among operating, investing, and financing cash flow activities

A business engages in three types of business activities:

- Operating activities
- Investing activities
- Financing activities

The statement of cash flows reports cash receipts and payments related to these three activities. The major classes of cash receipts and payments are shown in Exhibit 11-1.

Operating activities create revenues, expenses, gains, and losses—*net income*, which is a product of accrual-basis accounting. The statement of cash flows reports on operating activities; thus, it reports principal revenue-generating activities, i.e., transactions and other events that

Exhibit 11-1 | Major Classes of Cash Receipts and Cash Payments on the Statement of Cash Flows

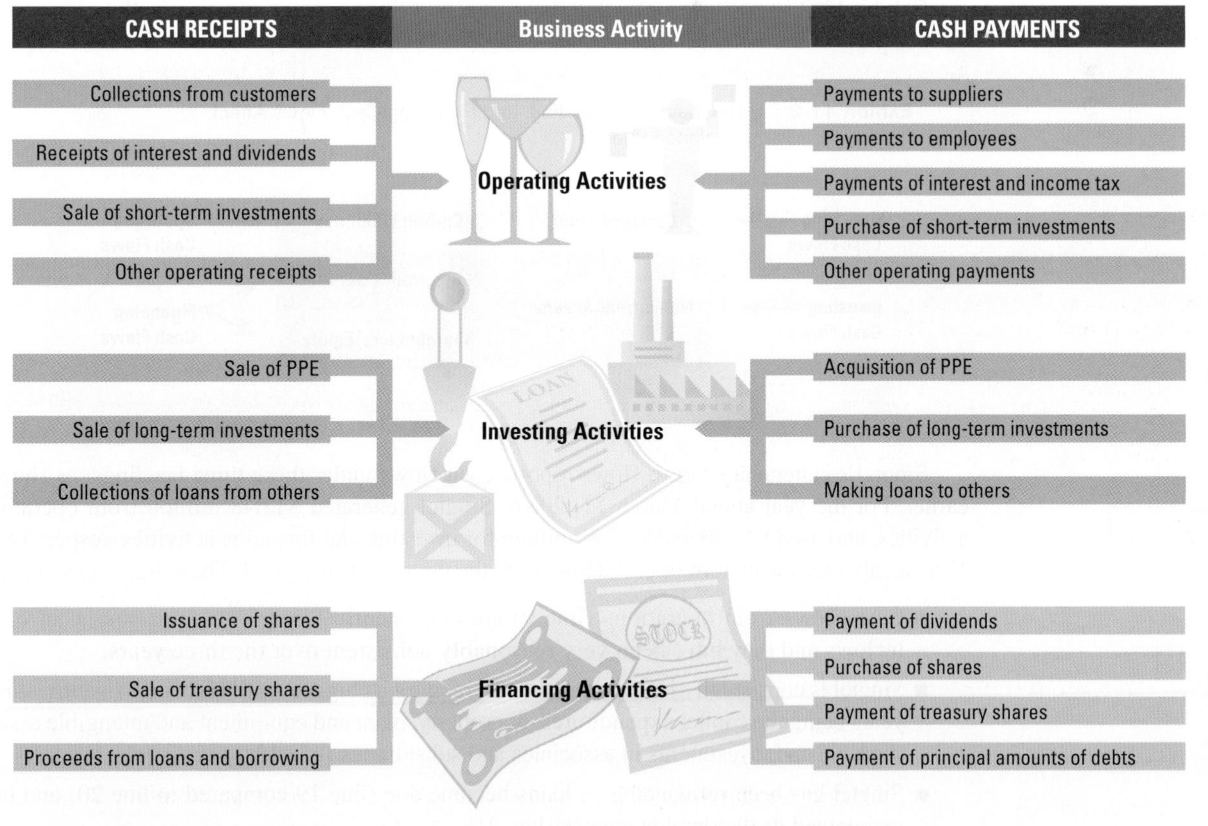

enter into determining profit or loss. Operating activities are the most important of the three categories because they reflect the core of the organization. *A successful business must generate most of its cash from operating activities.*

Investing activities increase and decrease noncurrent assets, such as PPE, intangible assets, and investments in other companies. Purchases and sales of these assets are investing activities. Investing activities are important for a company's medium- and long-term operations, as they represent the extent to which investments have been made for resources intended to generate future income and cash flows.

Financing activities obtain cash from, and pay cash to, investors and creditors. Issuing shares, borrowing money, buying and selling treasury shares, and paying cash dividends are financing activities. Paying off a loan is another example. Financing cash flows relates to noncurrent liabilities and shareholders' equity. These activities are important to help readers predict claims on future cash flows by providers of capital to the entity.

Stop & Think

Royal Dutch Shell borrowed €1 billion from Rabobank. The term of the loan requires Shell to make a full payment in three years' time amounting to €1.1 billion, inclusive of interest. How should the cash outflow of €1.1 billion be reported on Shell's cash flow statement?

Answer:

The €1.1 billion outflow actually consists of two components, €1 billion for the loan principal repayment and €0.1 billion for the interest payment. Shell would report a cash outflow of €1 billion under cash flows from financing activities and €0.1 billion interest payments under cash flows from operations.

Exhibit 11-2 shows how operating, investing, and financing activities typically relate to the various parts of the Balance Sheet.

Exhibit 11-2 How Operating, Investing, and Financing Cash Flows Affect the Balance Sheet

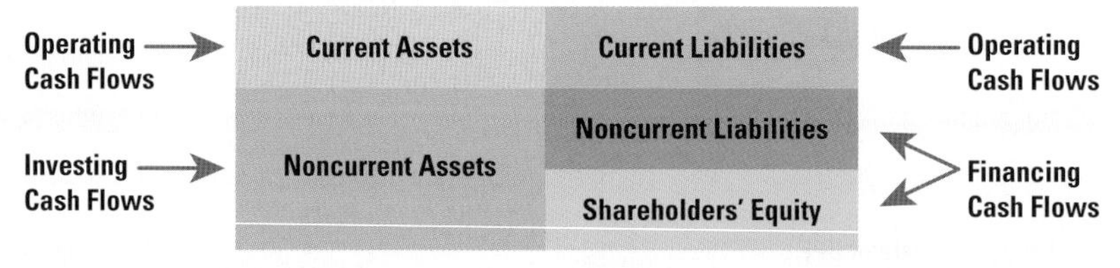

Singtel's statement of cash flows reports cash flows under these three headings, as shown earlier. For the year ended March 31, 20X6, Singtel generated $4,648 million from operating activities, and used $2,740 and $2,044 million for investing and financing activities, respectively. You can also see the pattern of cash flows over the three years provided. These figures show that:

- Cash flows from operations (line 9) are consistently Singtel's largest source of cash inflows and they have been very reasonably consistent over the three years.
- Singtel is consistently investing in the future, with its biggest cash flow item over the three years being the capital expenditures on property, plant and equipment and intangible assets (line 11) and investments in associates and subsidiaries (line 12).
- Singtel has been refinancing as loans become due (line 19 compared to line 20) and has maintained its dividend payments (line 21).

You may see some companies' cash flow items not being categorized in the same way we have done it in Exhibit 11-1, which is the most common way of classifying cash flow items. *IAS 7* allows for alternative classifications, "in a manner which is most appropriate to its business . . . in a consistent manner." *IAS 7* provides guidance on some of these alternatives:

- Interest paid, usually categorized as an operating cash flow item, may be classified as financing cash flow items or investing cash flows.
- Interest and dividends received, usually classified as operating cash flow items, may be classified as investing cash flow items.
- Dividends paid, usually categorized as a financing cash flow item, may be classified as cash flow from operations.
- Taxes paid, usually categorized as an operating cash flow item, may be classified as investing or financing activities (if it can be tied to an individual transaction that gives rise to such activities).

For the purposes of learning cash flow items, we will use the "usual" classifications of cash flow items, i.e., interest paid, interest and dividends received, taxes paid as operating cash flows, and dividends paid as financing cash flows. But remember that when you look at companies' real financial statements, you may see alternative placements of these items.

Two Formats for Operating Activities

IAS 7 requires an entity to report cash flows from operating activities using one of two methods:

1. **Indirect method**, which reconciles from net income to net cash provided by operating activities.
2. **Direct method**, which reports all cash receipts and cash payments from operating activities.

How do the two methods differ? The two methods use different computations, but they produce the same figure for cash flows from *operating activities*. The two methods do not affect *investing* or *financing activities*, which are prepared similarly to the direct method, by the reporting of major classes of cash receipts and payments in their respective activities.

A simple analogy provides a good explanation of the two methods. Suppose you are given a series of numbers: 2, 3, 5, 7, and 8, which totals 25. You are then asked to sum the prime numbers in the sequence. There are clearly two methods of doing this. You could identify the prime numbers, in this case 2, 3, 5, and 7 and sum them, and the answer would be 17. This is the direct method, where you identify the items (or cash flows) and then add them up. Alternatively, since you know the total of the series was 25, and 8 is the only number that is not a prime number, you could arrive at the same answer by making use of this total, i.e., 25 – 8 = 17. The indirect method makes use of a total (in cash flow terms, it would be your net income, a total of revenues less expenses in your Income Statement) and adjusts for items that are not prime, to arrive at the same answer. Note that 25 is not prime, neither is 8, but yet you get the 17 as the sum of prime numbers in the sequence.

IAS 7 actually advocates for the direct method because it provides information which may be useful in estimating future cash flows that is not available under the indirect method. However, this is not heeded by most companies which mostly prepare their cash flow statements using the indirect method.

The following summarizes the differences between the indirect and direct methods:

Indirect Method		Direct Method	
Net income	$600	Collections from customers	$2,000
Adjustments:		*Deductions:*	
Depreciation, etc.	300	Payments to suppliers, etc.	(1,100)
Net cash provided by operating activities	$900	Net cash provided by operating activities	$ 900

same

Exhibit 11-3 TRF's Income Statement

	A	B	C
1	**The Roadster Factory, Inc. (TRF) Income Statement**	**Year Ended December 31, 20X7**	
2	**(In thousands of $)**		
3	Revenues and gains:		
4	Sales revenue	$ 303	
5	Interest revenue	2	
6	Gain on sale of PPE	8	
7	Total revenues and gains		$ 313
8	Expenses:		
9	Cost of goods sold	$ 150	
10	Salary and wage expense	56	
11	Depreciation expense	18	
12	Other operating expense	17	
13	Income tax expense	15	
14	Interest expense	7	
15	Total expenses		263
16	Net income		$ 50
17			

Exhibit 11-4 TRF's Balance Sheet

	A	B	C	D
1	**The Roadster Factory, Inc. (TRF) Comparative Balance Sheets**	**12 Months Ended**		
2	**(In thousands of $)**	**Dec. 31, 20X7**	**Dec. 31, 20X6**	**Increase (Decrease)**
3	**Assets**			
4	Current:			
5	Cash	$ 34	$ 42	$ (8)
6	Accounts receivable	96	81	15
7	Inventory	35	38	(3)
8	Prepaid expenses	8	7	1
9	Notes receivable	21	—	21
10	PPE, net	343	219	124
11	Total	$ 537	$ 387	$ 150
12	**Liabilities**			
13	Current:			
14	Accounts payable	$ 91	$ 57	$ 34
15	Salary and wage payable	4	6	(2)
16	Accrued liabilities	1	3	(2)
17	Long-term debt	160	77	83
18	**Shareholders' Equity**			
19	Ordinary share capital	162	158	4
20	Retained earnings	119	86	33
21	Total	$ 537	$ 387	$ 150
22				

We shall begin with the indirect method since it is the more common method that you are likely to see in financial reports. Singtel's cash flow from operations was prepared using the indirect format. To illustrate the statement of cash flows, we use The Roadster Factory, Inc. (TRF), a dealer in auto parts for sports cars. The Income Statement and Balance Sheet for TRF are shown in Exhibits 11-3 and 11-4, respectively.

PREPARE CASH FLOWS FROM OPERATING ACTIVITIES USING THE INDIRECT METHOD

3 **Prepare** cash flows from operating activities using the indirect method

Earlier you read that *IAS 7* describes operating activities as principal revenue-generating activities, i.e., transactions and other events that determine the profit or loss of an entity. Under the indirect method, this is exactly how we start cash flows from operating activities. The operating section begins with the net income, taken from the Income Statement (see Exhibit 11-3), and is followed by "Adjustments to reconcile net income to net cash provided by operating activities." These adjustments include items that are *not* cash flows, just like our simple analogy earlier uses the number 8 (from the series of 2, 3, 5, 7, 8) to determine the sum of the prime numbers. Let's discuss these adjustments.

To make it easier for our discussion, let's have a look at a template for the preparation of cash flow from operating activities using the indirect method (see Exhibit 11-5).

Exhibit 11-5 | Template for Cash Flows from Operating Activities: Indirect Method

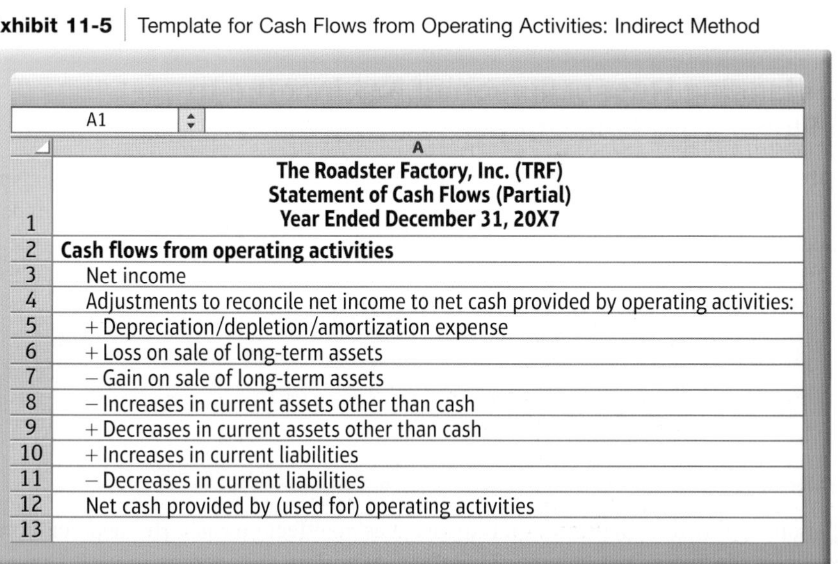

	A
1	**The Roadster Factory, Inc. (TRF)** **Statement of Cash Flows (Partial)** **Year Ended December 31, 20X7**
2	**Cash flows from operating activities**
3	Net income
4	Adjustments to reconcile net income to net cash provided by operating activities:
5	+ Depreciation/depletion/amortization expense
6	+ Loss on sale of long-term assets
7	– Gain on sale of long-term assets
8	– Increases in current assets other than cash
9	+ Decreases in current assets other than cash
10	+ Increases in current liabilities
11	– Decreases in current liabilities
12	Net cash provided by (used for) operating activities
13	

Proceed as follows to prepare the statement of cash flows from the operating activities (or "CFO") section of the statement of cash flows by using the indirect method:

Step 1 Start with net income from TRF's Income Statement (Exhibit 11-3). The indirect method always starts with a summary number from the Income Statement. We use net income in our example here, but sometimes you may see companies using pre-tax income. If a company starts the indirect method with profit before tax, it will need to show a separate line on "income taxes paid" after Step 5.

Step 2 From the Income Statement (Exhibit 11-3), add back depreciation, depletion, and amortization expense, and remove any gains (or add back losses) on the sale of long-term assets.

Step 3 Examine the Balance Sheet (Exhibit 11-4) and identify the changes in current assets and current liabilities (usually referred to as "changes in working capital"), except for cash and cash equivalents.

Step 4 Deduct increases in current assets other than cash and add decreases in current assets other than cash.

Step 5 Deduct decreases in current liabilities and add increases in current liabilities.

If you have completed the five steps using the exhibits above, you will probably have obtained something like Exhibit 11-6 below.

Exhibit 11-6 | Statement of Cash Flows: Operating Activities by the Indirect Method

	A	B	C
1	**The Roadster Factory, Inc. (TRF)** **Statement of Cash Flows (Partial, Indirect Method)**	**Year Ended** **December 31, 20X7**	
2	**(In thousands)**		
3	**Cash flows from operating activities:**		
4	Net income		$ 50
5	Adjustments to reconcile net income to net cash		
6	provided by operating activities:		
7	Ⓐ Depreciation	$ (18)	
8	Ⓑ Gain on sale of PPE	(8)	
9	Ⓒ Increase in accounts receivable	(15)	
10	Ⓒ Decrease in inventory	3	
11	Ⓒ Increase in prepaid expenses	(1)	
12	Ⓒ Increase in accounts payable	34	
13	Ⓒ Decrease in salary and wage payable	(2)	
14	Ⓒ Decrease in accrued liabilities	(2)	27
15	Net cash provided by operating activities		$ 77
16			

Understanding Reconciliation of Net Income to Cash Flows from Operations

Ⓐ Depreciation, Depletion, and Amortization Expenses. These expenses are added back to net income to convert net income to cash flow. In fact, all noncash expenses are added back, including any impairment charges reported on the Income Statement (see Chapter 7's discussion on impairment of assets). Let's see why. Depreciation is recorded as follows:

	A	B	C	D
1		Depreciation Expense	18,000	
2		Accumulated Depreciation		18,000
3				

Depreciation, recorded as Depreciation Expense, has no effect on cash. But depreciation, like all other expenses, decreases net income. Therefore, to convert net income to cash flows, we add depreciation back to net income. The add-back cancels the earlier deduction.

Example: Suppose you had only two transactions, a $1,000 cash sale and depreciation expense of $300. Cash flow from operations is $1,000, and net income is $700 ($1,000 – $300). To go from net income ($700) to cash flow ($1,000), we add back the depreciation ($300). Depletion and amortization are treated like depreciation.

Have another look at Singtel's statement of cash flows at the start of this chapter. You will see that Line 5 was the addition of depreciation and amortization back to net profit, the first step under the indirect method.

Ⓑ Gains and Losses on the Sale of Long-term Assets. Sales of long-term assets are *investing* activities. However, the resulting gains (or losses) from the sales have been included in the determination of income. Therefore, to avoid double counting, we will need to adjust the net income. Losses are added back to net income, and gains are deducted from net income. For TRF, we deduct the $8 gain on sale of PPE (shown on the Income Statement) away from net income under the indirect method.

In the Singtel's example, you can see line 6 removes gain (and adds back loss) from the sale of long-term assets back to profit as part of the indirect method.

Ⓒ Changes in the Current Asset and Current Liability Accounts. Most current assets and current liabilities result from operating activities. For example, accounts receivable result from sales, inventory relates to cost of goods sold, and so on. Changes in the current accounts are adjustments to net income under the indirect method. The reasoning is as follows:

1. *An increase in another current asset decreases cash.* It takes cash to acquire assets. Suppose you make a sale on account. Accounts receivable are increased, but cash isn't affected yet. Exhibit 11-4 reports that during 20X7, The Roadster Factory's Accounts Receivable increased by $15,000. To compute cash flow from operations, we must subtract the $15,000 increase in Accounts Receivable, as shown in Exhibit 11-6. The reason is this: We have *not* collected this $15,000 in cash. Similar logic applies to all the other current assets. If they increase, cash decreases.
2. *A decrease in another current asset increases cash.* Suppose TRF's Accounts Receivable balance decreased by $4,000. Cash receipts caused Accounts Receivable to decrease, so we add decreases in Accounts Receivable and the other current assets to net income.
3. *A decrease in a current liability decreases cash.* Payment of a current liability decreases both cash and the liability, so we subtract decreases in current liabilities from net income. In Exhibit 11-6, the $2,000 decrease in Accrued Liabilities is *subtracted* to compute net cash provided by operations.
4. *An increase in a current liability increases cash.* The Roadster Factory's Accounts Payable increased. That can occur only if cash was not spent to pay this debt. Cash payments are therefore less than expenses and TRF has more cash on hand. Thus, increases in current liabilities increase cash.

In the Singtel example, the working capital adjustments were summarized in line 7. Singtel's actual statement of cash flows shows increases and decreases in current assets and current liabilities as adjustments to profit using the indirect method.

A Closer Look

As mentioned earlier, you may see some companies start with "net income before tax" rather than "net income after tax" at the top of their statement of cash flows. This is typically because of a requirement to explicitly disclose how much a company pays for tax during the year. If we have done this for TRF, we would have the following CFO:

	A	B	C
1	**The Roadster Factory, Inc. (TRF)** **Statement of Cash Flows (Partial, Indirect Method)**	**Year Ended** **December 31, 20X6**	
2	**(In thousands)**		
3	**Cash flows from operating activities:**		
4	Net income before tax		$ 65
5	Adjustments to reconcile net income to net cash		
6	provided by operating activities:		
7	Depreciation	$ 18	
8	Gain on sale of PPE	(8)	
9	Increase in accounts receivable	(15)	
10	Decrease in inventory	3	
11	Increase in prepaid expenses	(1)	
12	Increase in accounts payable	34	
13	Decrease in salary and wage payable	(2)	
14	Decrease in accrued liabilities	(2)	27
15	Income tax paid		(15)
16	Net cash provided by opearting activities		$ 77
17			

In this example, the income tax paid equals income tax expense because there were no income tax payable balances at either the beginning or ending of the year. Had there been any income tax payable balances, they would affect the income tax paid and not be included in the changes in working capital adjustments. See Exhibit 11-14? (later) for calculations of income tax paid.

Evaluating Cash Flows from Operating Activities. Let's step back and evaluate TRF's operating cash flows during 20X7. TRF's operations provided net cash flow of $77,000. This amount exceeds net income, which is one sign that TRF was able to translate profitability to cash generations.

If you want to immediately compare the indirect method above with the direct method, you can take a detour to pages 649–655, and then return here to continue with the other cash flow activities.

PREPARE CASH FLOWS FROM INVESTING ACTIVITIES

4 **Prepare** cash flows from investing activities

Cash flows from investing activities (or "CFI") basically revolve around the cash inflows and outflows related to long-term assets of the entity. Exhibit 11-1 showed us that the major classes of cash receipts include sale of PPE and other noncurrent assets, sale of long-term investments, and collections of loans to others; the outflows are typically for acquisition of PPE and other noncurrent assets, purchase of long-term investments, and making loans to others.

Most of the data for this section are from TRF's Balance Sheet (refer to Exhibit 11-4). Let's calculate the cash flow items under this category (remember, you don't have shortcuts like the CFO's indirect method for CFI).

Computing Purchases and Sales of PPE. Companies keep a separate account for each item of PPE. But for computing cash flows, it is helpful to combine all the PPE items into a single summary account. Also, we subtract accumulated depreciation and use the net figure. It's easier to work with a single PPE account.

To illustrate, observe the following:

- TRF's Balance Sheet reports beginning PPE, net of accumulated depreciation, of $219,000. The ending balance is $343,000 (Exhibit 11-4).
- TRF's Income Statement shows a depreciation expense of $18,000 and an $8,000 gain on sale of PPE (Exhibit 11-3).

TRF's purchases of PPE during the year totaled $196,000 (we shall take this as given). How much, then, are the proceeds from the sale of PPE? To do this, you must remember that (1) proceeds less book value of assets sold are equal to gain on disposal, and (2) the change in net PPE is caused by addition of new PPE, depreciation charge for the period, and the book value of PPE sold. So, let's first determine the book value of the PPE sold, as follows:

PPE, Net

Beginning balance	+	Acquisitions	−	Depreciation	−	Book value of assets sold	=	Ending balance
$219,000	+	$196,000	−	$18,000		−X	=	$343,000
						−X	=	$343,000 − $219,000 − $196,000 + $18,000
						X	=	$54,000

The sale proceeds are $62,000, determined as follows:

Sale proceeds	=	Book value of assets sold	+	Gain	−	Loss
X	=	$54,000	+	$8,000	−	$0
X	=	$62,000				

The PPE T-account provides another look at the computation of the book value of the assets sold.

PPE, Net

Beginning balance	**219,000**	**Depreciation**	**18,000**
Acquisitions	**196,000**	Book value of assets sold	54,000
Ending balance	**343,000**		

If the sale had resulted in a loss of $3,000 instead, the sale proceeds would be $51,000 ($54,000 – $3,000), and the statement of cash flows would report $51,000 as a cash receipt from this investing activity.

Computing Purchases and Sales of Investments, and Loans and Collections. The cash amounts of investment transactions can be computed in the manner illustrated for PPE. Investments are easier because there is no depreciation, as shown in the following equation:

Investments (amounts assumed for illustration only)

Beginning balance	+	Purchases	–	Book value of investments sold	=	Ending balance
$100,000	+	$50,000		–X	=	$140,000
				–X	=	$140,000 – $100,000 – $50,000
				X	=	$10,000

The Investments T-account provides another look (amounts assumed).

Investments

Beginning balance	100,000		
Purchases	50,000	Book value of investments sold	10,000
Ending balance	140,000		

The Roadster Factory has a long-term receivable, and the cash flows from loan transactions on notes receivable can be determined as follows (data from Exhibit 11-4):

Notes Receivable

Beginning balance	+	New loans made	–	Collections	=	Ending balance
$0	+	X		–0	=	$21,000
		X			=	$21,000

Notes Receivable

Beginning balance	0		
New loans made	21,000	Collections	0
Ending balance	21,000		

Exhibit 11-7 shows the statement of cash flows, and Exhibit 11-8 summarizes the cash flows from investing activities, highlighted in color.

Exhibit 11-7 Statement of Cash Flows: Investing Activities

	A	B	C
1	**The Roadster Factory, Inc. (TRF) Statement of Cash Flows (Partial)**	**Year Ended December 31, 20X7**	
2	**(In thousands)**		
3	**Cash flows from operating activities:**		
4	Acquisition of PPE	$ (196)	
5	Loan to another company	(21)	
6	Proceeds from sale of PPE	62	
7	Net cash used for investing activities		(155)
8			

Exhibit 11-8 Computing Cash Flows from Investing Activities

Receipts									
From sale of PPE	Beginning PPE, net	+	Acquisition cost	−	Depreciation	−	Book value of assets sold	=	Ending PPE, net
	Cash received	=	Book value of assets sold	+ or −	Gain on sale / Loss on sale				
From sale of investments	Beginning investments	+	Purchase cost of investments	−	Cost of investments sold	=	Ending investments		
	Cash received	=	Cost of investments sold	+ or −	Gain on sale / Loss on sale				
From collection of notes receivable	Beginning notes receivable	+	New loans made	−	Collections	=	Ending notes receivable		
Payments									
For acquisition of PPE	Beginning PPE, net	+	Acquisition cost	−	Depreciation	−	Book value of assets sold	=	Ending PPE, net
For purchase of investments	Beginning investments	+	Purchase cost of investments	−	Cost of investments sold	=	Ending investments		
For new loans made	Beginning notes receivable	+	New loans made	−	Collections	=	Ending notes receivable		

If you look at Singtel's cash flow from investing activities, you will see that it has been investing in new PPE and intangible assets (line 11), as well as making investments in other companies (line 12). There are some buying and selling of financial assets investments (lines 13 and 14), but they are relatively small compared to lines 11 and 12.

PREPARE CASH FLOWS FROM FINANCING ACTIVITIES

5 **Prepare** cash flows from financing activities

Cash flows from financing activities (or "CFF") are those that relate to the capital structure and owners of the entity. Financing activities affect long-term liabilities and equity accounts such as Notes Payable, Bonds Payable, Long-Term Debt, Share Capital, Paid-in Capital in Excess of Par, Treasury Shares, and Retained Earnings. Most of the data are from the Balance Sheet (see Exhibit 11-4).

Exhibit 11-1 showed us that the major classes of cash receipts include issuance of shares, proceeds from selling treasury shares, loans, and borrowings; and the outflows include repurchase of shares ("share buy-back") either for cancellation or treasury, and repayment of loans and borrowings. Let's work out TRF's cash flows from financing activities.

Computing Issuances and Payments of Long-Term Debt. The beginning and ending balances of Long-Term Debt, Notes Payable, or Bonds Payable come from the Balance Sheet. If either new issuances or payments are known, the other amount can be computed. The Roadster Factory's new debt issuances total $94,000 (take this amount as given). Debt payments are computed from the Long-Term Debt account (see Exhibit 11-4).

Long-Term Debt (Notes Payable, Bonds Payable)

Beginning balance	+	Issuance of new debt	−	Payments of debt	=	Ending balance
$77,000	+	$94,000		−X	=	$160,000
				−X	=	$160,000 − $77,000 − $94,000
				X	=	$11,000

Long-Term Debt

		Beginning balance	77,000
Payments	11,000	Issuance of new debt	94,000
		Ending balance	160,000

If the $94,000 new debt issuance information was not given, we would have naturally assumed that TRF had simply borrowed an additional $83,000 (i.e., $160,000 ending balance less $77,000 beginning balance).

Computing Issuances of Shares and Purchases of Treasury Shares. These cash flows can be determined from the share capital accounts. For example, cash received from issuing shares is computed from Share Capital and Capital in Excess of Par. We use a single summary Share Capital account as we do for PPE. The Roadster Factory data are as follows:

Share capital

Beginning balance	+	Issuance of new shares	=	Ending balance
$158,000	+	$4,000	=	$162,000

Share Capital

		Beginning balance	158,000
		Issuance of new shares	4,000
		Ending balance	162,000

This $4,000 would have been the net impact of the issuances and repurchases of shares. You could have been told in the question that the issuance of shares for the period was $20,000. You would have noticed that TRF must have bought back some shares, otherwise $158,000 + $20,000 would not equal $162,000. In such situations, TRF must have bought back $16,000 worth of shares, either for treasury or cancellation.

Computing Dividend Declarations and Payments. If dividend declarations and payments are not given elsewhere, they can be computed. For TRF, this computation is as follows:

Retained Earnings

Beginning balance	+	Net income	−	Dividend payments	=	Ending balance
$86,000	+	$50,000		−X	=	$119,000
				−X	=	$119,000 − $86,000 − $50,000
				X	=	$17,000

The T-account also shows the dividend computation.

Retained Earnings

		Beginning balance	86,000
Dividend payments	17,000	Net income	50,000
		Ending balance	119,000

Our completed statement of cash flows from financing would look something like that shown in Exhibit 11-9.

Exhibit 11-9 | Statement of Cash Flows: Investing Activities

	A	B	C
1	**The Roadster Factory, Inc. (TRF)** **Statement of Cash Flows (Partial)**	**Year Ended** **December 31, 20X7**	
2	**(In thousands)**		
3	**Cash flows from financing activities:**		
4	Proceeds from issuance of long-term debt	$ (94)	
5	Proceeds from issuance of shares	(4)	
6	Payment of long-term debt	(11)	
7	Payment of dividends	(17)	
8	Net cash provided by financing activities		70
9			

Exhibit 11-10 summarizes the cash flows from financing activities, highlighted in color.

Exhibit 11-10 | Computing Cash Flows from Financing Activities

Receipts							
From borrowing—issuance of long-term debt	Beginning long-term debt	+	Cash received from issuance of long-term debt	−	Payment of debt	=	Ending long-term debt
From issuance of share	Beginning share capital	+	Cash received from issuance of new shares	−	Share cancellations	=	Ending share capital
Payments							
Of long-term debt	Beginning long-term debt	+	Cash received from issuance of long-term debt	−	Payment of debt	=	Ending long-term debt
To purchase treasury share	Beginning treasury share	+	Purchase cost of treasury shares			=	Ending treasury share
Of dividends	Beginning retained earnings	+	Net income	−	Dividend payment	=	Ending retained earnings

For Singtel, you can see that it has both proceeds from and payments for loans and borrowings during the year (lines 19 and 20). The other significant item in the cash flow from financing section is the dividend payment (line 21).

Stop & Think

Classify each of the following as an operating activity, an investing activity, or a financing activity as reported on the statement of cash flows prepared by the *indirect* method.

a. Issuance of shares
b. Borrowing
c. Sales revenue
d. Payment of dividends

e. Purchase of land	i. Sale of equipment
f. Purchase of treasury shares	j. Cost of goods sold
g. Paying bonds payable	k. Purchase of another company
h. Interest expense	l. Making a long-term loan to another company

Answers:

a. Financing	g. Financing
b. Financing	h. Operating
c. Operating	i. Investing
d. Financing	j. Operating
e. Investing	k. Investing
f. Financing	l. Investing

Completing the Statement of Cash Flows (Indirect CFO)

Now that we have prepared all three categories of cash flow activities, it is time to complete the cash flow statement. Let's assemble what we have done into one single statement and calculate the net cash flows from the three cash flow activities (see Exhibit 11-11). This is often a very stressful time, because if we have done our work carefully, we sure want our net cash flows to reconcile the change in cash on the Balance Sheet.

Exhibit 11-11 Statement of Cash Flows: Indirect Method

A1

	A	B	C
1	**The Roadster Factory, Inc. (TRF)** **Statement of Cash Flows**	**Year Ended** **December 31, 20X7**	
2	**(In thousands)**		
3	**Cash flows from operating activities:**		
4	Net income		$ 50
5	Adjustments to reconcile net income to net cash		
6	provided by operating activities:		
7	(A) Depreciation	$ 18	
8	(B) Gain on sale of PPE	(8)	
9	(C) Increase in accounts receivable	(15)	
10	(C) Decrease in inventory	3	
11	(C) Increase in prepaid expenses	(1)	
12	(C) Increase in accounts payable	34	
13	(C) Decrease in salary and wage payable	(2)	
14	(C) Decrease in accrued liabilities	(2)	27
15	Net cash provided by operating activities		77
16	**Cash flows from investing activities:**		
17	Acquisition of PPE	$ (196)	
18	Loan to another company	(21)	
19	Proceeds from sale of PPE	62	
20	Net cash used for investing activities		(155)
21	**Cash flows from financing activities:**		
22	Proceeds from issuance of long-term debt	$ 94	
23	Proceeds from issuance of shares	4	
24	Payment of long-term debt	(11)	
25	Payment of dividends	(17)	
26	Net cash provided by financing activities		70
27	**Net (decrease) in cash**		$ (8)
28	Cash balance, December 31, 20X6		42
29	Cash balance, December 31, 20X7		$ 34
30			

As you can see, we did a pretty a good job! The net cash flows for the period show a decrease of \$8,000, which explains why TRF's cash went from \$42,000 to \$34,000. What does the statement of cash flow tell us? TRF was able to generate cash flow from operating activities, which is used (together with some borrowings) to expand its investments in new PPE. Reflect on TRF's financial position (its Balance Sheet, Exhibit 11-4) and financial performance (its Income Statement, Exhibit 11-5). While they were your source data for the cash flow statement, the insights you get from the cash flow statement clearly supplement what you already have.

Noncash Investing and Financing Activities

Companies sometimes make investments that do not require cash. They may also obtain financing other than cash. Alternatively, they may sell assets for noncash considerations, akin to "swapping" one asset for another. Our TRF working example has none of these noncash investing and financing transactions. Now suppose TRF issued shares valued at \$300,000 to acquire a warehouse. The Roadster Factory would journalize this transaction as follows:

	A	B	C	D
1		Warehouse Building	300,000	
2		Share Capital		300,000
3				

This transaction would not be reported as a cash payment because TRF paid no cash. But the investment in the warehouse and the issuance of shares are important. These noncash investing and financing activities can be reported in a separate schedule under the statement of cash flows. Exhibit 11-12 illustrates noncash investing and financing activities (all amounts are assumed).

Exhibit 11-12 Noncash Investing and Financing Activities (All Amounts Assumed)

	A	B
1		**Thousands**
2	**Noncash Investing and Financing Activities:**	
3	Acquisition of building by issuing shares	\$ 300
4	Acquisition of land by issuing note payable	70
5	Payment of long-term debt by issuing shares	100
6	Total noncash investing and financing activities	\$ 470
7		

For example, Singtel provided this additional note regarding a noncash transaction.

ADAPTED EXCERPTS FROM SINGTEL'S NOTES TO THE ACCOUNTS

Noncash Transactions

In March 2016, Singtel received a dividend distribution of S\$60 million from NetLink Trust, a wholly owned associate of Singtel, which was offset against an amount due to NetLink Trust.

In October 2014, Singtel sold certain infrastructure assets to NetLink Trust for an aggregate consideration of S\$280 million. The aggregate consideration paid by NetLink Trust was financed by an interest-bearing loan from Singtel.

Source: From Singtel, Annual Report, 2016, page 136.

Now let's apply what you've learned about the statement of cash flows prepared by the indirect method.

Mid-Chapter Summary Problem

Lucas Corporation reported the following Income Statement and comparative Balance Sheets, along with transaction data for 20X7:

	A	B	C
1	**Lucas Corporation Income Statement**	**Year Ended December 31, 20X7**	
2	Sales revenue		$ 662,000
3	Cost of goods sold		560,000
4	Gross profit		102,000
5	Operating expenses		
6	Salary expenses	$ 46,000	
7	Depreciation expense—equipment	7,000	
8	Amortization expense—patent	3,000	
9	Rent expense	2,000	
10	Total operating expenses		58,000
11	Income from operations		44,000
12	Other items:		
13	Loss on sale of equipment		(2,000)
14	Income before income tax		42,000
15	Income tax expense		16,000
16	Net income		$ 26,000
17			

	A	B	C	D	E	F
1	**Lucas Corporation Comparative Balance Sheets**	**December 31**				
2	**Assets**	**20X7**	**20X6**	**Liabilities**	**20X7**	**20X6**
3	Current:			Current:		
4	Cash and cash equivalents	$ 19,000	$ 3,000	Accounts payable	$ 35,000	$ 26,000
5	Accounts receivable	22,000	23,000	Accrued liabilities	7,000	9,000
6	Inventories	34,000	31,000	Income tax payable	10,000	10,000
7	Prepaid expenses	1,000	3,000	Total current liabilities	52,000	45,000
8	Total current assets	76,000	60,000	Long-term note payable	44,000	—
9	Long-term investments	18,000	10,000	Bonds payable	40,000	53,000
10	Equipment, net	67,000	52,000	**Owners' Equity**		
11	Patent, net	44,000	10,000	Share capital	52,000	20,000
12				Retained earnings	27,000	19,000
13				Less: Treasury shares	(10,000)	(5,000)
14	Total assets	$ 205,000	$ 132,000	Total liabilities and equity	$ 205,000	$ 132,000
15						

Transaction Data for 20X7:			
Purchase of equipment	$ 98,000	Issuance of long-term note payable to purchase patent	$ 37,000
Payment of cash dividends	18,000	Issuance of long-term note payable to borrow cash	7,000
Issuance of shares to retire bonds payable	13,000	Issuance of shares for cash	19,000
Purchase of long-term investment	8,000	Sale of equipment (book value, $76,000)	74,000
Purchase of treasury shares	5,000		

Requirement

Prepare Lucas Corporation's statement of cash flows (indirect method) for the year ended December 31, 20X7. Follow the four steps outlined below. For Step 4, prepare a T-account to show the transaction activity in each long-term Balance Sheet account. For each PPE, use a single account, net of accumulated depreciation (for example: Equipment, Net).

Step 1 Lay out the template of the statement of cash flows.

Step 2 From the comparative Balance Sheet, determine the increase in cash during the year, $16,000.

Step 3 From the Income Statement, take net income, depreciation, amortization, and the loss on sale of equipment to the statement of cash flows.

Step 4 Complete the statement of cash flows. Account for the year-to-year change in each Balance Sheet account.

Answer

	A	B	C
1	**Lucas Corporation Statement of Cash Flows**	**Year Ended December 31, 20X7**	
2	**Cash flows from operating activities:**		
3	Net income		$ 26,000
4	Adjustments to reconcile net income to		
5	net cash provided by operating activities:		
6	Depreciation	$ 7,000	
7	Amortization	3,000	
8	Loss on sale of equipment	2,000	
9	Decrease in accounts receivable	1,000	
10	Increase in inventories	(3,000)	
11	Decrease in prepaid expenses	2,000	
12	Increase in accounts payable	9,000	
13	Decrease in accrued liabilities	(2,000)	19,000
14	Net cash provided by operating activities		45,000
15	**Cash flows from investing activities:**		
16	Purchase of equipment	$ (98,000)	
17	Sale of equipment	74,000	
18	Purchase of long-term investment	(8,000)	
19	Net cash used for investing activities		(32,000)
20	**Cash flows from financing activities:**		
21	Issuance of shares	$ 19,000	
22	Payment of cash dividends	(18,000)	
23	Issuance of long-term note payable	7,000	
24	Purchase of treasury share	(5,000)	
25	Net cash provided by financing activities		3,000
26	**Net increase in cash**		**16,000**
27	Cash balance, December 31, 20X6		3,000
28	Cash balance, December 31, 20X7		$ 19,000
29	**Noncash investing and financing activities:**		
30	Issuance of long-term note payable to purchase patent		$ 37,000
31	Issuance of shares to retire bonds payable		13,000
32	Total noncash investing and financing activities		$ 50,000
33			

Long-Term Investments

Bal. 10,000	
8,000	
Bal. 18,000	

Equipment, Net

Bal. 52,000	
98,000	76,000
	7,000
Bal. 67,000	

Patent, Net

Bal. 10,000	
37,000	3,000
Bal. 44,000	

Long-Term Note Payable

	Bal. 0
	37,000
	7,000
	Bal. 44,000

Bonds Payable

	Bal. 53,000
13,000	
	Bal. 40,000

Share Capital

	Bal. 20,000
	13,000
	19,000
	Bal. 52,000

Retained Earnings

	Bal. 19,000
18,000	26,000
	Bal. 27,000

Treasury Shares

Bal. 5,000	
5,000	
Bal. 10,000	

PREPARE CASH FLOWS FROM OPERATING ACTIVITIES USING THE DIRECT METHOD

6 **Prepare** cash flows from operating activities using the direct method

The direct method is the method advocated by *IAS 7* because it provides clearer information about the sources and uses of cash. But very few companies use this method because it requires more computations than the indirect method. Here's an example of a CFO prepared using the direct method.

Cochlear is an Australian-listed company that helps people with difficulties in hearing. Its statement of cash flows is presented using the direct method, which reports the major inflows and outflows of cash from and for operating activities, similar to the items depicted in Exhibit 11-1.

ADAPTED EXCERPTS FROM COCHLEAR'S 2016 STATEMENT OF CASH FLOWS

For years ended 30 June, in thousands of Australian Dollar (A$)

Cash flows from operating activities	**2016**	**2015**
Cash receipts from customers	1,105,512	919,280
Cash paid to suppliers and employees	(834,884)	(694,288)
Grant and other income received	5,461	3,250
Interest received	454	297
Interest paid	(10,745)	(7,627)
Income taxes paid	(80,685)	(32,211)
Net cash provided by operating activities	185,113	188,701

Source: From Cochlear, Annual Report, 2016, page 56.

We shall continue to use The Roadster Factory (TRF) to illustrate the preparation of cash flow from operating activities using the direct method. The direct method will require you to actually calculate each (major class of) cash inflow and cash outflow.

Compute Operating Cash Flows by the Direct Method

To compute operating cash flows by the direct method, we use the Income Statement and the *changes* in the Balance Sheet accounts. Exhibit 11-13 illustrates the process. We reproduce the Income Statement for TRF in Exhibit 11-14 and its comparative Balance Sheet in Exhibit 11-15 for ease of reference.

Exhibit 11-13 | Direct Method of Computing Cash Flows from Operating Activities

RECEIPTS / PAYMENTS	Income Statement Account	Change in Related Balance Sheet Account	
RECEIPTS:			
From customers	Sales Revenue	+ Decrease in Accounts Receivable − Increase in Accounts Receivable	
Of interest	Interest Revenue	+ Decrease in Interest Receivable − Increase in Interest Receivable	
PAYMENTS:			
To suppliers	Cost of Goods Sold	+ Increase in Inventory − Decrease in Inventory	+ Decrease in Accounts Payable − Increase in Accounts Payable
	Operating Expense	+ Increase in Prepaids − Decrease in Prepaids	+ Decrease in Accrued Liabilities − Increase in Accrued Liabilities
To employees	Salary (Wage) Expense	+ Decrease in Salary (Wage) Payable − Increase in Salary (Wage) Payable	
For interest	Interest Expense	+ Decrease in Interest Payable − Increase in Interest Payable	
For income tax	Income Tax Expense	+ Decrease in Income Tax Payable − Increase in Income Tax Payable	

*We thank Professor Barbara Gerrity for suggesting this exhibit.

Exhibit 11-14 | The Roadster Factory's Income Statement

	A	B	C
1	**The Roadster Factory, Inc. (TRF)** **Income Statement**	**Year Ended December 31, 20X7**	
2	**(In thousands of US$)**		
3	Revenues and gains:		
4	Sales revenue	$ 303	
5	Interest revenue	2	
6	Gain on sale of PPE	8	
7	Total revenues and gains		$ 313
8	Expenses:		
9	Cost of goods sold	$ 150	
10	Salary and wage expense	56	
11	Depreciation expense	18	
12	Other operating expense	17	
13	Income tax expense	15	
14	Interest expense	7	
15	Total expenses		263
16	Net income		$ 50
17			

Exhibit 11-15 | TRF's Balance Sheets

	A	B	C	D
1	**The Roadster Factory, Inc. (TRF) Comparative Balance Sheets**	**12 Months Ended**		
2	**(In thousands of US$)**	**Dec. 31, 20X7**	**Dec. 31, 20X6**	**Increase (Decrease)**
3	**Assets**			
4	Current:			
5	Cash	$ 34	$ 42	$ (8)
6	Accounts receivable	96	81	15
7	Inventory	35	38	(3)
8	Prepaid expenses	8	7	1
9	Notes receivable	21	—	21
10	PPE, net	343	219	124
11	Total	$ 537	$ 387	$ 150
12	**Liabilities**			
13	Current:			
14	Accounts payable	$ 91	$ 57	$ 34
15	Salary and wage payable	4	6	(2)
16	Accrued liabilities	1	3	(2)
17	Long-term debt	160	77	83
18	**Shareholders' Equity**			
19	Ordinary share capital	162	158	4
20	Retained earnings	119	86	33
21	Total	$ 537	$ 387	$ 150
22				

Computing Cash Collections from Customers. Collections start with sales revenue (an accrual-basis amount). The Roadster Factory's Income Statement (Exhibit 11-14) reports sales of $303,000. Accounts receivable increased from $81,000 at the beginning of the year to $96,000 at year-end, a $15,000 increase (Exhibit 11-15). Based on those amounts, cash collections equal $288,000, as follows. We must solve for cash collections (X):

Accounts Receivable

Beginning balance	+	Sales	−	Collections	=	Ending balance
$81,000	+	$303,000		−X	=	$96,000
				−X	=	$96,000 − $81,000 − $303,000
				X	=	$288,000

The T-account for Accounts Receivable provides another view of the same computation.

Accounts Receivable

	Debit		Credit
Beginning balance	81,000		
Sales	303,000	Collections	288,000
Ending balance	96,000		

Accounts Receivable increased, so collections must be less than sales. All collections of receivables are computed this way. Let's turn now to cash receipts of interest revenue. In our example, The Roadster Factory earned interest revenue and collected cash of $2,000 (because there was no interest receivable in the beginning and at the end of the period). The amounts of interest revenue and cash receipts of interest often differ, and Exhibit 11-13 shows how to make this computation, when necessary.

Computing Payments to Suppliers. This computation includes two parts:

- Payments for inventory
- Payments for operating expenses (other than interest and income tax).

Payments for inventory are computed by converting cost of goods sold to the cash basis. We use Cost of Goods Sold, Inventory, and Accounts Payable. First, we must solve for purchases. All the amounts come from Exhibits 11-14 and 11-15.

Cost of Goods Sold

Beginning inventory	+	Purchases	−	Ending inventory	=	Cost of goods sold
$38,000	+	X	−	$35,000	=	$150,000
		X			=	$150,000 − $38,000 + $35,000
		X			=	$147,000

Now we can compute cash payments for inventory (Y), as follows:

Accounts Payable

Beginning balance	+	Purchases	−	Payments for inventory	=	Ending balance
$57,000	+	$147,000		−Y	=	$91,000
				−Y	=	$91,000 − $57,000 − $147,000
				Y	=	$113,000

The T-accounts show where the data come from. Start with Cost of Goods Sold.

Cost of Goods Sold

Beg. inventory	**38,000**	**End. inventory**	**35,000**
Purchases	147,000		
Cost of goods sold	**150,000**		

Accounts Payable

Payments for inventory	113,000	**Beg. bal.**	**57,000**
		Purchases	**147,000**
		End. bal.	**91,000**

Accounts Payable increased, so payments for inventory are less than purchases.

Computing Payments for Operating Expenses. Payments for operating expenses other than interest and income tax are computed from three accounts: Prepaid Expenses, Accrued Liabilities, and Other Operating Expenses. All TRF data come from Exhibits 11-14 and 11-15.

We can assume that the beginning prepayments will be used in the period and the ending prepayment is what we paid for during the year. Similarly, we can assume that the beginning accrued liabilities will be paid for during the year, and the ending balance will remain owing.

Prepaid Expenses

Beginning balance	+	Payments	−	Expiration of prepaid expense (assumed)	=	Ending balance
$7,000	+	X	−	$7,000	=	$8,000
		X			=	$8,000 − $7,000 + $7,000
		X			=	$8,000

Accrued Liabilities

Beginning balance	+	Accrual of expense at year-end (assumed)	–	Payments	=	Ending balance
$3,000	+	$1,000		–X	=	$1,000
				–X	=	$1,000 – $3,000 – $1,000
				X	=	$3,000

Other Operating Expenses

Accrual of expense at year-end	+	Expiration of prepaid expense	–	Payments	=	Ending balance
$1,000	+	$7,000		X	=	$17,000
				X	=	$17,000 – $1,000 – $7,000
				X	=	$9,000
Total payments for operating expenses					=	$8,000 + $3,000 + $9,000
					=	$20,000

The T-accounts give another picture of the same data.

Prepaid Expenses

Beg. bal.	**7,000**	**Expiration of prepaid expense**	**7,000**
Payments	8,000		
End. bal.	**8,000**		

Accrued Liabilities

		Beg. bal.	**3,000**
Payment	3,000	**Accrual of expense at year-end**	**1,000**
		End. bal.	**1,000**

Other Operating Expenses

Accrual of expense at year-end	**1,000**		
Expiration of prepaid expense	**7,000**		
Payments	9,000		
End. bal.	**17,000**		

Total payments for operating expenses = $20,000 ($8,000 + $3,000 + $9,000)

Now we can compute Payments to Suppliers as follows:

Payments to Suppliers	=	Payments for Inventory	+	Payments for Operating Expenses
$133,000	+	$113,000	+	$20,000

Computing Payments to Employees. It is convenient to combine all payments to employees into one account, Salary and Wage Expense. We then adjust the expense for the change in Salary and Wage Payable, as shown here:

Salary and Wage Payable

Beginning balance	+	Salary and wage expense	–	Payments	=	Ending balance
$6,000	+	$56,000		–X	=	$4,000
				–X	=	$4,000 – $6,000 – $56,000
				X	=	$58,000

Salary and Wage Payable

		Beginning balance	**6,000**
Payments to employees	58,000	**Salary and wage expense**	**56,000**
		Ending balance	**4,000**

Computing Payments of Interest and Income Taxes. The Roadster Factory's expense and payment amounts are the same for interest and income tax (because interest payable and tax payable balances are zero), so no analysis is required. If the expense and the payment differ, the payment can be computed as shown in Exhibit 11-13.

Let's put the direct method of cash flow from operations all together.

	A	B	C
1	**The Roadster Factory, Inc. (TRF)** **Statement of Cash Flows (Partial, Direct Method)**	**For Year Ended** **December 31, 20X7**	
2	**(In thousands of $)**		
3	**Cash flows from operating activities:**		
4	Receipts:		
5	Collections from customers	$ 288	
6	Interest received	2	
7	Total cash receipts		$ 290
8	Payments:		
9	To suppliers	$ (133)	
10	To employees	(58)	
11	For income tax	(15)	
12	For interest	(7)	
13	Total cash payments		(213)
14	Net cash provided by operating activities		77
15			

As you can see, the cash flow from operating activities is $77,000, the same result obtained earlier using the indirect method (Exhibit 11-6). Remember both methods give you the same cash flows from operating activities; they are just derived differently, one by identifying the actual cash flows, and the other by a reconciliation of net income to CFO.

Stop & Think

Fidelity Company reported the following for 20X7 and 20X6 (in millions):

At December 31	20X7	20X6
Receivables, net	$3,500	$3,900
Inventory	5,200	5,000
Accounts payable	900	1,200
Income taxes payable	600	700

Year Ended December 31	20X7
Revenues	$23,000
Cost of goods sold	14,100
Income tax expense	900

Based on these figures, how much cash did:

- Fidelity collect from customers during 20X7?
- Fidelity pay for inventory during 20X7?
- Fidelity pay for income taxes during 20X7?

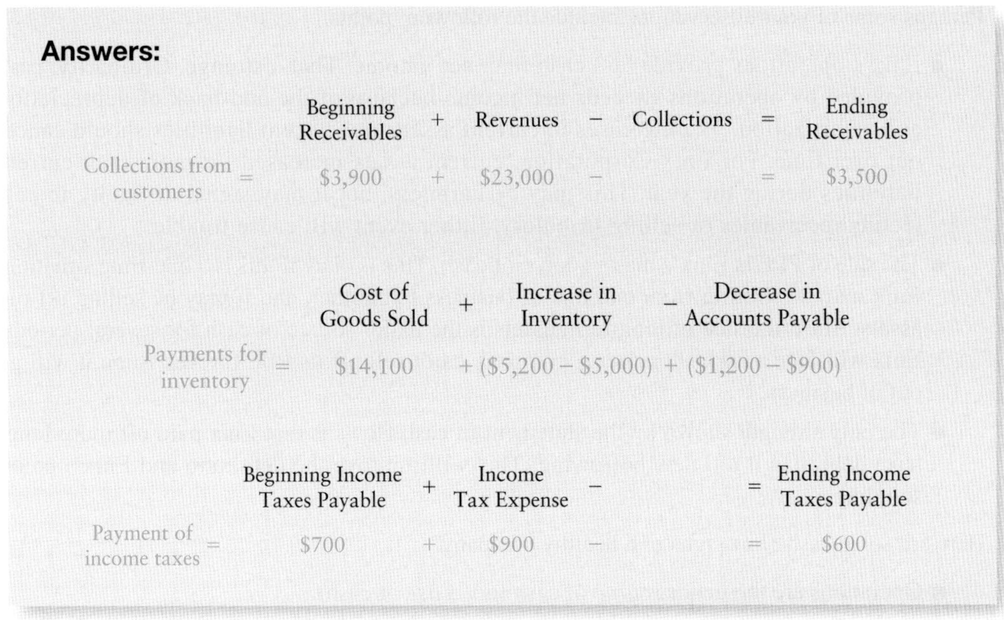

Answers:
Beginning Receivables + Revenues − Collections = Ending Receivables
Collections from customers = $3,900 + $23,000 − = $3,500
Cost of Goods Sold + Increase in Inventory − Decrease in Accounts Payable
Payments for inventory = $14,100 + ($5,200 − $5,000) + ($1,200 − $900)
Beginning Income Taxes Payable + Income Tax Expense − = Ending Income Taxes Payable
Payment of income taxes = $700 + $900 − = $600

EVALUATE A COMPANY'S ABILITY TO GENERATE CASH FLOWS

Analysts find the statement of cash flows more helpful for spotting weaknesses than for gauging successes. Why? Because a *shortage* of cash can throw a company into bankruptcy, but lots of cash doesn't ensure success. What do you think of the following statement of cash flows?

7 Evaluate a company's ability to generate cash flows

	A	B	C
1	**Enix Corporation** **Statement of Cash Flows**	**Year Ended** **June 30, 20X6**	
2	**(In millions of $)**		
3	**Operating activities:**		
4	Net income		$ 35,000
5	Adjustments for noncash items:		
6	Depreciation	$ 14,000	
7	Net increase in current assets other than cash	(24,000)	
8	Net increase in current liabilities	8,000	(2,000)
9	Net cash provided by operating activities		33,000
10	**Investing activities:**		
11	Sale of property, plant and equipment	$ 91,000	
12	Net cash provided by investing activities		91,000
13	**Financing activities:**		
14	Borrowing	$ 22,000	
15	Payment of long-term debt	(90,000)	
16	Purchase of treasury shares	(9,000)	
17	Payment of dividends	(23,000)	
18	Net cash used for financing activities		(100,000)
19	Increase (decrease) in cash		$ 24,000
20			

Perhaps some of your observations include the following points:

- Enix's operations provide less cash than net income. That's strange. Ordinarily, cash provided by operations exceeds net income because of the add-back of depreciation and amortization. The increases in current assets and current liabilities should cancel out over time. For Enix Corporation, current assets increased far more than current liabilities during the year. This may be harmless, but it may signal difficulty in collecting receivables or selling inventory. Either event will cause trouble.
- The sale of PPE is Enix's major source of cash. This is okay if this is a one-time situation. Enix may be shifting from one line of business to another, and it may be selling off old assets. But if the sale of long-term assets is the major source of cash for several periods, Enix will face a cash shortage. A company can't sell off its PPE forever. Soon it will go out of business.
- The only strength shown by the statement of cash flows is that Enix paid off more long-term debt than it did new borrowing. This will improve the debt ratio and Enix's credit standing.

Here are some cash-flow signs of a healthy company:

- Operations are the major *source* of cash (not a *use* of cash).
- Investing activities include more purchases than sales of long-term assets.
- Financing activities are not dominated by new loans and borrowings.

DECISION GUIDELINES

Evaluating Cash Flow Activities

Cash flows offer insights into how a company is performing. If you see a company exhibiting the following cash flow patterns over a few years, the explanations provided in the table may give you additional insight about the company.

CFO	CFI	CFF	Possible Explanation
+	+	+	Building up cash reserves, possibly looking for an acquisition.
+	–	–	Operating cash flow being used to buy long-term assets and reduce debt.
+	+	–	Operating cash flow and sale of long-term assets being used to pay down debt.
+	–	+	Operating cash flow and borrowed money being used to expand.
–	+	+	Operating cash flow problems covered by sale of long-term assets, borrowing, and contributions from shareholders.
–	–	+	Rapid growth through purchase of long-term assets, shortfalls in operating cash flow.
–	+	–	Sales of long-term assets is financing operating cash flow shortages.
–	–	–	Using cash reserves to sustain operating cash flow short-falls and pay creditors.

Free Cash Flow

Throughout this chapter, we have focused on cash flows from operating, investing, and financing activities. Some investors want to know how much cash a company can "free up" for new opportunities. **Free cash flow** (Fcf) is the amount of cash available from operations after paying for capital expenditures (typically investments in new PPE). Free cash flow can be computed as follows:

$$\text{Free cash flow} = \begin{array}{c}\text{Net cash provided}\\ \text{by operating activities}\end{array} - \begin{array}{c}\text{Cash payments for}\\ \text{investments in PPE}\end{array}$$

Singtel provided its free cash flow in its annual report as follows.

ADAPTED EXCERPTS FROM SINGTEL'S 2016 ANNUAL REPORT

Free Cash Flow (in $million)	2016	2015	2014
Cash flow from operations	4,648	5,787	5,350
Cash capital expenditure	(1,930)	(2,238)	(2,102)
Free Cash Flows	2,718	3,549	3,249

Source: Singtel, Annual Report, 2016, page 100.

Note that you would normally not know the amount of cash payments for capital expenditure. In such a situation, you can use the total long-term asset payments (line 13 of Singtel's statement of cash flows).

Cash Realization Ratio

One cash flow ratio that is becoming more popular is the **cash realization ratio**. This basically measures how much of net profit is reflected in actual cash generated from operations. It can be calculated as a ratio of CFO over net profit. Singtel's cash realization ratio is therefore:

$$CRR = \frac{CFO}{Net\ Profit}$$

2016	$\frac{4,648}{3,858} = 1.20$
2015	$\frac{5,787}{3,785} = 1.53$

A number greater than 1 is considered a good ability to realize cash from profits. Exhibit 11.16 shows how Singtel performed in comparison to other major companies in the telecommunication industry, such as Softbank and Telefónica. You can see that Singtel's cash-realization ratio has decreased from 1.53 in 2015 to 1.20 in 2016. It is lower than Softbank and Telefónica. While this may not be an immediate concern, a continuous decline in the cash-realization ratio would lead to deterioration in an entity's ability to generate cash.

Exhibit 11-16 | Cash Realization Comparisons

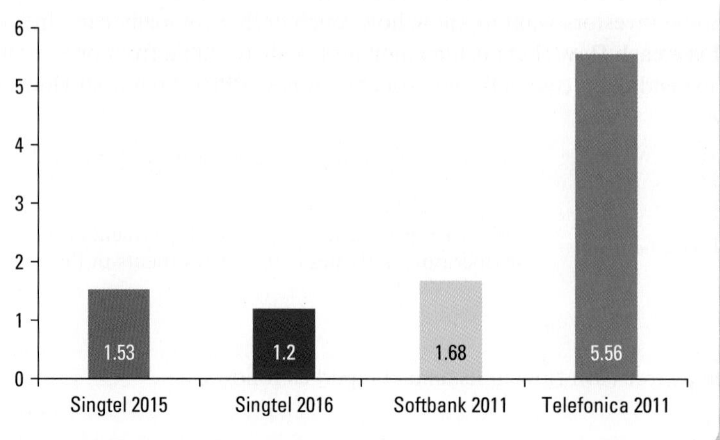

Examining Cash Flow Patterns

A company's cash flows should be examined over a period of time, not just at the end of one fiscal year. One simple but insightful cash flow analysis is to simply plot the cash flow patterns over a number of years. Exhibit 11-17 shows Singtel's cash flow patterns for the past five years. We have also plotted net profit for the years for comparison.

Exhibit 11-17 | Singtel's Cash Flow Patterns 2012–2016

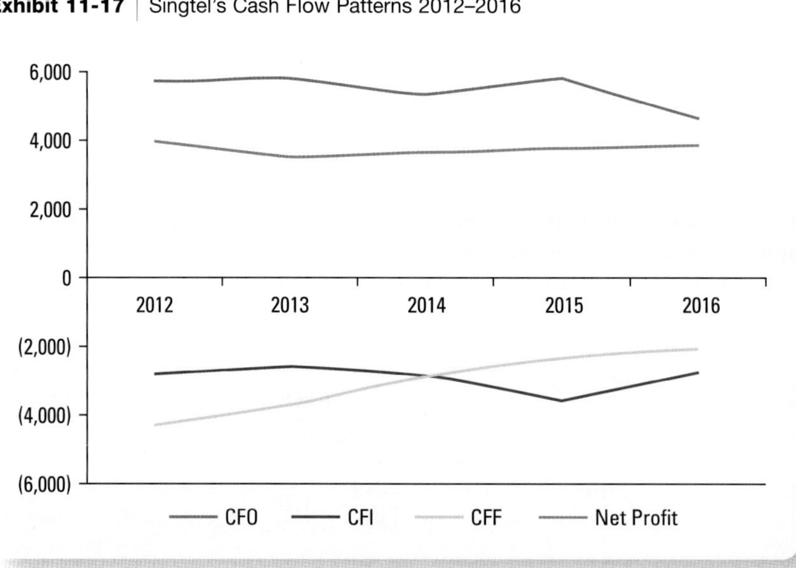

Stop & Think

What observations can you make from Singtel's cash flow patterns from X to Y?

Answers:

- There has been little growth in Singtel's net profit over the five years.
- Cash flows from operating activities are on a downward trend, from $5,710 million in 2012 to $4,648 million in 2016.
- Cash used for investing activities is stable at about $2,500 million, with the exception of 2015 when Singtel used over $3,500 million for investing activities.
- Cash used for financing activities has been getting smaller. When examined together with its dividends (which has remained relatively constant), the only other possible explanation is that Singtel has been raising funds either through borrowings or issuance of shares.

If you compare Singtel's cash flow patterns, presented in Exhibit 11-17, with a company like Vodafone, presented in Exhibit 11-18, you will see that Singtel's cash flows are more stable than Vodafone's.

Exhibit 11-18 | Vodafone's Cash Flow Patterns 2012–2016

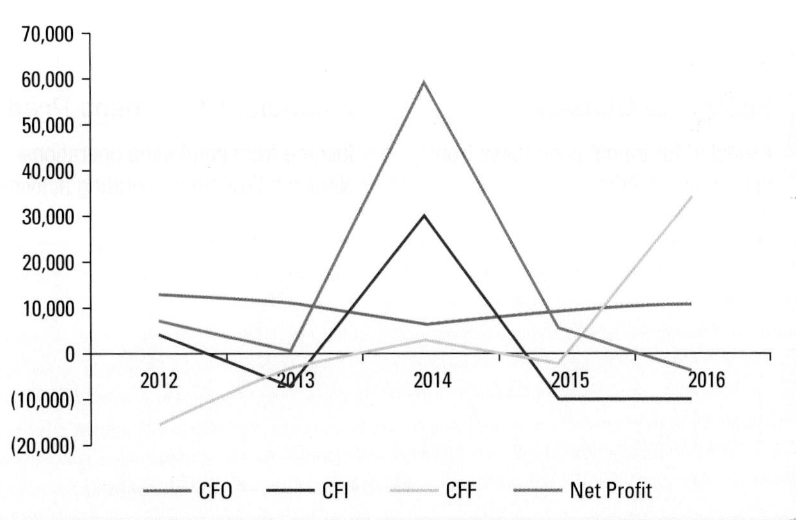

DECISION GUIDELINES

INVESTORS' AND CREDITORS' USE OF CASH-FLOW AND RELATED INFORMATION

Jan Childres is a private investor. Through years of experience she has devised some guidelines for evaluating both share investments and bond investments. Childres uses a combination of accrual-accounting data and cash-flow information. Here are her decision guidelines for both investors and creditors.

➤ INVESTORS

Questions	Factors to Consider	Financial Statement Predictor/Decision Model
1. How much in dividends can I expect to receive from an investment in shares?	Expected future net income Expected future cash balance Future dividend policy	Income from continuing operations Net cash flows from CFO, CFI, and CFF Current and past dividend policy
2. Is the share price likely to increase or decrease?	Expected future net income Expected future cash flows from operating activities	Income from continuing operations Income from continuing operations Net cash flow from operating activities
3. How much free cash does the company have at its disposal to pursue additional business opportunities?	Cash flows from operations	CFO – Capital expenditure
4. How much cash did the company generate out of its profits?	Cash Realization Ratio	$\frac{\text{CFO}}{\text{Net profit}}$

➤ CREDITORS

Question	Factor to Consider	Financial Statement Predictor
Can the company pay the interest and principal at the maturity of a loan?	Expected future net cash flows from operating activities	Income from continuing operations/ Net cash flow from operating activities

End-of-Chapter Summary Problem

Adeva Health Foods, Inc., reported the following comparative Balance Sheet and Income Statement for 20X7.

	Adeva Health Foods, Inc. Comparative Balance Sheets	December 31	
1			
2		20X7	20X6
3	Cash	$ 19,000	$ 3,000
4	Accounts receivable	22,000	23,000
5	Inventories	34,000	31,000
6	Prepaid expenses	1,000	3,000
7	Equipment, net	90,000	79,000
8	Intangible assets	9,000	9,000
9		$ 175,000	$ 148,000
10			
11	Accounts payable	$ 14,000	$ 9,000
12	Accrued liabilities	16,000	19,000
13	Income tax payable	14,000	12,000
14	Notes payable	45,000	50,000
15	Share capital	31,000	20,000
16	Retained earnings	64,000	40,000
17	Treasury share	(9,000)	(2,000)
18		$ 175,000	$ 148,000
19			

	Adeva Health Foods, Inc. Income Statement	Year Ended December 31, 20X7
1		
2	Sales revenue	$ 190,000
3	Gain on sale of equipment	6,000
4	Total revenue and gains	196,000
5	Cost of goods sold	85,000
6	Depreciation expense	19,000
7	Other operating expenses	36,000
8	Total expenses	140,000
9	Income before income tax	56,000
10	Income tax expense	18,000
11	Net income	$ 38,000
12		

Assume that Berkshire Hathaway Inc. is considering buying Adeva. Berkshire Hathaway requests the following cash-flow data for 20X7. There were no noncash investing and financing activities.

a. Collections from customers

b. Cash payments for inventory

c. Cash payments for operating expenses

d. Cash payment for income tax
e. Cash received from the sale of equipment (Adeva paid $40,000 for new equipment during the year.)
f. Issuance of shares
g. Issuance of notes payable (Adeva paid off $20,000 during the year.)
h. Cash dividends (There were no share dividends.)

Provide the requested data. Show your work.

Answers

a. Analyze Accounts Receivable (let X = Collections from customers):

Beginning	+	Sales	−	Collections	=	Ending
$23,000	+	$190,000	−	X	=	$22,000
				X	=	$191,000

b. Analyze Inventory and Accounts Payable (let X = Purchases, and let Y = Payments for inventory):

Beginning Inventory	+	Purchases	−	Ending Inventory	=	Cost of Goods Sold
$31,000	+	X	−	$34,000	=	$85,000
		X			=	$88,000

Beginning Accounts Payable	+	Purchases	−	Payments	=	Ending Accounts Payable
$9,000	+	$88,000	−	Y	=	$14,000
				Y	=	$83,000

c. Start with Other Operating Expenses, and adjust for the changes in Prepaid Expenses and Accrued Liabilities:

Other Operating Expenses	− Decrease in Prepaid Expenses	+ Decrease in Accrued Liabilities	=	Payments for Operating Expenses
$36,000	− $2,000	+ $3,000	=	$37,000

d. Analyze Income Tax Payable (let X = Payment of income tax):

Beginning	+	Income Tax Expense	−	Payments	=	Ending
$12,000	+	$18,000	−	X	=	$14,000
				X	=	$16,000

e. Analyze Equipment, Net (let X = Book value of equipment sold. Then combine with the gain or loss to compute cash received from the sale.)

Beginning	+	Acquisitions	−	Depreciation	−	Book Value Sold	=	Ending
$79,000	+	$40,000	−	$19,000	−	X	=	$90,000
						X	=	$10,000

Cash Received from Sale	=	Book Value Sold	+	Gain on Sale
$16,000	=	$10,000	+	$6,000

f. Analyze Share Capital (let X = Issuance) of shares

Beginning	+	Issuance	=	Ending
$20,000	+	X	=	$31,000
		X	=	$11,000

g. Analyze Notes Payable (let X = Issuance) of notes payable:

Beginning	+	Issuance	−	Payment	=	Ending
$50,000	+	X	−	$20,000	=	$45,000
		X			=	$15,000

h. Analyze Retained Earnings (let X = Dividends) payments

Beginning	+	Net Income	−	Dividends	=	Ending
$40,000	+	$38,000	−	X	=	$64,000
				X	=	$14,000

REVIEW | Statement of Cash Flows

Quick Check (Answers are given at the end of the chapter.)

1. All of the following activities are reported on the statement of cash flows except

a. financing activities.
b. operating activities.
c. investing activities.
d. marketing activities.

2. Activities that create long-term liabilities are usually

a. noncash investing and financing activities.
b. investing activities.
c. financing activities.
d. operating activities.

3. Activities affecting long-term assets are

a. marketing activities.
b. financing activities.
c. investing activities.
d. marketing activities.

4. In 20X6, PMW Corporation borrowed $120,000, paid dividends of $35,000, issued 10,000 shares for $46 per share, purchased land for $250,000, and received dividends of $20,000. Net income was $160,000, and depreciation for the year totaled $8,000. How much should be reported as net cash provided by operating activities by the indirect method?
   a. $205,000
   b. $168,000
   c. $230,000
   d. $152,000

5. Activities that obtain the cash needed to launch and sustain a company are
   a. investing activities.
   b. financing activities.
   c. marketing activities.
   d. income activities.

6. The exchange of shares for land
   a. would be reported as noncash investing and financing activities.
   b. would be reported as financing activities.
   c. would not be reported on the statement of cash flows.
   d. would be reported as investing activities.

Use the following Montana Company information for questions 7–10.

Net income	$50,000	Increase in accounts payable	$ 10,000
Depreciation expense	12,000	Acquisition of equipment	35,000
Payment of dividends	2,000	Sale of treasury shares	4,000
Increase in accounts receivable	9,000	Payment of long-term debt	16,000
Collection of long-term notes receivable	6,000	Proceeds from sale of land	42,000
Loss on sale of land	15,000	Decrease in inventories	3,000

7. Under the indirect method, net cash provided by operating activities would be
   a. $81,000.
   b. $73,000.
   c. $79,000.
   d. $57,000.

8. Net cash provided by (used for) investing activities would be
   a. $(1,000).
   b. $(13,000).
   c. $1,000.
   d. $13,000.

9. Net cash provided by (used for) financing activities would be
   a. $(14,000).
   b. $(18,000).
   c. $14,000.
   d. $2,000.

10. The cost of land
    a. must have been $42,000.
    b. must have been $57,000.
    c. must have been $27,000.
    d. cannot be determined from the data given.

11. Sweet Treat Ice Cream began the year with $80,000 in accounts receivable and ended the year with $60,000 in accounts receivable. If sales for the year were $700,000; the cash collected from customers during the year amounted to
    a. $760,000.
    b. $700,000.
    c. $720,000.
    d. $680,000.

12. Nassau Farms, Ltd., made sales of $760,000 and had cost of goods sold of $410,000. Inventory decreased by $10,000 and accounts payable decreased by $12,000. Operating expenses were $180,000. How much was Nassau Farms's net income for the year?
   a. $172,000
   b. $170,000
   c. $168,000
   d. $350,000

13. Use the Nassau Farms data from question 12. How much cash did Nassau Farms pay for inventory during the year?
   a. $410,000
   b. $400,000
   c. $422,000
   d. $412,000

Accounting Vocabulary

cash equivalents (p. 633) Highly liquid short-term investments that can be converted into cash immediately.

cash flows (p. 633) Cash receipts and cash payments (disbursements).

cash realization ratio (p. 659) An entity's ability to generate cash from net or operating profit. Calculated as cash flows from operations divided by net profit.

direct method (p. 637) Format of the operating activities section of the statement of cash flows; lists the major categories of operating cash receipts (collections from customers and receipts of interest and dividends) and cash disbursements (payments to suppliers, to employees, for interest and income taxes).

financing activities (p. 636) Activities that obtain from investors and creditors the cash needed to launch and sustain the business; a section of the statement of cash flows.

free cash flow (p. 659) The amount of cash available from operations after paying for capital expenditures such as investments in PPE.

indirect method (p. 637) Format of the operating activities section of the statement of cash flows; starts with net income and reconciles to cash flows from operating activities.

investing activities (p. 636) Activities that increase or decrease the long-term assets available to the business; a section of the statement of cash flows.

operating activities (p. 635) Activities that create revenue or expense in the entity's major line of business; a section of the statement of cash flows. Operating activities affect the Income Statement.

statement of cash flows (p. 633) Reports cash receipts and cash payments classified according to the entity's major activities: operating, investing, and financing.

ASSESS YOUR PROGRESS

Short Exercises

S11-1. ***(Learning Objectives 1, 2, 3: Explaining the purposes of the statement of cash flows)*** State how the statement of cash flows helps investors and creditors perform each of the following functions:

LO 1 2 3

   a. Predict future cash flows.
   b. Evaluate management decisions.

S11-2. ***(Learning Objectives 1, 2, 3: Explaining the purposes of the statement of cash flows)*** Fondue Ltd. has experienced an unbroken string of nine years of growth in net income. Nevertheless, the company is facing bankruptcy. Creditors are calling all of Fondue's loans for immediate payment, and the cash is simply not available. It is clear that the company's top managers overemphasized profits and gave too little attention to cash flows.

LO 1 2 3
■ **writing assignment**

Requirement

1. Write a brief memo, in your own words, to explain to the managers of Fondue Ltd. the purposes of the statement of cash flows.

LO 3

S11-3. *(Learning Objective 3: Evaluating operating cash flows—indirect method)* Examine the statement of cash flows of Watches, Inc.

A1

	A	B	C
1	**Watches, Inc.** **Consolidated Statement of Cash Flows (Adapted; in millions)**	**Year Ended December 31, 20X6**	
2	**Cash flows from operating activities:**		
3	Net income	$ 983	
4	Adjustment to reconcile net income to net cash		
5	provided by operating activities:		
6	Depreciation and amortization	278	
7	Change in assets and liabilities, net of acquired businesses:		
8	Accounts receivable	(587)	
9	Other current assets	(200)	
10	Accounts payable	(98)	
11	Accrued expenses and other liabilities	(298)	
12	Unearned revenue	31	
13	Income taxes payable	(333)	
14	Other, net	33	
15	Net cash used in operating activities		(191)
16	**Cash flows from investing activities:**		
17	Purchase of property and equipment	$ (1,991)	
18	Purchase of investments	(26,603)	
19	Sale of investments	24,108	
20	Acquisitions of other companies	(454)	
21	Net cash used in investing activities		(4,940)
22	**Cash flows from financing activities**		
23	Proceeds from the issuance of shares, net	$ 1,043	
24	Other, net	473	
25	Net cash provided by financing activities		1,516
26	Other, net		22
27	Net increase (decrease) in cash and cash equivalents		(3,593)
28	Cash and cash equivalents at beginning of year		5,194
29	Cash and cash equivalents at end of year		$ 1,601
30			

Suppose Watches' operating activities *provided*, rather than *used*, cash. Identify three things under the indirect method that could cause operating cash flows to be positive.

LO 1 2
■ writing assignment

S11-4. *(Learning Objectives 1, 2: Using cash-flow data to evaluate performance)* Top managers of Tranquility Inns are reviewing company performance for 20X6. The Income Statement reports a 25% increase in net income over 20X5. However, most of the increase resulted from an exceptional gain from a lawsuit Tranquility Inns has last won against a competitor. The Balance Sheet shows a large increase in receivables. The cash flows statement, in summarized form, reports the following:

Net cash used for operating activities	$(60,000)
Net cash provided by investing activities	40,000
Net cash provided by financing activities	35,000
Increase in cash during 20X6	$ 15,000

Requirement

1. Write a memo giving Tranquility Inns's managers your assessment of 20X6 operations and your outlook for the future. Focus on the information content of the cash flow data.

LO 3

S11-5. *(Learning Objective 3: Reporting cash flows from operating activities—indirect method)* Beautiful Atlantic Transportation (BAT) began 20X6 with accounts receivable, inventory, and prepaid expenses totaling $59,000. At the end of the year, BAT had a total of $56,000 for these current assets. At the beginning of 20X6, BAT owed current liabilities of $21,000, and at year-end current liabilities totaled $33,000.

Net income for the year was $13,000. Included in net income were a $3,000 loss on the sale of land and a depreciation expense of $9,000.

Show how BAT should report cash flows from operating activities for 20X6. BAT uses the *indirect* method.

S11-6. ***(Learning Objectives 2, 3: Identifying items for reporting cash flows from operations—indirect method)*** Cocoa Clinic, Inc., is preparing its statement of cash flows (*indirect* method) for the year ended March 31, 20X6. Consider the following items in preparing the company's statement of cash flows. Identify each item as an operating activity—addition to net income (O+) or subtraction from net income (O−)—an investing activity (I), a financing activity (F), or an activity that is not used to prepare the cash flow statement by the indirect method (N). Place the appropriate symbol in the blank space.

	a. Decrease in accrued liabilities
	b. Issuance of shares
	c. Gain on sale of building
	d. Loss on sale of land
	e. Depreciation expense
	f. Increase in inventory
	g. Decrease in accounts receivable
	h. Increase in accounts payable
	i. Purchase of equipment
	j. Decrease of prepaid expense
	k. Collection of cash from customers
	l. Net income
	m. Retained earnings
	n. Payment of dividends

LO 3

S11-7. ***(Learning Objective 3: Computing operating cash flows—indirect method)*** Ether Corporation accountants have assembled the following data for the year ended June 30, 20X6.

Net income	$?	Cost of goods sold	$117,000
Payment of dividends	5,700	Other operating expenses	34,000
Proceeds from the issuance of shares	27,000	Purchase of equipment	44,000
Sales revenue	230,000	Increase in current liabilities	8,000
Decrease in current assets other than cash	36,000	Payment of note payable	32,000
Purchase of treasury shares	7,000	Proceeds from sale of land	29,000
		Depreciation expense	12,000

Prepare the *operating activities section* of Ether's statement of cash flows for the year ended June 30, 20X6. Ether uses the *indirect* method for operating cash flows.

LO 3 4 5

S11-8. ***(Learning Objectives 3, 4, 5: Preparing a statement of cash flows—indirect method)*** Use the data in Short Exercise 11-7 to prepare Ether Corporation's statement of cash flows for the year ended June 30, 20X6. Ether uses the *indirect* method for operating activities.

LO 4

S11-9. ***(Learning Objective 4: Computing investing cash flows)*** Motorsports of Madrid, Inc., reported the following financial statements for 20X6:

	Motorsports of Madrid, Inc. Income Statement	Year Ended December 31, 20X6
2	**(In thousands)**	
3	Service revenue	$ 800
4	Cost of goods sold	340
5	Salary expense	50
6	Depreciation expense	40
7	Other expenses	180
8	Total expenses	610
9	Net income	$ 190

	Motorsports of Madrid Comparative Balance Sheets	December 31, 20X6 and 20X5				
2	**(In thousands)**					
3	**Assets**	**20X6**	**20X5**	**Liabilities**	**20X6**	**20X5**
4	Current:			Current:		
5	Cash	$ 28	$ 11	Accounts payable	$ 48	$ 43
6	Accounts receivable	54	43	Salary payable	26	24
7	Inventory	77	89	Accrued liabilities	16	19
8	Prepaid expenses	6	5	Long-term notes payable	69	54
9	Long-term investments	54	79			
10	PPE, net	229	188	**Shareholders' Equity**		
11				Share capital	48	38
12				Retained earnings	241	237
13	Total	$ 448	$ 415	Total	$ 448	$ 415

Compute the following investing cash flows (enter all amounts in thousands):

a. Acquisitions of PPE (all were for cash). Motorsports of Madrid sold no PPE.

b. Proceeds from the sale of investments. Motorsports of Madrid purchased no investments.

LO 5

S11-10. ***(Learning Objective 5: Computing financing cash flows)*** Use the Motorsports of Madrid data in Short Exercise 11-9 to compute the following (enter all amounts in thousands):

a. New borrowing or payment of long-term notes payable. Motorsports of Madrid had only one long-term note payable transaction during the year.

b. Issuance of share capital or retirement of shares. Motorsports of Madrid had only one share capital transaction during the year.

c. Payment of cash dividends (same as dividends declared).

LO 6

S11-11. ***(Learning Objective 6: Computing operating cash flows—direct method)*** Use the Motorsports of Madrid data in Short Exercise 11-9 to compute the following (enter all amounts in thousands):

a. Collections from customers

b. Payments for inventory

LO 6

S11-12. ***(Learning Objective 6: Computing operating cash flows—direct method)*** Use the Motorsports of Madrid data in Short Exercise 11-9 to compute the following (enter all amounts in thousands):

a. Payments to employees

b. Payments of other expenses

LO 4 5 6 7

S11-13. ***(Learning Objectives 4, 5, 6, 7: Preparing and analyzing a statement of cash flows—direct method)*** Horse Heaven Farm began 20X6 with cash of $180,000. During the year, Horse Heaven earned service revenue of $600,000 and collected $480,000 from customers. Expenses for the year totaled $330,000, with $300,000 paid in cash to suppliers and employees. Horse Heaven also paid $138,000 to purchase equipment and a cash dividend of $47,000 to shareholders. During 20X6, Horse Heaven borrowed $25,000 by issuing a note payable. Prepare the company's statement of cash flows for the year. Format operating activities by the *direct* method. Calculate Horse's free cash flow and cash realization ratio.

S11-14. ***(Learning Objective 6: Computing operating cash flows—direct method)*** Middleton Golf Club has assembled the following data for the year ended September 30, 20X6: LO 6

Cost of goods sold	$105,000	Payment of dividends	$ 8,000
Payments to suppliers	90,000	Proceeds from issuance of shares	18,000
Purchase of equipment	43,000	Sales revenue	214,000
Payments to employees	75,000	Collections from customers	204,000
Payment of note payable	16,000	Payment of income tax	15,000
Proceeds from sale of land	62,000	Purchase of treasury shares	5,800
Depreciation expense	7,000		

Prepare the *operating activities section* of Middleton Golf Club's statement of cash flows for the year ended September 30, 20X6. Middleton uses the *direct* method for operating cash flows.

S11-15. ***(Learning Objectives 4, 5, 6, 7: Preparing and analyzing a statement of cash flows—direct method)*** Use the data in Short Exercise 11-14 to prepare Middleton Golf Club's statement of cash flows for the year ended September 30, 20X6. Middleton uses the *direct* method for operating activities. Calculate Middleton's free cash flow and cash realization ratio. LO 4 5 6 7

Exercises MyLab Accounting

Select A and B exercises can be found within MyLab Accounting, an online homework and practice environment. Your instructor may ask you to complete select exercises using MyLab Accounting.

Group A

E11-16A. ***(Learning Objectives 2, 3: Identifying activities for the statement of cash flows—indirect method)*** Cooper-Fowler Investments specializes in low-risk government bonds. Identify each of Cooper-Fowler's transactions as operating (O), investing (I), financing (F), noncash investing and financing (NIF), or a transaction that is not reported on the statement of cash flows (N). Indicate whether each item increases (+) or decreases (−) cash. The *indirect* method is used for operating activities. LO 2 3

	a. Net income
	b. Payment of long-term debt
	c. Accrual of salary expense
	d. Cash sale of land
	e. Purchase of long-term investment
	f. Acquisition of building by cash payment
	g. Purchase of treasury shares
	h. Issuance of shares for cash
	i. Decrease in accrued liabilities
	j. Depreciation of equipment
	k. Sale of long-term investment
	l. Issuance of long-term note payable to borrow cash
	m. Increase in prepaid expenses
	n. Payment of cash dividend
	o. Loss on sale of equipment
	p. Decrease in merchandise inventory
	q. Acquisition of equipment by issuance of note payable
	r. Increase in accounts payable
	s. Amortization of intangible assets

LO 2 3

E11-17A. ***(Learning Objectives 2, 3: Classifying transactions for the statement of cash flows—indirect method)*** Indicate whether each of the following transactions records an operating activity, an investing activity, a financing activity, or a noncash investing and financing activity.

	A	B	C	D	E	F	G	H
1	a.	Cash	50,000		g.	Depreciation expense	11,000	
2		Accounts receivable	8,000			Accumulated		11,000
3		Service revenue		58,000	h.	Treasury shares	7,800	
4	b.	Bonds Payable	46,000			Cash		7,800
5		Cash		46,000	i.	Land	84,000	
6	c.	Cash	74,000			Cash		84,000
7		Share capital		10,000	j.	Equipment	18,000	
8		Capital in excess of par		64,000		Cash		18,000
9	d.	Dividends payable	17,200		k.	Salary expense	23,000	
10		Cash		17,200		Cash		23,000
11	e.	Loss on disposal of equipment	1,200		l.	Furniture and fixtures	24,200	
12		Equipment, net		1,200		Cash		24,200
13	f.	Cash	6,800		m.	Building	158,000	
14		Long-term investment		6,800		Note payable, long-term		158,000
15								

LO 3

■ **writing assignment**

E11-18A. ***(Learning Objective 3: Computing cash flows from operating activities—indirect method)*** The accounting records of North East Distributors, Inc., reveal the following:

Net income	$39,000	Depreciation	$18,000
Collection of dividend revenue	7,900	Decrease in current liabilities	19,000
Payment of interest	12,000	Increase in current assets	
Sales revenue	14,000	other than cash	25,000
Loss on sale of land	23,000	Payment of dividends	7,800
Acquisition of land	43,000	Payment of income tax	15,000

Requirement

1. Compute cash flows from operating activities by the *indirect* method. Use the format of the operating activities section of Exhibit 11-6. Also evaluate the operating cash flow of North East Distributors. Give the reason for your evaluation.

LO 3

E11-19A. ***(Learning Objective 3: Computing cash flows from operating activities—indirect method)*** The accounting records of Abundant Fruit Traders include these accounts:

Cash

Debit		Credit	
May 1	90,000		
Receipts	440,000	Payments	445,000
May 31	85,000		

Accounts Receivable

Debit		Credit	
May 1	1,000		
Receipts	540,000	Collections	440,000
May 31	101,000		

Inventory

Debit		Credit	
May 1	3,000		
Purchases	438,000	Cost of sales	336,000
May 31	105,000		

Equipment

Debit		Credit	
May 1	185,000		
Acquisition	5,000		
May 31	190,000		

Accumulated Deprec.—Equipment

Debit		Credit	
		May 1	55,000
		Depreciation	5,000
		May 31	60,000

Accounts Payable

Debit		Credit	
		May 1	14,500
Payments	327,000	Purchases	438,000
		May 31	125,500

Accrued Liabilities

Debit		Credit	
		May 1	19,000
Payments	32,000	Receipts	26,000
		May 31	13,000

Retained Earnings

Debit		Credit	
Quarterly		May 1	63,000
Dividend	16,000	Net Income	20,000
		May 31	67,000

Requirement

1. Compute Abundant's net cash provided by (used for) operating activities during May. Use the *indirect* method. Does Abundant have trouble collecting receivables or selling inventory? How can you tell?

E11-20A. *(Learning Objectives 3, 4, 5, 7: Preparing and analyzing the statement of cash flows—indirect method)* The Income Statement and additional data of Newbury Travel Products, Inc., follow:

	A	B	C
1	**Newbury Travel Products, Inc.** **Income Statement**	**Year Ended** **December 31, 20X6**	
2	Revenues:		
3	Service revenue	$ 283,000	
4	Dividend revenue	8,000	$ 291,000
5	Expenses:		
6	Cost of goods sold	103,000	
7	Salary expense	78,000	
8	Depreciation expense	26,000	
9	Advertising expense	4,500	
10	Interest expense	2,600	
11	Income tax expense	8,000	222,100
12	Net income		$ 68,900
13			

Additional data:

a. Acquisition of PPE was $222,000. Of this amount, $170,000 was paid in cash and $52,000 by signing a note payable.
b. Proceeds from sale of land totaled $28,000.
c. Proceeds from issuance of shares totaled $90,000.
d. Payment of a long-term note payable was $18,000.
e. Payment of dividends was $13,000.
f. From the Balance Sheets:

	A	B	C
1		**December 31**	
2		**20X6**	**20X5**
3	**Current assets:**		
4	Cash	$ 30,000	$ 10,800
5	Accounts receivable	42,000	59,000
6	Inventory	30,000	91,000
7	Prepaid expenses	9,400	8,700
8			
9	**Current liabilities:**		
10	Accounts payable	$ 38,000	$ 27,000
11	Accrued liabilities	18,000	99,000
12			

Requirements

1. Prepare Newbury's statement of cash flows for the year ended December 31, 20X6, using the *indirect* method.
2. Evaluate Newbury's cash flows for the year, including its free cash flow and cash realization ratio. In your evaluation, review all three categories of cash flows and give the reason for your evaluation.

LO 3 4 5

E11-21A. ***(Learning Objectives 3, 4, 5: Interpreting a statement of cash flows—indirect method)*** Donald is reviewing his nephews' cash flows. Huey, Dewey, and Louie all report the same income number ($22,000) and bought the same equipment ($84,000) during the year. Explain how Huey, Dewey, and Louie fund their respective PPE purchase. Whose cash flow would you rate as the best? The worst?

	A	B	C	D
1		**Huey**	**Dewey**	**Louie**
2	Cash flows from operating activities			
3	Net income	$ 22,000	$ 22,000	$ 22,000
4	Depreciation and amortization	10,000	10,000	10,000
5	Increase in current assets	(23,000)	(3,000)	(12,000)
6	Decrease in current liabilities	(12,000)	(5,000)	(2,000)
7		(3,000)	24,000	18,000
8	Cash flows from investing activities:			
9	Acquisition of PPE	(84,000)	(84,000)	(84,000)
10	Sales of PPE	10,000	38,000	90,000
11		(74,000)	(46,000)	6,000
12	Cash flows from financing activities:			
13	Issuance of shares	98,000	63,000	16,000
14	Payment of debt	(22,000)	(38,000)	(24,000)
15		76,000	25,000	(8,000)
16	Net increase (decrease) in cash	$ (1,000)	$ 3,000	$ 16,000
17				

LO 4 5

E11-22A. ***(Learning Objectives 4, 5: Computing investing and financing amounts for the statement of cash flows)*** Compute the following items for the statement of cash flows:

a. Beginning and ending PPE, Net, are $112,000 and $106,000, respectively. Depreciation for the period was $10,000, and purchases of new PPE were $34,000. PPE were sold at a $4,000 loss. What were the cash proceeds of the sale?

b. Beginning and ending Retained Earnings are $48,000 and $74,000, respectively. Net income for the period was $59,000, and share dividends were $8,000. How much were cash dividends?

LO 6

■ **writing assignment**

E11-23A. ***(Learning Objective 6: Computing cash flows from operating activities—direct method)*** The accounting records of Princeton Pharmaceuticals, Inc., reveal the following:

Payment of salaries and wages	$36,000	Net income	$64,000
Depreciation	20,000	Payment of income tax	25,000
Decrease in current liabilities	23,000	Collection of dividend revenue	12,000
Increase in current assets other than cash	24,000	Payment of interest	18,000
Payment of dividends	8,000	Cash sales	34,000
Collection of accounts receivable	50,000	Loss on sale of land	5,000
		Acquisition of land	38,000
		Payment of accounts payable	59,000

Requirement

1. Compute cash flows from operating activities by the *direct* method. Also evaluate Princeton's operating cash flow. Give the reason for your evaluation.

LO 4 5 6

E11-24A. ***(Learning Objectives 4, 5, 6: Identifying items for the statement of cash flows—direct method)*** Selected accounts of Avril Antiques show the following:

Salary Payable

		Beginning balance	10,000
Payments	30,000	Salary expense	28,000
		Ending balance	8,000

Buildings

Beginning balance	80,000	Depreciation	20,000
Acquisitions	120,000	Book value of building sold	119,000*
Ending balance	61,000		

*Sale price was 150,000.

Notes Payable

		Beginning balance	234,000
Payments	67,000	Issuance of note payable for cash	74,000
		Ending balance	241,000

Requirement

1. For each account, identify the item or items that should appear on a statement of cash flows prepared by the *direct* method. State where to report the item.

LO 4 5 6 7 ■ writing assignment

E11-25A. ***(Learning Objectives 4, 5, 6, 7: Preparing and analyzing the statement of cash flows—direct method)*** The Income Statement and additional data of Cobbs Hill, Inc., follow:

	A	B	C
1	**Cobbs Hill, Inc.** **Income Statement**	**Year Ended** **April 30, 20X6**	
2	**Revenues:**		
3	Sales revenue	$ 232,000	
4	Dividend revenue	11,000	$ 243,000
5	**Expenses:**		
6	Cost of goods sold	108,000	
7	Salary expense	46,000	
8	Depreciation expense	31,000	
9	Advertising expense	11,500	
10	Interest expense	2,100	
11	Income tax expense	9,000	207,600
12	Net income		$ 35,400
13			

Additional data:

a. Collections from customers are $14,000 more than sales.
b. Payments to suppliers are $1,500 less than the sum of cost of goods sold plus advertising expense.
c. Payments to employees are $3,000 more than salary expense.
d. Dividend income, interest expense, and income tax expense equal their cash amounts.
e. Acquisition of PPE is $145,000. Of this amount, $100,000 is paid in cash and $45,000 by signing a note payable.
f. Proceeds from sale of land total $30,000.
g. Proceeds from issuance of shares total $94,000.
h. Payment of long-term note payable is $18,000.
i. Payment of dividends is $9,500.
j. Cash balance, April 30, 20X5, was $20,000.

Requirements

1. Prepare Cobbs Hill, Inc.'s statement of cash flows and accompanying schedule of noncash investing and financing activities. Report operating activities by the *direct* method.
2. Evaluate Cobbs Hill's cash flows for the year, including its free cash flow and cash realization ratio. In your evaluation, review all three categories of cash flows and give the reason for your evaluation.

LO 4 5 6

E11-26A. ***(Learning Objectives 4, 5, 6: Computing amounts for the statement of cash flows—direct method)*** Compute the following items for the statement of cash flows:

a. Beginning and ending Accounts Receivable are $25,000 and $21,000, respectively. Credit sales for the period total $63,000. How much are cash collections from customers?

b. Cost of goods sold is $78,000. Beginning Inventory was $27,000, and ending Inventory balance is $29,000. Beginning and ending Accounts Payable are $11,000 and $8,000, respectively. How much are cash payments for inventory?

Group B

LO 2 3

E11-27B. ***(Learning Objectives 2, 3: Identifying activities for the statement of cash flows—indirect method)*** Rogers-Carter Investments specializes in low-risk government bonds. Identify each of Rogers-Carter's transactions as operating (O), investing (I), financing (F), noncash investing and financing (NIF), or a transaction that is not reported on the statement of cash flows (N). Indicate whether each item increases (+) or decreases (−) cash. The *indirect* method is used for operating activities.

	a. Sale of long-term investment
	b. Issuance of shares for cash
	c. Increase in accounts payable
	d. Amortization of intangible assets
	e. Loss on sale of equipment
	f. Payment of long-term debt
	g. Cash sale of land
	h. Purchase of treasury shares
	i. Net income
	j. Acquisition of building by cash payment
	k. Decrease in merchandise inventory
	l. Depreciation of equipment
	m. Decrease in accrued liabilities
	n. Payment of cash dividend
	o. Purchase of long-term investment
	p. Issuance of long-term note payable to borrow cash
	q. Increase in prepaid expenses
	r. Accrual of salary expense
	s. Acquisition of equipment by issuance of note payable

LO 2 3

E11-28B. ***(Learning Objectives 2, 3: Classifying transactions for the statement of cash flows—indirect method)*** Indicate whether each of the following transactions records an operating activity, an investing activity, a financing activity, or a noncash investing and financing activity.

	A	B	C	D	E	F	G	H
1	a.	Equipment	15,700		h.	Cash	85,000	
2		Cash		15,700		Share capital		15,000
3	b.	Dividends payable	18,200			Capital in excess of par		70,000
4		Cash		18,200	i.	Furniture and fixtures	25,500	
5	c.	Salary expense	19,500			Cash		25,500
6		Cash		19,500	j.	Cash	71,000	
7	d.	Building	145,000			Accounts receivable	16,000	
8		Note payable, long-term		145,000		Service revenue		87,000
9	e.	Dividends payable	17,300		k.	Cash	9,200	
10		Cash		17,300		Long-term investment		9,200
11	f.	Depreciation expense	8,000		l.	Loss on disposal of equipment	1,400	
12		Accumulated depreciation		8,000		Equipment, net		1,400
13	g.	Bonds payable	48,000		m.	Land	20,400	
14		Cash		48,000		Cash		20,400
15								

E11-29B. ***(Learning Objective 3: Computing cash flows from operating activities—indirect method)*** The accounting records of Central Distributors, Inc., reveal the following:

LO 3
■ writing assignment

Net income	€41,000	Depreciation	€16,000
Collection of dividend revenue	6,800	Increase in current liabilities	24,000
Payment of interest	15,000	Decrease in current assets other than cash	29,000
Sales revenue	13,000	Payment of dividends	7,100
Loss on sale of land	18,000	Payment of income tax	12,000
Acquisition of land	44,000		

Requirement

1. Compute cash flows from operating activities by the *indirect* method. Use the format of the operating activities section of Exhibit 11-6. Also evaluate the operating cash flow of Central Distributors. Give the reason for your evaluation.

E11-30B. ***(Learning Objective 3: Computing cash flows from operating activities—indirect method)*** The accounting records of Finest Fruit Traders include these accounts:

LO 3

Cash

Oct 1	11,000		
Receipts	537,000	Payments	446,000
Oct 31	102,000		

Accounts Receivable

Oct 1	8,000		
Receipts	538,000	Collections	537,000
Oct 31	9,000		

Inventory

Oct 1	4,000		
Purchases	437,000	Cost of sales	434,000
Oct 31	7,000		

Equipment

Oct 1	188,000		
Acquisition	7,000		
Oct 31	195,000		

Accumulated Deprec.—Equipment

		Oct 1	52,000
		Depreciation	9,000
		Oct 31	61,000

Accounts Payable

		Oct 1	14,000
Payments	328,000	Purchases	437,000
		Oct 31	123,000

Accrued Liabilities

		Oct 1	12,000
Payments	28,000	Receipts	22,000
		Oct 31	6,000

Retained Earnings

		Oct 1	66,000
Quarterly Dividend	18,000	Net Income	35,000
		Oct 31	83,000

Requirement

1. Compute Finest's net cash provided by (used for) operating activities during October. Use the *indirect* method. Does Finest have trouble collecting receivables or selling inventory? How can you tell?

■ writing assignment

E11-31B. *(Learning Objectives 3, 4, 5, 7: Preparing and analyzing the statement of cash flows—indirect method)* The Income Statement and additional data of Norton Travel Products, Inc., follow:

	A	B	C
1	Norton Travel Products, Inc. Income Statement	Year Ended December 31, 20X6	
2	**Revenues:**		
3	Service revenue	€ 235,000	
4	Dividend revenue	8,300	€ 243,300
5	**Expenses:**		
6	Cost of goods sold	102,000	
7	Salary expense	62,000	
8	Depreciation expense	33,000	
9	Advertising expense	4,300	
10	Interest expense	2,400	
11	Income tax expense	7,000	210,700
12	Net income		€ 32,600
13			

Additional data:

a. Acquisition of PPE was €180,000. Of this amount, €145,000 was paid in cash and €35,000 by signing a note payable.
b. Proceeds from sale of land totaled €49,000.
c. Proceeds from issuance of shares totaled €34,000.
d. Payment of long-term note payable was €16,000.
e. Payment of dividends was €9,000.
f. From the Balance Sheets:

	A	B	C
1		December 31	
2		20X6	20X5
3	**Current Assets:**		
4	Cash	€ 32,000	€ 13,300
5	Accounts receivable	41,000	57,000
6	Inventory	48,000	87,000
7	Prepaid expenses	9,100	8,200
8			
9	**Current Liabilities:**		
10	Accounts payable	€ 32,000	€ 17,000
11	Accrued liabilities	14,000	43,000
12			

Requirements

1. Prepare Norton's statement of cash flows for the year ended December 31, 20X6, using the *indirect* method.
2. Evaluate Norton's cash flows for the year, including its free cash flow and cash realization ratio. In your evaluation, review all three categories of cash flows and give the reason for your evaluation.

E11-32B. *(Learning Objectives 3, 4, 5: Interpreting a statement of cash flows—indirect method)* Daisy is reviewing her nieces' cash flows. April, May, and June all report the same income number (€12,000) and bought the same equipment (€98,000) during the year. Explain how April, May, and June fund their respective PPE purchase. Whose cash flow would you rate as the best? The worst?

	A	B	C	D
1		April	May	June
2	Cash flows from operating activities			
3	Net income	€ 12,000	€ 12,000	€ 12,000
4	Depreciation and amortization	14,000	14,000	14,000
5	Increase in current assets	2,000	(8,000)	3,000
6	Decrease in current liabilities	3,000	(20,000)	4,000
7		31,000	(2,000)	33,000
8	Cash flows from investing activities:			
9	Acquisition of PPE	(98,000)	(98,000)	(98,000)
10	Sales of PPE	105,000	20,000	30,000
11		7,000	(78,000)	(68,000)
12	Cash flows from financing activities:			
13	Issuance of shares	18,000	106,000	74,000
14	Payment of debt	(26,000)	(20,000)	(35,000)
15		(8,000)	86,000	39,000
16	Net increase (decrease) in cash	€ 30,000	€ 6,000	€ 4,000
17				

E11-33B. ***(Learning Objectives 4, 5: Computing investing and financing amounts for the statement of cash flows)*** Compute the following items for the statement of cash flows: LO 4 5

a. Beginning and ending PPE, Net, are €102,000 and €98,000, respectively. Depreciation for the period was €13,000, and purchases of new PPE were €30,000. PPE were sold at a €6,000 gain. What were the cash proceeds of the sale?

b. Beginning and ending Retained Earnings are €46,000 and €70,000, respectively. Net income for the period was €49,000, and share dividends were €10,000. How much were cash dividends?

E11-34B. ***(Learning Objective 6: Computing cash flows from operating activities—direct method)*** The accounting records of One Stop Pharmaceuticals, Inc., reveal the following: LO 6 ■ **writing assignment**

Payment of salaries and wages	€40,000	Net income	€25,000
Depreciation	18,000	Payment of income tax	9,000
Increase in current liabilities	10,000	Collection of dividend revenue	8,000
Increase in current assets other than cash	33,000	Payment of interest	14,000
Payment of dividends	7,000	Cash sales	36,000
Collection of accounts receivable	80,000	Gain on sale of land	6,000
		Acquisition of land	35,000
		Payment of accounts payable	52,000

Requirement

1. Compute cash flows from operating activities by the *direct* method. Also evaluate One Stop's operating cash flow. Give the reason for your evaluation.

E11-35B. ***(Learning Objectives 4, 5, 6: Identifying items for the statement of cash flows—direct method)*** Selected accounts of Ezra Antiques show the following: LO 4 5 6

Salary Payable

		Beginning balance	14,000
Payments	20,000	Salary expense	42,000
		Ending balance	36,000

Buildings

Beginning balance	100,000	Depreciation	22,000
Acquisitions	155,000	Book value of building sold	117,000*
Ending balance	116,000		

*Sale price was 160,000.

Notes Payable

		Beginning balance	244,000
Payments	72,000	Issuance of note payable for cash	90,000
		Ending balance	262,000

Requirement

1. For each account, identify the item or items that should appear on a statement of cash flows prepared by the *direct* method. State where to report the item.

E11-36B. *(Learning Objectives 4, 5, 6, 7: Preparing and analyzing the statement of cash flows—direct method)* The Income Statement and additional data of Happy Life, Inc., follow:

	A	B	C
1	**Happy Life, Inc.** **Income Statement**	**Year Ended** **November 30, 20X6**	
2	**Revenues:**		
3	Sales revenue	€ 223,000	
4	Dividend revenue	10,500	€ 233,500
5	**Expenses:**		
6	Cost of goods sold	102,000	
7	Salary expense	42,000	
8	Depreciation expense	19,000	
9	Advertising expense	14,000	
10	Interest expense	4,500	
11	Income tax expense	8,000	189,500
12	Net income		€ 44,000
13			

Additional data:

a. Collections from customers are €17,500 more than sales.
b. Payments to suppliers are €1,100 more than the sum of cost of goods sold plus advertising expense.
c. Payments to employees are €1,800 less than salary expense.
d. Dividend income, interest expense, and income tax expense equal their cash amounts.
e. Acquisition of PPE is €158,000. Of this amount, €110,000 is paid in cash and €48,000 by signing a note payable.
f. Proceeds from sale of land total €24,000.
g. Proceeds from issuance of shares total €88,000.
h. Payment of long-term note payable is €14,000.
i. Payment of dividends is €8,000.
j. Cash balance, November 30, 20X5, was €22,000.

Requirements

1. Prepare Happy Life, Inc.'s statement of cash flows and accompanying schedule of noncash investing and financing activities. Report operating activities by the *direct* method.
2. Evaluate Happy Life's cash flows for the year, including its free cash flow and cash realization ratio. In your evaluation, review all three categories of cash flows and give the reason for your evaluation.

LO 4 5 6

E11-37B. ***(Learning Objectives 4, 5, 6: Computing amounts for the statement of cash flows—direct method)*** Compute the following items for the statement of cash flows:

a. Beginning and ending Accounts Receivable are €22,000 and €17,000, respectively. Credit sales for the period total €62,000. How much are cash collections from customers?

b. Cost of goods sold is €79,000. Beginning Inventory balance is €28,000, and ending Inventory balance is €25,000. Beginning and ending Accounts Payable are €12,000 and €14,000, respectively. How much are cash payments for inventory?

Challenge Exercises

E11-38. ***(Learning Objectives 3, 6: Computing cash-flow amounts)*** Tip Top, Inc., reported the following in its financial statements for the year ended May 30, 20X6 (in thousands):

	A	B	C
1		**20X6**	**20X5**
2	**Income Statement**		
3	Net sales	$ 23,948	$ 21,648
4	Cost of sales	18,062	15,423
5	Depreciation	256	228
6	Other operating expenses	3,857	4,245
7	Income tax expense	563	478
8	Net income	$ 1,210	$ 1,274
9	**Balance Sheet**		
10	Cash and equivalents	$ 16	$ 15
11	Accounts receivable	603	614
12	Inventory	3,140	2,872
13	Property and equipment, net	4,346	3,436
14	Accounts payable	1,551	1,371
15	Accrued liabilities	935	632
16	Income tax payable	197	193
17	Long-term liabilities	480	468
18	Share capital	515	445
19	Retained earnings	4,427	3,828
20			

Requirement

1. Determine the following cash receipts and payments for Tip Top, Inc., during 20X6: (Enter all amounts in thousands.)

a. Collections from customers
b. Payments for inventory
c. Payments for other operating expenses
d. Payment of income tax
e. Proceeds from issuance of shares
f. Payment of cash dividends

LO 3

E11-39. ***(Learning Objective 3: Using the Balance Sheet and the statement of cash flows together)*** Delorme Specialties reported the following at December 31, 20X6 (in thousands):

	A	B	C
1		**20X6**	**20X5**
2	From the comparative Balance Sheet:		
3	Property and equipment, net	€ 10,590	€ 9,360
4	Long-term notes payable	4,600	3,080
5	From the statement of cash flows:		
6	Depreciation	€ 1,950	
7	Capital expenditures	(4,090)	
8	Proceeds from sale of property and equipment	740	
9	Proceeds from issuance of long-term note payable	1,250	
10	Payment of long-term note payable	(80)	
11	Issuance of shares	389	
12			

Requirement

1. Determine the following items for Delorme Specialties during 20X6:

a. Gain or loss on the sale of property and equipment

b. Amount of long-term debt issued for something other than cash

Quiz

Test your understanding of the statement of cash flows by answering the following questions. Select the best choice from among the possible answers given.

Q11-40. Paying off bonds payable is reported on the statement of cash flows under

a. investing activities.
b. operating activities.
c. financing activities.
d. noncash investing and financing activities.

Q11-41. The sale of inventory for cash is reported on the statement of cash flows under

a. noncash investing and financing activities.
b. financing activities.
c. investing activities.
d. operating activities.

Q11-42. Selling equipment is reported on the statement of cash flows under

a. operating activities.
b. investing activities.
c. financing activities.
d. noncash investing and financing activities.

Q11-43. Which of the following terms appears on a statement of cash flows—indirect method?

a. Collections from customers
b. Cash receipt of interest revenue
c. Payments to suppliers
d. Depreciation expense

Q11-44. On an indirect method statement of cash flows, an increase in a prepaid insurance would be

a. added to increases in current assets.
b. included in payments to suppliers.
c. added from net income.
d. deducted to net income.

Q11-45. On an indirect method statement of cash flows, an increase in accounts payable would be

a. added to net income in the operating activities section.
b. deducted from net income in the operating activities section.
c. reported in the investing activities section.
d. reported in the financing activities section.

Q11-46. On an indirect method statement of cash flows, a gain on the sale of PPE would be
a. reported in the investing activities section.
b. ignored, since the gain did not generate any cash.
c. added to net income in the operating activities section.
d. deducted from net income in the operating activities section.

Q11-47. Select an activity for each of the following transactions:
1. Receiving cash dividends is a/an ________________ activity.
2. Paying cash dividends is a/an ________________ activity.

Q11-48. Click Camera Co. sold equipment with a cost of $22,000 and accumulated depreciation of $10,000 for an amount that resulted in a gain of $2,000. What amount should Click report on the statement of cash flows as "proceeds from sale of PPE?"
a. $10,000 **c.** $20,000
b. $14,000 **d.** Some other amount

Questions 49–57 use the following data. Sheehan Corporation formats operating cash flows by the *indirect* method.

	A	B	C
1	**Sheehan's Income Statement for 20X6**		
2	Sales revenue	$ 178,000	
3	Gain on sale of equipment	10,000*	$ 188,000
4	Cost of goods sold	115,000	
5	Depreciation	7,500	
6	Other operating expenses	25,000	147,500
7	Net income		$ 40,500
8			

*The book value of equipment sold during 20X6 was $22,000.

	A	B	C	D	E	F
1		**Sheehan's Comparative Balance Sheet at the end of 20X6**				
2		**20X6**	**20X5**		**20X6**	**20X5**
3	Cash	$ 5,500	$ 3,000	Accounts payable	$ 8,000	$ 9,000
4	Accounts receivable	5,000	13,000	Accrued liabilities	6,000	4,000
5	Inventory	11,000	10,000	Long-term debt	25,000	10,000
6	Plant and equipment, net	97,000	71,000	Share capital	18,000	9,000
7		$ 118,500	$ 97,000	Retained earnings	61,500	65,000
8					$ 118,500	$ 97,000
9						

Q11-49. Which of the following items would *not* be found in Sheehan's cash flow from operating activities section of the cash flow statement?
a. Gain on sale of equipment **c.** Increase in inventory
b. Depreciation **d.** Increase in share capital

Q11-50. How do Sheehan's accrued liabilities affect the company's statement of cash flows for 20X6?
a. They don't, because the accrued liabilities are not yet paid
b. Increase in cash provided by operating activities
c. Increase in cash used by investing activities
d. Increase in cash used by financing activities

Q11-51. How do accounts receivable affect Sheehan's cash flows from operating activities for 20X6?

a. Increase in cash provided by operating activities
b. Decrease in cash provided by operating activities
c. Decrease in cash used by investing activities
d. They don't, because accounts receivable result from investing activities

Q11-52. Sheehan's net cash provided by operating activities during 20X6 was

a. $30,000.
b. $55,000.
c. $35,000.
d. $46,000.

Q11-53. Which of the following items would *not* be found in Sheehan's cash flow from investing activities section of the cash flow statement?

a. Profit from the sale of PPE
b. Proceeds from the sale of PPE
c. Purchase of other long-term assets (if any)
d. Purchase of PPE

Q11-54. The book value of equipment sold during 20X6 was $22,000. Sheehan's net cash flow from investing activities for 20X6 was

a. net cash used of $23,500.
b. net cash used of $53,000.
c. net cash used of $50,000.
d. net cash used of $44,000.

Q11-55. Which of the following items would *not* be found in Sheehan's cash flow from financing activities section of the cash flow statement?

a. Proceeds from disposal of PPE.
b. Proceeds from bank loan.
c. Payment of dividends.
d. Shares bought back.

Q11-56. Sheehan's largest financing cash flow for 20X6 resulted from

a. payment of dividends.
b. purchase of equipment.
c. sale of equipment.
d. issuance of shares.

Q11-57. Sheehan's net cash flow from financing activities for 20X6 was

a. net cash used of $50,000.
b. net cash used of $20,000.
c. net cash provided of $9,000.
d. net cash used of $44,000.

Q11-58. Sales totaled $830,000, accounts receivable increased by $60,000, and accounts payable decreased by $40,000. How much cash did the company collect from customers?

a. $730,000
b. $810,000
c. $890,000
d. $770,000

Q11-59. Income Tax Payable was $5,500 at the end of the year and $4,000 at the beginning. Income tax expense for the year totaled $60,500. What amount of cash did the company pay for income tax during the year?

a. $60,500
b. $62,000
c. $64,500
d. $59,000

Problems MyLab Accounting

Select A and B problems can be found within MyLab Accounting, an online homework and practice environment. Your instructor may ask you to complete select problems using MyLab Accounting.

Group A

LO 2 3 4 5

P11-60A. ***(Learning Objectives 2, 3, 4, 5: Preparing an Income Statement, Balance Sheet, and statement of cash flows—indirect method)*** Vintage Automobiles of Dubai, Inc., was formed on January 1, 20X6. The following transactions occurred during 20X6:

On January 1, 20X6, Vintage issued its shares for $440,000. Early in January, Vintage made the following cash payments:

a. $190,000 for equipment
b. $210,000 for inventory (seven cars at $29,000 each)
c. $18,000 for 20X6 rent on a store building

In February, Vintage purchased two cars for inventory on account. Cost of this inventory was $90,000 ($45,000.00 each). Before year-end, Vintage paid $56,000 of this debt. Vintage uses the FIFO method to account for inventory.

During 20X6, Vintage sold eight cars for a total of $496,000. Before year-end, Vintage collected 80% of this amount.

The business employs five people. The combined annual payroll is $125,000, of which Vintage owes $8,000 at year-end. At the end of the year, Vintage paid income tax of $12,500.

Late in 20X6, Vintage declared and paid cash dividends of $13,000.

For equipment, Vintage uses the straight-line depreciation method, over five years, with zero residual value.

Requirements

1. Prepare Vintage Automobiles of Dubai, Inc.'s Income Statement for the year ended December 31, 20X6.
2. Prepare Vintage's Balance Sheet at December 31, 20X6.
3. Prepare Vintage's statement of cash flows for the year ended December 31, 20X6. Format cash flows from operating activities by using the *indirect* method.

P11-61A. ***(Learning Objectives 2, 4, 5, 6: Preparing an Income Statement, Balance Sheet, and statement of cash flows—direct method)*** Use the Antique Automobiles of Dubai, Inc., data from Problem 11-60A.

Requirements

1. Prepare Vintage's Income Statement for the year ended December 31, 20X6.
2. Prepare Vintage's Balance Sheet at December 31, 20X6.
3. Prepare Vintage's statement of cash flows for the year ended December 31, 20X6. Format cash flows from operating activities by using the *direct* method.

P11-62A. ***(Learning Objectives 2, 3, 4, 5: Preparing the statement of cash flows—indirect method)*** Morgan Software Corp. has assembled the following data for the years ending December 31, 20X6 and 20X5.

A1

	A	B	C
1		December 31	
2		20X6	20X5
3	**Current Accounts:**		
4	Current assets:		
5	Cash and cash equivalents	$ 130,700	$ 40,000
6	Accounts receivable	70,900	63,400
7	Inventories	7,600	81,000
8	Prepaid expenses	3,200	1,400
9	Current liabilities:		
10	Accounts payable	$ 57,300	$ 55,400
11	Income tax payable	18,700	16,200
12	Accrued liabilities	15,200	27,500
13			

Transaction Data for 20X6:			
Acquisition of land by issuing long-term note payable	$201,000	Purchase of treasury shares....	$10,700
Stock dividends	31,400	Loss on sale of equipment	5,000
Collection of loan..................	10,600	Payment of cash dividends	9,300
Depreciation expense	17,000	Issuance of long-term note payable to borrow cash.....	34,500
Purchase of building.............	97,000	Net income..........................	6,500
Retirement of bonds payable by issuing ordinary shares ...	64,000	Issuance of ordinary shares for cash	36,500
Purchase of long-term investment........................	44,600	Proceeds from sale of equipment	81,000
		Amortization expense..........	5,000

Requirement

1. Prepare Morgan Software Corp.'s statement of cash flows using the *indirect* method to report operating activities. Include an accompanying schedule of noncash investing and financing activities.

LO 2 3 4 5 7
■ writing assignment
■ spreadsheet

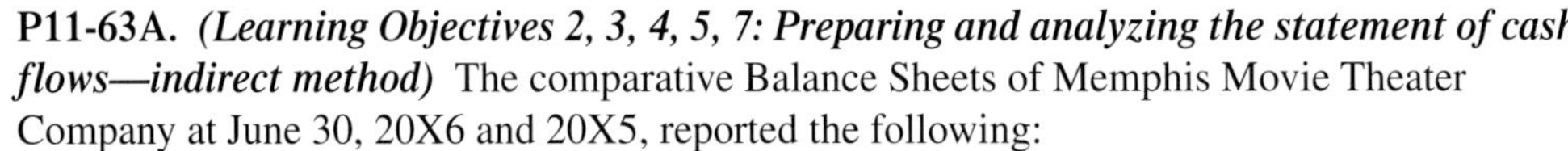

P11-63A. ***(Learning Objectives 2, 3, 4, 5, 7: Preparing and analyzing the statement of cash flows—indirect method)*** The comparative Balance Sheets of Memphis Movie Theater Company at June 30, 20X6 and 20X5, reported the following:

	A	B	C
1		June 30	
2		20X6	20X5
3	**Current assets:**		
4	Cash and cash equivalents	$ 67,300	$ 28,000
5	Accounts receivable	15,400	26,100
6	Inventories	64,100	62,500
7	Prepaid expenses	3,300	8,200
8	**Current liabilities:**		
9	Accounts payable	$ 57,100	$ 56,400
10	Accrued liabilities	38,700	18,200
11	Income tax payable	9,200	10,500
12			

Memphis Movie Theater's transactions during the year ended June 30, 20X6, included the following:

Acquisition of land by issuing note payable	$100,000	Sale of long-term investment....	$12,700
Amortization expense...........	9,000	Depreciation expense	15,700
Payment of cash dividend......	29,000	Cash purchase of building.....	44,000
Cash purchase of equipment	79,000	Net income...........................	54,000
Issuance of long-term note payable to borrow cash.....	42,000	Issuance of share for cash......	24,000
		Dividend	11,000

Requirements

1. Prepare Memphis Movie Theater Company's statement of cash flows for the year ended June 30, 20X6, using the *indirect* method to report cash flows from operating activities. Report noncash investing and financing activities in an accompanying schedule.

2. Evaluate Memphis Movie Theater's cash flows for the year, including its free cash flow and cash realization ratio. Review all three categories of cash flows and give the reason for your evaluation.

LO 2 3 4 5
■ writing assignment
■ spreadsheet

P11-64A. *(Learning Objectives 2, 3, 4, 5: Preparing the statement of cash flows—indirect method)* The 20X6 and 20X5 comparative Balance Sheets and 20X6 Income Statement of Affordable Supply Corp. follow:

	A	B	C	D
1	**Affordable Supply Corp. Comparative Balance Sheets**			
2		**December 31**		**Increase**
3		**20X6**	**20X5**	**(Decrease)**
4	Current assets:			
5	Cash and cash equivalents	$ 17,300	$ 4,000	$ 13,300
6	Accounts receivable	45,700	44,500	1,200
7	Inventories	61,400	47,000	14,400
8	Prepaid expenses	1,800	3,900	(2,100)
9	PPE:			
10	Land	69,100	22,600	46,500
11	Equipment, net	53,100	49,500	3,600
12	Total assets	$ 248,400	$ 171,500	$ 76,900
13	Current liabilities:			
14	Accounts payable	$ 35,200	$ 26,900	$ 8,300
15	Salary payable	24,000	13,100	10,900
16	Other accrued liabilities	22,100	23,700	(1,600)
17	Long-term liabilities:			
18	Notes payable	51,000	34,000	17,000
19	Shareholders' equity:			
20	Share capital, no-par	88,600	65,900	22,700
21	Retained earnings	27,500	7,900	19,600
22	Total liabilities and shareholders' equity	$ 248,400	$ 171,500	$ 76,900
23				

	A	B	C
1	**Affordable Supply Corp. Income Statement**	**Year Ended December 31, 20X6**	
2	**Revenues:**		
3	Sales revenue		$ 450,000
4	**Expenses:**		
5	Cost of goods sold	$ 186,900	
6	Salary expense	76,300	
7	Depreciation expense	17,900	
8	Other operating expense	49,900	
9	Interest expense	24,200	
10	Income tax expense	29,200	
11	Total expenses		384,400
12	Net income		$ 65,600
13			

Affordable Supply had no noncash investing and financing transactions during 20X6. During the year, there were no sales of land or equipment, no payment of notes payable, no retirements of shares, and no treasury shares transactions.

Requirements

1. Prepare the 20X6 statement of cash flows, formatting operating activities by using the *indirect* method.
2. How will what you learned in this problem help you evaluate an investment?

■ writing assignment
■ spreadsheet

P11-65A. ***(Learning Objectives 2, 4, 5, 6: Preparing the statement of cash flows—direct method)*** Use the Affordable Supply Corp. data from Problem 11-64A.

Requirements

1. Prepare the 20X6 statement of cash flows by using the *direct* method.
2. How will what you learned in this problem help you evaluate an investment?

LO 2 4 5 6 7
■ writing assignment

P11-66A. ***(Learning Objectives 2, 4, 5, 6, 7: Preparing and analyzing the statement of cash flows—direct method)*** Ramirez Furniture Gallery, Inc., provided the following data from the company's records for the year ended May 31, 20X6:

- **a.** Credit sales, $586,500
- **b.** Loan to another company, $12,400
- **c.** Cash payments to purchase PPE, $72,200
- **d.** Cost of goods sold, $313,500
- **e.** Proceeds from issuance of ordinary shares, $7,200
- **f.** Payment of cash dividends, $48,400
- **g.** Collection of interest, $4,700
- **h.** Acquisition of equipment by issuing short-term note payable, $16,000
- **i.** Payments of salaries, $79,000
- **j.** Proceeds from sale of PPE, $22,700, including $6,900 loss
- **k.** Collections on accounts receivable, $428,600
- **l.** Interest revenue, $3,600
- **m.** Cash receipt of dividend income, $8,800
- **n.** Payments to suppliers, $369,000
- **o.** Cash sales, $191,400
- **p.** Depreciation expense, $40,200
- **q.** Proceeds from issuance of note payable, $24,600
- **r.** Payments of long-term notes payable, $83,000
- **s.** Interest expense and payments, $13,500
- **t.** Salary expense, $75,900
- **u.** Loan collections, $11,800
- **v.** Proceeds from sale of investments, $9,600, including $4,400 gain
- **w.** Payment of short-term note payable by issuing long-term note payable, $94,000
- **x.** Amortization expenses, $3,200
- **y.** Income tax expense and payments, $38,400
- **z.** Cash balance: May 31, 20X5, $19,200; May 31, 20X6, $12,700

Requirements

1. Prepare Ramirez Furniture Gallery, Inc.'s statement of cash flows for the year ended May 31, 20X6. Use the *direct* method for cash flows from operating activities. Include an accompanying schedule of noncash investing and financing activities.
2. Evaluate 20X6 from a cash-flow standpoint. Give your reasons.

LO 3 4 5 6

P11-67A. ***(Learning Objectives 3, 4, 5, 6: Preparing the statement of cash flows—direct and indirect methods)*** To prepare the statement of cash flows, accountants for Daisy Electric Company have summarized 20X6's activities in two accounts as follows:

Cash

Beginning balance	49,600	Payments on accounts payable	402,000
Sale of long-term investment	14,600	Payments of dividends	47,900
Collections from customers	661,800	Payments of salaries and wages	143,600
Issuance of shares	61,000	Payments of interest	26,600
Receipts of dividends	16,900	Purchase of equipment	31,000
		Payments of operating expenses	34,500
		Payment of long-term note payable	41,500
		Purchase of treasury shares	22,400
		Payment of income tax	17,000
Ending Balance	37,400		

Share Capital

		Beginning balance	74,200
		Issuance for cash	61,000
		Issuance to acquire land	80,800
		Issuance to retire note payable	20,000
		Ending balance	236,000

Daisy's 20X6 Income Statement and Balance Sheet data follow:

	A	B	C
1	**Daisy Electric Company Income Statement**	**Year Ended December 31, 20X6**	
2	**Revenues:**		
3	Sales revenue		$ 689,200
4	Dividend revenue		16,900
5	Total revenue		706,100
6	**Expenses and losses:**		
7	Cost of goods sold	$ 334,000	
8	Salary and wage expense	135,800	
9	Depreciation expense	19,000	
10	Other operating expense	23,700	
11	Interest expense	29,100	
12	Income tax expense	14,500	
13	Loss on sale of investments	22,100	
14	Total expenses and losses		578,200
15	Net income		$ 127,900
16			

	A	B
1	**Daisy Electric Company** **Selected Balance Sheet Data**	**December 31, 20X6**
2		**Increase (Decrease)**
3	Current assets:	
4	Cash and cash equivalents	$ (12,200)
5	Accounts receivable	27,400
6	Inventories	59,700
7	Prepaid expenses	600
8	Long-term investments	(36,700)
9	Equipment, net	12,000
10	Land	80,800
11	Current liabilities:	
12	Accounts payable	(8,300)
13	Interest payable	2,500
14	Salary payable	(7,800)
15	Other accrued liabilities	(10,200)
16	Income tax payable	(2,500)
17	Long-term note payable	(61,500)
18	Share capital	161,800
19	Retained earnings	80,000
20	Treasury shares	(22,400)
21		

Requirements

1. Prepare the statement of cash flows of Daisy Electric Company for the year ended December 31, 20X6, using the *direct* method to report operating activities. Also prepare the accompanying schedule of noncash investing and financing activities.
2. Use Daisy's 20X6 Income Statement and Balance Sheet to prepare a supplementary schedule of cash flows from operating activities by using the *indirect* method.

P11-68A. ***(Learning Objectives 3, 4, 5, 6: Preparing the statement of cash flows—indirect and direct methods)*** The comparative Balance Sheets of Ibrahim Design Studio, Inc., at June 30, 20X6 and 20X5, and transaction data for fiscal year 20X6 are as follows:

	A	B	C	D
1	**Ibrahim Design Studio** **Comparative Balance Sheets**			
2		**June 30**		**Increase**
3		**20X6**	**20X5**	**(Decrease)**
4	Current assets:			
5	Cash	$ 28,900	$ 21,000	$ 7,900
6	Accounts receivable	48,800	31,700	17,100
7	Inventories	78,400	80,700	(2,300)
8	Prepaid expenses	3,100	2,200	900
9	Long-term investment	10,300	5,600	4,700
10	Equipment, net	74,000	73,300	700
11	Land	33,100	94,500	(61,400)
12		$ 276,600	$ 309,000	$ (32,400)
13	Current liabilities:			
14	Notes payable, short-term	$ 14,000	$ 19,000	$ (5,000)
15	Accounts payable	29,400	40,400	(11,000)
16	Income tax payable	13,200	14,400	(1,200)
17	Accrued liabilities	3,700	9,400	(5,700)
18	Interest payable	3,400	2,400	1,000
19	Salary payable	1,000	4,400	(3,400)
20	Long-term note payable	47,200	94,000	(46,800)
21	Share capital	59,400	52,000	7,400
22	Retained earnings	105,300	73,000	32,300
23		$ 276,600	$ 309,000	$ (32,400)
24				

Transaction data for the year ended June 30, 20X6:

- **a.** Net income, $81,700
- **b.** Depreciation expense on equipment, $14,900
- **c.** Purchased long-term investment, $5,700
- **d.** Sold land for $54,900, including $6,500 loss
- **e.** Acquired equipment by issuing long-term note payable, $15,600
- **f.** Paid long-term note payable, $62,400
- **g.** Received cash for issuance of shares, $3,400
- **h.** Paid cash dividends, $49,400
- **i.** Paid short-term note payable by issuing shares, $6,000

Requirements

1. Prepare the statement of cash flows of Ibrahim Design Studio, Inc., for the year ended June 30, 20X6, using the *indirect* method to report operating activities. Also prepare the accompanying schedule of noncash investing and financing activities. All current accounts except short-term notes payable result from operating transactions.
2. Prepare a supplementary schedule showing cash flows from operations by the *direct* method. The accounting records provide the following: collections from customers, $246,700; interest received, $1,700; payments to suppliers, $119,600; payments to employees, $42,900; payments for income tax, $13,900; and payment of interest, $4,900.

Group B

P11-69B. ***(Learning Objectives 2, 3, 4, 5: Preparing an Income Statement, Balance Sheet, and statement of cash flows—indirect method)*** Slick Automobiles of Dubai, Inc., was formed on January 1, 20X6. The following transactions occurred during 20X6: LO 2 3 4 5

On January 1, 20X6, Slick issued its shares for €350,000. Early in January, Slick made the following cash payments:

- **a.** €150,000 for equipment
- **b.** €180,000 for inventory (five cars at €35,000 each)
- **c.** €16,000 for 20X6 rent on a store building

In February, Slick purchased six cars for inventory on account. Cost of this inventory was €288,000 (€48,000 each). Before year-end, Slick paid €198,400 of this debt. Slick uses the FIFO method to account for inventory.

During 20X6, Slick sold six vintage autos for a total of €438,000. Before year-end, Slick collected 90% of this amount.

The business employs three people. The combined annual payroll is €90,000, of which Slick owes €6,000 at year-end. At the end of the year, Slick paid income tax of €15,000.

Late in 20X6, Slick declared and paid cash dividends of €17,000.

For equipment, Slick uses the straight-line depreciation method, over five years, with zero residual value.

Requirements

1. Prepare Slick Automobiles of Dubai, Inc.'s Income Statement for the year ended December 31, 20X6.
2. Prepare Slick's Balance Sheet at December 31, 20X6.
3. Prepare Slick's statement of cash flows for the year ended December 31, 20X6. Format cash flows from operating activities by using the *indirect* method.

P11-70B. ***(Learning Objectives 2, 4, 5, 6: Preparing an Income Statement, Balance Sheet, and statement of cash flows—direct method)*** Use the Slick Automobiles of Dubai, Inc., data from Problem 11-69B. LO 2 4 5 6

Requirements

1. Prepare Slick's Income Statement for the year ended December 31, 20X6.
2. Prepare Slick's Balance Sheet at December 31, 20X6.
3. Prepare Slick's statement of cash flows for the year ended December 31, 20X6. Format cash flows from operating activities by using the *direct* method.

LO 2 3 4 5

P11-71B. ***(Learning Objectives 2, 3, 4, 5: Preparing the statement of cash flows—indirect method)*** Newton Software Corp. has assembled the following data for the year ended December 31, 20X6 and 20X5:

	A	B	C
1		December 31	
2		**20X6**	**20X5**
3	**Current Accounts:**		
4	Current assets:		
5	Cash and cash equivalents	€ 66,400	€ 36,000
6	Accounts receivable	23,000	64,200
7	Inventories	89,500	84,000
8	Prepaid expenses	3,300	2,300
9	Current liabilities:		
10	Accounts payable	57,300	55,700
11	Income tax payable	28,000	16,300
12	Accrued liabilities	15,800	7,400
13			

Transaction Data for 20X6:

Acquisition of land by issuing long-term note payable	€198,000	Purchase of treasury shares	€14,400
Dividends	31,600	Loss on sale of equipment	3,000
Collection of loan	11,000	Payment of cash dividends	18,800
Depreciation expense	17,000	Issuance of long-term note payable to borrow cash	34,000
Purchase of building	159,000	Net income	58,000
Retirement of bonds payable by issuing ordinary shares	71,000	Issuance of ordinary shares for cash	74,200
Purchase of long-term investment	49,900	Proceeds from sale of equipment	12,900
		Amortization expense	6,000

Requirement

1. Prepare Newton Software Corp.'s statement of cash flows using the *indirect* method to report operating activities. Include an accompanying schedule of noncash investing and financing activities.

LO 2 3 4 5 7

■ writing assignment

■ spreadsheet

P11-72B. ***(Learning Objectives 2, 3, 4, 5, 7: Preparing and analyzing the statement of cash flows—indirect method)*** The comparative Balance Sheets of Marmaduke Movie Theater Company at June 30, 20X6 and 20X5, reported the following:

	A	B	C
1		June 30	
2		**20X6**	**20X5**
3	**Current assets:**		
4	Cash and cash equivalents	€ 8,700	€ 18,000
5	Accounts receivable	15,400	22,100
6	Inventories	64,100	61,500
7	Prepaid expenses	16,300	8,200
8	**Current liabilities:**		
9	Accounts payable	€ 58,100	€ 55,400
10	Accrued liabilities	58,700	48,200
11	Income tax payable	6,200	10,100
12			

Marmaduke's transactions during the year ended June 30, 20X6, included the following:

Acquisition of land by issuing note payable	€115,000	Sale of long-term investment....	€13,400
Amortization expense............	6,000	Depreciation expense	15,600
Payment of cash dividend......	34,000	Cash purchase of building.....	59,000
Cash purchase of equipment	45,600	Net income............................	50,000
Issuance of long-term note payable to borrow cash.....	26,000	Issuance of shares for cash	13,000
		Share dividend......................	9,000

Requirements

1. Prepare Marmaduke Movie Theater Company's statement of cash flows for the year ended June 30, 20X6, using the *indirect* method to report cash flows from operating activities. Report noncash investing and financing activities in an accompanying schedule.
2. Evaluate Marmaduke's cash flows for the year, including its free cash flow and cash realization ratio. Review all three categories of cash flows and give the reason for your evaluation.

P11-73B. ***(Learning Objectives 2, 3, 4, 5: Preparing the statement of cash flows—indirect method)*** The 20X6 and 20X5 comparative Balance Sheets and 20X6 Income Statement of King Supply Corp. follow:

A1

	A	B	C	D
1	**King Supply Corp. Comparative Balance Sheets**			
2		**December 31**		**Increase**
3		**20X6**	**20X5**	**(Decrease)**
4	Current assets:			
5	Cash and cash equivalents	€ 17,600	€ 5,000	€ 12,600
6	Accounts receivable	45,500	44,500	1,000
7	Inventories	79,100	67,500	11,600
8	Prepaid expenses	2,100	6,000	(3,900)
9	PPE:			
10	Land	69,100	21,900	47,200
11	Equipment, net	53,100	49,200	3,900
12	Total assets	€ 266,500	€ 194,100	€ 72,400
13	Current liabilities:			
14	Accounts payable	€ 35,800	€ 25,600	€ 10,200
15	Salary payable	22,000	15,600	6,400
16	Other accrued liabilities	22,900	24,200	(1,300)
17	Long-term liabilities:			
18	Notes payable	50,000	37,000	13,000
19	Shareholders' equity:			
20	Share capital, no-par	88,600	64,300	24,300
21	Retained earnings	47,200	27,400	19,800
22	Total liabilities and shareholders' equity	€ 266,500	€ 194,100	€ 72,400
23				

	A	B	C
1	**King Supply Corp. Income Statement**	**Year Ended December 31, 20X6**	
2	Revenues:		
3	Sales revenue		€ 448,000
4	Expenses:		
5	Cost of goods sold	€ 185,300	
6	Salary expense	76,800	
7	Depreciation expense	17,500	
8	Other operating expense	49,700	
9	Interest expense	24,900	
10	Income tax expense	29,800	
11	Total expenses		384,000
12	Net income		€ 64,000
13			

King Supply had no noncash investing and financing transactions during 20X6. During the year, there were no sales of land or equipment, no payment of notes payable, no retirements of shares, and no treasury share transactions.

Requirements

1. Prepare the 20X6 statement of cash flows, formatting operating activities by using the *indirect* method.
2. How will what you learned in this problem help you evaluate an investment?

spreadsheet

P11-74B. ***(Learning Objectives 2, 4, 5, 6: Preparing the statement of cash flows—direct method)*** Use the King Supply Corp. data from Problem P11-73B.

Requirements

1. Prepare the 20X6 statement of cash flows by using the *direct* method.
2. How will what you learned in this problem help you evaluate an investment?

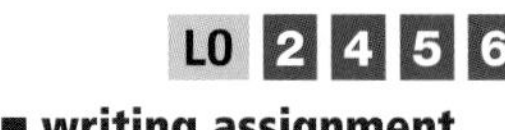

P11-75B. ***(Learning Objectives 2, 4, 5, 6: Preparing the statement of cash flows—direct method)*** Dunleavy Furniture Gallery, Inc., provided the following data from the company's records for the year ended December 31, 20X6:

a. Credit sales, €568,000
b. Loan to another company, €13,800
c. Cash payments to purchase PPE, €60,900
d. Cost of goods sold, €383,700
e. Proceeds from issuance of ordinary shares, €8,000
f. Payment of cash dividends, €49,000
g. Collection of interest, €5,200
h. Acquisition of equipment by issuing short-term note payable, €17,500
i. Payments of salaries, €94,700
j. Proceeds from sale of PPE, €23,300, including €7,000 loss
k. Collections on accounts receivable, €407,000
l. Interest revenue, €4,300
m. Cash receipt of dividend income, €5,000
n. Payments to suppliers, €388,200
o. Cash sales, €202,000
p. Depreciation expense, €41,100
q. Proceeds from issuance of note payable, €20,300
r. Payments of long-term notes payable, €70,000
s. Interest expense and payments, €14,700
t. Salary expense, €92,600

u. Loan collections, €13,100
v. Proceeds from sale of investments, €12,200, including €3,800 gain
w. Payment of short-term note payable by issuing long-term note payable, €69,000
x. Amortization expenses, €4,200
y. Income tax expense and payments, €37,800
z. Cash balance: December 31, 20X5, €50,000; December 31, 20X6, €17,000

Requirements

1. Prepare Dunleavy Furniture Gallery, Inc.'s statement of cash flows for the year ended December 31, 20X6. Use the *direct* method for cash flows from operating activities. Include an accompanying schedule of noncash investing and financing activities.
2. Evaluate 20X6 from a cash-flow standpoint. Give your reasons.

P11-76B. ***(Learning Objectives 3, 4, 5, 6: Preparing the statement of cash flows—direct and indirect methods)*** To prepare the statement of cash flows, accountants for Spencer Electric Company have summarized the 20X6 activity in two accounts as follows:

Cash

Beginning balance	71,500	Payments on accounts payable	399,500
Sale of long-term investment	20,000	Payments of dividends	27,600
Collections from customers	661,600	Payments of salaries and wages	143,300
Issuance of shares	22,200	Payments of interest	27,100
Receipts of dividends	16,800	Purchase of equipment	31,700
		Payments of operating expenses	34,900
		Payment of long-term note payable	41,300
		Purchase of treasury shares	26,300
		Payment of income tax	18,600
Ending Balance	41,800		

Share capital

		Beginning balance	73,200
		Issuance for cash	22,200
		Issuance to acquire land	61,700
		Issuance to retire note payable	17,000
		Ending balance	174,100

Spencer's 20X6 Income Statement and Balance Sheet data follow:

	A	B	C
1	**Spencer Electric Company Income Statement**	**Year Ended December 31, 20X6**	
2	**Revenues:**		
3	Sales revenue		€ 647,200
4	Dividend revenue		16,800
5	Total revenue		664,000
6	**Expenses and losses:**		
7	Cost of goods sold	€ 404,600	
8	Salary and wage expense	150,500	
9	Depreciation expense	16,400	
10	Other operating expense	30,500	
11	Interest expense	24,900	
12	Income tax expense	16,100	
13	Loss on sale of investments	16,700	
14	Total expenses and losses		659,700
15	Net income		€ 4,300
16			

	A	B
1	**Spencer Electric Company** **Selected Balance Sheet Data**	**December 31, 20X6**
2		**Increase (Decrease)**
3	Current assets:	
4	Cash and cash equivalents	€ (29,700)
5	Accounts receivable	(14,400)
6	Inventories	(12,900)
7	Prepaid expenses	(6,000)
8	Long-term investments	(36,700)
9	Equipment, net	15,300
10	Land	61,700
11	Current liabilities:	
12	Accounts payable	(7,800)
13	Interest payable	(2,200)
14	Salary payable	7,200
15	Other accrued liabilities	(10,400)
16	Income tax payable	(2,500)
17	Long-term note payable	(58,300)
18	Share capital	100,900
19	Retained earnings	(23,300)
20	Treasury shares	(26,300)
21		

Requirements

1. Prepare the statement of cash flows of Spencer Electric Company for the year ended December 31, 20X6, using the *direct* method to report operating activities. Also prepare the accompanying schedule of noncash investing and financing activities.
2. Use Spencer's 20X6 Income Statement and Balance Sheet to prepare a supplementary schedule of cash flows from operating activities by using the *indirect* method.

P11-77B. ***(Learning Objectives 3, 4, 5, 6: Preparing the statement of cash flows—indirect and direct methods)*** The comparative Balance Sheets of Salim Design Studio, Inc., at June 30, 20X6 and 20X5, and transaction data for fiscal year 20X6 are as follows:

	A	B	C	D
1	**Salim Design Studio** **Comparative Balance Sheets**			
2		**June 30**		**Increase**
3		**20X6**	**20X5**	**(Decrease)**
4	Current assets:			
5	Cash	€ 28,900	€ 2,400	€ 26,500
6	Accounts receivable	59,000	22,300	36,700
7	Inventories	98,200	40,400	57,800
8	Prepaid expenses	3,500	2,500	1,000
9	Long-term investment	10,000	5,000	5,000
10	Equipment, net	74,900	73,600	1,300
11	Land	58,100	98,900	(40,800)
12		€ 332,600	€ 245,100	€ 87,500
13	Current liabilities:			
14	Notes payable, short-term	€ 13,200	€ 20,200	€ (7,000)
15	Accounts payable	42,300	41,300	1,000
16	Income tax payable	13,300	14,400	(1,100)
17	Accrued liabilities	97,400	9,300	88,100
18	Interest payable	3,500	2,500	1,000
19	Salary payable	400	3,100	(2,700)
20	Long-term note payable	48,700	94,200	(45,500)
21	Share capital	79,700	51,600	28,100
22	Retained earnings	34,100	8,500	25,600
23		€ 332,600	€ 245,100	€ 87,500
24				

Transaction data for the year ended June 30, 20X6:

a. Net income, €73,500
b. Depreciation expense on equipment, €14,000
c. Purchased long-term investment, €5,000
d. Sold land for €33,700, including €7,000 loss
e. Acquired equipment by issuing long-term note payable, €15,300
f. Paid long-term note payable, €60,800
g. Received cash for issuance of shares, €21,200
h. Paid cash dividends, €47,900
i. Paid short-term note payable by issuing shares, €7,000

Requirements

1. Prepare the statement of cash flows of Salim Design Studio, Inc., for the year ended June 30, 20X6, using the *indirect* method to report operating activities. Also prepare the accompanying schedule of noncash investing and financing activities. All current accounts except short-term notes payable result from operating transactions.
2. Prepare a supplementary schedule showing cash flows from operations by the *direct* method. The accounting records provide the following: collections from customers, €272,700; interest received, €1,400; payments to suppliers, €130,900; payments to employees, €40,000; payments for income tax, €12,600; and payment of interest, €5,300.

APPLY YOUR KNOWLEDGE

Decision Cases

LO 3 4 5
■ writing assignment

Case 1. *(Learning Objectives 3, 4, 5: Preparing and using the statement of cash flows to evaluate operations)* The 20X7 Income Statement and the 20X7 comparative Balance Sheet of T-Bar-M Camp, Inc., have just been distributed at a meeting of the camp's board of directors. The directors raise a fundamental question: Why is the cash balance so low? This question is especially troublesome since 20X7 showed record profits. As the controller of the company, you must answer the question.

	A	B
1	**T-Bar-M Camp, Inc. Income Statement**	**Year Ended December 31, 20X7**
2	**(In thousands)**	
3	**Revenues:**	
4	Sales revenue	$ 436
5	**Expenses:**	
6	Cost of goods sold	$ 221
7	Salary expense	48
8	Depreciation expense	46
9	Interest expense	13
10	Amortization expense	11
11	Total expenses	339
12	Net income	$ 97
13		

	A	B	C
1	**T-Bar-M Camp, Inc. Comparative Balance Sheets**	**December 31**	
2	**(In thousands)**	**20X7**	**20X6**
3	**Assets**		
4	Cash	$ 17	$ 63
5	Accounts receivable, net	72	61
6	Inventories	194	181
7	Long-term investments	31	0
8	Property, plant and equipment	369	259
9	Accumulated depreciation	(244)	(198)
10	Patents	177	188
11	Totals	$ 616	$ 554
12	**Liabilities and Owners' Equity**		
13	Accounts payable	$ 63	$ 56
14	Accrued liabilities	12	17
15	Notes payable, long-term	179	264
16	Share capital, no par	149	61
17	Retained earnings	213	156
18	Totals	$ 616	$ 554
19			

Requirements

1. Prepare a statement of cash flows for 20X7 in the format that best shows the relationship between net income and operating cash flow. The company sold no PPE or long-term investments and issued no notes payable during 20X7. There were *no* noncash investing and financing transactions during the year. Show all amounts in thousands.
2. Answer the board members' question: Why is the cash balance so low? Point out the two largest cash payments during 20X7. (Challenge)
3. Considering net income and the company's cash flows during 20X7, was it a good year or a bad year? Give your reasons.

Case 2. *(Learning Objectives 1, 2: Using cash-flow data to evaluate an investment)* Applied Technology, Inc., and Four-Star Catering are asking you to recommend their shares to your clients. Because Applied and Four-Star earn about the same net income and have similar financial positions, your decision depends on their statements of cash flows, summarized as follows:

	Applied		Four–Star	
Net cash provided by operating activities:		$ 30,000		$ 70,000
Cash provided by (used for) investing activities:				
Purchase of PPE	$(20,000)		$(100,000)	
Sale of PPE	40,000	20,000	10,000	(90,000)
Cash provided by (used for) financing activities:				
Issuance of shares		—		30,000
Paying off long-term debt		(40,000)		—
Net increase in cash		$ 10,000		$10,000

Based on their cash flows, which company looks better? Give your reasons. (Challenge)

Ethical Issue

Copenhagen Motors is having a bad year. Net income is only €37,000. Also, two important overseas customers are falling behind in their payments to Copenhagen, and Copenhagen's accounts receivable are ballooning. The company desperately needs a loan. The board of directors is considering ways to put the best face on the company's financial statements. Copenhagen's bank closely examines cash flow from operations. Daniel Peavey, Copenhagen's controller, suggests reclassifying as long-term the receivables from the slow-paying clients. He explains to the board that removing the €80,000 rise in accounts receivable from current assets will increase net cash provided by operations. This approach may help Copenhagen get the loan.

Requirements

1. Using only the amounts given, compute net cash provided by operations, both without and with the reclassification of the receivables. Which reporting makes Copenhagen look better?
2. Identify the ethical issue(s).
3. Who are the stakeholders?
4. Analyze the issue from the (a) economic, (b) legal, and (c) ethical standpoints. What is the potential impact on all stakeholders?
5. What should the board do?
6. Under what conditions would the reclassification of the receivables be considered ethical?

Focus on Financials: | Nestlé

This case spans all 12 chapters and is based on the consolidated financial statements of Nestlé. As you work with Nestlé throughout this course, you will develop the confidence and ability to use the financial statements of other companies as well.

Refer to Nestlé's financial statements in Appendix A. If you wish, you can obtain the full annual report from www.nestle.com/investors. You may find the information overwhelming for now, but try to spot the key principles that we have discussed in this chapter. It will get progressively easier as you gain familiarity with the elements of the financial statements.

Requirements

1. By which method does Nestlé report cash flows from operating activities? How can you tell?
2. Suppose Nestlé reported net cash flows from operating activities using the direct method. Compute these amounts for the year ended December 31, 20X6 (ignore the statement of cash flows, and use only Nestlé's Income Statement and Balance Sheet).
   a. Collections from vendors, customers, and others. Assume that all sales are on account.
   b. Payments to suppliers. Assume all inventory is purchased on account, and that all cash payments to suppliers are made from accounts payable.
3. What is Nestlé's main source of cash? Is this good news or bad news to Nestlé's managers, shareholders, and creditors? What is Nestlé's main use of cash? Good news or bad news?
4. Calculate Nestlé's free cash flow and cash realization ratio for 20X6 and 20X5.

Group Projects

Project 1. Each member of the group should obtain the annual report of a different company. Select companies in different industries. Evaluate each company's trend of cash flows for the most recent two years. In your evaluation of the companies' cash flows, you may use any other information that is publicly available—for example, the other financial statements (Income Statement, Balance Sheet, statement of changes in equity, and the related notes) and news stories from magazines and newspapers. Rank the companies' cash flows from best to worst and write a two-page report on your findings.

Project 2. Select a company and obtain its annual report, including all the financial statements. Focus on the statement of cash flows and, in particular, the cash flows from operating activities. Specify whether the company uses the direct method or the indirect method to report operating cash flows. As necessary, use the other financial statements (Income Statement, Balance Sheet, and statement of changes in equity) and the notes to prepare the company's cash flows from operating activities by using the other method.

Quick Check Answers

1. *a*
2. *c*
3. *c*
4. *b* ($160,000 + $8,000)
5. *b*
6. *a*
7. *a* ($50,000 + $12,000 − $9,000 + $15,000 + $10,000 + $3,000)
8. *d* ($6,000 − $35,000 + $42,000)
9. *a* (−$2,000 + $4,000 − $16,000)
10. *b* ($42,000 + $15,000)
11. *c* ($80,000 + $700,000 − $60,000)
12. *b* ($760,000 − $410,000 − $180,000)
13. *d* ($410,000 − $10,000 + $12,000)

12 Financial Statement Analysis

SPOTLIGHT | Nestlé www.nestlé.com

In 2016, Nestlé celebrated its 150th anniversary. From its humble beginning of making condensed milk, Nestlé now has over 2,000 brands under its umbrella, from coffee, snacks, baby food, and bottled water, to ice cream, pet care, and weight management products. Nestlé has assets of 132 billion Swiss Francs (CHF) and sales were just below CHF 90 billion. As a shareholder or potential investor, how would you evaluate Nestlé's financial performance and financial position? What analysis techniques can we use for financial analysis? How do we make sense of the numbers?

Jiradet ponari/123RF

The objective of financial reporting, through financial statements and other disclosures, is to help users make economic decisions. One of the primary tools available to you is a process we call financial statement analysis. This includes examining year-on-year changes, component and common-size analysis, as well as using the common financial ratios to help you make an economic decision on the financial position and financial performance of an entity.

In this chapter, we cover this process, using the financial statements of Nestlé Group, whose annual report is reproduced, in parts, in Appendix A. You can see Nestlé's financial statements summarized below.

	A	B	C	D
1	Nestlé Group Consolidated Income Statement	For the year ended Dec. 31		
2	**(Adapted, in millions of Swiss Francs, CHF)**	**2016**	**2015**	**2014**
3	Sales	89,469	88,785	91,612
4	Other revenue	317	298	253
5	Cost of goods sold	(44,199)	(44,730)	(47,553)
6	Distribution expenses	(8,059)	(7,899)	(8,217)
7	Marketing and administration expenses	(21,485)	(20,744)	(19,651)
8	Research and development costs	(1,736)	(1,678)	(1,628)
9	Other trading and operating income	453	204	264
10	Other trading and operating expenses	(1,597)	(1,828)	(4,175)
11	Operating profit	13,163	12,408	10,905
12	Financial income	121	101	135
13	Financial expense	(758)	(725)	(772)
14	Taxes	(4,413)	(3,305)	(3,367)
15	Income from associates and joint ventures	770	988	8,003
16	Profit for the year	8,883	9,467	14,904
17				

This chapter covers the basic tools of financial analysis. The first part of the chapter shows how we can evaluate Nestlé from year to year and how to compare it to other companies that are in the same industry. For this comparison, we can use other fast moving consumer goods (FMCG) companies around the world, including Procter and Gamble (P&G) and Unilever. The second part of the chapter discusses the more commonly used financial ratios. You have seen many of these ratios in the earlier chapters. However, we are yet to use all of them in a comprehensive analysis of a company.

By studying all these ratios together:

- You will learn the basic tools of financial analysis.
- You will enhance your ability to assess operations of a business.

Regardless of your chosen field—marketing, management, finance, entrepreneurship, or accounting—you will find these analytical tools useful as you move through your career.

	A	B	C	D
1	**Nestlé Group Consolidated Balance Sheet**	**At December 31**		
2	**(Adapted, in millions of Swiss Francs, CHF)**	**2016**	**2015**	**2014**
3	Cash and cash equivalents	7,990	4,884	7,448
4	Short-term investments	1,306	921	1,433
5	Inventories	8,401	8,153	9,172
6	Trade and other receivables	12,411	12,252	13,459
7	Prepayments and accrued income	573	583	565
8	All other current assets	1,361	2,641	1,884
9	Total current assets	32,042	29,434	33,961
10	Property, plant and equipment	27,554	26,576	28,421
11	Intangible assets and goodwill	53,404	52,008	54,357
12	Financial assets and other investments	16,428	14,094	14,142
13	All other non-current assets	2,473	1,880	2,569
14	Total non-current assets	99,859	94,558	99,489
15	Total assets	131,901	123,992	133,450
16				
17	Short-term borrowings	12,118	9,629	8,810
18	Trade and other payables	18,629	17,038	17,437
19	Accruals and deferred income	3,855	3,673	3,759
20	Provisions	620	564	695
21	All other current liabilities	2,295	2,417	2,194
22	Total current liabilities	37,517	33,321	32,895
23	Long-term borrowings	11,091	11,601	12,396
24	Provisions and other payables	5,027	4,330	5,003
25	All other non-current liabilities	12,285	10,754	11,272
26	Total non-current liabilities	28,403	26,685	28,671
27	Total liabilities	65,920	60,006	61,566
28	Share capital	311	319	322
29	Treasury shares	(990)	(7,489)	(3,918)
30	Retained earnings	82,870	88,014	90,981
31	Other equity items	(16,210)	(16,858)	(15,501)
32	Total equity	65,981	63,986	71,884
33	Total liabilities and equity	131,901	123,992	133,450
34				

	A	B	C	D
1	**Nestlé Group Consolidated Cash Flow Statements**	**For the year ended Dec. 31**		
2	**(Adapted, in millions of Swiss Francs, CHF)**	**2016**	**2015**	**2014**
3	Profit for the year	8,883	9,467	14,904
4	Adjustments (summarized)	6,699	4,835	(204)
5	Operating cash flows	15,582	14,302	14,700
6	Investing cash flows	(6,123)	(4,153)	(3,072)
7	Financing cash flows	(6,184)	(12,235)	(10,637)
8	Currency adjustments/retranslations	(169)	(478)	42
9	Net cash flows	3,106	(2,564)	1,033
10	Cash and cash equivalent at beginning of the year	4,884	7,448	6,415
11	Cash and cash equivalent at end of the year	7,990	4,884	7,448
12				

A1			
Nestlé Group Consolidated Changes in Equity	**For the year ended Dec. 31**		
(Adapted, in millions of Swiss Francs, CHF)	**2016**	**2015**	**2014**
Equity at beginning of the year	63,986	71,884	64,139
Profit for the year	8,883	9,467	14,904
Other comprehensive income	741	(3,938)	1,900
Dividend paid	(7,369)	(7,374)	(7,219)
Other equity transactions	(260)	(6,053)	(1,840)
Equity at end of the year	65,981	63,986	71,884

LEARNING OBJECTIVES

1. **Perform** basic (horizontal and vertical) analysis of financial statements
2. **Prepare** common-size financial statements
3. **Perform** financial ratio analysis to make business decisions
4. **Use** financial ratios and other information to make investment decisions

It Starts with the Big Picture

Financial analysis involves more than just doing the math. Thorough analysis of the financial position and results of operations of a company begins with understanding the business and industry of the company—the big picture. This usually entails quite a bit of reading and research, using all kinds of media—the business press, trade journals, and other publications. You can often gain free access to this information via popular finance websites that you can research on the Internet, such as Google Finance, Yahoo Finance, MSN Finance, Bloomberg, Reuters, and many others.

There are also some "for pay" websites (such as the Motley fool, http://www.fool.com, and Dun & Bradstreet's Hoovers, http://www.hoovers.com) or subscription services (such as Standard and Poor's Capital IQ, www.capitaliq.com) through which industry and company analyses may be purchased. Learning about what's happening in the industry, markets, general economic conditions, trends in product development, and specific company strategies puts the numbers in context and helps you understand why they turned out as they did. After all, accounting data should paint a picture of the results of implementing a particular business strategy. Once we have an understanding of the big picture, we can start to dig deeper into the numbers, and they will make more sense.

It is also impossible to evaluate a company effectively by examining only one year's numerical data. This is why (in Chapter 4), we noted that *IAS 1—Presentation of Financial Statements* requires all financial statements to have comparative figures of at least two periods.

Nestlé's financial statements for the last three financial years (2014–16) were shown at the beginning of this chapter. In fact, most financial analysis covers trends of three to five years. Since one of the goals of financial analysis is to predict the future performance of an entity, it makes sense to start by mapping the trends of the past. You saw an example of this with Singtel's cash flow trends in Chapter 11. This is particularly true of Income Statement data such as net sales and net income.

Let's start our examination of Nestlé with two basic analysis techniques: horizontal analysis and vertical analysis.

PERFORM BASIC (HORIZONTAL AND VERTICAL) ANALYSIS ON FINANCIAL STATEMENTS

Horizontal Analysis

1 **Perform** basic (horizontal and vertical) analysis of financial statements

Many decisions hinge on the trend of revenues, expenses, income from operations, and so on. Have revenues increased from last year? By how much? It is a good idea to start with a broad perspective of how Nestlé has performed in the last 3 years. We can simply look at the absolute numbers for sales and operating profit (or total assets or other totals), or we can show it visually. The graphs in Exhibit 12-1 show Nestlé's three-year trend of sales revenue and operating profit.

Exhibit 12-1 | Sales and Operating Profit of Nestlé

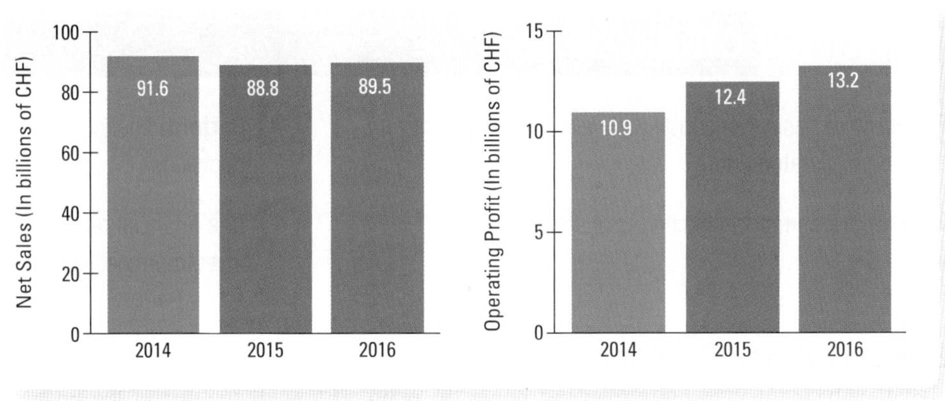

It looks like Nestlé's sales have dropped somewhat, but it was able to increase its operating profit!

Suppose you are looking at another company and its sales have increased by $50,000. In isolation, this fact is not very helpful, but knowing the long-term percentage change in net sales helps a lot. It is better to know that net sales have increased by 20% than to know that the increase is $50,000. It's even better to know that percentage changes in net sales for the past several years have been rising year on year.

The study of percentage changes from year to year is called **horizontal analysis**. Computing a percentage change takes two steps:

1. Compute the amount of the change from one period (the base period) to the next.
2. Divide the amount of change by the base period amount.

Let's apply this to Nestlé's sales and operating profit for the year 2016 and 2015 (CHF 89,469 compared to CHF 88,785, and CHF 13,163 compared to CHF 12,408, respectively). For sales, the amount change is an increase of CHF 684, and for operating profit, an increase of CHF 755. Expressed as percentages, they represent an increase of 0.77% in sales and an increase of 6.08% in operating profit. As you can see, the percentages give a better context than just the actual sales or actual operating profits.

	2016	2015	Increase/(Decrease) Amount	Percentage
Sales	89,469	88,785	684	0.77%
Operating profit	13,163	12,408	755	6.08%

If we extend this horizontal analysis to Nestlé's Income Statement, you will see something like this below in Exhibit 12-2.

Exhibit 12-2 Horizontal Analysis of Nestlé's Income Statements

	A	B	C	D	E
1	**Nestlé Group Consolidated Income Statement**	**For the year ended Dec. 31**		**Increase/(Decrease)**	
2	**(Adapted, in millions of Swiss Francs, CHF)**	**2016**	**2015**	**Amount**	**Percentage**
3	Sales	89,469	88,785	684	0.77%
4	Other revenue	317	298	19	6.38%
5	Cost of goods sold	(44,199)	(44,730)	(531)	(1.19%)
6	Distribution expenses	(8,059)	(7,899)	160	2.03%
7	Marketing and administration expenses	(21,485)	(20,744)	741	3.57%
8	Research and development costs	(1,736)	(1,678)	58	3.46%
9	Other trading and operating income	453	204	249	122.06%
10	Other trading and operating expenses	(1,597)	(1,828)	(231)	(12.64%)
11	Operating profit	13,163	12,408	755	6.08%
12	Financial income	121	101	20	19.80%
13	Financial expense	(758)	(725)	33	4.55%
14	Taxes	(4,413)	(3,305)	1,108	33.52%
15	Income from associates and joint ventures	770	988	(218)	(22.06%)
16	Profit for the year	8,883	9,467	(584)	(6.17%)
17					

Horizontal analysis does not provide you with answers as to why other income increases by 122.06% and other expenses decreases by 12.64%. You will need to carefully study the notes to the financial statements and make an assessment if these 2016 amounts are likely to repeat in the years beyond. You would want to check if there are likely to be changes in the income from associates and joint ventures and also the reasons why the tax expenses vary so much from 2015 to 2016. As an investor, you would want to assess if these items are likely to have a further impact in future operations. Horizontal analysis provides that first step in seeing how the numbers move from one year to the next.

Similarly, studying changes in Balance Sheet accounts can also enhance our understanding of the current and long-term financial position of the entity. Exhibit 12-3 looks at a few Balance Sheet changes that transpired for Nestlé in 2016.

Exhibit 12-3 Horizontal Analysis of Nestlé's Balance Sheets

Nestlé Group Consolidated Balance Sheet	At December 31		Increase/(Decrease)	
(Adapted, in millions of Swiss Francs, CHF)	2016	2015	Amount	Percentage
Cash and cash equivalents	7,990	4,884	3,106	63.60%
Short-term investments	1,306	921	385	41.80%
Inventories	8,401	8,153	248	3.04%
Trade and other receivables	12,411	12,252	159	1.30%
Prepayments and accrued income	573	583	(10)	(1.72%)
All other current assets	1,361	2,641	(1,280)	(48.47%)
Total current assets	32,042	29,434	2,608	8.86%
Property, plant and equipment	27,554	26,576	978	3.68%
Intangible assets and goodwill	53,404	52,008	1,396	2.68%
Financial assets and other investments	16,428	14,094	2,334	16.56%
All other non-current assets	2,473	1,880	593	31.54%
Total non-current assets	99,859	94,558	5,301	5.61%
Total assets	131,901	123,992	7,909	6.38%
Short-term borrowings	12,118	9,629	2,489	25.85%
Trade and other payables	18,629	17,038	1,591	9.34%
Accruals and deferred income	3,855	3,673	182	4.96%
Provisions	620	564	56	9.93%
All other current liabilities	2,295	2,417	(122)	(5.05%)
Total current liabilities	37,517	33,321	4,196	12.59%
Long-term borrowings	11,091	11,601	(510)	(4.40%)
Provisions and other payables	5,027	4,330	697	16.10%
All other non-current liabilities	12,285	10,754	1,531	14.24%
Total non-current liabilities	28,403	26,685	1,718	6.44%
Total liabilities	65,920	60,006	5,914	9.86%
Share capital	311	319	(8)	(2.51%)
Treasury shares	(990)	(7,489)	(6,499)	(86.78%)
Retained earnings	82,870	88,014	(5,144)	(5.84%)
Other equity items	(16,210)	(16,858)	(648)	(3.84%)
Total equity	65,981	63,986	1,995	3.12%
Total liabilities and equity	131,901	123,992	7,909	6.38%

From total assets perspective, you can see that Nestlé has grown 6.38%, from CHF 123,992 to CHF 131,901, as a result of increases in both current assets and non-current assets. In particular, cash has the biggest percentage increase of 63.60%. Short-term borrowings increased by 25.85%, accompanied by a decrease in long-term borrowings of 4.40%. Note that the largest decrease in quantum is retained earnings (CHF 5,144), but percentage wise, it has only dropped by 5.84%. This is why you will need to balance your review of horizontal analysis between the quantum and percentage since a large base may result in a smaller percentage change, and similarly, a small base may result in a very big percentage change.

A word of caution: you should not show a percentage change when the numbers swing from negative to positive or vice versa. In such cases, while you can mathematically calculate the percentage difference, they are not meaningful and not shown. For example, if you had a loss of \$100 last year and you now have a profit of \$150, you can't possibly use a percentage to describe the change. For these instances, you should put the notation "n.m." to stand for not meaningful.

Stop & Think

Have another look at Exhibits 12-2 and 12-3. Are the biggest percentage items always the most important items that cause changes in the Income Statement or Balance Sheet from one year to another? Can you always ignore small changes, such as anything that is less than 5%?

Answer:

The largest percentage change in Nestlé's Income Statement was 122.06% for "other trading and operating income" (CHF 249). However, this amount is only the fifth highest change by amount. In comparison, the third largest amount change was CHF 684 for increase in sales, but it was only 0.77% in percentage terms. The 0.77% change would probably be more significant for Nestlé's performance than the 122.06% change.

Similarly, on the Balance Sheet, the smallest percentage change was CHF 159 (1.30%) change in "trade and other receivables." However, this is likely going to be more important than say, a CHF 56 (9.93%) change in provisions.

Thus, smaller percentage changes do not always mean they can be ignored. Similarly, a percentage change may be very substantial just because there was a small base.

Trend Analysis

Trend percentages are a form of horizontal analysis. Trends indicate the direction a business is taking. How have revenues changed over a five-year period? What trend does net income show? These questions can be answered by trend percentages over a representative period, such as the most recent five years.

Trend percentages are computed by selecting a base year whose amounts are set equal to 100%. The amount for each following year is stated as a percentage of the base amount. To compute a trend percentage, divide an item for a later year by the base-year amount.

$$\text{Trend \%} = \frac{\text{Any year's amount}}{\text{Base year's amount}}$$

Remember that income from operations (or operating profit) is often viewed as the primary measure of a company's earnings quality. This is because operating income represents a company's best predictor of the future net inflows from its core business units. Net income from operations is often used in estimating the current value of the business.

Nestlé's operating profit for the last 5 years is as follows:

(In millions, CHF)	2016	2015	2014	2013	2012
Operating profit..........................	13,163	12,408	10,905	12,408	13,388

We want to calculate a trend for the five-year period 2012 through 2016. The first year in the series (2012) is set as the base year. Trend percentages are computed by dividing each year's amount by the 2012 amount. The resulting trend percentages follow (2012 = 100%):

	2016	2015	2014	2013	2012
Operating profit..........................	98	93	81	98	100

Overall, Nestlé's operating income has been lower than 2012 (the highest in the five-year series). It dropped to a low of 81% in 2014 but has steadily climbed back to the same level as 2013.

You can perform a trend analysis on any item you consider important. Trend analysis using Income Statement data is widely used for predicting the future. Horizontal and trend analyses highlight changes over time. It is a basic technique that will get you started in financial statement analysis.

Vertical Analysis

Vertical analysis (or component analysis) shows the relationship of financial-statement items relative to a total, which is the 100% figure. All items on the particular financial statement are reported as a percentage of the base. For the Income Statement, total revenue (sales) is usually the base. Suppose under normal conditions a company's net income is 8% of revenue. A drop to 6% may cause the company's share price to fall. Let's apply this to Nestlé's Income Statement.

Exhibit 12-4 shows the vertical analysis of Nestlé's Income Statement as a percentage of revenue.

Exhibit 12-4 Vertical Analysis of Nestlé's Income Statements

	A	B	C	D	E
1	**Nestlé Group** **Consolidated Income Statement (Adapted)** **For the year ended Dec. 31**				
2	**(In millions of Swiss Francs, CHF)**	**2016**	% sales	**2015**	% sales
3	Sales	89,469	100.00%	88,785	100.00%
4	Other revenue	317	0.35%	298	0.34%
5	Cost of goods sold	(44,199)	(49.40%)	(44,730)	(50.38%)
6	Distribution expenses	(8,059)	(9.01%)	(7,899)	(8.90%)
7	Marketing and administration expenses	(21,485)	(24.01%)	(20,744)	(23.36%)
8	Research and development costs	(1,736)	(1.94%)	(1,678)	(1.89%)
9	Other trading and operating income	453	0.51%	204	0.23%
10	Other trading and operating expenses	(1,597)	(1.78%)	(1,828)	(2.06%)
11	Operating profit	13,163	14.71%	12,408	13.98%
12	Financial income	121	0.14%	101	0.11%
13	Financial expense	(758)	(0.85%)	(725)	(0.82%)
14	Taxes	(4,413)	(4.93%)	(3,305)	(3.72%)
15	Income from associates and joint ventures	770	0.86%	988	1.11%
16	Profit for the year	8,883	9.93%	9,467	10.66%
17					

Some observations from the above vertical analysis are as follows:

- Cost of sales was 50.38% of revenue in 2015, but it has decreased a percentage point to 49.40% in 2016. This indicates Nestlé's ability to manage cost of sales.
- In general, distribution expenses, marketing and administration expenses, and research and development costs were slightly higher in 2016 compared to 2015 as a percentage of sales.
- Consequently, the operating profit has increased from 14% to 15%. One percentage point may look small, but it translates to a 700 million CHF increase in operating profit for Nestlé.
- As a percentage of sales, taxes have gone up from 3.72% to 4.93%.
- Overall, for each CHF of sales in 2016, Nestlé made about 10% in net profit, and this was slightly down from 2015.

We could do a similar vertical analysis on the Balance Sheet. If you want to see the composition of total assets, then let total assets be 100% and express all assets as a percentage of total assets. However, if you are zooming in on the composition of current assets, then let current assets be 100% and examine only components of current assets. A common way to visualize

Stop & Think

Perform a vertical analysis for the common-size percentages for the following Income Statement:

Net sales	$150,000
Cost of goods sold	60,000
Gross profit	90,000
Operating expense	40,000
Operating income	50,000
Income tax expense	15,000
Net income	$ 35,000

Answer:

Net sales	100%	(= $150,000 ÷ $150,000)
Cost of goods sold	40	(= $ 60,000 ÷ $150,000)
Gross profit	60	(= $ 90,000 ÷ $150,000)
Operating expense	27	(= $ 40,000 ÷ $150,000)
Operating income	33	(= $ 50,000 ÷ $150,000)
Income tax expense	10	(= $ 15,000 ÷ $150,000)
Net income	23%	(= $ 35,000 ÷ $150,000)

vertical analysis is to depict the items as a pie chart. For a pie chart to be effective, you would want to show no more than 7 slices and combine all other smaller items together. Exhibit 12-5 shows an example of component analysis of Nestlé's assets using a pie chart.

Exhibit 12-5 Vertical Analysis of Nestlé's Assets Using a Pie Chart

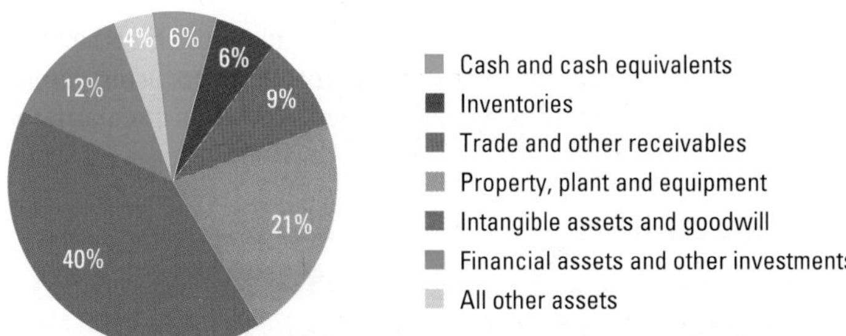

PREPARE COMMON-SIZE FINANCIAL STATEMENTS

Benchmarking

2 **Perform** common-size financial statements

As you have seen throughout the textbook, when we do financial analysis, we normally benchmark the financial numbers and ratios to other similar companies. **Benchmarking** simply means comparing one entity to another. Usually benchmarks are selected because they direct competitors in the same industry or market, peers in the broader market, or just any other "aspiration" entities. You may be running a small retail shop, but if you aspire to do just as well as Amazon or department stores like Marks and Spencer, then go ahead, you can always benchmark your own company's performance against specific companies. The most important aspect of benchmarking, however, is that it gives you context in which you could interpret your data.

A Closer Look

You could also research industry averages on various websites. For example, http://www.bizstats.com/industry-financials.php offers some basic financial ratio information from 251 industries and sub-sectors. In addition, your university library may have subscriptions to Dun & Bradstreet's *Industry Norms and Key Business Ratios*, Standard & Poor's *Capital IQ*, or Risk Management Association's *Annual Statement Studies*. There are also many others, but they typically require you to subscribe or purchase the information. In this chapter, relevant industry benchmarks are obtained from S&P's *Capital IQ* at the time of writing.

Suppose you are a financial analyst for a large investment bank. You are considering investing in one of two different companies in the same industry, say Nestlé, Unilever, or P&G. A direct numerical comparison of these companies' financial statements is not meaningful, in part because of differing currencies and size differences. One company may be so much larger than the others. One of the techniques you could use, called **common-size financial statements**, is basically an extension of vertical analysis.

We can modify Exhibit 12-4 to report only percentages (no currency amounts) for two or more companies. When compared side-by-side, such common-size financial statements aid the comparison of different companies because all amounts are stated in percentages, thus expressing the financial results of each comparative company in terms of a common denominator. Currency and size differences are eliminated when you do a common-size comparison.

Exhibit 12-6 presents the common-size Income Statements of Nestlé, Unilever, and P&G. To make common-size comparisons meaningful, you often have to synchronize the items in the two (or more) financial statements and simplify. For example, one company may separate selling and distribution expenses from administrative expenses, but another may combine them as selling, general, and administrative expenses. Another difference could be where one company provides analysis of its expenses by function and another company provides it by nature (we discussed function vs. nature in Chapter 4). Sometimes, you may only be able compare the key line items. Exhibit 12-6 offers the broad expense categories for our comparisons of the three FMCG companies.

Note that Nestlé reports in Swiss Francs (CHF), Unilever in euros (EUR) and P&G in US dollars (USD), and yet we are able to arrive at some comparative numbers using common-size analysis. This is one of the major advantages of using percentages rather than comparing actual amounts.

Exhibit 12-6 Common-size Income Statements

A1

	A	B	C	D
1	**Common-size Income Statements**	**Nestlé 2016**	**Unilever 2016**	**P&G 2016**
2	Sales	100.00%	100.00%	100.00%
3	Cost of goods sold	(49.40%)	(51.19%)	(50.40%)
4	Gross profit	50.60%	48.81%	49.60%
5	Other operating income and expenses	(35.89%)	(34.01%)	(29.02%)
6	Operating profit	14.71%	14.80%	20.58%
7	Interest expense	(0.85%)	(1.11%)	(0.89%)
8	Tax expense	(4.93%)	(3.65%)	(5.12%)
9	Other non-operating income and expenses	1.00%	0.48%	1.66%
10	Profit for the year	9.93%	10.52%	16.24%

As you can see from Exhibit 12-6, Nestlé has the highest gross profit margin, but the lowest operating profit margin and net profit margin. This means both its operating and nonoperating income and expenses are higher than Unilever and P&G. Looking at the bottom-line performance, we can see that Unilever is slightly better than Nestlé, but P&G's performance is about 5 percentage points better than Nestlé and Unilever.

Mid-Chapter Summary Problem

Perform a horizontal analysis and a vertical analysis of the comparative Income Statement of Hard Rock Products, Inc., which makes metal detectors. State whether 20X7 was a good year or a bad year, and give your reasons.

	A	B	C
1	**Hard Rock Products, Inc. Comparative Income Statements Years Ended December 31, 20X7 and 20X6**		
2		**20X7**	**20X6**
3	Total revenues	$ 275,000	$ 225,000
4	Expenses:		
5	Cost of goods sold	194,000	165,000
6	Engineering, selling, and administrative expenses	54,000	48,000
7	Interest expense	5,000	5,000
8	Income tax expense	9,000	3,000
9	Other expense (income)	1,000	(1,000)
10	Total expenses	263,000	220,000
11	Net income	$ 12,000	$ 5,000
12			

Answer

The horizontal analysis shows that total revenues increased 22.2%. This was greater than the 19.5% increase in total expenses, resulting in a 140% increase in net income.

	A	B	C	D	E
1	**Hard Rock Products, Inc. Horizontal Analysis of Comparative Income Statements Years Ended December 31, 20X7 and 20X6**				
2		**20X7**	**20X6**	**Increase (Decrease) Amount**	**Percent**
3	Total revenues	$ 275,000	$ 225,000	$ 50,000	22.2%
4	Expenses:				
5	Cost of goods sold	194,000	165,000	29,000	17.6
6	Engineering, selling, and				
7	administrative expenses	54,000	48,000	6,000	12.5
8	Interest expense	5,000	5,000	—	—
9	Income tax expense	9,000	3,000	6,000	200.0
10	Other expense (income)	1,000	(1,000)	2,000	n.m.*
11	Total expenses	263,000	220,000	43,000	19.5
12	Net income	$ 12,000	$ 5,000	$ 7,000	140.0%
13					

*n.m., not meaningful. Percentage changes are typically not computed for shifts from a negative to a positive amount and vice versa.

The vertical analysis shows decreases in the percentages of net sales consumed by the cost of goods sold (from 73.3% to 70.5%) and by the engineering, selling, and administrative expenses (from 21.3% to 19.6%). Because these two items are Hard Rock's largest dollar expenses, their percentage decreases are quite important. The relative reduction in expenses raised 20X7 net income to 4.4% of sales, compared with 2.2% the preceding year. The overall analysis indicates that 20X7 was significantly better than 20X6.

	A	B	C	D	E
1	**Hard Rock Products, Inc.** **Vertical Analysis of Comparative Income Statements** **Years Ended December 31, 20X7 and 20X6**				
2		**20X7** **Amount**	 **Percent**	**20X6** **Amount**	 **Percent**
3	Total revenues	$ 275,000	100.0%	$ 225,000	100.0%
4	Expenses:				
5	Cost of goods sold	194,000	70.5	165,000	73.3
6	Engineering, selling, and administrative expenses	54,000	19.6	48,000	21.3
7	Interest expense	5,000	1.8	5,000	2.2
8	Income tax expense	9,000	3.3	3,000	1.4**
9	Other expense (income)	1,000	0.4	(1,000)	(0.4)
10	Total expenses	263,000	95.6	220,000	97.8
11	Net income	$ 12,000	4.4%	$ 5,000	2.2%
12					

**Number rounded up.

PERFORM FINANCIAL RATIO ANALYSIS TO MAKE BUSINESS DECISIONS

3 **Perform** financial ratio analysis to make business decisions

Financial ratios are a major tool of financial analysis. We have discussed the use of many ratios in financial analysis in various chapters throughout the book. A ratio expresses the relationship of one number to another. Suppose your Balance Sheet shows current assets of $100,000 and current liabilities of $50,000. The ratio of current assets to current liabilities is $100,000 to $50,000. We can express this ratio as 2 to 1, or 2:1, or some may even say current ratio is at 200%. In any case, what we really mean is that the current ratio is 2.

Many companies include selected financial ratios in a special section of their annual reports or post them online on their "investor relation" websites. For example, Nestlé's corporate website, under the Investor tab, provides a link to its "Annual Review" where a number of ratios are shown and discussed. Similarly, on the Unilever website (https://www.unilever.com/investor-relations/annual-report-and-accounts/) you can see a list of key ratios highlighted. Alternatively, you may visit various information websites, such as Moody's, Standard & Poor's, Risk Management Association, Reuters, and others, for their coverage of companies' news and financial information, including financial ratios. You are more likely to find more coverage on larger multinational companies than on smaller ones. For example, you can check out Reuters' coverage of Nestlé at http://www.reuters.com/finance/stocks/financialHighlights?symbol=NESN.S.

The financial ratios we discuss in this chapter are classified as follows:

1. Efficiency ratios
2. Financial strength ratios
3. Profitability ratios
4. Investment ratios

Sometimes you may find different ratio classifications and even slightly different formulas for the ratios we are about to discuss. For example, Reuters classify ratios into efficiency, effectiveness, financial strength, profitability, and valuation ratios. Don't be alarmed by any differences; as long as you calculate the ratios consistently, there is always value to financial statement analysis. A weighing scale that is slightly inaccurate can still tell you which item in a room is the heaviest or lightest.

Exhibit 12-7 gives the Income Statement and Balance Sheet data of Ikon Furniture, an independent furniture and homewares retailer. We will work with this exhibit as our running example on how to perform financial statement analysis and compare the financial ratios to an industry average. At the end of each section, we will also show you the financial ratios of Nestlé for discussion.

Exhibit 12-7 Comparative Financial Statements

A1

	A	B	C
1	**Ikon Furniture, Inc.** **Comparative Income Statements** **Years Ended December 31, 20X7 and 20X6**		
2		**20X7**	**20X6**
3	Net sales	$ 858,000	$ 803,000
4	Cost of goods sold	513,000	509,000
5	Gross profit	345,000	294,000
6	Operating expenses:		
7	Selling expenses	126,000	114,000
8	General expenses	118,000	123,000
9	Total operating expenses	244,000	237,000
10	Income from operations	101,000	57,000
11	Interest revenue	4,000	0
12	Interest (expense)	(24,000)	(14,000)
13	Income before income taxes	81,000	43,000
14	Income tax expense	33,000	17,000
15	Net income	$ 48,000	$ 26,000
16			

A1

	A	B	C
1	**Ikon Furniture, Inc.** **Comparative Balance Sheets** **December 31, 20X7 and 20X6**		
2		**20X7**	**20X6**
3	**Assets**		
4	Current Assets:		
5	Cash	$ 29,000	$ 32,000
6	Accounts receivable, net	114,000	85,000
7	Inventories	113,000	111,000
8	Prepaid expenses	6,000	8,000
9	Total current assets	262,000	236,000
10	Long-term investments	18,000	9,000
11	Property, plant and equipment, net	507,000	399,000
12	Total assets	$ 787,000	$ 644,000
13	**Liabilities**		
14	Current Liabilities:		
15	Notes payable	$ 42,000	$ 27,000
16	Accounts payable	73,000	68,000
17	Accrued liabilities	27,000	31,000
18	Total current liabilities	142,000	126,000
19	Long-term debt	289,000	198,000
20	Total liabilities	431,000	324,000
21	**Shareholders' Equity**		
22	Share capital, no par	186,000	186,000
23	Retained earnings	170,000	134,000
24	Total shareholders' equity	356,000	320,000
25	Total liabilities and shareholders' equity	$ 787,000	$ 644,000
26			

Efficiency Ratios

For companies that buy or make goods for sale, the ability to sell inventory and collect receivables is critical. In this section, we discuss a number of ratios that measure an entity's ability to collect cash. We have previously introduced some of the ratios here in earlier chapters (receivable turnover, inventory turnover, and payable turnover in Chapters 5, 6, and 9). Let's start with the components of a cash conversion cycle.

Inventory Turnover. Companies generally strive to sell their inventory as quickly as possible. The faster inventory sells, the sooner cash comes in. **Inventory turnover** (discussed in Chapter 6) measures the number of times a company sells its average level of inventory during a year. A fast turnover indicates ease in selling inventory; a low turnover indicates difficulty. A value of 6 means that the company's average level of inventory has been sold six times during the year, and that's usually better than a turnover of 3. But too high a value can mean that the business is not keeping enough inventory on hand, which can lead to lost sales if the company can't fill orders. Therefore, a business strives for the most profitable rate of turnover, not necessarily the *highest* rate.

To compute inventory turnover, divide the cost of goods sold by the average inventory for the period. We use the cost of goods sold—not sales—in the computation because both cost of goods sold and inventory are stated at cost. Ikon Furniture's inventory turnover for 20X7 is:

Formula	*Ikon's Inventory Turnover*	Industry Average
$\text{Inventory turnover} = \dfrac{\text{Cost of goods sold}}{\text{Average inventory}}$	$\dfrac{\$513{,}000}{\$112{,}000} = 4.6$	4.2

Cost of goods sold comes from the Income Statement (Exhibit 12-7). Average inventory is the average of beginning ($111,000) and ending inventory ($113,000) (see the Balance Sheet, Exhibit 12-7). Inventory turnover varies widely with the nature of the business. For example, a fast-food chain restaurant, such as Pizza Hut, Taco Bell, KFC, or Long John Silver's, is likely to have a high turnover ratio because it turns around its inventory into sales in a short time. This may be a necessity because food spoils quickly. On the other hand, a furniture retailer turns its inventory over only a few times a year, as most of the inventory is kept for a while on shop floors and warehouses, waiting for customers to purchase. In this case, Ikon's inventory turnover is slightly above the industry average. To evaluate inventory turnover, compare the ratio over time. A sharp decline suggests the need for corrective action.

Inventory turnover can also be expressed in number of days. If you divide 365 days by Ikon's inventory turnover ratio of 4.6, this is equal to about 79 days, compared to the industry average of 87 days. This ratio is called the **inventory resident period** (or days supply on hand, days inventory on hand, or something to that effect).

Accounts Receivable Turnover. Receivable turnover measures the ability to collect cash from customers. In general, the higher the ratio, the better. A low receivable turnover indicates ineffectiveness in collecting dues from customers. However, a receivable turnover that is too high may indicate that credit is too tight, and that may cause you to lose sales to good customers.

To compute accounts receivable turnover, divide net sales by average net accounts receivable. The ratio tells how many times during the year average receivables were turned into cash. Note that we would normally exclude non-trading revenue and receivables. For example, we would only include revenue from trading activities and not interest revenue or dividend income. Similarly, we would only include trade receivables and not other receivables such as loans to employees. Ikon Furniture's accounts receivable turnover ratio for 20X7 is:

Formula	*Ikon's Accounts Receivable Turnover*	Industry Average
$\text{Accounts receivable turnover} = \dfrac{\text{Sales Revenue}}{\text{Average accounts receivable}}$	$\dfrac{\$858{,}000}{\$99{,}500} = 8.6$	6.2

Average net accounts receivable can be derived by adding beginning ($85,000) and ending receivables ($114,000), then dividing by 2. Ikon's receivable turnover of 8.6 times per year is a little faster than the industry average. Why the faster collection? Ikon may be a hometown store that sells to local people and businesses who typically settle their bills on time.

Similarly, we can also convert receivable turnover into days and refer to it as the **receivable collection period**, also known as days sales outstanding, or days sales in receivables, or something similar. For Ikon, on average, it takes 42 days to collect cash from its receivables. This is better than the home furnishing industry's average of 59 days.

Accounts Payable Turnover. Businesses buy their supplies and raw materials on credit, and take time to pay their accounts payable. A high account payable turnover ratio means a business pays its suppliers very quickly, and a low payable turnover means a longer time period for payments to suppliers. Generally, a lower payable turnover is better than a higher one, as the business is making full use of the credit terms extended by its creditors. However, a business can't stretch the payable period too far because no one would supply the business if it continued to be delinquent on its payments.

To compute **payable turnover**, divide cost of goods sold by the average accounts payable for the period. Again, we would only include trade-related payables and exclude items such as interest payable, short-term loan, tax payable, and so forth. Average accounts payable for the period is $73,000 + $60,000 divided by 2. Ikon Furniture's payable turnover for 20X7 is:

Formula			*Ikon's Accounts Payable Turnover*	Industry Average
Accounts payable turnover	=	$\frac{\text{COGS}}{\text{Average net accounts payable}}$	$\frac{\$513{,}000}{\$70{,}500} = 7.3$	3.7

It seems that Ikon pays its creditors faster than the industry average. Perhaps as a small store, it was not given as liberal a credit term as other major players in the home furnishing industry. If we express this ratio in days, the **payable outstanding period** (or days payable outstanding) is 50 days (365/7.3), whereas the industry average is about 99 days (365/3.7).

Cash Conversion Cycle. If we put the inventory resident period, receivable collection period, and payable collection period together, we can get a rough idea of how long it takes for a business to sell its inventory, collect payments, and make its payments to suppliers. This is what we call the **cash conversion cycle**.

Ikon's cash conversion cycle is thus inventory resident period + receivable collection period − payable outstanding period, or 79 + 42 − 50 = 71 days. The home furnishings' cash conversion cycle is much faster at 87 + 59 − 99 = 47 days, primarily due to the long payable outstanding period. In general, a shorter cycle is better than a longer cycle; in fact it can even be a negative number. Here's an example of HP (Hewlett-Packard)'s disclosure on its cash conversion cycle. Note that HP uses slightly different terminology and 90-day averages instead of 2-year averages that we use in this chapter.

ADAPTED EXCERPTS FROM HP INC'S ANNUAL FILING

Management utilizes current cash conversion cycle information to manage our working capital level. The table below presents the cash conversion cycle as of October 31, 2016, and October 31, 2015.

	As of October 31		
	2016	**2015**	**2014**
Days of sales outstanding in accounts receivable	30	35	33
Days of supply in inventory	39	39	35
Days of purchases outstanding in accounts payable	(98)	(93)	(86)
Cash conversion cycle	(29)	(19)	(18)

continued on the following page

The sum of days' sales outstanding in accounts receivable ("DSO") and days' supply in inventory ("DOS") less days' purchases outstanding in accounts payable ("DPO") is known as Cash Conversion Cycle.

The DSO is used to account for the average number of days of outstanding receivables. We can calculate the DSO by dividing ending accounts receivable, net of allowance for doubtful accounts, by a 90-day net revenue average. The DOS also accounts for the average number of days from procurement to the sale of a product. It is computed by dividing the ending inventory by a 90-day average of cost of goods sold.

The DPO is used to compute the average number of days for outstanding accounts payable balances. It is calculated by dividing ending accounts payable by a 90-day average of cost of goods sold.

Source: HP Inc., Annual Filing 2016, page 45–46

Stop & Think

Use the following information to calculate Nestlé's Cash Conversion Cycle for 2016 and 2015. What is your assessment of Nestlé's trading efficiency?

Nestlé (in CHF Millions)	2016	2015	2014
Sales	89,469	88,785	91,612
COGS	44,199	44,730	47,553
Invetories	8,401	8,153	9,172
Trade receivables	10,023	9,696	10,283
Trade payables	18,629	17,038	17,437

Answer:

Inventory turnover and resident period 2016 = 44,199/average of 8,401 and 8,153 = 5.34 times; and 365/5.34 = 68.35 days

Inventory turnover and resident period 2015 = 44,730/average of 8,153 and 9,172 = 5.16 times; and 365/5.16 = 70.69 days

Receivables turnover and collection period 2016 = 89,649/average of 10,023 and 9,696 = 9.07 times; and 365/9.07 = 44.02 days

Receivables turnover and collection period 2015 = 88,785/average of 9,696 and 10,283 = 8.89 times; and 365/8.89 = 41.07 days

Payable turnover and payment period 2016 = 44,199/average of 18,626 and 17,038 = 2.48 times; and 365/2.48 times = 147.27 days

Payable turnover and payment period 2016 = 44,730/average of 17,038 and 17,437 = 2.59 times; and 365/2.59 times = 140.66 days

Cash conversion cycle 2016 = 68.35 days + 40.22 days − 147.27 days = −38.70 days

Cash conversion cycle 2015 = 70.69 days + 41.07 days − 140.66 days = −28.91 days.

Nestlé has a very good cash conversion cycle. The time it took to pay suppliers is longer than the time it took to sell inventory and collect cash, resulting in a negative CCC. There is a limit, however, on how long Nestlé can practically delay payment to its suppliers. Suppliers may increase their prices or even refuse to supply Nestlé if they have to wait for a long time for payments.

Asset Turnover Ratio. Another way to examine efficiency would be to assess the amount of resources used to generate sales or revenue. This can be done on a total assets basis, or sometimes on a fixed assets (i.e., PPE) basis. This ratio is calculated by dividing sales or revenue by average total assets.

Formula	*Ikon's Asset Turnover* 20X7	20X6	Industry Average
$\text{Asset Turnover} = \dfrac{\text{Sales}}{\text{Average total assets}}$	$\dfrac{\$858{,}000}{\$715{,}500} = 1.2$	$\dfrac{\$803{,}000}{\$644{,}000} = 1.2$	0.9

*Using 20X6 ending figures only

Ikon has been able to generate $1.2 worth of sales for every $1 of assets in 20X6 and 20X7. Its assets turnover is higher than the industry average of 0.9.

Financial Strength Ratios

Financial strength ratios are indicators of an entity's abilities to meet its financial obligations, either in the short-term or the long-term. Short-term indicators are usually called **liquidity ratios** and long-term ones are usually called **solvency ratios**. Let's look at these indicators in turn.

In any financial year, a business has current assets at its disposal and has current liabilities to settle. **Working capital** is the term we use to describe what a business has to work with during the year, i.e., current assets less current liabilities. Generally, the higher the working capital, the better. Too much of it, however, means the business is not utilizing its current assets effectively, as cash, inventory, and receivables do not earn much income. Some businesses may operate on very little working capital, especially if they have a very strong cash conversion cycle. Consider two companies with equal working capital:

	Company Jones	Smith
Current assets	$100,000	$200,000
Current liabilities	50,000	150,000
Working capital	$ 50,000	$ 50,000

Both companies have working capital of $50,000, but Jones' working capital is as large as its current liabilities. Smith's working capital is only one-third as large as current liabilities. Jones is in a better position because its working capital is a higher percentage of current liabilities. Two decision-making tools based on current assets and current liabilities data are the *current ratio* and the *quick ratio*.

Current Ratio. The most common ratio evaluating current assets and current liabilities is the **current ratio**, which is simply current assets divided by current liabilities. The current ratio measures the ability to pay current liabilities with current assets (as discussed in Chapter 5).

The current ratios of Ikon Furniture, Inc., at December 31, 20X7 and 20X6, follow, along with the average for the home furnishing industry:

Formula	*Ikon's Current Ratio* 20X7	20X6	Industry Average
$\text{Current ratio} = \dfrac{\text{Current assets}}{\text{Current liabilities}}$	$\dfrac{\$262{,}000}{\$142{,}000} = 1.85$	$\dfrac{\$236{,}000}{\$126{,}000} = 1.87$	1.6

Ikon's current ratio decreased slightly during 20X7. In general, a higher current ratio indicates a stronger financial position. The business has sufficient current assets to maintain its operations. What is an acceptable current ratio? The answer depends on the industry. The norm for companies in most industries is around 1.5, as reported by the Risk Management Association. Ikon Furniture's current ratio of 1.85 is better than the home furnishing industry average of 1.6.

Quick Ratio. A more refined version of current ratio is known as the **quick ratio** (also known as the **acid-test ratio**). It tells us whether a business could pass the "acid test" of paying all its current liabilities if they came due immediately. The quick ratio uses a narrower base to measure liquidity than the current ratio does.

To compute the quick ratio, we add cash, short-term investments, and net current receivables (accounts and notes receivable, net of allowances) and divide by current liabilities. Inventory is excluded because they are less liquid, as businesses may be unable to convert inventory to cash immediately. This is why sometimes you see this shortcut in measuring quick ratio: (Current Assets − Inventory) ÷ Current Liabilities.

Ikon Furniture's quick ratios for 20X7 and 20X6 follow:

Formula	*Ikon's Quick Ratio* 20X7	*Ikon's Quick Ratio* 20X6	Industry Average
$\text{Quick ratio} = \dfrac{\text{Cash + Short-term investments + Net current receivables}}{\text{Current liabilities}}$	$\dfrac{\$29{,}000 + \$0 + \$114{,}000}{\$142{,}000} = 1.01$	$\dfrac{\$32{,}000 + \$0 + \$85{,}000}{\$126{,}000} = 0.93$	1.3

The company's quick ratio improved during 20X7 and is lower than the industry average. It seems like Ikon is holding more inventory than other companies in the industry.

Use the following information to calculate Nestlé's short-term financial strength ratios for 2016 and 2015. What is your assessment of Nestlé's liquidity?

Nestlé (in CHF Millions)	2016	2015
Current assets	32,042	29,434
Current liabilities	37,517	33,321
Inventories	8,401	8,153

Answer:

Working capital 2016 = 32,042 − 37,517 = negative working capital of CHF 5,475 million.

Working capital 2015 = 29,434 − 33,321 = negative working capital of CHF 3,887 million.

Current ratio 2016 = 32,042 / 37,517 = 0.85
Current ratio 2015 = 29,434 / 33,321 = 0.88
Quick ratio 2016 = (32,042 − 8,401) / 37,517 = 0.63
Quick ratio 2015 = (29,434 − 8,153) / 33,321 = 0.64

Nestlé is working under a negative capital and has a current ratio well below 1.5. This is usually an indicator of financial weakness. However, recall that Nestlé has a negative cash conversion cycle, which makes it less necessary to have large current assets to meet its current liabilities. We could also calculate quick ratio using its alternative form if we had the breakdown of the items instead of just the total current assets: Cash + Short-term Investment + Receivables / Current Liabilities.

Debt Ratio. Suppose you are a bank loan officer and you have received $500,000 loan applications from two similar companies. The first company already owes $600,000, and the second owes only $250,000. Which company gets the loan? All else being equal, you will probably approve the loan application from Company 2, because it owes less.

This relationship between total liabilities and total assets is called the **debt ratio**, which gives an indication of the degree of **leverage** or **gearing** of a company. The debt ratio tells us the proportion of assets financed with debt (see Chapter 9). A debt ratio of 1 reveals that debt has financed all the assets. A debt ratio of 0.50 means that debt finances half the assets. The higher the debt ratio, the greater the pressure to pay interest and principal. The lower the ratio, the lower the risk. You can also express debt ratio as a percentage.

The debt ratios for Ikon Furniture in 20X7 and 20X6 follow:

Formula	*Ikon's Debt Ratio* 20X7	*Ikon's Debt Ratio* 20X6	Industry Average
$\text{Debt ratio} = \dfrac{\text{Total liabilities}}{\text{Total assets}}$	$\dfrac{\$431{,}000}{\$787{,}000} = 0.55$	$\dfrac{\$324{,}000}{\$644{,}000} = 0.50$	0.62

Capital IQ reports that the average debt ratio for home furnishing companies is about 0.62 (or 62%), with relatively little variation from company to company. Ikon' 55% debt ratio indicates a fairly low-risk debt position compared with the industry average of 62%.

An alternative way to describe the level of an entity's leverage is the **debt-to-equity** ratio. Recall that the accounting equation is Assets = Liabilities + Equity. If you know the debt ratio (i.e., liabilities over assets), you can easily work out an entity's debt-to-equity ratio. If total assets are $787,000 and total liabilities are $431,000, equity must be $356,000. The debt-to-equity ratio is thus $431,000 over $356,000, or 1.21 times. A debt-ratio of 0.55 is equivalent to a debt-to-equity ratio of 1.21.

Times-Interest-Earned Ratio. Analysts use another ratio—the **times-interest-earned ratio** (or interest coverage ratio)—to relate income to interest expense. To compute the times-interest-earned ratio, divide income from operations (operating income) by interest expense. This ratio measures the number of times operating income can cover interest expense and is also called the **interest-coverage ratio**. A high ratio indicates ease in paying interest; a low value suggests difficulty.

Ikon' times-interest-earned ratios are:

Formula	*Ikon's Times-Interest-Earned Ratio* 20X7	*Ikon's Times-Interest-Earned Ratio* 20X6	Industry Average
$\text{Times-interest-earned ratio} = \dfrac{\text{Income from operations}}{\text{Interest expense}}$	$\dfrac{\$101{,}000}{\$24{,}000} = 4.21$	$\dfrac{\$57{,}000}{\$14{,}000} = 4.07$	5.8

The company's times-interest-earned ratio increased in 20X7. This is a favorable sign but it is lower than the industry's average interest coverage ratio. This means there are some risks that any shortfall in profitability may negatively affect Ikon's ability to pay interest to its creditors.

A Closer Look

There are many other versions of these ratios, depending on which textbook, website, rating agency, or financial institution you read or follow. For example, some would consider "debt" in debt ratio to be more specific than total liabilities. They would prefer to interpret debt as "interest-bearing liabilities," and exclude other items such as accounts payable, accrued liabilities, unearned revenue, and so forth because these liabilities do not bear interest. When you think of your own "debt," you would naturally think of your tuition loan or motor vehicle loan, and not your outstanding telephone bill, or that your friend paid for your lunch last week!

Similarly, there are numerous additional refinements one could employ. For example, when interest payments are capitalized (under IAS 23—Borrowing Costs, briefly discussed in Chapter 7), these payments will not be shown as an expense. These analysts, in calculating times-interest-earned, prefer to add any capitalized interest to the interest expense shown on the Income Statement on the ratio's denominator. To them, the ability to pay interest does not depend on whether the interest is expensed or capitalized.

Stop & Think

Use the following information to calculate Nestlé's long-term financial strength ratios for 2016 and 2015. What is your assessment of Nestlé's solvency?

Nestlé (in CHF Millions)	2016	2015
Total assets	131,901	123,992
Total liabilities	65,920	60,006
Total equity	65,981	63,986
Operating profit	13,163	12,408
Interest expense	758	725

Answer:

Debt ratio 2016 and 2015 = 65,920/131,901 = 0.50 times and 60,006/123,992 = 0.48 times

Debt to equity ratio 2016 and 2015 = 65,920/65,981 = 1.00 times and 60,006/63,986 = 0.94 times

Times interest earned 2016 and 2015 = 13,163/758 = 17.37 times and 12,408/725 = 17.11 times

Long-term measures generally do not fluctuate much from one year to another unless there is a major change in an entity's capital structure. Nestlé funds its assets from roughly equal amounts shareholder funds and creditors. Interest-bearing loans are a small part of total liabilities, which why it has a very high (and healthy) ability to pay interest expenses.

Profitability Ratios

The fundamental goal of a business is to earn a profit, and so the ratios that measure profitability are reported widely. Profitability ratios may be expressed in decimals or percentages. For example, 0.10 is equal to 10%, 0.25 equals 25%, etc. As investors are accustomed to seeing returns in percentages, we will use % for profitability ratios. You will also see that we use the term "return" for many of the profitability ratios. In this context, returns simply mean any measure of profit, usually net profit.

Gross Profit, Operating Profit, and Net Profit Margin. These ratios show the percentage of each sales dollar earned as gross, operating, and net profit. If the company does not explicitly have a line on its Income Statement as operating profit (or profit from operations), you can use earnings before interest and tax (EBIT) as a surrogate for operating profit. In fact, when you did the common-size analysis in Exhibit 12-6, you were already calculating operating profit margins and net profit margins.

The margin-related ratios for Ikon Furniture are:

Formula	*Ikon's margin-related ratios* 20X7	20X6	Industry Average
Gross Profit Margin $= \dfrac{\text{Gross profit}}{\text{Sales}}$	$\dfrac{\$345{,}000}{\$858{,}000} = 40.2\%$	$\dfrac{\$294{,}000}{\$803{,}000} = 36.6\%$	31.6%
Operating Profit Margin $= \dfrac{\text{Operating profit}}{\text{Sales}}$	$\dfrac{\$101{,}000}{\$858{,}000} = 11.8\%$	$\dfrac{\$57{,}000}{\$803{,}000} = 7.1\%$	7.9%
Net Profit Margin $= \dfrac{\text{Net profit}}{\text{Sales}}$	$\dfrac{\$48{,}000}{\$858{,}000} = 5.6\%$	$\dfrac{\$26{,}000}{\$803{,}000} = 3.2\%$	5.6%

Companies strive for a high rate of net income (sometimes referred to as **return on sales**). The higher the percentage, the more profit is being generated by sales dollars. Ikon Furniture's gross, operating, and net profit margins have improved in 20X7. Ikon was able to generate gross profit and operating profit margins above the industry averages, and its net profit margin matches the home furnishing industry's average.

Return on Total Assets. The **return on total assets** (ROA) (introduced in Chapter 7), measures a company's success in using assets to earn a profit. There are some variations in the numerator for this ratio. Some textbooks advocate the use of net profit, others use net profit but with interest expenses added back, or operating profit, or earnings before interest and tax. We will use net profit in this text. Average total assets is the denominator, which is the total of beginning and ending balances ($787,000 and $644,000) divided by 2. On occasions when we don't have access to beginning balances (e.g., we don't have Ikon's beginning balances for 20X6), we can use the ending balance instead of the average. We will show Ikon's ROA after discussing ROE in the next section.

Return on Equity. A popular measure of profitability is the **return on ordinary shareholders' equity**, often shortened to *return on equity* (ROE). This ratio shows the relationship between net income and ordinary shareholders' investment in the company—how much income is earned for every $1 invested by the ordinary equity shareholders (see Chapter 10). Naturally, if a company does not have preference shares (like Ikon Furniture), we do not have to worry about excluding preference dividends and preference equity. We would simply take the total return figure and divide it by the average total equity in our calculations.

A Closer Look

You may be wondering why we specifically single out ordinary equity for this ratio. Recall that preference shares have a predetermined, fixed return in the form of preference dividends to the preference shareholders. Thus, after paying for the preference dividends, profits are available to ordinary shareholders.

For companies with preference shares, you will need to exclude preference dividends from the numerator and preference capital (both paid-in preference capital and any capital in excess of par for the preference capital). The formula to use when you are analyzing ROE for a company with preference shares will thus be:

$$\frac{\text{Net income} - \text{Preference dividend}}{\text{Average of total equity} - \text{Preference equity}}$$

Let's see Ikon Furnitures' ROA and ROE for 20X7 and 20X6. For 20X6, we will use ending balances only as we do not have information about Ikon's 20X6 beginning balances (i.e., the ending 20X5 numbers) to calculate averages. Ikon Furniture has no preference shares and thus has no preference dividends. All of its equity is therefore ordinary. Average equity for 20X7 uses the beginning and ending balances [($320,000 + $356,000)/2 = $338,000].

Formula	Ikon's ROA and ROE 20X7	20X6	Industry Average
Return on asset = $\frac{\text{Net profit}}{\text{Average total assets}}$	$\frac{\$48,000}{\$715,500} = 6.7\%$	$\frac{\$26,000}{\$644,000} = 4.0\%$	4.0%
Return on equity = $\frac{\text{Net profit}}{\text{Average equity}}$	$\frac{\$48,000}{\$338,000} = 14.2\%$	$\frac{\$26,000}{\$320,000} = 8.1\%$	8.6%

*Using 20X6 ending figures only

Ikon improved its ROA and ROE significantly in 20X7, generating 6.7% return on assets and 11.8% return on equity. The home furnishings' industry averages are only 4% and 8.6%, respectively. Observe that Ikon's return on equity (14.2%) is higher than its return on assets (6.7%). All businesses that have liabilities will have higher ROE than ROA. In fact, the higher the debt ratio, the higher the leverage. Companies that finance operations with significant debt are said to be highly leveraged. All is well when profits are greater than are necessary to meet interest payments. However, as the global financial crisis has taught us, highly leveraged companies are the first ones to fall when there is a drop in profitability. If revenues drop, debts must still be paid. Therefore, leverage is a double-edged sword. It increases profits during good times but compounds losses during bad times.

Stop & Think

Use the following information to calculate Nestlé's profitability ratios for 2016 and 2015. What is your assessment of Nestlé's profitability?

Nestlé (in CHF Millions)	2016	2015	2014
Sales	89,469	88,785	91,612
Gross profit	45,270	44,055	44,059
Operating profit	13,163	12,408	10,905
Net profit	8,883	9,467	14,904
Total assets	131,901	123,992	133,450
Total equity	65,981	63,986	71,884

Answer:

Gross profit margin 2016 and 2015 = 45,270/89,469 = 50.60% and 44,055/88,785 = 49.62%

Operating profit margin 2016 and 2015 = 13,163/89,469 = 14.71% and 12,408/88,785 = 13.98%

Net profit margin 2016 and 2015 = 8,883/89,469 = 9.93% and 9,467/88,785 = 10.66%
Return on assets 2016 = 8,883/average of 131,901 and 123,992 = 6.94%
Return on assets 2015 = 9,467/average of 123,992 and 133,450 = 7.35%
Return on equity 2016 = 8,883/average of 65,981 and 63,986 = 13.67%
Return on equity 2015 = 9,467/average of 63,986 and 71,884 = 13.94%

While Nestlé has done better in gross profit margin and operating profit margin, the lower net profit in 2016 has resulted in lower net profit margin, lower return on assets, and lower return on equity.

Analysts use a technique called *DuPont Analysis* to better understand how ROE is achieved. This technique is made popular by the DuPont Corporation, which started using this analysis back in the 1920s. The DuPont Analysis breaks down ROE into three components: profitability, efficiency, and leverage. Mathematically, the Dupont Analysis uses the following formula:

ROE	=	Net Profit Margin	×	Asset Turnover	×	Equity Multiplier
		$\frac{\text{Net Profit}}{\text{Sales}}$		$\frac{\text{Sales}}{\text{Assets}}$		$\frac{\text{Assets}}{\text{Equity}}$

The focus is not on the ROE itself but on how it is achieved via these three components. ROE may go up, but it may be due to additional leverage instead of superior margin or improved efficiency. Applying the formula to Nestlé will show the following:

DuPont ROE Analysis		20X7	20X6
Net Profit Margin	$= \frac{\text{Net Profit}}{\text{Sales}}$	$\frac{8{,}883}{89{,}449} = 9.9\%$	$\frac{9{,}467}{88{,}785} = 10.7\%$
Asset Turnover	$= \frac{\text{Sales}}{\text{Assets}}$	$\frac{89{,}449}{131{,}901} = 67.8\%$	$\frac{88{,}785}{123{,}992} = 71.6\%$
Equity Multiplier	$= \frac{\text{Assets}}{\text{Equity}}$	$\frac{131{,}901}{65{,}981} = 199.9\%$	$\frac{123{,}992}{63{,}986} = 193.8\%$
		DuPont ROE = 13.5%	DuPont ROE = 14.8%

We can see that ROE has gone down because of decrease in profitability and efficiency, despite the increase in leverage.

Investment Ratios

Investors buy shares to earn a return on their investment. They pay close attention to how much each share they own is generating profit, cash, and dividends, and the market price for each share. Let's look at some common ratios that can help you decide if your investment is performing well.

Earnings per Ordinary Share. Earnings per ordinary share, or simply earnings per share (EPS), is the amount of net income earned for each outstanding ordinary share (see Chapter 10). EPS is probably the most widely quoted of all financial statistics. It's also the only ratio that appears at the bottom of the Income Statement (required by *IAS 1—Presentation of Financial Statements*) and the only financial ratio that has an accounting standard (*IAS 33—Earnings per share*).

Earnings per share is computed by dividing net income available to ordinary shareholders by the weighted-average number of ordinary shares outstanding during the year. Preference dividends are subtracted from net income because the preference shareholders have a prior claim to their dividends. Ikon has 10,000 ordinary shares outstanding and no preference shares (and thus has no preference dividends). The firm's EPS ratios for 20X7 and 20X6 can be calculated as:

		Ikon's Earnings per Ordinary Share	
Formula		20X7	20X6
Earnings per share of share capital	$= \frac{\text{Net income} - \text{Preference dividends}}{\text{Weighted-average number of ordinary shares outstanding}}$	$\frac{\$48{,}000 - \$0}{10{,}000} = \$4.80$	$\frac{\$26{,}000 - \$0}{10{,}000} = \$2.60$

Ikon Furniture's EPS increased 85% during 20X7, and that's good news. The Ikon shareholders should not expect such a significant boost every year. Most companies can only expect to increase their EPS by a few percentage points annually.

A Closer Look

If you pay closer attention to the denominator in the EPS formula, you will notice that it is labeled "weighted-average number of ordinary shares outstanding." This means we are not using a simple arithmetic average but need to take into account how long a certain number of shares have been outstanding. For example, if you started the year on January 1, 20X6, with 10,000 shares and on November 1, 20X6, issued an additional 6,000 shares (total 16,000), the weighted average would be 11,000 (i.e., 10,000 × 10/12 months) + (16,000 × 2/12 months) shares for the period. For listed companies, there may be other equity transactions such as stock dividends, stock splits, and purchase of treasury shares that change the weighted-average of ordinary stock outstanding.

In addition, *IAS 1* and *IAS 33* require two versions of EPS: basic and diluted earnings per share. The latter takes into account potentially dilutive financial instruments such as convertible bonds, convertible preference shares, and stock options. This is beyond the scope of this text.

Price/Earnings Ratio. The **price/earnings ratio** shows how much an investor is willing to pay for each unit of earnings. This ratio, abbreviated P/E, appears in every financial section of newspapers and online financial databases. The P/E ratio makes use of the **earnings per share (EPS)** ratio we calculated earlier.

Calculations for the P/E ratios of Ikon Furniture, Inc., follow. Suppose the market price of Ikon's ordinary share was $60 at the end of 20X7 and $35 at the end of 20X6. Share prices can be obtained from a company's website, a financial publication or website, or a stockbroker.

	Ikon's Price/Earnings Ratio	
Formula	20X7	20X6
$\text{P/E ratio} = \dfrac{\text{Market price per ordinary share}}{\text{Earnings per share}}$	$\dfrac{\$60.00}{\$4.80} = 12.5$	$\dfrac{\$35.00}{\$2.60} = 13.5$

Given Ikon Furniture's 20X7 P/E ratio of 12.5, we would say that the company's share is selling at 12.5 times earnings. Each $1 of Ikon's earnings is worth $12.50 to the stock market. The P/E ratio reflects the market's overall expectation of a company's performance. The more optimistic the market is, the higher the P/E ratio. The home furnishing average PE ratio is about 14.3 times earnings.

Dividend Yield. Dividend yield is the ratio of dividends per share of stock to the share's market price. This ratio measures the percentage of a share's market value returned annually to the shareholders as dividends. For investors looking for a steady stream of dividend payouts, dividend yield is a very important ratio to consider in their investment decisions.

Ikon Furniture paid annual cash dividends of $1.20 per share in 20X7 and $1.00 in 20X6. The market prices of the company's ordinary share were $60 in 20X7 and $35 in 20X6. The firm's dividend yields on ordinary share are:

Formula			Dividend Yield on Ikon's Share Capital 20X7	20X6
Dividend yield on ordinary share*	=	$\frac{\text{Dividend per ordinary share}}{\text{Market price per ordinary share}}$	$\frac{\$1.20}{\$60.00} = 2.0\%$	$\frac{\$1.00}{\$35.00} = 2.9\%$

*Dividend yields may also be calculated for preference shares.

Preference shareholders pay special attention to this ratio because they invest primarily to receive dividends. The same formula can be adjusted to calculate dividend yield only for preference shareholders: dividend per preference share divided by market price per preference share.

An investor who buys Ikon Furniture ordinary shares for $60 can expect to receive around 2% of the investment annually in the form of cash dividends. Dividend yields vary widely, from 5% to 8% for mature, established firms (such as P&G and Unilever) down to the range of 0% to 3% for younger, growth-oriented companies.

Book Value per Ordinary Share. Book value per ordinary share is simply ordinary shareholders' equity divided by the number of ordinary shares outstanding. Ordinary equity equals total equity less preference equity.

Ikon Furniture has no preference shares outstanding. Calculations of its book value per ordinary share follow. Recall that 10,000 ordinary shares were outstanding.

Formula			Book Value per Share of Ikon's Share Capital 20X7	20X6
Book value per ordinary share	=	$\frac{\text{Total shareholders' equity} - \text{Preference equity}}{\text{Number of ordinary shares outstanding}}$	$\frac{\$356{,}000 - \$0}{10{,}000} = \$35.60$	$\frac{\$320{,}000 - \$0}{10{,}000} = \$32.00$

Book value indicates the recorded accounting amount for each ordinary share outstanding. Many experts believe book value is not useful for investment analysis because it bears no relationship to market value and provides little information beyond what's reported on the Balance Sheet. But some investors do base their investment decisions on book value. Specifically, they would rank shares by the ratio of market price to book value. The lower the ratio, the more attractive the share. These investors are called "value" investors, as contrasted with "growth" investors, who focus more on trends in net income. The home furnishing industry's price to book value is about 1.4 times.

Investors often extend this ratio by comparing it to the current price for each share. For example, if the book value per share is $2 and the current market price is $6, we can say the "price to book" is 3 times.

Putting it All Together

What does the outlook for the future look like for Ikon Furniture? If the company can stay on the same path it has followed for the past two years, it looks bright. It appears that its earnings per share are solid, and its margins, ROA, and ROE ratios are all above average for its industry. From the standpoint of liquidity and leverage, it also appears to be in good shape, with higher liquidity, excellent debt and interest coverage, and lower debt ratios than its industry. The company's P/E ratio of 12:1 is below the industry average, and it pays a 2% dividend. All of these factors make Ikon Furniture shares look like a good investment.

Using the Statement of Cash Flows

You may have noticed that the ratios we described earlier are all based on Income Statement and Balance Sheet. What about cash flows? We covered Free Cash Flow and Cash Realization Ratio earlier (in Chapter 11), but in general, cash flow ratios have received less attention and coverage than they deserve. Fortunately, they are not a whole new set of ratios! Cash flow ratios are usually alternative versions of the ratios we discussed earlier, with the emphasis changed to cash from operations (CFO). Here are some of the cash flow ratios you could use:

Standard ratios discussed earlier	Cash flow version	Variation from standard ratios
Current ratio	CFO coverage ratio	CFO ÷ current liabilities
Debt ratio	CFO solvency ratio	CFO ÷ total liabilities
Net profit margin	CFO margin ratio	CFO ÷ sales revenue
Times-interest-earned	CFO interest ratio	(CFO + interest paid) ÷ interest paid

USE OTHER INFORMATION TO MAKE INVESTMENT DECISIONS

Economic Value Added (EVA®)

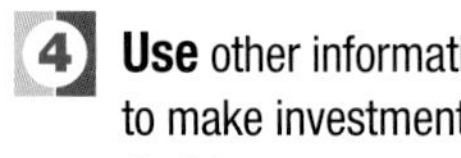

4 Use other information to make investment decisions

The top managers of Coca-Cola, Quaker Oats, and other leading companies use **economic value added (EVA®)** to evaluate operating performance. EVA® combines accounting and finance to measure whether operations have increased shareholder wealth. EVA® can be computed as follows:

$$\text{EVA}^{®} = \text{Net income} + \text{Interest expense} - \text{Capital charge}$$

$$\text{Capital charge} = \left(\begin{array}{c} \text{(Beginning balances)} \\ \text{Notes payable} + \text{Current maturities of long-term debt} + \text{Long-term debt} + \text{Shareholders' equity} \end{array} \right) \times \text{Cost of capital}$$

All amounts for the EVA® computation, except the **cost of capital**, come from the financial statements. The EVA model uses net income, but adjusted for certain expenses (such as non-cash expenses and even marketing expenses). For simplicity, we shall use net income as a starting point and make some simple adjustments. The cost of capital is a weighted average of the returns demanded by the company's shareholders and lenders. Cost of capital varies with the company's level of risk. For example, shareholders would demand a higher return from a start-up company than from Nestlé because the new company is untested and, therefore, more risky. Lenders would also charge the new company a higher interest rate because of its greater risk. Thus, the new company has a higher cost of capital than Nestlé.

The cost of capital is a major topic in finance classes. In the following discussions we assume a value for the cost of capital (such as 10%, 12%, or 15%) to illustrate the computation of EVA®.

The idea behind EVA® is that the returns to the company's shareholders (net income) and to its creditors (interest expense) should exceed the company's **capital charge**. The capital charge is the amount that shareholders and lenders charge a company for the use of their money. A positive EVA® amount suggests an increase in shareholder wealth, and so the company's shares should remain attractive to investors. If EVA® is negative, shareholders will probably be unhappy with the company and sell its shares, resulting in a decrease in the share price. Different companies tailor the EVA® computation to meet their own needs.

Let's apply EVA® to Nestlé. For the income measure, we shall use net profit but add back impairment losses and depreciation, i.e., CHF 8,883 + 3,772 + 1,736 = CHF 14,391 million. We can continue to calculate Nestlé's EVA® as follows, assuming a 10% cost of capital.

$$\text{Nestlé's EVA}^{®} = \begin{matrix}\text{Adjusted}\\ \text{net}\\ \text{income}\end{matrix} + \begin{matrix}\text{Interest}\\ \text{expense}\end{matrix} - \left[\begin{pmatrix} & \text{(Beginning balances)} & \\ \begin{matrix}\text{Short-term}\\ \text{borrowings}\end{matrix} + & \begin{matrix}\text{Long-term}\\ \text{debt}\end{matrix} + & \begin{matrix}\text{Shareholders'}\\ \text{equity}\end{matrix}\end{pmatrix} \times \begin{matrix}\text{Cost of}\\ \text{capital}\end{matrix}\right]$$

$$= \underbrace{14{,}391 + 758} - (9{,}629 + 11{,}601 + 63{,}986) \times 0.10]$$

$$= 15{,}149 - \underbrace{85{,}216 \times 0.10}$$

$$= \underbrace{15{,}149 - 8{,}522}$$

$$= 6{,}627$$

By this measure, Nestlé's operations added CHF 6,627 million of value to its shareholders' wealth after meeting the company's capital charge. This performance is considered very strong, especially given the tough economic conditions around the world.

OTHER ISSUES IN FINANCIAL STATEMENT ANALYSIS

Limitations of Ratio Analysis

Business decisions are made in a world of uncertainty. As useful as financial ratios are, they aren't a cure-all. Consider a physician's use of a thermometer. A reading of 40° Celsius (or 104.0° Fahrenheit) tells a doctor something is wrong with the patient, but that doesn't indicate what the problem is or how to cure it.

In financial analysis, a sudden drop in any ratio may signal that something is wrong, but that doesn't identify the problem. A manager must analyze the figures to learn what caused the ratio to fall. The manager must evaluate all the ratios in the light of factors such as increased competition or a slowdown in the economy. Business models and strategies would also help explain the financial ratios you calculate. For example, you would expect a company selling luxury goods to have higher profit margins than another selling household goods. Sales turnover for the latter, however, would be significantly higher than for the former.

Legislation, international affairs, scandals, and other factors can turn profits into losses. To be useful, ratios should be analyzed over a period of years to consider all relevant factors. Any one year, or even any two years, may not represent the company's performance over the long term.

You must also remember that the numbers on the financial statement are a result of the company's applications of accounting standards that require significant judgment and often rely on estimates and assumptions. There may also be differences in accounting standards in one region versus other. For example, Sinopec (China's largest oil company) financial statements are prepared under Chinese Accounting Standards (CAS) and Tata Motors' under Indian GAAP. For introductory accounting courses, we may assume that the differences are minimal. Analyzing the numbers without consideration of the accounting policies that resulted in those numbers is like the old adage, "garbage in, garbage out."

Red Flags in Financial Statement Analysis

Recent accounting scandals have highlighted the importance of *red flags* in financial statement analysis. The following conditions may mean a company is very risky:

- *Earnings Problems.* Have income from continuing operations and net income decreased for several years in a row? Has income turned into a loss? This may be okay for a company in a cyclical industry, such as an airline or a home builder, but companies usually cannot survive losses in consecutive years.
- *Decreased Cash Flow.* Cash flow validates earnings. Is cash flow from operations consistently lower than net income? Are the sales of PPE a major source of cash? If so, the company may be facing a cash shortage.
- *Too Much Debt.* How does the company's debt ratio compare to that of major competitors and to the industry average? If the debt ratio is much higher than average, the company may be unable to pay debts during tough times.
- *Inability to Collect Receivables.* Are receivables resident periods growing faster than for other companies in the industry? A cash shortage may be looming.
- *Buildup of Inventories.* Is inventory turnover slowing down? If so, the company may be unable to move products, or it may be overstating inventory as reported on the Balance Sheet. Recall from the cost-of-goods-sold model that one of the easiest ways to overstate net income is to overstate ending inventory.
- *Trends of Sales, Inventory, and Receivables.* Sales, receivables, and inventory generally move together. Increased sales lead to higher receivables and require more inventory in order to meet demand. Strange movements among these items may spell trouble.

The Decision Guidelines feature summarizes the most widely used ratios.

DECISION GUIDELINES

USING RATIOS IN FINANCIAL STATEMENT ANALYSIS

Milla and Ryssa operate a financial services firm. The two sisters manage other people's money and do most of their own financial statement analysis. Suppose they are analyzing a company on behalf of their clients and want to find out the company's efficiency, financial strength, performance, and suitability as an investment. They use the standard ratios we have covered in this chapter.

Ratio	Computation	Information Provided
Measure efficiency of a company's operations:		
1. Inventory turnover	$\frac{\text{Cost of goods sold}}{\text{Average inventory}}$	Indicates the salability of inventory—the number of times a company sells its average level of inventory during a year. Can be expressed in days as inventory resident period.
2. Accounts receivable turnover	$\frac{\text{Sales revenue credit sales}}{\text{Average net accounts receivable}}$	Measures the ability to collect cash from customers. Can be expressed in days as receivables collection period.
3. Payable turnover	$\frac{\text{Cost of goods sold}}{\text{Average accounts payable}}$	Measures the frequency of payments to trade creditors. Can be expressed in days as payable payment period.

Ratio	Computation	Information Provided
4. Cash conversion cycle	Receivable collection period + Inventory resident period − Payable outstanding period	Indicates the speed at which an entity is able to convert cash from its inventory and receivables, less the time it takes to settle accounts payable.
5. Asset turnover	$\frac{\text{Sales}}{\text{Average total assets}}$	Measures the ability to use assets to generate revenue.
Measure financial strengths (short-term and long-term):		
6. Current ratio	$\frac{\text{Current assets}}{\text{Current liabilities}}$	Measures the ability to pay current liabilities with current assets.
7. Quick ratio	$\frac{\text{Sales}}{\text{Average total assets}}$	Shows the ability to pay all current liabilities if they come due immediately. Sometimes calculated as (current assets – inventory) divided by current liabilities.
8. Debt ratio	$\frac{\text{Total liabilities}}{\text{Total assets}}$	Indicates percentage of assets financed with liabilities or debt.
9. Times-interest-earned ratio	$\frac{\text{Income from operations}}{\text{Interest expense}}$	Measures the number of times operating income can cover interest expense. Also called interest coverage ratio.
Measure profitability:		
10. Gross/Operating/Net profit margin	$\frac{\text{Gross or Operating or Net profit}}{\text{Net sales}}$	Shows the percentage of each sales dollar earned as income. Variants include gross profit, operating profit, and net profit.
11. Return on total assets (ROA)	$\frac{\text{Net income}}{\text{Average total assets}}$	Measures how profitably a company uses its assets. For the numerator, alternative formulas exist (net income plus interest expense, operating profit, or earnings before interest and tax).
12. Return on ordinary shareholders' equity (ROE)	$\frac{\text{Net income} - \text{Preference dividends}}{\text{Average ordinary shareholders' equity}}$	Gauges how much income is earned for on ordinary shareholder equity.
Analyze shares as potential investment:		
13. Earnings per ordinary share (EPS)	$\frac{\text{Net income} - \text{Preference dividends}}{\text{Weighted-average number of ordinary shares outstanding}}$	The amount of net income on a per-ordinary-share basis.
14. Price/earnings (P/E) ratio	$\frac{\text{Market price per ordinary share}}{\text{Earnings per share}}$	Indicates the market price for one currency unit of earnings.
15. Dividend yield	$\frac{\text{Dividend per ordinary share (or preference)}}{\text{Market price per ordinary share (or preference)}}$	Shows the percentage of a share's market value returned as dividends to shareholders in each period.
16. Book value per ordinary share	$\frac{\text{Total shareholders' equity} - \text{Preference equity}}{\text{Number of ordinary shares outstanding}}$	Indicates the recorded accounting amount for each ordinary share outstanding.

End-of-Chapter Summary Problem

The following financial data are adapted from the annual reports of Artisan Corporation:

	A	B	C	D	E
1	**Artisan Corporation Four-Year Selected Financial Data Years Ended January 31, 20X6, 20X5, 20X4, and 20X3**				
2	**Operating Results***	**20X6**	**20X5**	**20X4**	**20X3**
3	**Net Sales**	$ 13,848	$ 13,673	$ 11,635	$ 9,054
4	Cost of goods sold and occupancy expenses				
5	excluding depreciation and amortization	9,704	8,599	6,775	5,318
6	Interest expense	109	75	45	46
7	Income from operations	338	1,445	1,817	1,333
8	Net earnings (net loss)	(8)	877	1,127	824
9	Cash dividends	76	75	76	77
10					
11	**Financial Position**				
12	Merchandise inventory	1,677	1,904	1,462	1,056
13	Total assets	7,591	7,012	5,189	3,963
14	Current ratio	1.48:1	0.95:1	1.25:1	1.20:1
15	Shareholders' equity	3,010	2,928	2,630	1,574
16	Average number of ordinary shares outstanding				
17	(in thousands)	860	879	895	576
18					

*Dollar amounts are in thousands.

Requirement

1. Compute the following ratios for 20X4 through 20X6, and evaluate Artisan's operating results. Are operating results strong or weak? Did they improve or deteriorate during the three-year period? Your analysis will reveal a clear trend.
   a. Gross profit margin
   b. Net profit margin
   c. Earnings per share
   d. Inventory turnover
   e. Times-interest-earned ratio
   f. Return on shareholders' equity

Answer

	20X6	20X5	20X4
1. Gross profit margin	$\frac{\$13,848 - \$9,704}{\$13,848} = 29.9\%$	$\frac{\$13,673 - \$8,599}{\$13,673} = 37.1\%$	$\frac{\$11,635 - \$6,775}{\$11,635} = 41.8\%$
2. Net profit margin	$\frac{\$(8)}{\$13,848} = (0.06)\%$	$\frac{\$877}{\$13,673} = 6.4\%$	$\frac{\$1,127}{\$11,635} = 9.7\%$
3. Earnings per share	$\frac{\$(8)}{860} = \$(0.01)$	$\frac{\$877}{879} = \$1.00$	$\frac{\$1,127}{895} = \$1.26$
4. Inventory turnover	$\frac{\$9,704}{(\$1,677 + \$1,904)/2} = 5.4$ times	$\frac{\$8,599}{(\$1,904 + \$1,462)/2} = 5.1$ times	$\frac{\$6,775}{(\$1,462 + \$1,056)/2} = 5.4$ times
5. Times-interest-earned ratio	$\frac{\$338}{\$109} = 3.1$ times	$\frac{\$1,445}{\$75} = 19.3$ times	$\frac{\$1,817}{\$45} = 40.4$ times
6. Return on equity	$\frac{\$(8)}{(\$3,010 + \$2,928)/2} = (0.3\%)$	$\frac{\$877}{(\$2,928 + \$2,630)/2} = 31.6\%$	$\frac{\$1,127}{(\$2,630 + \$1,574)/2} = 53.6\%$

Evaluation: During this period, Artisan's operating results deteriorated on all these measures except inventory turnover. The gross profit percentage is down sharply, as are the times-interest-earned ratio and all the return measures. From these data it is clear that Artisan could sell its merchandise, but not at the mark-ups the company enjoyed in the past. The final result, in 20X6, was a net loss for the year.

REVIEW | Financial Statement Analysis

Quick Check (Answers are given at the end of the chapter.)

Analyze the Odyssey Company's financial statements by answering the questions that follow. Odyssey owns a chain of restaurants.

A1

	A	B	C
1	**Oullette Company Consolidated Statements of Income (Adapted) Years Ended December 31, 20X7 and 20X6**		
2	**(In thousands, except per share data)**	**20X7**	**20X6**
3	Revenues:		
4	Sales by Company-operated restaurants	$ 13,200	$ 11,100
5	Revenues from franchised and affiliated restaurants	4,500	3,700
6	Total revenues	17,700	14,800
7	Expenses:		
8	Cost of goods sold	3,300	3,108
9	Payroll and employee benefits	3,200	3,000
10	Occupancy and other operating expenses	2,900	2,800
11	Franchised restaurants—occupancy expenses	949	850
12	Selling, general, and administrative expenses	1,820	1,730
13	Other operating expense, net	510	855
14	Total operating expenses	12,679	12,343
15	Operating income	5,021	2,457
16	Interest expense	370	345
17	Other non-operating expense, net	140	168
18	Income before income taxes	4,511	1,944
19	Income tax expense	1,820	820
20	Net income	$ 2,691	$ 1,124
21	Per-ordinary-share basics:		
22	Net income	$ 2.69	$ 1.15
23	Dividends per ordinary share	$ 0.50	$ 0.24
24			

	A	B	C
1	**Oullette Company** **Consolidated Balance Sheets** **December 31, 20X7 and 20X6**		
2	**(In thousands, except per share data)**	**20X7**	**20X6**
3	**Assets**		
4	**Current Assets**		
5	Cash and equivalents	$ 690	$ 455
6	Accounts and notes receivable	780	840
7	Inventories	140	120
8	Prepaid expense and other current assets	580	440
9	Total current assets	2,190	1,855
10	**Other Assets**		
11	Investments in affiliates	1,150	1,055
12	Goodwill, net	1,780	1,590
13	Miscellaneous	990	1,100
14	Total other assets	3,920	3,745
15	**Property and Equipment**		
16	Property and equipment, at cost	28,800	26,500
17	Accumulated depreciation and amortization	(8,850)	(7,900)
18	Net property and equipment	19,950	18,600
19	Total assets	$ 26,060	$ 24,200
20	**Liabilities and Shareholders' Equity**		
21	**Current liabilities**		
22	Accounts payable	$ 520	$ 675
23	Income taxes	70	14
24	Other taxes	230	180
25	Accrued interest	189	196
26	Accrued restructuring and restaurant closing costs	110	385
27	Accrued payroll and other liabilities	890	795
28	Current maturities of long-term debt	365	305
29	Total current liabilities	2,374	2,550
30	Long-term debt	8,700	9,500
31	Other long-term liabilities and minority interests	690	520
32	Deferred income taxes	1,005	1,015
33	**Shareholders' Equity**		
34	Preference shares, no par value; authorized—140.0 million shares;		
35	issued—none	—	—
36	Ordinary shares, $0.01 par value; authorized—2.0 billion shares;		
37	issued—1,400 million shares	14	14
38	Additional paid-in capital	1,786	1,662
39	Unearned ESOP compensation	(85)	(101)
40	Retained earnings	21,741	19,550
41	Accumulated other comprehensive income (loss)	(815)	(1,570)
42	Ordinary shares in treasury, at cost; 400 and 420 million shares	(9,350)	(8,940)
43	Total shareholders' equity	13,291	10,615
44	Total liabilities and shareholders' equity	$ 26,060	$ 24,200
45			

1. Horizontal analysis of Odyssey's Income Statement for 20X7 would show which of the following for Selling, General, and Administrative expenses?
   a. 1.05
   b. 0.95
   c. 0.68
   d. None of the above

2. Vertical analysis of Odyssey's Income Statement for 20X7 would show which of the following for Selling, General, and Administrative expenses?
   a. 0.144
   b. 0.138
   c. 0.103
   d. None of the above

3. Which item on Odyssey's income statement has the most favorable trend during 20X6–20X7?
   a. Total revenues
   b. Food and paper costs
   c. Net income
   d. Payroll and employee benefits

4. On Odyssey's common-size Balance Sheet, Goodwill would appear as
   a. up by 11.9%.
   b. $1,780 million.
   c. 10.06% of total revenues.
   d. 0.068.

5. A good benchmark for Odyssey Company would be
   a. Volvo.
   b. Whataburger.
   c. Microsoft.
   d. All of the above.

6. Odyssey's inventory turnover for 20X7 was
   a. 61 times.
   b. 25 times.
   c. 17 times.
   d. 72 times.

7. Odyssey's acid-test ratio at the end of 20X7 was
   a. 0.06.
   b. 2.83.
   c. 0.92.
   d. 0.62.

8. Odyssey's average collection period for accounts and notes receivables is
   a. 17 days.
   b. 32 days.
   c. 15 days.
   d. 2 days.

9. The average debt ratio for most companies is 0.64. Odyssey's total debt position looks
   a. risky.
   b. safe.
   c. middle-ground.
   d. cannot tell from the financials.

10. Odyssey's return on total revenues for 20X7 was
    a. $2.69.
    b. $1.16.
    c. 10.33%.
    d. 15.2%.

11. Odyssey's return on shareholders' equity for 20X7 was
    a. 10.3%.
    b. 15.2%.
    c. 22.5%.
    d. $2,691 million.

12. On May 31, 20X7, Odyssey's ordinary shares sold for $30 per share. At that price, how much did investors say $1 of the company's net income was worth?
    a. $30.00
    b. $1.00
    c. $10.99
    d. $11.15

13. On May 31, 20X7, Odyssey's ordinary shares sold for $30 per share and dividends per share were $0.50. Compute Odyssey's dividend yield during 20X7.
    a. 4.1%
    b. 2.9%
    c. 5.0%
    d. 1.7%

14. How much EVA® did Odyssey generate for investors during 20X7? Assume the cost of capital was 5% and use unadjusted net income.
    a. \$2.045 million
    b. \$1.943 million
    c. \$3.061 million
    d. \$2.691 million

Accounting Vocabulary

asset turnover ratio. (p. 719) An indicator of the efficiency with which a company is deploying its assets in generating revenue.

benchmarking (p. 711) The comparison of an entity to another entity (competitor or peer) or against industry averages, with the objective of providing context to the evaluation of the entity.

book value per ordinary share (p. 727) Ordinary shareholders' equity divided by the number of ordinary shares outstanding. The recorded amount for each ordinary share outstanding.

capital charge (p. 729) The amount that shareholders and lenders charge a company for the use of their money. Calculated as beginning balances of (Notes payable + Loans payable + Long-term debt + Shareholders' equity) × Cost of capital.

cash conversion cycle (p. 717) The length of time it takes a company to convert cash from its inventory purchases and receivables. Calculated as inventory resident period plus receivable collection period less payable outstanding period.

common-size financial statement (p. 712) A financial statement that reports only percentages (no dollar amounts).

cost of capital (p. 728) A weighted average of the returns demanded by the company's shareholders and lenders.

current ratio (p. 719) Current assets divided by current liabilities. Measures a company's ability to pay current liabilities with current assets.

debt ratio (p. 721) Ratio of total liabilities to total assets. States the proportion of a company's assets that is financed with debt.

debt-to-equity (p. 721) A measure of indebtedness; the amount of liabilities (or interest-bearing liabilities) as a proportion of total equity.

dividend yield (p. 726) Ratio of dividends per share to the share's market price. Tells the percentage of a share's market value that the company returns to shareholders as dividends.

earnings per share (EPS) (p. 726) Amount of a company's net income earned for each ordinary share outstanding.

economic value added (EVA®) (p. 728) Used to evaluate a company's operating performance. EVA combines the concepts of accounting income and corporate finance to measure whether the company's operations have increased shareholder wealth. EVA = Net income + Interest expense – Capital charge.

gearing (p. 721) A measure of indebtedness of an entity, also known as leverage, typically measured by the proportion of assets financed by liabilities (or alternatively only interest-bearing liabilities).

gross profit margin (p. 723) The amount of gross profit earned from each currency unit of sales.

horizontal analysis (p. 706) Study of percentage changes in comparative financial statements.

interest-coverage ratio (p. 721) Another name for *times-interest-earned ratio*.

inventory resident period (p. 716) The average length of time (in days) to sell inventory, based on *inventory turnover*. Part of *cash conversion cycle*.

inventory turnover (p. 716) Ratio of cost of goods sold to average inventory. Indicates how rapidly inventory is sold. Can also be expressed in days *(inventory resident period)*.

leverage (p. 721) The degree of external financing of an entity. Earning more income on borrowed money than the related interest expense, thereby increasing the earnings for the owners of the business.

liquidity ratios (p. 719) Financial strength ratios that focus on short-term obligations, typically current liabilities.

net profit margin (p. 723) The amount of net profit earned from each currency unit of sales. Also called *return on sales*.

operating profit margin (p. 723) The amount of operating profit earned from each currency unit of sales.

payable outstanding period (p. 717) The average length of time (in days) to pay account payables, based on *payable turnover*. Part of *cash conversion cycle*.

payable turnover (p. 717) Ratio of cost of goods sold to average payables. Indicates how quickly trade creditors are paid. Can also be expressed in days (payables outstanding period).

price/earnings ratio (p. 726) Ratio of the market price of an ordinary share to the company's earnings per share. Measures the value that the share market places on one currency unit of a company's earnings.

quick ratio (p. 720) Ratio of the sum of cash plus short-term investments plus net current receivables to total current liabilities. Tells whether the entity can pay all its current liabilities if they come due immediately. Also called the *acid-test ratio*.

receivable collection period (p. 717) The average length of time (in days) to collect receivables, based on *receivable turnover*. Part of *cash conversion cycle*.

return on ordinary shareholders' equity (p. 723) Net income minus preference dividends, divided by average ordinary shareholders' equity. A measure of profitability. Also called *return on equity (ROE)*.

return on sales (p. 723) Another name for *net profit margin.*

return on total assets (p. 723) Net income divided by average total assets. This ratio measures a company's success in using its assets to earn income for the persons who finance the business. Also called *return on assets (ROA).*

solvency ratios (p. 719) Financial strength ratios that focus on both short-and long-term obligations.

times-interest-earned ratio (p. 721) Ratio of income from operations (or earnings before interest and tax) to interest expense. Measures the number of times that operating income can cover interest expense. Also called the *interest-coverage ratio.*

trend percentages (p. 709) A form of horizontal analysis that indicates the direction a business is taking.

vertical analysis (p. 710) Analysis of a financial statement that reveals the relationship of each statement item to a specified base, which is the 100% figure.

working capital (p. 719) Current assets minus current liabilities; measures a business's ability to meet its short-term obligations with its current assets.

ASSESS YOUR PROGRESS

Short Exercises

S12-1. ***(Learning Objective 1: Performing horizontal analysis of revenues and net income)*** Fitzgerald Corporation reported the following amounts on its 20X6 comparative Income Statement: LO 1

(In thousands)	20X6	20X5	20X4
Revenues	$10,727	$9,832	$9,411
Total expenses	6,325	6,099	5,772

Perform a horizontal analysis of revenues and net income—both in dollar amounts and in percentages—for 20X6 and 20X5.

S12-2. ***(Learning Objective 1: Performing trend analysis of sales and net income)*** Fenton, Inc., reported the following sales and net income amounts: 

(In thousands)	20X6	20X5	20X4	20X3
Sales	$12,010	$9,680	$8,470	$8,240
Net income	635	515	390	310

Show Fenton's trend percentages for sales and net income. Use 20X3 as the base year.

S12-3. ***(Learning Objective 2: Performing vertical analysis to correct a cash shortage)*** Craft Software reported the following amounts on its Balance Sheets at December 31, 20X6, 20X5, and 20X4: LO 2

(In thousands)	20X6	20X5	20X4
Cash	$ 7,800	$ 2,250	$ 2,000
Receivables, net	36,400	22,500	24,000
Inventory	270,400	198,000	148,000
Prepaid expenses	10,400	18,000	12,000
Property, plant and equipment, net	195,000	209,250	214,000
Total assets	$520,000	$450,000	$400,000

Sales and profits are high. Nevertheless, Craft is experiencing a cash shortage. Perform a vertical analysis of Craft Software's assets at the end of years 20X6, 20X5, and 20X4. Use the analysis to explain the reason for the cash shortage.

LO 3

S12-4. ***(Learning Objective 3: Comparing common-size Income Statements of two companies)*** Hartigan, Inc., and Pintal Corporation are competitors. Compare the two companies by converting their condensed Income Statements to common size.

(In millions)	Hartigan	Pintal
Net sales	$10,850	$8,700
Cost of goods sold	6,499	6,029
Selling and administrative expenses	3,125	1,688
Interest expense	54	35
Other expenses	33	43
Income tax expense	432	209
Net income	$ 705	$ 696

Which company earned more net income? Which company's net income was a higher percentage of its net sales? Explain your answer.

LO 4

S12-5. ***(Learning Objective 4: Evaluating the trend in a company's current ratio)*** Examine the financial data of Jacob Corporation.

Year Ended December 31	20X6	20X5	20X4
Operating Results			
Net income	$ 220	$ 120	$ 119
Per ordinary share	$1.23	$0.93	$0.63
Percent of sales	15.6%	17.6%	19.6%
Return on average shareholders' equity	14.0	17.0	20.0
Financial Position			
Current assets	$ 560	$ 455	$ 445
Current liabilities	360	333	356
Working capital	200	112	89
Current ratio	1.56	1.37	1.25

Show how to compute Jacob's current ratio for each year 20X4 through 20X6. Is the company's ability to pay its current liabilities improving or deteriorating?

LO 4

S12-6. ***(Learning Objective 4: Evaluating a company's acid-test ratio)*** Use the Gargantua, Inc., Balance Sheet data below.

Requirements

1. Compute Gargantua, Inc.'s acid-test ratios at December 31, 20X6 and 20X5.
2. Use the comparative information from the table on the bottom of the following page for Horner, Inc., Isaacson Company, and Jona Companies Limited. Are Gargantua, Inc.'s acid-test ratios for 20X6 and 20X5 strong, average, or weak in comparison?

	A	B	C	D	E
1	**Gargantua, Inc. Balance Sheets (Adapted)**				
2				**Increase (Decrease)**	
3	**(Dollar amounts in millions)**	**Dec 31, 20X6**	**Dec 31, 20X5**	**Amount**	**Percentage**
4	**Assets**				
5	**Current Assets**				
6	Cash and cash equivalents	$ 1,203	$ 903	$ 300	33.2%
7	Short-term investments	7	84	(77)	(91.7)
8	Receivables, net	246	256	(10)	(3.9)
9	Inventories	91	81	10	12.3
10	Prepaid expenses and other assets	203	343	(140)	(40.8)
11	Total current assets	1,750	1,667	83	5.0
12	Property, plant and equipment, net	3,619	3,396	223	6.6
13	Intangible assets	1,089	841	248	29.5
14	Other assets	824	718	106	14.8
15	Total assets	$ 7,282	$ 6,622	$ 660	10.0%
16	**Liabilities and Shareholders' Equity**				
17	**Current liabilities**				
18	Accounts payable	$ 977	$ 884	$ 93	10.50%
19	Income tax payable	39	69	(30)	(44)
20	Short-term debt	121	115	6	5.2
21	Other	70	73	(3)	(4)
22	Total current liabilities	1,207	1,141	66	5.8
23	Long-term debt	3,544	2,982	562	18.8
24	Other liabilities	1,177	1,046	131	12.5
25	Total liabilities	5,928	5,169	759	14.7
26	**Shareholders' equity**				
27	Share capital	—	—	—	—
28	Retained earnings	1,513	1,629	(116)	(7.1)
29	Accumulated other comprehensive (loss)	(159)	(176)	17	9.7
30	Total shareholders' equity	1,354	1,453	(99)	(6.8)
31	Total liabilities and shareholders' equity	$ 7,282	$ 6,622	$ 660	10.0%
32					

Company	Acid-Test Ratio
Horner, Inc. (Utility)	0.73
Isaacson Company (Department store)	0.68
Jona Companies Limited (Grocery store)	0.72

LO 4

S12-7. ***(Learning Objective 4: Computing and evaluating cash collection cycle)*** Use the Gargantua 20X6 Income Statement shown here and the Balance Sheet from Short Exercise 12-6 to compute its cash conversion cycle for the year 20X6. Identify all components of the cash conversion cycle clearly.

	A	B	C
1	**Gargantua, Inc.** **Statements of Income (Adapted)**		
2	**(Dollar amounts in millions)**	**Dec 31, 20X6**	**Dec 31, 20X5**
3	Revenues	$ 9,550	$ 9,086
4	Expenses:		
5	Cost of goods sold	2,230	2,248
6	Payroll and employee benefits	2,134	2,004
7	Occupancy and other operating expenses	2,776	2,784
8	General and administrative expenses	1,175	1,131
9	Interest expense	154	136
10	Other expense (income), net	12	(32)
11	Income before income taxes	1,069	851
12	Income tax expense	288	252
13	Net income	$ 781	$ 599
14			

Do these measures look strong or weak? Give reasons for your answer.

LO 4

S12-8. ***(Learning Objective 4: Measuring ability to pay long-term debt)*** Use the financial statements of Gargantua, Inc., in Short Exercises 12-6 and 12-7.

Requirements

1. Compute the company's debt ratio at December 31, 20X6.
2. Compute the company's times-interest-earned ratio for 20X6. For operating income, use income before both interest expense and income taxes. You can simply add interest expense back to income before taxes.
3. Is Gargantua's ability to pay liabilities and interest expense strong or weak? Comment on the value of each ratio computed for questions 1 and 2.

LO 4

S12-9. ***(Learning Objective 4: Measuring profitability)*** Use the financial statements of Gargantua, Inc., in Short Exercises 12-6 and 12-7 to compute these profitability measures for 20X6. Show each computation.

a. Gross, operating, and net profit margins.
b. Return on total assets.
c. Return on ordinary shareholders' equity.

LO 4

S12-10. ***(Learning Objective 4: Computing EPS and the price/earnings ratio)*** The annual report of Tri-State Cars, Inc., for the year ended December 31, 20X6, included the following items (in millions):

Preference share outstanding, 6%	$425
Net income	$510
Number of ordinary shares outstanding	100

Requirements

1. Compute earnings per share (EPS) and the price/earnings ratio for Tri-State Cars' shares. Round to the nearest cent. The price of a Tri-State Car share is $57.12.
2. How much does the stock market say $1 of Tri-State Cars' net income is worth?

S12-11. ***(Learning Objective 4: Using ratio data to reconstruct an Income Statement)*** A skeleton of Athol Country Florist's Income Statement appears as follows (amounts in thousands): LO 4

	A	B
1	**Income Statement**	
2	Net sales	$ 7,500
3	Cost of goods sold	(a)
4	Selling expenses	1,511
5	Administrative expenses	328
6	Interest expense	(b)
7	Other expenses	154
8	Income before taxes	1,046
9	Income tax expense	(c)
10	Net income	$ (d)
11		

Use the following ratio data to complete Athol Country Florist's Income Statement:

a. Inventory turnover was 4 (beginning inventory was $748; ending inventory was $726).
b. Net profit margin is 12%.

S12-12. ***(Learning Objective 4: Using ratio data to reconstruct a Balance Sheet)*** A skeleton of Athol Country Florist's Balance Sheet appears as follows (amounts in thousands): LO 4

	A	B	C	D
1	**Balance Sheet**			
2	Cash	$ 85	Total current liabilities	$ 1,900
3	Receivables	(a)	Long-term debt	(e)
4	Inventories	762	Other long-term liabilities	720
5	Prepaid expenses	(b)		
6	Total current assets	(c)		
7	PPE	(d)	Share capital	185
8	Other assets	2,100	Retained earnings	3,515
9	Total assets	$ 7,400	Total liabilities and equity	$ (f)
10				

Use the following ratio data to complete Athol Country Florist's Balance Sheet:

a. Debt ratio is 0.50.
b. Current ratio is 1.40.
c. Acid-test ratio is 0.45.

S12-13. ***(Learning Objective 4: Analyzing a company based on its ratios)*** Take the role of an investment analyst at Standard Chartered. It is your job to recommend investments for your client. The only information you have is the following ratio values for two companies in the graphics software industry. LO 4

Ratio	Graphit.net	Data Doctors
Days' sales in receivables	44	50
Inventory turnover	6	10
Gross profit percentage	69%	60%
Net income as a percent of sales	13%	14%
Times interest earned	17	11
Return on equity	36%	28%
Return on assets	15%	20%

Write a report to the Standard Chartered's investment committee. Recommend one company's shares over the other. State the reasons for your recommendation.

LO 5

S12-14. ***(Learning Objective 5: Measuring economic value added)*** Compute economic value added (EVA®) for Beverly Software. The company's cost of capital is 5%. Net income was $780,000, interest expense $408,000, beginning long-term debt $720,000, and beginning shareholders' equity $3,080,000. Use unadjusted net income in your calculations. Round all amounts to the nearest thousand dollars.

Should the company's shareholders be happy with the EVA®?

Exercises MyLab Accounting

Select A and B exercises can be found within MyLab Accounting, an online homework and practice environment. Your instructor may ask you to complete select exercises using MyLab Accounting.

Group A

LO 1

E12-15A. ***(Learning Objective 1: Computing year-to-year changes in working capital)*** What were the dollar amount of change and the percentage of each change in Wilderness Lodge's working capital during 20X6 and 20X5? Is this trend favorable or unfavorable?

	20X6	20X5	20X4
Total current assets	$280,000	$330,000	$350,000
Total current liabilities	125,000	160,000	170,000

Which company appears to have the strongest financial position? Explain your reasoning.

LO 1 ■ spreadsheet

E12-16A. ***(Learning Objective 1: Performing horizontal analysis of an Income Statement)*** Prepare a horizontal analysis of the comparative Income Statements of Sensible Music Co. Round percentage changes to the nearest one-tenth percent (three decimal places).

A1

	A	B	C
1	**Sensible Music Co.** **Comparative Income Statements** **Years Ended December 31, 20X6 and 20X5**		
2		**20X6**	**20X5**
3	Total revenue	$ 855,000	$ 915,000
4	Expenses:		
5	Cost of goods sold	$ 403,000	$ 409,000
6	Selling and general expenses	233,000	262,000
7	Interest expense	9,300	10,600
8	Income tax expense	84,000	85,000
9	Total expenses	729,300	766,600
10	Net income	$ 125,700	$ 148,400
11			

LO 1

E12-17A. ***(Learning Objective 1: Computing trend percentages)*** Compute trend percentages for Palm Valley Sales & Service's total revenue and net income for the following five-year period, using year 0 as the base year. Round to the nearest full percent.

(In thousands)	Year 4	Year 3	Year 2	Year 1	Year 0
Total revenue	$1,441	$1,226	$1,122	$1,018	$1,040
Net income	106	101	88	75	90

Which grew faster during the period, total revenue or net income?

E12-18A. ***(Learning Objective 2: Performing vertical analysis of a Balance Sheet)*** Fore Golf Company has requested that you perform a vertical analysis of its Balance Sheet to determine the component percentages of its assets, liabilities, and shareholders' equity.

	A	B
1	**Fore Golf Company** **Balance Sheet** **December 31, 20X6**	
2	**Assets**	
3	Total current assets	$ 41,230
4	Property, plant and equipment, net	112,290
5	Other assets	36,480
6	Total assets	$ 190,000
7		
8	**Liabilities**	
9	Total current liabilities	$ 46,930
10	Long-term debt	104,690
11	Total liabilities	125,700
12		
13	**Shareholders' Equity**	
14	Total shareholders' equity	38,380
15	Total liabilities and shareholders' equity	$ 190,000
16		

E12-19A. ***(Learning Objective 3: Preparing a common-size Income Statement)*** Prepare a comparative common-size Income Statement for Sensible Music Co., using the 20X6 and 20X5 data of Exercise 12-16A and rounding to four decimal places.

LO 3
■ spreadsheet

E12-20A. ***(Learning Objective 3: Preparing a common-size Income Statement)*** Compare the 20X6 common-size Income Statement you performed earlier in E12-19A. How does this compare to Nestlé's vertical analysis in Exhibit 12-4? You may need to combine a few line items to make the common-size statements comparable.

LO 3
■ **writing assignment**

E12-21A. ***(Learning Objective 4: Computing five ratios)*** The financial statements of Smith News, Inc., include the following items:

LO 4
■ spreadsheet

	Current Year	Preceding Year
Balance Sheet:		
Cash	$ 26,000	$ 32,000
Short-term investments	14,000	20,000
Net receivables	50,000	73,000
Inventory	94,000	76,000
Prepaid expenses	9,000	8,000
Total current assets	193,000	209,000
Total current liabilities	129,000	96,000
Income Statement:		
Sales revenue	$490,000	
Cost of goods sold	274,000	

Requirement

1. Compute the following ratios for the current year:
   - **a.** Current ratio
   - **b.** Acid-test ratio
   - **c.** Receivable collection period
   - **d.** Inventory resident period
   - **e.** Payable outstanding period
   - **f.** Cash conversion cycle

LO 4
■ writing assignment
■ spreadsheet

E12-22A. ***(Learning Objective 4: Analyzing the ability to pay current liabilities)*** Barney Furniture Company has requested that you determine whether the company's ability to pay its current liabilities and long-term debts improved or deteriorated during 20X6. To answer this question, compute the following ratios for 20X6 and 20X5:

a. Current ratio
b. Acid-test ratio
c. Debt ratio
d. Times-interest-earned ratio

Summarize the results of your analysis in a written report.

	20X6	20X5
Cash	$ 21,000	$ 53,000
Short-term investments	32,000	15,000
Net receivables	117,000	127,000
Inventory	243,000	272,000
Prepaid expenses	18,000	4,000
Total assets	500,000	531,000
Total current liabilities	247,000	312,000
Long-term debt	27,000	134,000
Income from operations	191,000	160,000
Interest expense	39,000	45,000

LO 4

E12-23A. ***(Learning Objective 4: Analyzing profitability)*** Compute four ratios that measure the ability to earn profits for Harper Decor, Inc., whose comparative Income Statements follow:

A1

	A	B	C
1	**Harper Decor, Inc. Comparative Income Statements Years Ended December 31, 20X6 and 20X5**		
2		**20X6**	**20X5**
3	Net sales	$ 120,000	$ 100,000
4	Cost of goods sold	64,000	52,000
5	Gross profit	56,000	48,000
6	Selling and general expenses	21,000	18,000
7	Income from operations	35,000	30,000
8	Interest expense	4,000	2,000
9	Income before income tax	31,000	28,000
10	Income tax expense	10,000	8,000
11	Net income	$ 21,000	$ 20,000
12			

Additional data:

	20X6	20X5	20X4
Total assets	$104,000	$100,000	$83,000
Ordinary shareholders' equity	$ 72,000	$ 70,000	$69,000
Preference dividends	$ 3,000	$ 2,000	$ 1,000
Ordinary shares outstanding during the year	$ 10,000	$ 9,000	$ 4,000

Did the company's operating performance improve or deteriorate during 20X6?

LO 4
■ writing assignment

E12-24A. ***(Learning Objective 4: Evaluating a share as an investment)*** Evaluate the ordinary share of Regal Distributing Company as an investment. Specifically, use the three ordinary share ratios to determine whether the ordinary share increased or decreased in attractiveness during the past year.

	20X6	20X5
Net income	$ 84,000	$ 59,000
Dividends to ordinary shares	22,000	23,000
Total shareholders' equity at year-end (includes 90,000 ord. shares)	320,000	520,000
Preference shares, 5%	80,000	80,000
Market price per ordinary share at year-end	$ 24.50	$ 17.50

LO 5

E12-25A. ***(Learning Objective 5: Using economic value added to measure corporate performance)*** Two companies with different economic-value-added (EVA®) profiles are Barton Oil Pipeline Incorporated and Crompton Bank Limited. Adapted versions of the two companies' financial statements are presented here (in millions):

	Barton Oil Pipeline Inc.	Crompton Bank Limited
Balance Sheet data:		
Total assets	$ 4,338	$14,000
Interest-bearing debt	$ 1,257	$ 13
All other liabilities	2,675	2,605
Shareholders' equity	406	11,382
Total liabilities and equity	$ 4,338	$14,000
Income Statement data:		
Total revenue	$11,000	$ 3,800
Interest expense	75	6
Net income	$ 190	$ 1,230

Requirements

1. Before performing any calculations, which company do you think represents the better investment? Give your reason.
2. Compute the EVA® for each company and then decide which company's shares you would rather hold as an investment. Assume both companies' cost of capital is 8.5% and use unadjusted net income in your calculations.

Group B

LO 1

E12-26B. ***(Learning Objective 1: Computing year-to-year changes in working capital)*** What were the euro amount of change and the percentage of each change in Ricardo Lodge's working capital during 20X6 and 20X5? Is this trend favorable or unfavorable?

	20X6	20X5	20X4
Total current assets	$420,000	$320,000	$260,000
Total current liabilities	190,000	150,000	120,000

LO 1
■ writing assignment

E12-27B. ***(Learning Objective 1: Performing horizontal analysis of an Income Statement)*** Prepare a horizontal analysis of the comparative Income Statements of Fashion Music Co. Round percentage changes to the nearest one-tenth percent (three decimal places).

	A	B	C
1	**Fashion Music Co. Comparative Income Statements Years Ended December 31, 20X6 and 20X5**		
2		**20X6**	**20X5**
3	Total revenue	€ 1,104,000	€ 919,000
4	Expenses:		
5	Cost of goods sold	€ 489,000	€ 400,450
6	Selling and general expenses	299,000	269,000
7	Interest expense	25,500	14,500
8	Income tax expense	107,500	86,850
9	Total expenses	921,000	770,800
10	Net income	€ 183,000	€ 148,200
11			

LO 1

E12-28B. ***(Learning Objective 1: Computing trend percentages)*** Compute trend percentages for Andover Valley Sales & Service's total revenue and net income for the following five-year period, using year 0 as the base year. Round to the nearest full percent.

(In thousands)	Year 4	Year 3	Year 2	Year 1	Year 0
Total revenue	€1,465	€1,279	€1,091	€1,030	€1,045
Net income	116	108	78	66	80

Which company appears to have the strongest financial position? Explain your reasoning.

LO 2

E12-29B. ***(Learning Objective 2: Performing vertical analysis of a Balance Sheet)*** Epsilon Golf Company has requested that you perform a vertical analysis of its Balance Sheet to determine the component percentages of its assets, liabilities, and shareholders' equity.

	A	B
1	**Epsilon Golf Company Balance Sheet December 31, 20X6**	
2	**Assets**	
3	Total current assets	$ 46,000
4	Property, plant and equipment, net	212,000
5	Other assets	39,000
6	Total assets	$ 297,000
7		
8	**Liabilities**	
9	Total current liabilities	$ 54,000
10	Long-term debt	110,000
11	Total liabilities	164,000
12		
13	**Shareholders' Equity**	
14	Total shareholders' equity	133,000
15	Total liabilities and shareholders' equity	$ 297,000
16		

LO 3
■ spreadsheet

E12-30B. ***(Learning Objective 3: Preparing a common-size Income Statement)*** Prepare a comparative common-size Income Statement for Fashion Music Co. using the 20X6 and 20X5 data of Exercise 12-27B and rounding to four decimal places.

LO 3
■ writing assignment

E12-31B. ***(Learning Objective 3: Preparing a common-size Income Statement)*** Compare the year 20X6 common-size Income Statement you performed earlier in E12-21B. How does this compare to Nestlé's vertical analysis in Exhibit 12-4? You may need to combine a few line items to make the common-size statements comparable.

LO 4
■ spreadsheet

E12-32B. ***(Learning Objective 4: Computing five ratios)*** The financial statements of Advent News, Inc., include the following items:

	Current Year	Preceding Year
Balance Sheet:		
Cash	$ 65,000	$ 91,000
Short-term investments	13,000	25,000
Net receivables	79,000	82,000
Inventory	93,000	75,000
Prepaid expenses	6,000	12,000
Total current assets	256	285,000
Total current liabilities	133	97,000
Income Statement:		
Sales revenue	$498,000	
Cost of goods sold	278,000	

Requirement

1. Compute the following ratios for the current year:
   - **a.** Current ratio
   - **b.** Acid-test ratio
   - **c.** Receivable collection period
   - **d.** Inventory resident period
   - **e.** Payable outstanding period
   - **f.** Cash conversion cycle

LO 4
■ writing assignment
■ spreadsheet

E12-33B. ***(Learning Objective 4: Analyzing the ability to pay current liabilities)*** Fred Furniture Company has requested that you determine whether the company's ability to pay its current liabilities and long-term debts improved or deteriorated during 20X6. To answer this question, compute the following ratios for 20X6 and 20X5. (Round your answers to two decimal places.)

- **a.** Current ratio
- **b.** Acid-test ratio
- **c.** Debt ratio
- **d.** Times-interest-earned ratio

Summarize the results of your analysis in a written report.

	20X6	20X5
Cash	€ 27,000	€ 47,000
Short-term investments	33,000	4,000
Net receivables	120,000	135,000
Inventory	238,000	271,000
Prepaid expenses	22,000	8,000
Total assets	590,000	510,000
Total current liabilities	187,000	332,000
Long-term debt	147,000	84,000
Income from operations	191,000	169,000
Interest expense	41,000	43,000

LO 4

E12-34B. ***(Learning Objective 4: Analyzing profitability)*** Compute four ratios that measure the ability to earn profits for Collins Decor, Inc., whose comparative Income Statements follow:

	A	B	C
1	**Collins Decor, Inc.** **Comparative Income Statements** **Years Ended December 31, 20X6 and 20X5**		
2		**20X6**	**20X5**
3	Net sales	$ 274,000	$ 227,000
4	Cost of goods sold	135,000	116,000
5	Gross profit	149,000	111,000
6	Selling and general expenses	60,000	49,000
7	Income from operations	89,000	62,000
8	Interest expense	9,000	6,000
9	Income before income tax	80,000	56,000
10	Income tax expense	28,000	18,000
11	Net income	$ 52,000	$ 38,000
12			

Additional data:

	20X6	20X5	20X4
Total assets	$249,000	$239,000	$227,000
Ordinary shareholders' equity	$106,000	$104,000	$102,000
Preference dividends	$ 17,000	$ 15,000	$ 13,000
Ordinary shares outstanding during the year	19,000	17,000	11,000

Did the company's operating performance improve or deteriorate during 20X6?

LO 4
■ writing assignment

E12-35B. ***(Learning Objectives 4: Evaluating a share as an investment)*** Evaluate the ordinary share of Basic Distributing Company as an investment. Specifically, use the three ordinary share ratios to determine whether the ordinary share increased or decreased in attractiveness during the past year.

	20X6	20X5
Net income	$ 92,000	$ 98,000
Dividends to ordinary shares	28,000	13,000
Total shareholders' equity at year-end (includes 90,000 ord. shares)	575,000	525,000
Preference shares, 5%	90,000	90,000
Market price per ordinary share at year-end	$ 24.00	$ 25.16

LO 5

E12-36B. ***(Learning Objective 5: Using economic value added to measure corporate performance)*** Two companies with different economic-value-added (EVA®) profiles are Houle Oil Pipeline, Inc., and Johnson Bank Limited. Adapted versions of the two companies' financial statements are presented here (in millions):

	Houle Oil Pipeline, Inc.	Johnson Bank Limited
Balance Sheet data:		
Total assets	$ 4,338	$14,451
Interest-bearing debt	$ 1,250	$ 5
All other liabilities	2,900	2,585
Shareholders' equity	188	11,861
Total liabilities and equity	$ 4,338	$14,451
Income Statement data:		
Total revenue	$10,900	$ 3,700
Interest expense	80	9
Net income	210	1,180

Requirements

1. Before performing any calculations, which company do you think represents the better investment? Give your reason.
2. Compute the EVA® for each company and then decide which company's shares you would rather hold as an investment. Assume both companies' cost of capital is 11.0% and use unadjusted net income in your calculations.

Challenge Exercises

E12-37. ***(Learning Objectives 2, 3, 4: Using ratio data to reconstruct a company's Balance Sheet)*** The following data (dollar amounts in millions) are taken from the financial statements of Floor 1 Industries, Inc.:

Total liabilities	$12,600
Pref. share	$ 0
Total current assets	$11,900
Accumulated depreciation	$ 1,700
Debt ratio	70%
Current ratio	1.40

Requirement

1. Complete the following condensed Balance Sheet. Report amounts to the nearest million dollars.

		(In millions)
Current assets		
Property, plant and equipment		
Less: Accumulated depreciation		
Total assets		
Current liabilities		
Long-term liabilities		
Shareholders' equity		
Total liabilities and shareholders' equity		

E12-38. ***(Learning Objectives 2, 3, 4: Using ratio data to reconstruct a company's Income Statement)*** The following data (dollar amounts in millions) are from the financial statements of County Corporation:

Average shareholders' equity	$3,400
Interest expense	$ 800
Preference shares	$ 0
Operating income as a percent of sales	25%
Rate of return on shareholders' equity	12%
Income tax rate	40%

Requirement

1. Complete the following condensed Income Statement. Report amounts to the nearest million dollars.

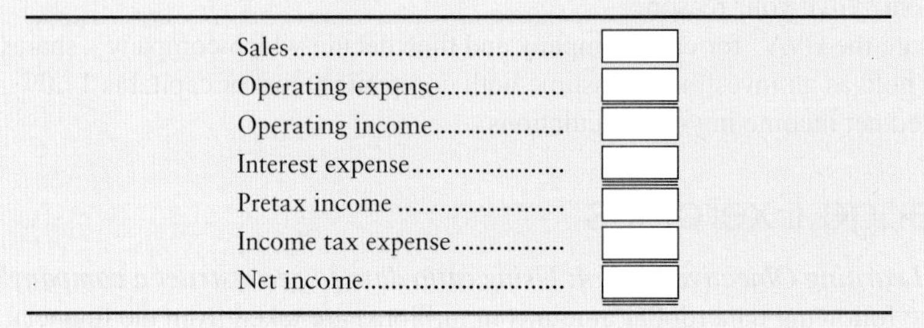

Sales	
Operating expense	
Operating income	
Interest expense	
Pretax income	
Income tax expense	
Net income	

Quiz

Use the Fatima Bell Corporation financial statements that follow to answer questions 12–39 through 12–50.

	A	B	C	D
1	**Fatima Bell Corporation** **Consolidated Statements of Income**	**(In millions, except per share amounts)**		
2		**Year ended December 31**		
3		**20X6**	**20X5**	**20X4**
4	Net revenue	$ 42,810	$ 35,299	$ 30,968
5	Cost of goods sold	34,010	29,111	26,061
6	Gross profit	8,800	6,188	4,907
7	Operating expenses:			
8	Selling, general, and administrative	3,342	3,000	2,581
9	Research, development, and engineering	575	556	542
10	Special charges	—	—	502
11	Total operating expenses	3,917	3,556	3,625
12	Operating income	4,883	2,632	1,282
13	Investment and other income (loss), net	172	212	(78)
14	Income before income taxes	5,055	2,844	1,204
15	Income tax expense	1,108	912	472
16	Net income	$ 3,947	$ 1,932	$ 732
17	Earnings per ordinary share:			
18	Basic	$ 1.34	$ 0.94	$ 0.42
19				

	A	B	C
1	**Fatima Bell Corporation Consolidated Statements of Financial Position**		
2		**December 31**	
3	**(In millions)**	**20X6**	**20X5**
4	**Assets**		
5	Current assets:		
6	Cash and cash equivalents	$ 4,301	$ 4,138
7	Short-term investments	830	512
8	Accounts receivable, net	3,402	2,401
9	Inventories	427	410
10	Other	1,638	1,213
11	Total current assets	10,598	8,674
12	Property, plant and equipment, net	1,517	932
13	Investments	6,613	5,323
14	Other non-current assets	301	144
15	Total assets	$ 19,029	$ 15,073
16	**Liabilities and Shareholders' Equity**		
17	Current liabilities:		
18	Accounts payable	$ 7,702	$ 6,002
19	Accrued and other	3,676	3,044
20	Total current liabilities	11,378	9,046
21	Long-term debt	301	302
22	Other non-current liabilities	1,701	1,167
23	Commitments and contingent liabilities (Note 7)	—	—
24	Total liabilities	13,380	10,515
25	Shareholders' equity:		
26	Preference share and capital in excess of $0.02		
27	par value; shares issued and outstanding: none	—	—
28	Ordinary share and capital in excess of $0.05		
29	par value; shares authorized: 6,000; shares		
30	issued: 3,240 and 2,989, respectively	7,801	7,004
31	Treasury share, at cost; 175 and 124 shares,		
32	respectively	(6,333)	(4,404)
33	Retained earnings	4,321	2,054
34	Other comprehensive loss	(104)	(50)
35	Other	(36)	(46)
36	Total shareholders' equity	5,649	4,558
36	Total liabilities and shareholders' equity	$ 19,029	$ 15,073
37			

Q12-39. During 20X6, Fatima Bell's total assets

a. increased by 26.2%.
b. increased by $9,390 million.
c. increased by 20.8%.
d. both a and b.

Q12-40. Fatima Bell's current ratio at year-end 20X6 is closest to

a. 9,390.
b. 1.2.
c. 0.9.
d. 20.8.

Q12-41. Fatima Bell's acid-test ratio at year-end 20X6 is closest to

a. 0.75.
b. 0.68.
c. 0.45.
d. $8,533 million.

Q12-42. What is the largest single item included in Fatima Bell's debt ratio at December 31, 20X6?

a. Investments
b. Cash and cash equivalents
c. Share capital
d. Accounts payable

Q12-43. Using the earliest year available as the base year, the trend percentage for Fatima Bell's net revenue during 20X6 was

a. 121%.
b. up by 21.3%.
c. up by $11,842 million.
d. 138%.

Q12-44. Fatima Bell's common-size Income Statement for 20X6 would report cost of goods sold as

a. 130.5%.
b. up by 16.8%.
c. 79.5%.
d. $34,010 million.

Q12-45. Fatima Bell's cash conversion cycle during 20X6 was

a. 102.7 days
b. –44.3 days
c. 91.7 days
d. 100.9 days

Q12-46. Fatima Bell's receivable collection period during 20X6 was

a. 29 days.
b. 25 days.
c. 21 days.
d. 117 days.

Q12-47. Fatima Bell's long-term debt bears interest at 11%. During the year ended December 31, 20X6, Bell's times-interest-earned ratio was

a. 137 times.
b. 144 times.
c. 148 times.
d. 150 times.

Q12-48. Fatima Bell's trend of net profit margin is

a. declining.
b. worrisome.
c. stuck at 20.8%.
d. improving.

Q12-49. How many ordinary shares did Fatima Bell have outstanding, on average, during 20X6? Hint: Compute earnings per share.

a. 2,946 million
b. 5,258 million
c. 5,244 million
d. 2,965 million

Q12-50. The book value per share of Fatima Bell's ordinary share outstanding at December 31, 20X6, was

a. $5,649.
b. $1.84.
c. $1.96.
d. $2.08.

Problems MyLab Accounting

Select A and B problems can be found within MyLab Accounting, an online homework and practice environment. Your instructor may ask you to complete select problems using MyLab Accounting.

Group A

P12-51A. ***(Learning Objectives 1, 4: Computing trend percentages, return on sales, and comparison with the industry)*** Net sales, net income, and total assets for Canberra Shipping Company for a five-year period follow:

(In thousands)	20X8	20X7	20X6	20X5	20X4
Net sales	$672	$518	$378	$330	$320
Net income	39	35	51	38	30
Total liabilities	315	277	265	229	210

Requirements

1. Compute trend percentages for each item for 20X5 through 20X8. Use 20X4 as the base year and round to the nearest percent.
2. Compute the net profit margin for 20X6 through 20X8.
3. How does Canberra Shipping's net profit margin compare with that of the industry? In the shipping industry, rates above 5% are considered good, and rates above 7% are outstanding.

P12-52A. ***(Learning Objectives 3, 4: Preparing common-size statements; analyzing profitability; making comparisons with the industry)*** Top managers of McDonough Products, Inc., have asked for your help in comparing the company's profit performance and financial position with the average for the industry. The accountant has given you the company's Income Statement and Balance Sheet and also the following data for the industry:

	A	B	C
1	**McDonough Products, Inc. Income Statement Compared with Industry Average Year Ended December 31, 20X6**		
2		**McDonough**	**Industry Average**
3	Net sales	$ 720,000	100.0%
4	Cost of goods sold	504,000	57.3
5	Gross profit	216,000	42.7
6	Operating expenses	180,000	29.4
7	Operating income	36,000	13.3
8	Other expenses	7,200	2.5
9	Net income	$ 28,800	10.8%
10			

	A	B	C
1	**McDonough Products, Inc. Balance Sheet Compared with Industry Average December 31, 20X6**		
2		**McDonough**	**Industry Average**
3	Current assets	$ 486,400	72.1%
4	PPE, net	118,400	19.0
5	Intangible assets, net	21,760	4.8
6	Other assets	13,440	4.1
7	Total	$ 640,000	100.0%
8			
9	Current liabilities	$ 248,320	47.2%
10	Long-term liabilities	139,520	21.0
11	Shareholders' equity	252,160	31.8
12	Total	$ 640,000	100.0%
13			

Requirements

1. Prepare a common-size Income Statement and Balance Sheet for McDonough Products. The first column of each statement should present McDonough Products' common-size statement, and the second column should show the industry averages.
2. For the profitability analysis, compute McDonough Products' (a) gross profit margin (b) operating profit margin, and (c) net profit margin. Compare these figures with the industry averages. Is McDonough Products' profit performance better or worse than the average for the industry?

3. For the analysis of financial position, compute McDonough Products' (a) current ratio, (b) quick ratio, and (c) debt ratio. Compare these ratios with the industry averages. Is McDonough Products' financial position better or worse than the average for the industry?

LO 4
■ writing assignment

P12-53A. ***(Learning Objective 4: Calculating cash conversion cycle).*** You are analyzing the effectiveness of the trading operations of AVN Limited. Extracts of its financial statements are provided below.

	A	B	C
1	**AVN Limited** **Selected information from financial statements**		
2		**20X7**	**20X6**
3	Sales	$ 176,000	$ 150,000
4	Cost of sales	83,000	73,000
5	Receivables, net	24,000	18,000
6	Inventory	16,000	12,000
7	Payables	20,000	16,000
8			

Requirement

1. Calculate AVN's cash conversion cycle for 20X7. What is your assessment of AVN's cash conversion cycle?

P12-54A. ***(Learning Objective 4: Computing effects of business transactions on selected ratios)*** Financial statement data of Greenland Engineering include the following items:

Cash	$ 25,000	Accounts payable	$101,000
Short-term investments	38,000	Accrued liabilities	37,000
Accounts receivable, net	82,000	Long-term notes payable	160,000
Inventories	149,000	Other long-term liabilities	37,000
Prepaid expenses	6,000	Net income	96,000
Total assets	674,000	Number of ordinary shares outstanding	52,000
Short-term notes payable	41,000		

Requirements

1. Compute Greenland's current ratio, debt ratio, and earnings per share. (Round all ratios to two decimal places.)
2. Compute the three ratios after evaluating the effect of each transaction that follows. Consider each transaction *independently*.
   a. Borrowed $130,000 on a long-term note payable.
   b. Issued 40,000 ordinary shares, receiving cash of $400,000.
   c. Paid short-term notes payable, $25,000.
   d. Purchased merchandise of $48,000 on account, debiting Inventory.
   e. Received cash on account, $14,000.

P12-55A. *(Learning Objective 4: Using ratios to evaluate a share investment)* Comparative financial statement data of Bloomfield Optical Mart follow:

LO 4

	A	B	C
1	**Bloomfield Optical Mart** **Comparative Income Statements** **Years Ended December 31, 20X6 and 20X5**		
2		**20X6**	**20X5**
3	Net sales	$ 695,000	$ 595,000
4	Cost of goods sold	376,000	284,000
5	Gross profit	319,000	311,000
6	Operating expenses	127,000	142,000
7	Income from operations	192,000	169,000
8	Interest expense	37,000	51,000
9	Income before income tax	155,000	118,000
10	Income tax expense	40,000	53,000
11	Net income	$ 115,000	$ 65,000
12			

	A	B	C	D
1	**Bloomfield Optical Mart** **Comparative Balance Sheets** **December 31, 20X6 and 20X5**			
2		**20X6**	**20X5**	**20X4**
3	Current assets:			
4	Cash	$ 38,000	$ 40,000	
5	Current receivables, net	217,000	149,000	$ 140,000
6	Inventories	298,000	285,000	181,000
7	Prepaid expenses	9,000	25,000	
8	Total current assets	562,000	499,000	
9	Property, plant and equipment, net	284,000	276,000	
10	Total assets	$ 846,000	$ 775,000	710,000
11				
12	Total current liabilities	$ 281,000	$ 267,000	
13	Long-term liabilities	241,000	236,000	
14	Total liabilities	522,000	503,000	
15	Preference shareholders' equity, 5%, $10 par	70,000	70,000	
16	Ordinary shareholders' equity, no par	254,000	202,000	195,000
17	Total liabilities and shareholders' equity	$ 846,000	$ 775,000	
18				
19				

Other information:

1. Market price of Bloomfield ordinary share: $82.20 at December 31, 20X6, and $52.96 at December 31, 20X5.
2. Ordinary shares outstanding: 20,000 during 20X6 and 18,000 during 20X5.

Requirements

1. Compute the following ratios for 20X6 and 20X5:
   - **a.** Current ratio
   - **b.** Inventory turnover
   - **c.** Times-interest-earned ratio
   - **d.** Return on assets
   - **e.** Return on common shareholders' equity
   - **f.** Earnings per share
   - **g.** Price/earnings ratio

2. Decide whether (a) Bloomfield's financial position improved or deteriorated during 20X6 and (b) the investment attractiveness of Bloomfield's ordinary shares appears to have increased or decreased.
3. How will what you have learned in this problem help in the evaluation of an investment?

LO 4 5
■ writing assignment

P12-56A. ***(Learning Objectives 4, 5: Using ratios to decide between two share investments; measuring economic value added)*** Assume that you are considering purchasing shares as an investment. You have narrowed the choice to DVR.com and Express Shops and have assembled the following data.

Selected Income Statement data for the current year:

	DVR	Express
Net sales	$605,000	$520,000
Cost of goods sold	450,000	383,000
Income from opeations	90,000	75,000
Interest expense	–	17,000
Net income	62,000	40,000

Selected Balance Sheet and market price data at end of current year:

	DVR	Express
Current assets:		
Cash	$ 22,000	$ 38,000
Short-term investments	10,000	14,000
Current receivables, net	182,000	167,000
Inventories	210,000	181,000
Prepaid expenses	21,000	8,000
Total current assets	445,000	408,000
Total assets	981,000	935,000
Total current liabilities	362,000	333,000
Total liabilities	673,000	700,000
Preference shares, 5%, $150 par		30,000
Ordinary shares, $1 par (100,000 shares)	100,000	
$5 par (15,000 shares)		75,000
Total shareholders' equity	308,000	235,000
Market price per ordinary	$ 6.10	$ 55.00

Selected Balance Sheet data at *beginning* of current year:

	DVR	Express
Balance Sheet:		
Current receivables, net	$144,000	$195,000
Inventories	205,000	199,000
Total assets	853,000	908,000
Long-term debt	–	299,000
Preference share, 5%, $150 par		30,000
Ordinary share, $1 par (100,000 shares)	100,000	
$5 par (15,000 shares)		75,000
Total shareholders' equity	260,000	221,000

Your strategy is to invest in companies that have low price/earnings ratios but appear to be in good shape financially. Assume that you have analyzed all other factors and that your decision depends on the results of ratio analysis.

Requirements

1. Compute the following ratios for both companies for the current year and decide which company's shares better fit your investment strategy.
   a. Acid-test ratio
   b. Inventory turnover
   c. Receivables resident period
   d. Debt ratio
   e. Times-interest-earned ratio
   f. Return on ordinary shareholders' equity
   g. Earnings per ordinary share
   h. Price/earnings ratio
2. Compute each company's economic-value-added (EVA®) measure and determine whether the companies' EVA®s confirm or alter your investment decision. Each company's cost of capital is 10%. Use unadjusted net income in your calculations.

Group B

P12-57B. ***(Learning Objectives 1, 4: Computing trend percentages, return on sales equity, and comparison with the industry)*** Net sales, net income, and total assets for Salvador Shipping Limited for a five-year period follow:

(In thousands)	20X8	20X7	20X6	20X5	20X4
Net sales	$656	$538	$381	$330	$320
Net income	37	33	50	38	30
Total liabilities	309	275	262	237	210

Requirements

1. Compute trend percentages for each item for 20X5 through 20X8. Use 20X4 as the base year and round to the nearest percent.
2. Compute the net profit margin for 20X6 through 20X8, rounding to three decimal places.
3. How does Salvador Shipping's net profit margin compare with that of the industry? In the shipping industry, rates above 5% are considered good, and rates above 7% are outstanding.

P12-58B. ***(Learning Objectives 3, 4: Preparing common-size statements; analyzing portability; making comparisons with the industry)*** Top managers of Walsh Products, Inc., have asked for your help in comparing the company's profit performance and financial position with the average for the industry. The accountant has given you the company's Income Statement and Balance Sheet and the following data for the industry:

LO 3 4
■ writing assignment
■ spreadsheet

A1

	A	B	C
1	**Walsh Products, Inc. Income Statement Compared with Industry Average Year Ended December 31, 20X6**		
2		**Walsh**	**Industry Average**
3	Net sales	$ 910,000	100.0%
4	Cost of goods sold	655,200	57.3
5	Gross profit	254,800	42.7
6	Operating expenses	218,400	29.4
7	Operating income	36,400	13.3
8	Other expenses	13,650	2.5
9	Net income	$ 22,750	10.8%
10			

	A	B	C
1	**Walsh Products, Inc.** **Balance Sheet Compared with Industry Average** **December 31, 20X6**		
2		**Walsh**	**Industry Average**
3	Current assets	$ 415,800	72.1%
4	PPE, net	101,520	19.0
5	Intangible assets, net	20,520	4.8
6	Other assets	2,160	4.1
7	Total	$ 540,000	100.0%
8			
9	Current liabilities	$ 209,520	47.2%
10	Long-term liabilities	114,480	21.0
11	Shareholders' equity	216,000	31.8
12	Total	$ 540,000	100.0%
13			

Requirements

1. Prepare a common-size Income Statement and Balance Sheet for Walsh Products. The first column of each statement should present Walsh Products' common-size statement, and the second column should show the industry averages.
2. For the profitability analysis, compute Walsh Products' (a) gross profit margin, (b) operating profit margin, and (c) net profit margin. Compare these figures with the industry averages. Is Walsh Products' profit performance better or worse than the average for the industry?
3. For the analysis of financial position, compute Walsh Products' (a) current ratio, (b) quick ratio, and (c) debt ratio. Compare these ratios with the industry averages. Is Walsh Products' financial position better or worse than the average for the industry?

LO 4

P12-59B. *(Learning Objective 4: Calculating cash conversion cycle)* You are analyzing the effectiveness of the trading operations of CMI Limited. Extracts of its financial statements are provided below.

	A	B	C
1	**CMI Limited** **Selected information from financial statements**		
2		**20X8**	**20X7**
3	Sales	€ 1,545,000	€ 1,365,000
4	Cost of sales	855,000	730,000
5	Receivables, net	104,000	107,000
6	Inventory	89,000	75,000
7	Payables	93,000	69,000
8			

Requirement

1. Calculate CMI's cash conversion cycle for 20X8. What is your assessment of CMI's cash conversion cycle?

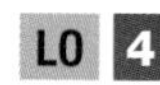

P12-60B. ***(Learning Objective 4: Computing effects of business transactions on selected ratios)*** Financial statement data of Tunisia Engineering include the following items:

Cash	€ 26,000	Accounts payable	€106,000
Short-term investments	34,000	Accrued liabilities	34,000
Accounts receivable, net	87,000	Long-term notes payable	165,000
Inventories	145,000	Other long-term liabilities	32,000
Prepaid expenses	8,000	Net income	98,000
Total assets	677,000	Number of ordinary	47,000
Short-term notes payable	48,000	shares outstanding	€106,000

Requirements

1. Compute Tunisia's current ratio, debt ratio, and earnings per share.
2. Compute the three ratios after evaluating the effect of each transaction that follows. Consider each transaction *independently*.
   a. Borrowed €110,000 on a long-term note payable.
   b. Issued 20,000 shares of ordinary shares, receiving cash of €360,000.
   c. Paid short-term notes payable, €28,000.
   d. Purchased merchandise of €42,000 on account, debiting Inventory.
   e. Received cash on account, €18,000.

P12-61B. ***(Learning Objective 4: Using ratios to evaluate a share investment)*** Comparative financial statement data of Schmid Optical Mart follow:

A1

	A	B	C
1	**Schmid Optical Mart Comparative Income Statements Years Ended December 31, 20X6 and 20X5**		
2		**20X6**	**20X5**
3	Net sales	$ 680,000	$ 585,000
4	Cost of goods sold	374,000	281,000
5	Gross profit	306,000	304,000
6	Operating expenses	130,000	143,000
7	Income from operations	176,000	161,000
8	Interest expense	30,000	49,000
9	Income before income tax	146,000	112,000
10	Income tax expense	40,000	45,000
11	Net income	$ 106,000	$ 67,000
12			

	A	B	C	D
1	**Schmid Optical Mart Comparative Balance Sheets December 31, 20X6 and 20X5**			
2		**20X6**	**20X5**	**20X4**
3	Current assets:			
4	Cash	€ 32,000	€ 36,000	
5	Current receivables, net	211,000	154,000	€ 134,000
6	Inventories	291,000	288,000	188,000
7	Prepaid expenses	6,000	30,000	
8	Total current assets	540,000	508,000	
9	Property, plant and equipment, net	288,000	278,000	
10	Total assets	€ 828,000	€ 786,000	704,000
11	Total current liabilities	€ 280,000	€ 293,000	
12	Long-term liabilities	240,000	231,000	
13	Total liabilities	520,000	524,000	
14	Preference shareholders' equity, 3%, $5 par	65,000	65,000	
15	Ordinary shareholders' equity, no par	243,000	197,000	198,000
16	Total liabilities and shareholders' equity	€ 828,000	€ 786,000	
17				

Other information:

1. Market price of Schmid ordinary share: €78.12 at December 31, 20X6, and €59.10 at December 31, 20X5.
2. Ordinary shares outstanding: 19,000 during 20X6 and 17,000 during 20X5.

Requirements

1. Compute the following ratios for 20X6 and 20X5:
   a. Current ratio
   b. Inventory turnover
   c. Times-interest-earned ratio
   d. Return on ordinary shareholders' equity
   e. Earnings per ordinary share
   f. Price/earnings ratio
2. Decide whether (a) Schmid's financial position improved or deteriorated during 20X6 and (b) the investment attractiveness of Schmid's ordinary shares appears to have increased or decreased.
3. How will what you have learned in this problem help in the evaluation of an investment?

LO 4 5
■ writing assignment

P12-62B. ***(Learning Objectives 4, 5: Using ratios to decide between two share investments; measuring economic value added)*** Assume that you are considering purchasing shares as an investment. You have narrowed the choice to CDROM and E-shop Stores and have assembled the following data.

Selected Income Statement data for current year:

	CDROM	E-Shop
Net sales (all on credit)	$595,000	$514,000
Cost of goods sold	453,000	386,000
Income from operations	88,000	69,000
Interest expense	—	12,000
Net income	66,000	37,000

Selected Balance Sheet and market price data at the *end* of the current year:

	CDROM	E-Shop
Current assets:		
Cash	€ 24,000	€ 41,000
Short-term investments	5,000	15,000
Current receivables, net	185,000	165,000
Inventories	219,000	187,000
Prepaid expenses	21,000	11,000
Total current assets	454,000	419,000
Total assets	978,000	928,000
Total current liabilities	363,000	332,000
Total liabilities	663,000	693,000
Preference shares, 6%, $150 par		30,000
Ordinary shares, $1 par (100,000 shares)	100,000	
$5 par (10,000 shares)		50,000
Total shareholders' equity	315,000	235,000
Market price per ordinary share	€ 8.84	€ 70.68

Selected Balance Sheet data at the *beginning* of the current year:

	CDROM	E-Shop
Balance Sheet:		
Current receivables, net	€143,000	€190,000
Inventories	202,000	195,000
Total assets	843,000	914,000
Long-term debt	–	300,000
Preference share, 6%, €150 par		30,000
Ordinary share, €1 par (100,000 shares)	100,000	
€5 par (10,000 shares)		50,000
Total shareholders' equity	259,000	220,000

Your strategy is to invest in companies that have low price/earnings ratios, but which appear to be in good shape financially. Assume that you have analyzed all other factors and that your decision depends on the results of ratio analysis.

Requirements

1. Compute the following ratios for both companies for the current year and decide which company's shares better fit your investment strategy.
   - **a.** Acid-test ratio
   - **b.** Inventory turnover
   - **c.** Receivables resident period
   - **d.** Debt ratio
   - **e.** Times-interest-earned ratio
   - **f.** Return on ordinary shareholders' equity
   - **g.** Earnings per share
   - **h.** Price/earnings ratio
2. Compute each company's economic-value-added (EVA®) measure and determine whether the companies' EVA®s confirm or alter your investment decision. Each company's cost of capital is 12%. Use unadjusted net income in your calculations.

APPLY YOUR KNOWLEDGE

Decision Cases

LO 5

Case 1. ***(Learning Objective 5: Assessing the effects of transactions on a company)*** Suppose Nestlé is having a bad year in 20X4, as the company has incurred a $4.9 billion net loss. The loss has pushed most of the return measures into the negative column and the current ratio dropped below 1.0. The company's debt ratio is still only 0.27. Assume top management of the company is pondering ways to improve the company's ratios. In particular, management is considering the following transactions:

1. Sell off the cable television segment of the business for $30 million (receiving half in cash and half in the form of a long-term note receivable). The book value of the cable television business is $27 million.
2. Borrow $100 million on long-term debt.
3. Purchase treasury share for $500 million cash.
4. Write off one-fourth of goodwill carried on the books at $128 million.
5. Sell advertising at the normal gross profit of 60%. The advertisements run immediately.
6. Purchase trademarks from other companies, paying $20 million cash and signing a one-year note payable for $80 million.

Requirements

1. Top management wants to know the effects of these transactions (increase, decrease, or no effect) on the following ratios of Nestlé:
   - **a.** Current ratio
   - **b.** Debt ratio
   - **c.** Times-interest-earned ratio
   - **d.** Return on equity
   - **e.** Book value per ordinary share

■ **writing assignment**

2. Some of these transactions have an immediate positive effect on the company's financial condition. Some are definitely negative. Others have an effect that cannot be judged as clearly positive or negative. Evaluate each transaction's effect as positive, negative, or unclear. (Challenge)

■ **writing assignment**

Case 2. ***(Learning Objective 4: Analyzing the effects of an accounting difference on the ratios)*** Assume that you are a financial analyst. You are trying to compare the financial statements of CNH Global, an international company that uses international financial reporting standards (IFRS), to those of Caterpillar, Inc., which uses US GAAP. Caterpillar, Inc., uses the last-in, first-out (LIFO) method to account for its inventories. IFRS does not permit CNH Global to use LIFO. Analyze the effect of this difference in accounting methods on the two companies' ratio values. For each ratio discussed in this chapter, indicate which company will have the higher (and the lower) ratio value. Also identify those ratios that are unaffected by the FIFO/LIFO difference. Ignore the effects of income taxes, and assume inventory costs are increasing. Then, based on your analysis of the ratios, summarize your conclusions as to which company looks better overall.

Case 3. *(Learning Objectives 2, 4: Identifying action to cut losses and establish profitability)* Suppose you manage Europe Vacations, a travel agency specializing in European tour destinations that lost money during the past year. To turn the business around, you must analyze the company and industry data for the current year to learn what is wrong. The company's data follow:

	A	B	C
1	**Europe Vacations, Inc. Common-Size Balance Sheet Data**		
2		**Outward Bound**	**Industry Average**
3	Cash and short-term investments	3.0%	6.8%
4	Trade receivables, net	15.2	11.0
5	Inventory	64.2	60.5
6	Prepaid expenses	1.0	0.0
7	Total current assets	83.4%	78.3%
8	Fixed assets, net	12.6	15.2
9	Other assets	4.0	6.5
10	Total assets	100.0%	100.0%
11			
12	Notes payable, short-term, 12%	17.1%	14.0%
13	Accounts payable	21.1	25.1
14	Accrued liabilities	7.8	7.9
15	Total current liabilities	46.0	47.0
16	Long-term debt, 11%	19.7	16.4
17	Total liabilities	65.7	63.4
18	Ord. shareholders' equity	34.3	36.6
19	Total liabilities and shareholders' equity	100.0%	100.0%
20			

	A	B	C
1	**Europe Vacations, Inc. Common-Size Income Statement Data**		
2		**Outward Bound**	**Industry Average**
3	Net sales	100.0%	100.0%
4	Cost of sales	(68.2)	(64.8)
5	Gross profit	31.8	35.2
6	Operating expense	(37.1)	(32.3)
7	Operating income (loss)	(5.3)	2.9
8	Interest expense	(5.8)	(1.3)
9	Other revenue	1.1	0.3
10	Income (loss) before income tax	(10.0)	1.9
11	Income tax (expense) saving	4.4	(0.8)
12	Net income (loss)	(5.6)%	1.1%
13			

Requirement

1. On the basis of your analysis of these figures, suggest four courses of action Europe Vacations might take to reduce its losses and establish profitable operations. Give your reason for each suggestion. (Challenge)

Ethical Issue

Turnberry Golf Corporation's long-term debt agreements make certain demands on the business. For example, Turnberry may not purchase treasury shares in excess of the balance of retained earnings. Also, long-term debt may not exceed shareholders' equity, and the current ratio may not fall below 1.50. If Turnberry fails to meet any of these requirements, the company's lenders have the authority to take over management of the company.

Changes in consumer demand have made it hard for Turnberry to attract customers. Current liabilities have mounted faster than current assets, causing the current ratio to fall to 1.47. Before releasing financial statements, Turnberry's management is scrambling to improve the current ratio. The controller points out that the company owns an investment that is currently classified as long-term. The investment can be classified as either long-term or short-term, depending on management's intention. By deciding to convert an investment to cash within one year, Turnberry can classify the investment as short-term—a current asset. On the controller's recommendation, Turnberry's board of directors votes to reclassify long-term investments as short-term.

Requirements

1. What is the accounting issue in this case? What ethical decision needs to be made?
2. Who are the stakeholders?
3. **■ writing assignment** Analyze the potential impact on the stakeholders from the following standpoints: (a) economic, (b) legal, and (c) ethical.
4. **■ writing assignment** Shortly after the financial statements are released, sales improve; so, too, does the current ratio. As a result, Turnberry's management decides not to sell the investments it had reclassified as short term. Accordingly, the company reclassifies the investments as long term. Has management acted unethically? Give the reasoning underlying your answer.

Focus on Financials: | Nestlé

Refer to Nestlé's consolidated financial statements in Appendix A (available on www.pearson-globaleditions.com/Harrison).

Requirements

Use the consolidated financial statements and the data in Nestlé's annual report (Appendix A) to evaluate the company's comparative performance for 2016 versus 2015.

1. Does Nestlé appear to be improving or declining in the following dimensions?
   - **a.** The ability to pay its current liabilities
   - **b.** The ability to sell inventory and collect receivables
   - **c.** The ability to pay long-term debts
   - **d.** Profitability
   - **e.** The ability to generate cash flows
   - **f.** The potential of the company's shares as a long-term investment. You may want to obtain Nestlé's current share price to support your answer. (Challenge)
2. **■ writing assignment** What is your opinion of the company's outlook for the future? Would you buy the company's share as an investment? Why or why not? (Challenge)

Group Projects

■ writing assignment

Project 1. Select an industry you are interested in, and use the leading company in that industry as the benchmark. Then select two other companies in the same industry. For each category of ratios in the Decision Guidelines featured earlier in this chapter, compute at least two ratios for all three companies. Write a two-page report that compares the two companies with the benchmark company.

Project 2. Select a company in the retail industry and obtain its financial statements. Convert the Income Statement and the Balance Sheet to common size and compare the company you selected to the industry averages. You can assume the home furnishings' industry averages you have seen in this chapter are representative of the retail industry as a whole.

Quick Check Answers

1. *a* ($1,822/$1,731)
2. *c* ($1,822/$17,710)
3. *c* ($2,694 – $1,128)/$1,128 = 138.8%
4. *d* ($1,780/$26,060)
5. *b*
6. *b* {3,302/[(140 + 120)/2]} = 25.4 ≈ 25 times
7. *d* [($690 + $780)/$2,374 = 0.62]
8. *a* ($780 + $840)/2 / ($17,710 / 365) = 16.7 ≈ 17 days
9. *b* (Debt ratio is ($26,060 − $13,291)/$26,060 = 0.49. This debt ratio is lower than the average for most companies, given in the chapter as 0.64.)
10. *d* ($2,694/$17,710 = 0.152)
11. *c* ($2,694/ [($13,291 + $10,615) / 2] = 0.225)
12. *d* ($30/$2.69)
13. *d* ($0.50/$30)
14. *a* [$2,694 + $372 − ($305 + $9,500 + $10,615) × 0.05] = $2,045

MyLab Accounting

For online homework, exercises, and problems that provide you with immediate feedback, please visit www.myaccountinglab.com.

Glindex

A

B

C

D

E

F

G

H

I

J

L

Q

R

S

T

U

V

W

Company Index

Note: Company names in bold are real companies.